Withdrawn

AFRICAN AMERICAN NATIONAL BIOGRAPHY

AFRICAN AMERICAN
NATIONAL
BIOGRAPHY

Editors in Chief

Henry Louis Gates Jr.
Evelyn Brooks Higginbotham

VOLUME 1
Aaron–Brown, Ruth

OXFORD
UNIVERSITY PRESS
2008

OXFORD
UNIVERSITY PRESS

Oxford University Press, Inc., publishes works that further
Oxford University's objective of excellence
in research, scholarship, and education.

Oxford   New York
Auckland   Cape Town   Dar es Salaam   Hong Kong   Karachi
Kuala Lumpur   Madrid   Melbourne   Mexico City   Nairobi
New Delhi   Shanghai   Taipei   Toronto

With offices in
Argentina   Austria   Brazil   Chile   Czech Republic   France   Greece
Guatemala   Hungary   Italy   Japan   Poland   Portugal   Singapore
South Korea   Switzerland   Thailand   Turkey   Ukraine   Vietnam

Copyright © 2008 by Oxford University Press

Published by Oxford University Press, Inc.
198 Madison Avenue, New York, NY 10016

www.oup.com

Oxford is a registered trademark of Oxford University Press

The Library of Congress Cataloging-in-Publication Data

African American National Biography / Henry Louis Gates Jr., Evelyn Brooks
Higginbotham, editors in chief.
p. cm.
Includes bibliographical references and index.
ISBN-13: 978-0-19-516019-2 (series)
1. African Americans—Biography—Encyclopedias.   2. African Americans—History—
Encyclopedias.   I. Gates, Henry Louis.   II. Higginbotham, Evelyn Brooks, 1945–
E185.96.A4466 2008
920'.009296073—dc22

2007044671

3 5 7 9 8 6 4 2

Printed in the United States of America
on acid-free paper

EDITORIAL AND PRODUCTION STAFF

Dedicated to
John Hope Franklin
Richard Gilder
Donald and Susan Newhouse

In Memory of John Wesley Blassingame Sr.

CONTENTS

xvi · CONTENTS

PREFACE

When I was an Assistant Professor of Afro-American Studies and English at Yale in the late 1970s and early 1980s, I met the great historian John Wesley Blassingame Sr. every morning for breakfast at the Naples Pizza Shop. Situated near the geographical center of the Yale campus, Naples had become the actual center of African American intellectual life at Yale by the time I returned there in 1975, after graduate school at the University of Cambridge—all because John Blassingame, for reasons that he took to his grave, preferred Naples to every other restaurant in New Haven.

Every morning John and I would meet, sometimes alone, sometimes with other colleagues such as the economists Donald Brown and Gerald Jaynes, the philosopher KWAME ANTHONY APPIAH, the historian Peter Ripley, the sociologist Hardy Frye, and the anthropologist John Brown Childs—all regulars during their time at Yale. (Throughout the *African American National Biography*, subjects profiled elsewhere are indicated by SMALL CAPS.) We talked about everything from last night's basketball game to contemporary politics to historical events. We argued as though our lives depended on it over questions such as whether BOOKER T. WASHINGTON and W. E. B. DU BOIS could have forged a strategic alliance or whether "Booker T." was an "Uncle Tom." While I was in the process of ascertaining the race of HARRIET E. WILSON, African American literature's first woman novelist, it was to Blassingame, at Naples, that I would bring the results of my research and whose counsel I would seek about new leads to pursue. It was there that we celebrated with a slice of pepperoni pizza and a glass of beer when Blassingame became satisfied that Wilson was, as I had expected and as she claimed to be, a black woman and a novelist.

Blassingame was the first African American scholar to write a full-length study of the history of slavery from the viewpoint of the slaves themselves. Using slave narratives, which at painstaking length he attempted to authenticate, "Blass" (as we called him, with enormous affection and respect) re-created the morals and manners and the life and times of what he termed, brilliantly, "the slave community." And it was at Naples that he and I would plot—fantasize about, actually—the future of the fledgling field of Afro-American Studies in the decades ahead.

Upon one thing we agreed early on: we had to find a way to map the field with reference works, sophisticated reference works such as biographical dictionaries; encyclopedias of history and culture; scholarly editions of texts; collected works of authors who had published essays primarily in periodicals; collected-papers projects for major canonical figures like Washington, Du Bois, MARCUS GARVEY, and FREDERICK DOUGLASS; bibliographies; and concordances—in short, all of the foundational reference works that, taken together, bring a field of study into the realm of the scholarly. It is upon reference works such as these that any discipline of study is constructed and through which a field is defined, and "Afro-Am" (as we called it then) was no exception. Indeed, we were determined that we would be part of the generation that eliminated forever the curse of scholars of African American Studies: that each successive generation was forced to reinvent the proverbial wheel, repeating the research undertaken by earlier scholars, of which we remained unaware. It was nothing less than a textual legacy of memory that we hoped to leave to our colleagues and contemporaries, and to our intellectual heirs. So we embarked upon projects, major and minor, with alacrity and a sense of excitement difficult for our students today—who now take reference works and research collections such as these for granted—even to begin to understand.

The *African American National Biography* was born out of Oxford University Press's partnership with the American Council of Learned Societies, which resulted in the *American National Biography (ANB)* and was originally conceived as a complement to the *ANB*. In 2001 Casper Grathwohl at OUP asked me to select a figure included in the *ANB* about whom Americans should know more, and then to write an essay about her or his accomplishments for the book *Invisible Giants* (2002). When I looked for my first and second choices through whom to fulfill this assignment—JAMES MCCUNE SMITH and WILLIAM SANDERS SCARBOROUGH—I was surprised to find they were not among the many thousands of biographies in the *ANB*. As I searched more widely for other African American historical figures, I realized that a second biographical dictionary would be necessary to cover all of the African American figures essential to narrating the complex story of American history. When I suggested the idea to Grathwohl and to my coeditor, Evelyn Brooks Higginbotham, they quickly agreed to embark upon this project. The result is the *African American National Biography*.

Henry Louis Gates Jr.
Cambridge, Massachusetts, October 2007

INTRODUCTION

The impulse to collect and codify the lives and achievements of African Americans has a long and curious history. Faced with allegations that blacks were innately inferior intellectually to Europeans and therefore fit by nature only to be slaves, opponents of slavery during the Enlightenment seized upon a novel idea. They decided that a most efficacious way to refute these spurious and quite dangerous charges was to marshal dramatic biographical evidence about the lives and times of blacks who had distinguished themselves in some way, but especially in the arts and sciences. Accordingly, since 1808, when the antislavery activist Abbé Henri Christophe Grégoire published *De la littérature des Nègres*, well over three hundred black biographical dictionaries have been published—their rather colorful titles ranging from *God's Image in Ebony* (1854) and *The Colored Aristocracy of St. Louis* (1858), to *Progress of a Race* (1897), *Negro Stars in All Ages of the World* (1890), and *The African Abroad* (1913).

Given that its origins were deeply and directly political, the genre of the black biographical dictionary lent itself readily to hyperbole and wishful thinking, sometimes for patently ideological reasons, and sometimes because imagination had to do the work of research and historical fact. JOEL AUGUSTUS ROGERS's *World's Great Men of Color* (1947) is one of the best examples of an overly zealous researcher making unsubstantiated claims of African descent in regard to such well-known historical figures as Alessandro de' Medici, John VI of Portugal, and Robert Browning. Still, a surprising number of African Americans have only survived as part of the historical record because some enterprising and well-intentioned foe of slavery or advocate of the Negro's equal rights made a concerted effort to record what they did and how they did it as one of the stories in one of these curious biographical dictionaries, thereby countering claims about what was possible for a Negro to achieve "by nature." In the story of the collective life of the race, as narrated through the achievements contained in these individual lives, would be proof that the person of African descent was fit to be something more than a slave. We might think of this as antislavery (and, later, civil rights) agitation by biography.

If Rogers's work represents an extreme form of the genre in which almost everybody who did anything historically significant in the West turns out to have been recently descended from one African or another, at the other extreme stand biographical dictionaries created by white scholars, in which blacks have traditionally been dramatically underrepresented. Until its most recent edition, the *Dictionary of American Biography* included only 120 African Americans, while *Notable American Women* (*NAW*) included only 41 black women. (The most recent edition of *NAW*, however, has made significant progress in correcting this problem.) Clearly, a "comprehensive biographical dictionary based on scholarly research," as RAYFORD WHITTINGHAM LOGAN and Michael R. Winston put it in their seminal *Dictionary of American Negro Biography* (*DANB*, 1982), was urgently needed to fill this hole in the official historical record, and the supremely scholarly dictionary—consisting of 626 entries—that Logan and Winston produced began to do just that.

The study of history itself has changed considerably since the 1980s, when Logan and Winston edited the *DANB*. When that dictionary was published, African American Studies had just begun to emerge as a vibrant field of study in the academy, despite the fact that black historians had been publishing pioneering scholarly research at least since W. E. B. DU BOIS earned his PhD in History at Harvard in 1895 (his thesis was published a year later).

In the last three decades, historical methodology has increasingly explored and accepted new types of evidence, such as slave narratives and oral testimony, and these have given rise to new interpretive frameworks that focus on the significance of broad social movements, rather than merely the "great man" or "great woman" theory of historical agency. More recently, attention to popular culture has provided a wealth of insight into the lived experience of persons who, like most slaves and women, did not necessarily leave many written records. But most important of all, without a doubt, are the Internet and digitization projects such as those being undertaken by Ancestry.com and Google, which are scanning millions and millions of pages of original historical documents, manuscripts, and books, and have resurrected a multiplicity of names of individuals known only to their peers, now long gone. These digitization projects have rescued the historically obscure from a certain purgatory; they were lost and now are found. Or, more accurately, students and scholars can now "find" these people and begin to piece together the stories of their lives because their names and their accomplishments have been preserved in some historical document: a will, a tax record, a birth or death certificate, a deed—documents that we can retrieve in seconds and then study through the magic of the world wide web. So many broad conclusions about what actual human beings did or felt in any given historical period—and we are thinking here of the whole of American history, not just African American history—will have to be reconsidered, inductively, based upon the emergence of this veritable Alexandrine library of historical data.

★　★　★

With the idea of supplementing the *American National Biography* (*ANB*) and at the same time updating Logan and Winston's volume, and relying on the revolution in research in African American Studies since 1982, we launched with Oxford University Press the largest black biographical dictionary project to date—the *African American National Biography* (*AANB*). In 2004 we published the book *African American Lives* to introduce readers to a sample of the 4,100 biographies that fill the pages of these eight printed volumes.

If choosing the 600 biographies that filled *African American Lives* proved a daunting task, selecting more than 4,000 entries for the full-length *African American National Biography* was much more so. This aspect of the project was a constant negotiation between the editors and our contributors—a debate that lasted until the very last entry was sent to the printer and no time remained to discuss the historical importance of this individual or that, and whether that individual would be included in this incarnation of the project, and who might be the best person to write his or her biography. From the beginning, though, we realized that even an eight-volume reference work would, necessarily, omit important historical actors, especially since the digital revolution is enabling the continual rediscovery of people whose identities and accomplishments have been suspended for decades, even centuries, in the amber of dusty, obscure archives. To confront the issue, we, along with Casper Grathwohl, the reference publisher at Oxford, designed an online component of *AANB*. Eventually, this "online edition" became the centerpiece of OUP's reference program in African and African American history and culture, the online *African American Studies Center*. Working with a database that currently includes more than 12,500 names of African Americans, the online *AANB* will continue to grow well beyond the 4,100 biographies published in this edition. Initially we plan to add 2,000 new biographies online, and this work is well underway.

The editors of *AANB* decided to include entries on living subjects, which departs from the editorial policy of projects like the *ANB* and the *Dictionary of National Biography*. We did so to enable *AANB* to capture the unprecedented contributions of African Americans since

World War II, and especially since the civil rights era. Thus the *AANB* includes not only deceased twentieth-century figures like MARY MCLEOD BETHUNE, LOUIS ARMSTRONG, PAUL ROBESON, and FLORENCE GRIFFITH JOYNER, but also COLIN POWELL, TONI MORRISON, HANK AARON, QUINCY JONES, OPRAH WINFREY, and HARRY BELAFONTE. Living subjects also include several presidential cabinet secretaries, federal judges, congressional leaders, and candidates for the presidency of the United States; Nobel and Pulitzer Prize winners; musicians, artists, and entertainers in every genre; Olympic and world-champion athletes; as well as prominent writers, activists, religious leaders, scientists, inventors, and educators.

The sheer scope of *AANB*, however, also enabled us to unearth the stories of unheralded African Americans, many of whom had never before appeared in a biographical dictionary. *AANB* is thus a work of recovery, meant to place individuals of specific historical significance (or notoriety) side by side on the page with those outstanding figures about whom most of us know something, so that readers can encounter the lives not just of MARTIN LUTHER KING JR. or MALCOLM X, but also the first African American woman poet, the slave LUCY TERRY; the frontierswoman Stagecoach Mary (MARY FIELDS); MAJOR TAYLOR, a world-champion cyclist and the first black international athletic superstar; and the Alabama midwife, MARGARET CHARLES SMITH, who delivered more than 3,500 babies between 1948 and 1976.

AANB is a work that tells the story, for the first time, of the broadest swath of the black people who, together, created our collective history—people whose contributions marked and were confined to their place and time, and people whose contributions have transcended their place and time. In a significant sense, the simplicity and serendipity of arranging subjects in alphabetical order serves as a powerful educational tool. Readers curious about the writer JAMES BALDWIN may find equally fascinating the adjacent entries on MARY LOUISE BALDWIN, the principal of the famed all-white Agassiz School in Cambridge, Massachusetts, and VERNON JOSEPH BAKER, winner of the Medal of Honor for his heroism as a soldier in World War II. Those interested in the history of music and hip-hop will undoubtedly be drawn to the entry on SNOOP DOGGY DOGG, but we hope that they will find equally fascinating the nearby entry on VALAIDA SNOW, a jazz musician and singer who is one of two *AANB* subjects to have been interned in a Nazi concentration camp (the other being LIONEL ROMNEY).

As the largest act of biographical and historical recovery in the history of African American Studies, the *AANB* is full of colorful characters like Colonel ALLEN ALLENSWORTH, who founded an all-black town in California in 1808; MARY ELLEN PLEASANT, a legendary woman of influence and political power in Gold-Rush and Gilded-Age San Francisco; ALICE OF DUNK'S FERRY, who died in Philadelphia at the age of 116, a female slave and an Episcopalian; and RICHARD POTTER, "a celebrated Ventriloquist and Professor of Legerdemain," who owned a two-hundred-acre estate in Andover, Massachusetts, before his death in 1835. Even Joel A. Rogers—most appropriately—is in our collection of distinguished black lives, along, of course, with the great historical figures of our people. And, indeed, the strength of *AANB* is that, taken together, the lives recorded here tell a richer and fuller story of black life in America than was ever possible. Consider the life of the Honorable THEOPHILUS B. MORTON, "a great race man and leader among the people," as his contemporary biographer put it. As a messenger to a district judge in San Francisco, Morton was a person of vital importance to his community, but someone whose contributions to American history had long been forgotten. T. B. Morton will now be remembered forever for all he did for his people, no matter how modest those contributions might seem in the twenty-first century, when black people have achieved so very much. The number of individuals in *AANB*, the depth of coverage of the marvelously colorful and sometimes quirky people whose lives actually make up the "Black Experience in America," is astonishing, even to its editors. Their stories, long buried in those dusty archives that contain the raw material of history, will never be lost again. And that is what scholarship in the field of African American Studies should be all about.

★ ★ ★

The literary critic and biographer ARNOLD RAMPERSAD demonstrated in an important essay published in the *Yale Review* several years ago that the biographical impulse among African Americans—as measured by the publication of life histories of black individuals by black authors—has been surprisingly limited. Few blacks, Rampersad found, had written full-length biographies of black subjects. On the other hand, African Americans excelled at writing autobiographies, starting with autobiographical slave narratives. Extraordinarily, many black authors have published autobiographies as their first books; usually, one writes an autobiography after one is established as a public figure, someone about whose life general readers might naturally be curious. But in the black literary tradition, writers have often used autobiographies to establish themselves as public figures. One need think only of MAYA ANGELOU's canonical *I Know Why the Caged Bird Sings* to illustrate the point. Moreover, many black authors have embraced the form so thoroughly that they have published multiple autobiographies, texts that at times contradict important facts asserted in a previous autobiography. FREDERICK DOUGLASS and W. E. B. Du Bois are probably the two best examples of this practice.

Though there have been many attempts over the last two hundred years to put in place a biographical record of African American lives, now, thanks to Oxford University Press, we can at long last publish the definitive black biographical database, recording and updating the contributions of an unprecedented number of historically significant African Americans, individual subjects whose contributions to American history have long deserved to be preserved. As we have seen, black biographical dictionaries have often operated as important and iconographic acts of hero-production and hagiography, as testaments to the intellectual capacities of "the Negro." Nurses and churchmen, clubwomen and fraternal orders, free citizens and slaves, sleeping-car porters and freemasons—each provided their piece of the collective biographical history of their contemporaries and peers. But the *AANB* stands upon the foundation that the pioneering editors of these biographical dictionaries constructed. The *AANB* is heir to the tradition that they, collectively, so nobly and fearlessly created.

The *AANB* would also not have been possible without the efforts of the more than 1,700 contributors whose expertise and desire to tell these great stories appears on every page. The incredible diversity of subjects covered in the *AANB* is a testament to the broad range of our contributors, including professors and graduate students, as well as independent scholars and freelance writers. The participation of writers from Canada, the Caribbean, Europe, and Africa reflects the deep interest in African American history throughout the world.

It is impossible for us to thank the countless individuals who made *AANB* possible, but special appreciation goes to Casper Grathwohl and Anthony Aiello at OUP and to Steven Niven at Harvard's Du Bois Institute for their unwavering commitment and excellent editorial skills throughout the project's existence. We would also like to thank Karen Dalton, Kate Tuttle, John Bollard, Donald Yacovone, and many others who contributed to this important project through the Du Bois Institute. Finally, we wish to thank the individuals and foundations that so generously supported the research, writing, and publication of *AANB*, without whom this massive undertaking would have been impossible. The American Council of Learned Societies wholeheartedly supported this "expansion" of the *American National Biography* and assisted us in innumerable ways, especially during the phase that culminated with the publication of *African American Lives*. Additional thanks go to Harriet

Zuckerman, William Bowen, and the Mellon Foundation; Richard Gilder and James Basker at the Gilder-Lehrman Foundation; Donald and Susan Newhouse, members of the National Advisory Board of the Du Bois Institute; Alison Bernstein, Irma McClaurin, and Monica Hilliard at the Ford Foundation; and Anthony Appiah, Harry Lasker, and the Educational Netcasting Corporation.

Henry Louis Gates Jr.
Evelyn Brooks Higginbotham
Editors in Chief

EDITORIAL NOTE

Work on the *African American National Biography* (*AANB*) began early in 2002 in the Barker Center at Harvard University with the compilation of a database containing the names of 12,500 African Americans. These ranged from ESTEBAN, who in 1528 was the first African to set foot in North America, to the tennis star SERENA WILLIAMS, born in 1982. By September 2002, HENRY LOUIS GATES JR. and EVELYN BROOKS HIGGINBOTHAM had assembled a ten-member editorial board of eminent scholars and selected John K. Bollard as the *AANB*'s first managing editor. Bollard created a collegial and intellectually stimulating work environment at the *AANB* offices established at 69 Dunster Street in Cambridge, and instituted the highest standards for all who would work for the project. He was assisted by three associate editors and senior writers: Sholomo Ben Levy, Steven J. Niven, and Lisa Rivo. Over eighteen months, this team completed the first stage of *AANB*, the *African American Lives* project. In addition to writing eighty entries for *African American Lives* and more than two hundred biographies for the full *AANB*, Levy, Niven, and Rivo solicited and edited contributions from a wide range of scholars and writers.

In the summer of 2005 the *AANB* underwent a major reorganization, with Kate Tuttle serving as executive editor until August 2006. Together, Tuttle and Niven in the Harvard offices of the *AANB* and Anthony Aiello at Oxford University Press in New York reorganized the project staff, created a board of seventeen subject-area experts to assist the editors in chief and senior editorial staff in the review and approval of entries, added renowned scholars to the advisory board to ensure that we were keeping an eye on both the forest and the trees, and somehow assigned, collected, reviewed, revised, approved, and edited more than three thousand new biographies in the last three years of the project. The final year of the project proved the most challenging. In August 2006 Steven Niven followed Kate Tuttle as the Harvard-based *AANB* executive editor.

The editorial staff of the *AANB* has made a special effort to ensure that a number of topics received due coverage in these pages, notably the role of African Americans before the nineteenth century and in the exploration of the frontier and westward expansion; the sustained and memorable, but often neglected, role of blacks in science, medicine, and technology; and the contributions in every sphere and historical period by African American women. While 28 percent of our entries are biographies of women, we expect that this figure will be higher in the growing online edition of the *AANB*. In some categories, the numbers of women are even higher: 38 percent of our activists and 44 percent of our writers are women. Slightly more than half of all of the educators featured in the *AANB* are women.

The full diversity of all 4,100 subjects can be gleaned from the list indexes arranged by a variety of topics, including subject category, occupation, and realms of renown; place of birth; and medal and award winners. Nearly all entries also contain a Further Reading section, which lists relevant biographical sources and, where available, obituaries and manuscript collections. Any autobiographies by the subject of the entry are listed first in the Further Reading section.

The *AANB* reflects the perseverance, creativity, and achievements of black Americans over five centuries. Legal and extralegal impediments—such as slavery, segregation, and racial violence—limited, but could not fully prevent African Americans' participation in our national life. Thus, while there would be no African American Chairman of the Joint Chiefs of Staff until COLIN POWELL in the 1990s, Powell built on the efforts of black military figures

from the Revolutionary War (including JOHN REDMAN, CRISPUS ATTUCKS, PRINCE ES-
TABROOK, CATO CARLISLE, SCIPIO AFRICANUS, and PRIMUS HALL); the Civil War (among
them J. R. CLIFFORD, ROBERTS SMALLS, ANDRE CAILLOUX, PRINCE RIVERS, BRUCE ANDER-
SON, JOHN LAWSON, and WILLIAM CARNEY); as well as HENRY O. FLIPPER, the first black
graduate of West Point; the Buffalo Soldiers CATHY WILLIAMS, CHARLES VEALE, JOHN
DENNY, and SAMUEL GARLAND; and the twentieth-century military leaders CHARLES
YOUNG, BENJAMIN O. DAVIS SR., BENJAMIN O. DAVIS JR., CHARITY ADAMS EARLEY, HAZEL
JOHNSON-BROWN, and HARRIET M. WEST WADDY. The famed pediatric neurosurgeon BEN
CARSON and the U.S. Surgeon General DAVID SATCHER likewise built on the legacy of the
slave physicians CESAR and ONESIMUS and the nineteenth-century medical pioneers
DANIEL HALE WILLIAMS and WILLIAM WARRICK CARDOZO.

And when ROSA PARKS refused to give up her seat on a Montgomery, Alabama, bus in
December 1955, she followed a precedent set by, among others in these volumes, BAYARD
RUSTIN, JACKIE ROBINSON, BENJAMIN DAVIS JR., HOMER PLESSY, IDA WELLS-BARNETT,
Congressman ROBERT BROWN ELLIOT, SOJOURNER TRUTH, JAMES W. C. PENNINGTON, and
DAVID RUGGLES. Ruggles refused to give up his seat in a New Bedford, Massachusetts, rail-
car in 1841, a year after the railway was established in that town. Even the seemingly
twenty-first-century cause of reparations for slavery, as advocated by DEADRIA FARMER-
PAELLMANN, has its precedent in the remarkable work of CALLIE HOUSE, born a slave in
1861, a leading light in the Slave Mutual Relief, Bounty and Pension Association, which
boasted 300,000 members in 1915. A similar pattern emerges in the categories of sports
and entertainment. TIGER WOODS stands on the shoulders of fellow golfers TED RHODES
and CHARLIE SHIPPEN; the NFL coaches TONY DUNGEE and LOVIE SMITH owe a debt to
pioneering college coaches such as EDDIE ROBINSON of Grambling State; CHRIS ROCK follows in a long line of comedians that includes BILL COSBY, RED FOXX, and MOMS MABLEY.

The *AANB* also acknowledges those African Americans who paid the greatest price, losing their lives solely because of their color. Among these are two slave women named CELIA,
one from Florida and one from Missouri, both executed for killing their masters in self-
defense; the Reconstruction politicians CHARLES CALDWELL and NOAH PARKER, both assassinated in Mississippi in 1875; and ANTHONY P. CRAWFORD and SAM HOSE, lynching
victims during the "nadir," as the historian RAYFORD W. LOGAN has described it, of American race relations between 1880 and 1915. You will also find entries on the victims of racist
resistance to the post–World War II Second Reconstruction: EMMETT TILL, MEDGAR
EVERS, VERNON DAHMER, JIMMY LEE JACKSON, MALCOLM X, and MARTIN LUTHER KING
JR. The youngest subjects in the *AANB* and also the most tragic are ADDIE MAE COLLINS,
DENISE MCNAIR, CAROLE ROBERTSON, and CYNTHIA WESLEY, victims of the 1963 church
bombing in Birmingham, Alabama. For the first time in any biographical dictionary, each of
these young women, memorialized in SPIKE LEE's documentary *4 Little Girls* (1997), has a
separate entry.

Tom Wolejko at Harvard and Jody Benjamin and Ryan Abrecht at OUP worked wonders
during the final months of production, locating contributors to remind them of their due
dates, making sure the most crucial entries were submitted, and ensuring the most efficient
and timely flow of entries among contributors, subject editors, executive editors, copyedi-
tors, and proofreaders. In the final seven months of production, Donald Yacovone, research manager at the Du Bois Institute, and Julie Wolf of QWERTY Editorial Inc. joined
the editorial staff to ensure that we met our goal of at least 4,000 high-quality entries by
June 2007.

Anthony Aiello, *AANB*'s co-executive editor at OUP, joined the project in 2004 and was
involved with all aspects of development and production: coordinating the efforts of the
various teams and offices involved in completing *AANB*, maintaining the project schedule
and budget, reviewing manuscripts, managing the art research and image acquisition, and

otherwise acting as the point of contact for everyone working on *AANB*. Responsibility for the copyediting, proofing, and printing of *AANB*'s nearly 4,100 entries lay primarily with Martin Coleman and Nancy Tan. Coleman's unflappability and expertise with managing encyclopedia production was most welcome throughout the always difficult editing and composition of a project of such scope, and Tan's completion of the final production stages was a superhuman effort. Coleman and Tan's constant vigilance and attention to detail ensured that entries met our editorial demands for accuracy and excellence while also making sure that production goals and publication deadlines were being met.

★   ★   ★

Working with Professors Gates and Higginbotham has been a privilege and an honor. The passion they bring to this vitally important work and the excellence they have demanded of the project staff and the scholars and experts who have contributed to *AANB* have made each day its own learning experience, as we have tackled large issues such as whom to include and whom to exclude and why, of race, of naming; and smaller issues like the length of entries, the handling of bibliographies, or whether to hyphenate "African American." Through it all, the *AANB* has been a communal effort that we hope will open doors to previously unexplored spaces in American history.

Steven J. Niven
Anthony Aiello
Executive Editors

AFRICAN AMERICAN NATIONAL BIOGRAPHY

AARON (1811?–), a former Virginia slave who became an antislavery lecturer, used no last name. Almost nothing is known about him outside of the record contained in his episodic, forty-eight page memoir. He did not provide any information about his parents other than that "hard work and hard usage . . . killed them." (*Light and Truth*, 6) He recorded that he had lived in Maryland and Kentucky, but that for most of his time as a slave he lived in Virginia, owned by a master with seven other slaves, three of whom were female. Aaron's owner proved especially cruel, preferring to personally punish his slaves rather than send them out for a whipping. During the summer he forced his three female slaves to work all day and then spend the entire night cooling him and his family with fans while they slept. Aaron was forbidden to go to church, although he often did so despite his master's commands and received beatings for his disobedience or would be locked up in a cellar for days without food or water. Aaron did not indicate when or what particular incident prompted him to run away when he was twenty-nine or thirty years of age, but he did reveal that he left a wife behind when he fled from Virginia to Lancaster, Ohio, a small town southeast of Columbus.

Aaron remained in Lancaster for about four years before his former owner learned of his whereabouts and sent slavecatchers to retrieve him. To outfox his pursuers, Aaron said that he walked backward through a swamp, leaving footprints that would lead his pursuers in the wrong direction. He was imprecise about his travels while escaping further north—perhaps to protect the few who aided him—but said that by the time he published his memoir he had traveled in twelve Northern states and one hundred miles through Canada. His experience in the North, probably during the early 1840s, affirmed the message of the black abolitionist movement that most Northerners hated slavery and the slave. "I have traveled through about all of the free States," he said. "I have been mobbed in a great many places" (*Light and Truth*, 41). Sometime after his departure from Ohio, he was shunned from Elizabethtown, New Jersey, and probably would have died from exposure if not for one family that allowed him to sleep in a barn. In most towns, he found that even abolitionist families treated him coldly, preferring that he freeze to death rather than sleep in their homes.

After leaving New Jersey, he conducted an extensive antislavery tour of New England. Probably traveling mostly by foot, Aaron wandered from Massachusetts to Maine, from Connecticut to Rhode Island, seeking a place to speak, meals, donations, and a warm spot by a fireplace to sleep. His travels appeared to begin well in Foxboro, Massachusetts. He encountered sympathetic Universalists, possibly led by Reverend Charles W.

Mellen, who "treated me like a brother, minister and all" (*Light and Truth*, 4) and even helped pay for the publication of his memoir in 1845. Eventually, he succeeded in speaking in thirty-two churches and in numerous halls, schools, and private homes, many undoubtedly arranged by friends he had made in the antislavery community. George Benson, William Lloyd Garrison's brother-in-law, for instance, accompanied Aaron to Providence, Rhode Island. In Portland, Maine, he addressed an audience of seven to eight hundred people, very likely the largest he attracted.

But most of his New England tour only revealed the depth of the region's racial prejudice. At one point, Aaron's lecturing had brought him somewhere between forty-eight and seventy-five dollars, which, when he arrived in Providence, he placed in the hands of a white tavern owner for safekeeping. When Aaron retrieved his cash the next morning, only twenty-five dollars remained. Aaron heard of a wealthy white man from the city who traveled south every winter, each time taking a different black boy with him as a servant. Although every year the man claimed his servant had died during his visit, he in fact had sold all of them into slavery. In Hallowell, Maine, Aaron learned that the city could boast of at least fifty-two solid antislavery families, but none would give him a place to sleep or a scrap of food. In Braintree, Massachusetts, the birthplace of John Quincy Adams, Aaron discovered a minister who had recanted his abolitionism after marrying a woman from the South who owned 160 slaves: "slavery is not so bad as he formerly thought it was" (*Light and Truth*, 35).

Aaron had gained great familiarity with the Bible (although he could not read), the antislavery movement, and antislavery politics. While he condemned most of the North as steeped in racial animosity and hypocrisy—"wolves clothed in sheep's clothing"—he spoke knowledgeably and approvingly about the Liberty Party, a small antislavery political party with strongholds in southeastern Massachusetts, parts of northern New England, and western New York, Michigan, and Ohio. It was, to Aaron, a trusted enemy of slavery: "it makes the abolition of slavery the paramount vital interest of this nation . . ." (*Light and Truth*, 11–12). His tour brought him to countless hamlets, where he would seek assistance and an opportunity to talk about his experience in slavery. Unable to write, he used his travels to find people willing to write portions of his memoir for him, usually a widow or a wife whose husband was away at work. More often than not, when the husband returned from work, he would chase Aaron from his house. Aaron's reliance upon others to write his text accounts for its meandering quality and constant shifts between the first and third person narrator. But it also allowed him to support his stances with quotations from newspapers, books, poems, the Bible, political leaders, white abolitionist leaders, and other slaves, including an account of Toussaint L'Ouverture and a portion of the slave narrative of MOSES GRANDY's, which concludes his brief work.

The first page of the memoir reveals an image of Aaron, a woodcut of a slight, dark-skinned man in what appears to be a turban. How true a representation it is cannot be known, but the depiction clearly sought to present the author as a respectable, perhaps foreign-born—if not slightly exotic—individual worthy of sympathy and support. Perhaps sold at some of Aaron's later appearances, the pamphlet was aimed at white audiences and drew upon the authority of the printed word to serve as irrefutable evidence of the evils of slavery and racial prejudice.

Further Reading:
Aaron. *Light and Truth of Slavery. Aaron's History* (1845).

LAURA MURPHY

AARON, Hank (5 Feb. 1934–), baseball player and executive, was born Henry Aaron in the Down the Bay section of Mobile, Alabama, the third of eight children of Herbert Aaron and Estella (maiden name unknown). His parents had left the Selma, Alabama, area during the Depression for greater opportunity in Mobile's shipbuilding industries. In 1942, as the family grew and Down the Bay became more crowded with wartime job seekers, the Aarons moved to a rural suburb of Toulminville. Working as a boilermaker's apprentice, Herbert Aaron suffered through the frequent layoffs that plagued black shipyard workers before wartime demand dictated full employment. Ever resourceful, Herbert Aaron bought two lots in Toulminville, hired carpenters to frame out the roof and walls of a house, and set about with his family to find materials to finish the property. The Aarons continued to live in the house even as Henry achieved superstardom.

Making balls from such scavenged materials as tape and tin cans and using them by himself or in frequent games with his playmates, young Henry loved baseball. His younger brother Tommie became a professional player, later joining Hank on the Milwaukee Braves in 1962. While the big leagues were still a dream, Henry was developing the skills and techniques of success by tossing bottle caps into the air and hitting them with a broomstick. This regimen encouraged him to hit with his weight shifted to his front foot, a stance that resulted in the consistently good contact between ball and bat that set him apart from other hitters. From his earliest playing days,

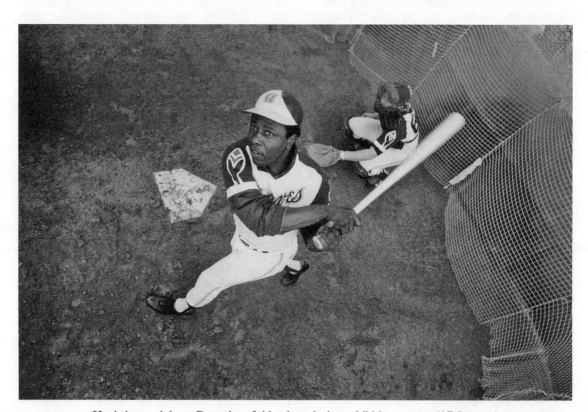

Hank Aaron, Atlanta Braves' outfielder, bats during exhibition season. (AP Images.)

players and coaches wondered at the size and strength of Aaron's wrists. Henry's notable qualities were not limited to his batting stance, however. Herbert Aaron had instilled in his son qualities of pride, determination, and respect exercised without attracting attention. Henry later recounted that, when he left home to play baseball, his father told him that "nobody would want to hear what I had to say until I proved myself" (Aaron and Wheeler, 17).

After JACKIE ROBINSON broke the color barrier in the major leagues in 1947, the thirteen-year-old Henry skipped school to listen to Brooklyn Dodgers broadcasts on a pool-hall radio. Five years later he left Alabama for Indiana to play for the Indianapolis Clowns in the Negro American League. Aaron's world expanded even further when the Major League Boston Braves purchased his contract from the Clowns in 1952. Having just missed out on signing Willie Mays, the Braves front office acted quickly with Aaron and sent him to their Class C Northern League farm team in Eau Claire, Wisconsin. Despite bouts of homesickness and the difficulties of playing shortstop in the minor leagues, he fared well in Eau Claire. He hit .336 to finish second in the league, earning a trip to spring training in 1953 with the parent Braves club, now moved to Milwaukee. Reassigned to second base, Aaron was sent to the Class A Sally League team in Jacksonville after manager Ben Geraghty learned that he was willing to become the first black player in the league. Along with outfielder Horace Garner and shortstop Felix Mantilla, Aaron integrated the Deep South league. Geraghty respected and supported Aaron, who hit a league-leading .362 and won the Most Valuable Player award. That winter, Aaron began playing the outfield.

During the summer of 1953, Aaron met Barbara Lucas and enjoyed spending time with her family. The couple married on 6 October, and a daughter was born a year later. Four other children followed.

When the Braves left fielder Bobby Thomson broke his leg during spring training for the 1954 season, Aaron was given the opportunity to start in his place. He responded by hitting .280 and winning the job permanently. Clearly, the Braves had a bona fide major leaguer. During that first season, the Braves traveling secretary Donald Davidson began calling Henry "Hank," and the name stuck. At the end of the season, Aaron requested a change from the number five he had been wearing, and in 1955 he began wearing number forty-four, the number he made famous.

Aaron performed well in 1955 and even better in 1956, when he hit .328 and won the National League batting title. Disappointment dominated his mood at season's end, however, when the Braves lost the pennant to the Dodgers in the final series. Determined to win the pennant his team had lost the previous year, Aaron had, arguably, his best year ever in 1957. Hitting a dramatic home run to win the pennant and playing solidly as the Braves defeated the New York Yankees to take the World Series, he won the National League's Most Valuable Player award.

Many observers wondered why Aaron, although the best hitter in baseball, was not regarded as an American superstar, as were Mickey Mantle and WILLIE MAYS. The issue is complex. Mantle's great popularity during the period might be attributed to his racial identity as a white man and to the greater opportunity for publicity afforded to those who played in New York. Mays enjoyed far greater adulation than Aaron, perhaps because of his more outgoing personality. At least part of the answer seems to lie in Aaron's personality: quiet, steady, workmanlike, balanced. Such steadfastness shouts no claims, calls no attention to itself. It exists; it endures.

Hank played well season after season and his home run totals accumulated, but the Braves suffered increasingly lean years following their glory days in Milwaukee, particularly after the club moved to Atlanta in 1966. Although Aaron experienced racist attitudes and behavior all his life, the tenor of abuse shifted once it was realized he had a chance to break Babe Ruth's career home run record. For some whites, the idea of a black man replacing Ruth as the home run king was too much to bear.

Pressures multiplied. Divorced from his first wife early in 1971, he married his second wife, Billye Williams, widow of the civil rights activist Dr. Sam Williams, late in 1973. During the 1973 season he hit a remarkable forty home runs in only 392 at bats, but threats on Aaron and his family increased. The FBI assigned agents to accompany Billye and the children. Aaron was often forced to eat by himself, and after he had received a particularly venomous death threat, he warned teammates not to sit next to him in the dugout. Somehow, though, he managed to concentrate on the game that he loved. Hank's friend Congressman JOHN LEWIS suggests that "Hank was shattering something. Sometimes I believe that maybe some force or some power gives you that extra ounce of grace" (Tolan, 169). Perhaps the example of his father and Jackie Robinson and the words of MARTIN LUTHER KING JR. gave Aaron the power to use his bat as his voice in overcoming racism in the United States.

Aaron broke Ruth's record on 8 April 1974, with his 715th home run. He increasingly used his place in the spotlight to press for greater equality, and in Atlanta he spoke his mind with increasing force. Buoyed when FRANK ROBINSON became the first black manager in Major League Baseball in 1975, Aaron stressed the need for more African American managers and executives. However, Atlanta's chilly reaction to his push for black front-office candidates led Aaron to endorse a trade to the American League Milwaukee Brewers in 1975. After two seasons, he retired with 755 home runs. Aaron's home run record would last for 33 years until August 2007, when BARRY BONDS of the San Francisco Giants struck his 756th home run.

In 1977 the Braves owner Ted Turner hired Aaron as an executive with responsibilities in the Braves farm system—the network of affiliated minor league teams that provides players for the major league team. As a Braves executive, Aaron served as an advocate for African American candidates and worked to eliminate racial barriers in sports, in part through partnerships with the NAACP, Operation PUSH, and Big Brothers/Big Sisters. He continued to work with such activists as ANDREW YOUNG and JESSE JACKSON in establishing baseball, as not only America's national pastime, but also as a leading force in creating a more just society.

Further Reading
Baseball-related documentation and clippings files relating to Hank Aaron's career are housed in the archives of the National Baseball Hall of Fame in Cooperstown, New York.
Aaron, Hank, with Furman Bisher. *Aaron, r.f.* (1968; rev. ed. as *Aaron*, 1974).
Aaron, Hank, with Lonnie Wheeler. *I Had a Hammer: The Hank Aaron Story* (1991).
Poling, Jerry. *A Summer Up North: Hank Aaron and the Legend of Eau Claire Baseball* (2002).
Tolan, Sandy. *Me and Hank: A Boy and His Hero, Twenty-Five Years Later* (2000).

PETER VALENTI

AARON, Jesse (1887–1979), wood carver, sculptor, and folk artist, was born Jesse James Aaron in Lake City, Florida, to descendants of slaves and Seminole Indians. Aaron attended school for less than one year before he was sent to work as a contract laborer for local farms. Trained as a baker when he was twenty-one years old, he found he enjoyed the creativity it required. He opened several bakeries, worked as a cook at Gainesville's Hotel Thomas from 1933 to 1937, and then cooked for a variety of fraternities and hospitals in Florida. Aaron also worked as a cook aboard the Seaboard Air Line Railroad during this time.

Aaron married Leeanna Jenkins, and when the family settled in northwest Gainesville in the 1930s they opened a nursery. From this point until 1968, when Aaron became a folk artist at the age of eighty-one, it is difficult to determine what is fact and what has been embellished in his story. Some sources state that Aaron had carved since the 1940s, while others tell a story that involves an important turning point that opened the field of art to him. The latter, more dramatic account states that the family made a living with the nursery until 1968, when, unable to pay for a cataract operation for his wife, Jesse was forced to sell the nursery. This appears plausible, since the artist recounted to numerous interviewers that he was worried about his ability to pay for his wife's eye surgery. As Aaron told the story, he was awakened in the middle of the night on 4 July 1968 by a voice commanding him to "Carve wood!" And carve wood he did, until his death in 1979. He made wood sculptures at such a prodigious rate that, decades after his death, his carvings were still widely available for purchase.

Aaron was particular in his selection of the wood for his art. He said that his carving tools and chain saws brought out the forms and shapes that he saw inside the wood itself. He would hunt through swamps and forests for appropriate wood pieces for carving. He sculpted animal shapes and animal and human faces from Florida cypress, hardwoods, dogwood, and cedar. Aaron used both an abstract and a folk-inspired naturalistic style. Some of his works are humorous and include resin-molded noses and eyes attached to the wood pieces. Other works borrow totem pole motifs with animal figures stacked on top of one another. Some appear as if a child constructed the piece, including the use of animal legs extending from the center of the animal's anatomy. Aaron carved both large- and small-scale works. Most pieces average one to three feet in height, but he did smaller pieces as well as extremely large garden pieces. He displayed his finished carvings in his front yard, which doubled as his gallery, marked by the handmade sign on the lawn that read "Jesse J. Aaron Museum, Jesse J. Aaron, sculptor." Tourists as well as locals browsed his property selecting wood sculptures for purchase. As Aaron's fame grew, so did his outdoor display area. He used a scarification technique on his trees, which involved cutting into the bark to allow later growth to create patterns and shapes in the treated areas. His home museum was featured on CBS News and in newspapers including the *Christian Science Monitor*.

"J.J.," as Aaron was known to his friends and fellow artists, worked in untreated hardwoods. The first cut he made used a chain saw, and the shaping and carving followed with hammers and woodworking tools. Many of Aaron's sculptures featured discovered objects such as old clothing, pipes, and special paints he would make from turpentine, brown tempera, and local mud. The paints were used for decoration while the overall wood remained unpainted. He also cast eyes and attachments for the wood from polyester resin.

Aaron's work was classified as folk art, sometimes called "outsider" or "intuitive" art. The critic Roger Cardinal used the term "outsider art" to describe works created by artists not recognized by the trained art community. This type of art is also called "self-taught" or "naive" art. Artists assigned to these categories have not been trained in art schools and tend to use nontraditional materials in their work; many turn to art late in life. Many outsider artists prefer natural and organic matter, and they attribute their creativity to spiritual and divine inspiration. The southern United States has a tradition of wood carving, and art historians have claimed that certain elements of Aaron's work suggest an intuitive borrowing of features found in native African woodcrafts.

Aaron was known as a practical man. Florida locals tell a story that Aaron found himself without a jack after having had a flat tire on his way to an art exhibition. Aaron purportedly took several of his wood sculptures and used them to lift the truck while he changed the tire. The story concludes with several drivers stopping to purchase the makeshift jacks before he had the tire changed.

Aaron continued to carve even when he could no longer search the swamps and forests for wood. As he grew older, he used assistants to collect wood, and many people brought their own choices of wood to his home. Aaron refused to carve most wood pieces, claiming he could not "interpret" them fully.

Despite the relatively short period of time in which he worked as an established artist, Aaron was recognized as an important carver and sculptor. He was awarded a grant from the National Endowment for the Arts, and from the 1970s on his works have been included in exhibits at Florida State University in Tallahassee, the Corcoran Gallery of Art in Washington, D.C., the New Orleans Museum of Art, and the High Museum of Art in Atlanta, Georgia. The University of Florida at Gainesville was the first to invite Aaron to display his work in a solo exhibition in 1970, and his carvings were displayed in 2003 at the Mennello Museum of American Folk Art in Orlando.

Further Reading

Arnett, Paul, and William Arnett, eds. *Souls Grown Deep: African American Vernacular Art of the South,* vol. 1: *The Tree Gave the Dove a Leaf* (2000).
Fine, Gary Alan. *Everyday Genius: Self-taught Art and the Culture of Authenticity* (2004).
Johnson, Jay, and William C. Ketchum Jr. *American Folk Art of the Twentieth Century* (1983).
Purser, Stuart R. *Jesse J. Aaron, Sculptor* (1975).
Ricco, Roger, Frank Maresca, and Julia Weissman. *American Primitive: Discoveries in Folk Sculpture* (1988).
Rosenak, Chuck, and Jan Rosenak. *Museum of American Folk Art Encyclopedia of Twentieth-century American Folk Art and Artists* (1990).
Russell, Charles, ed. *Self-Taught Art: The Culture and Aesthetics of American Vernacular Art* (2001).
Thomison, Dennis. *The Black Artist in America: An Index to Reproductions* (1991).
Yelen, Alice Rae, et al. *Passionate Visions of the American South: Self-taught Artists from 1940 to the Present* (1993).

PAMELA LEE GRAY

AARONS, Charlie (1845 or 1847–?), slave, wagon driver, steamboat laborer, and sawmill worker, was born in Petersburg, Virginia, the son of Aaron and Louisa. Aarons had two siblings, but neither their names nor the surnames of his parents have been recorded. Considering that Charlie's father's first name was Aaron, Charlie probably adopted his father's first name as his own surname upon emancipation. The historian Eugene D. Genovese has argued that after the Civil War many former slaves rejected the surnames assigned to them when they were in bondage and adopted new ones, often choosing surnames—"entitles" the slaves called them—that connected them to their fathers or to other relatives. Some celebrated their newfound liberty by creating new surnames such as Freedman or Justice. Genovese notes that in the first decade of emancipation, freedmen and freedwomen changed their surnames frequently so that, as one freedwoman put it, if "the white folks get together and change their minds and don't let us be free anymore, then they have a hard time finding us" (447).

All that is known about Charlie Aarons's life can be found in the oral history interview of him recorded by the Federal Writers' Project, an agency of President Franklin Roosevelt's New Deal, in August 1937. At that time Aarons told an interviewer that he had been between eighteen and twenty—"a man able to do a man's work"—at the time of the surrender of the Confederacy in 1865. A number of historians have noted that the Federal Writers' Project interviews with former slaves should be used with caution. Oftentimes the respondents provided their white interviewers with inaccurately positive accounts of their time in bondage; African Americans in the Jim Crow South of the 1930s still had to tread carefully in their everyday dealings with white folks. White interviewers and Federal Writers' Project staff also on occasion rewrote parts of the interviews to conform to the white Southern contention that slavery had been a benign institution. The interview with Charlie Aarons, for example, is subtitled: "Ex-slave Says He Loved Young Marster John."

Aarons did indeed recall his love for one of his masters, John Harris, and also noted that Harris loved him as well. The entire transcript of Aarons's interview, however, provides a more complex narrative of his life. When Charlie was ten years old, his first master, J. H. White, a store owner in Petersburg, sold him to a speculator in slaves named Jones, who brought the youngster to Mobile, Alabama, which at that time had a thriving trade in slaves. The cotton boom of the 1840s and 1850s resulted in a doubling of slave prices; children aged eight to twelve years old could fetch upwards of four hundred dollars in the slave markets. Charlie never saw his brother, sister, or parents again. In the interview eight decades later, he described his fear at being placed on a block at the Mobile slave mart and his anxiety at hearing various masters bid for him. Aarons was eventually purchased by Jason Harris, who ran a cotton slave-labor camp near Newton Station in Jasper County, Mississippi.

Harris was in Charlie Aarons's view a "pretty rough master" who provided miserly rations to his sixty or so male and female slaves, who worked in the fields from six in the morning until six at night. When asked if his master or mistress ever taught him to read or write, Aarons replied ruefully, "No, madam, only to work." Punishments and beatings of slaves by Harris's white overseer and black drivers were also common. Although Aarons's duties included driving mule wagons filled with cotton long distances from his plantation home, he claimed that he never attempted to run away, such was his fear of being caught and beaten by patrollers and the "nigger dogs" sent to track down runaways.

When the Civil War began in 1861 Aarons went to the front with his master's son John Harris, whom he looked after while also caring for Harris's horses and tents. Both men survived the battle and siege of Vicksburg, Mississippi, unscathed, as did the Harris plantation. Aarons's white interviewer did not ask

Aaron some direct questions that an African American interviewer might have—for example, how he felt upon being freed, or what he thought about Reconstruction. A clue to Aarons's political allegiances can be found, however, in his response to a question about having seen Jefferson Davis, the first and only president of the Confederacy, in Mobile. After replying that he had seen Davis in Mississippi after the war, Aarons's "face lit up," according to his interviewer, when he recalled that he had seen another president: "Yes, madam, I saw President [and former Union general Ulysses S.] Grant," who "came through Mobile from New Orleans, and my there was a big parade that day." When asked his opinion of another Republican president, Abraham Lincoln, Aarons, a longtime Baptist, replied that the Bible says "there was a time for slavery" when "people had to be punished for their sin, and then there was a time for it not to be, and the Lord had opened a good view to Mr. Lincoln, and he promoted a good idea."

Aarons's interview also revealed that he moved to Mobile, Alabama, after the war to work in a Yankee camp, where he drove wagons for the Union troops for a salary—his first ever—of fourteen dollars a month plus room and board. Aarons also worked as a laborer on steamboats on the Mississippi and, in his final working years, as a laborer in a sawmill at Oak Grove, Alabama. As of 1937 Aarons was a widower; he had been married four times, and he also survived his two sons, whose names are not known. Two of his daughters, Carrie Johnson of Kushla, Alabama, and Ella Aarons of Mobile, were still living at that time. In his late eighties Aarons expressed his view that "all people should be religious" and that "the present day folks are bad and wicked, and don't realize anything like the old folks." It is not known when Aarons died.

Further Reading
Interview of Charlie Aarons by Mary A. Poole, Oak Grove, Alabama, 4 Aug. 1937, in George P. Rawick, ed., *The American Slave: A Composite Autobiography*, supplement, series 1, vol. 1, *Alabama Narratives* (1977). Also available at http://memory.loc.gov/ammen/snhtml/mesnibibNarrators1.html#top.
Genovese, Eugene D. *Roll Jordan Roll: The World the Slaves Made* (1974).
Musher, Sharon Ann. "Contesting 'the Way the Almighty Wants It': Crafting Memories of Ex-Slaves in the Slave Narrative Collection," *American Quarterly* 53.1 (2001).

STEVEN J. NIVEN

ABBOTT, Anderson Ruffin (7 Apr. 1837–29 Dec. 1913), surgeon, was born in Toronto, Upper Canada (now Ontario), the son of Wilson Ruffin Abbott, a businessman and properties investor, and Mary Ellen Toyer. The Abbotts had arrived in Toronto around 1835, coming from Mobile, Alabama, via New Orleans and New York. Wilson Abbott became one of the wealthiest African Canadians in Toronto. Anderson received his primary education in Canadian public and private schools. Wilson Abbott moved his family to the Elgin Settlement in 1850, providing his children with a classical education at the famed Buxton Mission School. Anderson Abbott, a member of the school's first graduating class, continued his studies at the Toronto Academy, where he was one of only three African Americans. From 1856 to 1858 he attended the preparatory department at Oberlin College, afterward returning to Toronto to begin his medical training.

At age twenty-three Abbott graduated from the Toronto School of Medicine, having spent four years under the tutelage of ALEXANDER T. AUGUSTA, a black physician. Abbott became a licentiate of the Medical Board of Upper Canada in 1861, and in 1863 he petitioned U.S. Secretary of War Edwin Stanton and was commissioned as an assistant surgeon, assuming the rank of captain.

From 1863 to 1866 Abbott served in the Washington, D.C., area, first at Camp Barker, a "contraband camp" that accommodated runaway slaves, under the command of his former mentor, A. T. Augusta. The establishment of Freedmen's Hospital in Washington, D.C., in 1863, the first public hospital for African Americans in the United States, has been attributed to the work of these two doctors. When Augusta was transferred to another post, Abbott assumed the position of executive in charge of the contraband hospitals in Washington; these hospitals provided medical care to emancipated slaves and to soldiers. In 1864 he moved to Abbott's Hospital in the Freedmen's Village, the Union-controlled estate in northern Virginia seized from Robert E. Lee.

While in Washington, Abbott met Abraham Lincoln. In a memoir he described the stir that he and Augusta made during a White House reception in the winter of 1863–1864. After Lincoln's assassination in April 1865, Mary Todd Lincoln gave Abbott the plaid shawl that Lincoln had often worn about town.

At the end of the Civil War, Abbott signed a contract with the Freedmen's Bureau to serve at the Freedmen's Hospital in Washington, where he remained until his resignation on 5 April 1866.

Returning to Canada, Abbott resumed his medical studies at Toronto University, standing for the primary examination for the degree of medicine in 1867. In 1869 he was made a member of Ontario's College of Physicians and Surgeons. From 1869 to 1871 he continued to practice and for a time was acting resident at the Toronto General Hospital.

In 1871 Abbott married Mary Ann Casey, with whom he would have three sons and four daughters, five of whom survived infancy. He also moved that year to Chatham, Ontario, to practice medicine, remaining there until 1881. Abbott held numerous public positions in Chatham: he was president of the Wilberforce Educational Institute (1873–1880); coroner of the County of Kent (1874), possibly the first person of African descent to hold such a position in Canada; associate editor of the *Missionary Messenger*, the organ of the British Methodist Episcopal Church (1874); president of the Chatham Literary and Debating Society; president of the Chatham Medical Society (1878); and chief templar of the Masonic lodge.

For Abbott, intellect was the noblest part of human nature, an ideal that directed much of the remainder of his life and work. While continuing to practice medicine, he became known in North America and abroad as a champion of education and of the rights of African Americans, as well as a civic leader and orator. In Chatham, Abbott was active in the fight against segregated schools; at Wilberforce, a predominantly African Canadian school, he strove to ensure that the students received a good classical education.

In 1881 Abbott moved his family to Dundas, Ontario, where through his medical practice he continued to be involved in local educational and civic affairs, even though the population was primarily white. He served as an officer of the Dundas Mechanics' Institute as a high school trustee, as a warden for St. James Anglican Church, and as a registrar of the St. James Guild.

The Abbotts left Dundas in 1889, moving to Oakville, Ontario, where they remained for one year before returning to Toronto. In the spring of 1890 Abbott, though still residing in Toronto, was elected a member of the predominantly white James S. Knowlton Post No. 532 of the Grand Army of the Republic, New York State; he was made surgeon of the post in 1892 and appointed aide-de-camp to the commanding officer of the Department of New York. Abbott's appointment gave him the distinction of becoming the highest-ranking man of African descent in the organization (Henry S. Robinson).

When the renowned cardiologist DANIEL HALE WILLIAMS left Provident Hospital and Training School in Chicago in 1894, Abbott, who had been residing in Chicago with his family since 1891, was persuaded to come out of retirement and accept the position of medical superintendent for the facility. As a holder of medical licenses in both Illinois and Michigan, Abbott was able to practice in the United States. He remained at Provident for about three years, apparently resigning in the spring of 1897 for business reasons. An astute businessman like his father, Abbott had acquired several properties. The Abbotts remained in Chicago until they returned to Toronto around 1900.

An avid writer, lecturer, and poet, Abbott expounded on such topics as Darwinism, race, the medical profession, and the integration of schools. Over the years, in addition to writing for the *Missionary Messenger*, he contributed to such papers as the *Chatham Planet*, *Dundas Banner*, and *New York Age*. He died in Toronto, leaving a legacy in the field of medicine and in literary circles.

Further Reading

Abbott's papers are held in the Metropolitan Toronto Reference Library.

Hill, Daniel G. *The Freedom-Seekers: Blacks in Early Canada* (1981).

Robinson, Gwendolyn, and John W. Robinson. *Seek the Truth: A Story of Chatham's Black Community* (1989).

Robinson, Henry S. "Medical History: Anderson Ruffin Abbott, MD, 1837–1913," *Journal of the National Medical Association* 72 (1980): 713–716.

DALYCE NEWBY

ABBOTT, Cleveland Leigh (9 Dec. 1894–16 April 1955), Tuskegee athletic coach, was born in Yankton, South Dakota, to Elbert B. Abbott, a stonemason, and Mollie (Brown) Abbott. Abbott grew up in Watertown, South Dakota, attending Watertown public schools, where he was a superior student and athlete. He graduated from high school in 1912 with an unheard-of sixteen Arrow letters in athletics.

Abbott entered South Dakota State College in Brookings, South Dakota, in the fall of 1912, selecting a dairy science major and joining the athletic program. His outstanding athletic and academic performance attracted the attention of the college president Ellwood Perisho, an acquaintance of BOOKER T. WASHINGTON. Washington promised Abbott a job at Tuskegee, contingent on his continued scholastic excellence. Abbott did not disappoint, maintaining his high marks and earning fourteen athletic letters in four years: in track, football, baseball, and basketball. In this last, he played center, captained the team, and was named All Northwestern Center. In football he helped the team to fifteen wins with only six losses in three seasons. He also anchored the track team.

Although Washington died during Abbott's junior year, his successor honored the memorandum of agreement for Abbott's employment. Abbott began at Tuskegee as an agricultural chemist under the direction of GEORGE WASHINGTON CARVER, and as assistant athletic coach in the fall of 1916. On leave from Tuskegee during World War I, he completed officers' training at Fort Des Moines, Iowa, in 1917 and served on the front lines in France, achieving the rank of major. After his discharge he took graduate work at Kansas State College and served briefly on the faculty of Kansas Vocational School in Topeka, where he coached and was commandant of cadets. Subsequently he took graduate work at Harvard. In 1919 Abbott married Jessie Scott of Iowa, whom he had met while representing South Dakota State College at the Drake College Relays in Des Moines; they would have no children. Abbott returned to Tuskegee in 1923 as the school's athletic director and head football coach, positions he would hold for thirty-two years.

During his long career at Tuskegee, Abbott built an outstanding men's athletic program, successful in all sports, bringing home many titles and honors. In 1954 he became the first coach in black college football to claim 200 victories. Perhaps his most important achievement, however, was his pioneering athletic program for women, especially in track and field. From 1935 until 1955 Abbott's Golden Tigers won fourteen national team outdoor titles in track and field, eight of them consecutively. Tuskegee's individual athletes won forty-nine indoor and outdoor titles, and six achieved membership on Olympic track-and-field teams.

Despite national discriminatory practices that separated black collegiate athletic programs from mainstream collegiate athletics, Abbott was widely respected and was frequently consulted by representatives of national programs. He served two times on the U.S. Olympic Track and Field Committee and was among the founders of the Southern Intercollegiate Athletic Conference Basketball Tournament. Many of Abbott's students became champions in their own right, including ALICE COACHMAN, the first African American woman to win a gold medal. (She won the 1948 Olympic Games high-jump title in London.) In 1956, Mildred McDaniel repeated that win at the Helsinki Olympics. Abbott's coaching style and care for his students influenced countless individuals and many coaches, including EDWARD S. TEMPLE, who coached the great WILMA RUDOLPH and patterned his program after Abbott's.

Beloved by his students, Major Abbott, as they called him, passed away on 16 April 1955 and was buried in Tuskegee, Alabama's University Cemetery. With the new appreciation of African American collegiate athletics, many posthumous honors came to Coach Abbott. In 1968, his South Dakota alma mater established its own Athletic Hall of Fame, and Cleveland Abbott was the second man inducted. His wife traveled to South Dakota to accept the honor. In 1992, Abbott was inducted into the SAIC Hall of Fame, and in 1994 to the Alabama Sports Hall of Fame. In 1996, he was inducted into the USA Track and Field Hall of Fame. Most recently, in 2007, he was nominated for admission to the South Dakota Hall of Fame, a statewide organization located in Chamberlain, South Dakota, that honors notable South Dakotans.

Further Reading
Dunkle, Amy, with V. J. Smith. *The College on the Hill: A Sense of South Dakota* (2003).

BETTI CAROL VANEPPS-TAYLOR

ABBOTT, Israel Braddock (11 May 1843–6 May 1887), carpenter, newspaper editor, and state representative during Reconstruction, was born free, of "unmixed African blood," in New Bern, North Carolina, to Israel B. Abbott and Gracie Maria Green. His father died in 1844, and Abbott was raised by his mother and maternal grandmother, Hannah, the wife of Bristow Rue (Rhew). His mother's second husband was Nelson Brown, with whom she had a daughter, Hannah Cora, and stepsons Samuel H. Brown and George M. Brown. She married her third husband, the Reverend Joseph Green, a Methodist Episcopal Zion Church minister, in 1854. When Abbott was four, his grandmother contributed one dollar toward his education, and he attended a school taught by Mrs. Jane Stevens. He went to school regularly until age ten, when he began serving two years as apprentice to a carpenter, completing his trade with his stepfather, Joseph Green. As the Civil War began in 1861, Abbott was required to work on con-

structing Confederate fortifications. Friends soon secured him work as a servant to a Confederate officer, Lieutenant Alexander Miller, of the Second North Carolina Infantry Regiment. Abbott escaped by forging a pass and running away. In December 1861 he reached New Bern, where he hid until the Union army arrived in spring 1862. His legendary escape made him a sought-after speaker in churches and other institutions in the black community.

The 1870 census erroneously lists Abbott as age thirty. He was, in fact, twenty-seven, a house carpenter residing in Ward 6, with real estate valued at $300 and a personal estate of $400. His wife, Susan, age twenty-four, is listed as "keeping house" for their four children. The 1880 census reveals that Abbott and his wife had seven children: James E. (16), Ann M. (14), Hannah C. M. (12), Gracy B. (10), Israel B. Jr. (7), Susan (4), and Dodge William (b. June 1880); all but the last two attended school that year. Abbott was active in Craven County's black community, where he was widely known and respected. He was a leader of the Abraham Lincoln and Frederick Douglass Equal Rights League and president of the New Bern Council, which had five hundred members. The black community embraced the Republicans, and significant numbers of black Republicans were elected to public office. In 1867 Abbott was appointed to a state Republican executive committee and campaigned for a constitutional convention and adoption of a constitution. In June 1868 the first state legislature under the new constitution convened, and Abbott was elected assistant doorkeeper of the house of representatives—an important, nonlegislative position. On 1 January 1870, the seventh anniversary of the Emancipation Proclamation, he was chosen orator and, according to the *Daily Examiner* of 19 February 1874, delivered "an admirable and highly complimented address." In 1872 he helped to establish and became president of the Young Men's Intelligent and Enterprising Association, which promoted business opportunities, schools, and academies for the black population.

After the Civil War, the Ku Klux Klan and other secret societies seeking to reestablish white supremacy terrorized blacks and white Republicans. In 1870 North Carolina's General Assembly passed a law, named after the Republican senator T. M. Shoffner, enabling the governor to declare martial law and call out the militia against insurrections. That year the Republican governor William Woods Holden commissioned Abbott as second lieutenant in the state militia under the Shoffner Act. Abbott also represented Ward 6 of Craven County at Republican conventions. In 1870 he ran against Captain G. B. Willis for the North Carolina House of Representatives and lost by two votes. He then served as the county's deputy sheriff and a Superior Court crier. In 1871 he was an opposition candidate for the Republican convention. The following year he was elected to the North Carolina House of Representatives by a large majority, serving there for two years. When his term as state representative ended in 1874, he remained a force in party politics. In the mid-1870s he also served a term on New Bern's Board of Aldermen. He was a delegate in 1880 to the Republican National Convention that nominated James Garfield for president and was chair in 1884 of the Replublication State Convention. Abbott was a passionate reformer, a good speaker, debater, and shrewd politician, and in his role as convention chair his executive abilities shone as he presided over "representatives disposed to be unruly" (*New Bern Daily Journal*, 7 May 1887, 1). He was praised by the *Daily Examiner* on 19 February 1874 for "getting votes where, seemingly, there are none to be had."

Abbott belonged to several black fraternal organizations, and in 1877 he joined the Good Samaritan Order. In October 1878 he was elected as the order's grand chief and subsequently was reelected five or six times. In 1880, with his friend GEORGE HENRY WHITE, a fellow Republican leader, Abbott began publishing and coediting *Good Samaritan,* a black weekly newspaper. In 1881 he led a strike for higher wages by black residents of James City who worked as servants and laborers—including in cotton fields across the river in New Bern, which meant the additional personal expense of taking private boats or ferries to work. The strike failed largely because New Bern's black population did not support the James City residents. In *James City: A Black Community in North Carolina,* Joe Mobley mentions a story by Abbott in the *Good Samaritan* urging black workers to join labor unions. On 18 September 1881 Abbott addressed the strikers in Red Church on West Street and was vilified in the white press. On 21 September, Abbott and E. E. Tucker founded a Laborers Union—which, notably, included women—to ensure that "each receives a reasonable compensation for his or her services" (Watson, 520). In 1886 Abbott ran for Congress as an Independent against the black Republican incumbent, JAMES EDWARD O'HARA. This split vote enabled the white Democratic challenger, Furnifold Simmons, to win.

The Interment Book for Greenwood Cemetery in New Bern records that Abbott died on Friday, 6 May 1887, at 6:00 A.M., five days short of age forty-four, of "Brites Disease Kidneys." Good Samaritan Lodge No. 18 appointed a committee of remembrance: FREDERICK DOUGLASS, Mary A. Green, S. S. Latham, and Merritt Whitley, who wrote an obituary describing Abbott as "indefatigable in his efforts to advance the Order in the State of North Carolina . . . a devout husband, a kind father, a good citizen, and a true Samaritan" (*New Bern Weekly Journal,* 26 May 1887). His tombstone inscription reads: "He was . . . a loyal and progressive leader of his race." Many years later, an obituary in the *Chicago Defender* (6 Nov. 1926, 2) for one of his sons states that Abbott was a man "whose name is among the pioneers of North Carolina."

Further Reading

Anderson, Eric. *Race and Politics in North Carolina, 1872–1902: The Black Second* (1981).

Foner, Eric. *Freedom's Lawmakers*, rev. ed. (1996).

Justesen, Benjamin R. *George Henry White: An Even Chance in the Race of Life* (2001).

Watson, Alan D. *A History of New Bern and Craven County* (1987).

ALICE BERNSTEIN

ABBOTT, Robert Sengstacke (28 Nov. 1868–29 Feb. 1940), newspaper publisher, was born Robert Abbott in Fort Frederica, St. Simons Island, off the coast of Savannah, Georgia, the son of Thomas Abbott and Flora Butler, former slaves who operated a grocery store on St. Thomas Island. Thomas Abbott died the year after Robert was born, and Robert's mother moved to Savannah, where in 1874 she married John Herman Henry Sengstacke. Sengstacke was the son of a German father and a black American mother and, although born in the United States, was reared in Germany. He returned to the United States in 1869 and pursued careers in education, the clergy, and journalism. In the latter role Sengstacke became editor of the *Woodville Times*, a black community weekly newspaper that served Savannah-area residents. Abbott's admiration for his stepfather inspired him to add the name Sengstacke to his own and to attempt to become a publisher in his own right.

Abbott's first newspaper job was as a printer with the white-owned *Savannah Echo.* He soon decided to obtain a college education; after attending several other institutions, Abbott enrolled at Hampton Institute in Virginia in 1889 at the age of twenty-one. Hampton, founded by the Congregationalists and supported by northern philanthropists, was both a trade school and an academic institution for African Americans. Abbott completed training as a printer in 1893, then culminated his undergraduate career with a bachelor's degree in 1896, after nearly seven years at Hampton. His experience there included opportunities to hear two charismatic black speakers, FREDERICK DOUGLASS and IDA B. WELLS-BARNETT, who influenced him to seek a leadership role in the development of civil rights for black Americans. After graduating from Hampton, Abbott moved to Chicago, where in 1899 he earned a law degree from Kent College of Law, the only black in his class of seventy students. Abbott, however, was never admitted to the bar. For the next few years he tried to establish a career as a lawyer in several midwestern cities without success; eventually he returned to Woodville to teach in a local school.

In 1905, at the age of thirty-seven, Abbott returned to Chicago and began publication of his own newspaper, the *Chicago Defender.* He chose Chicago as the base for his paper because of its large black population (more than thirty thousand), though at the time the black newspaper field in Chicago was extremely crowded, with three established local weeklies and the availability of two other well-respected journals, the *Indiana Freeman* and the *New York Age.* The title "Defender" represented his pledge that the paper would defend his race against the ills of racism.

Abbott's first number of the *Defender* was virtually a one-man production operated from rented desk space in a real estate and insurance office with furnishings that included a folding card table and a borrowed kitchen chair. But with an initial investment of twenty-five cents (for paper and pencils) and the help of his landlady's teenage daughter, he was able to launch a publishing enterprise that became one of the most influential newspapers in the United States. Within ten years the *Defender* was the nation's leading black newspaper, with an estimated circulation of 230,000.

Despite his early exposure to the printing trade and newspaper publishing, Abbott was seen by many of his contemporaries as an unlikely candidate for success as a newspaperman. He was not an articulate speaker, but he had a strong talent for gathering rumor, hearsay, and other information and turning them into human-interest stories. Abbott also proved a master at upstaging his competitors. Proclaiming his paper to be "the only two-cent weekly in the city" and focusing front-page coverage on sensational and crime news, Abbott steadily increased his paper's readership. The *Defender*'s most significant contribution, however, was perhaps its crusade to encourage black migration from the former slave states of the South to Chicago and other midwestern cities.

The campaign, launched during World War I, was instrumental in bringing thousands of blacks to the North in search of better jobs, housing, and educational opportunities. For Abbott the migration was part of a plan to increase the *Defender*'s circulation and give him an opportunity to penetrate the black readership markets in the South. Several southern cities so resented the effectiveness of the *Defender*'s campaign that they banned its distribution. The *Atlanta Constitution* wrote that the migration cost the South "her best labor" force and that the region's economy suffered greatly. It has been estimated that nearly thirty-five thousand blacks moved to Chicago from the founding of the *Defender* in 1905 to 1920, more than doubling the city's African American population.

An indirect result of the heavy influx of black migrants to Chicago was a race riot in 1919 that highlighted the tensions between whites and blacks in the city. Abbott was appointed to the Commission on Race Relations, charged with determining the causes of the riot. Although the commission's report implicated the *Defender*'s strong stance for black civil rights as a contributing factor in the riots, Abbott signed the document.

The *Defender* was a fearless champion for the cause of racial equality for African Americans. Abbott enumerated his policies as the elimination of racial prejudice in the United States, the opening of trade union membership to blacks, black representation in the president's cabinet, equal employment opportunities for blacks in the public and private sectors, and black employment in all police forces nationally. He also sought the elimination of all school segregation and the passage of federal civil rights legislation to protect against breakdowns in desegregation laws at the state level as well as to extend full voting rights to all Americans. These policies found a ready market, and the *Defender*'s growth during World War I allowed it to open and maintain branch offices in several major U.S. cities as well as one in London. During the war Abbott publicly asked why blacks should fight for the United States on foreign battlefields while being denied basic rights at home, a stance that provoked investigations by the federal government. In 1918, just two months short of his fiftieth birthday, Abbott married Helen Thornton Morrison; they had no children.

In the decade following World War I, the *Defender*'s circulation began to fall with the arrival of a new competitor, the *Chicago Whip*, and the onset of the Depression years. The *Defender* generally supported Republican politics, although in 1928 Abbott opposed Herbert Hoover in favor of the Democratic candidate Alfred E. Smith. During the 1930s, perhaps because of the 1919 riots and the impact of the Depression, the *Defender* took a more moderate stance regarding racial matters. The period also took a personal toll on Abbott, and he suffered several financial reversals. By 1935 circulation had declined to seventy-three thousand. After his mother died in 1932, Abbott began to travel extensively and attempted during the mid-1930s an ill-fated venture into magazine publishing with *Abbott's Monthly*.

Following a costly divorce from his first wife in 1932, Abbott married Edna Brown Dennison in 1934 but soon fell into ill health. In 1939 he gave control of the *Defender* to his nephew John H. Sengstacke, son of his half brother Alexander. Abbott died at his home in Chicago the following year. He left behind a newspaper that had pioneered new territory for the black press, becoming the first national paper to have an integrated staff and to be unionized. In 1956, under John Sengstacke's leadership, the *Defender* became a daily newspaper, soon to become the flagship publication of the nation's largest black newspaper chain.

Further Reading
Abbott's papers are in the *Chicago Defender* Archives in Chicago.
Ottley, Roi. *The Lonely Warrior* (1955).
Wolseley, Roland E. *The Black Press U.S.A.* (1971; 2d ed., 1990).

CLINT C. WILSON

ABD AL-RAHMAN, Ibrahima (1760?–1829), a military leader in Africa, a slave in Mississippi, was born into the rising Bari family of the Fulbe people in the fabled but real African city of Timbuktu. His name is sometimes written as Abdul Rahahman and Abder Rahman. The Fulbe people were prominent leaders in West African jihads from the eighteenth to the twentieth centuries and, though enslaved, the most persistent adherents to Islam in the Americas. Abd al-Rahman's father and family had moved south to territory soon to be called Futa Jallon in the highlands of present-day Guinea after he and non-Muslim allies wrested power from their animist opposition between 1776 and 1778. Well into the twentieth century the military Bari-Soriya and religious Karamoko Al-fiya families, usually peacefully, traded rule over their people and lands.

For about a century Futa Jallon was the strongest nation in the area. In its capital Timbo, Abd al-Rahman was educated in Fula-Muslim schools to read and write Arabic and to fight his people's enemies. The city's teachers instructed many important West African Muslim students, teachers, and leaders. At least three of the latter were stolen away to the New World and gained some renown there: BILALI, born in Timbo, became a de facto imam in Georgia; Samba, taken with Abd al-Rahman to Natchez, Mississippi, maintained his Muslim traditions and gave his children Muslim names; and the student-teacher LAMINE KEBE (a Serahule), was returned to Africa after enslavement in Georgia in 1835.

In 1788, in his early twenties, married, a father, and a respected cavalry officer, Abd al-Rahman commanded a troop charged with reopening trade to the coast. After an apparent victory, he and fifty of his men were ambushed and taken to the Gambia River where they were sold as slaves. Including a stop in Dominica, his six-month passage across the Atlantic Ocean ended in Spanish New Orleans. After a month there he was sold up the Mississippi to Thomas Foster of Spanish Natchez. Soon, however, Abd al-Rahman recovered his land legs and ran away. Weeks later he returned, presumably having not found allies or escape beyond the plantation. Nevertheless, though he was forced to adjust to his circumstances, Abd al-Rahman had his limits. He was called Prince by his master in deference, it seems, to his proud manner, antipathy to labor, and to his early, undoubtedly discounted argument that he was of royal blood.

Abd al-Rahman became a kind of slave foreman and was favorably noticed because of his seriousness, honesty, and religiosity. Though he listened politely to Christian preachers, he adhered to his Muslim obligations. Abd al-Rahman appreciated some Christian principles and practices, but declared, according to Cyrus Griffin, a sympathetic Natchez newspaper editor: "the [New] Testament very good law; you [Christians] no follow it; you no pray often enough; you greedy after money . . . you want more land, more neegurs; you make neegur work hard, make more cotton. Where you find dat in your law?" Not finding a Muslim to marry, he settled down with a recently purchased Baptist woman, Isabella, around 1794.

His own narrative of his place in Futa Jallon might have been forever overlooked but for the arrival in Natchez in 1807 of a medical doctor named John Coates Cox. Cox was the only European known to have sojourned in Abd al-Rahman's hometown of Timbo in the 1780s, and for six months as a patient he had even been within Abd al-Rahman's own family compound. The two men recognized one another at first sight. Cox corroborated the slave's high African status and emphasized it in his attempts to persuade his purchaser to free him.

After the doctor's death in 1816, his son also tried to free Abd al-Rahman. Both were unsuccessful. Abd al-Rahman's managerial skills (as well as his wife's obstetrical talents) had become indispensable to Foster and their growing plantation. Finally in 1826, having become something of a local celebrity, a father of nine children, and an old man by then relieved of his heavier duties, Abd al-Rahman decided to write home in Arabic—the only written language he knew. His letter was sent to Morocco—the only Muslim nation with which the United States had diplomatic relations. Cyrus Griffin sought the American Colonization Society's (ACS) assistance. Two years later, a surprising response came to the U.S. State Department asking for the Muslim man's freedom and transportation to Morocco. Foster agreed, providing the old man would leave the United States as soon as arrangements could be made. But he came up with a surprising caveat. Instead of quickly getting rid of Abd al-Rahman via a riverboat to New Orleans and out to sea, Foster wanted his proud African to be taken north and east so that he might be awed by and would report to his people about the urbanization, wealth, and productivity of the United States.

Abd al-Rahman was happy about being freed, but he was unhappy that no provision had been made for his wife and children. Showing something of their respect for him, sympathetic Natchezians raised enough money to redeem his wife. In late March 1828 he and Isabella were shipped up the Mississippi and Ohio rivers. From the time they arrived in Cincinnati to the time they left Virginia for Liberia on 7 February 1829, Abd al-Rahman, then aged sixty-four or sixty-five, a black man in a geographically extended, largely white world, was in constant motion. He was not awed by the cities, their prodigal materialism, or their mechanical progress. Instead, he became the chief campaigner in an attempt to redeem his children through donations in the North, comparable to the lesser campaign Natchez neighbors had completed to buy his wife.

In newspaper accounts composed in all the major coastal cities, Abd al-Rahman, though at some level begging, displayed a splendid dignity wherever he went. He appeared at the White House, Congress, the offices and homes of wealthy American Colonization Society members, street corner rallies, school campuses, and—most extraordinarily—public marches and meetings with African American leaders in opposition to the ACS. President John Quincy Adams donated to his cause, as did dignitaries and common people alike in Philadelphia, New York, New Haven, Hartford, Springfield, Worcester, Boston, and Providence. The Reverend Thomas Gallaudet, founder of the first school for the deaf, became one of his most ardent supporters. It was the Colonizationist Gallaudet who prevailed upon the artist Henry Inman to produce a wonderful crayon portrait of the remarkable freedman. JOHN RUSSWURM, one of the founders of *Freedom's Journal*, the first African American edited newspaper, met and soon followed Abd al-Rahman to

Africa. DAVID WALKER, soon to be the author of the strongest and one of the earliest publications opposing slavery by an African American, toasted Abd al-Rahman in Boston. (This was in a time, 1828, at which William L. Garrison and other white abolitionists had not yet begun their fight against slavery. Indeed, Garrison donated to the ACS in that year.)

Commentators admired Abd al-Rahman's dignity, seriousness, and apparent spirituality as he sought money to purchase and free his children. Colonizationists assisting his travels hoped that he would increase interest in their plans to send other freed or troublesome people to Liberia. Businessmen hoped that he would improve African trade. Ministers hoped that their help and advice might convert him and other Muslims to Christianity. Abd al-Rahman's literacy led potential donors to seek samples of his writing. Some of his writings were presumed to be the Lord's Prayer but they were, in fact, variations on the first chapter of the Quran or were short autobiographical statements.

Abd al-Rahman became a kind of hero in the Northeast, but an anti-slavery villain in the old Southwest. Foster, his former owner, was incensed by his eloquent Prince's progress through cities that he had wanted his freed slave to be awed and dumbfounded by. In the election year of 1828 Foster and Natchez and New Orleans newsmen, former allies, and others, saw in Abd al-Rahman's travels a political rather than a charity-seeking campaign engineered by anti–Andrew Jackson (the incumbent's Democratic rival) and antislavery Adams supporters.

Ultimately Abd al-Rahman managed to raise only half of the exorbitant prices that Foster demanded for his children, but he was able to pay for passage for him and his wife to Africa. (Coincidentally, the future first president of Liberia, JOSEPH J. ROBERTS, crossed the Atlantic Ocean on the same ship. It is not known whether the two men met.) Immediately upon sighting the coast of Africa, Abd al-Rahman reconfirmed his adherence to the faith of his fathers.

Shortly after landing in mid-March 1829 Abd al-Rahman corresponded with his family in still-distant Timbo. Although he looked forward to revisiting his homeland with Isabella, his plans were cut short by his death in July. A year later, however, Isabella was able to greet the eight children and grandchildren whom her husband's heroic efforts had redeemed.

Further Reading
Alford, Terry. *Prince among Slaves* (1977).
Austin, Allan D. *African Muslims in Antebellum America: A Sourcebook* (1984).
Austin, Allan D. *African Muslims in Antebellum America: Transatlantic Stories and Spiritual Struggles* (1997).
ALLAN D. AUSTIN

ABDUL, Raoul (7 Nov. 1929–), classical singer, author, gay rights activist, and former literary assistant to writer LANGSTON HUGHES, was born in Cleveland, Ohio. Abdul's father, Hamid Abdul, was from Calcutta, India, and his mother, Bernice (Shreve) Abdul, was able to trace her ancestry back to the pre-Revolutionary War era. Abdul got his start in theater at a young age, participating in children's theater by age six. He attended John Hay High School and, after graduation, worked as a journalist for the *Cleveland Call and Post*. He would later go on to earn a diploma from the Vienna Academy of Music in 1962. He also studied at Harvard University, the New School for Social Research, the Cleveland Institute of Music, New York College of Music, and the Mannes College of Music.

In 1951, at age twenty-two, Abdul relocated to New York City. There he began studying music and was a singer in a number of classical and operatic performances with such notables as WILLIAM WARFIELD and MARIAN ANDERSON. He sang at Vermont's Marlboro Music Festival in 1956 and the Vienna Music Festival in 1962. He made his Carnegie Hall debut in 1967, in a recital of German lieder, with John Wustman accompanying on piano. He later had operatic roles in the first American stage productions of Carl Orff's *Die Kluge* and sang the title role in Darius Milhaud's *Les malheurs d'Orphée*. He also appeared in seventeen performances of Mozart's *Così fan tutte* and twelve performances of Gian Carlo Menotti's *Amahl and the Night Visitors* at Cleveland's Karamu House. He appeared in other concerts on tours in the United States, Canada, Austria, Netherlands, Hungary, and Germany.

In 1958 he organized the Coffeehouse Concerts, Harlem's first subscription series of chamber music concerts. He remained director of the series until 1963. Abdul began his most notable working relationship in 1961 with the poet and writer Langston Hughes. Abdul worked as a literary assistant to Hughes and became a close friend to the writer. He was Hughes's assistant until Hughes's death in 1967.

In the 1960s Abdul began working as a writer, editor, and critic, employing his wide knowledge of the arts in books and periodicals. In 1970 he published his first book, *3,000 Years of Black Poetry*, co-edited with Alan Lomax. Over the next few years he edited *The Magic of Black Poetry* (1972) and authored the volumes, *Famous Black Entertainers of Today* (1974) and *Blacks in Classical Music: A Personal History* (1977). His articles appeared in *Anthology of the American Negro in the Theatre* (1967) and *The Negro in Music and Art* (1967). He also wrote the column "The Cultural Scene" for *Associated Negro Press* and was cultural editor for the *New York Age*. He gave lectures and master classes at universities across the United States and abroad.

Abdul was also a gay rights pioneer. His lectures on famous gays in the African American community at Riverside Church and elsewhere became legendary. He was active for more than five decades in organizations devoted to gay rights, including the Stonewall Mattachine Society and One Incorporated. He was honored for his activism with several awards, including a "Lift Every Voice" Legacy Award and the New York organization Black Pride's Griot Award. Abdul's life companion, Richard Mayer Haber, was an attorney, writer, and philanthropist, and became a master's candidate in anthropology at Columbia University at age seventy-one. Haber died in 2001.

Abdul began giving private voice lessons in his home in New York in the 1970s, with a teaching method based on the Austrian singing technique he learned while studying in Vienna. He was for a time the entertainment editor for the *New York Amsterdam News*.

BRENNA SANCHEZ

ABDUL-JABBAR, Kareem (16 Apr. 1947–), basketball player, was born Ferdinand Lewis Alcindor, the son of Ferdinand Lewis "Al" Alcindor, a police officer with the New York Transit Authority, and Cora Alcindor, a department-store price checker. The almost thirteen-pound baby arrived in Harlem one day after the major league debut of JACKIE ROBINSON in Brooklyn; as with Robinson, fiercely competitive athletics and the struggle against racial injustice would define much of his life.

From a young age, Alcindor was introspective and intense. He had an artistic sensibility, drawn in part from his father, a stern and silent cop who played jazz trombone and held a degree from Juilliard. An only child in a strictly Catholic household, he moved from Harlem at age three to the Dyckman Street projects on the northern tip of Manhattan, a racially mixed, middle-class community. In third grade he was startled to see a class photo that featured him not just towering over his classmates as expected, but standing out by the color of his skin. "Damn, I'm dark and everybody else is light!" Alcindor recalled thinking years later (Abdul-Jabbar, *Giant Steps*, 15). In fourth grade, his parents shipped him to an all-black boarding school outside Philadelphia, where he was taunted for his intellectual leanings. But in his one year at Holy Providence School, he developed street toughness and also launched his first hook shot, a weapon that would become his aesthetic and athletic trademark.

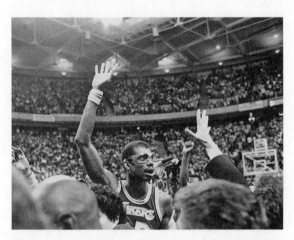

Kareem Abdul-Jabbar, after setting a new NBA regular season scoring record of 31,421 points, acknowledges cheering fans during a game against the Utah Jazz in Las Vegas, Nevada, 6 April 1984. (AP Images.)

Back in New York from fifth grade on, Alcindor began to grow into his coordination. By eighth grade, he was a sinewy six feet, eight inches; by tenth grade, he was a seven footer with astonishing agility. At Power Memorial, an all-boys Catholic school where his teams lost only one game in his final three years, Alcindor never fit neatly into the jock stereotype. He read widely, joined the debate team, and began to frequent New York's jazz clubs. On the court, though, the Renaissance man reigned. His game was at once graceful and ferocious. Coach Jack Donohue opened up the world for his sensitive star, bringing him to NBA games at Madison Square Garden. There the coach pointed with particular reverence to the inspired and unselfish play of the Celtics center BILL RUSSELL. Donohue's influence was not completely positive, however. At halftime of an unusually lethargic performance during Alcindor's junior year, the fiery coach tore into his prodigy, telling him he was acting "just like a nigger!" (*Sports Illustrated*, 27 Oct. 1969). The wound from that remark festered for many years.

That summer Alcindor's growing awareness of racism sharpened when he participated in the journalism workshop of the Harlem Youth Action Project. At one point he covered a press conference by MARTIN LUTHER KING JR., a moment commemorated in a photograph in *Jet* magazine. He also witnessed five days of rioting in Harlem after a white policeman shot a black teenager. "Right then and there I knew who I was and who I had to be," he said in a *Sports Illustrated* profile (31 Mar. 1980). "I was going to be black rage personified, black power in the flesh."

The summer of 1964 also proved defining in his association with WILT CHAMBERLAIN. Eleven years Alcindor's senior and established (along with his rival Russell) as the dominant big man in the NBA, Chamberlain took the high school kid under his considerable wing. He loaned Alcindor jazz albums, invited him to his apartment to play hearts, and ferried him in his Bentley up to Saratoga to watch Chamberlain's prize thoroughbreds run. At one point the two played a memorable game of H-O-R-S-E, a matchup of trademark hook shots by Alcindor and fadeaways by Chamberlain that would have been captured on film in a better world.

After another scintillating high school season, Alcindor enrolled at the University of California, Los Angeles (UCLA), winner of the last two national championships. Although NCAA rules then forbade freshmen to play varsity sports, Alcindor served immediate notice by scoring thirty-one points and leading the freshman team to an emphatic fifteen-point victory over the storied varsity. The next year, under the dignified tutelage of the coaching legend John Wooden, Alcindor launched a collegiate career for the ages. In his very first game he broke the school scoring record with fifty-six points. He earned three consecutive All-America honors, leading the Bruins to three straight national titles and a glittering record of 88–2. Having reached his full height of seven feet, two inches, Alcindor had become a complete player.

A menacing shot blocker, he intimidated on defense, and his devastating hook shot and ferocious inside moves were almost impossible to stop. So powerful was his impact on the game that the NCAA outlawed the dunk after his freshman year (though it was reinstated ten years later).

Never satisfied with a one-dimensional life, Alcindor broadened his horizons by studying martial arts with Bruce Lee, and by reading *The Autobiography of MALCOLM X*. Having dismissed what he considered to be the repressive Catholicism of his childhood, he developed a deep connection to Islam. After his junior year in the summer of 1968, he studied in a New York mosque and became a devout follower of Hamaas Abdul-Khaalis. That same summer, Alcindor decided to boycott the Olympic Games, refusing to play for a country that, he felt, denied fundamental rights and respect to black people. He publicly supported the "black power" salutes of sprinters TOMMIE SMITH and John Carlos on the medal podium in Mexico City, earning him a mound of hate mail when he returned to UCLA for his senior year.

In 1969, shortly before he graduated with a BA in History, Alcindor polished off his college basketball career with a 37-point, 20-rebound performance in UCLA's victory over Purdue in the NCAA championship game. He became the first pick in the NBA draft, selected by the Milwaukee Bucks, an expansion team that had managed a grim 27–55 record in its first season. For six years he toiled in Milwaukee, a period marked by brilliance on the court and tumult off it. Averaging 28.8 points per game, he won Rookie of the Year honors in 1969–1970 and sparked the Bucks to a dramatic turnaround with a 56–26 record. Perhaps never before or since has one person's impact on a professional team been so profound. The next year, teaming with the newly acquired OSCAR ROBERTSON, Alcindor led his team to an NBA championship. Though criticized by the media as an aloof giant, his impact on the game was undeniable. He averaged 31.7 points and 16 rebounds per game, and earned the first of six Most Valuable Player (MVP) awards, a figure unmatched in NBA annals.

His connections to Islam and Abdul-Khaalis became increasingly public. The religious mentor chose Alcindor's bride in 1971 (Habiba Brown) and the name Kareem Abdul-Jabbar (meaning "generous and powerful servant of Allah"), which became legal a few months later. In one off-season, the NBA's most dominating player studied Arabic at Harvard; another year he traveled to the Middle East. In 1972–1973 he was followed by NBA security guards after six of Abdul-Khaalis's relatives, including four of his children, were murdered by Black Muslim extremists. (A few years later Abdul-Khaalis was sentenced to forty years in jail for his involvement in a hostage-taking incident, during which a reporter was killed.)

On the court Abdul-Jabbar's excellence was undiminished (MVP awards again in 1972 and 1974), but off-court strains were evident. He separated from his wife shortly after the birth of his first daughter in 1973, though they later had two more children. (He subsequently had two additional children with other women.) Abdul-Jabbar had a falling out with Chamberlain over the latter's claim in an autobiography that black women were sexually inferior and his public support of President Richard Nixon. Then in the 1974–1975 season, Abdul-Jabbar got poked in the eye and responded by slamming his fist into a backboard support, breaking two bones in his hand, and taking him away from the game, his oasis. At year's end, the Bucks accommodated his demands for a trade, shipping him to the Los Angeles Lakers in return for four players.

Abdul-Jabbar's first years back in California were marked by more of the same: overpowering play (MVP awards in 1976 and 1977) coupled with a brooding court mien that earned him few friends. In the first game of the 1977–1978 season, he was widely criticized for responding to an elbow by Milwaukee's Kent Benson with a devastating punch that sidelined Benson with a concussion and Abdul-Jabbar with another fractured hand. Increasingly, the game's best player was regarded as an outcast. "No man is an island," opined the legendary *Los Angeles Times* columnist Jim Murray, "but Kareem gave it a shot."

In time, though, Abdul-Jabbar found his way back to shore, an American life that had a decided second act. In 1979–1980 the Lakers added the rookie point guard MAGIC JOHNSON, whose on-court exuberance was contagious. That year, with Abdul-Jabbar again earning MVP honors, the Lakers captured the NBA title. The Lakers became the dominant team of the 1980s, winning five titles with a stylish, fast-breaking brand of basketball known as "Showtime." In various ways Abdul-Jabbar seemed to soften. He displayed a deft comic touch in the 1980 movie *Airplane*, which opened up film and television roles for him in coming years. In 1983 he was visibly moved when fans around the country sent him jazz records after his treasured collection was destroyed in a house fire. Later that year he published *Giant Steps*, an unusually candid and cathartic autobiography. On the court he seemed almost impervious to age. In 1983–1984 he became the league's all-time leading scorer, eclipsing Chamberlain's record, appropriately enough, with his trademark shot, now widely known as a skyhook—"the most beautiful thing in sports," according to Bill Russell (*Time*, 20 Feb. 1989). Abdul-Jabbar seemed downright exuberant in 1984–1985 as the Lakers defeated the Celtics in the NBA Finals. Even pushing forty, bald and begoggled, he remained a force, helping the Lakers become the first repeat champions of the NBA in nineteen years in 1987 and 1988. So durable was he that when he played in his nineteenth and final All-Star game in 1989, he was older than seven of the twenty players in the accompanying NBA Legends Classic. When he finally retired a few months later, he had played more games, scored more points, and blocked more shots than anyone in league history. "In my opinion," the regal John Wooden said, "he is the most valuable player in the history of the game."

In his retirement, Abdul-Jabbar took to writing, including a highly reflective account of his final season, *Kareem*, and a history book, *Black Profiles in Courage* (1996), written with Alan Steinberg. He started a jazz label and remained involved in television and motion pictures. He initially professed a desire to stay away from basketball, but in a variety of broadcasting and coaching roles, including one year as an assistant coach for a high school team on an Apache Indian reservation and a return to the Lakers as an assistant coach in 2005, he began another long, graceful arc to the hoop.

Further Reading

Abdul-Jabbar, Kareem, with Peter Knobler. *Giant Steps* (1983).
Abdul-Jabbar, Kareem, with Mignon McCarthy. *Kareem* (1990).
Abdul-Jabbar, Kareem, with Stephen Singular. *A Season on the Reservation* (2000).
Smith, Gary. "Now, More Than Ever, a Winner," *Sports Illustrated* (23 Dec. 1985).

MARTY DOBROW

ABELE, Julian Francis (21 Apr. 1881–18 Apr. 1950), architect, was born in Philadelphia, Pennsylvania, the eighth of eleven children of Charles Sylvester Abele and Mary Jones, a washerwoman and milliner. Charles Able changed the spelling, although not the pronunciation, of his surname to Abele after mustering out of the Union army following the end of the Civil War. Charles, who worked as a carpenter and laborer at the U.S. Treasury Customs House, a sought-after patronage job, and as a porter, died when Julian was twelve. Mary Jones Able was a descendant of AB-SALOM JONES, the first African American Protestant Episcopal priest. Julian and his siblings were fourth generation Philadelphians and were expected by their parents to achieve recognition, marry well, and assume their rightful place in Olde Philadelphia society. Julian's oldest brother, Robert, was one of the first African American graduates of Hahnemann Medical College and a cofounder in 1907 of Mercy Hospital, the only Philadelphia hospital which would accept African Americans. Julian's oldest sister, Elizabeth, was a calligrapher and his sister Mary taught in a private school prior to marrying. His brothers Charles Jr. and Joseph worked as a sign maker and electrical engineer, respectively. His brother Ernest was considered a ne'er-do-well inventor, and Frederick, according to his grand niece, was "a little off the bean." Another brother, Harry, died as an infant, while two other brothers, Harry II and Thomas, died in their twenties. Julian was raised in a home where the fine arts were appreciated and family members knew the difference between a finale and a finial. Although Charles Jr. was the wealthiest family member, Robert inherited leadership of the family after his father's death. He paid Julian's tuition so his younger brother could pursue his dream to become an architect.

Abele followed his sisters and brothers to the Institute for Colored Youth (ICY), a private, preparatory school founded and supported by Philadelphia Quakers. ICY's principal, Fanny Coppin, whose educational innovations included fostering close relationships between faculty and students, mentored Julian personally, encouraging his ambition to become an architect and counseling him to enroll in the recently organized Pennsylvania Museum School of Industrial Art (PMSIA) after his 1897 graduation from ICY. During a period when the Franklin Institute and the School of Design for Women, both in Philadelphia, refused to enroll African Americans, Abele was admitted to the PMSIA without objection, and in 1898 he became one of the school's first recipients of a certificate in architectural design. Abele continued his architectural training at the University of Pennsylvania School of Architecture, where he won the respect of his peers and several awards for design and rendering and was also elected president of the Architectural Society. In 1902 he graduated with a BS in Architecture, becoming the school's first African American graduate and the second African American to earn a degree in Architecture, following ROBERT ROBINSON TAYLOR, an 1898 graduate of the Massachusetts Institute of Technology.

Abele's training included a continuing relationship with Philadelphia's T-Square Club, a professional organization founded in 1883 by thirteen Philadelphia architects. Admitted while a student at the University of Pennsylvania, Abele was the club's only African American member. In 1901, while a fourth-year student at the University of Pennsylvania, he had been awarded the T-Square Club Prize for superior performance. Thereafter Abele consistently earned first-place mentions, beating out more experienced architects in the club's annual competitions, which were held until 1925. Abele also showed his work at the architecture clubs of Pittsburgh and Toronto and at the Architectural League of New York.

While still a student, Abele was listed as an architect in the Philadelphia city directory, and until 1903 he worked evenings for the noted Philadelphia architect Louis C. Hickman. Soon after graduation, Abele went to Spokane, Washington, to design a house for his sister, Elizabeth Abele Cook, and her husband, John F. Cook. Already one of the most formally educated architects in the Commonwealth of Pennsylvania, he took the evening architectural design course offered by the Philadelphia Academy of Fine Arts, receiving a certificate in May 1903. Abele spent the next few years in Europe. And while he was not, as has been claimed, a graduate of L'Ecole des Beaux-Arts in Paris, he did travel throughout France and Italy, later exhibiting sketches completed during his European sojourn. On his application for membership in the American Institute of Architects, Abele listed travel to England, France, Germany, Switzerland, Italy, and Spain.

Abele's ribbon-winning, pen-and-ink sketches revealed a talented draftsman who "could delineate shadows with a grease pencil in so subtle a way that the observer got the impression of far more detail than Abele had actually drawn" (Maher, 372). Deeply fearful that an injury to his right hand would destroy his livelihood, Abele taught himself to draw with his left hand. Abele was also a landscape painter.

In 1906 Horace Trumbauer, known for the design of elegant mansions, hired Abele as a junior architect, making Abele the first African American architect employed by a white-owned firm. When he was promoted to senior designer two years later, Abele became responsible for siting buildings, collaborating with Trumbauer in choosing architectural styles, and creating the "look" for all commissioned buildings. Abele remained with Trumbauer until 1950, contributing to the design of more than two hundred buildings, twenty-one of which are listed on the National Register of Historic Places. After Trumbauer's death in 1938, Abele became head of the firm and, for the first time, was able to sign his own name to his designs.

A lifelong Francophile, Abele was a smart dresser and a sports and symphony fan. He shunned the spotlight, preferring, either by temperament or necessity, to remain in the background. On 6 June 1925 Abele married the Parisian Marguerite Bulle, a graduate of the Paris Conservatoire of Music. After nine years of marriage and three children, Marguerite ran off with a Polish émigré singer.

Under Trumbauer, Abele designed lavish homes, including Whitemarsh Hall (1916), a 150-room limestone home for Edward Stotesbury, a banker and Philadelphia's wealthiest citizen; Shadow Lawn (1927), a West Long Beach, New Jersey, mansion for Hubert Parson, the president of F. W. Woolworth & Company; and Marly (1931) in Washington, D.C., for the Dodge Brothers Motor Company heiress Delphine Dodge Baker. Abele designed the New York mansion of James Buchanan Duke, president of both the American Tobacco Company and the Southern Power Company, a building that is now New York University's Graduate Institute of Fine Arts. The Trumbauer firm's largest and most important work was commissioned by Duke for Duke University; Abele designed eleven Georgian-style buildings on the east campus and thirty-eight Gothic-style buildings on the west campus. While this represented more buildings than Henry Ives Cobb designed for the University of Chicago, Ralph Adams Cram designed for Princeton University, or Robert Robinson Taylor designed for Tuskegee Institute, there is no evidence that Abele ever set foot on Duke University's campus.

Abele contributed to the design of the Philadelphia Museum of Art, and after Trumbauer's death, he played a key role in the completion of the building. Typically, until recently, histories of Widener Library at Harvard University, which was designed by the firm of Horace Trumbauer, made no mention of Abele, one of the building's chief architects.

Julian Abele died on 18 April 1950 after suffering his second heart attack. He was buried in Eden Cemetery in Collingdale, a suburb of Philadelphia, near the mausoleums for Charles Eishenlohr, Peter Widener, and Thomas Develon Jr. that Abele had designed. The Corinthian-colonnaded Free Library of Philadelphia, which Abele designed in 1917, can be seen from his gravesite.

Further Reading
Adams, Michael. "A Legacy of Shadows," *Progressive Architecture* (Feb. 1991): 85.
Bond, Max. "Still Here: Three Architects of Afro-America—Julian Francis Abele, Hilyard Robinson and Paul R. Williams," *Harvard Design Magazine* (Summer 1997).
Maher, James. *Twilight of Splendor* (1975).
Tatman, Sandra L., and Roger W. Moss, eds. *Biographical Dictionary of Philadelphia Architects: 1700–1930* (1985).
Wilson, Dreck Spurlock, ed. *African American Architects: A Biographical Dictionary 1865–1945* (2003).
DRECK SPURLOCK WILSON

ABERNATHY, Juanita Jones (24 Dec. 1929–), civil rights activist, educator, and businesswoman, was born Juanita Odessa Jones in Uniontown, Alabama, the youngest of eight children of Ella Gilmore Jones and Alex Jones Sr., an influential and prosperous black farmer in Perry County, Alabama. When Alabama telephone and electric companies refused to provide service to the Jones homestead, Alex Jones Sr. and his brothers installed their own telephone lines and wired their own homes for electricity. One consequence of the family's financial independence was that Juanita was able to attend boarding school from age five until she graduated from high school in Selma, Alabama, where she had older sisters in attendance at the historically black Selma University. After high school, in 1947 Jones enrolled in Tennessee State University in Nashville, Tennessee, where she majored in business education with a minor in history and social studies. She returned to Alabama after earning a BS in 1951 and taught high school business courses in Beatrice, Alabama, where she also became secretary for the local chapter of the NAACP.

As secretary for the NAACP, Jones participated in voter registration efforts in Monroe County, Alabama, but after two years she gave up her teaching position in Beatrice. In 1954 she began teaching business courses at Tuskegee Institute High School in Tuskegee, Alabama. With a social consciousness already developed by her family's civic and community service, however, she continued to resist both the overt and subtle forms of racism that characterized the Jim Crow South during the 1950s and 1960s. From individual acts of resistance such as refusing to purchase groceries after being denied the same carry-out service as white patrons to later participation in virtually every major movement throughout the civil rights struggle, Jones continued to act on the belief, inculcated by her family, that she had a moral obligation to speak out against and challenge injustice.

Her work against racial discrimination and social injustice intensified after 1952, the year she married RALPH ABERNATHY, whom she had met when she was in the ninth grade. Four children—Juandalynn, Donzaleigh, Ralph David III, and Kwame Luthuli—were born to the marriage that lasted until Ralph Abernathy's death in 1990. As the wife of the minister who became one of the organizers of the Montgomery movement, top aide and confidant to MARTIN LUTHER KING JR., and successor to the presidency of both the Montgomery Improvement Association (MIA) and the Southern Christian Leadership Conference (SCLC), Juanita Jones Abernathy played important but often behind-the-scenes roles in the major movements organized by the SCLC after 1955. During the Montgomery bus boycott (1955–1956) she helped to organize and implement one of the first citizenship schools, conducting literacy classes before mass meetings. In 1956, like ROSA PARKS and SEPTIMA P. CLARK, she attended workshops at the Highlander Folk School in Monteagle, Tennessee.

In the early morning hours of 10 January 1957, while her husband was in Atlanta for the first meeting of the SCLC, the Abernathy home in Montgomery was bombed while she and her infant daughter Juandalynn were asleep. Fifteen minutes later she learned that her husband's church, First Baptist, had also been bombed. Before sunrise there were five bombings altogether in Montgomery, including the home of Robert Graetz, the white pastor of a black Lutheran congregation in the city. While police came to the Abernathy home after the bombing, they never entered the house and made no attempt to gather evidence.

As part of her continued civil rights activism, Abernathy faced violence again in the summer of 1966. As part of the Chicago Open Housing Movement, Abernathy and her husband, like Martin Luther King Jr. and CORETTA SCOTT KING, lived in an inner-city apartment building in the Lawndale section of that city. Both families not only lived in substandard housing to draw attention to the housing plight of blacks in that city, but also faced the violence of stone-throwing hecklers directed toward those who took part in peaceful demonstrations in Cicero, a predominantly white suburb of Chicago fiercely opposed to open housing legislation.

The Abernathy family moved to Atlanta in 1961. When Juanita Jones Abernathy was not participating in major national movements like Chicago in 1966, Memphis in 1967, and Charleston in 1968, she focused her energies on school desegregation, economic boycotts, and the integration of cultural organizations like the Atlanta Council for Visitors and events like the annual production of the Metropolitan Opera in Atlanta, which blacks were not allowed to attend. Over the next many years, using her business education background and acumen, she achieved a top sales position and an administrative position in Mary Kay Cosmetics and served as board member for a number of civic, educational, and business organizations.

A member of the founding board of directors for the Friends School of Atlanta, Abernathy went on to serve on the board of trustees for the Morehouse School of Religion, as secretary for the Metro Atlanta Rapid Transportation Authority (MARTA), as board member for the Fulton County Development Authority, the Atlanta Fulton County League of Women Voters League, and the Ralph David Abernathy Tower. As the widow of Ralph David Abernathy and CEO of the Ralph David Abernathy Foundation, she participated frequently in symposia and colloquia focused on issues of social justice, peace and human rights. In 2000, with DOROTHY HEIGHT and the civil rights attorney FRED D. GRAY, she served as panelist for a John F. Kennedy Jr. forum on the Montgomery bus boycott at Harvard University. Traveling nationally and internationally as a motivational speaker, she has addressed topics on religion, service, leadership, education, and the southern civil rights movement.

Further Reading
Abernathy, Donzaleigh. *Partners to History: Martin Luther King, Jr., Ralph David Abernathy, and the Civil Rights Movement* (2003).
Branch, Taylor. *At Canaan's Edge: America in the King Years, 1965–1968* (2006).
Hampton, Henry, and Steve Fayer. *Voices of Freedom: An Oral History of the Civil Rights Movement from the 1950s through the 1980s* (1990).
ALMA JEAN BILLINGSLEA BROWN

ABERNATHY, Ralph (11 Mar. 1926–17 Apr. 1990), clergyman and civil rights leader, was born David Abernathy near Linden, Alabama, the tenth of twelve children of farm owners Will L. Abernathy and Louivery Bell Abernathy. Abernathy spent his formative years on his family's five-hundred-acre farm in rural Marengo County in southwestern Alabama. His father's economic self-sufficiency and industry spared the family from most of the hardships of the Great Depression. "We didn't know that people were lining up at soup kitchens in cities all over the country," he would recall in his autobiography, *And the Walls Came Tumbling Down* (Abernathy, 6). Along with other family members, he attended Hopewell Baptist Church, where his father served as a deacon, and decided early to become a preacher, a commitment strengthened by a conversion experience at the age of seven. Abernathy attended high school at all-black Linden Academy, a Baptist-affiliated institution. Having little exposure to whites during his childhood, he remembered being "relatively unaware of racism or segregation" (Abernathy, 28).

In 1944 Abernathy was drafted into the armed services and enlisted as Ralph David Abernathy, a name given to him by his sister Manerva that he would use publicly for the rest of his life. Promoted to the rank of sergeant in the army, Abernathy served with his unit in France during the closing months of World War II, and he did not see combat before Germany's surrender. A bout of rheumatic fever prevented him from accompanying his unit to the Pacific theater, where, he later heard, nearly all of his comrades were killed in a battle on a Japanese-held island.

Returning to Alabama, Abernathy enrolled at Alabama State College in Montgomery. Elected president of the student council during his sophomore

Ralph Abernathy at National Press Club luncheon, 14 June 1968. (Library of Congress/U.S. News and World Report Collection/Warren K. Leffler, photographer.)

year, he led a strike against poor food in the student dining hall and the following year led another protest against substandard student housing. In 1948 Abernathy also chose the occasion of Mother's Day following his mother's death (his father had died several years earlier) to announce before the Hopewell congregation his call to the ministry. Soon afterward, he was ordained. He graduated from Alabama State College in 1950 with a BS in Mathematics. After serving briefly as a radio disc jockey during the summer of 1950, he spent a year in graduate studies in sociology at Atlanta University.

While in Atlanta, Abernathy attended a service at Ebenezer Baptist Church, where he heard a sermon by MARTIN LUTHER KING JR., who was finishing his summer duties as his father's assistant before returning to his studies at Pennsylvania's Crozer Theological Seminar. "I stopped to shake his hand and comment on his sermon," Abernathy later wrote. "At that meeting we both recognized in one another a kindred spirit" (Abernathy, 89).

Abernathy returned to Montgomery to become dean of men at Alabama State, while also serving as minister of a small congregation at Eastern Star Baptist Church in Demopolis. Soon afterward, however, he accepted a call from Montgomery's hundred-year-old First Baptist Church. In 1952 Abernathy married Juanita Odessa Jones (JUANITA ABERNATHY) of Uniontown, Alabama, a teacher at the Monroe County Training School in Beatrice, Alabama. The following year, the first of the couple's four children was born.

In 1954 King moved to Montgomery to assume the pastorate of Dexter Avenue Baptist Church, and the Abernathys quickly formed ties with King and his wife, CORETTA SCOTT KING: "Because of Jim Crow we could only have dinner at home. So the four of us had dinner every night, with Coretta preparing the meal one evening, Juanita the next. And usually conversations among the four of us would last way beyond midnight" (Abernathy, 129). According to Abernathy, the two preachers and their wives discussed plans to turn Montgomery "into a model of social justice and racial amity," but they did not begin to implement these plans until ROSA PARKS was arrested on 1 December 1955 for refusing a bus driver's order to give up her bus seat to a white man (Abernathy, 129). The next day, E. D. NIXON, a local NAACP leader and a Pullman car porter, called Abernathy to seek his help in rallying support for a bus boycott initiated by JO ANN ROBINSON of the Women's Political Council in Montgomery. Abernathy took the lead in mobilizing the city's black clergy and other local residents.

After the boycott got off to a successful start on 5 December, Abernathy became program chairman of the newly organized Montgomery Improvement Association (MIA)—a name he later took credit for suggesting—and King was elected the MIA's president. As the boycott continued during the following year, Abernathy became a key figure in the movement. He often spoke at mass meetings, sometimes giving fulsome introductions of King, who would later describe Abernathy as "my closest associate and most trusted friend" (King, *Autobiography* [1998], 64). Abernathy was one of more than one hundred boycott leaders arrested in February 1956 for violating Alabama's antiboycott statute. The willingness of the indicted leaders to go to Montgomery's jail to be arrested demonstrated their resolve and proved to be a turning point in the boycott. After King's conviction in March was appealed, the trials of Abernathy and the other defendants were postponed by a continuance. In November the U.S. Supreme Court ruled that bus segregation in Montgomery was illegal, and in the following month Abernathy joined King in riding the city's first desegregated bus.

In January 1957 Abernathy was among a group of black ministers who gathered in Atlanta to organize a regional group to sustain and expand the bus protests that had occurred in Montgomery and other southern cities. Although he was called away from the meeting owing to the bombing of the First Baptist Church and his parsonage, he returned to form an organization that eventually became the Southern Christian Leadership Conference (SCLC). King became president and Abernathy secretary-treasurer of the new group.

Abernathy accompanied King to most of the subsequent major events of the southern civil rights struggle, joining him in jail during the key campaigns in Albany, Georgia, in 1961 and 1962 and Birmingham, Alabama, in 1963. A year after King moved from Montgomery to Atlanta in order to be closer to SCLC's headquarters in that city, Abernathy followed him and, at King's urging, became pastor of Atlanta's West Hunter Street Baptist Church in August 1961. Abernathy shared King's firm commitment to nonviolence and traveled with him to Oslo, Norway, in 1964 to attend King's Nobel Peace Prize acceptance ceremony. In 1965 Abernathy was named at King's request to the new position of vice president at large of SCLC, clarifying his status as King's successor.

Abernathy continued to work closely with King during the Poor People's Campaign of 1968 and was at the Loraine Motel in Memphis when an assassin killed King on 4 April. Abernathy was the first person at King's side. He knelt down and tried to comfort the dying King while cradling his head: "Martin. It's all right. Don't worry. This is Ralph. This is Ralph."

After the assassination, Abernathy assumed the presidency of SCLC and continued the Poor People's Campaign. He later admitted, however, that he lacked many of King's attributes: "I didn't have as many degrees as he did and I didn't have his polish. In addition, my skin was darker, a more important factor in dealing with the white press than anyone would dare admit" (Abernathy, 499). The Resurrection City encampment of antipoverty protesters in Washington, D.C., could be sustained only until July 1968, when Abernathy and the remaining protesters were arrested. He served twenty days in jail. After this setback, Abernathy continued as SCLC's president, but the group's effectiveness declined as many of King's former associates departed. In 1977 Abernathy left SCLC to make an unsuccessful run to represent an Atlanta district in the U.S. House of Representatives.

Abernathy's post-SCLC years were marked by continued outspokenness on civil rights issues and some controversy. In the 1980s, he broke ranks with most black leaders to support Ronald Reagan's presidential candidacy. "Reagan promised me that he would make a jobs program a top priority for his administration," he later explained. When Abernathy's autobiography was published in 1989, he again sparked controversy by confirming reports of King's "weakness for women" (Abernathy, 470). Abernathy denied rumors that King had interracial affairs, saying: "He was never attracted to white women and had nothing to do with them, despite the opportunities that may have presented themselves" (Abernathy, 472). But he suggested that on the night of King's assassination, King may have been involved in a sexual assignation and argued with another lover. Members of King's family and some of his former SCLC associates publicly rebuked Abernathy, who defended himself by insisting that King's dalliances had already been revealed. The year following the publication of his autobiography, Abernathy died at the age of sixty-four.

Further Reading
Some of Ralph Abernathy's papers are included in the Southern Christian Leadership Conference collection, Library and Archives of the Martin Luther King Jr. Center for Nonviolent Social Change, Atlanta, Georgia. Portions are available on microfilm.
Abernathy, Ralph David. *And the Walls Came Tumbling Down* (1989).
Branch, Taylor. *Parting the Waters: America in the King Years, 1954–63* (1988).
Branch, Taylor. *Pillar of Fire: America in the King Years, 1963–65* (1998).
Garrow, David J. *Bearing the Cross: Martin Luther King, Jr., and the Southern Christian Leadership Conference, 1955–1968* (1986).
Obituary: *New York Times*, 18 Apr. 1990.

CLAYBORNE CARSON

ABRAHAM (fl. 1826–1845), also known as "Prophet," was a runaway slave who became a prominent leader among the Seminole. Nothing is known about his parents or childhood. Fleeing his master, Abraham escaped south into Florida, and was eventually adopted into the Seminole tribe, with whom he enjoyed considerable status. In 1826 he accompanied a tribal delegation to Washington, D.C., and became an influential counselor to Micanopy, a leading Seminole leader. The Seminole, or Florida Indians, once were a part both of the Muskogee (Creek) nation that had been driven out of Georgia by the early English colonists, and also of the Oconee and Yamasee tribes that had been driven out of the Carolinas following the Yamasee uprising of 1715. They had first settled among the Lower Creeks in the Florida Panhandle and created a haven for runaway slaves. Indeed, *Semino'le* is the Creek word for "runaway."

In 1818 Andrew Jackson led a command of American troops into Spanish Florida partly in an attempt to capture and return the runaway slaves to their masters. After the Florida purchase of 1819, southerners increased their demands for the return of their slaves, which the Seminole refused to do. Nonetheless, fugitive-slave hunters constantly raided Seminole villages and clashed with Indian and black warriors. Federal officials attempted to force the Seminole to surrender the fugitives by withholding rations and annuities, but the Seminole insisted that the blacks were their private property or had been welcomed into the tribe as full members.

Two years after the passage of the Indian Removal Act of 1830, Abraham served as an interpreter during the negotiations between the Seminole and James Gadsden for the Treaty of Payne's Landing. The treaty called for the removal of the tribe to Indian Territory but not before an exploration party was sent west to examine the region. Abraham served as the party's interpreter. After touring Indian Territory the party signed another treaty at Fort Gibson, agreeing to removal. Returning to their homeland, however, the party reported that while the land was suitable, the location was unacceptably close to the Plains Indians; the tribe rejected the treaty. The

Negro Abraham.

Abraham, a runaway slave who became a prominent counselor and interpreter among the Seminole in the early nineteenth century. (Library of Congress/Hughes & Meltzer.)

federal government then dispatched troops to enforce removal. Abraham became a leader of the runaway slaves fighting alongside the Seminole. On 3 February 1837, Abraham was induced to surrender and appeared at the camp of General Thomas S. Jesup carrying a piece of white cloth attached to a stick. Abraham entered Jesup's camp and, maintaining his dignity, walked to the general's tent, where he stuck the staff into the ground and waited for Jesup to appear.

According to the *Army and Navy Chronicle*, Abraham was "a cunning negro, of good consideration with the Seminoles." Although Abraham thought that he would be hanged for his part in the Seminole rebellion, federal officials realized that he could "do more than any other" to persuade those still fighting to surrender, and they used him as a peace mediator. On 6 March 1837 he served as the chief interpreter at a meeting held at Camp Dade at which the remaining leaders of the revolt, Jumper and Holahtochee, agreed to stop fighting and to report to Tampa Bay, Florida, for removal. Abraham continued to serve the government and in March 1838 was instrumental in convincing Alligator, one of the last warriors, to surrender. With Seminole resistance quelled, Abraham joined the other tribal members on their journey westward. On 25 February 1839 he, along with 195 other warriors, women, children, and former slaves, boarded the steamboat *Buckeye* for the trip to Indian

Territory, where he continued to serve as an interpreter in negotiations between Seminole and U.S. officials.

As with his early life, little is known of Abraham's later life or his place of death. The Seminole were among the more isolated of the southeastern Indians, and they maintained less contact with non-Indians than did other tribes; therefore, Abraham's ability to serve as a translator between the Americans and the Seminole made him a valuable addition to the tribe.

Further Reading
Army and Navy Chronicle 4.
Foreman, Grant. *Indian Removal: The Emigration of the Five Civilized Tribes of Indians* (1932).
Mahon, John K. *History of the Second Seminole War, 1835–1842* (1967).
McKenney, Thomas L. *Memoirs with Sketches of Travels* (1846).
Porter, Kenneth W. "The Negro Abraham," *Florida Historical Quarterly* 25 (1946): 1–43.

KENNY A. FRANKS

ABRAMS, Muhal Richard (19 Sept. 1930–), pianist and composer, was born in Chicago. He began studying piano at age seventeen and is largely self-taught, though in the late 1940s he studied briefly at Chicago Musical College and at Governors State University in Chicago. Abrams played his first professional gig in 1948, and during the early 1950s he wrote arrangements for the saxophonist King Fleming and other rhythm and blues groups. From 1957 to 1959 he was pianist, composer, and arranger for the hard-bop group MJT+3. Throughout the 1950s he also accompanied visiting soloists like MILES DAVIS, SONNY ROLLINS, Johnny Griffin, DEXTER KEITH GORDON, and MAX ROACH.

In the early 1960s Abrams and a group of young Chicagoans that included saxophonist EDDIE HARRIS and bassist Donald Garrett began to make plans for a rehearsal band. This initial attempt failed, but Abrams and Garrett revived the effort in 1961 and brought in the drummer Steve McCall and a cohort of adventurous players from Wilson Junior College—drummer Jack DeJohnette, saxophonists Roscoe Mitchell, Joseph Jarman, and Henry Threadgill, and bassist Malachi Favors. At first the music was quintessential hard bop; Abrams and Garrett had come from DuSable High School and cut their musical teeth playing with mainstream bop players like Harris and the saxophonist Johnny Griffin. But by 1963 they began to explore freer styles and, led by Abrams, established Experimental Band. There are no recordings of this music; descriptions from the time suggest abrupt rhythmic and dynamic shifts and unusual instrumental combinations. Abrams emphasized group improvisation within written arrangements that privileged rhythm and melody over European-rooted harmony. An example of how this group might have sounded can be found in Joseph Jarman's "Song for Christopher" on *As If It Were the Seasons* (Delmark, 1968), as described by Alyn Shipton: "Delicate flue and bell sounds are superseded by the vast energetic ensemble of the entire group, but from which detailed moments, featuring the flute, trombone, and other individual soloists consistently emerge" (810).

Abrams also exerted a profound influence over the lives and careers of his fellow musicians by encouraging them to broaden their education and to explore the other arts, with the goal of heightening their self-awareness and self-respect. He also encouraged band members to develop their own styles in sessions at clubs like the Wonder Inn and Fifth Jack's and in private homes. In 1965 Abrams, along with Philip Cohran, Jodie Christian, and McCall, formed the Association for the Advancement of Creative Musicians (AACM), a cooperative group that offered training and education for young, inner-city musicians and sought to "set an example of high moral standards" and "uphold the tradition of elevated, cultured musicians handed down from the past." Central to this tradition was "the right of the individual to express the individual's unique and personal approach to the music" (Mandel, 37). To help achieve these goals, Abrams established the AACM School of Music at the Abraham Lincoln Center in Chicago. The AACM produced concerts and performances at bars and clubs and created a close-knit fraternity of more than fifty musicians.

Abrams began his own recording career at the relatively advanced age of thirty-seven, releasing *Level and Degree of Light* for Delmark Records, followed two years later by *Young at Heart, Wise in Time*. Both albums focus on structured ensembles with pieces that range from blues to hard bop and to free playing, rooted in the AACM's essential philosophy. Abrams moved to New York City in 1976, and from the mid-1970s to the mid-1990s he recorded a series of albums for the Italian Black Saint label, along with two 1978 efforts for Novus Records (*Lifea Blinec* and *Spiral Live at Montreux*). The Black Saint recordings comprise his most important musical statements. They include duets like 1990's *Duets and Solos* as well as medium-size groups from sextets to nonets. Each of these albums also contains pieces by smaller ensembles drawn from the larger group, and all contain expressive and often unexpected music that swings.

Most impressive, though, are Abrams's compositions for big bands. Two albums in particular reveal this music in all its brilliance. *The Hearinga Suite* (1989) contains horn arrangements, cello playing by Diedre Murray, and a trumpet solo reminiscent of LOUIS ARMSTRONG. *Blu Blu Blu* (1990) is a joyful, stomping tribute to the pre-swing era bands of FLETCHER HENDERSON, DON REDMAN, and Benny Carter. The title cut has a wonderful bluesy swagger, while "One for the Whistler" evokes a DUKE ELLINGTON-like melancholy. All of these recordings feature the constantly shifting structures of sound, with improvisations rising from the ensemble and falling back in again, that are hallmarks of Abrams's writing. These recordings feature many veterans of the Chicago scene and longtime associates of Abrams, such as Threadgill, Mitchell, and the trombonist

GEORGE LEWIS. But they also highlight Abrams's role as a mentor to a wide range of younger musicians, such as saxophonists John Purcell, Patience Higgins, and Marty Ehrlich; trumpeters Eddie Allen and Baikida Carroll; and pianist Amina Claudine Myers. Between his work on these recordings and his efforts with the AACM, Abrams was a formative influence on dozens of the most creative artists in twentieth-century music, a role that has been widely recognized. In 1996 the Library of Congress chose his orchestra to open its concert season, and in 1990 Abrams was the first recipient of the prestigious Jazzpar Prize, awarded by the Danish government.

Abrams's compositions for classical orchestras and chamber groups represent an unjustifiably overlooked part of his career. These pieces have been performed by the Brooklyn Philharmonic Chamber Orchestra, the Kronos String Quartet, and the famed classical pianists Ursula Oppens and Frederic Rzewski. In 1991 the Friends of the Chicago Public Library and the Center for Black Music Research commissioned *What a Man*, in honor of the late Chicago mayor HAROLD WASHINGTON.

Abrams influenced the direction of jazz musically and institutionally. In addition to his seminal work in Chicago, he served as president of the New York chapter of the AACM, as a panelist for the National Endowment for the Arts and for the New York State Council on the Arts, and as a member of the board of directors of the National Jazz Service Organization and Meet the Composer. He taught at Columbia and Syracuse universities and served as a mentor for scores of important contemporary American musicians. His work for a wide variety of jazz ensembles is unsurpassed in its creative vision, and he refused to allow himself to be categorized, regarding himself not as a jazz or classical musician but simply as a musician. Abrams himself best summed up his musical philosophy: "Music has to touch you in some way . . . and that thing that touches you is the thing that a performer went down into him or herself to get" (Mandel, 36).

Further Reading
Giddins, Gary. *Visions of Jazz: The First Century* (1998).
Jung, Fred. "A Fireside Chat with Muhal Richard Abrams," *Jazz Weekly*, available online at http:\\www.jazzweekly.com.
Litweiler, John. *The Freedom Principle: Jazz after 1958* (1984).
Mandel, Howard. *Future Jazz* (1999).
Radano, Ronald M. *New Musical Figurations: Anthony Braxton's Cultural Critique* (1993).
Shipton, Alyn. *A New History of Jazz* (2001).

RONALD DUFOUR

ABRON, Lilia Ann (8 Mar. 1945–), chemical engineer and environmental engineering entrepreneur, was born in Memphis, Tennessee, the second of four daughters of Ernest Buford Abron and Bernice Wise Abron, both educators. Abron was educated in Memphis public schools and was a member of the National Honor Society. Abron divorced and had three sons, Frederick, Ernest, and David; she is occasionally credited as Lilia Ann Abron-Robinson.

Abron stayed close to home when she attended LeMoyne College, a historically black college in Memphis, Tennessee. She considered medical school, but she was persuaded by her advisor, Dr. Beuler, to pursue a career in engineering instead. Her decision was a risky one. She did not know of any African Americans with engineering degrees who were actually working as engineers; instead, she once said in an interview, they were often working in post offices. In 1966 Abron received her BS in Chemistry from LeMoyne College.

Abron pursued her graduate education at Washington University in St. Louis, Missouri. At Washington University Abron faced a different environment than the nurturing one she had known at LeMoyne. She was away from home for the first time, and although she had outstanding professors, the general atmosphere was very different. Abron had to adjust to larger class sizes, less personal attention, and classmates who were predominately white men. During this time, Abron began a consulting firm as a side business. After just thirteen months, in 1968, she received her MS in Sanitary Engineering, a degree that allowed her to eventually become an environmental engineer.

When she could not find a job after she completed her master's degree, Abron pursued doctoral studies at the University of Iowa. Minorities were being actively recruited by the university, and efforts were made to help her feel at ease. Cecil Lue-Hing served as her advisor and mentor. Abron was not only the first African American woman to earn a PhD in Chemical Engineering in 1971, but also the third woman to earn a doctorate in that department at the University of Iowa. After completing her doctorate, Abron worked as a professor at Tennessee State University, Vanderbilt University, Washington State University, and Howard University.

In 1978 Abron founded PEER Consultants, PC, an environmental and sanitary engineering consulting firm. PEER was awarded contracts from the Superfund program, the Boston Harbor cleanup, the Department of Defense for environmental policy work, and the Department of Energy through its Hazardous Waste Remedial Actions Program. *Engineering News-Record* magazine ranked PEER as a top engineering and design firm, its longevity remarkable in a field that saw many minority firms fail. PEER received the DoD Small Business/Environmental Restoration Excellence Award for work done over many years for the U.S. Air Force and the Air National Guard. Headquartered in Rockville, Maryland, PEER had offices in seven U.S. cities and eventually had a staff of one hundred workers.

In 1995 Abron founded PEER Africa Pty (Ltd) with co-owner Douglas Guy in Johannesburg, South Africa. After the official end of apartheid in South Africa in 1994 houses were needed for millions of people. PEER Africa designed energy-efficient homes— 40 to 50 percent more efficient than traditional homes—that could be built for less than $10,000.

PEER Africa worked on projects elsewhere in Africa, including Mali, Uganda, and Nigeria, as well as the Caribbean islands. In 1997 the United Nations Framework Convention on Climate Change praised PEER Africa's trademarked methodology, known as the PEER Africa Energy and Environmentally Cost Optimized Human Settlement Development Model. Two years later the United Nations presented Abron with an award for creating the innovative, environmentally friendly design for these South African homes.

In 1993 she was honored with the Distinguished Alumni Award at the University of Iowa, and she won the Alumni Achievement Award from Washington University in 2001 in recognition of both her professional and personal achievements in environmental engineering and of her contributions to the people of South Africa. In 2004 she was inducted into the Academy of Arts and Sciences representing the field of Engineering Sciences and Technologies. Honorees were chosen from American and foreign applicants to honor achievement in science, scholarship, the arts, and public affairs.

An active member of many professional organizations, Abron received professional engineering registrations in environmental engineering and chemical engineering and served on the Board of Registration of Professional Engineers for the District of Columbia and on the Engineering Advisory Board for the National Science Foundation. She held memberships in the American Society of Civil Engineers, American Association of University Women, the American Water Works Association, the Society of Sigma Xi, and the Water Environmental Federation.

Community involvement was always a priority for Abron. She served as president of the Jack and Jill of America Inc. chapter based in Washington, D.C., and as a board member for the Baptist Home for Children. In addition to being a vocal advocate for science education, Abron and PEER sponsored science-fair projects. Her success as an engineer and entrepreneur and her dedication to public service and education made Abron a mentor and role model to women, minorities, and students.

Further Reading

Eversley, Shelly. "A True Renaissance Woman: Lilia Abron, Ph.D, P.E.," *AWIS: Association for Women in Science Magazine* (Jul.–Aug. 1995).

SHERRI J. NORRIS

ABU BAKR AL-SIDDIQ (c. 1794–1841?), Islamic scholar, Jamaican slave, and author, was born in Timbuktu, Mali. When he was two years old his family moved to Jenné in the western Sudan, another major center of Islamic learning and a renowned Sahelian trade city. Heir to a long tradition of Islamic saints and scholars claiming descent from the Prophet Muhammad, he was part of one of several dynasties designated as Sherifian or *Shurfaa*. Abu Bakr was trained and certified in Jenné by several *ulama*, the highly intellectual stratum of Islamic teachers. He was in the process of becoming a cleric when he was captured. As was true for many Islamized Africans caught in the vortex of the Atlantic slave trade, Abu Bakr's itinerant life had pre-slave African and post-slave black Atlantic dimensions. His path shares the trajectory of many coreligionists from Muslim areas of the continent as well as of Christianized captives shipped to England, the Antilles, and North America. What is known about Abu Bakr comes to us through several autobiographical documents—in different English and Arabic versions—that he shared with contemporaries during and after his release from slavery in Jamaica. The first version came from a traveler to Jamaica, Richard Robert Madden, while others found their way to G. C. Renouard of Britain's Royal Geographical Society in 1836. A translation of another variant was rediscovered by the historian CHARLES HARRIS WESLEY, who published it in the *Journal of Negro History* in 1936. Each text is valuable in helping to reconstruct Abu Bakr's odyssey.

Abu Bakr claimed descent from a long line of literate and learned Muslim leaders. His father, Kara Muso (*Karamo* or *Karamoko* is Malinke for "learned man," from the Arabic *qalam*, or "pen"), was reputedly skilled in Koranic interpretation. Abu Bakr's paternal great-grandfather, 'Umar, was a *qa'id* (judge), and his maternal great-grandfather was designated as the king's witness (*shahid al-malik*) according to Ivor Wilks, possibly as a "jurisconsult." Abu Bakr frequently emphasized the critical importance that literacy had for him as a believer. This was clearly one of the cardinal virtues of his life.

His father died of fever soon after the family had moved to Jenné. Five years after his father's passing, with the sanction of his teacher, Abu Bakr traveled to visit his father's grave before journeying into the lands ruled by the Ashanti. At approximately age fourteen or fifteen, Abu Bakr was seized in the Asante (Ashanti) kingdom region of present-day Ghana and shipped to Jamaica in 1807 or 1808. He spent nearly three decades in slavery until he was emancipated in 1834.

During his captivity in Jamaica, Abu Bakr was the property of three owners. The first, a stonemason named Donellan, provided Abu Bakr's surname after he was bought by a man named Haynes, who baptized him as Edward Donellan. In 1823 he was purchased by Alexander Anderson, who so valued Abu Bakr's Arabic literacy that he engaged him as a bookkeeper for Anderson's business. Looking back in his narrative to his travails as a slave, Abu Bakr devoted special attention to reiterating the passionate piety that defined him as a believer, even as a chattel:

But for the bitterness of bondage, I have more to thank but those that brought me here. But praise be to God who has everything in his power to do as he thinks good, and no man can remove whatever burden he chooses to put on us. As he said, "Nothing shall fall on us except what he shall ordain, he is our Lord, and let all that believe in him put their trust in him" (Abu Bakr, "Life," 55).

Even in the depths of despair as a denizen of an island where life was short and days were long, Abu Bakr not only retained his faith but tenaciously hung on to the sacred language of the book, which remained inextricably linked in his consciousness with his ancestral lineage.

In 1834 Richard Madden, a sojourner in Jamaica, discovered that Abu Bakr was literate in Arabic and induced him to translate an autobiographical Arabic narrative of his life into phonetic spoken English, as Abu Bakr, now known as Edward Doulan (or Donellan) was not literate in the tongue of his overlord. Madden then incorporated the New World Muslim's memoir into his own compendium of reflections and letters treating the transformation of the economies and societies of Jamaica and Barbados from slavery to an apprenticeship system, a forerunner of what in the United States would be known as sharecropping and tenant farming. Madden negotiated Abu Bakr's sale and release from Anderson and also became persuaded that he should be repatriated to the western Sudan as soon as practicable. Prompted by Madden, John Davidson, a physician en route to Timbuktu, then began to explore this idea, actually going so far as to undertake a personal mission to western Sudan to make this possibility a reality. An auxiliary magistrate, Captain Oldrey, who had been involved in helping Abu Bakr earlier, continued to do so, and shortly thereafter, in 1835, Abu Bakr sailed to England under the guidance of Captain Oldrey, to whom he dictated another autobiographical account.

In late April 1836 the Reverend G. C. Renouard, foreign secretary of the Royal Geographical Society, stood before his colleagues to reveal several samples of Abu Bakr's thoughts, ranging from selections from the autobiographies to his geographical recollections of the regions of the western Sudan in which he had traveled and from which he had been taken in his youth. Those samples were later published in the Royal Society's journal as "Routes in North Africa." Meanwhile, Davidson sadly met his demise during a raid in West Africa, dying in Timbuktu, momentarily complicating the process of Abu Bakr's African return. By 1841, however, Britain's deputy ambassador to Morocco reported that Abu Bakr was residing in Jenné. After this safe return, Abu Bakr disappeared from view yet lives on in print.

Further Reading
Abu Bakr al-Saddiq. "The History of Abon Becr Sadika, known in Jamaica by the name of Edward Doulan," in Richard Robert Madden, *Twelve Months' Residence in the West Indies, during the Transition from Slavery to Apprenticeship. With Incidental Notices of the State of Society, Prospects, and Natural Resources of Jamaica and Other Islands* (1835).
Abu Bakr al-Saddiq. "The Life and History of Abou Bekir Sadiki, Alias Edward Doulan," discovered by Dr. Charles H. Wesley, "Documents," *Journal of Negro History* 21, no. 1 (Jan. 1936).
Afroz, Sultana. "The Jihad of 1831–1832: The Misunderstood Baptist Rebellion in Jamaica," *Journal of Muslim Minority Affairs* 21, no. 2 (2001).
Diouf, Sylviane A. *Servants of Allah: African Muslims Enslaved in the Americas* (1998).

Renouard, Rev. G. C. "Routes in North Africa by Abu Bekr es Siddik," *Journal of the Royal Geographical Society* 6 (1836).

Singleton, Brent. "The Ummah Slowly Bled: A Select Bibliography of Enslaved African Muslims in the Americas and the Caribbean," *Journal of Muslim Minority Affairs* 22, no. 2 (2002).

Wilks, Ivor. "Abu Bakr al-Siddiq of Timbuktu," in *Africa Remembered: Narratives by West Africans from the Era of the Slave Trade*, ed. Philip D. Curtin (1967).

DAVID H. ANTHONY III

ABU-JAMAL, Mumia (24 Apr. 1954–), a Philadelphia radio journalist who became an international icon in debates over race and the death penalty after he was convicted for the murder of a police officer, was born Wesley Cook to Edith and William Cook, migrants from the South. The family subsisted on welfare in the housing projects of North Philadelphia. As a boy Cook read avidly and sought enlightenment, attending services with his Baptist mother and Episcopalian father, then dabbling in Judaism, Catholicism, and the Nation of Islam. When he was about ten years old his father died of a heart attack, prompting him to assume a protective role toward his twin brother, Wayne, and younger brother, William.

The black liberation movement shaped Cook's coming of age. In a 1967 school class in Swahili, a Kenyan teacher assigned him the first name Mumia. In 1968, at age fourteen, he and some friends protested at a South Philadelphia campaign rally of the Alabama segregationist and presidential candidate George Wallace. Attacked by racist whites, he appealed to a police officer for help, who "kicked me in the face" and "kicked me straight into the Black Panther Party" (*Live from Death Row*, 173). In 1969 Cook helped found the Philadelphia chapter of the Black Panther Party for Self-defense and became its lieutenant of information. Under FBI surveillance, he worked summers for the *Black Panther* newspaper in New York City and Oakland, California, as a street seller, and he witnessed the 1970 police raid on the Black Panther offices in Philadelphia. In 1971 his girlfriend Fran Hart, a Panther, gave birth to Jamal, a son, prompting Cook to adopt the Arabic surname "Father of Jamal." The metamorphosis was complete from Wesley Cook to Mumia Abu-Jamal.

Dismayed by infighting within the revolutionary left, Abu-Jamal in the 1970s was a "bored, slightly petit bourgeois, burnt-out ex-Black Panther who distrusted organizations and still simmered in a stew of generational rebellion" (*Live from Death Row*, 175). Sympathetic teachers helped gain him admission to Goddard College in Vermont, where he volunteered on the campus radio station. There he married Hart, and they had a second child—Latifah, a daughter. But the relationship disintegrated, and he returned to Philadelphia without graduating from Goddard.

In 1974 Abu-Jamal began working on assignments for a variety of Philadelphia radio stations, sometimes using the name William Wellington Cole. In 1977 he

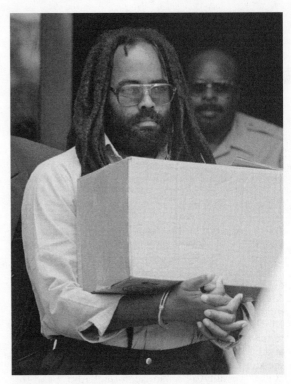

Mumia Abu-Jamal leaves Philadelphia's City Hall after a hearing on 12 July 1995. (AP Images.)

married a schoolteacher who took the name Marilyn Cook; she gave birth to a son, Mazi. Abu-Jamal's reporting aired on National Public Radio, National Black Network, Mutual Black Network, and Associated Press Radio, and he was elected president of the Philadelphia Association of Black Journalists. In January 1981—by then living with a third wife, Mydiya Wadiya Jamal—he was included on a list of "People to Watch" by *Philadelphia Magazine*.

It was as a reporter that Abu-Jamal came into contact with MOVE, a back-to-nature, armed, black nationalist religious group led by Vincent Leaphart, who had adopted the name John Africa. MOVE preached kindness and harmony while adopting a highly confrontational attitude toward police and the Philadelphia power structure—as well as neighbors irritated by MOVE's loudspeaker harangues and the stench of its many dogs' feces. Abu-Jamal increasingly viewed MOVE not as a deranged cult but as "idealistic, committed, strong, unshakable men and women who had a deep spirit-level aversion to everything this system represents" (Preface to *Death Blossoms*, 133). He was sharply critical of Mayor Frank Rizzo, a former police commissioner, and disputed Rizzo's account of the 1978 two-month police siege of MOVE's Powelton Village home, which led to convictions of nine MOVE members after an officer died during the conflict. Emulating MOVE, Abu-Jamal grew dreadlocks. He was impressed by Africa, who, representing himself, had won acquittal on bomb-building charges in a 1981 federal jury trial. However, Abu-Jamal lost his job at station WUHY when the station manager felt he was filing too many subjective reports about MOVE. Compelled to seek employment as a night-shift cabdriver, Abu-Jamal was robbed one night at gunpoint. He responded by purchasing a legally registered revolver.

At 3:55 A.M. on 9 December 1981, the twenty-five-year-old officer Daniel Faulkner, a Philadelphia policeman, stopped a Volkswagen Beetle driven by Abu-Jamal's younger brother, William Cook, on Locust Street in a downtown red-light district. An altercation ensued. Cook may have punched Faulkner. Then Faulkner bludgeoned Cook with a heavy-duty, police-issue flashlight. A black man ran across the street from an adjacent parking lot. Faulkner was shot in the back once, then again in the face at point-blank range. Abu-Jamal, twenty-seven years old, was found sitting on the curb, bleeding from a gunshot wound, a few feet from Faulkner's dead body. His taxicab was in the adjacent parking lot. He wore an empty holster, and beside him was his .38 caliber handgun with spent cartridges in all five cylinders. Standing against the wall was William Cook, who told Robert Shoemaker, the first officer at scene, "I had nothing to do with it." (*Commonwealth v. Mumia Abu-Jamal*, 19 June 1982, 31). To many, the conclusion was inescapable: Abu-Jamal was a cop killer. After a 1982 trial presided over by Judge Albert F. Sabo, a panel of ten white and two black jurors convicted Abu-Jamal of first-degree murder and sentenced him to death.

Initially the case remained obscure as it wound its way through the courts. An appeal filed by a public defender was denied by the Pennsylvania Supreme Court in 1989, and the U.S. Supreme Court refused review. In 1995, when Pennsylvania's Republican governor Tom Ridge signed Abu-Jamal's death warrant, making imminent his execution by lethal injection, Abu-Jamal suddenly rocketed to international prominence. Rallies were held, his photograph adorned T-shirts and posters, celebrities took up his cause, and journalists scrutinized trial transcripts. A new team of lawyers headed by Leonard Weinglass filed for post-conviction relief in Philadelphia.

One objection to the original trial's fairness was to the quality of the defense. Abu-Jamal and his family had hired Anthony E. Jackson, a young, progressive black lawyer. Since Abu-Jamal could not afford the bills, Jackson became, by consent, court appointed. However, Jackson had never been lead attorney in a capital case and had a reputation for substance abuse. Once it became apparent that he could not mount a compelling defense, he sought to withdraw, unsuccessfully. The court allowed Abu-Jamal to represent himself in jury selection but then ordered Jackson to resume as lead counsel because of the excessive time Abu-Jamal took to question potential jurors. Abu-Jamal persisted, demanding to represent himself and to have John Africa sit at his table. The court denied those requests. Abu-Jamal refused to cooperate with

Jackson thereafter and engaged in disruptive outbursts, prompting his removal from the courtroom on multiple occasions. Jackson, with few funds and little experience, faced Joseph McGill, a seasoned assistant district attorney, and Judge Sabo, a former law enforcement official who at retirement had presided over thirty-one death sentences, more than any other judge in the country. Jackson did not place a single character witness for Abu-Jamal on the stand in the penalty phase. Critics consider his closing arguments feeble.

A second disputed area is the forensic evidence. Police did not test Abu-Jamal's gun to see if it had been fired recently. Nor did they run a standard test to see if his hands had fired a gun. A medical examiner's report stated incorrectly that the bullet removed from Faulkner's brain was .44 caliber, but Jackson failed to direct the jury's attention to this discrepancy. Finally, no fingerprints were found on the weapon (though it is unusual to find identifiable prints on guns).

Abu-Jamal's supporters frequently conjectured that he may have been framed by police resentful of his support of MOVE and journalistic criticism of police. Vulnerable witnesses, they suggest, may have been pressured to provide perjured testimony. Cynthia White's story changed dramatically across four sessions with detectives. Robert Chobert, whose account also changed, was a convicted arsonist on probation who was driving a cab despite a DWI-suspended license. McGill, however, has observed that saintly witnesses are rarely found at night in red-light districts, and others pointed out that Abu-Jamal was a cabdriver at the time of his arrest, hardly a major thorn in the side of police. The most dubious witness's testimony pertained to a supposed hospital confession by Abu-Jamal. Officer Gary Wakshul, who traveled with Abu-Jamal in the van and remained with him at the hospital, claimed in 1982 to have heard Abu-Jamal say, "I shot the motherfucker and I hope the motherfucker dies." But two months before, at the actual time of the shooting, Wakshul filed a report stating, "The negro male made no comments" (Lindorff, 196).

Many critics, finally, doubted that the killing was deliberate and premeditated, even if Abu-Jamal did shoot Faulkner. In his 1982 cross-examination McGill introduced a 1970 news article in which Abu-Jamal, then fifteen years old and still named Wesley Cook, quoted the Chinese Communist Party chairman Mao Tse-tung's dictum "Political power grows out of the barrel of a gun." Critics note that this reference was meant to illuminate why police were murdering Black Panthers, not justify random attacks on police, and they find the introduction of the defendant's earlier political beliefs and affiliations into the trial to be prejudicial.

For twenty years Abu-Jamal maintained his innocence but refused to discuss the night of the shooting. In 2001 he claimed in a brief written account that he was shot by police while crossing the street to aid his brother, then lost consciousness. Meanwhile, his brother William Cook filed a 2001 affidavit stating that Kenneth Freeman, his business partner, who died in 1985, was in the Volkswagen but fled the scene, implying Freeman, rather than Abu-Jamal, may have shot Faulkner. Five witnesses told police in 1981 that they saw someone else fleeing, but critics point out that if someone other than Abu-Jamal was the killer, it strains credulity that Abu-Jamal and his brother would wait twenty years to mention it.

In 1995, just a few days before Abu-Jamal's scheduled execution, the death warrant was vacated. Judge Sabo, declining to recuse himself, presided over a 1995–1996 post-conviction relief hearing that the *Philadelphia Inquirer* described as overtly biased. When Governor Ridge signed a second death warrant in 1999, it, too, was vacated. Meanwhile, new revelations broke. In 2000 a court stenographer signed an affidavit that in 1982, on one of the first days of the trial, she overheard Judge Sabo (who died in 2002) say, "I'm going to help them fry the nigger" (Lindorff, 338).

In 1995 Abu-Jamal was housed at State Correctional Institute–Greene, a super-maximum death row prison in Waynesburg, Pennsylvania. Through distance learning he obtained a BA from Goddard College and an MA from California State University–Dominguez Hills. He published articles in the *Nation* and the *Yale Law Journal* and delivered recorded commencement addresses at several liberal arts colleges. In the early 1990s National Public Radio's *All Things Considered* canceled his scheduled commentaries, but they were published in *Live from Death Row* (1994), a book followed by *Death Blossoms: Reflections from a Prisoner of Conscience* (1997), *All Things Censored* (2000), *Faith of Our Fathers: An Examination of the Spiritual Life of African and African-American People* (2003), and *We Want Freedom: A Life in the Black Panther Party* (2004). In his writings Abu-Jamal maintains that mandatory exclusion of jurors who oppose capital punishment guarantees "pro-prosecution, pro-conviction, pro-death penalty" juries. He considers words like "corrections" and "penitentiaries" hypocritical, since prison is "a second-by-second assault on the soul, a day-to-day degradation of the self, an oppressive steel and brick umbrella" (*Live from Death Row*, 37, 64–65).

In 2001 the U.S. district judge William Yohn Jr. overturned Abu-Jamal's death sentence, saying jurors had been wrongly instructed. The Philadelphia district attorney appealed the ruling. Also in 2001 Abu-Jamal fired his legal team of Leonard Weinglass and Daniel Williams after Williams published a book that criticized "Free Mumia" supporters for insisting on his innocence rather than contesting the fairness of his trial. Eliot Lee Grossman and Marlene Kamish, his succeeding attorneys, required supporters to confirm Abu-Jamal's innocence and introduced the fantastic claim of Arnold Beverly, a man with an extensive criminal record and history of mental illness, that corrupt Philadelphia police hired him to kill Faulkner. In 2004 Abu-Jamal dropped Grossman and Kamish and made Robert Bryan lead attorney; the Beverly claim was abandoned.

In 2005 the Third Circuit Court of Appeals ruled that Abu-Jamal could appeal his case on three grounds: that jury selection was racially discriminatory; that improper comments to the jury by the prosecutor minimized the seriousness of returning a guilty verdict; and that Judge Sabo showed bias in the post-conviction relief hearings. The first two claims could lead to a new trial. The third could lead to a new evidentiary hearing. The court could also overturn Yohn's 2001 ruling, however, restoring Abu-Jamal's death sentence.

In 2006 the Parisian suburb of St. Denis named a street for Abu-Jamal, leading Congress to pass a resolution condemning the French city. Maureen Faulkner, the slain officer's widow, and Philadelphia's Fraternal Order of Police continued to insist upon Abu-Jamal's guilt and advocate his execution, but the public intellectual CORNEL WEST called Abu-Jamal "unjustly imprisoned for a crime he did not commit" (*Death Blossoms*, xii). Between these polarities of opinion fall critics of the trial's fairness who do not exonerate Abu-Jamal. The legal analyst Stuart Taylor has described Abu-Jamal as "guilty and framed," a killer subjected to a "grotesquely unfair" trial. The journalist Dave Lindorff hypothesized that Faulkner may have shot first or that Abu-Jamal might have fired in "a momentary paroxysm of anger and concern about his brother's safety," making the murder neither premeditated nor unprovoked (Lindorff, 61). Whether Abu-Jamal was the killer, whether his trial was fair, and whether he—or anyone else—deserves to be executed remained topics of sharp debate.

Further Reading

Abu-Jamal, Mumia. *Death Blossoms: Reflections from a Prisoner of Conscience* (1997).

Abu-Jamal, Mumia. *Live from Death Row* (1995).

Amnesty International. *United States of America: A Life in the Balance: The Case of Mumia Abu-Jamal* (2000).

Bisson, Terry. *On a Move: The Story of Mumia Abu Jamal* (2001).

Commonwealth v. Mumia Abu-Jamal, a.k.a. Wesley Cook. Trail Transcripts, Court of Common Pleas, Philadelphia County, Criminal County Division (1982).

Lindorff, Dave. *Killing Time: An Investigation into the Death Row Case of Mumia Abu Jamal* (2003).

Taylor, Stuart, Jr. "Guilty and Framed," *American Lawyer*, Dec. 1995, 74–85.

Williams, Daniel R. *Executing Justice: An Inside Account of the Case of Mumia Abu-Jamal* (2001).

CHRISTOPHER PHELPS

ACE, Johnny (9 June 1929–25 Dec. 1954), musician, songwriter, and rhythm and blues star, was born John Marshall Alexander Jr. in Memphis, Tennessee, the son of John Marshall Alexander and Leslie Newsome. His father earned his living in Memphis as a packer, but his lifework was as a commuting minister to two rural Baptist churches in eastern Arkansas. At LaRose Grammar School in South Memphis, John Jr., as his family called him, displayed both musical and artistic talent. He mastered the piano at home but was allowed to play only religious music. Along with his mother and siblings, he sang in the choir at Bethel

African Methodist Episcopal Church. Becoming restless at Booker T. Washington High School, John Jr. dropped out in the eleventh grade to join the navy and see the world. His sisters recalled military police coming to the house in search of their brother and thought of his brief period of enlistment in terms of weeks, ending in an "Undesirable Discharge" in 1947. His mother was furious. "I can't keep up with you," she scolded, "and *they* can't keep up with you."

It is possible that Alexander never had a job in the conventional sense, and he did not seek employment after his failed bit in the navy. He did, however, find kindred spirits on Beale Street, Memphis's famed nightlife center. Joe Hill Louis, "the Be-Bop Boy," may have started Alexander out as a professional musician, or the credit may belong to Dwight "Gatemouth" Moore, but by 1949 Alexander was the piano player with the Beale Street Blues Boys (later the Beale Streeters), a band that backed B. B. KING when he performed live. In 1950 Alexander wooed and married Lois Jean Palmer, a ninth-grader at Booker T. Washington High School, and moved her into his parents' home. A son was born to the couple that year and a daughter in 1952. Alexander's mother, who disapproved of his lifestyle and his occupation as a blues musician, embraced Alexander's wife and children but refused to let him sleep at the family home.

In 1952 David James Mattis, the program director at the Memphis all-black radio station WDIA (the "Mother Station of the Negroes"), founded Duke Records and changed Alexander's name to Johnny Ace. When Bobby "Blue" Bland could not sing a song scheduled for recording at the WDIA studio (it was subsequently revealed that Bland could not read), Mattis wrote new lyrics to an existing rhythm and blues hit, and Ace "faked out" a new melody. The result was "My Song," a "blues ballad" (*Billboard* called it a "heart ballad") that Ace sang in a vulnerable and innocent crooning style. Though the recording was poor, the charm of Ace's voice made it an immediate hit with its limited audience. "My Song" attracted the attention of the Houston entrepreneur Don D. Robey, a black man who owned Peacock Records and controlled a booking agency specializing in "chitlin circuit" venues. Robey became a partner and quickly the sole owner of Duke Records, moving the entire operation to Houston. He aggressively promoted Ace's "My Song" to the top of the rhythm and blues charts and groomed him as a national headlining rhythm and blues act, carefully cultivating the kind of polished, first-class, uptown image that BERRY GORDY JR. would later emulate at Motown.

Ace's career, which lasted less than two and a half years, produced eight rhythm and blues top-ten records, including three number one hits: "My Song" (1952), "The Clock" (1953), and "Pledging My Love" (1955). For the most part Ace lived the nomadic life of a road musician, with no permanent home or routine beyond a string of hotel stops, traveling coast to coast with a backup band and an opening act, the blues singer WILLIE MAE "BIG MAMA"

THORNTON. In 1954 Ace may have performed as many as 350 one-nighters, sometimes driving as far as 800 miles between shows. According to Evelyn Johnson, the head of the Buffalo Booking Agency and the closest thing to a personal manager that Ace had, Ace was shy, childlike, and unassuming. "Sweetest thing since sugar," she recalled, "but he didn't care about nuttin', honey." At a pawnshop in Florida he purchased a .22 caliber pistol to amuse himself and to alleviate the boredom of the road. On Christmas night 1954, while backstage during intermission at a "Negro Christmas Dance" at Houston's City Auditorium, Ace began "snapping" his pistol at the heads of people in his dressing room. According to Thornton, Ace then put the pistol to his own head and uttered his last words: "I'll show you that it won't shoot." Authorities ruled the cause of death to be "playing russian roulette—self inflicted."

Ace's last record, "Pledging My Love," first advertised in *Billboard* on the day of his death, represented neither rhythm nor blues, but nevertheless the slow ballad became a rhythm and blues triple-crown hit (number one in retail sales, radio airplay, and jukebox action), was the most-played rhythm and blues record of 1955, and generated more than half a dozen tribute records to the romantic legend of Johnny Ace. In addition the record crossed over to the pop charts to become a hit there as well. For the first time in the postwar era, white record buyers (primarily teens) chose a ballad by a solo black male singer signed to an independent rhythm and blues label as the unique and definitive performance of a popular song against which all subsequent performances were ruthlessly judged. Arguably, "Pledging My Love" represents the transitional record between rhythm and blues and rock and roll.

Johnny Ace died a rhythm and blues star and was resurrected a rock and roll legend. He has been called rock's first "casualty," "the first fallen angel," and "the colored James Dean." For disc jockeys he remains "the Late Great Johnny Ace."

Further Reading
Gart, Galen, and Roy C. Ames. *Duke/Peacock Records: An Illustrated History with Discography* (1990).
Salem, James M. "Death and the Rhythm-and-Bluesman: The Life and Recordings of Johnny Ace," *American Music* (Fall 1993): 316–367.
Tosches, Nick. *Unsung Heroes of Rock 'n' Roll* (1984).
                                                    JAMES M. SALEM

ADAIR, Thelma Cornelia (29 Aug. 1920–), Presbyterian educator and activist, was born Thelma Cornelia Davidson at Iron Station, North Carolina, one of five children of Robert James Davidson, a Baptist minister, schoolteacher, and principal, and Violet Wilson Davidson, a schoolteacher, mortician, and community organizer. Her grandfather, six uncles, and three brothers were all ministers, as would be her future husband. She grew up in Spindale, North Carolina, where her mother was a teacher and her father was principal and superintendent of Western Union Baptist Academy, and later in Kings Mountain, North Carolina, where her father served as a high school principal and as the pastor of several local churches. After her early years in public school, she enrolled in Lincoln Academy, a boarding school run by the American Missionary Society of the Congregational Church. Just before her thirteenth birthday, she enrolled in Barber-Scotia Junior College in Concord, North Carolina, a school of the "northern" United Presbyterian Church. She finished her college studies at the Methodist-affiliated Bennett College.

Adair's first full-time job was as a math, science, and history teacher at Mount Carmel Junior High School, a rural school located ten miles from Lancaster, South Carolina. She soon married Arthur Eugene Adair, a Presbyterian minister and missionary. Together they organized new churches and Sunday schools throughout North and South Carolina. The couple eventually had three children.

In 1942 the Adairs moved to New York City, where Eugene entered Union Theological Seminary and Thelma entered Columbia University Teachers College. At the request of Henry Sloane Coffin, president of Union Theological Seminary, Adair and her husband founded the Mount Morris Presbyterian Church in Harlem after a mostly white Presbyterian congregation had fled the neighborhood and abandoned its church building. The Adair family lived in an apartment in the church building for twenty-four years before they purchased a nearby brownstone. Adair eventually became one of the first women in that congregation to be ordained as an elder. She earned her MA from Columbia University Teachers College in 1945 and earned her EdD in Curriculum and Teaching in 1959; in 1977 Adair received the Distinguished Alumni Award from Columbia University Teachers College.

Most of Adair's professional career was spent as a professor of education at Queens College at the City University of New York, even while she continued an active life of service to her church and her community. She also lectured or taught at Maryville College, the College of Wooster, Dubuque University, the College of Idaho, Macalester College, Lafayette College, and New York University. She served as adjunct professor at Colgate-Rochester Divinity School, Princeton Theological Seminary, and Union Theological Seminary in New York. After thirty-one years of service, she retired from Queens College as professor emerita of early childhood education.

Adair then went on to organize and direct a number of noteworthy programs. She helped initiate the federal Head Start program for at-risk children, and she directed several programs in conjunction with the United Nations Educational, Scientific, and Cultural Organization Year of Education and with Peace Corps training programs, traveling to observe or consult throughout the Caribbean, Western Europe, East Asia, the Far East, and many African countries, including Cameroon, Egypt, Ethiopia, Ghana, Ivory Coast, Kenya, Liberia, Nigeria, Senegal, Sierra Leone, Uganda, and Tanzania. In 1944 she established Mount Morris New Life as a day care facility. In 1966 Adair became the first African American trustee of the Orphan Asylum Society in the City of New York, which operated the Graham Home for Children, an integrated orphanage in Hastings-on-Hudson. That same year she helped begin an integrated day camp as a cooperative project of the Mount Morris church and the Huguenot Memorial Church of Pelham Manor, New York. Adair also wrote or co-wrote several manuals for church schoolteachers, including *How to Make Church School Equipment: It's Easier Than You Think!* (1955), *When We Teach 4's and 5's* (1962), and *Parents and the Day Care Center* (1969).

Adair served on numerous Presbyterian Church agencies and boards. She served as president of the Black Presbyterian Caucus and on a national Special Committee on the Status of Women. Adair was vice president of the Board of Christian Education and was coordinator of educational strategy for the Board of National Missions. In 1974 the General Assembly of the United Presbyterian Church appointed Adair the chairperson of a special Consulting Committee on the Needs and Rights of Children, a position she held until 1976, at which time she resigned to become the first African American woman, and only the second woman ever, to be elected moderator of the General Assembly of the United Presbyterian Church, the denomination's highest elected office. As moderator, she represented the denomination on every continent except Africa, including a trip to Australia to celebrate the merger of the Methodist, Congregational, and Presbyterian churches as they came together to form the Uniting Church in Australia. On 11 December 1979, at the age of sixty-three, her husband, Eugene, died of a heart attack he had suffered during a meeting of the Presbytery of New York City.

After her year as moderator concluded, Adair continued her activity in the national leadership of the Presbyterian Church and served as a member of the General Assembly Council, as chair of the Global Mission Ministry Unit, as a member of the Evangelism and Church Development Unit, and as chair of the Presbyterian Senior Services of New York. Adair was one of the featured Presbyterian speakers on the 1989 *Protestant Hour* series of radio broadcast sermons. In 1991 she was one of three honorees named as a *Woman of Faith*, an award given to Presbyterian leaders whose lives "exemplify faith in God and commitment to the mission of the Presbyterian Church (U.S.A.)." She was a featured speaker at many regional and national gatherings of Presbyterian Women, and when the Covenant Network of Presbyterians was founded to promote a socially progressive stance for the Presbyterian Church, Adair agreed to serve on its board of advisers.

Adair held several important leadership roles in Church Women United (CWU), a national ecumenical Christian women's movement organized in conjunction with the National Council of Churches. In

1974 she was a leader in the CWU Asian Causeway, and in 1975 she served as a consultant for its Caribbean Causeway. Adair twice served as vice president, and from 1980 to 1984 she served as president of CWU, just the second African American to hold that position. Long active in that organization, she frequently chaired national conferences and served as adviser to the group's national board.

Adair later became active in the World Council of Churches. She was a cochairperson of the U.S. Committee on the Ecumenical Decade of Churches in Solidarity with Women, and in 1993 she was one of the planners and participants in the Reimagining Conference held in Minneapolis. In 1998 Adair and her daughter, Dr. Jeanne D. Adair, traveled to Zambia, and then on to Harare, Zimbabwe, where they served among the 125 U.S. delegates to the 1998 Ecumenical Decade Festival held 27–30 November in conjunction with the Eighth Assembly of the World Council of Churches. She also served on the advisory council of the National Council of Churches and was appointed to the International Board of Advisors of the United Nations Association of Haiti.

Adair became an advocate for health care and served on the Harlem Hospital Community Advisory Board. She worked with Harlem Hospital and the Columbia University School of Dental and Oral Surgery to establish a dental and medical clinic to serve the neighborhood's senior citizens, and in June 2002 the Thelma C. Davidson Adair Medical and Dental Center was opened in Harlem.

Adair served on the boards of the Frederick Douglass Creative Arts Center in New York City, Barber-Scotia College, Boggs Academy, Johnson C. Smith Seminary, the Inter-American University of Puerto Rico, and the Interdenominational Theological Center. Adair received numerous other honors, including an honorary degree and the Alumni Award for Meritorious Service in the Field of Education from Barber-Scotia College, an honorary degree from Middlebury College, and the United Negro College Fund Distinguished Award for Outstanding Service and Commitment to Higher Education.

Further Reading

The Presbyterian Historical Society in Philadelphia contains archival material related to Adair's service as moderator of the General Assembly, and Adair's work with Church Women United is documented in the Archives of the United Methodist Church at Drew University in Madison, New Jersey.

Basham, Beth, ed. *Women of Faith of the Presbyterian Church (U.S.A.), 1986 to 1996* (1997).

Cunningham, Sarah. "Thelma Adair: A Busy, Effective Moderator," in *A.D. 1977: The Magazine for the United Presbyterian Family* 6:4 (Apr. 1977).

Wilson, Agnes T. "Four Black Moderators," in *Periscopes 2: Black Presbyterians—Yesterday, Today, and Tomorrow: 175 Years of Ministry, 1807–1982* (1982).

Wilson, Frank T., Sr., ed. "Thelma Cornelia Adair—For People, Love, and Light," in *Black Presbyterians in Ministry* (1979).

DAVID B. MCCARTHY

ADAMS, Alton Augustus, Sr. (4 Nov. 1889–23 Nov. 1987), flutist, composer, bandmaster, music educator, journalist, and hotelier, was born in Charlotte Amalie, St. Thomas, Danish West Indies (later U.S. Virgin Islands) and is remembered as the U.S. Navy's first African American bandmaster. Adams was the son of Jacob Henry Adams, a carpenter, and Petrina Evangeline Dinzey, a tailor; both his parents were members of the black artisan class centered around St. Thomas's port. This culture celebrated music and literature and instilled the young Adams with values of hard work and self-education. Although professional musicians were unknown in the Virgin Islands in his youth, Adams dreamt of a musical career inspired by his deeply held belief that music was not just entertainment, but vital to community health.

Adams attended elementary school and apprenticed as a carpenter and then a shoemaker, choosing his trade based on the musical abilities of his master. Adams learned solfége from a neighbor and taught himself piccolo. He joined the St. Thomas Municipal Band under the direction of Lionel Roberts in 1907, and he quickly rose to the position of assistant bandmaster. With no school of music on the islands, he took correspondence courses in music theory and composition with Dr. Hugh Clarke at the University of Pennsylvania (eventually earning a bachelor's degree in 1931 from the University Extension Conservatory in Chicago). Adams's first compositions were performed by the Municipal Band, but by June 1910 he had resigned to form his own ensemble called the Adams Juvenile Band. This new group soon became part of the local community fabric by performing at social and charitable events and giving regular concerts on the city's bandstand at Emancipation Garden. Adams's first musical publication, *Doux Rêve d'Amour* for solo piano, appeared in 1912; and beginning in 1916 he contributed a series of idealistic monthly columns for the widely distributed *Jacobs' Band Monthly* (Boston), which cemented his national reputation. He married Ella Eugenia Joseph on 6 October 1917, and the couple had eight children.

Following the United States' purchase of the Virgin Islands from Denmark on the eve of American entry into World War I, Adams and his bandsmen were inducted into the navy on 2 June 1917, thus becoming the first African Americans to receive official musical appointments in the U.S. Navy most likely since the War of 1812; and Adams became the navy's first known black bandmaster. The all-black ensemble was to serve as a bridge between the islands' all-white naval administration and the predominantly black population. While some local leaders chose instead to protest this "naval rule," Adams chose to join with the new administration. His decision was controversial, but through cooperation Adams not only fulfilled his artistic dreams by becoming a professional musician, but also used his newfound authority as chief petty officer to influence the new administration for the benefit of his fellow islanders.

Adams's influence soon began to expand in both the navy and the community. He served as an officer of the local chapter of the Red Cross, helped found Charlotte Amalie's public library in 1920, started the islands' first public school music program in 1920, and ran a local newspaper, the *St. Thomas Times*, from 1921 to 1923.

At the suggestion of a 1924 Congressional committee sent to investigate conditions on the islands, Adams's naval band toured the U.S. East Coast in the summer of 1924, including stops in Washington, D.C., Philadelphia, New York, and Boston, to enthusiastic applause from both white and black audiences and vociferous praise from the black press. While in New York, Adams conducted the all-white Goldman Band in Central Park. In 1931 when a civilian administration displaced the navy, Adams's ensemble was transferred to Guantánamo Bay, Cuba. This move signaled the end of the band, separating Adams and his bandsmen from family, friends, and their ensemble's social purpose. Still strictly segregated, the navy kept the black bandsmen apart from white musicians and the band languished in administrative isolation.

Tragically, a 1932 fire that destroyed Adams's home on St. Thomas also claimed many of his music manuscripts. Only about a dozen works survived. His best known compositions are the *Virgin Islands March* (1919), *The Governor's Own* (1921), and *Spirit of the U.S.N.*, which was written for President Calvin Coolidge during the 1924 tour. Adams's music has received little attention from scholars of black music, in part because his compositions, except for his arrangements of *bamboula* dances and spirituals, contain few characteristics traditionally associated with African American music. Rather, Adams's music is in the classic march idiom of John Philip Sousa, his musical idol, and communicates palpable energy along with a discernible sense of patriotism.

Adams retired from active duty and joined the U.S. Naval Fleet Reserves in 1933. He returned to St. Thomas, soon resuming his work in the music programs of the public schools. In 1940 he again took on a newspaper editorship, this time for the *Bulletin* in St. Thomas, but he was recalled to active duty after Pearl Harbor was attacked by the Japanese in 1941. Sent back to Guantánamo in 1942, Adams assumed command of an all-white ensemble and reinstated eight former bandsmen, thus creating the navy's first official racially integrated band. The next year Adams and the other Virgin Islanders returned to St. Thomas and were again segregated as an all-black unit. This band would be transferred once more in 1944, this time to Puerto Rico. In 1945 Adams retired from the navy permanently.

Returning again to St. Thomas in 1945 after his military discharge, Adams became chairman of the governing committee of the St. Thomas Power Authority and deepened his belief in the economic determinism of equality. In 1947 he answered a call to increase the number of local hotel rooms by opening his home as the Adams 1799 Guest House. By 1952 Adams had become a charter member of the Virgin Islands Hotel Association. He was soon elected president, a position he held until 1971, again functioning as a liaison between the mostly white hotel owners and their workers, who were mostly black. During the 1950s and 1960s, Adams also served as a reporter, working as a stringer for the Associated Press and Associated Negro Press and contributing regular articles to GEORGE SCHUYLER's *Pittsburgh Courier*. Although he eschewed public office, Adams was closely involved with island politics as an adviser and editorial commentator. Adams also maintained friendships with a number of black American leaders including Schuyler, MAUD CUNEY-HARE, and W. E. B. DU BOIS.

In 1963 the Virgin Islands' legislature officially accepted the rededication of his "Virgin Islands March" to the people of the Virgin Islands, since the composition had long served as a native anthem. In 1982 the "Virgin Islands March" became the official territorial anthem of the Virgin Islands. Around 1983 Adams closed his guesthouse; he died four years later, only a few weeks after his ninety-eighth birthday. Among his many awards were an honorary doctorate from Fisk University (1978) and the Virgin Islands Medal of Honor (1983). Originally refused admission because of his race, Adams was inducted into the American Bandmasters Association posthumously in 2006.

Further Reading

Adams, Alton. *The Memoirs of Alton Augustus Adams, First Black Bandmaster of the United States Navy* (2008).

Clague, Mark. "Instruments of Identity: Alton Augustus Adams, Sr., the Navy Band of the Virgin Islands, and the Sounds of Social Change," *Black Music Research Journal* (Spring/Fall 1998).

Clague , Mark. "Adams, Alton Augustus," *International Dictionary of Black Composers* (1999).

Floyd, Samuel. "Alton Augustus Adams: The First Black Bandmaster in the United States Navy," *The Black Perspective in Music* (Fall 1977).

MARK CLAGUE
JOHN H. ZIMMERMAN

ADAMS, Carolyn (1944–), dancer and arts administrator, was born in New York City, the daughter of Julius J. Adams, a journalist who rose to managing editor of the *New York Amsterdam News,* and Olive A. Adams, an accomplished pianist. Her parents cultivated in her a deep appreciation of the arts, as well as a legacy of social activism that stayed with Adams throughout her life—both during her career as a dancer and after her retirement from the stage, when she helped found community-based arts centers for children in Harlem. The dance writer Muriel Topaz described the Adamses' home as a "center of social and political activity," and noted that the Global News Syndicate, an organization of black newspapers, was founded in their small apartment (Topaz, 30).

When she was eight years old Adams entered New York's progressive Ethical Culture School, an institution dedicated to the moral as well as intellectual development of its students. There she began to study dance, also receiving extensive training in piano and violin. As a child she auditioned for the renowned School of American Ballet (the academy associated with the New York City Ballet) but chose not to attend for fear that it would interfere with her other activities, and she opted instead for private training. After an injury briefly curtailed her dancing, Adams resumed her training with Nelle Fisher at Carnegie Hall, where she studied movement for actors and jazz. At age fifteen she began taking classes at the Martha Graham School, furthering her knowledge of a technique she had already begun learning back in the Ethical Culture School. Following her graduation from high school, Adams enrolled in the dance program at Sarah Lawrence College, headed by the esteemed Bessie Schönberg, a legendary figure who nurtured the careers of countless dancers and choreographers. Schönberg taught Adams technique, composition, and dance history. Additionally, thanks to another of her teachers, Karin Waehner, it was also during this time that Adams enjoyed her first professional experience, touring with *Les Grands Ballets Contemporains.*

The defining moment of Adams's career, however, happened almost by accident during the last semester of her senior year, when she drove her friends to an audition for the company of the modern dance choreographer Paul Taylor. Although Adams originally had not intended to try out, at the last moment she changed her mind, and made a significant impression on Taylor. Adams finished her BA before officially joining the company in September 1965, becoming the first black dancer in the group.

Adams remained with Taylor for seventeen years, originating dozens of roles in dances ranging from plotless to dramatic and becoming a role model for African American dancers at a time when few performed in white modern dance or ballet companies. Like Adams, Taylor had a good grounding in both ballet and Graham techniques (he had danced with her company), so the elements of his movement style were already ingrained in her body. In an interview with the dance historian Brenda Dixon Gottschild, the choreographer Meredith Monk—a former classmate of Adams's at Sarah Lawrence—described Adams's dancing as so fluid it was like she had "no bones" (Gottschild, 49). Equally important, Taylor encouraged individuality among his performers, and he created a working situation in which Adams was never stereotyped, and one in which her best qualities— lyricism, lightness, a quicksilver quality of movement, and extraordinary musicality—were allowed to shine.

Among Adams's repertory was the beautiful *Esplanade* (1975), one of Taylor's signature pieces, which featured passages of dazzling, joyful runs and leaps; the daughter in the disturbing *Big Bertha* (1970), in which a mechanical carnival doll reveals the dark underside of an American family; *Airs* (1978); and the gangster mistress in his version of *Sacre du Printemps* (1980). In his autobiography, *Private Domain*, Taylor praised Adams as both a dancer and as a human being, calling her "unmannered and

wondrous . . . an elegant nectar laced with warm delicacy, easy and effortless" (327).

Adams never lost the sense of social responsibility her parents had so carefully instilled in her. In an interview with *Dance Magazine* in November 1970, when she was still in her twenties and hitting the heights of her career, Adams spoke longingly of opening a performing arts center in Harlem. Three years later, she and her sister, Julie Strandburg (herself the head of Brown University's dance program), established the Harlem Dance Foundation. There, Adams not only trained students but also helped the most talented find much-needed scholarships. Her dedication to the community extended beyond choreography; she and the foundation fought vigorously to protect Harlem's architectural treasures, which were in danger of being demolished. In one instance Adams lay down in the street in front of bulldozers to prevent brownstones from being razed. She also went on to earn her realtor's license in order to combat destructive redlining.

Adams's concern for preserving dance history and for improving the quality of dance education led her—again with her sister—to bring another institution into being: the American Dance Legacy Institute, which they established in 1994. With the help of modern technology like the CD-ROM, as well as more traditional media like newspapers and video, she enlisted choreographers to document their dances so their knowledge could be disseminated to students and teachers throughout the country. In addition, the institute offered workshops and developed entire dance curricula for public school classrooms. In 1994 the American Dance Legacy Institute officially became a part of Brown University.

Adams became the director of the BFA program at the City College of New York, joined the faculty of the Juilliard School in 1983, and served as the director of both Jacob Pillow's education program and the New York State Education Department's summer program in modern dance. She and her sister also coauthored *American Education in the Arts: A Balancing of Visions for Cultural Transformation*, which was published in 1993.

In 1988 Adams married Robert Kahn, a former Paul Taylor dancer and Wall Street broker–turned–chef. The couple had two children, Sandra and Vitali. Through her inspirational dancing, widespread teaching, and social activism, Adams not only influenced a generation of dancers but has also helped affect the world beyond the stage.

Further Reading
Gottschild, Brenda Dixon. *The Black Dancing Body: A Geography from Coon to Cool* (2003).

Panel Discussion with Paul Taylor Dancers, on Paul Taylor Company Web site, available online at http://www.ptdc.org/dev/panel.php?id=51.

Taylor, Paul. *Private Domain* (1987).

Topaz, Muriel. "Carolyn Adams: A Lifelong Pursuit," *Dance Magazine* (July 1994).

KAREN BACKSTEIN

ADAMS, Elizabeth Laura (9 Feb. 1909–?), the first African American to publish an autobiography about conversion to Catholicism, was born in Santa Barbara, California, the only child of Lula Josephine Holden Adams, a painter, and Daniel Henderson Adams, a hotel headwaiter. Daniel and Lula Adams provided a comfortable, middle-class lifestyle for their daughter and raised her according to strict rules of courtesy, manners, and obedience. Shortly after Adams's birth the family moved to Los Angeles, where she attended an integrated primary school.

Adams and her parents fell victim to the influenza epidemic of 1918–1919. Mother and daughter returned to temperate Santa Barbara in 1920 at their doctor's recommendation and would suffer from chronic illness for the rest of their lives. Adams's father continued to work in Los Angeles for another four years and then died suddenly in 1924, shortly before he was to join the family in Santa Barbara. During this period friends of the family brought Adams and her mother to the Santa Barbara Mission, where "conversion came to me quickly and quietly—like the slumber that gently closes an infants eyes" (Adams, 106). Her parents, who raised her in the Methodist Episcopal Church, forbade her from joining the Catholic Church. She did not officially convert until 1928 or 1929, after graduating from high school and earning her mother's approval.

The family's financial standing plummeted after the death of Daniel Adams, and Adams had to give up her dream of going to college. During the 1930s she worked sporadically in domestic service and at secretarial jobs while caring for her ailing mother and struggling with her own health problems. She wanted to become a nun, but her obligation to her mother thwarted this ambition. Adams joined the Franciscan Tertiary instead, a secular "third order" that requires vows of moderation, temperance, and prayer and the commitment to remain in one's current marital state, whether married or unmarried (Kaplan, xix).

Adams published several poems, short stories, and autobiographical essays between 1930 and 1943. A shorter and slightly different version of *Dark Symphony* was serialized from October 1940 through March 1941 as "There Must Be A God . . . Somewhere" in the Catholic periodical *Torch*. The Catholic press's interest in Adams's work coincided with the church's attempt to convert African Americans in the 1930s and 1940s. Catholics viewed these efforts as domestic missionary work that could counter the growing radicalism in black communities (Kaplan, xlvi). The Catholic publisher Sheed & Ward released *Dark Symphony* in 1942; it sold ten thousand copies in its first four years and fifteen thousand copies total. White readers gave *Dark Symphony* high praise, commending its lack of bitterness and its educational value. Black critics, on the other hand, were skeptical of its optimism and its cautious handling of racism. For example, Theophilus Lewis, a writer for the radical black journal the *Messenger*, found Adams's descriptions of "petty discriminations" common and unremarkable,

whereas a white reviewer found these same passages "uncommon and inspiring" (Kaplan, xxii).

Adams may have been attracted to the Catholic Church because paradoxically this patriarchal, antidemocratic institution gave her a forum for self-expression that was denied her at home and in the Sunday school classes of her youth. Whereas the "religious people" in the black churches she visited commanded, "Don't question God!" (Adams, 70), the Catholic confessional offered "an ideal place . . . to ask questions of God" (128). In *Dark Symphony*, Adams constructs her life as a search for voice—for the freedom to ask questions and to find her own answers. The opening scene locates the narrative in the African American tradition, which originated with slave narratives, of a dual quest for literacy and freedom. Upon discovering a school as a toddler, Adams experiences a thirst for knowledge that would be central to her identity: "I pondered. Questioned. The questions flew out, then circled back like a boomerang—unanswered" (8). Adams revises the conversion narrative formula by replacing cycles of sin and repentance with cycles of questioning and silencing. Her spiritual journey also involves cycles of interracial spiritual communion and segregation, situating race at the center of her narrative.

Although Adams structures her narrative around experiences of racism and expresses an impulse to fight, she ultimately endorses her parents' philosophy of forgiveness and forbearance in the face of racism. Each time Adams tells a story about an encounter with racism she mitigates the sting by incorporating a sympathetic white character. However, *Dark Symphony* may not be as conciliatory as it seems at first glance. In her introduction to the 1997 reprint of *Dark Symphony*, Carla Kaplan argues that although Adams represents herself as "submissive and frail," the text "participates in the African-American heritage of double-voicedness" (xviii). For example, Adams quotes Harlem Renaissance writers rather than espousing radical views herself, and her stories about racism and family conflict often challenge her professions of forgiveness and obedience.

Adams relied on royalties from *Dark Symphony* in the 1940s and 1950s as she moved from job to job, struggled with her health, and attempted to write. Between 1944 and 1955 Adams requested at least twelve emergency advances on her royalties from Sheed & Ward, indicating a life plagued by illness and economic instability (Kaplan, xxiii). When her mother died on 21 June 1952, Adams relinquished all future claims on *Dark Symphony* for a onetime royalty of $375. She planned to live with a family and work and write, but this arrangement did not work out. Adams contacted Sheed & Ward in desperation once more in 1953, but the editor rejected her request (Kaplan, xxv). Adams then virtually slips out of the historical record. Kaplan's research indicates that she was living in Santa Barbara in 1970, but her death date is unknown (xxii).

Dark Symphony fits into the tradition of African American autobiography by demonstrating the centrality of religious experience to personal identity. The narrative links a spiritual quest with the quest for racial justice, basing the notion of equality on divine authority. *Dark Symphony* invites comparison to African American autobiographies of the 1930s and 1940s, including RICHARD WRIGHT's *Black Boy* and *American Hunger* (1945) and ZORA NEALE HURSTON's *Dust Tracks on a Road* (1942). Twenty-first-century readers may be interested in the tensions between writer and patron and between Adams's social critique and her desire—or pragmatic need—to connect to a white Catholic readership.

Further Reading
Adams, Elizabeth Laura. *Dark Symphony and Other Works,* ed. Carla Kaplan (1997).
Barton, Rebecca Chalmers. *Witnesses for Freedom: Negro Americans in Autobiography* (1948).
Brignano, Russell C. *Black Americans in Autobiography* (1984).
David, Jay. *Growing Up Black* (1968).
Kaplan, Carla. "Introduction: 'I Wanna March,'" in *Dark Symphony* (1997).
Scally, Sister Mary Anthony, R.S.M. *Negro Catholic Writers, 1900–1943: A Bio-Bibliography* (1945).
ERIN ROYSTON BATTAT

ADAMS, Dock (1838–Sept. 1898), militia leader, was born in Georgia to parents whose names have not been recorded. Some sources list his name as Doc Adams. He was probably born a slave, as were the vast majority of African Americans in Augusta's cotton-rich hinterlands in the late 1830s; the 1840 U.S. census lists fewer than two hundred free blacks in Richmond County. As a carpenter Adams, like other slave artisans, may have been able to hire out his time, and he may have saved enough money to purchase his freedom. In any case Adams joined the Union army during the Civil War, and he acquired enough money to purchase five hundred acres of land—worth three thousand dollars—near Nashville, Georgia, where he lived for a time after hostilities ended in 1865. By 1872 he had returned to Augusta, where he earned good wages working as a boss carpenter. Adams was also involved in the political life of Richmond County, making an unsuccessful bid for local office in 1872, the same year that he founded a black militia company, the Grant Guard Infantry, named in honor of President Ulysses S. Grant. Similar armed clubs had begun to emerge in various Southern black communities as a response to the armed terrorism of the Ku Klux Klan and other white paramilitary groups.

After Klan violence helped to "redeem" Georgia from Republican rule in the early 1870s, white Democrats in the state legislature imposed a poll tax that greatly reduced the number of eligible black voters. With black Georgians "unable to exercise their political opinion as they wished" (Foner, 570) and unwilling to be oppressed, Adams moved in 1874 to Hamburg, South Carolina, a small community in Aiken County directly across the Savannah River from Augusta. Unlike in Georgia, the Republican

Party remained in political control of South Carolina, which at that time had a majority black population. By 1874, however, the proliferation of white rifle clubs and other paramilitary organizations in Aiken County and in neighboring Edgefield and Barnwell counties signaled the growing determination of "straightout" Democrats in South Carolina to follow Georgia's lead by ending Republican rule, using violence if necessary.

In order to defend Hamburg's black residents against such violence, Adams resurrected the town's militia company, which had been founded in 1870 by the Republican governor Robert Scott and commanded initially by the Hamburg native PRINCE RIVERS. Since Rivers's appointment as Hamburg's trial justice the company had rarely mustered, but by 1876 Adams had enlisted around eighty militiamen, armed them with the best Winchester rifles, and had them perform drills on the streets of Hamburg on a regular basis. Local whites complained that Adams's men harassed them, prevented them from drinking at water fountains, and arrested them for trivial offenses. Most galling to Aiken County whites was Adams's demand that they give way on Hamburg's streets to allow his men to drill. Such behavior, one South Carolinian wrote, was an "insult [such] as no white people upon earth had ever to put up with before"—African Americans, of course, had been putting up with such behavior from whites for most of their lives prior to Reconstruction (Foner, 570).

Matters came to head on 4 July 1876 as Adams drilled his men on an abandoned street in Hamburg. Two young white farmers in a buggy approached them and ordered that they move aside to let their buggy through. Adams retorted that, at 150 feet wide, the street was wide enough for the men to pass without disrupting his drill; eventually, however, he ordered the militia to stand aside and let the buggy through. The following day one of the farmers submitted a complaint to Prince Rivers, demanding that the judge arrest Adams for obstruction of what the farmer called "his" road. Much to Adams's annoyance, Rivers did so, also charging Adams with contempt of court when he complained about the arrest at his arraignment. Rivers ordered Adams to stand trial on the following Saturday, 8 July.

In the meantime tensions escalated in Hamburg and the surrounding area, fueled by the intervention of the region's leading Democrat, the former Confederate general Matthew C. Butler, who also commanded an Edgefield County rifle club. On the day of Adams's trial Butler entered Hamburg at the head of a company of two hundred armed men and a cannon that he had procured in Augusta. Although he had no legal authority to do so, Butler demanded that the militia surrender its weapons and that Adams publicly apologize to the two white men. When Adams refused, the forty or so members of his militia retreated to their barracks, where Butler's men shot at them. The militia returned fire, killing one of the whites. Butler's troops responded by firing their cannon at the barracks, forcing the outnumbered black militiamen to flee. That night Butler's men killed Hamburg's black marshal and rounded up twenty-five African Americans, not all of them members of the militia. Although accounts differ in the details of what happened next, most agree that Butler's troops killed five of the prisoners in cold blood; eyewitnesses later testified that Butler personally selected the men to be killed. Later that night armed white mobs rode through Hamburg, attacking African Americans and setting fire to their homes and businesses. Dock Adams escaped unscathed.

The Hamburg massacre, as it came to be known, was a turning point in Reconstruction in South Carolina, and indeed in the South itself. In response President Grant, though reluctant to intervene militarily in the South, sent federal troops to South Carolina—an act that prevented widespread atrocities on the scale of those at Hamburg but did not entirely put an end to the violence. South Carolina blacks were outraged by events in Hamburg. Congressman ROBERT SMALLS viewed the incident as "a premeditated and predetermined . . . unwarranted slaughter," whose goal had been to "keep the negroes in their place" (Williamson, 271). Indeed, as Adams later testified to a U.S. Senate committee, the naked show of force by Butler's men at Hamburg had been overtly political: throughout the day they had repeatedly chanted, "This is the beginning of Redemption in South Carolina!" (Foner, 572). The Hamburg massacre also united nearly all South Carolina whites behind the Democrats in that year's election, which the Democrats won on the back of further acts of violence, fraud, and intimidation at the polls. The following year the redeemed South Carolina legislature elected Matthew Butler to the U.S. Senate. Charges against whites indicted for the Hamburg massacre were soon dropped.

After the end of Reconstruction, Adams lived out his final decades in relative obscurity. When he died peacefully in September 1898, one white newspaper used the occasion to place the blame for the violence of 1876 squarely on his shoulders: "Adams led his people against the whites, and they [Adams's militia] were shot down without mercy. . . . It was he who kept negroes constantly worked up, and he is responsible for so many of their lives being taken." A white Hamburg Republican offered a more accurate reading of Adams's role in the Hamburg massacre, namely that Adams's greatest fault was his skill in drilling his militia, which made him the target of Butler and his rifle clubs. Dock Adams's determination to keep the peace by meeting violence with violence was ultimately futile, however, given the white rifle clubs' vast superiority in weaponry and the unwillingness of the federal government to intervene as an honest broker between the two armed factions.

Further Reading
Foner, Eric. *Reconstruction: America's Unfinished Revolution, 1863–1877* (1988).
Holt, Thomas. *Black over White: Negro Political Leadership in South Carolina during Reconstruction* (1977).
Williamson, Joel. *After Slavery: The Negro in South Carolina during Reconstruction, 1861–1877* (1965).
Obituary: *Columbia (South Carolina) State*, 9 Sept. 1898.

STEVEN J. NIVEN

ADAMS, George (c. 1847–29 Sept. 1939), cowboy and rancher, may have been born into slavery and escaped from bondage before the Civil War, though information about his life prior to his arrival in southwest Texas in the 1870s is limited. Based on stories he later told to his co-workers it seems likely that Adams spent his early adult life working as a cowboy in the brush country region of Texas, probably south and west of San Antonio. Given the circumstance of his birth and the times in which George came of age, he never received a formal education. As recent historical scholarship has made clear, black cowboys on the Texas plains enjoyed greater freedoms than did African Americans living in more settled regions of the state. However, their freedoms were always tainted by the persistent racism that prevailed during the late nineteenth and early twentieth centuries. George Adams's life was a vivid example of the common experiences of African American cowboys working in South Texas between the 1870s and 1930s.

In the 1870s Adams migrated to southwest Texas, where he found work in the Trans-Pecos region on the 7D Ranch, located on Comanche Creek four miles east of Fort Stockton, Texas. Adams worked for this outfit until the owners of the Western Union Beef Company, which had purchased the 7D in 1890, sold their operation to John T. McElroy, who owned a large cattle operation in Reeves County, in 1899. Adams next worked for the T5 Ranch, also known as the Independence Cattle Company, located on Independence Creek at Independence Spring. The T5 was the first big ranch established in what would later become Terrell County. Perhaps because of the company's problems in paying its employees Adams's stint with the T5 was short-lived. In 1902 he signed on with the C. F. Cox Ranch, located in present-day Brewster and Terrell counties. Coleman Cox, a native of Arkansas and staunch Republican who had moved to Texas in the 1870s, had moved from Throckmorton County in north-central Texas to his eighty-thousand-acre ranch shortly after purchasing it in 1900. Cox established the headquarters of the ranch in Sanderson, a town in Terrell County with a population of 112 citizens. Though meager in size Sanderson represented the only connection to the "outside world." Adams lived and worked on the ranch for the remainder of his life.

Adams and Cox developed a close relationship that lasted thirty-five years. Cox grew to respect Adams and eventually considered him a part of his family. Their friendship was firmly established during Adams's early days on the ranch when he took advantage of Texas's homestead laws and claimed eight sections of land for Cox. Once Adams obtained free title to the land from the state, he sold it to his boss. In this way the Cox Ranch grew in size, and the two men became unofficial partners. During the Depression, Cox was unable to make his mortgage payments at the Sanderson bank. Just as the bank was ready to foreclose, Adams, who often received payment for his services in cattle and had managed over time to build up a sizable herd, put his own cattle up as collateral, and Cox's loan was renewed. Because of this act future generations of the Cox family were able to maintain ownership of the ranch.

For thirty-eight years Adams preformed the same basic work and enjoyed the limited forms of entertainment offered by ranch life. He rode fence lines, pulled cattle out from the mud of drying stock ponds, joined in round-ups, doctored livestock, and trained horses. For these services George's boss often paid him in cattle. By modern standards George's entertainments were few. He participated in the annual ranch rodeo held in Sanderson. Every year he led the rodeo parade, and at the rodeo grounds he and his co-workers would show off their skills as professional cowboys. Throughout the year Adams often played cards and checkers with members of the Cox family and other ranch hands.

Adams first lived in an old bunkhouse at the ranch but later moved to an old storeroom that was previously used for storing horse tack after Coleman Cox's death in 1937. Generally speaking Adams's diet was simple and consisted primarily of meat, beans, and bread. Two of his favorite dishes were biscuits and "por jo," a kind of tomato dumpling. Adams enjoyed the freedom that ranch life offered black cowboys in the late nineteenth and early twentieth centuries, though he remained aware of the racial barriers present within the region. He never joined white cowboys at social functions, dinners, or in conversations, unless they invited him—though it is true that his presence was almost always requested. He believed that the best way to overcome the realities of racial prejudices was to perform his ranching duties better than his white counterparts. This emphasis on outworking whites served to make African American cowboys some of the best cowhands to ride the open range, and Adams was no exception. According to interviews with individuals who knew him personally, Adams gained recognition from the men who worked with him. Among his contemporaries, his abilities to use a lariat and to break wild horses were discussed at greater length than was the color of his skin.

Adams died of pneumonia. He had never married and had no known relatives, and so only the members of the Cox family and his friends were left to mourn his loss. In a kind of final testimony to his life he was laid to rest in the Cedar Grove Cemetery at Sanderson, in an era when African Americans and whites were almost always interred in segregated cemeteries. Adams, however, was laid to rest in a white cemetery near the grave of his long-time friend Coleman Cox. George Adams's life illustrates the African American cowboy experience in the Southwest, but his story was also exceptional in many ways. Unlike other black cowboys Adams became in many respects his own boss and for all practical purposes a partner with a white rancher. He was able to remain a cowboy all his life and continued working until the week before his death. Many black cowboys were forced into non-ranching occupations when the cattle drives from Texas ended in the late 1800s. Adams had earned and retained the respect of the white population in Brewster and Terrell counties during his lifetime.

Further Reading
Barr, Alwyn. *The African Texans* (2004).
Downie, Alice E., ed. *Terrell County History: Its Past and Its People* (1978).
Howell, Kenneth W. "George Adams: A Cowboy All His Life," in *Black Cowboys of Texas*, ed. Sarah R. Massey (2000).
Obituary: *Sanderson Times*, 29 Sept. 1939.
KENNETH WAYNE HOWELL

ADAMS, Henry (16 Mar. 1843–?), emigrationist leader, was born Henry Houston in Newton County, Georgia, to enslaved parents whose names are not now known. Most of what is known of Henry Adams's personal life is derived from testimony he offered in 1880 to the United States Senate during a government investigation of the causes of mass African American emigration from the former states of the Confederacy.

Henry was given the surname Adams when a planter of that name brought him and his family to Desoto Parish, Louisiana, in 1850. He used that surname for the rest of his life. Upon the planter's death eight years later ownership of Henry and his family was transferred to a teenage girl, Nancy Emily Adams, who hired the family out to various plantations near the Texas-Louisiana border. Laboring alongside his father on the plantation of a man named Ferguson in Logansport, Louisiana, Henry Adams was separated from his mother, who worked on a distant plantation owned by a brother of Nancy Adams. Like many couples torn apart by the slave system, Henry Adams' parents reunited shortly after the end of the Civil War and the general emancipation that followed. While still a slave in Louisiana, Henry Adams married a woman named Malinda, with whom he had four children: Lucy, Rena, Josephine, and Henry. That marriage was also ended by the economic dictates of slavery when Malinda's owner took Henry Adams's wife and children with him to Texas.

Like his father, an independent-minded lay preacher, Henry Adams "feared God but not man" (Hahn, 318). Having already amassed "three horses and a fine buggey, and a good deal of money" while still a slave, Adams was determined after his emancipation in June 1865 to receive due payment for his labors (Painter, 72). Most former slaveowners were, however, unwilling to bargain with him for the oats he cut, the cotton he baled, or the rails he split, and so

Adams soon left for the city of Shreveport, Louisiana. There he made some money as a peddler on the road between Logansport and Shreveport, and witnessed the efforts of thousands of former slaves to reunite with their families and to try to make the best of freedom, in spite of harassment, violent intimidation, and unfair labor contracts and racist legislation—the notorious black codes—which threatened to return African Americans to a state of legal bondage. Adams attempted to eke out a living as a peddler, but was himself beaten and robbed.

Like other African Americans seeking to assert his newly-won right to a free and independent life, Adams joined the institution most likely at that time to ensure it, the United States Army, in the fall of 1866. He served with the Thirty-Ninth and, later, the Twenty-Fifth Infantry divisions throughout Louisiana, rising eventually to the rank of quartermaster sergeant and learning to read and write in the process. Upon leaving the military in September 1869 he returned to Shreveport with enough money to invest in property, which, in true Jeffersonian fashion, provided him with the independence to speak his mind. Soon Adams and other literate veterans began helping black tenants throughout Caddo Parish to challenge the unfair labor contracts devised by many white landowners. Although these efforts invariably failed in courts that were controlled by those same landowners, Adams's forthright manner and his increasing wealth earned him the enmity and resentment of powerful whites in Shreveport, who threatened to kill him. Adams nonetheless prospered financially throughout the early 1870s. A prodigious rail-splitter—he reportedly could chop and stack as many as seven cords of wood a day—Adams also succeeded in managing plantations, lumber yards, and a cotton-oil mill. He also built a lucrative sideline as a faith healer and herbalist.

The same independent means and character that made Adams so threatening to whites made him a natural leader among the Louisiana freed people. Despite his protests that he was only a humble woodchopper and rail-splitter with no involvement in politics, Adams served as president of the Shreveport Republican club and was central to get-out-the-vote efforts in the early years of Reconstruction, a role that again brought him death threats from whites. In 1873 Adams served on Shreveport's grand jury, which had a majority of African-American members. Yet since all the lawyers, judges, and other court officials were white, he soon learned that justice in the post-emancipation South was almost as colorbound as it had been during slavery. Blacks received disproportionately harsher sentences than did whites for committing the same crimes, and the law provided little protection for African Americans who suffered from unfair labor contracts designed to enrich their former owners.

Increasingly aware of the limits of Reconstruction, and foreshadowing the progressive era methods of W. E. B. DU BOIS, Adams also formed a secret committee to "look into affairs and see the true condition of our race, to see whether it was possible we could stay under a people who held us under bondage" (Hahn, 319). After traveling throughout nine southern states, he found that the answer to his question was an unequivocal *no*. Adams met with hundreds of freedmen in these states between 1870 and 1874 and found examples of white intimidation of black voters, unfair labor contracts, and outright violence against African Americans similar to that he had witnessed in Louisiana.

The emergence in the summer of 1874 of the White League, a statewide organization dedicated to removing all African Americans from political office in Louisiana, spurred Adams and his committee to action, and to the belief that the promise of citizenship offered by Reconstruction could only be realized outside the South. The several hundred members of Adams's Colonization Council petitioned President Ulysses S. Grant to provide land in the United States, Liberia, or some other country since it had become "utterly impossible to live with the whites in Louisiana" (Hahn, 319). The White League also put pressure on employers to fire Republican activists, including Adams, who on purely political grounds was dismissed from his job managing a major plantation. Thereafter he devoted his energies to building the Colonization Council to a membership of 69,000 by August 1877, when it again petitioned the president, now Rutherford B. Hayes, to support a plan to aid the emigration of African Americans from the South. Hayes, like Grant, paid no heed to the request.

In November 1878 Adams helped launch in Shreveport the Negro Union Cooperative Aid Association, which appealed to the black laborers and farmers of Louisiana to form a political convention that drew on the grassroots networks of religious, fraternal, and political networks to form a specifically black-nationalist response to the problems of the freed people. Although his own preference was for emigration to Liberia or some other part of Africa, Adams also encouraged the many thousands of southern black "exodusters" who, led by BENJAMIN "PAP" SINGLETON, sought a better life in Kansas and Indiana. In spite of—or perhaps because of—his own experiences in the Republican Party, Adams opposed the involvement of prominent ministers and established politicians in the emigrationist cause, preferring that the organization be composed "entirely of laboring people" (Hahn, 343). Though this stance gave his emigrationist movement a more democratic character, it also ensured that the Colonization Council and similar groups throughout the South would struggle to find the money needed to execute their plans. A yellow fever epidemic that afflicted Adams and many others in Louisiana in 1878 did not help matters.

Although the Colonization Council had urged blacks after 1876 to protest by boycotting the political process, Adams returned to political activism in the Louisiana elections of 1878. Violent intimidation of black and white Republicans alike and vote-rigging by the White League intensified in that election, but in spite of Adams's vocal protests to the attorney general of the United States, it became apparent that the federal government had largely abandoned the South to the white supremacist Redemptionist arm of the Democratic Party. In December 1878 Adams traveled to New Orleans in the hope of testifying before federal authorities about the violence and other election abuses he had witnessed in the previous month's elections. He continued to promote the idea of emigration to Liberia and to the increasingly more popular destination of Kansas, but was cut off from the base of his movement in northern Louisiana as well as from the mainstream leadership of the emigrationist cause. Although he found work in New Orleans in a variety of minor federal positions, he lacked funds and was unable to join several Colonization Council members who left for Liberia in 1881.

Adams disappears from the historical record in 1884. It is not known when or how he died. His significance lies in his efforts to promote the emigrationist cause among working-class rural black southerners during Reconstruction, a legacy upon which later black emigrationists, notably MARCUS GARVEY, would successfully build in the 1920s.

Further Reading
Hahn, Steven. *A Nation under Our Feet: Black Political Struggles in the Rural South from Slavery to the Great Migration* (2003).
Painter, Nell. *Exodusters: Black Migration to Kansas after Reconstruction* (1976; repr. 1986).
STEVEN J. NIVEN

ADAMS, John Henry, Jr. (21 Aug. 1878–5 Sept. 1948), artist, was born in Colquitt County, Georgia, son of John Henry Adams, a former slave and preacher in the Methodist Church, and Mittie Rouse. Many questions surround Adams's early life. While he reported in an *Atlanta Constitution* article (23 June 1902) that he came from a humble background, his father served parishes throughout Georgia. According to the *History of the American Negro and His Institutions* (1917), Adams Sr. was a man of accomplishment, leading black Georgians in a colony in Liberia for two years and receiving two honorary doctorates, from Bethany College and Morris Brown University. Educated in Atlanta schools, Adams claimed in the *Atlanta Constitution* article to have traveled to Philadelphia in the late 1890s to take art classes at the Drexel Institute of Art, Science, and Industry (later Drexel University). Drexel, established in 1891, opened its doors to a diverse student body. Even though the school's records do not show Adams's enrollment, it is likely that Adams reported the truth when he stated that he had studied under Howard Pyle, the famed illustrator and teacher who inspired a generation of American illustrators and who was at that time an instructor at Drexel. While the composition of Adams's drawings may have been inspired by Pyle's interest in dramatic narrative, the content of Adams's work is often closer in spirit to the socially progressive realist aesthetic of the Philadelphia newspaper illustrations of John Sloan, whose work, along

with that of other artists, was dubbed by the press the Ashcan School and considered radical for its depiction of the working class.

There is greater certainty concerning Adams's life from 1901 to 1908, as he returned to Atlanta and established the art department of the African Methodist Episcopal (AME) Church's Morris Brown College in 1901. Listed as "professor of art," Adams designed a curriculum that guided both male and female students through various media disciplines, including mechanical drawing, oil painting, watercolors, and charcoal, pastel, and pencil drawing. According to course catalogs, the art department, among the first at a historically black college, balanced traditional figure studies from plaster casts, still life, and out-of-doors landscape painting. Studio classes were supplemented by lecture series conducted by leading black scholars, including JOHN HOPE, W. E. B. DU BOIS, and the Congregational clergyman the Reverend HENRY HUGH PROCTOR. Adams's first naturalistic religious paintings, completed in 1902, earned the praise of the city's major newspaper, the *Atlanta Constitution*. Its editors reproduced Adams's biblical painting, *The Accused Woman*, in the paper's pages that same year and urged readers to see his works in person.

During his tenure at Morris Brown, Adams also began his best-known works, illustrations for the major African American journal of the era, *The Voice of the Negro*. From 1904 until 1907 he produced more than sixty drawings and political cartoons, as well as articles and poems for the *Voice*. Adams's drawing style for the *Voice* was both conservative and modern, reflecting his admiration for both BOOKER T. WASHINGTON and W. E. B. Du Bois. His drawings combined an interest in the Christian uplift and the Arts and Crafts–inspired aesthetics of Washington, as well as actively promoting positive images of African Americans based on self-determined ideas of beauty. In September 1906 the *Voice* began selling prints of his drawings, telling readers to place in their homes these "educative" works in order "to take the place of those meaningless white angels and black devils on our walls" (*Voice*, 622–623). One of these Adams prints, the editors of the *Voice* claimed, offered a black equivalent of the Gibson Girl, the favored motif of the popular white illustrator Charles Dana Gibson. Adams's political cartoons often recalled the vigorous marks of Thomas Nast's work. Those Adams drawings emphasizing moralizing racial uplift were quite similar to the work of Frank Beard. Not only was Beard a famous illustrator, but he was also widely known in the Atlanta black community for his drawings in Booker T. Washington's first autobiography, *An Autobiography: The Story of My Life and Work* (1900).

In addition to teaching at Morris Brown, painting, and working for the *Voice*, Adams found time to work on other projects. In 1905 he collaborated with *The Voice* contributor SILAS XAVIER FLOYD to create *Floyd's Flowers*, a Christian moralizing guide for black parents for which Adams produced more than eighty drawings. Then, in 1906, Adams supplied Du Bois with drawings for the short-lived *The Moon Illustrated Weekly*. The next phase of Adams's life as an artist, from 1908 to 1928, saw him leave Atlanta but continue to work for Du Bois. The *Atlanta Constitution* announced in 1908 that Adams planned a trip to Paris to visit the painter HENRY OSSAWA TANNER. Instead Adams moved to Florida in 1908, living most of the time in Jacksonville until the early 1930s, although he lived in Tampa during the late 1920s. In Florida he worked as a newspaper writer and photographer and created drawings for Du Bois's next publication, *The Horizon: A Journal of the Color Line*. The cover drawing for volume five of the 1909 *Horizon* showed Adams at his best, revealing how northern white patrons, in their refusal to see black progress, admired a white southern artist transforming a black man into a demeaning caricature. In 1910 Adams worked with Du Bois on his new venture, the NAACP's *The Crisis*, to which Adams contributed cover illustrations as well as political cartoons. By the late 1920s, when Adams's last drawings appeared in *The Crisis*, his style was considered old-fashioned and was replaced by the African-inspired modernism of artists such as AARON DOUGLAS.

In Adams's later years the Howard University artist and scholar JAMES AMOS PORTER stood almost alone in remembering Adams. Porter's important 1943 *Modern Negro Art* criticized the unevenness of Adams's style but recognized that he was an artist of considerable talent who deserved recognition. Porter seemed unaware that Adams was still alive. In 1948, twenty years after his last drawing appeared in *The Crisis*, Adams died quietly in a nursing home in Jacksonville, where he had returned two years earlier. Among the few places with Adams's works in their collections after his fame diminished were the Kenkeleba House in New York City, which had four oil portraits, and the Herndon Home in Atlanta, which had two Adams ink drawings.

Few modern artists experienced such fame and later obscurity as John Henry Adams Jr. During the first two decades of the twentieth century, Adams ranked high among the nation's leading African American artists, becoming perhaps the first nationally known black illustrator in America. Some thought his talent second only to Henry O. Tanner. Yet by the early 1930s Adams had vanished from the public eye.

Further Reading

Finding John Henry Adams's art and biographical information is challenging. The most accessible sources for seeing his art and reading his writings are microfilms of *The Voice of the Negro* (1904–1907) and *The Crisis* (Adams's drawings appear from 1910–1928).

Mellinger, Wayne Martin. "Ancestors: John Henry Adams and the Image of the New Negro," *The International Review of Art* 14 (1997).

Porter, James Amos. *Modern Negro Art* (1943, repr. 1992).

Powell, Richard. *Black Art and Culture in the 20th Century* (1997).

MICHAEL BIEZE

ADAMS, John Hurst (27 Nov. 1927–), bishop, civil rights leader, and educator, was born in Columbia, South Carolina, to Rev. Eugene Avery Adams and Charity Nash Adams. He and his three siblings, Avery, Charity, and Lucy Rose, were raised in a spiritual and intellectually stimulating home. His father, an African Methodist Episcopal (AME) minister and social activist, in the 1920s organized the first African American bank in Columbia and the first modern statewide civil rights organization in South Carolina. None of these activities went unnoticed by young John and they helped to define his later focus and commitments. Adams was educated in the segregated Columbia school system and graduated from BOOKER T. WASHINGTON High School. His undergraduate work was completed at Johnson C. Smith University in Charlotte, North Carolina, where he earned an AB degree in History in 1947. After studying at Boston University School of Theology, he received a bachelor of sacred theology (STB) in 1950. In 1956 he received his master of sacred theology (MTB) there. While at the university he befriended MARTIN LUTHER KING JR., who was pursuing a PhD in systematic theology. He became an apostle of King and his doctrine of non-violence. Adams also did some study at Harvard University in 1951 and at Union Theological Seminary in 1956.

As a seminary student Adams was assigned to the pastorate of Bethel AME Church in Lynn, Massachusetts, from 1950 until 1952. He served on the faculty at Payne Theological Seminary at Wilberforce University in Ohio from 1952 until 1956. After that he became President of Paul Quinn College in Waco, Texas, and also served as campus pastor to all the students. Adams married Dollie Deselle of New Orleans in 1956; together they would have three daughters. His wife would also go on to become a prominent church leader and hold a doctor of education degree from Baylor University in Waco, Texas.

In 1962 Adams went to Seattle, Washington, as pastor of First AME Church and began his ascent as a national leader. The members of the church were at first dismayed by this fiery young man who spoke out so bluntly about social conditions in the city—the segregated housing, de facto segregated schools, and discriminatory hiring practices—as well as by the style of his ministry. The white community labeled him a troublemaker. Not long afterwards, however, he became a leader of the civil rights movement in Seattle and earned the respect of both the black and white communities. His articulate assessment of the race problems and his passionate belief in the potential of the city ignited one of the most successful movements in the country. He was the key spokesman for black people in Seattle during the height of the civil rights movement. He chaired the Central Area Civil Rights Committee, which included the heads of all the local civil rights organizations, ranging from the Congress of Racial Equality (CORE), led by Walter Hundley; the NAACP, led by Charles Johnson and E. June Smith; and the Seattle Urban League, headed by

Edwin T. Pratt, who in 1969 would be murdered on the doorstep of his home. The Committee was forceful and unique because it presented a unified front pressing for citywide racial reform and it determined the local civil rights agenda.

In 1965 Adams co-founded the Central Area Motivation Program, the country's first "war on poverty" agency. Two years earlier he led a march downtown for equal employment, led the fight for an open housing ordinance in 1964, and in 1966 spearheaded the school boycott to force integration of the Seattle Public Schools. He served on the Model Cities Planning Board and watched the agency become an exemplar for the rest of the nation. His influence spread even further during his five years in Seattle when he was appointed in 1965 to Governor Daniel Evans' Urban Affairs Committee, United Good Neighbors Planning Committee, and the boards of the Council of Churches and the YMCA. Among his many commendations during this period were the Man of the Year Award, given by the Seattle chapter of B'nai B'rith in 1964, and the Man of the Year award from the Seattle Urban League in 1965.

Adams became pastor of Grant AME Church in the Watts section of Los Angeles in 1968, three years after the riot. He was appointed by Bishop Howard Thomas Primm of the Fifth Episcopal District. There he again became involved in local NAACP activities and led a freedom patrol based on his Seattle experience. His design, however, was program, not protest. He launched the Education Growth Organization and Black Church Ethnic Schools with a published curriculum that spread to six other churches in the city. With the purpose of developing pride and academic excellence, the Grant AME School for middle school students was held every Saturday morning with free breakfast and lunch. The curriculum included mathematics, English, and African American history. In 1972 Adams was appointed bishop of the Tenth Episcopal District (Texas), a position from which he continued his civil rights activism by escorting a student to integrate the Waco Public Schools, and by supporting student protests to integrate all public facilities in Waco. Recognizing the need for establishing communication across denominational lines he was instrumental in the founding of the Congress of National Black Churches in 1978.

From 1980 until 1988 Adams served as bishop of the Second Episcopal District (comprising Maryland, Washington, D.C., North Carolina, and Virginia) and began his pioneering efforts of expansion by facilitating the formation of thirty-five new congregations in his jurisdiction. His next four years were served as bishop of the Sixth Episcopal District (Georgia), where he welcomed four new congregations and continued his interest in civil rights. He resigned from the boards of the National Urban League and Southern Christian Leadership Conference in protest when the organizations' presidents supported the nomination of CLARENCE THOMAS to the U.S. Supreme Court.

Adams's final years in active ministry were spent in two southern AME districts. From 1992 until 2000 he was bishop of the Seventh Episcopal District (South Carolina), where he promoted the formation of ten new congregations and was a leader of the successful movement to remove the Confederate flag from the South Carolina State House. From 2000 to 2004 Adams served as bishop of the Eleventh Episcopal District (Florida, Barbados), where he encouraged the growth of eleven new congregations and oversaw the reorganization of fiscal affairs to eliminate indebtedness. He retired in 2005 and became adjunct professor at the Candler School of Theology at Emory University. His special and civic ministries comprised a vast array of social and educational activities, including membership on the boards of five colleges and universities and national boards of organizations dealing with racial, economic, and social problems. He was the recipient of over twenty-five awards for his service to the community.

Further Reading
Richardson, Larry Samuel. *Civil Rights in Seattle; a Rhetorical Analysis of a Social Movement* (1975).
Who's Who in America 2002, vol. 1 (c. 2001).
Who's Who in Religion, 1975–1976 (c. 1975).

MARY T. HENRY

ADAMS, John Quincy (4 May 1848–3 Sept. 1922), newspaper editor and publisher, civil rights leader, and Republican Party activist, was born in Louisville, Kentucky, the son of Henry Adams, a prominent minister and educator, and Margaret Corbin. Both of his parents were free persons of color. Following private schooling in Wisconsin and Ohio, Adams graduated from Oberlin College. After a brief teaching stint in Louisville, in 1870 he followed his uncle, Joseph C. Corbin, to work in Arkansas during Reconstruction. By 1874 Adams had risen from schoolteacher to assistant superintendent of public instruction. His lifelong activism in the Republican Party began in Arkansas; there he twice served as secretary to Republican state conventions, was elected as justice of the peace on the party ticket, and held the offices of engrossing clerk of the state senate and deputy commissioner of public works. The defeat of the Arkansas Republican Party in 1874 and the racial repression that followed led Adams to return to Louisville, where he again engaged in teaching.

Adams entered journalism in 1879 when he and his brother, Cyrus Field Adams, established the *Louisville Bulletin*, a weekly newspaper that served the Louisville African American community until 1885, when it was subsumed by the *American Baptist*. In 1880 Adams helped organize the National Afro-American Press Association, which held its first annual meeting in Louisville that year. Elected the organization's first president, he served from 1880 to 1882.

In 1886 Adams accepted an offer to join the staff of the St. Paul, Minnesota, *Western Appeal*, a black-owned weekly. Within a year he assumed the editorship and incorporated the Northwestern Publishing Company, which supported the expansion of the newspaper to include offices in Chicago, Louisville, Indianapolis, St. Louis, Dallas, and Washington, D.C. The *Western Appeal* prospered under his leadership; it was one of only nine African American newspapers established in the 1880s that survived until 1914. Its editorials consistently attacked racial discrimination and called for equal treatment both locally and nationally.

Adams helped organize resistance to racial discrimination in public accommodations and in the workplace in Minnesota through the establishment of the Minnesota Protective and Industrial League in 1887 and its successor, the Afro-American League of St. Paul, in 1889. He worked with T. THOMAS FORTUNE to found the National Afro-American League in 1890, serving on its first executive committee. The Afro-American Council, dominated by BOOKER T. WASHINGTON's accommodationist "Tuskegee machine," received his initial support in 1898. By 1903 the hostility of the council to civil rights activism in the North alienated Adams. Although he was not a leader in the National Association for the Advancement of Colored People (NAACP), he endorsed it by 1913 and broke with the Tuskegee faction. His editorials and civic activity continued to attack racial discrimination for the remainder of his life.

The other constant in Adams's public life was loyalty to the Republican Party. The *Western Appeal* consistently endorsed Republican candidates even as the party courted white southern votes by abandoning civil rights. Only President Warren G. Harding's acquiescence to segregation and lynching finally led Adams to question publicly his allegiance to the party.

Adams's influence peaked between 1890 and 1910. By 1913 the *Western Appeal* had closed its offices in Dallas, St. Louis, Louisville, Chicago, and Washington, D.C., and had shrunk to a local weekly. The paper and its editor remained influential in St. Paul, however, until his death. Adams was killed in an automobile accident in St. Paul. He was survived by his wife, Ella B. Smith, whom he had married in 1892; the couple had four children.

Even as he spent his life fighting the rising tide of racism during the Gilded Age, Adams demonstrated that the barriers to freedom were not insurmountable. His creation of a newspaper with offices in seven major cities, his leadership among African American journalists, and his advocacy of civil rights earned him a national reputation by 1900. He epitomized the African American middle class of the urban North. Light enough in complexion to pass for white, he edited a "race journal" supported by the African American community and dedicated to securing their civil rights.

Further Reading
No collection of Adams's papers exists, but the Minnesota Historical Society holds copies of his newspaper.

Spangler, Earl. *The Negro in Minnesota* (1961).

Suggs, Henry Lewis. "Democracy on Trial: The Black Press, Black Migration, and the Evolution of Culture and Community in Minnesota, 1865–1970," in *The Black Press in the Middle West, 1865–1985*, ed. Henry Lewis Suggs (1996).

Taylor, David V. "John Quincy Adams: St. Paul Editor and Black Leader," *Minnesota History* 43 (Winter 1973): 283–96.

Thornbrough, Emma Lou. "American Negro Newspapers, 1880–1914," *Business History Review* 40 (Winter 1966): 467–490.

Obituaries: *St. Paul Appeal*, 9 and 16 Sept. 1922.

WILBERT H. AHERN

ADAMS, John Quincy (1845–?), author of an autobiographical slave narrative, was born near Winchester, Virginia, to slave parents whose names are now unknown. Adams and his family were owned by George F. Calomese, a member of a prominent planter family. John Quincy Adams and his twin brother were one of four pairs of twins born to their mother, who had twenty-five children.

What we know of Adams's life comes from his autobiography, *Narrative of the Life of John Quincy Adams* (1872), which briefly traces Adams's life as a slave and as a freeman. Written in simple, plain language, the *Narrative* captures the tragedy of slavery in powerful ways. The most poignant events in Adams's early life involve the sale of family members and friends. In 1857 the sale of his twin brother Aaron and his sister Sallie left Adams "very sad and heart-broken" (Adams, 28). Though crushed by the loss, he maintained contact with Aaron for a time through correspondence: "Two or three years after I heard from my dear brother. He had been sold seven times, and was bought every time for a house servant. The last time he was sold a gentleman bought him in Memphis, Tennessee. There he lived for some time, and when he got a chance he wrote to us" (Adams, 28–29). The two then lost contact. In 1868, after a friend of John's had encountered Aaron in Memphis, Tennessee, the brothers were reunited. Appreciating that freedom meant that they could visit each other at will, the brothers had their rejoicing tempered by their failure to locate Sallie Ann. "But still I sorrow yet," Adams wrote. "My dear sister, Sallie Ann Adams, who was sold with brother Aaron, has not been heard from yet, but we still hope that God will bless us with that opportunity to meet her on earth. If not, this is our hope in the last days" (Adams, 31).

Adams's parents had instilled a deep faith in him and his siblings, which he carried throughout his life. Sunday church gatherings and biblical readings that promised salvation for the poor and oppressed were comforting to slaves. Religion also served to make slaves, including John Quincy Adams, keenly aware of their illiteracy. Possessing a strong desire to read and write from an early age, Adams augmented whatever instruction he received from his father, who could read, by listening to the conversations of his owners and acquiring whatever learning he could by stealth. "The man who would deprive another of learning to read and write, and learn wisdom does not fear God," Adams concluded. "They [slave owners] took my labor to educate their children, and then laughed at me for being ignorant and poor, and had not sense enough to know that they were the cause of it" (Adams, 12).

That anger toward the institution of slavery spurred Adams and his family to escape their plantation on 27 June 1862. As the Union general John W. Geary's division approached the Calomese plantation, the Adams family fled. General Geary, however, had issued orders that no one—white or black, free or slave—could leave Winchester. But Adams's father implored Geary to let him and his family through. Geary not only allowed them to continue on, but provided them with a pass to Pennsylvania. John Quincy Adams and his relatives moved from town to town, eventually settling in Harrisburg, where his father bought property, an extraordinary act for anyone fresh from slavery. Though his parents returned to Winchester following the war, John remained in Harrisburg, where he worked as a house servant for several employers. One of the elite whites whom he encountered frequently was General Geary, who was elected governor of Pennsylvania in 1866.

Adams was deeply philosophical about his escape from slavery. He wrote, "I do not know that I ever stole anything very valuable but one thing, and I think that every just man will say that I done right. In 1862 I stole John Q. Adams from Mr. George F. Calomese, of Winchester, Va. They valued me at $2,000. At that rate I stole $2,000" (Adams, 47). The act of "stealing himself" allowed Adams to find employment in various hotels as a bellhop and waiter. Most important for him, his wages allowed him to purchase books and pursue his lifelong interest in learning to read and write.

At the conclusion of his narrative, Adams included several personal letters of recommendation written by employers, friends, and attorneys who vouched for his integrity and for the veracity of his life story. In addition, Adams included the first clause of the Declaration of Independence, undoubtedly to draw his readers' attention to the phrase, "all men are created equal." Likewise Adams inserted the text of the three Reconstruction amendments to the U.S. Constitution: the Thirteenth, which ended slavery; the Fourteenth, which granted citizenship to African Americans; and the Fifteenth, which extended suffrage to black men. *Narrative of the Life of John Quincy Adams* is an important example of the genre of the slave narrative. It demonstrates much of what modern-day historians have sought to capture about the experience of slavery. In Adams's work we see not only the cruelty of slavery, but the slaves' heroic efforts to maintain their families, acquire education, and resist an institution that sought to degrade them to the level of commodities. We see their unquenchable thirst for freedom; there are no "contented slaves" in the story of John Quincy Adams.

Further Reading
Adams, John Quincy. *Narrative of the Life of John Quincy Adams, When in Slavery, and Now as a Freeman* (1872).

KEVIN D. ROBERTS

ADAMS, Numa Pompilius Garfield (26 Feb. 1885–29 Aug. 1940), physician and medical educator, was born in Delaplane, Virginia. Little is known about Adams's family and early life. He attended a country school run by his uncle, Robert Adams. Numa received additional instruction and inspiration from his grandmother Amanda, a midwife who shared with him the secrets of herbal medicine. When Numa Adams was thirteen, his family moved to Steelton, Pennsylvania. Soon Adams taught himself how to read music and purchased a used cornet, which he taught himself how to play.

After graduating from high school in 1905, Adams spent a year as a substitute teacher in Steelton and another year teaching seventh grade in Carlisle, Pennsylvania. These jobs helped him earn sufficient money to pay for his college education, and in 1907 he left Pennsylvania to enter Howard University in Washington, D.C. He soon joined the Lyric Orchestra, a dance band composed mostly of medical and dental students, which performed three to five nights a week. On other nights Adams supplemented his earnings by appearing with Louis Brown's orchestra.

Adams received his undergraduate degree magna cum laude from Howard in 1911, and the following year he earned a master's degree in chemistry from Columbia University. He moved back to Washington, D.C., to take a post as an instructor of chemistry at Howard. He remained on the faculty of Howard's chemistry department until 1919, rising through the ranks and becoming first assistant and then associate professor of chemistry. In 1918 Adams was named head of the department, but he did not find chemistry sufficiently satisfying to continue his career in it. In addition he may have been concerned about the limited salary that a professor at that time could get; he had married OSCEOLA MACARTHY in 1915, and they had one child.

In the fall of 1919 Adams resigned the chair of the chemistry department to pursue a medical career. The following spring he moved to Chicago and entered Rush Medical College. Adams again turned to music to help finance his education, but tastes had changed, and playing the cornet was no longer a marketable skill. Adams then purchased a saxophone and within three weeks had become sufficiently expert to join the Charley Cooke Orchestra. Attending classes during the day and performing every night, Adams relegated most of his studying to the commute of an hour and a half from Chicago to the dance hall where the orchestra played. This grueling schedule did not stop him from winning Rush's Smiley scholarship nor from finishing second in his medical class. He graduated in 1924 and was elected to Alpha Omega Alpha, a medical scholastic fraternity.

After a year's internship at a city hospital in St. Louis, Adams returned to Chicago and opened a private practice. He also served as assistant medical director of the Victory Life Insurance Company. In 1927 he returned to teaching, this time as an instructor in neurology and psychiatry at Provident Hospital.

In 1929 the quiet life he had established in Chicago ended when the president of Howard, MORDECAI JOHNSON, offered him the deanship of the university's medical school.

Even before Adams agreed to become the first African American dean of an approved medical school, he must have been aware of the difficulties that would face him. Although Howard had always been among the elite of the predominantly black medical schools, its budget was considerably smaller than that of many nonblack institutions. Howard had no endowment and subsisted entirely on tuition fees. Ten years earlier, Adams's predecessors had contemplated closing the school altogether.

Despite the obstacles and the mixed greetings that he received from the standing faculty—which included many white as well as black professors—Adams set to work charting a new path for Howard Medical School. Several of his actions in office proved controversial among the faculty. Traditionally the faculty members had worked their teaching schedules around other paid positions. Adams put an end to this system and enforced a daytime schedule of classes that would be more convenient for the students.

In another controversial move, Adams began a campaign to bring better-trained faculty to the medical school. In his first years he recruited a number of new faculty with doctorates in their disciplines. When interviewing new faculty members, Adams cared little for the reputation of the schools that a candidate had attended; rather, he paid particularly close attention to the candidate's course of study. Perhaps not surprisingly given his own background, he appeared to favor those who had a background in scientific research as well as in medicine. To attract the best candidates, Adams offered applicants a generous starting salary of $3,500, with a $500 increase each year up to $6,000. This move drew protest from the administrators at Nashville's Meharry Medical College, who argued that their school—then the only other black medical college in the country—would suffer because it could not match Howard's salaries.

Adams remained determined to provide Howard's medical students with the best possible education. Although the Depression forced him to withdraw his promise of raises, he continued his quest to mold Howard into an elite institution. During his ten years as dean, he steadily raised entrance requirements in the hope of improving the caliber of the student body. This policy, however, often resulted in fewer eligible students. One year, the school admitted a class of only twenty-six. Critics warned of loss of tuition revenues and reduction of opportunities for African Americans to enter the medical profession, but Adams's claim that this policy would produce better students was proven true toward the end of his tenure as dean. Previously, at least one student, and sometimes more, in each class had failed the annual board examinations, but the last four classes that Adams admitted while dean all passed.

In the final years of his deanship, Adams oversaw the integration of the Freedmen's Hospital with Howard University. Founded before the university, Freedmen's was operated by the U.S. Department of the Interior until the late 1930s. In 1937 the secretary of the department commissioned a study on the future of the hospital. On the basis of the study's recommendation, the department concluded that Howard Medical School should take over operation of the hospital. Even this change, which Adams oversaw, was not without its detractors; but despite protests, particularly from the city's Medico-Chirurgical Society, Freedmen's Hospital was transferred to Howard Medical School in 1940.

Adams died that same year in Chicago, after a long illness that many of his friends attributed at least in part to the strains of the deanship. He knew that he had antagonized many and endeared himself to few during his years as dean. Up to the end of his life, he continued to feel that his labors were unappreciated.

Further Reading
Cobb, William Montague. "Medical History," *Journal of the National Medical Association* 43 (1951).
Logan, Rayford. *Howard University: The First Hundred Years, 1867–1967* (1969).
Ludmerer, Kenneth M. *Learning to Heal: The Development of American Medical Education* (1985).
                                        SHARI RUDAVSKY

ADAMS, Ron (25 June 1934–), painter, graphic artist, printmaker, and publisher, was born in Detroit, Michigan, the son of Ned Adams, an electrician and occasional sign painter, and Laura. Adams first explored art making by mimicking his father, who, according to Adams, enjoyed drawing. After the divorce of his parents around 1944, Adams lived with his aunt and uncle, Claudia and Caleb Spivey. Although he sought to attend a program for gifted children at the Detroit Institute of Arts, his uncle vehemently prohibited it, preferring that Adams spend his free time working jobs such as delivering newspapers. Adams attended Northwestern High School in Detroit while continuing to live with the Spiveys until age fifteen, when he moved to his father's home.

After graduating from high school in 1951, Adams moved to Romeo, Michigan, a then rural town forty-one miles north of Detroit. There Adams worked at Graff Engineering, a small manufacturing company, and earned extra income on the weekends working on the farm of Victor Graff, the owner of Graff Engineering, during haying season. In 1951 Adams moved to Los Angeles; in 1955 he married Mary Black. The couple had a daughter, Rochelle Adams, and ultimately divorced in 1962. Adams worked on an assembly line for Mission Appliance Corporation and then for the Los Angeles Post Office while continuing his education; he studied graphic arts at the Los Angeles Trade Technical College (1955–1956), drafting at the Manual Arts Adult Night School in Los Angeles (1958), general engineering at Los Angeles City College (1959), and technical illustration and commercial art at Los Angeles Trade Technical College, where he received his certificate of trade proficiency in June 1963.

Adams had started working in 1962 as a technical illustrator for Hughes Aircraft Company in Los Angeles, and during his years there he continued his studies, this time in fine art, at the Otis Art Institute, Los Angeles, where he took courses in drawing, painting, and sculpture with Joseph Mugnaini and Arnold Meshes, who both became mentors for the young artist. In 1964 Adams was laid off from Hughes, whereupon he became a technical illustrator for Litton Industries in Woodland Hills, California. A year later Adams was laid off from Litton and was re-hired by Hughes. In 1965 he also studied drawing at the University of California, Los Angeles. Subsequently he began to exhibit his art, first at the Watts Art Festival in 1965, followed by exhibitions at the Los Angeles Municipal Gallery, Brockman Gallery, and the Downey Museum.

An affinity for Mexican muralists, such as José Clemente Orozco and David Alfaro Siqueiros, led Adams to move in 1966 to Mexico City, where he studied lithography and metal engraving at the University of Mexico. The following year the International Olympic Committee selected Adams to design a wide variety of materials, including posters, signs, murals, and other illustrations, for the 1968 Olympics in Mexico City.

In 1969 Adams moved back to Los Angeles and began working for Gemini Graphic Editions Limited (GEL) under the tutelage of Kenneth E. Tyler, the founder and owner. Then in its fourth year of operation, Gemini was becoming one of the preeminent artists' workshops and publishers of limited edition prints and sculptures in the United States. While at Gemini, Adams advanced from assistant printer to master printer in four years. As a printmaker, Adams worked with a wide range of highly recognized artists at the time, including Jasper Johns, Robert Rauschenberg, Ellsworth Kelly, and Frank Stella.

In 1973 Adams began working as a master printer at Ernest De Soto's Editions Press in San Francisco while maintaining a residence in Los Angeles. The following year he married Hazel Jaramillo, and they moved to Santa Fe, New Mexico, where he opened his own graphic workshop, Hand Graphics Ltd., with his wife and Robert Arber. Adams attracted several artists of note during the thirteen years of the workshop's existence, including Judy Chicago, Luis Jiménez, Fritz Scholder, R. C. Gorman, and the African Americans JOHN BIGGERS and CHARLES WHITE—two seminal figures in the graphic arts in the later twentieth century. Adams separated from his wife in about 1981.

The desire to return to creating his own art full time led Adams in 1988 to sell Hand Graphics and accept an invitation from Hampton University, a historically black university in Virginia, to be an artist in residence for the 1989–1990 academic year. While an

artist in his own right, Adams always recognized that printmaking, especially in the service of others, was a craft, albeit a highly skilled one. A pivotal work from this period was his large-scale color lithograph *Profile in Blue* (1988), which effectively summarized his life as a printmaker. In this work an African American printmaker—certainly a stand-in for the artist—sits on the bed of his press, ink roller in hand, and gazes into the distance.

The year 1987 marked the beginning of a long, intimate relationship between Adams and Arlene LewAllen and the foundation of LewAllen Contemporary, which became the preeminent modern and contemporary art gallery in Sante Fe. Four years after the beginning of his relationship with LewAllen, Adams divorced his wife, Hazel Jaramillo. Adam and LewAllen never married, and their relationship ended in 2002, the year LewAllen died of a brain aneurism. Two years later Adams moved to Atlanta, Georgia, where he continued to work as a professional artist.

Throughout Adams's career as an artist and printmaker, he was often engaged in a wide range of initiatives and projects that highlighted his long-standing role as an arts activist. These activities included his chairmanship of a committee he established in Sante Fe in 1985 to help provide artists with low-cost studios in a skyrocketing housing market.

Adams's career is also noted by numerous exhibitions that began in 1966 in venues that include, among others, the Museum of Fine Arts, Sante Fe (1987, 1992, 1995, 1996); Society of American Graphic Artists, New York (1986); Vanderbilt University Fine Arts Gallery in Nashville, Tennessee (2000); and the University of New Mexico Art Museum (1992). His art is in the collections of the Albuquerque Museum, New Mexico; the California Afro-American Museum, Los Angeles; the Hampton University Museum, Virginia; and the Smithsonian Museum of American Art, Washington, D.C.

Further Reading
Kimbrough, Blake T., and Marshall, Melvin A. *From Challenge to Triumph: African American Prints and Printmaking 1867–2002* (2003).
Taha, Halima. *Collecting African American Art: Works on Paper and Canvas* (1998).
Western Michigan University. *Progressive Proof: Celebrating Forty Years of Collecting at Western Michigan University* (2003).

JOSEPH S. MELLA

ADAMS-ENDER, Clara (11 July 1939–), military leader, nurse, educator, and entrepreneur, was born Clara Mae Leach Adams in Willow Springs, North Carolina. Her parents, Otha Leach and Caretha Bell, were sharecroppers, and she was the fourth of ten children. Her parents were staunch supporters of education and made sure that all of their children knew this. Her parents further instilled in the children a sense of self-respect and a belief that with knowledge they could do anything.

As a child growing up in a family of sharecroppers, Adams-Ender realized early that she wanted more out of life. Her perseverance in continuing her education while missing school to work the farm with her family was evident when she graduated second in her class at the age of sixteen. Although she enrolled in a nursing program, her first career choice was to be a lawyer. However, in 1956 her father believed that women went into nursing, not into law. So Adams-Ender entered the nursing program at North Carolina A&T.

Because of circumstances beyond her control, she withdrew from school a year later. The family tobacco farm hit on hard times, and it became necessary for her to work. Nevertheless she returned to the nursing program at North Carolina A&T and by the second semester found a way to pay for the rest of her training. She saw an army recruiting poster for nurses and met with the recruiters. She joined the army nursing corps, and the army paid for her junior and senior years of college. Just prior to graduating in 1961, Adams-Ender was commissioned as second lieutenant. After graduation she went to Fort Sam Houston in San Antonio, Texas, for basic military training.

Her duty station was Fort Dix, New Jersey, where she remained from 1961 to 1963, when she received a transfer to a base in the Republic of Korea. While Adams-Ender was in Korea her superiors came to recognize her natural skills as an administrator, a leader, and an instructor. In 1964 she was reassigned to the United States Army Training Center at Fort Sam Houston, where she took an advanced nursing course and served as a nursing instructor. Just prior to leaving Texas for the University of Minnesota to pursue a master of science degree in Nursing in 1967, she became the first woman in the army to receive an Expert Field Medical Badge.

After earning her degree in 1969, Adams-Ender was stationed at Walter Reed Army Medical Center in Washington, D.C., as an assistant professor. By this time she had attained the rank of captain. During her time at Walter Reed she moved quickly to the rank of major, soon followed by a promotion to lieutenant colonel. She then enrolled in the Army Command and General Staff College in Fort Leavenworth, Kansas. Completing her studies in 1976, she became the first African American woman and nurse to receive a master's degree in military art and science. After completing her studies, her next duty station was that of inspector general at Fort Sam Houston's Army Health Services Command.

In 1978 Adams-Ender was transferred to the Army Regional Medical Center in Germany. She worked tirelessly to run the intensive care unit (ICU), recruiting and training nurses for the unit and working to strengthen German-American relations among healthcare professionals. For her dedication and hard work Adams-Ender was promoted to the rank of full colonel in 1981. While stationed in Germany she met her husband, Heinz Ender, a German dentist; they married in 1981 and returned to the United States three months later.

Her next duty station took Adams-Ender to Fort Sheridan, Illinois, where she served as the chief of nurse recruiting and chief of the Army Nurse Corps division. Three years later Adams-Ender returned to Walter Reed Army Medical Center as chief of the department of nursing. By 1987 she was with the Surgeon General's Office as chief of the Army Nurse Corps and was promoted to brigadier general. In 1991 Adams-Ender became the deputy commander for the military district of Washington, D.C., and the commander of Fort Belvoir, Virginia.

Adams-Ender retired from military service in 1993 to become the CEO and president of CAPE (Caring for People with Enthusiasm), a management consulting firm in Lake Ridge, Virginia. Adams-Ender's military career spanned more than thirty years. She received numerous awards and honors, including the Distinguished Service Medal with oak-leaf cluster, the Legion of Merit, the Meritorious Service Medal with three oak-leaf clusters, the Army Commendation Medal, and Cross of Honor in Gold (from the German army).

Further Reading
Adams-Ender, Clara. *My Rise to the Stars: How a Sharecropper's Daughter Became an Army General* (2001).
Cheers, D. M. "Nurse Corps chief," *Ebony* (June 1989).
TERI B. WEIL

ADDERLEY, Cannonball (15 Sept. 1928–8 Aug. 1975), jazz saxophonist, was born Julian Edwin Adderley in Tampa, Florida, the son of Julian Carlyle Adderley, a high school guidance counselor and jazz cornet player, and Jessie Johnson, an elementary school teacher. The family moved to Tallahassee, Florida, where Adderley attended Florida Agricultural and Mechanical College High School from 1941 until 1944. He earned his bachelor's degree from Florida A&M in 1948, having studied reed and brass instruments with the band director Leander Kirksey and forming, with Kirksey, a school jazz ensemble. Adderley then worked as band director at Dillard High School in Fort Lauderdale, Florida, and jobbed with his own jazz group.

Adderley served in the army from 1950 until 1953, leading the Thirty-sixth Army Dance Band, to which his younger brother, the cornetist NATHANIEL "NAT" ADDERLEY, was also assigned. While stationed in Washington, D.C., in 1952, Adderley continued to play with his own group and furthered his musical studies at the U.S. Naval School of Music. Assigned to Fort Knox, Kentucky, he again led an army dance band. After his discharge, he returned to Fort Lauderdale to continue as the high school band director and as a jobbing musician.

Encouraged by the singer and saxophonist Eddie "Cleanhead" Vinson, Adderley moved to New York in 1955. After sitting in with OSCAR PETTIFORD at the Cafe Bohemia, he so impressed fellow musicians that he was asked to join Pettiford's band. Almost immediately, he signed a recording contract with EmArcy.

Julian "Cannonball" Adderley, jazz saxophonist and influential spokesperson for the black community, 1970. (AP Images.)

These early recordings display the influence of the altoists CHARLIE PARKER and Benny Carter. Although the bebop influence led Adderley to play long and sometimes highly chromatic solo lines, his deeply rooted interest in gospel and modern blues helped him create a distinctive voice.

In January 1956 Nat and Cannonball formed a quintet that toured nationally until 1957, when Cannonball joined the MILES DAVIS quintet. When the tenor saxophonist JOHN COLTRANE was added, this ensemble of the trumpeter Davis, Adderley, Coltrane, the bassist PAUL CHAMBERS, the drummer PHILLY JOE JONES, and both BILL EVANS and RED GARLAND on piano became the most influential group in jazz. The spectacular recordings in which Adderley and Coltrane vie for dominance, such as 1958's "Dr. Jekyll," and the modal jazz improvisations of the *Kind of Blue* session of 1959, such as "So What?" are recognized jazz masterpieces. This latter session introduced a new style, establishing modal jazz, improvisation based on a succession of scales rather than a progression of harmonies, as one of the mainstream techniques in jazz from that time forward.

In late 1959 Adderley left Davis and re-formed a quintet with his brother Nat. This group, with changing rhythm section personnel and the occasional addition of a second saxophonist (first Yusef Lateef and later Charles Lloyd), continued until Adderley's death and enjoyed considerable popular and critical success. Influenced by the work of ORNETTE COLEMAN in the early 1960s and the technological advances of electronic instruments that became a part of jazz shortly thereafter, the new Adderley brothers'

ensemble played a fusion of bebop, modal jazz, rock, and free jazz elements, sometimes called "soul jazz," that carried them on the crest of one avant-garde jazz wave of the 1960s. Their *Jazz Workshop* sessions, recorded live in San Francisco in 1962, display an early stage of this development, and their 1966 live album *Mercy, Mercy, Mercy!* which reflects this style, became one of the best-selling jazz records to that time. Their music appealed to fans of rock 'n' roll as well as to those of modern jazz, and the ensemble's tours often drew huge crowds not only in the United States but also in Japan, East and West Europe, and Great Britain. Speaking of his music, Adderley was quoted in 1966 as saying, "I'm aware that jazz is changing, and I have listened to and absorbed many influences. I feel that Ornette Coleman was a most important force. However, what I play today is a logical development of my own style."

Adderley married the actress Olga James in 1962. In the late 1960s he added soprano saxophone as a regular solo instrument in his performances. His mature playing was a masterful combination of elements: lessons learned from Charlie Parker, associations with Miles Davis, John Coltrane, and the keyboardist Joe Zawinul, and a natural affinity for black soul and gospel music. His solo lines and incisive sound were charged with an unerring sense of direction, a dazzling improvisatory technique, and a sense of timbral exploration married to a "downhome" feel for the blues. While on tour before his forty-seventh birthday, he suffered a stroke and died several weeks later in a hospital in Gary, Indiana.

Adderley's legacy is twofold: as a creative and compelling jazz artist of the later 1950s through the mid-1970s and as an influential spokesperson for this music and the black community. He served as a committee member for the National Endowment for the Arts, was a member of the Black Academy of Arts and Letters, and served on the jazz advisory panel of the John F. Kennedy Center for the Performing Arts. He hosted thirteen weeks of a television series, *90 Minutes*; appeared in a few motion pictures, including *Play Misty for Me* (1971), *Soul to Soul* (1971), and *Save the Children* (1973); made guest playing appearances on several television shows; and participated in many college workshops and seminars.

Among Adderley's honors are the Julian Cannonball Adderley Artist in Residence Program at Harvard University and several *Down Beat*, *Playboy*, and Encyclopedia of Jazz All Star and Poll Awards. Among his important and representative recordings are *Presenting Cannonball Adderley* (1955), *Somethin' Else* (1958), Miles Davis's *Milestones* (1958) and *Kind of Blue* (1959), *Mercy, Mercy, Mercy!* (1966), *Country Preacher* (1969), and *Inside Straight* (1973). A posthumously issued recording, *Big Man* (1975), composed jointly with his brother Nat, was based on the legend of JOHN HENRY with the blues singer JOE WILLIAMS in the title role. Adderley considered this one of the major achievements of his career. Among his many jazz compositions, several have entered the repertoire as standards, including "Sack o' Woe," "Domination," "Sermonette," and "Them Dirty Blues."

Speaking of Cannonball Adderley in 1993, Nat Adderley reflected:

I believe that a large part of what Cannonball did musically might have been missed or overlooked at the time he did it, because the concept of critical analysis of the music at that time was based more on alleged "European concepts" than on the total impact of what the music was. So it has only been in the last few years . . . that there has been a lot more consideration, a lot more interest, in what Cannonball did as students now study the solos. It has become much more evident that Cannonball was far superior in many areas than he was originally given credit for . . . many of the critics, I think, did not understand the infusion of Southern black gospel music and blues into what they considered a hallowed European classical tradition.

Further Reading

Adderley's papers, scores, and memorabilia are in the Black Archives Research Center of Florida Agricultural and Mechanical University in Tallahassee. Oral history material and recordings are preserved at the Institute of Jazz Studies of Rutgers University in Newark, New Jersey.

Baker, David. *The Jazz Style of Cannonball Adderley: A Musical and Historical Perspective* (1980).

Corey, Christiansen, and Tamara Danielsson. *In the Style of Cannonball Adderley, C Instruments Edition, Essential Jazz Lines Series* (2002).

Sheridan, Chris, comp. *Dis Here: A Bio-Discography of Julian "Cannonball" Adderley* (2000).

Obituary: *New York Times,* 9 Aug. 1975.

FRANK TIRRO

ADDERLEY, Nat (25 Nov. 1931–2 Jan. 2000), cornetist, trumpeter, bandleader, composer, arranger, and college educator, was born Nathaniel Adderley in Tampa, Florida, the second of two sons of Julian Adderley Sr. and Jessie Adderley. Julian Sr. was an educator who played trumpet and cornet, thus becoming Nat's first music teacher. Jessie was also a teacher. Nat's only sibling, JULIAN ADDERLEY JR., nicknamed "Cannonball" because of his rotund build, was three years older than his brother. The Adderleys moved from Tampa to Tallahassee, Florida, when Nat was a toddler so that Julian Sr. and Jessie could take teaching jobs at Florida A&M College (FAMC), a historically black school. The college changed its name to Florida A&M University (FAMU) in 1953.

Cannonball was the first of the two brothers to play trumpet. He later became more interested in the alto saxophone, leaving his trumpet to sit idle. Nat showed no interest in his brother's old horn and instead opted to develop his singing abilities. When Nat's voice began to change in 1946 as he matured, he decided to pick up and play his brother's trumpet, which he learned at an incredible pace. As a teenager he played with several music groups around Tallahassee and performed in his high school band. Around 1950 Nat decided to switch from trumpet to cornet,

although he did not completely abandon the former instrument. Nat loved the way his father played the cornet, attracted to the fatter and much earthier sound of the cornet over the sometimes-piercing sound of the trumpet. Local musicians attempted to deter Nat from switching to the cornet because of its almost nonexistent status in jazz music of the era. He played both instruments on several of his early professional recordings, but the cornet defined his long career.

Following high school Nat enrolled at FAMC, where he became a member of the school's world-famous "Marching 100" band and the school's symphonic orchestra. Under the leadership of the bandmaster, Dr. William Foster, considered the ultimate creator of progressive and imaginative marching and music pageantry, Nat was chosen as the trumpet's section leader and rank sergeant for the high-and-fast-stepping aggregation. Prior to graduation Nat joined the U.S. Army, where he played cornet in the Thirty-sixth Army Band. After a three-year stint in the military (1951–1953), Adderley returned to Tallahassee, where he re-enrolled at what had by then become FAMU. He earned a BA in Sociology with a minor in Music in 1954.

After graduation Nat's mother, Jessie, urged him to go to law school. She felt Nat would be an outstanding lawyer because of his penchant for arguing. Nat had other plans as word began to circulate throughout jazz circles about his profound sound and style of playing. The jazz great LIONEL HAMPTON invited Nat to join him on an upcoming international tour. Against his mother's wishes Nat accepted Hampton's invitation and headed to Europe. Returning to the United States in 1955, he and Cannonball, an FAMC graduate, "Marching 100" alumnus, and by then high school music teacher, decided to play together in New York. The two brothers showed up at the famous Café Bohemia, where the jazz greats HORACE SILVER (piano), OSCAR PETTIFORD (bass), and KENNY CLARKE (drums) were performing. Nat and Cannonball, with horns in hands, asked to sit in with the legendary musicians. The two brothers were well received by the group and the audience as they displayed a fresh, hot, soulful, and funky brand of jazz. Nat and Cannonball were a hit, and they soon were in high demand for club and recording sessions around New York. Nat played a gritty but straight-ahead hard bop, sometimes laced with soft staccato, soul, and funk licks. Although his mentors and influences were the likes of DIZZY GILLESPIE, MILES DAVIS, and CLARK TERRY, Nat displayed his own distinctive style.

Nat's first solo album, *That's Nat* on Savoy, was released in 1955. He played both trumpet and cornet. Nat was joined on this recording by Kenny Clarke (drums), Hank Jones (piano), and Jerome Richardson (tenor saxophone and flute). Nat and Cannonball's debut recording together was on *Introducing Nat Adderley* in 1955 on the EmArcy label. Nat was the leader for the recording date; Cannonball was a sideman. Soon afterward Nat and Cannonball formed a short-lived band; following its demise Nat performed with Woody Herman's band and then joined forces with the trombone great J. J. JOHNSON.

Nat reconnected musically with his brother in 1959 to anchor the Cannonball Adderley Quintet. The group made such an impression on the jazz scene that Miles Davis called record executives about the brothers, which resulted in the sudden elevation of their recording and performance career. For the next sixteen years the Cannonball Adderley Quintet was one of the best and most successful jazz ensembles in the world. The group released dozens of albums on labels such as Savoy, Blue Note, Riverside, Original Jazz Classics, Landmark, and Capitol. The jazz ensemble hit pay dirt in 1966 with the album *Mercy, Mercy, Mercy! Live at The Club*, which ushered in a new era of jazz, blending earthy sounds of soul, blues, funk, and gospel music. The album won a Grammy Award in 1968 for best instrumental jazz performance by a small group.

Nat was a major contributor to the success of the Cannonball Adderley Quintet. He composed or arranged many of its songs. His solos were uncanny, always painted with rich and soulful tones. Nat was also a shrewd businessman, often making the tough business decisions that kept the quintet on top. However, Nat never received the type of musical acclaim that his brother garnered. Sometimes jazz fans and critics took him for granted as he stood in his brother's musical shadow. During the Cannonball Adderley Quintet years Nat was leader for more than a dozen solo projects, but he always returned to play next to his brother. Perhaps Nat's greatest solo recording came in 1960, when he released the album *Work Song* on Riverside Records. The album's title song had a bluesy, hard-bop, call-and-response feel and featured the playing of the jazz guitarist WES MONTGOMERY. Through the years Nat wrote and arranged other compositions, including such classics as "Jive Samba," "Sermonette," and "The Old Country."

Nat performed with his brother until Cannonball's death in 1975. Nat then fronted his own jazz groups for more than two decades, which included work with the saxophonists Sonny Fortune and Victor Herring. He maintained a hectic national and international touring schedule that took his groups around the United States and to Europe, Japan, and Australia. He released several post-Cannonball albums, including *Don't Look Back, Hummin',* and *A Little New York Midtown Music.*

In the mid-1990s Adderley was named as an artist-in-residence at Florida Southern College in Lakeland, Florida, where he taught a music theory class. He had performed numerous times at the school's annual Child of the Sun Jazz Festival. Nat occasionally performed with the late R&B and pop balladeer LUTHER VANDROSS; the cornetist's only son, Nat Adderley Jr., served as the singer's pianist and musical director.

Health issues began to take a toll on Nat's career, forcing him to curtail touring and recording sessions.

His last two known recordings as a leader date from 1995, when he recorded a reprise of his and his brother's classic album *Mercy, Mercy, Mercy!* on Evidence Records and released the album *Live on Planet Earth* on Westwind Records. In 1997 Nat Adderley was inducted into the Jazz Hall of Fame in Kansas City. One of his last live performances was also in 1997, at the Playboy Jazz Festival at Hollywood Bowl in Los Angeles. Nat's right leg was amputated that year as a result of diabetes, the disease that led to his death at age sixty-eight. He was survived by his wife, Ann; daughter, Alison; and son, Nat Adderley Jr.

Over his fifty-year music career Nat performed in more than twenty countries and can be heard on well over one hundred albums, of which he was leader on about thirty. His legacy as one of jazz's most talented and successful cornetists, trumpeters, composers, and arrangers is well documented.

Further Reading
Down Beat (Feb. 1994, Mar. 1994, Mar. 1996).
Erlewine, Michael. *All Music Guide to Jazz* (1996).
Feather, Leonard. *The Encyclopedia of Jazz in the '60s* (1966).

Discography
The Adderley Brothers: The Summer of '55 (SVY-17063).
Work Song (RISA-1167-6; OJCCD-363-2).
Mercy, Mercy, Mercy, with Cannonball Adderley Quintet (Capitol Jazz 29915).
Live on Planet Earth (WW2088).

DONALD JAMES

AFRICANUS, Scipio (fl. 1777–c. 1780), Revolutionary War sailor, is known for his service on the Continental navy sloop *Ranger* under Captain John Paul Jones. A story passing as truth has been written about Scipio Africanus stating that he was a slave owned by Jones and accompanied him on the ships he commanded. In fact virtually nothing is known about Africanus except for the fact that he was a free man when he enlisted to serve on board the eighteen-gun *Ranger* for one year while she was building at Portsmouth, New Hampshire, sometime between March and July 1777.

While we know little about Scipio Africanus the man, some guesses as to his servitude and character may be ventured. That he was a slave prior to his naval service, as suggested by his first name, is likely. Classical Roman names such as Scipio, Cato, and Caesar were commonly given at birth by owners to slaves in New England. The original names of those enslaved from Africa were seldom learned by their white masters, likely because they were considered barbaric. It was much easier to give the newly enslaved their master's surname, and classical Christian names were both easier to pronounce and perhaps even helped to lend an air of dignity to the institution of slavery. Even when slaves gained their freedom, they usually retained their former master's surname. Of interest is Scipio's surname of Africanus. Perhaps it was bestowed upon him by a more enlightened master, in recognition of the Roman leader that conquered Africa. However, this was not the norm for slave owners, and it can be speculated that instead Scipio himself chose this surname upon being freed, possibly in contempt of his former master and surely in proud recognition of his own African heritage.

Despite the images conjured up by the name Scipio Africanus, that of a stately and imposing figure, historians can only speculate as to Africanus's position aboard the *Ranger*. Black sailors serving in the Revolution, including his shipmate CATO CARLISLE and others such as JAMES FORTEN and CAESAR TARRANT, served in a wide variety of shipboard positions. These ranged from the lowly cabin boy, often a slave owned by the ship's captain, to ordinary seaman, able-bodied seaman, and even as marines and pilots. It was a common belief that Africanus was Captain Jones's personal cabin boy. While this is possible there is no evidence to suggest such a position except for the erroneous statement by earlier historians that Scipio Africanus was Jones's slave. It is just as likely that Scipio may instead have served in a more skilled position. Blacks were a common presence in New England's maritime trade well before the war so their service in the navy during the war in a variety of capacities was neither unusual nor controversial. In Massachusetts a number of blacks served on the Continental navy frigate *Boston* in 1777, with Cato Austin operating the number one gun on the larboard watch, and Scipio Brown and Caesar Fairweather serving as ammunition handlers. Even in the southern colonies, where blacks were effectively barred from serving in the army, their service in the Continental and state navies was both frequent and varied in scope.

In order to follow the service of Scipio Africanus during the war, we must follow the career of Captain John Paul Jones and the *Ranger*, as Scipio's specific actions are unknown. The *Ranger* departed Portsmouth, New Hampshire, on her maiden voyage, after many delays in taking on men and material, on 1 November 1777. The sloop of war arrived in France after a voyage of a month, capturing several prizes along the way. The *Ranger* and her crew dallied in French ports until April 1778, during which time Captain Jones expended much effort in trying to gain command of a larger and more prestigious ship. His crew, Scipio Africanus and Cato Carlisle included, were left behind in a rather boring port and were employed in a variety of everyday maintenance chores. By the time Captain Jones came back to his ship, his crew was an unhappy lot. During this time the only highlight was *Ranger*'s encounter with a French naval squadron at Quiberon Bay. Here, for the first time ever, the stars and stripes of America was recognized and saluted by a foreign power, and Scipio Africanus and his fellow crew were there to witness the event.

The *Ranger* and her crew finally sailed to glory, and into the history books, on 10 April 1778 when the ship departed France for the hostile waters off England. In a campaign that made Jones an American hero, and struck terror into the heart of England, the *Ranger* captured several prizes and marauded in the Irish Sea, raiding Whitehaven Harbor and St. Mary's Isle. The crowning achievement came when Jones and his men captured the British twenty-gun sloop of war *Drake* in a battle that lasted an hour. Following these engagements the *Ranger* returned to France, where troubles between Jones and his men came to the fore. Upset with Captain Jones's treatment of one of his officers, as well as their extended service time and a lack of prize money from the ships they captured, seventy-seven crewmembers, styling themselves "Jovial Tars," petitioned the American commissioners in France. Among these petitioners was Scipio Africanus and the ship's other black sailor, Cato Carlisle. Eventually, the dispute was settled and Captain Jones left the ship and the *Ranger* returned home.

The final fate of Scipio Africanus is unknown. Perhaps he stayed aboard the *Ranger* for future cruises, or maybe he moved on to serve in the lucrative business of privateering. Whatever the case may be, his service in the Continental navy is indicative of the contribution made by black sailors who sailed the high seas during the American Revolution.

Further Reading

Knoblock, Glenn A. *"Strong and Brave Fellows"; New Hampshire's Black Soldiers and Sailors of the American Revolution, 1775–1784* (2003).

Morison, Samuel Eliot. *John Paul Jones; A Sailor's Biography* (1959).

Quarles, Benjamin. *The Negro in the American Revolution* (1961).

Sawtelle, Joseph G., ed. *John Paul Jones and the Ranger* (1994).

GLENN ALLEN KNOBLOCK

AGYEMAN, Jaramogi Abebe (13 June 1911–20 Feb. 2000), clergyman, community activist, denomination organizer, and black nationalist was born Albert Buford Cleage Jr., one of seven children of Pearl (whose maiden name is now unknown) and Albert Cleage Sr., in Indianapolis, Indiana. Shortly after Agyeman's birth, Cleage, Sr., a medical doctor, relocated with his family to Detroit, Michigan, where the father helped to establish the city's first African American hospital. After an undergraduate education that included a stay at Fisk University in Tennessee, Agyeman received his BA in Sociology from Wayne State University in 1937, serving as a caseworker for the Department of Public Welfare from 1931 to 1938. Subsequently Agyeman felt the call to ministry and obtained a Bachelor of Divinity degree from Oberlin College Graduate School of Theology in 1943. Also in 1943 Agyeman married Doris Graham, to which union was born two children, Kris and the renowned author PEARL CLEAGE. The couple divorced in 1955. He received ordination to the Congregationalist ministry (1943); pastored a Congregationalist church in Lexington, Kentucky (1942–1943); led the Church for the

Fellowship of All Peoples in San Francisco, an interracial congregation founded by HOWARD THURMAN (1943–1944); and served another Congregational church in Springfield, Massachusetts (1946–1951), where he was a strong supporter of the NAACP.

In 1951 Agyeman returned to Detroit to pastor the St. Mark's Community (Presbyterian) Church. In 1953 Agyeman and three hundred members seceded from St. Mark's to establish the Central Congregational Church. Like his father, Agyeman continued his involvement in community and civic activities. He worked closely with MARTIN LUTHER KING JR. on civil rights issues in the city in 1963.

It was the influence of past and present black nationalist and separatist personalities, however, that eventually caused division in Cleage's congregation and prompted the founding of a new denomination. MARCUS GARVEY, the early twentieth-century black leader, and the Nation of Islam leaders MALCOLM X and ELIJAH MUHAMMAD all shared certain ideas. They all believed that the inherently racist political-economic status quo would not afford blacks the opportunity to achieve freedom and empowerment. They also expressed the need to envision God in terms applicable to the struggles of black people and highlighted the pressing necessity for the African American community to be economically self-sufficient. This move toward black nationalism prompted opponents in the Central Congregational Church to ask for the intervention of the denomination (United Church of Christ) to deny funding to the local church should Agyeman not conform his teachings to those of the larger group. Agyeman, however, rebuffed attempts by the denomination to discuss his black nationalism and its theological legitimacy. He raised the principle of congregational autonomy and suggested that the denomination itself was leveling the charges under the guise of anonymous complaints. The dissidents withdrew from Central, according de facto victory to Agyeman and his supporters.

By 1967 Agyeman's black Christian nationalist theology had achieved systematic form. During the Easter season the pastor placed an eighteen-foot Black Madonna and Child portrait in the sanctuary. Initiating the Black Christian Nationalist Movement, in 1967 Agyeman renamed the church the Shrine of the Black Madonna, and in the early 1970s he formed the Pan African Orthodox Christian Church (PAOCC) denomination. Also, the leader dropped the name Albert Buford Cleage Jr. in favor of Jaramogi Abebe Agyeman, which can be translated as "Liberator, Blessed Man, Savior of the Nation." The PAOCC was intended to be an overarching organization, including African American fellowships from various denominations united around the theme of black liberation. Agyeman's Black Christian Nationalism taught that Jesus was of African lineage and had descended from one of ancient Israel's darker tribes. Therefore, Jesus was the Black Messiah who led nonwhite Israelites in revolt against white Roman oppres-

sors. Agyeman counseled that the power structure must be directly challenged by people who will not place their own individual desires over the well-being of the Black Nation and instead commit themselves to freeing black people throughout the world.

Agyeman shared with the major academic exponent of black theology, JAMES H. CONE, the basic understanding that a genuine embrace of Christianity required that people understand the indispensable necessity of standing in solidarity with the struggles of black people. Agyeman put forth his theology in two major books: *The Black Messiah* (1968) and *Black Christian Nationalism* (1972). Agyeman and his fellowship sponsored community-oriented programs, established a supermarket, and fostered other activities supporting black economic independence. In the political sphere they were instrumental in the use of the Black Slate to encourage black voting. They also assisted candidates in local and congressional races and helped to elect Detroit's first black mayor, COLEMAN YOUNG, and two members of the U.S. Congress.

The 1980s saw the decline of nationalist sentiment, religious or otherwise, in the African American community, adversely affecting membership in the PAOCC movement. Nonetheless, as of 2000 the PAOCC still had participating congregations in several cities, including Houston and Atlanta. Yet the influence of Agyeman and the Black Christian Movement extended beyond church membership. His teachings on the ethnic and political identities of ancient Israel influenced numerous scholars to ask piercing sociological questions regarding early Judaism and Christianity. Agyeman also stressed how important it is for theology and biblical studies to forthrightly address the concerns of blacks and others facing sociopolitical oppression.

Agyeman died in Calhoun Falls, South Carolina, in 2000.

Further Reading

Aaseng, Nathan. *African-American Religious Leaders* (2003).
McMickle, Marvin A. *An Encyclopedia of African American Christian Heritage* (2002).
Murphy, Larry G., J. Gordon Melton, and Gary L. Ward. *Encyclopedia of African American Religions* (1993).
Obituary: *New York Times*, 27 Feb. 2000.

SANDY DWAYNE MARTIN

AILEY, Alvin (5 Jan. 1931–1 Dec. 1989), actor, dancer, and choreographer, was born in Rogers, Texas, the son of Alvin Ailey, a laborer, and Lula Elizabeth Cliff, a cotton picker and domestic. Before Ailey was a year old, his father abandoned the family, leaving them homeless for close to six years. During that time Ailey and his mother made their way, often by foot, across the unforgiving terrain of the impoverished and bitterly racist Brazos Valley in southeastern Texas to seek shelter with relatives and find work in nearby fields.

Alvin Ailey. In 1958, Ailey founded the Alvin Ailey American Dance Theatre in New York City. Ailey choreographed an important body of work, including such signature pieces as *Revelations* and *Blues Suite*, that celebrated black worship and music and other African American themes in dance. (New York Public Library.)

A bright, curious child, Ailey joined his mother in the cotton fields as soon as he could carry a sack. He reveled in the sights and sounds of the gospel choirs and worshipers that he witnessed in the black Baptist churches of his youth. Ailey also became acquainted with the less pious side of life through those who spent Saturday nights dancing, drinking, and fighting in roadside bars and dance halls where blues musicians played over the constant drone of passing trains. Ailey had a photographic memory that allowed him to recall the body language of the people he saw in both bars and churches, memories he later drew on in his work.

In 1937 Ailey and his mother moved to Navasota, Texas, where they lived with Amos Alexander, a local black businessman. Alexander treated Ailey as a son and provided him with the only secure family environment he would experience. Ailey relished the stability of living in one place, eating regularly, going to the same school, and worshiping at the True Vine Baptist Church, but he developed a deep sense of obligation to Alexander and felt inferior to Alexander's own children. Ailey's 1961 autobiography, *Knoxville: Summer 1915*, is a moving account of his life in Navasota.

In 1942 Ailey's life changed dramatically. His mother moved to Los Angeles, determined to get one of the thousands of jobs being created by West Coast aircraft factories gearing up to handle the demands of World War II. Before his mother was hired as a night-shift worker for Lockheed, she and Ailey lived in a white section of the city, where she worked as a domestic and he attended a previously all-white school. Ailey's status as the only black student in the school reinforced his feelings of insecurity and inferiority. His love for dance was sparked by a class field trip to see Sergei Denham's Ballet Russe de Monte Carlo in 1943. Ailey had seen vaudeville shows, revues, and theater productions, but after seeing the Ballet Russe he attended as many dance events as he could. Among them was a presentation of the KATHERINE DUNHAM company. Dunham's spectacular productions of African and Caribbean dance styles had a tremendous influence on Ailey's concept of dance, theatricality, and the unique expressionism of ethnic dance.

In 1971, in his virtuoso solo *Cry*, Ailey immortalized his reaction to attending a white school and watching his mother scrubbing floors and hanging out laundry for white families. This piece, the first significant work created by Ailey for JUDITH JAMISON, was Ailey's tribute to his mother and "all black women—especially our mothers." Ailey always paid homage to his cultural heritage, and he created works based on experiences from different moments of his life. Of the seventy-nine works he created during his lifetime, his least successful dealt with subjects not drawn from his own experiences.

After moving to a racially mixed section of Los Angeles, Ailey attended Jefferson High School, which drew students of black and Hispanic heritage. He excelled in foreign language studies and distinguished himself as a gymnast. Intent on becoming a foreign language teacher, he entered the University of California, Los Angeles, in 1948 as a foreign language major.

By that time, however, he had started formal dance training under Lester Horton at the urging of his high school friend CARMEN DE LAVALLADE. A white man, Horton had founded the first multiracial dance company in America and developed his own modern dance technique. The breadth of movement and expression supported by the Horton technique appealed to Ailey. He also was intrigued by Horton's ability to fuse elements of theater and stagecraft in his works.

Ailey made his professional debut in Horton's company in 1950. He continued working toward his college degree until he decided to join Horton as a full-time dancer and teacher of the Horton technique. Late that year Horton died. With support from de Lavallade and the veteran Horton dancers James Truitte and Joyce Trisler, Ailey took over the artistic reins of the company, ran the school, and began to choreograph.

Ailey and de Lavallade were cast in the 1955 Twentieth Century–Fox motion picture *Carmen Jones*, directed by Herbert Ross. After filming was completed in 1954, Ross paired them in the Broadway-bound Truman Capote show *House of Flowers*. Their Broadway debut catapulted Ailey and de Lavallade into the limelight, but they continued to appear with Horton's company. Until 1960, Ailey remained an integral part of the effort to keep the company alive.

Living in New York City, Ailey studied dance with, among others, Martha Graham, Doris Humphrey, Donald McKayle, Karel Shook, and Charles Weidman. He also studied acting under Stella Adler. As a dancer Ailey moved with the power and grace of a lion. His physical strength, riveting presence, and ability to make movement appear to spring from within rather than as a result of the choreography set him apart from his peers. His total immersion in the roles he performed defined his approach to choreography and attracted gifted dancers to his productions.

Ailey's success on Broadway as a dancer and actor garnered him numerous theater awards and a secure future in musicals and theater. During this period, in addition to *House of Flowers*, Ailey appeared in *The Carefree Tree* (1955), HARRY BELAFONTE's 1956 production of *Sing, Man, Sing*, and LENA HORNE's 1957 *Jamaica*, the latter choreographed by Jack Cole. In 1958 Ailey drew on his memories of Saturday nights at the roadside bars to create the dance *Blues Suite*, which captured the parade of emotions experienced by people unable to escape the drudgery of hapless lives. Two years later he brought the charismatic Baptist preachers, fire-and-brimstone sermons, and gospel spirituals of his church to life in his signature masterpiece, *Revelations*. Noted for its spontaneity, *Revelations* has proven its universal appeal to audiences around the world. As a result, it remains the cornerstone of his company's outstanding repertoire. Ailey also appeared off-Broadway as an actor in *Call Me by My Rightful Name*, with Robert Duvall and Joan Hackett, and *Two by Saroyan*, and he made his Broadway debut in an acting role as CLAUDIA MC-NEIL's son in the 1962 production of *Tiger, Tiger, Burning Bright*.

Throughout his Broadway career Ailey never lost sight of his goal to establish a multiracial dance company with a repertoire representing the past and future of American modern dance and the unique qualities of black cultural expression. Ailey used the fees he earned on Broadway to fund his own company and recruited several Broadway dancers to join the Horton dancers he was assembling to create a concert group.

In 1958 Ailey presented the Alvin Ailey American Dance Theater in concert at New York City's Ninety-second Street YM-YWHA. Public and critical response was excellent and inspired Ailey and his dancers to continue building the company. To keep his dancers together, Ailey provided food and shelter when they were unable to find work between concert engagements. He also ran the company by himself, getting bookings, taking care of production details, promoting the troupe, and handling the company finances out of a shoebox. As financially strapped as the company was, Ailey refused to limit the company and its audiences to an all-Ailey repertoire. He often crossed the color line to empower those who shared his dream of establishing a dance company without racial limitations.

In 1960 the premiere of Ailey's *Revelations* created a sensation in the dance world, and the company's future began to take shape. That year Robert Joffrey commissioned Ailey to create a work for his ballet company, which brought Ailey in touch with the Joffrey company's backer, Rebekah Harkness. Harkness established a nonprofit foundation to sponsor broadly diverse projects within the field and cooperated with the U.S. Department of State Cultural Exchange Program to generate international recognition of American cultural achievements. The success of Ailey's *Feast of Ashes*, inspired by Federico García Lorca's *The House of Bernarda Alba* and set to an original Carlos Surinach score, put him in good stead with Harkness. Impressed by Ailey's fusion of dance styles and aware of the financial gridlock his company was in, Harkness allocated foundation funds to send Ailey's company on its first foreign tour.

In 1963 Harkness established the Harkness Ballet under the artistic direction of George Skibine. Ailey was invited to restage *Feast of Ashes*, which remained the property of the new company, and he was commissioned to create a new work for the company's inaugural season. As usual, Ailey applied the fees he earned to his own company. Although Harkness's wealth reinforced Ailey's personal insecurities, his commitment to his own company enabled him to accept her largesse.

Ailey's company ran out of money during its appearance at the First World Festival of Negro Arts in Dakar, Senegal, in 1966. Ailey managed to get his dancers to Barcelona, Spain, where his *Macumba*, set to Harkness music, was scheduled to premiere. Within a few hours of their arrival in Barcelona, Ailey had arranged for his dancers to be absorbed into the Harkness Ballet for the remainder of its European tour.

Although several of Ailey's dancers immediately found jobs with other companies, several joined the Harkness company for its summer workshop in Rhode Island. Jamison and Morton "Tubby" Winston stayed on for its subsequent American tour, but only Winston remained with the ballet company after Ailey's company resumed operation following a brief period of reorganization.

Ailey's relationship with Harkness remained strong, and his company continued to receive support from her foundation. Ailey always credited her for giving his company the opportunity to survive long enough to gain an international following in the world of dance.

With the exception of its brief period of reorganization, the Alvin Ailey American Dance Theater continued to build audiences around the world and offer more performances a year than any other American dance company. According to Jamison, whom Ailey named his successor before his death, the company covered most of its budget from almost year-round touring engagements in the United States and abroad.

Despite Ailey's achievements and enormous contributions to the world of dance, he remained unable to put aside his insecurities and accept his success. As a result, he felt undeserving of the many honors and awards that he received during his lifetime. His most significant awards included a Dance Magazine Award in 1975, the Spingarn Medal of the National Association for the Advancement of Colored People in 1976, the Capezio Award in 1979, the United Nations Peace Medal in 1982, the Samuel H. Scripps American Dance Festival Award in 1987, and a Kennedy Center award in 1988. The anxiety he felt over accepting awards often triggered long spells of depression and self-destructive behavior.

In 1980 Ailey was diagnosed as a severe manic-depressive during his hospitalization after he created a public disturbance. Although he continued to create significant new works for his company and others, Ailey began turning over his responsibilities for running the main company, its affiliated school, and a student repertory ensemble to others. However, he remained involved with developing an interactive, multidisciplinary summer workshop for inner-city children with interests in the arts.

Ailey, who never married, died in New York's Lenox Hill Hospital surrounded by his mother; Jamison; SYLVIA WATERS, director of the Alvin Ailey Repertory Ensemble; and Masazumi Chaya, assistant artistic director of the Alvin Ailey American Dance Theater.

Further Reading

Ailey's archive is housed at the Alvin Ailey American Dance Center in New York City.

Ailey, Alvin, with Peter Bailey. *Revelations* (1995).

Jamison, Judith, with Howard Kaplan. *Dancing Spirit* (1993).

West, Cynthia S'thembile. "Alvin Ailey: Signposts of an American Visionary." *African American Genius in Modern Dance* (1993).

Obituaries: *New York Times*, 2 Dec. 1989;*Dance Magazine*, Feb. 1990.

LILI COCKERILLE LIVINGSTON

AL-AMIN, Jamil Abdullah. *See* Brown, H. Rap.

ALBERT, Octavia Victoria Rogers (24 Dec. 1853–1890?), author and activist, was born in Oglethorpe, Georgia, the daughter of slaves. Details of her life are sketchy. Little is known of her parents

Octavia V. R. Albert collected interviews with former slaves in her book *The House of Bondage*, realistically describing their lives both before and after emancipation. (Schomburg Center.)

or her childhood beyond the date and place of her birth and the fact that she was born into bondage; thus, it is particularly intriguing that in 1870, only five years after the Thirteenth Amendment abolished slavery and one year after Atlanta University opened, seventeen-year-old Octavia was among the 170 students enrolled at that institution. Most of the little we know of her life comes from *The House of Bondage* (1890), the book that made her famous. From that source we learn that in 1873 she was teaching in Montezuma, Georgia, when she met her fellow teacher A. E. P. Albert. They married in 1874 and had one daughter.

Sometime around 1877 Albert's husband was ordained as a Methodist Episcopal minister, and the family moved to Houma, Louisiana, and later to New Orleans. It is not clear whether Octavia Albert ever worked professionally again. Most likely she did not, as it was rare for school systems, especially in the South, to employ married women, and because her husband quickly assumed a social prominence that would have discouraged her from being a wage earner.

A. E. P. Albert became a religious and political leader, held a degree in theology, was a trustee of New Orleans University, and served as editor of the *South-Western Christian Advocate*. As befitted her social position, Octavia Albert vacationed with her family at resorts such as the Bay St. Louis in Mississippi, attended lectures and receptions, and generally participated in the religious reform efforts deemed proper for a minister's wife. However, it is clear that she was not content with these activities, but she made her home a center of activity where people of all classes and conditions were welcome to study the Bible, learn to read and write, and discuss current events.

It was from just such community involvement that the idea was born for *The House of Bondage*. Albert's sympathies and interests had been increased by the frequent conversations she had with elderly former slaves, including Charlotte Brooks, who discussed with Albert her slavery experiences in Virginia and Louisiana. Albert announced that she intended to write Charlotte Brooks's story in—as closely as possible—Brooks's own words. Years later Albert stated, "My interest in, and conversations with, Aunt Charlotte, Aunt Sallie, Uncle John Goodwin, Uncle Stephen, and the other characters represented in this story led me to interview many other people [who gave] me additional facts and incidents about the colored people, in freedom as well as in slavery" (Albert, 120).

The full title of Albert's book reveals the grandness of her project: *The House of Bondage; or, Charlotte Brooks and Other Slaves: Original and Life-Like, as They Appeared in Their Old Plantation and City Slave Life; Together with Pen-Pictures of the Peculiar Institution, with Sights and Insights into Their New Relations as Freedmen, Freemen, and Citizens*. Some months after her death, Albert's *House of Bondage* was serialized in the *South-Western Christian Advocate*; it proved so popular that "letters poured in upon the editor from all directions, urging him to put it in book form" (Albert, v). The volume was published posthumously in 1890. The scope of Albert's project, covering rural and urban slavery and using oral testimonies, distinguishes her work from other studies of the period. In the 1880s slavery had once more become a popular topic for many writers, but most were of the so-called Plantation School, which considered the South a place of chivalry and slavery a benevolent, paternalistic institution. At the same time, many contemporary publications and politicians justified racial discrimination and increased violence against African Americans on the grounds that former slaves harbored deep hostility and plans for revenge and were without morals, self-discipline, or ambition. Declaring that "none but those who resided in the South during the time of slavery" (Albert, 1) could testify accurately to its horror, Albert set out to set the record straight by publishing interviews with former slaves, by describing their condition after slavery, and by celebrating the achievements they and their descendants had won despite great and increasing odds.

According to the historian John Blassingame, Albert was one of only a handful of experienced interviewers in the country and also "one of the most interesting" (Blassingame, lxi) in the country. Fascinating stories of slave life unfold in the dialogue between Albert and the interviewers. The major narrative is that of Charlotte Brooks; the half-dozen other extended accounts and the multitude of incidents in the lives of others they knew or had heard about serve primarily to supplement or emphasize the material that Brooks provides. Albert uses poetry, songs, speeches, and other material for documentation, for context, and for texture. Although she intended her work to combat negative stereotypes, Albert also emphasized another goal. It was vital, she argued, that the story of those who survived slavery and those who overcame racial oppression be treasured and transmitted to "our children's children," not only to set the record straight but to inspire African Americans. Her book posits "education, property, and character" as the "trinity of power" by which African Americans could gain their rightful places in society (Albert, 127).

Further Reading
Foster, Frances Smith. "Introduction to Octavia V. Rogers Albert," *The House of Bondage* (1988).
Blassingame, John, ed. *Slave Testimony: Two Centuries of Letters, Speeches, Interviews, and Autobiographies* (1977).
Majors, Monroe. *Noted Negro Women* (1893).

FRANCES SMITH FOSTER

ALBRIER, Frances Mary (21 Sept. 1898–21 Aug. 1987), civil rights activist and community leader, was born in Mount Vernon, New York, the daughter of Lewis Redgrey, a supervisor in a factory, and Laura (maiden name unknown), a cook. Following the death of their mother when Frances was three, Frances and her baby sister were reared by their paternal grandparents, Lewis Redgrey, a Blackfoot Indian, and Johanna Bowen, a freed slave, on their fifty-five-acre farm in Tuskegee, Alabama.

Frances attended Tuskegee Institute, where she studied botany under GEORGE WASHINGTON CARVER, who also advised her grandfather on productive farming techniques. In 1917 she enrolled at Howard University in Washington, D.C., studying nursing and social work. In 1920, following the death of her grandmother, Frances left college and moved to Berkeley, California, to join her father and stepmother. Two years later she married William Albert Jackson. They had three children. Jackson died in 1930, and in 1934 Frances married Willie Antoine Albrier, a Pullman Company club-car porter.

Because of precepts laid down by her grandmother and her teachers, Albrier was strongly motivated to improve the condition of black Americans. Imbued with the beliefs that education was essential in opening doors for African Americans and that those fortunate enough to become educated "owed something to the race," she made education a focus of all her activities. According to an oral history conducted in the 1970s, Albrier was admonished by her grandmother that "bitterness will kill you" and that she had to "fight and earn what you got . . . earn respect." From this Albrier "developed a sense of retaliation and fighting through the system."

Albrier's social action began during the 1920s, when she joined MARCUS GARVEY's Universal Negro Improvement Association, serving with the association's Black Cross Nurses and as vice president of its women's auxiliary. From 1926 to 1931 she worked as a maid and manicurist on the Pullman Company's Sunset Limited, supporting A. PHILIP RANDOLPH's efforts to organize the Brotherhood of Sleeping Car Porters. During the 1930s and 1940s, as a member and then as president of the American Federation of Labor's Women's Auxiliary of the Dining Car Cooks and Waiters, Albrier worked actively to bring black men and women into the discriminatory mainstream labor unions.

In 1940, as president of the Citizens Employment Council, Albrier led a successful "Don't Buy Where You Can't Work" movement, and in 1955, as secretary of a church-sponsored employment committee, she pushed again for black employment. From 1938 to 1943 she lobbied to hire black teachers in the Berkeley school system, first organizing the East Bay Women's Welfare Club to do research and outreach and then running for the Berkeley city council in 1939 to publicize the color barriers in the schools and local government. In 1943 Berkeley hired its first black teacher.

During the 1930s and 1940s Albrier assisted the East Bay Women's Welfare Club, the Association of Colored Women's Clubs, and the National Association for the Advancement of Colored People (NAACP) in their eventually successful effort to admit black women into the county hospitals' nurses training program and to permit them to live in dormitories. Albrier's friendship with MARY CHURCH TERRELL and MARY MCLEOD BETHUNE, both of whom taught her the value of black women's clubs, led Albrier to organize many such clubs, educating women on social and political issues and motivating them to community action.

During World War II Albrier broke other barriers. She was a pioneer in the Red Cross, qualified to drive in the motor corps and teach first aid classes. In 1942 she became the first black woman welder allowed to work in the Richmond Kaiser shipyards without a union card. African Americans were not allowed to become members of AFL unions, and because no separate black auxiliary existed in the Kaiser yards, Albrier complained directly to the manager, who permitted her to work without a union card. After an executive order was issued barring discrimination in union membership, a segregated auxiliary was organized, and in 1943 she joined the union. Suspecting that black postal employees suffered discrimination in work assignments, promotions, and general employee relations, Albrier left the shipyards in 1943 and went to work in the San Francisco post office. Shortly thereafter she organized the Postal Service Workers Club to deal with grievances related to discrimination.

Albrier saw Democratic Party politics as another way to fight for black rights. In 1938 she was the first woman elected to the Alameda County Democratic Central Committee, a position she held until 1962. She served as delegate to state party conventions and was a member of several local Democratic Party clubs, several of which she organized. She campaigned for state and national candidates, for fair employment and housing legislation, and for the election of black men and women to public office. An African American pharmacist from Berkeley, Byron Rumford, was elected to the California assembly in 1948, and in the 1960s blacks finally won seats on the Berkeley city council and school board.

Albrier's trip to Nigeria in 1960 to attend Nigerian independence ceremonies as a representative of the National Council of Negro Women was the crowning event of her life, symbolizing her commitment to the advancement of blacks worldwide. In line with her dedication to acknowledging black achievements, in 1958 and 1965 Albrier arranged the first window displays commemorating National Negro History Week in major downtown Oakland and San Francisco department stores. During the 1960s she spoke to schoolchildren on black history, and in 1968 she was president of the East Bay Negro Historical Society.

In the 1970s Albrier turned her attention to the elderly, taking a leading role in the development of Berkeley senior centers, speaking at seminars on aging, and serving as a delegate to the 1971 White House Conference on Aging. In 1967 the mayor of Berkeley appointed her to the seven-member Committee on Aging, and in 1972 she was named to the Herrick Hospital board of trustees, in each case becoming the first black appointee. In 1986 Albrier served as president of the Northern California Caucus on Black Aging.

From 1954 to 1978 Albrier received honors almost annually for her extraordinary community service, among them the NAACP West Coast Region "Fight for Freedom" Award (1954), the Woman of the Year Award (1966), the *Sun Reporter* Citizen of Merit Award (1967), a California assembly rules committee commendation for battling racial discrimination (1971), the California Congress of Parents and Teachers Honorary Service Award (1971), the National Congress of Negro Women's "Outstanding Woman of Northern California" Award (1973), the City of Berkeley Community Service Award (1976), and the Greyhound Corporation's "Woman of Tomorrow" Award (1978).

Albrier died in Berkeley, California. A soft-spoken but determined leader, she pioneered the cause of civil rights and participated actively in countless organizations aimed at encouraging African Americans to develop a sense of their own worth.

Further Reading

Albrier's papers are in the Bancroft Library, University of California, Berkeley.

Chall, Malca. "Determined Advocate for Racial Equality," in *The Black Women Oral History Project*, ed. Ruth Edmonds Hill, vol. 1 (1991).

Hill, Ruth Edmonds, and Judith Sedwick. *Women of Courage* (1984).

Painter, Charlotte, and Pamela Valoi. *Gifts of Age* (1985).

Obituaries: *San Francisco Chronicle* and *Daily Californian*, 28 Aug. 1987.

MALCA CHALL

ALBRIGHT, George Washington (1846–?), slave and state legislator, was born to unknown slave parents near Holly Springs in Marshall County, Mississippi, just south of that state's border with Tennessee. His parents were owned by different masters, and in 1857, when George was eleven, his father was sold and forced to move to Texas.

Later, when he was in his nineties, Albright recalled that he had learned to read and write as a child even though the state of Mississippi prohibited slaves from doing so. Historians have estimated that despite legal restrictions at least 5 percent of all slaves were literate on the eve of the Civil War, though literacy rates were probably lowest in rural, Black Belt communities like Holly Springs. In Albright's recollection, a state law required that any slave who broke this law be punished "with 500 lashes on the naked back, and [have his or her] thumb cut off above the second joint" (Rawick, 10). This somewhat exaggerated the actual statutory punishment, which as of 1856 required that slaves and free blacks who gathered in groups of five or more for the purpose of learning to read and write be given thirty-nine lashes. Because the state authorities did not monitor the punishment practices of individual owners, however, the number of lashes laid on—and any additional penalties, such as the severing of fingers—remained at the owner's discretion. Albright nonetheless learned to read and write, because his mother worked in the kitchen of her owner's house, where she listened as the white children of the plantation received their instruction; she in turn taught her own son, who later acquired a primer.

Albright recalled, however, that slave communication was greatly enhanced by what he called the "grapevine telegraph," through which slaves systematically conveyed news and information throughout the plantations. Despite the best efforts of planters to keep their slaves ignorant of the outside world, Albright and others learned, for instance, of John Brown's attack at Harpers Ferry and of the coming of the Civil War. Indeed, early in the war Albright's father ran away from his Texas plantation to join the Union forces but was killed at Vicksburg, Mississippi. At age fifteen, or perhaps a short while afterward, Albright himself joined "the fight for rights of my people," serving as runner for Lincoln's Legal Loyal League. The "4 Ls," as it was known, was a grassroots resistance movement that passed on information about the course of the war and President Lincoln's Emancipation Proclamation. Albright memorized various signals and passwords to ensure secrecy for the small gatherings in slave cabins that he addressed. Such acts of clandestine resistance worked to embolden slaves in Mississippi and elsewhere, who also learned how to assist the advancing Union army.

Active in this resistance network though he remained a slave, Albright continued his efforts to read and write. At nights he secretly read a copy of Harriet Beecher Stowe's *Uncle Tom's Cabin* that had been given to him by a white Northerner. After the war, in 1865, Albright attended a school founded in Marshall County by white Northerners, married one of his white teachers (whose name is not recorded), and trained to be a teacher himself. Albright's wartime resistance work and his literacy perhaps inevitably drew him into Reconstruction politics. In 1868 he worked to elect black delegates to Mississippi's constitutional convention, which established equal civil rights for both races and voting rights for black men, and in which an alliance of poor whites, blacks, and Republicans helped establish Mississippi's first system of publicly financed schooling for children of all races. Albright was among the state's first public school teachers for blacks. He taught at first under a shade tree, later in an old cabin, and finally in a church.

In 1873 Albright was elected to the Mississippi legislature on the Republican Party ticket headed by Adelbert Ames, a New England–born radical who became governor, and ALEXANDER K. DAVIS, a black lawyer who became lieutenant governor. The elections marked the high point of Reconstruction and black electoral power in Mississippi. Albright was, along with CHARLES CALDWELL, one of nine African Americans in the thirty-seven-member state senate, while fifty-five of the 115 members of the House of Representatives were also black. The elections also marked the high point of biracial political activism in the entire South for more than a century. Unlike counties in the Yazoo-Mississippi Delta, where blacks outnumbered whites by ten to one or more, Marshall County had only a slim black majority, which meant that Albright needed to secure the votes of a significant minority of whites. It was this radical combination of blacks and poor whites working for the common good, Albright believed, that so incensed the state's rich white planters. "No wonder the rich folks hate the memory of those legislatures to this very day," Albright remarked in 1937 (Rawick, 13).

The legislative achievements of Albright and his fellow black Republicans were significant. The Republicans enacted a state civil rights law, modeled on the 1875 federal law, that gave all of Mississippi's citizens equal rights before the law. They also expanded educational opportunities for both races, but especially for the black majority, for whom there had been no previous state provision of education. Most scholars now agree with Albright's assessment that the 1874–1875 legislature was fiscally responsible. In the view of one historian, Albright and his fellow Republicans gave Mississippi "a government of greatly expanded functions at a cost that was low in comparison with that of almost any other state" (Vernon Lane Wharton, *The Negro in Mississippi, 1865–1890*

[1947], 180). Prominent whites like John W. C. Watson, a Marshall County planter and former Whig, viewed the matter differently. Watson considered the Republican legislature corrupt and its black members unfit for public office. He described Albright as "very ignorant and wholly without qualifications" (*Mississippi in 1875*, 1003).

In 1875 a self-styled "taxpayers movement" formed throughout the state. Taking their cue from Watson and other so-called moderates, white Mississippians launched a campaign of violence and intimidation that left more than one hundred African Americans dead. In response Governor Ames attempted to establish and arm a biracial state militia to protect against marauding gangs of whites, and he appointed Albright to organize a militia in Marshall County. Though Ames called out these militias on only one occasion, the mere spectacle of armed blacks incensed white Mississippians. Albright recalled that his company "drilled frequently—and how the rich folks hated to see us, armed and ready to defend ourselves and our elected government!" (Rawick, 18). For his uncompromising attitude Albright was targeted by the Ku Klux Klan, who planned to kill him. He narrowly escaped with his life. Albright's colleague Charles Caldwell was not so lucky; he was executed by white vigilantes on Christmas Eve 1875, a few weeks after being reelected to the state senate.

Albright was also reelected to the senate, where he served until 1879. By then both houses of the legislature had been "redeemed" by conservative Democrats, who worked diligently to reassert white supremacy and curb black political power. That counterrevolution was cemented in Mississippi's constitution of 1890 that disfranchised all but a handful of blacks, as well as many illiterate poor whites. It is not known if Albright was still resident in his home state at that time. Like many former Reconstruction legislators he disappeared—or was forced to disappear—from public life. He eventually settled in Colorado, and he was last heard of in June 1937 when he was profiled in the *Daily Worker*, a Communist Party newspaper. In that article Albright recalled his childhood and Reconstruction, and he made clear his continuing militancy and passionate support for a biracial coalition of workers. He announced that he—like many blacks at that time—had abandoned the Republican Party because it had "turned against the common fellow" and was no longer the party of Ames and Lincoln (Rawick, 9). He now supported the Communist Party and commended its nomination of JAMES W. FORD as a vice presidential candidate. Following that interview Albright once again disappeared from the historical record.

Further Reading
Albright's narrative appears in George P. Rawick, ed., *The American Slave: A Composite Autobiography*, supplement, series 1, vol. 6, *Mississippi Narratives, Part 1* (1977), pp. 8–18. For information on Reconstruction in Marshall County, see *Mississippi in 1875: Report of the Select Committee to Inquire into the Mississippi Election of 1875* (1876).

Harris, William C. *The Day of the Carpetbagger: Republican Reconstruction in Mississippi* (1979).

STEVEN J. NIVEN

ALCORN, George Edward, Jr. (22 Mar. 1940–), physicist, inventor, and educator, was born in Indianapolis, Indiana, the eldest of two sons of Arletta (Dixon) Alcorn and George Alcorn, an auto mechanic. Little is known of his early life. George Alcorn Jr. earned a BA in Physics in 1962 from Occidental College in Pasadena, California, where he excelled both academically and athletically, earning eight letters in football and baseball. His educational pursuits took him next to Howard University, where he received a master's degree in Nuclear Physics after only nine months of study. During the summers of 1962 and 1963 Alcorn worked as a research engineer at the space division of North American Rockwell, where he computed trajectories and orbital mechanics for missiles, including the Titan I and II, the Saturn IV, and the Nova.

From 1965 to 1967 Alcorn researched negative ion formation with funded support from the National Aeronautics and Space Administration (NASA). Alcorn furthered his higher education at Howard University, earning his PhD in Molecular and Atomic Physics in 1967. He began working in the private sector soon after and by 1969 had married Maria DaVillier, with whom he had a son in 1979. His work in private industry sent him first to a position as a senior physicist at Philco-Ford and then to a position at PerkinElmer. Next Alcorn moved to IBM, where he worked as both an advisory engineer and an inventor. Meanwhile in 1973 Alcorn had begun teaching electrical engineering at Howard University, where he held teaching positions for several years, eventually rising to the rank of full professor. He held the same title at the University of the District of Columbia, again teaching electrical engineering.

In 1978 Alcorn's career path led him back to NASA. During his tenure there he invented the X-ray spectrometer. One of the best-known of his twenty inventions, this instrument is used to detect life on other planets and is said to have revolutionized radiology. The invention earned Alcorn the 1984 NASA–Goddard Space Flight Center (GSFC) award for inventor of the year. That same year Alcorn also received recognition from NASA's equal employment opportunity office both for recruiting minority women scientists and engineers and for helping minority businesses develop research programs. Although Alcorn's inventions may not be easily understandable or recognizable by the general public, his highly complex and extremely valuable technical contributions include:

Method of fabricating an imaging X-ray spectrometer
GaAs Schottky barrier photo-responsive device and method of fabrication
Dense dry-etched multilevel metallurgy with nonoverlapped vias

Method for forming dense dry-etched multilevel metallurgy with nonoverlapped vias
Hardened photoresist master image mask process

Among Alcorn's groundbreaking inventions is the fabrication of plasma semiconductor devices. The Institute of Electrical and Electronics Engineers called Alcorn's patent for the "Process for Controlling the Slope of a Via Hole" an important contribution to plasma etching, one that is now widely used by semiconductor manufacturing companies.

One of Alcorn's inventions while at NASA's GSFC brought him recognition in 1999 from *Government Executive* magazine. The magazine honored Alcorn with the Government Technology Award for developing the Airborne LIDAR Topographic Mapping System (ALTMS) in partnership with the Houston Advanced Research Center. The award was given to twenty-one programs out of the more than one hundred nominated, and only one other NASA facility received the honor that year. The ALTMS helps produce accurate elevation data and is used in such practical applications as floodplain mapping, highway design simulation, shoreline and erosion mapping, habitat assessments, and pipeline and utility surveys. Alcorn held numerous positions at NASA, including deputy project manager for advanced development, in which position he was in charge of developing new technologies for the space station Freedom; manager of advanced programs at NASA/GSFC from 1990 to 1992; and chief of Goddard's Office of Commercial Programs, which oversaw technology transfer, small business innovation research, and commercial use of space programs, from 1992 to 2005.

Alcorn's community service activities proved as wide ranging as his professional ones. A lifelong educator, Alcorn founded the Saturday Academy, a weekend honors program aimed at supplementing the science and math education of inner-city students. Howard University distinguished Alcorn in 1994 as a black achiever in science and technology at its Heritage of Greatness awards ceremony. Alcorn also worked with the Meyerhoff Foundation at the University of Maryland–Baltimore County (UMBC). Founded in 1988 by the UMBC president Freeman Hrabowski, the program encourages minorities to seek doctorates in science and engineering. In 2001 Congresswoman Donna M. Christian-Christensen recognized Alcorn for helping companies in the Virgin Islands apply NASA and other technological advances to their businesses. In 2005 Alcorn became assistant director of standards and excellence at the Applied Engineering and Technology Directorate.

Further Reading

Krapp, Kristine M. *Notable Black American Scientists* (1999).
"Physicists of the African Diaspora: George Edward Alcorn," accessible online at http://www.math.buffalo.edu/mad/physics/alcorn_georgeE.html.

PAMELA BLACKMON

ALDRIDGE, Ira (24 July 1807–10 Aug. 1867), actor, was born Ira Frederick Aldridge, the son of Daniel Aldridge, a minister, and Lurona (maiden name unknown). Although certain historical accounts record that Aldridge was born in Senegal, Africa, and was the grandson of the Fulah tribal chieftain, modern biographical scholarship has established that he was born in New York City. It is possible that he could claim Fulah ancestry, but his lineal descent from tribal royalty is unconfirmed. Extant evidence concerning Aldridge's life is sketchy, conflicting, or exaggerated, possibly owing in part to the aggrandizements of theatrical publicity.

As a young boy, Aldridge attended the African Free School in New York City. Although Aldridge's father intended for him to join the clergy, Aldridge showed an early attraction to the stage, excelling at debate and declamation. Around 1821 Aldridge tried to perform at Brown's Theatre (also known as the African Theatre), but his father forced him from the stage. English playbills later stated that Aldridge came via the African Theatre, New York, so Aldridge must have circumvented his father's objections before the theater was closed in 1823. Recognizing the slim prospects for an African American actor in the United States at a time of strong prejudices against blacks, Aldridge made plans to immigrate to England.

Aldridge became a dresser to the English actor Henry Wallack, who was performing in New York. Henry Wallack's brother, James, then employed Aldridge as a personal attendant while on passage to Liverpool. J. J. Sheahan, a friend of Aldridge's, wrote that James Wallack had planned to sponsor Aldridge and make money off his engagements, but when Wallack told a reporter that Aldridge was his servant, the two went their separate ways. (The often repeated account that Aldridge became the personal attendant of the British classical actor Edmund Kean and accompanied him back to England has been proved false.) Aldridge arrived in England in 1824, and although he announced his return to the United States a number of times throughout his career, he never went home.

Although it has been generally accepted that Aldridge made his debut in England in 1826 as Othello, playbills show that his first major engagement in London was at the Royal Coberg Theatre on 10 October 1825 under the name Mr. Keene. Aldridge, also dubbed the "African Roscius," acted under this name until around 1832. In his debut Aldridge played the royal slave Oroonoko in *The Revolt of Surinam*. During this engagement he also played in *The Ethiopian* and *The Libertine Defeated*. That the engagement was a success for Aldridge is evident in a playbill announcing his appearance in *The Negro's Curse*, a play written expressly for him. His biographers suggest that Aldridge rose to leading roles so quickly in part because of the novel appeal of having a "Man of Colour" in the cast. During the early part of Aldridge's career, many reviewers doubted the ability of a black actor, saying, for example, "Owing to the shape of his lips it is utterly impossible for him to

Ira Aldridge, the "African Roscius," as Othello, one of his best-known roles. European audiences embraced Ira Aldridge as one of the greatest tragedians of his time. Painting by Henry Perronet Briggs, c. 1830. (National Portrait Gallery/Smithsonian.)

pronounce English in such a manner as to satisfy the unfastidious ears of the gallery" (*The Times* [London], 11 Oct. 1825). Nonetheless, Aldridge was popular with audiences.

The prejudiced criticism demonstrated in the London press made it difficult for Aldridge, despite his popularity with the public, to establish a career in the city. He turned, therefore, to the British provinces, where he developed his craft over the next twenty-five years. In his first provincial engagement at Brighton, he played Oroonoko and, for the first time on record, Othello, making no great impression. He toured Sheffield, Halifax, Manchester, Newcastle, Edinburgh, Lancaster, Liverpool, and Sunderland. His repertoire consisted of *Othello, Oroonoko, The Slave, The Castle Spectre, The Padlock,* and *The Revenge. Othello* and *The Padlock* remained in his repertoire until his death.

In 1829 Aldridge appeared in Belfast, with Charles Kean playing Iago to Aldridge's Othello and Oroonoko to his Aboan. In 1830 Aldridge played his first "white" role, Captain Hatteraick in *Guy Mannering,* using white makeup and a wig. Afterward, Aldridge regularly played white roles, such as Shylock in *The Merchant of Venice* and Rob MacGregor in *Rob Roy.* In 1833 Aldridge played Dublin and for the first time crossed paths with Edmund Kean. Playing in an overlapping engagement, Kean saw Aldridge in the role of Othello and afterward recommended him to

the Royal Theatre at Bath, a prestigious provincial playhouse. Within three weeks Aldridge opened at Bath with his regular repertoire.

In 1833 Aldridge was invited to appear at the Theatre Royal Covent Garden, where he opened as Othello to Ellen Tree's Desdemona. The London press, however, was still unwilling, on the whole, to accept a black leading actor at its major theaters. A few critics found his performance commendable, but most agreed that Covent Garden was no place for a "curiosity" such as Aldridge. He had been scheduled to appear in two other roles at Covent Garden, but the performances were canceled for reasons that remain unclear. It is believed that the threats of critics perhaps convinced the Covent Garden manager, Pierre Laporte, that the "novelty" was not worth the financial risk. Whatever the reason for the cancellation, Aldridge's achievement is recorded by his biographers, who commented that his performance at Covent Garden "will forever be red-letter days in the history of world theatre and human progress, for . . . a lone Negro from an enslaved people challenged the great white actors in the very heart of their Empire" (Marshall and Stock, 135).

Rejected by London for a second time, Aldridge returned to the provinces for many successful years. In 1852 he began his first tour of the Continent. His success in Europe was unequaled by any other in his career. His first tour through Belgium, Hungary, Germany, Austria, and Poland lasted three years. In 1857 he toured Sweden, and afterward he continually toured the Continent, including Russia, until his death, returning to England periodically to play the provinces. It was on his first tour that he added the roles of Macbeth, King Lear, and Richard III to his repertoire and received great honors from the princes of Europe. The king of Prussia awarded him the Gold Medal of the First Class for Art and Sciences; in Vienna the emperor presented him with the Medal of Ferdinand; and he was made an honorary member of the Hungarian Dramatic Conservatoire in Hungary, the Imperial and Archducal Order of Our Lady of the Manger in Austria, and the Imperial Academy of Beaux Arts in St. Petersburg. After he played the major cities of Europe to royalty and accolades, it is no wonder that Aldridge preferred to tour Europe rather than the small provincial theaters of England. The racism in the United States and, to a lesser extent, England, was not present in other European countries at the time. As a result, Aldridge thrived in continental Europe, which judged him by his ability on the boards rather than by the color of his skin. In 1858, however, Aldridge finally found success at the Lyceum Theatre in London and in 1863 was granted British citizenship.

His biographers credit Aldridge with being "the first to show that a black man could scale any heights in theatrical art reached by a white man—and recreate with equal artistry the greatest characters in world drama" (Marshall and Stock, 335). Known for his versatility, Aldridge played both the greatest tragic characters of Shakespeare and the melodramatic slave characters of his early career with dexterity. A physically impressive man, Aldridge was known for his strong, clear voice and a style more realistic than that used by his contemporaries—so realistic that accounts by actors mention that Aldridge caused them to forget that they were on a stage, and the play became "naked, shattering reality." He was known as well for personalizing his roles, especially Othello; he studied and interpreted his roles with little consideration for the traditional interpretation. When he was abroad, he acted in English, while his supporting cast used the native language. One Russian actor who worked with Aldridge, Davydov, said that "his mimicry, gestures, were so expressive that knowledge of the English language for the understanding of his acting was not needed at all" (V. N. Davydov, *Razkaz o Proshlom* [1930], 98).

Aldridge was married twice, although we know very little about his wives. His first wife, the Englishwoman Margaret Gill, whom he married in 1832, died in 1864. He married his second wife, the countess Amanda Paulina von Brandt of Sweden, in 1865. Aldridge and his second wife had five children, one of whom died in infancy. Aldridge died in Lodz, Poland, while on his way to perform in St. Petersburg.

Further Reading

Hill, Errol. *Shakespeare in Sable* (1990).
Malone, Mary. *Actor in Exile: The Life of Ira Aldridge* (1969).
Marshall, Herbert. *Further Research on Ira Aldridge: The Negro Tragedian* (1970).
Marshall, Herbert, and Mildred Stock. *Ira Aldridge: The Negro Tragedian* (1958).
Obituary: *The Times* (London), 18 July 1867.

MELISSA VICKERY-BAREFORD

ALEXANDER, Archer (c. 1813–8 Dec. 1879), fugitive slave, was born near Richmond, Virginia, on a plantation owned by the Delaney family. Despite his memories of being well treated, his father, Aleck, was sold to pay his master's debts and taken south. Rev. Delaney justified Aleck's sale by claiming that the literate slave had shared ideas about freedom with other slaves in the neighborhood. When Rev. Delaney died in 1831, Alexander's mother, Chloe, was left to Mrs. Delaney, and eighteen-year-old Alexander was left to the master's son, Thomas. Chloe Alexander died six months after Thomas Delaney took her son with him to Missouri.

Delaney settled in western St. Charles County, Missouri, where Alexander married a local slave woman named Louisa. He later sold Alexander to Louisa's master, Jim Hollman, when he moved from the state, and the couple spent the next twenty years living with their growing family on the Hollman farm. Alexander was trusted with the management of the farm and was treated well, he believed, because of his faithful service to his master. However, a number of his ten children were sold away because, as his biographer explained, they had "behaved badly" (Eliot, 41).

During the early months of the Civil War, Jim Hollman and a group of local secessionists burned bridges in an attempt to delay the progress of Union forces toward the state capital at Jefferson City. Alexander, like most of his fellow slaves, was aware of the tumultuous political situation in Missouri and understood that his freedom was at stake. One night in February 1863 he walked five miles to inform a local Unionist neighbor that secessionists had cut the timbers under a railroad bridge over which Union troops would be passing. Alexander fell under suspicion after the sabotage scheme was thwarted, and he was forced to flee. Though slave hunters quickly captured him, he escaped and made his way to St. Louis, where he found work on the estate of the prominent Unionists Rev. William Greenleaf Eliot and his wife Abigail. Rev. Eliot was a Unitarian minister and an important St. Louis civic leader, having helped found both Washington University and the Western Sanitary Commission. According to Eliot, Alexander immediately impressed him with his strong work ethic, deep Christian faith, and stoic demeanor (61). Eliot knew of his employee's fugitive status and sought a thirty-day military protection permit and at the same time offered to purchase Alexander from his master. Hollman rejected the proposal and instead sent slave catchers to abduct Alexander, but Eliot was able to use his Union military connections to obtain his freedom. Alexander is sometimes credited with being the last slave to be captured under the Fugitive Slave Act of 1850.

Alexander spent a brief time working in Illinois until the passage of Missouri's gradual emancipation law of 1863. He then arranged for Louisa and their youngest daughter, Nellie, to escape from Hollman and join him in St. Louis. Five of the Alexanders' children also fled to St. Louis and their son, Tom, enlisted and died in the Union army. Alexander worked intermittently for the Eliots for the remainder of his life. A year after the war Louisa Alexander died under suspicious circumstances when she returned to the Hollmans to collect her few personal belongings. Soon after, Alexander married a woman named Judy.

Archer Alexander achieved fame both through William Greenleaf Eliot's biography of him, *The Story of Archer Alexander. From Slavery to Freedom, March 30, 1863*, and because his image was used by the artist Thomas Ball in his Freedmen's Memorial to Abraham Lincoln. The monument's troubled history began soon after Lincoln's assassination, when a former slave named Charlotte Scott offered the first $5 she earned as a freedperson for the purpose of honoring the fallen president. A Union general learned of Scott's gesture and encouraged the Western Sanitary Commission of St. Louis to administer a fund to be raised through contributions from former slaves, many of who were Union soldiers. The tribute was conceptualized as a representation of the freedmen's gratitude toward the former president for his efforts on their behalf.

The Western Sanitary Commission erected a more modest monument after it failed to raise a larger sum of money through combined efforts with other memorial funds. As a member of the commission, William Eliot viewed a marble sculpture in Thomas Ball's Italian studio and arranged with the artist to use his work for the freedmen's tribute. Ball's original statue depicted Abraham Lincoln granting freedom to a half-naked man wearing a liberty cap and passively crouching amidst the broken shackles of his enslavement. However, because the emancipated slave figure closely resembled the idealized images of the slave man so often used in abolitionist literature, the commissioners requested that Ball instead substitute the image of an actual man. This one would be physically breaking the shackles of slavery, thus suggesting agency in his own emancipation. Bell was given a photograph of Archer Alexander to use as his model. The final bronze statue depicts a nearly naked Alexander with his arm outstretched and fist clenched, kneeling at the feet of his emancipator. In spite of these alterations, the arrangement still suggests Lincoln's centrality to emancipation, rather than portraying the reality that Alexander, like most former slaves, was largely responsible for securing his own freedom.

FREDERICK DOUGLASS refrained from mentioning the crouching man in his public remarks at the 1876 dedication of the Freedmen's Monument in Washington, D.C.'s, Lincoln Park. Douglass is said to have privately commented that a standing figure would have better represented African American manhood. Erected at the end of Reconstruction, the Freedmen's Memorial quickly became one of the primary visual representations of emancipation in the nation's collective memory.

Archer Alexander died in St. Louis, Missouri. His well-attended funeral was presided over by William Greenleaf Eliot. Soon after, a monument was placed at the site of his capture as a fugitive; it read, "Archer Alexander. From Slavery to Freedom, March 30, 1863."

Further Reading

Eliot, William Greenleaf. *The Story of Archer Alexander. From Slavery to Freedom, March 30, 1863* (1885).
Savage, Kirk. *Standing Soldiers, Kneeling Slaves: Race, War, and Monument in Nineteenth-Century America* (1997).

DIANE MUTTI BURKE

ALEXANDER, Archie Alphonso (14 May 1888–4 Jan. 1958), engineer, was born in Ottumwa, Iowa, the son of Price Alexander, a janitor and coachman, and Mary Hamilton. The Alexanders were members of a tiny African American minority both in the town of Archie's birth and in Des Moines, Iowa, where they moved when he was eleven years old. In Ottumwa the Alexanders lived in the section of town inhabited by the poor, both black and white. In Des Moines they lived on a small farm on the outskirts of town. Since Iowa's public schools were not segregated, Alexander attended school with whites, and he graduated from Des Moines's Oak Park High School in 1905. Then—uncommon for the son of a janitor, whether black or white—he went on to further study. By working hard at part-time jobs, and with some help from his parents, Alexander attended Highland Park College and the Cummins Art School, both in Des Moines, before enrolling in 1908 at the College of Engineering at the University of Iowa in Iowa City. He was the College of Engineering's only black student, and upon entering, he allegedly was warned, bluntly but not unkindly, by one official that a Negro could not hope to succeed as an engineer. Continuing to support himself through a variety of part-time jobs, Alexander did well academically, pledged a fraternity, Kappa Alpha Psi, and also was a star as the first black member of the varsity football team. On the gridiron as a tackle he earned the title "Alexander the Great."

Upon graduation in 1912 Alexander found his adviser's gloomy warning confirmed. Every construction firm in Des Moines rejected his application for employment as an engineer. So Alexander took a job, for twenty-five cents an hour, as a laborer in the steel shop of the Marsh Engineering Company. There his eagerness and his ambition were not denied. When he resigned two years later to found his own engineering company, he was earning seventy dollars a week as the engineer in charge of bridge construction in Iowa and Minnesota for the March Engineering Company.

Starting modestly, often at jobs that attracted few, if any, other bidders, Alexander soon took on a white partner, George F. Higbee, with whom he had worked earlier at the Marsh Engineering Company. The partnership lasted from 1917 until 1925, when Higbee was killed in a construction accident. For the next four years Alexander ran the company alone, building mostly bridges and viaducts, his specialty, but also apartment buildings and sewage systems. He also built a new heating plant, a new power plant, and a tunnel that went under the Iowa River on the campus of his alma mater in Iowa City. Alexander, who still encountered prejudice and occasional hostility despite his unblemished engineering record, served as president of the Des Moines chapter of the NAACP and of the local Interracial Commission.

In 1929 Alexander took on as a junior partner a white engineer, Maurice A. Repass, a former classmate at the University of Iowa. Under the firm name of Alexander & Repass, the partners went on to complete projects in nearly every state and to build what *Ebony* magazine called the "nation's most successful interracial business." The best-known, though not the biggest, projects completed by the firm of Alexander & Repass were in the nation's capital: the Tidal Basin Bridge and Seawall, the K Street elevated highway and underpass from Key Bridge to Twenty-Seventh Street, N.W., and the Whitehurst Freeway around Georgetown.

Alexander married Audra A. Linzy of Denver in 1913. The couple had one child, who died in early childhood.

Like many black Americans until the election of Franklin D. Roosevelt as president in 1932, Alexander supported the Republican Party. But unlike most black voters, Alexander remained a lifelong Republican, even though it might have been politically as well as economically astute for him to have supported the Democratic Party during its era of dominance, especially since his engineering company did so much public work. But his politics never seemed to hurt his business, and in fact, he was eventually rewarded for his loyalty. Alexander was not just a member of the Republican Party but he was also an active member who twice, in 1932 and in 1940, served as assistant chairman of the Iowa Republican State Committee. In 1952 he was an early supporter of Dwight D. Eisenhower for president. Alexander's long years of dedication to the party were rewarded by his appointment, in April 1954, as governor of the Virgin Islands. The appointment was a disaster for all concerned, though, and it may even have hastened Alexander's death. Dogmatic, paternalistic, undemocratic, and with an openly stated contempt for the easygoing Virgin Islanders, Alexander was sometimes described as a "Midwestern Babbitt" who brought all the values of small-town America to the Caribbean. He lasted a strife-torn and acrimonious sixteen months before he was pressured to resign in August 1955.

Less than three years later, Alexander died at his home in Des Moines. In his will he left a trust fund for the support of his wife, the corpus of which was to go, upon her death, to the University of Iowa, Tuskegee Institute in Alabama, and Howard University in Washington, D.C., for engineering scholarships. In 1975 each of the three institutions received $105,000.

Further Reading
Alexander's papers are located at the University of Iowa, Iowa City.
Alexander, Archie Alphonso. "Engineering as a Profession," *Opportunity* (Apr.–June 1946).
Boyer, William W. *America's Virgin Islands: A History of Human Rights and Wrongs* (1983).
Wynes, Charles E. "'Alexander the Great,' Bridge Builder," *Palimpsest* 66 (May–June 1985).
Obituary: *Des Moines Sunday Register*, 5 Jan. 1958.
CHARLES E. WYNES

ALEXANDER, Arthur (10 May 1940–9 June 1993), soul and rhythm and blues singer and songwriter, was born Arthur Alexander Jr. in Florence, Alabama, to Arthur Alexander, a laborer and musician, and Fannie Scott Spencer. He was exposed to music at an early age by his mother and older sister, who sang in church, and by his father, who played weekend gigs as a bottleneck blues guitarist. After high school Alexander was working as a bellhop at the

Sheffield Hotel when he met Tom Stafford, a white R&B enthusiast who introduced him to what would become the nucleus of the Muscle Shoals–area studio scene: Dan Penn, Rick Hall, Spooner Oldham, and Billy Sherrill. The men, all then working for Rick Hall's Fame Music Stafford, found Alexander's songwriting abilities every bit as intriguing as his singing, and soon made sure that Alexander became part of Fame's writing operation. In 1958 Alexander and Henry Lee Bennett coauthored "She Wanna Rock," which was sold to Decca and recorded by the country singer Arnie Derksen. Two year later Alexander made his debut on record, cutting the earthy "Sally Sue Brown" for Judd Records under the pseudonym June (from "Junior") Alexander.

By 1962 Alexander had become a star. Following a short-lived separation from Fame, in 1961 Stafford convinced Hall to record Alexander singing the original "You Better Move On." This was the first session of note at Hall's new studio in Muscle Shoals, located in an old tobacco and candy warehouse, which went on to become one of the most productive (and hallowed) rooms in all of soul music. "You Better Move On" was an appropriately momentous beginning; its R&B-country hybrid (as much a function of Alexander's tastes as his white-backing band) laid the groundwork for the sound that would define an era through Stax and Atlantic recordings. Released on Dot, it proved tremendously popular as well, reaching the top twenty in the pop charts. Now under contract to Dot, Alexander scored a minor hit with the commercially minded "Where Have You Been," and then with "Anna (Go to Her)," a worthy follow-up to "You Better Move On." But he failed to meet the lofty expectations set by his debut and was released by Dot in 1965.

While Alexander's performing career may have been uneven, as a songwriter he was having far better luck. Steve Alaimo's 1963 version of "Every Day I Have to Cry Some" sold well, and Alexander was soon introduced to fans of the British Invasion by the Rolling Stones' cover of "You Better Move On" (1964) and the Beatles' early takes on "Anna" (1963). Numerous other artists would eventually record his compositions, including the Bee Gees, Dusty Springfield, the Drifters, and TINA TURNER.

After a three-year absence, which has been attributed to both illness and a variety of personal problems, Alexander signed to Sound Stage 7 in 1965. But he managed only four singles for the label between 1968 and 1970, further lending to his spectral standing in the music world. In 1971 he became a songwriter for Nashville's Combine Music, which employed Kris Kristofferson and Tony Joe White, and in 1972 he recorded a self-titled comeback album at American Studios in Memphis, bolstered by the support of many of his old Muscle Shoals colleagues. While considered a minor classic, neither the album nor its singles (including the excellent "Rainbow Road," Penn's telling of Alexander's story) performed well on the charts. A version of "Every Day I Have to Cry Some" provided Alexander with a minor hit in 1975, but after a few other abortive efforts he retired from music to drive a social services bus.

Alexander remained a cult figure to soul enthusiasts, however, as well as a songwriter's songwriter whose body of work ranks among the finest in American pop. It was this reputation that led the Elektra/Nonesuch producer Ben Vaughn to recruit Alexander for a nineties comeback. The result, 1993's *Lonely Just Like Me*, was a mix of old and new material that played to Alexander's melancholic strengths; like *Rainbow Road*, it featured contributions from many of Alexander's longtime peers and admirers. Tragically, Alexander passed away shortly after its release, when he had just begun touring in support of the well-received album. Alexander may have not lived to reap the rewards of his efforts, but at least the album served to remind audiences of a spectacular talent who had unjustly slipped into obscurity.

Penn, as sound an authority as there is on the history of southern soul, has said that "Arthur was the reason we all made it. He had the first Muscle Shoals hit and it was he that showed us anything was possible." Alexander's influence may have stretched well beyond his role in the genesis of one of the twentieth century's major musical movements. Alexander was a dazzling songwriter who refused to stay behind the scenes and a superb vocalist who insisted on interpreting his own material. Alexander's vision of the fully realized artist may have been his greatest gift to his acolytes in the British Invasion, his peers in the Muscle Shoals, and all of postwar American pop.

Further Reading
Guralnick, Peter. *Sweet Soul Music* (1986).
Younger, Richard. *Get a Shot of Rhythm and Blues* (2000).

Discography
Rainbow Road: The Warner Brothers Recordings (Warner Brothers 45581).
The Ultimate Arthur Alexander (Razor & Tie 22014).
NATHANIEL FRIEDMAN

ALEXANDER, Avery C. (29 June 1910–5 Mar. 1999), minister, civil rights leader, and member of the Louisiana House of Representatives, was born Avery Caesar Alexander in the town of Houma in Terrebonne Parish, Louisiana, to a family of sharecroppers. The names of his parents are not known. Seventeen years later, his family moved to New Orleans. Avery Alexander maintained an active life there and in Baton Rouge for the next seventy-two years.

Prior to his election to the Louisiana legislature, Alexander was employed as a longshoreman. At the same time, he pursued an education by taking night courses, receiving his high school diploma from Gilbert Academy in 1939. He became politically active by working as a labor union operative for a long-

shoreman's union, Local 1419. He also held the occupations of real estate broker and insurance agent.

Alexander received a degree in theology from Union Baptist Theological Seminary and became an ordained Baptist minister in 1944. As a minister, Avery joined the NAACP and became an activist in the civil rights movement. He was among the preachers present when the Southern Christian Leadership Conference (SCLC) was founded in New Orleans in 1957. He did not give up his loyalty to the longshoreman's union, however, and managed the union's welfare system in the late 1950s and early 1960s.

During the 1950s, while riding segregated streetcars in New Orleans, Alexander was known to throw the wooden screens separating the white section from the black section into the street. He later became active on the issue of bus employment discrimination and led a boycott that forced the New Orleans Public Service to hire African American bus drivers for the first time.

Although Alexander accomplished much throughout his life, his most famous undertaking was his

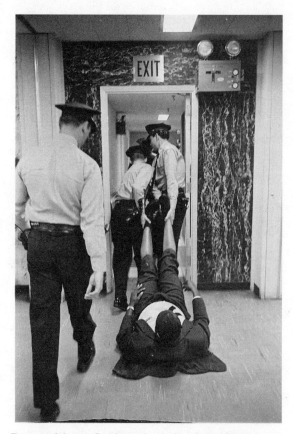

Reverend Avery C. Alexander, being dragged away from the City Hall cafeteria by the New Orleans police after he attempted to lead a sit-in protesting the city's racial policy, 31 October 1963. (AP Images.)

1963 attempt to integrate the public cafeteria in the basement of New Orleans City Hall. With a cohort of staunch supporters, Alexander entered the basement cafeteria to stage a lunch-counter sit-in. The protestors declared they would not leave the premises until they had either been served a sandwich or placed under arrest. When the white cafeteria workers told Alexander that they could not serve him, he recalled in *A House Divided*, a 1984 documentary, he replied, "I understand everything. But that's food, I'm hungry, and I want to be served." For five hours Alexander and the other protestors refused to leave the lunch counter.

Finally, white police officers pulled Alexander out of the cafeteria and, grabbing him by the heels, dragged him up the steps of city hall. Television footage showed Alexander's head banging on the staircase. As a whole, television coverage of the civil rights movement in New Orleans until this time had tended to ignore local police violence, concentrating instead on events in Birmingham, Montgomery, and Selma. The spectacle of Avery Alexander being dragged out of city hall, however, and the dramatic news coverage it spawned, galvanized the support of less-engaged citizens in New Orleans for civil rights.

Around the same time, Alexander voiced support for an economic boycott against a commercial district located on Dryades Street, where white storeowners had historically refused to hire African Americans. While the storeowners maintained their resistance, the black community changed its shopping patterns to support a commercial district where the boycotts had succeeded. As a result many of the Dryades stores went out of business.

In 1975 Alexander was elected as a Democrat to represent the 93rd District in the Louisiana House of Representatives, a position he held for the remainder of his life. In 1977 Avery Alexander joined nine other state legislators to establish the Louisiana Legislative Black Caucus, a major goal of which was to increase the proportion of African Americans in the state legislature. In the late 1980s the caucus was successful in reapportioning or redrawing Louisiana's legislative boundaries to increase the number of districts that would send African Americans to the state capitol. In addition to being a founding member of the Louisiana Legislative Black Caucus, Alexander also served as its chaplain. (The fact that he was a minister as well as a politician led to his being affectionately known as "The Rev.")

Alexander remained active in religious affairs throughout his life. He established a nondenominational church, the Church of All People, in 1990. His political activism continued into the last few years of the twentieth century. When David Duke, a former member of the Ku Klux Klan, tried to hold a rally in New Orleans, Alexander protested the event and was restrained by the police. In 1996 Avery walked on a Baton Rouge picket line to protest proposed changes to Louisiana's state affirmative action laws. The following year he spoke out against racist killings and the brutality of police officers against African Americans.

Both a minister and a politician, Avery Alexander was instrumental in forming civil rights coalitions of both religious and political leaders. For example, in August 1997, he joined with DICK GREGORY, ministers, and politicians from Mississippi and Michigan to form a national coalition to protest the unfair legal treatment of poor and minority members of society. The resulting summit that Alexander co-hosted in Detroit was entitled "Networking to Help the Hopeless to Obtain Equal Justice."

Though a protestor to the end, Alexander was also a statesman. He maintained his commitment to the Democratic Party and three times served as a delegate to the National Democratic Convention. Among his unfinished projects in the state legislature at the time of his death was a challenge to Louisiana's random drug-testing laws. When he died he was the most senior member of the Louisiana House of Representatives. A statue of Avery Alexander stands in a plaza across from the New Orleans city hall where he was arrested in 1963.

Further Reading
"In Memory of Louisiana State Representative Avery Alexander," *Congressional Record*, 11 Mar. 1999.
"Tribute to Reverend Avery C. Alexander," *Congressional Record*, 15 Mar. 1999.
Obituary: *New Orleans Times-Picayune*, 9 Mar. 1999.

NATHAN ZOOK

ALEXANDER, Clifford Leopold, Jr. (21 Sept. 1933–), lawyer, businessman, and secretary of the army, was born in New York City, the only child of Clifford Leopold Sr. and Edith McAllister. Alexander's father, a Jamaican native, became an apartment building manager of Harlem's Young Christian Association. His mother was from Yonkers, New York, where she worked for a real estate firm. Later she headed the New York City welfare department. She was the first African American woman to get elected to the Democratic Party's Electoral College. In this position she became a prominent figure in the broader civil rights struggle. Both parents inspired Alexander's later work to end racial discrimination.

Alexander spent his childhood in New York City. He received his early education at the Ethical Cultural School and Fieldston Schools in the Bronx. After graduating from high school, Alexander went to Harvard University. Here he met McGeorge Bundy, Harvard's Dean of Arts and Science and later national security advisor to presidents John F. Kennedy and Lyndon Johnson. Bundy would prove an early influence on Alexander's career path. Following in the footsteps of his mother, Alexander became the first African American student-body president. In 1955 he graduated cum laude from Harvard and received the university's Ames Award, which recognized students who played important and positive roles in their communities. During much of the late 1950s Alexander worked for Mutual Life Insurance Company, directing the complaints division. He also enrolled at Yale Law School, where in 1958 he received an LLB degree.

After finishing law school in 1958 Alexander served until 1959 with the 369th Field Artillery Battalion at Fort Six, New Jersey. In July 1959 he married the former Adele Logan, a fellow Fieldston student and Pulitzer nominee. The couple had two children, ELIZABETH [ALEXANDER] and Mark. After becoming a member of the New York Bar in 1959 he was appointed assistant district attorney in New York County, remaining in the office until 1961. Shortly thereafter he became an executive director of Manhattanville Hamilton Grange Neighborhood Conservation District of New York, where he worked to improve housing conditions for rental homes. Alexander also served as the executive director of Harlem Youth Opportunities Unlimited from 1962 to 1963. The program's goal was to help inner city youth in Harlem.

Alexander's life took a dramatic turn in 1963, when LOUIS B. MARTIN, then deputy chairman for the Democratic National Committee, called him to Washington to work in the Kennedy Administration. Accepting this political position, Alexander served for the National Security Council as a foreign affairs officer under the presidential assistant McGeorge Bundy from 1963 to 1964. In the same year, Alexander's political career began to flourish when he was appointed deputy special assistant to President Lyndon B. Johnson in 1964, and later became associate special counsel to President Johnson in 1965. He accepted the office of a deputy special counsel on the White House staff in 1966. From 1967 to 1969, as a special representative of President Johnson, he worked on the Voting Rights Act and headed the Equal Employment Opportunities Commission. He also led the delegation to ceremonies celebrating the independence of the Kingdom of Swaziland. Alexander stayed in the position of special representative until Senate Majority Leader Everett Dirksen accused him of pressuring employers to establish a work environment of equal opportunities for minorities and women. He resigned from his position in 1969.

Returning to his career as a lawyer, Alexander worked at the Washington law firm Arnold and Porter, LLP, from 1969 to 1975. Looking for new platforms to defeat white supremacy, Alexander in addition to his legal career was also a commentator, host, and co-producer on the TV program *Cliff Alexander: Black on White* from 1971 to 1976. Turning back to legal education, Alexander was for a short time a professor of law at Howard University from 1973 to 1974. In addition, he attempted unsuccessfully to win political office as the mayor of

the District of Columbia in 1974. Alexander continued his legal career as a partner of the lobbying firm of Verner, Liipfert, Bernhard, McPherson, and Alexander in 1975.

In 1977 President Jimmy Carter appointed Alexander as the nation's first African American secretary of the army, a position in which he served until the end of Carter's term in 1981. The Department of the Army honored Alexander with the Outstanding Civilian Award in 1980. As secretary of the army, Alexander prioritized contracts to minority businesses and reemphasized the need for an all-volunteer army. After resigning from this position and receiving the Distinguished Public Service Award in 1981, he became the president of his own consulting firm, Alexander and Associates, which focused on increasing the number of minorities in major corporations. One of the firm's most important clients was Major League Baseball, which had a poor record of minority hiring in front office and other administrative roles.

Alexander served on the boards of directors of several companies. He sat on the board of American Home Products Corporations, MCI Worldcom, IMS Health, Mutual of America, Dreyfus Investment Funds, and Dun & Bradstreet. He also served on the board of several non-profit companies in addition to being a member of the Board of Governors of the American Stock Exchange. His accomplishments in the field of law were honored with the Washington Bar Association Award in 1969, followed by the FREDERICK DOUGLASS Award in 1970 for dedicating his life to fighting racism.

Further Reading
Alexander, Clifford Leopold. "Black Memoir of the White House," *American Visions* (Feb. 1995).
Christmas, Walter. *Negroes in Public Affairs and Government* (1966).

ANTJE DAUB

ALEXANDER, Elizabeth (30 May 1962–), poet, educator, and cultural critic, was born in Harlem, New York, to CLIFFORD LEOPOLD ALEXANDER JR., a lawyer, political adviser, and business consultant, and Adele (Logan) Alexander, a historian, educator, and writer, and was raised in Washington, D.C. Alexander's childhood was characterized by the privileges of the black professional elite, which included travel, education, and involvement in the ongoing struggle for civil rights. She later described her father as a "race man" who worked to make things better for blacks. He was, according to one of her poems, HAJJ BAHIYAH "BETTY" SHABAZZ's lawyer. Her mother published on African American history. Alexander's poems and essays about her childhood describe loving parents, a connected extended family, and the creation of an enduring sense of racial affiliation.

Alexander received her BA from Yale in 1984, an MA from Boston University in 1987, and a PhD from the University of Pennsylvania in 1992. In Boston she studied with the poet and educator DEREK WALCOTT. Her first collection of poetry, *The Venus Hottentot* (1990), published in the *Callaloo* Poetry Series, attracted immediate acclaim. One of several creative works by African American women writers (including SUZAN-LORI PARKS and BARBARA CHASE-RIBAUD) to focus on the life and experiences of Saartjie Baartman—a South African (Xhosa) woman who was lured with false promises to Europe, where she was exhibited nude as a carnival freak, and whose genitals were subjected to scientific experiments—the volume also pays homage to a number of key black figures, including Alexander's West Indian paternal grandfather (Clifford L. Alexander Sr.), Nelson Mandela, ALBERT MURRAY, and JOHN WILLIAM COLTRANE, as well as to the figures named in the dedication: her parents and Derek Walcott.

Alexander began her academic career as an assistant professor of English at the University of Chicago (1991–1997). During this time Alexander won a National Endowment for the Arts creative writing fellowship (1992) and finished her PhD dissertation, "Collage: An Approach to Reading African American Women's Literature" (1992). She also worked with the friends and family of MELVIN DIXON and Tia Chucha Press to publish a posthumous volume of his poems, *Love's Instruments* (1995), for which she penned an introduction. Alexander expressed in this project and in her second volume, *Body of Life* (1996), the immense impact of the AIDS crisis on her life and work and on the black intellectual and artistic community. The collection places the poet in a network of black experience, family, and friends, and generally charts her movement from relative innocence to experience, ending with the deaths of friends with AIDS and of two of her grandparents.

That same year Alexander's verse-play, *Diva Studies*, was produced at Yale. Alexander and an excerpt from *Diva Studies* were featured in the journal *Callaloo*'s Emerging Women Writers special issue in 1996, alongside other noteworthy young African American women writers such as EDWIDGE DANTICAT, NATASHA TRETHEWEY, and Suzan-Lori Parks, thus suggesting her significance as a black woman writer at the turn of the twenty-first century. Her work, and that of the others in the issue, is celebrated by TRUDIER HARRIS in the introduction as "consciously expand[ing] our notions of the concept of African Americanness. . . . They are the descendants who have inherited a tradition, sifted through it for nourishment, and planted new seeds that will sprout new varieties of traditions" (*Callaloo*, Spring, 1996, 232–233).

In 1997 Alexander moved to Smith College, where she was the Grace Hazard Conkling poet-in-residence and the first director of the Poetry Center. She married Ficre Ghebreyesus in 1997; the couple had two sons. Upon leaving Smith in 1999 she moved

to Yale University's African American studies department as an adjunct associate professor. She also began teaching at the Cave Canem Poetry Workshop for African American writers. During this productive period, she published her third volume of poetry, *Antebellum Dream Book* (2001), as well as a collection of essays, *The Black Interior* (2004), and a fourth book of poetry, *American Sublime* (2005). She also participated in the launching of the journal *Meridians* as a member of the founding editorial board (2002). *Antebellum Dream Book* was named by the *Village Voice* as one of its Twenty-five Favorite Books of 2001, and the poet and critic Edward Hirsch proclaimed it "her best yet." The volume used the trope of dreaming to explore the personal and cultural unconscious depths of motherhood, race, and history. *The Black Interior* collected a number of essays that Alexander had published elsewhere between 1994 and 2000 and included three new pieces; the scope ranged from the role of *Jet* magazine as a conveyor of race pride to ANNA JULIA HAYWOOD COOPER as a black intellectual foremother. *American Sublime* was perhaps Alexander's most extended meditation on aesthetics, containing a section of *ars poetica* poems (that is, poetry on the art or nature of poetry itself), and sections invoking the blues, the story of the *Amistad* (the slave ship overtaken by the captive Africans in 1839), and American landscape painting. With this volume Alexander demonstrated her maturity as one of America's leading African American poets.

In the preface to her collection of essays *The Black Interior* Alexander wrote, "The work I do is culture work." Through her poetry, drama, and prose Alexander took the black civil rights legacy of her father and the black historical reclamation by her mother to the next level, imagining new possibilities for the black self, art, and African American culture. Recognition of the importance of her culture work came in 2005 when she was awarded a $50,000 Alphonse Fletcher Sr. Fellowship, for, according to the announcement, "work that contributes to improve race relations in American society and furthers the broad social goals of the U.S. Supreme Court's *Brown v. Board of Education* decision of 1954." Alexander's writing and teaching, deeply engaged in black history and culture and also inseparably interwined with America, continued to carry the struggle forward.

Further Reading

Jones, Meta DuEwa. Interview, *Writer's Chronicle* 39.2 (2006–2007).

Keenan, Deborah, and Diane LeBlanc. Interview, *Water-Stone Review* (2003), available online at http://www.waterstonereview.com/pdf/6/Alexander.pdf.

Pereira, Malin. "The Poet in the World, the World in the Poet: Cyrus Cassells' and Elizabeth Alexander's Versions of Post-soul Cosmopolitanism," *African American Review* 41.4 (Winter, 2007).

Phillip, Christine. Interview, *Callaloo* 19.2 (Spring 1996).

MALIN PEREIRA

ALEXANDER, Joyce London (1949–), magistrate judge, was born Joyce London in Cambridge, Massachusetts, to Oscar and Edna London. While attending Cambridge High and Latin School (now called Cambridge Rindge and Latin High School) Alexander was frequently elected as a class officer and eventually became the first African American president of the student council. After graduating from high school she entered Howard University in Washington, D.C., in the premedicine program. During her years at Howard the ongoing struggle for equality in the United States fueled Alexander's interest in the legal profession, and she decided to change her course of study from the medical to the political sciences, having also received an academic scholarship from the Boston NAACP.

While still at Howard, Alexander secured a job from the speaker of the U.S. House of Representatives Thomas P. "Tip" O'Neill. During her interview O'Neill informed Alexander that if hired she would learn a few things about political affairs, while earning a little extra spending money; Alexander assured O'Neill that she was there not "for fun or luxuries" but in order to pay for books and tuition. Impressed by her poise and candor, O'Neill hired her on the spot as his legislative aide.

Upon graduation from Howard University in 1969 Alexander enrolled in the New England School of Law in Boston, from which she graduated in 1972. She also took supplemental classes on federal jurisdiction and labor law at New York University. Her law school courses focused on political and community activism, and she was awarded the Reginald Heber Smith Community Lawyer Fellowship. The fellowship, lasting from 1972 to 1974, enabled Alexander to serve as a staff attorney with the Greater Boston Legal Assistance Project, where she dealt with cases involving juvenile defendants.

After completing her fellowship Alexander taught urban law and black politics at Tufts University and was legal counsel to the Youth Activities Commission of the City of Boston. She was active in many organizations, chairing the Massachusetts delegation for President Jimmy Carter at the Democratic National Convention and serving as a cofounder, first female president, and president emeritus of the Urban League of Eastern Massachusetts.

As an accomplished public speaker, Alexander frequently was the spokesperson for various agencies and was sought after by the press for interviews. She became the first African American woman in the nation and the first woman in Massachusetts to act as an on-camera legal editor for a major network affiliate when she was hired at WBZ-TV (CBS) in Boston. At the same time she served as assistant vice chancellor and general counsel of the Massachusetts Board of Higher Education.

President Carter nominated Alexander for a federal judgeship at the U.S. District Court for Massachusetts, and on 6 August 1979 she was sworn in as the first African American female United States magistrate judge. Critics voiced their displeasure about the nomination, citing her race, age (she was only thirty years old at the time), and gender. In 1989 in the federal courts in Massachusetts she created Kids, Courts & Citizenship, which was the first school-based education project in the Massachusetts court. The program allowed fifth-grade students to visit her courtroom, attend trial proceedings, and engage her and other court officials in conversations regarding the legal system. The program also encouraged students to participate in mock trials. Still a judge, during this time Alexander also cofounded and served as president of the Urban League of Eastern Massachusetts. From 1987 to 1988 she served as chairperson of the Judicial Council of the National Bar Association, an organization of black judges with more than 800 members.

Once again making history, on 2 January 1996 Judge Alexander became the first African American woman chief United States magistrate judge on the federal bench, and the first African American chief judge of any court in Massachusetts. Among her many accolades and awards, several stand out. Judge Alexander has received honorary doctor of law degrees from Northeastern University, New England School of Law, Bridgewater State College, Suffolk University Law School, Cambridge College, and North Carolina Central University. Judge Alexander was honored as a "living legend" by the Museum of Afro-American History in February 2004, was recognized for twenty-five years of service by the Federal Bar Association in May 2004, and was given the THURGOOD MARSHALL Award by the Judicial Council of the National Bar Association in August 2004. On 9 December 2006, Alexander married Johnny Ford, who served as mayor of Tuskegee, Alabama.

Further Reading
Reed, Pierce J. "Lady Justice: U.S. Magistrate Judge Joyce London Alexander," *New England Law Review* 38, no. 4 (2004).

KELLIE N. ADESINA

ALEXANDER, Kelly Miller (18 Aug. 1915–2 Apr. 1985), funeral home director and civil rights leader, was born in Charlotte, North Carolina, the youngest of the five children of Zechariah Alexander, a funeral home director, and Louise B. McCullough. Zechariah Alexander, the son of slaves, was a graduate of Biddle University (later Johnson C. Smith University), fought for the North Carolina Volunteer regiment during the Spanish-American war, and had worked as the Charlotte branch manager of the nation's largest black-owned business, C. C. SPAULD-ING's North Carolina Life Insurance Company. He also helped found the Charlotte branch of the NAACP during World War I and ran, unsuccessfully, for Charlotte city council in 1937. The Alexander home was thus one that emphasized service to the nation and to the race, as well as the virtues of self-discipline, self-reliance, and Christian faith. Zechariah

Alexander's political independence, rare in early-twentieth-century North Carolina, was largely a consequence of the freedom that came with running a business dependent primarily on black custom. Most black Tar Heels who worked for white employers in the Jim Crow era dared not be so outspoken.

From an early age it was clear that Kelly and his older brother Fred would follow in the Alexander family tradition of service and political activism. The young Kelly even practiced making speeches in front of a mirror. He also was a leader at Charlotte's Second Ward public high school, where he earned the nickname Shipwreck Kelly for his spirited, if sometimes reckless, performances as halfback on the football team. Upon his graduation from high school in 1933 Alexander studied first at the Tuskegee Institute in Alabama and then at the Renouard College of Embalming in New York City, where he trained to take over the family business alongside Fred. Before returning to Charlotte, however, Kelly worked as a jewelry salesman for a New York merchant. His travels throughout the South made him aware of the many indignities faced by African Americans who did not enjoy the economic protections of the Alexander Funeral Home or the Tuskegee Institute. Alexander and his white Jewish employer were barred from dining at most restaurants and hotels and were chased out of town by police officers on several occasions.

Alexander's experiences as a traveling salesman encouraged him to take an active role in the NAACP when in the mid-1930s he returned to North Carolina to work in the family funeral business. The Charlotte chapter—like most southern branches of the organization—had lain dormant since World War I. The coming of the New Deal, however, and particularly America's entry into World War II in late 1941 revived the NAACP's southern fortunes. At the forefront of these efforts in Charlotte, Kelly Alexander was elected president of both the city's branch and the statewide North Carolina Youth Council in 1940. The following year, while working as a reporter for a black Charlotte newspaper, Alexander met Margaret Gilreece, the May queen at Charlotte's Second Ward High School; the couple married five years later in April 1946 and had two sons, Kelly Jr. and Alfred.

The late 1940s and early 1950s marked a period of racial progress in North Carolina, at least in the large cities of the urban piedmont. Alexander was elected president of the North Carolina branch of the NAACP in 1948, and alongside several labor unions and crusading journalists like Durham's LOUIS AUSTIN he helped make the North Carolina chapter of the NAACP the nation's largest, with 120 branches and 30,000 members. As a result of the revitalized NAACP, black voter registration increased dramatically in Charlotte, Greensboro, Durham, and other cities. By 1954 there were six African American elected officials in the state, mostly on school boards, representing half of all blacks elected in the entire South. Kelly Alexander ran for Charlotte city council twice in the 1950s, though like his father two

decades earlier he failed in both races. Alexander's civil rights work was recognized at a national level in 1950 when he was elected to the NAACP board of directors and again in 1954 when he became an NAACP life member.

Alexander also had his critics, notably ROBERT F. WILLIAMS, president of the Monroe, North Carolina, NAACP chapter. Williams, a blunt-spoken World War II veteran, believed that civil rights progress had stalled in North Carolina. This was certainly true of public school integration; Governor Luther Hodges had successfully circumvented the Supreme Court's 1954 Brown ruling by using a token integration plan. By 1959 only a handful of black students had been assigned to traditionally white schools in Charlotte, Greensboro, and Winston-Salem, though Kelly Alexander had led by example by seeking to admit his own children to these schools. Williams and Alexander also clashed over Monroe's notorious "kissing case" in 1958, when Monroe had worked closely with New York Trotskyites to publicize the arrest at gunpoint, imprisonment, and beating of two black children, Hanover Thompson, who was ten years old, and David Simpson, who was eight. The boys' alleged "crime" had been to kiss an eight-year-old white girl. Alexander sympathized with the children's plight, but as a cold war liberal and a staunch defender of the free enterprise system, he appears to have been even more opposed to Williams's involvement with northern Communists. On a practical level Alexander feared that such ties would jeopardize the NAACP's recent gains in North Carolina. The growing division between the two men came to a head in the summer of 1959 when Alexander, supported by the north Carolina NAACP and the national executive secretary ROY WILKINS, removed Williams from the presidency of the Monroe chapter for suggesting that blacks should prepare to arm and defend themselves against white supremacist attacks.

Alexander was somewhat more supportive of the student-led lunch counter sit-in movement, which began in Greensboro in February 1960 and quickly spread to other North Carolina cities, including Charlotte. The vigor and righteous commitment of the young demonstrators was not unlike that of Robert Williams, but their nonviolent philosophy and public expression of Christian faith was much more attractive to Alexander. Though there were some tensions between these younger activists and the mainline NAACP leadership, the period from 1960 to 1965 was one of relative success for a broad-based civil rights movement in North Carolina. In Charlotte, Alexander worked with both radical black student protestors and conservative white businessmen to integrate most of the city's public accommodations by 1963, a year before the national Civil Rights Act required them to do so. North Carolina also enjoyed by far the highest black voter registration rate in the South in the early 1960s: 40 percent. It would require the passage of the 1965 federal Voting Rights Act, however, to secure a decisive electoral breakthrough.

That year Kelly's brother Fred became the first African American in the twentieth century to be elected to the Charlotte city council.

Such victories for the integrationist cause did not go unnoticed. On 22 November 1965, a few weeks after Fred Alexander's election victory, white supremacists firebombed the homes of four of Charlotte's leading civil rights activists: Kelly Alexander and his brother and neighbor Fred; the NAACP attorney JULIUS CHAMBERS; and Dr. Reginald Hawkins, a prominent dentist and longtime political campaigner. All four properties were badly damaged, but none of the occupants was injured. The bombings did, however, serve a positive purpose. A significant minority of whites in Charlotte, outraged at the damage to the city's reputation for tolerance, began to make common cause with Alexander and other black leaders. The city's leading white newspaper, the *Charlotte Observer*, condemned the violence and offered a reward for information about the perpetrators, though no one was ever arrested. White mayor Stan Brookshire organized a relief fund. Concern among the city's white businessmen was to some extent driven by a fear that violence would damage plans to attract new industries to Charlotte. Alexander understood this and began working closely with those leaders to ensure that African Americans, as well as whites, benefited from those new jobs.

The bombings also provided an opportunity for blacks and whites in the city to establish a school desegregation plan fully in the spirit of the 1954 *Brown* ruling. Led by Kelly Alexander and Julius Chambers, *Swann v. Charlotte-Mecklenburg Board of Education*, upheld by the U.S. Supreme Court in 1971, established an ambitious plan to achieve school desegregation through mandatory school busing. Throughout the 1970s and early 1980s the Charlotte school busing program was largely hailed as a success, particularly, as Kelly Alexander noted in an article in the *Crisis* in November 1975, compared to the violent white backlash in response to busing in northern cities like Boston. Alexander, who had been elected vice chair of the NAACP's national board in 1976, was elected chair in January 1984, at which point he stepped down as chair of the North Carolina conference of the NAACP, a position that he had held for thirty-six years. He was succeeded in that position by his son, Kelly M. Alexander Jr.

Kelly Alexander Sr. died at his Charlotte home, three days after giving a speech at a regional NAACP conference in West Virginia. In a statement announcing Alexander's passing, the NAACP executive director BENJAMIN HOOKS hailed him as a "fearless warrior who bowed to no foe." Although he was certainly a determined fighter for his cause, that assessment ascribes to Alexander a militancy that he rarely embraced or employed rhetorically. Rather, his work to end segregation in North Carolina was shaped primarily by the values that he shared with the white businessmen who ruled that state: belief in self-reliance and free enterprise, and faith in God and American patriotism. Kelly Alexander's skill lay in persuading whites that those values were fully compatible with racial equality.

Further Reading

The Kelly M. Alexander Papers (1915–1985) are held at the Special Collections Unit of the J. Murrey Atkins Library of the University of North Carolina at Charlotte.

Douglas, Davison M. *Reading, Writing, and Race: The Desegregation of the Charlotte Schools* (1995).

Gaillard, Frye. *The Dream Long Deferred* (1998).

Obituary: *New York Times*, 4 Apr. 1985.

STEVEN J. NIVEN

ALEXANDER, Raymond Pace (13 Oct. 1897–25 Nov. 1974), lawyer and judge, was the third of five children born to Hillard Boone Alexander, a laborer from Mecklenburg County, Virginia, and Virginia Pace, from Essex County, Virginia. Alexander's parents were born slaves, but were freed by the Thirteenth Amendment following the Civil War. In 1880 they migrated to Philadelphia, Pennsylvania, where they lived in the Seventh Ward, a community that would later be made famous by W. E. B. DU BOIS's seminal 1899 study *The Philadelphia Negro*. In 1903 Alexander's mother died of pneumonia. Because his father worked long hours, Alexander and his siblings moved to North Philadelphia to live with his maternal aunt, Georgia Chandler Pace. From the age of seven Alexander attended school and worked at various jobs, including dockworker, newspaper boy, general helper at the Metropolitan Opera House in North Philadelphia, Pullman porter, and, when he was in his early twenties, teaching assistant in economics.

Alexander graduated from John Hancock Elementary School and then attended the prestigious all-boys Central High School in Philadelphia, the second oldest high school in America. Alexander went on to receive his BS degree with honors in economics in three and a half years from the University of Pennsylvania. His economics professors wanted him to pursue a doctorate in economics, but Alexander decided instead to attend Harvard Law School. Becoming a lawyer, he believed, would offer him the best opportunity to fight racism and segregation in Philadelphia. Alexander recalled that at Harvard his "sense of injustice to Negroes other than myself spilled to the point of public protest" (Alexander). Harvard Law had radicalized him.

Having passed the Pennsylvania bar exam in July 1923, Alexander worked for a short time with a white attorney in Philadelphia before establishing his own firm later that same year. Alexander litigated criminal cases, personal injury suits, and public accommodation desegregation cases. In 1924 he filed his first civil rights suit, against Charles Starkosh, the white manager of the Aldine Theatre located in downtown Philadelphia. Edward Green, an African American, had bought two tickets to *The Ten Commandments*, but when he presented the tickets Starkosh switched them and gave Green two old ticket stubs and prohibited him from entering. This case reached trial in April 1925. The white employees corroborated Starkosh's story, and after a thirty-minute deliberation the jury acquitted Starkosh. Despite this early setback Alexander went on to win a number of civil rights cases, and with each victory his reputation and status grew. In 1925 Alexander married SADIE TANNER MOSSELL ALEXANDER, a University of Pennsylvania graduate and member of the "old black" elite in Philadelphia. Sadie Alexander was the first black woman to earn a PhD and JD from the University of Pennsylvania. The Alexanders had two daughters, Rae and Mary Elizabeth.

By the 1930s Alexander had begun to combine litigation with mass protests, and it was during that decade that he reached the apogee of his radicalism. In 1932 he litigated the Berwyn, Pennsylvania, school desegregation case. In March of that year the Berwyn school board built a new elementary school for white children; however, the black children's parents refused to send their children to a segregated school, so in June 1932 the black students initiated a school boycott that lasted for the next two years. In 1934 the boycott ended, and the schools desegregated.

Even though African Americans in northern cities voted in considerable numbers, the all-white power structure continued to deny them a fair share of city resources. From 1933 until 1937 Alexander mounted losing campaigns to become the first black judge in Philadelphia, defeats he blamed on both parties for refusing to support him. Between 1933 and 1948 Alexander switched parties three times, siding with whichever party gave him the best opportunity of becoming a judge and providing patronage to the black community. In this he was not alone; other black Philadelphia politicians, including CRYSTAL BYRD FAUSET, also switched between Republican and Democrat in those years. In 1948 a federal bench position in Philadelphia opened. Alexander campaigned hard for the position, but his opponent, WILLIAM HENRY HASTIE, a black attorney and longtime Democrat, had the advantage. Hastie was a lifelong Democrat and had more influence in the party. In spite of Alexander's civil rights work in Philadelphia and support from his peers, President Harry S. Truman appointed Hastie, because the Democratic Party was aware of Alexander's earlier party switching.

Though on the national level Alexander was not a major force, in Philadelphia he was instrumental in the 1951 Democratic Reform Movement. Alexander and white middle-class leaders formed a coalition to end the corrupt rule by the Republican Party, which had controlled Philadelphia politics since the Civil War. Alexander campaigned in the black sections of Philadelphia. In 1951 Alexander and the Democratic Party won the mayoral and city elections. Alexander was elected to the city council, upon which he served for the next eight years. In that role he was responsible for increasing the number of black city workers as well as improving public ser-

vices for African Americans. Alexander enjoyed working as a city councilman, but he wanted to be a judge. As his political clout increased, in 1959 a Court of Common Pleas judge position became available and he was appointed by the Democrat George Leader to the position, becoming the second black judge in Philadelphia.

As a judicial activist Alexander sought to use his position to improve people's lives. In the late 1950s he noticed a rise in juvenile delinquency and black poverty. He created the Spiritual Rehabilitation Program (SRP) to stop juvenile delinquency. The SRP was designed to assist first-time offenders and help them find employment. A variety of Christian denominations and Jewish organizations were supposed to fund the SRP, but black churches provided most of the funding. In 1962 Alexander organized the Community Legal Services (CLS) to provide legal representation to poor people.

Alexander served as judge during the civil rights movement as younger activists and new leaders such as CECIL B. MOORE, a rhetorically militant attorney and president of the local NAACP branch, emerged in Philadelphia. Moore organized pickets and boycotts in Philadelphia to increase the number of black workers. Alexander supported demonstrations in the South, but believed that they were unnecessary in Philadelphia. Rather, he remained committed to litigation and to coalitions with sympathetic whites, a strategy that by the 1960s had failed to eradicate institutionalized racism in Philadelphia.

During the late 1960s and 1970s, Alexander commented on the devastating effect of black poverty in Philadelphia. Like MARTIN LUTHER KING JR., he advocated a guaranteed income for poor Americans. Alexander castigated middle-class whites in Philadelphia for not doing enough to battle injustice. Similar to King, during the late 1960s Alexander recognized the impact chronic poverty had on the black community. Unfortunately, a number of white liberals abandoned the movement when their voices were still needed to address institutionalized racism and poverty. Alexander died of a heart attack in his office at city hall.

Further Reading

Raymond Pace Alexander's papers are housed at the University Archives at the University of Pennsylvania in Philadelphia. See especially his "Legal Education and Formative Influences in the Law" (Raymond Pace Alexander, UPT 50 A 374 Box 1, Folder 15).

Canton, David A. "The Origins of a New Negro Lawyer: Raymond Pace Alexander, 1898–1923," *Western Journal of Black Studies* 27, no. 2 (2003).

Leonard, Walter J. *Black Lawyers, Training and Results, Then and Now* (1977).

Mack, Kenneth W. "Law and Mass Politics in the Making of the Civil Rights Lawyer, 1931–1941," *Journal of American History* 93 (June 2006).

Segal, Geraldine R. *Blacks in the Law: Philadelphia and the Nation* (1983).

Smith, J. Clay, Jr. *Emancipation: The Making of the Black Lawyer, 1844–1944* (1993).

Obituaries: *Philadelphia Inquirer,* 25 Nov. 1974; *Philadelphia Tribune* and *Congressional Record,* 26 Nov. 1974.

DAVID A. CANTON

ALEXANDER, Sadie Tanner Mossell (2 Jan. 1898–2 Nov. 1989), attorney and civil rights activist, was born Sadie Tanner Mossell in Philadelphia, Pennsylvania, the youngest of three children of Aaron Albert Mossell Jr., an attorney, and Mary Louise Tanner. In 1899 Mossell's father deserted the family and fled to Wales. During elementary school Sadie and her mother divided their time between Mossell's grandparents' home in Philadelphia and an aunt and uncle's home on the campus of Howard University in Washington, D.C. When her mother returned to Pennsylvania, Mossell remained under the care of her aunt and uncle in Washington until she graduated from M Street High School.

Mossell entered the University of Pennsylvania in the fall of 1915 and majored in education. Her years as a student in an institution with so few women students and even fewer African Americans were extremely challenging. Yet, with her family's financial and emotional support, she prospered academically and graduated with honors in three years. In 1918 she received her BS from the University of Pennsylvania's School of Education. While her grades were high enough to gain her admittance to Phi Beta Kappa, the university did not select her for this honor for over fifty years.

Mossell completed her graduate work at the University of Pennsylvania, earning an MA in Economics in 1919 and being awarded the Frances Sargent Pepper Fellowship in Economics, one of five grants awarded to women in the Graduate School of Economics. On 15 June 1921 Mossell became the first African American woman in the United States to earn a PhD in Economics. Despite her academic accomplishments, Mossell could find no suitable work as an educator, since even the Philadelphia high schools refused to employ African American teachers. She faced similar roadblocks in the business world. Mossell was forced to go to North Carolina, where she worked for the black-owned North Carolina Mutual Life Insurance Company in Durham as an assistant actuary.

Although she first met RAYMOND PACE ALEXANDER while they were both students at the University of Pennsylvania, she did not marry him until after he completed his education. In 1920 Raymond became the first black graduate of the University of Pennsylvania's Wharton School of Finance and Commerce and graduated from Harvard Law School in 1923. The two were married on 29 November 1923 at the Tanner home in North Philadelphia.

Feeling unsatisfied with a life of domesticity, Alexander decided to go to law school. In 1924 she became the first black woman to enroll at the University of Pennsylvania School of Law. As in previous

Sadie Tanner Mossell Alexander received her PhD in Economics in 1921. (University of Pennsylvania/ Archives and Records Center.)

years, Alexander continued to face challenges stemming from the racist and sexist attitudes harbored by the law school administration, students, and outside institutions. In 1926 she became one of the first two black student contributors and associate editors elected to the *University of Pennsylvania Law Review.* The dean of the law school, however, refused membership to any black woman. He eventually relented when Alexander received the support of a faculty member. In 1927 Alexander became the first black woman to graduate from the University of Pennsylvania School of Law, to gain admission to the Pennsylvania Bar, and to practice law in Pennsylvania. Alexander entered practice at her husband's law firm, making Raymond and Sadie Alexander one of the first husband and wife legal teams in the United States. Such a partnership afforded her a smoother transition into the profession than would have been possible on her own.

At her husband's suggestion, Alexander arranged to be admitted to Orphans' Court in Philadelphia shortly after her admission to the Pennsylvania bar.

Orphans' Court cases afforded Alexander the opportunity to gain more trial experience than most female lawyers, of any race, in Philadelphia. She argued appeals before the full Orphans' Court bench, the Pennsylvania Supreme Court, and the United States District Court. She developed expertise in probate law, divorce, and domestic relations matters and became the firm's expert on estate and family law. In addition to her legal work, Alexander served in local government. In 1928 she became the first black woman to be appointed assistant city solicitor in Philadelphia. She served until 1930 and again from 1934 to 1938. She continued to work even after she became pregnant, giving birth to two daughters, Mary Elizabeth in 1934 and Rae Pace in 1936.

Alexander was also active in the JOHN MERCER LANGSTON Law Club. The organization was formed in 1925 as an alternative to the Philadelphia Bar Association, which prohibited any significant participation by African Americans. In 1932 Alexander, the only woman in the law club, helped to form a legal aid bureau to assist African Americans who could not afford to hire lawyers.

For years Alexander worked with her husband—who specialized in civil rights and criminal defense cases—to combat racial discrimination and segregation in Philadelphia movie theaters, hotels, and restaurants. They helped to draft the 1935 Pennsylvania state public accommodations law, which prohibited discrimination in public places. Later Alexander advocated for the integration of the University of Pennsylvania's faculty and the U.S. military.

Alexander was instrumental in the development of the National Bar Association (NBA), formed in 1925 as an alternative to the American Bar Association, which excluded blacks from membership. As one of the few female members of the organization, Alexander labored to highlight the role of black women in the law. She published a study on the status of African American women lawyers and found that the overwhelming majority of black women admitted to practice at the time were actively engaged in the law. Alexander was elected national secretary of the NBA on 26 November 1943 and remained in office until 1947.

Alexander became the first black woman appointed to a presidential commission when President Harry S. Truman selected her as a member of his Committee on Civil Rights in 1946. In 1948 the committee issued *To Secure These Rights*, a report on the need for more adequate means to protect civil rights. The report provided recommendations for increasing civil rights protections for all Americans, regardless of race, religion, or national origin. These recommendations became the basis for future civil rights policies and legislation, including the desegregation of the armed forces.

In addition to her duties as assistant city solicitor, Alexander played an active role in Philadelphia civic affairs. She served as a member of the Philadelphia Fellowship Commission from 1949 to 1965 and as its chairperson from 1965 until 1968. Alexander also chaired a special subcommittee charged with ensuring that a new version of the city's charter would contain provisions to safeguard equal opportunity and fair treatment in the city's administration. In 1952 Alexander drafted a portion of the charter that provided for the formation of the Philadelphia Human Relations Commission (HRC) and was subsequently appointed to be one of the nine commissioners on the HRC, which investigated allegations of employment discrimination in Philadelphia.

In 1959 Alexander opened her own law practice soon after her husband was appointed Philadelphia's first black judge. She continued to specialize in domestic relations and often took on clients who could not afford to pay her, considering such pro bono work "as much my duty as I consider it the duty of a physician to serve a dying patient" (Nier, 59). She worked diligently in her solo practice until 1974, when she joined the Philadelphia firm of Atkinson, Myers, and Archie as counsel.

In 1979 President Jimmy Carter appointed Alexander chair of the White House Conference on Aging. Throughout her life she remained active with a number of civil rights and social action organizations. She continued contributing to public life until 1983, when she was diagnosed with Alzheimer's disease. Alexander succumbed to this and other maladies at the age of ninety-one.

For over half a century, Alexander excelled as a pioneering lawyer, feminist, and civil rights activist by opening many of the doors of opportunity that were closed to African American women of her era. She "knew well that the only way [to] get that door open was to knock it down" (Hill, 80). In doing so, she dismantled racial and gender constructs of her time and created a new identity for women and African Americans by using the law as a tool for social change.

Further Reading

Sadie Alexander's papers are housed in the University of Pennsylvania Archives and Records Center in Philadelphia, Pennsylvania.

Hill, Ruth Edmonds. *The Black Women Oral History Project* (1991).

Mack, Kenneth W. "A Social History of Everyday Practice: Sadie T. M. Alexander and the Incorporation of Black Women into the American Legal Profession, 1925–1960," *Cornell Law Review* 87, no. 1405 (2002).

Nier, Charles Lewis. "Sweet Are the Uses of Adversity: The Civil Rights Activism of Sadie Tanner Mossell Alexander," *Temple Political and Civil Rights Law Review* 8, no. 59 (1998).

Segal, Geraldine R. *Blacks in the Law: Philadelphia and the Nation* (1983).

Smith, J. Clay, Jr. *Emancipation: The Making of the Black Lawyer 1844–1944* (1993).

Obituaries: *New York Times* and *Philadelphia Inquirer*, 3 Nov. 1989.

LIA B. EPPERSON

ALEXANDER, Virginia Margaret (4 Feb. 1900–24 July 1949), physician and public health provider, was born in Philadelphia, Pennsylvania, the fourth of five children of Hillard Boone Alexander, a horse trainer, and Virginia Pace Alexander. Born enslaved in 1856 to James and Ellen Alexander in Mecklenburg, Virginia, Alexander's father migrated to Philadelphia in 1880. Alexander's mother was born enslaved in 1854 to Thomas and Jenne Pace in Essex County, Virginia. She and her brother migrated to Philadelphia in 1880. In 1882 Hillard and Virginia were married. A working-class but respectable family, the Alexanders lived in the city's Seventh Ward with their three boys, RAYMOND PACE ALEXANDER, Milliard, and Schollie, and two girls, Irene and Virginia. Strong family values were instilled in the Alexander children at an early age. Church, education, and a solid work ethic were emphasized in the home. Shortly after the birth of the youngest child in 1903, Alexander's mother died of pneumonia. Faced with financial hardship, Alexander's father moved the family to North Philadelphia to reside with their maternal aunt. The Alexanders soon joined Zion Baptist Church, Philadelphia's third-largest African American church at the time.

The Alexander children persevered after the loss of their mother and excelled in school. The eldest, Raymond, began working on fishing docks after school to help support the family. Later, Alexander's father lost his livery stable business, placing an even greater economic strain on the family. Thirteen-year-old Virginia decided to leave school in order to work. Her father, determined that education would provide a better life for his children, refused to allow Virginia to relinquish her studies. She remained in school and graduated from high school in 1918 with an outstanding academic record. Following graduation she enrolled in the University of Pennsylvania, where she joined her brother Raymond as one of a few African American students.

In the early twentieth century, students of color at the University of Pennsylvania and at other predominantly white northern colleges experienced racism, discrimination, and isolation. Black students were not allowed to reside in dormitories, eat in cafeterias, or visit many of the social gathering places on campus. African American students at the university established their own support network, often through clubs and organizations. At the university Alexander joined Delta Sigma Theta Sorority, a public service organization for African American women that provided its members with social, cultural, and intellectual fellowship in the midst of an unreceptive racial environment. Because of her father's business failure, Alexander was responsible for her own educational expenses and worked as a clerk, maid, and waitress. In 1920 she was awarded a BA in education.

After college Alexander attended the Woman's Medical College of Pennsylvania, aided by a philanthropic friend. Alexander excelled in her studies and ranked second highest among medical aptitude test examinees. As one of only a handful of African American students, she faced myriad racially motivated incidents, such as professors who exhibited bigoted attitudes during class lectures. Nonetheless, she overcame these challenges and, once her studies were complete, sought entrance into the Philadelphia General Hospital internship program. The director of health at the hospital refused her admittance and indicated that he would continue to do so in spite of Alexander's impeccable credentials. Determined to succeed, Alexander instead sought entrance and was reluctantly accepted into the Kansas City General Hospital internship program. After completing the program in 1923, she returned to Philadelphia to begin diagnostic medical practice.

Armed with a desire to elevate the African American community through improved health conditions, she founded the Aspiranto Health Home in 1931. The private practice was established in her own home, where she cared for Philadelphia's poorest African Americans. In 1935 Dr. Helen Dickens, a fellow African American physician, joined Alexander's practice. Together they delivered babies and administered general medical care and emergency treatment. The clinic also offered parenting classes and postnatal recuperation to patients who often could not afford the services. Alexander did not allow her patients' inability to pay influence her decision to serve them. Never one to rest, Alexander pursued graduate study at Yale University School of Medicine, where she earned a master's degree in public health in 1937. Afterward she was appointed physician in charge of women's studies at Howard University in Washington, D.C. In this role she established a student health program and served as a medical adviser to the female students at the university until 1941.

When the United States entered World War II, Alexander became a medical volunteer. She was assigned by the U.S. Public Health Service in 1941 to treat poverty-stricken African American coal and iron miners in Birmingham, Alabama. The difficult conditions under which Alexander worked caused her to develop lupus, an autoimmune disease. After the war Alexander returned to her private practice in her Philadelphia home, where she specialized in obstetrics and gynecology. She delivered countless numbers of babies in Philadelphia, including Yolande Du Bois Williams, the granddaughter of W. E. B. DU BOIS. She worked tirelessly to aid families most in need. As a staff member of the Woman's Medical College Hospital, Pennsylvania Hospital, and Mercy-Douglass Hospital, Alexander remained a constant advocate for African American health. She once noted:

If we can reduce the incidence of death at both ends of Negro life in the United States, we can add greatly to the overall contribution which our group can make to the Nation as a whole. To do this, we will have to send physicians into sections which have no bright lights and little social enterprise, take public health information across the railroad tracks and, above all, give knowledge to Negro women who are going to become mothers (*Philadelphia Inquirer*, 31 July 1933).

Finding time to contribute to professional and civic associations, Alexander was a member of the Philadelphia County Medical Society, American Medical Society, and the YWCA Board of Directors. She was also a member of the Germantown Meeting, Society of Friends. She was a much-sought-after speaker on health issues in Philadelphia's African American community. She dedicated her life to improving medical care for African American women, children, and families, many of whom otherwise would have been neglected. She died in 1949 in Philadelphia from acute lupus.

Further Reading

The Virginia Margaret Alexander Papers are located in the University of Pennsylvania Archives.

Baker, Joseph. "Dr. Alexander's Work in Public Health Hailed," *Philadelphia Inquirer*, 31 July 1949.

"Can a Colored Woman Be a Physician?," *Crisis* (Feb. 1933).

Canton, David A. "The Origins of a New Negro Lawyer: Raymond Pace Alexander, 1898–1923," *Western Journal of Black Studies* 27, no. 2 (2003).

"Dr. Virginia M. Alexander," *National Library of Medicine: Changing the Face of Medicine*, available online at http://www.nil.gov/changingthefaceofmedicine.

Lyon, Marvin P., Jr. "Blacks at Penn, Then and Now," in *A Pennsylvania Album: Undergraduate Essays on the 250th Anniversary*, eds. Richard Slator Dunn and Mark Frazier Lloyd (1990).

Obituary: *Philadelphia Inquirer*, 25 July 1949.

LANESHA DEBARDELABEN

ALEXANDER-RALSTON, Elreta (21 Mar. 1919–14 Mar. 1998), lawyer and judge, was born in Smithfield, North Carolina, the youngest of the three children of Reverend Joseph C. Melton, a Baptist minister and teacher, and Alian A. Reynolds Melton. She received her early education in the public school system of Danville, Virginia, and at the age of fifteen graduated from the James B. Dudley High School in Greensboro, North Carolina. In 1937 she graduated from the neighboring North Carolina Agricultural and Technical College with a bachelor's degree in music. The following year, at the age of eighteen, she married Girardeau Alexander, a surgeon, and had a son, Girardeau Alexander III.

Alexander worked as a mathematics and history teacher and directed music in South Carolina and North Carolina for four years before deciding that music would not be her lifelong vocation. Instead she longed for a career in law, despite the profession's being largely a bastion of privileged white men. She enrolled in the Columbia University School of Law and was awarded the LLB degree in 1945, which gave her the distinction of being the first black woman accepted at Columbia law school and the first to graduate.

Alexander became the first black woman licensed to practice law in North Carolina, the first black woman to try a case—which she won—in the North Carolina Supreme Court, and the first black woman elected as a judge in the United States. During her twenty-one-year legal career she was actively involved in a myriad of cases that brought her wide acclaim. She once represented a group of citizens who brought suit against the Greensboro City Council for its attempt to block the re-zoning of a tract of land that would have permitted a private housing project for African Americans. The consequences of this suit also led to the election of the first black member to the Greensboro City Council and energized the movement to create more federal housing projects for low-income people. Alexander also served as the attorney for the incorporation of the first city-owned golf course in Greensboro that catered to African Americans.

In 1966 she wrote a book of poems, *When Is a Man Free?*. In 1968 she was elected district court judge for Guilford County, a position she held until 1981. Alexander was the only Republican woman elected in her district and the only black elected in the state. While on the bench she earned the nickname "Judge A" and was an early pioneer in what became known as first-offender programs and in applying community service in her various judgments. She also instituted what she called Judgment Day, a program in which youthful offenders were offered an opportunity a few weeks after a conviction to convince the judge of their progress toward rehabilitation. If the offender had stayed out of trouble, then the charges were dropped; if not, the offender suffered the consequences of his or her actions.

Alexander's brand of justice earned her many accolades and recognition by various national publications, but it also generated much resentment and prompted calls for her ouster. Each time she was successful in being elected and even switched her party affiliation from Democratic to Republican to win her seat. Having been elected to four consecutive terms, she retired from the bench, but she remained a highly respected jurist and attorney who was selected several times by Guys and Dolls, Inc., a public service organization that donates funds for scholarships for needy African American students, as the most admired black citizen of Greensboro, North Carolina.

In 1976 the Greensboro chapter of the National Conference of Christians and Jews awarded Alexander the Brotherhood Citation, and in 1977 the North Carolina Federation of Women's Clubs selected her as one of the twenty-five most distinguished women in the state. After the death of her husband in 1979, she married John D. Ralston, who had retired from the IRS appellate division. In 1981 she formed the law firm Alexander-Ralston, Pell & Speckhard. There she served as a successful trial attorney and senior partner in the firm.

Judge Alexander was an active participant in the affairs of her city and served as a member of the board of the Governor's School; the board of management of Hayes-Taylor YMCA; the advisory boards of the Henry Wiseman Kendall Center and the University of North Carolina at Greensboro; and the boards of visitors of Appalachian State University and Guilford

College. She was a member of the American Bar Association, the American Judicature Society, the American Trial Lawyers Association, and the Greensboro Chamber of Commerce, and she was twice a conferee of the President's Committee on Equal Employment and served as legal advisor for The Links, Inc., a nonprofit organization of women of color, from 1958 until 1966. Alexander-Ralston died in 1998.

Further Reading

"Elreta Alexander-Ralston," in *Paths toward Freedom* (1976).

Smith, Jessie Carney, ed. "Elreta Alexander-Ralston," in *Notable Black American Women* (1992).

ANDRE D. VANN

ALI, Muhammad (17 Jan. 1942–), world champion boxer and political activist, was born Cassius Marcellus Clay Jr. in Louisville, Kentucky, the eldest of two sons raised by Cassius Clay Sr., a sign painter and something of a frustrated artist, and Odessa Grady, a domestic. Young Clay began to take boxing lessons at the age of twelve because someone had stolen his bicycle and he was determined to exact revenge against the perpetrators. He never discovered who stole his bike, but he did blossom as a young fighter, taking instruction from the Louisville policeman Joe Martin. His brother, Rudolph Arnette Clay (Rudolph Valentino Clay in some sources and later Rahaman Ali), also took up boxing, but, lacking his brother's talent, never became a significant presence in the sport.

Clay became a gym rat, feeling that he could succeed in boxing as he never could in school. Although he showed no special ability in his first few years, he was extraordinarily determined. He was indeed a poor student, graduating from Central High School with a D-minus average, ranking 376 in a class of 391. But he became one of the most impressive amateur boxers in the country, winning six Kentucky Golden Gloves championships. He was the National Amateur Athletic Union (AAU) champion in 1959 and 1960 and won a gold medal as a light heavyweight in the 1960 Rome Olympics, although he almost did not go to the Olympics because he was afraid to fly.

His boyish good looks and his outgoing personality, combined with the gimmicks of his poetry and his good-natured bragging, made Clay famous after the Olympics, and he received a great deal more media attention than most amateur fighters. He turned professional immediately after returning from Rome and was managed by a syndicate of seven Louisville businessmen. He was skillfully guided by the wily veteran trainer Angelo Dundee, who did not try to change Clay's unorthodox style, which had always infuriated most of the old heads of boxing. Clay, like most highly touted young fighters, won all of his early fights against either second- or third-rate opponents or noted fighters whose skills had deteriorated, like ARCHIE MOORE. His most difficult fight of this "con-

Muhammad Ali defeats Sonny Liston for the heavyweight title in a first round knockout, 1965. (Library of Congress.)

tender" stage was against Doug Jones, in which Clay won a ten-round decision, although many at ringside thought he lost the fight. With his constant bragging, his poetry, and his zany antics, he won a national following, even appearing briefly in the 1962 film version of Rod Serling's *Requiem for a Heavyweight*.

At six feet three inches tall and over two hundred pounds, Clay astonished sportswriters with his hand and foot speed, his reluctance to punch to the body, his ability to defend himself while holding his hands at his waist, and his insistence on avoiding punches by moving his head backward instead of to the side. Clay modeled much of his style after his idol, the welterweight and middleweight champion SUGAR RAY ROBINSON. No heavyweight before Clay ever possessed such speed, quickness, or grace, and he attracted many people to boxing who would normally have had little interest in the sport, simply because they were enthralled with his style.

On 25 February 1964 in Miami, Clay fought as an underdog for the heavyweight title against SONNY LISTON, a former convict. Liston was thought to be virtually invincible because of his devastating one-round knockouts of the former champion FLOYD PATTERSON, the last heavyweight champion to weigh less than two hundred pounds. So few thought that the bragging Clay had a chance that rumors circulated that he would not even show up for the fight. Most thought the young braggart had no punch and no chin and would barely be able to withstand the hard-punching Liston. Clay, for his part, had been harassing Liston during most of the period before the fight, taunting him by calling him "the Bear" and "ugly" and banging on Liston's front door in the early morning hours, demanding that he fight him then and there. The weigh-in ceremony the morning of the fight was part theater of the absurd and part screwball comedy. Clay, wearing a robe that said "Bear Hunting," seemed as if he wanted to attack Liston and gave the appearance of being completely out of control. It was all an act on Clay's part to gain a psychological edge over his opponent.

More ominous, from the perspective of the fight's promoters and most of the general public, were rumors coming out of Miami that Clay was being seen with MALCOLM X, the charismatic minister of the Nation of Islam (NOI). This was probably the most feared and misunderstood religious sect of the time and certainly one of the most militant black organizations to emerge since the Depression. Clay had already joined the controversial group, but he did not announce his membership until after the fight with Liston. In part this was because he did not want the fight cancelled as the result of his religious conversion and in part because the Muslims did not want to be overly embarrassed by his defeat, which nearly all in the organization thought would happen, including the group's leader, ELIJAH MUHAMMAD. Malcolm X, however, was confident that Clay would win. He convinced the young boxer that the fight was a jihad, a symbolic war, both political and religious, between the crescent and the cross or between the black man who was for his people and the black man who represented white interests. The jihad image was a psychological device that Clay (and in many cases, his opponents) used to dramatize virtually all the major fights of his career, turning them into contesting forms of black political propaganda.

Clay stunned the sporting world by defeating the aging Liston fairly easily in seven rounds. After the fight Clay announced that he had not only joined the NOI but that he also had a new name, Muhammad Ali. The response from the boxing establishment, the sporting press, and the white public generally was hostile, even vitriolic. The NOI was largely seen, mistakenly, as an antiwhite hate group, something analogous to the Ku Klux Klan. Although there had been a few black jazz musicians who had converted to Islam, most of the public, black and white, knew little about the religion, and the NOI's highly racialized version of Islam further distorted the perceptions of most Americans. Never was an athlete so pilloried by the public as Ali was. Most sports journalists ridiculed his religion and refused to call him by his new name. The former champion Floyd Patterson went on a personal crusade against the NOI in his fight with Ali on 22 November 1965, which Patterson lost. Patterson later

became one of the few fighters to defend Ali publicly during his years of exile. No black athlete since the reign of JACK JOHNSON (1908–1915), the first black heavyweight champion, so enraged most whites and not a few blacks with his opinions and the way he chose to live his life.

He won a rematch with Sonny Liston in Lewiston, Maine, on 25 May 1965 in a bizarre first-round knockout, just two months after Malcolm X was gunned down in Harlem; yet these were soul-wrenching times for Ali because a scandal surrounding Elijah Muhammad had separated Ali from Malcolm X at the time of his mentor's assassination. Ali, probably one of the most unpopular fighters in history, spent most of the next year beating George Chuvalo in Toronto, Henry Cooper in London, and Karl Mildenberger in Germany. He also defeated ERNIE TERRELL in Houston, one of his few American fights during this period.

While Ali was abroad, the Selective Service changed his draft status from 1-Y (unfit for military service because of his low score on army intelligence tests) to 1-A (qualified for induction). Many saw this change as a direct response to intense negative public opinion concerning Ali's political views and the result of the escalation of the Vietnam War. In fact, after the Gulf of Tonkin incident, the passing score on the army intelligence tests was lowered, so that many other men besides Ali were affected. Ali refused to serve in the military on the grounds that it violated his religious beliefs. (Elijah Muhammad had served time in prison during World War II for refusing to enter the armed services and for sympathizing with the Japanese. WARITH DEEN MUHAMMAD, son of Elijah, also served time for refusing military service.)

In 1967 Ali was convicted in federal court of violation of the Selective Service Act and sentenced to five years in prison. He was immediately stripped of his boxing title, and every state athletic commission stripped him of his boxing license. For the next three and a half years, Ali, free on bond while appealing his case (which he eventually won on appeal to the U.S. Supreme Court on a technicality), was prohibited from boxing. He spoke on college campuses, became a darling of the antiwar movement, and inspired black athletes and activists such as the sports sociologist HARRY EDWARDS, who tried to organize a black boycott of the 1968 Olympics. The medal-winning track stars TOMMIE SMITH and John Carlos gave clenched-fist salutes during the playing of the National Anthem at those Games and were promptly sent home.

In 1970, with public opinion strongly against the Vietnam War and aided by growing black political power in several southern state governments, Ali was given a license to fight in Georgia. He returned to the ring on 26 October and defeated Jerry Quarry in three rounds. Although he was still a brilliant fighter, the long layoff had eroded his skills to some degree. He took far more punishment in the ring when he returned than he had before his hiatus. This was to have dire consequences for him as he grew older.

Ali had his biggest, most competitive and commercially successful fights in the 1970s. On 8 March 1971 he lost to the undefeated Philadelphian JOE FRAZIER in a close fifteen-round decision at Madison Square Garden in New York City, in what was the richest, most publicized sporting event in American history. The fight was so brutal that both men were hospitalized afterward, Frazier for several days. It was Ali's first defeat. He won the North American Boxing Federation title, a significant but lesser honor than the world's championship, in July 1971. He lost again in March 1973 against the former marine KEN NORTON in a twelve-round decision in which Ali's jaw was broken. Ali regained his North American Boxing Federation title from Norton in a highly disputed twelve-round decision six months later.

In January 1974 he fought Frazier again at Madison Square Garden. It was a nontitle match, as Frazier had lost his title to GEORGE FOREMAN. This time Ali won a close twelve-round decision. Ali finally regained the title in Kinshasa, Zaire, on 30 October 1974, when he knocked out Foreman in the eighth round of a fight where he was a decided underdog, most of the public thinking that Ali, at thirty-two, had passed his prime. Ali used a technique he called "Rope-a-Dope," where he leaned against the ropes and permitted Foreman to punch away at him; this approach, punctuated by Ali's punishing flurries at the end of each round, eventually fatigued the heavy-fisted younger champion. Ali was to use the technique in later fights, when he was too lazy to train, thus taking increasingly great punishment in the ring.

After regaining the title, Ali was lionized in the United States and enjoyed incredible popularity around the world. He became not only the most famous American Muslim but also the most famous Muslim anywhere and was the most photographed and publicized black man in history. He appeared in a film version of his life—*The Greatest* (1977)—based on his 1975 autobiography (edited by TONI MORRISON), joining JACKIE ROBINSON and JOE LOUIS as black athletes who starred in versions of their life stories on the screen. Ali also appeared on television programs and commercials. He even beat Superman in a special 1978 oversized issue of that comic. Part of this adulation and acceptance stemmed from the fact there was a general shift in attitude on the part of white sportswriters and the white public, but Ali himself tended to be less doctrinaire in his political and religious views as he grew older. And he was always gregarious and funny, something that lessened some of the white public's venom against him even when Ali was most demonized. Sometimes, his denigration of black opponents and his bragging seemed shrill and tasteless, as if he himself had grown weary of the act. He eventually embraced Wallace D. Muhammad's more ecumenical form of Islam when the NOI split into two factions following the death of Elijah Muhammad in 1975.

On 15 February 1978 an out-of-shape, uninspired Ali lost his title again to a young former marine and Olympic champion from St. Louis named Leon Spinks. Ali, however, managed to regain his title by beating Spinks on 15 September of the same year. In 1979, weary of the ring wars, his reflexes shot, his legs gone, and his appetite for competition slaked, Ali retired from the ring, only to do what so many great, aged champions do: come back. On 2 October 1980 Ali unsuccessfully challenged the heavyweight champion and his former sparring partner Larry Holmes, enduring a savage beating over ten rounds. His next fight was a ten-round decision loss to Trevor Berbick on 11 December 1981. After the Berbick fight, Ali retired for good, with a professional record of fifty-six wins, thirty-seven by knockout, and five losses. He was elected to the Boxing Hall of Fame in 1987.

Even before his retirement from the ring, Ali's speech was becoming slurred. After retirement he seemed to age, moving slowly and speaking with a thick tongue, his speech almost incomprehensible. He also suffered bouts of palsy. There is some debate as to whether Ali has Parkinson's disease or a Parkinson-like deterioration of his neurological system. Was this condition caused by the punishment he took in the ring in the later years of his career? It can certainly be safely said that his illness was aggravated by his ring career. By the end of the twentieth century, although Ali led a very active life, doing magic tricks, signing autographs, giving out copies of the Koran, traveling, and appearing at various public events, including, most famously, the lighting of the Olympic flame at the 1996 Games in Atlanta, he walked slowly and rarely talked.

Ali's private life was turbulent. He has married four times: to Sonji Roi (1964–1965), Belinda Boyd Ali (1967–1976), Veronica Porsche Ali (1977–1986), and Lonnie Ali, whom he married in 1986. He also had numerous affairs when he was younger. He has nine children, including one adopted son. Interest in Ali has been rekindled in recent years thanks to the Academy Award–winning documentary *When We Were Kings* (1996) and *Ali*, a Hollywood feature film released in 2001. Books continue to be written about him, and he has probably been the subject of more photographic books than any athlete in the twentieth century.

It is impossible to overestimate Ali's importance not only as a gifted athlete who dominated his sport for nearly two decades and helped make sports a multimillion-dollar television enterprise but also as a religious and political presence in American popular culture. He clearly made white America more aware not only of Islam but also of the growing militancy of black people who were discontent with the status quo. Ali clearly symbolized in the 1960s and 1970s the fact that blacks were redefining their relationship with whites as they were redefining themselves. Ali came to represent racial pride, strong religious principles, and youthful exuberance. In November 2005 Ali received the Presidential Medal of Freedom, the nation's highest civilian award.

Further Reading

Early, Gerald, ed. *The Muhammad Ali Reader* (1998).
Hauser, Thomas. *Muhammad Ali: His Life and Times* (1991).
Kram, Mark. *Ghosts of Manila: The Fateful Blood Feud between Muhammad Ali and Joe Frazier* (2001).
Mailer, Norman. *The Fight* (1975).
Oates, Joyce Carol. *On Boxing* (1987).
Olsen, Jack. *Black Is Best: The Riddle of Cassius Clay* (1965).
Plimpton, George. *Shadow Box* (1977).
Remnick, David. *King of the World: Muhammad Ali and the Rise of an American Hero* (1998).
Sheed, Wilfred. *Muhammad Ali* (1975).
Torres, Jose. *Sting like a Bee: The Muhammad Ali Story* (1971).

GERALD EARLY

ALI, Noble Drew (8 Jan. 1886–20 Jul. 1929), religious leader and founder of the Moorish Science Temple, was born Timothy Drew, the son of former slaves, in North Carolina. Much of his life is shrouded in mystery that he and his followers helped to create. He was apparently orphaned and claimed at various times that he was raised by Cherokee Indians and that he was a descendant of Bilali Mohammed, a heroic African Muslim Sufi who had been enslaved in the United States. Without parents and with little formal education, Drew may have joined a traveling circus and been influenced by such extravaganzas as the Barnum and Bailey pageant "The Wizard Prince of Arabia." He further claimed that at the age of sixteen he was taken by a gypsy woman to North Africa and there studied with a Moroccan mystic in the Essene Schools. As a test of his wisdom and worthiness, he was placed inside an Egyptian pyramid and miraculously found his way out, proving to all that he was a prophet. Having passed this test, he relates that he embarked on a pilgrimage to Mecca, where the sultan Abdul ibn Said gave him the name "Ali" and the sheiks presented him with a charter to teach Islam in America to those people of African descent who had been robbed of their true identity.

While much of Ali's biography may be fabricated, the story contains clues to his actual development and the origin of the ideas he would eventually propagate. His tale of exotic world travels, in fact, may describe an intellectual journey; the books he read and the people he encountered supplied the content of his eclectic ideology. Since he was born in the South after Reconstruction, it is reasonable to assume that his lot was similar to that of the 4 million black people of the period: poor and uneducated, with little opportunity for improvement. Thus, at an early age, Ali came to believe that the way to change one's future is to change one's past. In this way, Ali set the stage for future black cultural movements to reinterpret history as a means of racial empowerment.

The evidence suggests that Ali migrated north—as did nearly half the black population of the South between 1890 and 1930. He settled in Newark, New Jersey, where he worked as a railway expressman, attended Masonic lodges, worshipped with proselytes of a new Islamic sect called the Ahmadiyya Muslim Community, and joined the Theosophical Society, which included Mohammed Alexander Russell Webb, a prominent American convert to Islam and a proponent of Eastern religious thought. In 1913 Noble Drew Ali founded a congregation, the Canaanite Temple, in Newark. He claimed that before starting this organization he had met with Theodore Roosevelt at the White House, informed the president of his plan to convert "the Negro," and assured him that black Muslims would be loyal American citizens. According to Ali, Roosevelt responded by saying "Getting Negroes to accept Islam will be about as easy as getting horses to wear pants" (Evanzz, 62–63). There is no independent record that such a meeting ever took place.

By the 1920s the essential elements of Ali's doctrine had begun to coalesce. From the Judeo-Christian tradition, he emphasized the importance of Ruth, a Moabite woman who converted to Judaism and became a maternal ancestor of Jesus Christ. Morocco, Ali argued, was the ancient land of the Moabites, who, he believed, had olive skin tones like the blacks of America. Therefore, he proposed the term "Moorish American" as a replacement for "Negro," which did not connect a people with any particular land, language, religion, or history. "Asiatic Blackman," which he also coined, expanded the presumed ancestral homeland of black people from sub-Saharan Africa to include lands and peoples from the Middle East to India. From his limited knowledge of Islam, Ali found a god for the Moorish people in Allah.

The garb and ceremonies that Ali developed for his movement were influenced by the black Masonic tradition in America begun by PRINCE HALL in 1784. Modern observers who did not understand the historical context or cultural importance of these innovations often ridiculed the ceremonial dress, headwear, handshakes, passwords, and symbols that Ali used. Actually, such practices were quite common in both white and black lodges and secret societies. African Americans often took these organizations seriously, believing that such groups held the answers to questions about their true identity. Ali's experimentation with garb and culture prefigures the Black Power movement's adoption of African garb in the 1960s as a form of political expression.

In 1927 Ali codified his basic beliefs and published them as *The Holy Koran of the Moorish Science Temple*, also known as the *Circle Seven Koran*. While most of this text is derived from other wisdom literature, he introduced a number of practices, such as a diet that excluded meat and prohibitions on smoking and alcohol, that distinguished his movement from others of the time.

After several splits, power struggles, and doctrinal differences, Ali moved his headquarters to Chicago in 1925 and began referring to his growing organization

MOORISH SCIENCE TEMPLE OF AMERICA
OCTOBER 15. 16. 17. 18. 19. 20. 1928
PROPHET NOBLE DREW ALI . FOUNDER

Noble Drew Ali *(first row, standing in white jacket)*, in the cultural garb that he pioneered, standing before the Moorish Science Temple of America. (Schomburg Center.)

as the Moorish Holy Temple of Science. In 1928 it was renamed the Moorish Science Temple of America (MSTA); by that time it had more than thirty thousand members with seventeen branches in fifteen states and operated many small businesses. The addition of "America" in the title indicated that members of this group were trying to forge a kind of patriotic black nationalism that incorporated their American identity. Those who joined the organization were issued identity cards that described the bearer's nationality as "Moorish American." The card also read, "I am a citizen of U.S.A." There are reports of MSTA members who brandished these cards at white people as if to say, "I know who I am."

Noble Drew Ali taught that black people in America had had an intact Moorish culture, complete with a flag and tribal appellations. He claimed that these cultural markers were taken away after the American Revolution in order to subordinate black slaves to their white masters. Allegedly, Ali confronted President Woodrow Wilson with this information and de-

manded the return of the Moorish flag and the right of black people in America to add Bey and El to their surnames.

Ali's appointment of women to leadership positions within the organization was remarkably progressive. During the restructuring of the MSTA in 1928, M. Whitehead-El (also known as Dove-El) was made a "grand sheikess" over one congregation in Chicago and then elevated to the position of governor of several temples under her jurisdiction. Black women of this time were rarely given similar positions within black Christian denominations, and women within Islamic sects were traditionally excluded from such roles. Ali also supported changes that made the MSTA a more democratic organization and ultimately led to the local election of certain officers, many of whom were women. By the late 1920s the MSTA had become a political force in Chicago and played an important role in the election of OSCAR DE PRIEST to the U.S. House of Representatives in 1928, the first African American elected from a northern state.

Ali's demise and the subsequent decline of the MSTA coincided with the murder of Sheik Claude Greene. When Sheik Greene, who had publicly challenged Ali's management of the organization, was found murdered in his office at Unity Hall in March of 1929, Ali was immediately indicted as an accomplice to the crime—even though he and his wife, Pearl Jones Ali, were not in the city at the time of the assassination. Shortly after being released from police custody, Noble Drew Ali died at his home. While newspapers reported the cause of death as tuberculosis, members of the MSTA speculated that he had succumbed to injuries inflicted by the police or that MSTA members loyal to Greene had killed him.

Noble Drew Ali did not have any known heirs, but he left a legacy of African American interest in Islam that survived in the MSTA, in orthodox Sunni Muslim sects, and in other black nationalist organizations. He had a profound influence on W. D. Fard and ELIJAH MUHAMMAD, who were both members of the MSTA before they established the more militant Nation of Islam. Today, African Americans constitute one of the largest segments of the Muslim population in the United States.

Further Reading
The MSTA maintains a private archive of its material at its headquarters in Chicago. Primary documents about Noble Drew Ali also can be found in the files on the MSTA at the headquarters of the Federal Bureau of Investigation (also called the "Noble Drew Ali" file).
Clegg, Claude Andrew, III. *An Original Man: The Life and Times of Elijah Muhammad* (1997).
Evanzz, Karl. *The Messenger: The Rise and Fall of Elijah Muhammad* (1999).
Lincoln, C. Eric. *The Black Muslims in America* (1961).
Marsh, Clifton. *From Black Muslims to Muslims* (1996).
Turner, Richard Brent. *Islam in the African-American Experience* (1997).
Wilson, Peter Lamborn. *Sacred Drift: Essays on the Margins of Islam* (1993).

SHOLOMO B. LEVY

ALI, Rashied (1 July 1935–), jazz drummer, was born Robert Patterson in Philadelphia, Pennsylvania, the son of Poston Patterson. His talented pianist aunt was asked by the famous bandleader LIONEL LEO HAMPTON to tour with him, but as she was not yet finished with school her grandmother would not allow it. However, Ali liked what he heard emanating from his aunt's living-room rehearsals with a local group, especially the sounds from the drummer. Although he did not graduate, Ali's high school dances provided him the opportunity to hear such luminaries as the saxophonist CHARLIE PARKER and the big bands of Woody Herman and Stan Kenton. The young Rashied listened to the jazz drummers MAX ROACH and ART BLAKEY, but his earliest influences were his father's first cousins, the drummers

Bernard and Charlie Rice. Upon returning to Philadelphia after beginning his drumming career in the U.S. Army, Ali briefly studied at the Granoff School of Music.

Ali picked up invaluable experience learning to play strict-time backbeats and "grooves" behind Philadelphia "chitlin' circuit" rhythm and blues bands and the blues singers Big Maybelle and Dick Hart and the Heartaches. Ali gradually progressed to the Philadelphia/Wilmington, Delaware/Camden-Trenton, New Jersey, jazz scene with the organists Don Patterson and Jimmy Smith and the trumpeter LEE MORGAN. After touring Japan with the saxophone colossus SONNY ROLLINS in 1963 Ali moved to New York City and quickly became ensconced in the jazz capital's burgeoning avant-garde movement.

Variously referred to by music critics as "free jazz," "new wave," or "The New Thing," New York's downtown experimental music of the 1960s and early 1970s reflected the political, social, and cultural changes happening in America, especially within the African American community. As the title of Frank Kofsky's 1970 book *Black Nationalism and the Revolution in Music* implies, some writers of the time were attempting to conflate racial unrest with musicians such as the trumpeter DON CHERRY, the saxophonists PHAROAH SANDERS, ERIC DOLPHY, ORNETTE COLEMAN, Marion Brown, and ALBERT AYLER, the keyboardists/composers Paul Bley and SUN RA, and the drummers Sunny Murray, Beaver Harris, Andrew Cyrille, and Milford Graves, all of whom were radically challenging traditional melodic, harmonic, and rhythmic boundaries. This may have been for reasons more musical than political, however. Just as the bebop musicians of the 1940s deliberately crafted a technically complicated methodology to separate themselves from the preceding "swing" generation, the 1960s artists were determined to distance their style from its inherent 1950s post-bop or hard-bop roots in order to make their own distinctive statements and forge their own identifiable voices.

The champion of this movement was the saxophonist JOHN WILLIAM COLTRANE, whose successful sales at Impulse Records enabled him to recommend up-and-coming artists to the label. One of these was another Philadelphian, the saxophonist ARCHIE VERNON SHEPP, who provided Rashied Ali with his first major album release, *On This Night*, in 1965. Subsequently, Ali began working with John Coltrane in November 1965, and after a few engagements as a quintet together with Coltrane's legendary drummer Elvin Jones (documented on the 1965 album *Meditations*), Coltrane began his own "free jazz" period with his wife, ALICE MCLEOD COLTRANE, on piano, the mainstay bassist Jimmy Garrison, and Rashied Ali.

The relatively obscure Ali was now the drummer for arguably the premier group in jazz, and during the next two years, from 1965 to 1967, he toured the nation and the globe, recording and sharing Coltrane's passionate quest for new ways of making music, answering the leader's ongoing evolution with his own exceptionally idiosyncratic version of drum set playing. The final period of exploration for Coltrane with Rashied Ali produced the 1966 recordings *Live at the Village Vanguard Again* and *Cosmic Music*; the 1967 recordings *Stellar Regions, Interstellar Space, Expression*, and the last recorded live performance, in April 1967, *The Olatunji Concert*. *Interstellar Space* was perhaps the most controversial release from their collaboration, consisting of four saxophone and drum set duets, each titled for a planet. Unfortunately this multidirectional rhythmic approach could not be further pursued because of Coltrane's untimely passing later that year. Still in his early thirties, Ali worked for a while with Alice Coltrane, then expatriated to Europe, where he performed in Copenhagen, Germany, and Sweden. He had always admired the drummer PHILLY JOE JONES, and studied with him in England. Upon his return to New York in the early 1970s, Ali worked and recorded with the saxophonists JACKIE McLEAN, GARY LEE BARTZ, and Dewey Redman. While developing his leadership and organizational skills, he helped coordinate the New York Musicians Festival in 1972.

Finding the New York scene somewhat depressed, he wasted no time opening his own venue, Ali's Alley, in 1973. Originally a performance loft with a decidedly noncommercial booking policy concentrating on the avant-garde, his space eventually became a showcase for jazz across the stylistic spectrum. The club closed in 1979.

Ali's other trailblazing venture was his own artist-run label, Survival Records, which he founded at the same time as Ali's Alley. With this unusual amount of independence and control, he built a fine catalog of his own projects as a leader, along with some worthwhile releases from other artists. One important recording from Ali during this period was his own *Duo Exchange* with the saxophonist Frank Lowe. Survival's output was later rereleased on the Knitting Factory Classics imprint.

During the 1980s Ali performed with the saxophonists Makanda Ken McIntyre and David Murray. He recorded with the guitarist James "Blood" Ulmer, the tenor saxophonist George Adams, and the bassist Sirone in 1987. *Touchin' on Trane* with the bassist William Parker was recorded in 1991 and merited high praise from critics. Since the 1990s Ali has led a side project, Prima Materia, dedicated to preserving the spirit of Coltrane's music. Additionally, Ali was instrumental in encouraging young artists, including the respective saxophone and bass-playing sons of his mentors John Coltrane and Jimmy Garrison.

In addition to performing with his own Rashied Ali Quartet, he began performing duo concerts with the saxophonist Sonny Fortune, another fellow Philadelphian, in the 2000s. The pair sometimes played ninety minutes to a full two hours in exploration of a single composition. Festival organizer, promoter, independent label entrepreneur, club owner, and teacher by example, Rashied Ali devoted his life to pushing the envelope of jazz drumming.

Further Reading

Pareles, Jon. "Rashied Ali Quartet," *New York Times*, 6 Jan. 1988.
Patel, Mark. "Rashied Ali: 10 Questions," *One Final Note: The Jazz and Improvised Music Webzine* (6 June 2005).
Shteamer, Hank. "Rashied Ali," *All About Jazz/New York* 18 (Oct. 2003).

JIM MILLER

ALI, Salimah (Dec. 1954–), photographer, was born Joyce Allen at Harlem Hospital in New York, the oldest of four children, all of whose names were changed after her father converted to Islam in the late 1950s. In 1972 Ali graduated from Jamaica High School in Queens. Although a guidance counselor told Ali that as a young African American woman she would never attend college, she enrolled in LaGuardia Community College that fall. She concentrated on liberal arts until she took her first black and white photography course. Impressed by her negatives, Ali decided to pursue a degree in photography. At the time colleges and universities had only recently begun offering graduate and undergraduate degrees in photography. Ali applied to the Fashion Institute of Technology (FIT) in New York City in 1975. Although she possessed an exceptional portfolio and passed a required entrance exam three times, she was refused entry to the program because the administration did not believe a young African American woman was capable of producing such work. Ali was finally accepted when Dean Mentor of LaGuardia, also an African American woman, called FIT on her former student's behalf. Before she matriculated, Ali had given birth to Jamilah Aisha Allen. As a single mother, Ali had to balance raising her daughter, attending school, and supporting the household by working odd jobs. Her instructors provided a tremendous amount of support by allowing Ali to bring her daughter to class when she could not find a babysitter. In 1977 Ali graduated with an AA degree in Photography.

Ali's career began at a time when African American photographers were either "creating works purely for exhibition as fine art" (Willis, 171) or using photography to document the era's prevalent social issues such as the Black Power Movement. Few African Americans were involved in fashion and entertainment photography, and the number of African American women in these fields was even smaller. Understanding the limitations faced by African American women in the fashion industry, both in front of and behind the camera, Ali still chose to concentrate on entertainment photography. There she found many creative influences to sustain her drive, among them

Ozier Mohammed, GORDON PARKS, JAMES VAN-
DERZEE, and her own father. From the mid-1970s to
the mid-1980s she photographed numerous celebrities, including Earth, Wind & Fire, GRACE JONES,
EARTHA KITT, PATTI LABELLE, Bob Marley, and
STEVIE WONDER. During this time she also worked as
the photo editor for *Encore,* a national black news and
entertainment magazine.

In the mid-80s Ali continued to freelance as a photojournalist and documentary photographer, publishing in weekly newspapers like the *Amsterdam News*
and magazines such as *Essence* and *Ms.* The caliber of
Ali's work was such that the photographic historian
Jean Moutoussamy-Ashe profiled her in the biographical anthology *Viewfinders: Black Women Photographers* (1993). In the late 1990s Chris Hatch, the
photo editor for *Newsday,* gave Ali her first of many
assignments for daily newspapers; soon she would
also contribute to the *New York Times* and *USA Today.*
Aside from shooting for print publications, Ali also
worked as the still photographer for the African
American vampire movie *Def by Temptation* (1990)
and *A Litany for Survival: The Life and Work of Audre
Lorde* (1995), the critically acclaimed documentary
about the poet, teacher, and activist. While on the film
set, Ali shot the portrait of Lorde that would decorate
the cover of her book, *Sister Outsider* (1984). During
this time Ali also worked as an artist educator at the
Jamaica Center for Arts & Learning, which was
founded in 1972 to provide cultural programs for
Queens' underserved communities. While there she
taught the basics of black and white photography and
darkroom techniques to at-risk youth.

During the course of her thirty-year career Ali ex-
hibited extensively in many prestigious museums and
galleries, including the Museum of Fine Arts in
Boston; the Brooklyn Museum of Art, for its 2001
show Committed to the Image: Contemporary Black
Photographers; the Black Enterprise Gallery in New
York and the Studio Museum of Harlem for Self-
Portrait, an exhibition sponsored by *Black Enterprise
Magazine* in 1980 as a tribute to its black photographers; and the Bronx Borough President's Art
Gallery for Speaking of the Bronx, a project completed in 2006 by Image Griots, a Bronx-based
photography collective that documents various
Bronx neighborhoods. In addition the Schomburg
Center for Research in Black Culture commissioned
her and the photographer Jules Allen to shoot the
Twentieth-Century African Americans series, which
became part of the Center's permanent collection in
1999.

Ali's work has been featured in a number of books
about photography and women artists, including
*Patchwork of Dreams: Voices from the Heart of New
America* (1996), a book that celebrates the cultural
and artistic diversity of Queens-based artists; *The
Face of Our Past: Images of Black Women from Colonial
America to the Present* (1999); and *Committed to the
Image: Contemporary Black Photographers* (2001).

Ali's professional affiliations include the National
Association for Black Journalists (NABJ), the largest
organization of journalists of color, which provides
programs and services to and advocates on behalf of
black journalists; Kamoinge Inc., an artists' group
founded by the photographer Roy DeCarava in 1963
as a response to the negative and biased representation of African Americans in mainstream media; and
Image Griots.

Further Reading
Hine, Darlene Clark. *Black Women in America* (2005).
Hine, Darlene Clark, and Kathleen Thompson. *A Shin-
ing Thread of Hope* (1999).
Moutoussamy-Ashe, Jeanne. *Viewfinders: Black Women
Photographers* (1993).
Willis-Thomas, Deborah. *A Bio-Bibliography of Black
Photographers, 1940–1988* (1989).
Willis, Deborah. *Reflections in Black: A History of Black
Photographers, 1840 to the Present* (2000).
CRYSTAL AM NELSON

ALICE B. *See* Ella Speed.

ALICE OF DUNK'S FERRY (C. 1686–1802), oral
historian and centenarian, was born a slave in Philadelphia, Pennsylvania, to parents who were slaves brought
to the United States from Barbados. She was moved to
Dunk's Ferry in Bucks County, Pennsylvania, when
she was ten years old to be with her master, of whom
no information is available. There Alice lived as a slave,
collecting ferry fares for forty years of her life.

Alice was a spirited and intelligent woman. She
loved to hear the Bible read to her, but like most other
enslaved people she could not read or write. She also
held the truth in high esteem and was considered
trustworthy. Her reliable memory served her well
throughout her long life.

Many notable people of the time are said to have
made her acquaintance, like Thomas Story (founder of
the Association of Medical Superintendents of American Institutions for the Insane, which was the precursor to the American Psychiatric Association) and James
Logan (a statesman and scholar). She is even said to
have lit the pipe of William Penn, the man considered
to be the founder of Pennsylvania. Alice would comment on issues pertinent to the times as she collected
ferry fees from travelers. After a time she came to be
seen as a sensible, intelligent, and Christian woman,
and not just a functionary to be ignored. People
stopped to speak with her during their travels. She became a human storehouse for local information. As she
aged she told personal anecdotes of the people, events,
and places of young Philadelphia. Her early recollections told of Philadelphia when it was still wilderness
and Native Americans hunted wild animals in the
woodland. Her later recollections told of the early settlement of Philadelphia and other nearby areas. People
loved to hear her stories as they were usually about
their own family members, people of local note, and

others who were responsible for building up Philadelphia and its surrounding areas. Because she lived such a long life Alice personally experienced a momentous time in American history and was still alive to tell the tales to subsequent generations. Her stories helped to form a true history and folklore of Pennsylvania from the point of view of an honest common person.

Alice rode her horse from Dunk's Ferry to Christ Church in Philadelphia until she lost her sight at the age of 96. An excellent fisherwoman she still rowed her own boat and caught fish while blind. Her sight miraculously returned at the age of 100 or 102. There is no record of her having married or borne children. She died at Bristol in Bucks County at the age of 116. She remained a slave her entire life.

Alice was one of the first respected African American oral historians. A centenarian, she lived to see the birth and growth of an historic American city. As an oral historian she lived to tell generations of Americans about one of the birthplaces of modern day America. Her stories were not written down verbatim but rather passed from one generation to another. She herself is written about in many histories of Pennsylvania.

Further Reading

Cima, Gay Gibson. *Early American Women Critics* (2006).

Davis, W. W. H. *The History of Bucks County, Pennsylvania* (1905).

Gale Research. "Alice of Dunk's Ferry," in *Notable Black American Women Book 2* (1996).

Kaplan, Sidney. *The Black Presence in the Era of the American Revolution, 1770–1800* (1975).

Mott, Abigail. *Biographical Sketches and Interesting Anecdotes of Persons of Colour* (1826).

Stephens, Robert. "Part I," in *Six Part Investigation into a Family of Slavers, Traders & Thieves; Quakers & Anglicans; Colonialists, Royalists & Warmongers* (2003).

Watson. *Watson's Annals of Philadelphia and Pennsylvania*, vol. 1 (1857).

DARSHELL SILVA

ALLAIN, Théophile T. (1 Oct. 1846–2 Feb. 1917), businessman and politician, was born a slave in West Baton Rouge, Louisiana, to Sosthene Allain, a wealthy white planter, and one of Allain's slave mistresses, whose name is not recorded. Sosthene Allain appears to have favored his son, to whom he gave the nickname "Solougue," after a Haitian dictator of the 1840s and 1850s. In 1856, when Théophile was ten, his father called him to France to attend the christening of the son of Louis Napoleon III in Paris and also to travel with him to Spain and Britain. Théophile returned to the United States in 1859, where he studied with private tutors in New Orleans and at a private college in New Brunswick, New Jersey.

Although Allain had been born a slave, his education and foreign travel prepared him well for a leadership position in Louisiana business and politics after the Civil War. So, too, did his inheritance of the family plantation around that time. Upon returning to Louisiana from New Jersey in 1869, he began a lifelong interest in education by establishing schools for both blacks and whites. He also opened grocery businesses in West Baton Rouge and Iberville parishes and began cultivating and exporting rice and sugar, employing thirty-five laborers on his eight-hundred-acre plantation. Allain also secured a contract from the state of Louisiana to construct 150,000 yards of levees on the Mississippi River. By the early 1870s Allain's various business interests, including a cattle ranch, had secured him an annual income in excess of fifteen thousand dollars, making him one of the wealthiest people of color in Louisiana during Reconstruction.

Allain's burgeoning business ventures and his interest in expanding educational opportunities perhaps inevitably brought him to a career in politics. An active Republican, he won a seat in the Louisiana House of Representatives from West Baton Rouge Parish in 1870, but he was prevented from taking his seat because of alleged voting irregularities in his district. Allain won election to the house in 1872 and in 1874, was seated, and served with some distinction. Alongside his fellow Republicans and as chairman of the house appropriations committee he attempted to ease the burden of Louisiana taxpayers, while still maintaining state aid to education and other matters of government that had been neglected during slavery. Achieving that balance proved difficult, particularly in the wake of the worldwide depression that began in 1873 and greatly restricted the spending plans of all of the Southern state legislatures.

Allain also earned a reputation as something of a peacemaker in the Louisiana legislature, which was arguably the most contentious in the nation. The 1872 elections resulted in rival state legislatures in New Orleans—one Republican, supported by Allain and most African Americans, the other an alliance of white supremacist Democrats and conservative Republicans. The intensification of White League opposition to Republican rule also precipitated the infamous Colfax riot on Easter Sunday 1873, the single bloodiest episode during Reconstruction, which resulted in the death of more than a hundred African Americans in Louisiana's Red River Valley. In response to the Colfax riot and to the bitter divisions in the state legislature in 1873, Allain emerged as one of the most prominent black advocates of the unification movement, an effort by moderate white New Orleans businessmen and a few prominent people of color to seek a middle ground in Louisiana politics. The unification movement hoped to weaken both Northern Radical Republicans and the more extreme White League Democrats and to encourage an alliance of black and white businessmen to govern the state. The philosophy of black unificationists—most of whom were, like Allain, wealthy and of mixed race—prefigured that of BOOKER T. WASHINGTON in its emphasis on economic self-help and political moderation. The unification movement was short-lived, however, because the majority of black Louisianans, particularly the former slaves, distrusted the unification movement's white leaders and their mixed-race allies and because whites, particularly in rural and northern Louisiana, were in no mood to compromise. Although the Republicans narrowly won the 1874 elections—with Allain securing a seat in the state senate—the Colfax riot, among other atrocities, persuaded white Louisianans that violence and intimidation would eventually reclaim the state government from Republican rule.

Allain served in the Louisiana Senate from 1874 to 1876, the final two years of narrow Republican rule, during which his efforts to reform local government, build better roads and bridges, and repair levees on the Mississippi were defeated by Democrats and conservative Republicans determined to cut spending. He chaired the senate standing committee on elections, one of the more important assignments given the state's problems with voter fraud and intimidation, but he could do little to solve the problem of another contested state election in 1876. On that occasion the federal commission in Washington, D.C., brokered a compromise that secured the presidency for the Republican Rutherford B. Hayes, while allowing the Democrats to regain control of the contested Southern legislatures, including Louisiana's.

The end of Reconstruction did not end Allain's involvement in Louisiana politics, though the changed tenor of the times was made clear to him in 1879 when a barman on a steamer called the senator a "nigger" and refused to serve him a glass of water (Blassingame, 193). Allain participated in the Louisiana constitutional convention of 1879, where, along with P. B. S. PINCHBACK, he helped to establish Southern University, a state-funded institution for blacks only, which started in New Orleans and later moved to Baton Rouge. Some of Allain's fellow black politicians opposed the university's segregated status, but the senator, who served as vice president of the board of trustees, believed that Southern's free tuition would benefit African Americans of all backgrounds, not just the traditional Creole elite. In 1880 Allain left the senate but returned to the house, where he represented West Baton Rouge until 1890 and helped secure an appropriation of fourteen thousand dollars for Southern University. He displayed his pragmatism and political independence in 1886 by supporting a Democrat for Congress, for which he was briefly expelled from the Republican Party.

After Allain left the house in 1890 his financial resources went into decline. Some sources suggest that he lost his plantation, and others that he moved to Chicago to work for the Illinois Fish and Conservation Commission. Little is known about his personal life. He married Aline Coleman, a Louisianan who owned some property, and had six children, all of whom attended Straight University (later Dillard University) in New Orleans. By the time of Allain's death in February 1917, constitutional amendments had removed all African Americans from the state legislature and all but a handful from minor public offices. The educational establishments that Allain had helped to found and support in the 1870s and 1880s proved more durable, however, and the graduates of Straight, Southern, Leland, and other colleges eventually played a central role in restoring democracy to Louisiana in the second half of the twentieth century.

Further Reading
Information on Théophile T. Allain can be found in the Turnbull-Allain Family Papers, Manuscripts 4261, Louisiana and Mississippi Valley Collections, Louisiana State University, Baton Rouge, Louisiana.
Blassingame, John. *Black New Orleans, 1860–1880* (1973).
Vincent, Charles. *Black Legislators in Louisiana during Reconstruction* (1978).

STEVEN J. NIVEN

ALLEN, Anthony D. (15 June 1772–31 Dec. 1835), explorer and businessman, was born a slave in German Flats, New York. He was owned by the Dougal family and spent his youth in Schenectady. It is very likely his mother was a slave (New York did not abolish slavery until 1827); his father was a freeman and a mariner. Following the death of his master, he was purchased by another owner. After gaining his freedom in 1796, Allen arrived in Boston in 1800 and went to sea just as his father had done. Indeed, many African Americans living in Boston had ties to the maritime industry in some way. Like other black mariners, Allen faced the risk of reenslavement when he traveled to Southern ports. Once he was saved from imprisonment by one of the ship's owners, who paid $300 for his release.

Allen's years at sea between 1800 and 1810 provided him with unique experiences. He traveled to France where he saw Toussaint-Louverture, the black liberator of Haiti, and the Englishman Lord Nelson. He also traveled to China, India, Indonesia, Santo Domingo, Cuba, Jamaica, and Hawaii. He decided to leave ship while on the Hawaiian island of Oahu, and for a brief time he served as a steward to King Kamehameha I. In 1811 he was awarded a land grant by the high priest Hewahewa, a great honor since land grants were made only to chiefs and people who were highly respected in the kingdom. In 1812 Allen returned to sea, sailed to China, and then came back to Oahu to settle there permanently. Called "Alani" by the Hawaiian people, he was widely respected not only because of the land grant he had received but also because of his generosity—he supplied fresh meat and vegetables to the missionaries and befriended sailors who became sick aboard ship by providing them a place for rest and rehabilitation. He eventually married a Hawaiian woman who gave birth to three children: Peggy, Anthony Jr., and George Caldwell. There is evidence that Allen may have married a second wife, which was a common practice in Hawaii at the time. It is very likely that his second wife's name was Pehu, since this woman was mentioned twice in accounts by

Stephan Reynolds, a missionary and Allen's friend. Much of what we know about Anthony D. Allen can be attributed to the diaries and journals that were kept by missionaries like Reynolds (Scruggs, 42). For example, Maria S. Loomis wrote the following in 1820: "Among the residents of this island is a Black man native of Schenectady named Allen. He has been our constant friend . . . (and) he lives on a beautiful plain called Wyteta (Waikiki)."

By the time the first missionaries arrived in Hawaii in 1820 Allen was well established. Allen's developments on his six acres of land in Waikiki included a compound with eight or ten buildings. Some of the buildings were used for sleeping quarters, dining, cooking, storage, and for housing seamen who became ill on their journeys. According to missionary reports, Allen operated what could be considered the first Hawaiian hospital for American seamen. Many of the patients were brought to Allen's hospital for treatment and recuperation (Scruggs, 38–39); evidently he had learned some medical skills from Dr. Dougal in Schenectady.

Allen turned out to be an astute businessman and entrepreneur. Among his most successful ventures was as a farmer. He supplied fresh vegetables, eggs, milk, fowl, and meats. He also provided boarding for other people's cattle and horses. Another important part of his business was providing supplies for newly arrived ships in Honolulu's port. Reynolds reveals that Allen also ran a successful tavern that was popular among seamen. In the tavern could also be found the Hawaiian Islands' first bowling alley. Bowling, it seems, was a very popular recreational activity, as Reynolds stated in his journal in 1824 that "all the village is rolling at Allen's." In B. O. Wist's *A Century of Public Education in Hawaii*, Allen is recognized as the first individual to build a schoolhouse in Hawaii. Allen was literate and taught his own children to read and write at an early age.

Allen's daughter Peggy married Robert Moffet, a European American shoemaker in Honolulu. His other children went on to marry Hawaiian women and make lives for themselves in various enterprises. Anthony Allen Jr. moved to the island of Hawaii, and he became known as an expert catcher of wild bullock. He was also a valued friend of Prince Lot Kamehameha of Honolulu. George Caldwell Allen married Maria Lahilahi, the daughter of a Hawaiian woman and Don Francisco Marin, a Spanish adventurer and confidant of the king. Today, very little is known of what happened to subsequent descendants of Anthony D. Allen. Scruggs has stated that it is possible that "many do not even know they are of African ancestry" (Scruggs, 46).

Allen suffered a stroke in December 1835 and died on 31 December. Not only did Allen play a significant role in Hawaii's history but he is also considered to have been the best-documented person of African ancestry who lived in Hawaii during the early nineteenth century.

Further Reading
Scruggs, Marc. "Anthony D. Allen: A Prosperous American of African Descent in Early 19th Century Hawaii," *Hawaiian Journal of History* (1992).
Scruggs, Marc. "There Is One Black Man, Anthony D. Allen," in *They Followed the Trade Winds: African Americans in Hawaii* (2005).

MILES M. JACKSON

ALLEN, Aris Tee (27 Dec. 1910–8 Feb. 1991), physician and state legislator, was born in Beeville, Texas, the son of James and Mary Etta Whitby Allen. His parents separated when he was an infant. When Allen was six years old, his mother, feeling that he needed male guidance and discipline, sent him to San Antonio to be reared by his father, a hotel bellman. Even while attending elementary school, he was expected to earn his keep, selling newspapers, delivering clothes for a local tailor, and, at the age of twelve, serving as a hotel washroom attendant. Allen excelled in the classroom through primary and junior high schools. But apparently in his final year of junior high he left school after a classmate harassed him for wearing his father's clothing. He was soon hired as a busboy in a hotel dining room and within two years found employment as a waiter at a San Antonio hotel. By the spring of 1928 Allen had moved to Houston and found seasonal employment on the docks loading cotton bales onto freighters and found odd jobs as a domestic worker, chauffeur, waiter, and assistant to a clothing salesman. Becoming restless again, he moved north, where he had long heard that blacks had better opportunities.

Allen arrived in Chicago in the middle of the Great Depression but was fortunate to find work as a janitor's assistant, busboy, and chauffeur. By the spring of 1932 he was sweeping floors and making deliveries for a drugstore on Chicago's South Side. That fall he enrolled in night school in pursuit of his long-postponed high school diploma. Ever anxious to improve himself, Allen began taking every civil service examination that he could until he was informed of an opening in Washington, D.C., as an elevator operator. In the spring of 1934 he began the long drive to the nation's capital. In Washington he was assigned to the U.S. Department of Agriculture, where he worked days and attended high school night classes, completing two courses with good grades. In mid-August he transferred to the night shift and enrolled as a full-time high school day student.

In May 1938, at the age of twenty-seven, Allen finally earned his high school diploma, and the following fall he entered Howard University as a premedical student. During his third year at Howard, the U.S. entry into the war that had erupted in Europe was imminent. Enrolled as a reserve officer training candidate and accepted for preflight training, Allen considered joining the Ninety-ninth Pursuit Squadron, a black military air unit forming in Tuskegee, Alabama. But a friend convinced him that if the United States entered the war, physicians would be needed as well as pilots. Allen entered Howard Medical School, where, after the U.S. entry into the war, the curriculum was condensed to three years.

Before the war ended, Allen was released from his military obligation early when he agreed to practice medicine in Annapolis, Maryland, where there was a shortage of physicians. Once his practice was established, Allen married Faye Watson, a nurse in the Howard University medical clinic whom he had met while he was a student. She enrolled in medical school, and they became partners in their Annapolis medical office. Allen's medical practice was interrupted during the Korean conflict when he was called back into the air force to serve in the Flight Surgeon's Office at Vance Air Base near Enid, Oklahoma. Following his service he returned to Annapolis, resumed the practice of medicine, and became involved in community activities, including serving as president of the Parent Teacher Association at his children's school.

Allen was appointed by the governor of Maryland to the Anne Arundel County school board in the 1950s after the Supreme Court ordered the desegregation of public schools. He was often at odds with the county school superintendent, who favored gradual school desegregation. Allen was anxious to change the deplorable conditions of the black schools, particularly one that had no running water, where children wanting a drink or to wash their hands had to go to a nearby stream and get down on their hands and knees.

In 1966 Allen was elected to the Maryland House of Delegates as a Republican in a jurisdiction where Democrats outnumbered Republicans three to one. After two four-year terms in the house, he ran for a seat in the Maryland Senate but was defeated by 125 votes. He was subsequently elected chairman of the Maryland Republican Party, becoming the only black Republican state chairman in any of the fifty states, and in 1978 he was the first black to run for lieutenant governor of Maryland. Though he was defeated in his bid for state office, he was chosen to fill a vacancy in the state senate. Two years later he became the first African American in modern history to preside as secretary of the Republican National Convention.

In 1981 Allen resigned his seat in the Maryland Senate when President Ronald Reagan named him to serve as the director of the Bureau of Health Standards in the Health Care Financing Agency of the U.S. Department of Health and Human Services. While serving there, Allen, who had completed his medical school curriculum without finishing his bachelor's degree requirements, enrolled in night classes at Howard University. In the spring of 1985 the seventy-four-year-old Allen, who graduated from high school at twenty-seven, accepted his bachelor's degree. In 1990 Allen again won a seat in the house of delegates, where at the age of eighty he was its oldest member. Three months after his election Allen learned that he had terminal cancer and took his own life.

Further Reading

Bentley, Helen Delich. "The Death of a Pioneer," *Congressional Record*, 11 Apr. 1991.
May, Jude Thomas. *Achieving the American Dream: The Life of the Honorable Aris T. Allen, M.D.* (1990).
"The Odyssey of Aris Allen," *Annapolitan* (Apr. 1990).

HAROLD N. BURDETT

ALLEN, Debbie (16 Jan. 1950–), dancer, choreographer and actress, was born Deborrah Kaye Allen in Houston, Texas, to Andrew Allen, a dentist, and Vivian Ayers-Allen, a poet and librarian; her parents had two other children, the actress Phylicia Rashad, and Hugh Allen, better known as Tex. Although she exhibited an early interest in dance and desired to join the Houston Foundation for Ballet, she was denied admission when she applied in the 1950s in what her mother saw as a clear example of discrimination. Her parents were able to pay for private ballet lessons with the Ballet Russes. She later traveled and trained in Mexico City with the Ballet Nacional de Mexico. In 1964 she returned to Houston where she once again auditioned for the Houston Foundation for Ballet. This time she was not only accepted to the prestigious organization but was awarded a scholarship. Her talent won her the high school appelation of "Miss Versatile." After graduation she traveled to Washington, D.C., to attend Howard University, her sister Phylicia's alma mater. She graduated from Howard in 1971 with a BA in Classical Greek Literature, Speech, and Theater. During her time at Howard, she continued to develop as a dancer, working with the Michael Malone dance troupe.

In 1971 Allen moved to New York City, where she roomed with her sister while they both worked in a variety of acting roles. She performed in a wide variety of roles including Purlie in OSSIE DAVIS's *Purlie Victorious* and Beneatha in *A Raisin in the Sun*. In 1972 she became a principal dancer in GEORGE FAISON's Universal Dance Experience. In 1980 she earned a Tony Award nomination for the role of Anita in *West Side Story*; although she did not win the Tony, she did earn a Drama Desk Award for the role in that year. In the early 1980s Allen achieved her greatest recognition when she undertook the role of dance teacher Lydia Grant in the Broadway production of *Fame*. She later reprised the role in the television program of the same name, which ran from 1984 to 1987. The television role eventually earned her two Emmy Awards and a Golden Globe.

Despite her commitment to dance and acting, she eventually succumbed to the allure of direction and production. During Allen's tenure as Lydia Grant on Broadway and television, her sister earned a role on the popular situation comedy *The Cosby Show*. The show's originator and star, BILL COSBY, wanted Allen to direct an episode of the Cosby spin-off *A Different World*, based on the experiences of one *Cosby Show*–daughter attending a historically black college. Initially Allen resisted but in 1988 she accepted Cosby's offer and directed the series off and on throughout its duration. In the interim, she performed as Charity in *Sweet Charity* (1986) and was once again nominated for a Tony. She also performed in several specials, including *The Debbie Allen Show* and *Polly* (1989) and *Polly One More Time* (1990). Her tenure as director for *A Different World* eventually led to opportunities in the 1990s to direct other television shows such as *The Fresh Prince of Bel-Air* and *Quantum Leap*. She also choreographed the Academy Awards at least five times during the 1990s, and produced and directed *Stomping at the Savoy* at the Kennedy Center.

Among Allen's other television work are children's shows like *Brothers of the Knight* and *Dancing in the Wing* (2000) as well as programs such as *Cool Women* and *The Old Settlers,* which she directed and co-produced. She also directed episodes of series such as *Girlfriends*, *All of Us*, and *The Parkers*, and produced the film *Amistad* (1997). She had been inspired by William Owens's *Black Mutiny*, which told the story of the mutiny and trial of slaves captured after their mutiny aboard the schooner *La Amistad*. Working with acclaimed director Steven Spielberg and an all-star cast headed by Sir Anthony Hopkins and MORGAN FREEMAN, she served as executive producer of the film. During filming, the production encountered a series of problems, one of which was a lawsuit by writer BARBARA CHASE-RIBOUD, who claimed that the project plagiarized her own work on the subject.

Allen's first marriage was to record executive William Wilford, whom she divorced. She met husband Norm Nixon during the filming of *The Fish that Saved Philadelphia*; they married in 1984 and have two children, Vivian Nicole and Norm Jr., whom they call Thump.

Allen's work garnered her awards beyond Tony, Emmy, and Golden Globes. She was the first ever honoree of the Lena Horne Award for Career Achievement in 1995, and was also the recipient of a 1992 Essence Award and a 1995 Soul Train Lady of Soul Award. A member of the Black Filmmakers Hall of Fame, she has been given honorary doctorates from North Carolina School of the Arts and Howard University. Allen also served on the President's Committee on Arts and Humanities as well as the American Film Institute and the UCLA School of Theatre and Film. Allen opened The Debbie Allen Dance Academy in East Los Angeles with a design to teach dance as a cultural meaning. Students at the academy learn twelve different dance forms in what is meant to serve as a youth outreach opportunity as well as an educational one. The program also offers students the opportunity to study dance as a serious career.

Further Reading
"Allen, Debbie," *Encyclopedia of African American Cultural History*, vol. 5 (1996).
"Debbie Allen: On Power, Pain, Prime time," *Ebony* (March 1991).
Hine, Darlene Clark, ed. *Black Women in America: An Historical Encyclopedia* (1994).

DONNA WALLER HARPER

ALLEN, Elise Ford (29 July 1921–), editor and publisher, was born in Peoria, Illinois, to Dr. Cecil Bruce Ford and Florence Henderson Ford. She was the granddaughter of Major George Ford and a great-great-granddaughter of WEST FORD, who may have been the African American son of George Washington. Cecil Bruce Ford, a graduate of Meharry Medical College, was Peoria's first African American dentist, while Elise's mother, Florence, was a well-known seamstress. Elise Ford was baptized at the age of three at Bethel Methodist Church and attended the Peoria public school system with her siblings Bruce, Florence, and Harrison. Later Ford acted as her grandfather's secretary when he was the president of the Springfield chapter of the National Association for the Advancement of Colored People (NAACP), and wrote his correspondence as his eyesight failed in his later years.

The Ford oral history, which held that she was the three-times great-granddaughter of George Washington, was relayed to Elise by her grandfather at annual family reunions at Camp Butler. She was admonished not to discuss her heritage outside of the immediate family for fear of racial reprisals. She became the Ford family chronicler upon the death of Major Ford.

Elise Ford married James O. Allen in 1937, and the couple had eleven children. Her husband, a printer and inventor, started the Allen Printing Company in 1946, the first African American–owned printing establishment in Peoria.

During the early years of Allen's marriage, the civil rights movement swung into full force, with equal education at the forefront. This period would begin her long involvement as an advocate for the rights of the disenfranchised. In May of 1954 the U.S. Supreme Court in its landmark *Brown v. Board of Education* decision declared segregation in public schools unconstitutional; the Allen children attended a neighborhood school with a student body that was 80 percent minority. They had yet to be bused to the city's all-white neighborhoods. A firm believer that inequality could be fought through education, Allen became an active PTA member. She served as the first African American president of the PTA at McKinley Elementary and Roosevelt Junior High schools. This presidency would head the list of her numerous firsts as an African American.

In 1960 the Allen Printing Company became the Traveler Printing and Publishing Company. In 1966 Allen launched the *Traveler Weekly Newspaper*, becoming the first African American woman to edit and publish a newspaper in the state of Illinois. The newspaper started out as a single 8.5×11 sheet of paper with local news items and Allen's editorials but grew to tabloid size the following year. For the next four decades Allen would remain an important and influential voice for freedom and equality.

She also continued her civic work. From 1968 to 1973 she was the first African American to serve on the board of the Peoria Girl Scouts, receiving a certificate for "uplifting young black girls in the inner city of Peoria." She organized the first 4-H Club for black girls in the state. Discrimination was still a barrier for many African Americans trying to fight their way out of poverty and into a decent life, and, with this in mind, Allen ran for mayor in 1973. Much of the white populace considered her candidacy a joke, but many voters changed their minds after they heard Allen speak in debate, during which she demonstrated her understanding of the issues confronting the city and laid out solid, workable solutions that many of the other candidates lacked. Though Allen did indeed lose her bid as mayor, her run made her a household name, and the *Traveler Weekly's* circulation went statewide. A year later, in 1974, Allen was named Citizen of the Year by the Magnificent Gentlemen, Inc., a big brother organization, for her outstanding service to the community. Other awards came that same year: the Certificate of Achievement from the Peoria Commission on Human Rights, a commendation from the Peoria chapter of the National Organization for Women (NOW), and the Outstanding Business Women Award by the National Association of University Women.

That same year Allen continued her pursuit of equal protection under the law for all Americans, without regard to race, color, or creed. An African American mother of eleven had been sentenced to life in prison for killing her husband in self-defense. Allen reviewed the case with the public defender, interviewed witnesses, and began writing editorials in the *Traveler Weekly*, charging that the woman had not received a fair trail. The governor of Illinois, Dan Walker, read her editorials and later paroled the condemned woman. The power of Allen's insightful writing would lead to many more commendations from all over the state of Illinois.

As Allen knew, unchecked poverty kept the poor out of the mainstream society and made them easy targets for discrimination. To honor Allen's pursuit of quality education for minorities, a scholarship was established in her name in 1985, at the Roosevelt Magnet School. Her newspaper, the *Traveler Weekly*, has earned dozens of awards in the field of excellence in journalism. In humanitarian circles, she was presented numerous awards including the prestigious MARTIN LUTHER KING JR. Commemorative Leadership Award (1989). Elise Ford Allen's passion for equality for African Americans has earned her a place of honor in the realms of civil rights activists.

Further Reading

Allen-Bryant, Linda. *I Cannot Tell a Lie: The True Story of George Washington's African American Descendants* (2004).

Burton, Judith Saunders. "A History of Gum Springs, Virginia: A Report of a Case Study of Leadership in a Black Enclave," PhD dissertation (1986).

LINDA ALLEN-BRYANT

ALLEN, Ethel D. (8 May 1929–16 Dec. 1981), physician and politician, was one of three children born in Philadelphia, Pennsylvania, to Sidney S. Allen Sr., a Georgia native, Democratic committeeperson, and tailor with a seventh-grade education whose dream of becoming a doctor was realized by his daughter. Ethel's mother, the former Effie Jean Goodall, was a Democratic committeeperson born in Maryland who operated a tailoring business with her husband for many years. Ethel Allen became fascinated by medicine and the mysteries of life and death as a child while living in North Philadelphia, and she began to move toward medicine while studying at a Catholic institution, the then mostly white John W. Hallahan Girls Catholic High School, although her parents were Baptists.

Allen's intellectual curiosity led to intense scientific and medical inquiry, prompted by a visit to an uncle's dental practice, as well as by visits to a local physician who kept animal specimens in jars. Sheltered by her parents and an avid reader of political novels, Allen found refuge in the local library not far from her home near Twenty-third Street and Ridge Avenue. After attending national conventions in Philadelphia relating to her parents' political activities, Allen began to pattern herself after the famed black educator and activist MARY MCLEOD BETHUNE who advised President Franklin Roosevelt. Allen later told the *Philadelphia Inquirer Today* magazine, "Like most people thought about movie stars, I thought about politicians." She even managed the presidential campaign of a fellow student in high school, where she also learned how to play the piano and trumpet. By 1952, in fact, she had become involved in Dwight Eisenhower's presidential campaign by "scheduling appointments for the Philadelphia area," she said in the *Today* interview, likely a precursor to her gravitating toward the Republican Party.

Those experiences prepared her for local and state politics, but not before her medical career flourished once she enrolled in an all-black school, West Virginia State College (later West Virginia State University), where she hungered to learn more about African American culture. There she became a lifelong friend of the student Augusta A. Clark, who later became the second black woman on the Philadelphia City Council, with Allen's urging and support. Allen also excelled in Latin and drama. After graduation in 1946 with a bachelor's degree in biology, she was employed over the next dozen years as a research assistant for the pharmaceutical firm Rohm and Haas, as a chemist for the Atomic Energy Commission, and as an adviser to the Cheyney State College chapter of Delta Sigma Theta sorority, helping to find scholarships for college-bound students. Meanwhile, as she took graduate courses at Temple University from

1952 to 1954 and at the University of Pennsylvania in 1959, Allen applied to medical schools hoping to fulfill her lifelong dream of becoming a physician—just as the civil rights movement expanded.

Allen said that her father was initially ambivalent about her planned medical career because of the sexism and racism that a black woman would have to endure. In fact she spent more than five years applying to medical schools before the Philadelphia College of Osteopathic Medicine (PCOM) accepted her in 1959. There she encountered bigotry and chauvinism—particularly from white males in the student body—before graduating with a doctor of osteopathy degree in 1963.

By 1964 the quick-witted Allen had completed an internship at Grand Rapids Osteopathic Hospital in Grand Rapids, Michigan, after having been rejected at a number of institutions for an internship. She opened an office in Philadelphia at Fifteenth Street and Columbia Avenue, in the heart of black North Philadelphia. Once, while she was on a house call, thugs attempted to rob her at gunpoint, but she pulled her own handgun and forced them to exit the building naked.

Allen gained a reputation as a gritty, no-nonsense doctor and attracted the attention of community activists, some of whom were her patients. Several asked her to run for city council. Because of her political upbringing, her sensitivities related to racism and sexism, and her ambitions, she accepted the offer, defeating the three-term Democratic councilman Thomas McIntosh in November 1971 for the Fifth District seat. Allen had successfully switched aisles and became a powerful Republican with mayoral aspirations in a city known for its dominant Democratic base, often confronting the Democratic mayor Frank L. Rizzo (who later became a Republican) over such issues as funding to combat street gangs, rent control, affordable housing for her constituents, children's public health care, and even protecting the rights of street vendors.

Allen's initial foray into politics and primarily antipoverty stances during nearly two terms as a councilperson were especially noteworthy because she was a black Republican as well as an osteopathic physician, characteristics that media and political observers found fascinating. She sometimes joked about her uniqueness, calling herself a "BFR" or black female Republican. She was particularly concerned about issues that affected women, and in 1977 she traveled to China to monitor women's rights advances, an issue close to her heart in the United States.

A self-proclaimed practitioner of "ghetto medicine" who had a searing sense of humor, Allen contemplated national office after winning an at-large council seat, even giving President Gerald Ford a seconding speech at the National Republican Convention. Rising politically to become Secretary of the Commonwealth of Pennsylvania in 1979, Allen had already been named by *Esquire* magazine in 1975 as one of the nation's twelve outstanding women politicians, along with Representative SHIRLEY CHISHOLM, the first African American to run for president, an office that Allen briefly contemplated.

Allen's tenure as Pennsylvania's secretary—which followed the brief term of another black woman, C. DELORES TUCKER, who left the office amid controversy—lasted just nine months, because of charges that Allen had given speeches and received payment while she was supposed to be performing duties for the state. The Republican governor Richard Thornburgh dismissed her amid objections from civil rights groups claiming that his action was politically motivated. Though disappointed, Allen rebounded to take a position as a Philadelphia school district doctor with management responsibilities. She fought her own heart disease and cancer, which resulted in a mastectomy in 1975. She died at age fifty-two from heart disease. She was memorialized as the first black woman Philadelphia councilperson, as Secretary of the Commonwealth of Pennsylvania, and as a women's rights advocate and community activist. She was a tenacious fighter for the powerless, always mindful of racial and gender rights, despite the size and ferocity of her opposition.

Further Reading

Files of newspaper articles about Allen from the *Philadelphia Bulletin*, *Philadelphia Inquirer*, and *Philadelphia Daily News* are at Temple University's Urban Archives Center in Philadelphia.

Burkart, Kathryn W. "A Minority of One," *Philadelphia Inquirer Today*, 9 Sept. 1973.

Sims, Patsy. "I've Learned to Survive . . . ," *Philadelphia Inquirer*, 25 Jan. 1976.

Obituary: *Philadelphia Bulletin*, 18 Dec. 1981.

DONALD SCOTT SR.

ALLEN, Geri Antoinette (12 June 1957–), pianist and composer, was born in Detroit, Michigan, the daughter of Mount Vernell Allen Jr. She began studying classical piano at age seven but was also exposed to jazz at an early age. She met the trumpeter Marcus Belgrave when he was an artist-in-residence at her high school, Cass Technical; she studied jazz piano with him, and he became an important mentor, appearing on several of her later recordings. Allen also studied at the Jazz Development Workshop, a community-based organization.

After graduating from high school, Allen attended Howard University, where she was captivated by the music of THELONIOUS MONK and studied with John Malachi. In 1979 she earned a BA in Jazz Studies and taught briefly at Howard before moving to New York City, where she studied with the pianist Kenny Barron. She also met the jazz educator Nathan Davis, who invited her to enroll at the University of Pittsburgh; there she wrote a thesis on ERIC DOLPHY and earned an MA in Ethnomusicology in 1982. During her time in Pittsburgh she played in a trio led by the drummer Roy Brooks.

Allen returned to New York in 1982 and resumed her studies with Barron, rapidly making a name for herself among the more progressive young jazz leaders. She was a member of Oliver Lake's group Jump Up from 1982 to 1987, and between 1982 and 1984 she toured with a variety of prominent artists, including Brooks, the trumpeter LESTER BOWIE, the vibraphonist Jay Hoggard, the saxophonist Joseph Jarman, the flutist James Newton, and the singer Nancy Wilson. In 1984 she toured Europe with her own quartet and recorded *The Printmakers*, her first album as a bandleader, with Anthony Cox on bass and Andrew Cyrille on drums. The recording cemented her growing reputation among the jazz avant-garde. In 1985 she recorded *Home Grown*, featuring six of her own compositions, as well as a pair of Monk covers. Allen regularly featured her own writing, penning all of the compositions on *Open on All Sides in the Middle* (1986). This album had a funkier, more up-tempo feel than some of her later work, perhaps reflecting her contemporaneous involvement in the M-Base Collective, founded by the saxophonist STEVE COLEMAN. Allen appeared on two of that group's albums in 1985 and 1986, fitting easily into the dense ensembles and funky grooves.

Allen also freelanced widely throughout the late 1980s, playing with artists such as the saxophonists ARTHUR BLYTHE and Chico Freeman, the trumpeter WOODY SHAW, and the vibraphonist Hoggard. In 1987 she began a lengthy relationship with the bassist Charlie Haden and the drummer Paul Motian. The trio recorded several highly praised albums, including *Etudes* (1987), *Segments* (1989), *Live at the Village Vanguard* (1991), and *In the Year of the Dragon* (1991), all while touring extensively in the United States and Europe. These recordings contain many moments of breathtaking melodic beauty, as well as more experimental playing that helped showcase Allen's technical and stylistic range. She also played in a more conventional trio with the drummer Ralph Peterson and the bassist Essiet Essiet in the late 1980s; together these groups demonstrate Allen's ability to both play and compose across the entire spectrum of modern jazz piano, from post-bop to free jazz.

Allen's profile continued to rise with a string of acclaimed recordings in the 1990s. *The Nurturer* (1990) featured Belgrave on trumpet and Kenny Garrett on saxophone, and *Maroons* (1992) contained thirteen of Allen's own compositions. One of her former students, the trumpeter Wallace Roney, also appeared on *Maroons*. They were married in 1995 and had three children. In the fall of 1993 Allen toured Europe as a member of the singer BETTY CARTER's group, joining the drummer Jack DeJohnette and the bassist Dave Holland in the rhythm section and appearing on Carter's 1993 recording *Feed the Fire*. Also in 1993 Jazz at Lincoln Center commissioned a suite, *Sister Leola, an American Portrait*. In 1994 Allen appeared with the saxophonist ORNETTE COLEMAN's New Quartet at the San Francisco Jazz Festival, and she played on both versions of Coleman's *Sound Museum*

recordings. She was, in fact, the first acoustic pianist that the iconoclastic Coleman had worked with in thirty-five years, and her appearances provided still further evidence of her remarkable stylistic range. That same year she recorded *Twenty-one* with the bassist Ron Carter and the drummer TONY WILLIAMS, perhaps the most accomplished rhythm section in modern jazz. The recording again showcased her mastery of a broad range of the modern jazz piano vocabulary. In addition to several of her own compositions, it features the up-tempo "Lullaby of the Leaves," the gorgeous ballad "A Beautiful Love," and Monk's "Introspection."

In 1996 Allen appeared as MARY LOU WILLIAMS in Robert Altman's film *Kansas City*, and she was the first woman to win the Danish Jazzpar Prize. Under the auspices of this award she recorded a 1996 session, *Some Aspects of Water*, consisting of several trio pieces and larger selections accompanied by a Danish nonet, most notably the nineteen-minute title piece. Her 1997 session *Eyes in the Back of Your Head* is a mixture of solo pieces and duets with Roney or Coleman. *The Gathering* (1998) is a collection of atmospheric originals showcasing Allen's highly individual playing—a melodic, lightly percussive bridge between a fleet-fingered bop style and the more abrasive percussive approach of the avant-garde; it is a masterpiece of relaxed phrasing and intense feeling.

At the peak of her powers Allen suddenly found herself without a recording contract until the fall of 2004, when Telarc Records released *The Life of a Song*, a trio with the bassist Dave Holland and the drummer DeJohnette. The recording covers a wide stylistic range, from the slightly dissonant "LWB's House (The Remix)," a musical portrait of her family, to "In Appreciation: A Celebration Song," which has flavors of gospel and Motown and is dedicated to ROSA PARKS. "The Experimental Movement" is a tribute to the dancer and choreographer Jacquelyn Hillsman, and "Black Bottom" pays homage to Paradise Valley, the black neighborhood that was the center of Detroit's jazz community during Allen's formative years. Allen's imaginative rearrangements of BILLY STRAYHORN's "Lush Life" and of BUD POWELL's "Dance of the Infidels" are exclamation points to one of the great albums of the new millennium.

Allen has received broad recognition from her peers as a composer, soloist, and educator. In the early 1990s she taught at the New England Conservatory, and in 1995 she became a faculty member at Howard University. She received many awards and honors, including the EUBIE BLAKE Award from Cultural Crossroads. Allen's playing clearly reflects the boppish influences of Bud Powell and the quirky rhythms and phrasing of Thelonious Monk, and even a bit of CECIL PERCIVAL TAYLOR, but she also embraces the lyricism of HERBIE HANCOCK and Bill Evans, the conceptual freedom of Ornette Coleman, and even the more populist experiments of the M-Base Collective. She worked as an arranger for the singer Andy Bey on his album *American Song* (2003) and wrote and arranged material for the vocalist Mary Stallings. With BERNICE JOHNSON REAGON and Toshi Reagon she scored the HBO movie *Beah: A Black Woman Speaks*, a documentary of the life of the actress and civil rights activist Beah Richards. In "Time Line," Allen employs electric keyboards, synthesizers, and other electronic devices other electronic devices to explore the historical continuity of African music. Finally, the "Mary Lou Williams Project" is a trio effort with the drummer BILLY HART and the bassist Buster Williams. The group performed Williams's *Zodiac Suite* at Jazz at Lincoln Center in 2004 and performed excerpts from the suite at the Kennedy Center for the Mary Lou Williams Women in Jazz Festival. The suite was recorded and released on Mary Records in 2006. That same year Allen released a trio album with Ron Carter on bass and Jimmy Cobb on drums, along with the Atlanta Jazz Chorus, titled *Timeless Portraits and Dreams*, structured around a series of musical portraits of African American figures such as MARTIN LUTHER KING JR. and BILLIE HOLIDAY. In 2004 Allen was appointed director of jazz combos at the University of Michigan's department of jazz and contemporary improvisation.

Further Reading

Gourse, Leslie. *Madame Jazz: Contemporary Women Instrumentalists* (1995).

Holley, Eugene, Jr. "Geri Allen: Full Circle," *JazzTimes* (Jan. 1995).

Murph, John. "Mothership Connection," *JazzTimes* (Sept. 2004).

Palmer, D. "Geri Allen: Real Life Music Comes to Town," *Down Beat* 4, 6 (1988).

RONALD P. DUFOUR

ALLEN, James Latimer (7 Feb. 1907–1977), photographer, was born in New York City to Virginia Allen, a dressmaker who migrated from the British Virgin Islands in 1900, and an unidentified father. James attended Dewitt Clinton High School, where he discovered photography through the school's camera club, the Amateur Cinema League. The school was fertile ground for several members of the upcoming Harlem Renaissance, including the poet COUNTEE CULLEN, whose first published piece appeared in the school magazine, the *Magpie*. The artist CHARLES ALSTON also developed his talents as the art editor for the *Magpie* and leader of the art club. In 1923 Allen began a four-year apprenticeship at Stone, Van Dresser and Company, a white-owned illustration firm, where he received additional instruction in photography. Louis Collins Stone, the firm's owner and a portrait painter, and his wife seem to have taken a personal interest in Allen and in nurturing black talent. The writer and artist Richard Bruce Nugent also spent part of his adolescence in New York City, attended Dewitt Clinton, and was employed by this firm.

Following graduation from high school in 1925 Allen embarked on a career as an artist-photographer. With the support of patrons like ALAIN LEROY LOCKE and Carl Van Vechten, Allen opened a portrait studio at 213 West 121st Street in 1927 and quickly became the photographer of choice for the luminaries of the Harlem Renaissance. With subjects including Alston, Cullen, AARON DOUGLAS, W. E. B. DU BOIS, LANGSTON HUGHES, NELLA LARSEN, Locke, HAROLD JACKMAN, CHARLES SPURGEON JOHNSON, HALL JOHNSON, JAMES WELDON JOHNSON, JACOB LAWRENCE, NORMAN LEWIS, ROSE MCCLENDON, CLAUDE MCKAY, LOUISE THOMPSON PATTERSON, PAUL ROBESON, JOEL AUGUSTUS ROGERS, ARTHUR ALFONSO SCHOMBURG, EDNA LEWIS THOMAS, Van Vechten, and A'LELIA WALKER, Allen's roster of clients makes up the most comprehensive visual record of Harlem's cultural elite by an African American photographer. Carl Van Vechten, who was white, began his extensive body of photographs in 1932.

Allen created a visual image of the New Negro—the modern, urban, sophisticated, well-educated African American who exemplified the best that the race had to offer and refuted the claims of black inferiority that sustained white supremacist beliefs and Jim Crow policy. In his images well-groomed, well-dressed African American men and women posed in front of a simple gray backdrop are elegantly displayed as testaments to African American talent and achievement. Inscriptions on many of the photographic prints indicate that these portraits not only were meant for private display but also were exchanged between members of Harlem's social circles. The photographs seemed to have functioned as mutually reaffirming talismans of shared ideals and purpose in a world hostile to African American equality. This compelling vision was also deployed to promote the New Negro ideal among a national audience. Allen's portraits and his commercial images were consistently published in the leading Negro periodicals of the day, such as the *Crisis*, *Opportunity*, and the *Messenger*. *Opportunity*, the magazine of the National Urban League, featured Allen's photographs on their cover sixteen times between 1934 and 1942. His images provided a model of the New Negro that black leaders encouraged all African Americans to emulate.

Allen also enjoyed considerable recognition as a fine artist. He was one of four photographers who competed for the William E. Harmon Foundation Awards for Distinguished Achievement among Negroes established in 1926. The annual exhibition (1927–1931, 1933, and 1935) of submissions in the fine arts category was the chief venue open to African American artists. In 1930 Allen was awarded the Commission on Race Relations Prize for Photographic Work from the Harmon Foundation. This was a special award established that year specifically to honor photography. Allen won this prize again in 1931 and 1933. He was the only photographer included in the film *A Study of Negro Artists* produced by the foundation in 1934. Allen was featured in other key exhibitions, including the Exhibition of

Young Negro Artists in 1927, An Exhibition of Negro Art in 1935 at the Harlem YMCA, and the Exhibition of Fine Arts Productions by American Negroes, Hall of Negro Life, Texas Centennial in 1936 in Dallas. In 1930 he received a solo show, An Exhibition of Portraits by James L. Allen (A Group of New Portraits) at the Hobby Horse, a Harlem bookstore and café located at 113 West 136th Street.

With the onset of the Great Depression, Allen supplemented his income by taking photographs for the Harmon Foundation and the Harlem Art Workshop, thus producing an important archive of artworks and portraits of artists at work in their studios. He was employed as an instructor at the WPA-funded Harlem Community Art Center founded by the sculptor AUGUSTA SAVAGE in 1937. His documentation of activities there allowed Allen to work exclusively as a photographer and to maintain a studio, which he relocated to 2138 Seventh Avenue and then to 1858 Seventh Avenue until 1944.

Allen appears to have enlisted in World War II and was assigned to the Office of Strategic Services in Washington, D.C., where because of his prior experience he was tasked with processing film taken for intelligence purposes. Allen married around this time and never resumed his career as a photographer. He remained in Washington, working as a civil servant. When he died his personal archive was destroyed by his wife, who did not approve of his early profession. Surviving photographs by Allen can be found in the Moorland-Spingarn Research Center at Howard University, the Beinecke Rare Book and Manuscript Library at Yale University, the Schomburg Center for Research in Black Culture in New York, and the Harmon Foundation Collection at the National Archives and the Library of Congress. Allen, along with other photographers of his generation, reinvented the iconography of blackness and established a modern black aesthetic that symbolized the racial pride that African Americans felt during the interwar period.

Further Reading

Holloway, Camara Dia. *Portraiture and the Harlem Renaissance: The Photographs of James L. Allen* (1999).
Willis, Deborah. *Reflections in Black: A History of Black Photographers 1840 to the Present* (2000).
Wright, Beryl, and Gary Reynolds. *Against the Odds: African-American Artists and the Harmon Foundation* (1989).

CAMARA DIA HOLLOWAY

ALLEN, Macon Bolling (1816–15 Oct. 1894), lawyer and judge, was born A. Macon Bolling in Indiana; the names of his parents and the exact date of his birth are unknown. He changed his name to Macon Bolling Allen by an act of the Massachusetts legislature on 26 January 1844. Details of Allen's early life and education are sparse and contradictory. His birth name is given in some sources as Malcolm B. Allen, and his birthplace as South Carolina. Evidence suggests that he lived in Maine and Massachusetts as a young man. Maine denied his initial application to the Maine bar because of allegations that he was not a state citizen, but he purportedly ran a Portland business before 1844. It is known that he read law in the Maine offices of two white abolitionist lawyers, Samuel E. Sewell and General Samuel Fessenden, and that Fessenden promoted his admission to the Maine bar in 1844.

Allen became a member of the Maine bar later in 1844 after passing the law examination required of all nonresidents. He thus became the first African American licensed to practice law in the United States. When he was admitted to the Massachusetts bar in 1845, a Boston abolitionist newspaper, the *Liberator*, stated on 9 May 1845 that Allen had received a classical education and that he was a brilliant and energetic young man of exceptional character and deportment. Allen never practiced law in Maine, possibly because of its small African American population (only 1,335 in 1844); instead, after being admitted to the bar, he immediately moved (or perhaps returned) to Massachusetts.

Allen began practicing law in Massachusetts after his admission to the Suffolk County bar on 3 May 1845, making him the first African American admitted to that state's bar as well. He apparently experienced some difficulty in obtaining clients during the first year of his practice. In November 1845 Allen wrote the New Yorker John Jay Jr. (the chief justice's grandson) that New Englanders supported only famous, wealthy, or long-established attorneys; he wondered whether New York's lack of such a tradition and its large African American population offered better opportunities for a black lawyer. Undoubtedly some of Allen's difficulty stemmed from Boston abolitionists' public denunciation of Allen's refusal to support their petition pledging nonsupport for the government during the Mexican War. A bitter 1846 letter from Allen to the radical abolitionist William Lloyd Garrison explained both his strong sympathy with enslaved African Americans and his private and independent approach to the problem.

Allen's fortunes soon changed. He was appointed a justice of the peace by Massachusetts's Whig governors in 1847 and 1854; the first appointment made him the nation's first appointed African American judicial official. He remained in Charlestown, near Boston, where he practiced law and served as justice of the peace until after the Civil War.

In the late 1860s Allen joined a small cadre of northern African American lawyers and activists who migrated to the South—in Allen's case, to Charleston, South Carolina. There, in 1868, he joined ROBERT BROWN ELLIOT and WILLIAM J. WHIPPER, two African American lawyer-politicians, to form a law firm that attracted clients of both races. With offices at 91 Broad Street in Charleston, Whipper, Elliot, and Allen was the first known African American law firm in the United States. The firm's combination of legal talents and political influence enabled it to hire and train many other African American lawyers. Allen never gained high political office, as his law partners did—both were elected to the South Carolina legislature, and Elliot to the U.S. Congress in 1870 and 1872—though he ran for secretary of state as a Republican in 1872 and for the same position on MARTIN DELANEY's 1874 fusion ticket. In February 1873 the South Carolina legislature elected him a judge of the Inferior Court, to fill a vacancy left by George Lee, with whom Allen had competed for the original appointment. Allen was elected to probate court in 1876 and served with distinction through 1878.

Allen returned to law practice in Charleston, and little is known of his life after that. He died in Washington, D.C., leaving a widow (whose name is unknown) and a son, Arthur W. Macon.

Allen left a legacy as a pioneer in African American legal history that transcended time, space, and, to a large extent, racism—and which placed him in the forefront of the black struggle. His accomplishments in New England and South Carolina paved the way for the generations of black lawyers and activists who followed.

Further Reading
Carter, George E., and C. Peter Ripley, eds. *Black Abolitionist Papers, 1830–1865* (1981).
Finkelman, Paul. "Not Only the Judge's Robes Were Black: African-American Lawyers as Social Engineers during and after Slavery," *Stanford Law Review* 47 (1994): 161–209.
Smith, J. Clay. *Emancipation: The Making of the Black Lawyer, 1844–1944* (1993).
Obituaries: Charleston *Daily News and Courier*, 17 Oct. 1894.

JOHNIE D. SMITH

ALLEN, Red (7 Jan. 1908–17 Apr. 1967), trumpeter, was born Henry James Allen Jr. in Algiers, Louisiana, the son of Henry James Allen Sr., a trumpeter and leader of a brass band, and Juretta (maiden name unknown). Red Allen received instruction from his father and his two uncles, who were also trumpeters. Rehearsals were held at home, giving Allen the opportunity to hear New Orleans greats like LOUIS ARMSTRONG, BUDDY BOLDEN, OSCAR CELESTIN, BUNK JOHNSON, KING OLIVER, SAM MORGAN, and Kid Rena. Though surrounded by trumpet players, Allen played the violin and the alto horn before he settled on the trumpet. Soon after his tenth birthday he felt secure enough on the trumpet to become a member of his father's brass band. Allen learned to improvise by playing along with recordings. He varied the speed to change the pitch, thereby developing keen pitch perception.

In addition to playing with his father's band, Allen played riverboat gigs and freelanced until his nineteenth birthday in 1927, when he accompanied King Oliver's band to New York for an engagement at the Savoy Ballroom and for recordings for RCA Victor (*King Oliver, Vols. 1 & 2*). Allen returned to New Orleans for a stint with FATE MARABLE's riverboat

bands (1928–1929), returning to New York again in July 1929 to record *It Should Be You/Biffly Blues* (Victor 38073) and to work as sideman with Louis Armstrong on *I Ain't Got Nobody* (Okeh 8756). Allen worked in 1930 as sideman with JELLY ROLL MORTON on *Jelly Roll Morton and His Red Hot Peppers, 1927–1930, Vol. 1* for RCA Victor, and he recorded as leader on *Sugar Hill Function* (Victor 38140).

Other early recordings as lead trumpet, on such tunes as "It Should Be You," "Feeling Drowsy," "Dancing Dave," "Doctor Blues," and "Louisiana Swing," were made with members of the LUIS RUSSELL band from 1929 to 1932, which at the time included Albert Nichols, Charlie Holmes, J. C. HIGGINBOTHAM, and blues vocalist VICTORIA SPIVEY. Allen's work can be heard on *Luis Russell & His Louisiana Swing Orchestra* (1930, Columbia), *The Luis Russell Story* (1929, Parlophone), and *Song of the Swanee* (1930, Okeh 8780).

Allen's early improvisational style was characterized by sudden, odd turns of phrase, asymmetrical rhythmic construction, mixing of double-time flurries, long-held notes, contrasting dynamics, alternate fingerings of a single note, and a love of fast octave jumps (Schuller, 618–619). Although his style was heavily influenced by Louis Armstrong's, Allen's idiosyncratic rhythmic flexibility, glissandi, smears, tonguing, emotional conveyance, and technical fluency were unparalleled. Like Armstrong he challenged two- and four-bar phrasing, thinking more of playing through the changes. Several recordings made with Luis Russell—including "Saratoga Shout," "Doctor Blues," "Jersey Lightning," and "Song of the Swanee" on *The Luis Russell Story*, and "It Should Be You" and "Feeling Drowsy" on *Henry "Red" Allen, Vol. 1*—showcase Allen's style.

Allen's brilliance continued with his tenure in FLETCHER HENDERSON's band from 1932 to 1934 on tunes such as "Wrappin' It Up" and "Rug Cutter's Stomp" on *Fletcher Henderson* (1934), "Queer Notions" and "King Porter Stomp" on *The Fletcher Story, Vol. 4* (1933, Columbia), and *Wrappin' It Up* (1934, Decca 157). In 1935 Allen recorded *Ride, Red, Ride* (Columbia 30870) with the Mills Blue Rhythm Band, with whom he played from 1934 to 1937, and *Body and Soul* (Vocalion 38080). In 1937 he returned to Luis Russell's band, which was then accompanying Louis Armstrong, and found himself playing second to ROY ELDRIDGE. Eldridge had replaced Allen in Fletcher Henderson's band as well.

Allen left Russell's band in 1940 and went on to perform and record with musicians such as SIDNEY BECHET (*Egyptian Fantasy*, 1941, Victor 27337), Spike Hughes (*Spike Hughes and His All American Orchestra*, London Records), COLEMAN HAWKINS (1930–1941, CBS records), BILLIE HOLIDAY (*Billie Holiday: The Golden Years, Vol. 2*, Columbia), BUSTER BAILEY, Higginbotham, JAMES P. JOHNSON, KID ORY, and LIONEL HAMPTON. Allen also served as leader on *Get the Mop* (1946, Victor 201808). Other releases of the 1940s and 1950s include the compilation *Henry*

"Red" Allen, Vols. 1–4. Gunther Schuller further states, "Allen's stints with Coleman Hawkins in 1957 and Kid Ory in 1959, provided evidence of his growth as a trumpet soloist. Specifically, on 'I Cover the Waterfront' and 'I Got Rhythm,' one can hear creative and contrasting ideas and a rich and singing tone" (Schuller, 630). Allen himself described his experience of playing: it is "as if somebody [is] making your lip speak, making it say things he thinks" (Balliett, 13). In addition to his recordings, Allen appeared in three important TV jazz specials toward the end of his life: "Chicago and All That Jazz," "The Sound of Jazz," and "Profile of the Art." His career ended with the recording of two celebrated albums, *The Henry Allen Memorial Album/Mr. Allen—Henry Red Allen* and *Feeling Good.* He died of cancer in New York City.

Like many trumpeters of his time, Allen was influenced by Louis Armstrong. Unlike most of his peers, however, he developed a personal repertoire of performance concepts and effects that freed him from the musical constraints of the styles of both New Orleans and swing. That repertoire included a smooth legato articulation, a rhythm that was not tied to the fixed pulse, a wide range of dynamics, and a host of glissandi, growls, lip trills, rips, smears, and spattered notes. Allen thereby presaged the later avant-garde or free jazz movement, which extensively featured the performance techniques that Allen pioneered. His ability to transcend his immediate musical environment, as well as his originality and innovativeness on his chosen instrument, raised Allen to the stature of one of the best jazz performers of his era.

Further Reading
Balliett, Whitney. *Improvising* (1977).
Chilton, John. *Ride, Red, Ride: The Life of Henry "Red" Allen* (1999).
Evensmo, Jan. *The Trumpet and Vocal of Henry Red Allen, 1927–1942* (1977).
Hester, M. L. "Henry 'Red' Allen," *The Mississippi Rag* 12, no. 1 (1984).
Schuller, Gunther. *The Swing Era: The Development of Jazz, 1930–1945* (1989).
EDDIE S. MEADOWS

ALLEN, Richard (10 June 1830–16 May 1909), politician, was born a slave in Richmond, Virginia. His parents' names are not known. In 1837 Allen was taken to Harris County in Texas and was owned by J. J. Cain until the end of the Civil War in 1865. Allen married soon after the notification of his emancipation. He and his wife Nancy went on to have one son and four daughters. As a slave Allen was known to be a skilled carpenter; he is credited with designing and building a Houston mansion occupied by Mayor Joseph R. Morris. In 1867 Allen entered the political world as a federal voter registrar, and in 1868 he served as an agent for the Freedmen's Bureau and as a supervisor of voter registration for the Fourteenth District of Texas. Although he had not received a formal education, he was literate by 1870.

After attending several Republican Party meetings and, in 1869, being elected to the Texas legislature, Richard Allen evolved into one of the first and most engaged African American legislators. As a legislator Allen focused on the issues of education, law enforcement, and civil rights. In 1870 he unsuccessfully sought the Republican nomination for U.S. Congress. In 1873 he was reelected to the legislature, but the house instead seated his Democratic challenger, who had contested the election. In 1878 the Republican Party nominated Allen for lieutenant governor, making him the first African American to seek statewide office in Texas.

From 1881 to 1882 Allen served as quartermaster for the black regiment of the Texas militia, and from 1882 to 1885 he was storekeeper and then inspector and deputy collector of U.S. customs in Houston. As a political leader Allen took some unpopular positions, including his 1879 support for the Exoduster Movement, which encouraged African Americans to leave Texas and other Southern states for Kansas.

From 1872 to 1879 Allen served as a delegate to the National Colored Men's Convention. He served as a vice president in 1873 and as a chairman in 1879 of the African American state conventions that addressed concerns about civil rights, education, and economics. By 1883 African American politicians had consolidated their Republican power base; African Americans made up ninety percent of the party's membership. Allen became one of four delegates to attend the Republican National Convention in 1884.

Allen's achievements were not just political. In 1875 he presided over a Prince Hall Masonic lodge in Texas, and in 1877 he became the grand master for the state of Texas. He was also active in the labor movement, playing a key role in an 1890 labor dispute at the port of Houston. A civic leader, Allen spearheaded emancipation celebrations and served at Antioch Baptist Church as the superintendent of the Sunday school. He also served on the board of directors at Gregory Institute, Houston's first African American secondary school. Allen died in Houston and was buried in the city cemetery.

Further Reading
Barr, Alwyn. *Black Texans: A History of African Americans in Texas, 1528–1995* (1973).
Rice, Lawrence D. *The Negro in Texas 1874–1900* (1971).
Smallwood, James M. *Time of Hope, Time of Despair: Black Texans during Reconstruction* (1981).
WANDA F. FERNANDOPULLE

ALLEN, Richard (14 Feb. 1760–26 Mar. 1831), American Methodist preacher and founder of the African Methodist Episcopal church, was born into slavery to parents who were the property of Benjamin Chew of Philadelphia. He and his parents and three additional children were sold in 1777 to Stokely Sturgis, who lived near Dover, Delaware. There he at-

Richard Allen shown in a lithograph by Peter S. Duval, c. 1840. Allen was not only a religious leader but also a prominent secular leader and social activist in the northern free black community. (National Portrait Gallery, Smithsonian Institution/Art Resource, N.Y.)

tended Methodist preaching events and experienced a spiritual awakening. Allen, his older brother, and a sister were retained by Sturgis, but his parents and younger siblings were sold. Through the ministry of Freeborn Garretson, a Methodist itinerant preacher, Sturgis was converted to Methodism and became convinced that slavery was wrong. Subsequently, Allen and his brother were permitted to work to purchase their freedom, which they did in 1780.

For the next six years Allen worked as a wagon driver, woodcutter, and bricklayer while serving as a Methodist preacher to both blacks and whites in towns and rural areas in Maryland, Delaware, Pennsylvania, and New Jersey. By attending Methodist instructional meetings between 1777 and 1780, Allen became an exhorter and then a licentiate as early as 1780. After the American War of Independence, he traveled extensively in Delaware, Maryland, New Jersey, and Pennsylvania. In December 1784 he and HARRY HOSIER were the only two black preachers to attend the Christmas Conference in Baltimore, where the Methodist Episcopal Church was organized. He probably saw the Methodist leaders Thomas Coke, Bishop Francis Asbury, Richard Whatcoat, and Thomas Vasey at the conference. During 1785 he traveled the Baltimore circuit with Whatcoat.

At one point Asbury, the leader of American Methodism, invited Allen to become his traveling companion, an offer Allen accepted. In 1786 he preached to interracial groups of Methodists in Radnor, Pennsylvania, and at St. George's Church, Philadelphia. Assigned to preach at predawn meetings, Allen often preached four or five times a day and organized evening prayer groups. Unpaid by the church, he supported himself and later his family as a shoemaker. He married Flora (maiden name unknown) in 1791 and, after his first wife's death, was married a second time, in 1805, to Sarah (maiden name unknown). Allen and his second wife had six children.

In February 1786, while he was in Philadelphia, Allen organized a prayer-meeting society of forty-two members. His concern was to find and instruct "his African brethren," few of whom attended public worship. Noting the need for a place of worship for African Americans, he and his colleagues ABSALOM JONES, William White, and Dorus Ginnings found their efforts to meet this need opposed by the leadership of St. George's Church. In November 1787 black members of St. George's Church were pulled away from prayer and asked to leave, so Allen and Jones and their associates withdrew. Renting an unused store, Allen and Jones, with the help of Benjamin Rush and Robert Ralston, raised funds for a new building, which in 1794 became the St. Thomas African Episcopal Church of Philadelphia, the first independent black church in North America.

Allen, who remained a Methodist, purchased an abandoned blacksmith shop, moved it to Sixth Street near Lombard, and had it renovated. On 29 June 1794 Bishop Asbury dedicated the building as a church. For years Allen and his congregation thought the property, called Bethel Church, was theirs, only to be informed by successive elders at St. George's that Bethel Church was within their charge. In 1816, however, the Pennsylvania Supreme Court confirmed the independent existence of Bethel, and official contact between the two churches ceased.

Aware of friction between black and white Methodists in other places, Allen sent invitations to African churches to form an ecclesiastical organization. On 9 April 1816 sixty delegates from five black congregations met at Bethel Church and agreed to confederate. The result was the formation of the African Methodist Episcopal (AME) Church. Allen, who had been ordained deacon by Bishop Asbury in 1799, was ordained elder on 10 April 1816 and the next day was consecrated as bishop. The first *Discipline* was published in 1817, and the new organization's first General Conference was held in Philadelphia on 9 July 1820, with Bishop Allen presiding. For Allen, the Methodist emphasis on the simplicity of the Gospel, expressed through discipline and community, pointed the way to freedom from sin and physical slavery as well. His life and career, and the founding of Bethel Church, embodied this development and confirmed his role as a leader in the forefront of the black church movement.

Early in 1797 Allen, Jones, and JAMES FORTEN Sr. led black Philadelphians to petition the national government for the first time to revoke the Fugitive Slave Act of 1793 and to end slavery. In 1814, when it was feared that Philadelphia would be attacked by the British, Allen, Jones, and Forten raised the Black Legion of 2,500 men. Although Allen did not initially oppose voluntary emigration of blacks, as promoted by the American Colonization Society (formed in 1817), he came to see that large-scale emigration of free blacks would result in the abandonment of their brethren to slavery. In *Freedom's Journal* (2 Nov. 1827), Allen declared colonization a mistake. In 1830 he presided over the first meeting of the National Negro Convention Movement, which provided a structure for black abolitionism and organized the American Society of Free Persons of Color.

Allen led and participated in the formation of many organizations for the betterment of his people. The Free African Society established 12 April 1787 was the first black institution with the characteristics of a benevolent and reform organization. In 1795 a day school was operational in Bethel Church, and on 26 October 1796 the founding of a First Day school, or Sunday school, and a night school was reported. In 1804 Allen led in the creation of the Society for Free People of Color for Promoting the Instruction and School Education of Children of African Descent. From 1818 to 1820 he served as book steward of the Book Concern of the AME church. The creation of the Free Produce Society of Philadelphia, on 20 December 1830, was also his work. He chaired the first National Negro Convention from 20 to 24 September 1830, which was held at Bethel Church. In 1831 the address to the First Annual Convention of the People of Colour was signed by the Reverend Allen, in his role as president and senior bishop of the AME Church. In 1794 Allen and Jones had been cited by the mayor of Philadelphia for their services to the sick and dying during the yellow fever epidemic of 1793. Allen died in Philadelphia, but his contributions to religion, education, and culture live on in such institutions as the Allen Temple, Cincinnati, Ohio; Allen University, Columbia, South Carolina; and the Richard Allen Center for Culture and Art, opposite Lincoln Center, New York City.

Further Reading

Allen, Richard. *The Life, Experience and Gospel Labors of the Rt. Rev. Richard Allen* (1833, 1983).
George, Carol V. R. *Segregated Sabbaths: Richard Allen and the Emergence of Independent Black Churches 1760–1840* (1973).
Nash, Gary B. *Forging Freedom: The Formation of Philadelphia's Black Community, 1720–1840* (1988).
Raboteau, Albert J. "Richard Allen and the African Church Movement," in *Black Leaders of the Nineteenth Century* (1988).
Wesley, Charles H. *Richard Allen, Apostle of Freedom* (1935).

FREDERICK V. MILLS

ALLEN, Sarah (1764?–16 July 1849), churchwoman and reformer, and **Flora Allen** (?–11 March (1801), churchwoman and reformer, were, respectively, the second and first wives of RICHARD ALLEN, a bishop and founder of the African Methodist Episcopal (AME) Church. Although little is known of Flora Allen, she had probably met Richard Allen while attending Methodist class meetings and services at St. George's Methodist Church in Philadelphia. Known as a pious and respectable woman, Flora Allen helped her husband purchase a home at 150 Spruce Street in 1791 (as well as other properties, including those used by Allen's new church) and inaugurate the Bethel AME church in July 1794. White as well as black preachers celebrated her dedication to charity and hospitality. She died in Philadelphia after a long illness but is remembered as an early advocate of the independent black church. Sarah Allen was born Sarah Bass, a slave in Isle of Wight County, Virginia. She probably remained in bondage until the 1780s or 1790s, by which time she had moved to Pennsylvania. By the early 1790s, Sarah Bass's name appeared on the membership rolls of class meetings, the weekly preparation meetings required for those seeking membership in the Methodist Episcopal Church, nominally under the leadership of white preachers from St. George's Methodist Church in Philadelphia. Class lists also included Richard Allen and his first wife, Flora. Bass likely followed them out of the segregated white church and into Allen's fledgling AME organization. She also served an important role as a nurse and caregiver during Philadelphia's yellow fever epidemic, which claimed several thousand lives (including those of hundreds of African Americans) during the fall of 1793. The following year, when Richard Allen and ABSALOM JONES published their history of black involvement in yellow fever charity work, *A Narrative of the Proceedings of Black People During the Awful Calamity in Philadelphia*—which became the first copyrighted pamphlet by black writers in America—Sarah Bass's reform activities garnered special mention.

Bass married Richard Allen on 11 March 1801, after the death of his first wife. Bass had apparently been part of the AME congregation during the 1790s, although membership rolls are no longer extant. The couple had six children over the next two decades—Richard Jr., James, John, Peter, Sara, and Ann—and lived in Allen's home on Spruce Street (between present-day Fourth and Fifth streets). Sarah Allen also helped tend home at the Allen family's country property located in Delaware County, Pennsylvania, and purchased in 1808. Like Flora, Sarah became Richard's helpmeet, keeping a respectable home befitting her husband's stature as one of the leading black reformers of the age. She also cosigned property deeds with her husband, including a grant of property to the AME church. Finally, she was active in church and community benevolent activities, and helped found the Daughters of Conference, a group that aided black ministers attending AME conferences, and the Bethel Benevolent Society, a charitable organization that raised funds for AME families. Allen also supported women preachers, including JARENA LEE, who became the first black woman to preach at Bethel Church. According to Lee herself, Sarah Allen purchased the very first copy of Lee's autobiography, entitled *Religious Experience and Journal of Mrs. Jarena Lee*, in 1836.

In one sense, both Sarah Allen and Flora Allen represented the African American equivalent of the "Republican Mother." According to eighteenth-century theorists of American republicanism, women served a key role in the nation's moral life, inculcating the virtues of piety, sacrifice, and virtue in young men. Both of Richard Allen's wives were regarded as pillars of community and institution-building efforts among Northern free blacks, for they worked alongside their husbands to emphasize the significance of piety, moral uplift, and racial redemption. Nineteenth-century AME minister James Handy referred to Sarah Allen as a "matron"—someone who always sacrificed herself for the greater good of the black church and the free black community as a whole. Not until the era following the War of 1812 did a new generation of Bethel women, including Jarena Lee and Mary Still, chart new directions as public figures, seeking to become preachers, activists, and (later still) even ministers.

The great example of Sarah Allen's "matronly" self-sacrifice occurred before one of the AME churches' early conferences in Philadelphia. As ministers arrived at the Allens' house, Sarah expressed concern about their shabby appearance, with bare elbows showing through many of the men's garments. She quickly gathered together a sewing brigade of Bethel women, working all night to produce dignified clothing fit for leaders of the community. In another sense, Sarah Allen, like Flora Allen before her, represented the reality of most free black women's existence during the early national period. Unlike the idealized white Republican mother, free black women often worked both in and beyond the home to garner extra wages, particularly during the Bethel Church's earliest years. Indeed, although Richard Allen's many investment properties and personal savings later allowed Sarah Allen to live a comfortable existence as a free black woman, she still collected monies from Allen family rental properties following her husband's death. She was not, in other words, above working outside of the home. This image fit well with Bethel Church congregants, who before the 1830s comprised mostly day laborers and unskilled workers, with women as well as men helping their families survive the vicissitudes of life in northern cities. Jarena Lee was attracted to the AME church, she recalled, because of her acquaintance with a black female cook who spoke well of Richard Allen's church. For all of these reasons, subsequent generations of AME ministers, reformers and even bishops would hail Sarah Allen in particular as a founding mother of the black church. After Richard Allen died (26 Mar. 1831), she remained active in Bethel reform activities and aided fugitive slaves traveling through Philadelphia. After her own death, she was interred in the basement of Bethel Church with Richard Allen.

Further Reading

The Richard Allen Museum, Mother Bethel AME Church, Philadelphia has many exhibits and documents about the lives of Richard and Sarah Allen. An introduction is available online at: http://www.motherbethel.org/museum/.

Jones, Absalom, and Richard Allen. "A Narrative of the Proceedings of Black People During the Awful Calamity in Philadelphia," (1794), reprinted in Richard S. Newman et al. *Pamphlets of Protest* (2000).

Handy, James A. *Scraps of African Methodist Episcopal History* (1902).

Johnson, Charles Richard, and Patricia Smith, eds. *Africans in America* (1999)

Lee, Jarena. *Religious Experience and Journal of Mrs. Jarena Lee* (1836).

Newman, Richard S. *Black Founder: Richard Allen, African Americans and the Early Republic* (2008).

RICHARD S. NEWMAN

ALLEN, Thomas Cox (2 Apr. 1907–11 Sept. 1989), aviation mechanic and pilot, was born in Quitman, Wood County, Texas, the youngest of three children; both of his parents were teachers. Allen's father died when Thomas was three months old. His mother, Polly, continued to teach school and to run the family farm.

Allen became interested in flying in 1918, when an airplane made a forced landing in a pasture. The pilots paid the two young Allen brothers to guard the plane overnight so that its fabric and glue would not be eaten by cows. From this experience, Thomas Allen decided to become either an aviator or a mechanic.

In 1919, when Allen was twelve, the family moved to Oklahoma City, where his mother resumed teaching school. Allen often bicycled to a nearby airfield. In his teens, he persuaded the field owner to take a $100 saxophone as partial trade for flying lessons. He worked off the rest of the fee by helping the airplane mechanics. Eventually he earned enough to fly for five hours but could not afford the $500 bond needed to fly alone.

When Allen was seventeen, the ground crew dared him to fly solo while the instructor was away. The instructor saw the plane in the air and returned to the field in a rage as Allen landed. However, he was persuaded that the feat would be good advertising, in the racist belief that if he could teach a "Negro boy" to fly, he could teach anyone.

Soon after he had soloed, Allen hitchhiked to San Antonio, hoping to become an army aviator. He soon was made aware of the military's ban against African Americans. Instead, he became a mechanic's assistant at San Antonio's Stinson Field and subsequently held various jobs related to aviation mechanics in Texas and Kansas. By 1927 he had returned to Oklahoma

City, where he joined Tulsa-Oklahoma Airline, later known as Braniff.

In the spring of 1929 Allen met several of the organizers of the BESSIE COLEMAN Aero Club, founded in memory of the first black woman aviator, who had died in 1926. He moved to the Los Angeles area to join the group as a mechanic. Later that year he married Celine Smith; the couple had two sons.

In the late 1920s and early 1930s many pilots sought financial backing for transcontinental flights. White pilots found it easier to receive corporate backing than did African Americans, although there was a rumor of a $1,000 prize for the first black pilots to fly cross-country. With unemployment high during the Great Depression, Allen worked at whatever aviation job he could find. Over time he gained a reputation as a gifted mechanic, although his relations with the Aero Club's founder William J. Powell and other club members were often stormy.

Late in the summer of 1932, Allen was approached by JAMES HERMAN BANNING, the lead pilot for the Bessie Coleman Aero Club and the first black pilot to receive an American aviation license. Banning had access to a World War I surplus Eagle Rock aircraft with a fourteen-year-old engine, owned by Sam Moore and Arthur Dennis. He planned a transcontinental attempt, but he needed a mechanic and an additional investment of about $125 for fuel. Allen provided both the investment and the expertise.

With barely $100 left, Banning and Allen left Los Angeles on 18 September 1932. The team became known as the "Flying Hoboes." They planned to "hobo," begging for their meals and beds, which they hoped would raise enough money at each stop to continue across the country. Those who assisted them were asked to sign the "Gold Book" on the airplane's lower left-wing tip. They crossed the Rockies by a southern route over Arizona, New Mexico, and Texas. In Tulsa, Oklahoma, the oil company owner William Skully arranged credit for fuel from Tulsa to St. Louis. In St. Louis, trade school students provided needed repairs. In Pittsburgh the team agreed to drop fifteen thousand flyers for Franklin Delano Roosevelt's presidential campaign en route to New York. The Democratic Party financed that segment of the flight and rebuilt the plane in New York.

The Flying Hoboes landed in Valley Stream, Long Island, on 9 October 1932. Their flight time over three weeks totaled forty-one hours and twenty-seven minutes. They were feted by the New York mayor Jimmie Walker and in Harlem, but they were unable to locate the putative donor of the thousand-dollar prize.

On 10 November 1932 Allen and Banning started west. However, the plane was severely damaged when they were forced to land in a snowstorm not far from Pittsburgh. The *Pittsburgh Courier* financed their trip to Los Angeles by bus. They were unable to raise funds to retrieve the airplane before it was sold for scrap, with the "Gold Book" signatures eventually painted over. Banning and Allen dissolved their partnership in January 1933. Banning was killed in an airshow crash in February of that year.

Allen remained in Alhambra, California, and continued to work in the aviation industry. In the fall of 1939 he incorporated the Thomas C. Allen Aviation School in Los Angeles. According to a press release, the school planned to provide instruction in aviation mechanics "based on democratic principles" and was to accept students regardless of "race, creed or color." The emphasis was to be on safety and on training African Americans to join the aviation industry. It is likely that the outbreak of World War II subsumed the resources of the proposed school. During World War II, Allen ferried bombers for Douglas Aircraft. In 1949 Allen announced plans to become the first African American to make an around-the-world flight. Called the "People's Project," the flight was proposed without any corporate sponsorship and failed to raise sufficient backing.

Retiring from Douglas Aircraft in the 1960s, Allen moved back to Oklahoma City, where he was active as a volunteer with the Oklahoma Air and Space Museum in the 1980s. He died in Oklahoma City in 1989.

In 1992 Allen was inducted into the Oklahoma Aviation and Space Hall of Fame at the Kirkpatrick Science and Air Space Museum in Oklahoma City.

Further Reading
The Sam Moore Papers (1931–1936) at the Seaver Center, Natural History Museum of Los Angeles County, includes materials relating to the transcontinental flight.
Lynn, Jack. *The Hallelujah Flight* (1989).
Powell, William J. *Black Aviator: The Story of William J. Powell* (repr. 1994).
Obituary: *New York Times*, 13 Sept. 1989.

CAROLINE M. BROWN

ALLEN, William G. (c. 1820–?), abolitionist and educator, was born in Virginia, the son of a Welshman and a free mixed-race mother. After the death of both parents, a young Allen was adopted by a free African American family in Fortress Monroe, Virginia. Allen soon caught the eye of the Reverend William Hall, a New Yorker who conducted a black elementary school in Norfolk. Hall wrote Gerrit Smith, the well-known philanthropist and abolitionist from Madison County, New York, asking him to sponsor Allen's education. With Smith's support, Allen studied at the Oneida Institute, an interracial and abolitionist school in Whitesboro, New York, presided over by the abolitionist Beriah Green. In a letter written to Smith, Green mentioned Allen's good conduct, his accomplishments on the flute, and his service as clerk to Reuben Hough, the institute's superintendent and treasurer.

While attending the institute, Allen spent the summer of 1841 teaching in a school that Hiram Wilson, an Oneida Institute alumnus, had established among fugitive slaves in Upper Canada (Ontario). Allen supported the Liberty Party and the political abolitionists centered in upstate New York. Allen also participated in the black national convention movement, annual meetings organized by African Americans to discuss their common problems. Allen graduated from the Oneida Institute in 1844 and moved to Troy, New York, where he taught school and assisted HENRY HIGHLAND GARNET in editing the *National Watchman*, an abolitionist and temperance paper for African Americans. Three years later he moved to Boston, where he was employed as a law clerk by Ellis Gray Loring. While in Boston, Allen lectured on African American history, wrote *Wheatley, Banneker, and Horton* (1849), a collection of brief biographical sketches of PHILLIS WHEATLEY, BENJAMIN BANNEKER, and GEORGE MOSES HORTON, and served as secretary of the Boston Colored Citizens Association.

In 1850 Allen was appointed professor of Greek and of rhetoric and belles lettres at New York Central College in McGrawville, Cortland County. This interracial and coeducational institution, chartered in 1849 by the American Baptist Free Mission Society, was the only college in the country then employing African American faculty. In 1852 Allen became engaged to one of the white students, Mary King, the daughter of a former trustee. The engagement incensed the residents of Fulton, New York, King's hometown, and the couple, fearing mob violence, went to New York City, where they were secretly married in 1853.

Because of the racial antagonisms that their marriage had sparked, Allen resigned from the faculty of New York Central College, and he and his wife traveled to England in the spring of 1853. Allen attempted to earn a living in England by writing and lecturing on various literary and philosophical subjects. In 1854 Lady Byron engaged him to speak on behalf of penal reform. Allen also advocated moral reformatory schools and lectured against American slavery and prejudice. In 1853 his account of the problems caused by his marriage appeared under the title, *The American Prejudice Against Color: An Authentic Narrative, Showing How Easily the Nation Got into an Uproar*. Because of the warm reception he had received on a speaking trip to Ireland, Allen brought his family to Dublin in 1856; three of his seven children were born there. He published *A Short Personal Narrative* there in 1860.

The same year, Allen moved his family back to London, where he continued to lecture on Africa, educational reform, and abolitionism. In 1863 he became principal of the Caledonian Training School in Islington, established by the British abolitionist and philanthropist Harper Twelvetrees to meet the educational needs of the poor. The school closed after five years. Allen found it difficult to support his large family and appealed to friends of the abolitionist cause, such as Gerrit Smith, for assistance. The struggle to survive compounded the bitterness that he felt toward the American prejudice exhibited at the time of his marriage. About 1878 the Allens were living in a boardinghouse in Notting Hill, dependent on the charity of friends. Little is known of the circumstances of Allen's last years or of his death.

William G. Allen belongs to that cohort of nineteenth-century African Americans who, although free of slavery's yoke, encountered many obstacles in the North. Allen used the vehicle of education, first as a student and later as an instructor, to fight against racial restrictions in the United States. After moving to England, he continued to attack American slavery and racism, and his personal life was beset by many difficulties. Though he never achieved the public notoriety of FREDERICK DOUGLASS, nor was as actively involved in the American abolitionist movement as some other African Americans of his time, Allen's most notable contribution lay in his efforts to expose the connections between the institution of slavery and American prejudice.

Further Reading

Letters from Allen to Gerrit Smith are in the Gerrit Smith papers, George Arents Research Library, Syracuse University.
Blackett, R. J. M. "William G. Allen: The Forgotten Professor," *Civil War History* 26 (Mar. 1980).
Ripley, C. Peter, ed. *The Black Abolitionist Papers*, vol. 1 (1985).

MILTON C. SERNETT

ALLEN-NOBLE, Rosie (22 June 1938–), professor and educational administrator, was born Rosie Elizabeth Allen in Americus, Georgia, to Ulysses Grant Allen and Velma Douglas Allen. After completing a BS in Biology at Albany State College in Georgia, Allen-Noble taught in three Georgia high schools: the Vienna High and Industrial School (1960–1961), West Point High School (1962–1963), and Carver High School in Columbus (1963–1964). She also served as chairperson of the biology department at Columbia High School in Decatur, Georgia, from 1965 to 1970. Allen-Noble and Daniel Bernard Noble married in April 1964 and divorced in April 1968. They have one child, Antoinette Celine Noble-Webb.

While working on a master's degree in zoology at Atlanta University, Allen-Noble taught courses in biology, anatomy, and physiology at Spelman College, also in Atlanta (1965–1966). She completed the MS in 1967. From 1970 to 1976 she was an instructor of general biology and general physiology at Rutgers University in New Jersey, and from 1972 to 1978 she stood as visiting assistant professor of anatomy and physiology at Seton Hall University in South Orange, New Jersey. Allen-Noble completed her second MS, in Physiology, at Rutgers in 1974. Allen-Noble taught medical embryology, genetics, and physiology at New Jersey's College of Medicine and Dentistry from 1972 to 1987, and as an assistant professor she taught anatomy, physiology, microtechniques, and microscopic anatomy (histology) from 1976 to 1980.

In addition to teaching, Allen-Noble served as director of several science programs. In 1976 she led the science enrichment program (USEP) at Upsala College in East Orange, New Jersey. From 1978 to 1980 she acted as coordinator of medical technology programs at Fairleigh Dickinson University in Madison, New Jersey. Beginning in 1978 Allen-Noble directed the health careers programs at Montclair State College in Upper Montclair, New Jersey. She received awards for outstanding service from both Fairleigh Dickinson and Montclair State in 1982, and again from Montclair State in 1984–1985 and 1987. Moreover, she served on the President's Commission on Affirmative Action from 1980 to 1987.

Allen-Noble increasingly focused her efforts in the field of education, earning a doctor of education degree in 1991 from Rutgers's Graduate Program in Science Education. After completing this degree Allen-Noble joined the faculty at the Medical College of Georgia (MCG), where she taught in the Department of Cellular Biology and Anatomy and served as associate dean for Special Academic Programs. She continues to work with the school's educational outreach programs, in an effort to attract underrepresented minority and disadvantaged students to careers in the health and medical sciences and to ensure their success in undergraduate programs and on their medical school applications.

Beginning in 1996 Allen-Noble worked with the Health Professions Partnership Initiative, which teams MCG with nearby high schools, colleges, and universities that are generally attended by minority students. The program aims to strengthen students' science education and create a pipeline of well-qualified students to feed into medical schools and the health professions, as well as provide professional development resources for faculty members. The program has increased in size and has been successful in creating and sustaining educational diversity. It is particularly relevant in the wake of the Supreme Court's 1996 *Hopwood* decision, which declared affirmative action policies unlawful, and after which the MCG revoked scholarships specifically for minorities.

Further Reading
"Fewer Minorities Entering Medical Schools," *Shawnee News-Star*, 2 Nov. 1997.
Fincher, Ruth-Marie E., Wilma Sykes-Brown, and Rosie Allen-Noble. "Health Science Learning Academy: A Successful 'Pipeline' Educational Program for High School Students," *Academic Medicine* 77 (July 2002): 737–738.

GINNY CROSTHWAIT

ALLENSWORTH, Allen (7 Apr. 1842–14 Sept. 1914), soldier, minister, and social activist, was born in Louisville, Kentucky, the youngest of the six children of Levi Allensworth and Phyllis (maiden name unknown), slaves of the Starbird family. The Starbirds were respected members of the community and were partners in Wilson, Starbird, and Smith, a wholesale drug company based in Louisville. Levi died when Allen was an infant. Phyllis's other five children either had been sold down the Mississippi River or had escaped to Canada. Phyllis hoped that Allen could "even if partly educated, win his freedom" (Alexander, 9). Believing that God would play a role in his redemption as well, Phyllis named Allen after RICHARD ALLEN, the founder and first bishop of the African Methodist Episcopal (AME) Church. In Allen Allensworth's early years he was given to Thomas Starbird, Mrs. Starbird's son, as a companion.

When Thomas was sent to school, Allensworth's mother saw an opportunity for her son to become educated, even though it was a crime for a slave to do so. She instructed him to get "your 'Marse' Tom to play school with you every day he comes home; then you can learn to read and write like him" (Alexander, 8). Allensworth convinced Tom to do this, and the boys turned Tom's nursery into a classroom. Tom diligently relayed his school lessons to Allensworth every day. When this practice was revealed to Starbird, another home was found for Allensworth: he was put in the custody of Mr. and Mrs. Talbot, Quakers. This change was fortuitous for Allensworth, who was sent to the Sunday afternoon slave school at the St. Paul Protestant Episcopal Church, where slaves were taught the Ten Commandments, the Lord's Prayer, and to obey their masters. Furthermore, Mrs. Talbot also instructed him in spelling and reading. When Mrs. Starbird discovered that the boy was being taught to read, he was sold to John J. Smith, the owner of a large plantation in Henderson County, Kentucky. After saying goodbye to his mother, Allensworth left Louisville in the spring of 1854 aboard the steamer *Rainbow*. Before boarding the steamer he managed to purchase a copy of Noah Webster's blueback spelling book, a book second in popularity only to the Bible among slaves who could get either.

A short time after arriving Allensworth was discovered studying his book by Smith's wife and was punished. He also became friends with Eddie, a young orphan white boy. Ironically, Eddie was routinely punished for not completing his lessons. The two quickly formed an alliance and studied together whenever circumstances allowed.

Allensworth was not caught studying again; however, he was not able to avoid trouble altogether. When the Smiths left to visit their brother in Louisville, an overseer beat him severely. This inspired Allensworth to escape to Canada. Allensworth, thirteen years old, made it only a few miles away from the Smith farm before being caught. When the Smiths returned, Allensworth was sold downriver to New Orleans, where he was offered for sale at the auction house of Poindexter & Little with more than a thousand other slaves. In New Orleans, Allensworth was bought by Fred Scruggs, a horse racer. He became a jockey and returned to Louisville, Kentucky, where he remained the property of Scruggs until 1861, when the Civil War erupted.

In spring 1861 Scruggs made a business trip to Mobile, Alabama. He was unable to return because of the war, and Allensworth was shuffled between several masters over the next year. When the Confederate general Braxton Bragg's advance reached Louisville, Allensworth was invited to become a member of the hospital corps of the Forty-fourth Illinois and became a freeman. Soon after this, General William S. Rosecrans's Union forces moved on Bragg's position and forced a retreat. Nurse Allensworth reported for duty in Nashville, Tennessee, under Dr. Gordon of Georgetown, Ohio. On Dr. Gordon's advice, Allensworth enlisted in the navy in April 1863.

Immediately after reporting for duty aboard the gunboat *Queen City*, Allensworth was selected as a wardroom steward and was given thirty dollars a month. This was his first paid job as a freeman, and he advanced quickly thanks to his loyal service. For example, when two other African American members of the crew deserted, Allensworth decided to remain behind. As a direct result he became the captain's steward and was given a raise of five dollars a month. He was honorably discharged on 4 April 1865, days before the official end of the Civil War.

Two years later Allensworth and his brother William opened two restaurants in St. Louis, Missouri. This venture proved successful, and they attempted to expand their business. However, after being falsely accused of passing counterfeit currency, they sold both restaurants and left St. Louis. Allensworth returned to Louisville, where he found his mother and began supporting her. In addition he became both janitor and pupil at the Ely Normal School for freemen, organized by the American Missionary Society of New York. Allensworth remained at this school until the Freedmen's Bureau applied to the principal for a young man to go to Christmasville, five miles south of Louisville, to teach. Allensworth accepted the position and in 1868 took over this school.

Allensworth's congregation, the Fifth Street Baptist Church in Louisville, ordained him as its minister on 9 April 1871. Realizing his lack of biblical expertise, he enrolled in the Theological Institute at Nashville. From this point on Allensworth combined his skills as a teacher, preacher, and disciplinarian to develop churches, schools, and corporations with a view toward providing African Americans the moral and intellectual tools that he considered necessary for success as freemen. He built not only institutions but also an irreproachable reputation for integrity and intelligence. Allensworth had notable achievements in the Kentucky towns of Franklin, Georgetown, Elizabethtown, Louisville, and Bowling Green. Before accepting a post in Bowling Green he married Josephine Leavell (JOSEPHINE LEAVELL ALLENSWORTH) on 20 September 1877. They had one boy, who died shortly after birth, and two girls, who survived to adulthood.

While in Bowling Green, Reverend Allensworth became politically active. He was a Republican elector in 1880 and was a delegate to the Republican National Convention in 1880 and again in 1884. He fur-

ther increased his public stature by authoring five lectures: "Five Manly Virtues," "Humbugs and How They Live," "The Battle of Life and How to Fight it," "America," and "Character and How to Read It." Temporarily leaving his congregation, he embarked upon a tour of New England, supported by the Williams Lecture Bureau of Boston, Massachusetts. His lectures were hailed as extraordinary by newspapers from Kentucky to Boston.

Shortly after his mother died in 1878, Allensworth left Bowling Green and accepted a post as pastor of a Baptist church in Cincinnati, Ohio. There in 1882 an African American soldier brought it to Allensworth's attention that African American regiments were served by white chaplains. After learning that the chaplain of the Twenty-fourth Infantry was to retire in four years, Allensworth mobilized his friends to help him gain the chaplaincy. As a result, both Charles P. Jacob and Senator Joseph E. Brown met with President Grover Cleveland about the new chaplaincy. He became Chaplain Allensworth of the Twenty-fourth Infantry on 3 June 1886.

Allensworth served as chaplain until 1906. During this time he strove for the advancement and improvement of all enlisted men by designing an educational curriculum for servicemen at all levels of rank and responsibility. This curriculum was so successful that it was adopted throughout the U.S. Army. Through his powers of oration he won other smaller victories, such as convincing white officers to salute him. Allensworth emphasized that he would go out of his way to avoid a salute from a man who, having sworn to obey army regulations, would violate this oath. Allensworth called upon influential friends such as Congressman JOHN MERCER LANGSTON to draw attention to inequalities in the system of army deployment and appointment that made it impossible for an African American to be promoted from an African American regiment. His actions made promotion an official possibility for African American enlisted men. Allensworth's military career began winding down in 1900 when he injured his knee serving in the Philippines. Allensworth reinjured this knee in January 1901 and requested a transfer to Fort McDowell, California, where he had been recuperating. This transfer was granted. He served until 1906, when he was retired at his own request with the rank of lieutenant colonel, then the highest rank ever achieved by an African American in the U.S. Army.

After retiring, Allensworth and his family settled in Los Angeles. Though retired, Allensworth never ceased working for the advancement of African Americans. With the professor William Payne, the minister William Peck, and the real estate agent Harry Mitchell, Allensworth created an all-black community in Tulare County, California. The town was called Allensworth and in 1914 reached a peak population of approximately two hundred. As the community he founded reached its apex in prosperity, Allensworth's life ended suddenly when he stepped off a streetcar and was struck by a motorcycle.

Allen Allensworth began life with no advantages but worked tirelessly to succeed. Having illicitly obtained an education, he came to believe that inequality was a result of limited opportunity and nothing else, a belief reinforced by his success as a teacher, preacher, and chaplain. This attitude was embodied in the creation of California's first all-black community.

After Allen Allensworth's death, his town, Allensworth, prospered for a short time. However, when the Pacific Farming Company refused to provide water as promised, economic activity slowed. With the water table falling and the economy failing, the community began to collapse. After the Great Depression and World War II, Allensworth never recovered. In 1971 the town became Colonel Allensworth State Park, and many of the original buildings were restored. The park stands not only as a testament to Allensworth's life and lasting achievements but also as a reminder of the struggle of African Americans to create positive social environments during the nadir of race relations in the United States.

Further Reading
Alexander, Charles. *Battles and Victories of Allen Allensworth* (1914).
Radcliffe, Evelyn. *Out of Darkness: The Story of Allen Allensworth* (1998).
Wheeler, B. Gordon. "Allensworth: California's African American Community," *Wild West* (Feb. 2000).

JACOB ANDREW FREEDMAN

ALLENSWORTH, Josephine Leavell (3 May 1855–27 Mar. 1939), pianist, educator, and philanthropist, was born a slave in Trenton, Kentucky, to Mary Dickinson, also a slave, and Mr. Leavell, likely a scion of the white Benjamin Leavell family, pioneers of Trenton. According to family history, Josephine's father wanted to send her and her sister to Canada on the Underground Railroad, but their mother objected because of the danger and distance. Sometime between 1868 and 1875 Josephine attended the Nashville Normal and Theological Institute (also known as the Baptist Institute), a college for African Americans that was later renamed Roger Williams University. Daniel W. Phillips, a white Baptist minister, had started the school in 1864, teaching Bible classes to freed people in his home. The school was later acquired by Vanderbilt University and incorporated into its George Peabody campus, a teachers' college.

While at the Baptist Institute, Josephine studied music, particularly piano, and trained as a teacher. At the school she also met her fellow student ALLEN ALLENSWORTH, a traveling minister with the First District Baptist Association, who pastored several churches in southern Kentucky. Though Allen was thirteen years Josephine's senior, both had been born and raised in Kentucky and felt they had similar experiences. Allen was a former slave who as an adolescent had escaped bondage and joined Union soldiers during the Civil War. Josephine and Allen married on 20 September 1877 in Trenton, just as Allen accepted a pastorate with the State Street Baptist Church in Bowling Green, Kentucky.

Josephine was her husband's collaborator and partner as he moved from one church to the next, developing church-based Sunday schools and grade schools from Bowling Green, Kentucky, to Cincinnati, Ohio, for African American children who did not have access to public grade schools. The Allensworths firmly believed that churches had a responsibility to educate African Americans coming out of the era of slavery, and that uplifting the race was possible through a holistic approach to moral, spiritual, and academic education. In 1878 the Allensworths had their first child, Alpha, a son who died in infancy. They had two more children, Eva, born in 1880, and Nella, born in 1882.

That same year Allen learned that black regiments in the U.S. Army did not have black chaplains to serve their spiritual needs. He became aware of an opening with the 24th Infantry, an African American regiment, and began a personal campaign to get the job, soliciting support from prominent political friends. The U.S. Army offered him the position on 1 April 1886, giving him the rank of captain. On 1 July, his first day of duty, he reported to Fort Supply, the western Oklahoma base then responsible for policing and protecting grazing lands leased by cattlemen on Indian territories. Josephine, their two daughters, and her niece joined him two months later.

With children in tow, Josephine followed her husband to each station, including Fort Bayard in New Mexico, Fort Douglas near Salt Lake City, Fort Harrison in Montana, Fort Huachuca in Arizona, and the Presidio and Fort McDowell in San Francisco. While her husband served in the Philippines in 1899, she and their children stayed on the Presidio. Josephine helped Allen teach and develop Sunday school lessons, and she played the organ and piano during worship services. Her daughters later accompanied on violin and organ.

Many of the military stations were isolated from nearby towns, and when soldiers visited while off duty, they often garnered bad reputations for heavy drinking, carousing, and disrupting the peace. African American soldiers had won a probably undeserved reputation as the worst offenders. The Allensworths made it their cause to provide enlisted men and their families in the 24th Infantry with wholesome entertainment on base, so as to maintain good relations with the surrounding communities and keep a good image of the African American troops. Josephine often performed piano recitals for the men and their families. While at Fort Douglas, she also took on a job as telegrapher, the first African American in Salt Lake City to hold the position.

Josephine was revered and respected by the wives of enlisted men, though she and her husband made it a rule not to socialize with enlisted families, nor to let their children socialize with those of enlisted men. Because Allen was the sole black officer in the 24th Infantry, his family often could not socialize with the families of white officers, leaving Josephine and her children sometimes feeling isolated and alone (African American Museum and Library at Oakland vertical file, c.1975).

When the 24th Infantry was stationed in the Philippines, Josephine served as a treasurer of sorts for the wives of the enlisted men, collecting and distributing money the soldiers sent home to their families. The Reverend Allen Allensworth retired from the army with the rank of lieutenant colonel in April 1906, and the couple and their grown children settled in Pasadena, Los Angeles County, California. The Allensworths soon found that Southern California did not fully meet their expectations as a place free of racial discrimination. In 1908 Lieutenant Colonel Allensworth founded Allensworth, a black farming colony, with four other African American men. The town, located in California's San Joaquin Valley, prospered for several years, boasting its own elected government, law enforcement, and school district. Josephine served as the president of the town's first school board in 1910, and she organized the Women's Improvement Club, which developed a playground for the children of the colony.

Education was a cornerstone of the colony, and one of the first public buildings erected was a schoolhouse. In 1914 the townspeople approved a $5,000 bond to build a permanent school. Once the new school was completed, the original building was donated to Josephine. She then purchased a plot of land near the school and had the old schoolhouse moved there to house the town library. She named it the Mary Dickinson Memorial Library, after her mother. She, her husband, and other prominent townspeople donated books for the collection.

Josephine died at the age of 83 in Los Angeles County after living with her daughter Eva's family for about a decade. Though most of her work is overshadowed by the achievements of her husband, Josephine's contributions illustrate the essential role of women as partners of race-conscious men who pursued a vision of racial equity.

Further Reading
The African American Museum and Library at Oakland has a small but significant collection of papers related to Josephine Allensworth. See Vertical Files, B2, F1, F6 for an interview with Allensworth's granddaughters Josephine B. Smith and Louise Skanks Collier (c.1975).
Alexander, Charles. *Battles and Victories of Allen Allensworth* (1914).
Beasley, Delilah Leantium. *The Negro Trail Blazers of California* (1919).
Ramsey, Eleanor Mason. *Allensworth—A Study in Social Change* (1977).
Robinson, Jini M. *Allensworth Town Is Born Again* (1975).

VENISE WAGNER

AL-RAHMAN, Ibrahmia Abd. *See* Abd Al-Rahman, Ibrahima.

ALSTON, Charles Henry (26 or 28 Nov. 1907–27 Apr. 1977), artist and teacher, was born in Charlotte, North Carolina, the youngest of five children of the prominent Episcopalian minister Primus Priss Alston and his second wife, Anna (Miller) Alston. Nicknamed "Spinky" by his father, Charles showed his artistic bent as a child by sculpting animals out of the red clay around his home. His father died suddenly when Charles was just three. In 1913 his mother married a former classmate, Harry Pierce Bearden (uncle of ROMARE BEARDEN), and the family moved to New York City. Charles's stepfather worked at the Bretton Hotel as the supervisor of elevator operators and newsstand personnel, and over the years the family lived in comfortable brownstones in better neighborhoods.

Alston attended DeWitt Clinton High School, where he was art editor of the student newspaper the *Magpie* during the week, and he studied at the National Academy of Art on Saturdays. He turned down a scholarship to the Yale School of Fine Arts, choosing instead to work as a bellhop at Pennsylvania Station and attend Columbia University in New York. At Columbia he became a member of Phi Alpha Phi, the prestigious black fraternity whose members included at various times ADAM CLAYTON POWELL JR. and PAUL ROBESON. He also worked on the student newspaper the *Spectator* and drew cartoons for the *Jester*, the students' humor magazine. Alston also frequented nightclubs like Pod's and Jerry's or Mike's, turning his artistic eye on the energy of the jazz clubbers. *Opportunity* used his portrait of the popular dancer Lenore Cox for its cover. After he completed his undergraduate studies at Columbia, Alston became director of the boys' program at Utopian House, a community center that provided care for the children of working mothers, where one of his pupils was the young JACOB LAWRENCE.

In 1929 when he received a Dow Fellowship to pursue his graduate studies, Alston left Utopian House and its children's program to the management of GEORGE GREGORY. After earning his MA at Columbia in 1930, he became director of the library school at the Carnegie Art Workshop located at the 135th Street branch of the New York Public Library, which is now the Schomburg Center for Research in Black Culture. There Alston worked with the program supervisor and sculptor AUGUSTA SAVAGE, as well as with the author GWENDOLYN BENNETT and the artist AARON DOUGLAS. When the school lost its Carnegie funding, the New Deal's Works Progress Administration (WPA) sponsored its new quarters in part of an old stable that Alston had found for his own studio at 306 West 141st Street. Known simply as "306," it became a center for creative minds, black and white. The success of that center led to the formation of the Harlem Artists Guild in 1935, after 306 closed.

In the mid-1930s not only did Alston become the first African American supervisor of the WPA Federal Art Project Commission but he also established his reputation as an artist. His 1934 *Girl in a Red Dress* demonstrated his engagement with the cutting edge of art. As the art historian Richard J. Powell noted, the woman is "defiantly black, beautiful and feminine, yet also unsettled, mysterious and utterly modern" (Powell, 19). The two murals that Alston executed in 1936—*Magic and Medicine* and *Modern Medicine*—were exhibited at the Museum of Modern Art before they were moved, after a controversy quelled only by community support, to their permanent location in Harlem Hospital. The controversy stemmed from white reaction to Alston's portrayal of African magic alongside modern medicine. As NATHAN IRVIN HUGGINS noted in *Harlem Renaissance*, the panel *Magic and Medicine*

depicted the artist's conception of African magic. It has strong elemental and natural emphasis: animals, lightening, and the sun share the scene with dancing and conjuring Africans. Alston employed these obvious symbols—dancing, drums, fetishes, etc.—to embody the mural's message: modern medicine is better than primitive medicine. Nevertheless, the African panel was more effective—more romantic and magical—than those that depicted modern doctors in white smocks. (Huggins, 169)

Two Rosenwald Fellowships (1938–1939 and 1940–1941) enabled Alston to travel and work extensively in the southern United States, spending studio time at Atlanta University with HALE WOODRUFF. Alston's return to New York brought him back to commercial art as an illustrator for magazines such as *Mademoiselle, Fortune, Scribner's, Red Book*, and *Collier's*. The draft in World War II kept him stateside, and in 1942 Alston began working for the U.S. Office of War Information as an illustrator for a weekly series, "Negro Achievement," carried by 225 black newspapers. He married Myra Adala Logan in New York on 8 April 1944. He decided to pursue his prospering commercial art career and produced magazine covers and book jackets. While attending Pratt Institute under the GI Bill, Alston studied fine arts under the artist Charles Martin, who introduced Alston to the postimpressionist sculptor Alexander Kostellow, who introduced him to abstract expressionism. Alston continued his graduate studies at New York University.

In 1950 Alston became the first African American instructor to teach at New York's Art Students League. The 1950s brought Alston commissions for several murals: in Los Angeles, the Golden State Mutual Life Insurance Company, with Hale Woodruff; in New York, the Abraham Lincoln High School (Brooklyn) and the Museum of Natural History (Manhattan). He painted his abstract *Configuration* (1952) and the racially ambiguous couple of *Adam and Eve* (1954). During this period his work was exhibited in galleries throughout New York. Alston also taught at the Museum of Modern Art

(1956–1957) and participated in the MOMA art educator Victor D'Amico's teaching project at the World's Fair in Brussels. Alston's painting *The Family* was purchased and presented to the Whitney Museum of American Art.

In the 1960s Alston continued to produce signature work on African American families: figurative, colorful, and heavily sculptural in form. But as Beryl Wright pointed out in *African-American Art: 20th-Century Masterworks*, the catalog produced for a 1994 exhibit at New York's Michael Rosenfeld Gallery, Alston's oeuvre encompassed much more: his work "ranges from caricatures of Harlem nightclubbers, absorbing abstractions like *Untitled* (1952), paintings of protest and large public murals" (Wright, 63). Indeed, the turmoil of the early 1960s led Alston and other artists in 1963 to form the Spiral Group in New York, an attempt by African American artists to define their relationship to the civil rights struggles of students in the South. That group dissolved, but not before it produced the Spiral Black and White Exhibit on 5 June 1965 of work done only in black and white.

Alston's career continued to prosper throughout the 1960s and 1970s, from murals for several New York buildings to a bronze bust of MARTIN LUTHER KING JR. now in the permanent collection of the National Portrait Gallery of the Smithsonian. Alston was appointed full professor at the City College of New York in 1973, and in 1975 he received the first Distinguished Alumni Award from Columbia University. His final years were difficult: Alston's wife, Myra, battled cancer for several years, succumbing in January 1977. Three months later, on 27 April 1977, Alston himself died of the disease. His lifelong friend George Gregory eulogized Alston as a "man for all seasons: genteel and friendly, wise and with the power of perception—to see and feel things, people, his surroundings. Added to perspective and understanding, he lived his life by that Arista motto of character, service, and excellence" (Henderson, 26).

Further Reading

Henderson, Harry. "Remembering Charles Alston," in *Charles Alston: Artist and Teacher* (1990).
Huggins, Nathan Irvin. *Harlem Renaissance* (1973).
Michael Rosenfeld Gallery. *African-American Art: 20th-Century Masterworks*, essay by Beryl Wright (1993).
Powell, Richard J. "Re/Birth of a Nation," in *Rhapsodies in Black: Art of the Harlem Renaissance* (1997).

MARY ANNE BOELCSKEVY

ALSTON, Melvin Ovenus (7 Oct. 1911–30 Dec. 1985), educator and civil rights litigant, was born in Norfolk, Virginia, the son of William Henry "Sonnie" Alston, a drayman, and Mary Elizabeth "Lizzie" Smith, a laundress. The Alstons owned their home, and Melvin grew up in a middle-class environment. After attending Norfolk's segregated black public schools and graduating from Booker T. Washington High School, he graduated in 1935 from Virginia

State College, where he was honored for his debating and for excellence in scholarship. Following graduation he began teaching math at Booker T. Washington High School. Beginning in 1937 he served as president of the Norfolk Teachers Association, and he also held local leadership positions in the Young Men's Christian Association and the First Calvary Baptist Church.

Alston played a key role in an effort by black teachers in the Norfolk city public schools to challenge racial discrimination in their salaries. In 1937 the Virginia Teachers Association (VTA) and its local branch, the Norfolk Teachers Association, representing black teachers in the public schools, joined forces with the NAACP to organize a joint committee to pursue salary equalization—by which was meant that all teachers would be paid according to the white teachers' salary schedule rather than according to the lower black teachers' schedule. The NAACP supplied legal assistance, and the VTA established a fund of one thousand dollars to indemnify the lost salary of any teacher who was fired in retaliation for serving as plaintiff in a court case. In 1939 Alston's colleague Aline Elizabeth Black initiated but lost a case in state court to achieve salary equalization. Before her case could be appealed to the Virginia Supreme Court of Appeals, the school board declined to renew her contract, and when she lost her job, her lawyers concluded that she no longer had standing to sue. The joint committee paid Black her salary for the school year, and she went to New York, where she taught school and took classes toward a doctorate at New York University. With some reluctance Alston took her place in the litigation, guaranteed a similar indemnity of a year's salary if he lost his job as a consequence.

Alston's lawyers were the NAACP's big guns—THURGOOD MARSHALL, LEON A. RANSOM, and WILLIAM HENRY HASTIE—together with the Virginia attorneys OLIVER W. HILL and J. Thomas Hewin Jr. As a teacher, Alston sought a permanent injunction against the school board's racial discrimination in its salary schedule, and as a taxpayer he also challenged the city's discriminatory allocation of the state school fund. He and his attorneys lost the case in February 1940 in federal district court, but in June they won on appeal in the Fourth Circuit Court of Appeals, *Alston v. Board of Education of the City of Norfolk*. Pending a final resolution of the case, the court directed the school board not to distribute contracts for the coming year until July, so Alston could not be denied his job and no teachers could be required to waive their rights for that year.

The appeals court determined that the Norfolk school board had denied equal protection of the laws by paying, solely on the basis of race, black teachers lower salaries than white teachers. The court rejected the school board's contention that teachers, having signed contracts for the year, could not contest the terms to which they had agreed and, if they failed to sign, had no standing to sue. The court ruled that such waivers could not extend beyond the single year of the contract. Moreover, the appeals court overruled the district judge in the matter of whether the case concerned only Alston; rather, the court said, the case was a class action suit that affected all black teachers in the Norfolk system.

In October 1940 the United States Supreme Court let the decision stand. Alston's case proved to be one of the NAACP's more important victories in its campaign in the courts for equalization of salaries because it supplied a powerful precedent, both in law and in strategy, for similar suits in Virginia and in other southern states over the next ten years. The NAACP immediately altered its approach to a case then in progress in Florida, for example, and a 1942 out-of-court settlement in Richmond, Virginia, called for salary equalization in five annual increments. The Alston case led to litigation designed to achieve progress on other fronts, too—equal busing, equal facilities, and equal curricula—in the public schools of the South, and black Virginians achieved victories regarding each of those in the 1940s.

After two years away and no longer a litigant, Black retrieved her old job in 1941, while Alston undertook graduate work at Columbia University in New York. He earned an MS in Mathematics Education in 1942 and an EdD in the same field in 1945 with a dissertation on "Vitalized Verbal Problem Material in Algebra." During 1945 and 1946 Alston was perhaps the only teacher in the Virginia public schools, black or white, with a doctoral degree. In 1945 he married Doris Ruby Newsome. They had five children and an adopted daughter.

In 1946 Alston moved to Tallahassee, Florida, to take a position as professor of mathematics and head of the math department at Florida's black land-grant school, Florida Agricultural and Mechanical College. People who knew him there recalled him with great respect as someone with prodigious industry; his wife remembered him as a "workaholic." He served as college registrar from 1947 to 1948 and as dean of the School of Education from 1948 to 1953. Reflecting its new status as a university, the school changed its name in 1953 to Florida Agricultural and Mechanical University and reorganized its divisions into eight colleges. Alston served for a time as acting dean of the graduate school, and he was dean of the College of Education from its establishment in 1953 until he retired in 1969.

Alston then took a position at Southern Illinois University. From 1969 to 1974 he taught courses in secondary education and conducted research in local school systems. In declining health, he retired again and returned to Tallahassee, where he died.

Further Reading

The NAACP Papers in the Library of Congress include relevant material.

Lewis, Earl. *In Their Own Interests: Race, Class, and Power in Twentieth-Century Norfolk, Virginia* (1991).

Neyland, Leedell W., and John W. Riley. *The History of Florida Agricultural and Mechanical University* (1963).

Tushnet, Mark V. *The NAACP's Legal Strategy against Segregated Education, 1925–1950* (1987).
Obituary: *Tallahassee Democrat,* 1 Jan. 1986.

PETER WALLENSTEIN

AMAKI, Amalia (8 July 1949–), artist, art historian, curator, critic, and educator, was born Lynda Faye Peek in Atlanta, Georgia. Amaki, who legally changed her name in 1978, is the fourth of six surviving daughters of Mary Lee Hill, a homemaker, gardener, and quilter, and Norman Vance Peek, a landscape designer and gardener during the summer, and a cake and candy caterer during the winter. Early in her life and throughout her artistic career Amaki was influenced by her parents' penchant for recycling materials into creative forms.

Amaki's parents supported and encouraged her early artistic pursuits. Her mother enthusiastically showed Amaki's drawings to family friends and members of the community. Aware of Amaki's interest, the Reverend William Holmes Borders, a friend of the family and pastor of the Wheat Street Baptist Church where the Peek family worshipped, introduced ten-year-old Amaki to HALE ASPACIO WOODRUFF, a prominent painter who had taught at Spelman College in Atlanta between 1931 and 1946, and had painted a mural for the church.

When she was thirteen Amaki created a series of still lifes from burlap bags and yarn. Originally her father used burlap to make shopping and tote bags, and her mother used yarn in her sewn fabrics and quilts. Amaki's yarn and burlap wall hangings were framed and became part of a furniture display at Rich's Department Store in downtown Atlanta. A customer not only purchased the furniture but also bought Amaki's artwork.

Amaki attended David T. Howard High School in Atlanta where, while continuing to make art, she also studied journalism. In 1967 she enrolled at Georgia State University, where she received a BA in 1971 with a dual degree in Journalism and Psychology. During her tenure at the university she interned as a meteorologist and was a feature writer for the student newspaper, the *Signal.* In 1970 she won the prestigious Sigma Delta Chi Award for Outstanding Journalism from the Society of Professional Journalism.

In the 1970s, while employed as a reservations agent at the later defunct Southern Airways in Atlanta, Amaki traveled extensively throughout the United States, South America, Africa, and Europe. Her exposure to various cultures influenced her notions about American marginalization of racial and gender identities in her later positions as artist, curator, and teacher.

During this period Amaki continued to paint and take photographs. For years she was the family photographer at gatherings. Cognizant of Amaki's interest in both photography and painting, BENNY ANDREWS, a renowned painter and close friend, encouraged her to pursue a career in photography. He suggested that she "stop trying to paint photographs and learn something about photography." His comments persuaded her to decline offers to study painting at both Yale University and the University of California, Berkeley. Instead in 1976 she matriculated into the photography program at the University of New Mexico. Never completely relinquishing her interest in painting, Amaki was attracted to New Mexico, largely because of her admiration for the painter Georgia O'Keeffe, who resided in Abiquiu and whom Amaki would cite as an influence throughout her career.

At the University of New Mexico, Amaki's instructors included Betty Hahn, who taught Amaki the non-silver process, particularly cyanotype; Beaumont Newhall, who taught her the history of photography; and Garo Zareh Antreasian, an internationally renowned printmaker of lithographs, who taught Amaki drawing and critiqued her paintings. While in New Mexico, Amaki met eminent artists such as the painter Agnes Martin and the photographers Paul Caponigro, Ansel Adams, Linda Connor, and Minor White. In 1980 Amaki graduated with a BA in Photography and the History of Art.

In the spring of 1982, after residing in New Mexico and New York City as a freelance artist the previous year, Amaki returned to Atlanta. During the summer of 1982 she had a fortuitous meeting with Paul R. Jones, an Atlanta-based African American art collector. Amaki was introduced to Jones by Dan Moore, the founder and president of the Collections of Life and Heritage, Inc. (later the APEX Museum), to assist in cataloging Jones's collection. Jones had agreed to loan Moore part of his collection for an art exhibition at the main branch of the Atlanta-Fulton County Public Library, with the stipulation that Moore provide assistants to catalog Jones's extensive collection. Moore sent Amaki and two other recruits to Jones's home. Of the three recruits, only Amaki had a background in art and the stamina to tackle organizing Jones's massive collection, which at the time included artworks by African American, African, Southeast Asian, and South American artists. For the remainder of the summer Amaki alone completed the task, photographing and researching the artworks. This initial encounter between Jones and Amaki spawned a continuing professional relationship.

In the 1980s Amaki supplemented her art career with other jobs. She worked as an investigator for a bank, an employee for the Environmental Protection Agency, a contributing writer for *Art Papers,* an art critic for the Atlanta entertainment paper *Creative Loafing,* and an instructor of art history at Spelman and Morehouse colleges. During this period she was also enrolled in Emory University's Institute of Liberal Arts; she received an MA in Modern European and American Art in 1992 and a PhD in Twentieth-century American Art and Culture in 1994.

During the 1990s Amaki taught art history in Greater Atlanta–area institutions, including Morehouse College, Kennesaw State University, Spelman College, Atlanta College of Art, and North Georgia

College and State University. She also curated exhibitions on African American art, received numerous commissions to create art, published articles and essays on artists, and exhibited in numerous national group and solo exhibitions. Prior to her retrospective exhibition, in 2001 Amaki was appointed curator of the Paul R. Jones Collection at the University of Delaware and assistant professor of art, art history, and black American studies. In 2004 she curated an annual inaugural exhibition of Jones's African American art collection donated to the university and edited a book of the same title, *A Century of African American Art: The Paul R. Jones Collection*. The exhibition traveled to Spelman College, Montana State University, North Carolina A&T University, and the University of Louisiana at Lafayette. In addition to her curatorial role at the University of Delaware, Amaki was a professor of black American studies and taught art history courses. In the summer of 2004 Amaki was a visiting scholar at the Student Art Centers International (SACI) in Florence, Italy, where she taught photography.

In the summer of 2005, showcasing the art she had produced over thirty years, Amaki held a mid-career retrospective exhibition, Amalia Amaki: Boxes, Buttons and the Blues, at the National Museum for Women in the Arts. The exhibition was accompanied by a catalog of the same title and traveled to Spelman College Museum of Fine Art in the spring of 2006. By combining photography (including the cyanotype and digital techniques), painting, and found objects, Amaki created a multimedia array of commentaries about changing realities and perceptions. She reconstructed familiar and popular items—including boxes, buttons, beads, fans, quilts, replicas of the American flag, postcards, reproductions of women from magazine cosmetic ads, and photographs of African Americans, particularly female blues singers—into memorabilia embodying human emotions, identities, and concepts about beauty, gender, and race in American culture.

During the academic year 2005–2006 Amaki was scholar-in-residence at Spelman College, where she researched and coedited the book *Hale Woodruff, Nancy Elizabeth Prophet and the Academy,* published in 2007. In 2006 Amaki was promoted to full professor in the black American studies program at the University of Delaware while maintaining her position as curator of the Paul R. Jones Collection.

For her service and progressive contributions to enriching the community with African American art, Amaki received a 2002 Alumni Award of Distinction from Emory University, a 2006 Christi Award from Christina Cultural Art Center, and a 2006 Commendation from Governor Sonny Perdue of the state of Georgia.

Further Reading
Some of the information for this article was acquired during a telephone interview with Amaki on 2 August 2006 and in an e-mail dated 24 April 2007.

Barnwell, Andrea, Gloria Wade-Gayles, and Leslie King-Hammond. *Amalia Amaki: Boxes, Buttons and the Blues* (2005).
Fox, Catherine. "Visual Arts: Accentuating Positivity," *Atlanta Journal-Constitution*, 19 Feb. 2006.
Lewis, Samella Saunders. *African American Art and Artists* (2003).
Robinson, Jontyle, et al. *Bearing Witness: Contemporary African American Artists* (1996).

SHARON PRUITT

AMERICA, Richard F. (c. 1940–), author, educator, and economist, was born Richard Franklin America Jr. in Philadelphia, Pennsylvania, to Richard Franklin America Sr. and Arline America. In 1960 America received a BS in Economics from Pennsylvania State University and in 1965 an MBA from the Graduate School of Business at Harvard University. Afterward, he joined the Stanford Research Institute in Menlo Park, California, where he worked for the next four years as a Development Economist in the Urban and Regional Economics Group.

In April 1969 America published "What Do You People Want?" in the *Harvard Business Review*. In it he advocated major federal subsidies to facilitate economic equality and large-scale participation of blacks in the corporate world, and made suggestions as to how these goals might be accomplished, including the transfer of corporations to black shareholders and managers. The article offered a radical approach to policy pertaining to reparations and the economic development in the black community. However, America's unique suggestions for the most part went unnoticed in the mainstream reparations debate.

From 1968 to 1972 America served as a lecturer and director of Urban Programs at the Haas School of Business Administration at the University of California, Berkeley. Later he moved to Washington, D.C., to work in consulting and then in the federal government.

During this time America wrote extensively on the economic development of "Afro-America," a term that described a "social, political, and economic system" inclusive of every facet of the black community in the United States. In 1977 America expanded on this theme in *Developing the Afro-American Economy*, again addressing issues of economic equality and how to manage the development process. He discussed the idea of a "social debt" that whites owed blacks because of the benefits the former received directly or indirectly from slavery and discrimination. The resulting disparity between black and white median incomes was to be reduced through redistribution methods such as progressive taxation and development in the black community. America described the economic situation as one of "social monopoly" and suggested ways to apply antitrust laws to industries in which whites held an overconcentration of market power. He also addressed the major barriers to development such as crime and underfunded social services and other noncommercial activities, discussing how blacks could volunteer the funds needed to overcome these difficulties.

In the early 1980s the idea of "social debt" became an important issue within the National Economic Association (NEA). In 1969 Richard America, Marcus Alexis, Bernard E. Anderson, Robert S. Browne, Karl Gregory, Thaddeus Spratlen, Charles Z. Wilson, and others had founded the NEA, formerly called the Caucus of Black Economists. Its purpose was to increase blacks' participation in the field of economics and develop policy to address economic problems experienced in the black community. In addition the NEA published the *Review of Black Political Economy*, a journal previously published by the Black Economic Research Center, to advance policy that would "reduce racial economic inequality" around the world. America remained involved with the organization by writing for the *Review*, participating in the NEA conferences, and serving as president in 1985.

In 1990 America edited *The Wealth of Races: The Present Value of Benefits from Past Injustices*, a volume that incorporated many of the papers presented at NEA annual meetings in sessions organized and chaired by America. Included were estimates of the benefits whites received from slavery and discrimination as well as contributions to the discussions on reparations and other methods of achieving racial equality. This book was followed by *Paying the Social Debt: What White America Owes Black America* (1993), which again stressed the restitution that whites owed to blacks. Adding to his previous discussion on development, America examined issues such as drug use and crime that hindered economic advancement within the black community.

America continued on the theme of restitution in "Reparations and Public Policy," which appeared in the Winter 1999 issue of the *Review of Black Political Economy*. He wrote that, from 1619 to the present, whites had benefited economically from the unjust treatment of blacks. According to America, the majority of these benefits were enjoyed by those whose income lay in the top 30 percent of the income distribution for whites, and restitution was primarily owed to low-income blacks. The repayment of this debt was necessary to improve not only the economic conditions of many blacks but also for the overall health of the economy, as America argued in "Reparations and Higher Education," published in *Black Issues in Higher Education* (January 2000).

As a Professor of the Practice, Director of the Africa Initiative, and Director of Community Reinvestment, America taught courses in community reinvestment and economic development at the McDonough School of Business at Georgetown University in Washington, D.C. He also worked with business schools in Africa to improve education in management and development. America was an active member in Omega Psi Phi, the fraternity formed in 1911 by Frank Coleman, Oscar J. Cooper, Edgar A. Love, and ERNEST EVERETT JUST at Howard University in Washington, D.C. He continued to write on reparations, economic development, community reinvestment, and public policy, and later broadened his focus to include Africa, Latin America, and the Caribbean.

Further Reading
This essay is based on information drawn from personal interviews with the author.

JENNIFER VAUGHN

AMMI, Ben (12 Oct. 1939–), Hebraic scholar, author, anointed spiritual leader of the African Hebrew Israelites of Jerusalem, was born Ben Carter in Chicago, Illinois, the youngest of six children of Rena and Levi Carter. Little is known about Ben's mother and father.

As a young teenager, Carter was a gregarious person, very communicative, and he knew how to vocally motivate people. Growing up, he worked a variety of odd jobs, dusting chairs, collecting garbage, running errands, delivering groceries, and shining shoes.

Around 1959 he married Patricia Price, but nothing more has been documented about his wife or possible children. As things began to intensify during the Vietnam War, Carter joined the U.S. Army. By 1960, after serving about a year and a half of military duty, he was assigned to an army missile base in Chicago. Becoming more perceptive and grown-up, Carter began to display a working knowledge of world affairs. During these years the consciousness of African Americans began to change. African Americans nationwide began preaching Black Power and advocating African American solutions to African American problems.

In 1964 Carter worked as a metallurgist at Howard Foundry in Chicago. While working at the foundry, he studied Hebrew history with an individual by the name of Elder Buie. He learned about men who spoke of the connection between African Americans and the land of Israel, such as Prophet WILLIAM SAUNDERS CROWDY, who in 1896 founded the Church of God and Saints of Christ group. At this time Ben changed his name to Ben Ammi Ben Israel. Ammi felt that God had chosen a special people (African Americans) to be an example and guide for all people to follow. He explained that African Americans had indeed forced the anger of God as a direct result of walking opposite to his established order, which to him explained the unfortunate social conditions suffered by African Americans.

The Hebrew classes that Ammi attended began to grow in numbers. The classes were then moved to the second floor of an office building on 47th Street and Cottage Grove in Chicago. The new location was called Abeta Hebrew Culture Center. It was at this time that Ammi and everyone attending these classes began to refer to themselves as African Hebrew Israelites. In 1965, as his biblical knowledge continued to grow, Ammi split from Elder Buie's teachings and started instructing others at the Abeta Hebrew Culture Center. He spoke to the other members of Abeta about repatriation back into the Holy Land of Israel. He believed that African Americans could not stay true to the biblical scriptures while living in America and began his own quest to lead his followers. Thus, he started to lead a "back to Africa" movement among the members of Abeta. Even with this knowledge, leaving the confines of modern America seemed to be easier said than done. Many of his followers at first hesitated to leave their homes and jobs.

Despite the doubts and questions, Ammi stayed very positive and encouraging to the rest of the members of Abeta. As their date of departure grew near in 1967, he and his followers began to stock various supplies that they might need to survive in the jungle, activities that attracted police attention. During these volatile civil rights years, many organizations and African American individuals, such as the Black Panthers, the Student Nonviolent Coordinating Committee, and H. RAP BROWN and other activists were on the FBI's list as potential suspects. The FBI and the riots in Detroit in 1967 led the Chicago police to become wary of Ammi and the Hebrew Israelites of Abeta. Ammi and his followers were harrassed by whites and other African Americans regarding their plan to leave America.

Ammi claimed to have had a vision in which the archangel Gabriel revealed to him that African Americans descended from the biblical tribe of Judah. He led others to believe that the time had come for the biblical Israelites among the African Americans to return to Israel. As a result, in 1967 about 350 people from Chicago, along with Ammi, traveled to Liberia, West Africa, on their way to Israel. The reason for Ammi's decision to stop in Liberia was because in 1822 the West African country had already been chosen as a safe haven for African Americans escaping slavery. Their first settlement was about 100 miles from the capital city of Monrovia. Initially it was extremely difficult for them to adjust to living without Western comforts. Two years later only 39 of the original 350 people were still there.

Then, in 1969, the group finally settled in the southern region of Israel in a town called Arad and another small town in the Negev Desert called Dimona. By 1971 they had their immigrant status revoked and suffered many attempts at deportation, as they were not accepted into Israel because of the reason they gave for being there (to reclaim their homeland) and who they claimed to be (original Jews).

In 1973 the African Hebrew Israelites officially became the Original African Hebrew Israelite Community at Jerusalem. Into the early twenty-first century Ammi was the leader of twelve princes, ministers, and crowned brothers and sisters who administered the direction of the community. The group's children attended the Kingdom School in Holiness, and upon graduation, they continued study at an institute of higher learning called the School of the Prophets. The African Hebrew Israelites were completely vegan, abstaining from any meat or dairy products. Mothers delivered their babies at the House of Life, a communal clinic with its own medical staff. The community produced tofu, established health food restaurants, and operated an ice cream factory that manufactured nondairy ice cream. By 1977 the community had grown to 2,500 members. In 1986 forty-six members were deported on charges of living and working illegally in Israel, but in 1990 the Israeli government accorded the community legal recognition.

Ammi was responsible in the early 2000s for resettling more than five thousand individuals in Israel from Liberia, Ghana, Zaire, Benin, Zimbabwe, and Kenya, as well as the United States, St. Croix, and Bermuda. In 2005 he and members of the Southern Christian Leadership Conference inaugurated the Institute for a New Humanity from Chaos to Community, a conflict resolution center in Dimona, Israel. Making a guest appearance at the Million Family March in Washington, D.C., in 2000, Ammi was invited to speak at countless community centers, colleges, and universities. He was also the author of a collection of writings called the Resurrection Series. This included the books *God, the Black Man, and Truth* (1982); *God and the Law of Relativity* (1991); *The Messiah and the End of This World* (1991); *Everlasting Life . . . from Thought to Reality* (1994); *Yeshua the Hebrew Messiah or Jesus the Christian Christ?* (1996); and *An Imitation of Life* (1999).

Further Reading

Ahtur Yatsiliel Ben Nasik Immanuel. *Tree of Life: African Hebrew Israelites of Jerusalem, Absorbtion Manual* (2003).
Ben Ammi. Available online at www.kingdomofyah .com/Ben%20Ammi.htm.
HaGadol, Prince Gavriel and Odehyah B. Israel. *The Impregnable People: An Exodus of African Americans Back to Africa* (1993).

WILLIAM E. BANKSTON

AMMONS, Albert C. (23 Sept. 1907–2 Dec. 1949), jazz pianist, was born in Chicago. His parents' names are unknown; both were pianists. Albert was a teenage friend of MEADE LUX LEWIS. The two learned to play by following the key action of player pianos and by imitating more experienced musicians, including Hersal Thomas and Jimmy Yancey. Albert, having access to his parents' instrument, developed his skills faster than Lewis. Both men were particularly influenced by a tune called "The Fives," a blues tune involving strong, repetitive, percussive patterns in the left hand set against equally strong and percussive but less rigorously repetitive counterrhythmic patterns in the right. This piano blues style came to be known as boogie-woogie.

In 1924 Ammons joined a band in South Bend, Indiana. He married around this time, although details about his wife are unknown. His ultimately more famous and talented son, the tenor saxophonist GENE AMMONS, was born in 1925. At some point Ammons left for Chicago and then returned to South Bend to play in a big band at a whorehouse, the Paradise Inn. By 1927 he was playing in Detroit, and then he went back to Chicago. He continued to perform regularly while working as a driver at the Silver Taxi Cab company, where Lewis also was employed. They lived in the same rooming house as their fellow pianist PINE TOP SMITH, who taught Ammons "Pine Top's Boogie Woogie," the piece that named the style.

At some unspecified point Ammons led a band at the Dusty Bottom club in Chicago. He joined François Moseley's Louisiana Stompers in the summer of 1929 and played with William Barbee and His Headquarters from 1930 until 1931. Barbee, also a pianist, gave Ammons valuable lessons that expanded his stylistic range, and Ammons became somewhat comfortable playing in swing groups in the 1930s, although his repertoire remained limited by comparison with many other jazz pianists. He joined the drummer Louis P. Banks's Chesterfield Orchestra from 1931 until 1934, playing in clubs in Chicago and on a theatrical tour. He led a five-piece band, including the trumpeter Punch Miller, which played for weekend excursions to the South on the Illinois Central Railroad. In 1934 Ammons formed Rhythm Kings, which toward year's end began a two-year stand at the Club DeLisa. The group made recordings in February 1936, including "Nagasaki," on which Ammons broke away from the boogie-woogie style, and "Boogie Woogie Stomp," an arrangement of "Pine Top's Boogie Woogie" without Smith's vocal chatter and with the six-piece group rather than the piano alone. In April 1936 the Rhythm Kings' bassist, Israel Crosby, left to join the FLETCHER HENDERSON band. Soon thereafter the Club DeLisa began to present more complicated floorshows, and the music proved too difficult for Ammons. He was fired, and the job was given to his saxophonist, Delbert Bright.

Ammons played alone at the It Club, and in 1938 he led a band at the Claremont Club before traveling to New York to take part in the "Spirituals to Swing" concert at Carnegie Hall on 23 December. There he accompanied BIG BILL BROONZY on two numbers, including "Louise, Louise," and he formed a boogie-woogie piano trio with Lewis and PETE JOHNSON. Their enthusiastic reception furthered the public's developing passion for the boogie-woogie style, and the three pianists were catapulted to fame. With BIG JOE TURNER, the trio worked at Café Society in New York and the Hotel Sherman in Chicago, and they broadcast nationally. Ammons remained at the uptown location of Café Society in a duo with Johnson until 1942, when the two men began touring together.

In 1939 Ammons recorded a solo version of "Boogie Woogie Stomp" and his finest solo, "Shout for Joy," which the critic Jimmy Hopes commends for the rhythmic power of Ammons's left hand, Ammons's sense of structure, and the unusual final choruses, which are surprising within the context of the often predictable boogie-woogie style. A recording session

that same year with the Port of Harlem Jazzmen, including the trumpeter FRANKIE NEWTON, produced "Port of Harlem Blues," for which Ammons improvised an uncharacteristically delicate, high-pitched, tuneful, and nonpercussive blues melody. In 1941 he recorded with Johnson and the drummer Jimmy Hoskins, and he performed in the movie short *Boogie Woogie Dream*. The following year he recorded "Suitcase Blues" in memory of his early influence Thomas, who had recorded a version of it in 1925. "Bass Goin' Crazy," a playful performance also recorded in 1941, was equally percussive but altogether freer and more dissonant than Ammons's usual boogie-woogie style. Although he revived the name Rhythm Kings for recordings in 1944 that featured eminent swing musicians, the results were dull.

Sometime in the mid-1940s Ammons suffered a temporary paralysis of both hands. He resumed playing, mainly in Chicago, and in 1947 he recorded under the leadership of his saxophonist son. Ammons joined LIONEL HAMPTON at the beginning of 1949 and recorded "Chicken Shack Boogie." Having long suffered from alcoholism, he died in Chicago before year's end. His death date is commonly given as 2 December, but the brief and not necessarily reliable *Chicago Tribune* obituary of 4 December reports his death "yesterday."

Ammons was a somewhat more versatile pianist than his close friend Lewis and hence worked regularly with jazz groups. But he was never more than competent in this area and was no match for his colleague Johnson. Ammons's specific significance lies within the confines of the boogie-woogie piano style, in which Lewis and he are rated as the finest practitioners after Yancey. Later and indirectly Ammons's music reached a vast audience when the rhythm and blues, urban blues, and rock and roll styles adopted boogie-woogie piano patterns as part of their basic vocabulary.

Further Reading

Harrison, Max. "Boogie Woogie," in *Jazz*, eds. Nat Hentoff and Albert J. McCarthy (1959).
Hopes, Jimmy. "Boogie Woogie Man: A Bio-Discography of Albert Ammons," *Jazz and Blues* 1, no. 6 (1971): 4–7.
Newberger, Eli H. "Archetypes and Antecedents of Piano Blues and Boogie Woogie Style," *Journal of Jazz Studies* (Fall 1976): 84–109.
Page, Christopher I. *Boogie Woogie Stomp: Albert Ammons and His Music* (1997).
Pease, Sharon A. " 'Pine Top' Smith Influenced Early Piano Style of Swingin' Ammons," *Down Beat* (July 1937).
Travis, Dempsey J. *An Autobiography of Black Jazz* (1983).
Obituary: *Chicago Tribune*, 4 Dec. 1949.

BARRY KERNFELD

AMMONS, Gene (14 Apr. 1925–6 Aug. 1974), jazz tenor saxophonist, was born Eugene Ammons in Chicago, Illinois, the son of ALBERT AMMONS, a boogie-woogie pianist; his mother's name is unknown. Like several other prominent jazzmen, Gene studied music at Du Sable High School under Captain Walter Dyett. Initially he idolized LESTER YOUNG's improvising and even imitated Young's manner of playing with head and horn at a grotesquely tilted angle. During his third year in high school Gene began playing locally with the trumpeter King Kolax's band. At the semester's end he embarked on a cross-country tour with Kolax that included performances at the Savoy Ballroom in New York.

In 1944 the singer BILLY ECKSTINE formed a big band that included the tenor saxophonist CHARLIE ROUSE and the alto saxophonist CHARLIE PARKER. According to the group's pianist, John Malachi, Rouse was so smitten by Parker's playing that he was unable to concentrate on his own parts. Around August 1944 Rouse was fired. Ammons took Rouse's place on the recommendation of a friend, the Eckstine trumpeter Gail Brockman, who later participated in Ammons's early recordings as a leader. The group mainly recorded ballads featuring Eckstine's romantic voice, but it was also known as the first bop big band. That aspect of its musical personality is best preserved on two takes of "Blowin' the Blues Away," in which Ammons engages with the tenor saxophonist DEXTER GORDON in a magnificent battle of fast-paced blues improvisation. (Both men win.) Playing such as this exemplified Ammons's (and Gordon's) ability to draw a perfect balance between smooth tunefulness, a heady linear expression of harmony, and earthy honking and riffing.

While with Eckstine, Ammons acquired his nickname, "Jug." Evidently he had difficulty finding a straw hat big enough to fit, and the singer said, "You've got a head like a jug." From late 1944 onward Ammons was the principal instrumental soloist in a band teeming with up-and-coming bop musicians. He is featured on several records, including "I Love the Rhythm in a Riff" (1945), "Second Balcony Jump," "Cool Breeze," and "Oop Bop Sh'bam" (all from 1946), and in the movie *Rhythm in a Riff* (1946).

In Chicago in the first part of 1947, Ammons was featured alongside the trumpeter MILES DAVIS and the alto saxophonist SONNY STITT in jam sessions at the Jumptown Club, and he played in Stitt's octet at the Twin Terrace Café in March. Around May 1947, if not a couple of months before that, the Eckstine group split up. Ammons led small groups from mid-1947 onward. He had immediate success with the tuneful blues "Red Top" (1947), which had a second life when it was rereleased with lyrics overdubbed in 1953, but apart from this title his recordings of the late 1940s, including a session with his father on piano, are not among his best.

Ammons interrupted his band leading in late March or early April 1949 to replace Stan Getz in Woody Herman's Second Herd, with which he figured most prominently in "More Moon." Ammons left Herman at the beginning of September 1949, his place taken by the tenor saxophonist Billy Mitchell. Following directly in the tradition of "Blowin' the Blues Away," Ammons then formalized the saxophone battle in a quintet co-led by Stitt, who was now focusing on tenor as well as alto saxophone. They worked mainly at Birdland in New York from 1950 to 1951. Their finest recordings, made for the Prestige label, are two takes of "You Can Depend on Me" and three of "Blues Up and Down" (1950). The group continued intermittently until 1955. Around 1955 Ammons married Geraldine (maiden name unknown). They had two children. From 1955 to 1958 he led a number of ad hoc all-star blues and bop sessions for Prestige, one of which resulted in the outstanding album *Blue Gene* (1958).

Ammons has been rumored to be the composer of the blues theme "Walkin'," popularized by Miles Davis in 1954. Legally, "Walkin'" is credited to Ammons's manager, Richard Carpenter. There is no firm evidence that Carpenter appropriated it, although such actions have been commonplace in jazz. In any event, Ammons was not a significant jazz composer.

Ammons started using heroin sometime in the early 1950s (by his own account) and perhaps before that time; several of Herman's sidemen were notorious junkies. In 1958 he was convicted for possession of narcotics and sent to the Statesville Penitentiary near Joliet, Illinois. Paroled in June 1960, he recorded the album *Boss Tenor* but then returned to prison for violation of the condition of his parole that forbade him to perform in nightclubs. He served out the remainder of his sentence and in January 1961 resumed his career, recording the album *Boss Tenors* as co-leader with Stitt in August of that year. For engagements at McKie's Lounge in Chicago, Ammons was joined by Gordon in September and by Stitt and the saxophonist James Moody from late that year into February 1962.

During this period, 1960 to 1962, Ammons modified his style, placing less emphasis on his abilities as a bop improviser and more emphasis on African American gospel-influenced melodic gestures that were becoming popular in soul music. This reorientation led to a few modest hit singles, including his soulful instrumental rendering of the songs "Canadian Sunset" (from the Prestige *Boss Tenor* disk) and "Ca' Purange" (from the 1962 LP issued as *Bad! Bossa Nova* and also as *Jungle Soul*).

In June 1962 Ammons began using narcotics again and in September he was arrested. For this second conviction he spent seven years at Statesville, where, as previously, he kept his career alive by directing the prison band and playing every day. Meanwhile Bob Weinstock of Prestige, having recorded many sessions with Ammons from 1961–1962, released these gradually throughout the decade, effectively keeping Ammons's name before the public. Ammons was paroled in October 1969 and resumed his career with an engagement at the Plugged Nickel in Chicago, with Kolax playing trumpet. The following month a two-day recording session yielded two new albums, *The Boss Is Back* and *Brother Jug!*, the latter including a new hit single, Ammons's romantic instrumental rendering of "Didn't We." In March 1970 the New York State Liquor Board ruled against his performing in New York City, but he was able to work elsewhere and held a noted engagement in Chicago with the tenor saxophonists DON BYAS and Gordon in September 1970. He worked alongside EDDIE "LOCK-JAW" DAVIS in Chicago in May 1973. Ammons performed at the Ahus Jazz Festival in Sweden on 14 July 1974. Nine days later he entered Michael Reese Hospital in Chicago, where he died of bone cancer and pneumonia.

Further Reading

Burns, Jim. "Gene Ammons," *Jazz Journal* (23 Apr. 1970).

Feather, Leonard. "The Rebirth of Gene Ammons," *Down Beat* (25 June 1970).

Obituaries: *Chicago Tribune*, 7 Aug. 1974; *New York Times*, 8 Aug. 1974; *Chicago Defender*, 10 Aug. 1974; *Down Beat*, 10 Oct. 1974.

Discography

Porter, Bob, and Frank Gibson. "Gene Ammons: A Discography." *Discographical Forum* 6 (May 1968): 11–14; 7 (July 1968): 10–12.

BARRY KERNFELD

AMOS, Emma Veoria (1938–), painter and printmaker, was born in Atlanta, Georgia, to a family with a long line of educated and powerful women. Her grandmother, Emma, was a college-educated university professor in the 1890s, and her mother, India, was a similarly educated partner in the family drugstore with her father, Miles. Her paternal lineage included a grandfather who was the first black pharmacist in the state of Georgia. The family's social circle included such figures as BOOKER T. WASHINGTON and ZORA NEALE HURSTON. Along with her older brother, Larry, Amos attended schools in Atlanta's then-segregated public school system—first E.R. Carter Elementary and then Booker T. Washington High School.

Amos remembered wishing to be an artist from an early age, and eventually she enrolled in Ohio's Antioch College with a firm interest in the visual arts. She earned a BA from Antioch in Fine Arts as well as an etching diploma from London Central School of Art in 1959. After finishing her program in London, Amos returned to the United States, arriving in New York City in 1960. There she spent a year teaching at the prestigious Dalton School before she began working for the textile designer, Dorothy Liebes. From 1964 to 1966, Amos completed her MFA in Art Education at New York University (NYU), studying lithography with ROBERT BLACKBURN, and abandoning abstraction for figurative painting. At NYU, Amos also resumed her acquaintance with faculty member HALE WOODRUFF who invited her to join Spiral—a

historic group of black male artists including Norman Lewis, ROMARE BEARDEN, CHARLES HENRY ALSTON, and Merton Simpson with whom Amos exhibited until the group's dissolution in 1967.

Amos married Bobby Levine, an advertising director, in 1965. The birth of their first child, Nicholas, in 1967 prompted her to redirect her energies into printmaking rather than painting. In 1970, when her daughter India was born, and after suffering a near-miscarriage brought on by exposure to toxic printing inks and solvents, Amos turned full time to nontoxic pursuits such as quilting, illustration, and, in particular, weaving. Amos's interest in so-called craft and traditional "feminine" arts culminated in her co-production of *A Show of Hands*, a 1977–1978 "how-to" television show on crafts produced by WGBH in Boston.

As her children grew older, Amos returned to painting in the late 1970s, holding her first solo show at New York's Art Salon in 1979. The following year she began teaching at Rutgers' Mason Gross School of Art in New Jersey where she would become a full professor as well as chair of the Art Department. The 1980s, an enormously productive period for Amos, also marked her involvement in writing for and editing feminist publications such as *Heresies* and *M/E/A/N/I/N/G*. Her paintings from these years reveal both her shift to acrylic paint and her signature incorporation of either her own weavings, or African fabrics such as Kente cloth, into vibrant canvases that depict athletic figures running, dancing, and diving. By the late 1980s and through the mid-1990s these dynamic figures became completely freed from their terrestrial grounding, and they began to fall or fly through an unmoored, often fantastical space which continued to be edged with African fabrics—and thus literally and figuratively framed by Amos's interest in African cultures.

Along with her interest in African arts, Amos's career was distinguished by her longtime attention to the political dimensions of making images. Her art invariably treated subjects such as African American history and the visual representations of blacks, especially black women, within Western art. She also wrote and spoke extensively about issues of race and gender, as well as the obstacles facing black women artists.

Amos's interest in examining the objectionable ways in which nonwhite peoples were represented in the Euro-American visual tradition led her to include more collaged historical photographs or icons of Western art history within her canvases. She would appropriate these iconic images of art history only to deconstruct their racist and sexist meanings. She accomplished this deconstructive effect by highlighting the contemporary primitivism of German Neo-Expressionist painters such as A.R. Penck and Georg Baselitz in her *A.R. Pink Discovers Black* (1992) and *Which Way is Up Georg Baseless?* (1992). Amos also repainted Paul Gauguin's primitivistic Tahitian nudes, endowing them with agency, or revealing the racist stereotyping of the nonwhite body that occurs throughout Gauguin's oeuvre. In *Models* (1995), Amos considered the culturally specific norms of Western beauty and the exoticization of the non-Western body: Gauguin's model Te He Amana was whitened and juxtaposed with the figures of an African woman and a Greek *kouros*, the sculptural embodiment of Classical beauty—yet a sculptural form which was, ironically, closely related to West African sculpture. Here, as in her other paintings, Amos employed a bold, painterly *X* as a way to both invoke the repressive erasure of minority histories and to signal the remaking of identity in positive terms—a project that informed many of Amos's powerful and celebratory images.

Amos's work was shown in a major midcareer retrospective organized by the Ohio's College of Wooster in 1993, and this show was followed by a smaller 1994 exhibition at the New York gallery Art in General. The artist's paintings are held in the collections of the Museum of Modern Art, the Studio Museum in Harlem, and the Wadsworth Athenaeum.

Further Reading

Gouma-Peterson, Thalia. *Emma Amos: Paintings and Prints 1982–92* (1993).

hooks, bell. *Emma Amos: Changing the Subject. Paintings and Prints 1992–1994* (1994).

Murray, Al. "Interview with Emma Amos," *Smithsonian Archives of American Art* (1968). Available at http://www.aaa.si.edu/collections/oralhistories/transcripts/amos68.htm#top.

Patton, Sharon F. "Emma Amos: Art Matters," *Nka: Journal of Contemporary African Art* (Fall/Winter 2002).

LEORA MALTZ LECA

AMOS, Harold (7 Sept. 1918–26 Feb. 2003), scientist and educator, was born in Pennsauken, New Jersey, the second of nine children, to Howard R. Amos Sr., a Philadelphia postman, and Iola Johnson, who had been adopted by and worked for a prominent Philadelphia Quaker family who schooled her with their own children at home. This family remained lifelong friends of Iola and kept the young Amos family well supplied with books, including a biography of Louis Pasteur, which piqued Harold's interest in science in the fourth grade. Both Howard and Iola expected their children to be serious about their education and to excel academically. Harold, along with his siblings, took piano lessons and remained a competent amateur pianist. He also gained a reputation as an excellent tennis player.

Harold received his early education in a segregated school in Pennsauken, then graduated first in his class from Camden High School, in New Jersey. He later recalled that his love of teaching was awakened by the "wonderful teachers" that he had from first through twelfth grade. After graduation in 1936, Harold attended Springfield College in Springfield, Massachusetts, on a full academic scholarship at a time when

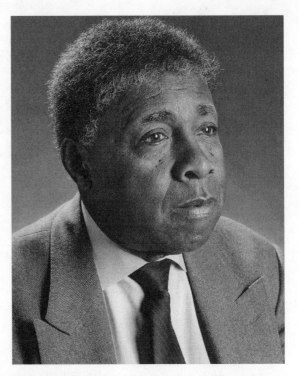

Harold Amos, a microbiologist who was Harvard Medical School's first black department chair and a mentor to hundreds of aspiring physicians, 1994. (AP Images.)

few such scholarships were offered to African Americans. Amos graduated summa cum laude in 1941, with a major in biology and a minor in chemistry. The following year he worked as a graduate assistant in the biology department at Springfield College, until he was drafted into the U.S. Army, where he served in the Quartermaster Corps as a warrant officer, personnel. He spent close to two years in England before the invasion of France and then served on the Continent until he was discharged in February 1946.

In the fall of 1946 Amos enrolled in the biological sciences graduate program at Harvard Medical School (Division of Medical Sciences), earning an MA in 1947 and a PhD in Bacteriology and Immunology in 1952, becoming the first African American to earn a PhD from the division. After spending a year as a Fulbright Fellow at the renowned Pasteur Institute in Paris, where he worked with the molecular biologist Georges Cohen, Amos returned to Harvard Medical School. With the exception of three subsequent sabbatical periods in France, he remained at Harvard for close to fifty years, rising through the ranks as a faculty member in the Department of Bacteriology and Immunology (now Microbiology and Molecular Genetics). Amos was made a full professor in 1969, named the Maude and Lillian Presley Professor of Microbiology and Molecular Genetics in 1975, and became professor emeritus in 1988. As chair of his department from 1968 to 1971 and again from 1975 to 1978, Amos was the first African American to head a department at Harvard Medical School. He was known particularly for his interest in and encouragement of students and young faculty.

In his role as chairman of the Division of Medical Sciences at Harvard Medical School from 1971 to 1975 and from 1978 to 1988, Amos provided creative, forward-looking leadership with fairness and diplomacy. The door to his office was almost always open, and he welcomed drop-in visitors. For decades, students and faculty found Amos personified the Division of Medical Sciences. He was an effective, inspiring, and inexhaustible supporter of all students, especially minorities, in science and medicine, and served, often in leadership positions, on numerous boards and advisory committees dedicated to these interests. Among others, Amos sat on the board of directors of the Josiah Macy Jr. Foundation, the Minority Medical Faculty Development Program Advisory Committee of the Robert Wood Johnson Foundation, the National Cancer Advisory Board, the President's Cancer Panel, and the Massachusetts Division of the American Cancer Society. As part of his interest in expanding the participation of minorities in research, he was an early advocate of the National Institute of Health's programs for minority college students.

Early in his career Amos intended to pursue research as an *E. coli* microbiologist, but, upon realizing that it was a field already crowded with competent senior scientists, he decided to study animal viruses and animal cells in culture. He was particularly interested in cells that could become malignant when infected with animal viruses and in sugar metabolism in cells. The body of scientific work that Amos carried out was eclectic in its scope and in the questions he asked, but it can be characterized as uncovering many facets of metabolism and of understanding how cells function and influence organisms. Amos pioneered approaches to studying how proteins and RNA in cells are affected by nutrients, including glucose, and hormones, such as insulin, from outside the cell.

Amos used cells in culture to understand how molecules get into cells and how entry is regulated during cell starvation or in plentiful conditions. He was particularly interested in how these influences controlled metabolism of RNA, work he did at an early time in the history of RNA biology. His work provided valuable information to other investigators, who studied the normal and abnormal control of cell division and how this could provide insights into understanding cancer. Major laboratories around the world were influenced by the careful and dependable work that he published. Between 1953 and the mid-1980s he was an author on over seventy scientific papers.

Amos was legendary for the continual contributions that he made to the work of his colleagues, his own students, and to untold numbers of other students with whom he talked and worked. He had a prodigious memory and an unusually creative approach, and he always asked insightful questions and offered clear suggestions to a myriad of other scientists who were fortunate enough to cross his path. In this way he created an aura of old-fashioned intellectualism in its best sense, and he contributed, behind the scenes, to literally thousands of scientific papers by other authors who directly benefited from his input. By reaching such a broad group of scientists—in terms of their levels of training or profession, their institutions, and the types of biological science they pursued—Amos helped usher in modern biology and modern biologists.

Amos described teaching as one of his primary responsibilities, and he was always accessible, quick to offer words of praise and encouragement, advice, and support. Even during his graduate school days, Amos was praised for his devotion to and competence as both a teacher and a mentor. He followed his students' careers and personal lives with enthusiasm, regularly communicating with countless medical and graduate students, many of whom held important positions in a broad range of fields, long after they had graduated. He had an unusual ability to capture people's strengths and to help develop them.

Amos never married but had a large circle of devoted friends, drawn from all walks of life and representing many phases and interests of his own life. He was well known as an enthusiastic Francophile, enjoyed using his fluent French, and appreciated French literature, music, and cuisine. Amos was a gracious and attentive host, organizing dinners at interesting restaurants or at his farm near Kezar Falls, Maine, to which he invited people whom he thought would enjoy meeting each other.

Amos was the recipient of numerous awards, including several honorary doctoral degrees, the Centennial Medal of the Harvard Graduate School of Arts and Sciences (2000), the first Charles Drew World Medical Prize from Howard University (1989), and the National Academy of Sciences' highest honor, the Public Welfare Medal (1995). He was named a Fellow of the American Academy of Arts and Sciences (1974), and elected to the American Association for the Advancement of Science (1991) and the Institute of Medicine of the National Academy of Sciences (1991). A modest man, few of his colleagues were aware of the full range of honors he had received.

Upon the occasion of his retirement from Harvard Medical School at the age of seventy, he noted that he "had to get back to work to try to do something useful with these few remaining years" (letter, October 1989). He accepted the position as the first national director of the Minority Medical Faculty Development Program (MMFDP) of the Robert Wood Johnson Foundation, serving until 1994. He developed a reputation for keeping in contact with and encouraging the MMFDP Fellows and their family members long after their tenure in the program, and for seeking alternative positions for applicants who were not awarded fellowships. Amos wrote to a friend less than a year before his death that he was "still working full-time in the lab and writing two manuscripts" on glycerol metabolism in mammalian cells (letter, March

2002). Amos died in Boston on 26 February 2003, shortly after suffering a stroke.

Harold Amos broke many barriers during his lifetime, in the scientific insights he directly and indirectly made possible, in his teaching and mentoring, and in his administrative contributions. Wherever he served, he was chosen because of his superior credentials. Amos's personable and accessible style in all aspects of his life and work succeeded in blending highly competitive academic work with the highest level of cultural appreciation and enjoyment, all with a profound degree of attention to collegiality and friendship.

Further Reading

Amos's 1972–2003 papers are housed at the Countway Library of Medicine, Harvard Depository of Rare Books.

Beecher, H. K. *Medicine at Harvard: The First Three Hundred Years* (1977).

Obituaries: *Boston Globe*, 4 Mar. 2003; *Harvard University Gazette*, 6 Mar. 2003.

THOMAS O. FOX
JOCELYN SPRAGG

AMOS, Wally (1 July 1936–), entrepreneur, author, and inspirational speaker, was born Wallace Amos Jr. in Tallahassee, Florida, to Ruby (maiden name unknown), a domestic worker, and Wallace Amos, a laborer at the local gasoline plant. Hard work, discipline, and religion were the cornerstones of Wally's strict childhood. The Christian faith was important to his parents, and they took him to church regularly. By the age of eight Wally had learned all the books of the Bible. In their tight-knit black community, Friday nights were reserved for community dinners where hearty southern fare was served: fried chicken, potato salad, black-eyed peas, and collard greens. Schooling options for black children were less abundant, however, so Ruby and several of her Methodist church members started a school, which Wally began attending at age ten. Wally's entrepreneurial spirit surfaced in his childhood when he started a roving shoeshine stand and delivered newspapers for the local *Tallahassee Democrat*.

In 1948 Wally's parents divorced, and his mother sent him to live with her sister Della in New York City. New York made a striking impression on Wally, who after coming from the segregated South was fascinated by the rich cultural diversity of his new classmates. In contrast to Wally's serious mother, Aunt Della was lighthearted and instilled the joy of laughter into Wally. Ruby eventually followed her son to New York, and they shared a two-bedroom apartment in Harlem. Deciding that he wanted to become a cook, Amos enrolled at the Food Trades Vocational High School. He split his time between his vocational training and his academic subjects. Amos's training included part-time work in food services at the Essex House Hotel in Manhattan. Despite working hard and being qualified, Amos was passed over for a promotion, as were his black colleagues.

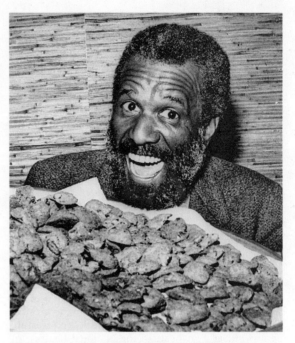

Wally Amos posing with cookies at a Tallahassee luncheon, 17 March 1983. (AP Images.)

Discouraged by the racism he had encountered, Amos dropped out of school to join the U.S. Air Force. He earned his GED High School Equivalency Diploma while in the Air Force, and he returned to New York four years later after being honorably discharged. In 1957 Amos started a new job as a stock clerk in the supply department at Saks Fifth Avenue, a New York department store. He worked hard and was promoted to manage the department, and the company paid for him to take retail and merchandising classes at New York University. In 1958 Amos married Maria (maiden name unknown); they had a son, Michael Anthony. Despite being given increasing responsibility, Amos felt that he was not being compensated adequately by Saks and decided to leave the company in 1961 with his wife expecting a second child.

Amos quickly found another job as a clerk in the mailroom of the William Morris Agency. Within a year of demonstrating his work ethic and managerial potential, he became the company's first black talent agent, in charge of the new rock-and-roll division. During his tenure at William Morris, Amos brought in Simon and Garfunkel and promoted clients including the Supremes, the Temptations, and MARVIN GAYE. In the shadow of his successful career and extramarital affairs, his marriage was faltering, and he divorced Maria and left their two children, Michael Anthony and Gregory, in her custody.

In 1967 Amos left William Morris and ventured out to Los Angeles with his new wife, Shirlee Ellis, and son, Shawn, to start his own talent agency. His start-up did not fare well, but his next venture proved more successful. Using his Aunt Della's recipe, Amos started baking chocolate-chip cookies. His cookies quickly became legendary, and inspired by a friend's suggestion, Wally started the Famous Amos Chocolate Chip Company in March 1975 with funds invested by Marvin Gaye, United Artists CEO Artie Mogull, and other friends. The first store was located on the Sunset Strip in Hollywood, and the demand for the company's cookies spread nationwide. Amos expanded the company over the next nine years, but managing the enterprise proved challenging. Outside investors infused cash into the ailing company on several occasions and retained a stake in the company, eventually leaving its founder with a minority share. In 1985 Amos's share had dwindled to 17 percent; after the company changed ownership a few more times, his stake in the company had eroded to zero, and he reluctantly agreed to disassociate himself from the company altogether. He signed a noncompete clause, effectively barring him from the cookie industry.

In 1977, his second marriage having ended, Amos moved to Hawaii and married for the third time, to his long-term girlfriend Christine (maiden name unknown); they had a daughter, Sarah. In 1979 he became the national spokesperson for Literacy Volunteers of America and became more involved in nonprofit organizations, including Cities in Schools, the Aloha United Way, and the Napoleon Hill Foundation. In November 1991, with the expiration of the noncompete clause, Amos started the Chip & Cookie Company. The owners of the Famous Amos Company launched a lawsuit charging that he had reneged on his previous agreement not to compete or use his likeness in association with food products. In 1993 an agreement was reached in which Amos would own his name for businesses not related to food and the rights of publicity to his name, and the Famous Amos Company would own the trademark rights to his name in association with foods. Amos had invested most of his financial resources into fighting the lawsuit and was burdened by debt. In spite of his financial woes he decided to start another cookie venture, the Uncle Noname Cookie Company. According to Amos, "The greater the pain, the harder the shock, the more hopeless the crisis, the more miraculous the outcome. Not only is every crisis resolved eventually; it is always resolved in the best possible way."

Amos has been a recurring guest on television shows, a product spokesman for corporations including Hush Puppies and United Airlines, and an inspirational speaker. His numerous awards include an honorary doctorate in education from Johnson and Wales University, the President's Award for Entrepreneurial Excellence, and the National Literacy Honors Award. He has also published several books, including his autobiography, and coauthored a self-help book with his son Gregory.

Further Reading
Amos, Wally, with Leroy Robinson. *The Famous Amos Story: The Face That Launched a Thousand Chips* (1983).

AYESHA KANJI

ANDERSON, Aaron (18??–?), sailor, was one of eight African American seamen to earn the Medal of Honor during the Civil War. Likely in his early twenties when he enlisted as a landsman (for which he was tasked with the simplest sail-handling and duties like manning the yardarm) in the Union navy from Pennsylvania, Anderson was probably born a free black and, because he was rated a landsman, had little or no prior seafaring experience.

Though few details of Aaron Anderson's military service are known, and virtually nothing of his private life, his exemplary service nonetheless serves to highlight the importance of the African American contribution to the Union navy in what was, up to that time, the nation's bloodiest war. Along with such men as JOACHIM PEASE, ROBERT SMALLS, and JOHN LAWSON, AARON ANDERSON was one of approximately eighteen thousand African Americans (eleven of them women) to serve in the Union navy from 1861 to 1865. Accounting for approximately 20 percent of the navy's enlisted force, these men and women came from such predominantly coastal states as Maryland, Massachusetts, New York, Pennsylvania, and New Jersey. Twenty-three hundred men alone came from Maryland, many of them experienced Chesapeake Bay sailors. Even inland states, such as Ohio and Kentucky, provided a healthy number of men with experience as river boatmen. When the war began, African Americans made up only 8 percent of the navy's strength. This number would peak at 23 percent from 1863–1864.

While segregation was the rule in the Union army for African American soldiers, the navy was less restrictive when it came to race relations. There had always been a tradition of black service in the navy, dating back to the days of the American Revolution, and the Civil War proved to be no different. Because of this, sailors like Aaron Anderson ate and slept with their white shipmates and were subject to the same naval code of discipline. Although conflicts between African American and white sailors aboard ship were not uncommon, records indicate that white sailors who took part in such fights were often disciplined on an equal basis with black sailors. Though instances of abuse of African American sailors at the hands of their white officers were not unknown, they do not seem to have been the norm. As to the positions held by African American sailors, most, like Anderson, served as landsmen. Black sailors also filled a wide variety of other ratings, including "ship's boy," coal-passer, fireman, steward, able-seaman, and ordinary seaman. One important aspect of African American naval service was the significant use of those men, such as ROBERT BLAKE, who were formerly enslaved. Referred to as contrabands, these men often acted as pilots and served to guide the Union navy through the small creeks and rivers in the South to attack Confederate positions. A major complaint of those blacks serving in the navy, however, was the inability to gain promotion to petty officer status. Despite their fine and in many cases heroic service, only a small number of men achieved such a promotion, in stark contrast to the men serving ashore as non-commissioned officers in the army's black regiments.

Whatever their rating, it is almost certain that every ship in the Union navy had at least one African American crewman. The majority of black sailors served on colliers, store ships, and other support vessels. Research has shown that anywhere from 63–100 percent of the men serving on these types of ships were of African American descent (Reidy, p. 5). The black presence in other ships, such as sloops of war, was considerably less. Examples of Union vessels crewed primarily by African Americans include the store-ship *Valparaiso* (43 of 46 men), the receiving ship *Vermont* (143 of 144 men), the paddle-wheel steamer *Stepping Stones* (32 of 34 men), and the gunboat *Glide* (30 of 38 men). In all of these cases, the few whites in each crew served as masters and in other officer positions.

Despite the perceptions of whites regarding their heritage, black sailors were in fact a welcome addition to the ships of the Union navy, always in competition with the army when it came to manpower needs. To be sure, navy admirals always preferred white crewmen. However, they also recognized the quality of their black enlistees and, unlike the army, utilized African Americans from the beginning of the war. Rear Admiral David Porter wrote to Rear Admiral A. H. Foote on 3 January 1863, "Don't be astonished at the lists of niggers I send you. I could get no men. They do first-rate," while Rear Admiral Samuel Du Pont wrote Secretary of the Navy Gideon Welles later that year that contrabands were "very useful, particularly as there is difficulty in obtaining men in the North ports" (Quarles, 229).

In regards to the service of Aaron Anderson, we know little of the details except for the act of bravery that made him the last African American naval Medal of Honor winner in the Civil War. Indeed it is because so little is known of Anderson that he is often the forgotten recipient among the African Americans who earned this high honor. While serving as a landsman on the store ship *Wyandank*, on 17 March 1865 he was part of a small boat crew sent on an expedition to clear Confederate positions in Mattox Creek, Virginia. According to his citation, Anderson "carried out his duties courageously in face of a devastating fire which cut away half the oars, pierced the launch in many places and cut the barrel off a musket being fired at the enemy" (*Medal of Honor*, 13). Earning the Medal of Honor alongside Anderson during the engagement was the *Wyandank*'s white boatswain's mate, Patrick Mullin.

After winning the Medal of Honor, Aaron Anderson disappears from history; his common name and a lack of naval records have made it impossible for historians to trace his whereabouts with any certainty. His meritorious naval service, however, dictates that he should always be remembered as a true American hero.

Further Reading
King, Lisa Y. "They Called Us Bluejackets," *International Journal of Naval History* 1.1 (Apr. 2002).
Quarles, Benjamin. *The Negro in the Civil War* (1953).
Reidy, Joseph P. "Black Men in Navy Blue during the Civil War," *Prologue Magazine* 33.3 (Fall 2001).
United States Navy. *Medal of Honor, 1861–1949: The Navy* (1950).

GLENN ALLEN KNOBLOCK

ANDERSON, Bruce (19 June 1845–22 Aug. 1922), Civil War soldier and Medal of Honor winner, was born in Mexico, Oswego County, New York. Unrecorded in the 1850 federal census, the names of Anderson's parents are confirmed to be unknown. However, likely candidates are Samuel and Mary Anderson, the only black or "mulatto" family recorded living in Oswego County in the 1840 (town of Granby) and 1850 (town of West Oswego) censuses. Samuel Anderson was a native of Bermuda, and his wife, Mary, was a New York native. Bruce Anderson does appear in the 1860 census, listed as a fourteen-year-old "mulatto" residing in Johnstown, New York, on the farm of Henry Adams and his daughter Margaret; he was likely a simple laborer. How he came to live with the Adams family is unknown, but Anderson would remain a resident in the area—except during the time of his Civil War service—for the remainder of his life.

While some African Americans served in units formed in Kansas, South Carolina, and Louisiana late in 1862, until adoption of the Emancipation Proclamation, the Lincoln administration refused to recruit black soldiers. Although a very small number of blacks such as Anderson and H. FORD DOUGLAS did serve in white units, northern racial prejudice precluded the general recruitment of black soldiers. But with falling recruitment rates and ballooning causality lists, the federal government was compelled to change course, recognize black patriotism, and recruit black troops. By mid-1863 black regiments had been formed in Massachusetts, Pennsylvania, and Ohio, but New York lagged behind and did not begin to form its own black units until the next year.

Sometime in 1863 or 1864 Bruce Anderson decided to enlist in the Union army. While military records do not give the date, his place of enlistment as a private in Company K of the 142nd New York Infantry Regiment was at Ephratah, New York, a short distance west of Johnstown. Although census records describe Anderson as "Mulatto" or "Black," he must have been rather light-skinned to have been allowed to assimilate into a white regiment; otherwise his recruitment would have been rejected, or he would have been immediately transferred to one of New York's all-black regiments, which began forming in 1864. By establishing himself in the 142nd, Anderson became a rare exception to Northern recruitment patterns. He also joined the nearly 180,000 African American troops fighting for the Union, and symbolized their exceptional valor.

Because it is unknown when Anderson joined his regiment, the full extent of his service remains a mystery. He might have taken part in the regiment's most notable actions at Cold Harbor, Petersburg, and New Market Heights from May to October 1864. He could have been enlisted as a replacement for casualties suffered in these battles, but he was a confirmed member of the regiment by November 1864 during its trench duty before the Confederate capital of Richmond, Virginia. In any case, Anderson became a private in the 142nd when it was assigned to the First Brigade, Second Division of General Alfred Terry's Provisional Corps in the Department of North Carolina in early December 1864 to aid in the reduction of Fort Fisher, one of the few remaining Confederate strongholds in the South.

Located at the mouth of the Cape Fear River, Fort Fisher stood guard over the Confederacy's sole remaining port of Wilmington, North Carolina. Made of earth and sand and armed with forty-seven cannons, twenty-five of them facing land and twenty-two pointed seaward, the fort proved formidable. In the first Union assault, conducted by General Benjamin Butler from 24 to 26 December 1864, Union forces were thwarted. The second attempt was led by General Terry, who well understood that a coordinated naval and ground attack was required to achieve victory. Union troops, including Anderson and the men of the 142nd, landed before the fort on 13 January 1864. Two days later an intense bombardment by Union naval forces knocked out nearly all of the fort's guns, while marine forces undertook an assault at the point where the sea and river sides of the forts met. Although the assault was unorganized and costly, it did serve to divert forces away from the main infantry assault on the river side of Fort Fisher. This assault began at 2:00 P.M. when an advance guard composed of men from the 142nd and other units in the Second Brigade armed themselves with axes and cut through the wooden palisades and abatis guarding the fort's outer works. Then they stormed the fort in the first assault wave, suffering heavy casualties. Among the men in this advance guard—a group sometimes referred to as a "forlorn hope" because their chances of returning alive were slim—was Anderson. Bravely volunteering to serve in the advance guard, Anderson not only exhibited supreme heroism but lived to tell about it. The fight for Fort Fisher lasted for nearly eight hours before the Confederates surrendered just before ten o'clock that evening. Casualties for the Union numbered just over thirteen hundred, while the Confederacy's were nearly double that number.

Anderson continued his service with the 142nd until the end of the war, participating in actions during the capture of Wilmington and Raleigh, North Carolina, and the surrender of General Joseph Johnston's Confederate army before leaving the service on 7 June 1865. Anderson's activities immediately after the Civil War are unknown, but it is likely he returned to New York. By 1880 Bruce Anderson was working as a farm laborer in Amsterdam, New York, living as a boarder at the house of a black family, John (b. 1840) and Alida (b. 1843) James, along with their son Edward (b. 1861) and grandson Harvey Howard (b. 1879). There he met his future wife, Julia James (b. 1855), and married her in 1884. By 1900 the couple had four children: Grace (b. 1886), Elizabeth (b. 1888), Edward (b. 1890), and Lena (b. 1893). Alida James, Julia's stepmother, also lived with the Anderson family.

Anderson remained in Amsterdam, living a quiet but respectable life. His heroism in the Civil War was not entirely forgotten; on 28 December 1914, at the age of sixty-nine, he received the Medal of Honor for his actions with the advance guard at Fort Fisher in January 1865. How the medal came to be awarded to Anderson at such a late date is unknown, but it was likely because of efforts by fellow townsmen, veterans, and local or state politicians. Anderson was not alone in receiving his medal so late; even WILLIAM HARVEY CARNEY, the "first" black Medal of Honor winner, did not actually receive his award until years after the close of the war. Racial discrimination likely played a role in the delays, but so did simple oversight and bureaucratic delays during the confusion that reigned at the war's end. For Anderson, however, the Medal of Honor, sadly, came just after the death of his wife, Julia; Anderson himself would die eight years later. Perhaps the least known of any decorated African American Civil War soldier, a Medal of Honor gravestone marks Anderson's burial site in Amsterdam's Green Hill Cemetery to ensure that his heroism will not be forgotten.

Further Reading
Quarles, Benjamin Arthur. *The Negro in the Civil War* (1989).

GLENN ALLEN KNOBLOCK

ANDERSON, Caroline Virginia Still Wiley (1 Nov. 1848–2 June 1919), physician, educator, and community worker, was born in Philadelphia, Pennsylvania. She was the eldest daughter of the abolitionist movement leaders WILLIAM STILL and Letitia George Still. In 1850 William Still became the head of the Philadelphia Underground Railroad and Vigilance Committee. He would later chronicle his experiences in the best-selling 1872 account, *The Underground Railroad*.

After completing primary and secondary education at Mrs. Henry Gordon's Private School, the Friends Raspberry Alley School, and the Institute for Colored Youth, Anderson entered Oberlin College. Although she was the youngest member of the graduating class of 1868, Anderson presided over the annual Ladies' Literary Society, a singular honor that had never been awarded to a student of African ancestry.

After graduating from Oberlin, Anderson returned home to teach drawing and elocution, and on 28 December 1869 she married Edward A. Wiley, a former slave and fellow Oberlin student. The ceremony took place in her parents' home, and the celebration that followed was in effect a reunion of former workers in the antislavery movement. ELIZABETH TAYLOR GREENFIELD, the first major American concert artist of African descent, performed music for sixty or seventy guests including ROBERT PURVIS, Dilwyn Parrish, H. M. Laing, SARAH MAPPS DOUGLASS, WILLIAM WHIPPER, and Lucretia Mott.

Edward Wiley died prematurely in 1874, and in the following year Anderson left Philadelphia with their two children, William and Letitia, to matriculate at Howard University College of Medicine in Washington, D.C. To support her young family, she also taught drawing and elocution at Howard.

There is sufficient evidence to indicate that Anderson had entertained thoughts of becoming a physician long before the death of her husband; possibly, as a student at the Institute for Colored Youth, where Sarah Mapps Douglass headed the girls' department. Douglass, a member of the Philadelphia Female Anti-Slavery Society and the first black woman to complete a medical course in the United States, believed that women should be educated for more than domesticity and made science, particularly physiology, an integral part of the curriculum for her female students. At Oberlin, Anderson had selected courses in chemistry, physiology, and anatomy. Back home in Philadelphia, she had attended lectures in physiology at the Woman's Medical College of Pennsylvania during the 1872–1873 winter sessions. Others who might have influenced Anderson's decision to pursue a career in medicine were her father's brother, JAMES STILL, a well-known medical practitioner in Medford, New Jersey, and his son, James Thomas Still, one of the first black graduates from Harvard Medical School who by 1874 had established an extensive practice in Boston.

At the end of her first year at Howard's medical school, Anderson returned to Philadelphia and matriculated at the Woman's Medical College of Pennsylvania, which had been founded by the Quakers in 1850. With philosophical underpinnings of liberalism and humanitarianism, this first American medical school for women would educate more black and Native American female doctors than any other predominantly white medical college in nineteenth-century America. Anderson graduated in the class of 1878 with one other student of African ancestry, Georgianna E. Young. They were the first black students to graduate from the school since 1867, when REBECCA COLE, the first black graduate from Woman's Medical College, was awarded an MD.

In 1879, after a yearlong internship at Boston's New England Hospital for Women and Children, Anderson established a practice in Philadelphia. A year later, on 17 August 1880, she married MATTHEW ANDERSON, a Presbyterian minister from Greencastle, Pennsylvania, who had studied at Oberlin College and seminaries at both Yale and Princeton. As a student at Princeton, he had been the first black student to live "in-residence." The couple had three daughters: Helen, Maude, and Margaret.

Less than a year after the marriage, on 10 June 1881, the Reverend Anderson organized the Berean Presbyterian Church, which spawned several enterprises, and his wife, "Dr. C. V.," as she was fondly called by the parishioners, played a major role in the development and operation of all of them, particularly the Berean Institute, established in 1899. In his groundbreaking sociological study of blacks in Philadelphia, W. E. B. DU BOIS observed that the church also conducted "a successful Building and Loan Association, a kindergarten, a medical dispensary, and a seaside home" and cited the Berean Presbyterian Church as one of two churches that were working "for the social betterment of the Negro" (Du Bois, 216–217). Later a bureau of mutual help, a type of placement service for students who had completed courses at the Berean Institute, was also created. As part of a continuing education program, each year the church sponsored two conferences that were held at the church and cottage and featured prominent speakers, both black and white, including BOOKER T. WASHINGTON, ALEXANDER CRUMMELL, Grover Cleveland, FRANCIS JAMES GRIMKÉ, and CHARLOTTE FORTEN GRIMKÉ. Occasionally, Anderson herself would present a paper.

Anderson was assistant principal, instructor of elocution, physiology, and hygiene, and supervisor of the dispensary at the Berean Institute. She was also manager of the seaside cottage and the bureau of mutual help, as well as the head of the Berean Woman's Christian Temperance Union. But her activities were not limited to those directly associated with the work that she and her husband had established. Anderson was often asked, and usually consented, to assume leadership for community projects such as organizing a Young Women's Christian Association for blacks or serving on the editorial board for *Who's Who in Philadelphia*, a collection of biographical sketches that was published in 1912. One contemporary described her as the "most intellectual woman" he had ever met.

In spite of commitments to church, community, and family, Anderson managed to maintain a private practice that was "evenly divided between white and colored people" (Richings, 412). She also treated patients at the City District and the Home for the Aged and Infirm Colored Persons, an institution established in 1864 and principally funded by prominent blacks and Quakers of Philadelphia. To meet the challenge of keeping informed of the rapidly changing developments in late-nineteenth- and early-twentieth-century medicine, Anderson assiduously retained her relationship with professional colleagues and participated in the meetings of the alumni association of the Woman's Medical College of Pennsylvania, serving as treasurer in 1888.

Anderson practiced medicine for more than thirty years, becoming a member of an elite group of American women: the first to demonstrate that gender and race prejudice in medicine need not be deterrents for black women who want to become physicians. Following a series of progressively debilitating strokes, she died at her home in Philadelphia.

Further Reading

Papers on Caroline Virginia Still Wiley Anderson are on file in the Archives and Special Collections/Black Women Physicians at Drexel University College of Medicine.

Du Bois, W. E. B. *The Philadelphia Negro: A Social Study* (1899, repr. 1967).

Hine, Darlene Clark. "Co-laborers in the Work of the Lord," in *"Send Us a Lady Physician": Women Doctors in America*, ed. Ruth Abrams (1985).

Peitzman, Steven J. *A New and Untried Course: Woman's Medical College and Medical College of Pennsylvania, 1850–1998* (2000).

Richings, G. F. *Evidences of Progress among Colored People* (1902).

GERALDINE RHOADES BECKFORD

ANDERSON, Cat (12 Sept. 1916–29 Apr. 1981), jazz trumpeter, was born William Alonzo Anderson Jr. in Greenville, South Carolina. Nothing is known of his parents, who died when he was four. Anderson grew up in Jenkins' Orphanage in Charleston, where as a boy he received the nickname "Cat" after scratching and tearing in a fight with a bully. He played in the orphanage's renowned bands, beginning on trombone and playing other brass and percussion instruments before taking up trumpet. From 1929 onward he participated in orphanage band tours, and in Florida in 1933 he formed the cooperative Carolina Cotton Pickers with fellow orphanage musicians. Returning to Charleston in 1934, they continued playing as the Carolina Cotton Pickers and then resumed touring.

Independent of the orphanage, Anderson held his first lasting affiliation with the Sunset Royals (c. 1936–1942). From 1942 to 1944 he worked in the big bands of LUCKY MILLINDER; the trumpeter ERSKINE HAWKINS, from which Anderson was quickly dismissed for upstaging Hawkins with his high-note trumpeting; LIONEL HAMPTON; Sabby Lewis; and Hampton again. In September 1944 Anderson joined DUKE ELLINGTON's orchestra. Anderson followed in the path of established trumpeting roles in the group, contributing an intense but understated and muted solo on his own composition "Teardrops in the Rain" (1945) and a vocalized plunger-muted solo on "A Gatherin' in a Clearin'" (1946). But his personal trademark was his ability to play in an astonishingly high range, of which the finest example is certainly "Trumpet No End" (1946).

Leaving Ellington in February 1947, Anderson led his own band until he rejoined Lewis briefly in 1949 and then Ellington in December 1950. Apart from a long absence in 1951, he remained with Ellington until November 1959. Notable recordings from this period include a plunger-muted solo on his own blues composition "Cat Walk" (1951) with the Coronets, a septet spun off from the big band; an improvised trumpet battle with CLARK TERRY and Willie Cook on "Duke's Jam" on the alto saxophonist JOHNNY HODGES's album *Ellingtonia '56* (1956); and a featured solo on "Madness in Great Ones" on Ellington's album *Such Sweet Thunder* (1957).

After leading another band and freelancing in Philadelphia, Anderson rejoined Ellington once again in April 1961. He is seen and heard in the film short *Duke Ellington and His Orchestra* (1962). In 1967 Ellington held a lengthy engagement at the Rainbow Grill in New York City with an eight-piece band that afforded Anderson an opportunity to demonstrate much more versatile trumpeting skills than his role as a high-note player normally allowed. Anderson remained in the orchestra until January 1971.

In 1971, finally tiring of incessant touring, Anderson became a freelancer on the West Coast, where he worked extensively as a studio musician. But he continued playing with jazz bands. He was a guest soloist with the bassist CHARLES MINGUS's group at the Newport Jazz Festival in July 1972, and on a European tour in the fall, Mingus featured Anderson in lengthy, plunger-muted solos on "Perdido." Anderson later played with the trumpeter Bill Berry's big band, and he participated in a few reunions with Ellington's band and with Hampton's, including the album *Lionel Hampton and His Jazz Giants '77* (1977) and some European tours with Hampton until 1979. Anderson also recorded his own album, *Cat Speaks* (1977). He died of cancer in Norwalk, California.

Before the Canadian trumpeter Maynard Ferguson emerged during the 1950s, Anderson was the undisputed master of freakish high-note trumpeting. Many Ellington aficionados prefer his stylistically derivative work, after the manner of LOUIS ARMSTRONG, COOTIE WILLIAMS, and others, to his personalized high-note displays, which were often sloppy, out-of-tune, and tasteless (for example, numerous versions of "Jam with Sam"). But on those occasions when it worked, as in the last minute of "Trumpet No End," Anderson's exhilarating trumpeting was nothing short of spectacular.

Further Reading

Chilton, John. *A Jazz Nursery: The Story of the Jenkins' Orphanage Bands of Charleston, South Carolina* (1980).

Dance, Stanley. *The World of Duke Ellington* (1970; repr., 1981).

Lambert, Eddie. "Cat Anderson: A Résumé of His Recorded Work," *Jazz Journal International* 35 (June 1982).

Obituaries: *New York Times*, 2 May 1981; *Jazz Journal International* 34 (July 1981).

BARRY KERNFELD

ANDERSON, Charles Alfred "Chief" (9 Feb. 1907–13 Apr. 1996), aviator and instructor of the Tuskegee Airmen, was born in Bryn Mawr, Pennsylvania, to Janie and Iverson Anderson, of whom little else is known. During his early childhood, he lived with his grandmother in Staunton, Virginia. There Anderson longed for an airplane so he could fly to see what was on the other side of the mountains that surrounded Staunton and the Shenandoah Valley. He frequently left home in search of airplanes that were rumored to have crashed in the valley. His constant disappearances frustrated his grandmother, and she sent him back to his parents. Once back in Pennsylvania, however, he continued leaving home in search of airplanes.

At the age of thirteen Anderson applied to aviation school, but was denied admission because he was African American. In 1926, at the age of nineteen, he used his savings and borrowed money from friends and relatives to purchase a used Velie Monocoupe, one of the first airplanes manufactured for private pilots. He appealed to white flight instructors and flight schools to teach him to fly, but no program would accept an African American student, but, persevering, he eventually found a school that would teach him basic ground school subjects and elementary aircraft maintenance. Anderson learned about aviation at the airport by listening to the pilots talk and watching airplanes take off and land. He spent six weeks practicing in his airplane learning on his own until he developed the courage to take off. On one of his early flights, Anderson hit a tree but remained undaunted and was successful in teaching himself to fly. In August of 1929 he earned his private pilot's license, and in 1932 he earned his air transport license—becoming the first African American to do so.

Earning the coveted air transport license, however, was not the means to productive employment in aviation that Anderson had anticipated. No airline or aviation company would hire him. Instead of using his piloting skills, he had to take a series of menial jobs, including caretaker for a boarding school and ditch digger.

It was while Anderson was employed as a ditch digger that he met Dr. ALBERT E. FORSYTHE, a prominent African American doctor who practiced in Newark and Atlantic City, New Jersey, and a pilot in his own right. Forsythe approached Anderson with the idea of using their mutual expertise in aviation to showcase African American potential in the burgeoning field of aviation. In July 1933 Anderson and Forsythe flew from Atlantic City, New Jersey, to Los Angeles, California, and back, making them the first African Americans to complete a round trip, transcontinental flight across the United States. This flight was accomplished without the aid of landing lights, parachutes, air-to-ground radios, or other modern instrumentation. In fact the only instruments they had were a compass and an altimeter, and they navigated the route using a road map.

The aviation duo also flew to Montreal, Canada, making them the first African Americans to fly internationally. In 1934 they promoted their "Pan American Goodwill Tour" of the Caribbean and South America in Forsythe's Fairchild 24, "The Spirit of BOOKER T. WASHINGTON" which he had purchased earlier that year. They first flew from Miami to the Bahamas, making them the first pilots to land an airplane in Nassau, which had no airport. Later in the tour, the plane crashed in Trinidad. Even with the unfortunate end of the airplane, the tour received worldwide attention and upon their return to the United States, the pair was honored in Newark, New Jersey, with a parade with more than 15,000 onlookers. Anderson would later recreate this historic flight on his eighty-sixth birthday.

Anderson married his childhood sweetheart, Gertrude Elizabeth Nelson, in 1933. The couple would have two sons, Alfred and Charles.

In the late 1930s Anderson offered flight instruction to African American youth and adults in Pennsylvania, and in 1939 he initiated the Civilian Pilot Training Program at Howard University in Washington, D.C. In 1940 he became an instructor in the Civilian Pilot Training Program at Tuskegee Institute (later Tuskegee University) in Alabama. He was the first pilot to fly an airplane into Tuskegee.

On 19 April 1941 First Lady Eleanor Roosevelt, wife of President Franklin Delano Roosevelt, visited Tuskegee Institute to learn more about infantile paralysis on behalf of her husband, who suffered with the disease. A Tuskegee Institute physician told her about the aviation program, and she requested a tour. She was introduced to Anderson and asked if he would give her a ride in his airplane. Against the adamant advice of her Secret Service staff, Anderson gave Eleanor Roosevelt a successful, forty-minute ride in his two-seater airplane.

In 1941 the first class of aviation cadets arrived at Tuskegee Institute to begin flight training. "Chief" Anderson was the key flight instructor for the primary phase of flight training for the Tuskegee Airmen, who became the first African Americans to serve as pilots in the U.S. military. His students included General BENJAMIN O. DAVIS, General DANIEL "CHAPPIE" JAMES, and the over 1,000 African American men who received flight instruction at Tuskegee Institute's Moton Field.

Anderson was a founding member of Tuskegee Airmen, Inc., an organization dedicated to remembering and honoring those first pilots, and Negro Airmen International. In 1988 he was awarded an honorary doctor of science degree from Tuskegee University. Known as the father of black aviation Charles Alfred "Chief" Anderson is noted for his persevering spirit in the field of aviation and his innumerable contributions to the legacy of the Tuskegee Airmen. Anderson died of cancer at his home in Tuskegee.

Further Reading
Cooper, Charlie. *Tuskegee Heroes* (1996).
Dryden, Charles. *A-Train: Memoirs of a Tuskegee Airman* (1997).
Obituary: *New York Times*, 17 Apr. 1996.

LISA M. BRATTON

ANDERSON, Charles W., Jr. (26 May 1907–14 June 1960), attorney, politician, and diplomat, was born in Louisville, Kentucky. He was the youngest of two children and the only son of Charles W. Anderson Sr., a physician, and Tabitha L. Murphy, a teacher.

Motivated by the high value that his parents placed on education, Charles W. Anderson Jr. entered Kentucky State College at age fifteen and attended from 1922 to 1925. He then transferred to Wilberforce University, one of the earliest universities established for African Americans. Although the reason for Anderson's transfer to Wilberforce University during the penultimate year of his undergraduate career is unclear, it is likely that he, like other black Kentuckians, was forced to pursue higher education outside of the state because of the still-standing *Plessy v. Ferguson* decision of 1896 authorizing separate but equal educational facilities. Higher educational institutions for blacks did not exist in Kentucky, and rather than wait for them to be created, Anderson moved to where the opportunities existed. After graduating from Wilberforce, Anderson attended Howard University's law school in Washington, D.C., and graduated with an LLB in 1930, at the age of twenty-three.

Anderson returned to Kentucky after graduation and passed the bar in 1932. Four years later, while working as a partner in his own firm of Anderson, Thomas & Walker, he helped to prepare the appeal of RAINEY BETHEA, a black man who was accused of robbing, raping, and murdering Lischia Edwards, a white woman, on 7 June 1936. Bethea's conviction was based on a variety of evidence, including fingerprints, possession of stolen goods, and no fewer than five confessions. He was convicted of rape and sentenced to death by hanging in accordance with Kentucky law. Although Bethea was initially accused of raping and murdering Edwards, the latter being a crime punishable by death in an electric chair, the Daviess County commonwealth attorney decided to drop the murder charges against Bethea and charge him solely with the crime of rape. By taking this step, the attorney all but eliminated the risk of having to decide between the competing punishments of death by hanging and death by electrocution in the case of a conviction.

Anderson and his legal team were not part of their client's initial defense, but they did volunteer to work on his appeal and lobbied to have the case overturned. The request was denied by the circuit court, led by the Daviess County commonwealth attorney, on the false grounds that Anderson and his team had inaccurately submitted Bethea's paperwork to the clerk of court. In anticipation of the court's negative response, Anderson and his team filed a writ of habeas corpus, which would allow them to petition the Daviess commonwealth for a new trial by arguing that the lower court had ruled against Bethea in error. This request was also denied. Bethea was hanged on 14 August 1936 in a public spectacle.

Unable to prevent Bethea's death through litigation, Anderson sought legislatively to end all future deaths by hanging. Later that year Anderson won a seat in the Kentucky House of Representatives as a Republican.

One of Anderson's first missions as state representative was to sponsor a bill that would repeal Kentucky's law mandating hanging for the crime of rape. The bill, which passed into law, stipulated that rape would carry the same sentence as other capital felonies, death by electrocution.

During his five two-year terms, Anderson succeeded in sponsoring many bills that became laws. For example, in an effort to combat his state's school segregation statute, one of Anderson's bills mandated that rural school districts offer secondary education to their black students. Moreover, the districts were required to pay each student $100, as well as transportation costs to a neighboring district in the event that students were unable to attend schools in their own home districts. Anderson similarly sponsored legislation entitling black students to $5,000 each if they were forced to enroll in a graduate degree program outside of Kentucky because one did not exist for them in the state. Finally, and perhaps as a tribute to his mother, Anderson helped to ensure that teachers were no longer required to forfeit their jobs upon marriage.

In 1946 Anderson resigned his seat in the Kentucky House of Representatives and accepted a position as Jefferson County's first black commonwealth assistant attorney. Unlike attorneys at the city and county levels, the new position gave Anderson the power he had lacked years earlier when defending Bethea. Among his duties was the ability to prosecute rape felonies and grant legal appeals. Anderson held the position until 1952.

It is not known whether Anderson was married or had any children. His life was cut short ten months after Dwight D. Eisenhower appointed him as an alternate U.S. delegate to the General Assembly of the United Nations on 21 August 1959. He died in Shelby County, Kentucky, when his car was struck by a train.

Further Reading

Kentucky Personnel Cabinet. *History of the Anderson Laureate*, available online at http://personnel.ky.gov/eeo/laureate.htm.
Ryan, Perry T. *The Last Public Execution in America*, available online at www.geocities.com/lastpublichang.
Wright, George C. A *History of Blacks in Kentucky: In Pursuit of Equality, 1890–1980*, vol. 2 (1992).
Wright, George C. *Racial Violence in Kentucky, 1865–1940: Lynchings, Mob Rule, and "Legal Lynchings"* (1990).
Wright, George C. *Life behind a Veil: Blacks in Louisville, Kentucky, 1865–1930* (1985).

TERESA A. BOOKER

ANDERSON, Charles William (28 Apr. 1866–28 Jan. 1938), politician and public official, was born in Oxford, Ohio, the son of Charles W. Anderson and Serena (maiden name unknown). After a public school education in his hometown and in Middletown, Ohio, Charles studied at Spencerian Business College in Cleveland and at the Berlitz School of Languages in Worcester, Massachusetts. Anderson's schooling continued informally as he matured into an intellectually accomplished and engaging man. His friend JAMES

WELDON JOHNSON noted Anderson's versatility, which included acute powers of observation and an ability to converse on many subjects, including "the English poets, the Irish patriots, [and] the contemporary leaders of the British Parliament" (Johnson, 219).

Anderson put these talents to good use after moving to New York City in 1886. He grabbed whatever opportunities that Republican Party politics offered ambitious black men, and he developed a ward heeler's capacity for keeping close track of voters, loaves, and fishes. By 1890 he had entered upon a succession of party and patronage positions that kept him busy through much of the rest of his life. Also in 1890 Anderson became president of the Young Men's Colored Republican Club of New York County and was appointed a gauger at the Internal Revenue Service. He served in that position until 1893, when he became private secretary to the New York State treasurer. In 1895 Anderson was named chief clerk of the state treasury, and in 1898 he became supervisor of accounts for the state racing commission, holding that post until 1905. In 1904 Anderson organized the New York City Colored Republican Club and worked for the reelection of Theodore Roosevelt. By then he had married Emma Lee Bonaparte.

Anderson's rise through the ranks seems to have been not simply because of party loyalty and personal charisma but also because he performed his jobs quite well. Theodore Roosevelt, one-time governor of New York, praised the "splendid efficiency" of Anderson's work for the racing commission and, in 1905, named him collector of internal revenue for the Second New York District. Explaining Anderson's appointment to this most visible position, BOOKER T. WASHINGTON contended that, given the widespread resistance to black officeholding, Roosevelt was "determined to set the example by placing a coloured man in a high office in his own home city, so that the country might see that he did not want other parts of the country to accept that which he himself was not willing to receive" (Harlan and Smock, vol. 1, 442). But the collectorship was not a position that could have been well served by any mere token appointee. The Second District included the financial heart of New York (and, consequently, of the nation), as well as the Manhattan docks. Anderson had charge of scores of deputy collectors, inspectors, and clerks, and he annually collected millions of dollars in revenue, eventually including income taxes. Anderson did good work, earning considerable support among the Wall Street elite. During this and his second collectorship, Anderson always kept his eye out for openings that might be filled by African Americans in the Internal Revenue Service, in other federal, state, and municipal agencies, and in the Republican Party. For instance, he helped arrange James Weldon Johnson's appointment to the consular service.

Though he had a hand in the passage of a state civil rights statute in 1895, Anderson's interest in developing practical opportunity and material reward for African Americans, rather than in more forthrightly agitating for racial justice, put him in sympathy with Booker T. Washington. The two were close allies as well as ideological soul mates. Washington helped secure the collectorship for Anderson, and Anderson became one of the most important cogs in the "Tuskegee Machine," the vehicle of patronage and discreet influence that Washington operated from his Alabama base, even as he counseled African Americans to put aside politics. As the machine's man in New York, Anderson traded political intelligence, gossip, and favors with Washington, who periodically forwarded an opossum from Alabama for Anderson's dinner table. Anderson egged Washington on in his struggles with critics like W. E. B. DU BOIS, recommending that Washington administer "a good thrashing" to "these young upstarts" (Harlan, 78). Indeed, Anderson did what he could to have Washington's adversaries dismissed from federal jobs, monitored the progress of the NAACP, and even played dirty tricks on NAACP supporters, such as planting stories of race mixing in white newspapers.

Anderson's excellent reputation as collector, which moved even Du Bois to recommend him for a diplomatic post, and his strong ties to the New York business community apparently kept him from immediately falling victim to Woodrow Wilson's hostility to black Republican officeholders. Anderson was not required to step down until March 1915, two years into Wilson's term as president. Anderson thereupon returned to state and party employ to wait out the interregnum. In 1915 he went to work for the New York State agriculture department, supervising inspectors and marketing operations in New York City. In 1916 and 1920 he was active among black voters during the GOP national campaigns. He returned to the higher reaches of federal patronage in 1923, when he was appointed collector of internal revenue for the newly created Third New York District. The district included his own neighborhood of Harlem. By 1928 the ailing Anderson had become less active in the day-to-day operations of the collectorship. He retired in 1934 and died in New York City four years later.

Anderson was the first important black politician in New York City and was certainly among the most powerful African American officeholders anywhere in the United States during the first decades of the twentieth century. His influence illustrated the growing importance of northern city-dwellers in black politics, as African Americans migrated out of the South and those that remained were marginalized by disfranchisement and the rise of "lily white" Republicanism. Anderson's career symbolizes, too, the significance in that era of the federal government and of the Republican Party to African Americans not simply as guarantors, though inconstant, of civil rights but also as providers of professional opportunity.

Further Reading

Harlan, Louis. *Booker T. Washington: The Wizard of Tuskegee, 1901–1915* (1983).

Harlan, Louis, and Raymond Smock, eds. *The Booker T. Washington Papers*, 14 vols. (1972–1989).

Johnson, James Weldon. *Along This Way: The Autobiography of James Weldon Johnson* (1933).

Meier, August. *Negro Thought in America, 1880–1915: Racial Ideologies in the Age of Booker T. Washington* (1963).

Osofsky, Gilbert. *Harlem: The Making of a Ghetto* (1966).

Obituary: *New York Times*, 29 Jan. 1938.

PATRICK G. WILLIAMS

ANDERSON, Eddie "Rochester" (18 Sept. 1905–28 Feb. 1977), radio and movie actor, was born Edward Lincoln Anderson in Oakland, California. Anderson was from a show business family. His father, "Big Ed" Anderson, was a vaudevillian, and his mother, Ella Mae (maiden name unknown), was a circus tightrope walker. As a youngster Eddie sold newspapers on the streets of Oakland, a job that, according to his own account, injured his voice and gave it the rasping quality that was long his trademark on radio.

Between 1923 and 1933 Anderson's older brother Cornelius had a career in vaudeville as a song and dance man, and Eddie, who had little formal education, joined him occasionally. With vaudeville dying, however, Eddie drifted toward Hollywood. In the depths of the Depression, pickings were slim. His first movie appearance was in 1932 in *What Price Hollywood?* For a few years he had only bit parts, but then he secured a major role in the movie *Green Pastures* (1936), playing the part of Noah, an old southern preacher. *Green Pastures* was a movie adaptation of a Marc Connelly play from stories by Roark Bradford. A rather lavish version of a simple Negro interpretation of the Bible, with heaven a giant "fish fry," the movie was considered to be the first since *Hallelujah* (1929) to treat with sympathy issues of concern to blacks.

After his performance in *Green Pastures*, Anderson was continually employed in Hollywood and made a great many movies. Very often he played minor roles, usually black stereotypes, but there were enough of them to provide a handsome living. For example, he had minor roles in *Show Boat* (1936) and *Gone with the Wind* (1939), in which he was so elaborately made up that few people recognized him. His talent for both comic and serious roles was readily apparent to the movie industry. In the year 1937 alone he appeared in six movies.

Anderson's rise to fame came through the role of Rochester on the *Jack Benny Show*. This radio program had been on the air since 1932, and Jack Benny had tried numerous comic personae—always purporting to be himself and not a fictional character—before settling on "the thirty-nine-year-old skinflint." Anderson joined the show in 1937. According to numerous scripts of later years, Benny "found" Rochester working as a Pullman porter and hired him as his personal valet. The truth was slightly different. Anderson was engaged for one show in which he played a train porter, and the sketch was so successful that five weeks later Benny decided to put in another porter scene featuring Rochester. These two shows worked so well that Benny decided to make Rochester a permanent part of his radio team. Rochester became his butler, valet, and general factotum.

By the early 1940s Anderson was earning more than $100,000 a year, making him the highest-paid African American in show business until Sidney Poitier began acting in the 1950s. A superb comic actor with exquisite timing, Anderson owed much of his success to his highly distinctive voice, often described as rasping or wheezing. Whatever the description, it was one of the classic voices of radio, instantly recognizable after two words—perhaps even after one syllable. Someone once suggested to Anderson that he have an operation to remove the "frog" in his throat, to which Anderson responded that if he had a frog in his throat he had no intention of having it operated on since it was a "gold-plated frog."

Because all the characters played themselves on the Benny show, many listeners came to believe that Rochester (as he was now called by everyone, even members of his own family) really was Benny's much-harried servant. Several listeners wrote in to complain about the low wages that Rochester was receiving and about the other intolerable burdens that he had to endure. Benny was forced to write back to many of these people and tell them that Rochester was really a well-paid actor named Eddie Anderson. During these years Anderson and his family lived in a mansion with a ballroom and were waited on by servants of their own. (He had married Mamie Sophie Wiggins in 1932; they had three children.) Anderson collected custom-built sports cars and raised thoroughbred horses. One of these ran in the Kentucky Derby in 1945.

Benny was, in fact, sensitive to the problem of using a "stock colored butler character," and to its racial implications. In the early 1940s he made an effort to eliminate any of Rochester's traits or habits that might appear to be racial stereotypes. For example, he removed all references to Rochester's eating watermelon or drinking gin. The racial issue was seldom raised in these years, least of all by Eddie Anderson, probably in part because it was always Benny, and not Rochester, who was the butt of the jokes.

Anderson stayed with the Benny radio program until it ended in 1955. He also appeared on Benny's television show until it ended in 1965; but in Benny's later television specials he was not a regular. By this time, feelings were running high against black stereotypes. When asked in a 1970 television appearance to re-create his old role as butler, he said, "Massa Benny, we don' do dat no mo" (Leslie Halliwell, *The Filmgoer's Companion* [4th ed., 1974], 22).

Throughout the radio years and beyond, Anderson continued his film appearances. In 1943 he had the lead in the successful movie version of the Harold Arlen and E. Y. Harburg stage musical *Cabin in the Sky*, which also featured ETHEL WATERS and LOUIS

ARMSTRONG. Directed by Vincente Minnelli, this film was considered notable for its humanized version of black American life. Anderson continued to have movie roles in the 1960s and had a splendid part as a taxi driver in Stanley Kramer's visual farce *It's a Mad, Mad, Mad, Mad World* (1963). On television he had a role in *Bachelor Father* (1962) and *Love, American Style* (1969). He also did a cartoon voice for the Harlem Globetrotters' television program.

Anderson's first wife died in 1954; his second marriage was to Eva Simon, but it ended in divorce. He died in Los Angeles.

Further Reading

Bogle, Donald. *Blacks in American Films and Television* (1988).
Harmon, Jim. *The Great Radio Comedians* (1970).
Landy, Eileen. *Black Film Stars* (1973).
Watkins, Mel. *On the Real Side: Laughing, Lying, and Signifying* (1994).
Obituary: *New York Times*, 1 Mar. 1977.

GEORGE H. DOUGLAS

ANDERSON, Garland (1886–31 May 1939), playwright and minister, was born in Wichita, Kansas. Little is known about his parents, although his mother is said to have been an active reformer and a poet. Anderson completed four years of school (the only formal education that he ever received) before his father moved the family to California to take a job as a janitor in the post office. The following year Anderson's mother died, and at age twelve he left home to become a newsboy, selling the *Telegraph Press* on the corner of Third and Market streets in San Francisco.

After working as a porter on the railroad, Anderson worked for the next fifteen years as a bellhop in various San Francisco hotels. During this period he also became a temporary convert to Christian Science. One afternoon in 1924 he saw a performance of Channing Pollack's moralistic drama *The Fool* and knew immediately that he had found the medium for his message to the world: He would write a play. He later said,

At first the idea seemed absurd. . . . No one realized more than myself that though I wanted to write this play, I had no training in the technique of dramatic construction; but I also realized that to shirk what I wanted to do could be likened to the outer shell of the acorn after it was planted in the ground saying to the inner stir of life for expression, "What are you stirring for? Surely you don't expect to become a great oak tree?" With this firm conviction I determined to write a play.

In three weeks of writing, between phone calls summoning him at the hotel where he worked, he completed *Don't Judge by Appearances* (later shortened to *Appearances*), the story of a black bellhop falsely accused of rape by a white woman—a bold topic in 1924 for a black author. At the play's denouement, however, the woman is revealed to be a mulatto who has been passing as white; this denouement was the only possible one in a year in which riots had threatened the Provincetown Playhouse in New York City because the black actor PAUL ROBESON had kissed onstage the hand of a white actress playing his wife in Eugene O'Neill's drama *All God's Chillun Got Wings*.

With the encouragement of the residents at the hotel where he worked, Anderson sent his play to the popular performer Al Jolson, who provided Anderson with the means to travel to New York City to seek his fortune. At a backers' audition at the Waldorf-Astoria Hotel, six hundred guests applauded the reading of the play by actor Richard B. Harrison, but they donated only $140 toward the production of *Appearances*.

Believing that "you can have what you want if you want it hard enough," Anderson wrote President Calvin Coolidge and persuaded Coolidge's secretary to grant him a meeting at the White House. Possibly as a result of the publicity surrounding that meeting, producer Lester W. Sagar took over Anderson's script in June 1925 and put the play into rehearsal with three African Americans in the cast of seventeen. Immediately, the white actress Nedda Harrigan resigned, refusing to perform on the same stage with a black actor (in previous Broadway shows, the black characters had been played by whites in blackface). Nevertheless, on 13 October 1925 at the Frolic Theater, *Appearances* opened. It was the first full-length play by a black playwright to be presented on the Broadway stage and the first Broadway play to incorporate both black and white cast members. Although it received tepid notices, the reviewers praised Anderson's entrepreneurial spirit. The drama ran for twenty-three performances, then toured major American cities until, on 1 April 1929, it returned to the Hudson Theatre in New York City to prepare for its opening at the Royale Theatre in London the following March.

In London the play became a *succès de curiosité*. Apparently Anderson's impeccable manners coupled with his unrelenting optimism attracted the British press, and he became somewhat of a celebrity. He was introduced to Queen Mary and was invited by the author John Galsworthy to speak at a meeting of PEN, the most prestigious literary club in London. Anderson also undertook a business venture, with the backing of a British industrialist, by establishing a chain of milk bars called Andy's Nu-Snack, thus introducing to Londoners cold malted milk. During his stay in England, Anderson met a white Englishwoman named Doris (maiden name unknown), whom he married in 1935 in Vancouver, Washington, one of the few states at that time to allow racially mixed marriages. She later published, under the name Doris Garland Anderson, her own account of the interracial marriage, the provocatively titled *Nigger Lover* (1938).

Although Anderson is said to have written two or three other plays, none was produced, and in his middle years he turned his energies to religion. In 1933 he published *Uncommon Sense: The Law of Life in*

Action, a text extolling the virtues of religious faith. In 1935 he became a minister in the New Thought movement at the Seattle Center of Constructive Thinking. During the last five years of his life he toured the United States, Canada, and England, lecturing on the topic, "You Can Do What You Want to Do If You Believe You Can Do It." Following his free lecture he offered—in the optimistic tradition of Elbert Hubbard, and later Dale Carnegie—a series of eight lessons (for fifteen dollars) on how faith in self and God can lead to good fortune. In 1936 a newspaper in Regina, Canada, observed: "He is the first Negro since BOOKER T. WASHINGTON to tour the country speaking to white people only. Seldom, he admitted, does a Negro ever appear to hear him. 'They are not interested,' he said rather sadly." He died in New York City.

Anderson sold a second script entitled *Extortion* to David Belasco in 1929, but it was never produced. Nor was his first play ever produced again. According to JAMES WELDON JOHNSON, *Appearances* "may not be an altogether convincing argument for the theories it advances, but the author himself is." Nonetheless, Anderson left his stamp on the Broadway stage. Because no New York critic complained about black and white actors appearing together on stage, within four months of the opening of Anderson's most notable play, Belasco produced *Lulu Belle* (1926), with ninety-seven black actors and seventeen white actors. Hence the production of *Appearances* marked the beginning of an integrated Broadway stage.

Further Reading

Anderson, Garland. *From Newsboy and Bellhop to Playwright* (1929).

Abramson, Doris. *Negro Playwrights in the American Theatre, 1925–1959* (1969).

Hatch, James V., and Omanii Abdullah. *Black Playwrights, 1823–1977: An Annotated Bibliography of Plays* (1977).

Hatch, James V., and Ted Shine, eds. *Black Theatre USA* (1974).

Peterson, Bernard L., Jr. *Early Black American Playwrights and Dramatic Writers* (1990).

JAMES V. HATCH

ANDERSON, Gloria Long (5 Nov. 1938–), physical organic chemist and pioneer F-19 synthetic organic chemist, was born in Altheimer, Arkansas, one of six children of parents who were sharecroppers. Her father, Charlie Long, had a third-grade education and her mother, Elsie Lee Foggie Long, a tenth-grade education. Gloria entered school at age four already able to read. She attended the segregated schools in Arkansas, which had all-black faculty who encouraged the students to succeed.

Anderson graduated from Altheimer Training (High) School in 1954 at the age of sixteen. She had no choice as to where to attend college, as going to college out of state was financially impossible, and at this time there were no affirmative action admissions to college so in-state student admissions would have

taken precedence over out-of-state black student admissions. At the time, Arkansas A&M, now called the University of Arkansas at Pine Bluff, was the only college in the state that accepted black students. For her freshman year, she received a partial scholarship from Arkansas A&M and her parents paid the difference; for her sophomore year she received a full Rockefeller scholarship on the condition that she maintain an A average. She got her only two Bs during that year, one in chemistry, a course she took on a dare. That she received even a B is remarkable because chemistry was not taught in her high school. Anderson then received a Rockefeller scholarship to complete her education. She majored in chemistry and in 1958 graduated first in her class of 237, with a grade point average of 2.96 out of 3.0. She did not want to teach after graduation, so she applied to graduate school and was accepted by Stanford University; she could not attend, however, because the school declined to offer any financial support. Instead she applied for an industrial job at the Ralston Purina Company but was not hired, possibly because of her race. As a result Anderson taught seventh grade for six months at Altheimer Training (High) School, but she disliked teaching young children.

Fortunately for her, the Russians launched *Sputnik* in 1957. The resulting panic compelled the federal government to invest heavily in science education. Kimuel Alonzo Huggins, chair of the chemistry department at Atlanta University, asked her to apply for admission to a master's degree program there for high school science teachers. She almost dropped out of the program when she married a high school teacher, Leonard Sinclair Anderson, on 4 June 1960 (the couple divorced in 1977) and because of the financial hardship that full-time study presented. She was encouraged by her thesis adviser and mentor Huggins to remain in the program, and he found financial support for her until she completed her degree in 1961. Her master's thesis, "Studies on 1-(4-Methylphenyl)-1,3-Butadiene," described a new three-step synthesis of butadiene, a gaseous hydrocarbon. That same year she gave birth to her son, Gerald. After graduation she taught at South Carolina State University in 1961–1962.

Anderson was encouraged to continue her graduate education by her next mentor, HENRY CECIL RANSOM MCBAY. McBay was instrumental in the lives of many black chemists from the 1930s to the 1990s. He hired her as a research assistant and chemistry instructor at Morehouse College, where she stayed from 1962 to 1964. She was then awarded a research teaching assistantship at the University of Chicago in 1965 to pursue a PhD. Thomas Cole, a black teaching assistant, became her role model, and she completed her degree in 1968. A portion of her dissertation, "F-19 Chemical Shifts for Aromatic Molecules," appeared in a 1968 issue of the *Journal of the American Chemical Society*.

McBay encouraged Anderson to apply for the position of chair of the chemistry department at

Atlanta's Morris Brown College, where she had been appointed an associate professor of chemistry, even though she was just out of graduate school. She got the position. While in Atlanta she did postdoctoral research with Charles L. Liotta at the Georgia Institute of Technology, and in 1984 she received a faculty research fellowship at the Rocket Propulsion Laboratory at Edwards Air Force Base in California.

Throughout her career Anderson successfully supported her research through grants from organizations like the National Science Foundation. She was a tireless proposal writer for her research and was able to obtain $271,614 for various research projects between 1969 and 1985. She was also able to obtain grants for Morris Brown for precollege programs and science improvement programs. Even though she was an avid researcher who spent most of her personal salary on supplementing her research, Anderson chose to remain at Morris Brown College, turning down offers to work at mainstream white universities.

She was eventually appointed Fuller E. Callaway Professor of Chemistry, an endowed professorship sponsored by the Callaway Trust to bring the salaries of Georgia professors up to the national average. Anderson continued her service to Morris Brown as a dean and acting president. She also improved the chemistry department at Morris Brown by hiring five chemistry professors with PhDs and by upgrading the program so it would be approved by the American Chemical Society, which included introducing modern scientific instrumentation to the chemistry labs.

During the 1980s Anderson focused her research on amantadienes, antiviral drugs, under the Minority Biomedical Support Program of the National Institutes of Health. In 1985 she investigated the synthesis of potential antiviral drugs as a United Negro College Fund Distinguished Scholar. She was also affiliated with BioSPECS of The Hague, Netherlands, as a research consultant.

Anderson was a member of the American Association for the Advancement of Science, the American Chemical Society, the National Science Teachers Association, the National Institute of Science, the Georgia Academy of Science, the New York Academy of Science, the American Association of University Professors, and Beta Kappa Chi, a scientific honor society.

Further Reading

Anderson, Gloria L., and Leon M. Stock. "Chemical Shifts for Bicyclic Fluorides," *Journal of the American Chemical Society* 90, no. 1 (3 Jan. 1968).

Sammons, Vivian Ovelton. *Blacks in Science and Medicine* (1990).

Warren, Wini. *Black Women Scientists in the United States* (1999).

JEANETTE ELIZABETH BROWN

ANDERSON, Ivie (10 July 1905–27 or 28 Dec. 1949), jazz singer, was born in Gilroy, California, the daughter of Jobe Smith. Her mother's name is unknown. Anderson's given name is sometimes spelled "Ivy." She studied voice at Saint Mary's Convent from age nine to age thirteen, and she sang in the glee club and choral society at Gilroy grammar and high school. While spending two years at the Nunnie H. Burroughs Institution in Washington, D.C., she studied voice under Sara Ritt.

Anderson performed in Los Angeles, California, around 1921, and in 1922 or 1923 she joined a touring version of the pioneering African American musical revue *Shuffle Along*, which brought her to New York City. She performed in Cuba in 1924, at the Cotton Club in New York City in 1925, and then in Los Angeles, where she was accompanied by the bands of Paul Howard, CURTIS MOSBY, and SONNY CLAY. In 1928 she sang with Clay's group in Australia. She starred at Frank Sebastian's Cotton Club in Los Angeles in April 1928 and then toured the United States as a solo singer.

Anderson spent twenty weeks with the pianist EARL HINES's big band at the Grand Terrace in Chicago, Illinois, from 1930 into early 1931. In February 1931 she joined DUKE ELLINGTON's orchestra, and during the next dozen years her career followed Ellington's incessant touring, mainly in America, but also for his first appearance in Europe in 1933. With Ellington she recorded "It Don't Mean a Thing (If It Ain't Got That Swing)" (1932), "Raisin' the Rent," "Stormy Weather," and "I'm Satisfied" (all 1933), and in 1933 she also performed "Stormy Weather" in a film short, *Bundle of Blues*. In 1937 she sang "All God's Chillun Got Rhythm" in the Marx Brothers' movie *A Day at the Races* (1937). Further significant recordings with Ellington include vocal versions of his instrumental themes "Solitude" and "Mood Indigo" (both 1940), "I Got It Bad and That Ain't Good" (1941)—also on a soundie (a film short for a video jukebox) of the same name, released in 1943—and "Rocks in My Bed" (1941). She left Ellington's band in 1942.

Anderson married Marque Neal, with whom she opened Ivie's Chicken Shack in Los Angeles. After divorcing Neal and selling the business, she married Walter Collins. The dates of the marriages are unknown. Having suffered for years from asthma, she died in Los Angeles. In what is evidently the most detailed and earliest obituary (its source unidentified), her date of death is given as 27 December 1949; all other sources give 28 December. Anderson was probably Ellington's most versatile singer and perhaps, after the extraordinary Swedish vocalist Alice Babs, his finest as well. She was a scat singer who imitated instrumental sounds, including the growling, trumpet-like vocalizations that ADELAIDE HALL had earlier introduced into Ellington's repertoire; she sang lively pop tunes, clearly enunciating lyrics that she delivered in a piercingly bright voice; and she sang ballads, in which setting her voice became full-bodied and took on a sultry quality. With her joyful delivery of "It Don't Mean a Thing," Anderson gave the forthcoming swing era its name and rhythmic spirit. Her affiliation with Ellington is also remembered especially for her understated but emotionally powerful rendition of the ballad "I Got It Bad and That Ain't Good." Ellington wrote of Anderson in his *Music Is My Mistress* (1973):

Although Ivie was not well known at that time [early 1930s], I soon found that she was really an extraordinary artist and an extraordinary person as well. She had great dignity, and she was greatly admired by everybody everywhere we went, at home and abroad. . . . She stopped the show cold at the Palladium in London in 1933. Her routine normally consisted of four songs, but while she was singing "Stormy Weather," the audience and all the management brass broke down crying and applauding. (124)

Further Reading

Collier, James Lincoln. *Duke Ellington* (1987).
Miller, Paul Eduard. "Ivie Joined the Duke for Four Weeks, Stays with Band for 12 Years," *Down Beat* (15 July 1942).
Placksin, Sally. *American Women in Jazz, 1900 to the Present: Their Words, Lives, and Music* (1982).
Schuller, Gunther. *The Swing Era: The Development of Jazz, 1930–1945* (1989).
Walker, Herbert E. "Ivy Anderson Quit Typing to Sing; She's a Star Now," *Chicago Defender*, 9 Feb. 1935.
Obituaries: *New York Times*, 30 Dec. 1949; *Pittsburgh Courier*, 7 Jan. 1950; *Metronome* 66 (Feb. 1950).

BARRY KERNFELD

ANDERSON, James, Jr. (22 Jan. 1947–28 Feb. 1967), U.S. Marine and Medal of Honor Recipient, was born in Los Angeles, California, the son of Mr. and Mrs. James Anderson Sr. Anderson attended and graduated from Carver Elementary School, located in Los Angeles, in 1958. After moving to Compton, he graduated from Willowbrook Junior and Centennial Senior High School. Anderson went on to attend Los Angeles Harbor College for approximately a year and a half.

Anderson left college and enlisted in the U. S. Marine Corps on 17 February 1966. He participated in recruit training with the First Recruit Training Battalion at the Marine Corps Recruit Depot in San Diego, California. After graduating from recruit training, Anderson was promoted to Private First Class in August 1966. Transferring to Camp Pendleton, California, Anderson attended infantry training with the Second Battalion of the Second Infantry Training Regiment.

Private Anderson arrived in Vietnam in December of 1966. There he served as a rifleman with Company F of the Second Battalion, Third Marines, Third Marine Division operating in Quang Tri Province. While engaged in a savage firefight with the Viet Cong on 28 February 1967 Private Anderson shielded his platoon mates from certain death by sacrificing his own life to smother a grenade blast. In an official statement, Anderson's comrade Private First Class Larry C. Herring commented, "I was trying to get my weapon to function when the next grenade came in. It fell about a foot in front of Anderson and he reached out and pulled the grenade into himself. . . . I feel that this man saved my life through his action of bravery and also the lives of the men around him." As a result of his actions in Quang Tri Province, Private First Class James Anderson Jr. was posthumously awarded the Congressional Medal of Honor for conspicuous gallantry, the highest decoration awarded in the U.S. military. He was also awarded the Purple Heart, the National Defense Service Medal, the Vietnam Service Medal with one bronze star, the Vietnamese Military Merit Medal, the Vietnamese Gallantry Cross with Palm, and the Republic of Vietnam Campaign Medal. He was survived by his parents, five sisters, and one brother.

Further Reading

The information in this biographical sketch was obtained courtesy of the U.S. Marine Corps History and Museums Division through the primary source documents present in James Anderson Jr.'s personal file. Documents were provided by the historian Annette Amerman per the author's request of 3 October 2006.
U.S. Marine Corps History Division biography of Anderson. Available at http://hqinet001.hqmc.usmc.mil/HD/Historical/Whos_Who/Anderson_J.htm

CHARLES EDWARD WILES IV

ANDERSON, Jervis (1 Oct. 1932–7 Jan. 2000), writer, was born Jervis Beresford Anderson in the rural village of Chatham, Jamaica, in the British West Indies, to Peter Anderson, a building contractor, and Ethlyn Allen, a homemaker. Peter Anderson enforced a strict Baptist upbringing on his son. Having passed a series of rigorous qualifying exams, within days after graduating from Kingston Technical School, a high school affiliated with the University of the West Indies, Jervis was hired as a trainee journalist at the *Daily Gleaner,* the most revered and influential newspaper on the island. He left its employ after a year—uncomfortable with the newspaper's conservatism and acquiescence to the colonial regime—and joined the writers' staff at *Public Opinion,* a weekly that advocated self-rule and was closely allied with the People's National Party. Having rejected the stern religion of his father and the unquestioning allegiance to the British Crown manifested by his school's headmaster, at his new position Anderson wrote numerous articles reflecting his maturing socialist, pro-independence stance. During the two years he was at *Public Opinion,* from 1956 to 1958, he crossed paths with the future Nobel laureate poet DEREK WALCOTT, the South African novelist Peter Abraham, the future Jamaican prime minister Michael Manley, and others who composed the region's literary and political avant-garde.

Seeking to expand his intellectual horizons, in 1958 Anderson left Jamaica to study literature at New York University (NYU). At NYU he was influenced by the pragmatist philosophy professor Sidney Hook, and earned a bachelor's degree in 1963 and a master's degree in 1966. While attending the university Anderson mingled in New York City's intellectual circles and managed to remain on friendly terms with feuding editors Norman Podhoretz at *Commentary* and Irving Howe at *Dissent,* to whose magazines he contributed articles mainly about African American culture and the black cultural elite. He later wrote articles and reviews for *The New Republic, The American Scholar,* the *New York Times, The New Leader,* and *The New York Review of Books,* among others. Anderson had worked for several months as director of research at the A. Philip Randolph Institute and was employed as a copy editor for the publisher John Wiley when editor William Shawn hired him in 1968 to write sketches for "The Talk of the Town" section of *The New Yorker.* For the next thirty years he worked as a staff writer there. Though for most of those years he was the only black staff writer at the magazine, he was appreciative of the fact that his editors did not restrict him to writing only about matters pertaining to lives of African Americans. In 1969 Anderson wed Eugenia Kemble, who worked in various positions as a trade union administrator; the marriage that ended in divorce ten years later. A member of the Authors Guild and the Society of American Historians, he was the recipient of a Guggenheim Fellowship in 1978.

Anderson's first bylined piece appeared in *The New Yorker* in 1972, followed later that year with a three-part series that profiled the life and times of trade unionist and civil rights activist A. PHILIP RANDOLPH, who in the 1920s and 1930s successfully organized African American railroad employees into the Brotherhood of Sleeping Car Porters. The series formed the basis of Anderson's critically acclaimed first book, *A. Philip Randolph: A Biographical Portrait* (1973), which earned him the Sidney Hillman Foundation Award. Similarly, the text of most of his next book, *This Was Harlem: A Cultural Portrait, 1900–1950* (1982), which tried to capture the spirit of the Upper Manhattan district in its heyday, was initially serialized in *The New Yorker* and mostly touted by reviewers. His attempt to demonstrate the relationship between crime and the availability of firearms that resulted in the 132-page *Guns in American Life* (1984), though not as widely received was, nonetheless, praised as a sobering reflection of a dark aspect of American culture. Anderson was intrigued by the interplay of external societal forces and what he called the "human character" of a resilient and vital African American culture, particularly those individuals who had a lasting impact on it.

In the 1980s and 1990s he wrote essays and profiles of persons for *The New Yorker,* most notably philosophy professor CORNEL WEST, poet COUNTEE CULLEN, jazz musician WYNTON MARSALIS, Episcopal bishop Paul Moore Jr., and writer Derek Walcott. A grant from the National Endowment for the Humanities in 1992 facilitated the publication of Anderson's last book, *BAYARD RUSTIN: Troubles I've Seen* (1997), a biography of the talented civil rights activist

and close lieutenant of A. Philip Randolph, and to whom MARTIN LUTHER KING JR. entrusted the responsibility of organizing the 1963 March on Washington. The book promptly ascended to the *New York Times* best-seller list.

Anderson retired from *The New Yorker* in 1998. With his reputation as a prominent intellectual firmly established, he chose to remain an active writer and scholar. In summarizing Anderson's professional achievements, a then–senior editor of the magazine and longtime friend, Hendrik Hertzberg, tried to convey a bit about his personality, observing that "he was courtly, a little solemn (except when he exploded in laughter, as he did frequently), deliberate, precise, and exceptionally tweedy" (Hertzberg, 28). One of his final works was a memoir of his life in Jamaica titled "England in Jamaica," published shortly after his death in *The American Scholar,* in which he related experiences that helped to shape the course of his career. His last-known project was a book-length biography on the early life of RALPH ELLISON, the celebrated novelist, whom he had interviewed in depth and profiled in *The New Yorker* in 1976, and whose writings he discussed in a public television documentary. Anderson's body was found in his New York City apartment nearly two weeks after he had died there, according to the attending medical examiner, of natural causes.

Further Reading
Anderson, Jervis. "England in Jamaica," *The American Scholar* (Spring 2000).
Hertzberg, Hendrik. "Postscript," *The New Yorker* (24 Jan. 2000).
Obituary: *New York Times,* 12 Jan. 2000.

ROBERT FIKES JR.

ANDERSON, John (c. 1831–?), fugitive slave and abolitionist, was originally named Jack Burton after his enslaver, a Missouri planter. His parents are unknown. Raised in his master's household, Anderson (the name he used in later life) eventually supervised other slaves and farmed his own small plot. In 1850 he married Maria Tomlin, a fellow slave from a nearby farm, and devoted himself to buying their freedom. In the meantime he had become accustomed to visiting Maria at her plantation and was growing impatient with the restrictions of slavery. His master tried to curb his wandering, but Anderson refused to submit to the lash. When this resulted in his sale to a planter on the far side of the Missouri River, Anderson resolved to run off.

On 3 September 1853, the third day of his escape, he encountered a planter, Seneca Digges, and four of his slaves. By Missouri law Digges had the legal authority to arrest any fugitive. When Digges ordered Anderson to come along to his house, the latter suddenly broke away. During the course of the pursuit Anderson encountered Digges and fatally stabbed him with a knife. With the help of the Underground Railroad, Anderson eventually made good his escape to Canada. Missouri authorities, outraged that a slave had murdered a white man, hired bounty hunters, who made several unsuccessful attempts to recover him. For the next seven years he lived quietly in Canada and took up the trade of mason and plasterer.

Then in April 1860 William Mathews, a Brantford, Ontario, magistrate, had Anderson charged with murder after a fellow fugitive named Wynnes, who had quarreled with Anderson, told the local sheriff that he was a wanted man in Missouri. However, no Missouri charges were presented and Anderson was released on a legal technicality. When the Canadian authorities finally had the paperwork, a warrant was issued and Anderson was rearrested that September. His case began to attract support, and Canadian abolitionists retained the services of a lawyer. At the hearing the only direct evidence that Anderson had murdered Digges came from a slave named Phil, whose testimony was given by way of a sworn deposition, as Phil would have been free as soon as he reached Canadian soil. Phil was the only eyewitness to the stabbing available to the prosecution. Anderson's lawyer, Samuel Black Freeman, should have objected to the deposition being admitted, but he did not, and shortly after the hearing he was criticized in the press for this tactical error. The facts of the assault were proven as was Digges's authority to apprehend the fugitive. Anderson was committed to be extradited to Missouri.

"The fate of Anderson is the general topic of conversation," wrote a correspondent to the leading provincial newspaper the Toronto *Globe* on 10 December 1860. "Should Anderson be given up, there will be such a burst of indignation as was never before heard in Canada." Canadians were, by and large, proud of their role in providing a haven for escaped slaves, and the prospect of sending Anderson to trial and almost certain death was politically abhorrent. Antislavery forces had warned that Article 10 of the Webster-Ashburton Treaty of 1842, which had normalized relations between Great Britain and the United States and provided for the extradition of criminals, could be used by Southern slaveholders to regain their lost property. By November 1860 the province's attorney general, John A. Macdonald, had artfully moved the issue into the courts by agreeing to fund a habeas corpus hearing. For the first time the interpretation of this clause would be directly before a court.

There was nervous expectation on 15 December 1860 when Anderson, described in the press as a short, powerful man with "an intelligent looking countenance," appeared before the Court of Queen's Bench to receive the verdict. Fifty Toronto police, nearly the entire force, were present and armed with muskets and bayonets to ensure that Anderson would not be freed by force. While one judge gave a ringing denunciation of slavery and denied that slave laws could ever be enforced in British territories, the majority, including the provincial chief justice, concluded that Anderson had resisted and

killed a man who had legal authority to detain him. Therefore, by the terms of the treaty, he should be returned to Missouri.

The decision in the Anderson case, coming only days before South Carolina seceded from the Union, alarmed many abolitionists, as Canada had been seen as a safety valve, the one place where fugitives could be safe; now it seemed that not even Canada was safe. Slaveholders, of course, were delighted with it. The Southern press seized on it as evidence that Britain would accommodate itself to the Confederacy. More thoughtful Northern writers noted that the case had sparked mass rallies across Canada in support of Anderson and that popular sympathy in British territories lay with the antislavery cause. A leading American abolitionist, Gerrit Smith, spoke in Toronto in January 1861 and asked if Canadians would permit Anderson to be returned to Missouri where he would be "seized by a mob and amidst fiendish exultations be burnt at the stake" (Toronto *Globe*, 19 Jan. 1861). Would Canadians act in the same spineless manner as did the Buchanan administration in Washington and accommodate slave owners? The overwhelming response from Smith's audience was "no."

So upset were abolitionist forces that British sympathizers, particularly the British and Foreign Anti-Slavery Society under the direction of Louis Alexis Chamerovzow, obtained a writ from a court in London ordering Anderson's attendance there. This imperial interference created indignation in Canada but was ultimately resolved when the writ was taken by a London bailiff to Toronto and served on the sheriff of Toronto. He ignored it, pending the next decision from the Canadian Court of Common Pleas, which ordered that Anderson be released. The English writ became a nullity. In order to ensure that he would not be subject to any more hearings, Anderson became the ward of British abolitionists and members of a new English organization, the London Emancipation Society, a group associated with William Lloyd Garrison, who invited him to come to England. His Canadian supporters, who were anti-Garrisonians, urged him to leave for his own safety. Anderson himself did not seem to notice that he had passed from one abolitionist faction to another. He was given a major reception in London on 2 July 1861 at Exeter Hall. Thereafter he traveled around England giving speeches.

Once there John Anderson was finally able to escape his unwanted role as a silent figure in the drama and express his own feelings, especially because for most of the period of his notoriety he was in jail and unable to talk with the press. He spoke at more than twenty-five rallies across southern England at which he described the repellent nature of Southern slavery. The antislavery movement in Britain, which had become moribund by 1860, was reinvigorated by the appearance of this personification of resistance to bondage. Under the direction of the Reverend Harper Twelvetrees, Anderson wrote an account of his life, his escape, and his legal tribulations in Canada. After some educational training, the London Emancipation Society decided to send

Anderson to Liberia, and he took ship for Monrovia on 24 December 1862. The details of his life from this point onward are unknown.

During its brief notoriety, the John Anderson case focused attention in Britain, the United States, and Canada on the question of how far non-slaveholding states would recognize the laws of slavery. The public indignation stirred up by the case illustrated the depth of moral repugnance felt outside the South toward slavery and suggested that public opinion in other countries would show little sympathy toward the nascent Confederacy.

Further Reading
Brode, Patrick. *The Odyssey of John Anderson* (1984).
Reinders, Robert C. *The John Anderson Case, 1860–1861: A Study in Anglo-Canadian Imperial Relations* (1975).
Twelvetrees, Harper, ed. *The Story of the Life of John Anderson, the Fugitive Slave* (1863, repr. 1971).
                                                PATRICK BRODE

ANDERSON, Leafy (c. 1887–Dec. 1927), religious leader, was born in Wisconsin. The names of her parents are not known, but there is evidence that she was of mixed African American and Native American heritage. "Mother Leafy Anderson," as she was known to her followers, claimed Mohawk as well as African American ancestry. Little is known of her childhood, but she already had become heavily involved in the Spiritualist movement by the time she reached her twenties. In 1913 Anderson established her first congregation, the Church of the Redemption, on State Street in Chicago. It was also known as the Eternal Life Christian Spiritualist Church, a name shared by many of her churches and by the first recorded organization of Spiritualist churches, also founded by Anderson.

Spiritualist churches were known for healing, prophecy, and especially for conveying messages from important spirits of the dead. The spirits that Anderson claimed to have contacted most often were Father John (or Jones), a prominent healer who she said had taught her to master evil; Queen Esther, a courageous woman of the Old Testament who had dared to petition the king on behalf of her people; and Black Hawk, a leader of the Sauk (Sac) Indians, whom she identified as the saint for the South, as White Hawk was for the North. Whether an actual person served as a model for White Hawk is not known, but Black Hawk, Queen Esther, and Father John were all real persons known to history.

Black Hawk was, by far, the most prominent of Anderson's spirit guides. The black Spiritual movement that Anderson promoted had some roots in nineteenth-century white Spiritualism with its séances and psychic arts. Indeed, nineteenth-century Spiritualists frequently contacted the spirits of American Indians, and Anderson quite possibly learned of Black Hawk and White Hawk from this earlier Spiritualist tradition. Anderson's churches, however, were not occult centers, and she vehemently denied connections between her movement and any form of "magic," especially voodoo. Anderson saw voodoo (or hoodoo) as an instrument for evil or a form of witchcraft. She viewed herself and the leaders of her churches as instruments of God.

Anderson and followers of her movement—as well as other similar black congregations—called themselves Spiritual, rather than Spiritualist, to disavow any connection to the occult. In the *Encyclopedia of African and African-American Religions* (2001), however, Claude F. Jacobs makes it clear that the more important reason was to distance themselves from racist white Spiritualists, who not only excluded black Spiritualists, but had begun to denounce them as frauds. Anderson combined elements of Spiritualism and Pentecostalism in her movement and also drew heavily on Roman Catholicism. Some congregations added elements from Quaker and Shaker doctrine, Judaism, Ethiopianism, astrology, and nineteenth-century scientific ideas, especially about disease. Anderson's theology was conservative in comparison with other early Spiritual congregations. She used familiar Protestant hymns and lessons based on biblical passages, especially the description of God as spirit from John 4:24, and the enumeration of spiritual gifts from 1 Corinthians 12.

Despite her conservative theological bent, reports associating her Spiritual churches with hoodoo and witchcraft resulted in occasional legal trouble for Anderson. It was sometimes difficult for her to obtain official recognition from cities and states where she tried to obtain charters for her churches and for the Eternal Life Christian Spiritualist Association, which she chartered in New Orleans in October 1920. There are unconfirmed reports of Anderson's arrest in New Orleans on charges related to occult practices, as well as a widely circulated, but perhaps apocryphal, story that her legal troubles ended when she gave a reading for the judge in her case and told him a number of things about his life that were not generally known.

Anderson's Spiritual movement, particularly because of its syncretistic nature, found especially fertile ground in New Orleans. When Anderson arrived there in 1920, she found a diverse population and religious traditions that already contained African, French, Spanish, and Caribbean influences. The Spiritualist churches that already existed in New Orleans were located primarily among French-speaking Creoles. Anderson introduced Spiritualism to New Orleans's non-Creole population, attracting people of all ethnicities and classes and both genders for worship, readings, training in healing and prophecy, and calling up spirits. This was true also for her Chicago congregations, as well as for other Spiritual churches she founded in Little Rock, Memphis, Pensacola (Florida), Biloxi (Mississippi), and Houston. The churches themselves were located in black neighborhoods, but the congregations were ethnically mixed, largely eliminating racial barriers.

The Spiritual movement also constituted one important way for black women to be freed from the male dominance in most black churches. Central beliefs in Anderson's Spiritualism included a democratic concept of equality among spirits, which must have been attractive to marginalized persons. Additionally, in the aftermath of the Civil War—as well as in the midst of the high incidence of fatal diseases and violent deaths common among blacks in the South at the turn of the twentieth century—Spiritualism provided a form of comfort that traditional religions could not offer to the bereaved. Communication with spirits provided proof of a life beyond the grave.

Skilled at fund-raising, Anderson charged hefty fees of those who could afford them, but she offered her services to the poor without charge, so she never amassed a fortune. When she died of a respiratory ailment in New Orleans in December 1927 at the age of forty, her estate consisted of only $36, two pianos, and six city lots with a total value of $8,800. Her niece, the Reverend A. Price Bennett, inherited—and in 1930 mortgaged and lost—Anderson's big three-story Eternal Life Christian Spiritual Church Number 12. That well-known institution on Amelia Street is no more, but Spiritual leaders actually trained by Anderson continued to operate churches and missionary societies into the 1980s.

In the early twenty-first century the black Spiritualist movement remained most prominent in New Orleans, but in 2007 there were records of black Spiritualist congregations in twenty-seven states and the District of Columbia. The Spiritual church sanctuaries resembled those in Catholic churches, and a number of the church's rituals celebrated Catholic saints. Séances were rare, but the spirit message session was an important part of worship, especially the "bless service" or "prophecy service." As of 2007, Black Hawk services were still common in contemporary black Spiritual churches, whose leaders also sometimes contacted Anderson's spirit.

Further Reading

Baer, Hans A. *The Black Spiritual Movement: A Religious Response to Racism* (1984).

Baer, Hans A., and Merrill Singer. *African-American Religion in the Twentieth Century: Varieties of Protest and Accommodation* (1992).

Jacobs, Claude F. "Black Spiritual Churches," in *Encyclopedia of African and African-American Religions*, ed. Stephen D. Glazier (2001).

Jacobs, Claude F., and Andrew J. Kaslow. *The Spiritual Churches of New Orleans: Origins, Beliefs, and Rituals of an African-American Religion* (1991).

SHERRY WRIGHT

ANDERSON, Marian (17 Feb. 1897–8 Apr. 1993), contralto, was born in Philadelphia, Pennsylvania, the daughter of John Berkeley Anderson, a refrigerator room employee at the Reading Terminal Market, an ice and coal dealer, and a barber, and Anne (also seen as "Annie" and "Anna," maiden name unknown), a former schoolteacher. John Anderson's various jobs provided only a meager income, and after his death, before Marian was a teenager, her mother's income as a laundress and laborer at Wanamaker's Department Store was even less. Still, as Anderson later recalled, neither she nor her two younger sisters thought of themselves as poor. When Marian was about eight, her father purchased a piano from his brother; she proceeded to teach herself how to play it and became good enough to accompany herself. Also as a youngster, having seen a violin in a pawnshop window, she became determined to purchase it and earned the requisite four dollars by scrubbing her neighbors' steps. When she attempted to teach herself this instrument as well, she discovered that she had little aptitude for it.

Anderson joined the children's choir of Union Baptist Church at age six. Noticing her beautiful voice and her ability to sing all the parts, the choir director selected her to sing a duet for Sunday school and later at the regular morning service; this was her first public appearance. Later she joined the senior choir and her high school chorus, where occasionally she was given a solo.

While she was still in high school, Anderson attempted to enroll at a local music school but was rejected with the curt statement, "We don't take Colored." She applied and was accepted to the Yale University School of Music, but a lack of finances prevented her from enrolling. Although she was not the product of a conservatory, Anderson was vocally prepared by Mary Saunders Patterson, Agnes Reifsnyder, Giuseppe Boghetti, and Frank La Forge. Over the years she was coached by Michael Raucheisen and Raimond von zur Mühlen, and she also worked briefly (in London) with Amanda Aldridge, daughter of the famous black Shakespearean actor IRA ALDRIDGE. Boghetti, however, had the greatest pedagogical influence.

Anderson's accompanists (with whom she enjoyed excellent relationships) were the African Americans Marie Holland and William "Billy" King (who, for a period, doubled as her agent), the Finnish pianist Kosti Vehanen, and the German pianist Franz Rupp. Between 1932 and 1935 she was represented by the Arthur Judson Agency and from 1935 through the remainder of her professional life by the great impresario Sol Hurok.

One of the happiest days of Anderson's life was when she called Wanamaker's to notify her mother's supervisor that Anne Anderson would not be returning to work. On another very happy occasion, in the late 1920s, she was able to assist in purchasing a little house for her mother in Philadelphia. Her sister Alyce shared the house; her other sister, Ethel, lived next door with her son JAMES DEPREIST, who became a distinguished conductor.

For many, including critics, an accurate description of Anderson's singing voice presented challenges. Because it was nontraditional, many simply resorted to the narrowly descriptive "Negroid sound." Others, however, tried to be more precise. Rosalyn Story, for example, has described Anderson's voice as "earthy darkness at the bottom . . . clarinet-like purity in the middle, and . . . piercing vibrancy at the top. Her range was expansive—from a full-bodied D in the bass clef to a brilliant high C" (Story, 38). Kosti Vehanen, recalling the first time he heard Anderson's "mysterious" voice, wrote, "It was as though the room had begun to vibrate, as though the sound came from under the earth. . . . The sound I heard swelled to majestic power, the flower opened its petals to full brilliance; and I was enthralled by one of nature's rare wonders" (Vehanen, 22). Reacting to his first encounter with Anderson's voice, Sol Hurok wrote, "Chills danced up my spine. . . . I was shaken to my very shoes" (Story, 47).

In 1921 Anderson, who was by then a well-known singer at church-related events, won the National Association of Negro Musicians competition. Believing that she was ready for greater public exposure, she made her Town Hall (New York City) debut in 1924. Disappointed by the poor attendance and by her own performance, she considered giving up her aspirations for a professional career. The following year, however, she bested three hundred other singers to win the National Music League competition, earning a solo appearance with the New York Philharmonic at Lewisohn Stadium.

In 1926, with financial assistance from the Julius Rosenwald Fund, Anderson departed for Europe for further musical study. After returning to the United States, she gave her first concert at New York City's Carnegie Hall in 1930. That same year she gave her first European concert, in Berlin, and toured Scandinavia. In 1931 alone she gave twenty-six concerts in fifteen states. Between 1933 and 1935 she toured Europe; one of her appearances was at the Mozarteum in Salzburg, where the renowned conductor Arturo Toscanini uttered the memorable line "Yours is a voice such as one hears once in a hundred years" (Anderson, 158). Another exciting experience took place in the home of the noted composer Jean Sibelius in Finland. After hearing Anderson sing, he uttered, "My roof is too low for you" and then canceled the previously ordered coffee and requested champagne. Sibelius also honored Anderson by dedicating his composition Solitude to her.

Anderson's second Town Hall concert, arranged by Hurok and performed on 30 December 1935, was a huge success. A one-month tour of the Soviet Union was planned for the following year but ended up lasting three months. Anderson was a box-office sensation as well in Europe, Africa, and South America. Her seventy U.S. concerts in 1938 still stand as the longest and most extensive tour for a singer in concert history. Between November 1939 and June 1940 she appeared in more than seventy cities, giving ninety-two concerts. Her native Philadelphia presented her with the Bok Award in 1941, accompanied by ten thousand dollars. She used the funds to establish the Marian Anderson Award, which sponsors "young talented men and women in pursuit of their musical and educational goals."

During 1943 Anderson made her eighth transcontinental tour and married the architect Orpheus H. Fisher of Wilmington, Delaware. The marriage was childless. In 1944 she appeared at the Hollywood Bowl, where she broke a ten-year attendance record. In 1946, six hundred editors in the United States and Canada, polled by Musical America, named Anderson radio's foremost woman singer for the sixth consecutive year. Anderson completed a South American tour in 1951 and made her television debut on the Ed Sullivan Show the following year. Her first tour of Japan was completed in 1953, the same year that she also toured the Caribbean, Central America, Israel, Morocco, Tunisia, France, and Spain.

Anderson sang the national anthem at the inauguration of President Dwight D. Eisenhower in 1957, and between 14 September and 2 December of that year she traveled thirty-nine thousand miles in Asia, performing twenty-four concerts under the auspices of the American National Theater and Academy and the U.S. State Department. Accompanying Anderson was the journalist Edward R. Murrow, who filmed the trip for his See It Now television series. The program, which aired on 30 December, was released by RCA Records under the title The Lady from Philadelphia. In 1958 Anderson served as a member of the U.S. delegation to the General Assembly of the United Nations. Three years later she sang the national anthem at the inauguration of President John F. Kennedy, appeared in the new State Department auditorium, and gave another concert tour of Europe. Her first tour of Australia was a highlight of 1962.

In early 1964 Hurok announced Marian Anderson's Farewell Tour, beginning at Constitution Hall on 24 October 1964 and ending on Easter Sunday 1965 at Carnegie Hall. The momentousness of the event was reflected in Hurok's publicity: "In any century only a handful of extraordinary men and women are known to countless millions around the globe as great artists and great persons. . . . In our time there is Marian Anderson." After the tour she made several appearances as narrator of Aaron Copland's Lincoln Portrait, often with her nephew James DePreist at the podium.

Although in her own lifetime Anderson was described as one of the world's greatest living contraltos, her career nonetheless was hindered by the limitations placed on it because of racial prejudice. Two events, in particular, that illustrate the pervasiveness of white exclusiveness and African American exclusion—even when it came to someone of Anderson's renown—serve as historical markers not only of her vocal contributions but also of the magnificence of her bearing, which in both instances turned two potential negatives into resounding positives.

In 1938, following Anderson's numerous international and national successes, Hurok believed that it was time for her to appear in the nation's capital at a major hall. She previously had appeared in Washington, D.C., at churches, schools, and civic organization

Marian Anderson with Eleanor Roosevelt. In a famous episode in 1939, the Daughters of the American Revolution denied Anderson permission to sing in Constitution Hall in Washington, D.C.—whereupon Mrs. Roosevelt arranged for Anderson to perform at the Lincoln Memorial. (National Archives/Joe McCary, Photo Response Studio)

meetings and at Howard University, but she had not performed at the district's premier auditorium, Constitution Hall. At that time, when negotiations began for a Marian Anderson concert to be given in 1939 at the hall owned by the Daughters of the American Revolution, a clause appeared in all contracts that restricted the hall to "a concert by white artists only, and for no other purpose." Thus, in February 1939 the American who had represented her country with honor across the globe was denied the right to sing at Constitution Hall simply because she was not white.

A great furor ensued, and thanks to the efforts of First Lady Eleanor Roosevelt and Secretary of the Interior Harold Ickes, the great contralto appeared the following Easter Sunday (9 April 1939) on the steps of the Lincoln Memorial before an appreciative audience of seventy-five thousand. She began the concert by singing "America" and then proceeded to sing an Italian aria, Franz Schubert's "Ave Maria," and three Negro spirituals—"Gospel Train," "Trampin'," and "My Soul Is Anchored in the Lord." Notably, she also sang "Nobody Knows the Trouble I've Seen." Commemorating the 1939 Lincoln Memorial concert is a mural at the Interior Department; it was formally presented in 1943, the year that Anderson made her first appearance in Constitution Hall, by invitation of

the Daughters of the American Revolution and benefiting United China Relief.

The second history-making event came on 7 January 1955, when Anderson made her debut at the Metropolitan Opera House in New York, becoming the first black American to appear there. Opera had always interested Anderson, who tells the story in her autobiography of a visit with the noted African American baritone Harry Burleigh, during which she was introduced to and sang for an Italian gentleman. When she climbed the scale to high C, the man said to Burleigh, "Why sure she can do Aida," a traditionally black role. On her first trip to England, Anderson had visited a teacher who suggested that Anderson study with her, guaranteeing that she would have her singing Aida within six months. "But I was not interested in singing Aida," Anderson wrote. "I knew perfectly well that I was a contralto, not a soprano. Why Aida?"

The international press announced Anderson's pending debut at the Met in October 1954. As the educator and composer Wallace Cheatham later noted, the occasion called for the most excellent pioneer, "an artist with impeccable international credentials, someone highly respected and admired by all segments of the music community" (Cheatham, 6). At the time there was only one such person, Marian Anderson. About Anderson's debut, as Ulrica in Giuseppe Verdi's *Un Ballo in Maschera, Time* magazine (17 Jan. 1955) reported that there were eight curtain calls. "She acted with the dignity and reserve that she has always presented to the public. . . . Her unique voice—black velvet that can be at once soft and dramatic, menacing and mourning—stirring the heart as always."

Anderson was a recipient of the Spingarn Medal (from the NAACP), the Handel Medallion (from New York City), the Page One Award (from the Philadelphia Newspaper Guild), and the Brotherhood Award (from the National Conference of Christians and Jews). She was awarded twenty-four honorary doctorates and was cited by the governments of France, Finland, Japan, Liberia, Haiti, Sweden, and the Philippines. She was a member of the National Council on the Arts and a recipient of the National Medal of Arts; in 1978 she was among the first five performers to receive the Kennedy Center Honors for lifetime achievement.

Several tributes were held in the last years of Anderson's life. In February 1977 the musical world turned out to recognize Anderson's seventy-fifth (actually her eightieth) birthday at Carnegie Hall. On 13 August 1989 a gala celebration concert took place in Danbury, Connecticut, to benefit the Marian Anderson Award. The concert featured the recitalist and Metropolitan Opera star JESSYE NORMAN, the violinist Isaac Stern, and the maestro Julius Rudel, conducting the Ives Symphony Orchestra. Because Anderson's residence, Marianna, was just two miles from the Charles Ives Center, where the concert was held, the ninety-two-year-old grand "lady from

Philadelphia" was in attendance. The Public Broadcasting Service (PBS) television station affiliate WETA prepared a one-hour documentary, *Marian Anderson*, which aired nationally on PBS on 8 May 1991. Anderson died two years later in Portland, Oregon, where she had moved to live with her nephew, her only living relative.

Many actions were taken posthumously to keep Anderson's memory alive and to memorialize her many accomplishments. The 750-seat theater in the Aaron Davis Arts Complex at City College of New York was named in her honor on 3 February 1994. The University of Pennsylvania, as the recipient of her papers and memorabilia, created the Marian Anderson Music Study Center at the Van Pelt–Dietrich Library. Of course, her greatest legacy is the singers who followed her. As the concert and opera soprano LEONTYNE PRICE, one of the many beneficiaries of Anderson's efforts, said after her death, "Her example of professionalism, uncompromising standards, overcoming obstacles, persistence, resiliency and undaunted spirit inspired me to believe that I could achieve goals that otherwise would have been unthought of " (*New York Times*, 9 Apr. 1993).

Further Reading
Anderson's papers and memorabilia are housed at the Van Pelt–Dietrich Library at the University of Pennsylvania.
Anderson, Marian. *My Lord, What a Morning* (1956).
Bogle, Donald. *Brown Sugar: Eighty Years of America's Black Female Superstars* (1980).
Cheatham, Wallace. "Black Male Singers at the Metropolitan Opera," *Black Perspective in Music* 16, no. 1 (Spring 1988): 3–19.
Sims, Janet. *Marian Anderson: An Annotated Bibliography and Discography* (1981).
Southern, Eileen, ed. *Biographical Dictionary of Afro-American and African Musicians* (1982).
Southern, Eileen, ed. *The Music of Black Americans: A History*. 2d ed. (1983).
Story, Rosalyn. *And So I Sing* (1990).
Vehanen, Kosti. *Marian Anderson: A Portrait* (1941; repr. 1970).
Obituaries: *New York Times* and *Washington Post*, 9 Apr. 1993.

ANTOINETTE HANDY

ANDERSON, Matthew (25 Jan. 1845–11 Jan. 1928), Presbyterian pastor, educator, and social reformer, was born in Greencastle, Pennsylvania, the son of Timothy Anderson and Mary Croog. One of fourteen children, he was raised in the comforts of a rural, middle-class home, less than thirty miles from historic Gettysburg. On a typical day of his youth, Matthew faced both the physical demands of farm life and the movement back and forth between two cultures. One, dominated by commerce and materialism, was uncharacteristically open to the Andersons, who owned lumber mills and real estate at a time when most black Americans were dehumanized and disenfranchised by chattel slavery. The other was a culture defined by close family ties and Presbyterian

piety. At home Matthew heard Bible stories and dramatic tales of runaway slaves; indeed, religious piety and the pursuit of racial freedom were dominant themes in his life. These early experiences inspired Matthew so deeply that, by the time he left Greencastle in 1863, he had decided on the ministry as his vocation. Study at Oberlin College in Ohio was the first step toward serving his religious faith and his vision of social and racial justice.

Shortly after graduation from Oberlin in 1874, Anderson entered Princeton Theological Seminary. He became the seminary's first African American in residence after he refused to live off-campus, which at that time was the custom for black seminarians. This refusal to accommodate himself to segregationist practices was the first of many assertive acts against unjust social and church practices. Anderson completed his theological studies in 1877 and then spent two years in part-time pastoral assignments in New Haven, Connecticut, where he took courses at Yale Divinity School. Anderson's time in New Haven marked the end of his "supply" (temporary) work and formal academic training.

While traveling to the South to do missionary work in October 1879, Anderson stopped in Philadelphia, Pennsylvania, to visit friends. It became, however, a permanent stop. On 17 August 1880 he married CAROLINE VIRGINIA STILL WILEY, daughter of the civic leader WILLIAM STILL and later the mother of their two children. Caroline, known as "Carrie" to friends, distinguished herself professionally by becoming one of the first black women to graduate from the Women's Medical College of Philadelphia in 1878. Together, Matthew and Caroline raised a family, were active in church and civic affairs, and collaborated on many programs until she died in 1919. Anderson was remarried the following year to Blanche Williams, a longtime associate.

In 1880 Anderson founded the Berean Presbyterian Church. In 1884 he established the Berean Building and Loan Association, a bank that has never—not even during the 1929 stock market crash—closed its doors. In 1899 he opened the Berean Manual Training and Industrial School. Each institution grew out of a need to provide services, skills, and support systems for the black community of Philadelphia during Reconstruction, when the country was being transformed from a slaveholding nation to a more pluralistic one. In addition, each institution bore the imprint of Caroline Anderson's medical training, whether in prenatal and vocational classes for women or in the establishment of the nurseries that she supervised within the Berean complex. Each of these institutions continued to thrive throughout the twentieth century.

Through the "Berean enterprise"—Anderson's general name for the complex of institutions that he established—Anderson continued a clergy tradition of activism within the African American community in Philadelphia, a tradition that had been established by the African Methodist Episcopal bishop RICHARD ALLEN and Reverend ABSALOM JONES in the late eighteenth century. Like them, Anderson formulated ideas and plans for improving the lives of blacks in particular but without excluding others. The name "Berean" represented two known references in Anderson's life and work. One came from studying Christian history and the early importance of the ancient city of Berea in northern Syria. The other reference was to Berea, Ohio, where in 1872 Anderson, then an uncredentialed but self-proclaimed evangelist, was confronted by church people who rejected his spiritual enthusiasm. Anderson was also known for his civic and intellectual leadership, for example, as an active member from 1901 to 1910 in the Universal Peace Movement, a Quaker organization opposed to slavery and war, and in the Afro-American Presbyterian Council, an organization started in 1893 for social fellowship and inspiration among black Presbyterians.

Anderson's Berean enterprise stood out like a signpost at a time when the course of Reconstruction presented savage attacks on black Americans. Anderson's initiatives bore added significance because they were taken at a time when the social order was undeniably antiblack and fervently racist. Moreover, the struggle for freedom, as Anderson saw it, was not simply the struggle for removing sinful barriers of racial discrimination; it also meant replacing the barriers with the pieties of religious, specifically Presbyterian, devotions. This was the ideal for Anderson, and the title of his only published book, *Presbyterianism: Its Relation to the Negro* (1899), symbolized his view of the interrelatedness of self and religion—in particular, the racial "self" as it defined the experiences of the black American. In the book's preface, Anderson outlined his work as a goal that would benefit all. He saw the doctrines of Presbyterianism as leading the oppressed black person into a state of "independence and decision of character necessary to enable him to act nobly and well his part as a man and a citizen of our great republic."

Another important illustration of Anderson's views is found in "A Private Investigation of Prevalent Conditions on the Panama Canal Zone," a report written in his seventy-fifth year in which Anderson continued to make personal statements about life events that, dominated by racial bigotry, contradicted positive (Presbyterian, he would say) human values. Anderson wrote the report while visiting the Canal Zone and traveling through much of the West Indies and Latin America in 1921. It was addressed to his Princeton seminary classmate and lifetime friend, the Reverend FRANCIS GRIMKÉ, informing him of the pattern of color prejudice that he saw in the zone. Anderson characterized these discriminatory policies as a "prodigious blunder" that diminished the great technical achievement of the Panama Canal. It was not always secular prejudice, however, that Anderson witnessed and protested against.

Anderson became increasingly involved in the Presbyterian Church's struggle to remain united after the Civil War, when some church policies toward the freed person threatened to divide blacks and whites, particularly in the church's debate over whether the Board of Home Missions and the Freedman's Board should remain separate organizations. Anderson believed that not enough money was being given to the Freedman's Board, and he eventually concluded that the two boards should be merged. Anderson's account of his role in this struggle is preserved in his book, in which he presents a record of his service as chairman of the Philadelphia Council of the Freedman's Board (1889–1890). In his account Anderson describes how he continually tried to raise the consciousness of the church's power structure, not just once, but over a period of time, through written appeals and involvement in the church's regional and national meetings. Several subsequent publications funded by the Presbyterian Church offer additional examples of Anderson's writing as the regional leader of Presbyterian clergy, most of whom were serving predominantly black congregations. By that time Anderson was no longer just a local leader; he was spokesman for the protest against a national Presbyterian Church policy that he and others believed violated the principles of the church's mission to the poor and believed diminished its potential for closing the gap between the races. Anderson died in Philadelphia.

Through the development of the Berean Presbyterian Church, the Berean Bank, and the Berean School, and through other reform activities, Matthew Anderson, defender of his Presbyterian faith and an articulate witness for social justice, created a legacy of hope and opportunity while leaving a permanent mark on community development in Philadelphia and the nation.

Further Reading
Anderson, Matthew. *Presbyterianism: Its Relation to the Negro* (1899).
Trotman, C. James. "Matthew Anderson." *American Presbyterians* 66, no. 1 (1988).
Trotman, C. James. "Matthew Anderson." *Princeton Seminary Bulletin* 9, no. 2 (1988).
Obituary: *Crisis* 35, no. 4 (Apr. 1928).

C. JAMES TROTMAN

ANDERSON, Michael (25 Dec. 1959–1 Feb. 2003), astronaut, was born Michael Phillip Anderson in Plattsburgh, New York, to Barbara and Andy "Bobby" Anderson. Because his father was a member of the United States Air Force, young Anderson moved regularly until the family settled in Spokane, Washington, in the 1960s. It was there that he attended public schools and became fascinated with America's space race. Michael would wear goggles when cutting lawns because he knew that he needed to protect his eyes in order to be an astronaut.

After high school Anderson went to the University of Washington, where in 1981 he received a bachelor of science degree in Physics and Astronomy, and then went to Creighton University, where he received a master of science degree in Physics in 1990. As an undergraduate he received pilot training at Vance Air Force Base in Oklahoma, and as a postgraduate he piloted KC-130 and T-38 transport and training aircraft and became a second lieutenant by the time he had more than four thousand hours of flight training. Anderson graduated from technical training at Keesler Air Force Base, Mississippi, in 1982, and completed his undergraduate pilot training at Vance Air Force Base, Oklahoma, in 1986. From 1988 to 1990 he was assigned to the Second Airborne Command and Control Squadron at Offut Air Force Base in Nebraska, where he became a KC-130 pilot. Anderson went on to serve as an aircraft commander and flight instructor pilot in the 920th Air Refueling Squadron at Wurthsmith Air Force Base in Michigan; this assignment lasted from January 1991 to September 1992. He then was an instructor pilot and tactics officer in the 380th Refueling Wing of Plattsburgh Air Force Base in New York, from September 1992 through February 1995.

In 1987 Anderson married his high school sweetheart, Sandra "Sandy" Hawkins. Michael and Sandy's first daughter, Sydney Anderson, was born in 1991, and their second daughter, Kaycee Anderson, was born in 1993. In 1994 the National Aeronautics and Space Administration (NASA) selected Anderson for astronaut training, and four years later on 16 January 1998 he was part of STS-89 (Space Transport System 89) aboard the space shuttle *Endeavor*. During its nine-day mission his vehicle docked with the Russian space station *MIR*, making Major Anderson the first and only African American to do so, because his was the fifth and final mission that docked with *MIR* before the Russian government decided to abandon the station. Shortly after that mission Anderson was promoted to the rank of lieutenant colonel and became the first and only African American ever to sit on the board of NASA that selects which candidates become astronauts.

NASA selected Anderson to be part of STS-107 (the 107th space shuttle mission), but the August 2002 mission was delayed when cracks were found in one of the shuttle's external fuel tanks. NASA grounded the entire fleet until all the shuttles were checked. On 16 January 2003 the space shuttle *Columbia* blasted off in what was considered a picture-perfect launch. Aboard were Payload Commander and Mission Specialist Michael Anderson (USAF), Commander Rick Husband (USAF), Pilot William McCool (USN), Mission Specialist Kalpana Chawla (USAF), Laurel Clark, MD (USN), Mission Specialist David Brown, MD (captain, USN), and Payload Specialist Colonel Ilan Ramon (Israeli Air Force). Eighty seconds into the launch NASA cameras picked up what appeared to be a foam tile coming off one of the solid rocket boosters, hitting the left wing. It appeared to be nothing out of the ordinary, and the sixteen-day mission continued, conducting more than eighty experiments.

After passing through the earth's atmosphere on the morning of Saturday, 1 February 2003, it became vividly clear to NASA that something had gone wrong. As *Columbia* blazed a preset descent from space over California and Texas, witnesses on the ground saw pieces of the shuttle streaking from it while NASA picked up *Columbia*'s onboard computers attempting to correct some sort of problem centered on the left wing. Television news cameras then recorded and broadcast around the world the fiery breakup of the spaceship over the skies of Texas. All seven astronauts perished.

Tributes, accolades, and memorial services abounded. The first official memorial service was on 4 February 2003, while Grace Community Church in Houston—the church of both Anderson and Rick Husband—held a nationally televised service on 5 February. At the National Cathedral in Washington, D.C., a memorial service was held the following day, at which the singer PATTI LABELLE sang "Way Up There," a song written especially for the fallen seven of *Columbia*. The Washington State Transportation Commission honored Anderson by renaming state route 904 in his name, while Creighton University honored him with a seven-foot statue. Arlington National Cemetery held another official memorial service on 7 March and dedicated a permanent plaque in honor of the courageous astronauts on 2 February 2004. NASA's Jet Propulsion Laboratory in Pasadena, California, proposed the idea of naming celestial bodies in the astronauts' honor, and on 6 August, after approval by the International Astronomical Union (the official clearinghouse for asteroid data), it honored the seven by naming after them seven asteroids that orbit the sun between Mars and Jupiter.

Further Reading
The main sources for this entry were personal interviews with the subject and his family by the author.
"Anderson Gave his Life to his Dream," *The St. Louis American* (6–12 Feb. 2003).
"Creighton University Honors Black Astronaut," *Jet* (5 July 2004).
"DeClue Family Member Is in Space," *The St. Louis American* (Jan. 29–4 Feb. 1998).
"Returning Astronaut Has Pizza on Order," *St. Louis Post-Dispatch*, 31 January 1998.
"Shuttle Probe Locating Left Wing's Breach," *Associated Press*, 30 April 2003.
"Silence, Then Shock: 7 Astronauts are Killed when *Columbia* Disintegrates" and "He'd Go Up Every Day if You'd Let Him," *St. Louis Post-Dispatch*, 2 February 2003.

DAVID DE CLUE

ANDERSON, Osborne Perry (27 July 1830–13 Dec. 1872), abolitionist, was born in West Fallowfield Township in Chester County, Pennsylvania, the son of Vincent Anderson, a free black man. Both Osborne and his father are listed in the U.S. census as "mulatto." Osborne's mother, according to family lore, was a white woman of Irish or Scottish descent. Osborne Anderson attended the public schools of

Chester County and may have studied at Oberlin College in Ohio in the 1850s, although the university has no official record of him doing so.

The most significant development in Anderson's early life was the passage by the U.S. Congress in 1850 of the Fugitive Slave Act, which made it a federal offense to harbor escaped slaves. Many free blacks in the North, as well as slaves who had escaped bondage and sought refuge in the free states, immediately made plans to flee to Canada, fearing that they would be captured by slave catchers and sold in the South. Anderson was among the forty thousand African Americans who fled to Canada in the decade following passage of the act. He settled in the community of Chatham, in the present-day province of Ontario, a popular destination for black emigrants. Among the nearly two thousand black settlers in Chatham at that time were Anderson's friend and former neighbor in Pennsylvania, MARY ANN SHADD (CARY). Anderson at first managed Shadd's uncle's farm, but by 1856 he was working with the Quaker-educated Shadd, who in 1853 had founded the *Provincial Freedman*, a newspaper for Ontario's black émigré community. He was employed at first as a subscription salesman, then as a printer, and he also wrote articles for the paper condemning both slavery and black emigration to Africa.

The *Provincial Freedman*'s uncompromising abolitionism and the militancy of Chatham's black community did not go unnoticed by John Brown, the radical white abolitionist who supported direct action tactics, including violence if necessary, to end slavery. In May 1858 Brown organized a direct action convention in Chatham at which Anderson served as one of two recording secretaries. Several prominent abolitionists invited to the meeting, notably FREDERICK DOUGLASS and HARRIET TUBMAN, did not attend, though others, including MARTIN DELANY, did. At the convention Delany and forty-five other delegates—thirty-four black and twelve white—elected Anderson as one of two members of congress for a future black state to be established in the southern Appalachians after the abolition of slavery. Some accounts suggest that Brown first discussed his plans for an armed raid on the federal arsenal at Harpers Ferry, Virginia (later West Virginia), at the Chatham meeting.

On 13 September 1859 Anderson left Canada to assist Brown in his planned attack on Harpers Ferry, which both men believed would help foment a general slave uprising in Virginia and the rest of the South. He was met by Brown himself on the Pennsylvania-Maryland border and traveled with him to a farm four miles from the federal arsenal where Brown and his allies had secretly been preparing for the raid for more than two months. Anderson, among the last of the conspirators to arrive, proved crucial to Brown's plans by thwarting a last-minute mutiny among twenty or so of Brown's followers, who were concerned that promised reinforcements had not yet arrived from Canada or other posts on the Underground Railroad. On 16 October 1859 "Chatham" Anderson, as he was known to Brown's men, chaired the final meeting of the insurrectionists before seventeen of them, including Anderson, DANGERFIELD NEWBY, and three other African Americans, set out for Harpers Ferry. That evening the raiding party captured the town's armory, arsenal, and rifle works with relative ease. Brown then sent Anderson and five other men to capture and hold as hostage Colonel Lewis W. Washington, a prominent local landowner and a descendant of President George Washington. Perhaps as many as 150 slaves in the nearby area were aware of the plot, and Anderson armed around 30 of them with pikes, spears, and muskets. Other slaves in the region assisted the revolt by burning and destroying their owners' property. Anderson's role in encouraging slaves to rebel resulted in his being named as the leader of the revolt in many of the first reports of the insurrection.

In spite of these early successes it quickly became apparent—as Frederick Douglass, among others, had warned—that Brown's forces were no match for the fifteen hundred members of the local militia and for federal troops led by Colonel Robert E. Lee. By the evening of Monday, 17 October, these forces had surrounded the firehouse at Harpers Ferry, where Brown was holding several hostages. Anderson, aided by Albert Hazlett and a fugitive slave named Shields Green, was in charge of guarding the arsenal. Green chose to join Brown in the firehouse, where he and eight of his comrades met the martyr's death that many of them had anticipated and welcomed. Six others, including Brown, were captured, tried, and executed.

Since Anderson was the sole survivor among the main participants of the raid, his account remains the best inside account that we have of those events. His seventy-two-page *A Voice from Harpers Ferry* is, however, misleading on some matters. Anderson suggests, for example, that he and Hazlett made their escape on the Monday afternoon, after seeing that Brown had been captured and in the hope of later securing his release. Most other accounts suggest that Brown was captured on the Tuesday, the morning after Hazlett and Anderson abandoned the arsenal. Most historians nonetheless accept as accurate Anderson's description of his perilous escape with Hazlett along the Shenandoah and Potomac rivers to Pennsylvania. Ten miles south of Chambersburg, Pennsylvania, the two men split up. Shortly afterward Hazlett, injured and exhausted, was captured, extradited to Virginia, and executed in January 1860. Anderson remained undetected and reached York, Pennsylvania, where he was assisted by WILLIAM GOODRIDGE, a veteran of the Underground Railroad—and also the owner of an actual railroad line—who helped him to reach Philadelphia. From there Anderson made his way to Cleveland, Ohio, and then back to Chatham.

The sole survivor of the Harpers Ferry raid, Anderson became instantly both a fugitive from federal justice and a hero to radical abolitionists. On 4 July

1860 he addressed a thousand people at a memorial service for the Harpers Ferry martyrs at Brown's farm in North Elba, New York, and devoted the rest of that year to writing *A Voice from Harpers Ferry*. Anderson's main reason for writing the volume was to counter the erroneous statements of journalists and government officials who claimed that all slaves in the vicinity of Harpers Ferry had opposed the insurrection. Following the outbreak of the Civil War in 1861 Anderson recruited black Canadians to fight for the Union cause, and he may also have fought in the Union army himself. After the war he moved to Washington, D.C., where he remained an active public speaker and worked as a messenger until his death in that city in 1872, aged forty-two. Like all of the Harpers Ferry rebels other than John Brown, Osborne Perry Anderson was largely forgotten in the century following his death. In 2000, however, Anderson's *Voice from Harpers Ferry* was made available to a new generation when it was republished with commentaries by the death-row prisoner MUMIA ABU-JAMAL, among others.

Further Reading

Anderson, Osborne Perry. *A Voice from Harpers Ferry* (1861).

Libby, Jean. *Black Voices from Harpers Ferry: Osborne Anderson and the John Brown Raid* (1979).

Stauffer, John. *The Black Hearts of Men: Radical Abolitionists and the Transformation of Race* (2002).

STEVEN J. NIVEN

ANDERSON, Peter (c.1822–1879), tailor, store owner, and newspaper editor, was born in Pennsylvania, to parents whose names and occupations are now unknown. Little is known about Anderson's early life except that he was a member of the Masonic Fraternity, ultimately gaining appointment as Deputy Grand Master of the Grand Lodge for the State of Pennsylvania. Anderson migrated west in the waning days of the California gold rush and in 1854 set up a tailor shop and clothing store in San Francisco. There he plunged into the city's small but energetic black community, a community linked by both the mining economy and by shared protest against injustices in the new state of California.

Anderson soon became a regular contributor to political discussions at the recently organized Atheneum Institute, a reading room and cultural center for black Californians. In January 1855 he and other prominent African Americans joined together to call for a Colored Citizens' Convention to protest racial discrimination in the state. Eventually Anderson would participate in every Colored Citizens' Convention held in California between 1855 and 1865.

Many African Americans profited from the state's mining economy, usually through small businesses such as barbershops, restaurants, or laundries. The money earned from such ventures allowed these pioneers to send for the wives and children they had temporarily left behind, and the state's black population quickly expanded. Despite California's status as a free state some Southern white migrants openly brought slaves to work in the gold fields. State law denied blacks the right to vote, send their children to public schools, or even testify in court, a prohibition upheld (and extended to Chinese immigrants) by the California supreme court in 1854 in *People v. Hall*.

During an 1855 meeting called to protest such discrimination Peter Anderson broached the idea of mass emigration to Sonora, Mexico. But when delegates gathered at the first State Convention of Colored Citizens in November 1855 they refused Anderson's call to endorse such a plan, instead focusing on testimony rights and public education demands. They also called for the development of a newspaper to help foster and sustain black political activism, an idea Anderson enthusiastically promoted to black San Franciscans after the conference. The first issue of the *Mirror of the Times* (1856–1858) appeared shortly before the second California Colored Convention, under the ownership of MIFFLIN WISTAR GIBBS and others.

During the turbulent years of the late 1850s Anderson established himself as a prominent voice in black politics. African Americans increasingly saw California as a hostile environment both because of the continued ban on black testimony and the infamous ARCHY LEE case. In 1858 the California State supreme court overturned a lower court's decision freeing Lee, a Mississippi-born slave, despite his residence in the state for over a year. African Americans rallied to his cause and after much legal wrangling, Lee eventually gained his freedom. In the midst of this conflict Anderson once again publicly endorsed emigration to Mexico, and though by this time there was greater interest in such ideas, the debate was cut short when news of a gold strike in Vancouver, Canada, reached California. Hundreds of African Americans headed north, including Archy Lee and Mifflin Gibbs, one of the editors of the struggling *Mirror of the Times*, which had ceased publication.

Anderson, meanwhile, remained in California, participating in continuing efforts to pressure the California legislature to reform its testimony laws and provide other civic opportunities to African Americans. In a letter to the *Weekly Anglo-African* (17 Dec. 1859) he complained that few remaining California blacks demonstrated an interest in politics. He noted that a restaurant occupied the old Atheneum Institute and that minstrel shows were being put on in the abandoned St. Cyprian African Methodist Episcopal (AME) Church of San Francisco. In 1859 Anderson and several allies created the Savings and Land Association, optimistically suggesting that with enough stockholders, blacks could acquire land for their own republic or state, but the arrival of the Civil War again dampened any real interest in Anderson's emigration plans.

For his part, Anderson recognized the political opportunities of the Civil War era and in 1862, after a stint as a reporter for the *Lunar Visitor*, a newspaper briefly published by the AME minister JOHN J. MOORE, he began publishing the *Pacific Appeal* under the slogan, "He who would be free, himself must strike the blow." Testimony rights emerged as the immediate focus of this weekly journal. By 1863 African Americans had finally gained the right to testify in California's courts and Anderson turned his political attention to education. He served on a San Francisco committee to press city officials for black children's schooling rights and regularly publicized other such efforts around northern California in the *Pacific Appeal*.

Anderson shared editorship of the *Pacific Appeal* with PHILIP A. BELL, an experienced abolitionist and journalist from New York who migrated west during the Civil War years. Bell used his significant political connections with African American leaders in the East to ensure that the *Pacific Appeal* maintained a national perspective on black politics. The newspaper also published social and business news from around the northern California region, creating an important network for black Californians.

Peter Anderson and Philip Bell increasingly quarreled however, and in 1865 Bell launched his own weekly newspaper, the *Elevator*, under the slogan "Equality Before the Law." Through their rival newspapers the editors regularly clashed over political strategy and partisan loyalty. Initially suspicious of the Republican Party, Anderson later came to insist that only strict Republican allegiance would ensure civil rights reforms. Regarded by some as arrogant he alienated other black leaders in northern California's political circles and soon his influence was eclipsed by Bell's. As early as the late 1860s Anderson was struggling to maintain regular publication of the *Pacific Appeal*. When he died in San Francisco the newspaper closed. Ultimately Anderson's commitment to civil rights protest and his rivalry with Bell demonstrates the political vitality of northern California's nineteenth-century black community.

Further Reading
Beasley, Delilah. *The Negro Trail Blazers of California* (1919).
Daniels, Douglas Henry. *Pioneer Urbanites: a Social and Cultural History of Black San Francisco* (1980).
Fisher, James Adolphus. "A History of the Political and Social Development of the Black Community in California, 1850–1950." PhD diss., State University of New York at Stony Brook, 1971.
Lapp, Rudolph M. *Blacks in Gold Rush California* (1977).

SUSAN BRAGG

ANDERSON, Regina (21 May 1901–5 Feb. 1993), librarian, Harlem Renaissance cultural worker, and playwright, was born Regina Anderson in Chicago, the daughter of Margaret (Simons) Anderson, an artist, and William Grant Anderson, a prominent criminal attorney. She was reared in a black Victorian household in Chicago's Hyde Park district, amply provided for by a father who counted W. E. B. DU BOIS, Theodore Roosevelt, and Adlai Stevenson among his friends and clients. Regina attended normal school and high school in Hyde Park, studying later at Wilberforce University and the University of Chicago, and eventually receiving a degree in Library Science from Columbia University's School of Library Science.

The Chicago of her youth and early adulthood struck her as provincial, yet it was flavored by migrants from the deep South and enlivened by the voice of IDA B. WELLS, whose writings on lynching gave Anderson an understanding of the link between race and violence, a subject of one of her Harlem Renaissance plays, *Climbing Jacobs Ladder* (1931). While the young woman scorned her parents' adherence to the genteel tradition, she inherited from their household a firm sense of self and a *savoir-vivre* that enabled her to move through different levels of society with ease and confidence. Following her parents' divorce, Anderson lived for a short time with her grandmother, then moved to New York in 1923, joining other "new women" and "new Negro women," who, empowered by their new voting rights, flocked to New York in search of personal emancipation. Anderson first settled in downtown Manhattan, living at a YWCA, and applied for a library position in the vast New York Public Library system. At the time without a degree, but with some experience working in libraries in Chicago, Anderson was placed in Harlem, at the 135th Street branch as assistant to the enlightened Ernestine Rose, a white woman who would make the branch an intellectual center for Renaissance Harlem.

Realizing that she herself was a victim of an educational system that had disregarded black contributions to America, and having never taken even a single course in black history, Anderson began to study African American history and culture in order to accommodate the interests of the library's black patrons. She perfectly understood the historical significance of her appointment and with inexhaustible energy set about building the collection of books, organizing groups for literary discussions featuring the younger generation of writers and artists, and the likes of LANGSTON HUGHES and COUNTEE CULLEN, who were hosted by an impressive volunteer corps that included ETHEL RAY NANCE, Regina's roommate. Nance later recalled her roommate's late-night reading activity, which produced notes on new and promising books, and her roommate's vigilant lookout for new and promising authors to bring to the library. Within a year of her residency in Harlem, she was instrumental in convincing CHARLES S. JOHNSON to organize the now-famous March 1924 Civic Club dinner which launched the Harlem Renaissance, a turning point in African American history and culture. If, as NATHAN HUGGINS suggested, Anderson had taken on the mission of getting to know herself through her race, it can also be said that she shared ARTHUR SCHOMBURG's mission of educating African Americans about themselves.

Recognizing the value of drama as a pedagogical tool, Anderson opened the basement of the library in 1924 for community theater, joining Du Bois in establishing the Crigwa (later Krigwa) Players, which would employ the theater as an extension of the aims of the *Crisis* Magazine. The Crigwa Players offered more serious fare than that provided by Harlem's Lafayette Theatre and, influenced by THOMAS MONTGOMERY GREGORY's Howard University Players and the revolutionary design of new Irish drama, it created additional outlets for writers and performers and attracted a loyal Harlem audience. With the demise of Krigwa, in 1928 Anderson herself spearheaded the founding of the Harlem Experimental Theatre, which opened the way for the founding of the American Negro Theatre (ANT). Relocated to St. Philip's Episcopal Church Parish House, the ANT established a tradition of theater-going that continued even into the early twenty-first century in the form of the community-based H.A.D.L.E.Y players, led by the octogenarian Gertrude Jeannette, a former member of the now-defunct American Negro Theatre, which also included SYDNEY POITIER and HARRY BELAFONTE as members. Working full time at the library, raising funds, and helping run the Harlem Experimental Theatre, under her pen name Ursula Trelling, Anderson composed a number of plays which saw production by the company, beginning with *Climbing Jacob's Ladder* in 1931.

The apartment that Anderson shared with Ethel Ray Nance and Luella Tucker at 580 St. Nicholas Avenue became an important salon, its significance captured in its alternate name, "Dream Haven." Firm believers in the importance of dialogue, the residents of Dream Haven brought together members of the younger generation, JEAN TOOMER, ERIC WALROND, AARON DOUGLAS, ZORA NEALE HURSTON and the older custodians of culture, CHARLES S. JOHNSON, ALAIN LOCKE, and W. E. B. Du Bois. Located in a newly integrated building, 580, where ETHEL WATERS also lived, faced the beautiful St. Nicholas Park and its roof, affording a splendid view of Harlem, the Mecca of the black world that all had come to love so much. "Dream Haven" embodied the wonderful friendship between Anderson and Nance that was to last many years after 1926, when Nance left New York and Anderson married William T. Andrews, an attorney and New York state assemblyman. They would have one daughter, Regina Ann.

A letter from W. E. B. Du Bois proved instrumental in helping Anderson secure a permanent position in the library after graduating from library school. Career advancement propelled the move from the 135th Street to downtown branches until 1936, when she began work at the Columbia branch, located on 115th Street near the university. In 1947 Anderson became supervisor of the Washington Heights branch and instituted discussion groups and a "Family Night" program that brought international and national notables to the neighborhood's mostly East European immigrant population. As responsive to the Washington Heights neighborhood as she had been to her Harlem clientele, Anderson established English as a second language classes in order to help immigrants make the transition to American life.

A cosmopolitan who enjoyed travel Anderson visited many countries in Europe, Asia, and Africa on behalf of women and human rights, while serving as vice president of the National Council of Women and the Urban League's representative to the United Nations Educational, Scientific, and Cultural Organization (UNESCO). In 1967 Anderson retired to her country home in Mahopac, New York, an area she and her family integrated, bringing large numbers of guests of color who received a warm welcome in the area. From their penthouse apartment atop 409 Edgecombe Avenue, home base over the years to WALTER WHITE, W. E. B. Du Bois, THURGOOD MARSHALL, and Aaron Douglas, she and Andrews remained important figures in Harlem's social and political life. With long memory, she was mindful of the radical thrust of her own aims for black theater and welcomed the revolutionary Black Arts Movement of the 1960s and 1970s. She was a consultant to New York Metropolitan Museum's controversial 1968 retrospective exhibition, *Harlem on My Mind*, a project that brought back vivid memories of "Dream Haven" and the Harlem of her earlier days The rediscovery of the Harlem Renaissance in the 1970s provided additional opportunities for Anderson to share her own memories of the period. She was a source for NATHAN HUGGINS's important study, *Harlem Renaissance* (1971), which initiated the modern reappraisal of the period.

In 1971 Anderson and her former Dream Haven mate, Ethel Ray Nance, completed a manuscript, *A Chronology of African-Americans in New York, 1621–1966*, a reflection of the "power of pride" in heritage that had energized 580 St. Nicholas Ave. Unpublished at the time of her death in 1993 the manuscript was foundational to the millennium exhibition and book, *The Black New Yorkers: The Schomburg Illustrated Chronology*, produced by the New York Public Library's Schomburg Center for Research in Black Culture, the successor to the 135th Street branch which Regina Anderson had nurtured.

Further Reading

The Schomburg Center in New York has a five-videocassette interview with Anderson conducted by Jean Blackwell Hutson in 1986 and a large photo collection covering the subject's personal, professional, and civic activities. It also holds committee reports she compiled for the Human Relations Committee of the National Council of Women of the United States.

Huggins, Nathan. *Harlem Renaissance* (1971).

Hull, Gloria. *Color, Sex, and Poetry: Three Women Writers of the Harlem Renaissance* (1987).

Levering Lewis, David. *When Harlem was in Vogue* (1979).

Marks, Carol, and Diana Edkins. *The Power of Pride* (1999).

Roses, Lorraine Elena, and Ruth Elizabeth Randolph. *Harlem's Glory: Black Women Writing, 1900–1950* (1997).

ONITA ESTES-HICKS

ANDERSON, T. J. (17 Aug. 1928–), musician, composer, arranger, teacher, scholar, and humanitarian, was born Thomas Jefferson Anderson in Coatesville, Pennsylvania, the only son and eldest of three children born to Thomas Jefferson Anderson Sr., a college professor and school principal, and Anita Turpeau Anderson, a teacher. Anderson's early years were spent in Washington, D.C., and Cincinnati, Ohio. His mother was a pianist who accompanied singers in church. She was his first musical mentor, providing encouragement from a very early age through music lessons on violin and trumpet.

Anderson attended James Monroe Elementary School in Washington, D.C., where he conducted a rhythm band and impressed Esther Ballou, a city supervisor of music, who told his mother, "the musical world will hear from your son." He later attended Benjamin Banneker Junior High in Washington, D.C. It was during his time in Washington that he discovered the Howard Theatre and the big bands of the likes of TINY BRADSHAW, LUCKY MILLINDER, FATS WALLER, JIMMIE LUNCEFORD, ERSKINE HAWKINS, DUKE ELLINGTON, and COUNT BASIE. Anderson also studied violin for six years with Louis van Jones, a member of the Howard University music faculty.

He later moved to Cincinnati to live with his maternal grandparents. His grandfather, the Reverend DAVID DEWITT TURPEAU, was a member of the Ohio House of Representatives, and his grandmother was a social activist. While in Cincinnati, Anderson attended Harriet Beecher Stowe Junior High School. He credits his music teacher Charles Keys as being very important in his training. He also continued to hear big bands and regularly attended several churches, including Methodist, Episcopal, and African Methodist Episcopal (AME), all chosen for the music.

In 1946 Anderson graduated from Horace Scott High School in Coatesville, Pennsylvania, where he was a member of the orchestra and the band. He performed on trumpet at the commencement ceremony, and his jazz band was honored. From 1946 to 1950, Anderson pursued undergraduate studies at West Virginia State College, graduating with a bachelor's degree in music in 1950. Two of his professors, Dr. Edward C. Lewis and Dr. Ahmed Williams, had great influence on him. In 1950 Anderson entered a graduate program in music education at Pennsylvania State University. He took composition courses with Professor George Ciega, whose encouragement prompted him to become a composer. He graduated in 1951 with a master's in music education.

Anderson began a teaching career at the secondary level as an instrumental music instructor for the High Point, North Carolina, public schools from 1951 to 1954. He also performed in the area with school groups and in a trio with JACKIE MCLEAN and DANNIE RICHMOND. Anderson spent the summer of 1954 studying composition with Dr. T. Scott Huston at the Cincinnati Conservatory of Music.

From 1954 to 1958, Anderson pursued doctoral studies in composition at the University of Iowa, graduating in 1958 with a PhD in music composition. His teachers at Iowa were Dr. Philip Bezanson and Dr. Richard Hervig, both of whom were important in his musical development. While pursuing his doctoral studies, Anderson continued his career as an educator, moving to historically black institutions of higher education. He taught at West Virginia State College in 1955–1956. On 16 June 1956 in Cincinnati, Ohio, Anderson married Lois Ann Fields. They went on to have three children. Upon completion of his doctoral studies, Anderson was appointed professor and chair of music at Langston University in Langston, Oklahoma, in 1958, and held that position until 1963. He then moved to Tennessee State University in Nashville, where he was a professor of music from 1963 to 1969.

In the summer of 1964, Anderson studied composition with the French composer Darius Milhaud at the Aspen School of Music. From 1969 to 1972, while serving as composer-in-residence for the Atlanta Symphony Orchestra, he orchestrated SCOTT JOPLIN's opera *Treemonisha*, which brought him worldwide recognition. During this same period, he was the Danforth Visiting Professor at Morehouse College.

In 1972, he moved to Tufts University in Medford, Massachusetts, as professor and chair of the music department, where in 1978 he was named Austin Fletcher Professor of Music, a position he held until 1990. In that year he retired from Tufts to devote his time to composing.

Anderson's teaching career in secondary and higher education spanned more than five decades, during which time he had an impact on thousands of students. When queried about his purposes in teaching, Anderson said:

Basically, my teaching focused on the personality of the student—what they were listening to and what they wanted to do. Those two things in particular. That's why . . . if you look over my students who are out there now, a variety of styles are represented. I believe in the freedom for them to choose and at the same time to incorporate skills as a composer. So those two things were the main focal points (telephone interview between author and Anderson, 6 July 2005).

Anderson's career as a composer spanned more than forty years, during which time he created more than eighty compositions that included music for instrumental solos, small ensembles, combinations, chamber orchestra, full orchestra, orchestra (chamber and full) with soloists or chorus, band, solo voice, voice with instrumental ensemble, vocal duet, choral music, and dramatic music. His works include "Pyknon Overture" (1958), "In Memoriam MALCOLM X" (1974), "Soldier Boy, Soldier" (1982), "Thomas Jefferson Anderson's Orbiting Minstrels and Contraband" (1984),

"Dear John, Dear Coltrane" (1989), "Bahia, Bahia" (1990), "Walker" (1992), "Huh! (What did you say?)" (1997), "Slip Knot" (2000), and "A Song for Elma Lewis" (2004).

Anderson has received more than thirty commissions, including those from the National Endowment for the Arts, the Fromm Foundation, ASCAP, Yo-Yo Ma, Meet the Composer, Robert Shaw, Symphony of the New World, and the Berkshire Music Center. He has been the recipient of numerous honors and awards, including those from the Rockefeller Foundation, the National Black Music Caucus, the John Simon Guggenheim Foundation, the National Association of Negro Musicians, the Mellon Foundation, the American Music Center, and the National Humanities Center. Anderson also received six honorary doctorates. In 2005 he was inducted into the American Academy of Arts and Letters, the highest formal recognition of artistic merit in the United States.

Anderson's compositional legacy is profound and eclectic, reflecting a deep mastery of African and African American musical aesthetics, traditions, and approaches as well as musical traditions from the East and the West. Regarding his intent as a composer, Anderson says:

Each piece has a different message, and what I try to do is write the best piece, technically and spiritually, that I can. And I don't mean spiritual in the religious sense. I mean spiritually in terms of roots to integrity and truth. That's what I'm talking about. So they are my children, so to speak. And what I try to do is bring forth what I knew. Let me put it this way: the goal is not to, say, incorporate. The goal is to use music as a part of—as an extension of my own personality. So if I have a piece that is influenced by jazz, I'm not trying to write a jazz piece, I'm writing a piece that is influenced by jazz but I'm trying to write a T. J. Anderson piece (telephone interview between author and Anderson, 6 July 2005).

Anderson's legacy is multidimensional, encompassing musical composition and arranging, teaching, and mentoring. He has served as an outstanding educator, as a leading spokesperson for issues related to black composers and scholars, and has been a major composer.

Further Reading
For additional biographical information, a list of compositions, commissions, reviews, memberships, awards, and honors information, see *The International Dictionary of Black Composers*, vol. 1, ed. Samuel A. Floyd Jr. (1999), 35–42.
"Black Composers and the Avant Garde: T. J. Anderson, Jr., Hale Smith, and OLLY WILSON," in *Black Music in Our Culture: Curricular Ideas on the Subjects, Materials, and Problems*, ed. Dominique-René De Lerma (1970).
"The Composer and His Relationship to Society: T. J. Anderson, David N. Baker, John Cater, John E. Price, and Herndon Spillman," in *Reflections on Afro-American Music*, ed. Dominique-René De Lerma (1973).
Hunt, Joseph. "Conversation with Thomas J. Anderson: Blacks and the Classics," *Black Perspective in Music* 1, no. 2 (1973): 156–165.

Discography
b Bop in 2 (Arizona University Recordings Contemporary Composer and Performer Series).
The Black Composers Series (The College Music Society CBS Special Products P19425–P19433).
Chamber Concerto (Remembrance) (Albany Records, Troy 303).
Chamber Symphony (Composers' Recordings, Inc. CRI-SD258).
"Don't Panic: 60 Seconds for Piano," on *Watermelon Revisited* (Wergo WER6649 2).
"Intermezzi," on *A City Called Heaven* (ACA Digital Recordings).
"It Won't Be the Same River," on *7 Cabaret Songs* (Capstone CPS8684).
Patterson, Willis C., ed. *The Second Anthology of Art Songs by African American Composers* (2002). Contains score and recording of *Words My Mother Taught Me*.
Songs of Illumination. Works by Hale Smith, Camille Nickerson, Thomas Kerr, Adolphus Hailstork, Stephen Newby, Howard Swanson, William Banfield, Evelyn Simpson-Curenton, and T. J. Anderson (Centaur CRC2357).
Variations on a Theme by M. B. Tolson New American Music, vol. 5, (Nonesuch Records, H-71303).
Videmus: Works by T. J. Anderson, David Baker, Donal Fox, Olly Wilson (New World Records, 80423-2).

LEONARD L. BROWN

ANDERSON, Webster (15 July 1933–30 Aug. 2003), Korean and Vietnam War veteran and Medal of Honor winner, was born in Winnboro, South Carolina, the son of Frizell Anderson, a carpenter, and Blanche Rabb Anderson, a homemaker. Webster's parents had seven children, daughters Frances, Alberta, Marjorie, and Marie, and sons Frizell Jr., Webster, Billy, and Larry.

In 1953, Anderson was drafted by the Army to serve in the Korean War. Although racism suffused the armed forces despite President Harry Truman's executive order to integrate the military, Anderson's initial Army experiences were largely positive. He would later tell his son Davis that joining the Army was "a good thing for him." He believed that his white commanding officers as much as his fellow soldiers "helped pave the way" for his military career (Anderson). Webster enjoyed a happy private life too, marrying Ida Davis in 1959. In their thirty-two years of marriage, before Ida's death in 1991, the couple had four children: daughters Vonnie and Tanetta, and sons Webster II and Davis. His children remember him as a good father even if, as son Davis laughingly recalls, "My father was always going to be a drill sergeant."

Following the Korean War, Anderson continued in the United States Army, serving in Battery A, 2d Battalion, 320th Field Artillery of the distinguished 101st Airborne Division as a staff sergeant and section chief. It was while his unit was operating at Tam Ky, Republic of Vietnam, on 15 October 1967, that Battery A's position was attacked by North Vietnamese infantry supported by automatic weapons, heavy mortars, and rocket propelled grenade launchers. When the enemy breached Battery A's position,

Anderson, with complete disregard for his personal safety, mounted the exposed parapet of his howitzer position and became the mainstay of the defense of the battery position. Sfc. Anderson directed devastating direct howitzer fire on the assaulting enemy while providing rifle and grenade defensive fire against enemy soldiers attempting to overrun his section gun position. While protecting his crew and directing their fire against the enemy from his exposed position, 2 enemy grenades exploded at his feet knocking him down and severely wounding him in the legs. Despite the excruciating pain and though not able to stand, Sfc. Anderson valorously propped himself on the parapet and continued to direct howitzer fire upon the closing enemy and to encourage his men to fight on. Seeing an enemy grenade land within the gun pit near a wounded member of his gun crew, Sfc. Anderson, heedless of his own safety, seized the grenade and attempted to throw it over the parapet to save his men. As the grenade was thrown from the position it exploded and Sfc. Anderson was again grievously wounded. Although only partially conscious and severely wounded, Sfc. Anderson refused medical evacuation and continued to encourage his men in the defense of the position. (Medal of Honor Citation, 1968)

After this action, Anderson was evacuated by helicopter for medical treatment by Colonel Patrick Brady. He would subsequently suffer the amputation of both legs and the loss of a portion of one arm. For his "inspirational leadership, professionalism, devotion to duty . . . gallantry and extraordinary heroism at the risk of his life above and beyond the call of duty" (Medal of Honor Citation) at Tam Ky, Anderson received the Medal of Honor. He and Brady, himself a Medal of Honor winner, became lifelong friends from that day forth.

Anderson's honorable service in two wars is worthy of recognition; in the Korean War Anderson learned the ways of a soldier, while in the Vietnam War he put all his experience to the best possible use and became a true leader of men. He would later tell his family that Vietnam was "a war we couldn't win," but that "it was my job" to fight wherever his country sent him. Anderson deserves continued recognition today not only as a Medal of Honor winner, but also as a man representative of the fine service rendered in the Vietnam War by African American career soldiers; too often black soldiers in the Vietnam War have been unfairly portrayed as men that "chose" to serve in Vietnam only as a means of avoiding a prison sentence back home.

While Webster Anderson endured the considerable difficulties involved in fighting in Vietnam, the obstacles he faced after the war were equally daunting; having lost both legs and part of an arm, his recovery and rehabilitation would be long and arduous, lasting from late 1967 into the early 1970s. A quiet and modest man, Anderson persevered through his rehabilitation period and, with the help of prosthetics, recov-

ered to live a long and productive life, operating a successful television repair business. As his son Davis recalls, "you name it, he did it . . . he walked five times a week on his prosthetics, could load and unload his own pontoon boat on his own, and, well, hell, would take off his prosthetics and crawl under the house to make repairs. He was six feet, four inches, but he could be as tall or short as he wanted to be and there wasn't anything he couldn't do." Indeed, Anderson's older children saw no change in their father's attitude; Vonnie remembered him "as the same father, only he was shorter," while Webster II recalls that "he was different physically, but still the same daddy." Ironically, Anderson's war-induced disabilities would also serve as an example to Webster and Ida's youngest son, Davis Anderson. Born in 1970, Davis was diagnosed with ligament cancer before he was a year old, forcing the amputation of a leg and its replacement with a prosthesis; in his father he found a role model to help him overcome his disability from the very beginning, providing love, discipline, and encouragement whenever it was needed.

Following his military career, Webster Anderson lived the rest of his life in Winnsboro, South Carolina, as one of its most distinguished citizens. After the death of his first wife Ida in 1991, he married his second wife Vickie in 1996. When not at work, he and his family traveled all around the world to Medal of Honor conventions, and he often spoke to veterans' organizations and at veteran hospitals before succumbing to cancer at the age of seventy.

Further Reading

All of the personal quotations reproduced above are from an interview conducted with Davis Anderson, the son of Webster Anderson, by the author on 2 February 2007.

Hane, Bobb. "Farewell the Hero," *The Herald Independent*, Winnsboro, South Carolina (4 September 2003).

Medal of Honor. *Vietnam War Medal of Honor Recipient Webster Anderson*, http://www.medalofhonor.com/WebsterAnderson.htm.

GLENN KNOBLOCK

ANDERSON, William T. (20 Aug. 1859–21 Aug. 1934), clergyman, army chaplain, and physician, was born a slave in Seguin, Texas. Little is known about his parents except that his mother was a slave, and during the Civil War she and William fled to Galveston, Texas. As a young boy, he joined the African Methodist Episcopal (AME) Church, which took on both local and national responsibility for the religious, intellectual, and social uplift of African Americans, often taking a leading role in promoting both secular and religious education. The AME Church, in fact, sponsored Anderson's education for three years at Wilberforce University in Ohio. The remainder of Anderson's education was financed by an Ohio sponsor, Stephen Watson, who was then the vice president of the London Exchange Bank of Madison County.

In 1886 Anderson received a theology certificate from Howard University and two years later graduated from the Homeopathic Medical College of Cleveland. Much later, he served as pastor for AME churches in Toledo, Ohio, Urbana, Illinois, Lima, Ohio, and Cleveland, Ohio, where he ministered to his largest congregation, St. John's.

A congressional act of 2 March 1867 had given the president of the United States the right to commission army chaplains. HENRY VINTON PLUMMER, in 1884, became the first black clergyman to be commissioned a chaplain to the Ninth Cavalry regiment, one of the units popularly known as Buffalo Soldiers. It was not until thirteen years later, in November 1897, that President William McKinley appointed Anderson to be a chaplain. He entered with the rank of captain into the Tenth Cavalry, another unit of Buffalo Soldiers. He was soon stationed at the Assinniboine headquarters in Montana. His religious programs were always well attended, and he organized a reading group, which sometimes discussed essays written by members of the group. His ministry at Fort Assinniboine ended in April 1898 when the Tenth Calvary departed for Camp Chickamauga in Georgia to prepare for the invasion of Cuba during the Spanish-American War.

For reasons that are unclear, Anderson failed to depart with his unit and did not rejoin his men until 25 July 1898 near Santiago, Cuba, where he cared for those who had contracted fever and dysentery. Immediately after his short stay in Cuba, Anderson and his regiment spent some months along the Gulf Coast of Alabama and Texas.

While languishing on the shores of the gulf, Anderson and his fellow troopers Herschel Cashin, Charles Alexander, HORACE W. BIVINS, and ARTHUR MCKINNON BROWN published *Under Fire with the Tenth Cavalry* (1899). Based on eyewitness accounts, this book traced the history of the unit's action and the steadfastness and bravery of black soldiers—both commissioned officers and enlisted men. *Under Fire with the Tenth Cavalry* revealed that in a private letter to JOHN EDWARD BRUCE of Albany, New York, Colonel Theodore Roosevelt praised the Ninth and Tenth Cavalry regiments for their courage during operations in Cuba.

Anderson and his regiment returned to Manzanillo, Cuba, in mid-1899, where they served as part of the army of occupation until April of 1902. He spent the next five years at Fort Mackintosh, Texas, and he also had a stint in Nebraska. In Cuba—and later in Nebraska—Anderson helped the enlisted men organize a regimental Young Men's Christian Association (YMCA) as a way for them to engage in self-help programs and to address issues such as racial inequality. In April 1907 Anderson's regiment was relocated to Fort William McKinley, near Manila in the Philippines, where he commanded the United States Morgue. Shortly after this assignment, he returned to the United States and was stationed at Fort Ethan Allen in Vermont. On 10 January 1910 he retired because of a disability that resulted from a fever he had contracted during his stay in Cuba.

Anderson returned to his home in Wilberforce and worked as an accountant and secretary to the bishop in the Third Episcopal District. In September 1916 he became the minister of Warren Chapel in Toledo, a church he had served for a short time in 1896 and 1897. He resigned from his ministry in September 1918 to offer his services to the Quartermaster Corps of the army. After the close of World War I, he led a drive to raise money for the defense of Dr. Leroy Bundy, a prominent leader of the East St. Louis black community who was charged with murder during the East St. Louis riot of 2 July 1917. He died in Cleveland in 1934, survived by his wife, Sada J. Anderson, who was also an active member of the AME Church and held several offices in the Women's Parent Mite Missionary Society. In the Cleveland area, an American Legion post was named for him.

Further Reading
Cashin, Herschel V., Charles Alexander, William T. Anderson, Arthur M. Brown, and Horace W. Bivins. *Under Fire with the Tenth U.S. Cavalry: Being a Brief, Comprehensive Review of the Negro's Participation in the Wars of the United States. Especially Showing the Valor and Heroism of the Negro Soldiers of the Ninth and Tenth Cavalries, and the Twenty-fourth and Twenty-fifth Infantries of the Regular Army . . .* (1899, repr. 1969).
Rudwick, Elliott. *Race Riots in East St. Louis, July 2, 1917* (1980).

SHERROW O. PINDER

ANDREWS, Benny (13 Nov. 1930–), artist, was born in Madison, Georgia, the second of ten children of Viola Perryman and George Andrews, sharecroppers. Benny Andrews grew up in a household where creativity was encouraged. With what little money they had, his parents bought pens and paper for their children and encouraged them to draw and tell stories. Although not formally trained as an artist, George Andrews painted throughout his life and received considerable recognition in his later years. As a teenager Benny Andrews attended Burney Street High School only sporadically, when weather conditions excused him from his work picking cotton in the fields. In 1948 he became the first member of his family to graduate from high school.

In 1948 Andrews moved to Atlanta and was awarded a 4-H club scholarship to attend one of Georgia's three black colleges. He entered Fort Valley State College in Fort Valley, Georgia, but dropped out two years later when his scholarship ran out. He joined the United States Air Force and fought in the Korean War until 1954, when he was honorably discharged. After hearing about the Art Institute of Chicago from an army artist, he applied, and with the help of the GI Bill he enrolled in September 1954. It was in Chicago that Andrews visited a museum for the first time. In Georgia, African Americans were prohibited from entering museums.

Although Andrews attended the Art Institute of Chicago at the height of Abstract Expressionism, his real interest lay in realism, particularly the American narrative tradition of artists like Norman Rockwell, Raphael Soyer, Thomas Hart Benton, and Andrew Wyeth. While attending art school and spending time in the streets of Chicago, Andrews developed the subject matter that would occupy him throughout his life: everyday people with ordinary jobs. He carefully recorded their clothes, gestures, and expressions, and though he was particularly interested in the African American experience, he was not limited to it. While at the Art Institute of Chicago, Andrews created *Janitors at Rest*, a milestone in his development, combining collage and painting. Andrews was, however, rejected by every show, organization, and club at the institute. While in Chicago he met and began living with Mary Ellen Jones Smith, a secretary.

In 1958, after graduating from the Art Institute of Chicago, Andrews moved to New York to try his hand as a professional artist. One week after arriving in New York City he and Mary Ellen Smith had a son, Christopher. Andrews painted at home while taking care of his son while Mary Ellen went off to work as a secretary. In New York he found support for his approach to realistic subject matter and collage, as well as inspiration in the concurrent trends in abstraction and figuration. Andrews was influenced by the pop art scene and by two southerners, Jasper Johns and Robert Rauschenberg, who incorporated found objects into their paintings. *Beggar Man* (1959) exemplifies his style in this period; it portrays a beggar holding out his hand asking for money. Andrews used torn, ragged paper in the painting to symbolize urban debris. The abstract, painted collage of a beggar is a metaphor for the difference between poverty in the rural South and in New York City. Andrews also regularly sketched and painted people on the streets and jazz musicians throughout the Bowery and Greenwich Village. In August 1959 he and Smith had another son, Thomas. They married that same year, and Andrews remained the children's primary caregiver.

Andrews began to show in 1959 at group exhibitions such as the Detroit Institute's Thirteenth Biennial of Painting and Sculpture. At a New York art fair that same year he met Paul Kessler, who offered him his first one-man show at Kessler's gallery in Provincetown, Massachusetts, in 1960. Andrews eventually made his way into the New York art scene, meeting and befriending other young, aspiring artists, and he was included in contemporary exhibitions, especially many abstract expressionist shows. But his connection with older artists such as Raphael Soyer, JACOB ARMSTEAD LAWRENCE, and Chaim Gross, social realists from the 1930s and 1940s, also had an impact. He became a member of the Forum Gallery, where he met many of these older artists and eventually had a one-man show, which was well received. Andrews continued his unique style and defied categorization; neither a realist nor an abstractionist, he drew on elements of both styles.

In the mid-1960s Andrews became increasingly interested in surrealism, particularly because of his own experience of trying to balance his life with his art and realism with abstraction. A third child, Julia, was born in June 1964, and the family moved into a five-thousand-square-foot loft. In 1965 Andrews's work was selected for the New York World's Fair. He was also awarded a John Hay Whitney Fellowship, which he used to travel back to his childhood home. His research there led to his Autobiographical Series, which focused on his black southern roots, a subject that he continued to explore throughout his life.

In the 1960s Andrews began to apply the lessons of the civil rights movement to his own world—the New York art scene. He was particularly upset that his gallery seemed to favor his use of white subject matter over black subject matter. Following the protests of black artists angry about the exclusion of African American curators and artists from Harlem on My Mind: Cultural Capital of Black America, 1900–1968—a 1969 exhibition at the Metropolitan Museum of Art—Andrews, along with Ed Taylor and Henri Ghent, formed the Black Emergency Cultural Coalition. The group protested the lack of black representation in major New York art institutions, such as the Metropolitan Museum of Art and the Whitney Museum of American Art. During this period Andrews emerged as a leader and spokesperson for social and artistic causes. Some critics labeled him a militant, which caused many galleries and collectors to turn away from his art well into the 1970s. Andrews himself pulled his work from commercial galleries and began a period of lecturing at universities and showing mainly in college and university galleries. He became a professor at Queens College in 1969. His efforts did eventually pay off; more black artists began to be shown in major New York City museums and galleries, and some black curators were hired in the 1970s. But Andrews also began to feel pigeonholed as a black artist who exhibited mainly in black art shows. However, he maintained his commitment to works with specific themes. Throughout the 1970s he worked mainly on a series titled The Bicentennial Series, portraying two hundred years of African American life. Although many artists in the 1970s were exploring the boundaries of art and experimenting with different styles, such as minimalism and earth art, Andrews continued in his personal style of painting, drawing, and collage. He also began to illustrate the novels of his brother, RAYMOND ANDREWS.

The 1980s brought new recognition to Andrews; America's artistic boundaries broadened to include more cultures and styles, and his work began to sell well, a development that experts credit to the growth of the black middle class in the 1980s. Andrews turned away from his political activism. His collages gained acceptance by a wider audience. In 1980 he was commissioned to paint a mural for the Hartsfield International Airport in Atlanta, and from 1982 to 1984 he served as the director of the visual arts program at the National Endowment for the Arts.

As director he instituted programs to help young artists, including a prison program in which he brought art lessons to prisoners. In 1986, following a ten-year separation, Andrews and his wife divorced. He then married his fellow artist Nene Humphrey. Several series—Portraits of . . . , America, Revival, and Music—occupied him into the 1990s.

During the 1990s Andrews turned his attention to exhibiting with members of his family. In 1990 he showed with his father in an exhibit called Folk: The Art of Benny and George Andrews, mounted by the Memphis Brooks Museum of Art in Tennessee. He also continued his interest in helping African American art institutions and young artists by starting a foundation that finds African American artists willing to donate their work. The foundation also runs workshops for young artists, teaching them how to break into the art world. In 2001 the Ogden Museum of Southern Art in New Orleans offered Benny Andrews and his family—his wife, Nene Humphrey; his father, George; and other family members—a permanent gallery within the facility.

Benny Andrews has traveled far in his life, from a sharecropper in the rural South to an established artist in New York City. His combinations of painting, drawing, and collage reflect his journey, capturing rural southern life, religious beliefs, and everyday people on the streets of New York. He also brings his extraordinary penmanship and his deep sensitivity and humanity to each artwork.

Further Reading
Brenson, Michael. "The Collages of Benny Andrews," *New York Times*, 4 Nov. 1988.
Fox, Catherine. "A Sharecropper's Son Goes the Distance," *Atlanta Constitution*, 20 May 1982.
Gruber, Richard J. *American Icons: From Madison to Manhattan, the Art of Benny Andrews, 1948–1997* (1997).
Tully, Judd. "Benny Andrews," *American Artist* 52 (Apr. 1988).

SARAH WOLOZIN

ANDREWS, Ludie (1875–1943?), nursing educator and administrator, was born in Milledgeville, Georgia, the daughter of a poor family about whom nothing is known. In 1901 Andrews applied to Spelman College's MacVicar Hospital School of Nursing. On her application, she asked for financial assistance, explaining that her family could not help her pay. Her mother had a large family to support and "an old flicted husband," who was not Andrews's father. Andrews also said that she had been married but did not currently live with her husband and expected no support from him. Letters praising Andrews and talking about her "good moral character" that came from the pillars of Milledgeville society proved instrumental in securing Andrews's admission.

In 1906 Andrews received her diploma from Spelman and set upon her life's work. During her training she resolved "that I wanted to work for my people, how or where this was to be done I did not know." She

did not have to wait long to find out. After caring for only two private cases—the bread and butter of black nurses in that time period—Andrews was offered the position of superintendent of Lula Grove Hospital and Training School for Colored Nurses and Patients.

Located in Atlanta, the school, which was run by a group of white physicians who served on the faculty of the Atlanta School of Medicine, was one of the few health facilities in the area open to African Americans. Andrews quickly developed a reputation for excellence both in administration and on the surgical floor. Howard Kelly, an internationally known surgeon and professor from Johns Hopkins University, helped cement that reputation after Andrews assisted him on an operation. At the end of the procedure, he proclaimed, "I have never been better served even by nurses that I myself have trained."

Knowing that white and black nurses had equal skills, Andrews started a crusade to allow black nurses to take the same state medical exam as white nurses in 1909. Some proposed that black nurses take a different test than their white counterparts. Andrews did not accept that suggestion, pointing out that this scenario would make it difficult for graduates of black nursing schools in Georgia to find jobs in other states. The state board then offered to issue her a license. Again Andrews refused, saying she wanted that opportunity for all black nurses. When the state board refused to change its policy, Andrews instituted legal proceedings, a case she eventually won.

When the city of Atlanta opened the 250-bed Grady Hospital in 1914, Andrews was a natural choice to serve as superintendent of colored nurses for the facility. Always cognizant of opportunities for women like herself, Andrews spearheaded the establishment of Grady Hospital's Municipal Training School for Colored Nurses in 1917. Grady had a nursing school, founded in 1892, but that institution allowed only white women to apply.

Once more, Andrews earned kudos from her physician colleagues. One doctor, W. B. Symmerall, said "her services were of the highest character; she showed ability in organization and in administration. I always found her thoroughly devoted to her duties; she had high ideals in regard to the work of her people and the nursing profession."

In 1920 Andrews not only won her case against the state medical board but she also received one of the more coveted positions in black nursing, the superintendency of Morehouse College's infirmary. As a faculty member, Andrews also taught home and community hygiene in the summer program for teachers and the school of social work. She did not restrict her message to students enrolled at Morehouse. A frequent lecturer on public health throughout the community, Andrews delivered a variant on that lecture in the Neighborhood Union. Her efforts in public health went beyond the theoretical. She served on the Tuberculosis Association, chairing its relief committee and helping to raise money for patients. She also was a member of an interracial committee that worked with troubled women who had ended up in prisons or in medical wards.

Andrews continued to champion the cause of black nurses throughout her life. She served on the committee of several nursing organizations as a representative of the National Association of Colored Graduate Nurses. In that capacity she lobbied for equal treatment of black nurses before the American Nursing Association, the National League of Nursing Education, and the National Organization for Public Health Nursing. In 1926 Andrews suggested to the American Nursing Association that it allow black nurses who could not join their local chapters because of discrimination to join the national group. Her lifetime of hard work on behalf of black nurses made Andrews a natural choice for the Colored Nursing Association's Mary Mahoney Award in 1943, which she received shortly before she died.

Further Reading

Carnegie, Mary Elizabeth. *The Path We Tread: Blacks in Nursing Worldwide, 1854–1994* (1995).
Hine, Darlene Clark. *Black Women in White: Racial Conflict and Cooperation in the Nursing Profession, 1890–1950* (1989).
Staupers, Mabel Keaton. *No Time for Prejudice: A Story of the Integration of Negroes in Nursing in the United States* (1961).
Thoms, Adah B. *Pathfinders: A History of the Progress of Colored Graduate Nurses* (1929).

SHARI RUDAVSKY

ANDREWS, Raymond (6 June 1934–26 Nov. 1991), writer, was born in Plainview, Georgia, in Morgan County, the fourth of ten children of George Cleveland Andrews, a sharecropper and self-taught folk artist, and Viola (Perryman) Andrews, also a sharecropper and, later, a newspaper columnist and the author of published short stories and an unpublished autobiography. Raymond's older brother, BENNY ANDREWS, would become an internationally known painter and printmaker. Raymond Andrews's paternal grandmother, Jessie Rose Lee Wildcat Tennessee, was the daughter of an African American mother and a Native American father. Although she married Eddie Andrews, an African American who died in 1917, Raymond Andrews's paternal grandfather was James Orr, a plantation owner's son.

In 1935 Andrews and his family moved to a small house near his grandmother's home on land owned by Orr. Then in 1943 the Andrews family moved to the nearby Barnett Farm to work as sharecroppers. The family endured the hardships of sharecropping, yet the Andrewses, unlike most of their neighbors, read newspapers and magazines and owned a radio.

Andrews started school in 1939; the first through the seventh grades for African American children were taught at Plainview Lower Church. Like most of the other students at Plainview, he only attended school when he did not have to work in the fields. Attending school also meant that Andrews and his schoolmates had to walk to and from school because Georgia did not provide school buses for black children. Andrews discovered that African Americans wrote books after reading about RICHARD WRIGHT's *Black Boy* in an issue of *Life* magazine, and became an avid sports fan after being inspired by JOE LOUIS's status as one of the nation's first African American celebrities. After completing seventh grade at Plainview Elementary, Andrews attended Burney Street High School, the African American secondary institution in the nearby city of Madison.

On 4 December 1949 Andrews, then fifteen, moved to Atlanta, for the first time riding a Greyhound bus and traveling more than five miles from home. Andrews resided at Atlanta's Butler Street YMCA, where another older brother, Harvey, also lived. During the day Andrews was employed as a hospital orderly; at night he attended BOOKER T. WASHINGTON High School and earned his diploma.

From 1952 to 1956 Andrews served in the U.S. Air Force, stationed in Korea. Following his discharge he attended Michigan State University for one year before moving to New York in 1957. The next year his brother Benny also moved to New York. Raymond Andrews held a variety of jobs while living in New York, including working as a reservations agent for KLM Royal Dutch Airlines. His position with the airline allowed him to travel to such European locations as the Netherlands and Switzerland. Andrews worked for the airline for eight years, quitting on his thirty-second birthday in 1966 in order to pursue his dream of becoming a professional writer. That same year Andrews's article about football in Plainview, "Yesterday: A Football Rebellion in Backwoods Georgia," was published in the 7 November issue of *Sports Illustrated*. One month later, on 28 December 1966 in New York City, he married Adelheid "Heidi" Wenger, who was also an airline agent. The couple divorced in 1980.

Although Andrews continued to work various jobs from 1967 to 1984, writing remained his priority. In addition to *Sports Illustrated*, his work appeared in magazines such as *Athens Magazine*, *Atlanta Review*, *Ataraxia*, *Catalyst*, and *Harper's* and in newspapers like the *Atlanta Journal-Constitution*. In 1978 his first novel, *Appalachee Red* (originally titled *Red, White, and Blue*), was published. The novel received Dial Press's first JAMES BALDWIN Prize for Fiction at a ceremony attended by Baldwin himself. After Andrews's impressive debut as a novelist, a number of literary critics hailed him as one of America's most promising novelists. Starting with *Appalachee Red*, Andrews published five books in a thirteen-year period, each illustrated by his brother, Benny Andrews. *Appalachee Red* was the beginning of his Muskhogean County trilogy, which included *Rosiebelle Lee Wildcat Tennessee* in 1980 and *Baby Sweet's* in 1983. His 1990 memoir *The Last Radio Baby* and two novellas, *Jessie and Jesus and Cousin Claire* in 1991, followed. A second memoir was published posthumously in the *Chattahoochee Review* in 1998.

Andrews left New York for Georgia in 1984, settling near Athens. In 1991, one month after the publication of his two novellas, Andrews, who was fifty-seven years old and in poor health, committed suicide. At the time of his death, he was writing another novel, *99 Years and a Dark Day*. He devoted his literary career to paying homage to his rural Georgia roots and providing glimpses into African American life in the South during the twentieth century.

From 28 September 2001 to 12 January 2002, the Robert W. Woodruff Library at Emory University in Atlanta mounted the exhibit "The Mother is Like a Vine in Thy Blood: Viola P. Andrews and the Andrews Family," which documented the family's history via their written and visual works.

Further Reading

Raymond Andrews's papers are housed in Emory University's Manuscript, Archives, and Rare Book Library, in Atlanta, Georgia.

Andrews, Raymond. *The Last Radio Baby: A Memoir* (1990).

Andrews, Raymond. "Once Upon a Time in Atlanta," *Chattahoochee Review* 18.2 (Winter 1998).

Camp, Lynn Robinson. *Morgan County, Georgia* (2004).

LINDA M. CARTER

ANGELOU, Maya (4 Apr. 1928–), writer, poet, and performer, was born Marguerite Annie Johnson in St. Louis, Missouri, the second of two children of Bailey Johnson, a doorman and a naval dietician, and Vivian Baxter Johnson, a card dealer who later became a registered nurse. Her parents called her "Rita," but her brother, Bailey, who was only a year older, called her "My Sister," which was eventually contracted to "Maya." When Maya was three years old, she and Bailey were sent to Stamps, Arkansas, to live with their paternal grandmother, Annie Henderson, whom Maya often referred to as "Mother."

Mrs. Henderson was a strong, independent black woman who owned a country store, in which Maya lived and worked. Maya was a bright student and an avid reader; she absorbed the contradictory messages of love emanating from the Christian Methodist Episcopal Church and of hatred, revealed in the pervasive mistreatment of blacks by their white neighbors. In 1935 Maya returned to live with her mother in Chicago, until it was discovered that the eight-year-old had been raped by her mother's lover, Mr. Freeman, in whose care she was often left. Freeman was murdered, probably by Maya's uncles, after she testified in court. The trauma of the attack, the trial, and the misplaced guilt she felt for the death of the man who had abused her trust caused Maya to withdraw into an almost complete silence. She was sent back to Arkansas, where for the next four years she rarely

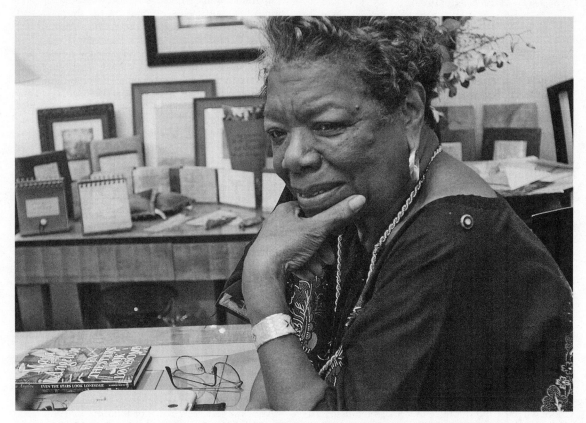

Maya Angelou at an interview in her New York apartment, 29 January 2002. (AP Images.)

spoke. By reading literature and poetry to her, Mrs. Bertha Flowers, a local, sophisticated black woman with impressive elocution, helped renew a love of language in a girl many believed to be mute.

At the age of thirteen Maya was at the top of her class when she and Bailey went again to live with their mother, who had by then moved to San Francisco. She attended George Washington High School and studied dance and drama at the California Labor School. She spent a summer with her father, but violent quarrels with his girlfriend compelled Maya to run away, preferring to live in an abandoned van for a month. In 1944 she temporarily dropped out of school and got a job as a streetcar conductor (becoming the first black woman in San Francisco to hold that position). As an adolescent she was almost six feet tall, insecure, desperate for affection, and confused about her sexuality. In this emotional state, she began an intimate relationship with a male acquaintance and became pregnant at the age of sixteen. Yet with indomitable determination she returned to school and graduated one month before giving birth to her only child, Clyde.

Angelou's journey to adulthood became the basis of her first and most celebrated autobiographical novel, *I Know Why the Caged Bird Sings* (1970), which was nominated for a National Book Award and named from a line in the poem "Sympathy," by PAUL LAURENCE DUNBAR. This book was soon followed by *Gather Together in My Name* (1974), which continues her odyssey. Angelou takes the reader through her postwar years as a single mother working as a cook at a Creole café in San Diego. She attempted to join the army and tried to retreat to Arkansas, the place of past comfort, only to learn that as an adult her lack of racial deference endangered her and those she loved. In 1947 her early efforts to become an entertainer led her into a world of drug use. During this period she became a madam for two lesbian demimondaines, and an abusive relationship with a man briefly plunged her into a life of prostitution. The narrative ends at the close of the 1940s with Angelou pulling her life together, as the religiously inspired title implies.

In 1950 Angelou began a three-year marriage to a former Greek sailor, Tosh Angelos ("Angelou" is a variant of his name), recounted in her third autobiographical volume, *Singin' and Swingin' and Gettin' Merry Like Christmas* (1976). Her singing and dancing career began to show promise when she became a calypso performer at the Purple Onion in San Francisco. This led to bookings in Chicago and ultimately at the Village Vanguard in New York. She moved to New York to study dance with PEARL PRIMUS and in 1954 landed a role in the George Gershwin opera *Porgy and Bess*, which toured Europe until 1955. When she returned to the United States, her career was progressing, but her failed marriage and frequent separations from her son evoked troubling memories of her own childhood. The book ends on a note of reconciliation and redemption as she sets out with her son on a Hawaiian cruise.

A fourth volume, *The Heart of a Woman* (1981), begins shortly after her return from Europe, when an old friend brings BILLIE HOLIDAY to Angelou's small San Francisco apartment for lunch. In this passage Angelou's skills as a writer are particularly evident. She recalls events with astonishing detail and relates them in an authentic and compelling style as her prose shifts between Standard English and the black vernacular she summons when its effect is most appropriate. Her ear for the particular speech patterns of her characters is evident in her re-creation of Billie Holiday's sassy and salty manner. These lively narrative qualities are sustained as the scene shifts to Brooklyn, where she moved in 1957 to appear in the off-Broadway play *Calypso Heatwave*. While in New York she joined the Harlem Writers Guild, whose members included JAMES BALDWIN, PAULE MARSHALL, and JOHN HENRIK CLARKE. This intellectual environment nurtured her literary interests and shaped her political activism. In 1960 she played a leading role in staging *Freedom Cabaret*, a revue she wrote to raise money to help MARTIN LUTHER KING JR. and the civil rights movement.

A few months later BAYARD RUSTIN nominated her to become the northern coordinator for the Southern Christian Leadership Conference. She held this position for a few months, but in May 1961 she was offered the role of White Queen in Jean Genet's Obie Award–winning play *The Blacks*, which had a cast that included JAMES EARL JONES and CICELY TYSON. However, soon after the production began, she left because of a monetary dispute with the director. Angelou's common-law husband at the time, the South African freedom fighter Vusumzi Make, did not want his wife to work, insisting that "no wife of an African leader can go on the stage" (Angelou, *The Heart of a Woman*, 205). Angelou found out that Make could not support the family without her income shortly before their move to Cairo, Egypt, in late 1961, when she discovered that they were being evicted from their Manhattan apartment.

In Cairo, Angelou became disillusioned by the chauvinism of black nationalists and defied her controlling, philandering husband by taking a job as the associate editor of the *Arab Observer*, an English-language newspaper. In 1963 she left Make and moved to Accra, Ghana, where she worked for the University of Ghana and became an editor of the *African Review* and a contributor to the *Ghanaian Times* and the Ghanaian Broadcasting Company. She arranged the itinerary for her friend MALCOLM X during his visit to Ghana, and she enjoyed a close relationship with the family of W. E. B. DU BOIS, who had expatriated from the United States to live in Ghana some years earlier. Angelou returned to the United States in 1966 to continue her career in the theater; however, James Baldwin urged her to pursue her writing. Angelou's penultimate final autobiographical volume, *All God's Children Need Traveling Shoes* (1986), recounts her sojourn in Africa. Her final autobiography, *A Song Flung Up to Heaven* (2002), documents the tumultuous events after

Angelou returned to America to help Malcolm X and the Organization of African-American Unity. Angelou describes in vivid detail the period between the assassinations of Malcolm X and Martin Luther King Jr., and brings us to the verge of her literary stardom.

David Levering Lewis has argued that Angelou's work is prominent within a grand tradition of African American autobiography extending from the slave narratives of FREDERICK DOUGLASS and HARRIET JACOBS, through the early modern memoirs of BOOKER T. WASHINGTON and the somewhat fictionalized autobiography of ZORA NEALE HURSTON, to the contemporary *Autobiography of Malcolm X*. While she incorporates the elements of triumphalism that one typically finds in the slave narratives and some of the determined individualism of the Horatio Alger genre, Angelou mingles Brer Rabbit savvy with resilient love to produce books that reveal harsh realities about race and gender in American life.

Most of her literary acclaim focuses on her autobiographies but Angelou has also published nine volumes of poetry, including *Just Give Me a Cool Drink of Water 'fore I Diiie* (1971), which was nominated for a Pulitzer Prize, and the noteworthy *And Still I Rise* (1978), which contains the very popular title poem and the often recited "Phenomenal Woman." In addition, she received a Tony Award nomination for her role in the Broadway play *Look Away* in 1973 and an Emmy Award nomination for her performance in ALEX HALEY's *Roots* in 1977. She became the first woman and the only African American to read a poem at a presidential inauguration when President Bill Clinton invited her to read "On the Pulse of Morning" in 1993. Two years later she was one of the few women to speak at LOUIS FARRAKHAN's Million Man March, where—despite her own unhappy relationships—she affirmed her hope for the black family.

When her eight-year marriage to the British builder Paul Du Fue ended in divorce in 1981, Angelou moved to North Carolina, where she became the Reynolds Professor of American Studies at Wake Forest University. She has remained a prolific writer, performer, and speaker well into her seventies.

Further Reading

Angelou, Maya. *All God's Children Need Traveling Shoes* (1986).
Angelou, Maya. *Gather Together in My Name* (1974).
Angelou, Maya. *The Heart of a Woman* (1981).
Angelou, Maya. *I Know Why the Caged Bird Sings* (1970).
Angelou, Maya. *Singin' and Swingin' and Gettin' Merry Like Christmas* (1976).
Bloom, Harold, ed. *Modern Critical Views: Maya Angelou* (1999).
Lupton, Mary Jane. *Maya Angelou: A Critical Companion* (1998).

SHOLOMO B. LEVY

ANSA, Tina McElroy (18 Nov. 1949–), novelist, journalist, and educator, was born in Macon, Georgia, the youngest child of Walter J. McElroy, an entrepreneur and business owner, and Nellie Lee McElroy, a teaching assistant. Ansa grew up surrounded by storytellers. Her grandfather was one, and the patrons of her father's neighborhood juke joint often shared the tales of their seedy lives.

This love of storytelling remained with Ansa as she pursued a BA in English at the historically black Spelman College in Atlanta. There, Ansa was introduced to the writing of ZORA NEALE HURSTON by her professor GLORIA WADE-GAYLES, an introduction that continued to shape Ansa's appreciation for the art of storytelling and folk tradition in the African American community, and one that would influence her own writing style tremendously. After completing her degree in 1971 Ansa became the first African American woman hired to work for the *Atlanta Constitution* (later the *Atlanta Journal-Constitution*). Ansa occupied several different positions during her years of employment with Georgia's most prominent newspaper, including copyeditor, makeup editor, layout editor, features editor, news reporter, and entertainment writer. Her work at the paper was the beginning of her career as a professional writer.

On 1 May 1978 Tina McElroy married Joneé Ansa, a cinematographer and graduate of the American Film Institute. After completing eight years at the Atlanta paper, Ansa accepted a position as an editor for the *Charlotte Observer* in North Carolina. In 1982 Ansa decided to market herself as a freelance journalist in order to free enough time to pursue a career in creative writing. She began to attend writing workshops and to submit her short fiction for publication, only to receive many rejection letters. Ansa returned to Georgia two years later and took residence on St. Simons Island, one of Georgia's famous Golden Isles.

Ansa published her first book-length project, *Not Soon Forgotten: Cotton Planters and Plantations of the Golden Isles of Georgia, 1784–1812*, for the Georgia Historical Society in 1987. The project piqued Ansa's interest in the history and legacy of her surroundings. Taking pride in the black folk life and history of the region, Ansa and her husband produced and directed the first of a now decades-old event in 1989; the Georgia Sea Island Festival is an attempt to preserve the cultural life and lore of the enslaved African communities that inhabited the rice, indigo, and cotton plantations along the Georgia coast.

Ansa's career as a novelist began to take shape shortly after attending a writing workshop in Macon with JOHN OLIVER KILLENS. Writers with Roots in Georgia, a local program that sponsored writers native to the state on the college lecture circuit, recruited Killens as a writer-in-residence at Mercer College. Ansa had long claimed Killens as her mentor, though she had never met him. Killens and Ansa's father attended high school together and graduated in the same class, so Ansa had known of Killens and his writing from a young age. Ansa revised a short story titled "Mamie" in the workshop with Killens; that story later became a chapter in her debut novel, *Baby of the Family* (1989).

Baby of the Family centers on the trials of young Lena McPherson, who is born with a caul, or thin membrane of the amniotic sac, over her face, an occurrence that according to African American folk beliefs signifies a connection to the supernatural. Ansa herself was born with a caul over her face and grew up hearing much of the lore surrounding the peculiarity of such a birth. In the book she explores the loss and disregard of tradition and the repercussions of such actions. The novel was named a Notable Book of the Year by the *New York Times* and also won the 1989 Georgia Authors Series Award.

In the fall of 1990 Ansa returned to Spelman as a writer-in-residence. She taught creative writing courses and continued to teach and supervise writing workshops at Emory University and Brunswick College. She also taught courses on mass media and communications. In 1993 Ansa published *Ugly Ways*, a novel that challenges the sanctity of motherhood by questioning what it means and what happens when women like Esther "Mudear" Lovejoy bring unorthodox convictions to the art of childrearing. Ansa and the actress Alfre Woodard negotiated a deal to bring *Ugly Ways* to the screen. Another work, *The Hand I Fan With* (1996), is the playful journey into the adult life of Lena McPherson, who continues to clash with the spirit world. In order to reconcile her mother's mishandling of her birth caul, and thus Lena's spiritual prowess, Herman—a hundred-year-old ghost—is sent to help Lena find her way. *The Hand I Fan With* received the 1996 Georgia Authors Series Award; Ansa is the only author to win the award twice. *You Know Better* (2002) confronts the divide between parents and children in the contemporary world, taking up the issue of what might be termed failed parenting in the African American community. All of Ansa's novels are set in the fictional town of Mulberry, Georgia, which is modeled after her beloved Macon. In a similar vein as TONI MORRISON, ALICE MALSENIOR WALKER, and Zora Neale Hurston, Ansa incorporates African American vernacular traditions and folklore as primary elements in her work. She calls her work "black-folkcentric," asserting that her stories begin and end with black folks (Ansa, 26).

Ansa's work has garnered critical attention at the Schomburg Center, the Richard Wright/Zora Neale Hurston Foundation, and the Smithsonian's African American Center. Ansa's feature articles, reviews, and editorials have appeared in the *Atlanta Journal-Constitution*, the *Los Angeles Times*, and other newspapers. Her essays, "Postcards from Georgia," have been featured on CBS' *Sunday Morning*. Interweaving the land, legends, and heritage of Georgia, Ansa's novels situate her not only as one of Georgia's most prominent women writers next to Flannery O'Connor and Alice Walker but also as a valuable link in a chain of African American literary women who infuse and thus preserve the ways of the folk in their writing.

Further Reading

Ansa, Tina McElroy. "Tina McElroy Ansa," in *I Know What the Red Clay Looks Like: The Voice and Vision of Black Women Writers*, ed. Rebecca Carroll (1994).

Cherry, Joyce L. "Tina McElroy Ansa," in *Contemporary African American Novelists: A Bio-bibliographical Critical Source Book*, ed. Emmanuel Nelson (1999).

Jordan, Shirley Marie. *Broken Silences: Interviews with Black and White Women Writers* (1993).

Mosby, Charmaine Allmon. "Tina McElroy Ansa," in *Contemporary Southern Writers*, ed. Roger Matuz (1999).

KAMEELAH L. MARTIN

ANTOINE, Caesar Carpetier (1836–Sept. 1921), Union army officer and politician, was born in New Orleans, the son of a West Indian midwife and a free black soldier who had served in the Corps d'Afrique with General Andrew Jackson in the War of 1812. His parents' names are not recorded. Family lore had it that Caesar's maternal grandfather, an African chief, had been enslaved and taken to America and that his paternal grandmother, Rose Antoine, had earned enough money from her work as a midwife to purchase her freedom. Rose Antoine also left each of her seven sons twenty thousand dollars in her will.

As a free black child in New Orleans, Antoine attended private schools—the public schools of the city were closed to blacks—and became fluent in both English and French. Upon leaving school as a teenager in the early 1850s he then apprenticed and worked as a barber, one of the more lucrative trades open to free blacks, until Union forces entered Louisiana in winter 1862. Within forty-eight hours of a Confederate move on Union positions, Antoine closed his barber shop to organize a company of black federal troops, Company I of the Seventh Regiment, Louisiana Militia. The company, in which Antoine served as captain, was also known as the Corps d'Afrique, perhaps in honor of his father's regiment. Antoine earned a reputation as one of the most accomplished black combat officers, though that did not prevent the Union general Nathaniel Banks from attempting to dismiss all black commissioned officers in Louisiana in mid-1864. C. C. Antoine, his brother Felix Antoine, and his friend P. B. S. PINCHBACK were among several black officers who resigned their commissions in protest.

Antoine's interest in political affairs appears to have begun at this time, and in January 1865 he was one of fifty delegates to the Convention of Colored Men of Louisiana, which met in New Orleans to demand political rights for the freedmen. Antoine also helped to launch a short-lived newspaper, the *New Orleans Black Republican*, which—perhaps surprisingly given Antoine's earlier resignation—was supportive of General Banks's tenure as Louisiana's military governor.

After the war and the failure of the *Black Republican*, Antoine moved to Shreveport, Louisiana, where he established a grocery and was elected as a delegate from Caddo Parish to the Louisiana constitutional convention, which met from 1867 to 1868. In the elections that followed in 1868 Antoine was elected to the state senate from Caddo Parish and quickly emerged as one of the leading black Republicans in the Louisiana legislature. Antoine's brother Felix was elected to the Louisiana House of Representatives the same year. In the senate Antoine worked to increase spending on higher education and to expand the powers of local government. His skills as a legislator were recognized in 1872 when he was elected lieutenant governor of Louisiana. He served briefly as acting governor and along with state representative THÉOPHILE ALLAIN was prominent in the unification movement of 1873, a doomed effort to forge a new moderate political coalition between wealthy white and black businessmen.

While he was lieutenant governor Antoine studied for and received a law degree at Straight University (later Dillard) in New Orleans and was appointed to the Caddo Parish school board in 1875. It is quite possible that Antoine again received the majority of Louisiana's votes for lieutenant governor in the controversial 1876 elections, which effectively left the state with two rival governments. Antoine and Stephen Packard, the Republican candidate for governor, were removed from office in 1877, however, as part of the compromise that elected the Republican Rutherford B. Hayes as U.S. president and ended Republican rule in Louisiana and other Southern states.

While serving in the senate and as lieutenant governor, Antoine's business interests prospered. In partnership with P. B. S. Pinchback he owned a newspaper, the *New Orleans Louisianian*, and a prosperous cotton brokerage. He also raised several racehorses, which he entered, with varying degrees of success, in several contests. After Reconstruction, Antoine fell on hard times, forcing his wife, whose name is not known, to petition President Hayes to find a federal position for her husband. She did not succeed, but in 1882 Antoine found work as president of the Cosmopolitan Insurance Association in New Orleans. Yet this company also fared poorly, no doubt in part because its officers no longer carried the political clout that they had enjoyed during Reconstruction.

In the 1890s Antoine returned to political prominence as vice president of the Comité de Citoyens, an organization opposed to Louisiana's newly enacted segregation and antimiscegenation laws. In 1892 the Comité raised funds to assist HOMER PLESSY's ultimately unsuccessful legal challenge to the constitutionality of the segregation laws. In 1896, the same year that the U.S. Supreme Court upheld the doctrine of "separate but equal" in *Plessy v. Ferguson*, Antoine attended the Republican National Convention.

Caesar Carpetier Antoine died in Shreveport, the owner of a small plantation and some real estate. His wealth and renown was greater than that of most African Americans in Louisiana at that time, but much less, surely, than he might have enjoyed had not Reconstruction—and Antoine's political career—ended so abruptly four decades earlier.

Further Reading

Information on Antoine can be found in The Honorable C. C. Antoine Scrapbook, Black Heritage Room, Southern University, Baton Rouge.

Blassingame, John. *Black New Orleans, 1860–1880* (1973).

Vincent, Charles. *Black Legislators in Louisiana during Reconstruction* (1976).

STEVEN J. NIVEN

APPIAH, Kwame Anthony (8 May 1954–), novelist, philosopher, and scholar was born in London, England, to Joe Appiah, a Ghanaian barrister and statesman, and Peggy Cripps, novelist and daughter of Sir Stafford Cripps, a British statesman. Not long after Appiah's birth, his family relocated to Ghana, where he attended primary school. After the political imprisonment of his father by then-president Kwame Nkrumah, Appiah returned to England. There he completed his secondary education at Bryanston, a British boarding school.

Influenced by his mother's affinity for the literary arts, Appiah read works of authors such as Chinua Achebe, D. H. Lawrence, and Tolstoy. Visitors to the Appiah residence included the Pan-Africanist authors and theorists C. L. R. JAMES and RICHARD WRIGHT. Appiah's multiethnic family and early fascination with literature helped shape his identity and his world view. In 1972 he entered Cambridge University, where he earned both a BA and a PhD in Philosophy in 1975 and 1982, respectively, becoming the first person of African descent to have earned a PhD in Philosophy from the university. As an undergraduate he met HENRY LOUIS GATES JR., with whom he would later collaborate on a number of projects.

In 1985 Cambridge University Press published Appiah's first book, his revised dissertation *Assertion and Conditionals*, which explores the idea that assertion is simply the articulation of belief systems, and an understanding of an assertion implies the understanding of the belief systems it expresses. Though his earlier work focused on semantics and logic, Appiah's later efforts were grounded in cultural identity and race. Published in 1992, *In My Father's House: Africa in the Philosophy of Culture*, a compilation of racially motivated and charged essays that explore notions of identity, race, and culture, is regarded as a philosophical classic on multiculturalism. A semi-autobiography together with cultural criticism and postcolonial theory, *In My Father's House*, is a well-known and respected book among most Africana Studies circles. Written in the 1980s, a time when race-based dialogue was uncommon and much less acceptable, *In My Father's House* explores African identity in the context of globalization. The book was honored by the the Modern Language Association and awarded the Annisfeld-Wolf Book Award and the African Studies Association's Herskovits Award.

Appiah, along with Amy Gutmann, a Princeton colleague, was awarded the North American Society Annual Book Award for Social Philosophy (1996), the American Political Science Association's Ralph J.

Bunche Award (1997), and the Gustavus Myers Award for the Study of Human Rights (1998) for their collaboration, *Color Conscious: The Political Morality of Race*, published in 1996. The foremost argument of *Color Conscious* is the social construction of race. Appiah and Gutmann emphasize that race is not a reputable biological construct. Despite its flawed foundations, however, racial identities are perfectly real and can be of legitimate significance—especially in racist societies.

Appiah's work includes book reviews, short essays, articles, poetic volumes, scholarly books, and mystery novels, most of which address issues of ethics and politics, personal and political identity, gender, nationalism, race, religion, and sexual orientation. Additionally Appiah co-authored a number of African American resource guides, including *The Dictionary of Global Culture Africana: The Encyclopedia of the African and African-American Experience* and the website Africana.com, both of which are collaborations with his long-time colleague and friend, Henry Louis Gates Jr.

Appiah held appointments at the University of Ghana, Cambridge University, and numerous institutions in the United States, including Yale (1981–1986), Cornell (1986–1989), Duke (1990–1991), Harvard (1999–2002), and Princeton (beginning in 2002). Appiah was named the Laurance S. Rockefeller University Professor of Philosophy at Princeton University in 2002. Additionally, he has taught courses ranging from epistemology to African American history. At Harvard, Appiah was on the board of the W. E. B. Du Bois Institute for African and African American Research. There he became an integral part of Harvard's black studies "Dream Team," which included Henry Louis Gates Jr., EVELYN BROOKS HIGGINBOTHAM, CORNEL WEST, and WILLIAM JULIUS WILSON.

Asserting that all people are teachers and students of each other, Appiah argues that, "through teaching I learn; I learn all the time. So it's as much for my sake as for the sake of my students (perhaps, even more for my sake, I don't know!) that I teach" (Dienst 2005). Correct answers, like identities, Appiah believed, are not fixed variables but rather fluid, complex realities that shift as much as they remain rooted and distinct. Instead of offering his students ready-made answers Appiah presented them with the necessary tools to allow them to make conscious decisions. Without telling them what to think he taught them how to reason critically. This, he believed, was the responsibility of an intellectual: to deepen understanding without dictating its application.

Kwame Anthony Appiah was an internationally renowned scholar who provided a wealth of intellectual resources for generations yet to come. With family ties that span the globe, Appiah was a cosmopolitan philosopher who specialized in identity, race, and culture. Reflected in his personal and professional life choices, Appiah was a man of converging identities. Born in London, raised in Ghana, and a citizen of the United States, he was the quintessential "citizen of the world."

Further Reading
Appiah, K. Anthony. *In My Father's House: Africa in the Philosophy of Culture* (1992).
Appiah, K. Anthony. *Color Conscious: The Political Morality of Race* (1996).
Attiyeh, Jenny. "In Defense of the Ivory Tower," *The Christian Science Monitor* (22 August 2002).
Poste, Danny. "Is Race Real? How Does Identity Matter?" *Chronicle of Higher Education*, vol. 48, issue 30 (5 April 2002).
Dienst, Karin. "Deepening the Conversation about Identity," *Princeton Weekly Bulletin*, vol. 94, no. 17 (21 February 2005).
Henry, Tanu T. "A Dream Team Defection: A Chat with K. Anthony Appiah," *AOL Black Voices* (2002).
NICOLE SEALEY

APPLEGATE, Joseph R. (4 Dec. 1925–18 Oct. 2003), linguist, educator, early computer language translator, Africanist, scholar of Arabic and Berber, was born in Wildwood, New Jersey, to Joseph Henry Applegate and Nancy Berkley Applegate. His father was a second-generation New Jersey resident, whose father was a Native American from Maine. Applegate's mother, whose father was also Native American, migrated from Virginia to Philadelphia, where Applegate's parents met around the time of World War I. Neither parent had more than an elementary school education. Hardworking and ambitious, they held high aspirations for their children. Applegate and his sister enjoyed the advantages of a small-town working-class upbringing, along with direct contact with black artists and entertainers who frequented the seaside summer boarding house their parents operated in Wildwood, New Jersey. Although the family was not affluent, Applegate's environment was sophisticated and urbane. He recalled awakening to the sounds of Louis Armstrong and Duke Ellington in the parlor composing music for their next performances. In the off-season, Applegate's father supported the family in small building contracting, especially plastering and bricklaying.

When Applegate was eleven or twelve, the family moved to Philadelphia, where he completed high school. A gifted language learner, he studied Latin in school and learned Yiddish and Italian from his friends in the diverse South Philadelphia community. Along the way, he picked up French without formal study. In 1941, at age sixteen, he received several academic scholarships and entered Temple University, majoring in Spanish education, with double minors in German and English.

By the time he graduated with a bachelor of science in Education in 1945, he had achieved an almost perfect score on the National Teacher's Examination. In February 1946, Applegate accepted a teaching position at Vaux Junior High School. By January 1947, he became the first African American to teach Spanish in the high schools of Philadelphia. Assigned to

Bok Vocational-Technical School, a commercial high school for girls, Applegate found himself carefully scrutinized because of both his age and gender. "I got annoyed . . . and I think that was part of the reason that I worked with the teacher's union and helped unionize . . . the public schools in Philadelphia" (Williams, 116). In September 1947, he transferred to William Penn Senior High School, where he taught until 1955.

Soon after beginning his teaching career, Applegate enrolled in the University of Pennsylvania part time. He also became involved in labor union organizing, encouraged by his parents' interest in politics. During their active participation in Republican Party organizational activities in Applegate's and his sister's formative years, their parents had taken both children to numerous political events. At the University of Pennsylvania, Hillary Putnam, the son of Samuel Putnam, the Communist Party activist and editor of *New Masses*, became one of Applegate's close friends. They both participated in campus politics. After completing his master's in Linguistics in 1948, Applegate continued at the University of Pennsylvania working toward a PhD in Linguistics. During his years at the university the Ford Foundation provided funds for the study of Asian and Near Eastern languages. As the language classifications were modified, the Afro-Asiatic group came to include the languages of North Africa, among them Arabic and Berber. The Ford Foundation, realizing the need for more analysis of the languages of North Africa, encouraged the Linguistics Department in that direction. Applegate, consequently, studied one of the Berber languages of Morocco. By 1955, he had completed his dissertation on *Shilha: A Descriptive Grammar with Vocabulary and Texts*. He was the first American to write on Berber. His study became the basis for later work on the Berber language group.

As graduation neared, the linguist Zellig Harris wrote the linguist Mark Hanna Watkins at Howard University to inquire about a position for Applegate (5 Jan. 1954, Watkins Archive). None was available. Therefore, in July 1955, Applegate and Noam Chomsky, who were both students of Harris, were invited to join the MIT machine translation project in the Research Laboratory of Electronics. At MIT, Applegate provided a mathematical description of the noun phrase and Chomsky the verb phrase, descriptions that continue to define the major structure of the English sentence in transformational generative grammar. They collaborated for four years. Chomsky remained at MIT, writing *Syntactic Structures* (1957), the defining text for transformational generative grammar.

By July, 1956, Applegate had been appointed as assistant professor of Modern Languages, to teach German to American students and English to foreign students. He assisted MIT in setting up its first language laboratory or "electronic classroom." According to Applegate, "I did not know until Clarence Williams contacted me, that I was the first full-time black faculty member at MIT—and I was not offered tenure" (interview with author, 6 June 2002, Washington, D.C.).

Applegate was, however, offered another opportunity that served as the pivotal juncture of his career. There were two factors that combined to change his life. One was the realization that machine translation of languages was less practical than expected and the second was that when Russia launched the space vehicle *Sputnik*, on 4 October 1957, the priorities of the American government changed. "The U.S. realized that it had fallen behind in part because of the lack of linguistic specialists." Congress then passed the National Defense Education Act, and the mastery of "critical languages" became a priority (interview with author, 26 June 1986, Washington, D.C.).

By July 1960, Applegate had accepted a grant from the U.S. Office of Education to continue research on the Berber languages. Until 1966, his university base was the Department of Near Eastern and African Languages at the University of California, Los Angeles (UCLA). There he became the first American to write on the Berber languages and to teach courses on them. Applegate's expertise allowed UCLA to become the only university in the United States where Berber languages could be studied. Almost immediately, though, Applegate traveled to Morocco, settling among the Riff cultural group in the mountains to study their language for almost a year (Williams, 120). He adapted quickly, finding the experience "rich," learning not only the language but also many cultural practices and principles, including how to ride camels, survive in the desert, and migrate yearly for agricultural and traditional reasons. Applegate's *The Structure of Riff* (1964) was the first analysis of the language. The same year, he wrote *The Structure of Kabyle* (1964), on the Berber language of Algeria, and compiled *The Berber Languages: A Selected and Annotated Bibliography* (1964). The following year, he published *A Reference Grammar of Kabyle* (1965), followed by *Spoken Kabyle* (1966), a textbook with tapes and visual materials, all for the Office of Education. Within several years, Applegate had produced a basic *Manual of Libyan Arabic* (1968) and a basic *Manual of Tamachek* (1968), both for the Peace Corps. He spent a summer with the Tuaregs, as they migrated from Northern Niger to Libya, in order to prepare instructional material on their language, Tamazight/Tamachek, for the Peace Corps.

By 1966, the position that had not been available at Howard University in 1955 had become available. Frank Snowden, the Dean of Arts and Sciences, invited Applegate to become an associate professor of Linguistics and to establish a language laboratory. He accepted. In 1967, however, he was invited to become director of the African Studies and Research Program, a position he held until 1969, by which time student nationalism called for a more African-centered approach (interview with author, 26 June 1986, Washington, D.C.). Beginning in 1969, Applegate served as a graduate professor of African Studies until his retirement in 2002. Modest about his own accomplishments, he is credited with the development of the PhD Program in African Studies, the first in the nation. At Howard, Applegate was seldom far from his labor organizing interests. For many years, he served as president of the Faculty Senate, and as a member of the Faculty Grievance and Ethics Committee. Well respected on and off campus, he did not hesitate to take Howard to court in support of faculty issues.

A major theme in Applegate's life was the importance of the use of technology for educational purposes. For many years, he produced a video series, *The African World*, to fill some of the gaps left by the series *The Africans*. After his retirement, he joined a laboratory where he continued to experiment with innovative methods of translating and teaching languages. Applegate authored eight books and more than eighteen articles. He could function in seventeen languages, eight of them from the Berber family. Among the others were Egyptian, Moroccan, Libyan, Modern Standard Arabic, Portuguese, Italian, and Greek. Well traveled in Africa and the Arabic world, he served as a positive ambassador for the United States. One of the highlights of his life was receiving a personal letter from CONDOLEEZZA RICE, the National Security Advisor, in 2002, in the aftermath of the destruction of the World Trade Center on 11 September 2001, requesting that he serve as a translator of Arabic documents for the American government (interview with author, 6 June 2002, Washington, D.C.). The opportunity of a lifetime was within reach, but never to be grasped. In a few short months, his health had declined. Near the end, he was placed in the Washington Home Hospice, where he died of pneumonia. There was no widow and no heirs.

Further Reading
"The African American Linguist Who Broke the Faculty Barrier at MIT," *The Journal of Blacks in Higher Education*, 17 (Autumn 1997).

Bernstein, Adam. "Professor Joseph Applegate Dies," *Washington Post*, 22 Oct. 2003.

Slater, Robert Bruce. "First Black Faculty Members at the Nation's Highest-Ranked Universities," *The Journal of Blacks in Highest Education*, 22 (Winter 1998–1999).

Unpublished interview with author, 26 June 1986, Washington, D.C.

Unpublished interview with author, 2 June 2002, Washington, D.C.

Williams, Clarence G., ed. "Joseph R. Applegate," *Technology and the Dream: Reflections on the Black Experience a MIT, 1941–1999* (2003).

MARGARET WADE-LEWIS

ARBOR, Jesse Walter (26 Dec. 1914–11 Jan. 2000), pioneer black naval officer, was born in Cotton Plant, Arkansas, a predominantly black community, one of twelve children of Tecora and Alexander Arbor. He had two sisters and nine brothers, and his ancestors had received land in the area when slavery

ended. Outgoing, humorous, and loquacious by nature, Arbor possessed a typically rural southern sense of place. During an oral history interview in the mid-1980s, he described Cotton Plant as, "A little place that only me and the Good Lord knows [with a population of] 1,661 up until the day I left, and there's never been that many since." Like his siblings, Arbor received a private school education. During his years in Arkansas he attended Arkadelphia–Cotton Plant Academy. Around 1930 the family left the farm area and moved to Chicago as part of a northerly migration of blacks seeking employment opportunities. Arbor's father worked as a carpenter, and his siblings attended Catholic schools. Because of his athletic prowess, several colleges sought to recruit Arbor in the early 1930s. He accepted a football scholarship at the all-black Arkansas Agricultural, Mechanical & Normal (AM&N) College, now, the University of Arkansas at Pine Bluff. A large, solidly built man, Arbor played right tackle on the football team and majored in the social sciences. He left school one semester short of a degree, after his football eligibility expired.

In 1935 Arbor observed that black professionals were not well paid, so he returned to Illinois and took a job at the Chicago Beach Hotel as doorman and receiving clerk. As he explained, he preferred pay to prestige. In 1939 he became a Pullman porter on trains that traveled widely about the country, then returned to Chicago to become a tailor. In September 1942—shortly before he would have been drafted into the Army—Arbor enlisted in the Navy. He went through recruit training at all-black Camp Robert Smalls, part of the large naval training station complex at Great Lakes, Illinois, north of Chicago. During World War II, Arbor advanced to quartermaster second class with responsibilities involving navigation, log keeping, and visual signaling. He was among the first blacks rated in that specialty. Arbor was stationed in the Boston area, where he served on board two coastal minesweepers and took an advanced navigation course in a Navy facility at Harvard University. In late 1943 Arbor's life changed dramatically when he was ordered to report back to Camp Robert Smalls to take part in the Navy's first officer training course for African Americans. Of the approximately one hundred thousand black sailors then in the Navy, Arbor and fifteen other men were chosen to begin the training in January 1944. The service-wide selection process included FBI background checks and recommendations on leadership ability. Almost all in the group had college experience, and a few had advanced degrees. In two and a half months, they went through a cram course that included training in such areas as navigation, communications, gunnery, propulsion machinery, seamanship, naval history, and the Navy disciplinary system.

The members of the training class concluded that they were part of a Navy experiment and they were determined to succeed or fail as a group, rather than compete with each other. Thus they pooled their knowledge in after-hours sessions. The men were not only in segregated Camp Robert Smalls but also separated from all other black trainees. At times the constant togetherness and the novelty of much of the material led to frayed nerves. Arbor and Dennis Nelson, one of the other officer candidates, often defused the tension with humor. The group did exceptionally well on exams. All sixteen passed the course in March 1944, but the Navy chose to commission Arbor and eleven others as ensigns; one man in the course, Charles Lear, became a warrant officer. The other three remained as enlisted men. Years later the pioneer officers received a distinctive group identity when they were retroactively named the Golden Thirteen.

Once they became officers, Arbor and Lear received assignments to the supply depot in Pearl Harbor, Hawaii; they were the first two black naval officers to be assigned overseas. The executive officer of the depot paved the way for their arrival by specifying that they should be treated with respect and no discrimination. Arbor's duties included an assignment as shore patrol officer and he delighted in wearing a .45-caliber automatic pistol on his hip as a badge of authority. Subsequently Arbor and Lear transferred to the island of Guam, which was gearing up for the planned invasion of Japan in 1945. The two served as troubleshooters in supply and logistics. As the senior black officer in the area, Arbor also served essentially as an unofficial adviser for black sailors. Once the war ended, Arbor left the service and returned to Chicago's South Side, where he resumed his work in the clothing business. He set up his own dry cleaning and tailor shop and in 1948 married Autry Brown, a schoolteacher in Memphis, Tennessee, whom Arbor had met during a trip there and who already knew other members of his family. They had three children: Jesse Jr., Deborah, and Brenda. Arbor's work in his shop continued until 1968, when a combination of urban renewal and concerns about his health led him to seek other employment. He applied to the Chicago Board of Education and was asked what he could do. As he did so often in life, Arbor gave a flip answer: "Run my mouth and boss like hell" (Stillwell, 188). He took a job running heating systems in various schools and performing administrative duties. He finally retired in 1984 at age seventy, but devoted much of his time to helping the Navy recruit minorities and met with later generations of black naval officers. He summed up his achievements by saying of the Golden Thirteen: "Having been one of the guinea pigs, I'm glad I had the endurance and fortitude to withstand the challenges we faced. . . . The black officers today express their appreciation when they see us" (Stillwell, 191). Arbor died in 2000.

Further Reading
Stillwell, Paul, ed. *The Golden Thirteen: Recollections of the First Black Naval Officers* (1993).
Obituary: *Chicago Tribune,* 14 Jan. 2000.

PAUL STILLWELL

ARCHER, Dennis (1 Jan. 1942–), lawyer, State Supreme Court Justice, mayor of Detroit, Michigan, and president of the American Bar Association, was born in Detroit to Ernest and Frances Archer, and was raised in Cassopolis, Michigan. Determined to raise himself from poverty, and encouraged by his parents to value education, Archer was steadfast in his studies. He graduated from Cassopolis High School in 1959 and entered Western Michigan University that fall. While attending Western Michigan he pledged Alpha Phi Alpha Fraternity, the first black collegiate fraternal organization. He graduated in 1965.

Archer had a desire to teach, so he relocated to Detroit and took a position in the Detroit schools teaching and assisting emotionally disturbed students. He met Trudy Duncombe, another young teacher, during this tenure, and they married on 17 June 1967. Although dedicated to education, Archer began to prepare himself for another level of public service when he entered law school at Detroit College of Law, taking courses in the evening while continuing to teach during the day. After his graduation in 1970 he passed the Michigan State Bar and began working for the Detroit-based firm of Gragg & Gardner. Within a year he was invited to join the firm of Hall, Stone, Allen, Archer & Glenn, ultimately becoming a partner. Despite having young children, Archer encouraged and supported his wife as she, too, pursued a law degree.

Archer and his wife became active in the southeastern Michigan Democratic Party and worked to help many African American and Democratic candidates win political office in the 1970s and 1980s. He assisted in the election of many Democrats, including Governor James Blanchard. Most notably, Archer served on the committee that assisted in the successful re-election of COLEMAN A. YOUNG as mayor of Detroit in 1977. He continued to practice law until 1986 when he was appointed by Governor James Blanchard as the first African American to sit on the Michigan State Supreme Court. Archer remained in that role for four years. When Coleman Young announced his intention to retire, Archer decided to step down from his seat on the Supreme Court and return to private practice in the hope of launching a campaign to run for the office. This move allowed the outgoing governor to appoint another African American, Conrad Mallet, to replace him, maintaining both an African American and a Democratic presence on the Court while Archer focused on becoming mayor of Detroit.

Criticized by African American residents of Detroit for courting the white and suburban vote during the 1993 mayoral election, Archer's personal appeal and broader message of change, unity, and hope gave him a 57–43 percent win over his opponent, Sharon McPhail, who had been handpicked by Coleman Young as his successor. The results of the election appeared to indicate that residents were prepared for a change from the type of government Coleman Young

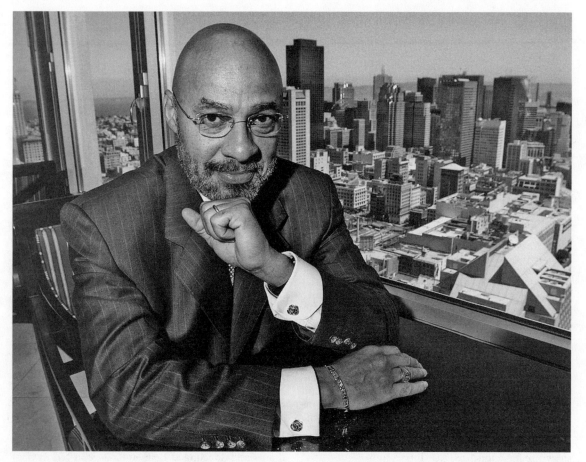

Dennis Archer, the first black president of the American Bar Association, San Francisco, 7 August 2003. (AP Images.)

represented—one heavily dependent on local union and African American residential support. After his inauguration Archer began working to reunite the city internally and to reestablish ties with suburban leaders previously estranged by his predecessor's political methods. This was a stark departure from the polemic politics of Young, who launched verbal attacks at suburban leaders such as Prosecutor Brooks Patterson and, near the end of his term, Governor Blanchard and others. Archer represented a corporate shift that, if used wisely, could transform the image of Detroit from a murder capital to a commerce capital. At this time Detroit had a national reputation for high crime, especially around Halloween, when random arson fires plagued the city for almost a week each year. Among his initiatives was a drive to increase police presence on city streets, decrease the number of fires, and reunite the metropolitan area.

Archer used the force of his position to begin a transformation of the city and its reputation. Under his leadership, business and commerce began to return to the city. The establishment of three casinos and the decision of the Compuware Corporation to relocate its headquarters to downtown Detroit gave rise to the new baseball and football stadiums, Comerica Park and Ford Field, which were funded by Comerica Bank, the Ilich Family and the Ford family respectively, a new city center, Campus Martius, and a successful bid to host Super Bowl XL. The Campus Martius project represented a shift in the city center and established a base for corporate headquarters, retail shops such as Ben and Jerry's Ice Cream, Border's Bookstores, and the Hard Rock Café, as well as activities such as ice-skating in winter and concerts in the summer. While serving as mayor, Archer held the position of president of the U.S. Conference of Mayors and was well respected by his peers.

After making his mark on the city's political and economic landscape, Archer expressed his longing for a more private life by not running for re-election in 2000. He left office in 2001 and was immediately appointed to the Board of Directors of Compuware—the first African American ever to hold this post. Archer later accepted the chairmanship of the Dickinson Wright law firm and was elected to a term as president of the American Bar

Association. A tribute to his desire to help others and another testament of his credibility, Archer was appointed in 2004 as independent guardian to ROSA PARKS as her health began to decline, a role he held until her death in 2005.

Further Reading
Greenberg, Michael R. *Restoring America's Neighborhoods: How Local People Make a Difference* (1999).
Doyle, Jack. *Taken for a Ride: Detroit's Big Three and the Politics of Pollution* (2000).
"Dennis Archer," *Newsmakers* (1994).

SIBYL COLLINS WILSON

ARCHER (ADAMS), Osceola Macarthy (13 June 1890–20 Nov. 1983), actor, director, educator, and artist advocate, was born Osceola Marie Macarthy in Albany, Georgia, of black, white, and Native American racial heritage. The daughter of a life insurance executive, Archer attended Fisk University Preparatory School in Nashville, Tennessee. She then enrolled at Howard University in Washington, D.C., in 1909, where she was a pupil of ALAIN LOCKE and the sociologist KELLY MILLER. Self-defined as a suffragette, in 1913, her senior year at Howard, Archer and twenty-one fellow female students cofounded one of the largest black fraternal organizations in the United States, Delta Sigma Theta, a sorority dedicated to community service and the mutual support of African American women. That same year Archer began to pursue her interest in drama by performing the title role in the Howard University Dramatics Club production of *The Lady of Lyon,* a Victorian romantic comedy known as a showcase for actors like Ellen Terry.

As a young actor, Archer entered a theatrical community that offered limited choices for African American women. Marrying her chemistry professor, NUMA P. G. ADAMS (who later became the first African American dean of the Howard Medical School), in 1915, Archer chose to put her artistic dreams on hold while she raised her only child, Charles Macarthy Adams. In 1919 Archer followed her husband to Chicago as he pursued his medical studies at the University of Chicago, and supported the family by working as a dress designer under her own label, Mrs. Adams. In 1932, as her son approached college age, Archer was encouraged by her husband to renew her professional dreams of a career on the stage as an actor and director.

During the time between Archer's university days and her return to acting, opportunities for blacks on the dramatic stage had begun to change. In 1917 Ridgeley Torrence's *Three Plays for a Negro Theater* opened the door for blacks on Broadway in non-musical roles. The emergence of the Lafayette Players, Anita Bush's company dedicated to the creation of a legitimate African American theater, set a precedent for a self-produced Negro Theater. And the heated debates between Alain Locke and W. E. B. DU BOIS over aesthetics served to redefine what African Americans might achieve in the theatrical arts. Half a generation after the first wave of African American actresses like FLORENCE MILLS, ADA WALKER, and DORA DEAN, Archer avoided having to take roles as a chorus girl in order to pursue the dramatic stage, and sought institutional training in dramatics.

Upon her arrival to New York City in 1932, however, Archer was refused admission to the Academy of Dramatic Arts because of her race. Searching for a theater school that accepted African American students, Archer enrolled in the Repertory Playhouse Associations' American Theater Wing School of Drama, founded by former members of the Moscow Art School. Graduating in 1934 at the age of forty-four, she adopted the stage name Osceola Archer. Archer soon received her first professional role in the avant-garde production of Dana Bernett's *Strange House.*

Setting her sights on the Broadway stage, Archer turned down two roles in her first season of auditioning, including John Houseman's *4 Saints in 3 Acts,* because she wanted her debut to be as a dramatic, rather than as a musical, actress. Soon, Archer won a role in Elmer Rice's *Between Two Worlds,* with Joseph Schildkraut. In 1935 Archer again found herself of Broadway, in Archibald MacLeish's *Panic,* with John O'Shaughnessy and Orson Welles. That same year, she toured with PAUL ROBESON in *The Emperor Jones.*

Although fortunate enough to have received two roles on Broadway during her first two years as a professional actress, Archer soon faced a slump in her career. Like many educated women of her time, Archer relied on her options in the field of education as fallbacks to the unstable world of the theater. In 1937 Archer completed a master's degree in Dramatic Art from New York University's School of Education, taking a position teaching drama and directing at Bennett College in North Carolina, where she also began to work on her next dream of being a director with her own theater company.

In 1939 Archer left Bennett College to again appear in *The Emperor Jones,* as well as to lay the foundations for her own company; her ambitions for a company ended, however, with the death of her husband in 1940. That same year, Archer relocated to New York City and began teaching and directing at the American Negro Theater, where she remained until 1949, training the next great generation of black theater professionals such as HARRY BELAFONTE, RUBY DEE, SIDNEY POITIER, OSSIE DAVIS, and Hilda Haines. Archer also taught at the American Theater Wing and the Harlem School of the Arts.

Archer was an actor, director, and teacher who forged strong careers in both the performing arts and in education. As a director she staged numerous plays for the American Negro Theater, the Putnam County Playhouse (where she is remembered as the first African American director of Summer Stock theater), and for various groups in and around New York City. As an actress she performed in five Broadway plays, numerous Off-Broadway productions, and at university and regional playhouses. She also appeared on the radio, as well as in television, commercials, and film, most notably in the made-for-television film *Rashomon* (1960) and in *An Affair of the Skin* (1963).

Dedicated to performing and directing the classics, Archer created a balance in her career that reflected both her artistic vision and her personal politics. She played roles in integrated casts at traditional white theaters, in addition to working with many African American companies and playwrights. Self-described as "a humanist against any separatism, especially on the stage," she was a staunch advocate for minorities' rights in the theater (interview, 1972). A member of four theatrical unions, she held positions on the equal rights committees of Actors Equity, the American Federation of Television and Radio Artists (AFTRA), Screen Actors Guild (SAG), and the Director and Writers Guild. In 1943, she was a member of the Executive Committee for the Stage Door Canteen, a New York City supper club that entertained military personnel during WWII. She also held positions of leadership with her sorority to continue her lifetime relationship to service and advocacy. In 1973, Delta Sigma Theta established the Osceola Award, which used her name to recognize distinguished achievements in the arts. In 1978 the Audience Development Committee (Audelco), an organization devoted to stimulating the arts in black communities, awarded Archer (along with the composer and pianist EUBIE BLAKE) an Outstanding Pioneer Award for a lifetime of service through art. Continuing her work until she was eighty-eight, Osceola Macarthy Adams Archer died at the age of ninety three.

Further Reading
Recording and transcript of 21 Feb. 1972 interview with Osceola Archer by James Hatch and Paula Singer is located at the Hatch-Billops Collection in New York City.
Obituary: *New York Times*, 24 Nov. 1983.

SUZI TAKAHASHI

ARCHEY, Jimmy (12 Oct. 1902–16 Nov. 1967), jazz trombonist, was born James H. Archey in Norfolk, Virginia. Nothing is known of his parents. He started playing the trombone in 1912, and from 1915 to 1919 he studied music at the Hampton Institute, spending his summers playing in a band led by the pianist Lillian Jones. After working in Quentin Redd's band on the Atlantic City boardwalk around 1922, Archey moved to New York City in 1923 and played with the trumpeter Lionel Howard's band at the Saratoga Club and the Capitol Palace. The next year he worked at Ed Small's, and from 1925 to mid-1926 he spent a year touring with the Lucky Sambo Revue and another few months with the Tan Town Topics. Starting in late 1926 he worked with the bands of John C. Smith and Arthur Gibbs and began a residency at the Bamboo Inn with Ed Campbell. In 1927 he played in the pianist Edgar Hayes's pit band at the Alhambra Theater, briefly toured with KING OLIVER in early June, and continued working at the Bamboo Inn with Campbell and then with Henri Saparo. In 1928 the pianist Joe Steele took over leadership of the Bamboo Inn band, and Archey remained with him into 1929. After leaving Steele he filled out the remainder of the year working with the bands of Charlie Skeete and Bill Benford. In April 1930 he once again toured with Oliver, and in June he joined LUIS RUSSELL's band for long engagements at the Saratoga Club, Connie's Inn, the Arcadia Ballroom, and other venues.

In early 1931 Archey worked for six months with Bingie Madison at the Broadway Danceland. But then he rejoined and remained with Russell's band—from October 1935 under the leadership of LOUIS ARMSTRONG—until early 1937, at which time he joined the singer Willie Bryant for regular appearances at the Apollo Theater. Archey stayed with Bryant until March 1939, when he left to begin a long residency at the Savoy Ballroom with Benny Carter. Carter's band was a favorite at the Savoy, but it occasionally played at other locations as well, among them the Apollo, Roseland Ballroom, Howard Theater, and Golden Gate Ballroom. In June 1940 Archey left Carter to work in the bands of ELLA FITZGERALD and Coleman Hawkins at the Savoy, but he was back with Carter in late January 1941 for a month-long engagement at Nick's in Greenwich Village. After a series of tours from March through September, Carter's group split up and Archey began a three-year period of freelancing, during which time he occasionally worked with CAB CALLOWAY and DUKE ELLINGTON. In 1944 and 1945 he was at the Zanzibar with CLAUDE HOPKINS, and from 1946 through 1948 he played sporadically at Billy Rose's Diamond Horseshoe with NOBLE SISSLE.

For almost twenty years Archey had found regular employment in big bands, usually playing lead trombone but rarely having the opportunity to establish a reputation as a jazz soloist. All that changed, however, in June 1947 when Rudi Blesh, producer of the *This Is Jazz* radio series, hired Archey as a permanent replacement for George Brunies. The half-hour broadcasts were aired weekly through 7 October, and Archey appeared on all the shows alongside widely respected jazzmen such as Wild Bill Davison, ALBERT NICHOLAS, SIDNEY BECHET, JAMES P. JOHNSON, Danny Barker, POPS FOSTER, and BABY DODDS. For part of the summer of 1947 Archey also took part in "Jazz on the River," Blesh's weekend chartered boat trips up the Hudson River. In February 1948 Archey made his first trip to Europe to play at the Nice Jazz Festival with Mezz Mezzrow in a band that also included the trumpeter Henry Goodwin, the pianist SAMMY PRICE, Foster, Dodds, and a young disciple of Bechet's, the clarinetist and soprano saxophonist Bob Wilber. After they returned home, Wilber decided to build a band of his own around Goodwin and Archey. In December 1948 Archey, Goodwin, and Foster, along with the young stride pianist Dick Wellstood and the drummer Tommy Benford, joined Wilber at the Savoy Café in Boston. Playing in a style associated with Bechet's New Orleans Feetwarmers, the personnel of Wilber's band remained intact until

April 1950, when Wilber himself left the group to form another band to open George Wein's new Storyville Club in Boston.

The leadership of the Savoy band was turned over to Archey, who replaced Wilber with the veteran Harlem clarinetist and saxophonist Benny Waters, whom both Archey and Goodwin had known since the 1920s. After their departure from the Savoy, Archey's band began a residency at Jimmy Ryan's on Fifty-second Street, where they remained until the spring of 1952, alternating with WILBUR DE PARIS's recently formed Rampart Street Paraders. After leaving Ryan's, Archey's band embarked on a European tour, but when that folded because of poor management, the band broke up. The men returned home, but Archey stayed on to play with EARL HINES's sextet, which was then also on tour. Back in New York, Archey resumed freelancing, frequently appearing at the Central Plaza, where, with Jimmy McPartland, Pee Wee Russell, and others, he was filmed for the 1954 documentary film *Jazz Dance*. From late 1954 to early 1955 Archey toured Europe again, this time as a sideman with Mezzrow, and from September 1955 through December 1962 he played with an all-star sextet under the alternate leadership of Muggsy Spanier and Hines. In 1963 he led his own bands on dates in the United States and Canada, and in February 1966 he toured Europe once more with the New Orleans All Stars, a stellar group assembled by the British trumpeter Keith Smith. Archey remained active professionally until his death in Amityville, New York.

Even from the beginning of his recording career, Archey was considered a reliable and forthright soloist, as is evidenced by the space accorded him by King Oliver, FATS WALLER, Joe Steele, James P. Johnson, and RED ALLEN on recordings made between 1927 and 1929. On the earlier of these his brash, blues-intoned style reflects that of KID ORY, whom he replaced in Oliver's band, but by late 1929 he had come under the influence of the more technically assured, rhythmically propulsive J. C. HIGGINBOTHAM, then the trombonist with Luis Russell's exciting new orchestra. Though lacking Higginbotham's inventiveness, Archey continued to play with a sprightly, robust earthiness for the remainder of his career. Between 1934 and 1939 he recorded with the Russell/Armstrong orchestra, Willie Bryant, and Benny Carter, but almost exclusively in the capacity of a sectionman. Starting in 1947, though, Archey was heard to advantage on small-band sessions led by MUTT CAREY, Wild Bill Davison, Punch Miller, and Tony Parenti and from 1949 through 1953 as a sideman with Sidney Bechet, Bob Wilber, SIDNEY DE PARIS, George Wettling, and WILLIE "THE LION" SMITH. Between 1954 and 1961 he worked and recorded with Muggsy Spanier and Earl Hines at Los Angeles clubs such as the Hangover and the Crescendo, and in 1966 he appeared on several albums by the touring New Orleans All Stars. Additionally, a number of Archey's band's weekly radio broadcasts from Jimmy Ryan's in 1952 have since appeared on record as well as on audio checks of Blesh's *This Is Jazz* series.

Nothing can be ascertained about Archey's private life, including whether he ever married or had children.

Further Reading
McCarthy, Albert. *Big Band Jazz* (1974).
Wright, Laurie, ed. *King Oliver* (1987).

Discography
Bruyninckx, Walter. *Swing Discography, 1920–1988* (12 vols., 1986–1989).
Bruyninckx, Walter. *Traditional Jazz Discography, 1897–1988* (6 vols., 1985–1988).
Rust, Brian. *Jazz Records, 1897–1942* (1982).

JACK SOHMER

ARCHIBALD, Nathaniel (2 Sept. 1948–), professional basketball player, was born Nathaniel Archibald in New York City, but he was known as "Tiny." Some say he was nicknamed after his father, "Big Tiny," while others believe that he was given that label because he was small in comparison with the other players on the basketball court. He was the oldest of seven children and was raised in the South Bronx's Patterson Housing Projects. At age fourteen, his father left the family and Archibald effectively became head of the household. His mother worked at a neighborhood supermarket called Alexander's to make enough money to care for the family. Basketball became Archibald's sanctuary from drugs and violence, which were rampant in his neighborhood and among his friends. Still, it wasn't easy for him to get himself on a team, as he was small, painfully shy, and lacked confidence on the basketball court. He tried out and failed to make his high school basketball team at DeWitt Clinton High School in his sophomore year and considered dropping out of school. However, Floyd Layne, a community sports director, later to be the head basketball coach for City College of Manhattan, knew the DeWitt Clinton coach and convinced him to give Archibald another chance. He made the team in his junior year, and by his senior year he had been named to the All-City team.

His grades were not good enough for him to attract scholarship offers from major college basketball programs, so Archibald went to Arizona Western Community College. After one year at Arizona Western, he was offered and accepted a scholarship to the University of Texas at El Paso, where he earned a bachelor of science degree and became a star for the school's basketball team. He averaged twenty points a game over three seasons. He won Honorable Mention All-American and WAC MVP in 1970. He continued to build his reputation during the postseason collegiate All-Star games in 1970, scoring 51 points in the Aloha Classic and averaging close to 40 points a game in five postseason exhibitions.

The NBA's Cincinnati Royals selected him in the second round of the 1970 draft. He became a starter in his rookie season when the veteran guard Flynn Robinson held out in a contract dispute. In his first season Archibald averaged 16 points a game. He became the floor leader in his second season, averaging 28.2 points a game, and was selected to the All-NBA Second Team at the end of the season.

Before the 1972–1973 season the Royals moved to Kansas City/Omaha and became the Kings. It was in his first season as a King that Archibald established himself. In 80 games, he averaged 34 points and 11.4 assists a game, becoming the only player in history to lead the league in both average points scored and assists in a single season. He was named to the All-NBA First Team at the end of that season.

Archibald played only 35 games in the 1973–1974 season because of an injured Achilles tendon, averaging 17.6 points a game. However, he played in all 82 games for the Kings in 1974–1975 and led the team to its first winning season since 1966. He averaged 26.5 points and 6.8 assists a game and was named to the All-NBA First Team at the end of the season. Moreover, the Kings made the playoffs that season but lost the Western Conference semifinals in six games to the Chicago Bulls. The following season Archibald averaged 24.8 points and 7.9 assists in 78 games and was again selected to the All-NBA First Team. The Kings suffered through a losing 1975–1976 season, and Archibald was traded to the New York Nets prior to the 1976–1977 season. However, he suffered a severe foot injury and missed most of the season. He was traded to the Buffalo Braves the next year, but tore an Achilles tendon and never played for the Braves. He was traded to the Boston Celtics before the 1978–1979 season. In the 1979–1980 season the Celtics had a 61-21 regular-season record, making the playoffs, but lost to Philadelphia in the Eastern Conference finals. Archibald led the league with 910 assists and was again named an NBA All-Star. In the 1980–1981 season Archibald directed the Celtics offense to a 62-20 record. He was named the All-Star Game MVP and was selected to the All-NBA Second Team at the end of the season, while leading the Celtics to the NBA championship. Archibald helped to get the Celtics back into the playoffs during the 1981–1982 season. He had eight assists per game, which was fourth best in the league. However, the Celtics lost to the Philadelphia 76ers in the Eastern Conference finals.

In the 1982–1983 season Archibald, who was now thirty-four years old, experienced a decline in his play. In 66 games he averaged only 27.4 minutes of playing time and had only 6.2 assists. He was cut by the Celtics at the end of the season and signed with the Milwaukee Bucks as a free agent for the 1983–1984 season. He retired after playing only 46 games for the Bucks.

In a fourteen-year career with the NBA, Archibald garnered 16,481 points, 6,476 assists, and was selected to six NBA All-Star games. He was elected to the Naismith Memorial Basketball Hall of Fame in 1991 and five years later was named to the NBA 50th Anniversary All-Time Team. After his retirement, Archibald returned to New York City, where he ran basketball schools for underprivileged children and earned a master of science degree in Adult Education

from Fordham University in 1990. He also worked as athletic director at the Harlem Armory homeless shelter until it closed in 1991. He served as both a physical education and health education teacher and career development counselor at PS 175/IS 275 in Manhattan, as executive director for the New York Urban Summer Career and Sports Academy, participated in numerous basketball clinics throughout the United States, and headed the Nate "Tiny" Archibald Basketball Camp at Riverbank State Park in New York. He was honored by Mayor DAVID N. DINKINS in 1993 for his work in New York City. He also served as the head basketball coach of the ABA Long Beach (California) Jam in 2004.

Further Reading

Devaney, John. *Tiny!: The Story of Nate Archibald* (1977).
Goldaper, Sam. *Hot Shots: Havlicek, Barry, Monroe, Archibald* (1975).
Greenfield, Jeff. *Tiny Giant: Nate Archibald* (1976).

ROBERT JANIS

ARMSTEAD, Robert "Bob" (8 Dec. 1927–9 Dec. 1998), coal miner who wrote the first published memoir of an African American coal miner, was born Robert Lee Armstead in Watson, West Virginia, to Queen Esther Armstead and James Henry Armstead. James worked in Alabama and West Virginia coal mines for fifty years. Bob received his formal education in all-black schools. The eighth of eleven children born and reared in coal camps, he learned early on that the family's well-being depended on his parents' extraordinary ability to feed and clothe so many on his father's meager income. His religious mother and authoritarian father instilled in their children a strong sense of responsibility, dedication to the family, and solid work ethic.

In 1929, when Bob was two years old, the family moved to Grays Flats, a segregated coal camp on the edge of Grant Town, West Virginia. In the late 1920s the Grant Town mine employed 2,200 men, 500 of whom were black. Armstead watched his father, a horse driver, collapse from exhaustion after working twelve- to fourteen-hour shifts for two dollars a day. His father's suffering, the use of mine guards on horseback to intimidate miners, and policies designed to keep miners poor left young Armstead with contempt for coal mine operators. Deeply aware of his poverty, he made sure to always carry change in his pockets and to keep what little money he had well hidden. Armstead wasn't paid for doing boyhood chores like carrying water, splitting wood, hunting and fishing for food, picking berries, and hoeing the family cornfield, so he solicited additional work from other coal camp residents. As a boy he loved camp life and kept his coal camp memories alive by telling and retelling stories from that time.

To cut labor costs and weaken the United Mine Workers of America (UMWA) in the mid-1930s, coal companies began to replace human labor with mining machines. The mechanization of the Grant Town mine left a disproportionate number of blacks without jobs. By 1941 James Armstead had lost his job and the company-owned family home. He found work driving horses in the deep Dakota mine outside Fairmont, while Bob Armstead attended one of the most notable black schools in West Virginia. Dunbar School, named for the poet PAUL LAWRENCE DUNBAR, included the only black high school in Marion County and had a K–12 enrollment of 600 students.

Although Bob Armstead worked various paying jobs as a teenager, he enjoyed boxing and dedicated himself to training as if it were one of his jobs. He left school in the eleventh grade and married the woman who was expecting his child. Following two years of low-paying jobs, he reconsidered working as a miner and, with the help of his father, joined the hundreds of men at the Consolidation Coal Company's Barnesville Shaft in Fairmont. Armstead's first day underground exhausted and thrilled him. Every coal mining process fascinated him. Above ground he continued to train as an amateur lightweight boxer, and from 1948 to 1951, scored thirty-three wins and only three losses; however, traveling mountain roads to tournaments, working, and trying to be supportive of his growing family proved too demanding. Although he quit boxing when he was twenty-four, Armstead served as a local referee for another six years. From 1950 to 1959 shutdowns and layoffs forced him to work at five different mines. During this difficult period his wife left the crowded Armstead home and relinquished care of their three children to Armstead and his family. On 24 December 1959 he married Zelda Gay Holloway. They lived apart from the family and reared two boys, Michael and Anthony.

From 1948 until his retirement in 1987 Armstead witnessed tragedy and death in the mines, but he never suffered a lost-time injury. He remained employed even as mechanization cut the workforce drastically. In addition to Barnesville Shaft, he worked at several West Virginia mines, including Everettville, Jordan, Grant Town, Loveridge, Four States, and Robinson Run. In a forty-year career, he was furloughed nearly five years due to layoffs, strikes, and mine shutdowns. In 1968 while at Loveridge mine, Bob earned his mine certification and joined a short list of African Americans in management. As a foreman he guided all-white crews in coal production. Just as he had earned a reputation for being an excellent machine operator on any equipment he tried, his crews also earned recognition as excellent coal producers. His closest encounter with death occurred in 1980 at Four States mine, when he rescued a machine operator who was buried under rock from a roof fall with his heavy tool belt snagged on a continuous mining machine lever. Armstead went in, cut the belt, and pulled the man out and away. Seconds later, tons of rock fell where they had been struggling. That second rock fall would have killed them both had Armstead not acted quickly.

Armstead retired from coal mining at the age of fifty-nine and, between part-time jobs, settled down to write his life story. His goal was to tell young people about camp life and to take readers underground to see how coal was mined through the years. What he did not realize was that he was writing a detailed history of sixty years of underground coal mining in northern West Virginia.

In May 1998 he approached the Fairmont writer S. L. Gardner when her feature on the Dakota mine appeared in the Fairmont *Times West Virginian*. Armstead impressed Gardner, an avid student of coal mining, with his never-before-published coal camp stories. Aware that no published memoir of a black coal miner existed, Gardner proposed a book project. The two worked closely with his writings and taped interviews until Armstead died of lung cancer in Morgantown, West Virginia. Assisted by the Armstead family, Gardner finished the book. *Black Days, Black Dust: The Memories of an African American Coal Miner* was published by the University of Tennessee Press in 2002 and was lauded as "an important historical work" (Pack, Lexington, Kentucky, *Herald Leader,* May 2002).

Bob Armstead's memoir has been adopted as required reading by black studies, Appalachian studies, and labor studies departments in colleges and universities nationwide. The success of *Black Days, Black Dust* honors two generations of hard-working African American men and establishes their place in history. It is also a testimonial to one man with a great gift for storytelling and teaching.

Further Reading

Armstead, Robert. *Black Days, Black Dust: The Memories of an African American Coal Miner,* as told to S. L. Gardner (2002).
Gardner, S. L. "Black Days, Black Dust: An Oral History of Life in the Coalfields," in *Traditions: A Journal of West Virginia Folk Culture and Educational Awareness,* vol. 9, no. 1 (2004).

S. L. GARDNER

ARMSTRONG, Henry (12 Dec. 1912–22 Oct. 1988), boxer, was born Henry Jackson Jr. near Columbus, Mississippi, the son of Henry Jackson. His mother, whose name is unknown, was a full-blooded Iroquois, and his father was of mixed Indian, Irish, and black ancestry. He was the eleventh child in a family of sharecroppers. When he was four years old his family moved to St. Louis, Missouri, where his father and older brothers worked in the food-processing industry. His mother died a few years later, after which he was reared by his paternal grandmother. Jackson graduated from Toussaint L'Ouverture Grammar School and Vashon High School, working during his school years as a pin boy at a bowling alley and becoming the inter-alley bowling champion in midtown St. Louis. He gained his first boxing experience by winning a competition among the pin boys.

Lacking funds to attend college, Jackson worked at a series of unskilled jobs. At the "colored" Young Men's Christian Association he came under the tutelage of a former boxer, Harry Armstrong, who gave

Henry Armstrong, boxer and Baptist minister, 15 July 1937. (Library of Congress/Carl Van Vechten.)

him the ring name of "Melody Jackson" after hearing him singing in the shower. He had several amateur fights in St. Louis and then left with Harry for Pittsburgh, where he trained to become a professional. Illnourished and badly trained, Jackson was knocked out in his first professional fight in July 1931, but he won his second on points. He returned to St. Louis and then with Harry went (probably in the fall of 1931) to Los Angeles, where he fought as an amateur boxer, using the name "Henry Armstrong."

Managed by Tom Cox, Henry Armstrong had almost a hundred amateur fights in California and won nearly all of them. Meanwhile, he set up a shoeshine stand and from 1931 to 1934 mainly earned his living by shining shoes. In 1932 Cox sold Armstrong's contract to Wirt Ross; the boxer became a professional again, losing his first two battles on points before becoming a consistent winner. A featherweight at five feet five and a half inches, Armstrong fought mostly in Los Angeles, with occasional trips to other California cities. In November 1934 he had his first major fight, losing a close decision in Mexico City to Baby Arizmendi, who claimed the world featherweight championship. In January 1935 Armstrong fought Arizmendi for the California-Mexico version of the featherweight title, but he lost. Later that year he beat the former flyweight champion Midget Wolgast in Oakland, California, and in August 1936 he defeated Arizmendi to claim the featherweight title. Armstrong won his last twelve fights in 1936, including a victory

over Mike Belloise, another featherweight contender. Late that year Ross sold his contract to the New York manager Eddie Mead; the actual cash for the sale was supplied by the entertainers Al Jolson and George Raft.

In 1937 Armstrong had twenty-seven fights and won them all, twenty-six by knockout, including several matches in New York City. On 29 October he knocked out Petey Sarron to win the world featherweight title at Madison Square Garden. This remarkable series of victories was followed in 1938 by fourteen consecutive wins, ten by knockout, and the acquisition of two more world titles. Armstrong challenged the lightweight champion Lou Ambers to a title fight, but Ambers's manager refused the match. Then, in an audacious move, Armstrong challenged the welterweight champion Barney Ross, and they met in Long Island City on 31 May. Armstrong trounced Ross on points in fifteen rounds and won the world welterweight title despite weighing only 133.5 pounds (less than the lightweight division limit). On 17 August at Madison Square Garden he defeated Ambers in fifteen rounds and won the lightweight title. Armstrong held the championship of three divisions until November, when he voluntarily relinquished the featherweight title, which he had never defended. He successfully defended his welterweight title twice that year against Ceferino Garcia and Al Manfredo.

Armstrong's manner of fighting was aptly described by the sportswriter and cartoonist Ted Carroll:

Armstrong's hurricane style . . . has amazed veteran ring observers for many reasons. Although he is forever pressing forward, he sheds punches with a peculiar movement of head and shoulders like the proverbial duck sheds water. His energy and endurance seem limitless as he . . . forces his opponents to break ground with a ceaseless barrage of punches tossed with power and precision from all angles.

Armstrong's style invariably resulted in action-filled, exciting fights.

Armstrong frequently was handicapped by the loss of points or rounds because of fouling. His headdown windmill style often resulted in low blows, butts, and other infractions. This problem cost him the lightweight title in his second fight with Ambers at Yankee Stadium on 22 August 1939, when the referee Arthur Donovan deducted five rounds for fouls. However, Armstrong successfully defended his welterweight title eleven times in 1939, including victories over Arizmendi, Davey Day, Lew Feldman, and Ernie Roderick.

Armstrong's amazing series of successes continued in 1940, including six more successful defenses of the welterweight title. Furthermore, he fought a draw with Ceferino Garcia for the middleweight title— 160-pound weight limit—in Los Angeles on 1 March, although he weighed only 142 pounds. Had he not been penalized two rounds by the referee George Blake for "rough tactics," Armstrong would have held a fourth world title.

At last, on 4 October 1941 at Madison Square Garden, Fritzie Zivic found the answer to overcoming Armstrong's style and captured the welterweight title. Zivic won decisively by throwing right uppercuts as Armstrong advanced, dramatically flooring the champion at the final bell, as the arena lights suddenly failed. In a return match on 17 January 1941, before a record crowd at the Garden, Zivic pummeled Armstrong even worse, stopping him in twelve rounds. Armstrong made a financially successful comeback in 1942 and continued boxing until 1945; although he won many fights, he was never again a serious title contender.

Armstrong lost his earnings to high living and excessive generosity. He served a brief stint in the army near the end of World War II and managed other fighters. Then he began to drink excessively before experiencing a religious conversion in 1949 and becoming a Baptist minister shortly afterward. He spent the remaining years of his life as an evangelist and founded and directed the Henry Armstrong Youth Foundation in Los Angeles. He had married Willa Mae Shandy in 1934; the couple had one child. Later, he married a second time, but his wife's name and the date of their marriage are unrecorded. In his later years Armstrong suffered from many medical problems, some of them boxing-related, such as cataracts and mental impairment. He died in Los Angeles. He was an inaugural inductee into the International Boxing Hall of Fame in 1990.

Further Reading

Armstrong, Henry. *Gloves, Glory, and God: An Autobiography* (1956).
Fleischer, Nat. *Black Dynamite*, vol. 2 (1938).
Obituary: *New York Times*, 25 Oct. 1988.

LUCKETT V. DAVIS

ARMSTRONG, Lil (3 Feb. 1898–27 Aug. 1971), jazz pianist, composer, and singer, was born Lillian Hardin in Memphis, Tennessee, the daughter of Dempsey Hardin, a strict, churchgoing woman who disapproved of blues music. Nothing is known of her father. At age six Lil began playing organ at home, and at eight she started studying piano. In 1914 she enrolled in the music school of Fisk University in Nashville, taking academic courses and studying piano and music theory. After earning her diploma, around 1917 she joined her mother in Chicago, where she found work demonstrating songs in Jones' Music Store. Prompted by her employer, in 1918 Hardin became house pianist for the clarinetist Lawrence Duhé's band at Bill Bottoms's Dreamland Ballroom, where she played with the cornetists "Sugar Johnny" Smith, FREDDIE KEPPARD, and KING OLIVER; the trombonist Roy Palmer; and other New Orleans musicians. Because she was still a minor, her mother picked her up every night after work.

In January 1920 Hardin joined a second Oliver-led band, and in May 1921 she went to San Francisco with Oliver's Creole Jazz Band for a six-month job at the Pergola Dance Pavilion. Hardin then went back to Chicago and a job at the Dreamland, resuming her former position with Oliver in the summer of 1922. In late August, LOUIS ARMSTRONG joined Oliver's group as second cornetist. Shortly thereafter Armstrong and Hardin began courting. However, while working at the Dreamland, she had married a singer named Jimmie Johnson, whose infidelities soon proved grounds for divorce. Eager to help free Armstrong from his own ill-advised first marriage, Hardin arranged divorces for both of them in 1923, and they were married in February 1924. They had no children. In 1923 King Oliver's Creole Jazz Band recorded thirty-seven performances, on which the pianist was limited to a strictly subordinate role in the rhythm section.

Even before they were married, Lil had begun trying to make Louis more sophisticated in his manners and dress, as well as urging him to leave Oliver. Louis, however, remained adamantly loyal to Oliver until mid-1924, when the band broke up following a long midwestern tour. Months of Lil's prodding had taken their toll, and, finally convinced that he should seek better avenues to showcase his own talent and reap its reward, Louis gave Oliver notice. In September he was offered a featured position in FLETCHER HENDERSON's orchestra at the Roseland Ballroom in New York. In October, Lil followed her husband east but soon returned to Chicago to lead her own band at the Dreamland. During this period, Louis Armstrong's reputation grew far beyond what it had been in Chicago, but by early November 1925 he was ready to leave New York, primarily because Lil wanted him to come home. By this time she was enjoying a successful run with her Dreamland Syncopators and encouraged the owners to pay a higher salary than usual to bring in Louis as a featured attraction.

Between November 1925 and December 1927 Lil Armstrong appeared on all of the Louis Armstrong Hot Five and Hot Seven recordings, forty-four titles in all. She also led one Hot Five date under her own name (as Lil's Hot Shots) in May 1926 and participated, along with Louis, on sessions with Butterbeans (JODIE EDWARDS) and Susie, ALBERTA HUNTER, and the Red Onion Jazz Babies. In July 1926 she also recorded with the New Orleans Bootblacks and the New Orleans Wanderers. In early 1929 she recorded with JOHNNY DODDS in both trio and sextet settings.

Although her command of the piano was marred by limited technique, swift, unswinging time, and a paucity of melodic ideas, Lil Armstrong was nevertheless a highly productive composer of jazz songs. It is difficult to ascertain exactly which songs she wrote independently of Louis Armstrong, but it can be assumed that she played an important role in transcribing and arranging certain melodic themes that he invented. Among the Hot Five and Hot Seven numbers for which she is given full or partial credit are "I'm Gonna Gitcha," "Droppin' Shucks," "King of the Zulus," "Jazz Lips," "Struttin' with Some Barbecue," "Hotter than That," and "Knee Drops." She also contributed "Gate Mouth," "Too Tight Blues," and "I

Can't Say," "Perdido Street Blues," "Papa Dip," and "Mixed Salad" to the 1926 Bootblacks and Wanderers sessions as well as "Pencil Papa," "Heah Me Talkin'," and "Goober Dance" to Dodds's 1929 dates. However, it must be said that her own contributions on piano, whether as soloist or accompanist, are invariably the least interesting elements of these recordings.

During the late 1920s Lil bought an eleven-room home in Chicago and real estate on Lake Michigan's Idlewild resort, properties she retained throughout her life. When Lil's job at the Dreamland ended in the spring of 1926, Louis joined CARROLL DICKERSON's orchestra at the Sunset Café while Lil worked in Hugh Swift's band and later toured with Freddie Keppard. During this time Lil also studied at the Chicago Musical College, and, after earning a degree in teaching, she studied at the New York College of Music, where she received her postgraduate degree in 1929.

Louis, who had started philandering while he was in New York, was beginning to tire of Lil's constant jealousy and pressure for him to better himself commercially. He began a serious relationship with another woman, Alpha Smith, around 1928. After numerous arguments with her husband, who had at last become successful, Lil finally sued for legal separation in August 1931, retaining her properties and receiving a considerable cash allowance. She eventually granted him a divorce and also won a suit against him for the rights to the songs they had co-composed. Lil never remarried, and she kept all relevant Louis Armstrong memorabilia, including letters, photos, and his old cornet, until her death.

Through the mid-1930s Lil Armstrong led both all-female and all-male bands of varying sizes in the Midwest, sometimes under the billing of Mrs. Louis Armstrong and Her Orchestra. She also broadcast regularly and appeared as a soloist in the *Hot Chocolates* and *Shuffle Along* revues. From 1936 Lil Armstrong lived in New York and worked as a house pianist for Decca Records, between 1936 and 1940 leading small jazz groups with such featured sidemen as JOE THOMAS, J. C. HIGGINBOTHAM, BUSTER BAILEY, and CHU BERRY. She also provided the accompaniments for the singers Blue Lu Barker, Rosetta Howard, Alberta Hunter, Frankie "Half Pint" Jaxon, PEETIE WHEATSTRAW, and others and participated in jazz dates under the leadership of RED ALLEN, Johnny Dodds, and ZUTTY SINGLETON. She emerges as a vivacious and entertaining singer on her own Decca recordings of 1936–1940. Among her compositions from this period are "My Hi-De-Ho Man," "Brown Gal," "Just for a Thrill," "Born to Swing," "Let's Get Happy Together," and "Everything's Wrong, Ain't Nothing Right." In late 1940 Armstrong returned to Chicago, where she worked throughout the next decade as a soloist in many local venues.

In early 1952 Armstrong went to Paris, where she recorded in a trio with SIDNEY BECHET and Zutty Singleton and also under her own name in 1953 and 1954. She worked primarily as a soloist in Paris but also spent some time in London before returning in

the late 1950s to Chicago. In December 1960 she recorded with Franz Jackson's band and in September 1961 led her own group for an album in the Riverside label's *Chicago: The Living Legends* series. In late October 1961 she participated in the telecast of *Chicago and All That Jazz*, an all-star jazz concert segment of NBC's *Dupont Show of the Week*. Little is known of Armstrong's activities after this point, but she probably continued appearing in clubs in Chicago and environs. Following Louis Armstrong's death in July 1971, a memorial concert was staged in his honor on 27 August at Chicago's Civic Center, and it was during her performance at this event that Lil Armstrong suffered a fatal coronary.

Further Reading

In 1960 or 1961 an oral interview with Lil Armstrong titled *Satchmo and Me* was released as Riverside RLP12–120.

Dahl, Linda. *Stormy Weather* (1984).

Giddins, Gary. *Satchmo* (1988).

Jones, Max, and John Chilton. *Louis: The Louis Armstrong Story 1900–1971* (1971; rev. ed., 1988).

Placksin, Sally. *American Women in Jazz* (1982).

Unterbrink, Mary. *Jazz Women at the Keyboard* (1983).

Obituary: *New York Times*, 28 Aug. 1971.

Discography

Bruyninckx, Walter. *Swing Discography, 1920–1988* (12 vols., 1985–1989).

Rust, Brian. *Jazz Records, 1897–1942* (1982).

JACK SOHMER

ARMSTRONG, Louis (4 Aug. 1901–6 Jul. 1971), jazz trumpeter and singer, known universally as "Satchmo" and later as "Pops," was born in New Orleans, Louisiana, the son of William Armstrong, a boiler stoker in a turpentine plant, and Mary Est "Mayann" Albert, a laundress. Abandoned by his father shortly after birth, Armstrong was raised by his paternal grandmother, Josephine, until he was returned to his mother's care at age five. Mother and son moved from Jane Alley, in a violence-torn slum, to an only slightly better area, Franklyn and Perdido streets, where nearby cheap cabarets gave the boy his first introduction to the new kind of music, jazz, that was developing in New Orleans. Although Armstrong claims to have heard the early jazz cornetist BUDDY BOLDEN when he was about age five, this incident may be apocryphal. As a child, he worked odd jobs, sang in a vocal quartet, and around 1911 bought a used cornet with his savings. He dropped out of school and got into trouble; in 1913 he was placed in the New Orleans Colored Waifs' Home for Boys, where Peter Davis, the music instructor, gave Armstrong his first formal music instruction. He left the home in June 1914. Although he was remanded to the custody of his father, he soon went to live with his mother and younger sister, Beatrice, whom Armstrong affectionately called "Mama Lucy."

Louis Armstrong, 1953, one of the earliest jazz trumpet virtuosos, who also revolutionized singing styles, late in his career. (Library of Congress.)

As a teenager, Armstrong played street parades, associated with the older musicians, and held various jobs, including delivering coal with a mule-drawn coal wagon. In his second autobiography, *My Life in New Orleans*, he relates the importance of these years in his development, particularly the influence of KING OLIVER:

At that time I did not know the other great musicians such as JELLY ROLL MORTON, FREDDY KEPPARD, . . . and Eddy Atkins. All of them had left New Orleans long before the red-light district was closed by the Navy and the law [1917]. Of course I met most of them in later years, but Papa Joe Oliver, God bless him, was my man. I often did errands for Stella Oliver, his wife, and Joe would give me lessons for my pay. I could not have asked for anything I wanted more. It was my ambition to play as he did. I still think that if it had not been for Joe Oliver jazz would not be what it is today. (99)

In 1918 Armstrong married Daisy Parker and began his life as a professional musician. Between November 1918 and August 1922 he played cornet at Tom Anderson's club as well as in the Tuxedo Brass Band, in FATE MARABLE's band on Mississippi River excursion paddle-wheel steamers, and incidentally in several New Orleans cabarets. His musical associates during these years were Oliver, Warren "BABY" DODDS, JOHNNY DODDS, JOHNNY ST. CYR, HONORE DUTREY, George "POPS" FOSTER, and EDWARD "KID" ORY.

Armstrong's rise to prominence began with his move to Chicago in August 1922, when Oliver invited him to come to the Lincoln Garden's Cafe as second cornet in Oliver's Creole Jazz Band. This group defined jazz for the local Chicago musicians and stimulated the development of this music in profound ways. Armstrong's first recordings were made with Oliver in 1923 and 1924; "Riverside Blues," "Snake Rag," "Mabel's Dream," "Chattanooga Stomp," and "Dipper Mouth Blues" are some of the performances that preserve and display his early mature work.

In 1924 Armstrong divorced his first wife and that same year married the pianist in Oliver's band, Lillian Hardin (LIL ARMSTRONG). She encouraged him to accept an invitation to play with the FLETCHER HENDERSON orchestra at the Roseland Ballroom in New York City. Armstrong's impact on this prominent name band was phenomenal. His solo style brought to the East a tonal power, creative virtuosity, and rhythmic drive that had not been a regular aspect of the Henderson band's performance practice. Armstrong's influence on Henderson, himself an arranger and pianist, and two of his fellow band members, in particular, the arranger and saxophonist DON REDMAN and the saxophone virtuoso COLEMAN HAWKINS, was partially responsible for the development of a new jazz idiom or style—swing. During his fourteen months with Henderson, Armstrong participated in more than twenty recording sessions and left memorable solos on "One of These Days," "Copenhagen," and "Everybody Loves My Baby," on which he cut his first, brief, vocal chorus. While in New York, Armstrong also recorded with CLARENCE WILLIAMS's Blue Five, a small combo that included the already famous saxophonist SIDNEY BECHET, and with the star blues singers MA RAINEY and BESSIE SMITH. With Henderson, Armstrong played trumpet, but in these small-group sessions he returned to cornet. For another two years he continued to use both instruments but finally retired his cornet for the brighter, more-focused sound of the trumpet.

Despite his growing stature among the jazz community, Armstrong was still but a sideman when he returned to Chicago in 1925. He immediately became the star of his wife's band at the Dreamland Cafe and soon joined Erskine Tate's orchestra at the Vendome Theater. In November 1925 he made his first recordings as a leader with a pickup group of old associates he called the "Hot Five"—his wife, Lil, on piano; Kid Ory on trombone; Johnny Dodds on clarinet; and St. Cyr on banjo. These recordings of the Hot Five and the Hot Seven (with the addition of bass and drums) are towering monuments of traditional jazz. "Cornet Chop," "Gut Bucket Blues," "Heebie Jeebies," "Skid-Dat-De-Dat," "Big Butter and Egg Man," "Struttin' with Some Barbecue," "Hotter Than That," and several others are numbered among the classics of this style, have entered the standard repertoire, and continue to be studied and performed regularly. In these recordings Armstrong established his eminence as a cornet and trumpet virtuoso and an unparalleled improviser, composer, and jazz vocalist. Melrose Brothers published notated transcriptions of some of his solos in 1927 immediately after the appearance of these recordings; these may be the first transcriptions from recorded performances ever published. The significance of this series of recordings is summarized by Gunther Schuller in his study *Early Jazz*:

The smooth rhythms of the earlier improvisations give way to stronger, contrasting, harder swinging rhythms. Double-time breaks abound. Melodic line and rhythm combine to produce more striking contours. This was, of course, the result not only of Armstrong's increasing technical skill, but also of his maturing musicality, which saw the jazz solo in terms not of a pop-tune more or less embellished, but of a chord progression generating a maximum of creative originality. . . . His later solos all but ignored the original tune and started with only the chord changes given. (Schuller, 102–103)

Armstrong's association with EARL "FATHA" HINES in 1927 led to another series of pathbreaking recordings in 1928, most notably "West End Blues," with a reconstituted Hot Five, and "Weather Bird," a trumpet and piano duet. In "West End Blues," Armstrong not only achieves an unprecedented level of virtuosity but also displays the beginnings of motivic development in jazz solos. In "Weather Bird," Hines and Armstrong partake in a rapid exchange of antecedent-consequent improvised phrases that set a pattern for future jazz improvisers who "trade fours and twos."

In 1929 Armstrong moved with his band from Chicago to New York for an engagement at Connie's Inn in Harlem. The floor show used a score by FATS WALLER that became a Broadway success as *Hot Chocolates* and featured an onstage Armstrong trumpet solo on "Ain't Misbehavin'." He also pursued many other endeavors, going into the recording studio to front his own band with Jack Teagarden and playing and singing in LUIS RUSSELL's group, which also featured the Chicago banjoist and guitar player Eddie Condon. Armstrong's singing style was unique in American popular music, especially when it was first presented to listeners on a broad scale through recordings of the 1920s.

One of his first vocal accomplishments was to introduce an improvisatory vocal-instrumental mode of singing called "scat singing" in his recordings of "Heebie Jeebies" and "Gully Low Blues" of 1926 and 1927, respectively. Although this method of singing nonsense syllables was common in New Orleans and had been used by others, it was Armstrong's recordings that were credited with the invention of this new device and that influenced hosts of later jazz singers. Contrasting with the classically oriented popular-song vocalists of the day, with the shouting-and-dancing stage singers of ragtime and minstrelsy, and with the loud and lusty belters of the classic blues, Armstrong's natural technique brought a relaxed but exuberant jazz style and a gravelly personal tone to popular singing. His 1929 recordings of "I Can't Give You Anything but Love" and "Ain't Misbehavin'" achieved great popular success. Armstrong continued to sing throughout his career and reached a pinnacle of popular success in 1964 when his recording of "Hello Dolly" became the best-selling record in America, moving to number one on the popular music charts.

From 1930 to the mid-1940s Armstrong was usually featured with a big band. In 1935 he joined forces with Joe Glaser, a tough-minded businessman who guided his career until 1969. Armstrong divorced Lil Hardin, marrying Alpha Smith in 1938. He later divorced her and was married a fourth and final time in 1942 to Lucille Wilson. He had no children with any of his wives. After World War II, Armstrong returned to performing with a small ensemble and played a concert in New York's Town Hall, with "Peanuts" Hucko (clarinet), Bobby Hackett (trumpet), Jack Teagarden (trombone), Dick Cary (piano), Bob Haggart (bass), and BIG SID CATLETT (drums), that inaugurated a new phase in his career. After the success of this "formal concert," Armstrong began to tour with a band labeled his "All Stars," ensembles of approximately the same size but with varying personnel selected from the ranks of established, well-known jazz musicians. Through Glaser's efforts, Armstrong and his All Stars became the highest-paid jazz band in the world. They toured successfully, sparking a renewed interest in Armstrong's recordings and earning him a place on the cover of *Time* magazine on 21 February 1949.

Throughout his long career Armstrong, as trumpeter, remained the leading figure among classic jazz musicians and rode many waves of public and financial success, but his historical impact as a jazz instrumentalist lessened as new styles developed and younger musicians looked elsewhere for leadership. Still, his solo trumpet playing remained superlative while other phases of his career, such as singing, acting, writing, and enjoying the fruits of his celebrity, gained prominence as time passed. Between 1932 and 1965 he appeared in almost fifty motion pictures, including *Rhapsody in Black and Blue* (1932), *Pennies from Heaven* (1936), *Every Day's a Holiday* (1937), *Doctor Rhythm* (1938), *Jam Session* (1944), *New Orleans* (1946), *The Strip* (1951), *High Society* (1956), *Satchmo the Great* (1957), *The Beat Generation* (1959), *When the Boys Meet the Girls* (1965), and *Hello, Dolly!* (1969). Beginning with broadcasts in April 1937, he was the first black performer to be featured in a network radio series, and he appeared as a guest on dozens of television shows starting in the 1950s.

Often unjustly criticized for pandering to the racist attitudes that prevailed in the venues where he performed, Armstrong was, in fact, a significant leader in the struggle for racial equality in America. He was a black artist whose work blossomed contemporaneously with the other artistic and intellectual achievements of the Harlem Renaissance and an important personage who spoke publicly in protest and canceled a U.S. State Department tour in 1957 when Governor Orval Faubus of Arkansas refused to let black children attend a public school. Armstrong firmly believed in equal opportunity as a right and in personal merit as the only measure of worth, and he was one of the first black jazz musicians to perform and record with white musicians (Hoagy Carmichael, Tommy Dorsey, Jack Teagarden, Bud Freeman, and Bing Crosby, among others). His artistry was such that he became a role model not only for black musicians but also for numerous aspiring young white musicians, most notably Bix Beiderbecke, Jimmy McPartland, Bobby Hackett, and Gil Evans.

Informally he became known as an "Ambassador of Goodwill," and Ambassador "Satch" toured Europe and Africa under the sponsorship of the Department of State during the 1950s. Armstrong amassed many honors in his lifetime—medals, stamps in his honor from foreign countries, invitations from royalty and heads of state, and critical awards such as the annual *Down Beat* Musicians Poll—but none seemed to hold greater significance for him than returning to his birthplace, New Orleans, in 1949 as King of the Zulus for the annual Mardi Gras celebration. Even though ill health plagued him in his last few years, Armstrong continued to work, appearing on television and playing an engagement at the Waldorf-Astoria Hotel in New York City during the last year of his life. He died in his home in Corona, Queens, New York.

Louis Armstrong and but three or four others are preeminent in the history of jazz. His importance in the development of this art form has gained greater, almost universal recognition in the years since his death as scholars and musicians reevaluate his contributions as a soloist, composer, bandleader, and role model. The measure of his impact on the social history of twentieth-century America also seems to be greater now as he gains recognition for his contributions to the Harlem Renaissance, for his actions as a thoughtful spokesperson for black Americans, as a significant writer of autobiography, as an entertainer of stature, and as a singer responsible for the development of major trends in American popular and jazz singing. His most accomplished biographer, Gary Giddins, wrote in *Satchmo*: Genius is the transforming agent. Nothing else can explain Louis Armstrong's ascendancy. He had no formal training, yet he alchemized the cabaret music of an outcast minority into an art that has expanded in ever-widening orbits, with no sign of collapse (26).

Further Reading
The papers of Louis Armstrong are preserved in the Louis Armstrong Archive at Queens College of the City University of New York, and virtually all of his recordings, some oral history material, and other related documents are at the Institute of Jazz Studies at Rutgers University in Newark, New Jersey.

Armstrong, Louis. *Satchmo: My Life in New Orleans* (1954).

Armstrong, Louis. *Swing That Music* (1936).

Collier, James Lincoln. *Louis Armstrong: An American Genius* (1983).

Friedwald, Will. *Jazz Singing: America's Great Voices from Bessie Smith to Bebop and Beyond* (1990).

Giddins, Gary. *Satchmo* (1988).

Gourse, Leslie. *Louis' Children: American Jazz Singers* (1984).

Jones, Max, and John Chilton. *Louis: The Louis Armstrong Story 1900–1971* (1971; rev. ed., 1988).

Schuller, Gunther. *Early Jazz: Its Roots and Musical Development* (1968).

Schuller, Gunther. *The Swing Era: The Development of Jazz 1930–1945* (1989).

Obituary: *New York Times*, 7 July 1971.

Discography
Westerberg, Hans. *Boy from New Orleans: A Discography of Louis "Satchmo" Armstrong* (1981)

FRANK TIRRO

ARMWOOD, Blanche (23 Jan. 1890–16 Oct. 1939), educator and activist, was the youngest of five children born to Levin and Maggie Armwood in Tampa,

Florida. Armwood's father was born a slave in Thomas County, Georgia, in 1855 and in the late 1870s became the first African American police officer in Tampa, Florida, and in 1895 became a deputy sheriff.

Armwood started her education at St. Peter Claver's Catholic School. She completed her studies in 1902 at the age of twelve and passed the Florida State Uniform Teachers' Examination. Since Tampa did not have a continuing education school for African Americans, the Armwoods sent Blanche to Spelman Seminary (later Spelman College), an all-female prep school for black women, in Atlanta, Georgia. There she studied English, Latin, and home economics, courses that would later prove an asset to her. Graduating from Spelman Seminary in 1906 with honors, summa cum laude, after four years of study, Armwood was the youngest in her class and began looking forward to attending college. However, because of her father's illness, she returned to Tampa. She immediately passed the Florida teacher's examination and started teaching first grade in the city's African American public schools. She quickly moved from teaching the primary grades to high school and took several summer classes in home economics from Florida Agricultural and Mechanical College, Columbia University, and the New York School of Social Sciences.

At age twenty-three Armwood married Daniel Webster Perkins, an attorney, on 23 November 1913. She resigned her position, having served seven and a half years in the school system and advancing from teacher to principal of the College Hill School in Tampa, and moved with her husband to his hometown of Knoxville, Tennessee. Within a few months, however, she discovered that her husband had an illegitimate son. History does not document her personal relationship with Perkins, but her religious beliefs and attitudes about marriage would not allow her to remain married. She eventually had the marriage annulled and in late 1914 returned to Tampa. That same year she was approached by the Tampa Gas Company and the Hillsborough County board of education to organize an industrial arts school that would specialize in domestic science. The school opened in January 1915, largely funded by the Tampa Gas Company. The Tampa School of Household Arts sought to help African American women properly perform their domestic duties by teaching them how to operate modern gas appliances. The school was such a success that more than two hundred women completed the training the first year. Armwood served as principal and head instructor for three years and was instrumental in the successful training of several hundred African American women and girls. She went on to open and organize a number of similar schools in other southern states. In the summer of 1917 New Orleans Gas and Light Company asked Tampa Gas Company to release Armwood to come to New Orleans to organize and operate its new school.

Armwood traveled throughout Louisiana, overseeing home demonstration agents. On 15 October 1917 she opened the largest school of domestic science in New Orleans for African American women and girls, New Orleans School of Domestic Science. She made numerous food demonstrations and in May 1918 published a cookbook called *Food Conservation in the Home*. In 1919, when she was twenty-nine years old, she met and married Dr. John C. Beatty, a dentist and graduate of Howard University Dental College, and four months later she resigned her position as supervisor of home economics. From 1919 until 1922 Armwood took on several projects, serving as spokesperson on women's voting rights, anti-lynching, and other civil rights issues. She joined the Republican Party, was recommended to serve as a national campaign speaker for the party, and went on to help create Republican clubs to teach African American women about politics and the voting process. She served on the presidential campaign for Warren G. Harding. Because of her dedication to the campaign, she was invited to the Marion, Ohio, home of Senator Harding to celebrate a Social Justice and Woman's Day affair.

In 1922 Armwood and her husband returned to Tampa, where she became the first executive secretary of the Tampa Urban League (TUL), a social welfare organization designed to help African Americans adjust to urban life. That same year the Hillsborough County school board appointed Armwood the first supervisor of African American schools, a position she held for eight years. During her tenure she purchased new school buildings, increased teachers' salaries, and extended the school year from six to nine months. She was influential in the 1926 opening of Booker T. Washington High School, which after four years became the first accredited African American school in the county. Armwood also held leadership positions in two major African American organizations, the Home Economics Department for the National Association of Colored Women (NACW) and the Louisiana chapter of the National Association for the Advancement of Colored People (NAACP). She also served as the state director of Florida's Anti-Lynching Crusades. During her time as executive secretary, Armwood assisted in opening the first library in an African American community, the Busy Merrymakers Women's Club, Helping Hand Day Nursery and Kindergarten for working mothers, and the Booker T. Washington Tampa chapter of the American Red Cross.

In the late 1920s Armwood's second husband was murdered by the family chauffeur amid unfounded rumors that she was involved in an affair with the driver. Devastated by the murder, Armwood threw herself into church work, where she met Edward T. Washington, a supervisor for the Interstate Commerce Commission. They were married in 1931, and soon afterward the couple relocated to Washington, D.C. Throughout the 1930s she labored for the NACW and NAACP. In 1934 Armwood enrolled in Howard University School of Law, earning her law degree in 1937 and graduating in 1938 with her juris doctorate degree, becoming the first African American woman born in Florida to earn a law degree. Her decision to become a lawyer was based on her commitment to the suffrage movement and the antilynching campaign. Her law degree helped divert her attention from activities having to do with racial uplift to the legal issues and fight against racism.

Armwood died suddenly at the age of forty-nine during a speaking engagement in the Northeast. It is not certain exactly what her illness was, but it was documented that she died from complications of many ailments, including phlebitis and exhaustion. Her life ended just when her career was starting a new phase. She was buried in the Armwood family plot at L'Unione Italiana Cemetery in Tampa, Florida. She was eulogized by Dr. BENJAMIN E. MAYS, then president of Morehouse College at the John Wesley AME Church in Washington, D.C. Having no children or dependants, she left a scholarship trust fund to her alma mater, Spelman College. Nearly a half century after her death, congressmen from Tampa and Tampa city officials paid tribute to her and in 1984 the Blanche Armwood Comprehensive High School opened in Seffner, Florida.

Further Reading
Alishahi, Michele. "'For Peace and Civic Righteousness': Blanche Armwood and the Struggle for Freedom and Racial Equality in Tampa, Florida," MA thesis, University of South Florida (2003).
Bilirakis, Michael. "Blanche Armwood: Tribute to the Late Blanche Armwood," *Congressional Record*, 2 Oct. 1984.
Burke, Mary. "The Success of Blanche Armwood," *Sunland Tribune*, Nov. 1989.
Davis, Elizabeth Lindsay. "Blanche Armwood," in *Lifting as They Climb* (1933).
Durham, John R. "Blanche Armwood: The Early Years," MA thesis, University of South Florida (1988).

LINDA WILSON-JONES

ARNETT, Benjamin William (6 Mar. 1838–9 Oct. 1906), African American religious, educational, and political leader, was born in Brownsville, Pennsylvania, the son of Samuel G. Arnett and Mary Louisa (maiden name unknown). Benjamin Arnett was a man of "mixed Irish, Indian, Scots, and African ancestry" (Wright, *Eighty-seven Years*, 79). He was educated in a one-room schoolhouse in Bridgeport, Pennsylvania. Arnett worked as a longshoreman along the Ohio and Mississippi rivers and worked briefly as a hotel waiter. His career as a longshoreman and waiter ended abruptly in 1858 when a cancerous tumor necessitated the amputation of his left leg. He turned to teaching and was granted a certificate on 19 December 1863. At that time he was the only African American schoolteacher licensed in Fayette County, Pennsylvania. For ten months during the academic year 1884–1885, Arnett served as a school principal in Washington, D.C. He returned to Brownsville in 1885, teaching there until 1887. Although largely self-educated, he also attended classes at Lane Theological Seminary in Cincinnati (later affiliated with McCormick Theological Seminary in Chicago). A man of many interests, Arnett was an occasional lecturer in ethics and psychology at the Payne Theological Seminary at Wilberforce University, a historian of the African Methodist Episcopal (AME) Church, a trustee of the Archaeological and Historical Society of Ohio, a member of the executive committee of the National Sociological Society, and was statistical secretary of the Ecumenical Conference of Methodism for the western section from 1891 to 1901.

Arnett's formal association with the AME Church began in February 1856. He was licensed to preach on 30 March 1865 and was ordained a deacon on 30 April 1868 in Columbus, Ohio. He became an elder on 12 May 1870 in Xenia, Ohio. As a delegate from the Ohio Annual Conference, Arnett attended the General AME Conference in 1872. He was appointed assistant secretary of the General Conference in 1876 and became general secretary in 1880. He was also elected financial secretary of the General Conference in 1880 and again in 1884. As financial secretary, he had primary responsibility for the publication of the annual *Budget* of the AME Church. Arnett's budgets contain not only detailed financial records but also personal observations and historical information. He continued as an editor of the AME *Budget* until 1904.

At the General Conference of 1888, Arnett was elected a bishop of the AME Church, the church's seventeenth bishop. He served the seventh episcopal district (South Carolina and Florida) from 1888 to 1892, the fourth episcopal district (Indiana, Illinois, and Iowa) from 1892 to 1900, the third episcopal district (Ohio, California, and Pittsburgh) from 1900 to 1904, and the first episcopal district (Philadelphia, New York, and New England) from 1904 to 1906.

An ardent Republican and active in party politics, Arnett was chaplain to the Ohio legislature in 1879 and to the Republican State Convention in Ohio in 1880. His most notable political accomplishment was his election (by eight votes) to the Ohio legislature to represent predominantly white Greene County in 1886. Arnett was the first African American legislator in Ohio to represent a predominantly white constituency. During his term in office he drafted a bill to abolish Ohio's discriminatory Black Laws and introduced bills to secure state funding for Wilberforce University, which at the time was near bankruptcy. While in the Ohio legislature, Arnett also established an enduring friendship with William McKinley Jr., and on behalf of the AME Church presented McKinley with the Bible used when he took the oath of office of the presidency in 1897. Arnett maintained close ties with McKinley and is said to have exerted considerable influence in Washington during the McKinley administration (1897–1901). He served as chaplain to the Republican National Convention in St. Louis in 1896.

Arnett enjoyed a considerable and deserved reputation as a public speaker and parliamentarian. He addressed the Republican State Convention in Denver in 1886 and the Centennial Celebration of the First

Settlement of the Northwest Territory in Mariti, Ohio, in 1888; he was invited to give commencement addresses at Wilberforce University in 1887 and at Claflin College, South Carolina, in 1889; and he presented the keynote address at the meeting of the Grand Army of the Republic in Chicago in 1900. He presided at the Parliament of Religion held at Chicago in September 1893 and at the Ecumenical Conference of Methodists held in London in September 1901. Arnett was vice president of the Anti-Saloon League of America and an active member of FREDERICK DOUGLASS's National Equal Rights League. Arnett was also active in the Masons and worked diligently on behalf of the Young Men's Christian Association.

Arnett married Mary Louise Gordon in 1858. The couple had seven children. Two of their sons, Benjamin William Arnett Jr. and Henry Y. Arnett, became ministers in the AME Church. Benjamin Jr. became president of Edward Waters College and Allen University. Henry became a pastor and presiding elder in the AME Church's Philadelphia and Delaware Conferences.

During Arnett's term in the Third Episcopal District (1900–1904), he established a ten-acre estate near Wilberforce University, called Tawawa Chimney Corner, where he hosted numerous visitors and amassed a large collection of African American literature. A number of volumes from Arnett's personal library were later acquired by W. E. B. DU BOIS; other volumes from Arnett's library are now a part of the ARTHUR A. SCHOMBURG collection of the New York Public Library. Arnett died of uremia in Wilberforce, Ohio.

Richard R. Wright Jr., in *Eighty-seven Years behind the Black Curtain*, describes his initial encounter with Arnett: "I was greatly impressed. Bishop Arnett, a handsome, clean-shaven man, was Northern born, very intelligent, unusually witty, an expert in church financing, author of half a dozen books and pamphlets, a distinguished and convincing orator, and a 'soul-stirring' preacher" (Wright, 92–94). This assessment was echoed by not a few of Arnett's contemporaries.

Arnett served as a bishop for more than eighteen years and had a considerable influence on church affairs. Perhaps his greatest contributions stem from his ability to mediate among various factions within the church and from his ability to successfully transcend racial, ethnic, and class boundaries. His published lectures, notably his 1888 centennial address "The Northwest Territory," show careful scholarship and a keen intellect.

Further Reading

Arnett's papers are in the Carnegie Library, Wilberforce University.

Coleman, Lucretia H. Newman. *Poor Ben: A Study of Real Life* (1890).

Wright, Richard R., Jr. *The Bishops of the African Methodist Episcopal Church* (1963).

Wright, Richard R., Jr. *Eighty-seven Years behind the Black Curtain* (1965).

Obituary: *New York Times*, 9 Oct. 1906.

STEPHEN D. GLAZIER

ARNOLD, Hendrick (?–1849), scout and pioneer of the West, was one of the free blacks in Texas who experienced some degree of freedom under four different governing entities—Spain, Mexico, the Republic of Texas, and the United States. Free blacks never constituted a large population in Texas in the eighteenth and nineteenth centuries. For example, a census in 1860 put the number of free blacks at four hundred, but later estimates by historians suggest that their numbers approached eight hundred. Despite their small numbers free blacks made a significant contribution to the early history of Texas. Hendrick Arnold played a pivotal role in the Texas Revolution (1835–1836) and beyond.

The date of Hendrick Arnold's birth is not known. He emigrated from Mississippi with his parents, Daniel and Rachel Arnold, in the winter of 1826. His father was likely white, while his mother was black; nothing else is known about them. The family joined the existing Stephen F. Austin colony of approximately three hundred families on the Brazos River and migrated with an additional nine hundred families between 1825 and 1829. Historical records indicate that by the fall of 1835 Hendrick Arnold had moved to the area of San Antonio, where he married a Tejana (Mexican) woman named Martina. She was the stepdaughter of Erastus "Deaf" Smith, another noteworthy figure in Texas history. Arnold had a daughter named Harriet in 1827, whose mother was one of his father's slaves. A second daughter named Juanita was born later, although the exact date is not known, likely from his marriage with Martina.

By the fall of 1835 Arnold was operating a gristmill in San Antonio. The social and political realities leading up to the Texas Revolution are summarized succinctly by the historian Harold Schoen: "It was as easy for the Negro as for the white man to place all his grievances, real and imaginary, at the door of the Mexican government, and when the outbreak of hostilities threatened his life and property and the safety of his family, all of which he held as dearly as his neighbors, he was willing to risk his life in their preservation" (Schoen, 26).

While Arnold and Deaf Smith (his father-in-law) were hunting buffalo in a frontier region north of present-day Austin, Mexican military forces successfully occupied San Antonio. On their journey home, when they were about five miles east of San Antonio, Smith and Arnold came upon a military encampment of Texans at Salado Creek commanded by Stephen F. Austin. Smith and Arnold volunteered as guides. A council of Texan officers met in December 1835 to consider moving on San Antonio, but they decided to postpone the attack.

When another Texan leader, Benjamin Milam, arrived at the encampment, he called for an immediate attack on San Antonio, an attack referred to by historians as the Siege of Bexar. Arnold was among the few known to have served as guides for Milam's military division. The start of the battle, however, was delayed because of Arnold's absence. It was only upon his return (from a hunting trip) that Milam's army of some three hundred expressed willingness to proceed with the attack. The Siege of Bexar was successful militarily, but Milam was killed. A leader of another military division, Francis Johnson, wrote the official report of the battle and specifically cited Arnold for his meritorious service. The Siege of Bexar was one of four major engagements of the war for Texas's independence. Later engagements involving the fall of the Alamo and Goliad were followed by final victory and Texas's independence after the Battle of San Jacinto on 21 April 1836. Arnold also served in the Battle of San Antonio, probably in a similar role as a scout. Historical records note that he was wounded sometime during his military service.

In 1836 Arnold petitioned the general council of the Texas provisional government for relief for his family, a common practice of Texas Revolution war veterans. He received a land grant a few miles northwest of the present site of Bandera, a relatively unexplored area less highly valued by others seeking land grants. Arnold successfully secured adjacent land for his grandmother, his father, and his brother. His brother appears to have been the only family member to settle on the land. Arnold died in a cholera epidemic in Bexar County in 1849 and was buried on the banks of the Medina River near his homestead.

Arnold's military service and his financial success are noteworthy given that the status of blacks deteriorated sharply under the Republic of Texas, whose constitution did not grant them full rights as citizens and allowed the practice of slavery. The Hendrick Arnold–Bertha Tryon Cemetery in Bandera, Texas, is named in his honor. A Texas state historical marker in San Antonio commemorates the Siege of Bexar and notes the contribution of Arnold, "free Negro & scout," to the Texas Revolution. The present-day Landmark Inn State Historical Site near Castroville, Texas, is located near the area where Arnold is believed to have settled near the Medina River.

Further Reading
Barr, Alwyn. *Black Texans: A History of African Americans in Texas, 1528–1995* (1996).
Jenkins, John, ed. *The Papers of the Texas Revolution, 1835–1836* (1973).
Schoen, Harold. "Free Negro in the Republic of Texas: The Free Negro and the Texas Revolution," *Southwestern Historical Quarterly* 40, no. 1 (July 1936).
Willett, Donald, and Stephen Curley. *Invisible Texans: Women and Minorities in Texas History* (2005).
                                        JACK BORDEN WATSON

ARNOLD, James (15 Feb. 1901–8 Nov. 1968), singer and guitarist known as "Kokomo," was born in Lovejoy Station, Georgia, a small railroad town in Clayton County, approximately twenty-five miles south of Atlanta. He was raised on a farm and learned some guitar from a relative named John Wigges, who was an accomplished knife-style guitarist. In 1919 Arnold moved to Buffalo, New York, where he

worked in a steel mill. After stops and similar jobs in Pittsburgh, Pennsylvania, and Gary, Indiana, Arnold moved to the Mississippi Delta in the late 1920s. He reportedly made a living as a bootlegger and throughout his life regarded his music as a sideline. He lived for a while in Glen Allan, Mississippi, and played with a partner named Willie Morris.

In 1930 Arnold made his recording debut as "Gitfiddle Jim" in a Memphis recording session for Victor. The two songs, "Rainy Night Blues" and "Paddlin' Madeline Blues," displayed the kinetic and speedy style for which he became known. "Rainy Night Blues," with its characteristic riff, presaged the classic "Dust My Broom." Arnold was a left-handed guitarist and often hummed while executing his manic slide runs.

Arnold settled in Chicago in the early 1930s, again taking jobs in steel mills. "Kansas" Joe McCoy recommended him to the Decca producer Mayo Williams. Arnold's first Decca recordings in 1934 produced a rare occurrence in blues: a double-sided hit. "Milk Cow Blues" and "Old Original Kokomo Blues" became Decca's first significant blues successes since 1930. Both songs were immeasurable influences on many blues and country artists who followed. A few of the most notable examples were ROBERT JOHNSON in his "Milk Cow Calf Blues," and Elvis Presley in his cover of the same piece in his original Sun Records sessions. Robert Johnson also adapted "Kokomo Blues" into his "Sweet Home Chicago."

Arnold's records sold very well and were widely heard throughout the South. Previously the recordings of important male blues singers such as SKIP JAMES and SON HOUSE enjoyed only modest and mostly regional success and were not appreciated on a wide scale until many years later. By comparison, Arnold's records were wildly successful immediately. His style was informed partly by the jazz music of the 1920s, with his deft slide guitar flourishes hinting at melodies from the great female singers and trumpeters of that era. Arnold was also influenced by the popular hokum bands of the time, and his slide playing could impart humor and a kazoo-like characteristic. It is probably no coincidence that there are similarities in his guitar playing to that of Hudson Whitaker, better known as TAMPA RED, who was also born and raised in Georgia.

Arnold made many records and tended to repeat themes and styles, as did many blues artists with great bodies of work. His living in several locales in the North allowed him to absorb the sophisticated jazz stylings of the cities and develop an articulation and wordplay in his singing not usually heard in blues singers in the South. His move to the Delta added grit and depth to his music before he finally settled in Chicago.

Arnold's influence on the great blues singers who followed cannot be overstated. Though he is largely unknown by many of today's blues fans, Arnold was a major influence on many great artists and provided both musical and lyrical archetypes. The "Dust My

Broom" lick alone shaped the career of ELMORE JAMES, who adapted it from Robert Johnson, who borrowed it from Arnold. Such borrowing was one of the great traditions in the blues. A version of "Kokomo Blues" was first recorded by Scrapper Blackwell in the late 1920s. For his own hit version of the song, Arnold supposedly adopted "Kokomo" from the brand of coffee; "Kokomo" also became Arnold's nickname. Arnold was strongly influenced by the singer and guitarist TOMMY JOHNSON.

Lyrically, there are many themes and word combinations heard in Arnold's songs that have made their way into the blues lexicon. A few examples are "I believe I'll dust my broom," asking for water and getting gasoline, and rolling and tumbling. Perhaps the most startling is the "Smokestack Lightning" reference heard in his version of "Stop, Look, and Listen," which also features a kind of yodeling. Certainly these topics and tactics were not lost on subsequent blues legends such as Robert Johnson, HOWLIN' WOLF, MUDDY WATERS, Elmore James, and MISSISSIPPI FRED MCDOWELL. Arnold's lyrics could be quite wry, and he adapted his "Dirty Dozens" from the traditional put-down songs called the "twelves." In addition to deep blues and novelty songs Arnold also recorded the interesting "Sissy Man Blues," in which the singer laments his willingness to settle for a "sissy man" if no woman can be found. This was surely a topic not often sung about.

Arnold's music was also widely heard by white country and hillbilly artists in the 1930s and influenced the burgeoning western swing style. The Decca recording artist Johnny Lee Wills, brother of Bob Wills, may have been the first to cover "Milk Cow Blues." Bob Wills himself later went on to cover the song, and his composition "Brain Cloudy Blues" owed much to the song. "Milk Cow Blues" became a staple in the hillbilly and rockabilly canon and has been recorded by many famous artists, including Presley, Ricky Nelson, and rock groups like the Kinks and Aerosmith, to name but a few.

Mayo Williams proceeded to record Arnold's catalog over the next four years, from 1934 to 1938. Arnold became embittered after recording some eighty-nine titles for Decca for very low fees. Thirty-eight songs were released, and Arnold received little in the way of royalty payments even though his records generated significant revenue for Decca. He left the label in 1938 and never recorded again. He played off and on in Chicago clubs until the late 1940s. When French researchers tracked him down in 1959, Arnold was working as a janitor at a steel mill and was reluctant to discuss his blues past. Arnold had never really wanted to make records and sought to live a simple life. He understood the temporal nature of the world and was not interested in the glitter and glamour. There are reports of his playing sporadically into the 1960s in Chicago. Kokomo Arnold's fast and rhythmic slide guitar playing, exuberant vocal styles, and prodigious output of recordings from 1934 to 1938 strongly contributed to the foundations of many of the giants of blues, country, and rock and roll who followed. This music would be strikingly different without his deep influence.

Further Reading

Calt, Stephen. Liner notes for *Bottleneck Guitar Trendsetters of the 1930s* (1992).
Harris, Sheldon. *Blues Who's Who* (1979).
Killian, Klaus. Liner notes for *Old Original Kokomo Blues* (1999).
Palmer, Robert. *Deep Blues* (1981).
Russell, Tony. *Blacks, Whites, and Blues* (1970).

Discography

Bottleneck Guitar Trendsetters of the 1930s (Yazoo Records L-1049).
Old Original Kokomo Blues (Wolf Records BC001).

MARK S. MAULUCCI

ARNOLD, Juanita Delores Burnett (27 July 1909–21 March 2005), schoolteacher and activist, was born in Tulsa, Oklahoma, the daughter of Eugene Lawrence Burnett, an oil worker, and Mary Jane McGowan Burnett, a seamstress. As a youth, Burnett survived the Tulsa Race Riot of 1921 and was a plaintiff in the subsequent legal case, *Alexander v. State of Oklahoma*. Burnett grew up in the Greenwood neighborhood of Tulsa, Oklahoma. In the early twentieth century, as Tulsa's economy boomed thanks to oil recently discovered in Oklahoma, Greenwood was a thriving enclave of African American businesses, schools, and churches. Her grandparents lived in Tulsa; her grandfather owned a grocery store and his family home. In a span of just a night and a day, from 31 May–1 June 1921, the lives and livelihood of the Burnett family and the Greenwood community were threatened when the Greenwood section of Tulsa was devastated by the Tulsa Race Riot.

Racial tension within Tulsa had been building for many years before the riot. Although the city's prosperity had earned it the nickname "Oil Capital of the World," Tulsa was rife with conflict surrounding the influx of immigrants and uneasy relations between prosperous African American business owners and poor white laborers. As in many cities across the United States during this period, the Ku Klux Klan was active in Tulsa, and African American residents of Greenwood were well aware of the constant threat of violence and retaliation. The riot was sparked by the publication of a front-page editorial in the *Tulsa Tribune*. The editorial accused a nineteen-year-old black shoeshine boy named Dick Rowland of assaulting Sarah Page, a white teenage girl, in the elevator of a building in downtown Tulsa—charges that were later dropped. Although the *Tribune* editors removed the article after the paper had run a few hundred copies, the inflammatory headline, "Nab Negro for Attacking Girl in Elevator," had already done its damage. When Tulsa police arrested Dick Rowland, a mob of thousands of white people thronged the courthouse ready to lynch the accused. A group of armed African American men gathered to protect

Rowland from mob vigilantism, a shot was fired, and the riot began.

In her oral account of the riots, recorded in 1999 by Eddie Faye Gates, an activist and member of the Tulsa Reparations Committee, Arnold recalled the growing anger and fear among African Americans in Greenwood as armed white men began to roam up and down her street. Many carried torches made from oil-soaked rags, which they used to set fire to homes and businesses. These men, Arnold believed, were "especially jealous of men like my father and grandfather who had nice homes and businesses." Her father was among the group of men who armed himself, ready to defend his family and his home. One white man whom Eugene Burnett had ordered off his property returned the next day, ready for further confrontation—but by that time, the Burnett family, along with many others, had fled northward to safety. As they did so, her parents assisted wounded and elderly black men and women who had fallen behind. Her grandfather's grocery store was spared with the help of several white salespeople who were also regular customers of the store. On 1 June 1921, they came to the store intending to guard it, warning the mob as it approached to stay away. According to Arnold's recollection, the men warned, "The man who owns this store is a good man. He worked hard for his property. He has done you and no one else any harm. You *will not* destroy the efforts of this man's hard work" (Gates, 1999).

Arnold's grandfather was one of the few lucky ones. The mob destroyed more than a thousand homes and business in the Greenwood area during the riot, leaving thousands homeless. The Burnett family home was among those destroyed. Estimates of the death toll from this, one of the worst race riots in U.S. history, have varied; once conservatively estimated at around one hundred, some historians now believe that at least several hundred people, mostly African American, were killed. Many of the victims were buried in unmarked mass graves.

After the riot, victims' attempts to seek legal justice met with stiff resistance from Tulsa's government, and the Ku Klux Klan further stifled any dissent. It was not until 1997, with the creation of the Tulsa Race Riot Commission, that the Oklahoma State government began to investigate the riot. The Commission gave its final report to the Tulsa City government and the Oklahoma governor and state legislature in 2001. The report recommended that five reparations be granted to the community of Greenwood, the survivors of the riot, and their descendants. These included reparation payments to survivors; reparation payments to survivors' descendants; the establishment of a scholarship fund for students affected by the riot; the creation of an economic development enterprise zone in the Greenwood District; and finally, the creation of a memorial and the reburial of human remains found in unmarked graves.

The Tulsa Reparations Coalition (TRC), an activist group that formed in 2001, took up the cause on behalf of the survivors to ensure that reparations would indeed be granted. On 24 February 2003, Juanita Arnold—along with more than one hundred other survivors—served as a plaintiff in *Alexander vs. State of Oklahoma*, a suit filed against the state of Oklahoma, the city of Tulsa, the chief of police of the city of Tulsa, and the City of Tulsa Police Department. However, despite the efforts of the TRC legal team, headed by Harvard Law professor Charles Ogletree, the drive to secure reparations was an uphill battle. On 9 March 2005, after a series of failed appeals and subsequent state court dismissals made on the grounds that the statute of limitations for filing complaints about the riot had passed, the TRC submitted a petition to the U.S. Supreme Court. On 16 May 2005, the U.S. Supreme Court dismissed their suit without comment.

Despite these setbacks, the fight has continued. In March 2007, Charles Ogletree appeared before the Inter-American Commission on Human Rights to file a petition on behalf of the survivors. The City of Tulsa, which had by this time established a Human Rights Commission, was also debating whether to build a Tulsa Race Riot museum. Greenwood itself experienced a slow economic rebirth, evidenced by several commercial establishments and churches, but the district has not recaptured its former economic success. However, with the help of people like Juanita Delores Burnett Arnold and other survivors of the Tulsa Race Riot, the Greenwood Cultural Center, built in the early 1970s, now helps preserve the memories of the place once known as the "Negro Wall Street of America."

Further Reading

Brophy, Alfred. *Reconstructing the Dreamland: The Tulsa Race Riot of 1921, Race Reparations, and Reconciliation* (2002).

Ellsworth, Scott. *Death in a Promised Land: The Tulsa Race Riot of 1921* (1982).

Gates, Eddie Faye. *Oral History Accounts of the Tulsa Race Riot of 1921 by Black Survivors*, http://www.tulsareparations.org/JArnold.htm (1999).

Madigan, Tim. *The Burning: Massacre, Destruction, and the Tulsa Race Riot of 1921* (2001).

ANDREA A. BURNS

ARRINGTON, Richard, Jr. (19 Oct. 1934–), mayor and educator, was born in rural Livingston, Alabama, to Richard Arrington Sr. and Ernestine Bell, sharecroppers. In 1940, when his father found work in a steel mill, the family moved to Fairfield, a suburb of Birmingham, Alabama. At Fairfield Industrial High School, Arrington took an interest in the study of history and also learned dry cleaning, a practical skill that he later used to finance his college education. In 1952, during his sophomore year at Miles College in Birmingham, he married his high school sweetheart, the former Barbara Jean Watts. Two influential professors persuaded him to major in biology, and he graduated with a bachelor's degree in 1955.

He went on to earn his master's degree in Biology in 1957 at the University of Detroit and in 1966 completed his PhD dissertation, "Comparative Morphology of Some Dryopoid Beetles," at the University of Oklahoma, where his popularity among zoology students and faculty, as well as his academic excellence, earned him the Ortenburger Award. He began teaching biology at Miles College in 1957 and became chairman of the department of natural science and academic dean. He also had part-time teaching appointments at the University of Oklahoma and the University of Alabama. From 1970 to 1979 Arrington was director of the Alabama Center for Higher Education (ACHE), an organization funded by the Ford Foundation that sought to enhance educational programs at the state's eight historically black colleges and universities.

Social reforms pushed by protesting blacks, as well as legislative measures like the 1965 Voting Rights Act to redress past discrimination, set the stage in Birmingham—the largest southern city where white resistance to desegregation seemed fiercest—for a black to attempt to become the city's first African American mayor. Arrington's high visibility in the black community, his record of accomplishment at Miles College and at ACHE, and his involvement in civic organizations moved his name to the top of the list of potential political candidates to represent the large and growing black population of Birmingham. These blacks, along with many whites, wanted to shed Birmingham's tarnished image and refashion the city as a modern urban place where opportunities in its expanding health-care, education, telecommunications, banking, and finance sectors pointed to a brighter future.

Initially contacted by a group of young men hopeful that he would agree to run for mayor, Arrington flatly rejected their proposal but later decided that a run for a seat on the city council was more feasible. Capitalizing on the voters' desire for a new generation of black leaders not handpicked by the white power structure, Arrington was easily elected to the city council in 1971 as its second black member and was reelected to a second four-year term in 1975. Arrington championed affirmative action in government hiring and contracts, as well as efforts to check police brutality—issues of greatest priority to his black constituency. Perceiving that he had a more realistic chance of capturing the mayor's office, in 1979 he won an extremely close election, thanks in part to carrying ten percent of the city's white vote. Thus Arrington became Birmingham's first African American mayor.

Over the next two decades, from 1979 to 1999, Arrington presided as mayor of Birmingham, a city's whose population grew increasingly black as whites retreated to the suburbs. He won reelections by delivering on his promise to increase substantially the number of blacks employed in city government—by the mid-1990s twelve of his twenty-three department heads were black, as were half of all city employees—

and to ease tensions between the black community and the police. Throughout his tenure as mayor Arrington enjoyed good relations with the city's predominantly white business community, which also helped to facilitate Birmingham's makeover as a progressive "New South" metropolis with a diverse and balanced economy, a far cry from the bygone era of dingy steel mills, shotgun houses, stifling racial segregation, and white racial hegemony.

There was, however, a low point in Arrington's twenty-year reign as mayor. Repeatedly accused of corruption and cronyism, in 1992 he was investigated for allegedly receiving a kickback of five thousand dollars from a Georgia architect and spent a night in jail for temporarily refusing to provide records related to the case. His critics also contended that Arrington failed to bridge the racial divide between blacks and whites in the city and that he was unable to attract businesses to its long-suffering downtown.

Arrington's 1985 address at the honors convocation at the University of Alabama at Birmingham (UAB) confirmed his appreciation of the history of the region and revealed his ambitious vision of the city's role in the New South. Reflecting on the strides that the city had made since the church bombings and street demonstrations of the 1960s, he told his audience, "we have tried never to move forward on a particular issue without being mindful of the lessons of our past. . . . The shifting and sharing of political power among all the people of this community has been a remarkable story in itself " (Arrington, 9).

Eventually the majority of city council seats were held by people loyal to Arrington. Hoping to ensure that his handpicked ally William Bell would succeed him as mayor—and with the endorsement of the Jefferson County Citizens Coalition (JCCC), the once-powerful local organization of black Democrats that he created in 1977—Arrington resigned in July 1999, three months before his term as mayor was due to expire. Bell, however, lost his bid to replace the long-serving mayor, and a new generation of black leaders—not as dependent on bloc voting and racial solidarity—began to take control of the city.

In the fall of 1999 Arrington commenced teaching as a visiting professor at UAB and worked on metropolitan planning and service projects at the university's Center for Urban Affairs. Perhaps to revitalize his faltering political machine (the JCCC) and to sway upcoming city council elections, in the summer of 2001 Arrington announced his intention to run for a sixth term as mayor, but shortly thereafter he dropped out of the race and quietly retired from the political scene.

Further Reading

Arrington, Richard, Jr. *Birmingham: The Reality of a New South Experience* (1985).

Franklin, Jimmy Lee. *Back to Birmingham: Richard Arrington, Jr., and His Times* (1989).

ROBERT FIKES JR.

ARROYO, Martina (2 Apr. 1936–), opera singer and college professor, was born in New York, the second child of Demetrio Arroyo, a mechanical engineer who moved to the United States from Puerto Rico at eleven years of age, and Lucille Washington Arroyo, a Charleston, South Carolina native. Her father studied engineering at the University of Florida and worked at the Brooklyn Navy Yard. With the exception of piano lessons from her mother and occasional singing at church, Arroyo received very little musical training during her childhood. Her family, however, ensured that films, concerts, plays, and other performances were a part of her upbringing.

After completing junior high school, Arroyo attended the Hunter College–operated special high school for gifted children. Her interest in opera, which took root during those years, developed from her experience with the Hunter College Opera Workshop. Upon listening to her performance of the "Jewel Song," a piece from Gounod's *Faust*, the workshop's director, Joseph Turnau, recognized potential in Arroyo. He introduced her to Thea Dispeker, who later became her manager, and Madame Marinka Gurewich, who would become and remain her voice teacher.

After graduating from Hunter High School, Arroyo proceeded to Hunter College, where she majored in romance languages and comparative literature. She graduated in 1954. Through the work of a guidance counselor and Turnau, Arroyo received special permission to enroll in Hunter's opera workshop, an opportunity not generally accorded undergraduates. During this time she began to attend Metropolitan Opera performances, particularly those of her favorite soprano, Renata Tebaldi.

Realizing that opportunities for African Americans in opera were limited, Arroyo prepared to be a teacher. Her musical aspirations, however, continued. While teaching high school in the Bronx, she took graduate courses at New York University, and continued her musical studies in the Hunter College Workshop and with Gurewich. Finding her schedule overwhelming, Arroyo, after one year of teaching, became, for two years, a caseworker for the New York City Welfare Department.

Arroyo had two careers at the Metropolitan Opera. The first one began on 14 March 1959, and ended on 2 January 1962; her second began on 6 February 1965. During her first career she sang comprimario and minor roles beginning with the offstage celestial voice in Verdi's *Don Carlo*. Other comprimario and minor roles were the third Norm and Woglinde in Wagner's *Götterdämmerung*, Woglinde in Wagner's *Das Rheingold*, Orlinde in Wagner's *Die Walküre*, and Forest Bird in Wagner's *Siegfried*. Arroyo's second career at the Metropolitan began when Rudolf Bing asked her, on two days' notice, to replace an ailing Birgit Nilsson in the title role of Verdi's *Aida*. Arroyo's success in this performance secured for her, the next day, a contract to perform major roles at the house.

Thanks to this classification, after *Aida*, she did thirteen major roles: Elisabetta in Verdi's *Don Carlo*; Cio-Cio-San in Puccini's *Madame Butterfly*; Leonora in Verdi's *Il Trovatore*; Elsa in Wagner's *Lohengrin*; Amelia in Verdi's *Un ballo in maschera*; Donna Anna in Mozart's *Don Giovanni*; Liu in Puccini's *Turandot*; Santuzza in Mascagni's *Cavalleria rusticana*; Elvira in Verdi's *Ernani*; Leonoro in Verdi's *La forza del destino*; Lady Macbeth in Verdi's *Macbeth*; Gioconda in Ponchelli's *La Gioconda*; and Maddalena in Giordano's *Andrea Chénier*.

Arroyo has also performed with the Vienna State Opera, Hamburg State Opera, Covent Garden, Teatro Colón in Buenos Aires, Argentina, Deutsche Oper Berlin, San Francisco Opera, Paris Opera, Lyric Opera of Chicago, San Diego Opera, Pretoria Opera in South Africa, Miami Opera, La Scala, and Canadian Opera Company. Roles performed away from the Metropolitan included Amelia in Verdi's *Simon Boccanegra*, Elena in Verdi's *I vespri siciliani*, Magna in Puccini's *La Rondine*, and the title roles in Puccini's *Tosca* and *Turandot*.

Arroyo performed in concert with the world's great orchestras and conductors. She was soloist with the New York Philharmonic for the world premiere of Samuel Barber's *Andromache's Farewell*, a work she subsequently introduced in Europe. She performed Karlheinz Stockhausen's *Momente* in Cologne and again with the Buffalo Philharmonic, Stockhausen conducting. She also premiered William Balcom's *Simple Stories*, performed in recital both nationally and internationally, and did master classes at the Salzburg Mozarteum and the Music Academy of the West.

Arroyo not only helped to open doors for other African Americans in opera, she became one of the first African American women to attain a high level of visibility in the lyric theater. While the social and political upheaval of the civil rights movement produced a community of African American women singers in opera, the movement did not produce a similar community of African American male singers who attained a high level of visibility in opera. Unlike that of their female counterparts, the African American male experience in opera is a story of individuals.

Arroyo was a six-term member, appointed by President Gerald Ford, of the National Endowment of the Arts and a member of the Carnegie Hall Board of Trustees. She remained a trustee emeritus of the Hunter College Foundation. She was inducted, in 2002, as a fellow of the American Academy of Arts and Sciences, and in 2004 London's Amici di Verdi awarded her the Verdi Medal in recognition of her many appearances in the United Kingdom. In the early years of the twenty-first century, Arroyo maintained studios at Indiana University, where she was a distinguished professor of voice, and in New York, where she taught the study and preparation of operatic roles under the auspices of the Martina Arroyo Foundation.

Further Reading

Abdul, Raoul. *Blacks in Classical Music* (1977).

Cheatham, Wallace McClain. "African American Women Singers at the Metropolitan Opera before Leontyne Price," *Journal of Negro History* 84 (Spring, 1999).

Gray, John. *Blacks in Classical Music* (1988).

Smith, Eric Ledell. *Blacks in Opera* (1995).

Southern, Eileen. *Biographical Dictionary of Afro-American and African Musicians* (1962).

Story, Rosalyn. *And So I Sing* (1990).

Turner, Patricia. *Afro-American Singers, an Index and Preliminary Discography of Opera, Choral Music and Song* (1977).

Turner, Patricia. *Dictionary of Afro-American Performers, 78 RPM and Cylinder Recordings of Opera, Choral Music and Song, c. 1900–1949* (1990).

WALLACE MCCLAIN CHEATHAM

ARTEMUS, John C. (1885–1964), carpenter, insurance agent, contractor and activist, was born in Edgefield, South Carolina in 1885. As a young boy, Artemus saw that discrimination and oppression was still very much alive in the South, even following Emancipation in 1865. His parents were sharecroppers; thus, they were subject to subordination through this system because it ultimately favored the owners of the land, not the workers. Although there were many important benefits to this agricultural arrangement, the sharecropping system was ultimately oppressive. Landlords exploited their positions by extending credit to the workers during times of bad weather and poor quality of crop and market price. The interest rates were often so high that workers were unable to pay them. Often, this meant landlords and sharecroppers were in much the same relationship as master and slave had been. It was precisely for this reason that Artemus grew up determined to fight for his family's welfare. However, when he confronted their landlord over unfair wages, he was evicted from his home.

Artemus moved to Columbia, South Carolina. Here, he worked a day job as a sales clerk while attending Benedict College at night. Benedict was founded in 1870 by the American Baptist Home Mission Society to provide an education to recently freed black Americans. While at Benedict College, Artemus learned the construction trade, specializing in carpentry and contracting. Artemus spent many years repairing homes and rental properties. He worked in neighborhoods across South Carolina—and across racial lines. He was one of the first black carpenters to work in white neighborhoods repairing homes.

Artemus eventually found a job as an insurance agent and assistant manager for North Carolina Mutual Life Insurance Company and stayed there for twelve years. However, after the Great Depression, he had cause to rethink his career. The numerous building projects undertaken under the auspices of the New Deal gave Artemus the chance to use his carpentry training. Artemus decided to try contracting in hopes that he could organize his own building projects. But, more importantly, he intended to hire other blacks as skilled labor. Unfortunately, black contractors were not eligible to compete for these new building projects. The exclusion of blacks in the job bidding process prompted Artemus to become one of the first black labor organizers.

Artemus, among others, organized Local 2260 of the United Brotherhood of Carpenters and Joiners to unionize blacks in the building trades in central South Carolina. First on Artemus's agenda was to fight for the rights of other black contractors. They fought for and won the inclusion of black union contractors and workers on major South Carolina construction projects. As the union's business agent and representative from 1939 to 1954 Artemus made sure that major companies, including DuPont, Fort Jackson, and other numerous housing contractors employed the skilled labor of black Americans.

While active in union organizing, Artemus also pursued a political agenda. A South Carolina court decision in 1947 opened up the primaries to black voters. In 1950 Artemus was the first elected treasurer of the Progressive Democratic Party, which was organized to enable blacks to participate in state and national elections. Artemus never stopped educating black voters on issues central to the elections. From 1952 until his death, he spent time as a poll manager helping acquaint black voters to the issues involved in voting.

His civil rights activism did not stop there. From 1951 to 1959 Artemus represented the black community as vice president at large of the South Carolina Federation of Labor Executive Board. His role was to oversee union actions and to maintain these actions under principles of justice and fairness. During this time there was still opposition to the integration of local union chapters. The responsibility of the Federation of Labor was to oversee this integration and ensure that black workers were offered the same choices as white workers. In 1963 Artemus's Local 2260 was responsible for breaking down many institutionalized racial barriers, eventually winning the integration of union locals. He died in 1964.

Throughout his life, Artemus fought for the civil liberties of black Americans. He never tired of teaching and proving that it was possible to overcome injustices. It was precisely because of the actions of individuals such as Artemus that the working environment in the South opened up to and incorporated contributions by black Americans.

Further Reading

African American Registry, retrieved from: http://www.aaregistry.com/african_american_history/1787/John _Artemus_an_ally_of_blue_collar_workers on August 12, 2007.

CHRISTINE SCHNEIDER

ARTER, Jared (27 Jan. 1850–1928), college president, educator, and minister, was born Jared Maurice Arter in Jefferson County, West Virginia, the son of

Jeremiah Arter, a slave and a miller by trade, and Hannah Frances Stephenson, a slave. When Arter was seven years old his father died in an accident at the mill. The plantation on which the family lived, the Little plantation, was located four miles from Harpers Ferry. In 1859 Arter witnessed the hanging of four men who participated in John Brown's raid at that city. This childhood memory sparked in him the desire to fight for equality; the schoolroom would be his battleground.

As a teenager Arter applied for a position as a bellboy, for which he would have to pass a test demonstrating his ability to read numbers. With help from his brother-in-law he mastered the skill sufficiently in one evening to pass the test. This accomplishment reinforced for Arter the notion that education would be his key to success. His desire to learn grew, and his mother seized the opportunity for Arter to receive an education and learn a trade by hiring him out to Mr. Ayers, a white businessman from New York, on the condition that her son receive academic instruction. Arter spent the next three and a half years working on a farm and learning basic skills in English. Within two years of completing his service, Arter had earned enough money to buy a house near Harpers Ferry for his mother, stepfather, and eight siblings.

In October 1873 Arter entered Storer College in Harpers Ferry (later part of Virginia Union University). The college was established under the Freewill Baptist doctrine and the Freedmen's Aid societies; it was the first African American college in West Virginia and had as its mission the training of African American teachers. While at Storer, Arter vowed to live a clean Christian life, abstaining from cigarettes, alcohol, and profanity. Shortly thereafter he received a license to preach. Arter spent the next six years at Storer teaching and studying. In 1879 he entered Pennsylvania State College as a freshman with William Adger; they were the institution's first African American students. In 1882 he entered Hillsdale College in Hillsdale, Michigan, as a sophomore and received a bachelor of philosophy degree in 1885. There he led a successful prohibition campaign to close a saloon in town and preached frequently on the subject of temperance. In 1887 Arter became an ordained gospel minister—which permitted him to complete the ecclesiastical duties of the Missionary Baptist denomination—and was hired as a teacher and minister at his alma mater back in Harpers Ferry. Arter stayed at Storer College for four years, setting the foundation for quality education. He married Emily Carter, a teacher, in 1890; they had three children.

In 1891 Arter entered the Chicago Theological Seminary and in 1894 graduated with a bachelor of divinity. He stayed in Illinois to pastor two Baptist churches, and in January 1895 he taught Latin, civil government, physics, and rhetoric at the American Baptist Home Mission Society. In 1900 Arter was asked to open a Bible school at the Cairo Mission, chartered as the J. S. Manning Bible School in Cairo, Illinois. The purpose of the school was to train men and women for missionary service. Emily Arter worked as an assistant teacher at the school.

In 1907 Arter experienced tragedies that tested his faith. His brother William died of pneumonia, two months later Emily Arter died after a long illness, and several months after her death their son Jared Jr. died from blood poisoning at the age of seven. Experiencing the deaths of three loved ones in such a short time caused Arter to reflect on his mission in life. In October 1907 Arter accepted the presidency of the West Virginia Industrial School Seminary and College in Hill Top.

From the beginning Arter motivated and inspired students and faculty. His leadership proved to be invaluable when the main building of the college burned in 1908. When Arter was asked what they should do, he replied, "Let us rise and build better" (Arter, 45). The day after the fire Arter gathered students, family, trustees, and the citizens of Hill Top for prayer, and they pledged that they would all persevere. In the interim, classes were held in a school that was once used to teach white children. A year after the fire Arter had procured fifty acres of land deeded to the college and five thousand dollars to begin reconstruction. In 1910 he married his second wife, the teacher Maggie Wall.

Arter oversaw the completion of a four-story brick structure before resigning in 1914. He stayed in the area to pastor the Baptist Church of Sun and to serve as principal of Fayetteville graded school until he was asked to return to Storer College Church, becoming pastor again in 1917. The church grew in membership, activity, and dues. Feeling that he had accomplished all he could, Arter retired on 9 October 1921. Shortly thereafter he was afflicted with a serious urinary tract infection, and although doctors told him that he needed surgery, Arter recovered and continued his works for education and benevolence until the end of his life.

Further Reading

Arter, Jared Maurice. *Echoes of a Pioneer Life* (1922).
Sernett, Milton C., ed. *African American Religious History: A Documentary Witness*, 2nd ed. (1999).
Mitchell, Henry H. *Black Church Beginnings: The Long-Hidden Realities of the First Years* (2004).

VALERIE A. GRAY

ARTIS, William Ellisworth (2 Feb.1914–1977), sculptor, ceramicist, and educator, was one of America's most prolific and respected three-dimensional artists in the mid-twentieth century. Born in Washington, North Carolina, to Elizabeth Davis and Thomas Miggett, he lived primarily with his father until the fall of 1926 when he relocated to Harlem and began living with his mother and her husband, George Artis. In New York he assumed the surname of his stepfather. He attended Haaren High School and went on to study sculpture and pottery at the AUGUSTA SAVAGE Studio of Arts and Crafts in the early 1930s, joining the ranks of JACOB ARMSTEAD LAWRENCE,

GWENDOLYN KNIGHT, ROMARE BEARDEN, Norman Lewis, and other notable artists whose initial studies included instruction under Savage. Artis was also a contemporary of his fellow sculptors SELMA HORTENSE BURKE and RICHMOND BARTHÉ, the latter the most exhibited and honored three-dimensional artist associated with the Harmon Foundation.

Artis won the JOHN HOPE Prize affiliated with the Harmon Foundation exhibition of 1933 for the terracotta *Head of a Girl,* which contributed to his receiving the Metropolitan Scholarship Award for Creative Sculpture to attend the Art Students League of New York in 1933–1934. At the league he studied with the French-born cubist sculptor Robert Laurent, a close colleague of the famed sculptor William Zorach, who also taught there. In 1935 Artis received a second John Hope Prize and went on to study at the Crafts Students League with Roberta Laber and at the Greenwich House Ceramic Center under Maude Robinson between 1936 and 1938. He was among the artists featured at the 1936 Texas Centennial exhibitions. Artis entered the New York State College of Ceramics in Alfred, New York, in 1940 for a year of instruction under Charles M. Harder and Marion L. Fosdick, after whom the Alfred University School of Art and Design Gallery was later renamed. Audrey McMahon of the College Art Association, who also served as regional director of the New York Works Project Administration/Federal Art Project, subsequently hired Artis to teach modeling and ceramics at the 135th Street branch of the YMCA in Harlem. He was later appointed director of the Boys' Work Department and instructed arts and crafts classes between 1937 and 1941; he also participated in a citywide mural project that targeted community centers and churches.

During World War II Artis served as a technical sergeant in the army, winning first prize in sculpture at the 1944 Atlanta University Annual Exhibition of Paintings, Sculpture, and Prints by Negro Artists of America while still enlisted. The prizewinning piece, *Woman with a Kerchief,* embodied the characteristics of the style for which he became well known—an elegantly executed head or bust of an unidentified subject with smooth, clean lines and serene expression. He received the prestigious Purchase Award from the International Print Society for his sculpture titled *African Youth* in 1945. Upon the completion of his military commitment, Artis received a Harmon Foundation Fellowship that subsidized brief residencies at six of the member institutions of the Historically Black Colleges and Universities (Spelman, Tuskegee, Talladega, Hampton, Fisk, and North Carolina Central) in the early months of 1946 to hold workshops demonstrating his ceramics techniques. That fall he reentered the ceramics program at New York State College for another year of study under Fosdick and Harder.

In 1947 Artis was awarded a Julius Rosenwald Fellowship to work at Tuskegee Institute and explore the use of Alabama clays in his ceramic work and to hold periodic open-studio sessions for student observation. He declined the opportunity, opting to briefly attend classes at Alfred University before enrolling at Syracuse University on the GI Bill. At Syracuse he came under the tutelage of the acclaimed Yugoslavian-born sculptor Ivan Meštrović and began to more vigorously explore abstract forms and functional adaptations in his work. Meštrović exposed him to Modernist techniques and composition and challenged him to investigate a range of visual stimuli, most notably contemporary documentary films. Artis moved away from production of busts and began creating works that referenced the entire human form, though not in an upright pose. He earned a BFA in 1950 and an MFA in Sculpture from Syracuse in 1951.

In the spring of 1947 he had received a second Atlanta University Art Annual Purchase Prize for a terra-cotta piece done in his signature style titled *Head.* Professional recognition continued in 1951 with his receipt of the National Sculpture Society Award and the Atlanta University Purchase Prize in Sculpture for a dramatic marble work of a crouched boy titled *Quiet One.* He spent a summer teaching on a South Dakota Native American reservation followed by one semester at Tuskegee Institute before matriculating at Nebraska State Teachers College, earning a second BA in art education in 1955. He did graduate study at Pennsylvania State University between 1956 and 1959, working concurrently during a portion of that time as associate professor of ceramics at Nebraska State Teachers College at Chadron from 1956 to 1965. His reputation continued to mount, and Artis won four additional Purchase prizes at Atlanta University over this period of time for *Head of Boy* in 1952, *Head of Young Lady* in 1959, *Young Mother* in 1962, and *Young Mother's Love* in 1963. In 1965 he received second prize in sculpture for *We Have Seen His Face.* Additionally, he won the annual Purchase Prize for a piece that was included in a group exhibition held at the Joslyn Museum of Art in Omaha, Nebraska, in 1962.

In the summer of 1965 Artis was hired by the metals specialist Alvin Pine to work at California State University, Long Beach, as assistant to the sculptor and Modernist jeweler Claire Falkenstein and the French sculptor of Polish origin Piotr Kowalski, two of the eight artists-in-residence awardees whose work was featured at that year's International Sculpture Symposium. Artis remained through the fall, continuing to assist both artists. The next fall he took a position as professor of art at Mankato State College in Minnesota, working there from 1966 until 1975. For his dedication and effectiveness as an instructor, he was named Outstanding Educator of America by the University of Minnesota in 1970, adding to the National Conference of Artists' Outstanding Afro-American Artist Award earned the same year. He was also presented with the Smith-Mason Gallery Award in 1971.

Over the course of his career, Artis received more than one hundred distinguished awards, commissions, and honors and had his work reviewed in *Time, Sculpture Review*, and the *Christian Science Monitor*. He was a member of several national professional organizations, including the American Ceramic Society, National Sculpture Society, National Art Educators Association, New York Society of Arts and Crafts, and College Art Association. His work appeared in more than thirty exhibitions including at the Museum of Modern Art, Whitney Museum of American Art, and High Museum of Art in Atlanta. Artis's work is in the permanent collections of many of the major art museums and galleries in the United States.

Artis was described by the artist Mary Parks Washington, a Spelman College student during the time Artis visited the campus and who was the subject of a bust he created around 1945, as hardworking, reclusive, quiet, and devoted to a male friend living in Paris. Artis died in 1977 of unknown causes.

Further Reading

Driskell, David Clyde. *Paintings by Ellis Wilson, Ceramics and Sculpture by William E. Artis* (1971).
Pendergraft, Norman E. *Heralds of Life: Artis, Bearden and Burke* (1977).
Reynolds, Gary A., and Beryl J. Wright. *Against the Odds: African-American Artists and the Harmon Foundation* (1989).

AMALIA K. AMAKI

ARTRELL, William Middleton (1836–28 Mar. 1903), temperance reformer, federal customs official, and educator, was born William Middleton Artrell, of one quarter African and three quarters European ancestry, at Nassau in the Bahamas. There Artrell benefited from a basic education on the British model, acquired experience as a schoolteacher, and became a staunch Episcopalian.

During the American Civil War the Bahamas prospered as a result of services to blockade runners, who transported British cargo in the short but dangerous voyage between the Bahamas and the Confederate coast. When the war ended, however, economic depression forced many Bahamians to seek work in the United States. In 1870 Artrell migrated to Key West, at that time a major port in Florida. Unlike most African Americans in the South, he had never been a slave. In 1870 Key West opened the Douglass School for African American children. Artrell became its first principal, and as a result he was sometimes called Professor Artrell. He was elected a Key West alderman in 1875 and received a patronage job as an inspector at the federal customs office in the following year.

From 1876 to 1885 Artrell received a series of promotions at the Key West customs office. In 1880 fellow Bahamians in Key West helped organize a petition against him, arguing that he was unpopular with local Republicans (this libelous charge was simply a tactic of his enemies). The Key West collector of customs indignantly rejected the charge against Artrell, saying it was "as false as it is malicious." Moreover, he

stated, Artrell was "the peer of any colored man in Florida." Three days later, leading African Americans in Key West convened at the Good Templar hall, with the Reverend Thomas Darley in the chair, to declare their "esteem" for the embattled Artrell (National Archives, Wicker to Lamphere, with attached report of the Darley meeting and cover letter). As a statistical and marine clerk in the customs office, Artrell's salary was $1,200. Later he was promoted to impost clerk at $1,500 per year.

Artrell is best known as a temperance reformer. A moderate drinker until late in 1874, he became a teetotaler and a prohibitionist. He came to believe that alcohol robbed black people of the opportunity for self-improvement and that the temperance movement offered them the possibility of escape from poverty and subjugation. He argues in a letter to the editor of the Philadelphia *Christian Recorder* that "the colored man cannot *afford* to waste his *time* and his *money* with drink. . . . It is highly necessary that the colored man should try and obtain riches in this world. It is a power for good, a lever that removes all obstacles." He adds, "There is no swifter way of obtaining it than by a temperate life" (10 Oct. 1878).

In 1875 Artrell applied to a fraternal temperance society called the Good Templars for a charter to organize a local lodge. Though blacks could always join Templar organizations in the northern states and overseas, Atrell was rejected by the southern white Templars because of his race. Reluctantly he instead organized a True Reformer fountain, a Jim Crow fraternal temperance society. Although he took office as assistant grand master of the grand fountain of Florida, Artrell rejected segregation in principle. In 1876, when a schism broke out in the international Good Templar organization, a British faction provided Artrell with a Templar charter. Liberated from the subordination to the southern white Templars, he appealed to biblical analogy to express his outrage: "Southern whites remind me forcibly of Pharaoh of old" (Artrell to J. G. Thrower, 15 Oct. 1876, in [Birmingham, England] *Good Templar's Watchword*, 27 Dec. 1876, quoted in Fahey, *Temperance & Racism*, 120). He did not exonerate the northern Templars. "The south, it seems, is willing to do all the dirty work, while the north quietly acquiesces." He added: "prejudice against the colored man is *the* great sin of the United States of America" (Artrell to editor, 16 Sept. 1878, in [Philadelphia] *Christian Recorder*, 10 Oct. 1878).

In 1878, having established a sufficient number of local lodges, African Americans organized a grand lodge of Florida, affiliated with the British faction of the Good Templar order. Although white Floridians were eligible to join, none did, so the grand lodge was segregated in practice, if not in theory. Artrell was elected grand worthy secretary, an office he occupied until 1884. The grand lodge was a small but durable organization with about a thousand members, equally divided between women and men, plus a small auxiliary for children. Most members lived at Jacksonville in the northeast, or at Key West in the far south of the state. In the latter city, Cubans organized a Spanish-speaking lodge. In 1883 Artrell represented Florida at an international Templar convention held in Canada. In 1884 Florida's *Journal of Proceedings* declared: "when our Grand Lodge has not been in session [Artrell] has been the Grand Lodge himself " (7–8). In that year Artrell's secretarial salary was $150.

When a Democrat entered the White House in 1885, Artrell lost his federal patronage job. As a result he left Key West for Jacksonville, where he taught and served as principal at a black school alternately called a graded school and Stanton Institute. While principal, he added an eighth grade. JAMES WELDON JOHNSON, one of his pupils, became well known as an African American intellectual. In his autobiography, he praised Artrell: "despite the fact that his education was not extensive, he actually knew what he was supposed to know and teach" (62). The job could not have paid much. Artrell concurrently worked as a tailor. During the yellow fever epidemic in 1888, he headed the Jacksonville relief society that aided African Americans. The general agent of the Slater fund said that Artrell "has done heroic service & won universal praise" (Garrison, 241).

After he moved to Jacksonville, Artrell headed the Templar grand lodge from 1885 to 1889. His election led to controversy with the supporters of his predecessor, Joseph E. Lee, a Republican politician, Jacksonville lawyer, and Baptist minister. In 1886 Artrell participated in the negotiations at Boston that reunited the British and American based Good Templar factions. He reluctantly accepted terms for reunion that included racial segregation. In the same year he served as director of the *Florida Templar* of Jacksonville, the only black-run temperance newspaper in the United States. Prestigious titles mattered less to Artrell than did the opportunity to recruit new members into his moral reform society. On one occasion he and wife endured a rain-soaked journey by steam ferry and mule-drawn dray to organize a small rural lodge at a Baptist church near Jacksonville, a winery expedition that ended with their return home at 2 A.M., only four hours before the Artrells began their next workday.

In 1894 James Weldon Johnson succeeded Artrell as Stanton's principal. At some point—the date is unclear, but 1897, when a new Republican president assumed office, seems likely—Artrell returned to Key West, where he resumed his career at the customs office. He held the office of deputy collector of the revenue until his death in 1903. He supplemented his government salary by working as a merchant tailor. His wife, Alexandrina Victoria Artrell, outlived him, and there is no record that they had any children.

Further Reading
Brown, Canter. *Florida's Black Public Officials, 1867–1924* (1998).
Fahey, David M. *Temperance & Racism: John Bull, Johnny Reb, and the Good Templars* (1996).
Fahey, David M. "The Good Templars and the African American Temperance Movement: W. M. Artrell of Florida," *Social History of Alcohol Review* 28.39 (1984).
Garrison, Curtis W. "Slater Fund Beginnings: Letters from General Agent Atticus G. Haywood to Rutherford B. Hayes," in *Journal of Southern History*, vol. 5, no. 2 (May 1939).
Johnson, James Weldon. *Along this Way: The Autobiography of James Weldon Johnson* (1933).

DAVID M. FAHEY

ASANTE, Molefi Kete (14 Aug. 1942–), scholar and author, was born Arthur Lee Smith Jr. in Valdosta, Georgia. He was the first son of Lillie Wilkson, a domestic worker, and Arthur L. Smith, a railroad worker. The family grew over the years and eventually included sixteen children.

Valdosta, a small southern town also known as the Azalea City, was the arena in which young Arthur first saw the abuses and injustices suffered by black people under segregation. He picked cotton during the summer to help his family, a task representing for him not only the injustices of the present but also the awful, backbreaking conditions that his ancestors had to endure for hundreds of years during slavery. While shining shoes at age eleven, he was spat upon by a white man, an experience he would later recall in describing his growing determination to fight against racism.

Identified early in life as possessing exceptional intellectual capabilities, Arthur could read at age four and was sought after by many parents in his neighborhood to tutor their children. His intellectual gift created the opportunity for him to leave Valdosta at age eleven to attend the Nashville Christian Institute, one of few black boarding schools in the United States at the time. Upon finishing high school in 1960 he attended Southwestern Christian College for two years before graduating from Oklahoma Christian College in 1964 with a BA in Communication. He received an MA in Communication from Pepperdine University in 1965 and a PhD in the same field from the University of California at Los Angeles in 1968. The title of his dissertation was "Samuel Adams' Rhetoric of Agitation during the American Revolution." While still in college, in 1964, Smith published his first book, *Break of Dawn*, a collection of poetry. In 1966 he married Ngena Scarber, with whom he had one daughter, Kasina Eka. The marriage, however, ended in divorce in 1979.

In 1968 Smith embarked on his academic career, with his first appointment at Purdue University as an assistant professor of communication. He was there only a short time before being lured back to UCLA, where he became associate professor of communication and director of the Center for Afro-American Studies between 1969 and 1973. It was during those critical years that Smith co-founded the *Journal of Black Studies*, created the African American Library, and wrote the curriculum for UCLA's MA program in African American studies. In 1973 Arthur Smith legally changed his name to Molefi Kete Asante. Molefi, a Suto name, means "One who remains to keep the traditions after a great disaster." Kete ("One who loves music and dance") and Asante (a common West African name, which typically means "I told you to leave me alone but you would not"), on the other hand, were given to him personally by the late Asantehene of Ghana, Opoku Wari II. That same year Asante left UCLA to join the faculty at SUNY Buffalo, where he served as professor and chair of the department of communication until 1982. From 1977 to 1979 he chaired SUNY's department of black studies. While in Buffalo, Asante met his second wife, the dancer, choreographer, and scholar Kariamu Welsh, with whom he had one son, Molefi Khumalo. After twenty years, their marriage ended in divorce in 2001.

Asante's next academic appointment, to Temple University as chair of its department of African American studies in 1984, provided him with the space to develop and implement fully his vision for the study of African people, culminating in 1988 with the creation of the world's first PhD program in African American studies. Such an initiative represented enormous progress, because the field's academic legitimacy had faced constant challenges since its inception in the late 1960s. Temple's PhD program in African American studies became an instant success, attracting hundreds of students from within the United States and around the world.

The program owed much of its success to Asante's paradigmatic vision. In 1980 Asante had published *Afrocentricity*, the first formulation of a theory that made him both famous and controversial. Afrocentricity's most fundamental concern is the conceptual disenfranchisement and invisibility of African people worldwide as a result of European intellectual hegemony and racism. At the heart of the Afrocentric idea lies the assertion that African people must operate as self-conscious cultural agents, no longer satisfied to be defined and manipulated from without, but more in control of their destinies through a positive and assertive self-definition. The criteria for this self-definition must be drawn from African culture. At its core Afrocentricity is a theory concerned with African epistemological relevance.

This first book on the topic was followed by two major theoretical works, *The Afrocentric Idea* (1987) and *Kemet, Afrocentricity, and Knowledge* (1990), in which Asante further expanded his theory on the centrality of the African experience for the proper study of African people. In addition to these key works of Afrocentric scholarship, Asante authored or edited more than sixty books, including the first *Encyclopedia of Black Studies* (2005), as well as hundreds of articles and chapters in books. In 1997 Asante decided, both because of personal reasons and because of growing intradepartmental conflict and pressure from an administration eager to change the philosophical orientation of the department, not to seek reelection as chair of the department of African American studies at Temple University.

A popular lecturer, Asante spoke at more than a 130 university campuses in the United States. His work has been translated into several languages, including French, Portuguese, and Spanish, and he lectured in England, France, Japan, China, Malaysia, Brazil, the Caribbean, and Africa. In 2003 Asante was the special guest of the South African president Thabo Mbeki. In addition to being an extraordinarily prolific scholar, Asante was also active in the black community as both activist and educator. Consistent with his deep belief in the importance of children's textbooks, Asante authored *African American History: A Journey of Liberation* (1995), the first African American high school text written by a black person. Asante also served as an Afrocentric educational consultant for school districts across the United States, as well as sitting on the boards of several Pan-African organizations. In 1993 he was honored as a traditional king in Ghana: Nana Okru Asante Peasah, Kyidomhene of Tafo. In 2002 Asante married Ana Yenenga, an African Costa Rican. During the first part of the twenty-first century he became the preeminent mentor of graduate students in African American studies when he supervised more than seventy-five doctoral dissertations. In 2003 he was appointed to the African Union's Steering Committee for the Conference of Intellectuals of Africa and Its Diaspora. In 2004 he was inducted into the Literary Hall of Fame for Writers of African Descent.

Further Reading
Molefi Kete Asante's papers are housed in the Amistad Research Center, Tulane University.
Mazama, Ama, ed. *The Afrocentric Paradigm* (2003).
Ziegler, Diana, ed. *Molefi Kete Asante and Afrocentricity: In Praise and in Criticism* (1995).

AMA MAZAMA

ASBERRY, Nettie J. (15 July 1865–17 Nov. 1968), classical pianist, civil rights activist, and social worker, was born Nettie Craig in Leavenworth, Kansas, the daughter of William P. Wallingford, an immigrant farmer from England, and Viola, his former slave. In 1837, prior to Nettie's birth, Wallingford moved his family from Kentucky and settled on the Platte purchase in Missouri. He was married three times and fathered seventeen children including six by Viola. Nettie, the youngest of these, was the only one born free. Information is scarce about Viola. After she was emancipated she rejected Wallingford's name and adopted Craig as her surname, likely because she was born on the Craig plantation in Kentucky. She took her children to Leavenworth, Kansas, where she married Taylor Turner. Her occupation was listed as a domestic. She died in Denver, Colorado, on 29 September 1906 at the age of seventy-six.

Nettie Craig began studying the piano at eight years of age, showing remarkable ability, and later composed her own music. At thirteen she served as secretary for a Susan B. Anthony woman's suffrage and abolitionist club. Few women of any race were attending college when Nettie attended the University of Kansas: "It was virtually unheard of for a black girl to do so in the reconstruction era following the Civil War" (*Tacoma News Tribune*, 1977). Believed possibly to be the first black woman in the nation's history to receive a PhD in any field, Nettie was granted a doctorate of music from the Kansas Conservatory of Music and Elocution in Leavenworth, Kansas, on 12 June 1883. In the 1880s, after working as a music teacher, choir director, and organist in Kansas City, Missouri, and Denver, Colorado, Nettie and her family were among the early settlers in the black town of Nicodemus, Kansas, where she was a music and school teacher.

In 1890, during her work in Kansas, she met and married Albert Jones, about whom little is known. They traveled by train to Seattle, Washington, where she was the first organist and musical director for the First African Methodist Episcopal (AME) Church. At the age of ninety-six, Nettie recalled their arrival in Seattle: "News of the great Seattle fire in 1889 aroused a lot of interest in the Midwest. Many disposed of their belongings and moved to Seattle. We arrived amid much bustle and excitement. It was a good time of friendship and good neighborliness" (*Tacoma News Tribune*, 1963). In 1893, after three years in Seattle, Jones tragically died, although the details of his death are unknown. She returned to her old hometown of Leavenworth, Kansas, where she was organist and musical director of Bethel AME Church. She taught music to students in Kansas City. After a few years of residence in Leavenworth, Nettie moved to Tacoma, Washington, where she continued her activities as organist and musical director for Tacoma's First AME Church. She then married Henry J. Asberry, a well-known businessman and proprietor of the Tacoma Hotel Barbershop.

Asberry was active in the NAACP, establishing branches in Tacoma, Seattle, and Spokane, Washington, Portland, Oregon, and other cities in Canada and Alaska. Asberry submitted the Tacoma charter application to the New York office and in 1913 her group became the first NAACP auxiliary established west of the Rocky Mountains. For a time she served as regional field secretary and later as the local branch secretary.

In 1916, in response to the film "Birth of a Nation," Asberry drafted a letter to the Tacoma newspapers protesting the movie's release and its racist portrayal of African Americans. "My blood was at the white-heat point. Instantly I began to hiss in my feeling of resentment at the series of infamous lies. People turned around and stared at me, but I had lost my equilibrium; I was in a fighting mood. . . . No one can witness the production of this movie and be the same as before he saw it. No city can afford to have the equilibrium of its people disturbed" (*The Tacoma Ledger*, 1916).

Asberry was well known for her ambitious participation in statewide women's clubs. In 1908, she helped organize the Cloverleaf Club, an art club for the exhibition of needlecraft and artwork of black women in Tacoma and the surrounding county. These women were determined to be a part of the 1909 Alaska-Yukon-Pacific Exposition in Seattle, where the club's exhibition earned them a gold medal. A handmade Battenburg lace opera coat Asberry and her sister Martha Craig Johnson made for the exhibit won a bronze medal, as did ceramics and paintings contributed by Mrs. Hiram Moore-Baker. In 1917, she started a number of clubs, all of which became charter members of the Washington State Federation of Colored Women's Organizations. The preamble to the organization's constitution declared: "We, the colored women of the State of Washington and Jurisdiction, feeling the need of united and systematic effort along moral, physical, and intellectual lines, in order to elevate our race, do hereby unite into a State Federation" (Bragg, 123). Asberry served as president of the Federation and was also a member of the Progressive Mother's Club of Tacoma and the Tacoma Inter-Racial Council. In 1918, Asberry served as auxiliary chairman of the Allen African Methodist Episcopal Red Cross Auxiliary. She devoted much of her senior life to social causes and volunteered countless hours of social work to those who needed assistance. When the United States entered the World War, her auxiliary did a lot of work for the men overseas. After the armistice was signed at the close of the war Asberry received a badge with two crosses for her services. She did not intend to devote her life to teaching. Later in life she answered the call to the endless need for social work. She said that although many people think of social workers as highly paid, many social workers gave countless volunteer hours.

Asberry was a member of the Baha'i faith for twenty-five years, an organization devoted to the unity of humanity. In this spirit she pursued "harmony between the races" (*Tacoma News Tribune*, 18 April 1976). She applied the principals of music, including beauty of form, harmony, and expression of emotion, and used them in a broader sense to heal the world's ills. Asberry died at the age of 103. A year later, in memory of her musical accomplishments and community work, the mayor of Tacoma, A. L. Rasmussen, proclaimed 11 May Dr. Nettie J. Asberry Day. In November 2004, The Asberry Cultural Club celebrated its fiftieth anniversary.

Further Reading
The Nettie J. Asberry Papers are in Special Collections at the University of Washington Libraries in Seattle. These contain correspondence, bulletins, notes, and minutes kept by her various organizations.
Bragg, L. E. *More Than Petticoats: Remarkable Washington Women* (1998).
Taylor, Quintard, and Moore, Shirley Ann Wilson. *African American Women Confront The West, 1600–2000* (2003).
Mumford, Esther Hall. *Seattle's Black Victorians 1852–1901* (1980).
Obituary: *Tacoma News Tribune*, 18 Nov. 1968.

ANTOINETTE BROUSSARD FARMER

ASHBY, Irving C. (29 Dec. 1920–22 Apr. 1987), jazz guitarist, was born in Somerville, Massachusetts, near Boston, the son of an apartment superintendent. His parents' names are unknown. The family was musical and closely in touch with the world of entertainment: "FATS WALLER used to come by the house all the time," Ashby told the writer James Haskins. Ashby taught himself to play guitar. At age fifteen he joined a band that played sophisticated arrangements for college dances, and, deeply embarrassed by his inability to read music, he began to learn chordal notation. He performed at a nightclub at Revere Beach while attending Roxbury Memorial High School. Ashby's abilities as a classical guitarist won him a scholarship at an open audition for the New England Conservatory of Music in Boston, but the school had no guitar teacher and thus the award went to the runner-up: "So that's the extent of my conservatory background—in and out the same day," he told the writer Harvey Siders (10). Having made his own ukulele at age twelve, Ashby helped to manufacture guitars at the Stromberg factory in Boston during a period when he was performing on a radio show on station WNAC.

When the guitarist CHARLIE CHRISTIAN came to prominence in 1939, he became the strongest influence on Ashby, who memorized all of Christian's recorded solos. While performing in Provincetown, Massachusetts, and planning to enter Boston University to study art and writing, Ashby accepted an offer to join LIONEL HAMPTON's band in California in fall 1940. Late in life Ashby regretted the move. He needed the money, but music was not his first choice for a career, and he felt—correctly, despite his considerable talent—that he never ranked with the greatest jazz guitarists. His recordings with Hampton include "Altitude" and "Fiddle-dee-dee," both from 1941. Sometime before the middle of that year he had an opportunity to play informally with Christian when the Hampton and Benny Goodman bands were staying at the same hotel in Chicago. Ashby left Hampton's band in 1942.

In Hollywood in January 1943 Ashby played in the group that accompanied Waller in the celebrated film *Stormy Weather*. Drafted, Ashby served in an army band. In 1946 he returned to Los Angeles, where he worked with the pianist Eddie Beal and participated in recording sessions as a sideman with the tenor saxophonist LESTER YOUNG, with the pianist André Previn (toward the start of Previn's career in jazz), with the bassist CHARLES MINGUS, and with the singers IVIE ANDERSON, LENA HORNE, and HELEN HUMES. He also sometimes participated as a leader. Around this time Ashby married Pauline (maiden name unknown), a schoolteacher; they had two daughters. He performed with the pianist ERROLL GARNER and the tenor saxophonist WARDELL GRAY at Gene Norman's Just Jazz concert in Hollywood in April 1947.

On 27 September 1947 Ashby replaced Oscar Moore in the singer and pianist NAT KING COLE's trio. After enjoying more than a year of touring, he encountered musical and personal problems early in 1949, when the conga and bongo player Jack Constanzo joined Cole's group. Ashby's best-known recording, "Bop Kick," is from this period, but unfortunately Costanzo's incongruous playing and Cole's new fascination with bop—a style to which Cole was unsuited—made this performance unsatisfying. Ashby nonetheless continued to admire Cole's talent greatly, and he stayed in the quartet through a European tour and the making of the film short *King Cole and His Trio*, both in 1950. Finally, around March 1951, Cole's gambling and tax problems provoked Ashby's resignation.

Ashby joined the bassist RAY BROWN in the pianist OSCAR PETERSON's trio for live performances, but Barney Kessel—who soon replaced Ashby in the trio—made studio recordings with Peterson late in 1951. Ashby recorded only a single session as Peterson's guitarist in January 1952. Among his work from this date is a solo in "Blue Moon." The highlight of Ashby's career came later the same year, when he joined Peterson, Young, ELLA FITZGERALD, and other stars for a European tour with Jazz at the Philharmonic: "That's what spoiled me; that's what ruined all other music for me" (Siders, 30).

Ashby then dropped out of the international and national jazz scene, with the exception of intermittent recordings—including sessions with the tenor saxophonist Illinois Jacquet (1955), the alto saxophonists EARL BOSTIC (1957) and WILLIE SMITH (1965), Peterson (1972), the pianist COUNT BASIE and the singer BIG JOE TURNER (1973), and the guitarist Mundell Lowe (1974)—and his own album *Memoirs* (1976). Ashby taught guitar in the Los Angeles area, worked in landscape design, and after moving to Perris, California, in 1969, delivered newspapers. His *Guitar Work Book* was self-published sometime in the early 1970s. He died at home in Perris.

Despite his doubts about his career, Ashby was a significant jazz guitarist who closely adhered to the model of Christian's innovative, single-note improvisational style—though unlike Christian, he also excelled as a chordal, rhythmic player.

Further Reading
Britt, Stan. *The Jazz Guitarists* (1984).
Siders, Harvey. "Irving Ashby: Playing with the Greats," *Guitar Player* 8 (Sept. 1974): 10, 27, 29–30.
Summerfield, Maurice J. *The Jazz Guitar: Its Evolution and Its Players*, 2d ed. (1980).
Obituary: *Los Angeles Times*, 2 May 1987.

BARRY KERNFELD

ASHE, Arthur (10 Jul. 1943–6 Feb. 1993), tennis player, author, and political activist, was born Arthur Robert Ashe Jr. in Richmond, Virginia, the son of Arthur Ashe Sr., a police officer, and Mattie Cunningham. Tall and slim as a young boy, Ashe was forbidden by his father to play football; he took up tennis instead on the segregated playground courts at

Arthur Ashe, on 1 July 1968, playing at Wimbledon as an amateur in the quarter finals against defending champion John Newcombe. (AP Photo.)

Brookfield Park, near his home. By the time he was ten years old he came under the tutelage of a local tennis fan and physician from Lynchburg, R. Walter Johnson. Johnson had previously nurtured the talents of ALTHEA GIBSON, who became the first African American to win Wimbledon, in 1957 and 1958, and his second protégé would prove no less successful.

Johnson was an exacting coach; he had his charges practice hitting tennis balls with broom handles to develop their hand-eye coordination. But his lessons extended beyond tennis; he also helped the young Ashe navigate an often hostile, segregated South. Johnson and Ashe's father (his mother died when he was six) instructed Arthur in the manners, discipline, and grace that would mark his carriage within and without the nearly all-white tennis world. When Arthur was fifteen, Johnson tried to enter him in an all-white junior tournament sponsored by the Middle Atlantic Lawn Tennis Association and held at Richmond's Country Club of Virginia, but the club refused his application. As a result, Ashe, who was ranked fifth in his age group in the country, was unable to earn a ranking from his own region.

In 1958 Ashe reached the semifinals in the under-fifteen division of the junior national championships. Soon afterward a tennis coach from St. Louis, Richard Hudlin, offered to take Ashe under his wing, and after completing his junior year in high school in Richmond, Ashe accepted. He moved in with Hudlin and his family and completed his schooling at Sumner High School in St. Louis, the alma mater of the African American comedian and activist DICK GREGORY. In 1960 and 1961 Ashe won the U.S. junior indoor singles title.

After graduating from high school, Ashe accepted a tennis scholarship to the University of California at Los Angeles (UCLA), where he became an All-American, led his college team to the National Collegiate Athletic Association championship, won the U.S. Hard Court Championship, and was named to the U.S. Davis Cup team. While at UCLA, he also spent time training with the tennis legends Pancho Segura and Pancho Gonzalez, who helped him develop the powerful serve and volley game that would become, along with his sheer athleticism, Ashe's trademark.

In 1965, while still in college, Ashe was ranked third in the world, and he beat the Australian Roy Emerson in five sets to win the Queensland championships at Brisbane, Australia. Graduating from UCLA in 1966 with a degree in Business Administration, Ashe entered a Reserve Officer Training Corps camp and finished second in his platoon for overall achievement at the end of the six-week course. He attained the rank of first lieutenant, serving in the military from 1967 to 1969. During this time he continued playing tennis, winning the U.S. Clay Court Championships in 1967. In 1968, while still an amateur and still in the U.S. Army, he defeated Tom Okker to win the first U.S. Open, one of the two most prestigious tennis tournaments in the world; with this victory he was ranked first in the world. Numerous wins followed, including three Davis Cups, the World Championships of Tennis in 1975 (a year in which he again became the world's highest-ranked player), and two additional Grand Slam championships—the Australian Open in 1970 and Wimbledon in 1975. At Wimbledon he became the first African American man to win at the All-England Club, beating Jimmy Connors. Ashe also won the doubles titles at the French, Australian, and Wimbledon championships.

John McPhee, whose book *Levels of the Game* (1969) chronicled Ashe's match with Clark Graebner, his opponent in the semifinal of the 1968 U.S. Open, considered Ashe a competitive genius. "Even in very tight moments, other players thought he was toying with them," McPhee wrote later in an appreciation piece in the *New Yorker* after Ashe's death. He continues:

They rarely knew what he was thinking. They could not tell if he was angry. It was maddening, sometimes, to play against him. Never less than candid, he said that what he liked best about himself on a tennis court was his demeanor: "What it is is controlled cool, in a way. Always have the situation under control, even if losing. Never betray an inward sense of defeat." And of course he never did—not in the height of his athletic power, not in the statesmanship of the years that followed, and not in the endgame of his existence.

Over the course of his career Ashe earned more than $1.5 million, becoming the sport's first black millionaire and one of his era's most visible African American athletes. Several companies, including Coca-Cola and Philip Morris, hired him to promote their products, and he worked for ABC television and HBO as a sports commentator. Ashe married Jeanne Marie Moutoussamy in 1977, and they had one daughter, Camera Elizabeth. In 1979, at the age of thirty-six, Ashe suffered a heart attack, which forced him to undergo bypass surgery and retire from playing competitive tennis. Still, one year after his operation he became the first and only African American to be named captain of the U.S. Davis Cup team, a position he held until 1985. Under his leadership the team won the international competition in 1981. In 1985 he became the first African American man elected to the International Tennis Hall of Fame.

Throughout his career and afterward Ashe spent considerable time and energy working for civil and human rights. He wrote eloquently about his complex position as a world-renowned success in a field dominated by whites; even as his moderation appealed to whites, he was occasionally criticized by more vocal black activists. "There were times, in fact, when I felt a burning sense of shame that I was not with other blacks—and whites—standing up to the fire hoses and the police dogs, the truncheons, bullets and bombs that cut down such martyrs as Chaney, Schwerner, and Goodman, Viola Liuzzo, MARTIN LUTHER KING JR., MEDGAR EVERS and the little girls in that bombed church in Birmingham, Ala.," he was quoted as saying in *The Black 100: A Ranking of the Most Influential African Americans, Past and Present* ([1993], 363). "As my fame increased, so did my anguish. I knew that many blacks were proud of my accomplishments on the tennis court. But I also knew that many others, especially many of my own age or younger, did not bother to hide their indifference to me and my trophies or even their disdain and contempt for me."

In 1973, after three years of trying, Ashe had received an invitation to play in the previously all white South African Open; twelve years later Ashe, the longtime friend of the still imprisoned Nelson Mandela, was arrested in South Africa for protesting apartheid. In 1992 he joined a group of protesters who were arrested in Washington, D.C., for objecting to the treatment of Haitian refugees by the George H. W. Bush administration. Ashe's concern for fairness and human dignity extended beyond race. In 1974 he helped found the Association of Tennis Professionals, a players' union, and served as president until 1979. He later became a board member of the United States Tennis Association, chairman of the American Heart Association, and a board member for the National Foundation for Infectious Diseases.

Always a bookish, thoughtful man, Ashe cultivated a second career as a writer and sports historian. Through his research, he managed to trace his own roots back ten generations on his father's side to a woman who, in 1735, was brought from West Africa to Yorktown, Virginia, on the slave ship *Doddington*. Ashe's benchmark three-volume history of black athletes in America, *A Hard Road to Glory*, was published in 1988.

Ashe suffered a number of serious health problems that ended his playing career but barely seemed to slow him down. He had a second heart attack in 1983, followed by emergency brain surgery in 1988; after the last operation rumors began to spread about his infection with HIV, the virus that causes AIDS. Although he kept his illness secret for nearly a decade, Ashe was forced to admit his diagnosis publicly when, on 7 April 1992, the newspaper *USA Today* threatened to print the story as soon as it could be confirmed. Because Ashe did not officially acknowledge his illness to the newspaper, he was able to put off publication of the story for a day and to inform friends, family members, and health officials of his condition. On 8 April, the day after *USA Today*'s initial phone call, Ashe held a press conference to break the news himself, reporting that the virus had been transmitted during blood transfusions associated with his second heart operation in 1983. The event prompted a worldwide outpouring of grief and a squall of commentary about the conflict between the press's responsibility to report the news and an individual's right to privacy. That year he helped raise $15 million for the Arthur Ashe Foundation for the Defeat of AIDS, and in part for this work he was named Sportsman of the Year by *Sports Illustrated*.

Ashe's death in New York City provoked a sense of loss that extended far beyond the boundaries of the tennis world or the borders of the United States. A memorial service held at the Richmond governor's mansion of DOUGLAS WILDER, the first African American governor of Virginia, attracted thousands of admirers from around the world. Wilder said that Ashe's "leadership may not be confined to athletics and sports alone, for he was totally committed to improving the lives of those yet to enjoy the full fruition of rights and opportunities in this country" (*New York Times*, 7 Feb. 1993).

Ashe's passing was mourned by many who saw in his example an unusual dignity and elegance, even in the face of a terrible disease. "Why, when we knew Arthur Ashe's health was precarious, did the news of his death from pneumonia last Saturday hit us like a ball peen hammer between the eyes?" wrote Kenny Moore in a cover story in *Sports Illustrated*. "Why did the announcement of this gentle man's passing force even the raucous Madison Square Garden crowd at the RIDDICK BOWE–Michael Dokes fight into unwonted reflection, never quite to return to the fray? In part, surely, we reel because, even with AIDS and a history of heart attacks, Ashe didn't seem to be sick.

He, of all men, hid things well. His gentility shielded us from appreciating his risk" (15 Feb. 1993, 12).

Further Reading

Ashe, Arthur, with Frank Deford. *Arthur Ashe: Portrait in Motion* (1975).
Ashe, Arthur, with Arnold Rampersad. *Days of Grace* (1993).
Ashe, Arthur, with Neil Amdur. *Off the Court* (1981).

McKAY JENKINS

ASHER, Jeremiah (13 Oct. 1812–27 July 1865), Civil War army chaplain and Baptist minister, was born in North Branford, near New Haven, Connecticut, to Ruel and Jereusha Asher. His paternal grandfather had been captured in the Guinea region of Africa at the age of four and was brought to America as a slave. Young Jeremiah grew up hearing fascinating tales of his grandfather's life, which included military service during the American Revolutionary War. Those stories would later inspire Asher in his own life.

Asher's father was a shoemaker who married a Native American woman from Hartford, Connecticut. Jeremiah grew up as a member of the only African American family in North Branford and was permitted to attend school along with white children. At the age of twelve he left school to help out his family financially, and over the next several years he worked as a farmhand, servant, and coachman. In 1833 he married Abigail Stewart of Glastonbury, Connecticut.

The young couple began their married life with much promise and soon joined the local Baptist church. After moving around Connecticut they eventually ended up in the Hartford area in 1839. His home church, the First Baptist Church of Hartford, was predominantly white and, as was the custom of the day, compelled African Americans to sit in segregated "Negro pews" during the worship service. White members had built a new pew for the congregation's black members, which Asher described as "the most objectionable one I had ever seen" (Asher, 44). The pew had high sides, about six feet tall, so that blacks sitting in it could not see, and perhaps more important, could not be seen. The black members were resentful but seemed reluctantly resolved to endure the new form of discrimination.

Asher, on the other hand, protested by boycotting church services, which encouraged other black members to do the same. That led the church to inquire why the black members were, in their words, "getting quite out of their place" (Asher, 45). Asher countered that they were not getting out of their place nor were they hard to please. Instead, they simply objected to the new pew and wished to sit in the gallery of the church. Writing later, he said, "I did not of course presume that black Christians had a right to sit below in their Father's house" (Asher, 45). Asher and other black members boycotted the church and, finally, after much going back and forth, the white pastor and

deacons met with Asher and black members in the private home of a black member. After hearing arguments from the blacks, the white pastor and deacons agreed to allow the blacks to sit "where they pleased in the galleries, and that was the end of this revolution" (Asher, 47).

Asher's experience in protesting the Negro pew led him to a deeper spiritual conviction and brought to light his leadership abilities. He went on to become a Baptist minister and helped to form a new church in Providence, Rhode Island. He served as pastor of that church for nine years, until he was called to Shiloh Baptist Church in Philadelphia. Shiloh was struggling financially, and so he determined to travel to England to raise money. With letters of support from other churches as well as the mayor's office, he set sail for Britain in 1849. Asher traveled across Britain, meeting with limited success initially, but eventually he was able to obtain support from local Baptist pastors. His British supporters encouraged him to publish an account of his life in order to raise more money, as well as to highlight racial prejudice in the United States. *Incidents in the Life of the Rev. J. Asher,* his autobiography, was published in London in 1850.

Asher's trip was a success, and he returned from England with enough money to pay off the church's debt. For the next eleven years he continued his work as pastor of Shiloh and served in various positions at the National Baptist Convention level. When the American Civil War broke out, Asher became interested in serving his country, much like his grandfather had done during the American Revolution. After Abraham Lincoln's Emancipation Proclamation went into effect on 1 January 1863, African Americans were permitted to join the Union army. No regular black officers were authorized, but provision was soon made for blacks to serve as chaplains. Although technically they were officers, they had no command authority and thus no possibility to serve over whites. Asher volunteered and was assigned to the Sixth United States Colored Infantry (USCT), one of only fourteen black chaplains to serve in the Union army.

The Sixth was sent to join the Army of the James in Virginia on 14 October 1863 and was put to work building fortifications around Yorktown. "The last month has been one of constant excitement and fatigue," Asher wrote. "The men having been working on the fortifications day and night, not excepting the Sabbath" (Redkey, 337). The Sixth eventually went on to see combat around Petersburg and Richmond. From an army hospital at Portsmouth, he noted, "There are in the hospitals here about five hundred sick and wounded colored soldiers . . . some few are without arms and legs." Wounded himself at the Battle of the Wilderness in May 1864, he spent time in the hospital recuperating.

Asher and the men of the Sixth were deployed to North Carolina and took part in the successful capture of Fort Fisher and the key port of Wilmington. From Wilmington they advanced into the interior of the state, joining forces with General William T. Sherman and participating in the capture of Raleigh and the surrender of General Joseph Johnston on 26 April 1865. In the aftermath of the war Asher and the men of the Sixth were assigned to occupation duty in the Wilmington area. He continued his chaplain duties and also helped the freedmen's schools teach the former slaves. Unfortunately, Asher soon fell victim to disease and died on 27 July 1865, the only black chaplain to die on duty. His remains were brought to Philadelphia, and he was buried at Olive Cemetery near Shiloh.

Further Reading
Asher, Jeremiah. *Incidents in the Life of the Rev. J. Asher* (1850).
Lamm, Alan K. *Five Black Preachers in Army Blue, 1884–1901: The Buffalo Soldier Chaplains* (1998).
Paradis, James M. *Strike the Blow for Freedom: The 6th United States Colored Infantry in the Civil War* (1998).
Redkey, Edwin S. "Black Chaplains in the Union Army," in *Civil War History,* vol. XXXIII, no. 4 (1987).

ALAN K. LAMM

ASHFORD, Emmett Littleton (23 Nov. 1914–1 Mar. 1980), baseball umpire, was born in Los Angeles, California, the son of Littleton Ashford, a truck driver, and Adele Bain. Ashford was two or three years old when his father abandoned the family, so he grew up under the strong influence of his mother, a secretary for the *California Eagle,* an African American newspaper published in Los Angeles. As a youth, Ashford exhibited the traits that marked him in adult life as a gregarious extrovert. At Jefferson High School he was a sprinter on the track team, a member of the scholastic honor society, and the first African American to serve as president of the student body and as editor of the school newspaper. He graduated from Los Angeles City College and attended Chapman College in nearby Orange from 1940 to1941. From 1944 until 1947 he served in the U.S. Navy.

Ashford began his umpiring career in 1941 by working recreation league, high school, college, and semiprofessional games. While in the navy in 1946, after hearing that JACKIE ROBINSON had broken the modern color line in organized baseball, Ashford first thought about an umpiring career and the possibility of reaching the major leagues. After the war Ashford added softball to his umpiring schedule and twice worked the National Softball Congress World Tournament. After the 1948 tournament—in which the team from Georgia initially opposed his presence on racial grounds but wound up insisting that he umpire the plate in the final game—he decided to give up his administrative job in the payroll and finance division of the Los Angeles post office to explore professional umpiring. With the assistance of the major league scout Rosey Gilhousen and after a four-game tryout in Mexico, Ashford was hired in July 1951 by the Class C Southwest International League, thereby becoming the first African American umpire in minor league baseball. He spent two seasons in Class C,

advanced in 1953 to the Class A Western International League, and in 1954 he reached the Class AAA Pacific Coast League (PCL), thanks to the support of the league president Clarence "Pants" Rowland, a former major league manager. Ashford spent twelve years in the PCL, three as umpire in chief (1963–1965), quickly becoming a favorite with fans because of his effervescent personality and flamboyant style. During the off-season he became the first African American to referee high school and college football and basketball games in southern California. He also conducted an umpiring clinic in Japan in 1958 under the auspices of the U.S. Air Force, and he umpired in the Dominican Republic winter league in 1959 and 1964.

After fifteen years in the minors, Ashford reached the major leagues at age fifty-one, when he was hired in September 1965 by the American League for the 1966 season. During a brief career terminated by the league's mandatory retirement of umpires at age fifty-five, he umpired the 1967 all-star game and the 1970 World Series. He retired in 1970, but he continued his umpiring activities by working Pacific Coast Conference college games, by serving as commissioner and umpire in chief of the professional-amateur Alaskan League, and by conducting clinics in Canada, Europe, and Korea. He also served from his retirement until his death as a special assistant to the commissioner of baseball, Bowie Kuhn, performing public relations duties on the West Coast. Married four times (1937, 1950, 1966, and 1979) and detached from his three children, Ashford never experienced the familial intimacy that he missed as a child.

Controversy dogged Ashford throughout his major league career. As the first African American to reach the major leagues in a capacity other than as a player, he received numerous threats and endured racial epithets. In addition, some fellow umpires criticized his flamboyant officiating style and resented his popularity with fans and sportswriters. Ashford's jocularity, his booming voice, and his exaggerated motions when making calls led many people to regard him as a clown who sacrificed judgment and accuracy for self-promoting showmanship. Others, especially some African Americans, considered his showboating to be a manifestation of a degrading STEPIN FETCHIT–like behavior that perpetuated negative stereotypes. Still others considered his elegant use of language, cultural interest in the arts and opera, and fashionable wardrobe (he wore cufflinks when umpiring) to be affectations intended to impress whites. Most pervasive were the charges that Ashford was a poor umpire who reached the majors solely to satisfy the civil rights advocates who championed his promotion.

The criticisms of Ashford, while not unfounded, were exaggerated. By the time that he reached the majors his umpiring skills had diminished, particularly when he called balls and strikes and when he followed batted balls into the outfield. But as some fellow umpires and Dewey Soriano, president of the PCL who had urged Ashford's promotion, argued,

Ashford was a hard-working, competent, thorough professional who was neither the best nor the worst in the league. Ashford's jovial demeanor, especially pronounced during arguments with players and managers, occasionally called to mind uncomplimentary racial stereotypes, but his personality was authentic, and his wit and charm facilitated his acceptance as a racial pioneer in sports officiating. His unconventional style clashed with the traditional conservative demeanor of veteran umpires, but it was natural rather than deliberate and presaged the more aggressive bearing and emphatic gestures that soon became the norm. Political pressures and the exigencies of the civil rights movement did boost his promotion, but his hiring had been long delayed by racist attitudes.

When asked why he gave up fifteen years of seniority with the U.S. Postal Service to become the first black umpire in minor and major league baseball, Ashford replied simply: "How many men go to their graves without ever doing what's in their hearts?" He was a courageous and determined man whose pioneering achievements spurred the racial integration of sports officiating at all levels of athletic competition. Even after his death in Los Angeles, Ashford, who always considered himself "an *umpire*, not a black umpire," achieved a historic first: his was the initial burial in the section of a cemetery in Cooperstown, New York, owned by the National Baseball Hall of Fame. In 1982 a Little League field in Los Angeles was named in his honor.

Further Reading
Gerlach, Larry R. *The Men in Blue: Conversations with Umpires* (1980).
Margulies, Alan. "The Entertainer," *Referee* (Sept. 1992).
Rust, Art. *"Get That Nigger Off The Field!": A Sparkling, Informal History of the Black Man in Baseball* (1976).
Obituaries: *Los Angeles Sentinel*, 6 Mar. 1980; *Los Angeles Times*, 7 Mar. 1980; *New York Times*, 4 Mar. 1980.
LARRY R. GERLACH

ASHLEY, Eugene, Jr. (12 Oct. 1930–7 Feb. 1968), Special Forces soldier in the Vietnam War and Medal of Honor winner, was born in Wilmington, North Carolina, the son of Eugene and Cornelia Ashley. Within a short time after the younger Eugene's birth, the family moved to New York City, likely to take advantage of greater opportunities for employment during the Depression years. Ashley graduated from Alexander Hamilton High School in 1948. With employment opportunities limited in the post–World War II era and meaningful jobs hard to come by, Ashley joined the United States Army on 7 December 1950.

During World War II black soldiers had fought in both the Pacific and European theaters in segregated units commanded by white officers. President Truman's 1947 Executive Order 9981, however, officially ended segregation practices in all branches of the U.S. armed forces. The tradition-bound services proved slow to change, and several years passed before actual practices were to comply with Truman's order. Even during the Korean War, African American soldiers like CORNELIUS CHARLTON fought for a time in segregated units. Indeed, Vietnam War soldiers, men like WEBSTER ANDERSON, Eugene Ashley, and thousands of other black enlisted men who entered the service in the 1950s would benefit from the social and racial changes made within the army at the very same time that the civil rights era was in full swing. African Americans gradually began to perceive service in the army as a desirable career choice.

Ashley's service in the army was varied both geographically and in the tasks he performed. Serving in Korea, Germany, Okinawa, and at several bases stateside, Ashley saw duty as an ambulance driver and infantryman. As he rose through the ranks, gained more training, and honed his skills, he worked as an antiaircraft gunner and later as a heavy weapons specialist, with experience in armor and airborne operations. In January 1968, his seventeenth year in the army, Ashley was sent to Vietnam as a sergeant first class, trained in operations and intelligence duties, and as operations sergeant in Special Forces (popularly known as the Green Berets) Airborne Detachment A-101, Company C, Fifth Special Forces Group, stationed at Camp Lang Vei under the command of Captain Frank Willoughby.

By the time Ashley arrived at Camp Lang Vei, the Americans' situation in Quan Tri province in South Vietnam had become perilous. Camp Lang Vei was located on Route 9 near the Laotian border, about six miles west of the marine base at Khe Sanh. A frontier outpost largely rebuilt by Captain Willoughby and his Special Forces detachment, it was first established in December 1966 and was said to have been ill-fated from the beginning. During the North Vietnamese assault and subsequent seventy-seven-day siege on the marine base at Khe Sanh, beginning on 21 January, Camp Lang Vei was in imminent danger, and subjected to mortar attack on 24 January 1968. By 6 February 1968, the camp was manned by twenty-four American Special Forces soldiers, with Sergeant First Class Eugene Ashley Jr. as lead intelligence sergeant, as well as fourteen South Vietnamese Special Forces (LLDB), a 161-man mobile strike force, nearly 300 Civilian Irregular Defense Group (CIDG) troops, and approximately 500 Laotian troops and civilians. The CIDG and Laotian troops often proved unreliable in battle, with the added danger that CIDG units were sometimes infiltrated by the North Vietnamese. The defense of Camp Lang Vei would fall primarily on the shoulders of the Green Berets, none more so than Eugene Ashley Jr.

Just after midnight on 7 February 1968, North Vietnamese Army (NVA) infantry and tank units began their assault on the outer perimeter of Camp Lang Vei—the NVA's first use of armor in the war. Despite a fierce defense on the outer perimeter by the mobile strike force and the destruction of three Soviet-built tanks, the NVA overwhelmed the perimeter defenders. Employing satchel charges, thermite and tear gas grenades, and flamethrowers, the NVA decimated the CIDG troops and within hours captured both ends of the camp. Outside the camp, Eugene Ashley lent support by directing mortar attacks, and when camp communications were cut, took on the added duty of directing air strikes on enemy positions using portable radio communications equipment. The NVA nearly succeeded in overtaking the underground command bunker using grenades and satchel charges. They also tried to bluff Captain Willoughby and the other defenders into surrendering by threatening to blow up the bunker; a number of LLDB men fell for this ruse, surrendered, and were summarily executed. The Americans remained and held the post. The defense of the camp was further imperiled when the Laotian troops refused to fight. Continuing to lead support efforts, Eugene Ashley mustered two Americans, Sergeant Richard Allen and Specialist Joel Johnson, and sixty Laotian troops to counterattack, but the effort failed when the Laotian troops bolted at the sound of NVA machine-gun fire. Joined by sergeants William Craig and Peter Tiroch, Ashley demonstrated determined leadership when he was able to muster more defenders who were retreating down Route 9, and attempted three more counterattacks on the command bunker. Each time, Ashley and his men were subjected to heavy machine-gun and automatic weapons fire, grenades, and satchel charges. Now close to his objective, Ashley led a fifth assault against the NVA; reflecting the legacy of the World War II Medal of Honor recipient Lieutenant JOHN FOX, Ashley directed air strikes against enemy forces very near to his own position. This final assault, combined with Ashley's directed air strikes, succeeded in driving the enemy off the high ground and thwarting the NVA attack. Later in the day, Special Forces commandos from Khe Sanh led a mission to reinforce Camp Lang Vei. The battle was over by late afternoon, with many of the wounded evacuated by marine helicopters. Sergeant First Class Eugene Ashley Jr., however, would not survive the attack. Severely wounded during his final assault, he was killed while being carried from the battlefield when an enemy mortar round landed nearby.

Ten Americans were killed or went missing and eleven were wounded in the battle that would later become known in Special Forces lore as "the night of the Silver Stars," so named because of the many Silver Star medals awarded to those who fought at Camp Lang Vei. However, the Silver Star was not the highest award earned for action at Lang Vei. Ashley was awarded the Medal of Honor for his resolute valor and the gallant charges that led to his death, and for saving many of his fellow soldiers. The Medal of Honor was presented by Vice President Spiro Agnew to Ashley's wife, Barbara, in a White House ceremony on 2 December 1969. Ashley is buried at Rockfish Memorial Park in Fayetteville, North Carolina. On 13 August 2001 the Eugene Ashley Jr. Memorial High School was dedicated in his honor in Wilmington, North Carolina.

Further Reading
Eugene Ashley High School. "About Ashley," http://www.nhcs.net/ashley.
Medal of Honor Citation. "Eugene Ashley, Jr.," http://www.aavw.org/served/homepage_ashley.html.
Phillips, William. *Night of the Silver Stars: the Battle of Lang Vei* (1997).
POW Network. *Bio, Hanna, Kenneth,* www.pownetwork.org/bios/h/h015.htm.

GLENN ALLEN KNOBLOCK

ASKIN, Luther B. (26 Dec. 1843–6 Apr. 1929), the first African American to integrate baseball, was born in Pittsfield, Massachusetts, the second son of Nelson Askin and Sarah Lloyd. In 1844 Nelson Askin moved to Florence, a mill village in Northampton, Massachusetts, to open a livery. Across the road was the Northampton Association of Education and Industry, a utopian community whose ideals and practices ensured an integrated membership. Although the association disbanded in 1846, many members stayed in Florence, including SOJOURNER TRUTH and DAVID RUGGLES; their influence marked the village as a "sanctuary" for all, regardless of religion, class, or race. But in 1849, when Sarah Askin arrived in Florence with her six children, Nelson had already sold off parts of his property, and shortly thereafter the livery was seized by creditors. By 1850 Nelson had abandoned Sarah. From then on, Sarah took in washing to support her children, who at the earliest opportunity left school to find work.

Luther Askin worked for more than fifty years in a brush shop, rising to foreman, in itself an accomplishment. He was also a stonecutter, carpenter, fireman, and musician. But his principal accomplishment was to play first base, from 1865 to 1866, for the Florence Eagle Base Ball Club. In 1872 Askin married Alice Lattimore of Moreau, New York. The couple remained in Florence for fifty-six years, raising five children. After Alice's death in 1928, Askin moved to Brooklyn to be with his daughters, where he died in 1929.

By every account, Askin led an unassuming life; the attention he received came about not from his own desire for recognition, but from an abiding need on the part of the people of Florence to celebrate the Eagle Base Ball Club. That Askin took pride in his seasons as an Eagle is evident, for his obituary lists his membership in the club before any other association. Yet no reference is made to his integration of the "Eagle nine." References to Askin's race can be found only in birth and census records or in accounts that address subjects other than the Eagles.

The papers of the Eagles' captain, Arthur G. Hill, show that he regarded Askin as "colored" (Hill, 1916). Although Askin's skin was light enough for his race to go unnoticed beyond the village, it is safe to assume that his teammates knew Askin's racial identify, as did most of Florence. Yet even in Florence the subject of Askin's integration of the Eagles went unmentioned for over a century. The reasons for this

Luther Askin, the earliest known black baseball player on an integrated team, photographed in his Nonotuck Fire Brigade uniform, c. 1878. (Collection of the Florence Business and Civic Association.)

silence may be found in the shifting identity of the Askin family, some of whom were variously referred to as "colored," "black," "mulatto," and one of whom, by the 1900s, identified himself as "white."

The drawing of the color line in baseball had its roots in the game's origins. In the 1840s, when amateur clubs were formed in New York City, baseball was a gentlemanly activity engaged in by professional men of the upper middle class. In time, the dockworkers of Brooklyn formed their own ball clubs and introduced a greater degree of competition, often offending the older clubs, who regarded "rough play" with distaste. Before the Civil War, blacks and whites had little social contact, and therefore no overt effort was required to segregate ball clubs. Blacks were playing baseball "as early as whites," along separate, "roughly parallel lines" (Seymour, *People's*, 532).

After the Civil War, "base ball fever" swept down upon the northeastern United States, and hundreds of amateur "nines" were formed. The limited pool of talent in Florence, with a population of only 1,400, partly explains why Catholics and Protestants, Irish mill workers, and Ivy League graduates played side-by-side. Also, the village's communitarian heritage, especially the Northampton Association, accounts for the heterogeneity of the Eagles. Even so, it would have been highly unusual for a black player to appear in "match games" arranged through invitations by clubs of adult white males. Yet this is what happened when Askin played for the Eagles.

The Eagles made their debut on 1 August 1865, defeating a team of Civil War veterans who called themselves champions of the "Army of the Potomac." In this, the Eagles' first official match, Askin played first base, qualifying him as "one of the original nine," and in most sources he is recognized as such.

The Eagles went undefeated from August 1865 to June 1866, and in each game Askin started at first base. The people of Florence had set their sights on winning the silver ball, a trophy symbolic of the championship of western Massachusetts. Crowds up to five thousand turned out; a pair of "sporting men" won seven hundred dollars at a single match, twice the annual salary of a millworker. The Eagles, who only the season before had taken the field barefooted and without uniforms, were altogether transformed. The club now wore fine uniforms, ordered balls for $3.50 apiece from New York, and had one hundred members, all of whom paid dues even if they did not play. It was as if the evolution of baseball had been compressed into the Eagles' first two seasons, transforming the game from a leisurely recreational activity to an intensely competitive sport.

On 9 June 1866, in the aftermath of the Eagles' first defeat (against the silver ball–champion Hampdens of Chicopee, no less), Askin was summarily dropped from the lineup. Whether the drive to win the silver ball brought about his demotion is difficult to say. All along, Askin was highly regarded for his fielding. In 1895 an anonymous player reminisced about Askin, calling him "Old Bushel Basket" because "the balls seemed to drop into his fingers and stay there as if a basket had held them" (Sheffeld, 186). In that reminiscence, there is a perplexing reference to a "sickness" that had, in some unspecified fashion, impaired Askin's performance. Yet a few weeks after his demotion, Askin scored seven runs for the Eagles' "second nine," so he was not so sick that he could not play.

In 1867, the year after Askin was dropped from the Eagles, the Pythians, a black team from Philadelphia, tested the baseball color line by applying for membership in the National Association of Amateur Base Ball Players. The National Association responded by putting in place a written ban against blacks, thus codifying the separate racial lines along which amateur ball clubs had evolved. Professional baseball, beginning with the National League in 1876, made little effort to address this situation. With rare exceptions, most notably the Walker brothers (MOSES FLEETWOOD WALKER and WELDY WALKER), who played in the American Association in 1884, segregation in professional baseball was the norm.

For years to come, local fans cited the Eagles as the amateur ideal, for compared to the Florence lads, it was said that all professional teams fell short. Some Eagles were well placed to cultivate their legend, having prospered as businessmen, politicians, journalists, and judges. Celebrations were staged in 1915 and 1916, the golden anniversaries of the club's founding and reign as champions. On both occasions Askin, then in his seventies, spoke on the evolution of baseball to a more "scientific" game. His remarks were reported, but no mention was made of the anomaly of his inclusion at reunions of an all-white team, nor did Askin pose for photographs. Like many African Americans of his era, Askin may have been deferential to the point of invisibility; or he may have chosen not to risk calling attention to his son, Luther Benjamin Askin, a bandleader in Lowville, New York, who had been passing for white for years.

Askin remained an unacknowledged pioneer of baseball integration until 1999, when Jim Ryan, a Florence centenarian, in the course of contributing to a local baseball history, recalled that he and Askin had "talked baseball" during the 1920s. During these encounters, Askin, then in his eighties, spoke to Ryan of his days with the Eagles. In reporting this, Ryan did not hesitate to identify the Askin family as black, for that was how the people of Florence had long regarded them. Other instances of integration in early baseball may yet be discovered, but finding them could be difficult, especially if a veil was drawn over the evidence, as with the Florence Eagles and Askin.

Further Reading
Papers that clarify the racial identity of the Askin family, especially the writings of Arthur G. Hill, are housed in the archives of the Florence Civic and Business Association, in Florence, Massachusetts.
Seymour, Harold. *Baseball: The Early Years* (1960).
Seymour, Harold. *Baseball: The People's Game* (1990).
Sheffeld, Charles A. *History of Florence Massachusetts* (1895).
Turner, Brian. "America's Earliest Integrated Team?" in *The National Pastime* (2002): 81–90.
Turner, Brian, and John S. Bowman. *The Hurrah Game: Baseball in Northampton 1823–1953* (2002).
BRIAN TURNER

ATKINS, Daniel (18 Nov. 1866–11 May 1923), United States Navy enlisted man, Spanish-American War combatant, and Medal of Honor recipient, was born in Brunswick, Virginia. Though nothing is known of his early life, it is likely that he was born to parents who had been formerly enslaved and who gained their freedom during the Civil War years. Perhaps because of his childhood proximity to the Atlantic Ocean and the major naval base at Norfolk, Virginia, Daniel Atkins joined the United States Navy around 1886.

The navy that Atkins joined in the 1880s was one in which opportunities for African Americans were steadily declining. In the years between the American Revolution and the close of the Civil War, black sailors served in a variety of shipboard posts, rated anywhere from cabin boy, cook, and steward to such higher positions as able-bodied seaman and gunner. In 1842 Senator John C. Calhoun attempted to have blacks banned from the navy altogether, but was unsuccessful. During the Civil War black sailors played a vital role in manning the Union navy, and a number of men, including JOACHIM PEASE, JOHN LAWSON, AARON ANDERSON, and ROBERT SMALLS were awarded the Medal of Honor for their courage under fire. However, in the postwar navy the situation of blacks in the service began to erode drastically, as the Reconstruction period came to an end and white supremacy reasserted itself in many of the nation's institutions. Because many of the navy's primary bases were located in the South and many naval officers were white southerners, black seamen began to experience the restrictions of a Jim Crow navy. While many white officers attempted to retain the accomplished black sailors in their charges, the restriction of blacks to steward- and commissary-related ratings had become unofficial U.S. Navy policy by the mid-1890s.

With regard to Daniel Atkins's naval service, few details are known. By early 1898 he was rated as ship's cook first class, a sure indicator of his years of service, as his next promotion would make him a petty officer. Atkins's shipboard duties would have included, as his rating suggests, not only preparation of food for his ship's crew but additional duties, such as procuring food supplies while the ship was in port and possibly assisting the captain's personal steward. As with all crew members of a ship of war, Daniel Atkins also had a battle station position (general quarters or GQ) during military operations, and he might have been employed as an ammunition passer, member of a gun crew, or lookout, to name a few possibilities. Though little is known about Atkins's service, one thing is clear: after years in the service, he was a respected and valued crew member, and subsequent events would bring that experience to bear to the utmost.

The month of February 1898 found Daniel Atkins aboard USS *Cushing* (TB-1) heading for Havana,

Cuba. Relations between Spain and America had deteriorated in the wake of Spanish efforts to crush an independence movement in its Cuban colony, prompting the United States to send vessels to patrol the waters of Cuba and the Florida Straits. The *Cushing* was the navy's first torpedo boat; commissioned in 1890, the ship weighed 116 tons and measured 140 feet long, was manned by 22 men, and carried three 6-pound cannons. With Daniel Atkins aboard, the ship was assigned to the North Atlantic Fleet Blockading Force in late 1897, performing picket duty and also serving as a courier boat. On 11 February 1898 the *Cushing* was steaming toward Havana in heavy seas when Ensign Joseph Breckinridge was washed overboard. Rushing to his aid and showing gallant conduct, Daniel Atkins and Gunner's Mate Third Class John Everetts attempted to save the officer in the stormy seas. While the efforts to save Breckinridge from drowning in the mounting seas were unsuccessful, Atkins's and Everetts's efforts did not go unheralded; both men were awarded the Medal of Honor for their actions aboard the *Cushing*. Daniel Atkins was one of eight African Americans to win the Medal of Honor in peacetime; in 1942, the award was restricted to valor shown in combat operations.

Following these heroics, Atkins probably stayed aboard his ship during the Spanish-American War and took part when it captured four small Spanish vessels in the Cays, and possibly served in an armed boat crew that helped capture and burn another small craft. The *Cushing* subsequently returned north in August 1898 to be stationed out of Newport, Rhode Island, before being sent to the Reserve Flotilla at Norfolk, Virginia, in 1901. As for Atkins, the remainder of his career is largely unknown. He would ultimately rise to the rank of chief commissary steward (CCS) and was probably still in the service in 1908 when blacks in the navy were once and for all restricted to the role of steward in preparation for the aptly named Great White Fleet's naval voyage around the world. From that time until 1920, and again from 1933 to 1942, African Americans joining the navy were restricted to the Steward's Branch, and from 1920 to 1933 they were banned from enlisting entirely.

Chief Commissary Steward Daniel Atkins, USN (Retired), died in Portsmouth, Virginia, and is buried in the Captain Ted Conaway Memorial Naval Cemetery in that town. A Medal of Honor gravestone marks his resting place.

Further Reading
Naval Historical Center. "Chief Commissary Steward Daniel Atkins, USN, (1866–1923)," available online at http://www.history.navy.mil/photos/pers-us/uspers-a/d-atkins.htm.

GLENN ALLEN KNOBLOCK

ATKINS, Jasper Alston (8 Aug. 1898–28 June 1982), civil rights lawyer, community activist, editor, and publisher, was born in Winston, North Carolina, the sixth and last son of nine children of Simon

Green and Oleona Pegram Atkins. His father was the founder and first president of the Slater Industrial Academy, later known as Winston-Salem State University. Atkins graduated from the Slater Academy in 1915 and then went to Fisk University in Nashville, Tennessee, graduating magna cum laude in chemistry in 1919.

When Atkins obtained his LLB cum laude at Yale University in 1922, he was the first African American to graduate with honors from that institution. While there, Atkins was a member of the debate team and served as a monitor of the Yale Law Library, where he oversaw the indexing of thirty-one volumes of the *Yale Law Journal*. In 1921 he was the first African American elected to the editorial board of the *Yale Law Journal*. Upon graduation, he was also the first black elected to the National Honorary Law Society, Order of the Coif.

In 1922 Atkins joined former Fisk schoolmate Carter Walker Wesley to form the law firm of Wesley & Atkins in Muskogee, Oklahoma, focusing primarily on the construction and brokerage business. Three years later he expanded his practice, relocating to Houston, Texas. There he continued in the firm of Wesley & Atkins, and then in 1931 added a third member, JAMES MADISON NABRIT JR., forming the new firm of Nabrit, Atkins & Wesley. Not satisfied to stay within the courts, Atkins joined Wesley in expanding their reach into the community activist sphere when he agreed to serve as an editor of their newly formed paper, the *Houston Informer and Texas Freedman*. A merger of two earlier publications, the *Texas Freedman*, which they had begun in 1893, and the *Houston Informer*, the paper ran from 1919 to 1931, expanding its readership across the state with calls for the repeal of Jim Crow laws, the hiring of blacks in the postal services, and the establishment of equal pay for black teachers, among other actions in support of the growing black communities. With the paper's growing appeal, Wesley expanded the initial publication into a chain of *Informer* papers published in towns across the state.

For five years, Atkins and Wesley, and later Nabrit, Atkins & Wesley worked with the NAACP on suits filed against the Houston Democratic Party for its practices preventing blacks from the voting in primary elections. One of these, *Nixon v. Herndon*, one of the so-called Texas White Primary cases, was eventually argued successfully in the U.S. Supreme Court in 1927. But, while the victory in this case outlawed prohibitions against black voters enacted by public officials and offices, it did not prevent the private sphere from discriminating against blacks. After the Texas Democratic Party argued that it was, in fact, a private institution (as opposed to an instrument of the state), the issue was taken back to the U.S. Supreme Court in 1932 with Dr. LAWRENCE A. NIXON, a black El Paso physician, again as the plaintiff. This case, *Nixon v. Condon*, was also resolved in favor of the plaintiff by a five-to-four vote. In its holding, the Court agreed that the Democratic Party

Committee was acting as an agent of the state and thus had violated the rights of its black citizens by preventing them from voting in primary elections, which in the Democratic-dominated South was tantamount to a general election.

Though happy with the verdict, Atkins and his fellow black lawyers derided the NAACP's own prohibitions against allowing even highly-qualified black lawyers, many of whom had built the cases and written the briefs, to argue their cases before the U.S. Supreme Court. Heretofore, the NAACP only countenanced the black lawyers arguing cases in the local or state jurisdictions, but sent its white legal teams to stand before the highest court in the land. Atkins and many other black lawyers began actively proselytizing for the permission to file briefs and join the NAACP in oral arguments. Texas civic leaders joined in the campaign, singling out Atkins as a prime candidate. William White, then head of the NAACP, received letters from Charles Houston and other Texas civic leaders, pointing out that "a man of Atkins's ability should be employed, since he is 'of our own nationality and from that fact, is more vitally interested in that which Negroes of the South desire'" (Meier, 936). Atkins's 1932 book *The Texas Negro and His Political Rights: A History of the Fight of Negroes to Enter the Democratic Primaries of Texas* details the long fight to gain voting rights in Texas and the vital roles played by black lawyers.

In 1935 Atkins and his partners bypassed the NAACP and took another white primary case, *Grovey v. Townsend*, before the U.S. Supreme Court. The case was not successful, but the move forced the NAACP to change its practices. The *Grovey v. Townsend* case was immediately followed by the NAACP case *Hollins v. State of Oklahoma*, in which NAACP leadership allowed the black lawyer and Howard Law School Dean CHARLES HAMILTON HOUSTON to argue its case before the court. Atkins noted, "Now that the NAACP has had a Negro lawyer for the first time in its history . . . before the Supreme Court, I trust that this will be the beginning of a new policy" (Meier, 942).

In 1936 Atkins left his law practice in Texas to help his brother, Frank, then president of Winston-Salem Teachers College, who had fallen ill. He took on the position of Executive Secretary for the College, a position he held until 1960. But Atkins's return to Winston-Salem did not signal a retreat from his long legacy of serving the community. He was a member of the Winston-Salem Housing Authority Board from its inception in 1941 until he resigned in 1958. He was a member of the Winston-Salem draft board from the outbreak of World War II until the Korean War. Then, after his retirement from Winston-Salem Teachers College in 1960, he returned to publishing as the executive editor of the Freedmen's Publishing company.

Nor did Atkins' legal work cease. Initially focusing on voting rights, he now turned his attention to discrimination in other arenas. In 1959 Atkins returned to the U.S. Supreme Court, where he led the successful prosecution of the *Wolfe v. State of North Carolina* case against racial discrimination on publicly owned golf courses. Atkins's legal expertise was sought again in 1968 and 1970. Initially serving as a plaintiff in *Atkins, Pro Se v. State Board of Higher Education of North Carolina* (1966–1970), and then as part of *Allen v. State Board of Higher Education of North Carolina* (1966–1973), Atkins helped dismantle segregated public education in North Carolina. Though the consent decree was not signed until 1985, three years after his death, it was a testament to Atkins's lifelong commitment to equality and opportunity.

Atkins died at the age of eighty-four. In 2003 the Lillian Goldman Law Library at Yale Law School welcomed the addition of his papers to its collection.

Further Reading

Jasper Alston Atkins' papers are housed in the Lillian Goldman Law Library of Yale University in New Haven, Connecticut. See "Guide to the Jasper Alston Atkins Papers (1922–1997): Manuscript Group 1811," comp. Mike Strom (2003).

Atkins, Jasper Alston. *The Texas Negro and His Political Rights: A History of the Fight of Negroes to Enter the Democratic Primaries of Texas* (1932).

Smith, J. Clay, Jr. *The Making of the Black Lawyer, 1844–1944* (1999).

Meier, August, and Elliot Rudwick. "Attorneys Black and White: A Case Study of Race Relations in the NAACP," *Journal of American History* 62.4 (Mar. 1976).

Finkelman, Paul. "Not Only the Judges' Robes Were Black: African-American Lawyers as Social Engineers," *Stanford Law Review* 47.1 (Nov. 1994).

Hine, Darlene Clark. "Blacks and the Destruction of the Democratic White Primary, 1935–1944," *Journal of American History* 62.1 (Jan. 1977).

JOY GLEASON CAREW

ATTAWAY, William Alexander (19 Nov. 1911–17 June 1986), writer, was born in Greenville, Mississippi, the son of William S. Attaway, a medical doctor, and Florence Parry, a teacher. His family moved to Chicago when Attaway was six years old, following the arc of the Great Migration, that thirty-year period beginning in the last decade of the nineteenth century during which more than 2 million African Americans left the South for the burgeoning industrial centers of the North. Unlike many of these emigrants, who traded the field for the factory and the sharecropper's shack for the ghetto, the Attaways were professionals at the outset, with high ambitions for themselves and their children in their new homeland.

Attaway attended public schools in Chicago, showing no great interest in his studies until, as a high school student, he encountered the work of LANGSTON HUGHES. He became, from that point on, a more serious student and even tried his hand at writing, composing scripts for his older sister's amateur drama club. After completing high school he enrolled at the University of Illinois, where he initially flourished not only academically but also athletically, becoming a collegiate tennis player.

His father's death while Attaway was still at college, however, derailed his academic career. As the Great Depression descended over America, Attaway dropped out of the university to wander the country, working as a seaman, à la Langston Hughes and CLAUDE MCKAY, a salesman, and a labor organizer, as well as in a variety of other odd jobs. He writes that "in Chicago I had all the advantages that a self-made man imagines are good for an only son. But after my father's death I rebelled and spent my time hoboing" (Bone, 132). After two years away from the university, he returned to finish his degree. During this period he experimented with one-act plays and short stories, publishing some of this work in newspapers and literary magazines. His first published short story, "Tale of the Blackamoor," appeared in 1936 in the little magazine *Challenge*, formed in 1934 to give another literary outlet for the new generation of African American writers. A drama, *Carnival*, was written and produced about the same time.

In the mid-1930s Attaway became involved in the Federal Writers' Project (FWP), a government initiative that provided work opportunities for unemployed writers during the Depression that was administered through the Works Projects Administration. Attaway helped write the Illinois section of the FWP's chief project, an American Guide Series, profiling the then forty-eight states. His work brought him into contact with some of the luminaries of contemporary African American literature also employed by the FWP, including RICHARD WRIGHT, Claude McKay, ARNA WENDELL BONTEMPS, MARGARET WALKER, RALPH WALDO ELLISON, and FRANK YERBY.

Moving to New York, Attaway entered the theater world with the assistance of his sister Ruth, who by now had achieved something of a reputation as a stage actress. He performed in several productions, including a 1939 traveling production of George S. Kaufman's *You Can't Take It with You*. In that year, he learned that his first novel, *Let Me Breathe Thunder*, had been accepted for publication by Doubleday. The novel, heavily influenced by John Steinbeck's *Of Mice and Men*, focuses on the adventures of two white hoboes during the Depression. It received limited critical attention and that mainly negative. It was generally thought to be too derivative and too heavily dependent upon mere reportage drawn from Attaway's own wanderings to be a successful work of literature.

His efforts did earn Attaway a two-year grant from the Julius Rosenwald Fund, which enabled him to work on a second novel. He completed and published in 1941 *Blood on the Forge*. This is a novel of an altogether different scope than his first, incisively portraying the collapse of traditional black folk culture in the relentlessly dehumanizing ghettos of the industrial, urbanized North. *Blood on the Forge* was well received critically but did not sell profitably, perhaps owing to the publication at about the same time of Richard Wright's *Native Son*, a novel that garnered immense critical and popular attention. The lack of commercial success of his second novel led Attaway to find new directions for his creative energy, most notably in writing songs and books about music and, eventually, scriptwriting for stage, screen, and television.

Attaway's songwriting was heavily influenced by calypso rhythms, and in 1957 he published the *Calypso Song Book*, containing many of the songs from which he drew inspiration. In the 1950s he made the acquaintance of HARRY BELAFONTE and collaborated with him and others in writing songs, authoring or coauthoring more than five hundred in his lifetime. Perhaps his most famous collaboration led to one of Belafonte's most popular hits, the "Banana Boat Song." Then, in 1967, Attaway published for children a compilation of representative popular music in America, including historical commentary, *Hear America Singing*.

Also, beginning in the 1950s, Attaway turned to writing for radio, film, and television, one of the first African American writers to do so. His work was featured in such television series as *Wide Wide World* and the *Colgate Comedy Hour*. He was one of the writers for an hour-long television special, airing in 1964, *One Hundred Years of Laughter*, showcasing, among the others, the African American comedians REDD FOXX, MOMS MABLEY, and FLIP WILSON in their first appearances on the small screen.

In 1962, at the age of fifty-one, Attaway married Frances Settele, from New York, at a ceremony held in his friend Belafonte's home. The couple had two children—a son, Bill, born in 1964, and a daughter Noelle, born in 1966. In the year of his daughter's birth, Attaway took his family to Barbados for a vacation and wound up staying eleven years among the people and the music he loved. Upon their return to America, the family settled in California, where Attaway spent the remaining years of his life writing screenplays.

Further Reading

Bone, Robert A. *The Negro Novel in America* (1965).
Gayle, Addison, JR. *The Way of the New World: The Black Novel in America* (1975).
Gloster, Hugh Morris *Negro Voices in American Fiction* (1948).
Hughes, Carl M. *The Negro Novelist* (1953).
Margolies, Edward. "Migration: William Attaway and *Blood on the Forge*," in *Native Sons: A Critical Study of Twentieth-century Negro American Authors* (1968).
Redding, J. Saunders. "The Negro Writer and American Literature," in *Anger and Beyond: The Negro Writer in the United States* (1966).

GEORGE P. WEICK

ATTUCKS, Crispus (c. 1723–5 Mar. 1770), probably a sailor, was the first to be killed in the Boston Massacre of 5 March 1770. Generally regarded to have been of mixed ancestry (African, Indian, and white), Attucks seems to have hailed from a Natick Indian settlement, Mashpee (incorporated as a district in 1763, near Framingham, Massachusetts).

The Boston Massacre. "The massacre perpetrated in King Street Boston on March 5th 1770, in which Messrs Saml. Gray, Saml. Maverick, James Caldwell, Crispus Attucks, Patrick Carr were killed, six other wounded, two of them mortally." Engraving by Paul Revere, 1770. (Library of Congress.)

While Attucks's life and background before the tragic event are uncertain, two reasonable conjectures stand out. First, he was a descendant of those Natick Indians converted to Christianity in the seventeenth century. One tribesman, John Attuck, was hanged on 22 June 1676 for allegedly conspiring with the Indian insurrection of that year. Second, it appears that Attucks may have once been a slave. The *Boston Gazette* of 2 October 1750 printed this notice: "Ran away from his Master, William Brown of Framingham on the 30th of September last, a mulatto Fellow, about twenty-seven years of age, named Crispus, 6 feet 2 inches high, short curled hair, his knees nearer together than common."

J. B. Fisher, who argues that Attucks had Indian blood, also claims that he became a crewman on a Nantucket whaler, owned by a Captain Folger, which was docked at the time of the Massacre in Boston harbor. A sailor, James Bailey, testified that the assaulting group, which Attucks headed, "appeared to be sailors." John Adams (1735–1826) said that Attucks "was seen about eight minutes before the firing at the head of twenty or thirty sailors in Cornhill. . . . He was a stout

fellow, whose very looks were enough to terrify any person. . . . He was about forty-seven years old."

The Bostonians' wrath had long been building against the stationing of the Fourteenth and Twenty-ninth British regiments in the town. On the evening of 5 March, Attucks dined at Thomas Symmonds's victualing house and, learning of the commotion taking place at the customshouse on King Street, joined a group headed in that direction. It is said that he and others had earlier threatened British soldiers at Murray's barracks. Attucks and his gang gathered cordwood sticks and wooden pieces from butchers' stalls, carrying these makeshift weapons over their heads as they approached the scene of the disturbance. John Adams, in remarks before the jury that tried the British soldiers for their role in the Massacre, stated that "Attucks appears to have undertaken to be the hero of the night, and to lead this army with banners." In his summation, Adams also said that "it is in this manner, this town has been often treated; a Carr from Ireland, and an Attucks from Framingham, happening to be here" to "sally out upon their thoughtless enterprises, at the head of such a rabble of negroes, &c., as they can collect together." Testimony at the soldiers' trial differed over whether Attucks had grabbed for the bayonet of Private Hugh Montgomery, causing a struggle that resulted in the shooting. John Adams tried to portray Attucks as the instigator, "to whose mad behavior, in all probability, the dreadful carnage of that night is chiefly ascribed." Adams added that Attucks's group was a "mob whistling, screaming, and rending like an Indian yell." Some witnesses, however, testified that Attucks was killed while leaning on his cordwood stick. Two shots to his breast caused the fatality.

After the massacre, the bodies of Attucks and James Caldwell, the two nonresident victims, were brought to Faneuil Hall. On 8 March a funeral procession of ten to twelve thousand people and numerous coaches accompanied the hearses of Attucks and three other victims to Granary burial ground, where all four coffins were buried in one grave.

Captain Thomas Preston, the British officer of the day who commanded the squad that fired upon the civilians, and eight soldiers were tried before the Suffolk Superior Court in Boston from 27 November to 5 December 1770. Preston and six of his men were acquitted, including William Warren, who was charged specifically with killing Attucks; two others were found guilty of manslaughter and were branded on the thumb after pleading benefit of clergy.

Crispus Attucks, apparently of African and Indian ancestry, was the first martyr of the American Revolution. Years later, in response to adoption of a new Federal Fugitive Slave Law in 1850, Attucks became a powerful symbol of black resistance to slavery and racism. His name was repeatedly invoked during the Civil War to recruit soldiers for the famed 54th Massachusetts Regiment. Other black military companies were named for him. In 1888 the city of Boston and the state of Massachusetts erected on Boston Common a memorial to Attucks and the other massacre victims.

Further Reading

Fisher, J. B. "Who Was Crispus Attucks?" *American Historical Record* 1 (1872): 531–533.

Quarles, Benjamin. *The Negro in the American Revolution* (1961).

Temple, Josiah H. *History of Framingham, Massachusetts, 1640–1885* (1887).

Wroth, L. Kinvin, and Hiller B. Zobel, eds. *Legal Papers of John Adams* (3 vols., 1965).

Zobel, Hiller B. *The Boston Massacre* (1970).

HARRY M. WARD

ATWATER, Ann (1 July 1935–), community activist, was born in Columbus County, North Carolina, the youngest of nine children of William Randolph George and Emma Jane Shaw, sharecroppers. While she was still quite young, Ann started working on the farm, where her parents taught her the values of hard work, discipline, and Christian compassion. When Ann was six, her mother died, but her father took on extra work at a nearby sawmill and managed to build an eight-room house for the family.

Ann attended Farmers Union High School in Whiteville, North Carolina, until the tenth grade. When she was fourteen she became pregnant and married the baby's father, French Wilson, who disappeared a month after the wedding. He reappeared shortly before the birth, but Ann lost the child. In 1952 the couple had a baby girl named Lydia. In 1953 Wilson secured a job at Central Leaf Tobacco Company in Durham and Ann and the baby soon followed. Despite Durham's reputation as "the capital of the black middle class," most blacks in the city remained poor, and Ann and French struggled with serious financial and emotional problems resulting from domestic violence.

Ann gave birth to another daughter, Marilyn, in 1956, but Wilson again disappeared. He soon surfaced with a better-paying job in Richmond, Virginia, but Ann refused to follow him, and the couple soon divorced. It was at this point that she dropped Wilson's name and adopted "Atwater," the surname of a man she had dated. Atwater continued working as a domestic for white families, supporting her two young daughters in a run-down section of Durham's Hayti neighborhood. In 1975 she married Willie Pettiford, a sanitation worker in nearby Wake Forest.

Although Atwater did not participate directly in Durham's early civil rights movement, she occasionally staged individual protests that at times had dire

Ann Atwater (left), and C. P. Ellis (right), waiting to see the premiere screening of the video documentary "An Unlikely Friendship" on 9 November 2001, Chapel Hill, North Carolina. The documentary recounts the friendship that formed between Atwater, a poor civil rights organizer, and Ellis, a Ku Klux Klan member, in Durham during a racially charged period in the early 1970s. (AP Photo.)

consequences. For example, shortly after learning of ROSA PARKS's refusal to move from a Montgomery bus seat in 1955, Atwater overheard her white employer making disparaging comments about blacks. Enraged, she confronted her boss and ended her tirade with a suggestion that black cooks might be spitting in the pots of their white employers. Unable to recall whether she quit or was fired, Atwater spent the next years working part-time jobs and struggling to support her two young daughters. By 1965 Atwater was forced to rely on welfare benefits after a doctor ordered her to quit domestic work because of her diabetes.

That same year, HOWARD FULLER, a Louisiana native raised in Milwaukee and one of the most talented black community organizers in North Carolina, successfully recruited Atwater to a new antipoverty effort begun by the North Carolina governor Terry Sanford in 1963, a year before President Lyndon Johnson launched his national War on Poverty. Howard Fuller had made Atwater's acquaintance as a result of community organizing drives conducted in low-income neighborhoods, under the auspices of Durham's antipoverty agency, Operation Breakthrough (OBT). Atwater quickly became one of the most effective and well-respected grassroots organizers in Durham and was widely recognized as a veritable expert on welfare and housing regulations. She worked with OBT and then for United Organizations for Community Improvement, a majority-female federation of low-income black neighborhood councils, which set the tone and agenda of black protest in Durham from the middle of the 1960s to the end of the decade.

In 1967 the *Carolina Times*, Durham's black weekly, named Atwater Woman of the Year. In 1968 she became the first black woman elected as vice president of the local Democratic Party. Although she embraced the tenets of nonviolent protest, she hinted that she was an expert at making the kinds of Molotov cocktails that exploded throughout Durham in the wake of MARTIN LUTHER KING JR.'s assassination in 1968. That same year she also joined Women-in-Action for the Prevention of Violence and Its Causes, a biracial women's organization established by Elna Spaulding to ease racial tensions in the city. Atwater was a key participant in the Black Solidarity Committee's seven-month boycott of Durham's white downtown merchants from 1968 to 1969. She also publicly supported Malcolm X Liberation University, a community-based black nationalist school founded in Durham after the black student takeover of the administration building at Duke University in 1969.

In 1971 Atwater and the Durham Ku Klux Klan leader Claiborne "C. P." Ellis formed an unlikely alliance. Wilbur Hobby, a white Durham labor leader, had secured a grant to establish a ten-day Save Our Schools community forum known as a "charrette" in order to ease a court-ordered school desegregation plan, and Ellis and Atwater reluctantly agreed to head the charrette. Ellis, a white maintenance worker and son of a textile worker, was initially quite hostile to Atwater, showing her the gun he carried in his car trunk.

However, Ellis soon realized that he and Atwater shared similar problems of poverty and disempowerment. He left the Klan, became a union leader at Duke University, and the odd couple remained friends for more than three decades. The militant black activist and former Klansman attracted national attention and were featured in the award-winning book *The Best of Enemies* (1996) and the award-winning documentary film *An Unlikely Friendship* (2003). When Ellis died of Alzheimer's disease in 2005, his children called Atwater to speak at his funeral, which she did. Upon learning of his death, Atwater commented on their enduring friendship: "At the end of 10 days, him and I fell in love, and we've been in love ever since until he closed his eyes on Thursday" (*News and Observer*). Atwater and Ellis did not have a romantic relationship, but had remained close friends throughout the years.

During the 1970s and 1980s Atwater worked at Head Start and at the Durham Housing Authority before declining health and a workplace injury forced her to retire in the early 1990s. Even in retirement and into her seventies, she continued her community work, teaching Bible classes at the local homeless shelter, securing funds to reopen a local recreation center, and assisting Durham's poor, who still called on her for assistance. She also remained active in local organizations, including the Durham Committee on the Affairs of Black People (one of the oldest black political machines in the South), the NAACP, and Mount Calvary United Church of Christ, where she served as deacon.

For more than four decades the issue of housing remained one of Atwater's central concerns. In the 1960s she took on the Durham Housing Authority director Carvie Oldham, earning the nickname "Roughhouse Annie," and managing to reverse regulations that excluded single mothers from public housing. One of her greatest triumphs was in the late 1960s, when she prevented the illegal eviction of thirty-five families that stood in the way of the construction of the Durham Expressway. She also served as president of the Birchwood Heights Homeowners Association, an innovative community of 200 homes created by the Durham Housing Authority in the 1970s, which allowed residents to make payments as rent until they became homeowners. However, the Birchwood Heights area was isolated, with no schools or community facilities nearby, and was plagued by drugs and violence. After the violent deaths of seven young adults during the period 1995–1996 Atwater and Reverend Paul Godshall founded the Birchwood Learning Center in 1996, which targeted unemployed teenage high school dropouts. Atwater also participated in New Hope, a ten-year project designed to end homelessness in Durham. In 2002 a charter school, the Ann Atwater Community School, was named after her, and one of New Hope's apartment buildings was also named after her in 2005.

Over the years Atwater has received countless awards and honors that filled an entire wall of her modest home. These included the Rosa Parks Award from the Durham Women in Community Service, the

MARY MCLEOD BETHUNE Award from the National Council of Negro Women, numerous Durham Mayor's and Human Relations Commission Awards, the Distinguished Service Award from the Durham NAACP, and the Martin Luther King Jr. Keep Your Dream Alive Award. Like so many low-income black women activists, Atwater received little monetary compensation for her work. Impoverished and in deteriorating health, Atwater, one of the city's most dedicated activists who never forgot the plight of the poor, was herself given assistance from several local and national church and community groups.

Further Reading

Much of the information for this entry was acquired during two interviews with Ann Atwater on 12 Jan. 1993 and 20 Feb. 2007.

Bloom, Diane. Producer and director, *An Unlikely Friendship,* thirty-five minute documentary video/DVD (2003).

Davidson, Osha Gray. *The Best of Enemies: Race and Redemption in the New South* (1996).

Greene, Christina. *Our Separate Ways: Women and the Black Freedom Movement in Durham, North Carolina* (2005).

Rochman, Bonnie. "Activist Mourns Ex-KKK Leader," *News and Observer,* 8 Nov. 2005.

Terkel, Studs. *Race: How Blacks and Whites Think and Feel about the American Obsession* (1992).

CHRISTINA GREENE

AUGUSTA, Alexander Thomas (8 Mar. 1825–21 Dec. 1890), physician, Civil War surgeon, and medical educator, was born free in Norfolk, Virginia, to parents whose names and occupations are unknown. Augusta received his early education from a Bishop Payne, defying a law that forbade African Americans to read or write. He continued to improve his reading skills while working as an apprentice to a barber. His interest in medicine led him to relocate to Baltimore, where he studied with private tutors. Eventually, Augusta moved to Philadelphia, Pennsylvania, to serve an apprenticeship. Although he was denied entry to the University of Pennsylvania, Augusta caught the attention of Professor William Gibson, who allowed the young man to study in his office.

In January 1847 Augusta married Mary O. Burgoin in Baltimore. They lived in California for three years before returning to the East Coast so that Augusta could pursue a medical degree. Denied access, despite his prior training in medicine, to the medical schools in both Philadelphia and Chicago, he applied to study in Canada. He was accepted by Trinity Medical College in Toronto, from which he graduated in 1856 with a bachelor of medicine degree. While studying in Toronto, Augusta supported himself and his wife by operating a store that offered services such as cupping and bleeding, as well as medicines. Mary Augusta worked as a dressmaker, and her skills were much sought after.

Records of Augusta's activities for the years between 1856 and 1861 are incomplete. He apparently ran the City Hospital and acted as a physician at Toronto's poorhouse, while possibly managing a private practice. There is further speculation that he was in charge of an industrial school for two years. He may also have spent some of this period in the West Indies, eventually returning to Canada.

With the onset of the Civil War, Augusta was eager to use his talents. In 1862 he journeyed to Washington, D.C., to take the examination for the volunteer medical service. Impatience prompted him to petition both President Abraham Lincoln and Secretary of War Edwin M. Stanton on 7 January 1863 with respect to a surgical appointment. In March he received a reply from the Army Medical Board denying his petition on the grounds that, first, he was of African descent and that, second, accepting him into the service would be a direct violation of Queen Victoria's Proclamation of Neutrality because as a Canadian resident he was "an alien and a British subject." In a letter to Lincoln and the Army Medical Board dated 30 March 1863, Augusta argued that the officials had misinterpreted his case. He explained that he had expected to serve the colored regiments, and that he was still a U.S. citizen despite having obtained his medical credentials in Canada.

On 1 April 1863 the board overturned its decision, finding Augusta "qualified for the position of surgeon in the Negro regiment now being raised." On 14 April 1863 Augusta was appointed a surgeon with the Seventh U.S. Colored Infantry, making him the first African American to receive a medical commission in the U.S. Army. Only seven other African Americans received such an appointment during the Civil War.

Serving from 1863 to 1864 as chief executive officer of Freedmen's Hospital, formerly called Camp Barker, Augusta was the first African American to head a U.S. hospital. In February 1864 several white physicians at the hospital petitioned the president to have Augusta permanently reassigned, because they refused to be subordinate to an African American. Augusta was then assigned to a recruiting office in Baltimore. When the Seventh U.S. Colored Troops were sent to Beaufort, South Carolina, Augusta went with them. He remained there until the end of the war.

Throughout most of Augusta's war service, the army paid him at the level of an enlisted Negro soldier, despite his holding the rank of major. This insult continued until Senator Henry Wilson of Massachusetts intervened on Augusta's behalf. The indignities that Augusta suffered during the war were not limited to the military, however. Average citizens were enraged at the sight of an African American in an officer's uniform. While journeying to Baltimore at one point during the war, Augusta was assaulted by a group of men and had to be rescued by police. When Augusta and his protégé, ANDERSON RUFFIN ABBOTT, attended the White House levee of 1863–1864, Abbott recorded that in full-dress regalia the two were "the synosure of all eyes."

Augusta's obstinacy scored a major victory for all African Americans residing in Washington, D.C., however. On his way to testify in a court-martial case on 1 February 1864, he was ejected from a streetcar when he refused to sit in the "Negroes Only" section. When he was forced to give an explanation for his tardiness to the judge advocate, the incident drew the attention of the Senate and became the subject of a debate resulting in the integration of all Washington streetcars.

On 13 March 1865 Augusta was brevetted lieutenant colonel in the U.S. Volunteer Corps "for meritorious and faithful service." He was the first African American to be awarded such rank. Following the war his services were retained by the medical division of the Bureau of Refugees, Freedmen, and Abandoned Lands, where he served as an assistant surgeon responsible for the Freedmen's Hospital in Savannah, Georgia.

Augusta, the highest-ranking African American to serve in the U.S. Civil War, mustered out of the army on 13 October 1866, returning to Washington, where he opened a medical practice. On 21 September 1868 he was appointed demonstrator of anatomy at the newly formed medical department at Howard University, making him the first African American to hold a faculty position at a U.S. medical school. While at Howard, Augusta held several professorships in anatomy. He was one of three faculty members to retain their positions in the medical department, despite severe salary cuts, when the nation and the university faced financial collapse in 1873. In 1877, after the medical faculty recommended to the trustees that Augusta switch positions with Dr. Daniel Lamb and become chair of materia medica rather than of anatomy, Augusta resigned and returned to private practice.

In 1869 Augusta and two other African American doctors were denied membership in the Medical Society of the District of Columbia, an association responsible for licensing and professional development. Frustrated with racist admission policies, Augusta helped found in 1884 the Medical-Chirurgical Society of D.C., the first African American medical society in the United States.

In 1870 Augusta became the attending physician at a smallpox hospital in Washington, also renewing his involvement with Freedmen's Hospital. By this time Freedmen's Hospital had become the teaching facility for Howard University's medical department. From 1870 to 1875 he served as a staff physician for the urino-genital diseases division, and from October 1875 to July 1877 he was the ward physician at the hospital. In 1888 he assumed the position of clinical lecturer on diseases of the skin. Augusta died in Washington, D.C.

Further Reading

Relevant material is available in the papers of Anderson Ruffin Abbott, the Abbott Collection, Metropolitan Toronto Reference Library.

Cobb, William Montague. "Medical History: Alexander Thomas Augusta," *Journal of the National Medical Association* 44, no. 4 (July 1952).

Greene, Robert Ewell. "Alexander T. Augusta," in *Black Defenders of America, 1775–1973: A Reference and Pictorial History* (1974).

Lamb, Daniel Smith. "Alexander Thomas Augusta, A.M., M.D.," in *Howard University Medical Department Washington, D.C.: A Historical, Biographical, and Statistical Souvenir* (1971).

Morais, Herbert M. *The History of the Negro in Medicine* (1967).

DALYCE NEWBY

AUNT CLARA. *See* Brown, Clara (Aunt Clara)

AUNT SALLY. *See* Campbell, Sarah (Aunt Sally) *or* Williams, Sally (Aunt Sally)

AUSTIN, Doris Jean (1949–Sept. 1994), novelist and columnist, was born in Mobile, Alabama. Raised primarily by her mother, Tommie Letitia Austin, and her grandmother, Rebecca Stallworth, Doris Jean was five years old when her family moved to Jersey City, New Jersey. Reverend Ercell Webb, her high school teacher, encouraged Austin to write, and Austin's early life in New Jersey provided a geographical and temporal backdrop for her only novel, *After the Garden* (1987).

Austin transformed the trials of her young adulthood into fodder for her writing. Before she was thirty, Austin's mother and grandmother had died of cancer, she had lived through two divorces, she had been diagnosed with and overcome cancer herself, and she had struggled with alcoholism. She also recovered the memory of the rape that she had survived when she was a child. Austin drew on these sources of pain for both her fiction and her nonfiction; in her contributions to *Essence* magazine, including "Holisitic Healing," "The 30-year Rape," and "The Men in My Life," Austin uses autobiographical writing as a way to begin discussions of larger issues, such as women's health and coping with sexual violence.

Published in 1987, Austin's novel *After the Garden* focuses on the narrative of the protagonist Elzina Tompkins, a young woman from an affluent neighborhood in Jersey City. In an interview with *Essence*, Austin described the text as not autobiographical, but explained that "I consciously wrote about *my* people— those who nurtured me—though the characters are composites, straight out of my imagination" (Guy-Sheftall, 28). In the novel, Elzina falls in love with Jesse James, a high school athletic star. Elzina becomes pregnant during her senior year of high school, dashing the hope of her grandmother Rosalie that Elzina will attend Tuskegee University. Jesse and Elzina marry and move in with Rosalie, and Austin's novel studies the dynamic of this intergenerational household.

An investigation of the workings of family, class, race, gender, and history, *After the Garden* met with generally positive reviews. Described as "a powerful first novel" in the *Library Journal*, *After the Garden* also received the praise of the *New York Times Book Review* critic Robert G. O'Meally, who lauded Austin's "courageous confrontation of character" (16 August 1987, 20).

In addition to contributing to *Essence*, Austin published articles in the *Amsterdam News* and the *New York Times Book Review*. Her short story "Room 1023" was published in the anthology *Streetlights: Illuminating Tales of the Urban Black Experience*, which Austin edited with Martin Simmons; the anthology was published in 1996, after Austin's death.

Austin was named a MacDowell Colony fellow and was awarded the DeWitt Wallace–Reader's Digest Award for Literary Excellence. She was known by some as a "writer's writer," and she was a good friend of the novelists ELIZABETH NUNEZ and TERRY MCMILLAN. Austin was a member of the Harlem Writer's Guild. She also cofounded (with others, including A. R. Flowers and B. J. Ashanti) the New Renaissance Writer's Guild in New York and subsequently served as its executive director.

From 1989 to 1994 Austin taught fiction workshops at Columbia University. She was living in New York and had begun work on a second novel when she died of liver cancer in 1994. After her death Terry McMillan established the Doris Jean Austin Writers Fellowship Award Program at the Frederick Douglass Creative Arts Center. Although her work is largely unstudied, Austin continues to be recognized as a talented novelist.

Further Reading

Andrews, William L., Frances Smith Foster, and Trudier Harris, eds. *The Oxford Companion to African American Literature* (1997).

Guy-Sheftall, Beverly. "Word Star," *Essence* (Oct. 1987).

Jones, Evora. "Doris Jean Austin," in *Contemporary African American Novelists*, ed. Emmanuel S. Nelson (1999).

King, Christine. Review of *After the Garden*, *Library Journal* (July 1987).

SARA E. HOSEY

AUSTIN, H. Elsie (10 May 1908–26 Oct. 2004), lawyer, diplomat, and activist, was born Helen Elsie Austin in Cincinnati, Ohio, the daughter of George J. Austin and Mary Louise Dotson Austin. Elsie Austin grew up in a family with a history of standing up for justice and equality. Her role model was her great-grandmother, the wife of one of the first black U.S. congressional representatives elected after the Civil War, who, when she was taunted by racist terror and threat of death by the Ku Klux Klan in Alabama because of her husband's role in politics, defied the Klan.

Austin expressed this courage and spirit as a child in Cincinnati's public schools; when she was eight years old and one of only two African American children in her class, she pointed out textbook errors that degraded the role of Africans in world history, and she listed many of the contributions made by Africans. After she spoke, she remembered later, there was an "electric silence" in the classroom. Her teacher, however, agreed with Austin and went on to discuss contributions made by African Americans and Africans.

Austin was one of six African Americans who integrated the undergraduate program at the University of Cincinnati in 1927, and in 1930 she became the first African American woman to graduate from the University of Cincinnati College of Law. After law school Austin practiced law in Ohio and Indiana and was the first black woman to serve as assistant attorney general in the state of Ohio and the first woman lawyer in the federal government's Senior Attorney Office of Emergency Management. In 1937 Elsie Austin received an honorary LLD degree from Wilberforce University in Ohio.

From 1939 to 1944 Austin served as president of Delta Sigma Theta, a service-based sorority of college-educated African American women. With more than nine hundred chapters worldwide, the sorority provides support and assistance in local communities in the United States and throughout the world, such as building and maintaining a maternity hospital in Kenya and in the United States operating Delta Academy, in which local Delta sororities work tutoring and mentoring African American students. In 1945 Austin wrote a play for high school students that went on to be produced in various communities through the Young Women's Christian Association (YWCA). The play, *Blood Doesn't Tell*, confronts the prejudicial thinking that African American blood is different and not suitable for blood donations. The drama portrays prejudice among schoolchildren and the community, discusses that prejudice, and educates students that all blood is the same.

In 1934 Elsie Austin joined the Baha'i community in Cincinnati. Founded in Iran in 1844, the worldwide Baha'i faith focuses on the principles of unity of God and humankind and denounces and works to abolish racism and prejudice. The community is led not by clergy but by a democratically elected spiritual assembly. In 1944 Austin was elected to the nine-member national governing body of the U.S. Baha'i community. In 1953 Austin met the head of the faith, Shoghi Effendi, on a pilgrimage to the Holy Land. Responding to a call among the community to establish new Baha'i communities, Austin resigned from the national board in the United States and settled in Tangier, Morocco. She lived there for five years, teaching school and traveling throughout Africa. From 1953 to 1958 she served on the Baha'i spiritual assembly in North and West Africa. During her membership in the Baha'i community, Austin served local spiritual assemblies in the United States, Nigeria, Kenya, and the Bahamas. She wrote numerous articles and pamphlets and reported on the 1957 Kenya Conference for the *Baha'i News*. She penned a pamphlet on the life of the Baha'i spiritual leader LOUIS GEORGE GREGORY, who was her mentor.

In 1960 Austin joined the U.S. State Department, and for the next ten years served as a cultural attaché with the United States Information Agency (USIA). She initiated the first USIA women's programs in Africa. These programs targeted women leaders and organizations in thirteen African countries. Austin received the Federal Women's Award in 1968 for her work, and in 1969 the University of Cincinnati honored her with a doctor of humanities degree.

Austin retired from the State Department in 1970, settled in Silver Spring, Maryland, and worked as a consultant in human relations and law. She worked with the Phelps Stokes Fund, which strives to build bridges of intercultural, interracial, and international understanding through educational initiatives. In 1974 Austin founded the African and American Women's Association, a nonprofit organization devoted to better understanding among the women of Africa and the Americas. While working with the Stokes Fund she lived and worked in Nigeria and helped the Nigerian government to build a nationwide judiciary system. In 1977 Austin attended the Baha'i International Teaching Conference in Kenya, and in 1975 she chaired the Baha'i delegation to the 1975 International Women's Conference in Mexico City. In 1982 Austin traveled to the People's Republic of China for the Stokes Fund. As part of a study team, she inspected schools and community educational services, and researched the education of minority groups in China.

The Baha'i World News Service's obituary of Dr. Austin cites a speech she gave during a 1998 gathering of Baha'is, in which Austin continued to urge action: "If we go about with faith, with intelligent protest, standing up and demonstrating what the right attitude and motivation is for human progress, we can cause progress," she said. In 2000 the University of Cincinnati named a scholarship in her honor. Austin died in San Antonio, Texas, at the age of ninety-six.

Further Reading
Burkett, Randal K., Nancy Hall, and Henry Louis Gates Jr., eds. *Black Biography, 1790–1950*. A Cumulative Index, vol. 1 (1991).
Hatcher, William S., and J. Douglas Martin. *The Baha'i Faith: The Emerging Global Religion* (1984).

Obituary: *Washington Post*, 26 Nov. 2004.

LINDA SPENCER

AUSTIN, Louis Ernest (24 Jan. 1898–12 June 1971), journalist, was born in Enfield, North Carolina, the year of the infamous Wilmington Race Massacre. His parents were William Louis Austin, owner of a barbershop, and Carrie Johnson. Louis Austin graduated from the Joseph K. Brick High School. His father, who never let any of his children work for whites, taught him in word and deed that no person was superior to him.

In Durham, Austin attended and graduated from the National Training School (later North Carolina Central University), which had been founded in 1910 by JAMES E. SHEPARD. Following graduation Austin sold life insurance for the North Carolina Mutual Life Insurance Company, founded in Durham in 1898 by black entrepreneurs. Austin also served as sports editor for Durham's black newspaper, the *Standard Advertiser*, founded in

1921 by Charles Arrant. In 1927, with the help of a loan from the Mutual affiliate Mechanics and Farmers Bank, Austin bought the paper, which was then known as the *Carolina Times*. Austin married Stella Louise Walker, and they had one daughter, Vivian, who after the death of her father took over as editor and publisher of the *Carolina Times*.

Austin's Christianity and his egalitarianism formed the foundation for his editorial positions. A longtime trustee of Saint Joseph's African Methodist Episcopal (AME) Church in Durham, Austin believed that it was his moral duty to speak the truth about the suffering and injustice inflicted upon African Americans. For twenty-seven years Austin served as president of the Interdenominational Ushers of North Carolina.

From the beginning Austin's editorials were forthright and resolute—the paper's motto was "The Truth Unbridled." For more than four decades Austin fought courageously against economic injustice, police brutality, racial segregation, and white supremacy. When in 1929 he published editorials in support of a black family under attack for purchasing a home in a white neighborhood, Austin received threatening phone calls, some promising to burn his house down. The Ku Klux Klan threw rocks and bottles at his house and burned a cross on his lawn. Austin once told an interviewer of an occasion when he was "ordered out of town" (he did not say by whom). Undaunted, Austin visited the man who had threatened him, "just to let him know that I would still be here any time he wanted me." That night a group of Austin's friends "gathered to stand guard and defend" him (Walker, p. 167). But Austin was not deterred by the threats of white racists—neither then nor later. Because Austin was so dismissive of whites' notions of racial etiquette, many whites viewed him as an anomaly and a radical who had little black support, but the truth was that his words and deeds made him a hero to many African Americans. Austin's outspokenness alienated advertisers, however, which meant that the newspaper struggled to remain solvent.

In 1933 Austin joined with the attorneys CONRAD PEARSON and Cecil McCoy in backing Thomas Raymond Hocutt's lawsuit against the white-only policy of the University of North Carolina at Chapel Hill. The NAACP lawyer WILLIAM HASTIE joined Pearson and McCoy in representing Hocutt. Because of a legal technicality and because of the refusal of the North Carolina College president James Shepard to submit Hocutt's transcript, the suit failed in state court. Nonetheless the case served as the beginning of the NAACP's legal battle to overturn segregated public education, culminating in 1954 with the *Brown v. Board of Education* decision.

Two years later in 1935 Austin helped found the Durham Committee on Negro Affairs to register black voters and increase black political influence in the city and the state. One of the original members of the executive committee, Austin worked for the Durham Committee for decades in various capacities. In 1953 he handled public relations for Rencher N. Harris's successful campaign to become the first black member of the Durham city council. Austin himself had unsuccessfully run for Durham city council in 1945.

During World War II, Austin capitalized on the nature of the war to press for equal rights for African Americans. In North Carolina, Austin was the leading proponent of the "Double V" strategy, coined by the *Pittsburgh Courier*, which encouraged blacks to fight for victory abroad while fighting for victory at home against the forces of white supremacy and racial oppression. Austin voiced the views of many African Americans when he spoke out against racial segregation and racial discrimination by the state and federal governments and by private businesses. After the outbreak of war in Europe in 1939 Austin—an avowed anti-imperialist—joined the chorus of black editors and columnists who saw little difference between German Nazism and British imperialism and thus urged the United States to stay out of the war. Austin demanded that the United States insist that Britain free its colonies: "We cannot fight a war on one hand to preserve the rights of free people while denying those rights to others" (*Carolina Times*, 14 Mar. 1942).

The *Carolina Times* joined other black newspapers to attack racial discrimination by the nation's armed forces and to fight for equal access for blacks in all service branches. In September 1940 Austin urged Congress to ensure that blacks would be included in all branches of the armed forces in the selective service bill then being debated.

After the Japanese attack on Pearl Harbor and America's entrance into the war, Austin regularly illuminated the contradictions between American policies to defeat the racist Nazis and racist violence at home against blacks. Austin renewed his criticism of segregation in the wake of violence that erupted in North Carolina as a result of racist discrimination by whites against black soldiers. In 1941 Austin backed A. PHILIP RANDOLPH's March on Washington movement, which succeeded in pressuring President Franklin D. Roosevelt to issue an executive order banning racial discrimination in hiring by defense contractors.

As president of the Durham branch of the NAACP, Austin helped establish the North Carolina State Conference of NAACP Branches, which provided a stronger and more united base to press forward in the fight for equal rights. During the war the North Carolina NAACP doubled the number of local branches and increased its membership to almost ten thousand.

Unlike some older black activists Austin sustained his position at the forefront of the movement for justice and equal opportunity during the modern civil rights movement of the 1950s and 1960s. He joined with a new generation of activists in supporting desegregation of public schools, lunch counters, and restaurants; equal access to employment opportunities; and voting rights. He continued to support litigation but also supported civil disobedience. After the *Brown* decision, Austin courageously criticized the White Citizens' Council as a latter-day KKK. He advocated boycotts of stores that refused to hire blacks. In 1963 he chastised black businessmen who failed to join picket lines in support of a boycott of white-owned stores. Moreover, the *Carolina Times* published the names of businesses that were being boycotted by the black community. Austin spoke out in favor of striking workers at Duke University, and he supported black citizens' rent strikes and actions against the city housing authority, which failed to address racial discrimination in public housing. He encouraged Howard Fuller, who led a local antipoverty agency in Durham called Operation Breakthrough, to confront a recalcitrant black upper class while battling powerful white leaders.

For more than half a century Louis Austin played an important role in African Americans' struggle for freedom. Courageous and forthright local leaders like Austin laid the foundation for the important victories produced by the postwar civil rights movement. Bridging the years before and after the landmark Supreme Court decision in *Brown v. Board of Education*, this intrepid journalist led voter registration campaigns, advocated integration of public education, lobbied for equal pay for black teachers and equal funding for black schools, publicized police brutality, and demanded equal employment opportunity for African Americans. Even in the year of his death, Austin was still speaking out for equity in education by challenging the policy wherein the boards of desegregating schools replaced black principals with whites.

Further Reading

The best primary sources regarding Austin are his editorials in the *Carolina Times*. The newspaper is available on microfilm from Duke University's Perkins Library.

Boyd, Harold Kent. "Louis Austin and the Carolina Times," MA thesis, North Carolina College at Durham, 1966.

Gershenhorn, Jerry. "*Hocutt v. Wilson* and Race Relations in Durham, North Carolina, during the 1930s," *North Carolina Historical Review* 78 (July 2001).

Gershenhorn, Jerry. "Double V in North Carolina: The *Carolina Times* and the Struggle for Racial Equality During World War II," *Journalism History* 32 (Fall 2006).

Walker, Harry J. "Changes in Race Accommodation in a Southern Community," PhD diss., University of Chicago, 1945.

Weare, Walter B. *Black Business in the New South: A Social History of the North Carolina Mutual Life Insurance Company* (1973).

Obituary: *New York Times*, 26 July 1971.

JERRY GERSHENHORN

AUSTIN, Lovie (19 Sept. 1887–10 July 1972), jazz singer, was born Cora Calhoun in Chattanooga, Tennessee. Nothing is known about her parents. In a 1950 article on Austin in *Down Beat*, the journalist George Hoefer wrote that "Lovie" was a nickname given to her by her grandmother. Hoefer further claimed that her grandmother "also brought up another little girl a few years younger then Lovie. Her name was BESSIE SMITH, and the two little playmates were parted before either of them began to get the blues." Lovie studied music theory and piano at Roger Williams University in Nashville and Knoxville College in Knoxville. Her career was launched in 1912, when she began touring the vaudeville circuit. At about this time she married a Detroit movie house operator, a union that lasted briefly. She then married the vaudeville performer Austin of the team Austin and Delaney. Lovie worked the vaudeville circuit as the piano accompanist of her husband's act. She then traveled with Irving Miller's *Blue Babies* revue. Other revues with which she was associated as director or producer were *The Sunflower Girls* and *The Lovie Austin Revue*. The latter had a long and successful run at New York City's Club Alabam. The former was a part of her experiences with the Theater Owners Booking Association (TOBA), a group of influential theater owners organized in 1920.

In the early 1920s Austin settled in Chicago, where she remained until the end of her life. She worked as house pianist for Paramount Records, accompanying such classic blues singers as IDA COX, MA RAINEY, ALBERTA HUNTER, and ETHEL WATERS. She was the pianist on Cox's first record and Rainey's first release. Other blues singers with whom she performed or recorded with were Bessie Smith, CHIPPIE HILL, Edmonia Henderson, Edna Hicks, HATTIE McDANIEL, Priscilla Stewart, Viola Bartlette, and Ozzie McPherson. As for her collaborating instrumentalists, the list includes the trumpeters LOUIS ARMSTRONG, LEE COLLINS, and Tommy Ladnier; the saxophonist WILLIAM "BUSTER" BAILEY; the clarinetist JOHNNY DODDS; the trombonist KID ORY; and the drummer BABY DODDS. She also recorded under her own name, Lovie Austin and Her Blues Serenaders. Her accompaniments were described as "sturdy and even-pulsed, yet rolling and rhythmic."

During the 1920s the piano was a vital rhythm accompaniment instrument. Not a solo improviser, Austin believed in collective improvisation. Although she often led small supporting ensembles (generally three members) for accompaniments, there was always a fullness of sound. Of her individual playing, a *Chicago Defender* journalist wrote, "percussive, pushing the beat along, filling in the bass parts with her right hand maintaining a steady flow of counter/melody." Austin's distinguishing features were "considerable skill and musical sophistication." Her many recordings with the Blues Serenaders are classics.

The pianist, composer, and arranger MARY LOU WILLIAMS throughout her career consistently recalled her impression of an early exposure to Austin's ge-nius. Williams indicated that as a child she visited a Pittsburgh theater and was fascinated and inspired by the female at the keyboard, Austin, who was writing down music with her right hand while accompanying the performance with her swinging left. Austin had done all of the orchestrations for the show. Behind schedule, she was at the same time arranging the music for the next act. In a later interview Williams recalled: "During this period, we didn't have very many readers and this woman was a master reader. I haven't seen a man yet that can compare with that woman" (*The Black Perspective in Music*, Fall 1980).

In Chicago, Austin worked as musical director for the Monogram Theater, where the leading black performers appeared. She remained in the post for twenty years and accompanied acts by Waters, McDaniel, BILL "BOJANGLES" ROBINSON, and others. Subsequently she worked in a similar capacity at both the Gem and the Joy theaters. Austin shared composition credits with Hunter on "Nobody Knows You When You're Down and Out" and "Down Hearted Blues." Other Austin compositions include "Bad Luck Blues," "Barrel House Blues," "Travelin' Blues," "Steppin' on the Blues," and "Frog Tongue Stomp." But there was little copyright protection, and she was deprived of many royalties.

As her New Orleans–style playing fell out of vogue, Austin worked as a security inspector at a naval defense plant during World War II. When Hoefer wrote his 1950 feature article on Austin, she was pianist for the Penthouse Studios at the Jimmy Payne School of Dance in Chicago. She recorded with Hill for Capitol Records in 1946 and with Hunter for Riverside Records in 1961, although her longest recording association was with the Paramount label. Austin officially retired in 1962 and died ten years later in Chicago. Her musical contributions remained overlooked until the revived interest in women in jazz in the 1970s and the subsequent publication of three books on women in the early days of jazz.

Further Reading
Handy, D. Antoinette. *Black Women in American Bands and Orchestras* (1981).
Hoefer, George. "Lovie Austin Still Active as a Pianist in Chicago," *Down Beat* (16 June 1950).
Shapiro, Nat, and Nat Hentoff, eds. *Hear Me Talkin' to Ya* (1955).
Obituaries: *Chicago Tribune*, 9 July 1972; *Living Blues*, Summer 1972; *Down Beat*, 12 Oct. 1972.

ANTOINETTE HANDY

AUSTIN, Oscar Palmer (15 Jan. 1948–23 Feb. 1969), Marine Corps soldier in the Vietnam War and Medal of Honor winner, was born in Nacogdoches, Texas, the son of Frank and Mildred Austin, and was raised in Phoenix, Arizona. A graduate of Phoenix Union High School, Austin was inducted for service in the U.S. Marine Corps during the height of the Vietnam War on 22 April 1968. Upon joining the marines, he was sent to boot camp at the Marine

Corps Recruit Depot in San Diego, California, and served as a member of the Third Recruit Training Battalion through July 1968. Austin subsequently received individual combat and infantryman training at Camp Pendleton, California, from August to September 1968 as part of the Second Infantry Training Regiment, following which, in October 1968, he was promoted to private first class. Later that month, on 15 October, he was sent to the Republic of Vietnam for his first tour of duty as a combat soldier as a member of Company E, Second Battalion, Seventh Marines, in the First Marine Division.

The role played by blacks in the marine corps during the Vietnam War was vital, and the conditions under which their service was performed mirrored in general the racial conditions that then existed in America. As marine corps historians have noted, "From the first commitment of troops until the last, black Marines were always present in Vietnam" (Shaw and Donnelly, 78). Unlike other wars, where blacks fought in segregated units, black marines fought side by side with their fellow marines who were white, and "the color of a man's skin was of no import to his role as a combat Marine" (Shaw and Donnelly, 78). Despite the fact that serious racial tensions between white and black marines often flared up at marine bases, especially at Camp Lejeune in North Carolina, and "that bigotry and prejudice were practiced in the Corps" (Shaw and Donnelly, 72), these issues often faded into the background in combat situations. Indeed, black marine corps combatants, numbering nearly 41,000 during the war, performed to such a high level that five soldiers would win the Medal of Honor. Among these men were JAMES ANDERSON JR., RODNEY MAXWELL DAVIS, Ralph Johnson, and Robert Jenkins Jr. Also in this class was Oscar Austin who, like his fellow Medal of Honor winners, died in the service of his country.

The month of February 1969 found Oscar Austin and the Seventh Marines stationed in vicinity of Da Nang in South Vietnam, an area noted for many hard-fought battles between the Americans and the Communist North Vietnamese. On the evening of 22 February, Austin's company was stationed six and a half miles west of Da Nang, where he served as an assistant machine gunner. In the early hours of 23 February, Austin's observation post came under severe fire from a ground attack by a large North Vietnamese army force. Grenade and small-arms fire predominated, and Austin's company was in a dangerous position. When Private First Class Oscar Austin observed that one of his fellow soldiers was wounded and in an exposed position, he

unhesitatingly left the security of his fighting hole and, with a complete disregard for his own safety, raced across the fire-swept terrain to assist the Marine to a covered location. As he neared the casualty, he observed an enemy grenade land nearby and, reacting instantly, leaped between the injured Marine and the lethal object, absorbing the effects of its detonation. As he ignored his painful injuries and turned to examine the wounded man, he saw a North Vietnamese Army soldier aiming a weapon at his unconscious companion. With full knowledge of the probable consequences and thinking only to protect the Marine, Private First Class Austin resolutely threw himself between the casualty and the hostile soldier and, in doing so, was mortally wounded. (Shaw and Donnelly, 100)

For his "indomitable courage . . . and selfless devotion to duty" on that Sunday morning in February 1969, Oscar Palmer Austin was posthumously awarded the Medal of Honor, the fourth black marine so honored in the war to that date (Shaw and Donnelly, 100). The medal was issued to Austin's parents in April 1970 at the White House in Washington, D.C., by Vice President Spiro Agnew.

Just like American soldiers in the nation's wars from the American Revolution through the Korean War, many of those fighting in Vietnam showed courage under extremely difficult circumstances, and Austin's heroism serves to exemplify their sacrifice. Oscar Austin has not been forgotten; not only was his name etched on the Vietnam Veterans Memorial Wall (panel 32W, row 088), but he was further memorialized when the *Arleigh Burke*–class Aegis destroyer *Oscar Austin* (DDG-79) was named in his honor and commissioned in 2000 by the United States Navy.

Further Reading
Leatherwood, Art. "Oscar P. Austin," in *The Handbook of Texas Online*, http://www.tsha.utexas.edu/handbook/online/article/AA/fause.html.
Shaw, Henry, Jr., and Ralph Donnelly. *Blacks in the Marine Corps* (2002).

GLENN ALLEN KNOBLOCK

AVERY, Byllye (20 Oct. 1937–), women's health advocate, was born Byllye Yvonne Reddick in Waynesville, Georgia, the daughter of L. Alyce M. Ingram, a schoolteacher. The name and occupation of her father is unknown. Although Byllye was born in Georgia, her family eventually settled in Deland, Florida, a town of five thousand people near Daytona Beach. Her mother, a graduate of Bethune-Cookman College, was a schoolteacher in nearby Perry, Florida. When Byllye was a teenager, her mother enrolled in a graduate program at New York University to earn a master's degree in education. Consequently, Avery's mother spent her summers in New York, away from her daughter, which was the only time in which she could take courses. Avery's father died during the last year of her mother's graduate studies.

Byllye attended Talladega College in Alabama and graduated in 1959 with a BA in Psychology. She soon married Wesley Avery, whom she had met at Talladega, in 1960. Byllye Avery eventually earned an MEd in Special Education from the University of Florida in 1969 and began working as head teacher in a children's mental health unit at the teaching hospital at the University of Florida in Gainesville.

Avery is often credited with starting the contemporary African American women's health movement in the United States. Given that she had no formal training or background in medicine or health care, Avery attributed her success to her personal experiences and her commitment to health issues. One major moment was the abrupt death of her husband from a massive heart attack in 1970 at the age of thirty-three, after which Avery was left with the responsibility of rearing their two children alone. The traumatic event forced her to think critically about preventive care and maintaining a healthy lifestyle.

Avery became active in health issues in the early 1970s. After a petition to open a Planned Parenthood clinic in Gainesville was rejected, Avery and four colleagues decided to establish and operate a clinic of their own. In 1974 they opened the Gainesville Women's Health Center, which was the first abortion and gynecological care clinic in the city. Continuing her interest in providing quality health care to women, in 1978 Avery helped found Birthplace, an alternative birthing center in Gainesville, where certified nurse-midwives assisted women with deliveries. Avery personally assisted in more than one hundred births at the center before her departure.

Recalling the negative attitudes toward sex that she encountered from her mother, Avery decided that she would not repeat the cycle with her own daughter. For her daughter's eleventh birthday Avery decided to celebrate it as a rite of passage marking her daughter's first menstruation, giving her a cake that read "Happy Birthday, Happy Menstruation!" Soon thereafter Avery conducted a workshop on menstruation and childbearing for students at her daughter's elementary school. Taking this public education project a step further, in 1987 Avery produced a video for the National Black Women's Health Project. The video, *On Becoming a Woman: Mothers and Daughters Talking Together*, encouraged open communication between mothers and daughters about the physical and emotional changes that occur during adolescence.

Avery's interest in the health of African American women developed at the most unlikely of places, the Comprehensive Employment Training Program (CETA), a job-training program for young women at Santa Fe Community College in Gainesville. While serving as the program's director, she observed and became increasingly concerned about the level of high absenteeism among the young African American women participants. She soon learned that many of the women were dealing with a multitude of issues, including hypertension, diabetes, raising many children, domestic violence, and sexual abuse. This realization spurred Avery to collect as much health information and statistics as she could possibly find. She was astounded by the health disparities between African American and white women and concluded that there is a "conspiracy of silence" concerning the poor health status of African American women (White, 6).

While serving on the board of directors for the National Women's Health Network in 1981, Avery conceived and started a two-year project called the Black Women's Health Project that focused on the health of African American women. Under the auspices of the project, Avery and twenty-two colleagues met to plan the Conference on Black Women's Health Issues, which was held in June 1983 at Spelman College in Atlanta. More than two thousand women attended the three-day event. Participants openly discussed pressing issues such as domestic violence, sexual abuse, obesity, diabetes, sexuality, childbirth, mental health, and overall well-being. The conference promoted a holistic, self-help approach to health that encouraged women to take charge of their own health through consciousness-raising groups and self-examination; it also emphasized the integration of physical wellness with spiritual and emotional well-being.

Prompted by the enthusiasm that was sparked among the conference's participants, the project officially became a free-standing organization based in Atlanta and was renamed the National Black Women's Health Project (NBWHP). The organization grew exponentially with the immediate founding of seventy-five self-help groups. By 1991 chapters had been formed in twenty-five states. The organization also began working with women in other countries, such as Belize, Jamaica, Brazil, Nigeria, and South Africa, through its SisteReach program. In 1990 the NBWHP opened an office in Washington, D.C., that focused on public policy advocacy.

In 1989 Avery was one of twenty prominent African American leaders, including DOROTHY HEIGHT, SHIRLEY CHISHOLM, FAYE WATTLETON, and MAXINE WATERS, who issued and signed a public statement entitled "We Remember: African American Women for Reproductive Freedom." The statement declared the group's support of reproductive freedom, broadening its very definition to include the right to have children; the right of access to contraceptive services, reproductive health information, and health care; and the right to safe and legal abortions. The statement addressed the effects of racism, poverty, and violence on the reproductive health of African American women. After many requests for reprints 250,000 copies of the brochure were subsequently circulated nationwide. The influential statement continues to appear in anthologies on women's rights and activism.

The recipient of many awards, Avery won a MacArthur Foundation Fellowship in 1989, as well as several honorary doctorates. Avery served as the first president of the National Black Women's Health Project until 1990. (In 2003 the organization changed its name to the Black Women's Health Imperative.) After stepping down as the NBWHP's president, Avery pursued other projects, including publishing a small book of inspirational affirmations, *An Altar of Words: Wisdom, Comfort, and Inspiration for African American Women*. In 2002 she founded the Avery Institute for Social Change in New York City, which focused on the health of people of color, with a special focus on affordable health care.

By showing the connections among race, ethnicity, economic circumstances, and health, Avery helped to create a viable health movement that addresses the pressing concerns of women of color. Her vision paved the way for other women's health activists of other racial and ethnic backgrounds, and the National Black Women's Health Project served as the model for other groups such as the National Latina Health Organization and the National Asian Women's Health Organization. Other African American groups, such as African American Women Evolving, built on the NBWHP's pioneering work. All of these groups fully embraced Avery's philosophy that women and people of color need not be experts in order to take charge of their health and well-being.

Further Reading
Silliman, Jael, Marlene Fried, Loretta Ross, and Elena Gutierrez. *Undivided Rights: Women of Color Organize for Reproductive Justice* (2004).
Simurda, Stephen J. "Byllye Avery: Guardian of Black Women's Health," *American Health* (March 1993).
Solinger, Rickie, ed. *Abortion Wars: A Half Century of Struggle, 1950–2000* (1998).
Springer, Kimberly, ed. *Still Lifting, Still Climbing: African American Women's Contemporary Activism* (1999).
White, Evelyn C., ed. *The Black Women's Health Book: Speaking for Ourselves* (1994).

KIMALA PRICE

AVERY, Margaret (c. 1950–), singer and actor, was born in Mangum, Oklahoma. Neither the exact date of her birth nor her parents' names are known. An only child, Margaret quickly developed a sense of independence that provided the foundation for a number of the strong characters she later played in her career as an actor. Her father's naval career took the family to San Diego, where Avery attended high school and performed in several drama competitions.

Upon graduation she enrolled in San Francisco State University, where she was inspired by Dr. MARTIN LUTHER KING JR.'s commitment to cultivating and mentoring the next generation of black leaders. She fostered King's notion of preparing African American youth for a brighter future by attaining her goal of becoming an elementary school teacher. Her interest in the stage never waned, however, despite the scarcity of roles for African American women, and she continued pursuing performance opportunities as a singer and drama student.

Eventually Avery moved to Los Angeles, where she worked as a substitute teacher while auditioning for television commercials. Pitching products such as mouthwash led to various stage roles and parts in several so-called black exploitation, or "blaxploitation," films, one of the few cinematic prospects available to black actors during the early 1970s. At this time Avery had her debut in television with roles in *Something Evil* (1972) and *Louis Armstrong—Chicago Style* (1976). She continued to be cast in feature films, including *Magnum Force* (1973) with Clint Eastwood and *Which Way Is Up?* (1977) with RICHARD PRYOR. Roles in the television series *A. E. S. Hudson Street* (1978) and in the made-for-TV movies

The Sky Is Gray (1980), *The Lathe of Heaven* (1980), and *For Us, the Living* (1983) honed her skills before the camera and increased her visibility to American audiences.

In 1985 the director Steven Spielberg brought ALICE WALKER's novel *The Color Purple* to the big screen. The film featured several performers who were newcomers to movies, including WHOOPI GOLDBERG and OPRAH WINFREY. Spielberg, who had directed Avery in a commercial years before, tapped her to play the role of Shug Avery, a chanteuse and mistress to DANNY GLOVER's character, known only as Mister. The part, reportedly turned down by the singer TINA TURNER, called for Avery to showcase the character's independent streak by standing toe-to-toe with Mister, while revealing the character's romantic streak by intimately kissing Goldberg's Celie. Avery's passionate performance earned her an Academy Award nomination for Best Supporting Actress.

In addition to subsequent appearances as a guest star in TV series including *The Cosby Show*, *JAG*, and *Walker, Texas Ranger*, as well as made-for-TV movies, Avery performed in various feature films, including *White Man's Burden* (1995), *Waitin' to Live* (2002), and *Second to Die* (2002). She also appeared as herself in the documentary *The Collaboration of Spirits: Casting and Acting "The Color Purple"* (2003).

Further Reading
Collier, Aldore. "Margaret Avery Says She 'Couldn't Buy a Job' Before *The Color Purple*," *Jet* (10 Mar. 1986).
"Margaret Avery: Anatomy of an Actress." *Black Stars* (Apr. 1976).
"Margaret 'Shug' Avery, Beyond *The Color Purple*!" *Essence* (May 1986).
"What a Sweet Role! The Role of 'Shug' in *The Color Purple* Brings Margaret Avery's Illustrious Career Back to Life." *Right On!* (May 1986): 46–47.

ROXANNE Y. SCHWAB

AYLER, Albert (12 July 1936–c. 5 Nov. 1970), composer and musician, was born in Cleveland, Ohio, the son of Edward Ayler, a semiprofessional violinist and tenor saxophonist, and Myrtle Hunter. Albert and his brother Donald, who later became a professional jazz trumpet player, received musical training early in life from their father. In second grade Albert performed alto saxophone recitals in school. He performed duets with his father (who also played alto saxophone) in church. Together they listened to a great deal of swing and bebop music, both on recordings and at jazz concerts.

From age ten to age eighteen Ayler attended Cleveland's Academy of Music, taking jazz lessons from Benny Miller. Throughout his mid-teenage years Ayler performed in young jazz and rhythm and blues bands. He also was a captain of his high school golf team; at the time, Cleveland's golf courses were largely segregated. While in high school Ayler spent two summers on the blues circuit, performing with LITTLE WALTER JACOBS. According to John Litweiler, the noted avant-garde jazz historian and critic, Ayler's knowledge of jazz standards and his mastery of bebop style gained him the nickname of "Little Bird" after the great CHARLIE PARKER.

Ayler entered the army in 1958, where he switched to tenor saxophone and traveled throughout Europe with a Special Services band based in France. Among the musicians with whom Ayler came into contact during this period were the bebop tenor saxophonists DON BYAS and DEXTER GORDON, as well as the KING OLIVER reedman ALBERT NICHOLAS. Europe in the late 1950s and early 1960s was a hotbed of activity in the fledgling free-jazz movement. Innovations such as abandoning chord changes, exploring sound for its own sake, and collective improvising—all recalling music's true roots—were ways of approaching free jazz's goal of "spiritual transcendence." Ayler's proximity to jazz clubs in Copenhagen and Paris allowed him to listen to and practice this emerging style when off duty.

Ayler remained in Europe immediately following his discharge in 1961, performing throughout Sweden with a bebop trio that was recorded live in 1962. That year he returned to Copenhagen, where he experienced his first studio recording date; the recordings that resulted from this session were released as *The First Recordings*, or *Something Different*, on Bird Notes. From that point on Ayler performed only his own music. He sat in with the avant-garde pianist CECIL TAYLOR's group at the Club Montmartre in the winter of 1962–1963. Ayler soon felt constrained by what he termed the "simplicity" of bebop and gravitated toward free performance. Ayler moved to New York in 1964, where he occasionally performed with Taylor and recorded an album in the winter of 1963–1964. He formed a quartet in New York in the summer of 1964 with the bassist Gary Peacock and the drummer Sunny Murray, picking up the trumpeter DON CHERRY in Europe. The quartet toured Sweden and Holland. Ayler married Arlene Benton in 1964; they had one daughter.

Ayler possessed a big, soulful sound very much in the style of rhythm and blues music. Wailing, braying, growling, buzzing—these are just a few terms that have been used to describe his playing. A thorough master of his instrument, Ayler was noted for bringing out multiple overtones in his sound through overblowing and manipulation. Characteristic of his playing were split tones, loud honks in the lower register, shrieks in the upper register, wide harsh vibrato, and extreme interval leaps.

Ayler used modes and scales, as well as sound for its own sake, in his emotional improvisation, which often featured simple motivic repetition based upon initially stated thematic material that would suddenly deviate from the established harmonic changes to collective improvisation. He played anything that came to his mind that possessed a connection with the material, developing relationships within a free context that were somewhat analogous to free association in psychology and stream-of-consciousness writing in literature. The social and philosophical aspects of his music assumed greater importance for Ayler than strict musical interpretation did. He once stated that his goal was to provide an atmosphere of spiritual transcendence for the audience (and for his fellow musicians) that would combine the collective cohesiveness of a New Orleans jazz band with a formal freedom arrived at individually.

Although Ayler received acclaim from critics, he was unable to gain a steady audience for his music, leaving him with a meager personal income. He performed and toured sporadically with his group throughout the 1960s, both in Europe and in the United States. Ayler played in studios and clubs in New York from 1965 to 1968. A member of the short-lived Jazz Composers Guild, Ayler performed his first major United States concert at New York's Town Hall in 1965 with his brother Donald. An appearance at the 1966 Newport Jazz Festival and a European Tour in November of that year highlighted the group's accomplishments.

A 1967 European tour included Ayler and his brother Donald, the violinist Michel Sampson, the bassist Bill Folwell, and the drummer Beaver Harris. Ayler performed college concerts with such musicians as Gary Peacock or HENRY GRIMES on bass; Beaver Harris, Sonny Murray, or Milford Graves on drums; and Cal Cobbs on piano or harpsichord. Ayler also occasionally performed on instruments such as alto and soprano saxophone, and even the bagpipes.

After returning from a European tour with his quintet in 1970, Ayler was reported missing in New York City. According to his companion, Ayler, in despair over family strife involving his brother Donald, had boarded the ferry to the Statue of Liberty and jumped off before the ferry reached Liberty Island. His body was found on 25 November in the East River near the Congress Street Pier in Brooklyn. The exact cause of death was unconfirmed.

Ayler, together with JOHN COLTRANE, ARCHIE SHEPP, and PHAROAH SANDERS, expanded the definition of jazz that was initiated by ORNETTE COLEMAN in the late 1950s, creating for future jazz musicians and audiences a much broader concept of improvised music.

Further Reading

Litweiler, John. *The Freedom Principle: Jazz after 1958* (1984).

Lyons, Len, and Don Perlo. *Jazz Portraits: The Lives and Music of the Jazz Masters* (1989).

Wilmer, Valerie. *As Serious as Your Life: The Story of the New Jazz* (1980).

Obituary: *New York Times*, 4 Dec. 1970.

Discography

Litweiler, John. "The Legacy of Albert Ayler," *Down Beat* 38, no. 7 (1971): 14–15, 29.

DAVID E. SPIES.

BABB, Valerie Melissa (6 May 1955–), writer, editor, and scholar, was born in New York City to Dorothy L. Babb and Lionel S. Duncan, both of whom were immigrants from the Republic of Panama. Her parents were part of the larger West Indian community, the "diggers" as many were called, who built the Panama Canal. Babb shared a close relationship with her mother, who instilled in her the value of an education.

Babb attended the Bronx High School of Science, a high school specializing in math and sciences and with some of the best English teachers, whose influence Babb credits for choosing this profession. After graduating from high school in 1973, she enrolled in Queens College of the City University of New York. She graduated with honors in 1977, earning a bachelor's degree in English with a minor concentration in Romance Languages. Babb went on to attend graduate school at the State University of New York at Buffalo, where she majored in English and pursued linguistics as a minor field of study. She earned a master's degree in 1979 and remained at SUNY Buffalo to earn her PhD in English in 1981. Babb's dissertation, "The Evolution of an American Literary Language," examined ways in which American writers used dialect, vernacular, and linguistic racial symbolism to create a literary language more appropriate for a national multicultural literature.

Babb accepted a tenure-track position as an assistant professor of English at Georgetown University in Washington, D.C., in 1981. In 1983 she published her first work of fiction, "A Panama Story," a short story that appeared in *Sargasso*. In 1987 she earned tenure, thus cementing her professional credentials. That same year, she gave birth to her first and only child, a son, Jaren.

At Georgetown, Babb produced *Black Georgetown Remembered*, a video documentary compiling the oral histories of members of the black Georgetown community. Intrigued by stories of this underrepresented community, Babb collaborated with the local historian and journalist Carroll Gibbs, who had developed a walking tour of Georgetown's black community. Based on her work with Gibbs, Babb outlined a preliminary script for a film on the history of black Georgetown. With Babb and Gibbs as narrators, the half-hour documentary premiered at the university in February 1989, in conjunction with Black History Month.

During the next two years, Babb served as associate professor of English at Georgetown, while extending the material in the video into her first published book, *Black Georgetown Remembered: A History of Georgetown's Black Community*. This documentary was published in 1991 and compiles the oral histories documenting the story of black presence in Georgetown from the first half of the twentieth century to the beginning of the twenty-first century.

Babb completed *ERNEST GAINES* in 1991. Part of Twayne Publishers' United States Authors Series, the book reviewed Gaines's work and examined his use of communal narrative to capture the oral storytelling in his native Louisiana. In doing so Babb revealed her own ongoing concern for the complexities of language, storytelling, and American culture. In 1994 her essay, "Old-fashioned Modernism: 'The Chaging Same' in Ernest Gaines's *A Lesson before Dying*," an excerpt from her book, appeared in *Critical Reflection on the Fiction of Ernest J. Gaines*, edited by David C. Estes.

In collaboration with Gay Gibson Cima, Babb co-authored the article "Questioning the Canon in a Multicultural Classroom," which appeared in *New Theatre Quarterly* in 1995. It is one of her many articles to appear in refereed journals and the only one specifically to demonstrate Babb's pedagogical approach to literature. That same year, she published her first of six book reviews, a critique of Sara Lawrence-Lightfoot's *I've Known Rivers: Lives of Loss and Liberation*, which appeared in *America*, and she earned a Keck fellowship from the Georgetown University American Studies Program.

In 1998, while teaching courses in American literature, women's studies, and American studies at Georgetown, Babb published her third book, the one that would anchor her position as a theorist of note, *Whiteness Visible: The Meaning of Whiteness In American Literature and Culture*. In it Babb investigated the language of "whiteness," not as a theory of race but as a social, political, and economic construct. Acting as both literary and cultural theorist, Babb deconstructed the idea of whiteness as necessarily representative of American culture. She combined cultural theory and material theory with close textual analysis to develop her own theory, namely that the term "America" has become synonymous with the concept of whiteness. Babb guided readers on a journey through the development of the American literary canon, concluding that America's propensity to conflate whiteness with being American is not only dangerous but also antithetical to the foundation of American literature. From literature of the seventeenth and eighteenth centuries, in which white voices dominate American literature, to literature of the early twentieth century, in which immigrants' voices emerge and challenge the implicit whiteness of American culture, Babb offered a new approach to reading and comprehending the language of the American literary canon.

Babb achieved the rank of full professor at Georgetown in 1998. During this time Babb also joined the faculty of the Bread Loaf School of English at Middlebury College in Vermont, where she devoted her summers to building the English curriculum. In 1999 Babb assumed the position of director of undergraduate studies at Georgetown.

In 2000 Babb left Georgetown University and accepted a position as professor in the English department at the University of Georgia. In this capacity Babb taught a variety of courses and served as editor of the LANGSTON HUGHES Review, the official publication of the Langston Hughes Society. In 2005 she earned a fellowship to participate in the Scholars-in-Residence Program at the Schomburg Center for Research in Black Culture. Upon her return to the University of Georgia in 2007 Babb became the first African American woman to hold the position of head of the English department.

Further Reading

Kazensky, Michelle, ed. "Valerie Babb," in *The Writers Directory* (2007).

Klebba, Caryn, ed. "Valerie Babb," in *Directory of American Scholars,* tenth ed. (2002).

Mallegg, Kristen, ed. "Valerie Babb," in *Who's Who among African Americans* (2006).

ONDRA KROUSE DISMUKES

BABY LAURENCE (24 Feb. 1921–2 Apr. 1974), jazz tap dancer, was born Laurence Donald Jackson in Baltimore, Maryland. His parents' names and occupations are unknown. He was a boy soprano at age twelve, singing with McKinney's Cotton Pickers. When the bandleader DON REDMAN came to town, he heard Laurence and asked his mother if he could take the boy on the road. She agreed, provided that her son was supplied with a tutor. Touring on the Loew's circuit, Laurence's first time in New York was marked by a visit to the Hoofers Club in Harlem, where he saw the tap dancing of HONI COLES, Raymond Winfield, Roland Holder, and Harold Mablin. Laurence returned home sometime later to a sudden tragedy; both of his parents had died in a fire. "I don't think I ever got used to the idea," he told Marshall Stearns in *Jazz Dance* in 1968. "They always took such good care of me."

Laurence and a brother formed a vocal group called The Four Buds and tried to establish themselves in New York. He worked in the Harlem nightclub owned by DICKIE WELLS—the retired dancer from the group Wells, Mordecai, and Taylor—who nicknamed him "Baby" and encouraged his dancing. Laurence frequented the Hoofers Club, absorbing ideas and picking up steps from EDDIE RECTOR, Pete Nugent, Toots Davis, Jack Wiggins, and Teddy Hale, who became his chief dancing rival. "I saw a fellow dance and his feet never touched the floor," the tap dancer Bunny Briggs said, recalling when he first saw Laurence dance in the 1930s. Laurence worked afterhours sessions, gigged around Harlem, Washington,

D.C., and Cincinnati, and began playing theaters such as Harlem's Apollo in the late 1930s. He performed with a group called The Six Merry Scotchmen (in some billings, the Harlem Highlanders), who dressed in kilts, danced, and sang JIMMIE LUNCEFORD arrangements in five-part harmony.

Around 1940 Laurence focused on tap dancing and became a soloist. Through the 1940s he danced with the big bands of DUKE ELLINGTON, COUNT BASIE, and Woody Herman, and in the 1950s he danced in small Harlem jazz clubs. Under the influence of the jazz saxophonist CHARLIE PARKER and other bebop musicians, Laurence expanded tap technique into jazz dancing. He performed with the jazz pianist ART TATUM, duplicating with his feet what Tatum played with his fingers. Through listening hard to Parker, DIZZY GILLESPIE, and BUD POWELL as well as jazz drummers such as MAX ROACH, Laurence developed a way of improvising solo lines and variations as much like a horn man as a percussionist. "He was more a drummer than a dancer," Whitney Balliett wrote in *New York Notes* (1976). "He did little with the top half of his torso. But his legs and feet were speed and thunder and surprise . . . a succession of explosions, machine-gun rattles and jarring thumps." Like musicians in a jazz combo, Laurence was also a fluent improviser who took solos, traded breaks, and built on motifs that were suggested by previous horn men. He was a master of dynamics who would start a thirty-two-bar chorus with light heel-and-toe figures, then drop in heavy offbeat accents and sprays of rapid toe beats that gave way to double-time bursts of rhythm.

Beset by drugs, alcohol, and financial troubles, Laurence stopped performing in the late 1950s. After a long illness he returned to Harlem in the early 1960s to work again in small jazz clubs. In 1960 he began a longtime engagement with CHARLIE MINGUS at the Showplace and that summer danced with Roach and Mingus in Newport, Rhode Island. Laurence was a sensation at the Newport Jazz Festival in 1962 in a legendary concert that included Nugent, Coles, and Briggs and marked the revival of tap dancing.

Laurence drifted into near oblivion in the late 1960s, dancing weekends in a restaurant in Gaithersburg, Maryland, with an excellent trio headed by the drummer Eddie Phyfe. By 1973 he reappeared in New York City, heading up the successful Sunday afternoon tap dancing sessions at the Jazz Museum. During this time he took in students, danced at the Palace with JOSEPHINE BAKER, did some television work, and gave one of his last triumphant performances at the Newport–New York Jazz Festival.

Laurence is regarded as an authentic jazz dancer who further developed the art of tap dancing by treating the body as a percussive instrument. "In the consistency and fluidity of his beat, the bending melodic lines of his phrasing, and his overall instrumentalized conception, Baby is a jazz musician," Nat Hentoff wrote in the album notes for *Baby Laurence—Dance Master,* a 1959 recording of Laurence's rhythmic virtuosity that demonstrates the inextricable tie between jazz tap dancing and jazz music.

Further Reading
Balliett, Whitney. *New York Notes: A Journal of Jazz, 1972–1975* (1976).
Stearns, Marshall, and Jean Stearns. *Jazz Dance: The Story of American Vernacular Dance* (1968).

Discography
Baby Laurence—Dance Master (Classic Jazz CJ30, recorded 1959, released 1977).

CONSTANCE VALIS HILL

BACON-BERCEY, June (23 Oct. 1932–), meteorologist, was born June Esther Griffin in Wichita, Kansas, the only child of James Griffin, an auto mechanic who put himself through law school and eventually became an attorney, and Cherrie MacSalles, a music teacher. The name she is known by, Bacon-Bercey, is a combination of the last names of her first two husbands. She was married to Walker Bacon, a doctor, from 1956 to 1967 and to John Bercey, a businessman, from 1968 to 1980. Encouraged by her parents, Bacon-Bercey became interested in science at a very young age, and in high school a physics teacher steered her toward a career in meteorology. Bacon-Bercey attended the University of California at Los Angeles, where she earned a BS in Mathematics and Meteorology in 1954 despite the attitude of many of her professors who felt that a woman was better suited to studying home economics. She continued on at UCLA and earned an MS in Mathematics and Meteorology in 1955, and armed with her degrees and her love of science and mathematics, she became the first black female professional meteorologist in the United States.

Bacon-Bercey joined the National Meteorological Center (NMC) as a meteorologist in 1956. In 1962 she left the NMC to work as a consultant for the Sperry Rand Corporation. As a Sperry Rand consultant she worked at the Atomic Energy Commission, where she monitored the effects of nuclear explosions in the atmosphere. It was also at the Atomic Energy Commission that she met her future husband, George W. Brewer, an atomic scientist.

From 1970 to 1973 Bacon-Bercey worked as a roving reporter for NBC in New York City and Buffalo, thus becoming the first black woman television meteorologist for the NBC affiliate in Buffalo, New York. Bacon-Bercey had predicted a heat wave, and when it happened as predicted, she was offered the job of meteorologist. The job served as a stepping-stone to other weather-related endeavors, including becoming the station's chief meteorologist and ultimately working with federal and state governments. In 1975 Bacon-Bercey left NBC to lecture on meteorology, speaking across the country. From 1975 to 1978 she worked for the National Weather Service (NWS) in Washington, D.C., as a meteorologist and broadcaster.

In 1979 she completed a master of public administration degree at the University of Southern Califor-

nia and joined the National Oceanic and Atmospheric Agency (NOAA) as a public affairs specialist, later becoming chief of television services. Bacon-Bercey's duties at NOAA included conducting weather briefings for ocean survey researchers, weather forecasters, and business and government officials, as well as the U.S. media. While working at NOAA in 1977 she won the top prize on the television game show the *$128,000 Question* and used most of the prize money to establish a scholarship fund, administered by the American Geophysical Union, for women who want to become meteorologists. In 1976 Bacon-Bercey rejoined the National Weather Service and moved to Redwood City, near San Francisco, where she worked primarily with pilots and air traffic controllers, did weather forecasting, and served as a training officer. She remained at the NWS for the rest of her career before retiring in 1989.

Not one to sit idly, Bacon-Bercey began working as a substitute teacher in the San Mateo public school system in 1990. She also continued to work as a consultant with private foundations, universities, various professional associations, and NOAA. In addition to other publications before and after retiring from meteorology, Bacon-Bercey contributed a lesson on weather titled "Weather Watch" to the Harcourt-Brace CD-ROM *Science AnyTime*. She has also taught in San Francisco Bay–area schools.

Throughout her career Bacon-Bercey was active in a variety of professional organizations, including the American Meteorological Association, Women in Science and Engineering, the American Geophysical Union, the American Association of Public Administrators, and the New York Academy of the Sciences. As a member of the American Geophysical Union she served on the Committee on Women and Minorities in Atmospheric Sciences. According to the American Meteorological Society, Bacon-Bercey was a founding member of the Board of Women and Minorities. The board's responsibilities include "increasing the participation of women and minorities in the atmospheric and related oceanic and hydrologic sciences; to recommend and develop programs and ideas for educational and professional opportunities for women and minorities; and to survey periodically the membership and report on the Society's character, demographics, and professional needs."

Bacon-Bercey was also actively involved in science and engineering fairs, believing that they are a wonderful way to encourage schoolchildren's interest in science and engineering and to recognize the students' accomplishments. She received a number of awards, including the 1972 Seal of Approval for Excellence in Television Weathercasting from the American Meteorological Society—she was the award's first female recipient. In 1984 Bacon-Bercey received NOAA's Certificate for Sustained Superior Performance; she later won an award for Outstanding Contribution to Furthering the Mission of NOAA from 1984 to 1992. In 2000 she was one of ten people recognized by the National Science Foundation and the National Aeronautics and Space Administration (NASA); she was recognized as a pioneer and role model in science and as a minority pioneer in atmospheric sciences.

Further Reading

Hall, Paula Quick. *A Day's Work?—A Life's Work!: A Visit with Some Women Whose Careers Began with Chemical, Civil, Electrical, Industrial, and Nuclear Engineering* (1987).

Workman, Bill. "Substitute Science Teacher Is a Meteorology Legend: Weather Pioneer June Bacon-Bercey Given More Honors," *San Francisco Chronicle*, 23 Mar. 2000.

ANNE K. DRISCOLL

BADGER, Roderick (4 July 1834–Dec. 1890), dentist, was born a slave in the Panthersville District of Dekalb County, Georgia. His mother (name unknown) was a slave, and his father, J. D. Badger, was a white dentist and also his master. Roderick had several brothers, including Robert and Ralph, all of whom had the same white father but different mothers. In many ways his life story can be seen as an example of the complex relationships between the races in the antebellum and postbellum South, where the black and white societies were supposed to be separate but where mixed-race children were common, growing ever more numerous in the decade leading up to the Civil War. As the son of his owner, Badger enjoyed the privileges associated with that status, including his eventual freedom and prosperity. However, his status as a mulatto and as a professional man did not protect him from many of the disadvantages of being a black man in the antebellum South.

Roderick learned the art of dentistry from his father. While working for his father during the week he was able to set aside Sundays as a day that he could work for himself. Saving the money he made on Sundays, he was able to obtain his freedom, although it is unclear whether his father liberated him or if he purchased his freedom. Some accounts indicate that his working on Sundays was not to buy his freedom but was to purchase his own tools to practice his trade. That his brothers also eventually became freemen implies that they were manumitted, not forced to buy their freedom. In any case, well before the advent of the Civil War, Badger was a free man of color. He married Mary A. Murphey, who was the daughter of a wealthy Georgia lawyer and was one of the black gentry. They had eight children between 1856 and 1879, two daughters and six sons, seven of whom lived beyond childhood, their first child Zora having died when she was one year old.

Badger and his family moved to Atlanta in 1856 where he set up his practice, becoming the first black dentist in the city. His practice was by all accounts highly successful, to the degree that he was the object of a hostile petition from white Atlanta businessmen in 1859. The petition, presented to the city council, named Badger as a "negro" businessman who unfairly took customers away from white businessmen. In response to the petition the council passed a rule that free blacks in the city of Atlanta would have to pay a fee of two hundred dollars to stay within the city limits. They were also imprisoned for five days, during which time they could be hired out to raise money to pay their fee. Every day that the fee was not paid the free person of color was to receive thirty-nine lashes. A second petition protesting Badger's prominence and practice was presented to the Atlanta ordinance committee in February 1861, though no record exists that the punitive ordinance was ever enforced.

With the onset of the Civil War, Badger served as an aide to a Confederate army colonel. When the colonel lost his watch during the campaign and Badger managed to retrieve it for him, the colonel gave the watch to Badger. It became a family heirloom. There is no indication in the record of whether or not he was pressed into this service with the colonel or entered it voluntarily. That he was a free man before the war and that he escaped from this service in 1864 with the arrival of the Union army in Georgia seem to indicate that he was an unwilling participant in the Confederate cause. Badger and his family fled to Chicago, where they waited out the rest of the war.

After the war Badger and his family returned to Atlanta, where he reestablished his practice, which included many prominent blacks in Atlanta. He also became active in assisting the freed people and joined the Republican Party. He served as a tutor at a school established for blacks at one of the local churches, and he was appointed an election official by Governor Bullock to help monitor the polls and make certain that blacks were allowed to practice their newly acquired right to vote. In 1879 he was elected for a three-year term to the board of trustees of Clark College (later Clark Atlanta University), making him the first black trustee of the college. Badger was able to amass considerable property in Atlanta, owning at least five other properties besides his office on Peachtree Street. He died on 27 December 1890 and is interred in the black section of the historic Oakland Cemetery in Atlanta.

Further Reading

Hornsby, Anne R. "The Accumulation of Wealth by Black Georgians, 1890–1915," in *Journal of Negro History* 74, no. 1 (1989).

Howard, W. P. "Atlanta as Left by the Enemy," in *Charleston Mercury* (19 Dec. 1864).

Robinson, Henry S. "Robert and Roderick Badger, Pioneer Georgia Dentists," in *Negro History Bulletin* 24, no. 1 (1961).

Sammons, Vivian Ovelton. *Blacks in Science and Medicine* (1990).

United States Congress Joint Select Committee on the Affairs in the Late Insurrectionary States. *Report of the Joint Select Committee appointed to inquire into the conditions of affairs in the late insurrectionary states, so far as regards the execution of laws and the safety of the lives and property of the citizens of the United States and Testimony Taken* (1892).

M. COOKIE E. NEWSOM

BAGNERIS, Vernel Martin (31 July 1949–), playwright, actor, director, singer, and dancer, was born in New Orleans, Louisiana, the third child of Gloria Diaz Bagneris and Lawrence Bagneris Sr. Bagneris's mother was a housewife and deeply religious woman who "quietly outclassed most people," and his father was a playful, creative man, a World War II veteran, and lifelong postal clerk. Bagneris grew up in the tightly knit, predominantly Creole Seventh Ward to a family of free people of color that had been in New Orleans since 1750. From the age of six he had a knack for winning popular dance contests, and during christenings and jazz funerals he learned more traditional music and dance. By the mid-1960s the once-beautiful, tree-lined neighborhood in which he was raised fell victim to the U.S. government's program of urban renewal, known colloquially as "Negro removal." A freeway overpass was constructed over a thriving neighborhood, inviting crime and eventually shuttering businesses and community. Trees were uprooted, homes were razed, the promenade was destroyed, and a neighborhood diaspora was in effect. Bagneris describes it thus: "Imagine the Champs-Elysées minus all trees, with a brooding highway held up by concrete poles and bare, unplanted dirt as its walkways." The Bagneris family moved to Gentilly, along with many other residents of the Seventh Ward.

Bagneris was in the advanced-placement track at St. Augustine High School, an institution committed to teaching dignity and respect to its young men, despite segregation in nearly every aspect of their lives in New Orleans. At fifteen years old, he and his compatriots were encouraged by the school leaders to quietly protest segregation at bowling alleys and drugstore counters citywide. Bagneris graduated in 1967, when overt instances of Jim Crow had diminished but seating was still segregated on public transportation, in restaurants and restrooms, and at water fountains. In the fall of 1967 he headed directly to a seminary to study for the priesthood where he stayed for three long days. "I didn't go there to meditate," said Bagneris. "I went to be of service. That was the confusion."

Fortunately, Xavier University, his older siblings' alma mater and one of the few predominantly black Catholic universities in the country, scrambled to enroll him. He declared sociology as his major, but during his sophomore year Bagneris was dragged to a theater audition by his girlfriend who was afraid to go alone. Bagneris was cast as Gremio in *The Taming of the Shrew*. His girlfriend was not cast. He was a naturally adept actor and made up his mind to pursue a career on the stage. Though he'd never even attended the theater before this audition, by his junior year he was writing, directing, and producing his own plays. The Free Southern Theatre, which began by touring rural, underprivileged areas in the South and eventually basing itself in New Orleans, performed two of Bagneris's plays before he had even graduated.

Bagneris was curious about avant-garde theater methods and, upon his graduation in 1972, traveled to Amsterdam to learn more about the Bread and Love experimental theater group. He returned to New Orleans and worked day jobs. He'd brought with him highly experimental European scripts and staged them in his hometown. He produced and directed Samuel Beckett's *Endgame* on a double bill with Eugène Ionesco's *The Lesson* in a photo gallery, was awarded an artist-in-residence grant by the Arts Council of New Orleans, and made a foray into a daring, wholly integrated theater company in the French Quarter called Gallery Circle. By 1972 he had won two Best Actor awards in New Orleans.

In 1976 Bagneris saw a play in New York City that would change his life: Will Holt's *Me and Bessie,* a one-woman show about the blues legend BESSIE SMITH. After seeing the show, Bagneris realized that there was a way to put New Orleans on the stage. It would require a year of research, oral histories, and interviews with his grandmother, all between gigs playing voodoo priests in independent movies and producing and starring in Edward Albee plays.

For six months Bagneris and his troupe prepared for a one-night-only production of *One Mo' Time,* a musical he had written based on black vaudeville performers in New Orleans. Their limited-run show quickly turned into three nights a week at the Toulouse Theatre in the French Quarter, with JAMES CARROLL BOOKER III playing piano in the lobby before each show. Then, by chance, a New York producer saw it and promised to move it to the city. In October 1979 *One Mo' Time* went to the Village Gate in New York, where it played for three and a half years, spinning a host of internationally touring companies, including a royal command performance in Britain for Queen Elizabeth II. The show earned a Grammy nomination for Best Cast Album in 1980 and was nominated for Society of West End Theatres (SWET) awards for Outstanding Achievement in a Musical, Best Musical, and Best Actress in a Musical in 1982.

Through *One Mo' Time* Bagneris met the dance masters HONI COLES and Charles "Cookie" Cook; however, he cites Pepsi Bethel of the P.B. Authentic Dance Ensemble, who had worked in independent black films during 1930s and 1940s, as his dance mentor. After their meeting, Bethel choreographed every show Bagneris directed. "My interest was not in preserving traditional musical theater. It just so happens that my culture has a lot of music and dance in it." It was Bagneris's father who, after seeing *One Mo' Time,* encouraged Bagneris to work on Creole themes. "I'm always being asked what I am. Even ALLEN TOUSSAINT asked me once, 'Where do you come from—Mars?' No, Allen, I'm from the 7th Ward."

After the success of *One Mo' Time,* Bagneris continued stage explorations with *Staggerlee* in 1985; *Further Mo',* the sequel to *One Mo' Time,* in 1990; and Cy Coleman's *The Life* on Broadway in 1998. In 1995 Bagneris received an Obie Award for *Jelly Roll!,* his portrait of jazz pioneer JELLY ROLL MORTON. Other notable performances include a 2004 revival of *Bubbling Brown Sugar* in which Bagneris starred with DIAHANN CARROLL. During this time he also worked in film, including *Pennies from Heaven* (1981), *Down by Law* (1986), and *Ray* (2004), the award-winning film adaptation of RAY CHARLES's life. In this film, Bagneris worked as choreographer and played the character Dancin' Al. Bagneris also played opposite OSSIE DAVIS in what was to be Davis's last film, the independent feature *Proud* (2004). *One Mo' Time* was revived on Broadway in 2002 and again in New Orleans in 2006.

Bagneris acted as the voice of numerous jazz figures on Public Radio International's *Riverwalk Jazz* program in 1993, re-creating the lives of BUNK JOHNSON, DANNY BARKER, Jelly Roll Morton, and others. In the program for a special performance in the new auditorium at the Library of Congress, Bagneris was proclaimed "a master of the American vernacular."

In October 2005, just two months after the devastation caused by Hurricane Katrina, Bagneris returned to live in New Orleans, ultimately settling in the French Quarter. He said:

It was an emotional choice to return to New Orleans. The whole thing was about feeling needed, to assure that certain things about your cultural history would be preserved. Besides, my heart has always been in New Orleans. Once you're dipped in it, you're *it*.

When Bagneris remounted *One Mo' Time* in New Orleans in December 2006, the three female cast members returned nightly to FEMA trailers that stood next to their damaged homes. But they performed brilliantly, as if there had been no devastation at all. "At times you think that performance—theater—is such a light, unnecessary thing but then you realize that it's not dessert, that it's an integral part of the meal after all."

Further Reading
Unless otherwise indicated, quotations are drawn from an interview between the author and Vernel Bagneris, 2 March 2007.
Bagneris, Vernel, and Leo Touchet. *Rejoice When You Die: The New Orleans Jazz Funerals* (1998).
Hay, Samuel A. *African American Theatre* (1994).
Woll, Allen L. *Black Musical Theatre: From Coontown to "Dreamgirls"* (1989).

WENDI BERMAN

BAILEY, Beryl Isadore Loftman (15 Jan. 1920–18 Apr. 1977), the first African American female linguist, early theorist in Pidgin and Creole linguistics, and educator, was born Beryl Isadore Loftman in Black River, Jamaica, West Indies. Her mother, Eliza Isadore Smith Loftman, was a teacher, and her father, James Henry Loftman, was an educator who became an inspector of schools. Because she was of the middle class, Beryl Loftman was expected to converse in Standard Jamaican English. Nevertheless, she valued the rhythm, music, and style of Creole:

"Though I was forbidden to speak Jamaican Creole in the home during my childhood, my use of Standard Jamaican English was restricted to the earshot of my parents, teachers. . . . With my playmates, brothers and sisters, household help, and the country folk, I conversed always in Creole" (Bailey, "Creole Languages," 3).

Loftman was the eldest of six children, and she and her siblings, Lucille, Myrtle, Kenneth, Seymour, and Howard (who died at six months), grew up valuing education. As an honor student at Wolmer's Girls School, in Kingston, Jamaica, Loftman continued her forays into Creole, prompting one of her teachers to question whether she "intended to go through life talking mathematics" (Bailey, *Jamaican Creole Syntax*, xiii). Loftman soon endeavored to become bidialectal, embracing Metropolitan English as a necessity for upward mobility, one of the factors that resulted in her placing first in Jamaica, with near-perfect scores, on both her junior and senior Cambridge examinations. These tests were sent from Great Britain to Jamaica, which was a British colony at the time, and their passage was required to complete one's education.

After completing Wolmer's with distinction in 1942, Loftman was qualified to accept teaching positions. (Wolmer's was the equivalent of an American community college, and provided the education needed to become a teacher in Jamaica.) Immediately she accepted an appointment to teach English composition and literature at the Bethlehem Training College in Malvern, Jamaica, a women's school operated by the Moravian Church. In 1946 she left Wolmer's to become an English teacher at Ardenne High School in Kingston, Jamaica. As a teacher, she became more aware of the complications her students faced attempting to maintain Jamaican Creole (their home language), while simultaneously mastering Metropolitan English; these issues prompted her interest in linguistics (Bailey, *Jamaican Creole Syntax*, xiii).

Loftman moved to New York City in 1948 and accepted a position as a secretary. That same year, she enrolled in the Columbia University School of General Studies, completing a bachelor's degree in History in February 1952, graduating summa cum laude. She then enrolled in the Graduate School of Arts and Sciences to begin her master's in linguistics, encouraged by Allen Walker Read, an American etymologist, lexicographer, and professor of linguistics at Columbia. She was also influenced by André Martinet, a French linguist who taught at Columbia from 1947 to 1955. Martinet suggested that she consider researching a comparative analysis of creoles for her master's thesis.

On 20 January 1952 Loftman married Neville Huntley Bailey, also of Jamaica, and had two daughters, Stephanie Abiodoun Bailey and Jennifer Ayaba Bailey. Neville Bailey, finding life in New York unfulfilling, returned to Jamaica to live in 1965. In December 1953 Beryl Bailey completed her master's degree in

Linguistics, with the thesis "Creole Languages of the Caribbean Area: A Comparison of the Grammar of Jamaican Creole with Those of the Creole Languages of Haiti, the Antilles, the Guianas, the Virgin Islands, and the Dutch West Indies." Her work represented a breakthrough in Creole studies, as Bailey was the first to maintain with strong evidence the notion of "sister Creoles." First, Bailey maintained that the Caribbean Creoles she analyzed in her thesis were genetically related, having as their African roots the Niger-Congo languages. Second, she classified them as having been lexified by (having gained the vocabularies of) either Germanic languages, principally English and Dutch, or Romance languages, principally French and Spanish. Third, Bailey advocated abandoning the term "Creole," utilizing instead "Afro-European languages" to describe those languages comprising the features of both African and Indo-European languages.

Although linguists have not embraced Bailey's "Afro-European" concept, many of the ideas she advanced have been accepted in the field. Because her thesis remains unpublished, linguists are generally unaware of the range of her ideas that are important to Pidgin and Creole linguistics. Over time, many of her ideas have become associated with the work of others. According to the Creolist William Stewart, "Creole Languages of the Caribbean Area" was Bailey's most significant contribution because of the range of its important theories, and its publication was overdue.

Devoutly religious, Bailey accepted employment with the American Bible Society as she continued her education toward the PhD in Linguistics from Columbia University. Although she spent the remainder of her life in the United States, she returned to Jamaica to conduct fieldwork in 1956 on a grant from the Research Institute for the Study of Man. From 1960 to 1962 she returned on a Junior Research Fellowship provided by the University of the West Indies. On a second fellowship from the Research Institute for the Study of Man, she gathered data for the *Language Guide to Jamaica*, the first full-length grammar of Jamaican Creole, prepared for Peace Corps volunteers and published in 1962. During the summer of 1963, she returned to Jamaica for a third time, completing the fieldwork stage of her dissertation project. While in Jamaica, she assisted Frederic G. Cassidy and Robert B. LePage as they collected data for their *Dictionary of Jamaican English*. Bailey received a Founder's Fellowship from the American Association of University Women (from 1962 to 1963) and a Senior Graduate Fellowship from the American Council of Learned Societies (from 1963 to 1964) in support of her research. In May 1964 Bailey completed her PhD, with the dissertation "Jamaican Creole Syntax: A Transformational Approach."

Among Bailey's major assets was her ability to communicate effectively across social class lines and the advantage of having native-speaker competency. Her most recognized contribution is her dissertation, published by Cambridge University Press in 1966. It was the first full-length description of the syntax of a Creole language and the first study to utilize the generative grammatical format outlined by the linguist Noam Chomsky in his 1957 book *Syntactic Structures*. Bailey became an assistant professor in the linguistics and behavioral program of Yeshiva University, New York, teaching there from 1964 to 1968. In 1966 she prepared a second book, *Jamaican Creole Language Course*, for the Peace Corps. After four years at Yeshiva she joined the linguistics program at Hunter College in 1968. When black studies became a university discipline, Hunter College initiated a department of black and Puerto Rican studies, selecting Bailey as the founding chair. She served in this position until 1977, when she contracted lung cancer; she died a few months later in New York City, at the age of fifty-seven.

During her brief career, Bailey published three books and twelve articles focusing on three issues: the structure of Creole languages spoken by African people in the Caribbean and the United States, second-language learning, and the development of processes for teaching "Metropolitan" English to speakers of Creole languages. Six of her articles focused on Black English as she connected the Caribbean Creoles and Black English to their African-language sources. Bailey emphasized through her research that Creoles and Black English were correct and independent linguistic systems and not "mistakes" within English. During the final decade of her career, Bailey also served as a consultant to the Department of Health, Education, and Welfare; Brooklyn College; the Ford Foundation; the American Bible Society; and the National Council of Churches.

At the end of her life, Bailey was dismayed that many citizens from her homeland opposed the promotion of the systematic analysis of Jamaican Creole. Likewise, many in the United States opposed the systematic analysis of Black English. She was a "foremother" whose research laid the groundwork for the expanded interest in both specialties after her death. Bailey continues to be regarded as one of the significant voices in developing both the theory and practice that has brought Pidgin and Creole studies and Black English/Ebonics studies to the center of linguist interest. In 1991 Marcyliena Morgan, a linguistic anthropologist at Stanford University, organized a panel called Racism, Linguistics, and Language in African America: Papers in Honor of Beryl Loftman Bailey, at the annual conference of the American Anthropological Association in Chicago.

Further Reading

Bailey, Beryl Loftman. "Creole Languages of the Caribbean Area," master's thesis, Columbia University (1953).

Bailey, Beryl Loftman. *Jamaican Creole Syntax: A Transformational Approach* (1966).

Holm, John. "Focus on Creolists (3): Beryl Loftman Bailey," *Carrier Pidgin* 10:3 (Sept. 1982).

Wade-Lewis, Margaret. "Beryl Bailey," in *African American Women: A Biographical Dictionary,* ed. Dorothy C. Salem (1993).

Wade-Lewis, Margaret. "Beryl Loftman Bailey: Africanist Woman Linguist in New York State," *Afro-Americans in New York Life and History* 17:1 (Spring, 1993).

Wade-Lewis, Margaret. "Beryl Bailey," in *Lexicon Grammaticorum: Who's Who in the History of World Linguistics,* ed. Harro Stammerjohann (1996).

Obituary: *New York Times,* 21 Apr. 1977.

MARGARET WADE-LEWIS

BAILEY, Buster (19 July 1902–12 Apr. 1967), jazz clarinetist and saxophonist, was born William C. Bailey in Memphis, Tennessee. Nothing is known of his parents. He attended the Clay Street School in Memphis, where he began studying clarinet at age thirteen. In 1917 he turned professional after joining the touring band of the famed blues composer W. C. HANDY, and it was during a trip to New Orleans with Handy that he first heard authentic jazz. In early 1919 he left Handy to move to Chicago, where he studied with Franz Schoepp, first clarinetist with the Chicago Symphony, and worked in Erskine Tate's Vendome Theatre Orchestra and doubled in FREDDIE KEPPARD's small jazz band at the Lorraine Gardens. In late 1923 or early 1924 Bailey replaced JOHNNY DODDS in KING OLIVER's Creole Jazz Band for an extensive tour that concluded with its return to the Lincoln Gardens in June 1924. In August 1922, while working with CARROLL DICKERSON at the Sunset Cafe, Bailey first met LOUIS ARMSTRONG, who had just come up from New Orleans to join the Oliver band. Following Armstrong by one week, on 6 October 1924 Bailey left Oliver and joined Armstrong in the FLETCHER HENDERSON Orchestra at New York's prestigious Roseland Ballroom. Bailey and Armstrong both made their first records with Henderson the next day, and on or about 16 October they backed up the blues singer MA RAINEY with a small contingent of Henderson men.

Bailey also recorded as a freelancer from the mid-1920s on; his most enduring association was with CLARENCE WILLIAMS's studio groups sporadically from 1925 to 1937. One of the most active jazz clarinetists of his time, Bailey appeared on hundreds of records throughout the prewar years as an accompanist to blues and vaudeville singers such as BESSIE SMITH, SIPPIE WALLACE, Maggie Jones, TRIXIE SMITH, ALBERTA HUNTER, EVA TAYLOR, and Coot Grant, as well as to jazz singers such as BILLIE HOLIDAY, Mildred Bailey, MAXINE SULLIVAN, UNA MAE CARLISLE, Jerry Kruger, Midge Williams, and Teddy Grace.

Although working with Henderson enabled Bailey to play with the best jazzmen of the day, including the trumpeters JOE SMITH and Tommy Ladnier, the trombonists Charlie Green and Jimmy Harrison, and the tenor saxophonist COLEMAN HAWKINS, Bailey increasingly took time off for engagements with other bands. In April 1929 he left Henderson, and in early

Buster Bailey, with John Kirby (left) at the Brown Derby in Washington, D.C., c. May 1946. (© William P. Gottlieb; www.jazzphotos.com.)

May he embarked on a European tour with the singer and band leader NOBLE SISSLE. After Bailey returned to the United States in late 1929, he worked in the bands of Edgar Hayes and Dave Nelson, rejoined Sissle for two years starting in 1931, and then returned to the Henderson fold in January 1934, leaving once more in November to join the Mills Blue Rhythm Band. Bailey stayed with that organization from December 1934 to October 1935, at which time he went back to Henderson and remained until February 1937, when he left permanently to begin a long and fruitful association with the former Henderson bassist JOHN KIRBY in Kirby's newly formed swing sextet.

Unquestionably because of his formal training, Bailey had developed a fluent clarinet technique early in his career. Indeed, had it not been for the racial temperament of the times, he might very well have gone on to perform in symphony orchestras. As he said many years later in an interview reprinted in *Hear Me Talkin' to Ya:*

One thing I'm happy to see is the integration that's been happening among musicians. . . . Years ago, if it had been like this when I came up I would be able to play with some symphony orchestra. I would have had more of an incentive to study because there would have been more of a prospect of my making a living the way I wanted to. Sure, we played concerts and overtures and numbers like that in the theatres, but when I started you couldn't even think, if you were a Negro, of making symphony orchestras.

On the evidence of his early jazz recordings, Bailey displayed a commendable technical assurance but lacked the passion and improvisatory skills of the foremost New Orleans clarinetists—SIDNEY BECHET, JOHNNY DODDS, and Jimmie Noone. He progressed rapidly, however, and his best performances of this early period are on the Henderson records of the late 1920s and mid-1930s. Bailey also appeared on scores of records with other bands—most notably the Red Onion Jazz Babies and the bands of Erskine Tate and Dave Nelson—and with a number of small groups in sessions organized by the prolific CLARENCE WILLIAMS. As busy as he was in the 1930s, Bailey always found time to participate in the small-band swing sessions that were common. Thus much of his characteristic work in those years can be found on the records of HENRY "RED" ALLEN, LIL ARMSTRONG, LEON "CHU" BERRY, ROY ELDRIDGE, LIONEL HAMPTON, Wingy Manone, Red Norvo, STUFF SMITH, WILLIE "THE LION" SMITH, and a host of others, including those under his own leadership.

It was with the John Kirby band, though, that Bailey finally found his most symbiotic musical setting. Except for Benny Goodman, perhaps no other jazz clarinetist could have executed the technically demanding parts written by Kirby and his trumpeter CHARLIE SHAVERS. The unique style of this group was well suited to Bailey's particular skills as a reader, technician, and the possessor of a legitimately sweet tone. Alternating swing versions of operatic arias and familiar classical themes with exotic original compositions and jazz standards, the Kirby sextet enjoyed successful engagements at many venues in New York, Chicago, and Los Angeles, as well as recording extensively for both commercial labels and for the Lang-Worth Radio Transcription Service. For the first time in his long career, the peripatetic, bustling nature of Bailey's earlier years with the big bands was now a thing of the past. Bailey remained a regular member of the Kirby band from 1937 through 1944 and occasionally appeared with the group for brief engagements in 1945 and 1946.

Buster Bailey spent most of his later years playing in and around New York. He worked with WILBUR DE PARIS from September 1947 to April 1949, and after a brief try at leading his own quartet he went with the trumpeter Red Allen in 1950 and with the trombonist "Big Chief" Russell Moore in 1952. A rare opportunity to perform theater music again presented itself in late 1953, when he joined the pit orchestra of *Porgy and Bess*. In 1954 he rejoined Allen for a job at the Metropole, but during this period he also started receiving calls for symphony rehearsals and concerts. Jazz festivals were becoming frequent venues in the late 1950s and early 1960s, and Bailey performed at several of them, often in the company of Allen. In 1961 he participated in the film *Splendor in the Grass* and began working with Wild Bill Davison

(1961–1963) and then with Red Richards's Saints and Sinners (1963–1964). Bailey joined Louis Armstrong's All Stars in July 1965 and was still with them at the time of his death in Brooklyn.

From the 1940s on, Bailey's most representative recordings were made with Red Allen, Armstrong, the Capitol Jazzmen, BUCK CLAYTON, Wild Bill Davison, Bobby Donaldson, Pee Wee Erwin, Leonard Gaskin, Coleman Hawkins, CLAUDE HOPKINS, Jonah Jones, Billy Kyle, Red Richards, REX STEWART, JOE THOMAS, and TRUMMY YOUNG. Also significant is the one album he made under his own name, *All About Memphis* (1958).

Further Reading
Bruyninckx, Walter. *Swing Discography, 1920–1988* (12 vols., 1985–1989).
Bruyninckx, Walter. *Traditional Jazz Discography, 1897–1988* (6 vols., 1985–1989).
Charters, Samuel B., and Leonard Kunstadt. *Jazz: A History of the New York Scene* (1962).
Dance, Stanley. *The World of Swing* (1974).
Rust, Brian. *Jazz Records, 1897–1942* (1982).
Schuller, Gunther. *Early Jazz* (1968).
Schuller, Gunther. *The Swing Era* (1989).
Shapiro, Nat, and Nat Hentoff, eds. *Hear Me Talkin' to Ya: The Story of Jazz by the Men Who Made It* (1955).
JACK SOHMER

BAILEY, DeFord (14 Dec. 1899–2 July 1982), musician, was born in Bellwood, Smith County, Tennessee, the son of John Henry Bailey and Mary Reedy, farmers. Bailey grew up in the rolling hills east of Nashville and as a child listened to what he later called the "black hillbilly music" played by his family. His grandfather Lewis Bailey was a skilled fiddler who won numerous local championships, and a family string band often appeared at local fairs and dances. DeFord's fascination with the harmonica, an instrument that was especially popular in Middle Tennessee, resulted from a childhood illness. When he was three he was stricken with polio and was bedridden for several years; to amuse himself he practiced the harmonica. Lying in bed and listening to the distant sound of trains, hunting dogs, and barnyard animals, DeFord became adept at working imitations of these into his playing, creating unorthodox "bent" notes and mouthing patterns into what would become a unique musical style. DeFord survived his illness, but it left him stunted and frail.

By 1918 Bailey had moved to Nashville, where he worked at a variety of jobs for wealthy white families. In his spare time he went to local theaters, where for the first time he heard professional entertainers, including the blues singers BESSIE SMITH and MA RAINEY. He soon adapted their songs to his harmonica, and in 1925 he entered a harmonica contest broadcast over a local radio station, WDAD. He won first place, embarrassing the management and forcing them to award two prizes, one for "each race." A short time later he met Humphrey Bate, a white harmonica player who was leading a string band that played for a large new Nashville radio station, WSM. Impressed with Bailey's playing, Bate recommended him to the station manager, George D. Hay, who invited Bailey to appear on the new Saturday night *Barn Dance* (later called the *Grand Ole Opry*). In June 1926 Bailey made his first documented appearance on the show.

Bailey, playing his solo nonchromatic harmonica, quickly became one of the most popular stars on the show. Radio fans, many of whom were unaware that Bailey was black, wrote hundreds of letters requesting his specialties, such as "The Fox Chase" and "Pan American Blues," in which he imitated a train. Hay made big plans for Bailey and told him that he was "nothing but a gold mine walking around on earth." Hay set up dates with several record companies, and Bailey did sides for Columbia (1927), Brunswick (1927), and Victor (1928). Surprisingly, the records did not sell well, and some were never even released to the public. The surviving eleven sides preserve the only documentation of Bailey playing in his prime.

Bailey became a familiar figure around Nashville, riding a custom-designed bicycle back and forth to work. In 1929 he married Ida Lee Jones; they had three children.

In 1932 the Grand Ole Opry started an Artists Service Bureau to help its radio entertainers set up tours and personal appearances. Bailey overcame his nervousness about traveling and went on tours with such Opry stars as the Delmore Brothers, the Fruit Jar Drinkers, Uncle Dave Macon, Robert Lunn, and later Bill Monroe and Roy Acuff. Though he continued to be a favorite on live shows—he had to play his harmonica through a big megaphone to be heard over primitive public address systems—Bailey often had trouble finding lodging in the segregated South. Hotels that welcomed the other Opry musicians often refused Bailey a room, forcing him to seek accommodation in the private homes of local blacks.

At about the time that the Opry started winning a national audience on network radio, Bailey left the show. In 1941 he was fired; the official reason was that he refused to learn any new tunes. In truth it was a complex dispute involving a struggle between two song-publishing organizations, ASCAP and BMI. In the 1920s Bailey had allowed his producer to publish and copyright his songs with ASCAP, and in 1941 ASCAP songs were banned from the airwaves as a result of a licensing disagreement between ASCAP and the major radio networks. Bailey was told that he could not play his old favorites such as "John Henry" and "Fox Chase," songs with which he had made his reputation. Confused, bitter, and angered by the new styles of music that he heard on the show, Bailey did not fight the firing, instead dropping entirely out of music. During this time he operated a shoeshine parlor in downtown Nashville, occasionally playing for friends but refusing to talk to journalists or historians about his early days.

By the late 1960s a new generation of fans began to see Bailey as a folk music hero. One of them, the Van-

derbilt student Dick Hulan, coaxed Bailey into playing at local coffeehouses and festivals. He refused offers to record again, however, and turned down chances to go to the Newport Folk Festival and to appear in films like Burt Reynolds's *W.W. and the Dixie Dancekings* (1975). In 1974 another young friend, David Morton, who worked with the Nashville Housing Authority, talked Bailey into returning to the Opry stage for an "Old Timers' Reunion." He returned to the Opry several other times before his death in Nashville.

Fans of country and folk music speak of Bailey as the genre's finest harmonica virtuoso. His songs are part of the standard repertoire, serving as an important link between rural nineteenth-century folk music and the more commercial music of the twentieth century. His struggle as the first black star in the nearly all-white world of country music has won the respect of generations.

Further Reading
Morton, David, and Charles Wolfe. *DeFord Bailey: A Black Star in Early Country Music* (1991).
Wolfe, Charles. *Grand Ole Opry: The Early Years* (1975).
                                        CHARLES K. WOLFE

BAILEY, Herman "Kofi" (1931–1981), graphic artist, painter, printmaker, and political activist, was born in Chicago in 1931. An only child, he attended Chicago public schools, moving briefly to Washington, D.C., to study at Howard University with ALAIN LEROY LOCKE, STERLING ALLEN BROWN, and JAMES AMOS PORTER. After one year he then enrolled at Alabama State College (later Alabama State University) to study under the sculptor, painter, and printmaker Hayward Louis Oubre, and he received a bachelor of arts degree. Bailey continued study at the University of Southern California (USC) as a student of CHARLES WHITE and the Hungarian-born Francis de Erdely. He earned the bachelor of fine arts degree in 1958 and the master of fine arts degree in 1960. At USC he worked as a graduate assistant for two years, introducing the students MEL EDWARDS and CALVIN BURNETT to the work of JOHN BIGGERS and other established African American graphic artists. Major influences on Bailey's career were Charles White, JACOB ARMSTEAD LAWRENCE, El Greco, Goya, and the Mexican muralists.

Bailey was mentored by W. E. B. DU BOIS, who shared his Pan-African ideology and penchant for experiencing the people and societies of the continent of Africa firsthand. Before embarking on numerous international travels, Bailey taught at Florida Agricultural and Mechanical University and Clark College (renamed Clark Atlanta University). He then continued studying and working in France, Switzerland, Mexico, Guyana, Nigeria, and finally Ghana, where he resided from 1962 to 1966. He was the official artist for the nation of Ghana before serving three years as the chair of the art department at the Kwame Nkrumah Ideological Institute, and he left the country when Nkrumah, the first prime minister and later president, was deposed.

Returning to Atlanta in 1967 as an artist-in-residence at Spelman College, Bailey worked with the MARTIN LUTHER KING JR. Poor People's Campaign, designing the poster that became the symbol of the 1968 March on Washington, as well as creating the Southern Christian Leadership Conference (SCLC) Hunger Poster. Convinced that representational art and noble depiction of "true Black life" were the best approaches to serving the African masses worldwide, Bailey was a prolific producer of drawings, paintings, and prints of portraits and figure-based works ranging from famous faces to cultural narratives. Epitomizing his sociopolitical consciousness, the imagery frequently contained a single figure that through personal or character reference emerged as a statement of the struggle against adversity, while also being an image of pride and solidarity. While he explored numerous materials—including inks, charcoal, graphite, pastels, oils, acrylics, watercolor, and mixed media—conté crayon became his signature drafting material, and lithography was his most common printmaking type.

Bailey's work has been shown in exhibitions at the Los Angeles County Museum of Art, the University of Southern California, the University of Ghana, the Ghana Institute of Art and Culture, Spelman College, the University of Delaware, Montana State University, Boston's National Center of Afro-American Artists, and Clark Atlanta University; and he has exhibited in Mexico, England, Canada, Brazil, Japan, Ivory Coast, Benin, Zaire, Uganda, and Nigeria. His work is in the permanent collections of the Paul R. Jones Collection at the University of Delaware, Spelman College Museum of Fine Art, and Clark Atlanta University Art Galleries, and in public and private collections in Algeria, Congo, Ghana, Nigeria, Guinea, Kenya, Tanzania, Uganda, Ivory Coast, France, England, Poland, Puerto Rico, Chile, Spain, Italy, Indonesia, and Hungary, as well as throughout the United States.

Further Reading
Lewis, Samella Saunders. *African American Art and Artists* (2003).

AMALIA K. AMAKI

BAILEY, Pearl (29 Mar. 1918–17 Aug. 1990), actress, singer, and entertainer, was born Pearl Mae Bailey in Newport News, Virginia, the daughter of the Reverend Joseph James Bailey and Ella Mae (maiden name unknown). Her brother Bill Bailey was at one time a well-known tap dancer.

While still in high school, Bailey launched her show business career in Philadelphia, where her mother had relocated the family after separating from Reverend Bailey. In 1933, at age fifteen, she won the first of three amateur talent contests, with a song-and-dance routine at the Pearl Theatre in Philadelphia, which awarded her a five dollar prize. In a second

contest at the Jungle Inn in Washington, D.C., she received a twelve dollar prize for a buck-and-wing dancing act. After winning a third contest at the famed Apollo Theater in Harlem, she began performing professionally—first as a specialty dancer or chorus girl with several small bands, including Noble Sissle's band, on the vaudeville circuits in Pennsylvania, Maryland, and Washington during the 1930s, then as a vocalist with COOTIE WILLIAMS and COUNT BASIE at such smart New York clubs as La Vie en Rose and the Blue Angel, and on the World War II USO circuit, during the 1940s.

Bailey made her Broadway debut as a saloon barmaid named Butterfly in the black-authored musical *St. Louis Woman*, which opened at the Martin Beck Theatre, 30 March 1946, and ran for 113 performances. Although the show was only modestly successful, she was praised for her singing of two hit numbers, "Legalize My Name" and "(It's) A Woman's Prerogative (to Change Her Mind)." For her performance, she won a Donaldson Award as the best Broadway newcomer. After several failed marriages, one to comedian SLAPPY WHITE, Bailey married the legendary white jazz drummer Louis Bellson Jr., in 1952; they adopted two children. Their marriage was reportedly a happy one. In later years, she frequently sang with her husband's band, and at one time toured with CAB CALLOWAY and his band.

After appearing in supporting roles in two predominantly white shows in 1950–1951, Bailey's first Broadway starring vehicle was *House of Flowers* (1954), a Caribbean-inspired musical. Bailey played the part of Mme. Fleur, a resourceful bordello madam, whose house of prostitution in the French West Indies is facing hard times, forcing her to resort to desperate measures to save it. The show opened at the Alvin Theatre, 30 December 1954, and had a run of 165 performances. Despite what the *New York Times* (30 Dec. 1954) called "feeble material," she was credited with "an amusing style" and the ability to "[throw] away songs with smart hauteur."

Bailey's most important Broadway role was as the irrepressible Dolly Levi (a marriage broker who arranges a lucrative marriage for herself) in the all-black version of *Hello, Dolly!*, which opened at the St. James Theatre in November 1967 for a long run, sharing the stage with the original 1964 Carol Channing version. The black version provided tangible evidence that roles originally created by white actors could be redefined and given new vitality from the perspective of the African American experience. Lyndon Johnson, who had used the show's title song as his campaign theme song in 1964, changing the words to "Hello, Lyndon!," saw the show when it came to Washington and was invited, along with his wife, Lady Bird, to join Bailey onstage for a rousing finale. For her performance, Bailey won a special Tony Award in 1968.

Bailey's most important film roles included *Carmen Jones* (1954), as one of Carmen's friends; *St.*

Louis Blues (1958), as the composer W. C. HANDY's Aunt Hagar; *Porgy and Bess* (1959), as Maria, the cookshop woman; *All the Fine Young Cannibals* (1960), as a boozing, over-the-hill blues singer; and *Norman . . . Is That You?* (1976), opposite the comedian REDD FOXX, as estranged parents of a gay son. Her voice was also used for Big Mama, the owl, in the Disney animated film *The Fox and the Hound* (1981).

A frequent performer and guest on television talk shows beginning in the 1950s, Bailey also hosted her own variety series on ABC, *The Pearl Bailey Show* (Jan.–May 1971), for which her husband directed the orchestra while she entertained an assortment of celebrity guests. She also appeared on television in "An Evening with Pearl" (1975) and in a remake of *The Member of the Wedding* (1982), in the role of Berenice. Bailey released numerous albums and was also the author of several books, including two autobiographies, *The Raw Pearl* (1968) and *Talking to Myself* (1971), and *Pearl's Kitchen* (1973), a cookbook.

In 1975 Bailey was appointed as a U.S. delegate to the United Nations. Other honors and awards included a citation from the New York City mayor John V. Lindsay; *Cue* magazine entertainer of the year (1969); the First Order in Arts and Sciences from the Egyptian president Anwar Sadat; the Screen Actors Guild Award for outstanding achievement in fostering the finest ideals of the acting profession; and an honorary Doctor of Humane Letters from Georgetown University (1977). She later earned a degree in theology from Georgetown.

During the later years of her life, Bailey was hospitalized several times for a heart ailment. She also suffered from an arthritic knee, which was replaced with an artificial one just prior to her death. She collapsed, apparently from a heart attack, at the Philadelphia hotel where she was staying (her home was in Havasu, Arizona); she died soon after at Thomas Jefferson University Hospital in Philadelphia.

Bailey was best known for her lazy, comical, half-singing, half-chatting style, expressive hands, tired feet, and folksy, congenial philosophy of life, which endeared her to audiences both black and white. The *New York Times* obituary (18 Aug. 1990) called her "a trouper in the old theatrical sense," who had "enraptured theater and nightclub audiences for a quarter-century by the languorous sexuality of her throaty voice as well as by the directness of her personality." At her funeral, Cab Calloway, who had starred with her in *Hello, Dolly!*, said that "Pearl was love, pure and simple love"; and her husband called her "a person of love," who believed that "show business" meant to "show love."

Further Reading

Bailey, Pearl. *The Raw Pearl* (1968).
Bailey, Pearl. *Talking to Myself* (1971).
Bogle, Donald. *Blacks in American Films and Television: An Illustrated Encyclopedia* (1988).
Bogle, Donald. *Brown Sugar: Eighty Years of America's Black Female Superstars* (1980).
Peterson, Bernard L., Jr. *A Century of Musicals in Black and White: An Encyclopedia of Musical Stage Works by, about, or Involving African Americans* (1993).

Obituaries: *New York Times*, 18, 24, and 25 Aug. 1990.
BERNARD L. PETERSON

BAILEY, Walter T. (11 Jan. 1882–Feb. 1941), architect, was born Walter Thomas Bailey in Kewanee, Illinois, to Emanuel Bailey and Lucy Reynolds. After attending Kewanee High School, Walter enrolled at the University of Illinois at Urbana-Champaign in 1900. There he studied in the architecture program, which was then part of the College of Engineering. The program at Illinois differed from those at most other architecture schools in the country: many schools followed in the tradition of the École des Beaux-Arts, emphasizing classical modes and principles of architecture, but the program at Illinois was influenced largely by German polytechnic methods of teaching. At Illinois, Bailey received an extensive education in the science of construction and in the history of architecture. Construction courses gave students both theoretical and practical training, while courses in the history of architecture taught them periods and styles such as Egyptian and Islamic, as well as classical.

As a student Bailey was active in various student groups on campus, including the Architects Club and the Twentieth Century Club. In October 1903 Bailey married Josephine L. McCurdy of Champaign, Illinois. The following spring he received a BS in Architecture, becoming the first African American to graduate from the architecture program at the University of Illinois and the first registered African American architect in the state of Illinois.

After graduating Bailey worked briefly as a draftsman for Henry Eckland, an architect in Kewanee, Illinois. In February 1904 Bailey moved back to Champaign to work as a draftsman in the firm of Spencer & Temple. The firm's principals, Nelson Strong Spencer and Harry R. Temple, were graduates of the architecture program at the University of Illinois. Bailey's obituary from the *Urbana Courier* states that Bailey assisted in the planning of the Colonel Wolfe School in Champaign, designed by Spencer & Temple and built in 1905. On 8 March 1905 Bailey's daughter Edyth Hazel was born. His second child, Alberta Josephine Bailey, was born on 16 August 1913. In September 1905 Bailey left Spencer & Temple to take on the position as head of the department of architecture at the Tuskegee Institute in Alabama.

From 1905 to 1914 Bailey oversaw the architecture program at Tuskegee while also undertaking his first independent commissions. Among his responsibilities were supervising the planning, design, and construction of all new buildings on campus and taking charge of the repairing and remodeling of older structures. During his tenure he designed White Hall, a girls' dormitory on campus, in 1908. He also designed two churches in nearby Montgomery, Alabama: St. John's African Methodist Episcopal Church in 1910 and the Old Ship African Methodist Episcopal Zion Church in 1912. Also in 1910 Bailey was awarded an honorary master's degree in architecture from the University of Illinois. He served as head of the department of architecture at Tuskegee until 1914, when he left to practice architecture full-time.

Bailey and his family moved from Tuskegee to Memphis, Tennessee, where he set up his own office and from which he undertook some of his largest and most important commissions. In 1923–1924 he designed the Fraternal Savings Bank and Trust Company building located on Beale Street, an affluent African American area of Memphis. Upon its completion Bailey moved his office to the building. In Little Rock, Arkansas, he designed the Mosaic State Temple building in 1922 and the Pythian Theater building in 1922–1923. In Hot Springs, Arkansas, a popular resort town, he designed the Pythian Bathhouse and Sanitarium in 1922–1923 and the Woodmen of the Union Bathhouse in 1924. In Nashville, Tennessee, he designed the Tennessee State Pythian building in 1924–1925.

In 1926 Bailey began plans for the National Pythian Temple to be located in Chicago, Illinois. Shortly before the National Pythian Temple was completed in 1928, Bailey moved his practice to Chicago, where he remained for the rest of his life. In Chicago, Bailey also designed an expansion of the First Church of Deliverance in 1939 and was hired by the Chicago Housing Authority to work as one of the architects on the Ida B. Wells Housing Project, completed in 1941. Early that year Bailey completed plans for the rebuilding of the interior of the Olivet Baptist Church. In February 1941 Bailey died as a result of complications developed from pneumonia.

Throughout his career Bailey designed buildings for an African American clientele. The Pythian Theater, Pythian Bathhouse and Sanitarium, Tennessee State Pythian building, and the National Pythian Temple were all structures commissioned by the Colored Knights of Pythias, a large, national African American fraternal order that grew to national prominence in the black community in the early twentieth century. The buildings that they commissioned served as places of African American social retreat or business. Additionally, the First Church of Deliverance and the Olivet Baptist Church were situated in an affluent African American part of Chicago and were both strong institutions of faith and community. These buildings, among others, exist as examples of architecture by African Americans for African Americans.

Further Reading

Portions of Bailey's correspondence are held by the Hot Springs National Park Administrative Archives, Hot Springs, Arkansas, and by the University of Illinois at Urbana-Champaign University Archives.

Taussig, Meredith, Timothy Barton, the Commission on Chicago Landmarks, and the Chicago Department of Planning and Development. *First Church of Deliverance, 4315 S. Wabash Avenue: Preliminary Staff Summary of Information* (1994).

Wilson, Dreck Spurlock, ed. *African-American Architects: A Biographical Dictionary, 1865–1945* (2004).

Obituary: *Urbana Courier*, 3 Feb. 1941.

MIKAEL D. KRIZ

BAKER, Augusta Braxton (1 Apr. 1911–23 Feb. 1998), storyteller, librarian, and author, was born Augusta Braxton in Baltimore, Maryland, the only child of two educators, Winford J. and Mabel Braxton. Her father later became a wood craftsman, and her mother retired from formal teaching to raise her daughter. Baker skipped at least two grades in elementary school and might have skipped more—she explained later in an interview with Robert V. Williams—if her father hadn't insisted that she be educated among her peers. Baker's maternal grandmother, Augusta Fax Gough, was an integral part of Baker's childhood and found that the only means of quieting the young Baker was to entertain her through storytelling. These beloved experiences with storytelling would become the catalysts for a career in storytelling and would inspire Baker to write children's literature.

At age sixteen Baker was admitted to the University of Pittsburgh. She did well with the academic material, despite the death of her father during her freshman year, but struggled with personal relationships since she was much younger than many of her peers. Raised in segregated Baltimore, Baker had difficulty establishing and maintaining relationships with white students. She met and married her first husband, James Baker, a graduate student in social work at the University of Pittsburgh. He was a fellow of the Urban League and assigned to establish the Albany Interracial Council in New York. Baker transferred to the Albany State Teacher's College, first pursuing a degree in education and later in library sciences.

Her experiences in confronting racial boundaries began at Albany State Teacher's College, where during her admission interview Baker was informed that she would do her practicum not at the affiliated high school attended by the professors' children, but instead at a local black elementary school. Clearly, Baker thought, Albany State Teacher's College was hesitant to admit her. In response she wrote to the administrative body at the University of Pittsburgh about the situation. Her husband, James Baker, also informed his supervisor, Eleanor Roosevelt, Franklin Delano Roosevelt's wife, about the college's decision to place Baker at a black elementary school, as opposed to the prestigious high school. The wife of then New York governor, Mrs. Roosevelt was able to pressure Albany State Teacher's College to admit Baker on the same terms that they admitted all other students. In addition, the University of Pittsburgh wrote a letter on Baker's behalf, demanding that she be admitted and receive the same treatment as the college's white students.

After graduating in 1933 with BAs in both Education and Library Science, she applied for a position with the New York Public Library (NYPL) system. As the Depression still gripped the country and few jobs existed, Baker's husband discouraged her from taking a job that might deny support from families in greater need. He believed that his well-paying job with the Urban League afforded his family a decent lifestyle during the harsh economic times. So for the next three years Baker labored at home as a devoted wife and mother of her only son, James H. Baker III. In February 1937 she received a letter from Anne Carroll Moore, head of the Children's Division at NYPL. Moore offered Baker a position as a children's librarian at the Harlem branch.

At the time, libraries were the cultural hubs in their communities, hosting plays, literary events, and community gatherings, and serving as a safe harbor for young adults who wished to escape the rough streets of Harlem. Baker was working closely with ARTHUR ALFONSO SCHOMBURG to establish and maintain black materials that were housed on the third floor of the library (Schomburg Collection). During these times Baker became acquainted with a young JAMES BALDWIN, who naturally gravitated to this section of library. He was often found among the stacks of black literature and culture; Baker was immediately notified. She was considered the authority on children in this unique environment, and was, in fact, called several times a day to collect children from other sections of the library. Admiring Baldwin's interests in African American history and literature, she became an advocate on the child's behalf. Though Dr. Schomburg was fairly permissive, the administration discouraged children in those sections reserved for adults, particularly in areas housing research material. Nevertheless, from time to time Baldwin was permitted to peruse the collection.

In 1953 Baker began working for the NYPL in an administrative capacity. She became the first black administrator as storytelling specialist and assistant coordinator of Children's Services of the NYPL. That same year she advised and helped establish the Children's Library Service for the Trinidad Public Library. Within a few years she began to publish her first set of children's books. She also began to promote her philosophies about negative versus positive images of African Americans in children's literature to a number of children's authors and book publishers, expressing her concerns about the psychological impact of such literature and advocating for it to be removed from the children's section of public libraries. Soon the types of books Baker encouraged began to be published widely. In addition to adding to her own collection, she began to compile a bibliography titled *Books about Negro Life for Children*, still widely used in many library systems around the world. She also organized and established the JAMES WELDON JOHNSON Memorial Collection at the Countée Cullen Regional Branch of the NYPL. In 1961 she was promoted to coordinator of children's services for the entire NYPL system, where she became one of the first to incorporate audiovisual materials into general circulation. She became a consultant for the children's program *Sesame Street* and in 1971 began broadcasting a weekly series, *The World of Children's Literature*, for WNYC Radio. Later she taught a number of courses in storytelling and children's literature at Syracuse University. She retired from the NYPL in 1974 and lived in Queens, New York, with her second husband, Gordon Alexander.

After serving fifteen years as a visiting lecturer for the state and local levels of the public school systems in South Carolina and the university, Baker conceded and, in 1980, accepted an appointment as storyteller-in-residence at the University of South Carolina. It was the first position of its kind at any university. She served on various advisory boards at the University of South Carolina and other institutions in the state in order to serve students of historically black colleges and universities, South Carolina State University, and Bennett College. Baker's honors include the Parents Magazine Medal, the Constance Lindsay Skinner Award from the Women's National Book Association, and a Distinguished Services Award from the Association of Library Services to Children of the American Library Association.

Further Reading

Augusta Braxton Baker's papers are housed in South Caroliniana Library, University South Caroliniana Society Manuscripts Collections, University of South Carolina, Columbia, South Carolina.

"Augusta Baker," in *Notable Black American Women*, book 1 (1992).

Williams, Robert V. "Interview with: Augusta Baker (AB)," University of South Carolina, Columbia South Carolina (7 May 1989).

DAMARIS B. HILL

BAKER, Bertram L. (10 Jan. 1898–8 Mar. 1985), first African American elected to political office in Brooklyn, New York, and a leader in the mid-twentieth century effort to integrate American tennis, was born on the Caribbean island of Nevis, then part of the British West Indies. His mother was Lillian de Grasse Baker, whose family had successful retail businesses on the island; his father was the Reverend Alfred B. Baker, a Wesleyan Methodist minister.

Tragedy struck in 1900 when Lillian Baker died of consumption. Bertram, an only child, would find comfort in the care of his maternal grandmother, Eliza de Grasse. In 1905 Baker's father left Nevis, accepting an offer to become founding pastor of the Ebenezer Wesleyan Methodist Church in Brooklyn. The Reverend Baker would later also found the Beulah Wesleyan Methodist Church in Manhattan.

In 1915 the Reverend Baker returned to Nevis to pick up his seventeen-year-old son Bertram, who had been working in a family-owned store and taking college preparatory courses on the neighboring island of St. Kitts. The father and son sailed together to

Brooklyn, where the younger Baker apparently harbored lingering resentments over his father's decision years earlier to leave him in Nevis. Despite his father's strong ties to the Wesleyan Methodist Church, Bertram began making plans to become an Episcopalian priest; but he was soon pulled in other directions.

Baker studied accounting with LaSalle Extension University, which offered correspondence courses, and was eventually hired as a bookkeeper with a Brooklyn chandelier-manufacturing firm. In 1920 he married Irene Louise Baker, a relative, who sacrificed her ambitions of becoming an artist to labor for decades as a homemaker and supportive wife. The couple would have two daughters, Lilian (who married and became Lilian Bemus) and Marian (who became Marian Howell). In 1924 Baker was naturalized as a U.S. citizen.

Believing that blacks in Brooklyn could only advance if they attained political power, Baker, in 1932, organized the United Action Democratic Association. Later in the decade he was appointed deputy collector of Internal Revenue, serving in Brooklyn's income tax audit section. In 1944, he was named confidential aide to the Brooklyn borough president John Cashmore.

Then came the accomplishment for which he would be recognized in local newspapers. In 1948 Baker won a seat on the New York State Assembly, becoming the first African American elected to office in Brooklyn. His victory set the stage for an explosive growth of black political power, which would occur later in the century as tens of thousands of blacks continued to migrate to Brooklyn from the Caribbean, Latin America, and Africa, as well as from other parts of the United States. Baker held his Assembly seat for 22 years.

Among Baker's notable legislative accomplishments was the passage in 1955 of the Baker-Metcalf law, which news articles described as the first piece of legislation in the country to bar housing discrimination. The act outlawed racial discrimination in the sale or rental of federally insured houses. Baker co-authored the bill along with George R. Metcalf, a white liberal Republican state senator from upstate New York. As chair of the Assembly's Education Committee in the 1960s, he withstood slanderous attacks from white conservatives who were angered by his support for school desegregation measures.

Baker practiced politics the old-fashioned way, dispensing patronage and aggressively fighting those who dared to challenge him. At the same time, he groomed the borough's first black judges and representatives to the city council and state senate, all nurtured by his United Action Democratic club.

Outside of New York party politics, Baker devoted much of his time to leading the American Tennis Association, the national organization of black tennis players, for which he served as executive secretary for three decades, until 1966. In that capacity he spearheaded the drive to desegregate American and international tennis competitions. ALTHEA GIBSON,

who broke down the racial barrier in tennis in the 1950s, credited Baker with helping initiate the process that enabled her to compete at Wimbledon. Gibson won the Wimbledon Singles Championship in 1957 and, upon her return to New York, celebrated at Baker's home in the Bedford-Stuyvesant section of Brooklyn and rode with him in a ticker-tape parade in Manhattan.

As for his métier of politics, Baker was one of a number of West Indian immigrants who made breakthroughs in the early 1900s. Among the other notable figures were Harlem politicians such as J. Raymond Jones, who emigrated from the Virgin Islands in 1918 and became the first black leader of the Manhattan Democratic Party in 1964, and Hulan Jack, who emigrated from St. Lucia in 1923 and became the first black borough president of Manhattan in 1954.

A number of scholars have postulated reasons for the political successes of Baker and other early immigrants. One possible explanation is rooted in New York political history. Many native-born blacks, from the mid-nineteenth century and into the twentieth century, remained loyal to the antislavery Republican Party of Abraham Lincoln. But in New York City, government was controlled by European immigrants in the Democratic Party, and black immigrants carried less psychological baggage related to the Civil War and thus were more easily able to form alliances with the white Democrats. The loyalty of native-born blacks to the Republican Party did not seriously begin to erode until the 1930s, when the Democratic president Franklin Delano Roosevelt pushed through New Deal social reforms that benefited urban blacks.

The twilight of Baker's career came in the late 1960s as he and other so-called Democratic machine politicians fell victim to the reform politics of the era. The grassroots movements of the 1960s spawned a new generation of activists in federally funded and other neighborhood organizations, which diluted Baker's power. Seeing the handwriting on the wall, he announced his retirement in 1970 and settled into a life of collecting books.

Baker was seen from a broad historical perspective, and his tenure was the first stage in a major demographic transformation of Brooklyn. In 1940, as he was ratcheting up the pressure on white Democratic bosses, blacks made up only 4 percent of Brooklyn's 2.6 million residents. By 2000 blacks were 34 percent of the total population, including tens of thousands of immigrants from the Caribbean, Africa, and Latin America. Moreover, by 2000 there were dozens of black elected officials representing Brooklyn in the U.S. Congress, in local, state, and federal courts, and in the city and state legislative bodies. Baker is thus regarded by whites and blacks as a "pioneer in Brooklyn politics" (Gerson, 22). During his retirement there was one piece of trivia in particular that Baker enjoyed relating. He would tell audiences, whether small ones at his home or larger ones at the Long Island Historical Society, that there was only one other person to have been born on the island of Nevis and to have served in the New York State Assembly: Alexander Hamilton.

In 1983, almost 60 years after becoming a U.S. citizen, Baker returned to his native island, which gained its independence from Great Britain. Weak and emotionally overwhelmed at being in the land of his birth, he gave a speech at a dedication of the rebuilt Alexander Hamilton House. He then went back to New York to live out his remaining months, pleased with the honors that came his way. In 1984 Baker received an honorary PhD from St. John's University.

Further Reading

Connolly, Harold X. *A Ghetto Grows in Brooklyn* (1977).
Gerson, Jeffrey. "Bertram L. Baker, the United Action Democratic Association, and the First Black Democratic Succession in Brooklyn, 1933–1954," *Afro-Americans in New York Life and History*, vol. 16, no. 2 (1992).
Gray, Frances Clayton, and Yanick Rice Lamb. *Born to Win: The Authorized Biography of Althea Gibson* (2004).
Holder, Calvin. "The Rise and Fall of West Indian Politicians," in *Political Behavior and Social Interaction: Caribbean and African American Residents in New York* (1970).
Kasinitz, Philip. *Caribbean New York* (1992).
Lewinson, Edwin R. *Black Politics in New York City* (1974).

Obituary: *New York Times*, 10 Mar. 1985.

RON HOWELL

BAKER, Ella (13 Dec. 1903–13 Dec. 1986), civil rights organizer, was born Ella Josephine Baker in Norfolk, Virginia, the daughter of Blake Baker, a waiter on the ferry between Norfolk and Washington, D.C., and Georgianna Ross. In rural North Carolina where Ella Baker grew up, she experienced a strong sense of black community. Her grandfather, who had been a slave, acquired the land in Littleton on which he had slaved. He raised fruit, vegetables, and cattle, which he shared with the community. He also served as the local Baptist minister. Baker's mother took care of the sick and needy.

After graduating in 1927 from Shaw University in Raleigh, North Carolina, Baker moved to New York City. She had dreamed of doing graduate work in sociology at the University of Chicago, but it was 1929, and times were hard. Few jobs were open to black women except teaching, which Baker refused to do because "this was the thing that everybody figures you could do" (Cantarow and O'Malley, 62). To survive, Baker waitressed and worked in a factory. During 1929–1930 she was an editorial staff member of the *American West Indian News* and in 1932 became an editorial assistant for GEORGE SCHUYLER's *Negro National News*, for which she also worked as office manager. In 1930 she was on the board of directors of Harlem's Own Cooperative and worked with the Dunbar Housewives' League on tenant and consumer rights. In 1930 she helped organize and in 1931 became the national executive director of the

Young Negroes' Cooperative League, a consumer cooperative. Baker also taught consumer education for the Works Progress Administration in the 1930s and, according to a letter written in 1936, divided her time between consumer education and working at the public library at 135th Street. She married Thomas J. Roberts in 1940 or 1941; they had no children.

Beginning in 1938 Baker worked with the National Association for the Advancement of Colored People (NAACP), and from 1941 to 1946 she traveled throughout the country but especially in the South for the NAACP, first as field secretary and then as a highly successful director of branches to recruit members, raise money, and organize local campaigns. Among the issues in which she was involved were the antilynching campaign, the equal-pay-for-black-teachers movement, and job training for black workers. Baker's strength was the ability to evoke in people a feeling of common need and the belief that people together can change the conditions under which they live. Her philosophy of organizing was "you start where the people are" and "strong people don't need strong leaders." In her years with the NAACP, Baker formed a network of people involved with civil rights throughout the South that proved invaluable in the struggles of the 1950s and 1960s. Among the more significant of her protégés was the Alabama seamstress ROSA PARKS. Baker resigned from her leadership role in the national NAACP in 1946 because she felt it was too bureaucratic. She also had agreed to take responsibility for raising her niece. Back in New York City, she worked with the NAACP on school desegregation, sat on the Commission on Integration for the New York City Board of Education, and in 1952 became president of the New York City NAACP chapter. In 1953 she resigned from the NAACP presidency to run unsuccessfully for the New York City Council on the Liberal Party ticket. To support herself, she worked as director of the Harlem Division of the New York City Committee of the American Cancer Society.

In January 1958 BAYARD RUSTIN and Stanley Levison persuaded Baker to go to Atlanta to set up the office of the Southern Christian Leadership Conference (SCLC) to organize the Crusade for Citizenship, a voter registration program in the South. Baker agreed to go for six weeks and stayed for two and a half years. She was named acting director of the SCLC and set about organizing the crusade to open simultaneously in twenty-one cities. She was concerned, however, that the SCLC board of preachers did not sufficiently support voter registration. Baker had increasing difficulty working with MARTIN LUTHER KING JR., whom she described as "too self-centered and cautious" (Weisbrot, 33). Because she thought that she would never be appointed executive director, Baker persuaded her friend the Reverend John L. Tilley to assume the post in April, and she became associate director. After King fired Tilley in January 1959, he asked Baker once again to be executive director, but his board insisted that her position must be in an acting capacity. Baker,

Ella Baker, speaking at the Jeannette Rankin news conference, 3 January 1968. (AP Images.)

however, functioned as executive director and signed her name accordingly. In April 1960 the executive director post of SCLC was accepted by the Reverend WYATT TEE WALKER.

After hundreds of students sat in at segregated lunch counters in early 1960, Baker persuaded the SCLC to invite them to the Southwide Youth Leadership Conference at Shaw University on Easter weekend. From this meeting the Student Nonviolent Coordinating Committee (SNCC) was eventually formed. Although the SCLC leadership pressured Baker to influence the students to become a youth chapter of the SCLC, she refused and encouraged the students to beware of the SCLC's "leader-centered orientation." She felt that the students had a

right to decide their own structure. Baker's speech "More than a hamburger," which followed King's and JAMES LAWSON's speeches, urged the students to broaden their social vision of discrimination to include more than integrating lunch counters. JULIAN BOND described the speech as "an eye opener" and probably the best of the three. "She didn't say, 'Don't let Martin Luther King tell you what to do,'" Bond remembers, "but you got the real feeling that that's what she meant" (Hampton and Fayer, 63). JAMES FORMAN, who became director of SNCC a few months later, said Baker felt the SCLC "was depending too much on the press and on the promotion of Martin King, and was not developing enough indigenous leadership across the South" (Forman, 216).

After the Easter conference weekend, Baker resigned from the SCLC, and after having helped Walker learn his job she went to work for SNCC in August. To support herself she worked as a human relations consultant for the Young Women's Christian Association in Atlanta. Baker continued as a mentor to SNCC civil rights workers, most notably ROBERT P. MOSES. At a rancorous SNCC meeting at Highlander Folk School in Tennessee in August 1961, Baker mediated between one faction advocating political action through voter registration and another faction advocating nonviolent direct action. She suggested that voter registration would necessitate confrontation that would involve them in direct action. Baker believed that voting was necessary but did not believe that the franchise would cure all problems. She also understood the appeal of nonviolence as a tactic, but she did not believe in it personally: "I have not seen anything in the nonviolent technique that can dissuade me from challenging somebody who wants to step on my neck. If necessary, if they hit me, I might hit them back" (Cantarow and O'Malley, 82).

After the 1964 Mississippi summer in which northern students went south to work in voter registration, SNCC decided to organize the Mississippi Freedom Democratic Party (MFDP) as an alternative to the regular Democratic Party in Mississippi. Thousands of people registered to vote in beauty parlors and barbershops, churches, or wherever a registration booth could be set up. Baker set up the Washington, D.C., office of the MFDP and delivered the keynote speech at its Jackson, Mississippi, state convention. The MFDP delegates were not seated at the Democratic National Convention in Washington, D.C., but their influence helped to elect many local black leaders in Mississippi in the following years and forced a rules change in the Democratic Party to include more women and minorities as delegates to the national convention.

From 1962 to 1967 Baker worked on the staff of the Southern Conference Education Fund (SCEF), dedicated to helping black and white people work together. During that time she organized a civil liberties conference in Washington, D.C., and worked with Carl Braden on a mock civil rights commission hearing in Chapel Hill, North Carolina. In her later years in New York City she served on the board of the Puerto Rican Solidarity Committee, founded and was president of the Fund for Education and Legal Defense, which raised money primarily for scholarships for civil rights activists to return to college, and was vice chair of the Mass Party Organizing Committee. She was also a sponsor of the National United Committee to Free ANGELA DAVIS and All Political Prisoners, a consultant to both the Executive Council and the Commission for Social and Racial Justice of the Episcopal Church, and a member of the Charter Group for a Pledge of Conscience and the Coalition of Concerned Black Americans. Until her death in New York City she continued to inspire, nurture, scold, and advise the many young people who had worked with her during her career of political activism.

Ella Baker's ideas and careful organizing helped to shape the civil rights movement from the 1930s through the 1960s. She had the ability to listen to people and to inspire them to organize around issues that would empower their lives. At a time when there were no women in leadership in the SCLC, Baker served as its executive director. Hundreds of young people became politically active because of her respect and concern for them.

Further Reading

Ella Baker's papers are in the Schomburg Center for Research in Black Culture of the New York Public Library.
Cantarow, Ellen, and Susan Gushee O'Malley. *Moving the Mountain* (1980).
Forman, James. *The Making of Black Revolutionaries* (1972).
Hampton, Henry, and Steve Fayer. *Voices of Freedom* (1991).
Ransby, Barbara. *Ella Baker and the Black Freedom Movement* (2003).
Weisbrot, Robert. *Freedom Bound* (1990).

Obituary: *New York Times*, 17 Dec. 1986.

SUSAN GUSHEE O'MALLEY

BAKER, Etta (31 Mar. 1913–), Piedmont-style guitarist, was born near Collettsville in the African American community of Franklin, an Appalachian hollow not far from the John's River in upper Caldwell County, North Carolina. Her grandfather Alexander Reid and father Boone Reid, both born in Franklin, played the banjo in the old-time clawhammer manner, with Boone going on to become an accomplished musician who also played fiddle, harmonica, and guitar, on which he used a two-finger-style approach. Boone Reid had absorbed many kinds of music of the mid-to-late nineteenth century, including Anglo-American dance tunes, lyric folksongs, ballads, rags, religious music, and published pieces that had drifted into folk tradition—popular Tin Pan Alley songs, old minstrel tunes, and Victorian parlor music. Boone and his wife Sallie, who sang, instilled their love of music in their eight children, a process that led eventually to the formation of a Reid family string band that played after supper and at local social events.

In January 1916 Reid moved his family to Chase City, Virginia, to farm tobacco. It is likely that he sometimes sold his crops in Durham, North Carolina, a tobacco-market center about 60 miles south. The storage warehouses there also served as a center of remarkable musical activity, and Reid probably ingested a great deal of music, perhaps even the finger-picked rags and reels of Reverend GARY DAVIS and BLIND BOY FULLER, as well as the newer form called blues. Around the time of this move Reid began teaching his barely three-year-old daughter Etta, perhaps his most persistent pupil, to play finger-style guitar. He found in her an eager student, expertly assimilating her father's instrumental styles and repertoire, although she was never able to master Reid's "fisting" clawhammer method on the banjo; she did in later years, however, begin to play a few of her father's banjo songs in a thumb-lead, finger-uppicking style.

The guitar technique that Etta learned from her father was to become known as "Piedmont blues," "East Coast blues," and more accurately, "the Piedmont style," since a great many musicians in the region had adopted the same method. This style consisted of a soft, syncopated melody produced by the index finger, and a relentless alternating bass pattern played with the thumb, which was also used to brush chords on the afterbeat. This style was particularly well suited to marches, cakewalks, reels, open-tuned parlor pieces, and, especially, ragtime tunes, but it did not lend itself whatsoever to the primary blues form. Indeed, roughly 85 percent of Etta Baker's repertoire consisted of "reels," named for an ancient Scottish dance and defined primarily on the basis of its rapid tempo (at least 120 beats per minute). Reels, also called "breakdowns" or "hoedowns," became an umbrella term for any kind of song played to a brisk, danceable tempo, subsuming other generic classifications in the process. When musicians began to insert partially flatted thirds and sevenths into these reels, many people—including Pink Anderson, FRED MCDOWELL, and BUKKA WHITE—came to think of them as "blues," which of course they were not. Consequently the term "Piedmont blues" is a misnomer; indeed the Piedmont style is an instrumental technique that has little to do with such genres as lyric folksongs, ballads, or religious music, all of which Etta played using it, or blues, which she did not, due to the form's requisite "slow-drag" tempo. Labels aside, Etta would later become an exemplar of both African American and Anglo American folk-musical traditions that existed in the mountains and Piedmont at least as far back as the Reconstruction era, if not before.

In 1923 the family moved back to Franklin, where Etta continued to play her music with her family and friends, especially her sister Cora, who also finger-picked the guitar, and her sister-in-law and first cousin Babe Reid, still another finger-style guitarist, and Babe's husband Fred (Boone's brother), who picked two-finger-style banjo. When Cora in 1931 married Theopolis ("The") Phillips, who played both guitar and banjo, an equally impressive extended family of musicians joined with the Reids, resulting in highly talented ensembles that played for "entertainments"—family get-togethers, house parties, and square dances—often alongside white mountain musicians who had for years been playing the same kinds of music in the same basic styles. Vocals were not a strong component of these events, which tended to focus on music for dancing, so Etta had few opportunities to develop her singing, so although she did sing a handful of blues tunes now and then.

Etta married Lee Baker in 1936 and moved down the mountain to Morganton, where she worked in a textile mill. She kept up with music during the next many years, often jamming with her nine children and of course with Cora, The, Fred, and Babe. She also began experimenting with songs from outside the family tradition, for example RAY CHARLES's "But On the Other Hand, Baby" and "One Mint Julep," but she always insisted that she'd learned most of her music from her father.

During a trip to Blowing Rock in early 1956 the Bakers attended a performance by the folksong revivalist Paul Clayton, who became impressed with Etta's playing after Lee persuaded his wife to pick a couple of tunes for the folks. Shortly thereafter, Clayton returned to the region to record Etta, her brother-in-law The, and her father Boone, the result of which was the seminal album *Instrumental Music of the Southern Appalachians* that influenced a great many revivalist guitar players.

Baker retired from her day-job in 1962 and began to devote time to her family, her gardening, at which she was also a master, and her music. After her husband Lee died in 1967 she became a semiprofessional musician, taking her regional style to schools, colleges, and innumerable concerts and festivals, including Wolf Trap, the 1982 Worlds' Fair, the John Henry Memorial Festival, and Merlefest.

In 1991 Baker was awarded an National Endowment for the Arts National Folk Heritage Fellowship, officially declaring her an American national treasure.

Further Reading

Biographical information on Etta Baker is based primarily on several tape-recorded interviews with the author, especially during 1980–1985, and liner notes to the albums listed below.

Lightfoot, William E. "The Three Doc(k)s: White Blues in Appalachia," *Black Music Research Journal* (2005).

Lightfoot, William E. "Etta Baker: One Dime Blues," *North Carolina Folklore Journal* (1995).

Lightfoot, William E. "Eight-Hand Sets and Holy Steps," *North Carolina Folklore Journal* (1990).

Lightfoot, William E. "Etta Baker and Cora Phillips," [Brown-Hudson Award Citation] *North Carolina Folklore Journal* (1982).

Wilson, Emily Herring. "One Dime Blues: Elizabeth Moore Reid, Cora Reid Phillips, Etta Reid Baker," in *Hope and Dignity: Older Black Women of the South* (1983).

WILLIAM E. LIGHTFOOT

BAKER, Frankie (30 May 1876–6 Jan. 1952), the inspiration for the "Frankie and Johnny" song, was born and raised in St. Louis, Missouri. Her parents were Cedric Baker and his wife Margaret (maiden name unknown), and she had three brothers: Charles, Arthur, and James. Charles, who was younger than Frankie, lived with her on Targee Street in 1900. In 1899 Baker shot and killed her seventeen-year-old "mack" (pimp), Allen "Al" Britt. St. Louis pianists and singers were soon thumping and belting out what would become one of America's most famous folk ballads and popular songs, "Frankie and Johnny," also known as "Frankie and Albert," "Frankie Baker," and "Frankie."

At age sixteen or seventeen Baker fell in love with a man who, unknown to her, was living off the earnings of a prostitute (this kind of man was known as an "easy rider," a term made famous by W. C. HANDY in his "Yellow Dog Blues"). When the prostitute, who had romantic relations with this man, discovered that he was also seeing Baker, she came to Baker's home one night and sliced the left side of her face. Baker received thirty-eight stitches and was left with a long scar.

Baker, emotionally broken by finding out her lover was involved with another woman, joined the "sporting life": that of pimps and whores, "hustlers and gamblers, brothels and taverns, musicians and other entertainers, and allied people and institutions." According to reports, she was quite successful. She dressed in fine clothes and jewelry and became a "queen sport" (Huston, 105) of the African American district around Targee Street.

> Frankie was a sporting lady
> A red light hung over her door
> She always paid fifty or sixty dollars
> For every suit that Johnny wore.
> He was her man
> But he done her wrong.
> (usual refrain, sometimes varied)
> (Buckley, 40)

After Baker met Al, a pianist, at the Orange Blossom's Ball at Stolle's Hall, he moved in with her at 212 Targee Street, where she roomed and did business. On occasion he beat her.

Problems arose when Baker found out that Al had another girl, an eighteen-year-old prostitute named Alice Pryor.

> Johnny says, "Listen now Frankie
> Don't want to tell you no lies
> I've lost my heart to another queen
> Her name is Nellie Bly."
> (Buckley, 52)

When he didn't come home on Saturday night, 14 October 1899, Baker went out and found him with Alice at the Phoenix Hotel.

> Frankie says to the barkeep
> "Have you seen my Albert nigh"
> The barkeep says to Frankie
> "He's with a woman called Alice Bly."
> (Buckley, 57)

After an argument, Baker returned home. Feeling ill she went to bed in the front bedroom, where she thought there was "more air" than in her customary room (David, 214). Al came in the next morning around 3:00 A.M., very angry, and their quarrel renewed. Claiming to be outraged that she was in the wrong room, he grabbed a lamp. She jumped up and stood by the bed. As he started after her with a knife, she pulled a pistol from under her pillow and shot him, the bullet going through his liver. He staggered to his parents' house at 32 Targee Street and was

taken to City Hospital, where he died in the early morning of 19 October.

> Frankie shot him once
> She shot him thru and thru
> "Please don't kill me, Frankie
> "You've shot me, that will do."
> (Buckley, 75)

A coroner's jury ruled that the killing was self-defense and justifiable homicide. On 13 November 1899 Baker was tried before Judge Willis B. Clark, Court of Criminal Correction, and acquitted.

Baker remained in St. Louis for about a year, drifted around some, and then settled in Omaha, Nebraska, where she was living in the early 1920s. Having heard about a "great flower show, the Rose Festival" (David, 216), in Portland, Oregon, she accepted an invitation from friends there to visit. By 1930 she was living in Portland and had "quit playing the game" (Terrett, *The World*), though she never married. She opened a shoe-shine parlor on Flanders Street and later worked as a chambermaid at the Royal Palm Hotel.

Illness struck in the 1930s, and within a few years Baker was unable to work. It appears that she spent much of her time playing solitaire in her home at 22 North Clackamas. She also collected items related to "Frankie and Albert/Johnny."

The 1933 release of the Paramount movie *She Done Him Wrong*, starring Mae West, stirred deep resentment in Baker, who thought it wrong that someone could profit from her story without paying her anything. She filed suit on 1 March 1935, but her lawyers decided that she could not win and withdrew the complaint.

Another opportunity came with the release in 1936 of Republic's movie, *Frankie and Johnnie*, starring Helen Morgan as Baker in an all-white cast. Baker's attorneys filed suit for $200,000 damages against Republic and others in April 1938. Depositions began in October 1939, but the trial itself was not held until February 1942.

One of the important witnesses was the famous radio personality and author Sigmund Spaeth, who was also known as the "Tune Detective" and the "Song Sleuth" because he had made a profession of tracking down song histories. Spaeth "lectured" the court for "nearly two days" (David, 228–229), severely damaging Baker's case. In *Read 'Em and Weep* (1926) he had written, "It is generally agreed that the beautifully honest story is a true one, and that the locale was St. Louis." Even though he had reaffirmed this belief in 1934, he testified otherwise as an expert witness in 1942, saying, "I've changed my mind" (David, 230). "Perhaps he had been mesmerized by money" (Harris, 38). It was believed that he had received $2,000 for his testimony.

Having a weak case and facing all-white defense witnesses and defense lawyers, as well as a white jury and judge, Baker lost. She was left penniless. Unable to work, she was on relief by 1949, when she was made the "first life member of Portland's Urban League," to which she had given "unfailing support" (David, 234).

Baker was found by a court to be mentally ill. She had a poor memory and a persecution complex, and she was belligerent—hallmark signs of Alzheimer's disease (though whether she suffered from this disease is not confirmed). Baker was committed to Eastern Oregon Hospital and Training Center, Pendleton, and was admitted there in April 1950. In less than two years she was dead. When she died in Pendleton, her body was sent to Los Angeles for burial.

Before 1912 the folk ballad was about Frankie and "Albert," which is easily understood as a mishearing of "Al Britt." The ballad may have been written by Bill Dooley, "one of the 'barroom bards' who collaborated with piano men in writing 'the topical, gay and ribald songs which emanated from the Negro quarter'" (David, 228). In 1912 a Tin Pan Alley version, "Frankie and Johnny," was published, music by Ren Shields and lyrics by the Leighton Brothers (Bert, Frank, William), who may have thought "Albert" dull and "Johnny" catchy. Since then "Johnny" has dominated. Shields's tune differs from the one usually sung, which was first published in 1912 as part of the tune for an unrelated song, "You're My Baby," music by Nat D. Ayer.

Bawdy elements, colorful incidents (often historically incorrect), the raggy blues tune, and a refrain that lends itself to dramatic, seriocomic renderings have all helped make "Frankie" immensely popular. Even so, the ballad's most important quality may be that it captures the spirit of a proud woman.

Further Reading
Buckley, Bruce Redfern. "Frankie and Her Men: A Study of the Interrelationships of Popular and Folk Traditions," PhD diss., Indiana University (1961).
David, John Russell. "Tragedy in Ragtime: Black Folktales from St. Louis," PhD diss., St. Louis University (1976).
Harris, Ellen. "They Done Her Wrong," *St. Louis*, Nov. 1999.
Huston, John. *Frankie and Johnny* (1930).
Terrett, Courtenay. "Frankie Still Mourns Her Man," *The World* (New York), 8 June 1930.

JOHN GARST

BAKER, General (6 Sept. 1941–), automobile worker and activist, was born General Gordon Baker Jr. in Detroit, Michigan, one of five children of General Gordon Baker Sr., an automobile worker, and Clara Baker, a housewife. Baker attended Southwestern High School in Detroit and went on to take classes at Highland Park Community College and Wayne State University. In the early 1960s he took a job with Ford Motor Company and continued to work in the automobile industry for almost forty years. In 1941 Baker's father had moved his family to Detroit from Georgia in search of a job in the booming war-production industries, taking part in the massive migration of African Americans from the rural

South to cities in the North during the first half of the twentieth century. Becoming an autoworker allowed Baker Sr. to dramatically improve his family's standard of living, especially in comparison to his prospects in the poverty-stricken South.

While his father sought a better life for his family through the relatively high pay of auto work, Baker Jr. demanded social and racial equality along with a fair wage. By the late 1950s he was involved in the civil rights movement, which grew rapidly among Detroit's large black population. He joined a group of black Wayne State University students organizing protests against businesses that practiced discrimination against African Americans and took its name, Uhuru, from a Swahili word for "freedom." Baker attended several speeches by MALCOLM X and participated in the July 1963 Walk to Freedom, led by MARTIN LUTHER KING JR., which brought 200,000 people to downtown Detroit. Baker also traveled to the August 1963 March on Washington. In 1965 he met the civil rights activist Marian Kramer. They worked together on many campaigns for social and economic justice, and continued to do so after their marriage in September 1978. They had eight children of their own and helped raise several of their nieces and nephews.

Baker was committed to a more confrontational and uncompromising approach to racial politics than the nonviolent civil rights movement associated with King. He was attracted to the philosophy of armed self-defense advocated by the NAACP activist ROBERT FRANKLIN WILLIAMS. Baker would gather with friends to listen to Williams's radio program, *Radio Free Dixie*, which Williams produced from exile in Cuba. He joined the Revolutionary Action Movement (RAM), a small but influential network of African American students and activists that adopted Williams's philosophy. In 1964 he made a clandestine trip to Cuba with a group of about eighty American university students in defiance of the travel ban declared by the United States. There he met Fidel Castro, Che Guevara, Williams, and other students and revolutionaries from Latin America, the Caribbean, Africa, and Asia. Baker returned committed to anti-imperialism and cognizant of the global impact of race on national and class divisions.

Baker's trip to Cuba would not be the only instance in which he openly defied the federal government. In 1965 Baker was drafted into the army and refused to serve in the Vietnam conflict, which he considered a justified struggle for national liberation. He responded to the draft board with a scathing letter denouncing the American military's repressive actions abroad and the role of American corporations in the exploitation of workers in Africa, Asia, and Latin America, which he linked to the treatment of African Americans within the United States. On his draft day, he passed a physical to prove that he was fit for service because he did not want to be mistaken for a pacifist or conscientious objector. Baker and others organized a simultaneous protest which, combined with his political beliefs, resulted in his dismissal as a security risk.

Baker's activism for civil rights and against imperialism converged with the workplace issues of the auto industry. He was particularly concerned with working conditions and racial injustice on the shop floor, where he felt black workers were unable to gain access to higher-paid skilled jobs and supervisory positions. In May 1968 a wildcat strike occurred at the Dodge motor company's main plant. Management fired seven workers accused of leading this strike, which the United Auto Workers (UAW) had not authorized. The five white workers involved were rehired, while Baker and another black worker were not. Baker and others used this as an opportunity to form the Dodge Revolutionary Union Movement (DRUM), a black workers' organization that fought for better working conditions, the desegregation of job classifications, and more blacks in the leadership structure of the UAW and the Chrysler Corporation. In 1969 DRUM became one part of the League of Revolutionary Black Workers, a conglomeration of several Revolutionary Union movements in the city that were committed to black nationalism, workplace rights, and a revolutionary anticapitalist perspective. The league emphasized the global nature of the struggle for racial equality and proclaimed the black working class the vanguard of revolutionary change. This movement incorporated economic and workers' rights issues into the local and national debate concerning civil rights for African Americans, linking the issues of race and class on the shop floor.

Baker's activism was not confined only to the 1960s. In 1976 he campaigned for state representative for his district on the Communist Labor Party ticket, garnering more votes than the Republican candidate but losing to the Democrat. Baker placed second in the Democratic primary of 1978 for the same position. Despite his open opposition to the UAW in the 1960s and 1970s, he saw the union as a means to make a difference on the shop floor. In 1986 he was elected unit president in UAW Local 600 and later worked for the local's staff. In 1990 he gave up his position with the union to return to work until he retired in August of 2003. He continued to organize against racism and economic injustice, campaigning for homeless rights, working for the Midwest Labor Library and Resource Center in Detroit, and traveling to give speeches about his experiences at union-sponsored conferences and on college campuses.

Further Reading
General Baker's papers were collected on microfilm by LexisNexis and published as *The Black Power Movement: Part 4, The League of Revolutionary Black Workers, 1965–1976,* ed. Ernie Allen Jr. (2004).
Georgakas, Dan, and Marvin Surkin. *Detroit: I Do Mind Dying,* rev. ed. (1998).

MICHAEL J. MURPHY

BAKER, George. *See* Father Divine.

BAKER, Harriet Ann (Aug. 1829–4 Mar.1913), evangelist and African Methodist Episcopal (AME) minister, was born a freewoman near Havre de Grace, Harford County, Maryland. One of seven children of William and Harriet Lego Cole, she was descended from a family that included a Native American maternal great-grandmother married to an Englishman, a maternal grandfather born in Guinea, and a paternal grandmother reputedly freed from slavery by a Baltimore court after enduring an unwarranted and savage beating while pregnant. In October 1845, when she was sixteen years of age, Harriet married William Baker, ten years her senior and a slave on the Edward Gallop plantation in Michaelsville, a nearby Maryland hamlet.

In 1847, when the couple learned of Gallop's plan to sell William to a slave dealer in Georgia, they fled north with their infant daughter. After a forty-eight-mile flight along the western bank of the Susquehanna River, they crossed into Columbia, Pennsylvania, a Lancaster County center of Underground Railroad activity. Despite being beset with racial tensions as manumitted and runaway blacks crowded into the commercially oriented town, Columbia, with its successful black population, nevertheless provided reasonable protection and numerous economic opportunities for ambitious workers and would-be entrepreneurs. The Bakers quickly found work, built a home, and settled into Columbia's vibrant black community, which at the time constituted 21 percent of the town's 4,100 residents.

Passage of the Fugitive Slave Act of 1850 dramatically altered life for the Bakers and other blacks throughout the southernmost free states. Emboldened slave catchers and owners promptly descended on Columbia to reclaim their property, and scores of black residents hurried north for increased safety. Baker's husband escaped to Boston for several months, but returned in December. In January the local magistrate committed him to jail as a runaway, wrongly accusing him of being involved in a riot in Lancaster City. His arrest purportedly made him the first victim of the act. An angry crowd of white abolitionists and irate blacks from the town's segregated Tow Hill area protested as officials transported William to Philadelphia, where a hearing ruled that he was to return with Gallop to Maryland. Harriet, with the help of white supporters, obtained an unsecured loan for $750 to purchase her husband's freedom. Over the next thirty years William Baker became a prominent figure in the economic and political life of Columbia's African American community.

Married life proved difficult for Baker. In twenty-six years she bore twelve children and saw seven die. To repay the debt incurred to free William, the Bakers had to refinance the house they had built in 1848. In 1863, soon after redeeming this second mortgage, a fire thought to be the work of Southern sympathizers completely destroyed the home. In the spring of 1872, her daughters Hannah Rebecca and Rulletta

Stephen, ages fifteen and thirteen, died within two weeks of each other. Nine years later a neighboring businessman was charged with raping eleven-year-old Eva, Baker's youngest child. Periodic bouts of assorted ailments, including heart, kidney, and liver illness, and even an accidental poisoning, plagued her.

Baker had experienced personal salvation in 1842, when at twelve or thirteen years of age, her mother tricked her into attending a prayer gathering at a vacant estate several miles outside Havre de Grace. The heartfelt and highly emotional prayers, songs, and praises of the assembled women combined with the extreme heat in the small building to overwhelm the skepticism of the youthful Harriet, who left believing that the heretofore unknown Jesus had saved her soul. During the subsequent decades, as Baker taught herself to read the Bible, she concluded that the Lord willed her to undertake a life of evangelism. Her husband, family, pastor, friends, and members of the church responded with vehement disapproval of a wife, mother, and a woman pursuing a life of evangelical activity. Baker, however, experienced a series of vivid dreams that deepened her feelings and intensified her prayers to abate the universal resistance she endured.

The death in 1872 of two of her daughters, Baker held, was providential and convinced her of the need to act. That winter she poured out her beliefs at a church meeting and boldly announced her intention to set forth in search of souls. The sincerity of her statement so disarmed the opposition that she began preparations for a new life, despite the lack of formal church approval. At the time Baker was forty-three years of age with an aging husband and three minor children at home, the youngest of whom was only two years old. During the following quarter century, while maintaining her residence in Columbia, Baker traveled throughout Pennsylvania and much of the Northeast. Affiliated with the Philadelphia Conference of the African Methodist Episcopal Church, which in the mid-1870s authorized her to preach, Baker labored in towns, small cities, and even such urban centers as New York, Baltimore, and Philadelphia. White and black churches of numerous evangelical denominations sought her out. These included Methodist Episcopal, Primitive Methodist, United Brethren, Baptist, Methodist Protestant, and AME Zion churches. She preached from pulpits, participated in camp meetings, conducted revivals, wrote hymns, led song services, and assisted at Sabbath schools. A highly effective and energetic minister of the gospel, she converted thousands of individuals, raised impressive sums of money, and aided pastors with the varied responsibilities of missionary work. In 1889 she became the pastor of a struggling church in Lebanon, Pennsylvania, the first woman to hold this position in the AME Church.

Harriet Baker's religious concepts were largely typical of conventional evangelical preachers of the day. Her printed sermons, an 1892 biography, and published letters of commendation from pastors stress her belief in standard biblical truths and of the need for personal conversion and sanctification through the workings of the Holy Spirit. The historian Bettye Collier-Thomas contends, moreover, that Baker's fundamentally orthodox sermons also subtly revealed a social message regarding the status of blacks and women. She maintains that Baker, particularly in "Behold the Man" and "Jesus Weeping over Jerusalem," used the story of Christ's rejection and passion in an autobiographical manner to assert the need for sinners to lead lives of holiness, no matter the pain caused by social alienation and opposition from earthly and church leaders.

Baker left Columbia following the death of her husband in the late 1880s and lived alternately with daughters in Bethlehem and Allentown, Pennsylvania. In 1900, at age seventy-one, she built at her own expense a two-story structure whose first-floor auditorium served as the Gospel Union or Bethel Mission (later St. James AME Zion Church), while the second story became her residence. For the next thirteen years Baker conducted weekly and Sunday services while continuing to travel throughout the region preaching special sermons, giving lectures, and leading revivals. These activities helped raise funds to support her and assist in paying the mortgage. The proceeds from the Reverend John H. Acornley's 1892 biography, *The Colored Lady Evangelist*, also served this purpose. Baker died at her Allentown home at eighty-three years of age, having labored for three decades to convert thousands to Jesus Christ. Evangelists whose lives and careers loosely paralleled those of Harriet Baker include AMANDA BERRY SMITH, JULIA A. J. FOOTE, MARY JANE BLAIR SMALL, and FANNY JACKSON COPPIN.

Further Reading

Harriet Baker seems not to have left any papers. The only thorough account of her life, written with her assistance, is a period biography by the Reverend John H. Acornley, *The Colored Lady Evangelist, Being the Life, Labors, and Experiences of Mrs. Harriet A. Baker* (1892). Period accounts of some of Mrs. Baker's activities in Columbia and during her years as an evangelist appear in *The Columbia Spy* and the *Christian Recorder*, the official organ of the AME church.

Collier-Thomas, Bettye. *Daughters of Thunder: Black Women Preachers and Their Sermons, 1850–1979* (1998).

Obituaries: Allentown *Democrat*, 3 Mar. 1913; Allentown *Morning Call*, 3 Mar. 1913.

JAMES CHRISMER

BAKER, Josephine (3 Jun. 1906–10 Apr. 1975), dancer, singer, and entertainer, was born in the slums of East St. Louis, Missouri, the daughter of Eddie Carson, a drummer, who abandoned Baker and her mother after the birth of a second child, and of Carrie McDonald, a onetime entertainer who supported what became a family of four by doing laundry. Poverty, dislocation, and mistreatment permeated

Josephine Baker at the Winter Garden Theater in New York, 11 February 1936. (AP Images.)

Baker's childhood. By the age of eight she was earning her keep and contributing to the family's support by doing domestic labor. By the time Baker was fourteen, she had left home and its discord and drudgery; mastered such popular dances as the Mess Around and the Itch, which sprang up in the black urban centers of the day; briefly married Willie Wells and then divorced him; and begun her career in the theater. She left East St. Louis behind and traveled with the Dixie Steppers on the black vaudeville circuit, already dreaming of performing on Broadway.

Baker's dream coincided with the creation of one of the greatest musical comedies in American theater, *Shuffle Along*, with music by EUBIE BLAKE and lyrics by NOBLE SISSLE. A constant crowd-pleaser with her crazy antics and frantic dancing as a comic, eye-crossing chorus girl, Baker auditioned for a role in the musical in Philadelphia in April of 1921, only to be rejected as "too young, too thin, too small, and too dark." With characteristic determination, she bought a one-way ticket to New York, auditioned again, and was rejected again, but she secured a job as a dresser in the touring company. On the road she learned the routines, and, when a member of the chorus line fell ill, she stepped in and became an immediate sensation. More than five hundred performances later, in the fall of 1923, the *Shuffle Along* tour ended, and Baker was cast in Sissle and Blake's new show, *Bamville*, later retitled and better known as *The Chocolate Dandies*. When the musical opened in New York in March of 1924, Baker not only played Topsy

Anna, a comic role straight out of the racist minstrel tradition, but also appeared as an elegantly dressed "deserted female" in the show's "Wedding Finale," foreshadowing the poised and polished performer of world renown she would become.

In the summer of 1925 Baker's dancing at the Plantation Club at Fiftieth Street and Broadway caught the eye of Caroline Dudley Reagan, a young socialite planning to stage a black revue in Paris in the vein of *Shuffle Along* or *Runnin' Wild*, the revue that introduced the Charleston in 1924. The company that came to be known as La Revue Nègre was long on talent, with such now legendary figures as the composer Spencer Williams, the bandleader and pianist CLAUDE HOPKINS, and the clarinetist SIDNEY BECHET, the dancer and choreographer LOUIS DOUGLAS, and the set designer Miguel Covarrubias. Baker joined the troupe as lead dancer, singer, and comic. When the performers arrived in Paris in late September 1925, opening night at the Théâtre des Champs Elysées was ten days away. During that brief time the revue was transformed from a vaudeville show, replete with the stereotypes expected by a white American public, into a music-hall spectacle filled with colonialist fantasies that appealed to the largely male, voyeuristic Parisian audience.

When La Revue Nègre opened to a packed house on 2 October 1925, it was an instantaneous *succès de scandale*. First, Baker stunned the rapt onlookers with her blackface comic routine, in which, seemingly part animal, part human, she shimmied, contorted her torso, writhed like a snake, and vibrated her behind with astonishing speed. Then she provoked boos and hisses as well as wild applause when, in the closing "Dance sauvage," wearing only feathers about her hips, she entered the stage upside down in a full split on the shoulders of Joe Alex. Janet Flanner recorded the moment in the *New Yorker*: "Midstage, he paused, and with his long fingers holding her basket-wise around the waist, swung her in a slow cartwheel to the stage floor, where she stood like his magnificent discarded burden, in an instant of complete silence. She was an unforgettable female ebony statue." Called the "black Venus" and likened to African sculpture in motion, Baker was seen both as a threat to "civilization" and, like *le jazz hot*, as a new life force capable of energizing a weary France mired down in tradition and in need of renewal.

Paris made "la Baker" a celebrity, embracing both her erotic yet comic stage persona and her embodiment of Parisian chic as she strolled the city's boulevards beautifully dressed in Paul Poiret's creations. Beginning in 1926 Baker starred at the oldest and most venerated of French music halls, the Folies-Bergère. Once again, she was a shocking sensation. Instead of the customary bare-breasted, light-skinned women standing in frozen poses onstage at the Folies, Baker presented the Parisian audience with a dark-skinned, athletic form clad in a snicker-producing girdle of drooping bananas, dancing the wildest, most electrifying Charleston anyone had ever witnessed.

As the young African savage Fatou, she captured the sexual imagination of Paris.

In 1928, sensing that her public was beginning to tire of her frenetic antics, Baker left Paris. During an extended tour of European and South American cities with her manager and lover, Giuseppe "Pepito" Abatino, she studied voice, disciplined her dancing, and learned to speak French. However, Baker's reception in such cities as Vienna, Budapest, Prague, and Munich was not what it had been in Paris. Protests broke out in hostile reaction to her nudity, to jazz music, and to her foreignness. Baker also encountered for the first time the racism she thought she had left behind in America, the racism against which she would campaign onstage and off for the rest of her life. By the time she made her triumphal return to Paris two and a half years later, she had transformed herself into a sophisticated, elegantly attired French star.

In the 1930s Baker's career branched out in new directions. Singing took on new importance in her performances, and in her 1930–1931 revue at the Casino de Paris she perfected her signature song, "J'ai deux amours," proclaiming that her two loves were her country and Paris. She began recording for Columbia Records in 1930. She starred in two films, *Zou-Zou* (1934) and *Princesse Tam-Tam* (1935), whose story lines paralleled her rags-to-riches life. In the first film she is transformed from a poor laundress to a glamorous music-hall star and in the second from a Tunisian goat girl to an exotic princess. In the fall of 1934 she successfully tackled light opera in the starring role of Offenbach's operetta *La Créole*.

One year later, hoping to enjoy the success at home she had earned abroad, Baker sailed with Pepito to New York and began four months of preparation for the Ziegfeld Follies of 1936. The reviews of the New York opening in January took hateful aim at Baker's performance. Belittling her success abroad with the explanation that in France "a Negro wench always has a head start," the reporter remarked that "to Manhattan theatergoers last week she was just a slightly buck-toothed Negro woman whose figure might be matched in any night-club show, and whose dancing and singing might be topped practically anywhere outside of Paris." Critics, black and white, resented her performing only French cabaret material rather than "Harlem songs." Newspapers also reported that Baker personally was snubbed, refused entrance to hotels and nightclubs. Reactions to this discrimination varied, with some condemning her for "trying to be white." The columnist ROI OTTLEY of the *Amsterdam News*, on the other hand, praised her efforts to overcome Jim Crowism, saying that "she was just trying to live ignoring color." He recommended that "Harlem . . . should rally to the side of this courageous Negro woman. We should make her insults our insults."

Disappointed by her reception in her homeland and saddened by the death from cancer of Pepito, Baker returned to Paris and to the nude revues at the Folies-Bergère. By then thirty years old, she wanted to marry and have children. She realized the first desire on 30 November 1937, when she wed Jean Lion, a rich and handsome Jewish playboy and sugar broker. After fourteen months of marriage, during which Baker did not become pregnant and Lion continued his wild ways, she filed for divorce, which was granted in 1942.

In June of 1940 German troops invaded Paris. Baker, who refused to perform either for racist Nazis or for their French sympathizers, fled to Les Milandes, her fifteenth-century château in the Dordogne, with her maid, a Belgian refugee couple, and her beloved dogs. Since September 1939 Baker had served as an "honorable correspondent," gathering information about German troop locations for French military intelligence at embassy and ministry parties in Paris. Once Charles de Gaulle had declared himself leader of Free France in a radio broadcast from London and called for the French to resist their German occupiers, Baker joined "*résistance*" and was active in it throughout World War II, working mostly in North Africa. For her heroic work she was awarded the Croix de Guerre, and de Gaulle himself gave her a gold cross of Lorraine, the symbol of the Fighting French, when he established headquarters in Algiers in the spring of 1943. Baker was a tireless ambassador for the Free France movement and for de Gaulle, performing for British, American, and French soldiers in North Africa and touring the Middle East to raise money for the cause. In recognition of the propaganda services she performed during this tour, she was made a sublieutenant of the Women's Auxiliary of the French Air Force. After the war de Gaulle awarded Baker the coveted Medal of Resistance.

Moving into the 1950s Baker harnessed her formidable energies behind two causes. The first was her own pursuit of racial harmony and human tolerance in the form of her "Rainbow Tribe." To demonstrate the viability of world brotherhood, with the orchestra leader Jo Bouillon, whom she had married in 1947, Baker adopted children of many nationalities, races, and religions and installed them at Les Milandes. In order to support the family that eventually numbered thirteen and to finance the massive renovation of the château and related construction projects, Baker returned to the stage. A quick trip to the United States in 1948 was as unsuccessful as the one twelve years earlier and left her convinced that, if possible, race relations there were even worse than before. This realization prompted Baker's second cause, the pursuit of civil rights for black Americans through the desegregation of hotels, restaurants, and nightclubs.

Traveling with a $250,000 Parisian wardrobe; singing in French, Spanish, English, Italian, and Portuguese; and performing with masterly showmanship, in 1951 Baker began an American tour in Cuba. When word of her success in Havana reached Miami, Copa City moved to book the star for a splashy engagement. Contract negotiations were long and difficult. Initiating what would become her standard demand with nightclubs, Baker insisted on a nondiscrimination clause. If management would not admit black patrons, she would not perform. The integrated audience for Baker's show at Copa City was the first in the city's history. Baker took her tour and her campaign against color lines from city to city—New York, Boston, Atlanta, Las Vegas, and Hollywood. And audiences loved her. *Variety* wrote, "The showmanship that is Josephine Baker's . . . is something that doesn't happen synthetically or overnight. It's of the same tradition that accounts for the durability of almost every show biz standard still on top after many years."

The pinnacle of Baker's civil rights efforts was reached in August 1963 when she was invited to the great March on Washington. Dressed in her World War II uniform, Baker stood on the platform in front of the Lincoln Memorial and spoke to the crowd of thousands, blacks and whites, demonstrating for justice and equality: "You are on the eve of victory. You can't go wrong. The world is behind you." Baker was among those arrayed around MARTIN LUTHER KING JR. as he delivered his "I have a dream" speech. Certainly, for Josephine Baker, that day was a dream come true.

The remaining years of Baker's life were not tranquil. Given her extravagant spending and generosity, financial problems continued to plague her. Jo Bouillon finally despaired of trying to raise so many children or to impose any fiscal responsibility and left Baker. In 1968 Les Milandes was sold, and Baker, who barricaded herself in the house with her children, was evicted. Such setbacks notwithstanding, she continued to give comeback performances, astonishing crowds with her ability to rejuvenate herself the moment she stepped on stage, the consummate star. Her final performance in Paris to a sold-out house on 9 April 1975 was no exception. The following day, just two months shy of her sixty-ninth birthday, Baker died of a cerebral hemorrhage brought on by a stroke. All of France mourned the passing of "la Joséphine." National television broadcast the procession of her flag-draped coffin through the streets of Paris and the funeral service at the Church of the Madeleine, where twenty thousand Parisians gathered to pay their respects.

In *Jazz Cleopatra: Josephine Baker in Her Time*, Phyllis Rose writes of Baker's "cabaret internationalism" as her "way of expressing a political position." A performer of consummate skill, Baker enthralled audiences for more than a half century. But personal adulation was not enough. Like PAUL ROBESON, HARRY BELAFONTE, LENA HORNE, BILL COSBY, and others, Baker put her prestige and popularity in the service of civil rights, racial harmony, and equality for all humanity.

Further Reading

Baker, Josephine, and Marcel Sauvage. *Les mémoires de Joséphine Baker* (1927).
Baker, Josephine, and Marcel Sauvage. *Les mémoires de Joséphine Baker* (1949).
Baker, Josephine, and Jo Bouillon. *Joséphine* (1976).
Colin, Paul. *Le tumulte noir* (1927).
Hammond, Bryan, and Patrick O'Connor. *Josephine Baker* (1988).
Rose, Phyllis. *Jazz Cleopatra: Josephine Baker in Her Time* (1989).
Obituary: *New York Times*, 13 April 1975.

KAREN C. C. DALTON

BAKER, LaVern (11 Nov. 1929–10 Mar. 1997), singer, was born in Chicago as Delores Williams. Nothing is known about her parents. Raised by her aunt, Merline Baker, also known as the blues singer MEMPHIS MINNIE, Baker started singing almost as soon as she could walk, both in her Baptist church and in the street. She grew up in poverty and sang for change on the downtown Chicago streets from the age of three. She started singing professionally as a teenager at the Club Delisa, decked out in downhome clothes and billed as "Little Miss Sharecropper." The "Sharecropper" sobriquet was a takeoff on the popular blues shouter "Little Miss Cornshucks," and although it garnered her attention at the time, she was embarrassed by it later in her life. She also appeared at different venues as Bea Baker.

At the age of seventeen, Baker moved to Detroit. By 1947 she was appearing regularly at the city's legendary Flame Show Bar. She was first heard on a commercial recording in 1949, singing with the Eddie Penigar Band for RCA Records. Over the next several years she recorded on different labels with two separate groups; with HOT LIPS PAGE and Red Sanders she recorded (as "Little Miss Sharecropper") on Columbia and on Okeh Records (as Bea Baker) with Maurice King and his Wolverines. Baker joined the Todd Rhodes Orchestra in 1952, taking the name LaVern Baker, and toured the national "chitlin' circuit" while recording with Rhodes for King Records.

Baker signed on with Ahmet Ertegun and Atlantic Records in 1953. At that point Atlantic was a strictly R&B and blues label whose other female star, RUTH BROWN, had a completely different voice and style from Baker's. Brown's hits like "Mama, He Treats Your Daughter Mean" and "Teardrops from My Eyes" were like most of Atlantic's successes of the era: black records made for black adults and strictly aimed at the R&B market, eschewing any attempt at gaining a white audience. Ertegun and the producer Jerry Wexler apparently had different designs for Baker.

Her first important Atlantic recording, "Soul On Fire," was a rewrite by Ertegun, Baker, and Wexler of the gospel standard "Journey to the Sky." Baker's simmering delivery and the record's gospel-tinged tension and release presaged the metaphorical fire to come. It served as a precursor of the crossover from rhythm and blues to rock and roll, a phenomenon that was to transform popular music in the 1950s.

Baker's first crossover pop hit was "Tweedle Dee" in 1955. An early example of the "white cover" phenomena, which reflected the pernicious racism of the era, "Tweedle Dee" was quickly covered and released by the white singer Georgia Gibb. Gibb's version was the bigger pop hit since it received massive airplay on the pop radio stations of the day. While Baker did appear singing the song on the Ed Sullivan Show, the "cover" practice (Gibbs later covered other Baker songs and ETTA JAMES's early hits as well) seriously curtailed some of the momentum of Baker and other R&B acts like FATS DOMINO and BIG JOE TURNER. Baker even unsuccessfully attempted to get Congress to change the copyright law to prevent the identical copying of arrangements. Two rhythm and blues hits, "Bop-Ting-A-Ling" (1955) and "Play it Fair" (1956) followed her first smash, but the release of "Jim Dandy" (1956) confirmed Baker's status as a rock and roll star.

Baker's crossover success brought her to the attention of pioneering deejay Alan Freed, who not only popularized the use of the term "rock and roll" on his New York radio show, but also became identified with the "new" music through the national multi-artist tours he promoted and the movies he produced and in which he starred. Baker's records epitomized his "big beat" sound, and she joined CHUCK BERRY, the Everly Brothers, Buddy Holly, Fats Domino, and LITTLE RICHARD on Freed's all-star shows throughout the country. She also starred in Freed's films *Rock, Rock, Rock* (1956) and *Mister Rock & Roll* (1957). The biggest hit of her career was the blues ballad "I Cried a Tear" (1958), which reached number three on the pop chart.

In a change of pace from her hits, Baker sang on what is arguably the best "BESSIE SMITH" album ever recorded: *LaVern Baker Sings Bessie Smith*. Produced by Nesuhi Ertegun and engineered by Tom Dowd, the album paired Baker with the hippest jazz musicians of the era, such as BUCK CLAYTON, Jerome Richardson, DANNY BARKER, and VIC DICKENSON, and she belted Bessie's tunes in her own inimitable style over the swinging arrangements of ERNIE WILKINS, Phil Moore, and Nat Pierce. While Bessie Smith was undoubtedly the greatest of blues singers, she lived in a time with limited recording resources; this was the album she might have made had she lived into the 1950s.

A television special from this period on the music of Harold Arlen showed some of the depth and breadth of Baker's talent and reflected her desire to broaden her range. She starred with Peggy Lee, Vic Damone, and Arlen in the *DuPont Show of the Week, Happy With the Blues: The Music of Harold Arlen*, broadcast on 24 September 1961. After sitting through the absurdity of a jungle set, the viewer was treated to Baker's seminal takes on "I've got a Right to Sing the Blues" and "Stormy Weather," as well as Lee's sultry "The Man That Got Away" and the definitive "I've Got the World on a String." She soon joined LOUIS ARMSTRONG's band as featured female singer and toured the world with him for the next two years.

Baker left Atlantic in 1964 and signed with Brunswick the following year. There she recorded

more R&B hits, the last of which was a funky duet with JACKIE WILSON, released in 1966, called "Think Twice." She joined a USO tour of Vietnam and the Far East in 1967. While on tour in 1969, she became ill and convalesced at a hospital on Subic Bay in the Philippines. The commander of the base was a fan and offered her a job running the Non-Commissioned Officers Club. She took the job and sang at the club for the next twenty years, completely dropping out of the music business in the United States.

Baker returned to the States for the first time in 1988 to sing at the Atlantic Records fortieth anniversary celebration, and once back in the country, she became active in the music business once more. In 1990 she recorded a song for the *Dick Tracy* soundtrack album, played dynamic gigs in New York and Washington, D.C., and was awarded a Career Achievement Award by the Rhythm and Blues Foundation. The offer of a lead role in the Broadway hit *Black and Blue* brought her back for good; she performed in the show for nine months in 1990. Tours of the United States and Europe followed in 1991, capped by an appearance with B. B. KING and Ruth Brown at the Montreux Jazz Festival in July. Her comeback was complete.

Baker suffered formidable health setbacks in 1993–1994, culminating in the loss of both her legs due to diabetic complications. She then embarked on what can only be described as one of the most inspiring comebacks in recent show business history. She relearned her material and started singing from a wheelchair. By 1995 she was back to captivating audiences, and in 1996 she made a triumphant performance before 10,000 people at the Newport Rhythm and Blues Festival. She had just learned to walk with artificial legs when she succumbed to heart failure in 1997. She was the second woman (after ARETHA FRANKLIN) inducted into the Rock and Roll Hall of Fame in 1991.

Further Reading

Ertegun, Ahmet, et al. *What'd I Say: The Atlantic Story, 50 Years of Music* (2001).
Wade, Dorothy, and Justine Picardie. *Music Man: Ahmet Ertegun, Atlantic Records, and the Triumph of Rock 'n' Roll* (1990).
Wexler, Jerry, and David Ritz. *Rhythm and the Blues: A Life in American Music* (1993).

Discography

LaVern Baker Sings Bessie Smith, Atlantic Records (1958).
LaVern Baker Live in Hollywood '91, Rhino (1991).
Soul On Fire: The Best of LaVern Baker, Atlantic (1991).

Obituary: *New York Times*, 12 Mar. 1997.

BARRY MARSHALL

BAKER, Lena (8 June 1900–5 Mar. 1945), the first woman executed by electric chair in Georgia, was born in Cuthbert, Georgia, to Queenie Baker, a sharecropper, and a father whose name is unknown.

Little is known about her early life. If typical of the African American experience in southwestern Georgia in the early 1900s Baker's childhood was probably one of long working hours and low expectations. Indeed, it was in the debt-ridden and desperate Georgia black belt of the early 1900s that W. E. B. DU BOIS discovered the "Negro problem in its naked dirt and penury" (Litwack, 114). In an attempt to escape from that world of debt and desperation, Baker began working at an early age, at first helping her mother chop cotton for a neighboring white family, the Coxes. Like other black women in the community, she also worked as a laundress and occasional domestic for white families in town. Despite the legacy of Cuthbert's most famous black educator, RICHARD R. WRIGHT, Baker attended school sporadically, when her labor was not needed by the her family or by the Coxes, and she did not return to school after the sixth grade.

Baker would also have been aware of the ever-present undercurrent of racial violence in Jim Crow-era Georgia. In addition to the notorious public lynching of SAM HOSE in 1899, more than 400 other African Americans were lynched by white mobs in that state between 1882 and 1920. Five black men were lynched in tiny Randolph County alone in that period, including a double lynching in Cuthbert in

Lena Baker, at the Georgia State Prison in Reidsville, Georgia, 23 February 1945. (AP Images/Georgia Department of Corrections, File.)

September 1916, when Baker was sixteen years old and which she may well have known about.

Baker regularly attended Cuthbert's Mount Vernon Baptist Church, where she sang in the choir, but she may also have been familiar with the region's many taverns, juke joints, and tent shows, which produced the likes of Columbus, Georgia's MA RAINEY, among others in their heyday before World War I. Some time in the mid-1920s, Baker and another black woman began to operate a small brothel in Cuthbert, catering to both black and white customers. After being arrested for prostitution and sentenced to several months in the workhouse, Baker returned to Cuthbert to work as a domestic and to raise three children, apparently without the assistance of their father, of whom nothing is known. Though she remained active in her church and choir, she was shunned by many in the black community who were unwilling to forgive her transgressions.

Isolated, she turned increasingly to alcohol. By the early 1940s her steady drinking had led Baker into the company of a fellow alcoholic, Ernest B. Knight, a white gristmill owner in his sixties with a reputation for casual violence. After Knight broke his leg in a fall, Baker began working for him, ostensibly to help him around his home. When rumors spread throughout Cuthbert that the couple were having a sexual affair—illegal under Georgia law—they were visited by the local sheriff, but not arrested. Knight's son also tried to end the affair by savagely beating Baker and later by threatening to kill her when Baker and Ernest Knight moved briefly to Tallahassee, Florida.

By early 1943 both Baker and Knight had returned to Cuthbert. Their relationship—violent, chaotic, and fueled by alcohol—continued. According to Baker's trial testimony, matters came to a head on the evening of 30 April 1943, when Knight forced her at gunpoint to come to his gristmill to drink and have sex. Baker resisted, but Knight threatened to beat and kill her. At some point during the following day Knight attempted to rape Baker, who resisted and managed to grab the pistol that he always wore strapped to his chest. Fearing for her life and seeing Knight holding an iron bar, Baker told a Randolph County court at her trial that she then fired the pistol in self-defense, killing Knight. Baker admitted her crime to the county coroner—a member of the white Cox family—was promptly arrested, and on 14 August 1944, an all-white, all-male jury found her guilty of the capital murder of Ernest Knight. The trial lasted only a few hours. Baker's attorney's appeals for clemency were swiftly dismissed, probably because the prosecution had made much of Baker's unsavory reputation and her conviction for prostitution.

On 5 March 1945 Lena Baker became the first woman to die in Georgia's electric chair. In her final statement she continued to insist that she had acted in self-defense and that she was ready to meet her God. The local white newspaper headlined the event "Baker Burns." To a considerable extent Lena Baker was a victim of unfortunate timing, as well as Georgia's racist criminal legal system. Two years after Baker's execution Rosa Lee Ingram, another African American woman from the southwest Georgia black belt, was also given the death sentence for her role in killing a white man in self-defense. In Ingram's case, however, pressure from the Civil Rights Congress, the Communist Party, the NAACP, and the *Pittsburgh Courier* persuaded the authorities to reduce her sentence to a life prison term and, eventually, to release her on parole. Five years later the U.S. Supreme Court ruled against the application of the death penalty in cases such as Baker's and Ingram's where there was such a clear element of self-defense.

Outside her own family Lena Baker's life and early death remained largely forgotten and ignored until the late 1990s, when some of her relatives, members of Mount Vernon Baptist Church, and anti–death penalty activists in Randolph County erected a permanent marker for her unmarked grave in Cuthbert Cemetery. They also began a campaign seeking a posthumous pardon for Baker from the state of Georgia, on the grounds that she had been a victim of abuse who had killed in self-defense. The campaign succeeded in August 2005, when the Georgia Board of Pardons and Paroles apologized for the state's refusal to grant Lena Baker clemency sixty years earlier.

Further Reading
Litwack, Leon. *Trouble in Mind: Black Southerners in the Age of Jim Crow* (1998).
Phillips, Lena Bond. *The Lena Baker Story* (2001).
                                                    STEVEN J. NIVEN

BAKER, Thomas Nelson, Sr. (11 Aug. 1860–25 Feb. 1940), philosopher and first African American to receive a PhD in Philosophy in the United States, was born enslaved of enslaved parents, Thomas Chadwick Baker, a Civil War veteran, and Edith (Nottingham) Baker, on Robert Nottingham's plantation in Northampton County, Virginia. Edith was the daughter of Southey and Sarah Nottingham of Northampton County. Thomas Nelson Baker was one of five children.

Describing the influences on his early intellectual life, Baker remembered:

My mother taught me my letters, although I well remember when she learned them herself. My first reading lesson was the second chapter of Matthew, the Bible being the only book we had. I never read a bad book in my life which is one of the blessings I got by being poor. I began to attend the common schools at eight and learned to love books passionately. I used to read through my recesses. Evenings I read the Bible to my parents and grandparents, while they listened with weeping eyes, thankful that I had received the great blessing of being able to read. (untitled newspaper, Hampton University Archives)

In 1872, when Baker was twelve, his father removed him from school so that he could work to help meet rent payments for the house that the family occupied. Baker worked for ten years as a farmhand, which led him to break all connections with books and schoolmates. However, once he came of age, his burning desire to get an education returned.

In 1881 Baker entered Hampton Institute in Virginia, where he studied for the next four years. During his first year Baker worked during the day and attended Hampton Institute's night school. During the last three years he attended the day school. After leaving, Baker taught for a year at schools in the Dismal Swamp, a region in southeast Virginia and northeast North Carolina.

In May 1886 Baker entered Mount Hermon School in Massachusetts (also known as the Reverend Dwight L. Moody's Boys' School), where he received training for entrance to college. Baker was one of only two black students there, but during his first year he acted as drillmaster. He graduated in June 1889.

Around 1890 Baker entered Boston University's liberal arts school, graduating with a BA in 1893. That year he went on to attend the Yale Divinity School, where he completed a bachelor of divinity degree in three years. Following this degree Baker studied philosophy and psychology from 1896 to 1900 at the Yale graduate school. Coupled with pastoral duties—for from 1896 to 1901 he was the minister of the Dixwell Avenue Congregational Church in New Haven, Connecticut, and was ordained there in 1897—he completed his PhD in Philosophy at Yale in 1903, becoming the first African American in the United States to receive a PhD in Philosophy.

Baker probably wrote much of his dissertation, "The Ethical Significance of the Connection between Mind and Body," while living in Pittsfield, Massachusetts, because in 1901 he had become the minister of the town's Second Congregational Church (the second minister in the church's history). He held this position until 1939, when he was made minister emeritus from 1939 to 1940. He was also the dean of clergymen in Pittsfield. In keeping with his high standing, in 1926 Baker had the honor of being the only black pastor to deliver an address at the mound of the unknown dead in Pittsfield Cemetery on Memorial Day.

On 18 September 1901, while he was still working on his dissertation, Baker married Elizabeth Baytop, an alumna of Hampton Institute and the daughter of Harry and Millie (Bright) Baytop, in Capahosic, Virginia. They had four children: Edith, Harry, Ruth, and Thomas Jr. All four excelled academically, with all four earning bachelor's degrees and some earning higher degrees.

Baker wrote various significant philosophical articles dealing with black values and ideals. Indeed, Baker's views concerning black aesthetics and black cultural identity constitute an early and significant philosophical precursor to the Harlem Renaissance and the 1960s Black Arts Movement. As early as May 1906, even before ALAIN LEROY LOCKE's *The New Negro* (1925), Baker, in *Alexander's Magazine*, forged a philosophical critique of racism and advanced an aesthetic alternative to the reigning white aesthetic of beauty. He argued, "not where we are, but what we are is the great and final question that should concern us" ("Not Pity but Respect," 111). For Baker, "It is the perversion of the aesthetical sense of physical beauty that the American Negro has struck his lowest depths of racial degradation" ("Ideals," 28). And in 1908, in the *Southern Workman,* Baker suggested a critical pedagogy that could create representational and semiotic diversity: "The pictures of the boys and girls in school are just what the Negro child needs to see. If there is to be any real race love, the Negro child must be taught to see beauty in the Negro type."

Baker was acutely aware of colonial hegemony and its inhumane manifestations. He maintained:

Everywhere the colored man sees built into the steamboats, trains and waiting rooms the teachings of Nietzsche: "All that is best is for my folk and for myself. If it is not given us, we take it. The best land, the purest sky, the best food, the most beautiful thoughts and the most beautiful women." (*Berkshire Eagle,* 1919)

Baker was also concerned with the symbolic reorientation of black consciousness. He argued that the watchword of black people should be "Not Pity but Respect." In short, by stripping away the identity of helplessness as imposed from the outside, black people could say to their oppressors in unequivocal terms that the "Jim Crow Negro" personality is dead, that they as black people stand within the domain of their own self-worth and self-value. Baker clearly understood the seriousness of the issue of black aesthetic symbolization; it was an issue of black survival within a racist, cultural, and institutional symbolic space designed to create a destructive black double consciousness, self-alienation, and somatic malediction.

Through his philosophical efforts to create a discourse of race pride and race identity, Thomas Nelson Baker became an important philosophical figure of the twentieth-century black intellectual vanguard. Baker died accidentally as a result of poisoning from illuminating gas and was buried at the Pittsfield Cemetery.

Further Reading

Materials by and about Thomas Nelson Baker can be found in the Baker file at the Hampton University Archives, Hampton, Virginia.

Baker, Thomas N. "Ideals," *Alexander's Magazine* (2 parts, Sept. and Oct. 1906).

Baker, Thomas N. "Not Pity but Respect," *Alexander's Magazine* (May 1906).

Yancy, George. "On the Power of Black Aesthetic Ideals: Thomas Nelson Baker as Preacher and Philosopher," *A.M.E. Church Review* (Oct.–Dec. 2001).

Obituaries: *Berkshire Eagle* 49, no. 207 (n.d.); *Yale University Alumni Records, 1940–1941* (1942).

GEORGE YANCY

BAKER, Vernon Joseph (17 Dec. 1919–), soldier and Medal of Honor recipient, was born in Cheyenne, Wyoming, to Manuel Caldera and Beulah Baker.

After the deaths of his parents, Vernon and his sisters, Irma and Katherine, were raised by their maternal grandparents, Joseph Samuel Baker, a retired brakeman for the Union Pacific Railroad, and Dora Lucas. Although his grandparents never officially adopted him, Vernon took the surname Baker and did not know his original surname until later in life. Baker was educated at various elementary and secondary schools, including two years at Father Flanagan's Boys Home in Omaha, Nebraska. Baker finally earned his high school diploma at Clarinda, Iowa, in 1939.

After graduation, Baker returned to Cheyenne, where he found work at the army depot at night doing maintenance, repair, and cleaning jobs. Baker was rejected on his first attempt to join the army. Finally in June 1942 he enlisted and was shipped to Fort Walters, Texas. While in Texas, Baker worked as the company supply clerk and was promoted from private first class to sergeant. His commanding officer noticed Baker's ability as a supply sergeant and assigned him to Officer Candidate School in Fort Benning, Georgia.

Following officer training, Baker was sent to the 370th Infantry Regiment as a second lieutenant and rifle platoon leader and was stationed at Fort Huachuca, Arizona. In October 1943 Baker was reassigned to the 360th Regimental Combat Team of the 92nd Infantry Division and was sent to Italy. In August 1944 his unit joined General Mark Clark's Fifth Army and engaged a veteran German army in fierce combat. Lacking proper equipment and training, the typical enlisted man held only a fourth-grade education, and the 92nd Infantry Division suffered a casualty rate of almost 25 percent from August 1944 until the final German surrender in Italy on 2 May 1945.

After nearly eighteen months of duty in Italy, Baker's platoon was ordered to assault Hill X and Castle Aghinolfi nearly three miles behind the vaunted German Gothic Line on 5 April 1945. During this action the platoon suffered a nearly 60 percent casualty rate. Baker was ordered to withdraw his battered platoon but was unable to do so because of intense German bombardment. Rather, he chose to fight the Germans almost single-handedly in order to save as many of his men as possible, and in the process he destroyed one machine-gun nest and a German observation tower. Along with another platoon member, Baker smashed two more gun emplacements and drew enemy fire away from attempts to withdraw his decimated unit.

The following morning, on 6 April 1945, Baker led the 360th and 361st Regimental Combat Teams through mine fields near Viareggio, Italy, to capture both of the original objectives of the mission. For these actions and the injuries he suffered while undertaking them Baker was awarded the Purple Heart, the Bronze Star, and the Distinguished Service Cross.

The 92nd Infantry Division pulled out of Italy in late 1945, but Baker remained there, staying in the army despite losing his officer's commission because he lacked a college degree. By the time Baker returned to Lincoln, Nebraska, in 1947 he had attained the rank of master sergeant and worked as a recruiting photographer. While in Lincoln he considered using the GI Bill to attend the University of Nebraska but instead chose to join the Eleventh Airborne, an all-black division. Baker trained at Fort Bragg, North Carolina, where he earned his jump wings and completed the army's noncommissioned officer school. Baker was promoted to first sergeant and assigned to Company K, 505th Infantry of the famed 82nd Airborne Division.

With the outbreak of hostilities in Korea in 1950, Baker volunteered for a tour of duty. He was denied because of his status as a Distinguished Service Cross winner but was later repromoted to lieutenant because of the wartime demand for officers. President Harry Truman had ordered the military desegregated in 1948, and Baker became one of the first black officers to command an integrated company. With the Korean armistice in 1953, Baker was mustered out of the airborne to the signal corps with his officer status revoked again.

After the war Baker was stationed in Tucson, Arizona, where he met Fern V. Brown, whom he married in June 1953. Brown was divorced and had twin four-year-old daughters, and she and Baker had one daughter, LaVerne, in December 1954 and adopted another daughter, Larise, in Korea in 1955. After returning from Korea, Baker was stationed at Fort Ord, California, where he served until he was transferred to Germany in 1967. Baker retired from the army in August 1968.

After retiring, Baker worked as a loan officer and an assistant field director with the American Red Cross. He was sent to Vietnam in 1969, where he worked in the field at Pleiku and Da Nang. Baker continued to work for the Red Cross until 1986. He retired after the death of his wife and moved to Spokane, Washington, so that he could pursue his lifelong love of big-game hunting. Baker was married a second time in 1993 to Heidy Pawlik, a German immigrant.

For his actions in Italy, Baker was awarded the Medal of Honor, the nation's highest award for military service, on 17 January 1997 by President Bill Clinton. Baker was one of only seven African Americans to receive this honor for their World War II service. At the time of the ceremony, Baker was the only recipient still living. The six other African Americans posthumously awarded the Medal of Honor were Private George Watson, Sergeant Edward A. Carter Jr., Private Willy F. James Jr., Sergeant Ruben Rivers, First Lieutenant Charles L. Thomas, and First Lieutenant JOHN FOX.

Further Reading
Baker, Vernon J., and Ken Olsen. *Lasting Valor* (1997).
Gibran, Daniel K. *The 92nd Infantry Division and the Italian Campaign in World War II* (2001).
Hargrove, Hondon B. *Buffalo Soldiers in Italy: Black Americans in World War II* (1985).

Motley, Mary Penick, ed. *The Invisible Soldier: The Experience of the Black Soldier, World War II* (1987).
JEFFERY OTHELE MAHAN

BALDWIN, James (2 Aug. 1924–30 Nov. 1987), author, was born James Arthur Baldwin in Harlem, in New York City, the illegitimate son of Emma Berdis Jones, who married the author's stepfather, David Baldwin, in 1927. David Baldwin was a laborer and weekend storefront preacher who had an enormous influence on the author's childhood; his mother was a domestic who had eight more children after he was born. Baldwin was singled out early in school for his intelligence, and at least one white teacher, Orrin Miller, took a special interest in him. At P.S. 139, Frederick Douglass Junior High School, Baldwin met black poet COUNTÉE CULLEN, a teacher and literary club adviser there. Cullen saw some of Baldwin's early poems and warned him against trying to write like LANGSTON HUGHES, so Baldwin turned from poetry to focus more on writing fiction. In 1938 he experienced a profound religious conversion at the hands of a female evangelist/pastor of Mount Cavalry of the Pentecostal Faith, which he later wrote about in his first novel, *Go Tell It on the Mountain* (1953), in his play *The Amen Corner* (1968), and in an essay in *The Fire Next Time* (1963). Saved, Baldwin became a Sunday preacher at the nearby Fireside Pentecostal Assembly.

In 1938 Baldwin entered De Witt Clinton High School in the Bronx; he graduated in 1942. There Baldwin was challenged intellectually and was able to escape home and Harlem. He wrote for the school magazine, the *Magpie*, and began to frequent Greenwich Village, where he met the black artist BEAUFORD DELANEY, an important early influence. Torn between the dual influences of the church and his intellectual and artistic private life, Baldwin finally made a choice. At age sixteen he began a homosexual relationship with a Harlem racketeer and later said he was grateful to the older man throughout his life for the love and self-validation he brought to the tormented and self-conscious teenager. As a preacher, Baldwin considered himself a hypocrite. At this same time, he discovered that David Baldwin was not, in fact, his real father and began to understand why he had felt deeply rejected as a child and had hated and feared his father. Fearing gossip about his homosexual relationship would reach his family and church, Baldwin broke with both the racketeer and the church. Now eighteen, he also moved away from home, taking a series of odd jobs in New Jersey and spending free time in the Village with artists and writers, trying to establish himself. He returned home in 1943 to care for the family while his stepfather was dying of tuberculosis. A few hours after his father's death, his youngest sister was born, named by James Baldwin, the head of the family. The Harlem riot of 1943 broke out in the midst of this family upheaval, all of which Baldwin described eloquently in *Notes of a Native Son* (1955).

After his stepfather's funeral Baldwin left home for the last time, determined to become a writer. In 1944 he met RICHARD WRIGHT, who helped him get a Eugene F. Saxon Fellowship to work on his first novel, then titled "In My Father's House." He gave part of the $500 grant to his mother and tried to start his literary career. Although Baldwin's first novel was rejected by two publishers, he began to have some success publishing book reviews and essays, establishing a name and a reputation. At the same time, he had difficulty extracting himself from the influence of Richard Wright, who became for Baldwin the literary father that he had to reject, as David Baldwin had been the punishing stepfather to be overcome. With what was left of the Rosenwald Fellowship he had received in 1948, Baldwin, frustrated by the fits and starts of his writing career and tired of America's racism, bought a one-way air ticket to Paris and left the United States on 11 November.

In Paris, Baldwin met writers such as Jean-Paul Sartre, Jean Genet, and Saul Bellow. He garnered notice as a critic with the essay "Everybody's Protest Novel," which came out in *Partisan Review* in 1949. Although mostly a critique of Harriet Beecher Stowe's *Uncle Tom's Cabin*, this was the first of a series of three essays in which Baldwin attacked his literary mentor, Wright. Baldwin followed with "Many Thousand Gone" in 1951 and, after Wright's death, "Alas Poor Richard" in 1961. But not until he took himself, his typewriter, and his BESSIE SMITH records to a tiny hamlet high in the Swiss Alps in 1951 did Baldwin begin to work in earnest on his first and best novel, *Go Tell It on the Mountain*. In this autobiographical family novel, fourteen-year-old John Grimes undergoes an emotional-psychological-religious crisis of adolescence and is "saved." *Go Tell It on the Mountain* explores the histories and internal lives of John's stepfather Gabriel, mother Elizabeth, and Aunt Florence, spanning the years from 1875 to the Depression and including "the Great Migration" from the South to Harlem. It was well received and was nominated for the National Book Award in 1954; Baldwin said in an interview with QUINCY TROUPE that he was told it did not win because RALPH ELLISON's *Invisible Man* had won in 1953 and America was not ready to give this award to two black writers in a row.

Baldwin won a Guggenheim grant to work on a second novel, published in 1956 as *Giovanni's Room*, about a homosexual relationship and with all-white characters in a European setting. Baldwin's American publisher turned it down for its honesty, so Baldwin had to publish *Giovanni's Room* first in London. It was a book Baldwin had to write, he said in an interview with Richard Goldstein, "to clarify something for myself." Baldwin went on to say, "The question of human affection, of integrity, in my case, the question of trying to become a writer, are all linked with the question of sexuality." The central character, David, a young American living in Paris, is forced to choose between his fiancée, Hella, and his male lover Giovanni. David rejects Giovanni, who is later tried and executed for the murder of an aging homosexual. Racked with guilt, David reveals his true homosexual nature and breaks his engagement, making Giovanni the injured martyr and moral pole in the novel.

Baldwin's first collection of essays, *Notes of a Native Son*, appeared in 1955. These autobiographical and political pieces made Baldwin famous as an eloquent and experienced commentator on race and culture in America. Here he says on his stepfather's funeral,

This was his legacy: nothing is ever escaped. That bleakly memorable morning I hated the unbelievable streets and the Negroes and whites who had, equally, made them that way. But I knew that it was folly, as my father would have said, this bitterness was folly. It was necessary to hold on to the things that mattered. The dead man mattered, the new life mattered; blackness and whiteness did not matter; to believe that they did was to acquiesce in one's own destruction. Hatred, which could destroy so much, never failed to destroy the man who hated and this was an immutable law. (Bantam ed. [1968], 94–95)

Baldwin returned periodically to the United States throughout the 1950s and 1960s, but never to stay. He first visited the South in 1957 and met MARTIN LUTHER KING JR. In 1961 he published the collection of essays *Nobody Knows My Name: More Notes of a Native Son*. By 1963 he was prominent enough to be featured on the cover of *Time* magazine as a major spokesman for the early civil rights movement after another collection of essays, *The Fire Next Time*, arguably Baldwin's most influential work, appeared. His first play, *Blues for Mr. Charlie* (1964), a fictionalized account of the 1955 Mississippi murder of fourteen-year-old EMMETT TILL, followed. In *The Fire Next Time* Baldwin effectively honed his prophetic, even apocalyptic rhetoric about racial tensions in America, fusing his themes of protest and love. During this period Baldwin had also published his third novel, *Another Country*, in 1962. His influence in national politics and American literature had reached a peak.

Another Country took Baldwin six years to complete; it eventually sold 4 million copies after a slow start with negative reviews. It is considered to be Baldwin's second-best novel. In it Baldwin portrays multiple relationships involving interracial and bisexual love through a third-person point of view. Again he looks for resolutions to racial and sexual tensions through the power of love. The characters, however, often have trouble distinguishing sex from love and sorting through their attitudes toward sex, race, and class. Though successful, the novel is somewhat unwieldy with nine major characters, dominated by the black jazz drummer Rufus Scott, who commits suicide at the end of the first chapter. The conclusion leaves readers with the hope that some of these troubled characters can achieve levels of self-understanding that will allow them to continue searching for "another country" within flawed and racist America. As the Nigerian writer Wole Soyinka wrote in 1989,

In the ambiguities of Baldwin's expression of social, sexual, even racial and political conflicts will be found that insistent modality of conduct, and even resolution, celebrated or lamented as a tragic omission—love. . . . James Baldwin's was—to stress the obvious—a different cast of intellect and creative sensibility from a Ralph Ellison's, a SONIA SANCHEZ's, a Richard Wright's, an AMIRI BARAKA's, or an ED BULLINS's. He was, till the end, too deeply fascinated by the ambiguities of moral choices in human relations to posit them in raw conflict terms. His penetrating eyes saw the oppressor as *also* the oppressed. Hate as a revelation of self-hatred, never unambiguously outward-directed. Contempt as thwarted love, yearning for expression. Violence as inner fear, insecurity. Cruelty as an inward-turned knife. His was an optimistic, greytoned vision of humanity in which the domain of mob law and lynch culture is turned inside out to reveal a landscape of scarecrows, an inner content of straws that await the compassionate breath of human love. (Troupe, 11, 17–18)

With the death of Martin Luther King Jr., and the change in the civil rights movement of the late 1960s from integrationist to separatist, Baldwin's writing, according to many critics, lost direction. The last two decades of his life he spent mostly abroad, particularly in France, which may have increased his distance from America in his work. In the essay collection *No Name in the Street* (1972), Baldwin discussed his sadness over the movement's waning. At the same time, he found himself the subject of attacks by new black writers such as ELDRIDGE CLEAVER, much like his own rejection of Richard Wright in the 1950s. *The Devil Finds Work* (1976) is Baldwin's reading of racial stereotypes in American movies, and *The Evidence of Things Not Seen* (1985), an account of the Atlanta child murder trials, was unsuccessful, although the French translation of this book was very well received. Baldwin also wrote a series of problematic novels in his later years: *Tell Me How Long the Train's Been Gone* (1968), *If Beale Street Could Talk* (1974), and *Just above My Head* (1979). In these novels Baldwin seems to go over the familiar ground of the first three novels: racial, familial, and sexual conflicts in flawed, autobiographical plots. He never again achieved the mastery of his first novel, *Go Tell It on the Mountain*, one of the key texts in all of African American literature and of American literature as a whole.

After Baldwin died on the French Riviera, his funeral was celebrated on 8 December 1987 at the Cathedral of St. John the Divine in New York, where MAYA ANGELOU, TONI MORRISON, Amiri Baraka, the French ambassador Emmanuel de Margerie, and other notables spoke and performed. Baldwin has generally been considered to be strongest as an essayist, though he published one outstanding novel, and weakest as a playwright because he became too didactic at the expense of dramatic art. His achievements and influence tended to get lost in the sheer productivity of his career, especially as his later work was judged not to measure up to his earlier work. After his death scholars were able to look at Baldwin's contribution with perspective and a sense of closure, and his literary stature grew accordingly.

Further Reading

Baldwin's personal papers and manuscripts are in the James Weldon Johnson Collection, Beinecke Rare Book and Manuscript Library, Yale University; the Berg collection at the New York Public Library; and the Schomburg Center for Research in Black Culture of the New York Public Library, among other repositories.

Books by Baldwin not mentioned above include *Going to Meet the Man* (1965), *A Dialogue: James Baldwin and* Nikki Giovanni (1971), *One Day When I Was Lost: A Scenario Based on* Alex Haley's *"The Autobiography of* Malcolm X" (1972), *A Rap on Race* (with Margaret Mead [1973]), *Little Man, Little Man: A Story of Childhood* (1976), *Jimmy's Blues: Selected Poems* (1983), *The Price of the Ticket: Collected Nonfiction* (1985), and *Perspectives: Angles of African Art*, ed. James Baldwin et al. (1987).

Campbell, James. *Taking at the Gates: A Life of James Baldwin* (1991).

Gates, Henry Louis, Jr. "The Welcome Table [James Baldwin]," in *Thirteen Ways of Looking at a Black Man* (1997).

Leeming, David Adams. *James Baldwin: A Biography* (1994).

Porter, Horace A. *Stealing the Fire: The Art and Protest of James Baldwin* (1989).

Standley, Fred L., and Nancy V. Burt, eds. *Critical Essays on James Baldwin* (1988).

Standley, Fred L., and Louis H. Pratt, eds. *Conversations with James Baldwin* (1989).

Troupe, Quincy, ed. *James Baldwin: The Legacy* (1989).

Weatherby, W. J. *James Baldwin: Artist on Fire* (1989).

Obituaries: *New York Times*, 2 Dec. 1987; *Washington Post*, 5 Dec. 1987; *New York Review of Books* 34 (Jan. 1988).

ANN RAYSON

BALDWIN, Maria Louise (13 Sept. 1856–9 Jan. 1922), educator, lecturer, and activist, was born in Cambridge, Massachusetts, the oldest daughter of Peter L. Baldwin, a Haitian mariner who became a Boston postman, and Mary E. Baldwin, a Baltimore native whose maiden name is now unknown. Baldwin was educated in Cambridge public schools, attending Sargent Primary School, Allston Grammar School, and Cambridge High School. After graduating from high school in 1874 she attended the Cambridge Teachers' Training School. Initially refused a job by the Cambridge school district, she looked elsewhere for employment and eventually took a position teaching elementary school in Chestertown, Maryland. Within a few years, however, she was back in Cambridge. Reportedly under pressure from the African American community, the Cambridge school district decided to offer her a job. In 1881 Baldwin accepted a teaching position at the Agassiz Grammar School on Oxford Street, where she would spend the remainder of her career.

As the only African American teacher at a school that was 98 percent white, Baldwin faced considerable challenges, but she soon earned the respect of the school community. She was especially beloved by her students, many of them the children of Harvard professors and other influential Cambridge residents. In 1889 she was appointed principal, and in 1916 she was promoted to "master" of the school, overseeing twelve white teachers and over 500 students. At the time Baldwin was the only African American in New England to hold such a position, and one of only two women masters in the Cambridge school district. Throughout her long career Baldwin was an educational innovator. She organized Cambridge's first Parent-Teacher Association, added art classes to the curriculum, and experimented with new methods of teaching math. Interested in the physical as well as the mental well-being of her students, she was the first master to hire a school nurse.

Though Baldwin worked primarily within a white world she remained deeply involved in Cambridge's African American community. She hosted a weekly reading group for black Harvard students in her home at 196 Prospect Street. One of these students, W. E. B. Du Bois, remained a life-long admirer of her work. Baldwin later served on the board of the Boston branch of the NAACP and lectured widely on issues relating to race and education.

Baldwin was also active in Cambridge and Boston civic life more generally. She audited classes at Harvard, was a founder and president of the League of Women for Community Service, and participated in local organizations including the Twentieth Century Club, the Boston Ethical Society, the Cantabriga Club, and the Unitarian Universalist Church. She socialized with members of the local elite including Elizabeth Agassiz, Edward Everett Hale, Thomas Wentworth Higginson, and Alice Longfellow. By the time of her death Baldwin had become a beloved local institution and widely acknowledged as one of the most distinguished educators of her era. Baldwin's most important legacy was her students, but she was memorialized in more tangible ways as well. In 1951 a dormitory at Howard University was named in her honor, and in 2002 the Cambridge School Committee renamed the Agassiz School the Maria L. Baldwin School.

Further Reading
Porter, Dorothy B. "Maria Louise Baldwin, 1856–1922," *Journal of Negro Education* (1952).
Wilds, Mary. *I Dare Not Fail: Notable African American Women Educators* (2004).

BRIALLEN HOPPER

BALL, Alice Augusta (24 July 1892–31 Dec. 1916), pharmacist, chemist, researcher, and instructor, was born in Seattle, Washington, one of four children of James P. Ball Jr., an attorney and photographer, and Laura Howard, a photographer and cosmetologist. Alice grew up in a remarkable family.

Her grandfather, JAMES PRESLEY "J. P." BALL SR., a photographer, was one of the first blacks in the country to master the new art of the daguerreotype. His famous daguerreotype gallery in Cincinnati, Ohio, displayed a well-publicized six-hundred-yard panorama of pictures and paintings depicting the horrors of slavery. Later he opened photography galleries in Minneapolis, in Helena, Montana, in Seattle, and in Honolulu. Alice Ball's father, in addition to being a photographer, also was a newspaper editor and lawyer and was credited with having a lasting effect on Montana history. The Balls lived in Montana for several years before moving to Seattle, and Ball's newspaper, the *Colored Citizen*, had "campaigned vigorously on Helena's behalf " during the battle between Helena and Anaconda for designation as the state capital. When Montana voters, including many blacks, selected Helena, "Ball claimed no small part in the result" (William L. Lang, "The Nearly Forgotten Blacks on Last Chance Gulch 1900–1912," *Pacific Northwest Quarterly* 70, no. 2 [April 1979]: 52).

Little is known of Alice Ball's early life except that she lived in Seattle and probably helped out in the busy family's Globe Photo Studio. Her grandfather, J. P. Ball Sr., suffered from rheumatism and sought relief in the warmer climate of Hawaii, where he died in 1904. The Honolulu city directory indicates that the Balls lived at two different residences between 1903 and 1905 and lists Alice's father's occupation as attorney at law, her mother's as photographer, and her two brothers', Robert and William, as stenographer and collector, respectively. Alice Ball attended the Central Grammar School in Honolulu and made a lasting impression on an eighth-grade classmate, John Pratt. Sixty years later he wrote in his memoir that "Alice Ball was brilliant, and later went far in chemistry" (John Scott Boyd Pratt, *The Hawaii I Remember* [1965], 18).

After graduating from Broadway High School in Seattle in June 1909, Alice Ball earned two degrees from the University of Washington: a pharmaceutical chemist (PhC) degree in 1912 and a bachelor of science in Pharmacy on 17 June 1914. A November 1914 alumni newsletter reported that Alice A. Ball was working on her master's degree in the department of chemistry at the College of Hawaii (later the University of Hawaii). On 1 June 1915 she graduated with her master of science in Chemistry as the first— and only—woman to do so in the history of the college (*Honolulu Star-Bulletin*, 1 Mar. 2000, p. A3). She also was the first black woman instructor at the college's chemistry department, where she taught from 1915 to 1916. Her college graduation photograph shows a beautiful, soft-featured woman with an air of seriousness. She could have easily been mistaken as Hawaiian, and in fact a 1925 *Honolulu Advertiser* article announced in bold front-page headlines: "Hawaiian Girl Heroine First Made Possible the Chaulmoogra Leprosy Cure."

Because of its disfiguring, stigmatizing, and incurable traits, few diseases have terrified mankind more than Hansen's disease. Once called leprosy, Hansen's disease was renamed for Dr. Gerharad Armauer Hansen, a Norwegian physician who identified the causative microorganism. For many centuries desperate physicians and patients had tried numerous treatments to combat the disease, including surgery, diet, X-rays, mercury, dyes, strychnine, and many other esoteric concoctions. All failed to cure the terrible disease, and most—except for one—offered little relief. Since the fourteenth century in China and even earlier in India, one substance had been used with moderate success to reduce the effects of Hansen's: chaulmoogra oil. Plain chaulmoogra, however, has a disagreeable taste and upsets the stomach, preventing patients from taking it long-term. For hundreds of years scientists had searched diligently for a way to administer chaulmoogra oil as an injection, but these early attempts failed because the virtually insoluble drug created painful muscle abscesses.

In 1916 Ball, then a twenty-four-year-old pharmacist and chemist, tackled the problem that had thwarted innumerable chemists, pharmacologists, and researchers working in some of the world's most sophisticated and well-equipped laboratories, and she accomplished what no other scientist had. She isolated an injectable ethyl ester of chaulmoogra oil. As a result she changed the lives of millions of Hansen's disease sufferers for almost a quarter of a century.

Perhaps it was Ball's chemical wizardry in analyzing the active principles of kava root for her master's thesis that impressed Dr. Harry T. Hollmann, acting assistant surgeon at the Kalihi Hospital and former medical assistant at the federal Leprosy Investigation Station on Kalaupapa, an isolation settlement on the island of Molokai. Hollmann related in a 1922 article in a leading medical journal how he had sought Ball's help: "I interested Miss Alice Ball, M.S., an instructress in chemistry at the College of Hawaii in the chemical problem of obtaining for me the active agents in the oil of chaulmoogra."

Tragically, Ball became ill, returned home to Seattle, and died at the age of twenty-four. After her untimely death, Arthur Dean, a PhD chemist, Alice's former thesis adviser, and then dean of the College of Hawaii, continued her work. However, by 1920 the chaulmoogra process became labeled in the professional literature as the "Dean Method." Unlike Dean, Hollmann did acknowledge Alice Ball's significant work in his 1922 article, which he gave a subheading: "Ball's Method of Making Ethyl Esters of the Fatty Acids of Chaulmoogra Oil." The article restored Alice Ball's name and achievements to the pages of history for the outstanding work that she had accomplished for Hansen's disease patients around the world.

Eighty-four years later, on 29 February 2000, Alice Ball was formally recognized for her breakthrough research in treating Hansen's disease when the governor of Hawaii proclaimed 29 February as Alice Ball Day in the state. A bronze plaque honoring Ball and her achievements was placed near a chaulmoogra tree on the University of Hawaii campus. In December 2006 the board of regents of the University of Hawaii honored Alice Ball by posthumously awarding her the Regents' Medal of Distinction, which is presented to individuals of exceptional accomplishment and distinction who have made significant contributions to the university, state, region, or nation or within their field of endeavor.

Further Reading
Hollmann, Harry T. "The Fatty Acids of Chaulmoogra Oil in the Treatment of Leprosy and Other Diseases," *Archives of Dermatology and Syphilology* 2 (1922).
Law, Anwei V. Skinsnes, and Richard A. Wisniewski, eds. *Kalaupapa National Historical Park and the Legacy of Father Damien: A Pictorial History* (1988).
Wermager, Paul. "Healing the Sick," in *They Followed the Trade Winds: African Americans in Hawaii,* ed. Miles M. Jackson (2004).

PAUL WERMAGER

BALL, Charles (1781?–?), fugitive slave, soldier, and slave narrative author, was born on a tobacco plantation in Calvert County, Maryland, the son of slave parents whose names are unknown. When Charles was four years old, his mother and siblings were sold to slave traders to settle their late master's debts; he never saw them again. Charles was sold to John Cox, a local slave owner, and continued to live near his father and grandfather. After the sale of Charles's mother, his father sank into a deep depression, eventually escaping from slavery on the eve of his purchase by a slave trader. Charles grew close to his octogenarian grandfather, a former African warrior who had arrived in Maryland about 1730.

Cox died when Charles Ball was twelve, and the young slave worked for his late master's father until he was twenty years old. During this time Ball married a slave named Judah who worked on a neighboring plantation as a chambermaid. Ball was the subject of a two-year lawsuit between a Mr. Gibson, who purchased him from the senior Cox, and Levin Ballard, who purchased him from Cox's children. Ball eventually worked for Ballard for three years before being sold to a slave trader from Georgia. Ball was separated from his wife and children without being allowed to say goodbye to them. He and fifty-one other slaves, bound by neck irons, handcuffs, and chains, were forced to travel on foot for more than a month from Maryland to Columbia, South Carolina. Ball recalled in his memoir, *Slavery in the United States: A Narrative of the Life and Adventures of Charles Ball* (1836), "I felt indifferent to my fate. It appeared to me that the worst had come, that could come, and that no change of fortune could harm me."

In South Carolina, Ball was auctioned to the owner of a large cotton plantation. Upon the marriage of his master's daughter, Ball moved to Georgia to serve her and her new husband in September 1806. After the death of his new master in a duel, however, the Georgia estate, along with its slaves, was leased in January 1807 for seven years to another man. Ball seems to have enjoyed an unusually close relationship with his new master, traveling with him to purchase cattle and horses from the Cherokee and to Savannah, Georgia, to buy supplies for the plantation, as well as exerting authority on the plantation as overseer. After his master died around May 1807, Ball was severely beaten by his mistress's visiting brothers. He made his first escape from slavery in August of that year.

Despite being caught and imprisoned in Virginia, where he escaped from jail, Ball successfully walked from Georgia to Maryland in a year, traveling by night and foraging for food. Reunited with his wife and children about May 1808, he worked as a freeman in Maryland then enlisted as a seaman and cook under Commodore Barney in December 1813. Ball was dispatched by the United States to negotiate with several hundred slaves who had escaped from slavery under British protection. Unsuccessful, Ball himself was given the opportunity to travel to Trinidad with the other "contraband." He declined on the basis that he was already free. Discharged in 1814 and widowed in 1816, Ball worked in Maryland and Washington, D.C. In 1820 he invested his savings in a farm and dairy near Baltimore. He married—this wife's name is unknown—and fathered four more children.

Ball's domestic happiness was destroyed in June 1830 when he was captured and returned to slavery by his former mistress's brother. In Milledgeville, Georgia, at the residence of his new master, Ball unsuccessfully sued for his freedom. Finally he managed to escape, only to be recaptured and sold. After a week Ball once again escaped, this time heading east instead of north, to Savannah. While loading cotton on a Philadelphia-bound ship, Ball persuaded a free black sailor to allow him to stow away on the ship. Hidden among bales of cotton and equipped with only a jug of water, bread, and molasses, Ball safely made the journey to Philadelphia, emerging, undetected, free once again. Upon his arrival he was assisted by an unnamed Quaker who provided him with clothing and lodging. After a few weeks Ball returned to his home in Baltimore, only to find that his wife and children, all of whom were legally free, had been captured and sold into slavery. He never saw them again. Afraid of being enslaved again, Ball moved to Pennsylvania, where he composed his memoirs.

Ball is best known as the subject of a popular and controversial slave narrative that was printed at least six times before the Civil War, including in an unauthorized, unattributed, abridged version, *Fifty Years in Chains* (1859). This novel-like account of slavery was popular not only for its subject's sensational adventures and its detailed descriptions of life in the South but also for its restraint. Acknowledging "the bitterness of heart that is engendered by a remembrance of unatoned injuries," Ball's ghostwriter, the Pennsylvania attorney Isaac Fischer, was careful to exclude "every sentiment of this kind" from his rendering of Ball's life. This editorial censorship, combined with Fischer's inclusion of anecdotes from sources other than Ball in the narrative, led both contemporary critics and recent scholars to question the authenticity of the text, and even the existence of its subject. Most agree, however, that despite its embroidery and its silences, the narrative tells the true story of a courageous man who refused to be broken by an inhuman system.

Further Reading

Ball, Charles. *Slavery in the United States: A Narrative of the Life and Adventures of Charles Ball* (1836).
Andrews, William L. *To Tell a Free Story: The First Century of Afro-American Autobiography, 1760–1865* (1986).
Davis, Charles T., and Henry Louis Gates Jr., eds. *The Slave's Narrative* (1985).
Starling, Marion Wilson. *The Slave Narrative: Its Place in American History* (1981).

JEANNINE DeLOMBARD

BALL, James Presley (J. P.) (1825–4 May 1904), daguerreotypist, photographer, and entrepreneur, was born in Virginia, the second of four children of William Ball and Susan Ball, who were free blacks. In his youth Ball was a stevedore who worked along the Ohio River. He may have learned daguerreotypy around 1840 from a Boston-based African American photographer named John B. Bailey in White Sulphur Springs, West Virginia. Ball settled in Cincinnati, a busy river town that was growing dramatically. One of Ball's earliest known works (early 1840s) is an outdoor scene, a half-plate daguerreotype of the Myers & Co. Confectioners in Cincinnati. It is a remarkably clear image featuring a horse and cart standing in the dirt street and a group of top-hatted men standing in front of the company building. This piece, like many of Ball's daguerreotypes, is enclosed in a brass mat and embossed "J. P. Ball/Cincinnati." Such works were frequently housed in navy- or red-velvet-lined leather or Union cases, a type of hinged case made of thermoplastic.

Between short-lived attempts at business in Cincinnati in 1845, 1847 (Ball's first Daguerrean Gallery of the West), and 1849, Ball was an itinerant artist in Pennsylvania and Richmond, Virginia, opening his first successful studio in Cincinnati on New Year's Day in 1851, about two years after he married Virginia Thomas. The business employed Ball's father, his brothers, Tom and Robert G., and his brother-in-law, Alexander Thomas, as well as the landscapist ROBERT S. DUNCANSON, who hand-tinted photographs at the studio, from the early to mid-1850s. In 1852 Ball's work was included in the Ohio Mechanics Institute Annual Exhibition in Cincinnati, and again in 1854, 1855, and 1857. By 1854 Ball employed nine men (including a white man) and averaged $100 a day in sales in his new Great Daguerrean Gallery of the West. That year Ball's first child, James Presley Ball Jr., was born, and an engraving of his studio was featured with a full-length article in *Gleason's Pictorial*. Ball's portrait daguerreotypes often featured frontal, three-quarter-length poses of husbands and wives, sisters, or a single subject against a plain background.

In 1855 Ball, an ardent abolitionist, commissioned a team of unknown African American artists to paint an enormous, 2,400-square-yard panorama, *Ball's Splendid Mammoth Pictorial Tour of the United States Comprising Views of the African Slave Trade; of Northern and Southern Cities; of Cotton and Sugar Plantations; of the Mississippi, Ohio, and Susquehanna Rivers, Niagara Falls, &C.* No longer in existence, the work depicted the slave trade from its inception in Nigeria to its height in the American South to freedom in Canada. Achilles Pugh, a Quaker, published a pamphlet describing each of the fifty-three scenes in detail. Thousands paid to see the work at the Ohio Mechanics Institute and Boston's Amory Hall, and Ball reportedly gave part of the proceeds to benefit children's schools.

After touring Europe and opening establishments in London (where his daughter Estella was born), Liverpool, and Paris, in 1856 Ball exhibited his European pictures in a new gallery he co-owned with another African American photographer, ROBERT JAMES HARLAN. Harlan had made a fortune in the Gold Rush in the West and used the funds to underwrite their business venture. Together the two won a bronze medal for a photograph and a diploma for a daguerreotype from the Ohio Mechanics Institute exhibition of 1857. The partnership dissolved after eighteen months, yet Ball continued to flourish as a portraitist. While few of his images of identified African Americans (such as FREDERICK DOUGLASS and Congressman JOHN ROY LYNCH) survived, a family album was found that contained sensitive *cartes-des-visite* of his mother, brothers, and brother- and sister-in-law and their children, as well as portraits of unidentified women and children.

In 1860 a tornado destroyed Ball's studio, but numerous white families contributed funds to set him up again in business, which achieved its greatest success during the Civil War. Ball photographed many Union soldiers and their families, using such features from conventional British painted portraits as the three-quarters pose for sitters and distinguishing props such as a Doric column, an elaborately carved Victorian chair, and theatrical drapery. Notable patrons included the singer Jenny Lind, the family of Ulysses S. Grant, General William Lytle, Congressman Timothy C. Day, the entrepreneur Samuel Pike, the artist Thomas D. Jones, the civil engineer R. C. Phillips, and the reverends Max Lilienthal and Moncure D. Conway.

In October 1862 Ball's wife, Virginia, violently attacked him because she suspected him of having an affair. She was arrested, and the couple divorced. In 1864 Ball married Fannie Cage. By the end of the war, Ball probably lost much of his business in the face of increased competition from other photographers as well as the declining patronage of former abolitionists.

Around 1871 he and his family moved south in search of greater opportunities for his photography business. They lived in Greenville, Mississippi, until 1875. From 1880 until 1886 he lived in Vidalia, Louisiana, and had a brisk real estate business. Ball and his children bought thirty-six plots of land and sold thirty-one of them between 1878 and 1889. Ball's son edited and published the weekly *Concordia Eagle* in Vidalia in the late 1870s and early 1880s. His granddaughters worked as dressmakers and milliners.

Ball next moved to Minneapolis. There he married Annie E. Ewing in July 1887 (it is not known what happened to his second wife) and was the official photographer for a celebration of the twenty-fifth anniversary of the Emancipation Proclamation in September of that year. A month later he served as delegate for a civil rights convention, then moved to Helena, Montana. There he and his son produced numerous cabinet cards, small photographic prints about the size of a postcard, of white civic and infantry groups, families, business partners, infants in their baptismal gowns, and children, women, and men with props such as cloth-covered tables, wooden gates, books, broken columns, hay bales, and bicycles. Some of these portraits feature painted backdrops of parlors or pastoral scenes, or frames with scroll or shell motifs. Notable sitters included the Montana senator Lee Mantle; Joe (a Chinese cook); an African American porter, William Irvin, in his Masonic uniform; and William Biggerstaff (a former slave), before and after his hanging for murder and in his coffin.

While most of Ball's images were studio work, he also photographed outdoor scenes, such as the Old Helena Library, a group portrait of the congregation of St. Paul's Church, and the cornerstone-laying ceremony of the state capitol. A popular citizen, in 1894 Ball served as a black delegate to the state Republican Party convention and as president of the Afro-American Club in Montana. That same year he also declined a nomination for the position of coroner.

Around 1900 Ball, with his daughter-in-law Laura and his son, who also worked as a lawyer, opened the Globe Photo Studio in Seattle and continued to practice commercial photography. Ball also sold advertisements for the *Seattle Republican* newspaper and organized Shriners' lodges in Seattle and Portland before seeking relief from crippling rheumatism in Hawaii around 1902. He died there two years later. He was cremated, and his remains were interred in Cincinnati.

Further Reading

Ball's work is in the collections of the Cincinnati Historical Society; the Cincinnati Art Museum; the International Museum of Photography and Film at George Eastman House, Rochester, New York; Montana Historical Society, Helena; Ohio State University, Columbus; Schomburg Center, New York Public Library; the University of Washington, Seattle; Library of Congress; Smithsonian Institution, National Underground Railroad Freedom Center; Haverford College; and Texas African American Photography Archive in Dallas, Texas.

Ball, James Presley. *Ball's Splendid, Mammoth Pictorial Tour of the United States* (1855).

Thompson, Lucille Smith, and Alma Smith Jacobs. *The Negro in Montana, 1800–1945: A Selective Bibliography* (1970).

Willis, Deborah. *J. P. Ball, Daguerrean and Studio Photographer* (1993).

Willis, Deborah. *Reflections in Black: A History of Black Photographers, 1840 to the Present* (2000).

Willis, Deborah, and Howard Dodson. *Black Photographers Bear Witness: 100 Years of Social Protest* (1989).

THERESA LEININGER-MILLER

BALL, William (fl. 1781), servant of Lieutenant Colonel William Washington (1752–1810), hero of the Battle of Cowpens in 1781, is a figure largely lost to history, known exclusively for a single act of heroism for which he has been sometimes celebrated as an early black American patriot and hero of the Revolutionary War.

Though slavery had been slow to find a foothold in Great Britain's New World holdings, by 1776 the practice had become widespread and existed in all thirteen colonies. Despite this—and despite the paradox of slaves who were noncitizens fighting in a war for national independence—black people were quick to join the national debate about the direction in which Americans ought to go. Sensing advantage, the British sought to exploit this moment by offering freedom to the slaves of the rebels in the southern colonies—hoping to arouse fears among slaveholders of slave revolts. Thousands of black men, however, joined the Patriots, even if their leaders did not always want them, and many fought in units alongside whites. When the British opened their southern campaign in May 1780, they hoped at once to appeal to what they considered a Loyalist stronghold and to again raise fears of the chaos of mass slave revolts. Perhaps the most important battle of the campaign was fought at Cowpens, South Carolina, on 17 January 1781, between Patriot forces under General Daniel Morgan (1736–1802) and an elite unit of redcoats commanded by the widely reviled and feared Colonel Banastre Tarleton (1754–1833).

Some dozen or more black men fought at Cowpens, but William Ball (his name may not even have been Ball, but rather Collin or Collins) was not a soldier. He is sometimes described as an orderly, a waiter, a servant, or a bugler, and even his race is an assumption based on his position. What little is known of him is this: sometime during the battle Ball's master, Lieutenant Colonel William Washington, rode out to meet Tarleton and his men. As Washington, a relative of George Washington's (1732–1799), searched for the British colonel, he was attacked and surrounded by Tarleton and two of his officers. Just as one of these raised his sword to strike, Ball appeared, fired his pistol, and wounded the officer. Tarleton and his fellows galloped away, and Washington was saved. This event was immortalized by John Marshall (1755–1835) in his multivolume biography of George

Washington and by William Ranney (1813–1857) in a highly romanticized painting in 1845. On 17 January 1981 the United States Post Office issued a stamp to commemorate Ball's valor.

Further Reading
Babits, Lawrence E. *A Devil of a Whipping: The Battle of Cowpens* (1998).

Fleming, Thomas J. *Downright Fighting: The Story of Cowpens* (1988).

Greene, Robert Ewell. *Black Courage, 1775–1783: Documentation of Black Participation in the American Revolution* (1984).

Marshall, John. *The Life of George Washington* (1804–1807).

JASON PHILIP MILLER

BALLARD, Butch (12 Dec. 1918–), jazz drummer, was born George Edward Ballard in Camden, New Jersey, the son of Asbury Ballard and Ada Brooks. Ballard was the oldest of seven children; at a year old he was brought to the Frankford section of Philadelphia, Pennsylvania, to live. For much of his life Ballard remained in the same neighborhood that he grew up in as a boy. Ballard's father was originally from Princess Anne, Somerset County, Maryland, before migrating to Philadelphia. The town of Princess Anne was established in 1733 and the family of Jarvis Ballard had a strong influence there. A number of the Ballard family slaves were listed on the Manokin Hundred poll tax list in the early 1700s. The poll tax lists were the record of the poll taxes levied on free males over the age of fifteen and slaves of both sexes over fifteen. During the colonial period, Maryland county officials collected taxes to cover the costs of government, the established church, and various county expenses such as maintenance of indigent residents, payment of jurymen, and the expenses for judges. It is unknown if Asbury Ballard is a descendant of the slaves of this family, but the possibility is strong. Ballard's mother, Ada Brooks, was from Philadelphia. Asbury Ballard worked his entire life for the Philadelphia water department; Ada remained at home with the children.

Butch Ballard was educated in the Philadelphia public school system, attended Northeast High School, and was a member of the school band. Ballard was about fifteen years old when he began taking drum lessons from Professor Coles, bandmaster of the O. V. Catto Elks Lodge at 16th and Fitzwater streets in Philadelphia. Lessons cost seventy-five cents. O. V. Catto's was a popular spot for African American teen and adult dances in the 1930s, and was named for the Philadelphian OCTAVIUS V. CATTO.

When Ballard was about sixteen years old, the Philadelphia band leader Herb Thornton had a job playing at a club near the drummer's church, the Second Baptist Church of Frankford. Butch Ballard snuck into the club and his friends goaded him into sitting in with the band on drums. Ballard said, "I was scared to death," but Thornton invited him to join his band a few weeks later (cited in Cloud Tapper, PhD diss.). Because the band practiced in South Philadelphia, Ballard had to haul all of his drums once a week to the station, take the train to Center City, then hop a trolley to the rehearsal. After high school Ballard and some of his other young musician friends in 1938 formed a band called the Celebrated Youth Band/Dukes Orchestra. In 1941 Butch Ballard married a native of Gary, Indiana, Jesse Davis, who had just moved to Frankford. That same year they both moved to Manhattan so Ballard could play with EDDIE "LOCKJAW" DAVIS at the celebrated and legendary Minton's Playhouse, at West 118th Street, and later with the COOTIE WILLIAMS's big band. With Williams's band, Ballard played the Apollo Theater and the famed Savoy Ballroom and took his first tour of the Deep South.

Having been raised in Philadelphia it never dawned on Ballard to check for signs that said "No Colored Served Here" when he reached a Mobile, Alabama, restaurant. Ballard said, "I'm trying to find bacon and eggs for how much it's gonna cost me, and someone says, 'Look up over your head and look at that sign.' Well, I noticed everyone around me was being served except me, and the waitress kept passing me by" (cited in Cloud Tapper, PhD diss.).

In 1943, while playing at the Earle Theatre in Philadelphia, Butch Ballard learned that the selective service was looking for him. He had been touring so much he had not gotten his draft notice. Signing on with the U.S. Navy, Ballard spent World War II with his ship's company band in the South Pacific until he was honorably discharged in 1945. As soon as the war ended, Ballard's music career soared into high gear with stints playing in LOUIS ARMSTRONG's band in 1946, ILLINOIS JACQUET's in 1947, and with the COUNT BASIE Orchestra in 1949. Big bands traveled mostly in Greyhound buses with the names of the bandleaders emblazoned on the sides of the bus; sometimes the band members rode in "nine-seater Chryslers or DeSoto's," Ballard remembered. "When you pulled into town, everybody would run to the hotel and say, 'Hey, the band's here!'" (cited in Cloud Tapper, PhD diss.). But racism was everywhere in the South; dances in the Carolinas were sometimes held in tobacco warehouses and African Americans were roped off from whites. In an Arizona theater Count Basie and Ballard were sitting in a practically empty movie theater trying to catch an afternoon matinee. An usher, not recognizing the famous band leader, asked them both to move to the balcony section reserved for blacks. Basie and Ballard received refunds and left.

In 1950 Ballard got a call from DUKE ELLINGTON, who wanted Ballard to go to Europe with him to back up SONNY GREER, Ellington's longtime drummer, whose drinking problem made him undependable. This three-month tour was a great opportunity. In 1953 Ballard became the Ellington Band's main drummer, making some classic recordings. Butch Ballard is one of the few men to have worked in both the Count Basie Orchestra and the Duke Ellington Band.

During the late 1950s Ballard led his own band in the Philadelphia area with noted local musicians. From 1960 to 1962 Ballard led the band that backed the singer EVELYN SIMMS in a nightclub called the Underground, at Broad and Spruce in downtown Philadelphia. The band included an up-and-coming young drummer-turned-comic named BILL COSBY. That same decade Ballard would back up NINA SIMONE, DINAH WASHINGTON, SONNY STITT, and many others at the famed Philadelphia jazz spot the Showboat.

In 1989 Butch Ballard toured Europe with the trumpeter Clark Terry's Spacemen and continued to play Europe every year, despite his advanced age (Ballard turned eighty-seven years old in December 2005). Ballard continued also to teach, lecture in public schools, and was the drummer for the big band the Philadelphia Legends of Jazz Orchestra.

Ballard's wife Jesse died of Alzheimer's disease in 1999 after fifty-eight years of marriage. They had no children. Aside from his musical career Butch Ballard served as the Democratic ward leader in his district, a neighborhood civil rights activist, and a dedicated trustee of his church. He lived on Plum Street, just a few blocks from where he grew up. Ballard said, "I've been very well blessed because I've been doing this all my life. I'm still doing it, and I'm going to keep on doing it until you come to my funeral. Getting up on stage and performing on my drums. I just love it" (Larry King, "Jazzman Keeps Up the Beat," *Philadelphia Inquirer*, 6 June 1990: NO4).

On 1 December 2006 Ballard was given the Mellon Bank Community Jazz Award at the Kimmel Center, sharing the stage with the saxophonist SONNY ROLLINS.

Further Reading

Cloud Tapper, Suzanne. *Children of the Earle Theater: The Philadelphia Jazz Community and the Jazz Aesthetic.* PhD diss., University of Pennsylvania (2003).

Hunter, Al, Jr. "Philly and All that Jazz. When Ellington Looked for Musicians, He Often Looked Here," *Philadelphia Daily News*, 26 Apr. 1999: p. 41.

King, Larry. "Jazzman Keeps Up the Beat," *Philadelphia Inquirer*, 6 June 1990: NO4.

Schermer, Victor L. "Butch Ballard: Legendary Philadelphia Jazz Drummer," 9 Jan. 2007. Available at http://www.allaboutjazz.com/php/article.php?id=24210.

Discography

Cootie Williams and his Orchestra (Classic Capitol Jazz Sessions, Jan., July, Sept. 1946).

Louis Armstrong and His Orchestra (SNAFU Victor LPM, 27 Apr. 1946).

Eddie "Lockjaw" Davis Quartet with Red Garland, (NYC, 1947).

Count Basie "Shoutin' Blues" (RCA, no date).

Johnny Hodges and His Orchestra (Paris sessions, Apr. and June, 1950).

Duke Ellington Orchestra. "I Got it Bad and that Ain't Good" (Raretone, NYC, 9 Feb. 1953); "Duke Ellington Plays Duke Ellington" (13–14 Apr. 1953).

Shirley Scott with Count Basie. "On the Street Where You Live" (NYC, 18 Dec. 1957).

The Complete Capitol Recordings of Duke Ellington (1953–1955) (Mosaic) Duke Ellington "Piano Reflections" (Capitol).

The Clark Terry Spacemen. "Squeeze Me" with Phil Woods. (13 Feb. 1989) (Chiaroscuro).

SUZANNE CLOUD

BALLARD, Florence (30 June 1943–22 Feb. 1976), singer and member of the Supremes, was born in Rosetta, Mississippi, the eighth child of Jessie and Lurlee Ballard. In 1953 the Ballards, following the Great Migration path taken by millions of African Americans, moved to Detroit, Michigan, where Jessie Ballard worked in an automobile factory until his death in 1959. The family lived in the Brewster-Douglass Projects, and Ballard's powerful singing voice distinguished her both in school and around the neighborhood. Two of her neighbors, EDDIE KENDRICKS and Paul Williams, who were members of the local singing group the Primes, told their manager, Milton Jenkins, about Ballard, and Jenkins was impressed enough to book Ballard—still in her teens—as a solo act at the Primes' performances.

This early connection between Ballard and the Primes is vitally important, both to Ballard's career and to the history of American popular music, for two reasons. First, the Primes would be renamed the Temptations in 1961 and go on to become one of the most popular groups in the country while recording for Detroit's then fledgling Motown Records. Second, under Jenkins's encouragement, Ballard put together a singing group of her own, initially a female counterpart to the Primes called the Primettes, formed in 1960. Ballard asked her friend MARY WILSON to join, and Wilson in turn recruited Diane Earle, soon to be known as DIANA ROSS. (Early versions of the group had a fourth member, first Betty McGlown and then Barbara Martin.) Ballard was the group's first lead singer, and the Primettes began rehearsals in the spring of 1959. Their performances, usually in conjunction with the Primes, soon gained them a local following, even though they were not consistently paid and the group's family and school obligations proved an obstacle to regular rehearsal.

In 1960 Diana Ross contacted her neighbor, WILLIAM "SMOKEY" ROBINSON, then working as a performer and songwriter at Motown Records, in hope of getting the Primettes a recording contract. The Motown chief BERRY GORDY JR., on the cusp of his label's reign at the top of popular music, liked the group, but he passed on signing them until they graduated from high school. Undeterred, the Primettes began visiting the Motown studios regularly, eventually recording background vocal accompaniment for several tracks. Later in 1960 they recorded a commercially unsuccessful single, "Tears of Sorrow," for Lupine Records.

In 1961 Gordy signed the Primettes to Motown. Their first single was "I Want a Guy," and soon after its release, Barbara Martin left the group. Remaining a trio, the Primettes, who changed their name in 1963 to the Supremes—Ballard's suggestion—cut several singles for Motown, none of which made any significant dent on the charts or on the radio. On these early recordings, Ross shared lead duties with both Wilson and Ballard, both of whom had arguably stronger voices. Gordy, however, chose to promote Ross as the group's lead singer, believing that her sweet vocals provided a better opportunity for success in a white marketplace.

In June 1965, after two years of little commercial success, "Where Did Our Love Go?" became the Supremes' first number one record, signaling the beginning of a run of chart dominance that put them on the highest plateau of success. Marked by the expert playing of the Motown house band the Funk Brothers and the spirited, gospel-based arrangements favored by the songwriting/production team Holland-LAMONT DOZIER-Holland, these mid-1960s singles, including "You Can't Hurry Love" and "You Keep Me Hangin' On," are definitive examples of the hugely successful "Motown sound," and Gordy's strategy of success among white audiences found its perfect vehicle in the sophisticated, nonthreatening trio. Like the rest of Motown's roster, the Supremes were sent through Motown's department of Artist Development, a kind of charm school run by the Motown label and housed in the company offices, where etiquette and fashion instructors helped craft Motown performers into polished performers capable of entertaining any sector of the public. Endorsements and television appearances followed, and the Supremes went from also-rans to perhaps Motown's primary success story.

Unfortunately, despite their success, serious divisions were brewing within the group. Both Wilson and (especially) Ballard resented Gordy's push of Ross as the star of the group, and Ballard also expressed concern over the fact that, as the Supremes racked up hit after hit, the group members remained relatively underpaid. Ballard's dissatisfaction with both the artistic direction and financial inequity of the Supremes' situation, plus the torrid pace of the Supremes' touring, began taking a toll on her, and she started to drink heavily and miss scheduled appearances. A somewhat ambiguous combination of these factors led to her forced removal from the group in 1967.

Ballard's post-Supremes life was marked by tragedy. She began a protracted legal battle in 1968, first against Motown and then against her attorney, which would bring her a large settlement only in 1975. She married the former Motown chauffeur Thomas Chapman in February 1968. This was a turbulent relationship that produced three daughters—Michelle, Nicole, and Lisa—and that temporarily fell apart in 1972. Musically, Ballard remained active, opening for BILL COSBY and WILSON PICKETT, and even singing at Richard Nixon's 1969 inauguration. She signed with ABC Records in 1968, producing an album's worth of Motown-esque performances, but her ABC tenure would be a short-lived commercial failure, a failure that Ballard felt Motown exacerbated through the ABC label head Larry Newton's long friendship with Berry Gordy (George, 166). By the early 1970s Ballard was abusing pills and alcohol, and she was in such serious financial straits that she and her family were forced to go on welfare and move into public housing, only five years after she left the Supremes.

In 1975 she finally received money from her lawsuits, reconciled with Thomas Chapman, moved into a new house in Detroit, and made appearances around the city, including a performance at the Ford Auditorium that received a standing ovation. Just as it appeared that the story of the original Supreme would turn away from tragedy, Ballard suddenly took ill and was rushed to the hospital. A day later, Ballard, her system weakened by years of drug abuse and hard times, died of cardiac arrest. Her ultimate legacy is twofold. On the one hand, she is a symbol of the great hope provided by Great Migration–era shifts in black socioeconomics. But on the other hand, the painful tragedy of her later life is a reminder of the limitations of even the brightest dreams of uplift and opportunity.

Further Reading
George, Nelson. *Where Did Our Love Go?: The Rise and Fall of the Motown Sound* (1985).
Hamilton, Andrew. "Florence Ballard," in *All Music Guide to Soul: The Definitive Guide to R&B and Soul*, ed. Vladimir Bogdanov (2003).
Posner, Gerald. *Motown: Music, Money, Sex and Power* (2002).
Whitall, Susan. *Women of Motown: An Oral History* (1998).

Obituary: *New York Times*, 23 Feb. 1976.

Discography
Florence Ballard. *The Supreme* (Spectrum Records 544517).
The Supremes. *Ultimate Collection* (Motown Records 530827).

CHARLES L. HUGHES

BALTIMORE, Jeremiah Daniel (15 Apr. 1852–29 July 1929), engineer, machinist, and inventor, was born in Washington, D.C., the son of the free blacks Thomas and Hannah Baltimore. Though his father was a Catholic, Jeremiah followed his mother's influence and adopted the Methodist religion. As a child Jeremiah was fascinated with engineering and science. He was known to have experimented often with such utilitarian things as tin cans, coffeepots, stovepipes, and brass bucket hoops.

Jeremiah was educated at the Sabbath School of the Wesley Zion Church in Washington, D.C., which was located on Fourth Street near Virginia Avenue and was founded in 1839 after black members left the Ebenezer Church. As part of his education Jeremiah also attended the school of Enoch Ambush, which

had begun operation in about 1833 in the basement of the Israel Bethel Church and remained open until 1864. Despite his attendance, Jeremiah left unable either to read or to write his own name.

Jeremiah experimented on his own and achieved his first major design in a steam boiler made out of stovepipes and old brass bucket hoops. The design was displayed at the Wesley Zion Sabbath School by the Reverend William P. Ryder. Jeremiah continued to improve upon his steam boiler, and his second design effort proved to be even more successful and was submitted to the United States Patent Office by Anthony Bowen. Bowen, a former slave, was born around 1805 in Prince George's County, Maryland, and moved to Washington, D.C., in 1826, where he became legally free four years later.

As a result of the exhibition of his second steam boiler an article about Baltimore appeared in the *Washington Sunday Chronicle* entitled "Extraordinary Mechanical Genius of a Colored Boy." Understanding the significance of this article, Baltimore sent a copy of the paper to President Ulysses S. Grant, who later gave him a card with the following words:

Will the Secretary of the Navy please see the bearer, J. D. Baltimore? I think it would be well to give him employment in one of the Navy Yards, where he can be employed on machinery. Please see statement of what he has done without instructions.

U. S. Grant

Once Baltimore presented the card to the secretary of the navy, George M. Roberson, he was immediately appointed as an apprentice in the department of steam engineering at the Washington navy yards. He encountered much unfair treatment and racial discrimination and after complaining was transferred to the Philadelphia navy yard.

While in Philadelphia, Baltimore attended the Franklin Institute and upon graduating was detailed to go to the naval station at League Island on the Delaware River, where he assisted in repairing four United States Monitors, which were iron, Civil War–era vessels. In Philadelphia he applied for positions at the Crump & Sons yard, a ship and engine building manufacturer, and also at Sellers & Brothers, a wire working manufacturer. Although denied employment at both yards because of his race, Baltimore persisted and applied for a position with Sellers & Brothers at least five more times until he was finally given a job. Unfortunately, ill health cut short his time there, and he soon returned to Washington, D.C. On 29 May 1872, not long after his return to Washington, he married Ella V. Waters, the daughter of Richard and Margaret Waters of Washington, D.C. After his marriage he opened a general repair shop in Washington.

Baltimore went on to have an extraordinary career. On 2 April 1880 he was appointed chief engineer and mechanician at the Freedman's Hospital in Washington, D.C. Established by the government after the abolition of slavery, the Freedman's Hospital later became the Howard University Medical School and Hospital. He also served as an instructor in metalwork at the Colored Manual Training School in Washington, D.C., and was a member of the Mechanic's Union in Washington, D.C. Furthering his own learning, Baltimore studied at the navy yard in Boston and at the government ordnance and armor-plate works at Bethlehem, Pennsylvania. He invented the pyrometer, a device used for measuring high temperatures, which was exhibited at the 1884 World's Fair in New Orleans. Baltimore died on 29 July 1929 of kidney failure and was buried on 1 August 1929 at the Columbian Harmony Cemetery in Washington, D.C.

Further Reading

"J. D. Baltimore, Esq.: Chief Engineer and Mechanician at the Freedman's Hospital—Engineer—Machinist—Inventor," *Freedman*, 20 Apr. 1889.
"A Leader of his Race: Interesting Career of Engineer J. D. Baltimore, a Protégé of President Grant," *Philadelphia Times*, 28 July 1892.
"A Negro Metallurgist," *Philadelphia Times*, 25 Nov. 1893.
Simmons, William J. *Men of Mark: Eminent, Progressive, and Rising* (1887).

KENYATTA D. BERRY

BALTIMORE, Priscilla (13 May 1801?–28 Nov. 1882), former slave, entrepreneur, steamboat worker, nurse, and church founder, was born in Bourbon County, Kentucky, in 1801 or 1804. Although her father was a white man and also her master, his name is unknown. Her mother, Lydia, was his slave. While she was still a child, Baltimore's father sold her to a trader who carried her to the St. Louis area. Over the next few years, she passed among several masters, including the New Orleans judge Joachim Bermudez, working as a house servant for French, Spanish, and Anglo-American households in Louisiana and eastern Missouri.

In New Orleans, Baltimore joined the Methodist Church. Her piety so impressed one preacher that he purchased her, then allowed her to hire her own time and buy her freedom. Baltimore worked as a chambermaid on steamboats and as a lying-in nurse. According to tradition, it took her seven years to earn the sum required. Her master returned part of the money along with her freedom papers.

Like many slaves sold away from their families, Baltimore immediately set out to find her mother. She found both her father and her mother, who was still his slave, not in Kentucky, where she had left them, but in Fredericktown, Missouri, not far from where she had once lived. It is reported that after upbraiding her father for his heartlessness, Baltimore purchased her mother's freedom. The two women moved to St. Louis, where Baltimore worked as a nurse and on steamboats. In 1833 she married a free African American named Lewis Coonce, but he died of cholera just three weeks later. The small estate Baltimore inherited from her husband included an eight-year-old boy. His inclusion in the inventory suggests that he was born to an enslaved mother and had been purchased by his father, but never formally manumitted. He became the first of Baltimore's foster children.

The following year, Baltimore purchased a house and lot on Seventh Street in St. Louis and went to work for John Daggett, a steamboat operator. There she met a boat hand named John Baltimore, and they married in 1835. It is unclear whether the Baltimores ever had children together, but in future years, their home was sometimes full of children. In 1835 a free African American woman sued Baltimore, claiming to own part of the property she had purchased. By 1840 the costs of the suit and her husband's debts had caused her to lose her home. In 1836 a mob murdered a free black boatman, Francis McIntosh, by chaining him to a tree and burning him alive about two blocks from Baltimore's house. These events contributed to the Baltimores' decision to move to the free state of Illinois. By 1840 the couple had joined a handful of free African Americans living in the American Bottom district of St. Clair County, just across the Mississippi River. They soon become substantial property owners in what grew to be Brooklyn, a black-majority village with a reputation as a refuge for fugitive slaves. One of Baltimore's foster children, Milton Carper, was the orphaned son of a neighbor murdered by slave catchers.

Baltimore expanded her entrepreneurial activities in Illinois, where she raised and sold vegetables and livestock and continued to work as a steamboat chambermaid, carrying on a side trade of selling pickles and preserves to passengers. She invested in house lots in nearby Belleville and contracted with carpenters to build houses, which she then sold. During this period, John Baltimore worked as a boat hand and sometimes as a butcher in the stockyards of East St. Louis.

In 1840 Baltimore met WILLIAM PAUL QUINN, a traveling evangelist and future bishop of the African Methodist Episcopal (AME) Church. When he sought lodging, she invited him to stay and preach. According to Bishop A. W. Wayman, the first AME Church in the West was organized in her home the following evening. This may also have been the occasion when, according to several reports, she crossed the Mississippi River to St. Louis one Sunday and recruited a few hundred slaves to hear Quinn preach. When the ferry operator balked at transporting slaves, demanding, "What security shall I have that you will return to your masters?" Baltimore answered, "I'll be their security" (*St. Louis Daily Globe Democrat*, 4 Dec. 1882). She was so well known and trusted that her word was enough.

Over the next years Baltimore became an important patron of the AME Church. The legal difficulties faced by free African Americans visiting the slave state of Missouri made her home a refuge. Quinn stayed with her whenever he came to St. Louis, relying on Baltimore to row him back to free soil at dusk.

When authorities in St. Louis attempted to imprison Bishop DANIEL ALEXANDER PAYNE in 1856 for illegal preaching, he, too, fled to Baltimore's home, sure of her protection. The 1850s, however, brought new tragedy to her life. Her husband raped a young girl living in their household, and when the girl found herself pregnant, she became his mistress. By 1856 John had decided to elope with the girl, who was expecting his second child. He began selling off livestock and other property and appropriated some $700 in cash from his wife's savings. She sued for divorce, asking the court to restore the property John had sold. She claimed she had earned all of it through her own labor, and John had no right to dispose of it. The court agreed, but it is unclear how much property she recovered.

With the outbreak of the Civil War, Baltimore, now divorced, returned to St. Louis. She worked as a nurse and devoted herself to St. Paul's AME Church. At one point, she single-handedly retired the church's five-thousand-dollar mortgage. Her devotion to the black community reached far beyond the church. She collected donations for Wilberforce University and joined the Daughters of the Tabernacle, one of the new fraternal organizations taking a leading role in postwar black civil society.

Vigorous and active to her last days, Baltimore outlived all of her kin and died quietly at home of old age. Her funeral drew enormous crowds and was among the largest St. Louis had ever witnessed. Mourners remembered her as "Mother" Baltimore, beloved for her generosity, kindness, and especially for her work building up the African American community.

Further Reading

Manuscript court case files: *Kitty Dickerson v. Priscilla Baltimore, John Baltimore, and Wilson Primm*, St. Louis Circuit Court–Chancery (Nov. 1835), Missouri State Archives, St. Louis; *Priscilla Baltimore v. John Baltimore*, St. Clair County Circuit Court (Aug. 1856), Illinois Regional Archives Depository, Carbondale.

Buchanan, Thomas C. *Black Life on the Mississippi: Slaves, Free Blacks, and the Western Steamboat World* (2004).

Clamorgan, Cyprian. *The Colored Aristocracy of St. Louis*, ed. with an introd. by Julie Winch (1999).

Obituaries: *St. Louis Daily Globe Democrat*, 30 Nov. 1882 and 4 Dec. 1882.

SHARON E. WOOD

BAMBAATAA AASIM, Afrika (10 Apr. 1960–), disc jockey, master of ceremonies, community leader, and rapper, was born Kevin Donovan in South Bronx, New York City. (No information on his parents is available.) Bambaataa, an early developer of hip-hop music, is credited with being the first rapper. In introducing hip-hop culture to a worldwide audience during the 1970s, he gained the reputation as one of the godfathers of the genre.

In his early years, Donovan organized the Savage Seven, a Bronx River Projects–area street gang,

which eventually became known as the Black Spades. After observing the negative impact of gang activities on his community, he endeavored to promote positive gang activities. In 1974 he established The Organization, later known as the Zulu Nation, a group of racially and politically aware rappers, B-boys (break dancers), graffiti artists, and others dedicated to peace, unity, and the pursuit of knowledge through music and hip-hop culture. Zulu Nation members came to include QUEEN LATIFAH, Monie Love, and the band De La Soul. Eventually rechristened the Universal Zulu Nation, the group established chapters in many countries and focused on numerous community initiatives, including designating the month of November as Hip-Hop History month. Donovan visited Africa in the late 1970s, in part inspired by the TV mini-series *Roots* (1977), based on ALEX HALEY's epic book. Later he changed his name to Afrika Bambaataa Aasim, which means "affectionate leader," as depicted in the movie *Shaka Zulu* (1986). On his return from Africa he continued to try to convince friends involved in gang life and violence to channel that energy into community uplift.

In emphasizing community involvement, Bambaataa focused on initiating block parties, informal gatherings that introduced break dancing contests, a dynamic feature of emergent hip-hop culture. Bambaataa maintained that offering young people an alternative and viable activity helped curtail gang violence in New York neighborhoods. The block parties also provided Bambaataa a reputation as one of the best DJs in the business. He owned a vast record collection, which he began while DJing at house parties in high school. Later, he used his broad knowledge of music to experiment with drum machines and computer sounds, which yielded "Planet Rock" in 1982, the first 12-inch single to fuse the burgeoning electro sound with the funk-based beats of hip-hop.

Bambaatta's expertise in DJing generated a following of artists, writers, and other musicians who attended his parties. By 1976 the popularity of DJing instigated DJ contests, and Bambaataa was instrumental

Afrika Bambaataa Aasim, speaking at a press conference in New York, 28 February 2006. (AP Images.)

in developing guidelines to choose the winners. His turntable techniques and musical proficiency garnered him a reputation as being one of the best DJs in hip-hop. His record debut as a producer came in 1980 with his band, Soul Sonic Force, recording "Zulu Nation Throwdown." The single became a rallying cry for the Zulu Nation, which by the late 1980s had become widely known.

He received production credit on other singles in the early 1980s and became a recording artist himself in 1982, when he signed with Tommy Boy records and released "Jazzy Sensation." He followed that with "Planet Rock," a single that became a hit on R&B charts that same year. The song combined electronic hip-hop beats with the main melody of "Trans-Europe Express," by Germany's Kraftwerk. It also included portions of other songs from records by Ennio Morricone and Captain Sky, thereby creating a new style of music, electro funk. "Planet Rock" went to number four on the R&B charts and joined the Sugarhill Gang's "Rapper's Delight" as one of the early classics of hip-hop. Bambaataa repeated his own success with the release later in 1982 of "Looking for the Perfect Beat" (with Soul Sonic Force).

With his newfound popularity, Afrika Bambaataa began branching out and working with musicians from other genres. In 1984, he recorded "Unity," with help from JAMES BROWN, and "World Destruction," featuring former Sex Pistol John Lydon (as Time Zone). That same year, he debuted an album, *Shango Funk Theology*, recorded as Shango, with Material personnel Bill Laswell and Michael Beinhorn. An LP-length single titled "Funk You!" appeared in 1985, after which Bambaataa recorded a second album, *Beware (The Funk Is Everywhere)* in 1986. He left Tommy Boy records in 1986 and signed with Capitol Records. His first album release for the label, in 1988, was *The Light*, recorded by Afrika Bambaataa & the Family, which included contributions from GEORGE CLINTON, UB40, Bootsy Collins, and Boy George. Three years later, Capitol released his next album, *1990–2000: Decade of Darkness*. It coincided with his career retrospective, *Time Zone*, released on his own Planet Rock Records. Bambaataa recorded sporadically during the 1990s but returned to the mainstream in 1997 with *Zulu Groove*. The new millennium brought the release of *Hydraulic Funk on Strictly Hype* (2000), and *Electro Funk Breakdown* followed in early 2001.

Bambaataa was a driving force in hip-hop. Frequently recognized as a pioneer at such venues as the annual Hip-Hop Music Awards, he also worked as a social activist. In 1991 he traveled around the world promoting hip-hop and giving concerts in England with Hip Hop Artists Against Apartheid to benefit the African National Congress. He also helped raise money for the Ansar (Muslim sect) community. Bambaataa's activities reflect the influence of people he admires, such as MALCOLM X and James Brown. He constantly stressed the importance of knowledge and enlightenment, and his ability to reach out and convey his art through music won him a devoted following.

Further Reading
Mitchell, Gail. "Afrika Bambaataa," *Billboard* (Aug. 2002).
Murphy, Bill. "Return of the Funk: Renegade," *Remix* (Nov. 2004).
Powell, Kevin. "Dead? Hip-Hop Culture Has Been Murdered," *Ebony* (June 2007).

JULUETTE BARTLETT PACK

BAMBARA, Toni Cade (25 Mar. 1939–9 Dec. 1995), writer, activist, screenwriter, and educator, was born Miltona Mirkin Cade to Walter and Helen Cade in New York City. Originally named for her father's employer, she renamed herself Toni in kindergarten, revealing an independent and imaginative streak at an early age. She took the surname Bambara after discovering it signed on a sketchbook in her great-grandmother's trunk in the attic; who this original Bambara was is now unknown. She legally changed her name in 1970. Bambara spent her childhood exploring Harlem, Bedford-Stuyvesant, Queens, and Jersey City with her brother, Walter. Through exploring these areas she developed her sharp eye for political activism and the power of the word, the tones of blues and jazz that she would translate into her written work (particularly through going to the Apollo Theater with her father), and listening to the stories told by those in her community. Raised in a family with few extended relatives, as a child she would often "adopt" the people she met in her neighborhood, including numerous "grandmothers."

Bambara worked for the Department of Social Welfare in New York City in the late 1950s as a social investigator with a goal of improving the living conditions of minority residents, and then went on to be the director of recreation in the psychiatry department of Metropolitan Hospital in New York City. After earning a BA in Theater Arts and English from Queens College in 1959 she studied acting and mime at the University of Florence in Italy and Ecole de pantomime Etienne Decroux in Paris in 1961. She then earned an MA in Modern American Literature from the City University of New York in 1964 while working as the program director of the Colony House Community Center. She served at the Venice, Italy, Ministry of Museums, pursued filmmaking in the United Kingdom, conducted doctoral work at the State University of New York in Buffalo, studied at the Commedia del' Arte in Milan, and attended KATHERINE MARY DUNHAM's Dance Studio. After teaching English at the City College of the City University of New York in the late 1960s she went on to teach at Rutgers University, Duke University, Spelman College, Barnard College, Atlanta University, Stephens College, and the School of Social Work.

Toni Cade Bambara, attending a national conference of African American writers at Howard University, 1976. (Moorland-Spingarn Research Center, Photograph by Calvin Reid.)

Bambara wrote her first story, "Sweet Town," as an undergraduate, and the piece won the John Golden Award for fiction. In 1970 she edited the pathbreaking anthology *The Black Woman*, which featured the work of NIKKI GIOVANNI, AUDRE LORDE, ALICE WALKER, PAULE MARSHALL, and Bambara's own writing. The anthology, published during the Black Arts Movement, helped to signal a body of feminist work by black women writers who would emerge during the 1970s and 1980s. In 1971 she published her second anthology, *Tales and Stories for Black Folks*, focused on African American folk heritage, with an emphasis on storytelling, and featuring tales that Bambara reportedly wished had been available to her when she was growing up. She then published two short story collections of her own work, *Gorilla, My Love* in 1972, which featured the renowned stories "My Man Bovanne," "The Lesson," "Black English," and "Raymond's Run," and *The Sea Birds Are Still Alive* in 1977, which featured the stories "The Organizer's Wife" and "The Apprentice." Bambara realized the political power of writing, and her work often featured strong black women as protagonists and a powerful sense of orality, urbanity, and musicality.

Traveling to Cuba, Vietnam, Brazil, and Guinea-Bissau in 1973 and 1975 with the North American Academic Marxist-Leninist Anti-Imperialist Feminist Women gave Bambara a deeper understanding of women's movements and grassroots organizing on an international level. Upon her return to the United States, she lectured extensively throughout the nation on political issues and founded the Southern Collective of African American Writers and the Pamoja Writers Collective after moving to Atlanta.

Although she was best known for her work in the short story genre, Bambara published a novel, *The Salt Eaters*, in 1980. Her mother's influence is illustrated by Bambara's dedication of the book to: "Mama, Helen Brent Henderson Cade Brehon, who in 1948, having come upon me daydreaming in the middle of the kitchen floor, mopped around me." Set in Claybourne, Georgia, the novel focuses on Velma Henry, a dispirited social and political activist who has attempted suicide, who finds herself in the hospital being cared for by Minnie Ransom, a traditional healer who works with people to mend their physical and psychical pain. This complex novel featured an experimental nonlinear writing style (which garnered mixed reviews), and focused on healing, spirituality, political and social change, personal empowerment, and environmental issues related to nuclear waste, all told with Bambara's signature bravura when dealing with matters of working-class struggle and race.

She also wrote screenplays, arguing that mainstream films, particularly those about people of color, were often racist. She wrote more than ten scripts and screenplays, many based on her own short stories: "Zora" in 1971; "Gorilla, My Love" and "The Johnson Girls" in 1972 (the latter produced in 1996); "Transactions" in 1979; "The Long Night" in 1981; "Epitaph for Willie" in 1982; "Tar Baby," based on TONI MORRISON's novel of the same title, in 1984; "Raymond's Run" in 1985; and "If Blessing Comes" in 1987.

She also collaborated with JULIE DASH and BELL HOOKS on *Daughters of the Dust: The Making of an African American Woman's Film* (1991), and then wrote an article on the film for *Black American Cinema* in 1993. In moving toward film Bambara took her political ideals with her, something made evident in her narrating and writing *The Bombing of Osage Avenue* in 1986, a film directed by LOUIS MASSIAH about the city of Philadelphia's police force shooting and then bombing the headquarters of MOVE, a black organization, which resulted in the destruction of sixty-one homes and the loss of eleven lives in May 1985. Bambara won an Academy Award for Best Documentary Film for this work, which was. Bambara and Massiah collaborated again on *W. E. B. Du Bois: A Biography in Four Voices*, which was released in early 1995. Each of the four acts was written and narrated by an African American author: Bambara, Wesley Brown, THULANI DAVIS, and AMIRI BARAKA. She also provided commentary for an *American Experience* documentary, *Midnight Ramble: OSCAR MICHEAUX and the Story of Race Movies*, which aired on PBS in 1994.

After battling colon cancer Bambara died in Philadelphia at the age of fifty-six, survived by her daughter, Karma Bene Bambara. *Deep Sightings and Rescue Missions*, a collection of Bambara's published and unpublished short stories, essays, and conversations, was published in 1996, and *Those Bones Are Not My Child*, a novel by Bambara based on the more than forty child abductions and murders that took place in Atlanta in the early 1980s, was published in 1999. Bambara, who was living in Atlanta at the time of the murders, had researched them for twelve years. Both books were edited and published after Bambara's death by Toni Morrison, who had long been a close friend.

While Bambara explored diverse media and genres, she never strayed from her portrayal of the sociopolitical aspects of black culture and communities, and continued to raise awareness of racial and feminist causes. Bambara was a major figure in twentieth-century African American literature, and her strongly held beliefs regarding the importance of political activism were evident in her immersion in civil rights issues around the world and her ability to translate her passion for this work onto the page and screen.

Further Reading
The Toni Cade Bambara papers are located at Spelman College in Atlanta.

Deck, Alice. "Toni Cade Bambara," in *Dictionary of Literary Biography*, eds. Thadious M. Davis and Trudier Harris (1985).
Guy-Sheftall, Beverly. "Commitment: Toni Cade Bambara Speaks," in *Sturdy Black Bridges: Visions of Black Women in Literature*, eds. Roseann P. Bell, Bettye J. Parker, and Beverly Guy-Sheftall (1979).
Tate, Claudia. *Black Women Writers at Work* (1983).

Obituaries: *New York Times*, 11 Dec. 1995; *Guardian* (London), 12 Dec. 1995; *Washington Post*, 13 Dec. 1995.

JENNIFER WOOD

BANKS, Charles (25 Mar. 1873–1923), banker and businessman, was born in a log cabin in Clarksdale, Mississippi, the son of Daniel Banks and Sallie Ann (maiden name unknown), poor farmers. Banks grew up in extreme poverty but was educated in the local public schools and later attended Rust University in nearby Holly Springs, Mississippi. Returning to Clarksdale, he speculated in land and cotton. After marrying Trenna A. Booze of Natchez, Mississippi, in 1893 Banks engaged her brother, Eugene P. Booze, as his apprentice, teaching Booze how to trade cotton and work his general store, Banks & Co. In 1904 Banks and Booze resettled in the black-owned town of Mound Bayou, Mississippi. Temporarily leaving the merchandising business, Banks established the Bank of Mound Bayou, owning roughly two-thirds of its stock and serving as cashier as well as operating

head. Several years later, in 1909, Banks and Booze founded the Farmer's Cooperative Mercantile Company. Capitalized at $10,000, the firm, which Booze managed, sold reasonably priced goods to area farmers until, for a variety of demographic as well as economic reasons, it closed its doors in 1922.

Located about halfway between Memphis and Vicksburg in the Mississippi delta, Mound Bayou was then one of the most promising examples of a new phenomenon in early twentieth-century American history: a town founded, run, and largely governed by African Americans. Established in 1886 by ISAIAH T. MONTGOMERY, Mound Bayou stood for two decades of economic and civic opportunity for black Americans. Though situated in the Deep South, the town epitomized BOOKER T. WASHINGTON's vision of self-help, and the bank of Mound Bayou—itself sufficiently unusual, since relatively few black-owned banks had been established in the United States by that time—enabled local residents to become economically independent of the larger white community. In 1907 Washington wrote a lengthy article in *World's Work* in which he praised Mound Bayou, the Bank of Mound Bayou, and Charles Banks in particular for the example and potential they demonstrated for all African Americans. Despite the bank's early success—by 1910 it had more than $100,000 in assets and was housed in a two-story building—the Bank of Mound Bayou failed in the recession of 1914. Within eighteen months Banks and Montgomery started a second bank, called Mound Bayou State Bank. This lending institution remained solvent for a decade but only partially met the community's demand for credit.

Banks and Montgomery, the wealthiest and most powerful figures in Mound Bayou, were principal spokesmen for Washington's policies and were instrumental in the founding and for many years the operation of Washington's National Negro Business League, established in 1900. Banks served as third vice president of the league from 1901 to 1905 and as first vice president from 1907 until his death. Banks was also organizer and president of the league's Mississippi branch and was politically active with the so-called Black and Tan Republicans in Mississippi.

Another of Banks's economic ventures was the Mound Bayou Loan and Investment Company, which he established and ran with WILLIAM THORNTON MONTGOMERY, Isaiah Montgomery's older brother. This chartered financial institution, which was capitalized at $50,000 and sold shares to the public, was founded to turn a profit but also to help keep the ownership of area farmland in the hands of African Americans. This was to be accomplished by covering defaulted mortgages of area farmers with capital raised locally, thus obviating the need to seek financial help elsewhere.

The most significant of Banks's ventures in Mound Bayou was the Mound Bayou Oil Mill and Manufacturing Company, an ambitious but ill-fated project whose failure crippled Banks financially and had a devastating effect on the town. Arguing that a cotton-seed-oil mill operation would further the Washingtonian goal of helping southern blacks become economically independent, Banks convinced the Mississippi chapter of the National Negro Business League to sponsor the venture, an apparently winning proposition given that the town's principal economic activity was growing cotton. The mill would thus enable Mound Bayou to become a producer of cotton products as well as cotton. Banks and Isaiah Montgomery began selling shares of stock in 1908, and construction of the plant began two years later. Unfortunately, there were serious problems from the outset. For one thing, Banks and Montgomery were unable to raise sufficient investment capital from local blacks and had only limited success in securing funds from wealthy white philanthropists. Banks ultimately convinced Julius Rosenwald, head of Sears, Roebuck & Company, to purchase $5,000 of oil mill bonds and to promise to lend the venture up to $250,000. This left the mill short of operating capital but with enough to finish construction. The mill was dedicated in November 1912. Banks's hope that the opening of the mill would increase the prospect of stock sales was realized, but still the operation was plagued by production problems. The economic recession of 1913–1914 exacerbated an already difficult situation and forced the partners to bring in B. B. Harvey, who invested in and then ran the mill. This turned out to be a death knell. Harvey, a white mill owner from Memphis, embezzled the profits and reneged on interest payments on a corporate loan from Rosenwald. Banks was unable to save the firm. Investors lost $100,000, and the virtually new factory building remained vacant for decades.

High cotton prices caused by World War I resulted in an upsurge of business activity, but after prices returned to prewar levels, the town's economic situation was in decline. Making matters worse was the dissolution of the partnership between Banks and Isaiah Montgomery in 1917 as a result of a political dispute. The town and Banks's fortunes were intimately connected. After he and Montgomery ceased to be partners, Montgomery consolidated his holdings and no longer supported broader town ventures. Banks, who had always been more concerned with racial solidarity than had Montgomery, continued his efforts to boost the town and thus saw his fortune plummet as the town's vitality flagged. In 1923, the year after the Farmer's Cooperative Mercantile Company, the town's largest retail outlet, failed, Banks died in virtual poverty. Little is known of his personal life or of the circumstances of his death.

Charles Banks was an important figure in post-Reconstruction America, and his career exemplified the interconnectedness of African American politics and black capitalism. Taking their cue from Booker T. Washington, African Americans in the South pursued the ideals of uplift and black capitalism. Mound Bayou, one of the most successful of a series of all-black towns on the frontier of the Trans-Appalachian West, was a prime example of this type of enterprise. Banks and Montgomery brought about this growth and development by skillfully attracting new settlers and outside financial assistance through an effective boosterism laced with black nationalism. As the historian Kenneth Hamilton has noted, Banks and Montgomery's joint speculative endeavors "made money, heightened racial pride, and built a black town."

Further Reading
Hamilton, Kenneth M. *Black Towns and Profit: Promotion and Development in the Trans-Appalachian West, 1877–1915* (1991).
Ingham, John N., and Lynne B. Feldman. *African-American Business Leaders* (1944).
Jackson, David H., Jr. *A Chief Lieutenant of the Tuskegee Machine: Charles Banks of Mississippi* (2002).
Mollison, W. E. "What Banks Managed by Colored Men Are Doing for Their Communities," *Colored America*, 12 Aug. 1907.

JOHN N. INGHAM

BANKS, Ernie (31 Jan. 1931–), Major League Baseball player and sports marketing executive, was born Ernest Banks in Dallas, Texas, to Eddie, a semiprofessional baseball player, WPA worker, and wholesale grocery employee, and Essie Banks, a homemaker. Raised in Dallas as the second child and first boy of twelve children, his mother said he "was a blessing to us all" (*Contemporary Black Biography*, 2002, 17). Ernie graduated from BOOKER T. WASHINGTON High School in Dallas in 1950 and later took courses at the University of Chicago, Northwestern University, and other colleges.

At Washington High, Banks excelled in baseball, basketball, and track and field (high jumping 5'11", broad jumping 19 feet). Once batboy for his dad's semipro team and on the Washington softball team, during high school summers he played in a barnstorming "summer time baseball troupe," the Amarillo Colts, earning $15 a game (*Current Biography*, 1959). After graduating from Washington in 1950, he was signed by Negro League star COOL PAPA BELL to play with the Kansas City Monarchs of the Negro American League for a $2,000 bonus. At season's end, JACKIE ROBINSON invited Banks to play with major league all-stars including ROY CAMPANELLA and LARRY DOBY. After serving in, and playing baseball for, the U.S. Army from March 1951 to 1953 in Europe during the Korean War, he finished the 1953 season with the Monarchs.

In 1953, Banks signed a contract with the Chicago Cubs, becoming their second black player (after Gene Baker), and the first to take the field, which he did on 14 September 1953. He and second baseman Baker became "the first black double-play combination in the majors" (Ashe, 19). "The major leagues, recently integrated, were eager to take advantage of the wealth of talent in the Negro leagues" (*Encyclopedia Britannica*, 2003). He was the second to last Negro League player, before HANK AARON, to go to the majors from the Negro Leagues. In his first short

Cubs season, he played ten games, hit two home runs, and batted .314; in 1954, he hit nineteen homers.

After becoming one of the first players to switch to a lighter bat, better for the slightly built, wrist-hitting six-foot one-inch right hander to whip around quickly, Banks's hitting improved significantly in 1955. From 1954 to August 1956 he also set a new-player record by playing 424 consecutive games. Starting for the Cubs at short in 1955, Banks hit forty-four home runs, a major league record for a shortstop; he also set a major league record by hitting five grand-slam home runs. In 1958, he broke his mark with forty-seven home runs, a twentieth-century record for the position. For four consecutive years (1957–1960) he hit over forty home runs, hitting his five hundredth homer (and sixteen hundredth RBI) on 12 May 1970 (*Contemporary Black Biography*, 2002, 18). He is regarded as "one of the finest power hitters in the history of the game" (*Encyclopedia Britannica*, 2003).

Banks was also one of the best defensive players, setting a record for highest fielding average (.985) for a shortstop in 1959, and winning the Gold Glove in 1960. "Informed baseball men are agreed that Banks is unquestionably the best shortstop in the business right now. He's a graceful, flowing fielder with wide range, strong arm, and good speed" (*Current Biography*, 1959). In 1962, at age thirty-one, he moved to first base because of leg injuries, and in 1969 he led National League first basemen in fielding average. He also played third base and the outfield occasionally.

In 1958 and 1959 Banks became the first National League player named Most Valuable Player two years in a row, achieving stats of 47 and 45 home runs, 129 and 143 RBIs, batting averages of .313 and .304, and slugging averages of .614 and .596 respectively. He was on the National League All Star teams thirteen times between 1957 and 1970. On retiring in 1971, he held most Cubs offensive records. Banks's accomplishments are more impressive because he played his entire career for the long-suffering Cubs and never appeared in a World Series.

Popular among fans for his performances and "an infectious enthusiasm for the game," including an unusual willingness to sign autographs, he was "known for his favorite saying: 'Let's play two today!'" (*Encarta Africana*, 1998), declared on a blistering hot day in July 1969 before the Cubs faded. His enthusiasm and professional demeanor earned admiration of players and fans alike. For those reasons and playing all nineteen of his major league seasons (1953–1971) with the Chicago National League ball club in the "friendly confines of beautiful Wrigley Field," he earned the nickname "Mr. Cub."

He ended his career with 512 home runs (the eighth highest career total at that time), 2,583 hits, 1,636 RBIs, and a .274 lifetime batting average. Between 1955 and 1960, he hit more home runs than any other player, including Hank Aaron, WILLIE MAYS, and Mickey Mantle, though his highest salary was $65,000 (*Contemporary Black Biography*, 18).

Banks's power hitting also improved Cubs attendance, from 750,000 in 1954 to over 1 million in 1958 (*Contemporary Biography*, 1959).

In 1977, Banks became only the third black player (after Jackie Robinson and Roy Campanella) elected to the Baseball Hall of Fame. He was only the eighth player elected in his first year of eligibility, and one of few elected without "ever playing in a post season game" (*Encyclopedia Britannica*, 2004). Known as "Number 14, Ernie Banks," his jersey number was the first the Cubs retired in 1982.

In 1963 Banks ran for Alderman in Chicago as an Independent but came in third after the machine Democrat and a Republican. In 1967, another alderman suggested replacing a Picasso sculpture in downtown Chicago with one of Banks instead. In the fall of 1968 he visited U.S. troops in South Vietnam for the United Service Organizations. In 1969 Chicago fans selected him the "Greatest Cubs Player" ever and he was named Chicagoan of the Year.

After his 1971 retirement as a player, Banks worked for the Cubs as coach, minor league instructor, "goodwill ambassador" for the team and for baseball, Cubs community relations consultant, and spokesman. In May 1973 the Cubs manager was thrown out of a game, and coach Banks briefly became the first black to manage a team, three years before FRANK ROBINSON managed the Cleveland Indians. When Cubs ownership changed from the Wrigley family to the Chicago Tribune company in 1981, Banks "was offered a lesser post" (*US News*, 20 Apr. 1987, 12). "I paid my dues to baseball, and its hurts to be out of the game," he noted, lamenting also the lack of progress in getting "blacks in top management." Yet he continued as an occasional Cubs goodwill ambassador.

Since 1945 the Cubs "hadn't won much . . . except accolades for their lovely if anachronistic old ballpark, where ivy clutters up the outfield wall and no light towers impale the sky" (*Christian Science Monitor*, 26 Sept. 1984). But in 1984, when the Cubs finally won their first divisional title in 40 years, they invited Banks to sit in the dugout for the play-offs (and again in 1989).

In the 1990s, he opened Ernie Banks International, a sports and events marketing firm. As a motivational speaker, he also established the Live Above and Beyond Foundation, a nonprofit organization that "assists children and senior citizens in building self-esteem" (*Contemporary Black Biography*, 19). In 1998 he received a Doctorate in Humanities from Missouri Valley College, in 1999 he was chosen among the hundred "Greatest Chicagoans of the Century" (*Jet*, 14 June 1999), and in 2001 he was named an Illinoisian of the Year.

Banks has served on the boards of Jackson Park Hospital, Big Brothers, Chicago YMCA, and Chicago Transit Authority. In retirement, he "might serve as a model for other players, as he carved out goals and interests of his own independent from the world of baseball" (*Contemporary Black Biography*, 19).

In 1958 Banks married Eloyce Johnson and had three children. In 1993, they divorced, and in a settlement Ernie lost eighty-five trophies, which sold together at auction for $82,000. In 1997 he married Liz Elizey of Chicago, president of Ernie Banks International.

Banks's inspiration to a generation of fans and future baseball players continued to be remembered fondly in Chicago and the nation at the beginning of the twenty-first century. This was particularly so in 2003, when the Cubs let another pennant slip away.

Further Reading
Banks, Ernie, and Jim Enright. *Mr. Cub* (1971).
Ashe, Arthur. *Hard Road to Glory: A History of the Afro-American Athlete Since 1946* (1988).
Libby, Bill. *Ernie Banks: Mr. Cub* (1971).
Salzman, Jack, David L. Smith, and Cornel West. *Encyclopedia of African-American Culture and History* (1996).
Smith, Jessie Carney. *Black Heroes of the Twentieth Century* (1998).

RICHARD SOBEL

BANKS, William Venoid (6 May 1903–24 Aug. 1985), radio and television pioneer, Masonic Christian Order founder, ordained Baptist minister, lawyer, community advocate, and business leader, was born on a sharecroppers' farm in Geneva, Kentucky, the son of Richard and Clara Banks, both tenant farmers. In June 1922 Banks graduated from the Lincoln Institute of Kentucky and moved to Detroit, Michigan, where he secured a job at the Dodge automobile main plant. He graduated from Wayne State University in 1926 and the Detroit College of Law in 1929. He briefly opened a criminal law practice, but after two years he discontinued his criminal work and invested in property during the Depression, while helping elect liberal Democrat and future Supreme Court justice Frank Murphy as Detroit's mayor in 1930.

In 1931 Banks was the head of the International Labor Defense League (ILDL), a legal organization known for defending numerous labor unions, which at that time were a hotbed for Communist activities. A year later he married a young, white, Jewish secretary named Rose Glassman. His wife's family disowned her, and she was often shunned by other whites because she had married a black man.

As the leader of the ILDL, Banks was considered a Communist sympathizer because he defended members of the Communist Party. In the late 1930s Banks resigned from his position but continued to practice law. In 1939, when war broke out in Europe, Banks purchased the Mackinaw Hotel in Mackinaw City, Michigan.

Banks's heart remained in serving others, and in 1948 he graduated from the Detroit Baptist Seminary and became an ordained Baptist minister in 1949. This same year Banks divorced Glassman. She was granted custody of their three children, Alterio, Harumi, and Tenicia, aged twelve, fourteen, and fifteen, respectively.

In 1950, realizing that the fraternal movement was an ideal vehicle with which to raise the economic status of blacks, Banks sold the Mackinaw Hotel and the thirty-two-story David Broderick Towers, which he owned as well. With a significant amount of the proceeds and some personal financing, Banks founded the International Free and Accepted Modern Masons (IFAMM) in Detroit. Banks served for thirty-five years as president and supreme grand master of IFAMM until the time of his death.

In 1957, acting upon his commitment to help black people, Banks organized and established several enterprises for young people, including the Universal Barber College, the Industrial College, and the International School of Cosmetology. Banks married Ruth Brown Dade, a Detroit schoolteacher, in August 1958; this second marriage was brief. In 1961 he married his law office secretary, Ivy Bird Morris.

In 1964 Banks led IFAMM to purchase a small radio station, whose call letters were changed to WGPR (or "Where God's Presence Radiates") on 107.5 FM. WGPR was the first black-owned and -operated radio station located in the city of Detroit. During the Detroit race riots of 1967, Banks witnessed majority-owned stations controlling the information that was provided and often airing misleading information for and about blacks.

By 1970 Banks had founded lodges in every state in the United States. By 1978 IFAMM had set up more than two thousand lodges in various states and countries, including in Africa, the West Indies, and South America.

By 1975 WGPR was generating more than $1 million in annual revenues. Although Banks realized television was a major force in the lives of blacks, he also knew there were no television stations owned and operated by blacks. So Banks pursued $2.5 million in assets needed to request a television broadcasting permit. When President Nixon heard about this request, he invited Banks to the White House and said that he would be watching Banks's progress. At the next WGPR board meeting, the board agreed to liquidate enough assets to gain approval of the license and begin construction of a station. One problem that arose was that the location for the proposed station would violate an international treaty regarding the spread of the signal into Canada. But U.S. congressmen Charles Coles Diggs Jr. and JOHN CONYERS JR. had the treaty altered to allow the signal intrusion. President Ford helped the station obtain FCC approval by helping Banks override Pentagon priority in transmitter tower construction. Banks enlisted the help of his eldest daughter, Tenicia Banks Gregory. She left her teaching position of twenty years to help him manage the TV station and became the first black female station manager in the United States. Later she became vice president of operations and remained in that capacity until after Banks died.

TV-62 went on the air on 29 September 1975, becoming the first black-owned and -operated television station in the United States. Making the necessary one-year advertising commitments for the FCC license were the following: the three major U.S. automobile manufacturers; Atlantic, CBS, and Warner Brothers recording studios; a few Fortune 500 companies; and several small black businesses. WGPR TV-62 was the first Detroit television station to offer twenty-four-hour programming. Many persons who trained at WGPR TV-62 moved on to lucrative positions at CNN, ABC, NBC, CBS, PBS, and other networks.

Banks received an honorary doctorate from Shaw University and a key to the City of Detroit from Mayor COLEMAN YOUNG. Dr. Banks helped bridge the gap between the generations, and in the October/November 1986 edition of *Dollars and Sense*, a little more than a year after his death, Banks was honored as a Distinguished American and Television Pioneer. Many people mentioned that he taught by example and left a legacy of dreams.

On 23 September 1994 the Masons announced the purchase of WGPR TV-62 by CBS for $24 million. Several black leaders and businesses that had supported Banks and WGPR TV-62 challenged the sale of the station to CBS and the transfer of the FCC license because of its historical significance in the community. The sale, however, was approved, and many viewed it as the end of an era in Detroit for all those who supported community-based programs in the interest of black people.

Further Reading

"Distinguished American: William V. Banks, Television Pioneer," *Dollars and Sense* (Oct./Nov. 1986).
Gregory, Sheila T. *A Legacy of Dreams: The Life and Contributions of Dr. William Venoid Banks* (1999).

SHEILA T. GREGORY

BANKS, Willie (11 Mar. 1956–), track-and-field athlete, was born William Augustus Banks III at Travis Air Force Base in northern California, the son of Georgia Corinthian, who worked in various factories and the school cafeteria, and William Augustus Banks II, a U.S. Marine. He attended Jefferson Junior High School (now Jefferson Middle School) and Oceanside High School, both in Oceanside, California. While at the latter institution, he was first recognized for his talent in both the high jump and the long jump events. However, it was not until his junior year—when the state decided to add the triple jump (sometimes referred to as the hop, step, and jump) to its competitions—that he found the area in which he most excelled. It turned out that his history teacher, Bill Christopher, was a former U.S. champion in the event himself. With his assistance, Banks quickly became a dominant triple jumper.

After graduating from high school in 1974, Banks attended the University of California, Los Angeles (UCLA). Two years into his collegiate career he was considered one of the favorites to compete for the United States at the Olympics in Montreal, but he finished fourth in the qualifiers in Eugene, Oregon—one place away from making the national team.

Banks finished his undergraduate degree at UCLA in 1978, having twice been the runner-up at the NCAA championships. He then began law school at UCLA. He earned the nickname the "Bouncing Barrister" for balancing his graduate studies while continuing to compete athletically.

In 1980 Banks secured a slot in the Olympics in Moscow, but the United States boycotted the games in protest of the Soviet Union's invasion of Afghanistan the previous year. He overcame the disappointment of not being to compete on track and field's biggest stage, and in 1981 he set the U.S. record in the triple jump at 56 feet 7.75 inches—a mark he later increased 6 additional times. He also began to build his legend as a transcendent performer. At an event in Stockholm, Sweden, in 1981 he instructed the spectators to clap their hands in unison as he began to make his jump; the crowd clapped faster and faster, in rhythm to his movement. The crowd loved this participation, and it seemed to help Banks. He set the European all-comers record. The drama of this accomplishment was heightened because his event had been long dominated by Soviet and Eastern European athletes. With his success and charm, Banks gained a special place among the world's most recognized amateur athletes, and his clapping tactic was imitated by many others in the years to come.

In 1984 Banks had another chance at Olympic glory—this time in the familiar environment of Los Angeles, but he suffered another setback, finishing sixth. A year later Banks not only rose above that frustrating result but achieved his greatest athletic success, setting the triple jump world record at 58 feet and 11.5 inches. His mark stood for nearly a decade. In recognition of his feat, that year he was given USA Track and Field's highest honor—the JESSE OWENS Award. In 1988 Banks made the Olympic team for the third time but again finished sixth after struggling to overcome an injury.

After his athletic career was over, Banks remained involved with USA Track and Field by serving stints as president of its alumni association, beginning in 2002, and chair of its athletes advisory committee. He also pursued business ventures under the name HSJ, Inc.—which stands for hop, skip, jump—including selling artificial athletic turf in Japan. In 2002 he founded the San Diego Sports Institute, a nonprofit organization that provides academic tutoring and athletic training to young boys and girls.

In 1986 he married for the first time. The couple had two children, Erin and Cori, and later divorced. In 1995 he married Hitomi Kamiya and adopted her two children, Yoshihiro and Yuki. Though he never achieved an Olympic medal, Banks is still remembered as one of the greatest triple jumpers in history. More than just a brilliant physical competitor, his charisma and personality made him an ambassador for American athletics abroad. Near the end of the cold war, at a time of global political unrest, he excelled in an event often dominated by the USSR. His reputation among track-and-field fans extended even farther than his world record.

Further Reading

Ashe, Arthur. *A Hard Road to Glory: A History of the African American Athlete: Track and Field* (1988).
Concannon, Joe. "Jumping Back to the Fore: 'Ambassador' Banks Returns for His Run at a Festival Crown," *Boston Globe* (July 1985).
Litsky, Frank. "Goals Keep Banks Jumping," *New York Times* (June 1985).

GERARD SLOAN

BANNEKER, Benjamin (9 Nov. 1731–19 Oct. 1806), farmer and astronomer, was born near the Patapsco River in Baltimore County in what became the community of Oella, Maryland, the son of Robert, a freed slave, and Mary Banneky, a daughter of a freed slave named Bannka and Molly Welsh, a freed English indentured servant who had been transported to Maryland. Banneker was taught by his white grandmother to read and write from a Bible. He had no formal education other than a brief attendance at a Quaker one-room school during winter months. He was a voracious reader, informing himself in his spare time in literature, history, religion, and mathematics with whatever books he could borrow. From an early age he demonstrated a talent for mathematics and for creating and solving mathematical puzzles. With his three sisters he grew up on his father's tobacco farm, and for the rest of his life Banneker continued to live in a log house built by his father.

At about the age of twenty Banneker constructed a striking clock without ever having seen one, although tradition states he may once have examined a watch movement. He approached the project as a mathematical challenge, calculating the proper sizes and ratios of the teeth of the wheels, gears, and pinions, each of which he carved from wood with a pocket knife, possibly using a piece of metal or glass for a bell. The clock became a subject of popular interest throughout the region and many came to see and admire it. The timepiece operated successfully for more than forty years, until his death.

After his father's death in 1759, Banneker continued to farm tobacco, living with his mother until she died some time after 1775. Thereafter he lived alone, his sisters having one by one married and settled in the region. They attended to his major household needs. His life was limited almost entirely to his farm, remote from community life and potential persecution because of his color, until the advent of new neighbors.

In about 1771 five Ellicott brothers of Bucks County, Pennsylvania, purchased large tracts of land adjacent to the Banneker farm and began to develop a major industrial community called Ellicott's Lower Mills (now Ellicott City, Maryland). They initiated the large-scale cultivation of wheat in the state, built flour mills, sawmills, an iron foundry, and a general store that served not only their own needs but also those of the region. They marketed their flour by shipping it from the port of Baltimore. Banneker met members of the Ellicott family and often visited the building sites to watch each structure as it was being erected, intrigued particularly by the mechanisms of the mills.

George Ellicott, a son of one of the brothers, who built a stone house near the Patapsco River, often spent his leisure time in the evenings pursuing his hobby of astronomy. As he searched the skies with his telescope, he would explain what he saw to neighbors who came to watch. Banneker was frequently among them, fascinated by the new world in the skies opened up by the telescope. Noting his interest, in 1789 young Ellicott lent him a telescope, several astronomy books, and an old gateleg table on which to use them. Ellicott promised to visit Banneker as soon as he could to explain the rudiments of the science. Before he found time for his visit, however, Banneker had absorbed the contents of the texts and had taught himself enough through trial and error to calculate an ephemeris for an almanac for the next year and to make projections of lunar and solar eclipses.

Banneker, now age fifty-nine, suffered from rheumatism or arthritis and abandoned farming. He subsequently devoted his evening and night hours to searching the skies; he slept during the day, a practice that gained him a reputation for laziness and slothfulness from his neighbors.

Early in 1791 Banneker's new skills came to the attention of Major Andrew Ellicott, George's cousin, who had been appointed by President George Washington to survey a ten-mile square of land in Virginia and Maryland to become the new site of the national capital. Major Ellicott needed an assistant capable of using astronomical instruments for the first several months of the survey until his two brothers, who generally worked with him, became available. He visited Ellicott's Lower Mills to ask George to assist him for the interim, but George was unable to do so and recommended Banneker.

At the beginning of February 1791 Banneker accompanied Major Ellicott to Alexandria, Virginia, the beginning point of the survey, and was installed in the field observatory tent where he was to maintain the astronomical field clock and use other instruments. Using the large zenith sector, his responsibility was to observe and record stars near the zenith as they crossed the meridian at different times during the night; the observations were to be repeated a number of nights over a period of time. After he had corrected the data he collected for refraction, aberration, and nutation and compared it with data in published star catalogs, Banneker determined latitude based on each of the stars observed. He also used the transit and equal altitude instrument to take equal altitudes of the sun, by which the astronomical clock was periodically checked and rated.

Banneker had the use of Major Ellicott's texts and notes, from which he continued to learn, and spent his leisure hours calculating the ephemeris for an almanac for 1792. In April, with the arrival of Major

Ellicott's brothers, Banneker returned to his home. He was paid the sum of sixty dollars for his services and travel. Ellicott was paid five dollars a day exclusive of room and board while his assistant surveyors were paid two dollars a day. Banneker still supported himself primarily with proceeds from his farm.

Shortly after his return home, with the assistance of George Ellicott and family, Banneker's calculations for an almanac were purchased and published by Baltimore printers Goddard & Angell as *Benjamin Banneker's Pennsylvania, Delaware, Maryland and Virginia Almanack and Ephemeris, for the Year of Our Lord, 1792 . . .* ; a second edition was produced by the Philadelphia printer William Young. The almanac contained a biographical sketch of Banneker written by Senator James McHenry, who presented Banneker's achievement as new evidence supporting arguments against slavery.

Shortly before the almanac's publication, Banneker sent a manuscript copy of his calculations to Thomas Jefferson, secretary of state, with a covering letter urging the abolition of slavery. Jefferson replied, "No body wishes more than I do to see such proofs as you exhibit, that nature has given to our black brethren, talents equal to those of the other colors of men, and that the appearance of a want of them is owing merely to the degraded condition of their existence. . . . No body wishes more ardently to see a good system commenced for raising the condition both of their body & mind to what it ought to be." The exchange of letters between Banneker and Jefferson was published as a pamphlet by the Philadelphia printer David Lawrence and distributed widely at the same time that the almanac appeared. Promoted by the abolitionist societies of Pennsylvania and Maryland, the almanac sold in great numbers.

Encouraged by his first success, Banneker continued to calculate ephemerides for almanacs that were published for the succeeding five years and sold widely in the United States and England. A total of at least twenty-eight editions of his almanacs were published, largely supported by the abolitionist societies. Although he continued to calculate ephemerides each year until 1804 for his own pleasure, diminishing interest in the abolitionist movement failed to find a publisher for them after the 1797 almanac.

Although he was not associated with any particular religion, Banneker was deeply religious and attended services of various denominations whenever ministers or speakers visited the region, preferring meetings of the Society of Friends. He was described as having "a most benign and thoughtful expression," as being of erect posture despite his age, scrupulously neat in dress. Another who knew him noted, "He was very precise in conversation and exhibited deep reflection." Banneker died in his sleep during a nap after having taken a walk early one Sunday morning a month short of his seventy-fifth birthday. He had arranged that immediately after his death, all of his borrowed texts and instruments were to be returned to George Ellicott, which was done before his burial

two days later. During his burial in the family graveyard on his farm, his house burst into flames and was destroyed. All that survived were a few letters he had written, his astronomical journal, his commonplace book, and the books he had borrowed.

The publication of Banneker's almanacs brought him international fame in his time, and modern studies have confirmed that his figures compared favorably with those of other contemporary men of science who calculated ephemerides for almanacs. Long thought lost, the sites of Banneker's house and outbuilding have been the subjects of an archaeological excavation from which various artifacts have been recovered. Banneker has been memorialized in the naming of several institutes and secondary schools. Without the limitation of opportunity because of his regional location and the state of science in his time, Banneker would undoubtedly have emerged as a far more important figure in early American science than merely as the first black man of science.

Further Reading
Most of Banneker's personal papers, correspondence, and manuscripts are privately owned.
Bedini, Silvio A. *The Life of Benjamin Banneker* (1972).
Tyson, Martha Ellicott. *Banneker, the Afric-American Astronomer: From the Posthumous Papers of Martha E. Tyson* (1884).

SILVIO A. BEDINI

BANNING, James Herman (5 Nov. 1899–5 Feb. 1933), aviator, was born in Oklahoma, the younger of the two children and only son of Riley and Cora Banning, of whom little else is known. In 1919 the family settled in Ames, Iowa, where Banning attended Iowa State College to study electrical engineering but soon became fascinated with the idea of flying and of gaining his pilot's license. After a year of college, Banning left and learned to fly in Des Moines, Iowa, where he was taught by an army aviator at Raymond Fisher's Flying Field. Banning did so well that he became the first black pilot to gain a pilot's license, CAA # 1324, issued by the U.S. Department of Commerce.

To earn a living—and to support his interest in flying—Banning formed and operated the J. H. Banning Auto Repair Shop in Ames from 1922 to 1928. In 1929 Banning was named the chief pilot of the BESSIE COLEMAN Aero Club, which was named for the pioneering black pilot, and which had been formed to encourage blacks to enter aviation. As chief pilot, he moved to Los Angeles, where Banning became a demonstration pilot, flying a 1926 two-seater Hummingbird biplane named "Miss Ames," after his hometown of Ames, Iowa, and advertising "FLY WITH BANNING" on the side. The Hummingbird was a small plane by today's standards, with a wingspan of just over thirty-three feet and an overall length of twenty-three feet six inches. Banning flew whenever and wherever he could, performing as a barnstormer or a stunt pilot, in air circuses, and even as a charter pilot, flying politicians to their various speaking stops during their campaigns for office. One of his most famous political passengers was the Illinois representative OSCAR STANTON DE PRIEST, who was the first African American elected to the U.S. Congress from a northern state.

Throughout the 1920s and 1930s aviators were trying to complete longer flights and set endurance records. Charles Lindbergh's solo flight across the Atlantic in 1927 was an inspiration for many pilots. In 1932 Banning and his mechanic, THOMAS COX ALLEN, an African American pilot in his own right, set off to fly from Los Angeles to New York. The plane they used, an Alexander Eaglerock biplane, was several years old and had been pieced together by the two men with spare parts, some of them from the junkyard. The Eaglerock, built by the Alexander Aircraft Company of Colorado, had been made famous during the 1920s as the preferred aircraft of barnstormers, who prized its relative stability. Banning and Allen's flight became known good-naturedly as that of the "Flying Hobos," since flying non-stop was beyond the technology of aviation at that time, and they needed to raise money for fuel and food for each new step of their trip every time they stopped. "The Flying Hobos" completed their coast-to-coast flight of 3,300 miles in forty-one hours and twenty-seven minutes of air time. However with all those stops to refuel, rest, and raise money, the entire trip actually took twenty-one days. Now Banning was well-known and popular as an aviator.

Banning's life ended in tragedy the following year, during an air show in San Diego. Banning had planned to perform a number of stunts and then take the stuntwoman Marion Daugherty up to 4,000 feet. From there she was to have made a parachute jump. But the flight school instructor at the Airtech Flying School denied him use of a plane, believing that Banning, as an African American, could not be a qualified pilot. Thus he was forced to be a passenger in a Travelair biplane, a two-seater with the passenger compartment in the plane's front and with no controls. The Travelair was—and still is—a fairly reliable aircraft; many from that era still exist. But it was being flown by a white navy pilot named Albert Burghardt, aviation machinist mate, second class, from San Diego Naval Air Station, who lacked flight experience. His only qualification for the assignment appears to have been his race. Burghardt, apparently trying to show off to his passenger, pulled the plane into a steep climb. It then stalled at approximately 400 feet and fell into a spin from which the pilot was unable to recover. To the horror of the thousands of spectators, the plane crashed. Banning was rushed to a hospital but never regained consciousness. He died an hour later and was buried in Evergreen Cemetery, in Los Angeles. Although Banning's life ended tragically, he left a bright legacy for African American aviators.

Further Reading
de Vries, Col. John A. *Alexander Eaglerock: A History of Alexander Aircraft Company* (1985).
Hart, Philip S. *Flying Free: America's First Black Aviators* (1996).
Haskins, Jim. *Black Eagles: African Americans in Aviation* (1997).
Lynn, Jack. *The Hallelujah Flight* (1989).

JOSEPHA SHERMAN

BANNISTER, Edward Mitchell (c. 1826–9 Jan. 1901), painter, was born in St. Andrews, New Brunswick, Canada, the son of Hannah Alexander, a native of New Brunswick, and Edward Bannister, from Barbados. While his birth date has generally been given as 1828, recent research has suggested that he was born several years earlier. After the death of his father in 1832, Edward was raised by his mother, whom he later credited with encouraging his artistic aspirations: "The love of art in some form came to me from my mother. . . . She it was who encouraged and fostered my childhood propensities for drawing and coloring" (Holland, *Edward Mitchell Bannister*, 17). His mother died in 1844, and Edward and his younger brother, William, were sent to work for a wealthy local family, where he was exposed to classical literature, music, and painting. Edward's interest in art continued, and an early biography of the artist reported that "the results of his pen might be seen on the fences and barn doors or wherever else he could charcoal or crayon out rude likenesses of men or things about him" (Hartigan, 71).

In the early 1850s Bannister settled in Boston, where he supported himself by working as a hairdresser. By 1853 he was employed by Madame

Edward Mitchell Bannister's *The Newspaper Boy*, 1869. (Art Resource/Smithsonian American Art Museum.)

Christiana Carteaux, a successful black entrepreneur who operated several beauty salons and sold her own line of hair products and who would later become his wife. Unable to persuade any of the local established artists to take a black man on as a pupil, Bannister studied art independently during this period. Despite these obstacles, he achieved some local recognition as a landscapist and portrait painter. In 1854 Dr. JOHN V. DeGRASSE, the first black doctor admitted to the Massachusetts Medical Society, gave Bannister his first commission, a harbor scene entitled *The Ship Outward Bound* (location unknown).

On 10 June 1857 Bannister and Carteaux were married, and by the following year Bannister had established himself as a full-time artist. His wife's financial and emotional support was critical to his success. As he recalled in later years, "I would have made out very poorly had it not been for her, and my greatest successes have come through her, either through her criticisms of my pictures, or the advice she would give me in the matter of placing them in public" (Holland, *Edward Mitchell Bannister*, 8). The couple was active in Boston's African American arts community and in the abolitionist movement. Bannister served as an officer of the Union Progressive Society and the Colored Citizens of Boston and was a delegate to the New England Colored Citizens Convention in 1859 and 1865.

In the 1860s Bannister began his professional artistic career in earnest. A listing in the Boston city directory identifies him as a portrait painter, and in 1862 he traveled to New York to study photography in order to enter into the lucrative daguerreotype business. Bannister advertised his services as a daguerreotypist in 1863 and 1864, but none of his photographs has been identified. During these years he also undertook his only formal art training, taking life-drawing classes at the Lowell Institute between 1863 and 1865 with the sculptor and anatomist Dr. William Rimmer. Few works survive from this period of Bannister's career, but his portraits of *Prudence Nelson Bell* (1864, private collection) and of *Robert Gould Shaw* (c. 1864, location unknown), the latter raffled to raise money for the families of black soldiers killed in the Civil War, are evidence both of his success as a portraitist and his ties to Boston's abolitionist and activist communities.

In 1869 Bannister left Boston and settled in Providence, Rhode Island, perhaps because of his wife's family ties to the area. He announced his professional arrival in the city by exhibiting two paintings, a portrait of the famous Boston abolitionist *William Lloyd Garrison* (location unknown) and *Newspaper Boy* (1869, National Museum of American Art [NMAA]), a sensitive portrait of one of the many young boys who sold papers on the streets of Boston. Although the racial identity of the fair-skinned child is uncertain, the painting is often discussed as one of Bannister's few known works dealing directly with African American subjects.

Upon moving to Providence, Bannister began to paint fewer portraits and more landscapes and sea scenes, the work for which he is primarily known today. While he never traveled to Europe, his work—like the work of many American painters—was strongly influenced by European art, particularly the landscape paintings of the Barbizon school. These loosely handled scenes of peasants and farm animals working in bucolic harmony touched a chord among many American landscape painters, and in works such as *Driving Home the Cows* (1881, NMAA) and *Hauling Rails* (1891, NMAA), Bannister created similarly idyllic images of pastoral landscapes. In *Haygatherers* (c. 1893, private collection), Bannister extended this poetic vision of rural life to a specifically American context, depicting African American women and children loading a cart with hay. The artist also painted many scenes of Rhode Island's coastline, which he observed from the decks of his small yacht, the *Fanchon*. In addition to his finished oil paintings completed in the studio, Bannister did many sensitively handled oil sketches and drawings, and these small works are among the freshest and most attractive of his works.

Like many nineteenth-century artists, Bannister viewed the depiction of the natural world as a spiritual endeavor. In a lecture delivered in 1886, he described the artist's role as "the interpreter of the infinite, subtle qualities of the spiritual idea centreing [sic] in all created things, expounding for us the laws of beauty, and so far as finite mind and executive ability can, revealing to us glimpses of the absolute idea of perfect harmony" (Hartigan, 77).

Bannister came to national attention when his painting *Under the Oaks* (location unknown) was awarded a first-prize medal at the Centennial Exhibition in Philadelphia in 1876. The only other African American artist represented at the exhibition was EDMONIA LEWIS, whose life-sized sculpture, *Death of Cleopatra*, caused quite a sensation. Bannister had submitted his work without any biographical detail, and he later recalled the surprise of the awards committee upon learning of his racial identity: "Finally when I succeeded in reaching the desk where inquiries were made, I endeavored to gain the attention of the official in change. He was very insolent. . . . I was not an artist to them, simply an inquisitive colored man; controlling myself, I said deliberately, 'I am interested in the report that *Under the Oaks* has received a prize; I painted the picture.' An explosion could not have made a more marked impression. Without hesitation he apologized, and soon every one in the room was bowing and scraping to me" (Hartigan, 70). A Boston collector, John Duff, purchased the painting for fifteen hundred dollars, a substantial sum of money at the time.

This success led to increased demand for his work and to his visibility and prominence in the local Providence art world. Bannister served on the first board of the new Rhode Island School of Design (RISD) and was a founding member of the Providence Art Club. Officially chartered in 1880, the club served as a center for Providence's artistic community, hosting lectures and social events and mounting regular exhibitions in the spring and fall. Bannister showed his work at the club's exhibitions for the remainder of his career and served regularly on the executive committee. His work was purchased both by African American patrons, such as JOHN HOPE, George Downing Jr., and Madame SISSIERETTA JONES, and by local white collectors, such as Isaac Bates and Joseph Ely.

While landscape and sea scenes remained Bannister's specialty, he made occasional forays into religious and history painting throughout his career. An account of Bannister's studio in the 1860s mentions a painting of *Cleopatra Waiting to Receive Marc Antony* (location unknown), and in the 1890s he painted several literary compositions, including a small oil sketch of *Leucothea Rescuing Ulysses* (1891, Newport Hospital, Rhode Island) and scenes from Edmund Spenser's *Faerie Queen*. Bannister's figure paintings are less confident in their execution than his landscapes, perhaps because of his lack of formal artistic training, but he continued to experiment artistically throughout his career. The late work *Street Scene* (late 1890s, Museum of Art, RISD), a brightly colored impressionist view of an urban thoroughfare, demonstrates Bannister's continued interest in experimenting with new styles and subjects even in the final years of his career.

Bannister died of a heart attack on 9 January 1901, while attending a prayer meeting at the Elmwood Street Baptist Church in Providence. In May of that year a memorial exhibition of his work, including 101 paintings, was mounted at the Providence Art Club. In the catalog the artist John Arnold recalled, "His gentle disposition, his urbanity of manner and his generous appreciation of the work of others made him a welcome guest in all artistic circles. . . . He was par excellence a landscape painter, the best our state has ever produced. He painted with profound feeling, not for pecuniary results, but to leave upon the canvas his impression of natural scenery, and to express his delight in the wondrous beauty of land, sea, and sky" (*Painters of Rhode Island*, 1996, 13).

Further Reading
Bannister's papers are at the Archives of American Art at the Smithsonian Institution, Washington, D.C.
Hartigan, Lynda Roscoe. *Sharing Traditions: Five Black Artists in Nineteenth-Century America* (1985).
Holland, Juanita. *Edward Mitchell Bannister, 1828–1901* (1992).
Holland, Juanita. "To Be Free, Gifted and Black: African American Artist, Edward Mitchell Bannister," in *International Review of African American Art* 12.1 (1995).

PAMELA M. FLETCHER

BAQUAQUA, Mahommah Gardo (c. 1824–?), abolitionist and slave-narrative author, was born in the commercial center of Djougou, West Africa, inland from the Bight of Benin in what would later be the republic of Benin. He was a younger son of a Muslim merchant from Borgu and his wife, who was from Katsina, the Hausa city in northern Nigeria—then known as the Sokoto Caliphate; his parents' names are now unknown. His home town, Djougou, was located on one of the most important caravan routes in West Africa in the nineteenth century, connecting Asante, the indigenous African state that controlled much of the territory that would become Ghana, and the Sokoto Caliphate. After a childhood in which he attended a Koranic school and learned a craft from his uncle, who was also a merchant and a Muslim scholar, Baquaqua followed his brother to Dagomba, a province of Asante. There he was captured in war in the early 1840s, but he was released when his ransom was paid. However, back home in Djougou, he was again taken captive, apparently kidnapped, in 1845, at about age twenty or twenty-one. Baquaqua was then sold south to Dahomey and eventually to a Portuguese ship trading at Ouidah and Popo and taken to Brazil.

In Brazil he was initially sold to a baker in Pernambuco, probably in the city of Olinda, near Recife. Because he attempted to escape and even plotted the assassination of his master, he was sold south to Rio de Janeiro, where a ship captain purchased him for employment as a cabin boy on various trading expeditions to southern Brazil and then in 1847 on a voyage to New York City, where his master was taking a consignment of coffee. Upon arrival in New York in June 1847, Baquaqua became the object of a legal dispute between abolitionist members of the New York Committee of Vigilance, who helped him jump ship, and his Brazilian master, who attempted to recover him through legal means. When two judges refused to free Baquaqua and declared that he was a foreign sailor who had deserted, Baquaqua's abolitionist supporters helped him to escape from jail in lower Manhattan and make his way to Boston, via Springfield, Massachusetts, on the Underground Railroad. From Boston he was sent to Haiti to avoid being arrested again.

Upon arrival in Port-au-Prince, Baquaqua became associated with the American Free Will Baptist mission. He remained under their patronage until he was in danger of being drafted into the Haitian army, which was involved in an abortive invasion of the Spanish colony to the east of Haiti on the island of Hispaniola. In late 1849 Baquaqua returned to the United States and enrolled in New York Central College, south of Syracuse, where he was a student until 1853. Baquaqua was one of the first Africans to be educated at an American institution of higher education.

Baquaqua knew most of the key abolitionists in upstate New York in the early 1850s, initially through his Baptist connections and then through his association with Gerrit Smith, the wealthy radical abolitionist who was elected to Congress in 1854 and subsequently ran for President of the United States on the Liberty Party ticket. Unlike most other abolitionists Baquaqua was preoccupied with returning to Africa. In pursuit of this goal he served as a member of the Baptists' Africa Mission, which in fact never sent a mission to Africa, despite Baquaqua's willingness to go and his speaking tours that were intended to raise funds for the mission. Baquaqua also tried to join the Mendi Mission of the Congregationalists, but was also unsuccessful in securing an appointment.

In 1854 Baquaqua traveled to Ontario, then known as Canada West, where he finished a fifty-six-page pamphlet about his life in Africa and his relatively brief experiences of slavery in Africa and Brazil. He wrote his autobiography in Chatham, Canada West, and published it in Detroit as *An Interesting Narrative. Biography of Mahommah G. Baquaqua, A Native of Zoogoo, in the Interior of Africa (A Convert to Christianity,) with a Description of That Part of the World; including the Manners and Customs of the Inhabitants* (1854). George Pomeroy, owner of the *Detroit Free Press* and founder of Wells Fargo, helped him to write and edit the manuscript.

His autobiography differs from the other "slave narratives" written in the United States and Canada in the 1840s and 1850s because of his description of Africa, the notorious "Middle Passage," and his captivity in Brazil. His account is valuable because it was one of the most detailed and fully authenticated accounts of Africa and the Atlantic crossing on a slave ship. Despite his conversion to Christianity, Baquaqua chose to keep his Muslim name and his cultural identification with the families of his father and mother, whose association with the Hausa and Dendi commercial networks of the African interior beckoned him to return to his homeland. Despite Baquaqua's speaking tours on the abolitionist circuits of New York and Pennsylvania, sales of his autobiography were not sufficient to enable him to secure passage to Africa. In early 1855, however, he was able to sail for Liverpool and remained in England until at least 1857, at which point he drops from the historical record. How and where he died, whether he married and had a family, are all unknown today.

Further Reading
Law, Robin, and Paul E. Lovejoy, eds. *The Biography of Mahommah Gardo Baquaqua: His Passage from Slavery to Freedom in Africa and America* (2006).

PAUL E. LOVEJOY

BAQUET, Achille (15 Nov. 1885–20 Nov. 1956), jazz clarinetist, was born in New Orleans, Louisiana, the son of Theogene V. Baquet, a cornetist, music teacher, and leader of the Excelsior Brass Band of New Orleans, and Leocadie Mary Martinez. Achille was the younger brother of the clarinetist GEORGE BAQUET. No information exists about the extent of Achille Baquet's formal education; however, he was probably exposed to some musical instruction at an early age by virtue of his musical family. Nevertheless, like so many other New Orleans musicians of that period, he was initially an "ear" musician before he began lessons with Santo Juiffre at the Orpheum Theater in New Orleans.

Later, while still a young man, Baquet developed a reputation of his own as a teacher of music fundamentals. Achille Baquet was both a successful teacher and an instrumentalist and was known to have been active both in early jazz bands and in brass bands when jazz was first developing in New Orleans. Although Baquet was a Creole, his light skin color allowed him to pass for white. Consequently, he was known to have performed with both black and white bands, including with "Papa" Jack Laine's, with Ernest Giardina's Ragtime Band, and with members of the Original Dixieland Jazz Band before it left New Orleans in 1916. In *Brass Bands and New Orleans Jazz* (1977), William J. Schafer maintains that Baquet, along with another Creole, the trombonist Dave Perkins, worked with Laine's bands to impose order on the members' ear playing, and in the process they taught many musicians to read music.

Baquet's most significant professional move came in 1918 when he answered the summons of the pianist Jimmy Durante to join him in New York City for an engagement at the Alamo Cafe on West 125th Street in Harlem. Durante, a ragtime pianist and singer, was assembling a New Orleans–style jazz band and had learned of Baquet from Nick La Rocca of the Original Dixieland Jazz Band. Durante's new group, known as the Original New Orleans Jazz Band, was a five-piece band that played at the College Inn on Coney Island and continued on at the Alamo for some years after Baquet left. In November 1918 the band recorded for the Okeh label and subsequently for the Gennett label in 1919 and 1920. Unlike his older brother, Baquet is not well represented on recordings; only a relatively small number have survived. But from his investigation of the Baquet brothers and of Achille's 1919 recordings for Gennett, Alan Barrell (*Footnote*, 1986) concludes that Achille possessed "an exceptional clarinet technique—beautifully mobile and accurate in hitting the notes."

Although Achille Baquet lived into his early seventies, whatever contributions he made as a jazz musician occurred during the formative years of his career. Durante's Original New Orleans Jazz Band was one of the earliest jazz bands to play New York, and contemporaries compared the band very favorably with La Rocca's Original Dixieland Jazz Band of that same period. Yet for reasons unknown, fame smiled on one and eluded the other. In addition, little is known of Baquet in his later years, other than that he moved to Los Angeles in 1920, where he became a member of Local 47 of the American Federation of Musicians. It is unknown whether he ever married or ever had children.

The recognition that was bestowed on some of his contemporaries from New Orleans somehow escaped Baquet, and he died in Los Angeles, one of the many largely uncelebrated early jazz musicians who failed to attain more than a parochial reputation. Still, enough evidence exists through his recordings—and from the testimony of those who knew both him and his playing—to place him among the founding generation of Creole musicians from New Orleans. By virtue of their participation as early performers at a time when few models existed, they, like Baquet, are regarded as pioneers in the development of early jazz.

Further Reading
Averty, Jean-Christophe. "A Look at Lizana," *Storyville* 146 (June 1991).
Barrell, Alan. "Back to Baquet," *Footnote* 17, no. 4 (Apr.–May 1986).
Barrell, Alan. "The Baquets—Some Concluding Notes," *Footnote* 18, no. 2 (Dec.–Jan. 1987).
Barrell, Alan. "B Is for . . . Baquet," *Footnote* 17, no. 3 (Feb.–Mar. 1986).

CHARLES BLANCQ

BAQUET, Dean P. (21 Sept. 1956–), journalist and the first African American editor of the *Los Angeles Times*, was born in New Orleans, Louisiana, one of five sons of Myrtle Baquet and Eddie Baquet Sr., prominent restaurant and bar owners. After years as a mail carrier, Baquet's father retired from the postal service, sold the family home, and opened a restaurant and bar, Eddie's Place, in 1966. At first the family moved into the restaurant's back rooms, with the brothers sharing one bed. The restaurant became famous for its authentic Creole cuisine, attracting such celebrities as BILL COSBY while still catering to the discriminating tastes of local residents. The Baquets, in fact, had long-established roots in the New Orleans community dating back 200 years, and many family members were local jazz musicians of note.

After graduating from the Catholic all-boys St. Augustine High School, Baquet attended Columbia University in New York City from 1975 to 1978, majoring in English literature. His first time outside of Louisiana, Baquet was homesick and returned during summers to New Orleans, where he interned at the *States-Item*. Baquet later told Joe Strupp, "Journalism was just an accident. It just happened, and I fell in love with it" (*Editor and Publisher*, 13 Dec. 2006). In 1978, after three years of college, he quit Columbia and joined the paper's staff full time.

Baquet began as a police reporter on the afternoon paper, working from five in the morning to the early afternoon and gathering news at city hall and the courts. Later Baquet and the reporter Jim Amoss served as the two members of the newspaper's investigative unit. Working to uncover corruption, Baquet revealed his talent as a journalist. Amoss said that Baquet would bite down on a story like a pit bull and not let go (*Editor and Publisher*, 13 Dec. 2006). His investigations exposed police shakedowns of prostitutes, organized crime, and racial discrimination in the New Orleans housing market. New Orleans' two newspapers merged in 1980, and Banquet continued with the New Orleans *Times-Picayune*, where he met Dylan Landis, his future wife and a noted author.

In 1984 Baquet started at the *Chicago Tribune*, where he continued as an investigative reporter. The paper elevated him to the position of associate metropolitan editor for investigation. Within four years Baquet had earned the Pulitzer Prize when he directed a team of three in a ten-month examination of corruption in Chicago's city council. The series of articles exposed a broad array of devices by which city aldermen exploited their offices for private gain.

From the *Tribune*, Baquet moved to the *New York Times* in 1990. Starting as a metropolitan reporter, he was assigned to the business desk as a special projects editor in 1992. He was soon back to in-depth investigations, and in 1994 he was again nominated for a Pulitzer for a fact-finding exposé of fraud and mismanagement at the health insurer Empire Blue Cross and Blue Shield.

The *New York Times*' executive editor Joseph Lelyveld appointed Baquet as deputy metro editor on a one-year trial basis. In 1995 Baquet became chief of the *Times*' national desk and ran a bureau noted for its open, collegial atmosphere and contented staff in a business often marred by hostility and resentment. In subsequent years at the *Times* and later the *Los Angeles Times*, Baquet showed himself consistently able to raise newsroom morale, get results, and maintain warm relations with reporters.

In 2000 John S. Carroll, the new executive editor at the *Los Angeles Times*, recruited Baquet from the *New York Times*, offering him the post of managing editor. Carroll was seeking to repair the paper's languishing reputation and credibility. Together Carroll and Baquet recruited top investigative reporters from across the country, and during the next five years the *L.A. Times* garnered a remarkable thirteen Pulitzers, including five in 2004. Critics claimed, however, that the paper was filled with long, tedious stories and focused more on the national and international beat while failing to report adequately on Los Angeles itself and its myriad cultural, ethnic, and minority enclaves.

The Tribune Company owned the *L.A. Times*, and as a publicly traded media corporation, its overriding concern was maintaining its profit margins. The *L.A. Times* consistently earned profits in the 15–20 percent range, which was insufficient for its owners, who were also preoccupied with the paper's loss of readers and advertising revenues, part of a nationwide trend. Between 2000 and 2005 the Tribune repeatedly ordered cuts, and the editorial staff was reduced from 1,200 to 960. Confronting demands for additional layoffs, Carroll resigned in 2005, citing his unwillingness to undermine the quality of journalism practiced by the paper.

Carroll handed the mantel of leadership to Baquet, making Baquet the first African American editor of a top U.S. newspaper. He was celebrated in the media and applauded by the *L.A. Times*' editorial staff, who appreciated his management skills and his commitment to upholding the quality of the paper's journalism. The conflict with the Tribune Company, however, was not resolved. Over the next fifteen months Baquet, along with the paper's publisher Jeffrey M. Johnson, became increasingly vocal about resisting the Tribune's demands for deeper cuts in bureaus and staff, and on 5 October 2006 Johnson was fired. Baquet stayed on, hoping to defend the paper. On 26 October 2006, at the convention of the Associated Press Managing Editors, he called upon his fellow editors to fight excessive demands for profits and cuts by newspaper owners. Such an appeal enhanced Baquet's reputation but was intolerable from the point of view of the *L.A. Times*' owners. Baquet was forced to resign on 7 November 2006. The *New York Times* quickly hired Baquet back, appointing him Washington bureau chief in March 2007.

Further Reading
Auletta, Ken. "Fault Line," *New Yorker* (10 Oct. 2005).
Strupp, Joe. "How Baquet Brothers Survived Setbacks in L.A. and NOLA," *Editor and Publisher*, 13 Dec. 2006.

RICHARD L. KAPLAN

BAQUET, George (1883–14 Jan. 1949), jazz clarinetist, was born in New Orleans, Louisiana, the son of Theogene V. Baquet, a music teacher and the leader of the Excelsior Brass Band of New Orleans, and Leocadie Mary Martinez. Baquet and his younger brother, ACHILLE BAQUET, were descendants of "downtown" Creoles, whose musical training was closely allied to the traditions of the French musical conservatory—a musical tradition held at that time to be far superior to that of the "uptown" jazz musicians. At age fourteen, Baquet was already playing E-flat clarinet with the Lyre Club Symphony Orchestra, a Creole ensemble with twenty to thirty pieces, directed by his father. Baquet later received additional training from the legendary Mexican-born clarinetist Luis "Papa" Tio, who, with his nephew LORENZO TIO JR., was among the founding members of the New Orleans school of clarinetists, a group that included JOHNNY DODDS, ALBERT NICHOLAS, OMER SIMEON, and BARNEY BIGARD.

Baquet is known to have played with the Onward Brass Band in 1900, with MANUEL PEREZ's Imperial Orchestra between 1901 and 1902, and with BUDDY BOLDEN and Frankie Dusen sometime before 1905. In 1902 he left New Orleans to tour with P. T. Wright's Nashville Student Minstrels, but he returned around 1905 to join the orchestra of John Robichaux, an uptown Creole and a rival of Buddy Bolden's, who led one of the most popular and successful pre-jazz ensembles of that period. During the years 1905 to 1914 Baquet was in great demand as a member of the Magnolia, Olympia, and Superior orchestras. He departed for Los Angeles in 1914 to join the Original Creole Orchestra—perhaps the first New Orleanians to expose a national audience to early jazz. Their music was jazz only in an embryonic sense. The element of ragtime was still strong, improvisation was minimal, and the feeling of rhythmic swing—so important in later jazz—was only partially developed. The group, which included the cornetist FREDDIE KEPPARD, played more vaudeville than dance venues; in Los Angeles they were even featured during the intermissions of prizefights. They toured extensively on the Orpheum Circuit, a chain of vaudeville theaters whose hub was the Orpheum in San Francisco. Fearing that their material would be copied and objecting to the low pay, Keppard supposedly refused Victor's offer to record them while in New York, thus allowing the Original Dixieland Jazz Band the distinction, a few months later, of becoming the first band to make a jazz recording.

Baquet moved to Philadelphia, Pennsylvania, in 1923 for an engagement with the Lafayette Players at the Dunbar Theater. He lived in Philadelphia for the next twenty-nine years, performing regularly for fourteen years at Wilson's Café on Walnut Street and also as a member of the Earle Theater Pit Orchestra. He was a venerated jazz senior among local musicians, but one who, on occasion, still recorded with nationally known artists. During this period Baquet appeared on recordings with the vocalists BESSIE SMITH and CLARA SMITH, and in July 1929 he recorded at least nine titles with JELLY ROLL MORTON's Red Hot Peppers during their sessions for RCA at RCA's Camden, New Jersey, plant.

A stroke in 1945 prompted Baquet's return to New Orleans, where he lived with his sister. Contrary to some earlier accounts, a second stroke occurred in New Orleans, not in Philadelphia, and he died there at Flint Goodridge Hospital.

Like his younger brother Achille, George Baquet became the focus of considerable legend over the years. He personally confirmed the assertion that he was one of the two clarinetists on the fabled Buddy Bolden cylinder, supposedly made in the early years of the century. Were it located, the much-sought-after cylinder might shed an entirely new light on the nature of early jazz, since it would predate the recordings of the Original Dixieland Jazz Band by more than twenty years. Baquet is also reputed to have been a teacher of SIDNEY BECHET and to have been the first to play the clarinet obligato in the New Orleans classic "High Society."

Baquet's contemporaries generally remember him as the possessor of a full, round tone and a legato style of playing associated with the first generation of jazz clarinetists from New Orleans. In his informative article in *Footnote*, Alan Barrell identifies Baquet and his generation as the progenitors of the modern reed sound of the 1930s ("B Is for . . . Baquet"). Barrell credits the New Orleanian Jimmie Noone (whose similar tone and full, legato style made him Baquet's replacement in the Original Creole Orchestra) with being the model for the young Benny Goodman, and he says that later reed players (among them Irving Fazola, Eddie Miller, and BARNEY BIGARD—all from New Orleans) were heavily influenced by Baquet's reed jazz style as they developed the new saxophone sound in orchestras led by DUKE ELLINGTON, Glenn Miller, Benny Goodman, and Bob Crosby.

Further Reading
Barrell, Alan. "Back to Baquet," *Footnote* 17, no. 4 (Apr.–May 1986).

Barrell, Alan. "The Baquets—Some Concluding Notes," *Footnote* 18, no. 2 (Dec.–Jan. 1987).

Barrell, Alan. "B Is for . . . Baquet," *Footnote* 17, no. 3 (Feb.–Mar. 1986).

Ramsey, Fred. "Vet Tells Story of the Original Creole Orchestra," *Downbeat* (15 Dec. 1940).

CHARLES BLANCQ

BARAKA, Amiri (7 Oct. 1934–), poet, playwright, educator, and activist, was born Everett Leroy Jones in Newark, New Jersey, the eldest of two children to Coyette Leroy Jones, a postal supervisor, and Anna Lois Russ, a social worker. Jones's lineage included teachers, preachers, and shop owners who elevated his family into Newark's modest, though ambitious, black middle class. His own neighborhood was black, but the Newark of Jones's youth was mostly white and largely Italian. He felt isolated and embattled at McKinley Junior High and Barringer High School, yet he excelled in his studies, played the trumpet, ran track, and wrote comic strips.

Graduating from high school with honors at age fifteen, Jones entered the Newark branch of Rutgers University on a science scholarship. In 1952, after his first year, he transferred to Howard University, hoping to find a sense of purpose at a black college that had eluded him at the white institution. It was at this point that a long process of reinventing himself first

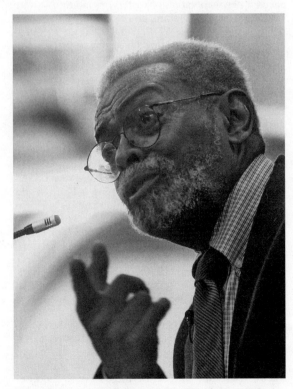

Amiri Baraka, speaking at the Newark Public Library in Newark, New Jersey, 2 October 2002. (Library of Congress.)

became evident; he changed the spelling of his name to "LeRoi" and told anyone who asked that he was going to become a doctor. Yet, he was more interested in pledging fraternities than getting good grades. In retrospect Jones blamed the college's "petty bourgeois Negro mentality" (*Autobiography*, 113) for his academic failure and came to regard black colleges as places where they "teach you to pretend to be white" (Watts, 22).

With his college ambitions dashed, Jones joined the air force in 1954, where he trained as a weatherman. He graduated at the top of his class and was stationed at Ramey Air Force Base in Puerto Rico. There he became an avid reader of Proust, Hemingway, Dostoyevsky, Sartre, and Camus. He subscribed to literary journals such as the *Partisan Review* and began to send his poems to publishers, who promptly rejected them. Jones claimed that his possession of left-leaning reading material was responsible for his dishonorable discharge from the military in 1957. Working as a stock clerk at the Gotham Book Mart in Manhattan, he resumed a friendship with Steve Korret, an aspiring writer in New York's Greenwich Village.

Through Korret, Jones was introduced to an avant-garde literary scene and a bohemian culture that profoundly altered his life. Allen Ginsberg, the doyen of the beat poets of the 1950s, became a mentor after Jones wrote him a letter on toilet paper to show how hip he was. Charles Olson, a leader of the ultramodern Black Mountain poets, influenced his writing, and even LANGSTON HUGHES, who occasionally gave readings in the Village accompanied by the bassist CHARLES MINGUS, encouraged him and nurtured a friendship that Jones cherished deeply. In 1958 Jones married, in a Buddhist temple, a white, Jewish woman, Hettie Cohen, the secretary of *The Record Changer*, a jazz magazine where Jones worked as the shipping manager. Together they had two children and published *Yugen*, a chic, though short-lived, literary magazine.

By the late 1950s Jones's poetry began to appear in such periodicals as *Naked Ear, Evergreen Review,* and *Big Table*, and in 1959 he founded a publishing company, Totem Press, which issued his first collection of poems, *Preface to a Twenty-Volume Suicide Note* (1961). Though his poetry at this point had a distinct blues idiom, it was not yet overtly political. That transformation was prompted by a visit to Cuba in 1960, where he saw artists as revolutionaries who advanced Cuban nationalism. This experience led him to view his own situation more critically. Soon after returning he began to write polemical essays such as "Cuba Libre," he became a street activist, and he urged his beat peers to strive for greater political relevance in their work. Jones then demonstrated that he was a serious student of history and music with the publication of *Blues People: Negro Music in White America* (1963). RALPH ELLISON remarked that "the tremendous burden of sociology which Jones would place upon this body of music is enough to give even the blues the blues" (Justin Driver, *New Republic*, 25

Apr. 2002), but most critics regarded the book as an important contribution.

In 1963 Jones tried his hand at playwriting and discovered that here, too, he had the Midas touch. *Dutchman*, a play about a "black boy with a phony English accent" who has a fatal encounter with an attractive white woman on a New York City subway, won an Obie in 1964, and became a sensation in many circles; it continues to be performed, and established Jones's new persona as an American firebrand. The following year, while at a book party surrounded by his cohorts from the Village, Jones received word that MALCOLM X had been assassinated up in Harlem. He later remembered this moment as an epiphany in which he realized that he was in the wrong crowd: "I felt that I had been dominated by white ideas, even down to my choice of wife" (*Village Voice*, 12 Dec. 1980). He left his wife and moved to Harlem, where he established the Black Arts Repertory Theater-School and soon became a leading black nationalist.

Jones's only novel, *The System of Dante's Hell*, was published in 1965, and much of the poetry he wrote during this period was a repudiation of his earlier life and career. In "Black Dada Nihilismus" he wrote, "Rape the white girls. Rape / their fathers . . . choke my friends," and in "The Liar" he reasoned, "What I thought was love / in me, I find a thousand instances / as fear." In "Black Art" he lays out his criteria for black poetry in lines such as "Poems are bullshit unless they are / teeth. . . . We want poems / like fists beating niggers out of Jocks / or dagger poems in the slimy bellies / of the owner-jews," and he speaks of his verses as a "poem cracking steel knuckles in a jewlady's mouth." Later, in an essay entitled "Confessions of a Former Anti-Semite," he acknowledged that during his "personal trek through the wasteland of anti-Semitism," his need to make an intellectual and political break with American liberals was unfortunately expressed as a venomous attack on Jews—who had earlier been his greatest liberal influences—and was often motivated by an unresolved anger toward his ex-wife. "Anti-Semitism," he wrote, "is as ugly an idea and as deadly as white racism" (*Village Voice*, 12 Dec. 1980).

The treatment of gays and homosexuality in Jones's work is highly problematic, as it is both complex and contradictory. Two of his early plays, *The Baptism*, set in a church, and *The Toilet*, set in a men's room, feature gay characters who can be interpreted sympathetically. According to Werner Sollors, "Homosexuality is viewed positively by Baraka both as an outsider-situation analogous to, though now also in conflict with, that of Blackness, and as a possibility for the realization of 'love' and 'beauty' against the racial gang code of a hostile society" (Sollors, 108). Ron Simmons argues that the gay tension is present in his work because Jones "never reconciled his homosexual past," a past that Jones alludes to in *The System of Dante's Hell* and ruminates about in "Tone Poem:" "Blood spoiled in the air, caked and anony-

mous. Arms opening, opened last night, we sat up howling and kissing. Men who loved each other. Will that be understood? That we could, and still move under cold nights with clenched-fists" (Simmons, 318). Jones concludes that race-conscious men could not safely sleep with men and be credible black nationalists. Yet, unlike ELDRIDGE CLEAVER, Jones did not see a contradiction in JAMES BALDWIN, who was explicit and unapologetic about his homosexuality. In "Jimmy!," a stirring eulogy to Baldwin he read at Baldwin's funeral in 1987, he credits Baldwin with starting the Black Arts Movement and pleads, "Let us one day be able to celebrate him like he must be celebrated if we are ever to be truly self determining. For Jimmy was God's black revolutionary mouth."

In 1966 Jones married Sylvia Robinson, a fellow poet. The following year he adopted the Swahili Muslim name Imamu Amiri Baraka (which means "spiritual leader, prince, blessed"), and she became Amina ("faithful") Baraka. Together they had five children. Baraka never fully embraced Islam as a religion and later dropped Imamu from his name. Rather he practiced "Kawaida," a form of cultural black nationalism that is an eclectic blend of Islamic, Egyptian, West African, and other traditions synthesized by MAULANA KARENGA, Baraka's mentor from about 1967 until Baraka became a Marxist in 1974. With the publication of *Home* (1966), especially the seminal essay "The Myth of 'Negro Literature,'" Baraka profoundly influenced a new generation of writers, including AUGUST WILSON, Haki Madhubuti, and SONIA SANCHEZ. As a political organizer in 1970, Baraka helped Kenneth Gibson to become the first black mayor of Newark, New Jersey, where Baraka had returned to live, and he was a principal organizer of the National Black Political Convention in Gary, Indiana, in 1972.

While serving a forty-eight week sentence in a Harlem halfway house in 1979, following a domestic dispute and a conviction for resisting arrest, Baraka began writing his autobiography, in which he characterizes some of the earlier sexist, racist, and specious ideological reasoning of the Black Power movement as little more than "nuttiness disguised as revolution" (*Autobiography*, 387). After becoming a Third World Marxist, the pace of both his writing and his activism slowed over the next two decades, during which he taught at several colleges, including Yale University, Rutgers University (where he was denied tenure), and at Stony Brook University, where he retired as Professor Emeritus in 1999. He received the American Book Awards' Lifetime Achievement Award in 1989, and in 2002 he was named Poet Laureate of New Jersey.

Yet controversy continued to dog him as the governor and state legislature introduced legislation to remove Baraka as laureate in reaction to his poem "Somebody Blew Up America," which questions whether Israel and President George W. Bush had foreknowledge of the 11 September 2001 terrorist attack on the World Trade Center in New York City. After months of legal wrangling, with Baraka refusing to rescind his comments, the state abolished the position of poet laureate in order to force his dismissal.

Further Reading

Baraka, Amiri. *The Autobiography of Leroi Jones* (1984, rpt. 1997).

Simmons, Ron. "Baraka's Dilemma: To Be or Not to Be?," in *Black Men on Race, Gender, and Sexuality*, ed. Devon Carbado (1999).

Sollors, Werner. *Amiri Baraka/LeRoi Jones: The Quest for a "Populist Modernism"* (1978).

Watts, Jerry Gafio. *Amiri Baraka: The Politics and Art of a Black Intellectual* (2001).

SHOLOMO B. LEVY

BARBADOES, James G. (c. 1796–22 June 1841) was an abolitionist and community activist. Nothing is known of the circumstances of his birth, early life, or education, although his surname may indicate West Indian origins.

Barbadoes emerged as an important figure in the small but influential African American community in Boston's West End by the mid-1820s. From 1821 to 1840 he operated a barbershop in Boston. He was a prominent member of the African Baptist Church and of African Lodge #459, the preeminent black fraternal organization in the nation. An amateur musician applauded for both his vocal and his instrumental talents, he performed regularly before local audiences. But he was best known as an "indefatigable political organizer."

In 1826 Barbadoes joined with the controversial essayist DAVID WALKER and several others to organize the Massachusetts General Colored Association (MGCA), which over the next few years led local protests, corresponded with race leaders throughout the North, supported the emerging African American press, and petitioned the U.S. Congress for an end to slavery in the nation's capital. Barbadoes served as secretary of the organization. He continued to hold a prominent place among Boston blacks in the 1830s. He was one of the founders and officers of the Boston Colored Temperance Society, which sought to convert local blacks to total abstinence from alcoholic beverages as a means of deflecting white criticisms and conserving community resources. He also represented Boston blacks at the 1833 and 1834 black national conventions.

After the conversion of William Lloyd Garrison to the cause of immediate abolition in 1830, Barbadoes became a devoted supporter and colleague of the Boston editor. He was one of the first African Americans to gain a prominent place in the new interracial antislavery movement that Garrison helped create. One of three blacks who attended the 1833 founding convention of the American Anti-Slavery Society (AASS) in Philadelphia, Pennsylvania, Barbadoes enthusiastically signed the organization's Declaration of Sentiments. He served on the board of managers of the AASS during its first four years. But he proved even more important to the movement at the local and regional levels. In 1833 Barbadoes helped bring the membership of the MGCA into the New England Anti-Slavery Society (NEASS), making the AASS affiliate a racially mixed body.

Barbadoes used this new forum to publicize the kidnapping and incarceration of free black sailors in southern ports, making his white colleagues aware of the problem for the first time. Barbadoes knew about the problem firsthand. His brother Robert had been imprisoned in New Orleans for five months in 1815 until word reached family and friends in Boston. In 1834 Barbadoes was named to the board of counselors of the NEASS. He remained active in the movement through the end of the decade. When the antislavery movement began to fracture in 1839–1840 over questions of political action and women's role, with many abolitionists viewing the Garrisonian positions as too extreme, Barbadoes emerged as one of Garrison's strongest defenders.

Throughout the 1830s Barbadoes, like Garrison, was a vocal critic of African colonization schemes, including the American Colonization Society's plan to resettle American blacks in Liberia. Yet in 1840, disillusioned by a lack of progress in the struggle for emancipation and equality in the United States, Barbadoes began to explore the possibility of migrating to a more hospitable location in the Caribbean. At first he promoted a venture in British Guiana (now Guyana), acting as secretary to a group of Boston blacks authorized by the colonial government to recruit African American settlers. Later in the year, contrary to the advice of many of his friends, Barbadoes and his family were among thirty Bostonians who migrated to St. Ann's Parish in Jamaica to participate in a venture devoted to the culture and manufacture of silk. It was sponsored by the Jamaica Silk Company, which had recently been organized by the Boston entrepreneur Samuel Whitmarsh. Barbadoes joined the enterprise "hoping to better his condition." But the venture developed slowly, and Barbadoes soon perceived that he had been duped by the flattering representations of company agents. Even worse, two of his children died of malaria, and Barbadoes himself soon succumbed to the disease. His widow, Rebecca, and their surviving children returned broken and destitute to their Boston home.

Further Reading

Dozens of documents relevant to Barbadoes's careers as an abolitionist and as an African American community activist are in issues of the *Liberator*, 1831–1841.

Child, David Lee. *The Despotism of Freedom; or, The Tyranny and Cruelty of American Republican Slave-Masters* (1971).

Hall, Douglas. *Free Jamaica, 1838–1865: An Economic History* (1959).

Logan, Rayford W., and Michael R. Winston, eds. *Dictionary of American Negro Biography* (1982).

Ripley, C. Peter, ed. *The Black Abolitionist Papers*, vol. 3, *The United States 1830–1846* (1991).

Obituaries: *Liberator*, 20 Aug. 1841; *Tenth Annual Report of the Massachusetts Anti-Slavery Society* (1842).

ROY E. FINKENBINE

BARBARIN, Paul (5 May 1899–17 Feb. 1969), jazz drummer, was born Adolphe Paul Barbarin in New Orleans, Louisiana, the son of Isidore John Barbarin, a coachman for undertakers, and Josephine Arthidore. The Barbarins were a distinguished musical family. Paul's father played alto horn with the Onward, Excelsior, and Tuxedo brass bands and recorded with Bunk Johnson in 1945. Paul's brothers were Louis, a drummer in New Orleans long associated with Papa Celestin; Lucien, also a drummer; and Willie, a cornetist. Barbarin's nephew was the jazz musician Danny Barker.

Having begun to play by using two forks on kitchen chairs, Barbarin was later arrested for drumming his sticks too loudly on the neighbor's steps; such was his skill that on his performing in court the judge dismissed the case, paid him fifty cents (his first professional income), and sent him home. Around 1915 he began working as a freight elevator operator to earn money for a drum set, and this purchase led to his accompanying Buddy Petit, SIDNEY BECHET, and Jimmie Noone. An astute observer, Barbarin retained and later recounted engaging memories of these early years of New Orleans jazz.

Going north to Chicago in 1917, he worked in the stockyards by day and as a musician by night. He joined the bassist BILL JOHNSON at the Royal Gardens early in 1918. The band included KING OLIVER and Noone. FREDDIE KEPPARD and Bechet also joined for a time. Barbarin toured into Canada with the Tennessee Ten, a musical comedy show, and he led a band in Connecticut before returning to Chicago to join Keppard briefly, then Noone. Barbarin and Noone married sisters. By his own account, Barbarin married Onelia Thomas in September 1922 while playing with King Oliver, although at that time Oliver's drummer was BABY DODDS. In any event Barbarin and his wife returned to New Orleans in 1923, initially staying with BARNEY BIGARD while the two men joined a band including LUIS RUSSELL and ALBERT NICHOLAS at Tom Anderson's Cabaret. Barbarin also began playing with the Onward and Excelsior brass bands, in which he marched with a snare drum before switching to bass drum. He later joined the Tuxedo Brass Band.

Nicholas, Bigard, Barbarin, and Russell left for Chicago late in 1924. All but Russell were to join Oliver at Lincoln Gardens, but the dance hall burned down and they began working only in February when Oliver introduced his Dixie Syncopators, now including Russell, at the Plantation Café. Bigard recalled that during this period Barbarin began using a gimmick of New Orleans drumming: he would pick up the snare drum during the last part of "Tiger Rag" and shout, "Hold that tiger" through the drum skins. Barbarin's drumming with the Dixie Syncopators was not well recorded except for a consistently prominent cymbal on many titles and clomping sounds from the temple blocks on "Wa-wa-wa" (1926). His contribution was nonetheless crucial.

This is nowhere more evident than in "Deep Henderson" (1926), when Barbarin, with a single chunky cymbal stroke, pulls the band back into place after Russell had allowed the rhythm to go astray in his piano solo.

Barbarin remained with Oliver until mid-1927, eventually touring to New York and then to Baltimore, where the band broke up. Barbarin and RED ALLEN went home to join the pianist WALTER PICHON at the Pelican Café in New Orleans. Later that same year Barbarin returned to New York to join Russell at the Nest Club. He remained in the band until early in 1932, in the process making recordings under Russell's own name (including "Muggin' Lightly," 1930); he also recorded under the leadership of LOUIS ARMSTRONG (including "St. Louis Blues," 1929), Oliver, Allen, and J. C. HIGGINBOTHAM, the last two being members of Russell's orchestra. Allen remembered the Russell band as "the most fiery band I ever heard. . . . It had the finest rhythm section, with POPS FOSTER on bass and Paul Barbarin on drums especially inspiring to the soloists."

After working in New York with lesser-known bands, including Pichon's and his own, Barbarin returned home to lead his Jump Rhythm Boys. He recorded with Russell again in New York in 1934 and then rejoined Russell's big band, with Armstrong taking over its leadership in 1935. Armstrong, "when discussing drummers, singled out Barbarin as an exceptional timekeeper." Recordings from this period capture Barbarin's drumming better than before. Additionally, on several titles from 1938, a decision evidently was made to feature Barbarin, whose musicality had generally been kept from the spotlight. Among these "Jubilee" offers solos based on military snare drum rudiments, juxtaposed with a conventional swing rhythm accompaniment, while "I Double Dare You" includes a classic example of syncopated New Orleans parade drumming in support of solos by the trombonist Higginbotham and the tenor saxophonist Bingie Madison. Ironically, this same year Barbarin was fired, his job given to BIG SID CATLETT.

At home once again, he led bands, joined Joe Robichaux's New Orleans Rhythm Boys, and worked with Pichon and Red Allen before leaving with Allen for a year in Chicago and on the West Coast (1942–1943). In Springfield, Illinois, he led a band in 1943, and he worked with Bechet in 1944, when his wife's illness brought him back home. Thereafter he was based in New Orleans, leading bands, playing in parades, and teaching at the Grunewald School of Music. He also worked with Art Hodes in Chicago in 1953 and performed in New York, Los Angeles, and Toronto. As a member of brass bands he was celebrated for the manner in which he danced while playing bass drum. He died while leading the Onward Brass Band in a carnival parade on Saint Charles Avenue in New Orleans.

The leading figure in one of the most distinguished musical families in New Orleans, Barbarin had a modest career as a composer. "Bourbon Street Parade" became a part of the standard repertoire in the revival of New Orleans jazz; he originally recorded it as a sideman with GEORGE LEWIS in 1951 and later on numerous occasions. As a leader, he recorded a number of his other compositions, including "The Second Line." His significance, though, was as a drummer, and he approached his own sessions as he would any other, filling a supportive, subsidiary role. In this manner he made his impact on jazz, particularly in affiliations involving Luis Russell.

Further Reading
Barker, Danny, and Alyn Shipton. *A Life in Jazz* (1986).
Bolton, Clint. "All Gone Now," *New Orleans Magazine* 5, no. 8 (1971).
Charters, Samuel Barclay. *Jazz: New Orleans, 1885–1963* (1963).
Norris, John. "Paul Barbarin," *Eureka* 1, no. 1 (1960).
Stagg, Tom, and Charlie Crump. *New Orleans: The Revival* (1973).

BARRY KERNFELD

BARBER, Jesse Max (5 July 1878–23? Sept. 1949), journalist, dentist, and civil rights activist, was born in Blackstock, South Carolina, the son of Jesse Max Barber and Susan Crawford, former slaves. Barber studied in public schools for African American students and at Friendship Institute in Rock Hill, South Carolina, where he graduated as valedictorian. In 1901 he completed the normal school course for teachers at Benedict College in Columbia, South Carolina, and afterward entered Virginia Union University in Richmond. There Barber was president of the literary society and edited the *University Journal*. In 1903 Barber earned a bachelor's degree and spent the summer after graduation as a teacher and traveling agent for an industrial school in Charleston, South Carolina.

By November 1903, Barber had moved to Atlanta to accept an offer from a white publisher, Austin N. Jenkins, to assist in launching a new literary journal, the *Voice of the Negro*, which was addressed to a national audience of African Americans. Initially listed as the journal's managing editor, Barber joined J. W. E. BOWEN of Gammon Theological Seminary as coeditor by March 1904. Bowen was a senior figurehead, however, and Barber served as the operative editor. Peter James Bryant, JOSEPH SIMEON FLIPPER, and HENRY HUGH PROCTOR, all prominent Atlanta pastors, were associate editors. The *Voice of the Negro* was a monthly periodical of high quality, carrying articles by such major figures as JOHN EDWARD BRUCE, W. E. B. DU BOIS, T. THOMAS FORTUNE, ARCHIBALD H. GRIMKÉ, PAULINE HOPKINS, KELLY MILLER, WILLIAM PICKENS, WILLIAM S. SCARBOROUGH, MARY CHURCH TERRELL, and FANNIE BARRIER WILLIAMS. Although the journal offered little fiction, it featured the poetry of WILLIAM STANLEY BEAUMONT BRAITHWAITE, BENJAMIN BRAWLEY, JAMES DAVID CORROTHERS, and

GEORGIA DOUGLAS JOHNSON, as well as the art of John Henry Adams and William E. Scott.

Barber and the *Voice of the Negro* were engaged in the struggle between, on the one hand, BOOKER T. WASHINGTON's advocacy of industrial education for African Americans and Washington's accommodationist approach to racial politics and, on the other hand, W. E. B. Du Bois's insistence on the full exercise of civil rights by African Americans and a classical education for a black elite. The first issue of the *Voice of the Negro* included an article by Booker T. Washington, and Washington's secretary, EMMETT JAY SCOTT, served as the journal's fourth associate editor until August 1904, leaving after Barber objected to Washington's editorial interference. The *Voice of the Negro*'s anti-Washington tone became more evident early in 1905 with the publication of W. E. B. Du Bois's attack on "hush money" used by Washington to control the black press, accompanied by an editorial attack on the "downright soulless materialism" of the Tuskegean's policies. Washington struck back with complaints to the journal's white owners, who had also published his autobiography, *Story of My Life and Work*. In September 1905 the *Voice of the Negro* endorsed the Niagara Movement organized by Du Bois, Barber, and others to protest African Americans' loss of civil rights. Four months later, the journal endorsed the Georgia Equal Rights League, which had similar objectives. *Voice of the Negro* was under attack by Washington-allied black journalists, such as BENJAMIN JEFFERSON DAVIS of the *Atlanta Independent* and T. Thomas Fortune of the *New York Age*. In June 1906 the journal's white owners offered the *Voice of the Negro* for sale just as it reached its maximum circulation of 15,000 in sales and subscriptions.

From 22 to 26 September 1906 white mobs swept across Atlanta, brutally attacking black people in the streets. Once white civilians were under control, the police entered the black community and disarmed its defenders. On 23 September John Temple Graves of the *Atlanta Georgian* telegraphed an account of the riot to the editor of the *New York World*, placing total blame on the African American community. Barber replied with a letter to the editor of the *World* blaming the racial sensationalism of venal politicians and the yellow journalism of men like Graves. Barber's letter was signed "A Colored Citizen," but white Atlantans discovered the name of its author and gave him a choice: leave town or face severe legal retribution. Barber fled the city, taking the *Voice of the Negro* with him to Chicago, where he continued its publication as *The Voice* for a year. In October 1907 the journal was sold to T. Thomas Fortune and ceased publication.

After the sale of *The Voice*, Washington's intervention cost Barber positions as editor of a newspaper, the *Chicago Conservator*, and as a teacher in Philadelphia. Barber discussed the possibility of launching a periodical for John E. Milholland's Constitutional League and addressed a session of the National Negro Political League, which was organized by WILLIAM

MONROE TROTTER, JOHN MILTON WALDRON, and Bishop ALEXANDER WALTERS in 1908 to challenge Republican hegemony among African American voters. In 1909 Barber attended the National Negro Conference in New York, which led to the founding of the NAACP. When Du Bois began editing the organization's journal, *The Crisis*, Barber served as a contributing editor for three years.

Choosing a career in which Washington could not pursue him, Barber entered the Philadelphia Dental School of Temple University in 1909. He graduated in 1912 and began practicing dentistry in the city. In 1912 Barber married Hattie B. Taylor, a Philadelphia public school teacher. After her death, he married another teacher, Elizabeth B. Miller.

Barber served as vice president and then president of the Philadelphia branch of the NAACP in its first decade. During the 1920s he was also a member of the NAACP's national board of directors. In 1922 Barber and T. Spotuas Burwell began a series of annual journeys to John Brown's grave in North Elba, New York, and organized the John Brown Memorial Association with the intention of garnering resources for a monument in honor of the famous abolitionist. As president of the association, Barber delivered the dedication address at a service at which its monument was unveiled in 1935. Barber continued to practice dentistry, and he engaged in little public activism after the dedication. Nine months after the death of his wife, Barber died in Philadelphia.

Further Reading

Aptheker, Herbert, ed. *The Correspondence of W. E. B. Du Bois* (1973–1978).

Bullock, Penelope L. *The Afro-American Periodical Press, 1838–1909* (1981).

Harlan, Louis, and Raymond Smock, eds. *The Booker T. Washington Papers* (1972–1989).

Johnson, Abby Arthur, and Ronald M. Johnson. *Propaganda and Aesthetics: The Literary Politics of Afro-American Magazines in the Twentieth Century* (1979).

Obituaries: *Philadelphia Independent*, 1 Oct. 1949; *Philadelphia Tribune*, 24 Sept. and 4 Oct. 1949.

RALPH E. LUKER

BARBOZA, Anthony (10 May 1944–), photographer, writer, and historian, was born Anthony Barboza in New Bedford, Massachusetts, to Lillian Barboza, a homemaker, and Anthony Barboza Sr., a Fuller Brush salesman. Anthony Jr. was one of eight sons, one of whom was also an award-winning photographer and two of whom were well-known journalists. Barboza began his career in 1964, when he studied under Roy DeCarava in New York City at the Kamoinge Workshop, cofounded in 1963 as a response to the negative and biased representation of African Americans in mainstream media, with DeCarava serving as Kamoinge's first director. The group, which continued into the twenty-first century as Kamoinge, Inc., used photography to document and celebrate African American experiences.

Between 1965 and 1968 Barboza served as a photojournalist in the United States Navy. Upon opening his commercial photo studio in New York City a year after being discharged, he began shooting images in virtually all genres: commercial, documentary, editorial, and entertainment. He became one of the most widely published African American photographers, whose work has appeared in more than fifty publications worldwide, including *Ebony, Esquire, Essence, Life, National Geographic, Vanity Fair,* and *Vogue.* He has also photographed advertising campaigns for clients such as Adidas, Coca-Cola, HBO, SPIKE LEE Productions, and the United Negro College Fund. A survey of his work, however, demonstrates an interest in fine art portraiture, specifically of African American cultural and political icons.

Barboza paid homage to the tradition of Harlem Renaissance photographers, particularly JAMES AUGUSTUS JOSEPH VANDERZEE, one of the era's most popular studio photographers, whose work embodied and depicted the Great Migration's new, cosmopolitan African American culture, but in contrast to Barboza's subjects, primarily featured everyday, black New Yorkers. From 1975 to 1980 Barboza photographed a number of famous artists, musicians, and writers whose significant contributions to the African diaspora's cultural legacy went largely ignored by the dominant culture. AMIRI BARAKA, JAMES BALDWIN, ROMARE BEARDEN, and Miriam Makeba are only a small selection of the portraits included in the series that Barboza self-published as *Black Borders* (1980). His brother the journalist and author Steven Barboza and the poet NTOZAKE SHANGE—whose portrait is included in the book—contributed text to *Black Borders,* the publication of which was made possible by a grant from the National Endowment for the Arts. The New York State Council of the Arts awarded Barboza two additional grants while he was compiling the series.

In 1982 at the Studio Museum in Harlem, Barboza opened Introspect, a retrospective exhibit including a cross-range of his portraiture. The museum later compiled this work into the monograph also titled *Introspect* (1982). During the course of his long career, Barboza continued to artistically explore the personal yet contentious themes of his first book, the invisibility of African Americans and the pain of having their dreams denied and fears confirmed. Selections of this evolving body of work have been exhibited throughout the United States as well as in Taiwan and Germany; many pieces are also part of the permanent collections of more than ten museums, among them the Brooklyn Museum, the Museum of Modern Art in New York, the Schomburg Center for Research in Black Culture, and the Studio Museum in Harlem.

Barboza's dedication to photography extended beyond shooting and exhibiting his work; from the early 1970s he served the photographic community in a variety of capacities. He was a panelist-judge for the New York State Council of the Arts, the National Endowment for the Arts, and the Massachusetts Council of the Arts. He also lectured for several institutions, including the International Center of Photography, the School of the Museum of Fine Arts, the Rochester Institute of Technology, New York University's Tisch School of the Arts, and the Rhode Island School of Design. In 2001 Barboza served as assistant curator of the Brooklyn Museum's critically acclaimed show Committed to the Image: Contemporary Black Photographers. President of Kamoinge, Inc., as of 2005, he continued to operate into the twenty-first century his commercial studio in New York City, where he began *Black Dreams/White Sheets*, a project depicting blacks living in a dream state in America, with a planned publication date of 2009.

Further Reading

Barboza Studio, available online at http://www.barboza studio.com.
Kamoinge, available online at http://www.kamoinge.com.

CRYSTAL AM NELSON

BARÈS, Basile Jean (9 Jan. 1845–Sept. 1902), composer and pianist, was born in New Orleans, Louisiana, to Augustine Celestine, a slave, and Jean Barès, a white French-born carpenter. He was baptized at the age of one month in Saint Mary's Roman Catholic Church in the French Quarter. Basile Barès was born a slave of Adolphe Périer, the French-born owner of a music emporium, where Barès learned to tune pianos. Barès worked at this Royal Street business while receiving piano instruction under Eugène Prévost, former director of the Orleans Theater and the French Opera of New Orleans, and instruction in composition under C. A. Predigam. Barès played both piano and saxophone and composed for piano.

Barès's first-known published piece of sheet music, "Grande polka des Chasseurs à Pied de la Louisiane," was copyrighted to him in 1860, despite the illegality of this action because he was a sixteen-year-old slave. Very few slaves are known to have published works under their own names, and this could be the reason Barès was identified only by his first name as author on the sheet music. He is also known to have published and performed under the name Basile Périer while a slave, publicly using the surname Barès only after 1865. Despite previous suggestions that his use of the surname Périer may have meant that he was the son of his owner, recent evidence strongly suggests that this was not the case (Sullivan).

Barès took several business trips to Paris while working for the Périer business, where he remained employed once emancipated by the war. During a four-month visit in 1867, possibly his first, he performed frequently at the Paris International Exhibition. In the 1870s he began working in the New Orleans music shop of Louis Grunewald, whose music business became an empire in the burgeoning world of sheet-music publication. Grunewald published at

least eight of Barès's compositions, including the 1875 "Les variétés du Carnaval," a collection of five dance pieces for piano. Between 1869 and the late 1880s Barès published at least nineteen dances for piano, many with carnival themes, such as the "Galop du Carnaval" in 1875. Because his published compositions do not include many that he had composed and performed publicly, the exact number of his compositions is unknown. At least twenty-eight published works are known to exist in a variety of Louisiana archives, including those of Tulane University and the Historic New Orleans Collection. Xavier University holds an unpublished composition as well as his autographed photograph taken while in Paris. More of Barès's published music is available today than for any other black composer of his era.

Barès's music could be heard in theaters, concert halls, ballrooms, and private homes; his compositional style has been given many labels, including popular, art, concert, salon, and classical. Because modern notions of separating popular music from high-culture music did not exist then, his pieces were used more flexibly within the musical climate of the city. His compositions were based on European models and published usually with French titles and, at times, lyrics. Barès reportedly loved France and things French. His existing published works are mostly dance numbers, including polkas, waltzes, quadrilles, and mazurkas. Some music scholars have suggested that forms used in these pieces contain elements later used in jazz.

In New Orleans, where he spent most of his life and career, Barès frequently performed with other Creole musicians of color, who were also local free blacks, including Victor-Eugène Macarty and Samuel Snaër. Some of these performances were benefits for groups favoring black male suffrage as well as for the Freedmen's Orphan Asylum. Creoles of color in New Orleans experienced tightening racial restrictions during Reconstruction and the late nineteenth century. The relative autonomy that free people of color had experienced in New Orleans before the Civil War, especially when compared with that of other American cities, began to disintegrate. It was in this changing climate that Barès lived and worked. New Orleans's Creole of color musicians could first use the Théâtre d'Orléans for their performances after the Civil War ended, but only during the off-season between May and October when the French and French-Creole population frequently fled the hot and sickly city. When the theater, which relied on the patronage of the large free black community of the city, tried to reinforce its strict segregation rules in 1875, Barès and other Creole of color musicians staged a boycott that helped cause serious financial problems for the theater. The repertoire at such performances varied greatly. Original compositions by Barès, such as "Magic Bells" and "Fusées musicales," were interspersed with pieces arranged from popular French and Italian operas. This would have been a common practice during all musical stage performances of the place and time, regardless of race, as original compositions were mixed with popular opera pieces.

Barès was recruited to play for both white and black audiences, including accompanying EDMOND DÉDÉ. On his return to New Orleans from his home in France, the famous New Orleans–born Creole of color violinist, composer, and orchestra leader performed a series of concerts in 1893 with Barès at the piano. Barès also helped many prominent white composers arrange vaudeville and opera orchestrations, and he led a string band for whites' carnival balls. Barès published no music after his 1884 "La Louisianaise: Valse brillante." This is likely because of a general decline in interest in locally composed French songs—fashions were moving toward more American musical styles—but could also be because of the increased segregation and limitations on blacks in Jim Crow New Orleans. Barès died in New Orleans, leaving one son and three daughters.

Further Reading
Blassingame, John W. *Black New Orleans, 1860–1880* (1973).
Sullivan, Lester. "Composers of Color of Nineteenth-Century New Orleans: The History behind the Music," in *Black Music Research Journal* 8 (1988).
Trotter, James M. *Music and Some Highly Musical People* (1878).

ANN OSTENDORF

BARKER, Danny (13 Jan. 1909–13 Mar. 1994), jazz guitarist and banjoist, vocalist, and author, was born Daniel Moses Barker in New Orleans, Louisiana, to Moses Barker, a drayman, and Rose Barbarin Barker. Barker grew up in New Orleans with a largely absent Baptist father of rural origins and a mother whose familial connections to the Barbarin family, famed in New Orleans music, rooted him in the city's Creole of Color musical community. His childhood experiences immersed him in the cultures of both sides of his family: rural Protestant and urban Roman Catholic.

Barker's uncle, the drummer PAUL BARBARIN (composer of the jazz standard "Bourbon Street Parade"), started Danny on drums; after trying the clarinet, Danny decided to play multiple string instruments: guitar, banjo, and ukulele. A teenaged Barker played in "spasm bands," children's bands that featured rudimentary instruments often created from discarded objects. Playing ukulele, Barker led a spasm band named the Boozan (Creole patois for "Good Times") Kings, which played for tips from white and black barroom audiences. He later played banjo professionally in New Orleans before moving to New York in 1930 and finding work as a rhythm guitarist. In 1931 he married Louisa Dupont, and the couple had one child, Sylvia Barker. Barker played in numerous big bands, including that of LUCKY MILLINDER (1937–1938) and Benny Carter (1938) before joining CAB CALLOWAY's Orchestra (1939–1946). While with Calloway, Barker

recorded his observations of working and traveling with the band. During this period Barker played in some of the most famous recordings and music film shorts featuring the Calloway orchestra, including "Blues in the Night" (1940) and "Minnie the Moocher" (1941). A few years earlier Barker had appeared as a musician in OSCAR MICHEAUX's 1933 film *The Girl From Chicago*.

The stress of long and regular absences from his wife and daughter induced Barker to leave Calloway's band and seek other ways to support his family. Sylvia Barker remembers her mother singing blues songs while doing the dishes at night whenever her father was on tour, and Danny and other musicians encouraged her to record. Louisa Barker first recorded with Danny and others in 1938, at which time the producer gave her the professional name of "Blu Lu." Two of their risqué songs, both written by Danny, gained special notice: "Don't You Feel My Leg (Don't You Make Me High)" (1938) and "I Got Ways Like the Devil" (1938). The former earned Barker a Grammy Award in the mid-1970s after Maria Muldaur covered the song.

The Barkers were signed to the Apollo Record label in 1946, and they toured into the late 1940s. Finding little commercial success, however, and wishing to resettle in New York City, Barker sought different ways of earning a living. He created King Zulu Records and released what are likely the earliest commercial recordings of New Orleans Mardi Gras Indian songs: "Chocko Mo Feendo Hey" and "My Indian Red" in the early 1950s. Barker found success as a songwriter when, among other triumphs, Johnny Mercer and NAT KING COLE both recorded versions of Barker's "Save the Bones for Henry Jones" (1947).

Barker played in bars both as a solo artist and in small groups. He was a regular in the Dixieland Revival movement in New York, playing at Ryan's and Condon's. Fluent in many styles, Barker also appeared with BILLIE HOLIDAY in the 1957 *Sound of Jazz* television program. Other artists Barker performed and recorded with included LEAD BELLY, JELLY ROLL MORTON, LOUIS ARMSTRONG, and WYNTON MARSALIS. He also initiated his own research project into the early history of New Orleans jazz. Barker started the "Jazzland Research Guild" in the early 1950s and asked his musician friends to fill out a survey and participate in his collecting efforts. According to his daughter Sylvia, few of Barker's black peers took him seriously, largely because of his race. Though stung by the lack of cooperation from his fellow musicians, Barker nevertheless cooperated with the many white authors who approached him regarding the same history. Barker is featured prominently in Nat Hentoff's *Hear Me Talking to You* (1955).

Playing in Greenwich Village and other New York City venues brought Barker into contact with many authors; a few were moved by his stories of New Orleans and jazz history and offered to provide him with room and board in a New York City hotel while he wrote. This arrangement ended quickly, however, when Barker balked at the creative interference of his would-be patrons. Nevertheless, his writing continued until late in life and flourished following his return to New Orleans in 1965. Barker collaborated with the sociologist Jack Buerkle to produce *Bourbon Street Black*, a study of African American musicians. The music historian Alyn Shipton worked with Barker to compile his stories and transcriptions of interviews into *A Life in Jazz*, a blend of autobiography and fiction. The urban folk revival brought renewed interest in Barker's banjo work, and it was at least in part by playing at venues such as the popular Newport Folk Festival that Barker began to consider the importance of honoring jazz musicians with their own New Orleans festival.

Barker enjoyed playing traditional New Orleans jazz and studying its history. He worked as an assistant to the curator of the New Orleans Jazz Museum Club for the next several years, and he served as grand marshall of the Onward Brass Band from 1965 until 1972. These activities made Barker a central figure in plans for the first jazz festivals in the city, precursors to the New Orleans Jazz and Heritage Festival.

Barker was largely responsible for the revival of brass band music in New Orleans after he formed and mentored the Fairview Baptist Church Christian Marching Band in the early 1970s. He had formed the band in response to Reverend Andrew Darby's request that he help keep neighborhood children occupied. The Fairview Church Band served as an incubator for many of the musicians who would lead the brass band revival in the city during the last decades of the twentieth century. Barker had once observed that "no kids want to dance to their grandparents' music," (personal interview, 1993) and so he supported these musicians in developing their own interpretations of the music.

Barker recorded with several traditional New Orleans jazz bands. He also fully developed his vocal performance style and recorded a 1988 solo record for Orleans Records that captured his impish sense of humor. Barker would mug for audiences and wear loud clothes when playing solo, when accompanying Blue Lu, or as leader of Danny Barker and his Jazz Hounds. He drew inspiration from the vaudeville and film star BERT WILLIAMS and developed a comic persona similar to that of the comedian whose films he had watched so eagerly as a child. In the last decade of his life Barker had become a cultural icon in his hometown, and he received national honors in 1991 when he was named a National Endowment for the Arts Jazz Master.

Barker's health deteriorated quickly after he was diagnosed with cancer. He did not want to have a jazz funeral because he felt that the tradition had been warped. Despite his wishes, musicians convinced the family to allow one, and Barker received one of the best attended jazz funerals in the city's history.

Further Reading
Much of the information in this essay stems from numerous personal interviews with the Barker family:

Danny Barker (1991–1993); Louisa Barker (1993–1996); Sylvia Barker (1994 and 1996).
Barker, Danny. "A Memory of King Bolden," *Evergreen Review* 37 (1965).
Barker, Danny, and Alyn Shipton. *A Life in Jazz.* (1988).
Barker, Danny, and Alyn Shipton, eds. *Buddy Bolden and the Last Days of Storyville* (2001).
Buerkle, Jack V., and Danny Barker. *Bourbon Street Black: The New Orleans Jazzmen* (1974).
Hentoff, Nat. *Hear Me Talkin to You* (1955).

Obituaries: *New York Times*, 15 Mar. 1994, and (New Orleans) *Times-Picayune* 14 Mar. 1994.
MICHAEL MIZELL-NELSON

BARKLEY, Charles (20 Feb. 1963–), professional basketball player, was born Charles Wade Barkley in Leeds, Alabama, in 1963. Barkley was raised by his mother, Charcey Glenn, who supported the family by cleaning homes, and his grandmother, Johnnie Mae Edwards, who worked in a meat factory. In high school the five-foot-ten-inch Barkley harbored ambitions to play in the National Basketball Association (NBA) despite failing to make the varsity squad in the tenth grade. However, Barkley persevered by putting in long hours on the practice court and by honing his vertical leaping ability. During his senior year in high school, Auburn University offered Barkley (who then stood six feet four inches) a basketball scholarship.

At Auburn, Barkley earned the first of many nicknames he would garner throughout his career: the "round mound of rebound." He earned this nickname because he weighed three-hundred pounds and was able to consistently out-rebound taller opponents. Barkley caught the eye of NBA scouts by starting at center and using his "God-given ability to rebound." However, he never averaged more than fourteen points per game in college.

Nonetheless, the Philadelphia 76ers decided to take a chance on the "round mound of rebound," making him the fifth pick in the 1984 NBA Draft. Widely considered the best NBA Draft ever, the 1984 Draft saw Barkley passed up for other outstanding players such as MICHAEL JORDAN and Hakeem Olajuwon before landing with the 76ers. When Barkley joined his new team, he was unsure of his scoring ability; he was also unsure of his ability to adjust to big city life. He was quickly schooled by NBA legends JULIUS "DR. J" ERVING and Moses Malone; they instructed him to invest his money wisely and get rid of most of his seven cars.

As an NBA player, Barkley more than met his goal of "scor[ing] ten points a game and get[ting] ten rebounds a game." During his first three years in the league, he was leading the NBA in rebounding and averaging over twenty points per game. From 1984 to 1992 Barkley played for the 76ers and became a household name, both for his scoring and rebounding as well as for his run-ins with bad-tempered fans and the media. Perhaps the most famous of these run-ins was in New Jersey, where he attempted to spit at a heckler who hurled a racial epithet at him; instead, he accidentally hit a young girl in the stands.

By 1992 Barkley had grown tired of the mediocrity of the 76ers players and hungered for a chance at the one prize that had eluded him: an NBA championship. Furthermore, Barkley's consistent outspoken opinions frustrated the 76ers' management. Throughout his eight years in Philadelphia, Barkley had publicly commented on everything from American racism to the idea that athletes should not have to be role models. Barkley's opinions were consistently in newspapers, on sports talk radio, and most famously on a 1993 Nike advertisement where he unapologetically proclaimed: "I am not a role model."

The 76ers rid themselves of the outspoken Barkley by trading him to the Phoenix Suns for Jeff Hornacek and Andrew Lang after the 1991–1992 season. Barkley seemed to be reenergized by the trade. Barkley was the highest scorer on the legendary 1992 Olympic "Dream Team" that dominated the Olympic field and won the gold medal. The 1992–1993 NBA season proved to be Barkley's most memorable, as he led the Suns to sixty-three victories and garnered his first and only appearance in the NBA finals, where the Suns lost to Jordan's Chicago Bulls in six games. Throughout the series Barkley turned in consistent play, posting respectable numbers in scoring, rebounds, and assists.

Although the Suns nearly made it to the NBA Finals again in 1993–1994, Barkley never again returned to the NBA Finals, even though he continued his torrid pace of rebounding and scoring. He would make one last run at the championship when he was traded to the Houston Rockets after the 1995–1996 season. He recommitted himself to conditioning and offered to come off the bench for a Houston Rockets team that included NBA superstars Olajuwon and Clyde Drexler. However, a career of battling bigger, stronger players had taken a toll on his body and he was not the same player he had once been. Barkley admitted he was a "good player, not a great player" at that stage in his career.

Despite the fact that Barkley never won a championship, he is still remembered as one of the best players in NBA history and his career statistics reflect that. As of 2007, he was one of only four players to have accumulated 23,000 points, 12,000 rebounds, and 4,000 assists. He was a fixture on the NBA All-Star team and was named one of the NBA's 50 greatest players in 1996. Barkley's career averages of twenty-three points per game and almost twelve rebounds a game are a tribute to his consistency and hard work on the court.

Off the court Barkley was an outspoken and persistent critic of racism and consistently fought for the rights of lower income families. He donated $3 million to Alabama schools, arguing that everyone should have a good education available. Barkley considered running for governor of his home state of Alabama as an independent and wrote several books, including *Outrageous* (1994), *I May be Wrong, but I Doubt It* (2002), and *Who's Afraid of a Large Black Man?* (2005), detailing his views on race, class, and the state of America. Barkley was also a basketball commentator for TNT and did not rule out a return to basketball on the administrative side, stating that he would "love to be a GM [general manager]" of an NBA team. Barkley lived in Arizona with his wife Maureen and daughter Christiana.

Further Reading
Casstevens, David. *Somebody's Gotta Be Me: The Wide, Wide, World of the One and Only Charles Barkley* (1994).
Tulumello, Mike, and Dave Cruz. *Breaking the Rules: A Season with Sports' Most Colorful Team, Charles Barkley's Phoenix Suns* (1997).

DANIEL A. DALRYMPLE

BARKSDALE, Don (31 Mar. 1923–8 Mar. 1993), basketball player and track athlete, was born Donald Angelo Barksdale in Oakland, California, the son of Agee Barksdale, a Pullman porter, and Desiree Barksdale, a homemaker. Barksdale grew up in a predominantly black neighborhood and played sports as a youngster at San Pablo Park, just four blocks from his home. Dutch Redquist, the director of the playground, helped him develop his skills. JACKIE ROBINSON, the great UCLA athlete who broke the color barrier in Major League Baseball, visited the park and became another of Barksdale's mentors. Barksdale also accompanied his father to meetings of the Brotherhood of Sleeping Car Porters where he listened to black activists such as A. PHILIP RANDOLPH.

While Barksdale was a gifted athlete, he never played high school basketball. The Berkeley High School basketball coach refused to have more than one black player on the team, so Barksdale, who entered high school in 1937, was cut in three consecutive years by the school's coach. Barksdale continued to develop his skills playing recreational basketball. He lettered in track and field for three straight years and competed in the long jump, high jump, and triple jump. Upon graduation in 1940, his athletic skills earned him an invitation to compete in basketball and track and field at Marin Junior College (later the College of Marin) in Kentfield, California, where he led Marin to two California State Junior College championships. In the middle of the 1942–1943 season, Barksdale accepted a scholarship to the University of California, Los Angeles (UCLA). He played only five basketball games for the UCLA Bruins before he was drafted into the army, but in one of the games he played, Barksdale scored eighteen points and helped UCLA defeat the University of Southern California for the first time in forty-two consecutive games.

In the fall of 1942 Barksdale was stationed at Camp Ross in California and was a member of an army service team. In 1944–1945 he scored 780 points and the following season hit for 1,288, the highest point total in the history of armed forces basketball. In 1946–1947 Barksdale returned to UCLA and led the Bruins in scoring with 368 points, averaging 14.7

points per game. In 1947 he made several All-America teams, the first African American so honored.

At the end of the 1947 season Barksdale decided to extend his basketball career by playing with the Oakland Bittners, a team that played by rules governed by the Amateur Athletic Union (AAU). Technically, AAU players were not paid to play but worked for a company that also sponsored a basketball team. Barksdale himself did not work for Lou Bittner but rather owned a Blue 'n Gold beer distributorship, becoming the first African American to own a distributorship for this company. He also worked as a disc jockey. Some of the most successful of the AAU teams were sponsored by the Phillips Petroleum Company, the Caterpillar Company, and the Goodyear Tire and Rubber Company. The Oakland Bittners, by comparison, were a much smaller operation. The owner, Lou Bittner, had a tax consulting and insurance business, as well as a passion for sports. Barksdale chose to play for the Bittners instead of a professional team because in the late 1940s all the professional teams were east of the Mississippi River and paid rather small salaries. Moreover, only a few African Americans played in these leagues, and then only briefly, reflecting the racism prevalent in the country as a whole. Given these realities, the Bittners were a good fit for Barksdale, and the team had some of the best basketball talent from California's Bay Area.

By 1947 Barksdale measured six feet six inches and weighed two hundred pounds. He jumped well and had a feathery jump shot, and in the 1947–1948 season, he led the American Basketball League in scoring with a 16.7 scoring average. On 7 January 1948 Barksdale made history when he became the first African American athlete to play in an integrated athletic contest in Oklahoma. In front of an overflow crowd in Bartlesville, the Bittners beat the Phillips 66ers 45-41, the first home-court loss for them since 1944. Barksdale scored 17 points and held Bob Kurland, Phillips's great center, to 5 points.

In March 1948 all the outstanding AAU teams gathered in Denver for the annual AAU national basketball tournament. The stakes in this tournament were especially high because the top three teams would earn the right to play in a tournament to decide who would represent the United States in the 1948 Olympics. While Oakland lost in the semifinals to Phillips, the Bittners, with Barksdale scoring twenty-one points, won the game for third place. Barksdale was named to the AAU All-America team and earned a trip to Madison Square Garden to play in the tournament to select the U.S. Olympic basketball team. After the tournament, the U.S. Olympic Basketball Committee named Barksdale as one of the fourteen players to represent the United States in the 1948 London Olympics. This made him the first African American basketball player to compete in the Olympics.

Prior to sailing to London, Barksdale trained with the Phillips 66ers, who won the Olympic tournament and placed five players on the team. To raise money for the trip, the Olympic committee scheduled three exhibition games between the Phillips 66ers and the Kentucky Wildcats, the second-place team in the tournament, who also had five players on the Olympic team. On 9 July 1948 the two teams met in Lexington, Kentucky, and Barksdale became the first African American to play on an integrated team in the Bluegrass State. Barksdale did not allow an anonymous death threat or the refusal of Lexington hotels to allow him to stay with his team to affect his play, and he and Bob Kurland each scored thirteen points to give Phillips the victory. In 1948 the United States Olympic basketball team won the gold medal, and this brought an extremely eventful year in Barksdale's life to a close.

The 1949 AAU basketball tournament was held in Oklahoma City, Oklahoma. In the championship game, the Oakland Bittners edged the Phillips 66ers 55-51 as Barksdale led all scorers with 17 points. Oakland's victory ended Phillips's streak of six consecutive AAU championships. Because of segregation, neither Barksdale nor Dave Minor, also an African American, was allowed to stay with their teammates while they stayed in Oklahoma. Nonetheless, when Barksdale was named to the all-tournament team, the crowd gave him a loud ovation.

The following year Lou Bittner dropped his team sponsorship and Barksdale played for the Oakland Blue 'n Gold. The team lost in the finals of the National AAU Tournament to Phillips although Barksdale won All-America honors for a third time. In March 1951 he led the United States to a victory in the Pan American Games, for which the AAU had the responsibility of organizing the U.S. basketball team. He played his last AAU game in the 1951 tournament when the Blue 'n Gold was upset in the second round. Despite his team's loss, Barksdale was named an AAU All-America for the fourth time. In 1951 Barksdale signed a professional contract with the Baltimore Bullets, along with Dave Minor becoming the team's first black players. He played with the Bullets from 1951–1953 and with the Boston Celtics from 1952–1955. In four years he averaged eleven points per game, and in 1953 he was the first African American to play in the NBA All-Star game.

Because of foot and ankle problems, Barksdale retired from basketball in 1955 and returned to Oakland, where until the 1960s he owned the Sportsman and Showcase nightclubs and also worked as a popular disc jockey in the Bay Area until the 1970s. Later he worked as a scout for the Golden State Warriors. In 1962 he married Jewell Jackson. The Barksdales had two sons, Donald and Derek, before divorcing in 1975. In 1982 he created the Save High School Sports Foundation to help make high school sports affordable for children in the Bay Area. The organization raised more than a million dollars by holding Celebrity Waiter Luncheons, for which he recruited celebrities such as WILLIE MAYS, DANNY GLOVER, and Carol Channing. Barksdale died in 1993 of cancer of the esophagus. He was inducted into the UCLA Hall of Fame in 1987, the Bay Area Hall of

Fame in 1996, and the Pacific Ten Hall of Fame in 2005.

Further Reading
Grundman, Adolph H. *The Golden Age of Amateur Basketball: The AAU Tournament, 1921–1968* (2004).
Thomas, Ron. *They Cleared the Lane: The NBA's Black Pioneers* (2002).

Obituary: *New York Times,* 11 Mar. 1993.

ADOLPH GRUNDMAN

BARNES, Ernie (15 July 1938–), football player and painter, was born Ernest Eugene Barnes Jr. in Durham, North Carolina, the son of Ernest Barnes Sr., a tobacco worker, and Fannie Mae Geer, who worked for a local legal official. On occasion Barnes talked with Mr. Fuller, his mother's employer, and from him learned about culture, art, and classical music.

Before the landmark Supreme Court case *Brown v. Board of Education* in 1954 it was uncommon for African Americans in North Carolina to have access to museums or other sources of information about ancient or world cultures. Segregation and racial inequalities in schools and other public institutions deprived most back children of avenues for artistic pursuits. Despite such constraints, Barnes's mother exposed her son to as much culture and art as she could: he studied dance and horn and percussion instruments as well as the visual arts. By the time Barnes completed high school he had already been exposed to the great masters of the classical arts. An awkward adolescent, Barnes was overweight, tall, and painfully introverted, characteristics for which he was frequently ridiculed. His only refuge, aside from the protection of his mother, was the vast openness of creativity. Barnes felt safest in the company of his sketchbook and drawing implements. Once the schoolchildren recognized that his skill for drawing overshadowed his shyness and his weight, he was no longer ridiculed; in fact, he became the center of attention.

As his talent grew, so did his body. Standing head and shoulders above most of his high school classmates, Barnes became involved in extracurricular sports. In 1952 he started playing football; he excelled on the field and off, becoming a team leader. He graduated from high school with offers of several college scholarships. Barnes accepted an athletic scholarship at North Carolina College (later North Carolina Central University), where he played football and studied to become an artist.

After college his large stature and presence on and off the field gained the attention of the American Football League (AFL). Barnes was drafted by the Baltimore Colts as a lineman in 1959. Although he had joined the ranks of well-paid and famous athletes, Barnes maintained his love for art. He returned to Durham to create his first notable painting, *The Bench.* This piece fused his experience of the world of sports with his emergence into the world of painting. The AFL was Barnes's introduction to the lucrative yet brutal world of professional sports in which this affable southerner was confronted with the truculent racist discourse of white America. During the civil rights movement in the 1960s Barnes was developing as a football player as well as an artist. Recognizing that neither painting nor any other form of art was commonly associated with a 263-pound lineman, Barnes was unsure if he would be accepted by his fellow teammates. Much to his surprise, however, he and his art were well received.

Barnes's professional football career ended in 1966, but his painting career continued. Reflectively, Barnes reconnected with his beginnings, his time as a professional athlete, and his heritage as an African American. From a wellspring of memories, Barnes created a lasting body of work, gaining widespread acclaim through word of mouth and showings at small social events. Barnes was sponsored, supported, and promoted by country clubs and sportswriters from the Midwest to New York. Blending its creator's memories of the football field, the civil rights struggles, and his love of music and black culture, Barnes's work was featured as set decoration on the television program *Good Times* and in other venues. In 1984 Barnes married Bernadine Gradney, a Los Angeles schoolteacher; the couple had five children. Ernie Barnes was able to sustain his career by staying true to his love of art and by contributing to the education of children through the promotion of learning and the arts. In 2003 he returned to Durham to Hillside High, his alma mater, to talk to the students about using the power of creativity to enrich their lives, an example of the importance Barnes placed on community outreach and on helping children appreciate the arts.

Further Reading
Barnes, Ernie. *Autobiography: From Pads to Palette* (1995).
Kirkpatrick, C. D. "Art Helps Build Hillside Dreams," *Herald Sun,* 15 Aug. 2003.
Nakao, Annie. "Barnes Draws from Life but It's No Still Life," *San Francisco Chronicle,* 12 Sept. 2002.
Robertson, Dale. "Football Helped Barnes Blend Colors, Career," *Houston Chronicle,* 30 Jan. 2004.

HASAAN A. KIRKLAND

BARNES, Samuel Edward (25 Jan. 1915–21 Jan. 1997), pioneer black naval officer, was born in Oberlin, Ohio, one of five children (two boys and three girls) of James and Margaret Barnes. James, from North Carolina, was a chef at Oberlin College, and Margaret, from Kentucky, ran a family laundry. Soon after they married, Barnes's parents settled in Oberlin to raise their family because of the community's liberal atmosphere. They were aware of the role the town had played as a way station on the Underground Railroad for fugitive slaves in the nineteenth century. Barnes received the bulk of his education in Oberlin. He graduated from high school there in 1932 and was elected to the National Honor Society. In 1936 he graduated from Oberlin College with a bachelor's degree in Physical Education. He was an outstanding athlete who played end on the college's football team and starred on the track team. He established a school record in the broad jump, ran the 100-yard dash, 220, 440, and was part of the mile relay team.

From 1936 to 1941 Barnes was on the staff of church-affiliated, all-black Livingstone College in Salisbury, North Carolina. He was director of athletics, head basketball and football coach, dormitory supervisor, and assistant to the dean of the college. As he recounted in an oral history many years later, Barnes avoided contact with whites as much as possible. He went by his initials to avoid being addressed by his first name. Whites addressed him as "Professor" to avoid having to attach the word "Mister" before his last name.

From 1941 to 1942 Barnes was the boys' work secretary at a YMCA in Cincinnati, Ohio, before enlisting in the Navy in September 1942. He was honor man—deemed by his seniors to be the top-performing member—of his company in recruit training at the Great Lakes Naval Training Station, north of Chicago. His next assignment as an enlisted man was in the physical training section at Camp Robert Smalls, the segregated site of training for black naval personnel at Great Lakes. In December 1943 Barnes married Olga Lash of Salisbury, North Carolina. They had three children, Olga Michele Welch, Margaret Nadine "Alexa" Donaphin, and Michael David Lash Barnes.

In January 1944, shortly after his marriage, Barnes joined fifteen other enlisted petty officers at Camp Robert Smalls to form the first training course for black officers in the history of the U.S. Navy. The sixteen men were culled from a population of approximately one hundred thousand black sailors. Included in the selection process were detailed background checks by the FBI. Almost everyone in the group had college experience, and a few had advanced degrees. In two and a half months, they went through a cram course that included training in such areas as navigation, communications, gunnery, propulsion machinery, seamanship, naval history, and the navy disciplinary system. The members of the training class concluded that they were part of an experiment on the part of the navy and were determined to succeed or fail as a group, rather than compete with each other. Thus they pooled their knowledge in after-hours sessions. All sixteen passed, but only thirteen became officers—twelve ensigns and one warrant officer. The other three students remained as enlisted men. Years later the pioneering officers became known collectively as the Golden Thirteen. Barnes's sister Margaret was among the first black women officers of the Women's Army Corps (WAC) commissioned by the army during World War II.

After receiving his commission in March 1944, Ensign Barnes remained at Great Lakes until the spring of 1945. During that time he was in charge of physical training and recreation for the three camps that trained black sailors. In April 1945 he became officer in charge of Logistics Support Company #123, which was trained at Camp Peary, Williamsburg, Virginia. In May 1945 the company went overseas, first to Eniwetok Atoll in the Marshall Islands and later to Okinawa in the Ryukyus chain. The men of his all-black company were stevedores, involved in loading and unloading ships in anticipation of the planned invasion of the Japanese home islands. One of the few white officers who welcomed Barnes on Okinawa was Lieutenant (junior grade) Stephen Belichick, whom Barnes had known from his college years in Ohio. Belichick's son Bill later coached the Cleveland Browns and New England Patriots of the National Football League.

Once World War II ended, Barnes, by now a lieutenant (junior grade), returned to the United States and left active service in 1946. He returned to Oberlin College to do graduate work toward his master's degree, which he received in 1949. In 1947 he had begun a long career at Howard University in Washington, D.C., one of the nation's foremost traditionally black schools. At various times he was assistant football coach, head boxing coach, head wrestling coach, and head track coach. In 1956 he completed a doctorate in Sports Administration from Ohio State University. From 1956 to 1970 Barnes was Howard's director of athletics and head of the men's physical education department. In 1957 and 1958 during a one-year sabbatical from Howard, he went to Iraq on behalf of the U.S. State Department. While there he worked as a "sports ambassador," teaching Iraqi students about American coaching techniques.

Barnes was a member of the National Collegiate Athletic Association (NCAA) Council from 1965 to 1970. From 1971 to 1973 he was secretary-treasurer of the NCAA, the first black person to be an officer of the organization. After leaving Howard University, Barnes moved on to the Federal City College in Washington, D.C., to work for two years as interim director of athletics. In 1974 he became chairman of the division of health and physical education for the District of Columbia Teachers College. He remained in that capacity when the University of the District of Columbia was formed by the merger of D.C. Teachers College and two other schools. He retired in 1984 but remained active in the community. Among other pursuits, he worked with the Navy's Recruiting District Advisory Committee in Washington. He helped get a junior Naval Reserve Officer Training Corps program established in a Washington high school and was instrumental in working with the Washington Redskins in establishing companies of Navy recruits named for that professional football team. Among his many honors, Barnes was selected in 1986 as a charter member of the Oberlin College Athletic Hall of Fame. He died in Washington, D.C., in 1997.

Further Reading

Reminiscences of Dr. Samuel E. Barnes, Member of the Golden Thirteen (1993). This volume is comprised of interviews conducted in 1986 and 1988 and was published by the U.S. Naval Institute in Annapolis, Maryland.

Stillwell, Paul, ed. *The Golden Thirteen: Recollections of the First Black Naval Officers* (1993).

Obituary: *Washington Post*, 24 Jan. 1997.

PAUL STILLWELL

BARNES, William Harry (4 Apr. 1887–15 June 1945), physician, otolaryngologist (an ear, nose, and throat specialist), inventor, and administrator, was born in Philadelphia, Pennsylvania, the son of George W. Barnes, a laborer, and Eliza Webb. Barnes and his two sisters lived poverty-stricken lives on Lombard Street, in a very poor area of the city. Barnes decided at an early age to become a physician, a decision unheard of and regarded in his neighborhood as preposterous. His parents tried to discourage him from pursuing what to them seemed an impossible dream for a poor black youth, hoping rather that he would focus on finding realistic employment. Nevertheless determined, Barnes walked ten miles every day to and from school and from his after-school work as a porter and messenger for jewelry shops. During summers he worked as a porter in hotels. Seeing those who lived a far different and more elegant life than his own inspired him to work himself out of poverty. In 1908 Barnes graduated from Philadelphia's Central High School with a collegiate bachelor of arts degree and decided to compete for a four-year scholarship to medical school offered by the University of Pennsylvania. He spent the entire summer of 1908 in serious study, took the competitive examination, passed it, and became the first African American to win that scholarship. Four years later, in 1912, Barnes received an MD and began a year's internship at Douglass and Mercy hospitals in Philadelphia. Also that year he married Mattie E. Thomas; they had five children.

Barnes soon established several long-term relationships with hospitals and other medical facilities in and outside of Philadelphia. From 1913 to 1945 he was an ear, nose, and throat staff physician at Douglass Hospital. In 1921 he was chief of otolaryngology at Jefferson Medical School Hospital in Philadelphia. From 1913 to 1922 and again in 1931 he was lecturer in bronchoscopy at Howard University Medical School in Washington, D.C. At this time he was also a registrant of the American College of Surgeons. In 1918 Barnes served as acting assistant surgeon for the U.S. Public Health Service. In spite of a heavy schedule of professional responsibilities and a professionally stultifying racial environment, he managed to develop and maintain a growing private medical practice between 1922 and 1945. In 1922, against the advice of friends, associates, and relatives, he limited his medical practice to diseases of the ear, nose, and throat, making him the first black medical specialist in the United States. In the early 1930s he organized and headed the Department of Bronchoscopy at Mercy Hospital. He found time to do postgraduate work at Douglass and Mercy hospitals (1921), the

University of Pennsylvania (1924, 1926), the University of Paris, and the University of Bordeaux (1924). In addition to formal coursework he also underwent advanced medical training in bronchoscopic technique with internationally known specialists, such as Sebileau and Baldenbeck in Paris, Moure in Bordeaux, Unger in New York, and Schatz and Lukens in Philadelphia. Barnes was the first black physician to master the technique of bronchoscopy. He was also the first black granted certification by an American medical certifying board, the American Board of Otolaryngology (1927), and therefore the first black physician officially recognized as a medical specialist in the United States.

Barnes was a medical and community activist who worked hard to increase the flow of medical information and its accessibility to the African American community. In addition he made great efforts to upgrade medical practice and standards among black physicians. One of his highest priorities was to improve general living conditions within black communities because he was acutely aware of the connection between decent housing and good public health. He was the thirty-seventh president of the National Medical Association (1935–1936), a parallel organization created by black physicians in 1895 because they were denied membership in the American Medical Association. Barnes was an active participant in NMA annual meetings, which he turned into teaching forums by presenting papers and demonstrating surgical procedures. In 1931 Barnes founded the Society for the Promotion of Negro Specialists in Medicine, and from 1931 to 1933 he served as the organization's executive secretary. A member of Philadelphia's Zoar Methodist Church, where he regularly taught Sunday school and was president of the board of trustees for fifteen years, Barnes organized a well-baby clinic and taught first aid. At other churches in the community he also set up and taught first-aid classes. He founded the Zoar Community Building and Loan Association and served as its president from 1925 to 1945. A proponent of integration in public housing, he was one of the original members of the Philadelphia Housing Authority and served as its assistant secretary-treasurer from 1937 to 1945.

Barnes was a medical innovator. Between 1913 and 1938 he invented the hypophyscope, an instrument for seeing the pituitary gland by accessing it through the sphenoidal sinus; invented a lingual tonsillectome, a specialized scalpel used in performing tonsillectomies; developed a surgical modification of the Myles lingual tonsillectomy procedure; developed surgical procedures for more effectively treating tonsillar abscesses; and created improved medical record-keeping procedures for patient records. He was an early riser and a practitioner of strict punctuality. When chairing meetings he would begin at the appointed time regardless of who was, or was not, present. His surgical operations were often scheduled for seven o'clock in the morning, to the annoyance of his staff and nurses.

Barnes belonged to and was an officer in many civic and professional organizations, including the American Medical Association, once black membership became possible in the late 1920s and early 1930s; the American Board of Otolaryngology; the Negro Specialists Society, of which he was executive secretary from 1931 to 1938; the Philadelphia Academy of Medicine and Allied Sciences, of which he was president for three years in the early 1930s; the NAACP; and the Citizen's Republican Club, where he was president of the Forum Commission in the 1930s. He died in Philadelphia.

Barnes was an indefatigable worker who involved himself in every aspect of medical and community life. His personal motto, which he often expressed, was "failure comes from within." In his view, therefore, failure could be controlled and eliminated. He proved by his own example that despite growing up in poverty and despite the existence of racial barriers, one could achieve lofty goals. Having done that, Barnes actively tried to help as many other people as possible obtain better lives for themselves.

Further Reading

Barnes, William Harry. *National Medical Association Journal* 47 (1955).
"The President Elect." *National Medical Association Journal* 26 (1934).
Sammons, Vivian Ovelton. *Blacks in Science and Medicine* (1990).

BILL SCOTT

BARNETT, Claude Albert (16 Sept. 1889–2 Aug. 1967), entrepreneur, journalist, and government adviser, was born in Sanford, Florida, the son of William Barnett, a hotel worker, and Celena Anderson. His father worked part of the year in Chicago and the rest of the time in Florida. Barnett's parents separated when he was young, and he lived with his mother's family in Oak Park, Illinois, where he attended school. His maternal ancestors were free blacks who migrated from Wake County, North Carolina, to the black settlement of Lost Creek, near Terre Haute, Indiana, during the 1830s. They then moved to Mattoon, Illinois, where Barnett's maternal grandfather was a teacher and later a barbershop owner, and finally to Oak Park. While attending high school in Oak Park, Barnett worked as a houseboy for Richard W. Sears, cofounder of Sears, Roebuck and Company. Sears offered him a job with the company after he graduated from high school, but Barnett's mother insisted that he receive a college education. He graduated from Tuskegee Institute with a degree in Engineering in 1906. His maternal grandfather and BOOKER T. WASHINGTON, founder and head of Tuskegee Institute, were the major influences on Barnett's life and values. He cherished the principles of hard work, self-help, thrift, economic development, and service to his race.

Following graduation from Tuskegee, Barnett worked as a postal clerk in Chicago. While still employed by the post office, in 1913 he started his own advertising agency, the Douglas Specialty Company, through which he sold mail-order portraits of famous black men and women. He left the post office in 1915 and in 1918, with several other entrepreneurs, founded the Kashmir Chemical Company, which manufactured Nile Queen hair-care products and cosmetics. Barnett became Kashmir's advertising manager and he toured the country to market its products and his portraits. He helped to develop a national market for Kashmir and also pioneered the use of positive advertisements. Traditional advertisements featured an unattractive black woman with a message that others should use the company's products to avoid looking like her. In contrast, Barnett used good-looking black models and celebrities with positive messages about the beauty of black women. He visited local black newspapers to negotiate advertising space and discovered that they were desperate for national news but did not have the resources to subscribe to the established newswire services. Barnett recommended that the *Chicago Defender*, founded by ROBERT ABBOTT in 1905 and the most widely circulated black newspaper during the early twentieth century, establish a black news service. The newspaper rejected his proposal since it had enough sources for its own publication and feared harming its circulation by providing competitors with material.

In March 1919, with backing from Kashmir's board of directors, Barnett started the Associated Negro Press (ANP) in the company's office. In 1926 the Kashmir Chemical Company dissolved under legal pressure from Procter and Gamble, which made a similar line of products called Cashmere. Barnett was now free to devote his attention fully to ANP. During this era black newspapers published weekly, so ANP evolved as a mail service rather than as a wire service, thereby making it affordable to subscribers. Moreover, the major wire services did not offer much information about African Americans. Barnett began ANP with eighty subscribers, including almost all the black newspapers and several white papers. He charged $25 to join ANP and a monthly fee of $16 to $24, depending on whether newspapers received dispatches once or twice a week. Subscribers agreed to credit ANP for articles featured in their newspapers, to provide ANP with news about their communities, and to forfeit membership if they failed to pay for the service within sixty days.

The staff produced about seventy pages of copy a week, including news stories, opinion pieces, essays, poetry, books reviews, cartoons, and occasionally photographs; the copy was then mimeographed and sent to subscribers. It did not cost much to operate ANP. The service mined news stories from various sources, such as black newspapers, the white press, special correspondents, and news releases from government agencies, foundations, organizations, and businesses, creating one of the most comprehensive files of news stories about African Americans. Barnett wrote some of the stories himself under the pen name

Albert Anderson, a combination of his middle name and his mother's maiden name. Because subscribers usually were late in paying their fees, Barnett struggled to keep ANP afloat. Sometimes he took advertising space in the newspapers in lieu of news service fees. His companies, first Associated Publishers Representatives and later the National Feature Service, then sold the space to advertisers, offering advertisers lower rates than they would get if they placed advertisements directly with the newspapers.

In 1932 Barnett became one of the first graduates to serve on Tuskegee Institute's board of trustees. He also served as president of the board of trustees of Provident Hospital in Chicago, director of the Supreme Liberty Life Insurance Company, member of the Red Cross's national board of governors, and trustee of the Phelps-Stokes Fund. During the late 1920s and early 1930s he headed the Republican Party's publicity campaign for the black vote. Some of his ANP subscribers became upset by his stories that favored the Republicans. After Franklin D. Roosevelt's election to the presidency in 1932 and First Lady Eleanor Roosevelt's growing popularity among African Americans, Barnett ended his relationship with the Republican Party.

Barnett married the popular concert singer and actress ETTA MOTEN (BARNETT) in 1934. She had three daughters from a previous marriage. Barnett managed her career until 1942, when she assumed the lead role in the Broadway show *Porgy and Bess* and began to require the attention of a full-time agent. Also in 1942, Barnett became special assistant to the secretary of agriculture, Claude R. Wickard, a position that he held with successive secretaries until 1952, when the Republicans regained the White House with the election of Dwight D. Eisenhower. During his tenure with the Department of Agriculture, Barnett was a strong advocate for black tenant farmers and sharecroppers and sought to make it possible for them to own land. He also tried to improve the condition of black farmers through federal aid for health, education, and insurance programs. He was particularly interested in strengthening black agricultural colleges.

During World War II, ANP employed eight people at its Chicago headquarters and had almost two hundred subscribers. The news service opened an office in Washington, D.C., and later one at the United Nations in New York City. Barnett penned many articles about segregation in the military and pressed the federal government to accredit black journalists as war correspondents. His advocacy of racial equality played an important role in President Harry S. Truman's decision in 1948 to desegregate the military.

With an expanding African independence movement after World War II, Barnett secured more than one hundred African newspapers as subscribers to ANP. In 1959 he organized the World News Service to provide copy to subscribers in Africa. Barnett traveled to Africa more than fifteen times to solicit subscribers and to collect material for articles on black

progress. He and his wife became avid collectors of African art and were much-sought-after speakers on Africa to African American civic, fraternal, and religious organizations. Although he had no formal training as a newsman, Barnett helped to develop a generation of black journalists. Most of his featured columnists wrote for the benefit of a large black audience rather than for pay.

With the rise of the civil rights movement during the late 1950s, many white newspapers began to cover the black community in the United States. News organizations started hiring black correspondents, most of whom had broken into the industry with ANP. Barnett had established a means for the black press to secure national and later international news about black people. ANP, with its motto "Progress, Loyalty, Truth," set professional standards for the black press and nurtured black journalists who were well prepared to move into mainstream media with the success of the civil rights movement. Increased competition, persistent financial problems, and failing health forced Barnett to close ANP and to retire in 1963. He made several more trips to Africa and began writing an autobiography. He died of a cerebral hemorrhage at his Chicago home.

Further Reading

The Archives and Manuscript Department of the Chicago Historical Society house Barnett's papers and ANP files. Most of this material is available on microfilm.

Evans, Linda J. "Claude A. Barnett and the Associated Negro Press." *Chicago History* 12, no. 1 (Spring 1983): 44–56.

Hogan, Lawrence D. *A Black National News Service: The Associated Negro Press and Claude Barnett, 1919–1945* (1984).

Silverman, Robert Mark. "The Effects of Racism and Racial Discrimination on Minority Business Development: The Case of Black Manufacturers in Chicago's Ethnic Beauty Aids Industry." *Journal of Social History* 31, no. 3 (Spring 1998): 571–597.

Obituary: *New York Times*, 3 Aug. 1967.

ROBERT L. HARRIS JR.

BARNETT, Etta Moten (5 Nov. 1901–2 Jan. 2004), actor, singer, and philanthropist, was born Etta Moten in Weimar, Texas, the only daughter of Reverend Freeman F. Moten and Ida Norman Moten. The ten-year-old Etta took an active part in church, singing in the choral group and instructing Sunday-school lessons. Standing on a makeshift step stool, in order to be at the same height level as the rest of the choir, she shared her voice with the congregation.

After high school Barnett wedded Lieutenant Curtis Brooks. During their seven-year marriage, she had four children, one of whom died at birth. Following in the footsteps of her college-educated parents, she attended the University of Kansas in the 1920s; however, in order to receive her education, Barnett had to sacrifice her conventional family life. She divorced her husband and left her three daughters under her parents' supervision while she attended school. On weekends she cared for her children at her parents' house, but during the week Barnett was a full-time student, earning a degree in voice and drama in 1931. Once an unhappy wife but dedicated mother of three, Barnett changed her fate at a time when many people thought change for women, especially black women, was impossible.

Barnett sang with the EVA JESSYE Choir of New York after she finished her education. On the way to New York she met her future second husband, CLAUDE BARNETT, father of the Associated Negro Press. Claude, dazzled by Etta's ambition, wrote introductory letters to his New York acquaintances to smooth her entrance into the theater scene. Soon after she arrived in New York Etta joined the Broadway cast of *Fast and Furious* (1931). Her performance earned her a place in the touring cast of *Zombie* (1932), which coincidentally played in Chicago, where Etta became reacquainted with her future husband, Claude. Due to his affiliation with national newspapers, he also had connections in Hollywood; Etta headed to the West Coast.

Entering the ranks of the film industry, Barnett dubbed songs for actresses, including Barbara Stanwyck and Ginger Rogers, without getting recognition in the credits. However, she became famous for her on-screen portrayal of a widow in *Gold Diggers* (1933), singing "My Forgotten Man." Because her role was not that of the stereotypical housekeeper or nursemaid, Barnett's performance gave credence to the idea that black actors could portray realistic characters, something many Americans at the time considered impossible. Her role in the film sparked interest and pride among African Americans around the nation, and the black press anointed her "The New Negro Woman." In addition, *Gold Diggers* won Barnett national acclaim for her musical talent: she was the first black woman to perform at the White House, reprising her song from the film at Franklin D. Roosevelt's birthday party in 1934.

In her next film, *Flying Down to Rio* (1933), with Fred Astaire and Ginger Rogers, Barnett appeared with large fruit placed strategically in her hair, a style that many people mistakenly believed originated with Carmen Miranda, as she sang "The Carioca." Her performance of the musical number increased her fame when the Academy Awards panel nominated the piece for best song. A dynamic duo, Etta and Claude Barnett married in 1934, and Etta's three daughters moved to their mother's new Chicago residence.

Barnett returned to New York to play the role of Bess in *Porgy and Bess* in 1942. According to Barnett, Gershwin sought her to fill the role in 1935, when he initially produced the show. However Barnett, a lush contralto, politely declined the role since Gershwin had composed the part for a soprano voice. Yet Barnett did play Bess in the production's longest stint, starting in New York in 1942 and traveling throughout the United States and Canada until 1945. Among

Barnett's other Broadway credits are *Sugar Hill* (1931) and *Lysistrata* (1946). SIDNEY POITIER charmingly described her as "the most incredible, amazing, voluptuous, dignified, and sensual actress to grace the Broadway stage in my lifetime" (Kinnon, "Etta at 100," 62).

Though she enjoyed a successful career in film and theater, Barnett's influence reached beyond the artistic sphere and into the world of activism and philanthropy. Beginning in 1947 African governance and culture became a part of Etta and Claude life as they traveled to the continent several times on behalf of three United States presidents during the movement for African independence. In March of 1957 Etta interviewed MARTIN LUTHER KING JR. about Ghana's independence celebration. Though her husband died in 1967, she carried on their support of African progress for the next thirty-seven years. In the 1950s she broadcast her own radio show, *I Remember When*, to listeners in thirty-eight states. Various organizations, such as the African American Institute, the National Council for Negro Women, the DuSable Museum of African American History, and the Chicago Lyric Opera, received her support and membership. In 1979 her legendary work earned her a place in the Black Filmmakers Hall of Fame.

At the age of ninety-six, Barnett remarked, "I've always said that the only difference between a rut and a grave is the depth, and I'm not ready for either one" (Kinnon, "Etta Moten Barnett," 52–54). Having lived a long, fulfilling life Etta Moten Barnett died of pancreatic cancer in Chicago's Mercy Hospital at the age of 102. Barnett's diverse acting roles, her portrayal of Bess, and her philanthropy have left a lasting impression on American culture.

Further Reading

Kinnon, Joy Bennett. "A Diva for All Times," *Ebony* (2004).

Kinnon, Joy Bennett. "Etta at 100: Etta Moten Barnett, Pioneer Actress, Singer, and Activist, Celebrates Centennial," *Ebony* 57 (2001).

Kinnon, Joy Bennett. "Etta Moten Barnett: Still on the Case at 96," *Ebony* (1997).

Laskas, Jeanne Marie. "Her Heart Keeps on Singing," *Good Housekeeping* 226, issue 2 (1998).

"Pioneer Actress-Singer Etta Moten Barnett Celebrates 100th Birthday in Chicago." *Jet* 100 (Dec. 2001).

Obituaries: (London) *Independent*, 7 Jan. 2004; *Variety*, 12 Jan. 2004; *Jet*, 26 Jan. 2004.

ALLISON KELLAR

BARNETT, Ida B. Wells. *See* Wells-Barnett, Ida Bell.

BARNETT, Marguerite Ross. *See* Ross-Barnett, Marguerite.

BARRETT, Janie Porter (9 Aug. 1865–27 Aug. 1948), educator, school founder, and social welfare advocate, was born in Athens, Georgia, the daughter of Julia Porter. Various biographical accounts indicate that Barrett's parents were former slaves, while others speculate that her father was white. Little is known about either parent. During her early childhood, Barrett resided in the home of the Skinners, a white family whom her mother served as housekeeper. After her mother's marriage to a railway worker, Barrett remained with the Skinners, who encouraged her to further her education.

Though the Skinners suggested that she move north, Barrett, at her mother's urging, attended Hampton Institute in Virginia, graduating in 1884. While at Hampton she became convinced that it was her duty as an educated black woman to work assiduously for the betterment of all African Americans. That belief led her to teach in Dawson, Georgia, and at LUCY CRAFT LANEY's Haines Normal and Industrial Institute in Augusta, Georgia, prior to securing a teaching position at Hampton in 1886. In 1889 she married Harris Barrett, a cashier at Hampton Institute. They had four children.

While rearing her own children, Barrett decided to share her skills with some neighborhood girls. Beginning with Tuesday afternoon sewing classes in her home for a few girls, she soon formed a club for "improving the homes and the moral and social life of that community." People of all ages and of both genders were actively involved in developing skills designed to improve the quality of their lives. In time, because of the overwhelming response to the club and its activities, Barrett sought larger quarters.

Janie Porter Barrett established an informal day-care school at her home in Hampton, Virginia. In 1890, it became the Locust Street Social Settlement, the first settlement house for African Americans. (Austin/Thompson Collection, by permission of Hampton University Museum and Archives.)

In 1902 the Barretts constructed a building on their property to house the Locust Street Settlement, as the club was then called, the first of its kind in Virginia. An auxiliary group of prominent community members raised funds to pay the club's basic expenses and to expand its programs. Northern philanthropists also contributed to the expansion. In 1903 the Barretts added a kindergarten to the growing list of services, and by 1909 the Locust Street Settlement House included five girls' and women's clubs and four boys' clubs. Students and staff from Hampton Institute provided instruction in arts and crafts, domestic arts, and agricultural science.

Barrett enjoyed a continuing relationship with Hampton Institute that resulted in a commitment by staff, faculty, and students to her social service and self-help projects. In 1907 the institute supplied stationery and other support to the Virginia State Federation of Colored Women's Clubs, founded at that year's Hampton Negro Conference. Barrett served as the federation's first president.

After an encounter with an eight-year-old black girl who had been incarcerated, Barrett convinced the federation to adopt as its primary project the establishment of a rehabilitative home for "wayward colored" girls. In 1915 members founded the Industrial Home School for Delinquent Colored Girls at Peake in Hanover County, Virginia, set on a 147-acre farm. Initially Barrett served as secretary of the school's interracial board of trustees. Following her husband's death in 1915, however, Barrett accepted the position of superintendent.

Under her leadership the school gained national prominence and was able to secure a state subsidy and private donations. Largely owing to Barrett's innovative administrative efforts, including the introduction of social welfare principles that nurtured the girls and guided their lives in new directions, the Russell Sage Foundation ranked the school among the top five of its kind in the United States. The reformatory school's program stressed the personal and educational development of the residents rather than punishment for their past behavior. Many of the students flourished in the environment, where good conduct was rewarded and practical skills for living were taught. The girls received vocational training that included sewing, housekeeping, and laundering. The program was designed to provide an eighth-grade education. Those who earned good deportment records for two years were eligible for parole. After their release, contact was maintained with the girls through the school's publication and through personal communication from Barrett.

The school's many accomplishments and success stories brought Barrett numerous awards. Notable among her recognitions was the 1929 William E. Harmon Award for Distinguished Achievement among Negroes. The award was given by the Harmon Foundation, established in 1922 by the philanthropist William E. Harmon. Because of her national reputation as an expert in child rehabilitation, President Herbert Hoover invited Barrett in 1930 to participate in the White House Conference on Child Health and Protection.

Although kept busy by the school's management, Barrett remained active with the federation and with the National Association of Colored Women (NACW), serving as chairperson of the NACW executive board from 1924 to 1928. She also served on local boards such as that of the Richmond Urban League and, in keeping with her promotion of interracial cooperation in matters relating to racial uplift and equality, was a member of the Commission on Interracial Cooperation. The school's board, with its interracial membership, reflected Barrett's commitment to work with whites to achieve the school's goals.

Barrett remained superintendent of the Industrial Home School for Delinquent Colored Girls until her retirement in 1940. She left the school, now a model institution for those seeking to steer young black females away from delinquent behavior, to return to Hampton, Virginia, where she remained until her death. In honor of her achievements, the school that she had led for nearly twenty-five years was renamed the Janie Porter Barrett School for Girls.

Further Reading

Neverdon-Morton, Cynthia. *Afro-American Women of the South and the Advancement of the Race, 1895–1925* (1989).

Whitman, Alden. *American Reformers* (1985).

CYNTHIA NEVERDON-MORTON

BARRIER, Eric (Eric B.) (1965–), DJ, producer, and member of Eric B. and Rakim, was born in East Elmhurst, Queens, New York. In his youth Barrier showed a musical aptitude, playing trumpet and guitar before devoting his energy to DJ-ing, a form which—by the mid-1970s—was a cornerstone of the burgeoning hip-hop movement arising in New York City's boroughs. Barrier's turntable talents eventually landed him a job as the mobile DJ for New York radio station WBLS while in high school. It was also during this period that Barrier met William Griffin Jr., a young MC who had adopted the name and stage persona of "Rakim Allah" in 1984 to signal his growing commitment to the Five-Percent sect of the Nation of Islam, a controversial but influential sect that promoted a broadly Afrocentric blend of political and spiritual advancement. A prodigiously talented lyricist, Rakim's complicated, sophisticated rhymes found their perfect complement in the busy, jazz-inflected soundscapes favored by his new partner.

In 1985 Eric B. and Rakim made their partnership official, releasing their debut single—"Eric B. Is President" backed by "My Melody"—for small, Harlem-based Zakia Records in 1986. Rakim soon became one of hip-hop's most respected lyricists, but the duo's first single was a celebration of its other member, spotlighting Barrier's pioneering work as DJ and producer. This DJ-centric focus was in keeping with much early hip-hop, but remains ironic in light of Rakim's rising reputation. Barrier used multiple, overlapping samples, a style of "noize" whose juxtapositions created a multilayered, occasionally jarring collection of rhythms and melodic snippets; in short order this approach became preeminent within the genre. Eric B. was particularly fond of JAMES BROWN samples, using Brown's stabbing style and deeply polyrhythmic arrangements to construct his own post-industrial symphonies, whose dissonance was perfectly matched by Rakim's thoughtful, politicized rhymes. Mixing the sonic blasts of Barrier's turntables, with Rakim's "knowledge-dropping" rhymes, Eric B. and Rakim's music quickly distinguished itself.

Their 1987 debut full-length recording, *Paid in Full*, fulfilled the promise of their early singles with an album's worth of the explosive creative energy that marked their early work. Still praised as one of hip-hop's greatest works, *Paid in Full* includes "I Know You Got Soul," a hit built around a funk track by James Brown associate Bobby Byrd (which the writer Steve Huey suggests "kicked off hip-hop's fascination" with Brown-related samples), and "Paid in Full," whose rhythm track was later sampled on numerous occasions (Huey, 158–159). The album also included three tracks on which Eric B. is featured without Rakim, displaying his dizzying prowess on the "wheels of steel."

Their second album, *Follow the Leader*, followed in 1988, and its artistic and commercial success solidified Eric B. and Rakim's place at hip-hop's pinnacle. The title single is perhaps Rakim's greatest moment as an MC, a mind-altering journey through time and space, and more Rakim-less examples of Barrier's "turntablism" are featured on the record. As was evident on all their recordings, but particularly on the single "Follow the Leader," which is arguably their masterpiece, the duo displayed a deep jazz sensibility, a mindset reflected in their choice and manipulation of backing tracks, but more significantly by both members' innovative approach to their craft. Both Eric B. and Rakim envisioned a limitless creative palette for their art, within which they were able to reimagine the possibilities and limitations previously inscribed within rap music, and even popular music more generally. While many of their records are highly danceable (thanks to Barrier's fondness for funk and soul), their artistic aim exceeds this benchmark. This boundary-busting style proved revolutionary: Rakim's lengthy, literate rhymes raised the stakes for all future MCs, and Eric B.'s turntable hurricanes provided perfect soundtrack for the genre's burst of desperate creativity. During this period, the group's devotees—including KRS-ONE and Public Enemy—made acclaimed, popular music that followed Eric B. and Rakim's groundbreaking example. After *Follow the Leader* the duo recorded the 1989 hit "Friends" with the R&B singer Jody Watley, and Barrier established production and management companies in 1992.

Though their first two albums proved an insurmountable legacy, even for such a talented partnership, both 1990's *Let the Rhythm Hit 'Em* and 1992's *Don't Sweat the Technique* have their highlights. The former features "In the Ghetto," an urgent call to arms built around a restless rhythm track, and the latter includes "Know the Ledge," on which Rakim sounds a note of caution about the perils of life in urban black America. Nonetheless as hip-hop entered a period dominated by the West Coast–based "gangsta" movement, the challenging collages of Eric B. and Rakim seemed increasingly out of place, even though the group's esteem within all sectors of the rap community remained high. The 1992 release of *Don't Sweat the Technique* completed the duo's contract with MCA Records, which had begun in 1988, and—in the ensuing confusion over the direction of their career, particularly over the possibility of each recording a solo album—they broke up.

For the next several years, legal disagreements prevented either member from capitalizing on their previous success. Although Rakim would stage a successful comeback in the late 1990s, Barrier's subsequent career was less storied. His legendary reputation and track record helped him score various unremarkable production jobs throughout the 1990s, including a brief partnership with the gangsta virtuoso DR. DRE, and he released a 1995 solo effort that met with little critical or commercial success. Despite Eric B.'s subsequent lack of chart presence, his legacy was felt throughout the hip-hop world, as his groundbreaking redefinition of sample-based hip-hop tracks (combined with the virtuosic lyrics of his collaborator Rakim) continued to inform and influence the genre and culture.

Further Reading

Chang, Jeff. *Can't Stop Won't Stop: A History of the Hip-Hop Generation* (2005).

George, Nelson. *Hip Hop America* (1998).

Huey, Steve. "Eric B. and Rakim," in *All Music Guide to Hip-Hop*, ed. Vladimir Bogdanov (2001).

Wang, Oliver. *Classic Material: The Hip-Hop Album Guide* (2003).

CHARLES L. HUGHES

BARROW, Peter (1841–1906), slave, Civil War soldier, politician, and Baptist minister, was born Peter Barnabas Barrow, a Virginia slave. The month and day of his birth are unknown. It is believed that he was born near Petersburg, Virginia, and may have been taken to Mississippi or Alabama with his owner. In 1864 Barrow joined Company A, 66th U.S. Colored Infantry and in 1865 became a sergeant. A year later Barrow was discharged because of an injury he received. He went on to teach school at Vicksburg, Mississippi.

Barrow, who was most likely self-educated, served as a member of the Mississippi House of Representatives for Warren County, Mississippi, from 1870 to 1871. From 1872 to 1875 he served in the Mississippi State Senate. He migrated to Spokane, Washington, in 1889 and settled there in the city's African American community. Barrow and other African Americans were determined to thrive by establishing businesses, seeking political rights, creating jobs, and developing churches. Barrow served as the president of a land de-

velopment company established to help build a colony of black rural workers. Land was purchased at a location called Deer Lake in Stevens County, Washington, "[f]or the purpose of giving the Negroes of Spokane an opportunity to make good on the farm, and to prove their worth as farm laborers." Therefore, "a band of Spokane colored folks has organized a development company, bought 140 acres of land near Deer Lake and will start this spring to develop the land with Negro labor only. No similar company exists in the United States" (Franklin, 24–26).

Shortly after arriving in Spokane, Barrow engaged in the city's political and religious affairs, in which he earned respect from both blacks and whites of the community. One of the political organizations he was involved with was the John Logan Colored Republican Club, which he founded in 1889 or 1890. One of the purposes of the club was to decide on which candidates to endorse for political offices. This club was made up of some of Spokane's most prominent black citizens, including Fred E. Wilson, Charles Scrutchins, and Rudolph B. Scott. During a particular club meeting, the members debated which candidate to endorse as their congressional representative. They discussed the possibility of two representatives, John L. Wilson and Judge George Turner, who went to the U.S. Senate in 1897. The club finally adopted a resolution that read as follows:

The present congressman, John L. Wilson has failed to give the Negro the proper consideration in our [judgment] as a Congressman from the State of Washington and failed to acknowledge the receipt of letters from our people in matters of gigantic importance, and has failed to comply with the resolution adopted in the last convention of the state. (Franklin, 24–26)

The club's resolution stated that Wilson's conduct was inappropriate for a congressman due to his "entering into an altercation and again into a free fight." Therefore the club endorsed Judge Turner as its candidate. Wilson, however continued to serve in the House of Representatives until 1895, at which time he went to the U.S. Senate. In 1894, unhappy with the lack of response to African American issues from the Republicans, Barrow unsuccessfully ran for the state legislature on the Populist ticket. He remained with the radical party through the tempestuous election of 1896 and eventually became a presidential elector for Spokane and Whitman Counties.

After residing in Spokane for only a year, Barrow, his wife, and a few African American citizens helped found the first black church in the city. This group of citizens gathered "to consider the propriety of organizing a church." Barrow served as pastor of Calvary Baptist Church from 1895 until he traveled to attend a church convention in Tacoma, Washington, in 1906 and died there, most likely in a streetcar accident.

Further Reading

Franklin, Joseph. *All Through the Night: The History of Spokane Black Americans 1860–1940* (1989).

Taylor, Quintard. "The Emergence of Black Communities in the Pacific Northwest: 1865–1910," *Journal of Negro History* (Autumn 1979).

FLORENCE COLEMAN

BARROW, Willie Taplin (7 Dec. 1924–), social activist and spiritual adviser, was born Willie Taplin in the small rural town of Burton, Texas, the daughter of Nelson Taplin, a Baptist preacher, and Octavia, a Methodist congregant. A member of a large extended family, Barrow fondly recalled an upbringing steeped in strict traditional family values and old-time southern religion. She lived with her parents, six siblings, both sets of grandparents, and a great-grandmother in the family home, and they were sometimes joined by a cousin or two in need of temporary housing. The family lived together, worked together, and went to church together. Although they had limited economic resources, they grew the food that they needed on the family farm, and though she came to understand the family's poverty in later years, Barrow said that she never knew hunger as a child.

Barrow discovered her activist voice and spirit early in life. Under the state-sponsored segregation that plagued the South, she was required to travel miles from home to attend a black public school. When she spied a yellow school bus preparing to pick up white children in a nearby community in the late 1930s, however, Barrow organized her schoolmates and staged a protest. It was her first taste of confrontational politics. The sweetness of her victory placed her on a "warrior's" path that served her for decades to come.

Upon graduating from high school in 1941, Barrow decided to study the ministry and moved from the South to the West Coast to pursue her calling. With limited funds and no expectation of financial support from her family, she joined thousands of other African Americans and women who were joining the war industries, accepting full-time employment at the Kaiser Shipyards in Portland, Oregon, where she worked the night shift and learned how to be a welder. Barrow enrolled in the Warner School of Theology in Portland as a full-time day student. Despite these challenges, Barrow persevered. She continued to hone her organizing and leadership skills as she pursued her desire to do God's work. Before moving to Chicago to continue her studies at the Moody Bible School in 1958, Barrow organized the first Black Church of God in Portland. In the mid-1960s she went to Liberia to complete her divinity studies at the University of Monrovia, which later presented her with an honorary doctor of divinity degree.

In 1945 Barrow married Clyde Raymond Barrow. This too became part of her enduring legacy. The couple remained married for fifty-three years, until Clyde's death in 1998. Willie Barrow chronicled her successful marriage in her book *How to Get Married and Stay Married* (2004). She also decided that she wanted to be a mother. She first adopted a child, then she gave birth to a son, and she eventually accepted the role of "godmother" for more than two hundred children.

From 1953 through 1965 Barrow served as a field organizer for MARTIN LUTHER KING JR. and was part of the historic Selma to Montgomery march. She trained new recruits, organized boycotts and rallies, and encouraged participation in voter registration drives. In 1962 she joined forces with the Reverend JESSE JACKSON SR. to organize a new effort, Operation Breadbasket, an outgrowth of the economic arm of the Southern Christian Leadership Conference (SCLC) dedicated to social uplift and economic empowerment in the African American community. Operation Breadbasket was the model for People United to Serve Humanity (PUSH), founded by Jackson in 1971. Barrow maintained a lifelong affiliation with PUSH. Her leadership and organizing skills were easily transferred to the new civil rights organization. However, she faced gender restrictions, as she was asked to train a succession of young male leaders but was never given the opportunity to lead. She challenged the leadership of PUSH and was subsequently named national executive director, chairperson, CEO of operations, and co-chairperson of the Rainbow-PUSH Coalition.

Affectionately called the "Little Warrior," Barrow took the lead role in many social movements, including the student and civil rights movements, the labor movement, the peace movement, and—as a result of the loss of her son Keith Barrow to AIDS—the fight for gay and lesbian rights. An activist at home and abroad, Barrow fulfilled the role of associate pastor and minister of justice for the Vernon Park Church of God in Chicago, was the first executive director of the statewide Coalition against Hunger in Illinois, and traveled to Vietnam during the height of the war in search of peace. She served as campaign director and road manager for Jackson's presidential campaigns in 1984 and 1988. A lifelong member of the National Council of Negro Women, the National Political Congress of Black Women, and the National Urban League, Barrow left an indelible mark of activism on every community in which she served.

Further Reading

Barrow, Willie. *How to Get Married and Stay Married* (2004).

Reid-Merritt, Patricia. *Sister Power: How Phenomenal Black Women Are Rising to the Top* (1996).

PATRICIA REID-MERRITT

BARRY, Marion Shepilov, Jr. (6 Mar. 1936–), four-time mayor of Washington, D.C., was born on a cotton plantation near the Delta hamlet of Itta Bena in northwestern Mississippi to sharecroppers Marion Barry Sr. and Mattie Barry. In 1940 Barry Sr. died, and in 1944 Barry, his mother, and his sister moved to Memphis, Tennessee, where Mattie worked as a maid and married Dave Cummings, a butcher. The combined family, which eventually included nine members, lived in a narrow, wooden "shotgun" house in South Memphis, one of four black enclaves in the city. Barry slept on the couch and rose early each morning to chop wood for the stove. He stuffed cardboard in his shoes to fill the holes and sold his sandwiches to other kids at school for pocket money. A bright, industrious child, he eventually became one of the first African American Eagle Scouts in Memphis. In the summer he traveled with his mother and sisters to pick cotton in Arkansas and Mississippi.

Barry graduated from BOOKER T. WASHINGTON High School, one of two black high schools in Memphis, in 1954. He then became the first in his family to attend college, choosing the predominantly black LeMoyne College in Memphis. After joining Alpha Phi Alpha fraternity, Barry headed the school chapter of the NAACP. At this time, he adopted the middle name of "Shepilov" by picking the name out of a newspaper story about Dmitri Shepilov, a high-ranking member of the Soviet Communist Party. He graduated in 1958 and then earned a master's degree in chemistry at Fisk University in Nashville. He organized the Fisk NAACP and participated in sit-ins at Nashville restaurants. Barry subsequently finished three years as the only black student in the chemistry doctoral program at the University of Tennessee but did not complete his degree. He then taught at the all-black Knoxville College. Increasingly involved with civil rights, Barry abandoned academe in 1964 to become immersed in the civil rights movement full time. Barry briefly worked as the first chair of the Student Nonviolent Coordinating Committee (SNCC) and was a member of the SNCC executive committee. In 1965 he moved to Washington, D.C., to work as an SNCC field secretary. He left SNCC in 1967.

Barry became a familiar figure in Washington as he agitated for civil rights. He gained particular fame for his efforts on behalf of poor blacks. In 1971 Barry was elected to serve on Washington, D.C.'s first school board, and he became board president in 1972. When Congress granted the District of Columbia limited home rule in 1973, Barry won a seat on the first D.C. city council in 1974 as the highest vote getter. He won reelection in 1976, and in 1978 he won election as mayor of Washington, D.C.

Barry inherited an unwieldy bureaucracy, a budget deficit that topped $100 million, and a government beholden to Congress for part of its revenues; Congress could veto any council decision and held approval power over the D.C. budget. To much acclaim, he balanced the budget in his first term and initially reduced the deficit.

Barry served two more terms before leaving office in 1990 as mayor; however, rumors of drug use dogged him. His 1986 reelection victory came despite allegations of drug use and womanizing, as well as such chronic and highly visible problems as soaring city budget deficits, a dramatic increase in drug-related homicides, and the conviction of top city officials on corruption charges. Many black Washington, D.C., residents saw Barry as the victim of a white conspiracy to destroy him and voted for him in response to racial politics. On 18 January 1990, when his former girlfriend Rasheeda Moore cooperated in an FBI sting investigation, Barry was filmed smoking crack cocaine and was arrested. Shortly afterward Barry entered the Hanley-Hazelden Clinic in West Palm Beach, Florida, for treatment for health concerns that included alcohol abuse. Barry and his press secretary were silent about any cocaine abuse. A planned absence of a month stretched to seven weeks when Barry transferred from Hanley-Hazelden to Fenwick Hall, a drug-treatment facility in South Carolina.

On 15 February 1990 Barry was indicted on three felony counts of lying to a grand jury about his drug use and on five misdemeanor counts of cocaine possession. Black newspapers and radio shows portrayed the mayor as the victim of a white federal conspiracy to dethrone him, and the FBI came under severe attack for using heavy-handed tactics to entrap him. Meanwhile, the media, notably the *Washington Post*, bashed Barry in editorials and daily exposés of the criminal investigation. Barry abandoned his reelection plans after conviction on a misdemeanor for cocaine possession. He served six months in prison.

Always a popular politician in racially polarized D.C., Barry won a seat on the city council in 1992. He won a landslide victory to a fourth mayoral term in 1994. In May 1996 Barry abruptly took a leave from his mayoral duties to seek help at a retreat in rural Maryland and then at a more distant church facility near St. Louis, raising suspicions that his substance abuse problems had resurfaced. Barry's hiatus occurred not long after he underwent surgery for prostate cancer, and he described himself as suffering from physical and spiritual exhaustion. He retired from politics in 1998 and aborted a run for city council in 2002 after another drug incident. In April 2002 police working near an open-air drug market in the Buzzard Point section of Southwest Washington found a small rock of crack cocaine in Barry's car. Park police said that the officer who approached Barry's Jaguar saw the driver ingest something and noticed a powdery substance under Barry's nose. The incident attracted a lot of publicity but nothing more. Supporters worried publicly that Barry had relapsed into drug usage, but in 2004 Barry won the Ward 8 city council seat with 96 percent of the vote. Barry's legal troubles continued, however, when in March 2006, he received three years' probation after pleading guilty to two misdemeanor charges for failing to file tax returns for the year 2005.

Barry was married three times, first in 1972 to Mary M. Treadwell; this marriage ended in divorce in 1977. He then married Effi Slaughter in 1978; this marriage produced a son, Marion Christopher Barry, in 1983 but ended in divorce in 1991. In 1994 he married Cora Masters, but this marriage, too, ended in divorce in 2002.

Further Reading

Agronsky, Jonathan I. Z. *Marion Barry: The Politics of Race* (1991).

Barras, Jonetta Rose. *The Last of the Black Emperors: The Hollow Comeback of Marion Barry in a New Age of Black Leader* (1998).

CARYN E. NEUMANN

BARTHÉ, Richmond (28 Jan. 1901–6 Mar. 1989), sculptor, was born in Bay St. Louis, Mississippi, the son of Richmond Barthé and Marie Clementine Roboteau, a seamstress. His father died when Barthé was one month old. Barthé began drawing as a child and first exhibited his work at the county fair in Mississippi at age twelve. He did not attend high school, but he learned about his African heritage from books borrowed from a local grocer and publications given to him by a wealthy white family that vacationed in Bay St. Louis. This family, which had connections to Africa through ambassadorships, hired Barthé as a butler when he was in his teens; he moved with them to New Orleans. At age eighteen Barthé won first prize for a drawing he sent to the Mississippi County Fair. Lyle Saxon, the literary critic for the *New Orleans Times Picayune*, then attempted to register Barthé in a New Orleans art school, but Barthé was denied admission because of his race.

In 1924 Barthé began classes at the School of the Art Institute of Chicago, his tuition paid by a Catholic priest, Harry Kane. Living with an aunt, Barthé paid for his board and art supplies by working as a porter and busboy. During his senior year Barthé began modeling in clay at the suggestion of his anatomy teacher, Charles Schroeder. His busts of two classmates were shown in the Negro History Week exhibition. These works, along with busts of the Haitian general Toussaint-Louverture and the painter HENRY OSSAWA TANNER (first exhibited at a children's home in Gary, Indiana), were included in the Chicago Art League annual exhibition in 1928, the year of Barthé's graduation.

Barthé achieved wide recognition for his bronze busts and figures in the 1930s and 1940s. Within a year after his move to New York City in February 1929, he completed thirty-five sculptures. He continued his education at the Art Students League with fellowships from the Rosenwald Foundation (1929–1930). Barthé's first solo exhibitions (favorably reviewed by the *New York Times*) were in 1934 at the Caz-Delbo Gallery in New York, the Grand Rapids Art Gallery in Michigan, and the Women's City Art Club in Chicago, followed by exhibitions in New York at Delphic Studios (1935), Arden Galleries (1939), DePorres Interracial Center (1945), International Print Society (1945), and Grand Central Art Galleries (1947). He also exhibited in numerous group shows at various institutions, including the Harmon Foundation (1929, 1931, and 1933), the New York World's Fair (1939), the Whitney Museum annual exhibitions (1933, 1940, 1944, and 1945), the Metropolitan Museum of Art's *Artists for Victory* (1942), and the Pennsylvania Academy of Fine Arts' annual exhibitions (1938, 1940, 1943, 1944, and 1948).

Many of Barthé's early works, such as *Masaai* (1933), *African Woman* (c. 1934), and *Wetta* (c. 1934), depict Africans. Barthé dreamed of visiting Africa, stating, "I'd really like to devote all my time to Negro subjects, and I plan shortly to spend a year and

Richmond Barthé explored African and African American themes in many of his sculptures, such as *The Blackberry Woman*, bronze, 1932. (Whitney Museum of American Art.)

a half in Africa studying types, making sketches and models which I hope to finish off in Paris for a show there, and later in London and New York" (Lewis, 11), but he never traveled to the continent. Other works by Barthé, such as *Feral Benga, Stevedore*, and *African Man Dancing* (all 1937), were among the first sculptures of black male nudes by an African American artist.

In the mid-1930s Barthé moved from Harlem to midtown Manhattan for a larger studio and to be closer to major theaters, as many of his clients were theatrical celebrities. Among his portrait busts are *Cyrina* (from *Porgy and Bess*, c. 1934), *Sir John Gielgud as Hamlet* (commissioned for the Haymarket Theatre in London, 1937), *Maurice Evans as Richard II* (1938, in the Shakespeare Theatre in Stratford, Connecticut), and *Katherine Cornell as Juliet* (1942). Barthé later produced busts of other entertainers, such as JOSEPHINE BAKER (1950) and PAUL ROBESON *as Othello* (1975).

Barthé's largest work was an eight-by-eighty-foot frieze, *Green Pastures: The Walls of Jericho* (1937–1938), which he completed under the U.S. Treasury Art Project at the Harlem River Housing Project. His other public works of art include portraits of Abraham Lincoln, in New York (1940) and India (1942); Arthur Brisbane, in Central Park; GEORGE WASHINGTON CARVER, in Nashville (1945), and BOOKER T. WASHINGTON, at New York University (1946).

Many of Barthé's busts, such as *Birth of the Spirituals* (1941) and *The Negro Looks Ahead* (1944), are imbued with a calm spirituality. Barthé described his representational work as an attempt to "capture the beauty that I've seen in people, and abstraction wouldn't satisfy me. . . . My work is all wrapped up with my search for God. I am looking for God inside of people. I wouldn't find it in squares, triangles and circles" (Reynolds and Wright, 154). A strong believer in reincarnation, the artist often called himself an "Old Soul" who had been an artist in Egypt in an earlier life.

In the 1940s Barthé received numerous awards, beginning with Guggenheim fellowships in 1941 and 1942. In 1945 he was elected to the National Sculpture Society (sponsored by the sculptor Malvina Hoffman) and the American Academy of Arts and Letters. He also received the Audubon Artists Gold Medal of Honor and the James J. Hoey Award for interracial justice. The sculptor was also active in several artists' organizations: the Liturgical Arts Society, the International Print Society, the New York Clay Club, and the Sculptors Guild. He also had solo exhibitions at the South Side Art Center in Chicago (1942); the Sayville Playhouse on Long Island (1945); the Margaret Brown Gallery in Boston (1947); and Montclair Art Museum in New Jersey (1949).

In 1950 Barthé received a commission from the Haitian government to sculpt a large monument to Toussaint-Louverture; it now stands in front of the Palace in the Haitian capital, Port-au-Prince. In 1947 Barthé had moved to Jamaica, where he remained through the late 1960s. His most notable works from this time are the General Dessalines monument in Port-au-Prince (1952) and a portrait of Norman Manley, the prime minister of Jamaica (1956). The Institute of Jamaica hosted Barthé's solo show in 1959. In 1964 the artist received the Key to the City from Bay St. Louis. He then sculpted contemplative black male nudes, such as *Meditation* (1964), *Inner Music* (1965), and *Seeker* (1965).

Barthé left the West Indies in 1969 because of increasing violence there and spent five years traveling in Switzerland, Spain, and Italy. He then settled in Pasadena, California, and worked on his memoirs. In 1978 he had a solo exhibition at the William Grant Still Center in Los Angeles and was subsequently honored by the League of Allied Arts there in 1981. He died in Pasadena. Following his death, a retrospective was held at the Museum of African American Art (1990). Barthé's work toured the United States with that of RICHARD HUNT in the Landau/Traveling Exhibition *Two Sculptors, Two Eras* in 1992. His work, which was eventually collected by the Metropolitan and Whitney museums in New York City, the Smithsonian Institution in Washington, D.C., and the Art Institute of Chicago, among many others, continues to be featured in exhibitions and survey texts on African American art.

Further Reading
Lewis, Samella. *Two Sculptors, Two Eras* (1992).
Reynolds, Gary A., and Beryl J. Wright. *Against the Odds: African American Artists and the Harmon Foundation* (1989).

THERESA LEININGER-MILLER

BARTHOLOMEW, Dave (24 Dec. 1920–), bandleader, songwriter, producer, and arranger, was born Dave Louis Bartholomew in Edgard, Louisiana, to Louis Bartholomew, a musician, and Marie Rousell, a housekeeper. Louis played Dixieland tuba in Kid Harrison's and Willie Humphrey's jazz bands. He moved the family to New Orleans while Dave was in high school. Young Dave became interested in performing music after watching his father play. He first took up the tuba but switched to the trumpet because it would allow him a place in the popular marching bands of New Orleans. As a high school student he enjoyed the tutelage of Peter Davis, LOUIS ARMSTRONG's teacher. Bartholomew honed his skills on the New Orleans scene in the late 1930s. He moved in and out of various jazz and brass bands in Louisiana, including Marshall Lawrence's Brass Band, Toots Johnson's Band, and Claiborne Williams's Band. The pianist Fats Pinchon asked Bartholomew to join his group in 1939. Shortly afterward Pinchon left to take another job, allowing Bartholomew to become bandleader. In 1941 he married Pearl King with whom he would have three children.

World War II soon intervened, and Bartholomew was drafted into the army in 1942. The military offered him an opportunity to continue his musical education. He served in the 196 AGF band, where he learned to write and arrange songs. After the war Bartholomew returned to New Orleans with a newfound confidence and a desire for success. He put together a new band and soon became known as the premier bandleader in the city. The Bartholomew group frequented such New Orleans clubs as the Greystone, Club Rocket, the Starlight, the Robin Hood, Al's Starlight, and the Dew Drop. It played a hard-driving rhythm and blues steeped in the Dixieland tradition and its changing lineup featured the cream of Crescent City musicians, including the saxophonists Alvin "Red" Taylor and Lee Allen, and the drummer Earl Ball. Bartholomew played and occasionally sang, although in early 1947, he hired Theard Johnson as a lead vocalist.

Bartholomew's early studio efforts included recordings of "High Society" and "Stardust." He scored a minor regional rhythm and blues hit in 1949 with "Country Boy." Over the next several years Bartholomew continued to issue solo recordings with a rollicking New Orleans R&B flavor, from the social commentary of "The Monkey" (1954) to the risqué romp of "My Ding-a-Ling" (1952). CHUCK BERRY scored a number-one hit twenty years later with a cover of the latter song.

Bartholomew's meeting with Lew Chudd, president of Los Angeles's Imperial Records, shifted his career in a different direction. Chudd hired the bandleader as a producer and a talent scout, empowering him to recruit new talent and using his band to back solo artists. Bartholomew experienced his biggest recruiting success with the pianist ANTOINE "FATS" DOMINO, whom he hired in 1949. He produced and arranged Domino's most famous performances, including "The Fat Man," "Ain't that a Shame," "Blue Monday," "I'm Walkin'," and "Blueberry Hill." The last three cracked *Billboard's* Top Ten in 1956 and 1957. His strong commercial sense failed him only occasionally. He believed, for instance, that the eventual multimillion seller "Blueberry Hill" would fail.

Bartholomew exercised a firm hand in the studio and crafted a clean, tight sound from his players. His self-proclaimed "Big Beat" sound helped Domino to become the most successful black rock 'n' roller of the 1950s. Noting current popular music trends, Bartholomew began sweetening Domino's records with strings and female voices while still preserving his original sound. The Bartholomew-Domino collaboration remained lucrative, turning out hits into the early 1960s when, like many other rhythm and blues artists, Domino suffered from shifts in the music industry as a result of the British Invasion.

Bartholomew and Domino shared songwriting credits on most of the pianist's 1950s and early 1960s output. The producer told interviewers that he and the performer worked out tunes in the studio, but it is likely that Bartholomew took the primary role in composing Domino's songs. Although this work earned him his greatest financial gains and some notoriety, Bartholomew also produced a variety of hit records for other artists. He sat behind the board for many high-charting singles, including Lloyd Price's "Lawdy Miss Clawdy" (1952), Shirley & Lee's "Let the Good Times Roll" (1957), and Smiley Lewis's "I Hear You Knocking" (1952) and "One Night" (1956).

During the 1960s Bartholomew moved away from production work and focused on live performances. He played with his orchestra and toured some with Domino. A shrewd businessman, Bartholomew carefully managed his money, buying commercial and residential real estate in the New Orleans area, and retaining a portion of his huge song catalog. Some music writers credited him with ownership of over 4,000 songs, although in 2007 Broadcast Music Incorporated (BMI) listed his song credits at 425. He established Broadmoor Records in the late 1960s. He also created three music publishing companies.

The last few decades of the twentieth century found Bartholomew in semiretirement, still performing and recording occasionally, but writing music constantly. In 1968 his wife, Pearl, died. Two years later he married Rhea Douse. They had two children and Douse brought three children from a previous marriage. Bartholomew was inducted into the Rock and Roll Hall of Fame in 1991 and the Songwriters Halls of Fame in 1998. The Rhythm and Blues Foundation, composed of musicians and industry executives, honored Bartholomew with its Pioneer Award in 1996. When Hurricane Katrina devastated New Orleans less than ten years later, he relocated to Balch Springs, Texas, a Dallas suburb.

Although he was the key figure behind 1950s New Orleans R&B, Bartholomew's emphasis on production and songwriting, as opposed to making records under his own name, as well as Fats Domino's formidable persona, contributed to his relative anonymity in the public consciousness. His influence on popular music, however, was immense. Hundreds of millions of records were sold bearing his songs and numerous artists covered his tunes. These acts included Elton John, the Rolling Stones, Paul McCartney, Hank Williams Jr., Bob Seger, the Fabulous Thunderbirds, Dave Edmunds, Cheap Trick, Elvis Costello, and Joe Cocker. Bartholomew was not only a critical figure in the history of twentieth-century New Orleans music but his songs and productions also helped to shape the transition from rhythm and blues into rock 'n' roll.

Further Reading

Berry, Jason, Jonathan Foose, and Tad Jones. *Up from the Cradle of Jazz: New Orleans Music since World War II* (1986).
Broven, John. *Rhythm and Blues in New Orleans* (1974).
Hannusch, Jeff. *I Hear You Knockin': The Sound of New Orleans Rhythm and Blues* (1985).

ZACHARY J. LECHNER

BARTZ, Gary Lee (26 Sept. 1940–), musician and composer, was born in Baltimore, Maryland, to Floyd Bartz, a railroad employee and club owner, and Elizabeth E. Bartz, a club owner. Bartz grew up in West Baltimore during an era when the music scene in that city was thriving. The hub of African American entertainment in Baltimore was found on Pennsylvania Avenue, although there were numerous clubs throughout the city owned by African Americans. At the age of six Bartz heard his first CHARLIE PARKER recording at his grandmother's house. Bartz recalled this formative moment: "Not knowing what the music was, what the instrument was or who was playing, I thought it was the most beautiful thing I ever heard, I said right then, I want to do whatever that is" (Ouellette, 31). When Bartz was eleven, he began to play the alto saxophone, influenced to take up the instrument by his love of Parker and LOUIS JORDAN.

Bartz's parents were instrumental in nurturing his musical career. While Bartz was in his early teens, his father would take him around to different clubs in Baltimore. He would tell both local musicians and those who toured through town about his son's musical abilities. At the Comedy Club in Baltimore, Bartz's father touted his son's abilities to saxophonist SONNY STITT, and Stitt invited Bartz to play with him. Immediately after the session, the two developed a friendship.

Bartz graduated high school from Baltimore City College in 1958. After graduation, Bartz moved to New York, at the age of seventeen, to attend the Juilliard School of Music. Skillful at playing music by ear, he wanted to learn to read music. He continued his musical education outside the classroom by frequenting cabarets on the Lower East Side to hear musicians such as Chet Baker, RED GARLAND, Donald Byrd, LEE MORGAN, YUSEF LATEEF, and HANK MOBLEY.

Bartz continued his studies at Juilliard for two years. In 1959 he left school but continued his informal musical training by playing with many seasoned and up-and-coming musicians including CHARLES MINGUS, John Gilmore, Lee Morgan, Donald Byrd, Freddie Hubbard, and PHILLY JOE JONES in New York City. In 1960 Bartz's father bought the North End Lounge, which was located at 1869 N. Gay Street in Baltimore. His parents managed the club, and it became a venue in which Bartz could perfect his playing. Bartz began commuting to Baltimore from New York to work in his father's club on weekends.

In the meantime, Bartz organized a band. In 1961 the Gary Bartz Quartet began to perform regularly at the North End Lounge. In 1962, Bartz married Rosa Lindsay at the Douglass Memorial Church in Baltimore, in a ceremony officiated by the Reverend Marion C. Bascom. From 1962 to 1964 he played with the Charles Mingus Jazz Workshop, where he worked with ERIC DOLPHY and met McCOY TYNER. While still in his early twenties, he took his first professional job with the MAX ROACH–ABBEY LINCOLN group in 1964.

Bartz's father hired ART BLAKEY to play at his club. He had heard that John Gilmore was leaving Blakey's group, and he called his son to come to Baltimore to sit in. Bartz made his recording debut on Blakey's *Soul Finger* album. He established himself as a solid musician and was considered by his peers as one of the best alto players since CANNONBALL ADDERLEY. Bartz became a leading sideman, playing with some of the top musicians in the field. His musical range allowed him to incorporate hard bop, acoustic hard bop, avant-garde, funk, fusion, soul, and R&B into his repertoire.

Bartz worked with Art Blakey's Jazz Messengers from 1965 to 1966. But by 1967 Bartz was recording regularly as a group leader for Prestige and Milestone records. In 1968 Bartz worked with McCoy Tyner and his Expansions band as the alto saxophonist. Working with Tyner was another high point in Bartz's life. Tyner's strong connection with JOHN COLTRANE was important to Bartz and his development as an up-and-coming saxophonist. In 1970 Bartz, along with Ron Carter, Andy Bey, and others created the group Harlem Bush Music. Bartz also formed his own band later that year, called Ntu Troop ("Ntu" is the Bantu word for "unity"). This ensemble fused African folk music, hard bop, vanguard jazz, soul, and funk, synthesizing these musical styles into a dynamic musical form. Keeping busy as a musician, Bartz also continued to tour with the Max Roach band.

In 1970, after hearing promising things about Bartz's musical talent, MILES DAVIS hired Bartz and featured him as a soloist on his *Live Evil* recording. He worked with Davis's fusion group from 1970 to 1971. Throughout his career, Bartz recorded with several music labels, including Milestone, Prestige, Capitol, Atlantic, and Steeple Chase. By the late 1970s Bartz was doing studio work in Los Angeles with the vocalist and producer Phyllis Hyman and the producer, bandleader, and drummer Norman Connors. In 1977 his album *Music Is My Sanctuary* was regarded as one of the best fusion recordings of that era.

In the 1980s Bartz collaborated with the writer, producer, and percussionist Mtume with the release of "Music," a single from his album *Bartz* (1980), which was a spirited blend of musical genres. He collaborated with jazz vocalist Leon Thomas on *Precious Energy* in the late 1980s. From the early 1980s until 1988 Bartz wandered around until he recorded *Reflections on Monk* in 1988. Bartz further developed his musical talents by combining various musical idioms as he became one of the favorite jazz innovators of the 1990s, continuing to make recordings throughout the decade.

Despite Bartz's numerous recordings, he was troubled by the music industry's control over musicians and their work. He noted in an interview that "a creative musician is counterproductive to the record industry. They don't want creative musicians; they want clones" (Nahigian and Enright, 4). Bartz understood that the music industry did not have musicians' best interests in mind, but instead was concerned with promotions and sales of music, and that the only means for musicians to control their livelihood in the industry was to create and own their own labels and retain rights to their music. To gain total control of his musical creativity, "to empower himself," and to "take this great black music back for the musicians," Bartz's created his own label in 1999, called OYO (Own Your Own) Recordings. In 2001 he joined the faculty of the Oberlin Conservatory of Music in Ohio as visiting professor of Jazz Saxophone. In 2005 Bartz released *Live at the Jazz Standard Vol. 1: Soulstice*, *Live at the Jazz Standard Vol. 2*, and *Soprano Stories*, all of which were released through the OYO label. That same year he won a Grammy for Best Jazz Instrumental Album, Individual or Group for his playing on McCoy Tyner's album *Illuminations*. Bartz continues to perform as special guest with the McCoy Tyner Trio nationally and internationally.

Further Reading
Cook, Richard, and Brian Morton. *The Penguin Guide to Jazz Recordings,* 8th ed. (2006).
Nahigian, Alan, and Ed Enright. "Gary Bartz: Take Back the Music," *Down Beat* (Sept. 1998).
Ouellette, Dan. "Saxophone Hand," *Down Beat* (March 2000).
Rogers, John. "Gary Bartz," *All About Jazz* (July 2005).
VIVIAN NJERI FISHER

BASIE, Count (21 Aug. 1904–26 Apr. 1984), jazz pianist, composer, and bandleader, was born William James Basie in Red Bank, New Jersey, the son of African American parents Harvey Lee Basie, an estate groundskeeper, and Lillian Ann Chiles, a laundress. Basie was first exposed to music through his mother's piano playing. He took piano lessons, played the drums, and acted in school skits. An indifferent student, he left school after junior high and began performing. He organized bands with friends and played various jobs in Red Bank, among them working as a movie theater pianist. In his late teens he pursued work in nearby Asbury Park, but he met with little success. Then, in the early 1920s, he moved to Harlem, where he learned from the leading pianists of the New York "stride" style, WILLIE "THE LION" SMITH, JAMES P. JOHNSON, LUCKEY ROBERTS, and especially FATS WALLER, his exact contemporary.

Basie remained undecided between a stage or musical career. Until 1929 he alternately combined playing in Harlem nightclubs and theaters (on piano and organ) and touring with bands for vaudeville and burlesque troupes, which took him as far from New York as New Orleans, Kansas City, and Oklahoma. In Kansas City, during a layover in 1927 or 1928, Basie was stricken with spinal meningitis. After recovering, he worked solo jobs and eventually joined WALTER PAGE's Blue Devils, a major regional dance band. The Blue Devils featured the southwestern boogie-woogie

style of relatively spare blues-based melodies, effortless dance rhythms, and "swinging" syncopation (all hallmarks of the later Basie band style). Basie worked at devising arrangements for the band, assisted by the trombonist-guitarist EDDIE DURHAM. Basie's ability to read and write music improved over the years, but he continued to rely on staff and freelance arrangers. At this time Basie lost interest in the musical stage and dedicated himself to dance music.

Kansas City, a wide-open hub of speakeasies, gambling, and prostitution, offered an active job market for black musicians who specialized in the aggressively swinging southwestern (or Kansas City) blues style. While with the Blue Devils, Basie blended this style with his New York "stride" piano background, and in 1929 he was hired by BENNIE MOTEN, who led the most successful Kansas City band of the time. Basie later called this move both the greatest risk and the most important turning point of his career. The Moten band toured extensively and played to large crowds in Chicago and New York.

About 1930, while working as Moten's second pianist and arranger, Basie married Vivian Wynn, but they soon separated and later divorced. Also in 1929 or 1930, he met a young chorus dancer, Catherine Morgan. She and Basie married in 1942 and had one daughter.

During a touring break in 1934, Basie took some Moten band musicians to Little Rock, Arkansas, for a longer-term job at a single location, after which the Moten band broke up. Back in Kansas City, Basie worked as a church organist and was preparing to join Moten's newest group when the bandleader died unexpectedly in 1935.

Count Basie, at the Aquarium in New York City, c. 1947. (© William P. Gottlieb; www.jazzphotos.com.)

Since 1928 Basie had called himself "Count" in imitation of royal nicknames used by other Harlem musicians, but only on taking over the Moten band did he bill himself by that name. Basie soon had the best players from the Moten unit working for him at the Reno Club in Kansas City. This nucleus included the trombonists Dan Minor and Eddie Durham, who was the band's chief arranger during its early years; the tenor saxophonists Herschel Evans and LESTER YOUNG, a key innovator in jazz history; and the inimitable blues vocalist JIMMY RUSHING.

To many listeners, however, the heart of the band was its superb rhythm section: on drums, JO JONES, a keenly knowledgeable musician who revolutionized both big band and small group drumming; on guitar, CLAUDE WILLIAMS, who was replaced in 1937 by Freddie Green (the mainstay of the Basie group for five decades); and on bass, Walter Page, former leader of the Blue Devils. These three men, in concord with Basie's own idiomatic piano work, synchronized their playing with unmatched skill, lightening and shading the driving, four-to-a-bar Kansas City beat, and infusing the band's ensemble play with supple, flowing, danceable rhythms.

In 1935 the white writer, critic, and record producer John Hammond heard a Basie radio broadcast and made arrangements to give the band national exposure. Expanding the group to thirteen men, Basie took his musicians to Chicago, where six of them made their first, classic recordings under the pseudonym (for contractual reasons) Jones-Smith, Inc. In New York City the band played at the Roseland Ballroom and recorded for Decca Records, with which the inexperienced Basie signed a demanding, long-term contract that paid no royalties. Included in the larger band's initial recordings was Basie's signature tune, "One O'Clock Jump," which featured the leader's slyly spare opening piano solo and the repeated, haunting melody played by the band. By this time BUCK CLAYTON's often muted trumpet solos had become another of the band's features, while Ed Lewis on trumpet, Earle Warren on alto saxophone, and Jack Washington on baritone saxophone anchored those instrumental sections. The band later formed an association with Columbia Records, which continued into the 1940s.

The Basie orchestra had come to New York City at the height of the big band era, but the group's relaxed, unembellished, freely swinging style reportedly puzzled those mostly white East Coast listeners who were enthusiasts of the strictly disciplined, thoroughly professional Benny Goodman orchestra. Hammond worked with Basie to tighten the band's section work and solo presentations. Such New York musicians as the trombonists DICKY WELLS and BENNY MORTON and the trumpeter Harry Edison were hired. BILLIE HOLIDAY, who already had forged her own deeply personal jazz singing style, became the band's first woman vocalist, to be replaced a year later by HELEN HUMES. They each joined Jimmy Rushing, who solid-ified his position as the leading male blues singer of the big band era. The changes paid off in the late 1930s with successful stints at New York's Famous Door and Savoy Ballroom ("the home of happy feet"), followed by engagements in Chicago and San Francisco.

Basie later recalled that by 1940 "what that name [Count Basie] stood for now was me and the band as the same thing." The band undertook almost constant tours throughout the country and continued its prolific recording work. Among bandleaders Basie was matched only by DUKE ELLINGTON as a careful, tenacious master of a group of disparate individual artists. Both men were ambitious leaders who defined the basic sounds of their groups, and each of them was ready to step back and allow great freedom to their soloists. But although Ellington was a composer of major stature, Basie was the more successful in integrating his band into the lucrative, white-dominated entertainment industry of the 1940s through the 1970s.

With the start of World War II, Basie, like many other bandleaders, had to cope with myriad difficulties; some of these included restrictions on travel, the musicians' union's two-year recording ban, and above all the military draft's continual disruption of the band's roster. Basie again showed great skill in choosing talented replacements, at different times bringing in the trombonist J. J. JOHNSON, the trumpeter Joe Newman, the tenor saxophonists Lucky Thompson, Paul Gonsalves, and ILLINOIS JACQUET, and the drummer SHADOW WILSON, among others. All through the 1940s the orchestra worked at choice locations such as New York's Ritz-Carlton and Philadelphia's Academy of Music, while it also maintained nearly continuous nationwide touring. After the recording ban was lifted at the end of 1943, the band resumed making records until the close of the decade. In addition, the Basie group was featured in several Hollywood films—*Reveille with Beverly, Crazy House,* and *Top Man* (all 1943)—and made frequent appearances on Kate Smith's national radio show.

Following the war Basie continued to revise personnel and shuffle arrangers; he allowed younger players like WARDELL GRAY on tenor saxophone and CLARK TERRY on trumpet to introduce a few new bebop ideas. But by the late 1940s the band had become relatively unadventurous. That development coincided with waning public interest in swing-era orchestras, and in 1950 Basie was forced to disband.

Basie remained active for more than a year with a sextet that showcased Gray, Terry, and the clarinetist Buddy DeFranco. In 1952, at the urging of singer BILLY ECKSTINE, he assembled a new orchestra, which eventually would include Marshall Royal as first alto saxophonist and rehearsal director; the highly original trumpeter THAD JONES; the tenor saxophonists Frank Foster, Frank Wess, Paul Quinichette, and EDDIE "LOCKJAW" DAVIS; Basie's longtime rhythm colleague Freddie Green; the drummer Gus Johnson, soon replaced by Sonny Payne; and the blues and ballad singing of JOE WILLIAMS. Birdland, then the most thriving club for jazz in New York, served as an effective home base, though the band often played the Blue Note in Chicago and the Crescendo in Los Angeles as well.

This edition of the Basie orchestra placed new emphasis on arrangers and precisely played ensembles. The arrangers Neal Hefti, ERNIE WILKINS, QUINCY JONES, and "the two Franks" (Foster and Wess) played key roles in making the band sound more appealing to a wider audience. The Basie orchestra now served a varied range of popular tastes, recording with celebrity singers such as Frank Sinatra and Tony Bennett, and featuring everything from Wild Bill Davis's crowd-pleasing arrangement of "April in Paris," to popular television theme songs, to jazz versions of rhythm and blues hits. In 1963 the Basie orchestra was featured in four best-selling albums, including two instrumental records arranged by Quincy Jones. Such popularity had not been attained by any big band since World War II, and, with rock music coming to dominate the record industry, it was a feat not to be duplicated.

Basie and his musicians had made the first of thirty successful European tours in 1954, and in 1963 they made the first of eight trips across the Pacific Ocean. Frequent national tours continued, usually reaching the West Coast twice each year. By 1961, when it performed at one of President John F. Kennedy's inaugural celebrations, the band had become part of America's official culture. Further appearances at the White House culminated in a reception for Basie in 1981, which celebrated a Kennedy Center honor for his contributions to the performing arts. In 1982 he was given a tribute, sponsored by the Black Music Association, at New York's Radio City Music Hall.

Six years earlier, in 1976, Basie had suffered a heart attack that kept him away from the band for half a year. After returning, he continued the band's touring on a reduced schedule, while remaining active at work in the recording studios. But various illnesses further weakened him, and a year after his wife's death, he died in Hollywood, Florida.

Basie's unique ability to inspire a large jazz band with the rhythmic drive and ease of 1930s Kansas City small combos, to select and lead an ever-changing roster of talented and complementary musicians, to adapt to rapidly evolving and diverse musical tastes while maintaining artistic integrity, to integrate his band into the mainstream of American entertainment, and to give the band matchless worldwide exposure all show him to have been one of the major figures in twentieth-century American music.

Further Reading
Basie's memorabilia and papers are still in private hands, although they have been pledged to the Hampton University Library, Hampton, Virginia.

Basie, Count, with Albert L. Murray. *Good Morning Blues* (1985).
Dance, Stanley. *The World of Count Basie* (1980).
Schuller, Gunther. *The Swing Era* (1989).
Sheridan, Chris. *Count Basie: A Bio-Discography* (1986).
Obituary: *New York Times*, 27 Apr. 1984.

BURTON W. PERETTI

BASKETT, James F. (16 Feb. 1904–9 July 1948), actor, was born in Indianapolis, Indiana, the only son of Elizabeth Baskett, a homemaker, and John Baskett, a barber. He was among the first students to attend Arsenal Technical High School in Indianapolis, where he studied pharmacology. A lack of funds, though, forced him to forsake his plans to make that his career.

On a visit to Chicago as a teen, however, he was asked to fill in for a sick performer in a show and developed an interest in acting. On the stage, Baskett toured as singer, actor, and comic under the name Jimmie (sometimes Jimmy) Baskette for most of the top African American companies of the period. He performed with Henry Drake and Ethel Walker's touring variety troupe in *Go Get 'Em* (1926) and *Look Who's Here* (1927) and with the prolific Salem Tutt Whitney and J. Homer Tutt's Smart Set company in *Deep Harlem* (1929). He moved to New York where he performed with the Lafayette Players. He also appeared in *Hot Chocolates* (1929), with music by FATS WALLER, and in *Lew Leslie's Blackbirds of 1930*, for which EUBIE BLAKE composed the music. He performed in BILL "BOJANGLES" ROBINSON's revue, *Hot from Harlem* (1932), which opened at the prestigious Palace Theatre and toured the vaudeville circuit through 1934 after being renamed *Goin' to Town* in its second year. Baskett also appeared in several low-budget independent films, often called "race films," geared for African American audiences, including *Harlem Is Heaven* (1932), *Gone Harlem* (1939), and *Comes Midnight* (1940). He also served as a straight man for comedians at the Apollo Theater and traveled to Los Angeles in that capacity with DEWEY "PIGMEAT" MARKHAM, where they performed with great success in the early 1940s. Baskett relocated to Los Angles with his wife, Margaret, and there he met Freeman Gosden of the *Amos 'n' Andy* show and subsequently joined the cast of radio's immensely popular, long-running comedy in 1943. He played the fast-talking lawyer Gabby Gibson, whose popularity came to rival that of the main characters', a role he continued until his death in 1948.

In 1945, in answer to an ad for voice actors, Baskett auditioned for the role of a talking butterfly in *Song of the South*, Walt Disney's planned adaptation of Joel Chandler Harris's *Uncle Remus* stories. Disney was so impressed with Baskett's talents that he cast him, ahead of many better-known black actors, in the lead role of Uncle Remus, the performance for which he is best known. In the 1946 film, set not long after the Civil War, the elderly Uncle Remus lives on a plantation and helps the owner's young son adjust to rural life and to the extended absence of his father by telling him exemplary tales of the adventures of Brer Rabbit, a trickster character, as he evades the attempts of Brer Fox and Brer Bear to catch and eat him. The film was Disney's first live-action feature, although Uncle Remus's stories were animated in Disney's usual style. In addition to playing Uncle Remus, Baskett also provided the voice for Brer Fox, who, like his radio character, was a fast talker. His delivery was so rapid, in fact, that even Disney's best animators had a difficult time matching the character's mouth movements to Baskett's dialogue. When Johnny Lee, who voiced Brer Rabbit, left on a USO tour, Baskett even provided some of that character's dialogue in one scene.

For his performance, the Board of Governors of the Academy of Motion Picture Arts and Sciences presented him with a Special Award statuette inscribed "For his able and heartwarming characterization of Uncle Remus, friend and storyteller to the children of the world." The board had serious reservations about giving him the award, however, because of the stereotypical nature of the role, until the actor-humanitarian Jean Hersholt threatened to make a scene at the award ceremony if Baskett did not receive the award. He thus became the first African American male to be honored by the academy. In the film he also sang "Zip-A-Dee-Doo-Dah," which won the Oscar for Best Song. The film was commercially successful in its original release and in several subsequent rereleases. At the time of its release, some black newspapers praised it for potentially furthering race relations, but over the years it drew the criticism of various African American groups over the stereotypical depiction of its black characters. As a result, Buena Vista, Disney's distribution company, announced in 1970 that it was withdrawing the film for good. In 1972, however, it was rereleased and grossed twice as much at the box office as it did in its initial release. It earned even more in a 1986 release, but this was its last public screening in the United States, and Disney has not issued it in video format.

After his success in *Song of the South*, Baskett continued to work on the *Amos 'n' Andy* show, despite serious health problems which sometimes interfered with the live broadcasts. In 1947 the producer Jean Dalrymple began planning a revival of Marc Connelly's Pulitzer Prize–winning play, *The Green Pastures*, with James Baskett to star as De Lawd. Baskett's declining health led to repeated postponements of the project, however, and his 1948 death in Hollywood from heart disease ultimately caused it to be canceled entirely.

Further Reading

Cohen, Karl F. *Forbidden Animation: Censored Cartoons and Blacklisted Animators in America* (1997).
Wiley, Mason, and Damien Bona. *Inside Oscar: The Unofficial History of the Academy Awards* (1996).

Obituary: *New York Times*, 14 July 1948.

RICHARD J. LESKOSKY

BASQUIAT, Jean-Michel (22 Dec. 1960–12 Aug. 1988), painter, was born in Brooklyn, New York, the son of Gerard Basquiat, an accountant originally from Haiti, and Matilde Andradas, of Puerto Rican descent. A precocious draftsman from childhood, Basquiat received little formal artistic training. The last school he attended was the experimental City-as-School program in Manhattan, where he befriended his fellow artist Al Diaz.

Before quitting school altogether in 1978, Basquiat created SAMO (meaning "same old shit"), which was variously a pseudo-religion, a fictional logo, a nom de plume, and a persona. Basquiat and Diaz spray-painted original aphorisms with a copyright symbol next to the word SAMO on walls and in alleys in lower Manhattan. Their mock epigrams and mottoes included "SAMO as an end to mindwash religion, nowhere politics, and bogus philosophy," "SAMO saves idiots," and "plush safe he think, SAMO." Whereas other graffiti artists such as Fab 5 Freddy, Futura 2000, and Rammellzee painted multicolored and elaborately designed "tags" on subway cars and alleyways, Diaz and Basquiat focused on their concepts and text-based work rather than aesthetics. In the 11 December 1978 issue of the *Village Voice*, Basquiat and Diaz identified themselves as SAMO; soon thereafter, they parted ways.

Aside from his SAMO work, Basquiat drew and painted his own art on any available surface he could find, including refrigerator doors; he also made postcards and t-shirts, which he sold on the street. Using oil and acrylic paints, oil paint sticks, and collage materials, he blended roughly drawn visual elements and text. When asked about his subject matter, Basquiat re-

Jean-Michel Basquiat painted *Native Carrying Some Guns, Bibles, Amorites on Safari* in 1982. Six square feet, the painting is done in acrylic, oil, and oil paint-stick on canvas with exposed wood supports. (The Hermes Trust, Isle of Man.)

sponded that he painted "royalty, heroism, and the streets." Black male figures, skulls, crowns, and hobo symbols proliferated in his paintings. He sometimes included references to his personal heroes, such as the musician CHARLIE PARKER and the boxer JOE LOUIS, as well as art-historical references such as Leonardo da Vinci's sketchbooks. Basquiat used words not as expanded captions but as crucial components in the composition and meaning of the work, sometimes repeating words or crossing them out, as in *Horn Players* (1983, Eli and Edythe L. Broad Collection, Los Angeles). In this painting, the artist painted Charlie Parker's name and the word "ornithology" (referring to the musician's nickname "the Bird") several times on the canvas, overlaid with more paint and next to his painted images of the musician. Basquiat once said, "I cross out words so that you will see them more; the fact that they are obscured makes you want to read them."

In 1980 Basquiat painted a large mural for his first group exhibition, the Times Square Show. Organized by Colab (Collaborative Projects Incorporated), the exhibition featured several artists early in their careers, including Jenny Holzer, Kenny Scharf, and Kiki Smith. The following year Basquiat took part in numerous exhibitions in New York, such as New York/New Wave at P.S.1, along with the artists Robert Mapplethorpe and Andy Warhol, and Beyond Words: Graffiti Based-Rooted-Inspired Works at the Mudd Club. The Galleria d'Arte Emilio Mazzoli in Modena, Italy, held Basquiat's first one-man exhibition in the spring of 1981.

In 1980 the New York art dealer Annina Nosei began selling Basquiat's work and offered him her gallery basement to use as his studio. Despite this unusual arrangement (Nosei was criticized for having Basquiat "on exhibit"), she exposed Basquiat's art to several important collectors and gave him his first U.S. one-man exhibition in 1982. Although Basquiat changed dealers often in his short career, he maintained steady relationships with the Los Angeles dealer Larry Gagosian and Bruno Bischofberger, who was based in Switzerland and was the artist's international representative.

Basquiat was the youngest artist in the prestigious Documenta 7 exhibition in Kassel, Germany (1982), and in the 1983 Biennial Exhibition at the Whitney Museum of American Art. The Museum of Modern Art included him in their International Survey of Recent Painting and Sculpture at MOMA (1983).

He continued to gain recognition when, in 1983, he became a close friend of Andy Warhol, who was also represented by Bischofberger. At the suggestion of the dealer, the two artists collaborated on several paintings in 1985. Warhol painted or silk-screened corporate logos such as those of GE and Arm & Hammer along with other images including Felix the Cat. Basquiat painted over and around Warhol's work with his repertoire of motifs and words. Their paintings, exhibited in New York at the Tony Shafrazi Gallery that same year, received mixed reviews. One *New York Times* critic wrote that Basquiat was an art

world mascot and that Warhol used him to regain his own popularity. Warhol and Basquiat ended their friendship following the exhibition.

An article on Basquiat written by Cathleen McGuigan for the *New York Times Magazine* (10 Feb. 1985) exposed him to a popular audience but also posed questions about the consequences of an inflated art market on such a young career. Some critics claimed that Basquiat became more interested in making art that would satisfy his collectors than in creating innovative work. But many of his last works featured new developments, such as very dense accumulations of words and images, as in *Untitled (Stretch)* (1985, estate of the artist), or starkly powerful compositions, as exemplified by *Riding with Death* (1988, private collection), which shows a dark human skeleton riding a white skeleton of a horse.

Basquiat died of a drug overdose in New York at the age of twenty-seven. His death at such an early age commanded reflection in the art world, an environment where artistic ideals had been replaced by greed and the pursuit of fame due to a period of auspicious wealth and soaring art prices. Basquiat, who never hid his career aspirations, was hailed as the first African American art star. Bearing the burden of this title, he was sometimes viewed as an exotic novelty or as a traitor to his race in the predominantly white art world. But Basquiat refused to be labeled. He said, "I don't know if my being black has anything to do with my success. I don't think I should be compared to black artists but all artists."

Although not an organized movement, Basquiat and other painters grouped as "neo-expressionists"— including Julian Schnabel, Georg Baselitz, and Susan Rothenberg—returned a sense of bravura and improvisation to painting that harked back to the abstract expressionists. Influenced by pop art, Basquiat's wordplay and use of signs and symbols aligned him with other postmodern artists, particularly those like Robert Longo who combined specific and sometimes edited images inspired by the mass media to convey meaning. Basquiat also maintained a very personal vision in his work, painting his heroes (boxers and jazz musicians), his artistic influences (da Vinci and Warhol), and episodes from his own life (drug use and racism) in his idiosyncratic style. His poetic means of combining text with imagery and social issues with personal experiences resonates in the work of several contemporary artists such as GLEN LIGON and LORNA SIMPSON.

Further Reading
Basquiat, Jean-Michel, with Bruno Bischofberger. *Jean-Michel Basquiat* (1999).
Hoban, Phoebe. *Basquiat: A Quick Killing in Art* (1998).
Marshall, Richard, ed. *Jean-Michel Basquiat* (1992).
Tate, Greg. "Nobody Loves a Genius Child." *Village Voice*, 14 Nov. 1988: 31–35.
Wines, Michael. "Jean-Michel Basquiat: Hazards of Sudden Success and Fame." *New York Times*, 27 Aug. 1988.

N. ELIZABETH SCHLATTER

BASS, Charlotta (Oct. 1880–Apr. 1969), journalist, activist, and vice presidential candidate, was born Charlotta Amanda Spears in Sumter, South Carolina, the sixth of eleven children of Hiram Spears and Kate (maiden name unknown). The details of her childhood are unknown, but sometime before her twentieth birthday she went to live with her brother in Providence, Rhode Island, and began work at the *Providence Watchman*, selling ads and helping in the office. After ten years, suffering from exhaustion, she went for a rest to California on the advice of her doctor.

At the beginning of what was to have been a two-year stay, Spears went against her doctor's orders and took a job at the *Eagle*, a newspaper with a largely black readership. Her job was to sell advertising and subscriptions. However, when the newspaper's editor, John Neimore, became ill, he began to turn the operations of the *Eagle* over to Spears. When he died, the paper's new owner put Spears in charge, in May 1912. Spears continued to publish news of black society but increasingly dealt with social and political issues in the paper she renamed the *California Eagle*. Her commitment to righting the wrongs of society quickly became apparent.

In 1912 Joseph Bass joined the paper as an editor. Bass had been one of the founders of the *Topeka Plain Dealer,* and he shared Spears's concerns about injustice and racial discrimination. The two were soon married and ran the paper together for the next two decades. Among the targets of their passionate attacks was D. W. Griffith's film *The Birth of a Nation,* which perpetuated the worst kind of racial stereotyping in order to glorify the Ku Klux Klan. (The Klan tried to

Charlotta Bass, as a candidate for vice president on the Progressive Party ticket, 1952. (Los Angeles Public Library.)

sue the paper for libel in 1925, but the suit was unsuccessful.) The Basses powerfully championed the black soldiers of the Twenty-fourth Infantry who were unjustly sentenced in a 1917 race riot that took place in Houston, Texas. They also filled their newspaper with support for the SCOTTSBORO BOYS, nine young men who were framed and convicted of rape in Scottsboro, Alabama, in 1931. The Basses also strongly endorsed labor leader A. PHILIP RANDOLPH in his battle against racial discrimination in railroad employment.

Away from the newspaper, Bass helped found the Industrial Business Council, which fought discrimination in employment practices and encouraged entrepreneurship among black people. In an effort to defeat housing covenants in all-white neighborhoods, she formed the Home Protective Association. In 1919 she attended the Pan-African Congress in Paris, organized by W. E. B. DU BOIS, and during the 1920s was co-president of the Los Angeles chapter of MARCUS GARVEY's Universal Negro Improvement Association.

After Joseph Bass died in 1934, Charlotta Bass continued to run the *California Eagle* on her own. She also became more active in local and national politics. In 1940 the Republican Party chose her as western regional director for Wendell Willkie's presidential campaign. Three years later she became the first African American member of the Los Angeles County Superior Court grand jury. In 1945 Bass ran for the L.A. city council as a "people's candidate" in a landmark election for black Angelenos. Although she lost the race, her progressive platform and powerful campaigning united diverse black organizations throughout the city's Seventh District. Her campaign also laid the groundwork for later, more successful, African American candidates, notably the future L.A. city councilman and mayor TOM BRADLEY.

The immediate postwar years in the United States were marked by a growing demand for African American civil rights, which was met by an upsurge in Klan activity and other forms of racial violence. In her newspaper and in her political activities, Bass took an unyielding stand against these horrors. When blacklisting hit Hollywood, she spoke out in favor of the "Hollywood Ten," a group of screenwriters who had refused to testify before the House Un-American Activities Committee (HUAC) about alleged Communist infiltration of the film industry. She herself was called before the California equivalent of HUAC, the Tenney Committee, which she denounced as "fascist."

Believing that neither of the major parties was committed to civil rights, Bass left the Republican Party in the late 1940s to become one of the founders of the Progressive Party. Nearing the age of seventy, she campaigned heavily for the party's presidential candidate, Henry Wallace, in the 1948 election. Leaving the *California Eagle* in the early 1950s, she traveled to wherever she felt her voice might make a difference for the causes that she believed in. She went to Prague, Czechoslovakia, to support the Stockholm Appeal to ban the bomb at the peace committee of the World Congress. Like other members of the American left at the time, notably PAUL ROBESON, she traveled to the Soviet Union and commented on its apparent lack of racial discrimination.

In 1950, she ran for California's Fourteenth Congressional District, but lost again. Bass nonetheless believed that her campaign had been successful in raising the issues she felt were important. This realization led her to accept the Progressive Party's nomination for vice president of the United States in 1952, making her the first black woman to run for national office. Bass was a consistent thorn in the side of her Republican opponent, Senator Richard Nixon, attacking him fiercely throughout the campaign. Her platform called for civil rights, women's rights, an end to the Korean War, and peace with the Soviet Union. By the early 1950s, however, the Progressive Party was perceived by many Americans to be too closely linked to the Communist Party. Some of those links were real; others the result of McCarthyite hysteria. Either way, Bass and her running mate fared poorly, even among African Americans in those states that allowed blacks to vote. Nationally, the Progressive Party won only 0.2 percent of the vote.

In 1960 Charlotta Bass wrote an autobiography entitled "Forty Years: Memoirs from the Pages of a Newspaper." During her years of retirement, she maintained a library in her garage for the young people in her neighborhood. It was a continuation of her long fight to give all people opportunities and education. She died in Los Angeles.

With remarkable dedication, Charlotta Bass used her role as editor of the oldest black-run newspaper on the West Coast to crusade against injustice and inequality. She may never have won an election, but, as she said in her 1952 campaign, "Win or lose, we win by raising the issues."

Further Reading
Bass's unpublished manuscript "Forty Years: Memoirs from the Pages of a Newspaper" is available at the Southern California Library for Social Studies and Research in Los Angeles and the Schomburg Center for Research in Black Culture of the New York Public Library.
Gill, Gerald R. " 'Win or Lose—We Win': The 1952 Vice Presidential Campaign of Charlotta A. Bass," in *The Afro-American Woman: Struggles and Images* (1981).
Streitmatter, Rodger. *Raising Her Voice: African American Women Journalists Who Changed History* (1994).
Obituary: *Los Angeles Sentinel,* 17 Apr. 1969.
KATHLEEN THOMPSON

BASS, George Houston (23 Apr. 1938–19 Sept. 1990), playwright, academic, director, and producer, was born in Murfreesboro, Tennessee, near Nashville. One of nine children Bass grew up in a

segregated area of the capital, the son of Clarence Bass, a Baptist minister, and Mabel Dixon Bass, a retired schoolteacher and health-care worker. The atmosphere of his childhood home was closely knit and disciplined; life revolved around education and religion. Bass earned his bachelor's degree in Mathematics with honors from Fisk University in 1959. While a senior, he met the Harlem Renaissance writer ARNA BONTEMPS, then a Fisk librarian, who brokered the student's formative literary partnership with LANGSTON HUGHES. Bass then attended Columbia University's Graduate School of Business (1959–1960) to study finance, but quit because of what he felt was endemic racism in the academic and social milieu. He received an MA from New York University's Film School (1964) and attended Yale School of Drama (1966–1968) as a recipient of the John Golden Playwriting Fellowship.

The literary partnership between Hughes and Bass began in 1959 when Hughes visited Tennessee on a lecture tour. In exchange for financial support for studies at Columbia, Bass conducted research and performed various administrative tasks while living in the writer's Harlem brownstone. For five years Hughes's influence granted his protégé ample opportunity to mingle with the luminaries of the New York artistic and social scene, including his lifelong friend Carl Van Vechten, the musicians Noble Sissle and Eubie Blake, as well as the Nigerian dissident Wole Soyinka. Bass also traveled extensively with his mentor and attended theater rehearsals for Hughes's play *Black Nativity* (1961), a fusion of Christian scripture, poetry, and song. As a dramatist Hughes had already garnered praise for such pieces as *Mulatto* (1935), a successful Broadway production. Concerned about the prospective difficulties that a career playwright would face, Hughes urged Bass to consider film school instead. Although he was unable to secure steady employment as a film studies graduate, Bass found work as a freelance writer and director. In 1964 he received the Rosenthal Award from the American Society of Cinematologists for the most creative script written by a young American.

Aside from Hughes, Bass also worked with DAISY BATES, author of the memoir *The Long Shadow of Little Rock* (1962), and VINNETTE CARROLL, Broadway's first black woman director. When Hughes died in 1967 Bass nurtured the writer's legacy as literary executor of the estate. That same year *The Game*, a film adaptation of one of Bass's plays, won the Plaque of the Lion of St. Mark at the Venice Film Festival. From 1964 until 1970 Bass was artistic director of the Jacob Riis Amphitheatre in New York. From 1968 to 1969 he served as associate producer and story editor of *On Being Black*, a set of nationally broadcast teleplays for WGBH-TV in Boston. Bass also spent time as artistic director of the Black Arts Theater in New Haven, Connecticut.

In 1969 Bass was hired as a lecturer at Brown University to teach classes in English and theater. He eventually secured full tenure as a professor of theater arts and African American studies in 1985. There he met Ramona Wilkins, a theater student originally from New York, whom he married in 1974. They had three children: Kwame, Khari, and Ayana.

Bass is perhaps most renowned as the originator and artistic director of the Rites and Reason Theater (originally the Black Theater, 1970), a research organ of the Africana Studies Department at Brown. From 1973 onward he collaborated with his colleague, the historian Rhett S. Jones, to conceive of the research-to-performance method, an interdisciplinary approach to interpreting black culture through the dual prisms of dramatic theory and innovative artistic practice. Beginning in 1988 he teamed with Karen Allen Baxter, a respected producer and the theater's present managing director, to plan projects for both Rites and Reason and other black companies nationwide. As a scholar Bass was concerned with the revivification of folk history, mythology, and communal rituals through art. He produced and directed more than fifty of his and other playwrights' works while at Brown, the first of which was his historical play *Black Masque* (1971). Other notable works from his oeuvre include *Malacoff Blue* (1976), *De Dey of No Mo'* (1980), and *Brer Rabbit Whole* (1984). Brown's George Houston Bass Performing Arts Space, christened at Commencement in 1991, was named in honor of the founder of New England's oldest continually operating black theater.

The diversity of African American vernacular traditions and the centrality of religion in everyday life emerged as key themes in Bass's work. He demonstrated his appreciation for folklore by editing, along with the critic HENRY LOUIS GATES JR., *Mule Bone: A Comedy of Negro Life* (originally written in 1931). Hughes and his contemporary ZORA NEALE HURSTON had composed this controversial play together, but they became embroiled in a major feud before the work could reach fruition. This work was published in full and subsequently produced for the first time in only in 1991, with Bass and Gates serving as consultants. Apart from resurrecting *Mule Bone*, analyzing and anthologizing Hughes's poems and plays, and searching for a suitable literary biographer for Hughes (Bass ultimately chose Arnold Rampersad), Bass maintained his lifelong commitment to Hughes by co-founding the Langston Hughes Society in 1981 and editing its official publication, *The Langston Hughes Review*.

Bass's vision of a modern black theater focused upon the tension between community values and individual choices. It also integrated traditional forms with more contemporary, experimental approaches and themes. Formal recognition for his artistic achievements included a John Hay Whitney Fellowship (1963), a Harlem Cultural Council Grant (1969), a Howard Foundation Fellowship (1977), a Fulbright Research Scholarship (1977), and a Ford Foundation Travel and Study Grant (1978). In 1967 Yale School of Drama honored its respected alumnus by staging George Bass Day, a festival of his short works. Bass died of a heart attack at Miriam Hospital in Providence, Rhode Island.

Further Reading
Griffin, Sharon. "Artist in Residence—One Writer's Journey of Affirmation: Poet Langston Hughes Helped Brown's George Bass Uncover His Creative Contours," *Providence Journal*, 28 June 1987.
Peterson, Bernard L., Jr. *Contemporary Black American Playwrights and Their Plays: A Biographical Directory and Dramatic Index* (1988).
Obituary: *New York Times*, 21 Sept. 1990.

NANCY KANG

BASSETT, Angela (16 Aug. 1958–), actress, was born Angela Evelyn Bassett in the Bronx, New York, to Betty Bassett, a social worker, and a father whose name and occupation are unknown. Soon after Angela's birth her parents divorced, and she moved with her mother and sister to St. Petersburg, Florida. Bassett first thought of a career in acting after a 1974 school trip to Washington, D.C., where she saw JAMES EARL JONES perform in *Of Mice and Men* at the Kennedy Center.

After graduating from Boca Ciega High School in St. Petersburg in 1976, Bassett won a scholarship to

Angela Bassett, accepting her award for Outstanding Supporting Actress in a Motion Picture for *The Score*, at the 33rd Annual NAACP Image Awards Ceremony at the Universal Amphitheatre in Los Angeles, 23 February 2002. (AP Images.)

study at Yale University. She earned her BA in African American Studies in 1980 and a master of fine arts from the Yale School of Drama in 1983. After Yale, Bassett did a stint as a photo researcher for *U.S. News and World Report* while also pursuing theater roles in New York and performing at the Yale Repertory Theatre. Under the mentorship of the director Lloyd Richards, Bassett acted in the playwright AUGUST WILSON's *Ma Rainey's Black Bottom* and *Joe Turner's Come and Gone* in 1985 and 1988 respectively. She soon moved to television roles, first as a prostitute in *Doubletake* (1985) and next as a news reporter on FX (1986).

In 1991 Bassett caught Hollywood's attention as Cuba Gooding Jr.'s mother in JOHN SINGLETON's *Boyz in the Hood*. She also had a minor role in John Sayles's *Passion Fish* (1992). She followed by playing BETTY SHABAZZ opposite DENZEL WASHINGTON in *MALCOLM X* (1992), but her career took off with her role as TINA TURNER in *What's Love Got to Do with It?* (1993). Bassett earned critical praise for her physical transformation to portray the famously sculpted singer. The performance earned Bassett a Golden Globe for Best Actress—the first African American to win the award—as well as an Oscar nomination for best actress.

After her pivotal role as Turner, Bassett reportedly never had to audition for a film. In 1994 the author TERRY MCMILLAN handpicked her to star in both *Waiting to Exhale* (1995) and *How Stella Got Her Groove Back* (1998). Critics singled out Bassett for her performances in both films, but it was in *Stella* that she attacked both race and gender stereotypes through her portrayal of a forty-year-old divorced executive and mother who falls in love with a twenty-year-old Jamaican. In 2001 the independent film producer Lee Daniels offered her the opportunity to star in his *Monster's Ball*, which became critically acclaimed, but Bassett turned it down. A self-described private person, she publicly voiced her refusal to play Daniels's Leticia Musgrove, telling *Newsweek* magazine that she "wasn't going to be a prostitute on film" (Samuels, 54), and that she did not want to play to stereotypes about black women and sexuality. HALLE BERRY took the role, for which she won an Academy Award in 2001.

In 1997 Bassett married Courtney B. Vance, an actor she had met while studying at Yale. Having battled infertility for years, Bassett and Vance used a surrogate to have two children in January 2006.

Bassett mixed her traditional acting roles with more unique projects, such as *Vampire in Brooklyn* (1995) and *Strange Days* (1995), in the latter playing one of the few black female science fiction characters in film. In 2002 she reunited with Sayles (and returned to her native Florida) to star in his ensemble film *Sunshine State*. Staying true to her passions, Bassett continued her notable portrayals of powerful and courageous black women. She played ROSA PARKS in a television movie directed by JULIE DASH, *The Rosa Parks Story* (2002), for which Bassett earned the

NAACP Image Award and was nominated for an Emmy for outstanding lead actress. In 2007 Bassett was cast to costar with Don Cheadle in *Toussaint*, a biographical film about the Haitian revolutionary Toussaint L'Ouverture. Devoted to children's assistance and charities, Bassett served as an active ambassador of UNICEF; she was appointed in 2003 along with her husband. She also supported the Royal Theater Boys and Girls Club in St. Petersburg.

Further Reading

Bassett, Angela, and Courtney B. Vance. *Friends: A Love Story* (2007).
Collier, Aldore. "Angela Bassett Talks About Love, Marriage, the Twins and the Joys of Motherhood," *Ebony* (May 2006).
Samuels, Allison. "Angela's Fire," *Newsweek* (July 2002).

LINDA CHAVERS

BATEMAN, Mildred Mitchell. *See* Mitchell-Bateman, Mildred.

BATES, Daisy (11 Nov. 1914–4 Nov. 1999), journalist and civil rights activist, was born Daisy Lee Gatson in Huttig, Arkansas, to parents she would never know. She may also have had four brothers. Bates learned as a child that three white men had attempted to rape her mother, who died while resisting them. Realizing that a black man in Arkansas could not successfully prosecute whites for murder, and fearing reprisals if he attempted to do so, Daisy's father left town shortly afterward, leaving his infant daughter with his friends Orlie and Susie Smith, who adopted her. Daisy enjoyed the close love and attention that came from being an only child, but the Smiths could not protect her from the most pernicious manifestations of white supremacy in Jim Crow Arkansas: verbal and physical abuse from whites, substandard education, and minimal economic opportunities. Her childhood was also scarred by the presence in town of one of her mother's murderers, though Daisy, the image of her mother, exacted a kind of revenge by staring at and haunting the man referred to in her memoirs as the "drunken pig."

At the age of fifteen she met the twenty-eight-year-old Lucius Christopher "L. C." Bates, a journalist then working as an insurance agent. The couple courted for several years and married in 1942, moving to Little Rock, Arkansas, to establish the *Arkansas State Press*, a weekly newspaper for the black community. They had no children.

During World War II, the *State Press* exemplified the increasing determination of southern blacks to challenge their second-class citizenship. In 1942, for instance, its reporting of a white policeman's cold-blooded murder of a black soldier on the streets of Little Rock prompted white advertisers to withdraw their financial support of the paper in protest. The Bateses persisted in exposing police brutality, however, and by the end of the war the *State Press*'s campaigns

Daisy Bates, at her home in Little Rock, Arkansas, 11 September 1997. A portrait of her late husband L. C. Bates hangs on the wall behind her. (AP Images.)

had persuaded the Little Rock authorities to hire black policemen to patrol African American neighborhoods. The paper's crusading reputation greatly increased its circulation among blacks throughout Arkansas but also earned the Bateses the enmity of conservative whites. In 1946, for example, Daisy and L. C. were sentenced to ten days in prison for publishing an article criticizing the conviction of labor activists, but the couple was later released on bond, and the Arkansas Supreme Court quashed their sentences.

In 1952 the Arkansas NAACP recognized Daisy Bates's tireless campaigning for civil rights by electing her its president, a post that placed her at the forefront of desegregation efforts two years later, when the U.S. Supreme Court delivered its *Brown v. Board of Education* decision. Commentators believed that Arkansas under Governor Orval Faubus, a racial moderate, might lead the region in compliance with the school desegregation ruling, and that progressive Little Rock would lead Arkansas. After 1955, however, the Court's implementation decree, *Brown II*, emboldened segregationist whites. *Brown II* required local authorities to desegregate with "all deliberate speed," a phrase that white-dominated school boards, including Little Rock's, interpreted as a signal to delay and obstruct integration. In 1956 Bates responded to white delaying tactics by urging readers of the *State Press* to support *Cooper v. Aaron*, an NAACP lawsuit recommending the speedy integration of the Little Rock schools.

In September 1957 the Little Rock school board finally unveiled its plan to enroll nine black students in the previously all-white Central High School, but even that token effort enraged whites. Working-class whites were particularly aggrieved that their children would be integrated while the children of wealthier whites would not. Tensions were raised further on the first day of classes, when Governor Faubus enlisted the Arkansas National Guard to surround the school. Warning that "blood would run in the streets" if blacks entered the building, Faubus had essentially used military force to deny the "Little Rock Nine" their constitutional right to attend an integrated school. Such defiance encouraged other whites to resist violently. Someone threw a rock through Bates's window, threatening dynamite next. And when one of the students, Elizabeth Eckford, attempted to enter the school alone, white mobs jeered at, spat at, and physically threatened the fifteen-year-old.

Throughout the tension, Daisy Bates served as the main adviser and confidante of the children and their parents. She paid for private bodyguards, held strategy sessions in her home, tutored the children during the three weeks that the state of Arkansas refused to do so, and helped handle the demands of the world media. On 25 September 1957, after President Dwight Eisenhower had federalized the National Guard and sent one thousand Screaming Eagles paratroopers from the 101st Airborne Division to enforce the law, Bates escorted the students through the front door of Central High School. In the year that followed, she continued to act as a mentor for the students when they braved intimidation and assaults, and also when they fought back, as one student did when she emptied a bowl of hot chili on the head of a white youth who taunted her. Bates's defiance and the courage of the students earned them the NAACP's Spingarn Medal in 1958.

The successful, albeit minimal, integration of Central did not end conflicts between Bates and the Little Rock authorities. In October 1957 she resisted a local ordinance that required organizations to provide the city clerk with financial records and the names of staff and officers. Other municipalities used such information to harass and punish NAACP members, and Bates argued that compulsory disclosure of these records infringed citizens' rights to freedom of association. The local court duly convicted Bates of violating the ordinance in 1957, but that conviction was reversed in 1960 by a unanimous U.S. Supreme Court ruling, *Bates v. Little Rock*.

After the Little Rock crisis, Bates faded from the national spotlight but remained active in civil rights. She spoke at the 1963 March on Washington, worked in the Johnson administration's War on Poverty, and led a community revitalization project in rural Arkansas. In 1984 the University of Arkansas awarded her an honorary degree. Many other awards followed. The city of Little Rock named an elementary school in her honor in 1987, and she even carried the Olympic torch en route to Atlanta in 1996. She received her greatest honor posthumously, when President Bill Clinton, a fellow Arkansan and friend, awarded Bates and the Little Rock Nine the Congressional Gold Medal. As the Nine received their honors from the president in November 1999, Bates lay in state in the Arkansas Capitol, a few feet away from the spot where Governor Faubus had predicted blood in the streets in 1957.

Popular histories of the civil rights era often depict Daisy Bates as the epitome of virtuous, nonviolent resistance and grace under pressure, largely on the strength of her brave, motherly shepherding of the Little Rock Nine. Indeed she was nonviolent in her approach, but she was also a realist. Her journalism was confrontational. She challenged police brutality and, from the time she learned of her mother's murder, found it "hard to suppress certain feelings, when all around you see only hate" (Tyson, *Robert F. Williams and the Roots of Black Power*, 153). Such feelings were not unreasonable given that the Ku Klux Klan raised three fiery crosses on her lawn and that white supremacists bombed her home several times. In 1959 she was at first equivocal about the case of ROBERT WILLIAMS, a North Carolina NAACP leader who advocated that blacks arm themselves in self-defense. After the NAACP Executive Secretary WALTER WHITE promised Daisy an extra $600 a month to help the ailing *State Press*, however, she agreed to support White's campaign to censure Williams. That decision reflected Bates's pragmatism—white advertisers had withdrawn support from the *State Press*, and the paper would soon fold. Daisy Bates was certainly courageous, but like others in the civil rights movement—and like activists in all eras—she recognized that success often requires compromise.

Further Reading
There are three main manuscript sources for information on Bates. In 1966 she donated papers related to the Little Rock crisis to the State Historical Society in Madison, Wisconsin. Twenty years later, she donated papers to the Special Collections Library of the University of Arkansas in Fayetteville. For her tenure as president of the Arkansas NAACP, see the Papers of the NAACP in the Library of Congress, Washington, D.C.

Bates, Daisy Lee. *The Long Shadow of Little Rock* (1962).
Kirk, John A. *Redefining the Color Line: Black Activism in Little Rock, Arkansas, 1940–1970* (2002).
Jacoway, Elizabeth, and C. Fred Williams. *Understanding the Little Rock Crisis* (1999).
Obituary: *New York Times*, 5 Nov. 1999.
STEVEN J. NIVEN

BATES, Peg Leg (11 Oct. 1907–8 Dec. 1998), tap dancer and entrepreneur, was born Clayton Bates in Fountain Inn, South Carolina, the son of Rufus Bates, a laborer, and Emma Stewart, a sharecropper and housecleaner. He began dancing when he was five. At age twelve, while working in a cotton-seed gin mill, he caught and mangled his left leg in a conveyor belt. The leg was amputated on the kitchen table at his home. Although he was left with only one leg and

a wooden peg leg that his uncle carved for him, Bates resolved to continue dancing. "It somehow grew in my mind that I wanted to be as good a dancer as any two-legged dancer," he recalled. "It hurt me that the boys pitied me. I was pretty popular before, and I still wanted to be popular. I told them not to feel sorry for me." He meant it. He began imitating the latest rhythm steps of metal tap-shoe dancers, adding his own novelty and acrobatic steps. He worked his way from minstrel shows and carnivals to the vaudeville circuits. At fifteen, after becoming the undisputed king of one-legged dancers, able to execute acrobatic, graceful soft-shoe dancing and powerful rhythm-tapping all with one leg and a peg, Bates established a professional career as a tap dancer.

In 1930, after dancing in the Paris version of Lew Leslie's *Blackbirds of 1928*, Bates returned to New York to perform as a featured tap dancer at such famous Harlem nightclubs as the Cotton Club, Connie's Inn, and Club Zanzibar. On Broadway in the 1930s he reinvented such popular tap steps as the Shim Sham Shimmy, Susie-Q, and Truckin' by enhancing them with the rhythmic combination of his deep-toned left-leg peg and the high-pitched metallic right-foot tap. As one of the black tap dancers able to cross the color barrier, Bates joined performers on the white vaudeville circuit of Keith & Loew and performed on the same bill as BILL "BOJANGLES" ROBINSON, Fred Astaire, and Gene Kelly. In 1949 Bates sang and danced the role of the swashbuckling pirate Long John Silver in the musical review *Blackouts*. "Don't give up the ship, although you seem to lose the fight; life means do the best with all you got, give it all your might," he sang in the Ken Murray musical that played for three years at the Hollywood and Vine Theatre in Hollywood, California. Wearing a white suit and looking as debonair as Astaire, Bates made his first television appearance in 1948 on *This Is Show Business*, a show hosted by Clifton Fadiman and Arlene Francis, performing high-speed paddle-and-roll tapping and balancing on his rubber-tipped peg as though it were a ballet pointe shoe. On the *Ed Sullivan Show* in 1955, Bates strutted his stuff as he competed in a tap challenge dance, countering Hal LeRoy's wiggly steps with airy wing steps. "You're not making it easy," Bates chided as he tossed off heel clicks and soared into a flash finish with trenches (in which the body leans forward on the diagonal and the legs kick high to the back). Bates made more than twenty appearances on the *Ed Sullivan Show*, last appearing in a tap challenge dance with "Little Buck" on 22 August 1965.

While television gave him greater fame than ever before, Bates continued to pursue a variety of performance venues. In 1951 he invested his earnings and, with his wife, Alice, purchased a large turkey farm in New York's Catskill Mountains and converted it into a resort. The date of his marriage to Alice is not known, but the marriage lasted until her death in 1987. They had one child. The Peg Leg Country Club, in Kerhonkson, New York, flourished as the largest resort in the country that was owned and operated by a black person, and it catered to a largely black clientele and featured hundreds of jazz musicians and tap dancers. "During the prejudice years, country clubs were not integrated," said Bates, "and I started thinking how blacks might like to have a country resort just like any other race of people." After selling the property in 1989, Bates continued to perform and teach. He appeared before youth groups, senior citizens, and handicapped groups, spreading his philosophy of being involved in spite of life's adversities and encouraging youngsters to be drug-free and pursue an education. "Life means, do the best you can with what you've got, with all your mind and heart. You can do anything in this world if you want to do it bad enough," he often said.

Bates's tap dancing was melodically and rhythmically enhanced by the combination of his deep-toned peg, made of leather and tipped with rubber, with the higher-pitched metallic tap shoe. He was also accomplished in acrobatics, flash dancing (that is, executing spectacularly difficult steps involving virtuosic aerial maneuvers), and novelty dancing. He consistently proved himself beyond his peg-legged specialty, surpassing many two-legged dancers to become one of the finest rhythm dancers in the history of tap dancing.

In 1992 Bates was master of ceremonies at the National Tap Dance Day celebration in Albany, New York, where he received a Distinguished Leadership in the Arts award. In 1991 Bates was honored with the Flo-Bert Award by the New York Committee to Celebrate National Tap Dance Day. Bates died in Fountain Inn, South Carolina, just a mile and a half from the place where he lost his leg.

Further Reading
Hill, Constance Valis. "Tap Day to Receive a Peg Leg Flourish." *Albany Times Union*, 22 May 1992.
Frank, Rusty. *Tap! The Greatest Tap Dance Stars and Their Stories, 1900–1955* (1990, 1994).
Obituary: *New York Times*, 8 Dec. 1998.
CONSTANCE VALIS HILL

BATH, Patricia (4 November 1942–), doctor of ophthalmology, inventor, medical researcher, and advocate for social equity in health care, was born in Harlem, New York, the daughter of Rupert and Gladys Bath. A one-time merchant marine and global traveler, her father emigrated from Trinidad, taking a position as the first black motorman for the New York City subways, and her mother, a descendant of African slaves and Cherokee Indians, Bath tells her biographers, "was a housewife who worked as a domestic after we entered middle school. . . . She scrubbed floors so I could go to medical school" (Davidson). A brilliant student, Bath attended New York's Charles Evans Hughes High School and in 1959 was selected for a National Science Foundation summer program at Yeshiva University. Working on a cancer research team, Bath demonstrated the future potential of her work in science and medicine and

was recognized as one of *Mademoiselle* magazine's Merit Award winners in 1960.

Bath graduated, in 1964, with highest honors from Hunter College in New York City, receiving her bachelor's degree in Chemistry and Physics. A year later, when she entered Howard University's medical school, she was awarded fellowships by the National Institutes of Health and the National Institute of Mental Health. During the summer of 1967 Bath researched children's health in Yugoslavia, and in 1968 she served as medical coordinator for MARTIN LUTHER KING JR.'s Poor People's Campaign, which sponsored a mass march on Washington, D.C., to bring needed attention to poverty in America. Both experiences enhanced Bath's commitment to international medicine and equitable health care. After completing her medical degree with honors, Bath returned to New York to pursue more specialized medical training. Between 1968 and 1973 she completed an internship at Harlem Hospital (1968–1969) and was the first African American resident training in ophthalmology and corneal transplant at Columbia University (1969–1970) and New York University (1970–1973). While completing postgraduate work at Columbia, she married, and in 1972 she had a daughter, Eraka.

While interning at Harlem Hospital, Bath observed that, while half the patients at the Harlem Hospital eye clinic were blind or visually impaired, she saw very few blind patients at Columbia. To test her observation, Bath conducted a study and found that the rate of blindness among blacks was indeed twice that among whites. Concluding that blacks lacked access to adequate eye care, Bath initiated what she called Community Ophthalmology, training volunteers to visit underserved people at day care and senior centers to provide eye exams and identify and treat eye problems. Community Ophthalmology and providing eye care for the underserved would remain one of Patricia Bath's lifelong concerns and ambitions.

Bath and her daughter moved to Los Angeles in 1974 so that she could join the faculties of UCLA and Charles R. Drew University as assistant professor of surgery and ophthalmology. After just one year, she became the first woman faculty member in the Department of Ophthalmology at UCLA's Jules Stein Eye Institute. In 1977 Bath traveled to Nigeria and became the chief of ophthalmology at Mercy Hospital. Between 1977 and 1978 she was on the White House Council for National and International Blindness Prevention Program, and by 1983 she cofounded and chaired the ophthalmology residency training program at Drew/UCLA—becoming the first woman in the country to hold such a position. Between 1976 and 1978 Bath and three colleagues founded the American Institute for the Prevention of Blindness (AIPB), which is funded through donations of time from surgeons and donations of equipment from manufacturers. An international organization, the AIPB aims to provide eye care to people who otherwise would not be able to afford it, including making preventive medicines and treatment available to children.

In the 1980s Bath began developing a new technology to be used in the surgical removal of cataracts. Almost everyone who lives long enough will eventually develop cataracts, one of the leading causes of blindness. For years surgeons removed cataracts and replaced them with artificial lenses, but the traditional surgery was highly invasive. Bath became convinced that a laser could be used to remove cataracts more accurately and less invasively. Despite discouragement and difficulties, Bath persisted, doing much of her research in Germany so that she could work with the most advanced medical laser equipment available and expedite the inventive process. Ultimately successful in designing a laser probe, she applied for a United States patent in 1986. Her first patent, number 4,744,360, was issued two years later for an instrument known as the laserphacoprobe, which uses a powerful beam of light to break up and destroy the cataract. Continuing to improve her invention—which began to be used throughout the country and the world—Bath eventually received three more patents in the United States, and she also holds patents in Japan, Canada, and five European countries. Bath was the first African American woman doctor to receive a patent for a medical invention.

When she retired in 1993, Bath became the first woman elected to the UCLA Medical Center's honorary medical staff, but her global advocacy for the extension of eye care to the poor and underserved was only beginning. She became a pioneer in the field of telemedicine, which uses electronic communications to provide medical services to remote areas where people have limited access to health care. While holding positions in telemedicine at Howard University Hospital and at St. George's University in Grenada, she served as a consultant to an Internet firm, eBio-Care.com and continued to direct the AIPB.

Dr. Bath's medical innovations, including her patented laser equipment and new methodologies for removing cataracts, as well as the organizational changes she has brought to eye care through Community Ophthalmology and the American Institute for the Prevention of Blindness, have saved the vision of thousands around the globe. Her career has been marked by firsts both for women and for African Americans. Bath's contributions to science, medical technology, and socially conscious health care in the second half of the twentieth century cannot be overstated. She was elected to the Hunter College Hall of Fame in 1988 and was named a Howard University Pioneer of Academic Medicine in 1993.

Further Reading

Davidson, Martha. "The Right to Sight: Patricia Bath," Lemelson Center Invention Features, Smithsonian Institution (March 2005). Available online at http://invention.smithsonian.org/centerpieces/ilives/bath/bath.html

Sullivan, Otha Richard. *Black Stars: African American Women Scientists and Inventors* (2001).

PAMELA C. EDWARDS

BATSON, Flora (16 Apr. 1864–1 Dec. 1906), singer, was born in Washington, D.C. Though her father's name is unknown, evidence suggests that he was a Union soldier. After her father died from injuries sustained during the Civil War, Batson moved with her mother, Mary Batson, to Providence, Rhode Island. She attended school and studied music in Providence; by the age of nine she was a featured soloist at Bethel Church as well as at other local churches in the Rhode Island and Boston, Massachusetts, region.

Batson's professional career began to blossom at a time when several black women were achieving renown as classically trained singers. Nellie Brown Mitchell, SISSIERETTA JONES, MARIE SELIKA—all classical singers and contemporaries of Batson—stood in stark contrast to the Jim Crow stereotypes that prevailed in a nation only recently rid of institutionalized slavery. In the early 1880s Batson was the featured soloist at People's Church in Boston. She also toured with Redpath's Lecture Lyceum Bureau, a popular booking agency in the Boston area, sang for Storer's College at Harpers Ferry, West Virginia, and beginning in 1883 became a featured singer with the temperance movement while under the management of Thomas Doutney.

In 1883 Batson came to the attention of James G. Bergen (named in some sources as Col. John Bergen), the owner of the Bergen Star Concert Company (sometimes called the Tennessee Star Concert Company). Bergen was known for promoting black talent in New England during the late 1800s, and his roster of artists included Sidney Woodward, Sissieretta Jones, Nellie Brown Mitchell, Carrie Melvin, and HARRY T. BURLEIGH. Bergen, who was white, also had a romantic interest in Batson, and although sources disagree on exactly when the nuptials occurred (the most oft-cited dates are the year 1885 and 13 December 1887), the two were married until 1896. Unusual for the time, their consensual, interracial union was covered by newspapers in the United States and abroad.

Batson's relationship with James Bergen and the Bergen Star Concert Company positioned her for international renown. Her major appearances during this period include her performance with Adelaide Smith and Sam Lucas at New York City's Steinway Hall in 1885 and her triumphant Philadelphia debut during that same year. The watershed moment of Batson's career came when she stepped in at the last minute to substitute for Nellie Brown Mitchell, who up until that point had been the leading soprano of the Bergen Company. A scheduling conflict prevented Mitchell from appearing at a concert in Providence, and Batson, singing in her stead, received rave reviews. From that point in 1885 Batson became the undisputed star of Bergen's Concert Company.

By 1887 Batson had become nationally known and the press had dubbed her the "Double-voiced Queen of Song" because of her vocal range, which extended from baritone to soprano. Her repertoire, equally broad in its range, included concert and operatic selections, dramatic pieces, ballads, and popular songs. She was most often requested to sing ballads such as "The Last Rose of Summer" and "The Cows Are in the Corn." The public frequently expressed its affection for her with necklaces, crowns, earrings, and other bejeweled gifts. Batson took pride in wearing these during her performances, and an extant portrait published in several sources shows her adorned in her trademark jewels and tiara.

While black prima donnas of the late nineteenth century enjoyed wide acclaim, they also endured a press that frequently compared them to their white counterparts. In newspapers, Batson was dubbed the "colored Jenny Lind" after the world-famous Swedish coloratura soprano who dominated the concert stage in the 1850s. The press also called Batson the "Patti of her race," a comparison to Adelina Patti, the Italian-born prima donna who came to fame in the late 1800s. Because these comparisons were so commonplace, it no doubt created confusion since another black singer and contemporary of Batson's, Sissieretta Jones, was also widely known as "the Black Patti."

Batson made no fewer than three world tours throughout the course of her career. She traveled to Europe, China, Japan, Africa, Great Britain, Australia, India, Fiji, and New Zealand. She sang for numerous dignitaries and crowned heads of state including Queen Victoria of Great Britain, Pope Leo XIII, the royal family of New Zealand, and Queen Lili'uokalani of Hawaii.

In 1896 Batson's relationship with James Bergen and the Bergen Star Concert Company came to an end. Sources differ, however, as to the exact reasons for this dissolution. Some sources claim that Batson herself severed their relationship, while others suggest that Bergen's death occurred at about this time. In either case, Batson signed with a new manager in 1896, Gerard Millar, who was an African American basso.

Batson and Millar toured and performed together and were the featured duo in the South Before the War Company. The two also sang with the Orpheus McAdoo Minstrels and Vaudeville Company, a career change indicative of the public's increasing appetite for popular and comedic forms of entertainment during the years surrounding the turn of the twentieth century. Batson and Millar were eventually married. Soon after her death, Millar published *Life, Travels, and Works of Miss Flora Batson, Deceased Queen of Song*.

Although she turned to vaudeville during the later years of her career, Batson favored performing for churches and charitable causes until the end of her life. A deeply religious woman, she gave her last concert at Bethel African Methodist Episcopal Church in Philadelphia. At the time of her sudden death in Philadelphia, Flora Batson was considered one of the leading singers of her time.

Further Reading

Live, Travels, and Works of Miss Flora Batson, Deceased Queen of Song (1906?) is part of the Music Collection of the Boston Public Library. Copies are also available at the Library of Congress and at Brown University.

Southern, Eileen. "Flora Batson Bergen," in *Biographical Dictionary of Afro-Americans and African Musicians* (1982).

Story, Rosalyn. *And So I Sing: African American Divas of Opera and Concert* (1990).

Wright, Josephine. "Black Women in Classical Music in Boston During the Late Nineteenth Century: Profiles of Leadership," in *New Perspectives on Music: Essays in Honor of Eileen Southern* (1992).

TERESA L. REED

BATTEY, Cornelius Marion (C. M.) (26 Aug. 1873–1927), photographer and educator, was born in Augusta, Georgia, to Florida and Robert Battey, both laborers. He was living in New York City by his late teens and had become one of the most famous African American photographers in the country by 1900, although nothing is known about his educational background. In 1900 Battey married Anna H. Stokes, who gave birth to two daughters, Edyphe F. (born 1901) and Antoinette (born 1908). Affiliated with studios in Cleveland and New York, his primary base, he enjoyed a lucrative career as a studio and commercial photographer with a respected reputation among Americans and Europeans. He was superintendent of the Bradley Studio in New York with such clientele as Sir Thomas Lipton and Prince Henry of Prussia, and was a partner in Battey and Warren Studio in the city.

Battey made classic photogravure portraits of the Tuskegee Normal and Industrial Institute founder and president BOOKER T. WASHINGTON, c. 1890 and 1908; the statesman and abolitionist leader and publisher FREDERICK DOUGLASS, c. 1895; the educator and Virginia congressman JOHN MERCER LANGSTON, c. 1890; the poet PAUL LAURENCE DUNBAR, c. 1905; and the scholar W. E. B. DU BOIS, 1908, along with numerous other statesmen, writers, performers, and national leaders. A selection from this body of portraiture of distinguished male figures was published in *Our Heroes of Destiny*, later titled *Our Master Minds*. He also photographed Margaret Murray, the wife of Booker T. Washington, in 1914. The same year, he created a tender portrayal of his second wife, *"You"—Portrait of Mrs. C. M. Battey*, inscribed with the following: "Where the Birth of Love Was First Drawn / Into the Rosy, Reluctant Auroras of Life" and "This is a character / sketch of *my* Pal taken / by her husband."

In 1905 Booker T. Washington petitioned George Eastman, one of the institution's benefactors, to finance a chair in photography that would be a catalyst for student creative development toward professional art careers as well as provide technical training and a staff post for institutional documentation. Eastman agreed to provide funds, and Battey was offered the position. He appeared well educated and was reputed for his integrity, work ethic, and high standards. Battey stood out further as being a member of an elite group of photographers who succeeded at multitasking across the spectrum of photographic branches, techniques, and subjects.

Battey and first wife, Anna, had divorced by the fall of 1910, and soon after he married the photographer Elizabeth Rahn, with whom he had two children, a daughter Muriel (born in 1908) and a son Champlin (born 1911).

Battey arrived on Tuskegee's campus in January 1917, two years after Washington's death and during the presidential term of Washington's successor, ROBERT RUSSA MOTON, who offered only lukewarm support to the board-initiated program. As head of the photography division, Battey was the official photographer for the Institute as well as chair and instructor of the photography curriculum. Needing students to jump-start the department, he embarked upon a recruitment campaign. He seized the opportunity at a Tuskegee "Men's Meeting" (a male convocation), during which he announced his pilot course and encouraged those with an artistic temperament to visit his office the following day. PRENTICE HERMAN POLK, an evening student at the time, was the first to respond. Polk became his best-known student, having a distinguished career as a portrait photographer and assuming the leadership of the division at Tuskegee, where he also served as the official photographer for fifty years.

Battey produced sensitive portrayals of the campus community, placing particular artistic emphasis on the treatment of classroom scenes, student activities, and college rituals. In his first year he photographed the commencement ceremony by depicting it as a regal processional of young men in dark suits and hats and parasol-carrying young women wearing floor-length white gowns. He made equally sensitive photographs of well-dressed, poised, and attentive students engaged in various course instructions, posed in the gardens, and gathered outside buildings between sessions. One of his famous student subjects was WILLIAM LEVI DAWSON, who went on to organize the School of Music at Tuskegee in 1931. Battey's photographs of campus dignitaries, important visitors, various structures, the Tuskegee band, and other scenes in Macon County, Alabama, contributed to the comprehensive nature of his work as the official photographer. Battey headed up the program until his death in 1927.

Ellie Lee Weems and Elise Forrest Harleston were among the students who, like Polk, went on to have exemplary careers in the field. Weems, a fellow Georgian, operated a studio in Atlanta and later in Jacksonville, Florida. Harleston, from Charleston, South Carolina, was encouraged by the genre and portrait painter EDWIN AUGUSTUS HARLESTON, her future husband, to study further under Battey. She later opened a studio in Charleston.

The recipient of awards in American and European galleries, Battey was featured in the NAACP's *Cri-sis* magazine in 1917 and did cover photographs for *The Crisis,* the National Urban League publication *Opportunity Journal,* and *The Tuskegee Messenger.* At the time of his death, Battey was in the process of inventorying, packing, and shipping his negatives to South Carolina where he had planned to retire.

Further Reading

Battey photographs are in the collections of Tuskegee University in Tuskegee, Alabama; Library of Congress in Washington, D.C.; and Schomburg Center for Research in Black Culture in New York City.

Appiah, Kwame Anthony, and Henry Louis Gates Jr. *Africana: The Encyclopedia of the African and African American Experience* (1999).

Willis, Deborah. *Reflections in Black: A History of Black Photographers 1840 to the Present* (2000).

AMALIA K. AMAKI

BATTEY, Earl (5 Jan. 1935–15 Nov. 2003), baseball player, was born Earl Jesse Battey Jr. in Los Angeles, California, to Esther (maiden name unknown) and Earl Battey Sr. His parents—particularly Esther who, from 1938 to 1948, was a catcher on women's softball teams such as the Watts All-Stars, the Ebonettes, and the MacAfee All-Stars—encouraged him to play baseball as a youngster. As a freshman at Los Angeles's Jordan High School, Battey made the team, only to sit the bench for the first six games of the season as a backup outfielder. When the starting catcher split his finger during a game, however, coach Norm Forester looked to Battey, his only nonpitcher left on the twelve-man roster, to fill in. Battey turned out to be so good as catcher that he kept the position even after the previous catcher recovered. At six feet, one inch tall and 205 pounds, the thick, slow-footed Battey was a natural for his position, with a powerful arm that he attributed to practicing with a punching bag. While in high school Battey developed his skills by playing for an adult men's team, the Watts Giants, against such future major leaguers as Duke Snider, Bob Lemon, and Irv Noren. He was also aided by the coaching of his uncle, Clifford Prelow, a former Brooklyn Dodgers prospect, and BIZ MACKEY, a former Negro League catcher and manager who moved to Los Angeles when Major League Baseball's integration precipitated the dissolution of the Newark Eagles.

While in high school Battey was better known as a basketball player than as a baseball player. After graduating in 1953, however, he turned down offers from the Harlem Globetrotters and UCLA to sign with the Chicago White Sox. His early years in baseball presented several major challenges, both professional and personal. Arriving for spring training in Florida in 1954, Battey encountered overt segregation and racism for the first time when he was prevented from eating in white restaurants or attending jazz concerts with whites. Though he took these injustices in stride, at other times his temper was problematic. For instance, that season he punched the opposing team's catcher, incurring a fine of two hundred dollars. Professionally, Battey spent his time in the White Sox organization frustrated and undervalued. Elevated to the major leagues for five games at the end of the 1955 season, he returned for only four the next, spending most of 1956 in the minor leagues at Toronto and part of 1957 with Los Angeles of the Pacific Coast League.

Battey established himself as Chicago's backup catcher in 1957, though he batted only .174 in forty-eight games and improved only slightly over sixty-eight games the next season. Battey handled his backup role positively, using his time to study the game and work with Hall of Fame manager and catcher Al Lopez on improving defensively. "I never got discouraged," he said later. "It's different sitting on the bench for a contender than it would be for a second-division club" (Baseball Hall of Fame file). Indeed, in 1959 the White Sox reached the World Series, only to lose to the relocated Los Angeles Dodgers in six games. They did so with little help from Battey, who logged only twenty-six games while batting .219 and was the only Chicago player not to play in the World Series.

In 1960 Battey was traded to the Washington Senators. He was initially dismayed to leave the American League's championship team for its last-place team. Yet Washington's haplessness provided him with the opportunity to play every day. When he arrived in Washington it was clear that he had much work to do. According to Senators coach Clyde McCullough, a former major league catcher himself, "When we first got Battey he was raw as a pound of uncooked hamburger." But after 1960, a season in which Battey hit .270 with 15 home runs over 137 games as the starting catcher, McCullough could say that "from a mechanical standpoint he's the best [catcher] in baseball" (Los Angeles Times, 17 Feb. 1961). Manager Cookie Lavagetto even credited Battey with being the driving force behind Washington's climb from eighth to fifth place in the American League.

Battey soon established himself as the most dependable catcher in baseball, catching more games in the first half of the 1960s than anyone else and playing at least 131 games in every season. His record during this time is incredible considering the daunting string of injuries that he suffered, including dislocated fingers, chronic knee problems, two broken cheekbones, and a goiter that helped make him sixty pounds heavier than his officially listed playing weight. During the 1965 World Series he ran neck-first into an overhanging crossbar at Dodger Stadium while chasing a pop foul. Unable to speak above a whisper or turn his neck to the left, he nevertheless played effectively in the remaining four games of the series, throwing out five would-be base stealers, including the great MAURY WILLS twice.

The Washington Senators relocated prior to the 1961 season, becoming the Minnesota Twins. "I like it here," Battey commented on his new home. "People are friendly, business opportunities are good and I can't think of a better place to play ball" (Baseball Hall of Fame file). He thrived in Minnesota, hitting a career high .302 in 1961. Despite trade rumors the following season, Battey continued to excel at and behind the plate, foiling twenty-four would-be base stealers and picking off thirteen runners. As a result he won his third consecutive Gold Glove and earned his first of four appearances at the All-Star game over the next five years. In 1965 Battey garnered the most votes of any American League All-Star, picked at the time by fellow ballplayers.

The acclamation of his colleagues represented the respect with which Battey was regarded, both as a player and as a person. With his sharp sense of humor and friendly demeanor Battey became one of the most popular players in the Minnesota clubhouse. Teammate Tony Oliva later recalled, "When I came into the league as a rookie, I spoke little English. But he spoke Spanish and he helped me out. . . . He took me under his wing" (Star-Tribune, 18 Nov. 2003).

After a 1964 season in which many speculated that he was washed up, Battey fought through thirteen separate injuries to bat .297 over 131 games, finish tenth in the Most Valuable Player voting, and help lead the Twins to the World Series. Despite his strong defensive performance in that series, Battey hit only .120 in the Twins' seven-game loss. Looking back at the end of his career, Battey stated, "What I remember most is the 1965 season, the World Series and all that—I guess that was the best thing that ever happened to me in baseball" (Baseball Hall of Fame file).

After the 1965 season Battey's fortunes were in clear descent. Off the field, in January 1966 he was sentenced to five days in jail for failing to file state income tax returns from 1961 to 1964. Nearly two years later he was fined one thousand dollars and was put on three years of probation for nonpayment of federal income taxes during that time. On the field his production dwindled to only .255 over 115 games in 1966. He retired in 1967 after playing only forty-eight games and batting a meager .165. Despondent over a bright career cut short by injuries, he sat at his locker after his final game repeating, "What a way to go." After clearing up his legal troubles in late 1967 he announced plans to return for the 1969 season, but they never materialized.

Battey's life after baseball was dedicated to helping children. After working during his baseball days as a sports and physical fitness promoter for General Mills, he became the baseball consultant for Consolidated Edison in 1968. The position entailed accompanying five thousand poor children to forty games at Yankee Stadium or Shea Stadium, at which he would answer questions over a loudspeaker concerning baseball strategy. Despite the significant cut in pay that this role required, Battey commented, "It's worth it. I always enjoyed working with children" (Baseball Hall of Fame file). He held his position for twenty-three years before coaching the Bethune Cookman College baseball team in Daytona Beach, Florida, from 1980 to 1982. While coaching there he earned a degree, and then he moved on to coach high school baseball and teach special education in Ocala, Florida. Battey also served as a scout for the Seattle Mariners during this time.

In 2000 Battey was named the all-time greatest catcher in Minnesota Twins history. Until his death from cancer on 15 November 2003 he continued to follow baseball avidly. According to A. J. Pierzynski, Minnesota's starting catcher at the time, "All he wanted to talk about was baseball. He was so ill, but all he wanted to do was talk about baseball" (*Pioneer Press*, 18 Nov. 2003). Battey left behind a wife, Sonia, and five children, as well as a legacy of greatness as a player and a man. As former teammate and Hall of Famer Harmon Killebrew said, "He was the best catcher I ever played with. Few realize how great a player he was. He was a leader on and off the field. He was a first-class guy" (*Star Tribune*, 18 Nov. 2003).

Further Reading
There is a file with information on and interviews with Earl Battey at the National Baseball Hall of Fame Library, Cooperstown, New York.
Shatzkin, Mike, ed. *The Ballplayers* (1990).
Thorn, John, and Pete Palmer, eds. *Total Baseball* (1989).

Obituaries: *Saint Paul Pioneer Press* and *Minneapolis Star-Tribune*, 18 Nov. 2003.

CHRISTOPHER DEVINE

BATTLE, Effie Dean Threat (12 Mar. 1881–3 July 1963), educator, poet, and community activist, was born in Okolona, Chickasaw County, Mississippi, the only child of former slaves Mary Johnson Threat and George W. Threat. Though illiterate, her mother understood the value of education. She took in laundry and sold eggs and vegetables to save for her daughter's education. After completing studies at the Okolona Public School in 1894, Battle continued her education at Rust College in Holly Springs, Mississippi, graduating with an AB degree in 1900. She was teaching away from home when she learned that WALLACE BATTLE had come to Okolona to establish an industrial school. Although she was in line to become principal of a Greenwood, Mississippi, school she chose to return home in 1902 to help with the development of the Okolona Industrial School. She married the school's founder the following year. They had five children.

Along with her role as the wife of the president of Okolona Industrial School, Battle taught math. She also devoted time to writing poetry, some of which was published in newspapers and magazines, and which was sometimes used to raise funds for the school when she traveled north to do readings. Battle's love of writing poetry led to the publication of a well-received, eighteen-page volume of ten of her poems under the title *Gleanings From Dixie Land in Ten Poems* (c. 1914).

When her husband took a leave in 1925 and subsequently resigned from the presidency of Okolona In-

dustrial School in 1927, Battle assumed the position of acting president. She operated the school in that capacity until 1933, when a permanent replacement was named. Although she was offered the position of dean of the Teacher Training School, she decided that she could not continue at the school in a subordinate position.

After her departure from Okolona, Battle relocated to the Bedford-Stuyvesant and later Crown Heights sections of Brooklyn, New York. Her poetry continued to win her renown as she did readings and was published in newspapers. Her poem "June" was published in *Modern American Poetry* by Galleon Press in 1934. Battle's earlier work, *Gleanings From Dixie Land in Ten Poems*, received praise from JAMES WELDON JOHNSON, author of the *Autobiography of an Ex-Colored Man* (1912). After receiving a copy of her collection in 1934, he informed Battle that he was placing it in the Francis Collection, a collection for private use by his classes in creative literature at Fisk University. In August 1937 she received a monetary award when she won first prize in a poetry contest on radio station WHN in New York. "Going to See the President," an illustrated poem, was included in an exhibit at the 1939 World's Fair called *The Big Book of Poetry*, presented by the National Poetry Center, Radio City, New York. Battle also participated in church and other programs for which she held poetry readings and spoke about the experiences she and her husband had as educators and school administrators in the South. She kept abreast of conditions at Okolona Industrial School and regularly participated in its annual Founder's Day program.

Battle was an early member of the Women's Service League of Brooklyn, an organization founded in the 1930s by ADDIE HUNTON, a former YWCA official and club woman activist. The organization was dedicated to promoting an active interest in the civic and social problems of the black community and of black women in particular. During the years that she was a member, Battle served the organization as corresponding secretary, recording secretary, and historian.

Battle died in Brooklyn. In 1996 her book of poetry, *Gleanings from Dixie Land*, was republished as part of a collection entitled *Six Poets of Racial Uplift*, with an introduction by Gayle Pemberton.

JOANNE H. EDEY-RHODES

BATTLE, Kathleen (13 Aug. 1948–), lyric coloratura soprano, was the youngest of seven children born in Portsmouth, Ohio, to Grady Battle, a steelworker from Alabama who belonged to a gospel quartet, and Ollie Layne Battle. Together with her six older siblings, Kathleen Deanna Battle experienced the gospel music of her African Methodist Episcopal Church from a very early age. Battle studied at Portsmouth High School with Charles Varney and began piano lessons at the age of twelve.

She considered using her National Achievement Scholarship, which she was awarded in 1966, to study

Kathleen Battle, performing at the opening gala for the Muhammad Ali Center in Louisville, Kentucky, 19 November 2005. (AP Images.)

mathematics at the University of Cincinnati, but she graduated instead from the University of Cincinnati's College-Conservatory of Music with a degree in music education in 1970. The following year, Battle received a master's degree from the same institution. After graduation, Battle worked as a music teacher for fifth- and sixth-graders in a Cincinnati inner-city school for two years. While teaching, she continued to audition as a performer, and in 1972 Thomas Schippers, conductor of the Cincinnati Symphony, selected Battle to sing at Italy's Spoleto Festival of Two Worlds, where she sang Brahms's *German Requiem*. The performance received unanimous commendation and served as a career watershed. Confident, she began to appear with the best American and European orchestras.

In 1974 the conductor James Levine chose her to sing the "Mater Glorioso" in Mahler's eighth symphony at Cincinnati's May Festival, an event that began a long-lasting professional association. Battle then went to New York to work as an understudy for Carmen Balthrop, who had the leading role in Scott Joplin's *Treemonisha*. In 1975 she made her debut at the New York City Opera as Susanna in Mozart's *The Marriage of Figaro*, and two years later Battle first appeared at the Metropolitan Opera under Levine's direction as the Shepherd in Richard Wagner's *Tannhäuser*. Critics acclaimed her performances and praised her voice, which maintained its integrity at both ends of a two-and-one-half octave range, from low A to high E. Her successful New York debut established her as one of the Metropolitan's favorite artists. She also sang in the best opera houses around the world and worked with internationally renowned directors. Battle attained star status with supporting roles that usually did not produce divas, such as Zerlina in Mozart's *Don Giovanni* and Sophie in Richard Strauss's *Der Rosenkavalier*. While she particularly specialized in Mozart roles, her repertoire was di-

verse, and included Baroque music and African American spirituals. In spite of being one of the few African Americans in a predominantly white milieu (she shared this lonely status with LEONTYNE PRICE and JESSYE NORMAN), Battle's presence in a cast became a guarantee of success.

The recipient of several honorary degrees from, among other institutions, her alma mater, the University of Cincinnati; Westminster Choir College in Princeton, New Jersey; Ohio University; Xavier University in Cincinnati; Amherst College; and Seton Hall University. She was also a five-time Grammy Award winner: 1986 Best Classical Soloist Performance for *Kathleen Battle Sings Mozart*, 1987 Best Opera Recording for Richard Strauss's *Ariadne Auf Naxos*, 1987 Best Classical Soloist Performance for *Kathleen Battle—Salzburg Recital*, 1992 Best Classical Vocal Performance for *Kathleen Battle at Carnegie Hall*, and 1993 Best Opera Recording for Handel's *Semele*. Battle often teamed up with the most distinguished artists of her time. She appeared in concert with conductors such as Herbert von Karajan, Riccardo Muti, Seiji Ozawa, Claudio Abbado, Sir Georg Solti, Lorin Maazel, and Sir Neville Marriner. She performed with tenors Luciano Pavarotti and Plácido Domingo, violinist Itzhak Perlman, trumpeter WYNTON MARSALIS, and saxophonist GROVER WASHINGTON JR. These partnerships were documented on numerous CD recordings, many of which were bestsellers. In 1984 Battle performed Mozart's "Coronation" Mass, conducted by Herbert von Karajan in the Vatican. In spite of her success, Battle always sought new challenges. In 1988 she accepted the role of Cleopatra in the first Met production of Handel's *Julius Caesar*, a difficult and almost unknown opera.

Yet with success Battle also acquired a reputation for being difficult and a perfectionist. She enraged managers across the globe and cancelled events at the last moment because she felt her requests had not been satisfied. In 1993, for example, she walked out of a Met production of *Der Rosenkavalier* over disagreements with the conductor Christian Thielemann. Battle was as loved by audiences as she was dreaded by the people who worked backstage and by some of her colleagues. This aspect of her personality received particular public attention in 1994 when she was fired from the Met production of Donizetti's *La Fille du Régiment* for acting unprofessionally. The termination ensued after Battle's insistent complaints against one of her co-stars. All future Met offers also were withdrawn, a decision that drew nearly unanimous consensus from opera house managers around the world. Scores of media articles portrayed Battle as fussy and unreliable, or, at best, as an apparent example of the insecurities that beset opera singers. Nevertheless, Battle emerged undamaged and her recording and recitals remained popular. Her fees for recitals exceeded forty thousand dollars per event. Her opera appearances in the United States became a rarity, however.

Battle's dismissal from the Metropolitan prompted the artist to expand her repertoire to more accessible material. Before then, Battle had made only one brief foray outside classical music for a 1993 duet with pop superstar Janet Jackson. Battle's newer focus on popular music, including gospel material, Gershwin songs, Vangelis's theme music for NASA's Mission to Mars program, folk songs, and lullabies, led her to record crossover albums such as *So Many Stars* (1995), *Grace* (1997), and *Classic Battle: A Portrait* (2002). Mixing classic arias, sacred music, and popular songs, these works have been instant successes. In 2000 Battle's voice was featured in the update of the Disney classic *Fantasia,* in the segment entitled "Pomp and Circumstance," and in 2004 she sang on the soundtrack of Zhang Yimou's *House of Flying Daggers.* Although Battle did not often talk about racial matters, in 1995 she recorded *Honey and Rue,* a song cycle about the African American experience, which she commissioned from composer André Previn and Nobel Prize winner TONI MORRISON. In 1999 she was inducted into the NAACP Image Hall of Fame.

Further Reading

Pniewski, Tom. "Bravo Battle," *World and I* (Aug. 1998).

Story, Rosalyn. *And So I Sing: African-American Divas of Opera and Concert* (1990).

Discography

Classic Battle: A Portrait (Sony, 2002).

Grace (Sony, 1997).

So Many Stars (Sony, 1995).

Bel Canto: Italian Opera Arias (Deutsche Grammophon, 1993).

Baroque Duets (Sony, 1992).

LUCA PRONO

BATTLE, Wallace Aaron, Sr. (10 May 1872–6 Sept. 1946), educator, industrial school founder, and Episcopal Church school field secretary, was born in Hurtsboro, Russell County, Alabama, one of thirteen children of former slaves, Jeanetta (Redden) and Augustus Battle Sr.

Battle's parents sent him to the district school when he was eight years old. He had not progressed far in his education when, at the age of sixteen, he joined his older brother, Augustus Aaron Battle Jr., and two sisters at Talladega College in Talladega, Alabama. Only prepared to enter the third grade, he attended class with eight-year-olds. Wallace was so determined to move forward in his education that he completed three grades in one year. He remained in attendance at Talladega College from 1889 to 1898. In the later years of his college preparatory studies there, he taught during the summers at Duke Station, Calhoun County, Alabama. He also became involved with teaching in Mission Sunday Schools that were set up for the poor some distance from Talladega. It was during the course of this experience that he set his goal of establishing an industrial school. Soon after

entering Talladega's freshman college class, Battle decided to leave Talladega for Berea College in Berea, Kentucky.

Founded in 1855 by John G. Fee, Berea was the first interracial and co-educational college in the South. It was based on the philosophy of promoting understanding and kinship among all people. The school had a profound effect on Battle, who sustained himself by working on campus in various capacities, including that of the school's bell ringer, and through small loans from one of his teachers at Talladega. His attention to punctuality gained him recognition on the campus, and when it came time to graduate, he was chosen as one of the speakers. The experience of losing his place in his speech and fumbling his lines taught him to never write a speech to be read but instead to study his subject matter so that the words would come to him as needed. He graduated from Berea in June 1901 with an AB degree and was subsequently awarded an AM degree in 1907. During the course of his life, Battle also attended summer sessions at the Universities of Illinois and Wisconsin, and at New York University.

After graduating from Berea, he spent a year helping Augustus Jr. with his work as principal of the Anniston Industrial College in Anniston, Alabama. Battle was in charge of the normal and college preparatory department as well as the industry department. His experience at Anniston helped to prepare him for the founding of his own school in the fall of 1902.

Okolona, a town of 4,000 inhabitants in Chickasaw County, Mississippi, was chosen as the site for the establishment of the school that Battle had conceived of years before. He organized a local board of trustees consisting of six African Americans and two whites. The Okolona Industrial School, later Okolona College, was founded on 2 September 1902 and opened at a church with five teachers and 39 students on 1 October 1902. They moved to the school's permanent site, which initially consisted of a 60-acre farm, in November of the same year. Within the first nine months, $3,000 was raised and 205 students representing 4 states and 35 towns and cities had been enrolled. The curriculum was made up of a variety of industrial and academic courses.

In 1903, Battle married EFFIE DEAN THREAT BATTLE, a graduate of Rust College. They became the parents of five children, Thelma, Wallace Jr., Marie (Annie Marie), Madelon (Madeline), and another child who died in infancy. Battle's wife assisted him with the development of the school. Over time, Okolona's board expanded to include some prominent members and the school gained recognition and support from a number of private and institutional sources, including Andrew Carnegie and the General Education Board.

Battle authored *The Mississippi Letter,* a quarterly school publication that was distributed around the country. He served as president of the Mississippi State Teacher's Association for four years, and he was the founder and first president of the Welfare League of Okolona. During World War I, Battle acted as a spokesperson on behalf of liberty bonds and sought to boost morale in Mississippi. The school became a Student's Training Camp. His war effort coupled with the rigors of operating the school led to ill health, and Battle became a victim of the flu pandemic. He spent six months recuperating on the Gulf Coast of Mississippi and another three months out of state.

In order to secure the future of the Okolona Industrial School, it was put under the management and ownership of the Protestant Episcopal Church in October 1918 with Battle retaining the presidency. By the time he resigned in 1925, the school's property had increased to 380 acres, with 300 students, 12 buildings, and a value of $250,000. Battle settled on a farm in New Jersey for two years where he taught night school during the winters. In 1927, the Episcopal Church asked him to assume the newly created position of field secretary of the American Church Institute for Negroes. The appointment made him the first African American general staff officer of the National Council of the Episcopal Church. Among his duties was oversight of the church's nine schools and colleges in eight southern states.

In 1932, Battle was awarded a fellowship of $1,500 from the Julius Rosenwald Fund to investigate the possibilities for black immigrants in Brazil. In the same year, he was awarded an honorary LittD degree from his alma mater, Berea College. Battle remained in his position with the Episcopal Church until his retirement in 1940. Between that time and his death in 1946, he spent his retirement years in Chaplin, Connecticut.

Berea honored Battle posthumously on 12 October 2006 with the John G. Fee Award for his distinguished service to his community and his vision of education.

JOANNE H. EDEY-RHODES

BAUGH, John (10 Dec. 1949–) linguistics professor, was born in Brooklyn, New York, to Barbara Ardis Goore, an elementary school teacher and principal, and John Gordon Baugh VI, a director of projects at Hughes Aircraft Company in El Segundo, California. Baugh, the eldest of their three children, had an early fascination with language that grew in part from observing the complexity of linguistic differences around him. In due course Baugh decided to focus on linguistics in part because of experiences derived from a familial move in 1958 to Los Angeles. The Baughs relocated to a working-class, multiethnic neighborhood where many residents were learning English as a second language. He was also influenced by later experiences when the family moved to the western San Fernando Valley in 1960, where they were one of the few African American families in a mainly upper-middle-class, white, affluent community.

While attending Chatsworth High School in suburban Los Angeles, California, between 1964 and 1967, Baugh once joined white students in ridiculing the strong southern accent of a math teacher from Alabama; the teacher was white and knew well that many of the affluent white students who populated the school belittled his intellect. That linguistic experience was later reinforced for Baugh across the country in Philadelphia at Temple University; in a public-speaking class, he noticed that most African American and Puerto Rican students got Ds and Fs on their speeches, while the majority of working-class white students received Bs and Cs. He came to believe that it was because of the linguistic dexterity afforded him by his background that he earned an A in the class. In high school Baugh combined a mathematics major with a minor in auto mechanics. In college he began by studying accounting, but he found the issue of linguistic differences so fascinating that he changed his major to speech and communication, focusing on rhetoric, persuasion, and argumentation.

During this time, Baugh read a now famous article titled "The Logic of Nonstandard English," written by William Labov, who would later be his dissertation supervisor. Labov compared the logical constructs of middle-class African American speech with the nonstandard grammar of teenage gang members and was able to show that from a logical point of view, the teenagers were more coherent semantically than the more educated African Americans. This article, which fascinated Baugh, was his formal introduction to the study of linguistics. Baugh earned his BA in Speech and Rhetoric at Temple University in 1972. He then studied at the University of Pennsylvania, earning an MA in Linguistics in 1976 and a PhD in Linguistics in 1979. His doctoral dissertation was titled "Linguistic Style Shifting in Black English."

Throughout his academic career, Baugh sought to advance distinguished scholarship of and by people of African descent, beginning with linguistic science, and eventually extending to all academic disciplines in his administrative roles, including traditional studies and preprofessional training in medicine, law, and various professional endeavors. His academic appointments have been in linguistics, as well as the fields of psychology, anthropology, education, English, African American studies, sociology, and foreign language education. A thorough list of his research interests bridges theoretical and applied linguistics, with particular attention to matters of policy and social equity in the fields of education, medicine, and law—fields where fluency in the dominant language has clear social advantages. Some of his research explores the ways that linguistic variation reinforces social stratification in the United States, Austria, Brazil, Hungary, South Africa, and the United Kingdom. His work also examines the evolution and dissemination of English and other European languages in postcolonial contexts worldwide, particularly with respect to linguistic profiling—discrimination based on the sound of an individual's voice regarding various traits, such as race, sex, age, sexual orientation, region, and class in advanced industrialized societies.

While completing his graduate studies, Baugh worked as a lecturer and assistant professor at Swarthmore College in Pennsylvania from 1975 to 1979. In 1980 he began teaching at the University of Texas at Austin as an assistant professor and later as an associate professor with appointments in linguistics, anthropology, and foreign language education. He was a visiting scholar at the Center for Applied Linguistics in Washington, D.C., during the 1982–1983 academic year. In 1983 Baugh married Charla Larrimore; they had three children, Chenoa, John, and Ariel, and later two grandchildren—Braden and Brynja.

During the 1988–1989 academic year, Baugh was a research fellow at the Center for Advanced Study in the Behavioral Sciences in Stanford, California, and in 1990 he became a professor at Stanford University in Palo Alto, California, with appointments in education and linguistics. It was there that Baugh conducted research on what had become his most famous study, leading to the creation of the term "linguistic profiling." When Baugh had first arrived in Palo Alto to begin his time at the Center for Advanced Study in the Behavioral Sciences, he noticed a disturbing trend as he was trying to find a place to live. When he telephoned a landlord about an available rental property, he was often invited to look at it, but when the landlords saw him in person, they told him there must have been a mistake; no places were available. Baugh concluded that his identity as an African American had been concealed over the telephone. His resulting research eventually led him to detailed exploration of what he came to call linguistic profiling. In 2002 the Ford Foundation provided Baugh with a three-year, $500,000 grant.

Baugh received many honors and awards throughout his career. In addition to receiving various research and teaching awards, he was principal investigator, National Science Foundation: Linguistic Diversity, Literacy and Related Consequences for Human Health and Environmental Change (1991–1993). The U.S. Department of Housing and Urban Development named him Pioneer of Fair Housing, in support of advancing civil rights nationally (2004). Baugh is the author of numerous scholarly articles, including publications in *American Speech, Annual Review of Anthropology, Du Bois Review,* and *Journal of English Linguistics.* He also contributed to a number of books on Black English. His authored books include *Beyond Ebonics: Linguistic Pride and Racial Prejudice* (2000), *Out of the Mouths of Slaves: African American Language and Educational Malpractice* (1999), and *Black Street Speech: Its History, Structure and Survival* (1983), for which he won the Choice Outstanding Academic Book Award in 1984.

Baugh's interest in promoting the education of people of African descent and low-income students led him to become a founding member of the highly successful Eastside College Preparatory School in East Palo Alto (after East Palo Alto's only high school closed in 1976). The school was founded in 1996 and became fully accredited in 2003. One hundred percent of its graduates have gone on to pursue higher education. In 2005 Baugh was the first appointed MARGARET BUSH WILSON Professor in Arts and Sciences, named in honor of the prominent civil rights attorney and emeritus trustee, and director of the African and African American studies program at Washington University in St. Louis. He also received appointments at Washington University in the departments of psychology, anthropology, education, English, and linguistics.

Further Reading

Baugh, John. *Beyond Ebonics: Linguistic Pride and Racial Prejudice* (2000).

Baugh, John. *It Ain't about Race: Some Lingering (Linguistic) Consequences of the African Slave Trade and Their Relevance to Your Personal Historical Hardship Index* (2006).

Baugh, John. *Out of the Mouths of Slaves: African American Language and Educational Malpractice* (1999).

BETHANY K. DUMAS

BAYLEY, Solomon (c. 1771–c. 1839), was born a slave near Camden, in Kent County, Delaware. Bayley wrote in his *Narrative* that his grandmother was a "Guinea woman" who had been transported from West Africa to Virginia when she was only eleven years old and sold to "one of the most barbarous families of that day." Despite this, she gave birth to fifteen children and "lived to a great age" (38). Bayley's mother had been born and raised with the same Virginia family. She had had several children with her husband, Abner, by the time her master and mistress died and one of their daughters and her husband moved to Delaware, taking the black family. A few years later Solomon Bayley was born, one of thirteen children.

Bayley grew to manhood in Kent County, Delaware. He took a slave named Thamar as his wife and they had two children. When the wife of the couple who owned them died, and her husband moved back to Virginia in 1799, Bayley and his family, along with his mother and father and siblings, were transported to Hunting Creek, which later became Alexandria, Virginia. Under Delaware law, slaveholders taking slaves out of the state were not permitted to put them up for immediate sale, but soon after they arrived the owner sold the entire family. Moreover, they were scattered in all directions, "some to the east, some west, north and south" (39). About one year after the sale, Bayley's father, brother, and sister were sold and taken to the Caribbean. His mother was more fortunate. She ran away with Bayley's infant brother, and made it to freedom in New Jersey.

In his reminiscence, Bayley explained that, shortly after arriving in Virginia, he began legal proceedings to secure his freedom. Not only did Delaware law prohibit his immediate sale, but a Virginia statute, passed in 1795, gave persons illegally detained as slaves the right to sue for their freedom. If they did not have enough money to launch a suit, they would be assigned counsel and allowed to sue in forma pauperis (as a poor person). "I employed lawyers," Bayley wrote, "and went to court two days, to have a suit brought to obtain my freedom" (2). Two days before the trial date, he was "taken up and put on board a vessel out of Hunting Creek, bound to Richmond." Jailed and cast into irons, he was "brought very low." After some time, he was put into one of three wagons owned by his new master and began a journey toward the mountains. "Now consider, how great my distress must have been," he later confessed, "being carried from my wife and children" (2).

At this point, Bayley decided to run away. Waiting for the right moment, he slipped off the wagon and hid in some bushes until the other wagons had passed. He then set out across the countryside heading back toward Richmond. Thinking he would surely perish, he ran at night and with the aid of "a dreadful wind," thunder, lightning, and rain, he avoided capture. Twice slave catchers with their trained hunting dogs came close, but the rain covered up his scent. From Richmond, Bayley made it to Petersburg, remaining there three weeks before going down the James River in a small boat with another runaway. When they reached Chesapeake Bay, his companion was detected, captured, and after trying to escape by jumping over the side of a boat, was bludgeoned to death with an oar. Bayley, however, escaped detection. Having instructed his wife if they were ever parted to run away and meet him at a specific location on the Eastern Shore (perhaps the farm of an antislavery white or free black family), Bayley miraculously found his wife and his two children. Together, they set out to the North and freedom.

When Bayley and his family returned to Kent County in 1799, the white man who had illegally sold him and his family in Virginia confronted Bayley and threatened to enslave him again; Bayley, in turn, threatened to take him to court. In the end the two compromised; if Bayley paid the man eighty dollars, a fraction of his market value, he would be allowed to go free. Bayley agreed, purchased himself, and finally, as he put it, "the yoke was off my neck" (18). In freedom, the ambitious and energetic Bayley learned the trade of coopering. With the demand for barrels high, and his wages higher than those of many whites, he was able to save enough to purchase his wife and children. He made his final purchase in 1813, buying his son, described by the auctioneer as a "likely young negro," for $360 and one shilling. Several white men, including one whom Bayley described as a "great man," assisted him, paying him for his security bond and asking another bidder to allow Solomon to purchase his son.

During the Second Great Awakening in the early nineteenth century, Bayley experienced a religious conversion. He joined the Methodist Episcopal Church, became one of its most devout members, and, when one minister suggested it was a sin not to sanctify his marriage in the eyes of God, he married his wife (he was in the process of purchasing her freedom at the time) in a church ceremony. Bayley felt so strongly about his new faith that he gave up working as a cooper because the wooden barrels he made were used for whiskey. Following his conversion, he became a farm laborer and spent a good deal of time as a lay preacher.

In 1820 Robert Hurnard, a British abolitionist visiting Delaware, heard stories about Bayley's remarkable escape and invited him to talk about his life. Upon his return to England, Hurnard wrote to Bayley, asking him to write a memoir and some letters about his life. Hurnard learned that Bayley had placed his two daughters, Margaret and Leah, "out in the service of respectable families" (vi) but they, along with his son, Spence, had died prematurely. Although advanced in life, Bayley enjoyed good health, as did his wife, who was four years older.

In 1824 Bayley's recollections were published in England, with Hurnard promising to "transmit the whole of the profits of the publication to America, for the benefit of the aged couple" (viii). Although disjointed and containing lengthy Biblical quotations, *A Narrative* gives the reader a rare glimpse into the life of a runaway slave in the late eighteenth century. It emphasizes Bayley's fear, anxiety, and the remarkable obstacles confronting runaways. It also reveals the treachery of greedy whites, as well as the sympathy and support of those whites opposed to slavery. It also shows the primary importance of the black family, Christianity, and the triumph of human spirit over adversity.

In one of his letters, the self-taught Bayley observed that, for some time, he had followed the career of the Pan-Africanist PAUL CUFFE Sr. and was himself considering leaving the United States. In 1827 Solomon and Thamar Bayley decided to immigrate to Liberia, a fledgling colony in West Africa. Before departing, Bayley obtained a letter of commendation from Willard Hall, a U.S. District Court Judge and leader in the Delaware colonization movement, a group of whites who offered assistance to free blacks who wished to settle in West Africa; Hall wrote that despite his "unfavorable age" (Bayley was about fifty-six) "his character stands high not only among his people of colour, but among the most respectable of our citizens." The two former fugitive slaves then boarded the brig *Doris* out of Baltimore, and, along with eighty other passengers, mostly from New York and Maryland, they set sail via Norfolk, Virginia, for Liberia.

During the period when the Bayleys arrived in the Liberian capital of Monrovia, there were clashes between native inhabitants and the approximately twelve hundred settlers, and newcomers were dying from "the fever," or malaria. Nonetheless, the Bayleys cleared a seven-acre plot and began cultivating a small farm on the outskirts of Monrovia, near the St.

Paul's River. Solomon built a platform overlooking the river under a large tree, where, time permitting, he read and wrote. Following the death of his wife in 1833, Bayley published *A Brief Account of the Colony of Liberia*, which discussed the agricultural and commercial progress of the colony and the relationship between settlers and native Africans. He returned to the United States that year and visited a number of cities, but returned to Liberia, where he remarried and continued to farm, preach, and participate in community life until his death.

Further Reading

Bayley, Solomon. *A Narrative of Some Remarkable Incidents in the Life of Solomon Bayley, Formerly a Slave in the State of Delaware, North America* (1825).

Dalleo, Peter. "The Growth of Delaware's Antebellum Free African American Community," in *A History of African Americans of Delaware and Maryland's Eastern Shore*, ed. Carole Marks (1997).

Williams, William H. *Slavery and Freedom in Delaware, 1639–1865* (1996).

LOREN SCHWENINGER

BAYLOR, Elgin Gay (16 Sept. 1934–), basketball player and executive, was born in Washington, D.C., the son of a railroad brakeman. Little else is known about his parents. Baylor grew up in a poor section of the District of Columbia and played basketball at the all-black Spingarn High School, where he scored sixty-eight points in a single game to establish a new record for a D.C. high schooler. Although he was the first African American to make the all-metropolitan team, his poor grades discouraged college recruiters. Thus Baylor started his college career with a football scholarship at the tiny College of Idaho, which had only 450 students. Sam Vokes coached both football and basketball and decided that it made good sense to keep the talented Baylor off the football field. Baylor proceeded to average thirty-one points a game and made the NAIA All-American team, which recognizes the achievements of small-school athletes. After that year Baylor transferred to the University of Seattle. After sitting out the 1955–1956 season, Baylor finished third in scoring in the 1956–1957 season.

Baylor caught the attention of the nation's basketball fans in the 1957–1958 season when he averaged 32.5 points per game in the regular season to lead the nation in scoring. In the 1958 NCAA tournament, Baylor led Seattle to the championship game, where they fell to the University of Kentucky. Baylor elected to skip his senior season to enter the NBA with the Minneapolis Lakers.

Although the Lakers had won four NBA championships in the first half of the 1950s, they had descended into mediocrity when Baylor joined them in 1958. At six feet five inches tall and 225 pounds, Baylor was easily the most creative player in the NBA. Blessed with a great vertical leap and unbelievable body control, Baylor combined fakes and power that made him virtually unstoppable. As the rookie of the

Elgin Gay Baylor of the Los Angeles Lakers making a fast break past the Golden State Warriors' McCoy McLemore (32) during the season-opening game at San Francisco Civic Auditorium, October 1965. (AP Images.)

year Baylor led the Lakers to the 1959 finals, where they lost to the Boston Celtics. The following season Baylor set a new NBA single-game scoring record when he poured in sixty-four points against the Boston Celtics on 8 November 1959.

After struggling for several years, in 1960 the Lakers moved to Los Angeles. That same year the Lakers drafted Jerry West, another future NBA great who teamed up with Baylor to make the Lakers a frequent NBA finalist in the 1960s. In his first season in Los Angeles, Baylor averaged 34.8 points and scored 71 points on 15 November 1960 to break his own NBA record. After three years Baylor was one of the dominant players in the NBA and was the undisputed leader of the Lakers. Merv Harris of the *Los Angeles Herald Examiner* wrote, "Whenever Elgin wanted to play poker, they played poker. Wherever Elgin wanted to eat, they went to eat. Whatever Elgin wanted to talk about, they talked about."

As in the case of other black players, Baylor had to battle racism. When the Lakers played a game in Charleston, West Virginia, and a hotel refused to provide accommodations for Baylor and two teammates, the Lakers star boycotted the game. Active in the NBA Player's Association, he was one of the NBA stars prepared to boycott the 1964 All-Star game unless the league provided a pension program for the players.

In 1961–1962 Baylor had one of his finest seasons. Because he was required to fulfill U.S. Army reserve duty, Baylor played in only forty-eight regular season games, but he averaged an eye-popping 38.2 points per game. The Lakers took the Boston Celtics to the seventh game of the NBA finals only to lose in overtime. In the fifth game of the series Baylor set a new single-game play-off scoring record by sinking sixty-one points. He also snagged twenty-two rebounds. In 1962–1963 Baylor had another spectacular year, averaging thirty-four points and fourteen rebounds per game. The Lakers lost to the Celtics in the NBA finals but became the first NBA team to gross $1 million. By the 1963–1964 season Baylor's knees began to bother him, and during the following season, on 3 April 1965, his kneecap split and he severely damaged a knee ligament. Without Baylor the Lakers lost for the third time in four years in the NBA finals to the Boston Celtics.

Baylor fooled his doctors and managed to play in sixty-five games of the 1965–1966 season but averaged only 16.6 points per game. Once again the Lakers lost to the Celtics in the NBA finals. Baylor never fully recovered from his injury, which forced him to adjust his game and rely more on his jump shot than on the acrobatic moves that had been his trademark. Despite these limitations, Baylor was still an extraordinary player. In the 1966–1967 season Baylor averaged twenty-six points and made the all-NBA first team. The Lakers, however, were eliminated in the first round of the play-offs. The team bounced back in 1967–1968 when they won the Western Division but once again lost to their nemesis, the Boston Celtics, in the finals. Baylor finished second in the NBA in scoring with twenty-six points per game.

For the 1968–1969 season the Lakers added WILT CHAMBERLAIN to the tandem of Baylor and West. Baylor averaged 24.8 points and made the all-NBA team for the eighth time. In the NBA finals the Lakers jumped out to a three games to one lead over the Celtics but could not close the series, and Boston won yet another NBA championship. In 1969–1970 knee injuries limited Baylor to fifty-four games, but he still averaged 24 points. The Lakers advanced to the NBA finals against the New York Knicks, setting up one of the most memorable championship series in NBA history. In the seventh game, inspired by an injured Willis Reed, the Knicks trounced the Lakers. Injuries limited Baylor to two games in 1970–1971, and nine games into the 1971–1972 season he retired.

In the 1970s Baylor served as an assistant for the expansion team the New Orleans Jazz (1974–1976) and then was the Jazz head coach for three years (1976–1979). Baylor's teams registered a record of 86 wins and 135 losses. In 1986 the Los Angeles Clippers named Baylor vice president of basketball operations.

In the 1950s Elgin Baylor, along with BILL RUSSELL, Wilt Chamberlain, and OSCAR ROBERTSON, changed the way that basketball was played and opened the door to the NBA for other African American players. When he was free of injuries, Baylor was virtually unstoppable and scored with a variety of unpredictable shots. As an outstanding rebounder and passer, Baylor was a complete player whose creativity helped make the NBA one of America's most popular professional sports. In 1976 Elgin Baylor was inducted into the Naismith Basketball Hall of Fame. In 1996 he was named to the Fiftieth Anniversary NBA All-Time team. A ten-time all-NBA

player, Baylor scored 23,149 points for a 27.4 per-game average.

Further Reading
Lazenby, Roland. *The Lakers* (1993).
Pluto, Terry. *Tall Tales* (1992).
Thomas, Ron. *They Cleared the Lane: The NBA's Black Pioneers* (2002).
Whalen, Thomas J. *Dynasty's End: Bill Russell and the 1968–69 World Champion Boston Celtics* (2004).

ADOLPH GRUNDMAN

BAYNE, Thomas (1824–1889), dentist and politician, was born into slavery in North Carolina and was known as Samuel Nixon before his escape from bondage in 1855. Nothing is known about his parents. He was sold several times before being purchased by C. F. Martin, a dentist in Norfolk, Virginia. As Martin's slave, Nixon learned sufficient dentistry to serve as the doctor's assistant and to make dental house calls. He also developed bookkeeping skills and monitored the doctor's accounts.

In Norfolk, Nixon became involved with the Underground Railroad. Befriending the captains of many of the schooners sailing in and out of Norfolk, he often convinced them to hide fugitive slaves aboard ship and carry them north, usually to Philadelphia or to New Bedford, Massachusetts. After conducting many other slaves through the Underground Railroad, Nixon decided to become a passenger himself in March 1855. He and three other slaves disguised themselves and hid on board a schooner bound for Philadelphia. He left behind his wife, Edna (maiden name unknown), and one child, both of whom were owned by E. P. Tabb, a Norfolk hardware merchant. The ship landed in New Jersey, where Nixon was directed to Abigail Goodwin, a Quaker abolitionist. In a letter to a fellow abolitionist, Goodwin described Nixon as "a smart young man . . . well dressed in fine broad-cloth coat and overcoat, and has a very active tongue in his head," but she worried that "they will be after him soon."

Nixon then traveled to New Bedford, where he changed his name to Thomas Bayne and began a dentistry practice while maintaining contact with Underground Railroad agents like WILLIAM STILL of Philadelphia. Letters between Bayne and Still reveal that Bayne sometimes sheltered fugitives in his New Bedford home and that Still aided Bayne's advancement by sending medical and dental textbooks. In January 1860 Bayne thanked Still for his "Vigilance as a colored man helping a colored man to get such knowledge as will give the lie to our enemies." Bayne also gained renown in New Bedford as a speaker at abolitionist and temperance meetings, and he served on the New Bedford City Council in 1865.

At the end of the Civil War, Bayne returned to Norfolk, Virginia, to rejoin his family. He immediately became involved in politics, and in May 1865 he chaired a public meeting at which the participants passed eight civil rights resolutions under the title of *Equal Suffrage: Address from the Colored Citizens of Norfolk, Virginia to the People of the United States.* These resolutions pledged Virginia's loyalty to the Union, decried race discrimination as abhorrent to "patriotism, humanity, and religion," and demanded equal suffrage for black and white Americans. As a member of a committee that testified on behalf of rights for freedmen, Bayne appeared before O. O. Howard of the Freedmen's Bureau in December 1865. The following year he was among a delegation of black men from Virginia who met with President Andrew Johnson to articulate demands for civil and political rights, especially the right to vote. Bayne also testified before the Joint Committee on Reconstruction, where he urged that the rights of former slaves be protected and that Reconstruction reforms be enforced.

An important black leader in the Virginia Republican Party, Bayne served as vice president of the April 1867 state Republican convention held in Richmond, where he earned a reputation for his elegant dress and commitment to public education. He was subsequently elected as a delegate from Norfolk to the Constitutional Convention of the State of Virginia, which was charged with the task of drawing up a new state constitution that would qualify Virginia for readmission to the Union. Bayne was one of twenty-four black delegates to the convention, which met during the winter of 1867–1868. In the convention, Bayne adamantly insisted that the residual injustices of slavery be redressed. He fervently supported the proposed state constitution's Declaration of Rights, which stated that "all men are, by nature, equally free and independent, and have certain inherent rights . . . namely, the enjoyment of life and liberty, with the means of . . . obtaining happiness and safety." In the debate that surrounded that preamble, Bayne claimed the promises of the Declaration of Independence and the Constitution for black as well as white Americans, and he pledged himself to a constitution "that should not have the word black or the word white anywhere in it." He repeatedly argued that the harmful aftereffects of slavery could best be combated with the protection of black voting rights and equal citizenship rights.

Bayne recognized education as a priority for Virginia's black community. At the Virginia state convention he spoke out against the prejudice faced by many uneducated blacks with the reminder that white Virginians had "robbed the black man of his education, . . . taken the money and labor of the black man to support themselves in grandeur, and now they curse the black man because he is not a grammarian. They are like the hunter who shot the bird through both wings, and when it fluttered and fell, damned it because it would not rise." In reparation Bayne proposed that Virginia's constitution should ensure that "the free public schools in this State shall be open free to all classes, and no child, pupil or scholar shall be ejected from said schools on account of race, color, or any invidious distinction," but the measure was defeated as too radical.

Following the state convention, Bayne retained interest in public affairs, attending an all-black political convention in May 1869. Reconstruction soon ended in Virginia, however, and Bayne turned increasingly to his dentistry practice. As political opportunities for black Virginians diminished, Bayne sought to maintain a public profile by engaging in periodic bouts of traveling ministry, but these efforts were cut short by the senility that plagued his later years. In 1888 he was admitted to the Central State Lunatic Asylum in Norfolk, where he died. For Bayne, as for many other freedmen and freedwomen, the promise of Reconstruction's early days, during which he played an important role in post–Civil War politics, proved brighter than the long-term reality.

Further Reading
Aptheker, Herbert, ed. *A Documentary History of the Negro People in the United States,* vol. 2 (1968).
Foner, Eric. *Freedom's Lawmakers: A Directory of Black Officeholders during Reconstruction* (1993).
Still, William. *The Underground Railroad: A Record of Facts, Authentic Narratives, Letters &c.* (1872).
Taylor, Alrutheus A. *The Negro in the Reconstruction of Virginia* (1926).

CHANDRA M. MILLER

BEALS, Melba Pattillo (7 Dec. 1941–), journalist, author, and public speaker, was born Melba Joy Pattillo in Little Rock, Arkansas, the daughter of Howell "Will" Pattillo, a hostler's helper for the Missouri Pacific Railroad, and Dr. Lois Marie Peyton Pattillo, a junior high school English teacher who was among the first African Americans to attend the University of Arkansas (graduating in1954). In 1957, spurred by the 1954 Supreme Court ruling in *Brown v. Board of Education,* mandating public school desegregation, Beals, at the age of fifteen, became one of the first African American students—later known as the "Little Rock Nine"—to enroll in Central High School, then Arkansas' finest high school.

Prior to 1957 Beals's deepest anguish had been her parents' divorce when she was seven. She found solace in the hours she spent with her cherished grandmother, India Anette Peyton, while her mother worked and studied and her younger brother, Conrad, played. Convinced that the desegregation of Central High was key to the future of civil rights for her people, Beals tried to prepare herself. Yet despite her keen familiarity with the degradation and humiliation imposed by Jim Crow, nothing in her experience could inure her to the hostility and violence she faced. Aptly, her grandmother India had given her the work of Mohandas K. Gandhi, the Indian whose program of nonviolent resistance provided a practical means for fulfilling her destiny as a "warrior." The Bible, the primary source of her grandmother's teachings, gave the young Beals spiritual sustenance throughout her lengthy ordeal. Thus, she learned to conceal her terror, her disgust, and her physical pain, and to respond to monstrous assaults with a simple "thank you."

Ernest Green, a fellow member of the "Nine," became the first African American to graduate from Central High, but subsequent efforts by the National Association for the Advancement of Colored People (NAACP) to block Arkansas Governor Orville Faubus's plan to close all area high schools proved unsuccessful. At the same time, the Ku Klux Klan posted signs promising to pay for Beals's capture, dead or alive.

At age seventeen, Beals boarded a plane for San Francisco with little more than a promise from DAISY LEE GATSON BATES, president of the Arkansas State Conference of the NAACP, that Association members in Santa Rosa, California, would look after her. Having lost her grandmother, Beals was now forced to leave her mother and brother behind and begin the next phase of her life in the rural home of the McCabes, a white Quaker family that resembled her own solely in the wealth of love they shared. The transition to another predominantly white high school was made more difficult than necessary by her painful recollections of the brutality she had faced at Central High, and Beals found herself increasingly isolated and suffering a crisis in personal identity: the few black students had no interest in befriending her, and despite numerous offers she could not immerse herself in the white social set. A complete collapse of her physical and mental health led to one of her few trips home to Little Rock.

Although freedom in California was far from complete—Beals was denied admission to a Santa Rosa swimming pool—it had been sufficient to make a return to oppressive southern customs intolerable. Beals found it impossible to avert her eyes in the presence of whites or accommodate herself to segregated public seating, which were widely practiced customs in the South. Upon her return to California, Beals registered at Santa Rosa Community College but transferred to San Francisco State College (SFSC), a move that required her to forgo the comfort and warmth of the McCabes' home.

Her encounters with members of the educated black community in San Francisco quickly dashed her hopes for acceptance, and she found racism thriving among some of the white students on campus. Beals's refusal to reveal the role she had played in the Crisis of 1957 left her in the odd position of listening for the first time to a discussion of those events as an "outsider." Clearly, there were segregationists in California, too, even if they were not in the majority. Unable to find community with fellow blacks, Beals moved into a previously all-white women's residence club where, finally, she managed to establish tentative friendships. In 1962, despite her mother's pointed objections, she married Matt Beals, a white man, and reveled in life with her new husband.

Her daughter Kellie Joy was born in August 1963. That same month and far removed from the mounting struggle for civil rights, Beals watched the television coverage of MARTIN LUTHER KING JR., whom she had previously had the privilege of meeting, as he delivered his legendary "I have a dream" speech at the historic March on Washington. No longer pursuing her education, Beals rationalized that after enduring the trauma of desegregating Central High, she had earned time off from sociopolitical concerns; however, with the stillbirth of her second child, a wedge emerged between her and her husband, who soon abandoned both mother and child. For the first time in her life, Beals had to face the harsh economic reality that she and her daughter would survive only if they received public assistance. In 1968 they moved to a housing project, subsisting on welfare and food stamps. Encouraged by her surrogate father George McCabe, Beals decided, against all odds, to complete her education.

Beals's talent as a writer had not escaped the attention of her journalism teacher at SFSC, who encouraged her to submit an application for a program funded by the Ford Foundation. In 1971 Beals graduated from San Francisco State College and, leaving Kellie with her mother in Little Rock, enrolled in a master's degree program in broadcast journalism at Columbia University in New York City.

Her professional career began at KQED, the public television station in San Francisco. The following year, she accepted a position as an NBC newscaster with KRON-TV, also in San Francisco. Beals also published a number of articles for the *San Francisco Examiner*, *Essence*, and *People*. Her best-selling *Expose Yourself: Using the Power of Public Relations to Promote Your Business and Yourself* appeared in 1990 and soon became an industry standard work.

Beals offered gripping details of her experience as a student at Central High in *Warriors Don't Cry: A Searing Memoir of the Battle to Integrate Little Rock's Central High* (1994). Winner of the American Library Association's Notable Books Award (1995) and the Robert F. Kennedy Memorial Book Award (1995), this extraordinary volume remains a seminal account of early efforts to ensure quality public education for African Americans. A source of vital historical information and a testament to the raw courage of youthful conviction, *Warriors* revealed the buried truths behind events that brought a small city in a rural Southern state to the attention of the world. Although it took more than three decades for Beals to write and publish *Warriors*, she produced her second volume of memoirs, *White Is a State of Mind* (1999), in relatively short order, providing a helpful "update" of her experiences following her efforts to desegregate Central High.

Beals was a guest on many radio talk shows and appeared on C-Span's *Booknotes*, *Good Morning America*, *Nightline*, and *Oprah Winfrey*. In 1998 Beals—along with other members of the "Little Rock Nine"—was awarded the Congressional Gold Medal by President Bill Clinton. Founder of Melcon Communications, Beals developed a diversity seminar, "The Spirit of Diversity: Seeing Equal—Being Equal," designed to aid in the resolution of conflicts arising from racial and religious differences. In 2002 Beals was inducted into the Marin Women's Hall of Fame for her contributions to social change.

Further Reading
Beals, Melba Pattillo. *Warriors Don't Cry: A Searing Memoir of the Battle to Integrate Little Rock's Central High* (1994).
Beals, Melba Pattillo. *White Is a State of Mind* (1999).
Bates, Daisy. *The Long Shadow of Little Rock* (1962).

MARINELLE RINGER

BEAM, Joseph Fairchild (30 Dec. 1954–27 Dec. 1988), writer, poet, and activist, was born in Philadelphia, Pennsylvania, to Sun Fairchild Beam, a security guard, and Dorothy Saunders Beam, a teacher and school guidance counselor. Beam attended Philadelphia's public schools as well as the St. Joseph School for Boys (Clayton, Delaware), Malvern Preparatory (Paoli, Pennsylvania), and St. Thomas More (Philadelphia). In 1972, while still a teenager, Beam was honored with the Philadelphia School District's Volunteer Service Award. He later attended Franklin College in Franklin, Indiana, where he studied journalism and earned his BA in 1976. As an undergraduate Beam was active in the local Black Student Union and was a member of the Franklin Independent Men. He was also active in college journalism and radio programming and was awarded the Omega Psi Phi Fraternity Award for Broadcasting in 1974.

After graduation, Beam remained in the Midwest where he pursued a master's degree in communications. He returned to Philadelphia in 1979 and began working at Giovanni's Room, a local independent gay and lesbian bookstore. Beam continued the writing he had begun in college and was active in the struggle for social justice for the black gay community at the local and national level.

Beam's work appeared in many newspapers and publications, including *Au Courant, Black/Out, Blackheart, Changing Men, Gay Community News, The Painted Bride Quarterly, The Philadelphia Gay News, The Advocate, New York Native, Body Politic,* and *The Windy City Times.* Among his critically recognized short stories are "Brother to Brother" and "No Cheek to Turn." Beam also interviewed many of the influential community activists of his time, including AUDRE LORDE, BAYARD RUSTIN, and SONIA SANCHEZ. In these interviews, whose subjects often became life-long friends, Beam won praise for the style and beauty of his writing. Prefacing his interview with Audre Lorde, he wrote:

Audre Lorde is like a diamond. Multi-faceted, she is a mother, poet, novelist, publisher, socialist, feminist and lesbian. Sharp, she cuts through the bramble of political correctness and does not bite her tongue. Reflective, she shows not only where we are, but where we wish to be. (*Philadelphia Gay News*, 18–24 October 1996)

In 1984 Beam was recognized for outstanding achievement by a minority journalist by the Lesbian and Gay Press Association. In 1985, *The Philadelphia Gay News* awarded him its prestigious Lambda Award for Outstanding Achievement. Also in that year, Beam joined the Executive Committee of the National Coalition of Black Lesbians and Gays and became the editor of its journal, *Black/Out*. He also began to serve as a consultant for the Gay and Lesbian Task Force of the American Friends Service Committee.

1986 saw the publication of the work for which Beam is best known, *In the Life.* The first anthology of poetry and prose by and about black gay men, *In the Life* was groundbreaking and influential. Beam described the impetus for the volume, stating that "By mid-1983, I had grown weary of reading literature by white gay men. . . . None of them spoke to me as a black man. Their words offered the reflection of a sidewalk; their characters cast ominous shadows" (13). In this volume, to which he also contributed, Beam addresses many of the central themes that resonate throughout the pieces. With raw honesty, he confronts how the dominant culture renders black gay men invisible and describes the pain of being excluded by the African American community. *In the Life* features the work of nearly three dozen African American gay men who discuss issues of race, gender, and sexuality. In addition to describing the pain and costs of exclusion, prejudice, and invisibility, *In the Life* also highlights the beauty, character, and dignity of this community: "We are black men who are proudly gay. What we offer is our lives, our love, our visions. . . . We are coming home with our heads held up high" (18).

Soon after the publication of *In the Life,* Beam began a second anthology, *Brother to Brother,* named after his earlier, acclaimed short story. Beam died of an AIDS-related illness before he could finish *Brother to Brother,* so his mother, Dorothy, and friend, the poet ESSEX HEMPHILL, completed the book, which was published in 1991. *Brother to Brother* stands as yet another influential book that showcases essays, poetry, and other writing by black gay men. *In the Life* and *Brother to Brother* are lauded as critical, pioneering, and important books that document the lives and experiences of black gay men—who until *In the Life* were unrepresented in published work. These authors include Gilberto Gerald, A. Billy S. Jones, James Charles Roberts, and James S. Tinney.

Beam's life and legacy have been honored and continue to influence and inspire the work of others. The Joseph Beam Scholarship Prize, established by Beam's mother after his death, is awarded annually for any essay or literary work on gay, lesbian, or transgender issues written by an undergraduate or graduate student in the English department at Temple University in Philadelphia. The filmmaker MARLON RIGGS dedicated his critically acclaimed film *Tongues Untied* (1990) to Beam. The Joseph Beam Youth Collaborative in Philadelphia, a nonprofit educational organization, was founded in 2003 and works with and for lesbian, gay, bisexual, transgender, and questioning (LGBTQ) youth of color.

Further Reading

Many of Joseph Beam's papers are available at the Schomburg Center for Research in Black Culture in New York. The collection includes letters, conference materials, Beam's stories and essays, files of the National Coalition of Black Lesbians and Gays and its journal, *Black/Out*, and other documents, photos, and films.

Beam, Joseph, ed. *In the Life: A Black Gay Anthology* (1986).

Hemphill, Essex, ed. *Brother to Brother: New Writings by Black Gay Men* (1991).

BILLIE GASTIC

BEAMON, Bob (29 Aug. 1946–), track-and-field athlete, motivational speaker, and activist for youth, was born Robert Alfred Beamon in Jamaica, New York, to Naomi Brown Beamon and a father he never met. After his mother died from tuberculosis before Beamon's first birthday, his stepfather, James, assumed parental responsibility for Robert and his older, disabled brother Andrew. Robert's grandmother, Bessie Beamon, ultimately took over their care as a result of James's inadequate parenting skills. Rarely supervised, Beamon ran away from home when he was fourteen and joined a gang. When he struck a teacher who had attempted to break up one of Beamon's fights, he was expelled and charged with assault and battery.

Beamon's life might have become a tragedy if it weren't for a judge who was "thoughtful, compassionate, and obviously interested in helping kids" (*Second Chances*, 3). The judge took a chance and allowed Beamon to attend an alternative school in Manhattan for juvenile delinquents. Although teachers and the school were "tough," they taught Beamon a different kind of life. After leaving the alternative school, Beamon turned to athletics to escape his troubled past. In 1962, during junior high school, Beamon set a Junior Olympic record in the long jump of 24 feet 1 inch (Beamon, 62) and set his sights on going to the more academic Jamaica High School. The dean and head coach of the track team, LARRY ELLIS (who would later become the first black head track coach at Princeton and for the U.S. Olympic team), recognized Beamon's talent and "took Beamon under his wing," motivating him to dream and work toward his goals (*Second Chances*, 21). At the age of 16 Beamon set citywide track records in New York City and also set the New York State record for the long jump in 1965. That year he ranked second among U.S. high school athletes with a best jump of 25 feet 3½ inches and ranked first among triple jumpers with a best of 53 feet 3¾ inches (Schaap, 59). "Now, he had a purpose, an opportunity, encouragement from others and an Olympic dream" (*Second Chances*, 21).

Following graduation from Jamaica High School in January 1966, Beamon enrolled in North Carolina Agricultural and Technical College for less than a year before transferring to University of Texas–El Paso (UTEP), where he and fellow athletes faced racism from peers and local residents as well as the school's athletic director (*Booklist*, May 1999). In 1967, while Beamon was at UTEP, the track coach told a friend, "One day soon, Bob Beamon is going to make a jump that you won't believe and I won't believe" (*New York Times*, Nov. 2006).

Beamon set out to qualify for the 1968 Olympic long jump, but faced a problem. He had a strong tendency to foul (go over the "take-off" board, the board from which the jump begins). At the time Beamon's unofficial coach was his fellow track-and-field star and record holder Ralph Boston, who worked with Beamon to overcome his fouling problem. Nevertheless, Beamon ran into trouble during the Olympics by fouling in his first two attempts at qualifying for the finals. Prior to the third attempt, "Boston reminded him he could take off from farther behind the board and still reach the finals" (*New York Daily News*, June 2006) and Beamon adjusted himself accordingly for a successful jump. In the finals Beamon came just about as close to fouling as humanly possible: "The shadow of his takeoff shoe's toe lay for an instant over the foul line, but he left no mark on the telltale Plasticine [marking material]" (*Sports Illustrated*, June 1987). In addition, during his jump the wind blew behind him at exactly 2.0 meters per second, the maximum allowed.

After Beamon landed, the judges attempted to measure his jump, but the optical sighting device could not extend past twenty-eight feet. One of the judges exclaimed, "Fantastic, fantastic. . . . We will have to measure it with a tape" (*Sportstar Weekly*, Aug. 2006). As Beamon looked on, the officials measured the distance of the jump and announced it as 8.90 meters. Beamon did not understand what 8.90 meters measured to in feet, and so it took Boston telling Beamon that he had jumped 29 feet 2½ inches before Beamon realized the significance of what had just happened (*Sports Illustrated*, 66). Beamon immediately collapsed and broke into tears in the face of powerful emotions and was helped to his feet by teammates. It was later discovered that "he was suffering a cataplectic seizure as his muscles gave way under the emotion of it all" (*Sportstar Weekly*, Aug. 2006). The previous world record had been 27 feet 4¾ inches. In the thirty-three years prior to 1968, athletes had extended the world record by only 8½ inches past JESSE OWENS's 1935 record of 26 feet 8¼ inches, and Beamon was now first to jump over 28 feet and 29 feet. In January 1969 *Track and Field News* named him Track and Field Athlete of the Year for 1968 (Schaap, 115).

While Beamon's leap shattered the world record, his achievement was touched by controversy. Critics have pointed to Mexico City's high elevation and the maximum allowable wind as contributing factors in Beamon's achievement by allowing athletes to jump farther than normal. But Beamon's jump withstood the test of time, his record lasting for twenty-three years until 30 August 1991 when the American MIKE POWELL jumped 29 feet 4½ inches in the World Championships in Tokyo.

Beamon's life after the 1968 Olympics brought him mixed fortunes, and he never jumped as far as 27 feet again, though following a hamstring injury in early 1969, he did jump 26 feet 11 inches off his other leg in the Amateur Athletic Union championship in June 1969 (Schaap, 122). He was a fifteenth-round 1969 NBA draft pick by the Phoenix Suns, though a professional basketball career never materialized. In 1972 Beamon retired from track and graduated from Adelphi University, earning a degree in Cultural Anthropology. He received a master's degree in Counseling Psychology from San Diego State in 1975. He participated without distinction in professional track and field from 1973 to 1976. He worked for Home Federal Savings in San Diego and as a television commentator.

Beamon became an artist, developed and marketed a successful line of neckties, coached college track, and led the Youth Services division of the Parks and Recreation programs in the Miami-Dade County area in Florida. He was also involved in youth-centered civic work, worked as a philanthropist—organizing charity golf outings benefiting youth programs—and served as an advocate in the Florida Children's Court System for disadvantaged youth. Beamon warned that if children are being exposed to more and more violence, whether at school, on the streets, from television or in video games, and "parents are becoming less watchful over, and less involved with, their own kids. Families are far more fragmented and disconnected" (*Second Chances*, 4). He recognized the need to reach out to children in danger of becoming criminals and to show them there is a better way to live. He served as a national spokesperson for the Children's Courts and supported the fight against legislation that would prosecute juvenile offenders as adults.

Beamon is the owner of Bob Beamon Communications, Inc., and a professional speaker for Fortune 500 companies. In 1997 he married his fifth wife, Milana Walter Beamon, with whom he lived in Miami with his two daughters, Deanna, adopted with his previous wife in 1985, and Tameka. In 1999 he published his autobiography, *The Man Who Could Fly: The Bob Beamon Story*, with Milana. In 2000 he became the director of athletic development at Florida Atlantic University. A participant in the 1996 Atlanta Olympics opening ceremonies, he served on the board of the committee for the New York 2012 Olympic Bid. Elected to the U.S. Olympic Hall of Fame in 1983 (its first year of operation), he was also a member of the New York Track-and-Field Hall of Fame and was rated by ESPN as one of the top hundred athletes of the twentieth century.

Further Reading

Beamon, Bob, and Milana Walter Beamon. *The Man Who Could Fly: The Bob Beamon Story* (1999).
Beauregard, Sue-Ellen. "*The Man Who Could Fly: The Bob Beamon Story* (Young Adult Review)," *Booklist* (May 1999).
Justice Policy Institute and Children and Family Justice Center of Northwestern University School of Law. *Second Chances: 100 Years of the Children's Court, Giving Kids a Chance to Make a Better Choice* (May 2000).
"The Magic Leap," *Sportstar Weekly* (Aug. 2006).
Moore, Kenny. "Giants on the Earth (Bob Beamon's and Lee Evans's Records from 1968 Olympics Still Stand)," *Sports Illustrated* (June 1987).
Schaap, Dick. *The Perfect Jump* (1976).

RICHARD SOBEL

BEARD, Andrew Jackson (1849–10 May 1921), inventor, was born in Jefferson County, Alabama, the son of Milton Beard and Creasey Tatum, both former slaves on the Beard family plantation. He adopted the name of his former master at age fifteen after he was liberated by Union forces. A year later, he married Edie Beard, about whom nothing else is known. The couple raised three children: John, Jack, and Andrew Jr.; the latter died following graduation from high school. Like most former slaves, however, Beard was illiterate and remained so throughout his life.

After the Civil War, Beard worked as a sharecropper on his former master's farm until he was about eighteen years old and then moved to St. Clair County, Alabama. In 1872, he made a three-week journey from Birmingham to Montgomery on an oxcart that carried fifty bushels of apples, which he sold for approximately two hundred dollars. He eventually advanced from sharecropping to owning an eighty-acre farm outside Center Point, Alabama, where he raised his family and had tenant farmers. He built a wooden church, which also served as a schoolhouse, for his African American tenants, one family of which adopted his surname.

Beard, like many nineteenth-century inventors, was known as a "tinker," yet the term did not convey the intricacies of his work. He built and operated a flour mill in Hardwicks, Alabama, while he developed the concept for his earliest invention, a double plow. He received a patent on the device on 26 April 1881, which three years later he sold for $4,000. Following the sale of his double plow he returned to his birthplace and farmed for four years. He then received a patent for a plow or cultivator on 10 August 1886, which he sold for $5,200. At that point, he entered the real estate business; by this time his net worth was reportedly in excess of $30,000.

Despite receiving little recognition, African American inventors made many contributions, ranging from small cost-saving or safety devices to mechanical instruments that proved to be of vital importance to the industrial development of the nation. In 1889 Beard invented the rotary steam engine, which was promoted as being more efficient than conventional models at one-tenth the cost and having the ability to conserve 20 percent of steam without risk of explosion. He received a patent for the rotary engine on 7 May 1892. A year earlier Beard had unsuccessfully labored on the concept of a fish plate for a railroad, though he did not receive a patent.

Nineteenth-century African Americans often found employment with the railroad as firemen and switchmen, where they made significant contributions. For example, ELIJAH MCCOY, who studied mechanical engineering in Scotland, earlier worked as a fireman for the Michigan Central Railroad, where he invented a drip cup lubricating system in 1872. This lubricating device was modified for use in numerous other industries. Beard's employment with the Alabama and Chattanooga Railroad increased his exposure to mechanized instruments and led to his most significant invention, the automatic car-coupling, called the Jenny Coupler, which reduced the loss of life and limb. The job of hooking railroad cars had been done by individual workers, who had to climb down between two cars to insert the heavy iron pin that would hold the cars together. As the speed at which two cars could be brought together to be coupled was not mechanically controlled, the cars could crash together hard and fast. Many railroad workers were seriously injured—Beard himself reportedly lost a leg trying to couple two railroad cars together—and some even lost their lives. Aware of the grave danger faced by switchmen, who lacked insurance, he worked tirelessly, sometimes going without meals, to invent a safety device that made it unnecessary for switchmen to risk bodily harm as they connected train cars. On 23 November 1897, he received a patent for the Jenny Coupler, which sold for $50,000 to a New York company. This was followed by subsequent patents issued for improvements on 28 May 1901 and 31 May 1904. Another patent for improvements was assigned to the Beard Automatic Coupler Company on 19 December 1905. He later received recognition as an honorary member of the Master Car Builders Association and exhibited his invention at the association's convention in Atlantic City, New Jersey.

The facts of his later life remain unclear, but it is known that Beard rode a shiny buggy and had the image of a successful businessman, dressed in a vest and suit jacket and wearing eyeglasses. He acquired considerable landholdings and owned the Beard's Jitney (Taxi) Line in Birmingham, yet illiteracy coupled by unwise business decisions likely contributed to economic hardship in his final years. How he disposed of his considerable wealth is not known. Some reported that he donated several lots in Montgomery to support a school for African American children, and others indicated that he provided money to the same school in his will. In his latter years he fell upon hard times and was admitted to the Jefferson County Alms House in Birmingham, Alabama, where he died.

Further Reading
"Andrew Jackson Beard." *The National Cyclopedia* (1893).
Sluby, Patricia Carter. *The Inventive Spirit of African Americans: Patented Ingenuity* (2004).
Sullivan, Otha Richard. *African American Inventors* (1998).

ROLAND BARKSDALE-HALL

BEARD, Matthew (1 Jan. 1925–8 Jan. 1981), actor, was born Matthew Beard Jr. in Los Angeles, California, to Johnnie Mae Beard and Matthew Beard Sr. The oldest boy, he and his father were born on New Year's Day. Little is known about his parents, except that his father was a longtime minister in Los Angeles. Beard's father heard that there was an audition being held by Hal Roach, the creator and producer of the popular *Our Gang* film series, for a black child to replace Allen "Farina" Hoskins, who was growing too old for the role. Three hundred and fifty children auditioned, but director Bob McGowan was so impressed by little Matthew's confidence, nonchalance, expressive eyes, and contagious smile that he signed him up for five years without a screen test.

Matthew's younger sister, Betty Jane, preceded him in two earlier shorts. His other siblings and even his mother made later appearances in the series, but it was Matthew who became a regular in *Our Gang*, playing the role of Stymie from 1930 to 1935. Beard's first appearance in an *Our Gang* comedy was as Hercules in "Teacher's Pet" (1930). Beard was so curious and excited about being on a movie set that he constantly wandered around the studio examining the props and gimmicks. He interfered with the shoot so often that a frustrated Bob McGowan uttered, "This kid's beautiful, but he stymies me all the time" (Maltin and Bann, 259). Thereafter, his character was named Stymie.

Stymie may have gotten in the way, but he was also McGowan's favorite *Our Gang* kid. He wasn't alone. Beard was a crowd pleaser. His star power increased as he evolved from being a sidekick to a major player in *Our Gang*. Powered by an outsized personality and a charming, effervescent grin, he was a natural scene-stealer. Sporting his trademark oversized bowler hat that often sat askew on his shaved head, Beard's precociousness and comedic talent enabled him to transcend the stereotypes littering the *Our Gang* territory. DONALD BOGLE writes in his book *Toms, Coons, Mulattoes, Mammies, & Bucks* that race was not significant in the relationship between the black and white children despite the accepted notions and attitudes of the day. "Indeed, the charming sense of 'Our Gang' was that all the children were buffoons . . . forever plagued by setbacks and sidetracks as they set out to have fun, and everyone had his turn at being outwitted" (23). However, few could outsmart Stymie: "Stymie is one of the most self-reliant characters in the history of *Our Gang*. He can hold his own against any child or adult in the series just by using his wits, and never does he surrender his basic charm and appeal in the process" (Maltin and Bann, 106).

Beard delivered one-liners with a glint in his eye and the assurance of a seasoned pro. He mastered the art of deadpan expressions and hilarious double-takes. He was such an excellent performer that the studio nicknamed him "One-take Stymie." Beard later said, "A lot of my ability just came from the natural thing, that I guess was a gift from the Good Lord" (Maltin and Bann, 107). Beard proved he could be just as effective in dramatic scenes. It's hard not to feel Stymie's pain when he bursts into tears in "The Pooch" (1932) after being falsely accused of stealing the gang's beloved dog, Pete.

Beard remembered the Hal Roach lot as a special place filled with lots of fun and laughter. Between takes he observed many of the comedy stars of the era working on nearby sets. The one he watched the most, he remembered, was Stan Laurel, of Laurel and Hardy. "One day Laurel said, 'Well, give this kid a derby.' That's why it never fit me; it belonged to Stan Laurel!" (Maltin and Bann, 259). Later, Beard discovered that according to the English music hall tradition, the derby given to him by Laurel represented the crown of comedy. In later years Beard visited the ill comedian at his home in Santa Monica, California. Shortly before Laurel died Beard told him how much his friendship meant to him.

William Thomas, who played Buckwheat, eventually replaced Beard's Stymie. "They brought William out when I was beginning to get too large, and I just had that funny feeling. I heard the footsteps, but I didn't want to go" (Maltin and Bann, 156). The transition for Beard was difficult. As a movie star he received loving accolades from fans and attention from the director and such luminaries as Laurel and Hardy. But once he got home he had to survive the rough day-to-day existence that comes from living in poverty.

Beard went on to play minor parts (sometimes credited as Stymie Beard) in feature films including *Jezebel* (1938), *The Great Man Votes* (1939), *Stormy Weather* (1943), *Captain Blood* (1935), *Two Gun Man from Harlem* (1938), *Broken Strings* (1940), and *Way down South* (1939). *Two Gun Man from Harlem* and *Broken Strings* were so-called "race" films. After a time, though, Beard stopped acting. He dropped out of high school and began a drug habit that would last for decades. Almost thirty years later, a heroin addict, Beard checked himself into Synanon, a drug rehabilitation facility. He cleaned himself up and made a comeback, winning minor roles in feature films such as *Truck Turner* (1974) and *The Buddy Holly Story* (1978), along with television shows like *Sanford and Son*, *Good Times*, *Starsky and Hutch*, *Diff'rent Strokes*, and *The Jeffersons*.

Acting was not Beard's only passion. After his recovery, he traveled around the country lecturing and inspiring others as he shared his personal stories about drug abuse. Beard was married once, but the marriage may have been short-lived and in any event produced no children. In 1981 Beard suffered a stroke, contracted pneumonia, and died at the University of Southern California Medical Center. He was buried with his trademark bowler beside him.

Further Reading

Bogle, Donald. *Bright Boulevards, Bold Dreams: The Story of Black Hollywood* (2005).
Bogle, Donald. *Toms, Coons, Mulattoes, Mammies, & Bucks* (2001).
Maltin, Leonard, and Richard W. Bann. *The Little Rascals: The Life and Times of our Gang* (1977, 1992).
Richards, Larry. *African American Films through 1959* (1998).

WAYNE L. WILSON

BEARDEN, Romare (2 Sept. 1911–11 Mar. 1988), artist, was born Romare Howard Bearden in Charlotte, North Carolina, the son of R. Howard Bearden, a grocer, and Bessye Johnson. When Bearden was about four years old, the family moved to New York, settling in Harlem, where he went to public school and his parents developed a wide network of acquaintances among the Harlem jazz musicians and intellectuals of the day. His father later became an inspector for the New York Board of Health; his mother, a civic leader. Bearden finished high school in Pittsburgh, however, having lived there for a time with his grandmother. In 1932, after two years at Boston University, he transferred to New York University, where he created illustrations for the undergraduate humor magazine and earned a BS degree in Education in 1935. For the next two years he contributed political cartoons to the *Baltimore Afro-American*. Unable to find steady work, he enrolled at the Art Students League and studied drawing with the German emigré artist George Grosz in 1936–1937.

At about this time, Bearden joined the 306 Group, an informal association of black artists and writers—among them JACOB LAWRENCE and RALPH ELLISON—who met in the studio of his cousin, the painter CHARLES ALSTON, at 306 West 141st Street. From 1938 to 1942, now beginning to paint, Bearden supported himself as a full-time caseworker with the New York City Department of Social Services, a job to which he returned after World War II. In 1940, at the Harlem studio of a friend, Ad Bates, Bearden exhibited some of the work he had completed over the past four years, including paintings in oil and gouache, watercolors, and drawings. Taking his own studio on 125th Street, located over the Apollo Theater, he began work on a series of paintings that evoked the rural South of his childhood. Typical of the series is *Folk Musicians* (1941–1942), painted in a bold and dramatic style with flat planes and simplified, colorful figures.

While serving with an all-black regiment in 1944, Bearden mounted a solo exhibition at the "G" Place Gallery in Washington, D.C., which brought him to the attention of the influential New York dealer Samuel Kootz. Bearden's first exhibition at the Kootz Gallery, in 1945, was devoted to the *Passion of Christ* series, a group of semiabstract, cubist-inspired watercolors on paper. The exhibition was highly successful in terms of reviews and sales; *He Is Arisen*, purchased by the Museum of Modern Art in New York, was the first of Bearden's works to enter a museum collection. The following year, Kootz exhibited Bearden's painting *Lament for a Bullfighter*, inspired by García Lorca's poem "Lament for the Death of a Bullfighter." Inclusion of Bearden's works in the 1945 and 1946 annuals

Romare Bearden, acclaimed for his jazz and Cubism-inspired collages that portrayed all aspects of African American life. (Manu Sassoonian.)

at the Whitney Museum of American Art in New York and in the Abstract and Surrealist American Art show held at the Art Institute of Chicago in 1948 further boosted his growing reputation.

In 1951 Bearden went to Paris on the GI Bill to study philosophy at the Sorbonne. In addition to meeting the Cubist masters Pablo Picasso and Georges Braque, Bearden joined the circle of black artists and writers inspired by the concept of negritude. As he later admitted, however, the most significant thing he learned during his year in France was how to relate the black experience to universal experience. Between 1952, when he returned to New York, and 1954, the year he married the West Indian dancer Nanette Rohan, Bearden devoted himself mainly to music; some twenty of the songs he wrote in this period were published and recorded. Bearden then returned to painting and set up a new studio in lower Manhattan, on Canal Street, where he and his wife lived for the rest of his life. (They had no children.) In 1961 he showed some of his now wholly abstract oil paintings in the first of several solo exhibitions at the Cordier & Ekstrom Gallery, his dealers from that year on.

Bearden, who had described art in the journal he began keeping in 1947 as "a kind of divine play" (Schwartzman, 217), was increasingly drawn to collage, a way of "playing" with assortments of materials to create a whole and a medium much employed by the Cubists. He created his first signed collage, *Circus*, in 1961; three years later collage became his chief method of expression. The beginning of the civil rights movement and his participation in the discussions of the Spiral Group (which he cofounded in 1963) on the role of black artists in a time of new challenges coincided with this profound change in Bearden's art. In 1964 he created a series of small montages composed of fragments of reproductions cut from newspapers, magazines, or postcards and pasted onto a paper backing; these assemblages were then photographed and enlarged. The resulting *Projections*, as Bearden titled them, were exhibited that year at Cordier & Ekstrom. Later, arranged in series by subject matter, they were developed into true collages. One such sequence, titled *The Prevalence of Ritual*, includes individual panels representing "The Funeral," "The Baptism," and "The Conjur Woman." Another collage series evokes Harlem street life, as in

The Dove, a crowded assemblage of cutout figures set against a suggestion of city buildings. The bizarrely composite figures, the abrupt shifts in scale between heads and bodies, and the arbitrary spatial relationships convey the rich, kaleidoscopic variety of the scene. Other series recall the Harlem jazz world of the 1930s (*The Savoy*, for example) and southern life (the nostalgic *Train Whistle Blues*).

As Bearden developed his collage techniques into the 1970s, he began to incorporate more of his own painted touches, in acrylics or watercolors, as well as torn pieces of paper in various hand-painted colors and bits of fabric. Spaces were opened up and thus were easier to perceive. Coinciding with the start of annual visits to his wife's family home on Saint Martin, the artist's palette took on the lush colors of the Caribbean and the collage figures became overtly sensuous. One of these later collages, *The Block* (1971), a large six-panel composition, approached mixed-media work; with the accompaniment of taped gospel and blues music, children's voices, and actual street noises, it re-created the look, sounds, and "feel" of an urban street.

Besides working in collage, Bearden designed tapestries and posters; in 1968 he was represented in an international poster exhibition in Warsaw, Poland. He designed sets for the Alvin Ailey Dance Company in 1977 and continued to make prints, including the colored lithographs that illustrate a 1983 edition of the work of the Caribbean poet DEREK WALCOTT. He also created murals, such as *Quilting Time*, commissioned by the Detroit Institute of Arts and installed there in 1986. In it, the quilter and six onlookers form a frieze against a brilliantly hued tropical setting. The whole is a mosaic of glass tesserae, so combined and colored as to suggest the molding of bodies and the textures and folds of fabrics.

A large traveling retrospective of Bearden's work, organized by the Mint Museum in Charlotte, North Carolina, in 1980 and concluding its tour at the Brooklyn Museum in 1981, capped Bearden's career. Also in 1980 he taught at Yale University, one of several temporary teaching posts he held during the course of his career. Represented in every major museum in New York City and in others throughout the country, he is considered to have transformed collage, generally regarded as a minor art form, into a forceful means of expression with universal appeal. His biographer called him "An artist for all seasons and for all humankind" (Schwartzman, 305).

In addition to *The Painter's Mind: A Study of Structure and Space in Painting*, written with his longtime friend, the artist Carl Holty (1969), Bearden wrote (with Harry Henderson) *A History of Afro-American Artists from 1792 to the Present*, which was posthumously published in 1993. He and Henderson also wrote a book for young readers, *Six Black Masters of American Art* (1972).

Part of Bearden's legacy consists of his multiple roles as teacher; as art director of the Harlem Cultural Council, to which he was appointed in 1964; as organizer of the landmark exhibition, the Evolution of Afro-American Artists: 1800–1950, held at City College of New York in 1967; and as cofounder, in 1969, of the Cinque Gallery in New York, a showcase for younger artists from various minority groups. For these contributions, Bearden was inducted into the National Institute of Arts and Letters in 1966; he was honored by his home state in 1976 as recipient of the Governor's Medal of the State of North Carolina, and he also was awarded the National Medal of Arts in 1987. The Pratt Institute (1973) and Carnegie-Mellon University (1975) awarded him honorary doctorates. He died in New York City.

Further Reading

The Schomburg Center for Research in Black Culture of the New York Public Library is the primary source of archival material relating to Bearden: photographs, his sketchbook and notebooks, and correspondence. The center also maintains a collection of his posters as well as examples of his other work. The Archives of American Art in New York houses the Romare Bearden Papers.

Campbell, Mary Schmidt, and Sharon F. Patton. *Memory and Metaphor: The Art of Romare Bearden, 1940–1987* (1991).

Igoe, Lynn M., with James Igoe. *250 Years of Afro-American Art: An Annotated Bibliography* (1981).

Schwartzman, Marvin. *Romare Bearden: His Life and Art* (1990).

Obituary: *New York Times*, 13 Mar. 1988.

ELEANOR F. WEDGE

BEASLEY, Delilah Leontium (9 Sept. 1871–18 Aug. 1934), journalist and historian of the early West, was born in Cincinnati, Ohio, the eldest of five children of Daniel Beasley, an engineer, and Margaret (Heines) Beasley, a homemaker. Although little is known about her childhood, at the age of twelve Beasley published her first writings in the black-owned newspaper, the *Cleveland Gazette*. By the time she was fifteen she was working as a columnist for the *Cincinnati Enquirer*, becoming the first African American woman to write for a mainstream newspaper on a regular basis.

Beasley lost both parents as a teenager and was forced to take a full-time job working as a domestic laborer for the family of a white judge named Hagan. Her career then took several unusual turns as Beasley, who was described by biographer Lorraine Crouchett as "short, well-proportioned, and speaking in a shrill, light voice" (perhaps because of a chronic hearing problem), did not hesitate to embark on unconventional professional pursuits. She was often viewed as "eccentric and ahead of her time." After traveling to Elmhurst, Illinois, with the Hagans to work in their summer home, Beasley decided to relocate to Chicago, where she was employed as a masseuse. During this period she also studied medical gymnastics, scalp treatment, and physical therapy. Again and again she relocated in pursuit of her studies and interests: back to Ohio, to New York to work with pregnant women at the Buffalo Sanitarium, and eventually to Michigan, where she became head masseuse at a family resort. While continuing her work and studies in the health sciences Beasley used her free time to research African American history, taking advantage of the private libraries of friends and clients who allowed her access to valuable books. This began what would become Beasley's lifelong passion: a study of the undocumented history of African Americans in the West.

When she was in her early forties, in 1910, Beasley was invited to move to Berkeley, California, to work as a nurse and physical therapist with a former patient. Over the next eight years Beasley, who never married, dedicated herself completely to her research projects. Initially planning for a mere lecture series on the topic she conducted numerous interviews with local figures and traveled throughout the state to gather oral histories; she compiled tax documents and real estate and hospital records; she attended classes at the University of California, Berkeley; and she poured over newspaper archives at Berkeley's Bancroft Library.

While in California Beasley returned to her journalistic beginnings, penning in 1915 a well-received series of articles for the *Oakland Tribune* in protest of D. W. Griffith's movie *The Birth of a Nation*. This work won the journalist praise and recognition from the NAACP and helped to inspire a nationwide boycott of the film. Although she could have made a comfortable living as a masseuse at any time Beasley instead devoted her energies to historical research, earning just $10 a week for her *Tribune* column. After hearing her first lecture on the topic of pioneering black figures in the West, titled "My City of Inspiration—San Francisco," Beasley's friend, the minister David R. Wallace, convinced her to publish the findings as a book. Unable to find a publisher she placed herself into debt by borrowing the necessary funds from a colleague at the *Oakland Tribune*. She eventually published *The Negro Trail Blazers of California* in 1919, offering biographies of notable black figures from the era of slavery through statehood, as well as reports of the ongoing accomplishments of the black middle class. Although the book was the first such history of its kind, it received poor reviews from some historians, among them CARTER GODWIN WOODSON, who considered the work amateurish and flawed. Others, however, praised the book's groundbreaking documentation of positive contributions by black Americans.

In 1923 Beasley began writing a regular column for the *Oakland Tribune*, "Activities among Negroes," in which she condemned vociferously the use of derogatory terms like "nigger," "darkie," and "coon." Her efforts were far-reaching, and she even traveled long distances to make personal visits with editors in her campaign against such disparaging treatment. During the 1920s Beasley also became increasingly active in women's organizations. Always an adamant integrationist she was the only black female member of the press at the 1925 National Convention of Women Voters in Richmond, Virginia. She also worked with the League of Nations Association, the National League of Women Voters, and the World Forum on issues of civil rights and world peace. Following her retirement from the *Oakland Tribune* in 1925, she became particularly active in the women's club movement, herself becoming a trailblazing member of the National Association of Colored Women, and spearheading efforts to bring the group's 1925 national convention to Oakland. In addition she was a founding member of the Oakland branch of the National Urban League.

Throughout her life Beasley suffered from poor health due to heart disease, illnesses that eventually led to her death. Beasley's crowning work, *The Negro Trail Blazers of California*, was neglected for a time after its initial publication and was not resurrected until 1968, when it was reprinted by the California Historical Society and the San Francisco Negro Historical and Cultural Society.

Further Reading
Crouchett, Lorraine J. *Delilah Leontium Beasley: Oakland's Crusading Journalist* (1989).
Dannett, Sylvia G. L. *Profiles of Negro Womanhood* (1964).
Dillon, Richard H. *Humbugs and Heroes: A Gallery of California Pioneers* (1970).
Streitmatter, Rodger. *Raising Her Voice: African-American Women Journalists Who Changed History* (1994).

KRISTAL BRENT ZOOK

BEASLEY, Mathilda Taylor (Nov. 1832?–20 Dec. 1903), Catholic nun, was born Mathilda Taylor in New Orleans, Louisiana, to Caroline Taylor, a slave owned by James C. Taylor, whose surname he gave to his slaves. Her father, whose name is not known, was Native American. Little is known about Mathilda's early years, except that she learned to read and write and that she somehow received her freedom and moved to Savannah. There she began operating a secret school for African American children in the late 1850s, an enterprise for which she risked imprisonment because state laws prohibited education for blacks.

Taylor supported herself by working a variety of jobs in Savannah. In the 1860s she was employed at the Railroad House, a restaurant owned by Abraham Beasley, a prosperous free black man. In 1869 she married Beasley. His ventures included a produce market, a saloon, a boardinghouse, and, at times, the slave trade. The two had no children, and Mathilda Beasley was widowed in 1877. She inherited her husband's property, an estate that included five acres of land worth more than three hundred dollars.

In the 1880s Beasley departed for England to train as a nun. Upon her return she donated her husband's estate to the Sacred Heart Catholic Church of Savannah in order to establish the Saint Francis Home for Colored Orphans. The all-female orphanage began operation in 1887. Two years later Beasley founded the Third Order of Saint Francis, a religious order for black nuns. The community struggled to gain financial backing and remained a small group; in 1896 the Catholic directory listed five African American sisters and nineteen black orphan girls in Savannah. The group founded by Beasley built on earlier efforts by black Catholic women to establish religious communities. In 1829 MARY ELIZABETH LANGE founded the first such order, the Oblate Sisters of Providence.

In 1893 Beasley traveled to Philadelphia, Pennsylvania, where she visited Katherine Drexel, the wealthy heiress who had established the Sisters of the Blessed Sacrament for Indians and Colored People in 1890 as a means of evangelizing to those minority groups. Beasley requested both spiritual and financial aid from Drexel for her own religious order. Drexel briefly considered merging the two orders and transferring the Pennsylvania community to South Carolina, but she ultimately decided against such action, primarily because of racial issues. Beasley also communicated with a Cardinal Gibbons, requesting aid for the society in the form of new members. Her efforts continued, with requests to Father John Slattery, unofficial overseer of African American Catholic works in the United States. Her letters to Slattery included requests for books, more sisters, and any other aid that could be allotted to the struggling community.

Despite her efforts Beasley was unable to obtain the resources necessary to maintain the religious order. In 1898 the Third Order of Saint Francis was suppressed and the Saint Francis orphanage fell under the auspices of the Missionary Franciscan Sisters of the Immaculate Conception. Upon the order's dissolution Beasley retired to a small cottage adjacent to the orphanage; there she died during her prayers at the age of seventy-one. Though the religious order she founded failed to survive, Beasley's efforts continued the work of black Catholic women and helped to establish a precedent for African American nuns.

Further Reading

Davis, Cyprian. *The History of Black Catholics in the United States* (1990).

Obituary: *Savannah Morning News*, 21 Dec. 1903.

TONIA M. COMPTON

BEASLEY, Phoebe (3 June 1943–), artist and businesswoman, was born in Cleveland, Ohio, to George A. Beasley and Annette P. Beasley, both of whom worked at a local country club. Like many artists, she revealed considerable talent in childhood, excelling in school art classes and enjoying parental support for her creativity. She graduated from John Adams High School in Cleveland in 1961, and began her formal training at Ohio University, where she earned a BFA in Visual Arts in 1965. After graduation, she started teaching art at Cleveland's Glenville High School; she held this position from 1965 to 1969. During that time, she had a brief marriage in 1968 to Louis Evans, about whom little is known. They divorced in 1969.

In 1969 she moved to Los Angeles. After a year as a layout artist for Sage Publications, a leading publisher of social science books and journals, she became an advertising executive for KFI/KOST radio stations in Los Angeles. Beasley achieved enormous success in the field, securing several major accounts including McDonald's, Toyota, and Ford Motor Company. Beasley's enduring personal discipline enabled her to devote several hours a day to artwork on top of her corporate responsibilities, and she became accomplished in both advertising and art. She retired from the radio position in 1999 so she could focus primarily on art. Beasley found mainstream art institutions exclusionary and elitist: many white gallery owners bluntly expressed their unwillingness to feature African American art. Like most black artists in America, Beasley discovered early in her career the deeply ingrained racial biases of mainstream art institutions. White gallery owners repeatedly informed her of their unwillingness to carry works with African American subject matter.

In spite of the obstacles, Beasley developed a reputation as a leading African American artist of the late twentieth century. Resolved to use her art to communicate her observations about her own people, she created works with an African American focus while offering a deeper universal vision about the human condition.

Her first major breakthrough as an artist came through the efforts of basketball great BILL RUSSELL, who had seen her work in Los Angeles in 1970. In 1976 he arranged an individual show for her in Seattle's Polly Friedlander Gallery. Following that, Beasley exhibited her work in numerous individual and group shows in galleries and museums throughout the country. In addition to their representations in many public and corporate collections, her paintings have been acquired by several prominent private collectors, including African American luminaries OPRAH WINFREY, MAYA ANGELOU, BILL RUSSELL, and TAVIS SMILEY.

Her artwork demonstrated a unique personal style, combining figurative elements blended effectively with the abstract forms she learned as a student. Her early efforts in "hard edge" abstraction informed her mature paintings and collages, a fusion of European and American modernist styles marshaled to narrate episodes of African American history and culture. The artistic influences of her youth—Jackson Pollock, Oskar Kokoschka, and Willem de Kooning—were apparent in many of her figurally abstract paintings and energetic collages. Her skill in combining color and form with paint, tissue paper, found objects, and cloth provided her artworks with a compelling jazz-like rhythm reminiscent of the signature works of ROMARE BEARDEN. Her thematic focus revealed her sympathetic feeling for ordinary people engaged in the routine activities of life: sewing, reading, studying, cooking, waiting, and traveling. Her paintings simultaneously ennobled their subjects, encouraging audiences to view them with dignity and respect, in dramatic contrast to American popular culture's long history of racist caricature and stereotype. That vision reflected a profound humanism that built on the similar perspectives of several prominent figures of African American art, such as JACOB LAWRENCE, CHARLES WHITE, LOIS JONES, ELIZABETH CATLETT, and JOHN BIGGERS. Beasley's view of African American women was particularly striking; her engaging works with female subjects add an outstanding dimension to a theme pervading African American art since the nineteenth century.

Like many other African American artists of the twentieth and twenty-first century, Beasley's works often commented on institutionalized racism in the United States and the challenges of redressing it. *Executive Order 9981,* a mixed-media work on canvas, called dramatic attention to President Harry S. Truman's 1948 order that desegregated the United States military, fully three years after the Allied victory in World War II. Its bold composition and vibrant colors served to remind viewers to understand history and to appreciate both the progress and problems in implementing the ideals of a democratic society.

Beasley received the Presidential Seal of Official Artist from George H. W. Bush in 1989 and Bill Clinton in 1993; she was the only artist to be so honored twice. She also served as an official artist in President Clinton's administration. Her artistic excellence has brought her many public commissions, including service as an official artist of the 2000 Los Angeles Marathon and the 2000 Democratic National Convention. In 2005 she received an honorary Doctor of Fine Arts degree from her alma mater, Ohio University, where she delivered the commencement address to the graduating class.

Beyond her business and artistic successes, Beasley forged a durable commitment to civic activism in the Los Angeles area. From 1980 to 1984 she was president of the California Museum of African American Art, an institution founded by legendary art historian and artist SAMELLA LEWIS. She also served as a member of the Los Angeles County Arts Commission beginning in 1997, where her efforts advanced artistic creativity in the most populous county in the United States, through the commission's art grants program. In 1998 she began working with the Story Project Foundation, an organization dedicated to building confidence and encouraging literacy among teenagers through after-school programs and mentoring. Finally, in collaboration with Maya Angelou, Beasley published *Sunrise Is Coming After While* (1998), a limited-edition book of text and serigraphs interpreting the poems of LANGSTON HUGHES.

Further Reading

Bain, Terry. "Phoebe Beasley," in *St. James Guide to Black Artists,* ed. Thomas Riggs (1997).
Hanks, Eric, ed. *Masterpieces of African American Art: An African American Perspective* (2007).
Hanks, Eric, ed. *Timeless Textured Threads: Artwork by Phoebe Beasley* (2005).
King-Hammond, Leslie, ed. *Gumbo Ya Ya: Anthology of Contemporary African-American Women Artists* (1995).
Lewis, Samella, *African American Art and Artists* (2003).
PAUL VON BLUM

BEATTY, Talley (1919–29 Apr. 1995), choreographer, dancer, and teacher, was born in Cedar Grove, Louisiana, the son of a housepainter. His parents' names are unknown. In the small town of Cedar Grove, right outside Shreveport, Beatty's earliest dance influence was the legendary KATHERINE DUNHAM. According to the historian Joe Nash, a close friend and colleague of Beatty, Dunham invited him to "watch dances in progress" when he was eleven years old. Dunham was in rehearsal for Ruth Page's *La Guillablesse,* scheduled to open at the Chicago Civic Opera in 1933, and was trying to keep the young boy's playing from disrupting her work. Beatty danced onstage for the first time in the opera's 1934 season and emerged as a dancer of note after studying from 1937 to 1940 at Dunham's Studio de la Danse in Shreveport. He danced the role of a priest in Dunham's *Yanvalou,* a snakelike dance in honor of the voodoo deity Damballa, at the historic Negro Dance Evening, 7 March 1937, at the Ninety-Second Street Young Men's Hebrew Association in New York City.

Beatty toured with the Katherine Dunham Company for nineteen years. He was in the brief 1940–1941 run of *Cabin in the Sky* on Broadway and appeared in films with the Dunham company, including *Carnival of Rhythm* (1941), *Cuban Episode* (1942), *Flamingo* (1942), and *Stormy Weather* (1943). In the late 1940s he appeared in Maya Deren's innovative film *Choreography for Camera.* He danced in the 1946 revival of *Show Boat* with PEARL PRIMUS, Joe Nash, and Alma Sutton. He returned to New York around 1950. Beatty left Dunham's company to form a duo with the celebrated JANET COLLINS, who was the first black prima ballerina, from 1951 to 1954 at the Metropolitan Opera House.

Beatty's ballets have been classified as part of a jazz idiom; however, the movements are not vernacular, and they never fall into an unidentifiable heap of clichéd gesture. In fact his dances, which survive in the repertoire of the Philadelphia Dance Company, the Dayton Contemporary Dance Company, and the ALVIN AILEY American Dance Theater, are not only virtuoso tours de force but also transformative excursions into human need. Beatty's sagas of city living, depicted by fast-paced movement, convoluted interactions between text and subtext, and the tensions created by social challenges, are a testimony to his choreographic facility. Beatty's legacy is part of a long tradition of dance as social commentary and as a catalyst for social change.

The *New York Times* critic Anna Kisselgoff had this to say about his work in 1989: "What is a Beatty signature? It is primarily his genius for putting technical perfection at the service of emotional expression. Inventing a jazz idiom that has the continuum of classical dancing, he has composed dance poems of urban existence. Their structure is largely abstract, creating drama through pattern and composition." Despite the fact that Kisselgoff incorrectly labels the work as "a jazz idiom," probably because Beatty used classical jazz scores from the likes of MILES DAVIS, DUKE ELLINGTON, and BILLY STRAYHORN in his distillation of ideas and motifs, along with short, tight, isolated gestures to frame and accent large technical phrases, she is on target when she notes the structure of his dances. Beatty was a master craftsman of mood and innuendo. With just the right mix of gestural mapping, speed, rhythmic thrust, and abstraction, he created dances that challenged notions of dance patterning and stylistic classification.

Beatty's first major work, *Southern Landscapes* (1947), a response to Howard Fast's book *Freedom Road*, was reconstructed by the Philadelphia Dance Company in 1992. A ballet in four sections, *Southern Landscapes* comments on the rise of the Ku Klux Klan after the Civil War. Between 1947 and 1955 Beatty toured with his company, Tropicana, and created many memorable masterpieces, including *The Road of Phoebe Snow* (1959), which chronicles the journey of a luxury train that passes through the backyards of the United States witnessing people who are alienated from themselves and their communities, and *Come and Get the Beauty of It Hot* (1960), which takes audiences through a day in the lives of Harlemites. "Toccata," the opening segment of *Beauty*, is a collage of finger-popping, body-slapping moves atop technical ploys. Dancers take to their knees, twist in diverse directions, and end, hovering, in nearly upside-down balances; "Toccata" is often performed independently. The final section of *Beauty*, "Congo, Tango, Palace," which depicts the elegance and bravura of flamenco executed in a Spanish Harlem ballroom, is also performed as a solo work. The ballet, excerpted and in its entirety, is a staple of the Dayton Contemporary Dance Company. Other ballets that span Beatty's forty-eight years of dance making include *Tropicana* (1949); *Migration* (1964); *Bring My Servant Home* (1969), a tribute to MARTIN LUTHER KING JR.; *The Stack-Up* (1983); *A Rag, a Bone, and a Hank of Hair* (1985); and *Such Sweet Morning Songs* (1990).

In addition to his work on the concert stage as a dancer and a choreographer, Beatty created television specials, like Duke Ellington's "Black, Brown, and Beige" for CBS in 1974, and made movement for the Broadway show *Your Arms Too Short to Box with God*, which was nominated for a Tony Award in 1977. As a teacher Beatty also made his mark in the 1960s and 1970s. Students at the Alma Lewis School of Fine Arts in Boston and the FRED BENJAMIN Dance Company in New York as well as dance students in England, France, Sweden, and Israel had the opportunity to experience his rare gifts. Beatty had a wry sense of humor, an acute awareness of the human condition, and the courage to speak from his heart and soul. His death in New York City caused a silence in the dance world.

Declared a "living legend" in 1992 during the National Black Arts Festival in Atlanta, Georgia, and a recipient of the Samuel H. Scripps–American Dance Festival Award in 1993, Beatty was indeed a national treasure. He created more than fifty ballets that were performed by some fourteen companies in the United States, Europe, and western Asia. A member of Ballet Society (which became the New York City Ballet in 1933), Beatty not only defied the images ascribed to blacks during his time but also set a standard for performance that has become a model for contemporary dancers of all ethnic groups. Even when blacks were stereotyped as incapable of performing ballet, Beatty dared to dance and choreograph as he chose. A consummate ballet technician, he blended ballet with other ethnic styles. With the language of the body, he provided blueprints of everyday life for all humanity.

Further Reading

Barnes, Clive. "Dance: Beatty Winding Up City Center Season," *New York Times*, 21 May 1969.

Bartett, B. S. K. "Talley Beatty Company in Vivid Performance at John Hancock Hall," *Boston Globe*, 15 Jan. 1952.

Emery, Lynne Fauley. *Black Dance: From 1619 to Today*, 2d ed. (1988).

Long, Richard A. *The Black Tradition in American Dance* (1989).

C. S'THEMBILE WEST

BEATY, Powhatan (1839?–6 Dec. 1916), Medal of Honor recipient, actor, and playwright, was born in Richmond, Virginia, of unknown parentage. Beaty (sometimes spelled Beatty) was born a slave, but little else is known of his early years or how he came to be free. Beaty left Richmond in 1849 for Cincinnati, where he would spend the majority of his life, and became a farmer. Later, Beaty's education consisted of an apprenticeship to a black cabinetmaker in Cincinnati, as well as a tutelage under James E. Murdock, a retired professional actor and dramatic coach.

On 5 September 1862 Powhatan Beaty, along with 706 other African American men, was forced to join Cincinnati's Black Brigade after Confederate troops repeatedly threatened the city. The Black Brigade was one of the earliest, but unofficial, African American military units organized during the Civil War, but it did not engage in any military action since the city was never attacked. Instead, the brigade was tasked with building fortifications for the city and digging tunnels beneath the Ohio River in northern Kentucky, work that the white brigades were not asked to perform. Moreover, police officers had violently forced the men from their homes and places of work with billy clubs and bayonet points, and they were paraded through the streets of the city like prisoners. Despite the insulting experience with the Black Brigade, and the nation's formal repudiation of black service in the army, as the war between the North and the South began to escalate, so did Beaty's thirst for real military action. After the Lincoln administration

Powhatan Beaty, Civil War veteran, Medal of Honor recipient, actor, and playwright, c. 1900. (Library of Congress/Daniel Murray Collection.)

began allowing black recruitment, on 5 June 1863, at the age of twenty-four, Beaty enlisted as a private in the Union Army at Camp Delaware, Ohio, an all-black recruiting camp for African American enlistees. Beaty enlisted for three years and became a part of Company G, Fifth United States Colored Troops (USCT). Only two days later, he was promoted to first sergeant, one of the highest ranks an African American soldier could attain.

Beaty is best known for his role in the Battle of Chaffin's Farm (sometimes called Chapin's Farm), also known as the Battle of Fort Harrison or, more broadly, the Battle of New Market Heights, in Virginia on 29 September 1864. The Battle of New Market Heights was part of a larger effort by General Ulysses S. Grant to weaken Confederate Robert E. Lee's defenses in order to take back the city of Richmond and the surrounding area of Petersburg, Virginia. The clash primarily took place on New Market Road in Henrico County, later a suburb of Richmond, and the battle is most noteworthy because it resulted in the eventual and permanent possession of the fort by Union forces. Beaty's infantry was a part of the second wave of attacks in New Market Heights that took place at around 6 A.M. on 29 September 1864. The first wave was sent under the command of Union General Thomas Paine at around 5:30 A.M.

and consisted of 685 men, of which 365 died. After the white officers of his unit had all either been killed or wounded, Beaty, although wounded himself, took command of his company and led the soldiers into battle until he was ordered to retreat. During the retreat, he noticed that the color-bearer had been killed and that the flag was no longer in sight. Amidst increasing gunfire, Beaty returned to the scene of warfare and retrieved the flag. Beaty was awarded the Medal of Honor for his actions during this struggle, and his Medal of Honor citation states that he "took command of his company, all the officers having been killed or wounded, and gallantly led it" (Kelly, 284). Fourteen other African American soldiers received Medals of Honor for their valiant actions during this critical battle.

After the Civil War, Beaty briefly worked as a porter on the Mississippi River steamboat *City of Vicksburg*. Upon returning to Cincinnati, Beaty went back to cabinetmaking and again took up acting. In the 1870s he began to perform publicly, and near the end of the decade he attained some recognition for his theatrical performances. Earlier in his career, Beaty had played Spartacus in Robert Montgomery Bird's *The Gladiator* to favorable reviews in Cincinnati. Throughout the 1880s, he performed with the famed African American leading actress HENRIETTA VINTON DAVIS in Cincinnati, Washington, D.C., and Philadelphia. Beaty reportedly received high praise for his roles in *Macbeth*, *Richard III*, and *Ingomar, the Barbarian* in the *New York Globe*. In 1880 Beaty wrote a play about the transition from slavery to freedom titled *Delmar; or Scenes in Southland*. The play was performed publicly in 1881 with Beaty himself starring in the leading role as the plantation owner. While there are no official reviews of the play, according to Errol G. Hill, a newspaper commentator, the script "abounds in fine, dramatic situations" (Hill, 83). Finally, in 1888 Beaty became the drama director of the Literary and Dramatic Club of Cincinnati, a club that he had helped form.

Little is known about Beaty's life after 1890, but a historical marker that is a part of the Underground Railroad Heritage program states that he died on 6 December 1916, "leaving two sons, attorney and state representative A. Lee Beaty and John W. Beaty" (Grace, 50). As a testament to Beaty's important place in U.S. history, more specifically his involvement in the Civil War, House Bill 897, dated 10 February 2000, designates the Interstate Route 895 (Pocahontas Parkway) bridge over Virginia Route 5 the "Powhatan Beatty Memorial Bridge." Powhatan Beaty, along with many other prominent African American figures, is buried in the Union Baptist Cemetery in Cincinnati, the oldest African American religious burial ground still in use.

Further Reading

Claxton, Melvin, and Mark Puls. *Uncommon Valor: A Story of Race, Patriotism, and Glory in the Final Battles of the Civil War* (2006).

Claxton, Melvin, and Mark Puls. *Uncommon Valor: The Exploits of the New Market Heights Medal of Honor Winners* (2006).

Grace, Kevin, and Tom White. *Cincinnati's Cemeteries: The Queen City of Underground (OH)* (2004).

Hill, Errol G. *A History of African American Theatre* (2003).

Kelly, C. Brian, and Ingrid Smyer-Kelly. *Best Little Ironies, Oddities, and Mysteries of the Civil War* (2000).

Peterson, Bernard L. *Profiles of African American Stage Performers and Theatre People, 1816–1960* (2001).

MARLENE L. DAUT

BEAVERS, Louise (8 Mar. 1902–26 Oct. 1962), actress, was born in Cincinnati, Ohio, the daughter of William Beavers. Her mother's identity is not known. As a child Louise moved with her musically inclined family to California, where in 1918 she graduated from Pasadena High School. She then joined the Ladies' Minstrel Troupe for a year before being recognized by talent scouts.

Beavers, who would appear in more than one hundred motion pictures, began her Hollywood career by playing a maid to leading lady Lilyan Tashman in *Gold Diggers* (1923). Early on, maid was a role that Beavers had to play offscreen as well as on. From 1920 to 1926 she worked first as a dressing room attendant and then as the personal maid of the actress Leatrice Joy. In 1927 Beavers landed a major role in *Uncle Tom's Cabin*, followed in 1929 by roles in *Coquette* and *Nix on Dames*. In the early 1930s she earned critical notices for her handling of subservient roles in *Ladies of the Big House* (1932), *What Price Hollywood?* (1932), *Bombshell* (1933), and *She Done Him Wrong* (1933). Big-boned, dark-skinned, and usually smiling on the screen, Beavers was best known for playing the good-natured maid or housekeeper for such stars as Mae West, Claudette Colbert, and Jean Harlow.

Typecast as a maid for her entire career, Beavers was seen serving a cavalcade of other motion picture greats, including Clara Bow, Boris Karloff, Hedda Hopper, James Stewart, Joan Crawford, Spencer Tracy, Ralph Bellamy, Ginger Rogers, Joan Blondell, Jimmy Durante, Edward G. Robinson, Humphrey Bogart, Ronald Reagan, Jane Wyman, Rosalind Russell, Henry Fonda, Bing Crosby, John Wayne, Zero Mostel, Orson Welles, Marlene Dietrich, W. C. Fields, SIDNEY POITIER, June Allyson, Jack Lemmon, Debbie Reynolds, Lloyd Bridges, Natalie Wood, and PEARL BAILEY, among many others. As the film historian Donald Bogle has pointed out, Beavers came to epitomize the lovable, loyal, overweight "Mammy" figure seemingly capable of taking on all the troubles of the world. "She perfected the optimistic, sentimental black woman whose sweet, sunny disposition and kindheartedness almost always saved the day, the Depression era's embodiment of Christian stoicism and goodness, lending a friendly ear and hand to down-on-their-luck heroines, who knew that when the rest of the world failed them, Louise would always be there" (Bogle, 73).

Beavers's professional breakthrough came in her powerful portrayal of the businesslike, pancake-flapping Aunt Delilah to Claudette Colbert's Bea in *Imitation of Life* (1934), a sensitive performance acclaimed by both the white and black press; many critics felt that Beavers deserved an Oscar nomination. Yet what Beavers mostly won from that performance was the "Aunt Jemima" label that would stick to her forever. Despite her screen persona as a domestic, Beavers never cooked, though she did maintain a high-calorie diet to keep her weight up, and she took elocution lessons to cultivate a southern drawl. She married LeRoy Moore in the late 1950s.

Beavers was proud to be featured in two pioneering black-cast films produced by Million Dollar Productions, *Life Goes On* (1938) and *Reform School* (1939), even though in *Reform School* her role as a probation officer was a Mammy-type character. Of note is that, whereas in these films her respective characters were named "Star" and "Mother Barton," in other movies her names were usually associated with black servitude, such as "Lulu" in *The Expert* (1932), "Ivory" in *Ladies of the Big House* (1932) and *Women without Names* (1940), "Pearl" in *She Done Him Wrong*

Louise Beavers, appearing as the star in the motion picture *Prison Bait*, c. 1939. (Library of Congress.)

(1933), "Loretta" in *Bombshell* (1933), "Magnolia" in *Pick Up* (1933), "Imogene" in *Hat, Coat, and Gloves* (1934), "Florabelle" in *Wives Never Know* (1936), "Ophelia" in *Virginia* (1941), "Ruby" in *The Big Street* (1942), "Maum Maria" in *Reap the Wild Wind* (1942), "Mammy Jenny" in *Jack London* (1943), "Bedelia" in *Barbary Coast Gent* (1944), "Petunia" in *Seven Sweethearts* (1942), "Gussie" in *Mr. Blandings Builds His Dream House* (1948), and "Mammy Lou" in *Belle Starr* (1941). More typically, however, Louise Beavers was listed in movie credits—if at all—simply as "maid" (*Night World, Street of Women,* and *Young America,* all 1932), "cook" (*Made for Each Other,* 1939), "Mammy" (*Too Busy to Work,* 1932), "Aunt [so-and-so]" (Tina in *The Lady's from Kentucky,* 1939), or "Mamie" (*Make Way for Tomorrow,* 1937).

Ending the 1940s with *Tell It to the Judge* (1949), Beavers then starred in *Girls' School, The JACKIE ROBINSON Story,* and *My Blue Heaven* in 1950; *Colorado Sundown, I Dream of Jeannie,* and *Never Wave at a WAC* in 1953; *Goodbye, My Lady, Teenage Rebel,* and *You Can't Run Away from It* in 1956; *Tammy and the Bachelor* in 1957; *The Goddess* in 1958; and *All the Fine Young Cannibals* in 1960.

Beavers also played roles on television. Following on the heels of two other prominent black actresses who had starred on the popular television series *Beulah* (ETHEL WATERS and HATTIE MCDANIEL), Beavers decided to play the Henderson household's good-natured domestic. Her brief tenure, begun in 1952, lasted until the next year, when the show went off the air because she decided to leave the role. Her other television credits include *Star Stage* (1956), "The Hostess with the Mostest" on *Playhouse 90* (1957), and "Swamp Fox" on *Walt Disney Presents* (1959). Perhaps it was appropriate that, after nearly three decades and more than 116 films, Beavers's final role was the "Gilbert maid," serving Bob Hope and Lucille Ball in the 1961 madcap comedy *The Facts of Life.* She died the following year in Los Angeles.

The career of Louise Beavers serves as a critical reminder of how, in the early days of Hollywood, the stock roles available to black actresses progressed from merely inhabiting the background to representing a servile and gratuitous stereotype. Just as Aunt Delilah in *Imitation of Life* selflessly shares her pancake recipe with Bea rather than cash in on it herself, Louise Beavers exemplifies the legions of other early black actresses whose talents were subordinated to the self-serving biases of the dominant society.

Further Reading

Bogle, Donald. *Brown Sugar: Eighty Years of America's Black Female Superstars* (1980).

Loukides, Paul, and Linda K. Fuller, eds. *Beyond the Stars: Stock Characters in American Popular Film* (1990).

Nesteby, James R. *Black Images in American Films, 1896–1954: The Interplay between Civil Rights and Film Culture* (1982).

LINDA K. FULLER

BECHET, Sidney (14 May 1897–14 May 1959), clarinetist, soprano saxophonist, and composer, was born Sidney Joseph Bechet, the youngest of five sons and two daughters (three other children died in infancy) born to Omar Bechet, a shoemaker, and Josephine Michel in New Orleans, Louisiana. Bechet was raised as a middle-class Creole at the time when state law reclassified Creoles of color as Negro. The adoption of the black codes and de jure segregation had profound repercussions for the first generations of ragtime and jazz musicians in the Crescent City. Although Sidney spoke French in his childhood household and his grandfather, Jean Becher, was free and had owned property since 1817, Sidney Bechet identified himself as African American.

The Bechet family was decidedly musical. Sidney's father played the flute and trumpet for relaxation, and Sidney's brothers all played music as a hobby and developed skills in various trades for their vocations. Homer was a janitor and string bassist, Leonard a dentist and trombonist, Albert Eugene a butcher and violinist, Joseph a plasterer and guitarist. When he was only seven or eight years old, Sidney began playing a toy fife and soon began practicing on his brother's clarinet morning, noon, and night. He played in a band with his older brothers, but his family and other adult musicians quickly realized that Sidney was a prodigy whose technique outstripped that of some professionals.

Sidney's mother organized parties and hired professional bands to play in her home. When Sidney was just ten years old, she hired the great band of

Sidney Bechet, performing at an unknown location, possibly New York City, November 1946. (© William P. Gottlieb; www.jazzphotos.com.)

MANUEL PEREZ (who sent the equally legendary FREDDIE KEPPARD as a substitute) to play for her oldest son's twenty-first birthday. GEORGE BAQUET, the band's clarinetist, was late for the engagement, and Sidney, sequestered in another room, began playing his brother's clarinet as Baquet arrived. Sidney played well enough to cause Keppard to believe that it was Baquet warming up. As a result, Baquet began giving Sidney clarinet lessons. Bechet learned from him certain rudiments of clarinet playing, but he had already developed an unorthodox set of fingerings and refused to learn to read music. Bechet also studied with Paul Chaligny and ALPHONSE PICOU. His most important influence, however, came from "Big Eye" Louis Nelson. Nelson did not play in the academic style and specialized in the rougher "uptown" styles of the black players. Another lasting influence was the opera, which his mother took him to listen to. He especially liked the tenors (his favorite was Enrico Caruso), and the heavy vibrato that characterized his playing was in part modeled after them.

As Bechet began to play with professional organizations in parades, picnics, dance halls, and parties, he did not attend school regularly, despite his family's admonitions, and he reportedly ignored their advice about learning a trade other than music. At age fourteen he joined the Young Olympians, and soon he was playing with all the notable bands of New Orleans, including those led by Buddy Petit and BUNK JOHNSON. Bechet's family worried about the boy's exposure to the seamier aspects of musicians' nightlife. Yet, in this setting, Bechet developed into a soft-spoken and charming fellow who was very attractive to women. He also became a heavy drinker with a very short fuse and sometimes displayed a violent temper. As a teenager he was jailed for a violent incident. This odd mixture of musical virtuosity, charm, and violence would follow Bechet throughout his adult life.

Bechet went to Chicago in 1918, where he quickly found work within the various New Orleans cliques that dominated the scene. There he met and played for NOBLE SISSLE, JAMES REESE EUROPE, and WILL MARION COOK. Bechet's virtuosity and his ear for melodies and harmony were such that he amazed all three of these bandleaders, despite his not being able to read music, a skill normally required for these orchestras. In 1919 Bechet joined Cook's Southern Syncopated Orchestra, which brought him to New York, where his talents were much in demand. He then went to the British Isles with Cook's orchestra. British audiences received the orchestra warmly, and many critics singled out Bechet's playing as noteworthy. The most important review came from the Swiss conductor Ernst Ansermet, who wrote, in what was the first truly insightful critical article on jazz, that Bechet was an "extraordinary clarinet virtuoso" and an "artist of genius."

While in England, Bechet bought a soprano saxophone. The soprano saxophone was used very little in jazz, in part because of the severe intonation problems it presents, especially in the early models. But Bechet had a strong embouchure and a highly developed vibrato that allowed him to express himself with the instrument, and his supremacy as the greatest soprano saxophonist in jazz was not challenged until JOHN COLTRANE took up the instrument years after Bechet's death. The saxophone was perfect for Bechet, as its brassier and louder projection facilitated his natural inclination to take the melodic lead, usually the prerogative of trumpeters in the jazz ensembles of the 1910s and 1920s.

Bechet's stay in London ended when he was charged with assaulting a woman. Bechet pleaded not guilty, as did his codefendant, George Clapham. The stories of the two defendants and the two women involved conflicted, and Bechet hinted that his troubles with the police in England had racial overtones. He was sentenced to fourteen days of hard labor and was then deported on 3 November 1922.

Upon his arrival in New York, Bechet began to work in the theater circuit. He joined Donald Heywood's show *How Come*, in which Bechet played the role of How Come, a Chinese laundryman who was also a jazz musician. He was later billed as the "Wizard of the Clarinet" in theater bookings under Will Marion Cook's leadership. Bechet also began his recording career in New York, through CLARENCE WILLIAMS, a shrewd talent scout who helped supply black talent to record companies eager to cash in on the blues craze that followed MAMIE SMITH's hit record "Crazy Blues." In 1923 Bechet recorded his soprano saxophone on "Wild Cat Blues" and "Kansas City Man Blues" on Okeh Records. These records were listened to by thousands and served as models of jazz phrasing and improvisation for young musicians, including the likes of JOHNNY HODGES, HARRY CARNEY, and LIONEL HAMPTON. Bechet's success led to other recordings, where he accompanied singers such as Sara Martin, Mamie Smith, Rosetta Crawford, Margaret Johnson, EVA TAYLOR, and SIPPIE WALLACE. Bechet also began composing and made a big impression with his "Ghost of the Blues." He also wrote significant portions of *Negro Nuances*, a musical cowritten with Will Marion Cook and his wife, ABBIE MITCHELL. While the musical was not successful, Cook praised Bechet's compositions lavishly in the *Chicago Defender*.

In 1925 Bechet joined the *Black Revue*, featuring JOSEPHINE BAKER. The show took them to France, where they both became expatriates. Bechet continued working under the leadership of Noble Sissle and others. He also worked extensively in Germany, where he met Elisabeth Ziegler in 1926. He would eventually marry her in 1951, after both of them had married and divorced others. His original plans to marry Ziegler, after bringing her back to Paris in 1928, were spoiled. An argument between Bechet and the banjoist Gilbert "Little Mike" McKendrick began over a dispute about the correct harmonies to a song they had just played. By the end of the night the two were shooting at each other. Neither Bechet nor McKendrick was hit, but the pianist Glover Compton was shot in the leg, the dancer Dolores Giblins was shot in the lung, and an innocent bystander was shot in the neck. Bechet was sentenced to fifteen months in jail and was then deported.

He moved to Berlin and later returned to the United States after rejoining Noble Sissle's orchestra. In New York he led the New Orleans Feetwarmers with the trumpeter Tommy Ladnier. The group was short-lived, and Bechet briefly went into retirement from music and opened the Southern Tailor Shop in Harlem. In addition to tailoring, Bechet held jam sessions in the back room and cooked and served Creole cuisine. In 1934 Bechet returned to music once again at the behest of Noble Sissle. By the end of the 1930s the market for Bechet's style of jazz had lessened, but his cachet increased by the 1940s during the crest of the jazz revival. He played as either a bandleader or a star soloist throughout the United States. In 1949 he returned to Europe, eventually settling in France again, where he was the acknowledged patron saint of the European jazz revival. In 1951 he married Ziegler, with whom he lived for the rest of his life. He also had another home with a woman named Jacqueline, with whom he had a son, Daniel, in 1954. Bechet penned his most famous composition, "Petite fleur," in 1952, and in 1953 the Paris Conservatory Orchestra debuted his *La Nuit est une Sorcière*, a ballet in seven movements. With the help of two amanuenses, Joan Reid and Desmond Flower, Bechet also wrote *Treat It Gentle*, one of the most literarily ambitious jazz autobiographies.

Bechet, along with LOUIS ARMSTRONG, was among the first great jazz improvisers to liberate their solos from the rhythms and contours of the melody. Bechet's fame might have been even more widespread had the clarinet not fallen out of favor and the soprano saxophone been less obscure. He was the first to fashion legato melodies on the instrument and influenced such saxophone giants as Johnny Hodges and COLEMAN HAWKINS. He died before two of his disciples on the instrument, Steve Lacy and John Coltrane, popularized the instrument in the 1960s.

Further Reading

Bechet, Sidney. *Treat It Gentle* (1960).
Chilton, John. *Sidney Bechet: The Wizard of Jazz* (1987).
Obituary: *New York Times*, 15 May 1959.

SALIM WASHINGTON

BECK, Robert "Iceberg Slim" (4 Aug. 1918–30 April 1992), pimp-turned-novelist, autobiographer, essayist, and central figure of the black crime fiction movement that began in the 1960s, was born in Chicago, Illinois, as Robert Lee Maupin Jr., the only child of Mary Brown, a hairdresser, and Robert Maupin Sr., a hustler and one-time cook for Chicago mayor William "Big Bill" Thompson. In 1919, the year of the bloodiest race riots in Chicago's history, Robert Maupin Sr. tossed his infant son against a wall and abandoned the family. Beck survived, and Mary Brown supported her infant son by working as a door-to-door hairstylist. In 1924 she met Henry Upshaw, the owner of a cleaning and pressing shop, the only black business in Rockford, Illinois. Remembered by Beck as "the only father I had ever really known" (Iceberg Slim, 23), Upshaw provided Beck and his mother with a relatively stable middle-class life. However, in 1928, Brown left Upshaw to go to Chicago with a gambler named Steve, who abused the family for three years until Brown snuck out on him. After a short venture into the world of street hustling, Beck graduated at the age of fifteen in 1934 with a 98.4 average from Wendell Phillip High School, the first predominantly black high school in Chicago. Beck won an alumni scholarship to Tuskegee and attended BOOKER T. WASHINGTON's institution the same moment as fellow writer RALPH ELLISON. Beck and Ellison never knew one another, and emblematic of the distinct paths they would take as writers, Ellison left Tuskegee after two years for New York to become a novelist, and Robert Beck was expelled for bootlegging whiskey.

Returning to Chicago in 1936, Beck began his twenty-five-year career as a pimp and street hustler. He was known early in his career as Youngblood, but he earned the moniker of Iceberg Slim when a stray bullet knocked his hat off at a bar. Mistaking his cocaine-induced high for coolness-under-pressure, Beck's friend Glass Top gave him his legendary name. Robert Beck's early years as a pimp came at a moment when working-class blacks in Chicago and other urban centers were being increasingly isolated in inner-city ghettos with poor or substandard housing, and few job opportunities. Pimping was his attempt to transcend these social, racial, and spatial conditions. As he tells it in his autobiography: "I was still black in the white man's world. My hope to be important and admired could be realized even behind this black stockade. It was simple, just pimp my ass off and get a ton of scratch. Everybody in both worlds kissed your ass black and blue if you had flash and front" (Iceberg Slim, 117). For the better part of two and a half decades, Beck used the skills of sweet-talk, hustle, and muscle to earn enough money, or "scratch," to try to make his way out of the "black stockade" of the American ghetto. His criminal exploits landed him in prison five times, where he served a total of almost seven years. Beck was first incarcerated in 1936 at Wisconsin Green Bay State Reformatory on the charge of "carnal knowledge and abuse," and beginning in 1937, he served twenty-one months at Waupun State Penitentiary for grand theft. Beck returned to jail in 1946, where he served an eighteen-month sentence at Leavenworth on the charge of "white slavery" for sending a minor across state lines. In 1947 Beck was detained at the Cook County House of Corrections for armed robbery. He made a spectacular escape from the institution only to be recaptured and forced to serve out the rest of his sentence in 1960. Ironically, Beck never served any time for pimping.

The turning point in Beck's life came in 1960, when, after serving ten months in solitary confinement at Cook County House of Corrections, he decided to give up what is commonly known by the criminal underclass as "the Life." He moved to Los Angeles to make amends with his ailing mother, and even took the last name Beck, the name of his mother's husband, William Beck. With his common-law wife, Betty, Beck would have three daughters, Camille, Melody, and Misty, born in 1965, 1967, and 1970, respectively. In 1967, after trying a variety of jobs, including selling insecticides door to door, he submitted his autobiography to a Los Angeles–based paperback publisher, Holloway House. The manuscript would eventually become *Pimp: The Story of My Life* published in 1967. Because of the controversial title and content, Holloway House was unable to secure any advertising space for the book in mainstream venues like the *New York Times*, but the Holloway House founder and CEO, Bentley Morriss, a former Hollywood publicist, explored alternative ways of publicizing the book, and he secured guest appearances on television shows and at local universities for Beck.

Pimp became the best-selling book by a black American author ever, and its popularity inspired Beck to publish more. On the heels of *Pimp*, in 1967 he published *Trick Baby*, the story of a light-skinned African American named John Patrick O'Brian, nicknamed White Folks, whose ability to pass for white makes him one of the best con men in Chicago. Following in the literary tradition exemplified by JAMES WELDON JOHNSON's *The Autobiography of an Ex-Colored Man* (1912) and NELLA LARSEN's *Passing* (1929), among others, *Trick Baby* explores the possibilities and limits of racial passing as a viable form of overcoming racial oppression in America. In 1969 Beck published what is arguably his most powerful and sensitive work, *Mama Black Widow*, the story of a gay transvestite named Otis Tilson and his family. Based on taped interviews Beck conducted with Tilson months before his suicide and published the same year as the Stonewall Riot, *Mama Black Widow* is a haunting novel about the failed promises of the Great Migration and an extended meditation on the philosophies of nonviolence by the recently assassinated MARTIN LUTHER KING.

The subtle turn toward black politics in *Mama Black Widow* would come to full fruition in the only work published under the name Robert Beck, *The Naked Soul of Iceberg Slim* (1971). Dedicated to MALCOLM X, ANGELA DAVIS, and a number of members from the Black Panther Party, *Naked Soul* features a wide range of his political and personal thoughts, including a heartfelt letter to his biological father, a sketch of his visit to Black Panther headquarters in the Watts neighborhood of Los Angeles, and his theories on how hatred for the mother acts as the psychological motivation for pimping. Throughout the 1970s, Beck, continuing to use the pen name of Iceberg Slim, published three more best-selling books,

including *Death Wish*, a crime drama about the mafia (1976); *Long White Con*, a sequel to *Trick Baby* about the further of exploits of White Folks (1977); and *Airtight Willie and Me*, a collection of short stories (1979). In 1982 Robert Beck married Los Angeles native Diane Millman, a freelance typist/transcriber and a devoted fan of his work who had sent him a letter in 1980, and the woman with whom Beck remained until his death. Beck died in Culver City Hospital, later Brotman Memorial, on 30 April 1992 from complications stemming from diabetes, as Watts was aflame from the riots sparked by the acquittal of white police officers for the videotaped beating of motorist RODNEY KING. After his death, *Doom Fox*, the only book not published by Holloway House, was published by Grove Press in 1998.

Millions of copies of Beck's novels have sold in America's black communities, distributed through less traditional venues like barbershops, liquor stores, beauty salons, and other local black businesses. A hybrid of street slang, psychoanalysis, and crime narrative, Beck's stories about ghetto life from the inside made him a folk hero among many working-class African Americans. According to H. Bruce Franklin, in his important study of American prison fiction, Beck's autobiography about the plight of the criminal class in America places him in an African American literary tradition that extends from the slave narratives of FREDERICK DOUGLASS and HARRIET JACOBS to the prison and crime novels of CHESTER HIMES. The popular success of his work convinced Holloway House to proclaim itself the "world's largest publisher of the black experience novel," publishing hundreds of novels since the late 1960s that reflect the experiences of dispossessed urban minorities. Beck's literature paved the way for dozens of black writers, including DONALD GOINES, Odie Hawkins, Roosevelt Malloy, ROLAND JEFFERSON, Joe Nazel, and many others, and along with his protégé and fellow best-selling author Donald Goines, Beck is considered a literary godfather of hip-hop. His poetics and narratives have inspired the likes of ICE-T, ICE CUBE, DMX, TUPAC SHAKUR, SNOOP DOGGY DOGG, and JAY-Z.

Further Reading

Beck, Robert. *The Naked Soul of Iceberg Slim* (1971).
Franklin, H. Bruce. *The Victim as Criminal and Artist: Literature from the American Prison* (1978).
Graham, D. B. "Negative Glamor: The Pimp Hero in the Fiction of Iceberg Slim," *Obsidian* 1 (Summer 1975) .
Iceberg Slim. *Pimp: The Story of My Life* (1967).
Muckley, Peter A. *Iceberg Slim: The Life as Art* (2003).

JUSTIN DAVID GIFFORD

BECKWOURTH, Jim (26 April 1800?–1866?), mountain man, fur trapper and trader, scout, translator, and explorer, was born James Pierson Beckwith in Frederick County, Virginia, the son of Sir Jennings Beckwith, a white Revolutionary War veteran and the descendant of minor Irish aristocrats who became prominent Virginians. Little is known about Jim's mother, a mixed-race slave working in the Beckwith household. Although he was born into slavery, Jim was manumitted by his father in the 1820s. In the early 1800s, Beckwith moved his family, which reputedly included fourteen children, to Missouri, eventually settling in St. Louis. Some commentators suggest that Beckwith, an adventurous outdoorsman, was seeking an environment less hostile to his racially mixed family.

As a young teenager, after four years of schooling, Jim Beckwourth (as his name came to be spelled) was apprenticed to a blacksmith. Unhappy as a tradesman, he fled to the newly discovered lead mines in Illinois's Fever River region and then to New Orleans in search of greater adventure. Motivated by a lack of work and by the racism he encountered, Jim responded to a newspaper ad placed by the entrepreneurial fur traders Andrew Henry and William Henry Ashley. The ad called for "One Hundred MEN to ascend the Missouri to the Rocky Mountains"; Jim enlisted in 1824. The Ashley-Henry strategy, which Beckwourth emulated, combined direct beaver trapping with trading for furs at the Indian villages. He learned trapping and frontier skills alongside the legendary mountain men Jedediah Smith and Jim Bridger, becoming a crack shot and expert bowie knife and tomahawk handler. Beckwourth was present at the first Mountain

Jim Beckwourth, adventurer and explorer, in an undated photograph. (William Katz Collection.)

Man rendezvous at Henry's Fork on the Green River in 1825. He claimed to have been married briefly to two Blackfoot Indian sisters during this period.

While on a trapping expedition in the late 1820s, Beckwourth was captured by Crow Indians (Absaroke or Sparrowhawk people). How exactly Beckwourth came to live with the Crow remains unclear. During the years he lived with the tribe, Beckwourth became a valued Crow warrior and tribe member. He lived with a succession of Indian women and acknowledged one child, Black Panther or Little Jim. Beckwourth's tribal names—Morning Star, Antelope, Enemy of Horses, Bobtail Horse, Bloody Arm, Bull's Robe, and Medicine Calf—capture both the romance and the narrative value of his years living, hunting, and raiding with the Crow.

Leaving the tribe and the Ashley-Henry fur trading company behind in 1836, Beckwourth crisscrossed the Western frontier playing cards, prospecting, trapping, selling whiskey to Indians, stealing horses, brawling in saloons, and guiding settlers. Hired by the U.S. Army as a muleskinner, messenger, and scout during the Seminole War of 1837, he fought against the Seminole, a confederation of Native Americans and runaway slaves. Subsequently, Jim traveled the Southwest working as a fur trader and translator for Andrew Sublette and Louis Vasquez on the Santa Fe Trail and as a wagon loader at Bent's Fort in Taos. In 1842 Beckwourth opened a trading post with his current wife, Louise Sandoval, in what is presently Pueblo, Colorado. A few years later, abandoning yet another family, Beckwourth answered the siren call of California, where he survived as a horse thief (he claimed to have stolen over two thousand horses), a letter carrier, and from 1846 to 1847 as a guide for the American forces during the conquest of California.

The discovery of gold in 1848 brought Beckwourth to the Sierra mining camps. But while most forty-niners panned for gold, Jim invested in a more lucrative gamble: a passable travel route through the rugged mountain terrain. In 1850 he located the Beckwourth Pass near present-day Reno, Nevada. Capitalizing on his discovery, Jim built a wagon road servicing settlers and gold rushers and established a ranch and trading post in what came to be known as Beckwourth, California. A charming and personable host, Jim briefly reinvented himself as a hotel and saloonkeeper. The pass, which in its heyday accommodated ten thousand wagons annually, remained popular until the railroad supplanted wagon travel in 1855.

In 1858 Beckwourth traveled east to St. Louis, Denver, and Kansas City, until gold was discovered near Pikes Peak, Colorado. Beckwourth and his latest wife, Elizabeth Lettbetter, worked as shopkeepers in Denver, but Jim never quite adapted to city life; his marriage dissolved, and he subsequently married a Crow woman named Sue. The Colorado Volunteer Cavalry hired Beckwourth to locate Cheyenne and Arapaho Indian camps in 1864. Beckwourth's role in the subsequent Sand Creek Massacre permanently alienated him from the Indian tribes.

The facts of Beckwourth's life remain in contention. Even the year of his birth is debated among historians. Much of the historical perplexity is the result of obfuscations in the autobiography that Beckwourth dictated to Thomas D. Bonner in 1854. Most significantly, the autobiography omits any mention of Beckwourth's race. While it was Bonner who altered the spelling of the name "Beckwourth," Jim was responsible for confusing dates, omitting details, and lavishly embellishing the facts of his life, including his role in events, the number of rivals killed, money made, and battles waged. He may have taken as his own the heroic tales of other frontiersmen, including Edward Rose, who lived with the Crow a generation before Beckwourth. The book, published in 1856, put into print stories Beckwourth had been spinning for years. Storytelling was a valued skill and an important part of the period's oral tradition, and Beckwourth had spent a lifetime fashioning elaborate narratives with himself as the hero. The book found a ready audience among armchair travelers fascinated and titillated by the exoticism and liberation of frontier stories. Once the inaccuracies of his text were revealed, however, Beckwourth was quickly labeled a liar. As a result, many early historians wrote him off as an unreliable and purposeful braggart, while others, fueled by racism, attacked him on the basis of his "mixed blood." In the early twenty-first century, historians generally agree that much of the text's basic narrative can be believed and that it represents an invaluable documentary record.

An inveterate adventurer and explorer, Beckwourth looked and dressed the part. Dark-eyed, muscular, and taller than six feet, he often dressed in embroidered buckskin, Crow leggings, ribbons, earrings, and gold chains and wore his thick, dark hair loose to his waist or elaborately braided. Beckwourth was not, as has been claimed, completely illiterate. He spoke English with great skill, fluent French, some Spanish, and a number of Indian dialects. The elision of race in his autobiography has been compounded by numerous painted portraits that untruthfully depict him as very light-skinned and by the 1951 film *Tomahawk*, which cast Jack Oakie, a white actor, as Beckwourth.

Mystery still surrounds Beckwourth's death in Crow territory near the Bighorn River in 1866. While it is generally believed that he died of sickness or food poisoning, the rumor lingers that he was purposefully poisoned by the Crow after rejecting offers to rejoin the tribe.

Further Reading

Beckwourth, James P. *The Life and Times of James P. Beckwourth, Mountaineer, Scout, Pioneer, and Chief of the Crow Nation of Indians as told to Thomas D. Bonner* (1856).
Mumey, Nolie. *James Pierson Beckwourth: An Enigmatic Figure of the West, A History of the Latter Years of His Life* (1957).
Wilson, Elinor. *Jim Beckwourth: Black Mountain Man and War Chief of the Crows* (1972).

LISA E. RIVO

BEDOU, Arthur (Paul) (6 July 1880–June 1966), photographer and businessman, was born in New Orleans, where he remained professionally based throughout his sixty-plus-year career.

The leading African American photographer in New Orleans in the first half of the twentieth century, Bedou saw his reputation grow to national proportions as a result of his images of the life and travel of Tuskegee Normal and Industrial Institute (later Tuskegee University) President BOOKER T. WASHINGTON from the early 1900s through 1915. He photographed Washington at public-speaking engagements addressing crowds in Arkansas, Florida, Louisiana, Mississippi, South Carolina, Tennessee, Texas, Virginia, California, and numerous other locations during his final tour, which ended in 1915. He recorded Washington in transit by coach, train, and automobile in addition to his famous portraits of the education leader posed upon his horse.

As official photographer for the Institute, Bedou covered any number of events for the school. He recorded the 24 October 1905 celebration and parade in honor of President Theodore Roosevelt's visit to the campus (Roosevelt would later serve as a trustee), Tuskegee's twenty-fifth anniversary ceremony in 1906, and the delegation of officials and students from Barbados who attended the International Conference on the Negro held at Tuskegee in 1912. In addition to making formal photographs of administrators, faculty, alumni, and students in classrooms, work being done on buildings, and various other activities, he documented Washington hosting business, civic, political, religious, humanities, and academic dignitaries; and visiting school groups from Hawaii and Japan. Bedou also captured him attending events in the company of the educator and activist MARY MCLEOD BETHUNE, c. 1910; R. C. Houston Jr., president of Provident Savings Bank in Fort Worth, Texas; I. B. Scott, bishop of the African Methodist Episcopal Church; Dr. ELIAS CAMP MORRIS, president of the National Baptist Convention; ROSCOE CONKLING SIMMONS, editor of the *National Review;* and Charles S. Tator of the *New York Evening Post.*

Bedou was one of the earliest African American photographers to enjoy considerable financial success and to have his imagery considered for its artistic merit as well as technical proficiency. His private-studio clients included many of the city's elite and crossed all walks of life and ancestral heritage. Despite his reputation as a portraitist, he was equally regarded for documentation of the New Orleans Creole community, jazz musicians, and the Louisiana and Mississippi countryside. Some of the images reflecting his creative ability in camera work were a sensitively crafted photograph of a praline candy box with a portrait of two women from 1908; an outdoor scene titled *Color Waterfall View*, c. 1910; and a number of recorded views taken in Alabama, Florida, Kansas, Maryland, Massachusetts, Tennessee, and Virginia. He also took photographs at the home of FREDERICK DOUGLASS in the Anacostia neighborhood of Washington, D.C.

After Washington's death in 1915, and the founding of Xavier University by Mother Katherine Drexel in the same year, Bedou left Tuskegee and became the official photographer of the New Orleans school. On the business front, he was a founder of Peoples Life Insurance Company of Louisiana in 1922.

At Xavier, the first Catholic institution of higher learning for African Americans in the country, Bedou made numerous portraits of the Sisters of the Holy Family; full-body, standing poses of newly ordained Roman Catholic priests, c. 1934; and countless images of students at pivotal moments in their matriculation. He also recorded many campus views of buildings and monuments like the Goodridge School of Nursing. As was the case at Tuskegee, he expanded his lens toward residences, community buildings, churches, and portraits of African American students at other schools in the South from the late 1920s to the 1940s. He took the last photographs of MARCUS GARVEY in the United States before Garvey was deported to Jamaica and continued his extensive documentation of musicians, street festivals, and the diverse cultural demographics of the city.

From 1942 until his death in 1966, Bedou operated out of a studio at South Rampart and Common Streets in New Orleans. Many of his images of people associated with Tuskegee and Washington were unique because they included personal inscriptions to the president. Bedou's photography was placed in the permanent collections and archives of Xavier University, Tuskegee University, Atlanta History Center, Schomburg Center for Research in Black Culture, and numerous public and private collections.

Further Reading
Bedou, Arthur. *The Tuskegee Institute* (1911).
Coar, Valencia Hollins. *A Century of Black Photographers: 1840–1960* (1983).
Willis, Deborah. *Reflections in Black: A History of Black Photographers 1840 to the Present* (2000).
AMALIA K. AMAKI

BELAFONTE, Harry (1 Mar. 1927–), singer, actor, activist, and producer, was born Harold George Belafonte Jr. in Harlem in New York City, the son of Harold George Belafonte Sr., a seaman, and Melvine Love, a domestic worker. Belafonte Sr. was an alcoholic who contributed little to family life, other than occasionally hitting his spouse, and the young Harry was brought up almost exclusively by his mother. Harold and Melvine, who were both from the Caribbean, had a difficult time adjusting to life in New York, and after the Harlem race riots of 1935, Melvine and her son moved to her native Jamaica, where Harry spent five years shielded from American racism. When World War II broke out, the Belafontes returned to Harlem. Hoping for better conditions, the family would often try to pass for white. With white relatives on both the mother's and father's sides, they were all fair-skinned enough to be taken for Greek, Italian, or even Irish. Duty bound, Belafonte joined local gangs, drafted to help defend his white enclaves from neighboring blacks.

Belafonte attended school in Harlem, but struggled with dyslexia; by ninth grade he had had enough and dropped out. Soon thereafter he enlisted in the U.S. Navy and was assigned to an all-black unit. Because of his race—and his temper—Belafonte was assigned as a munitions loader, one of the most dangerous jobs on the home front. "The men who were stuck with munitions loading were very bitter, very angry," he recalls. "In our bitterness and anger we went out and got drunk. We wanted to beat up everybody we met, including each other" (Eldridge, 117–118). When feeling less pugilistic, Belafonte discovered a passion for politics. He enjoyed sitting in on discussions of race and racism in the United States and labored to understand pamphlets and essays by W. E. B. DU BOIS.

Belafonte met his first wife, Margurite Byrd, while his unit was stationed in Norfolk, Virginia. Byrd was studying psychology at the nearby Hampton Institute; she remembers their early relationship as "one long argument over racial issues" (Gates, 160). Belafonte and Byrd married in 1948 and had their first child, Adrienne, a year later. By this time, Belafonte had finished his tour of duty and moved his family to New York. Here, at Harlem's American Negro Theatre (ANT), Belafonte saw a play that sparked his interest in acting. With support from the GI Bill, he was soon enrolled in a workshop at the New School for Social Research, together with Marlon Brando, Tony Curtis, and Bea Arthur. Working as a janitor's assistant to help pay the bills, Belafonte volunteered backstage at the ANT. This quickly led to a role in a production of Sean O'Casey's *Juno and the Paycock*.

It was also at the ANT that Belafonte met SIDNEY POITIER, another black actor of Caribbean extraction, who became a lifelong friend and who, some say, stole Belafonte's career. The two were almost exact contemporaries and competed for many of the same roles. In a 1948 show called *Days of Our Youth*, Poitier was working as Belafonte's understudy. When Belafonte could not perform one night owing to his janitorial duties, Poitier filled in. A producer happened to be in the audience that evening and approached Poitier after the show. It was the actor's big break, the one that eventually landed him in Hollywood.

Belafonte soldiered on in the theater, but slowly began to turn his attention toward music. On a friend's suggestion he performed at amateur night at a midtown club called the Royal Roost and was immediately hired full time. His performance consisted of pop jazz standards, a repertoire Belafonte found less than edifying; after a year he called it quits. By this time he had saved up a tidy sum of money, and he used it to open a grill called the Sage in Greenwich Village. The restaurant folded after eight months, but during that time it had served Belafonte as a late-night rehearsal space. Belafonte began indulging his interest in folk music at the Sage, and, after it closed, he pursued his research at a more conventional

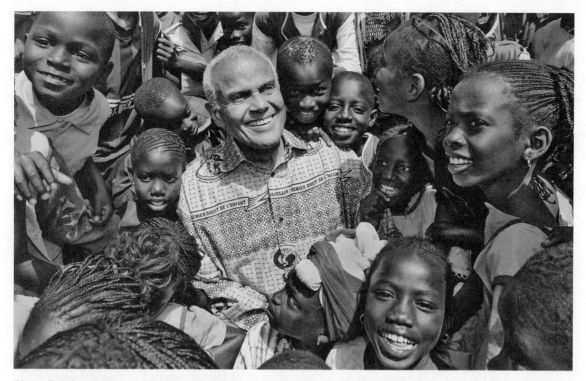

Harry Belafonte, singer, civil rights advocate, and Goodwill Ambassador for the U.N. Children's Fund, at a school in the Guediyawe district, Dakar, Senegal, 24 February 2004. (AP Images.)

venue, listening to field recordings in the Library of Congress.

In 1951 Belafonte brought his new act to the stage. Folk hardly seemed a promising genre at the height of the McCarthy era, when many of its left-leaning practitioners such as PAUL ROBESON and Pete Seeger were blacklisted, but success came quickly, with sell-out crowds at big-name clubs and a recording contract from RCA. Harry Belafonte's voice alone cannot account for his success, but combined with his stage persona—tight trousers, open shirt, and shiny, mocha skin—it wowed audiences. Belafonte sang the expected folk standards, but then veered off toward African, Caribbean, and even Hebrew songs like "Hava Nageela." (He claims most American Jews learned the tune from him.) In spite of his success, Belafonte suffered the same indignities as other black entertainers of the day and was routinely denied the right to eat or sleep at the same venues that paid dearly to book his act. But Belafonte was quick to have revenge; in 1954, after *Brown v. Board of Education* declared segregation unconstitutional, he cancelled his engagements in the South.

Belafonte released several folk albums, but it was not until 1956 that he fully embraced the Caribbean music that delighted his audiences. *Harry Belafonte—Calypso* proved an instant classic, and two songs in particular, "The Banana Boat Song (Day-O)" and "Jamaica Farewell," topped the charts. Some claimed

Belafonte had bastardized true Trinidadian calypso, but Belafonte was unapologetic about tailoring the music to American audiences. It was clearly an astute commercial move; in a year's time the album had sold 1.5 million copies, more than any previous record by a single artist.

As audiences grew and shows sold out, Belafonte resumed acting, taking roles in films and plays, including John Murray Anderson's Broadway revue *Almanac*, which earned him a Tony Award. Perhaps his most personally significant performance was in *Carmen Jones* (1954), an all-black film version of Georges Bizet's opera *Carmen* that also starred DOROTHY DANDRIDGE and PEARL BAILEY. Belafonte and Marguerite Byrd's second daughter, Shari, was born in 1954, but Belafonte's marriage ended in divorce in 1957. That same year he married Julie Robinson, a dancer with the KATHERINE DUNHAM Company, with whom he would later have a son, David, and a daughter, Gina. Initially, Belafonte's divorce slipped under the media's radar screen, but word of his remarriage eventually did get out, not least because his new bride was white.

Belafonte continued to act, including a role in 1957's *Island in the Sun*, a controversial tale of interracial love, but he found himself increasingly put off by Hollywood's ham-fisted attempts to deal with race. The scripts that came his way ranged from the shallow to the offensive, and Belafonte seemed unable to get any of his own ideas produced. In the 1960s he abandoned the cinema and engrossed himself in politics.

Belafonte had met MARTIN LUTHER KING JR. in 1956 during the Montgomery bus boycott and was immediately taken with King's passion and candor. At that first meeting, King seemed uncertain about the fate of the civil rights movement. He asked Belafonte for support, and over the next decade Belafonte lent his name and energy to the cause. He proved instrumental in rallying celebrities at home and abroad, forging political connections, and organizing fundraisers. Belafonte also devoted large sums of his own money, heavily insuring King's life and bailing out activists arrested during sit-ins and protest marches. When King was jailed in Birmingham, it was Belafonte who led the charge to raise the fifty-thousand-dollar bail. His efforts earned him a place on the board of directors of King's Southern Christian Leadership Conference. Over the years of their joint involvement, Belafonte and King developed a close personal friendship, which lasted until King's death in 1968.

After the civil rights movement began to wane, Belafonte shifted his focus to Africa. His appointment by President John F. Kennedy as a cultural adviser to the Peace Corps in 1961 had first sparked his interest, and through the coming decades he devoted boundless energy to campaigns for development aid and human rights. Chief among these was the anti-apartheid struggle in South Africa, which consumed Belafonte in the 1980s. In 1987 the United Nations Children's Fund recognized his efforts and made him a goodwill ambassador, a position he has used to draw attention to famine, war, and the plague of AIDS.

Belafonte's activism often drew on his connections in the entertainment world. For a week in 1968 he guest hosted Johnny Carson's *Tonight Show*, turning light entertainment into politics with guests like Robert F. Kennedy and Martin Luther King Jr. In his anti-apartheid efforts, he worked to introduce exiled South African musicians like Miriam Makeba and Hugh Masekela to listeners in the United States, and in 1988 he released *Paradise in Gazankulu*, his own album of South African–themed music. In 1985 Belafonte took a similar approach to relief efforts for famine in Ethiopia. Inspired by pop stars from the British Isles who launched Band Aid in 1984, Belafonte was the driving force behind "We Are the World," an American effort in 1985 which raised over $70 million in aid for Ethiopian famine victims.

Perhaps because his political and show-business interests have always been so entwined, Belafonte has never been forced to choose between the two. In the thick of the anti-apartheid movement, he resumed acting and found time to mount major concert tours. Earlier, at the height of the civil rights movement, Belafonte had begun what may be his most ambitious musical project, a series of records then called *Anthology of Negro Folk Music*. He wanted to showcase the richness and variety of the African American musical tradition with a collection that included work songs and spirituals, minstrel tunes and lullabies. But when recording was completed in 1971, the backers of the project, RCA and *Reader's Digest*, pulled out, citing lack of commercial prospects, and the tapes languished in RCA vaults. They were finally released in 2001 as *The Long Road to Freedom: An Anthology of Black Music* and were nominated for a Grammy Award for best historical album.

The release of *Long Road* topped off a flurry of show-business activity by Belafonte in the 1990s. In 1995 he starred in the independent film *White Man's Burden* and the following year played the gangster Seldom Seen in Robert Altman's *Kansas City*. Plans were afoot for Belafonte to produce yet another picture with an unusual take on race—a film version of *Amos 'n Andy*, the long-running radio and television show that was criticized by the NAACP, among others, for perpetuating racist stereotypes, but which nonetheless enjoyed a substantial audience among African Americans from the 1920s to the 1950s. After a short hiatus from film acting at the beginning of the twenty-first century, Belafonte returned to the big screen in 2006 with a role in Emilio Estevez's *Bobby*, a film about Senator Robert Kennedy.

Belafonte has also continued to play sold-out shows and has campaigned to raise awareness about prostate health among African American men and the need to curb gang violence. He provoked controversy, however, in a much-criticized 15 October 2002 appearance on CNN's *Larry King Live*, when he refused to apologize for his earlier denunciation of Secretary of State COLIN POWELL as President George W. Bush's "house slave." Powell called Belafonte's comments "an unfortunate throwback to another time and another place," but the entertainer insisted that the secretary of state was a "sell-out." Asked by King if the same term applied to CONDOLEEZZA RICE, Bush's national security adviser, Belafonte replied, "Yes. Absolutely. Absolutely. Even more so." Belafonte continued his polemics against the Bush administration in subsequent years. In January 2006, the Associated Press reported that during a meeting with Hugo Chavez, the president of Venezuela, Belafonte commented that Bush was "the greatest terrorist in the world."

In the final analysis, Harry Belafonte remains difficult to pigeonhole either as an activist or as an entertainer, but it hardly seems worth the effort. Whether his greatest achievements have taken place onstage or off remains open to debate; his success in both arenas does not.

Further Reading

Eldridge, Michael. "Remains of the Day-O." *Transition* 92: 110–137.

Gates, Henry Louis, Jr. *Thirteen Ways of Looking at a Black Man* (1997).

Ward, Brian. *Just My Soul Responding: Rhythm and Blues, Black Consciousness, and Race Relations* (1998).

CHRIS BEBENEK

BELINDA (c.1713–?), a former slave who achieved renown in the era of the American Revolution by laying claim to a portion of the wealth of her former master's estate, was born in the region of West Africa known as the Gold Coast (later Ghana). Her early years were spent in a village on the Volta River. According to her later memories, it was an Edenic existence. However, when she was about age twelve, the Atlantic slave trade shattered this bucolic world. She was captured in a slaving raid, permanently separated from her parents, marched overland to the coast, and sold to European slave traders. For several weeks she endured the horrific Middle Passage with some three hundred other Africans in chains, who were "suffering the most excruciating torment" (Carretta, 143).

In about 1732, after six or seven years in North America, Belinda became the slave of Isaac Royall Jr., a member of a prominent family of sugar planters on the Caribbean island of Antigua. She would serve him in bondage for nearly five decades. Royall had recently moved his family and slaves to Medford, Massachusetts, where he became the largest slaveholder in the colony. Belinda lived in his sizeable slave quarters in Medford, a rare experience for a New England slave. As the American Revolution neared, Royall became an outspoken Loyalist, an unpopular stance in radical Massachusetts. Fearing for his safety, he fled the colonies for Britain in April 1775, a few days after the battles of Lexington and Concord. With her master gone Belinda became the property of the state of Massachusetts, which manumitted her in 1778; unfortunately it appears that a son, Joseph, was sold away from her at the time of her manumission. She left Medford for Boston, where she and an invalid daughter, Prine, were living in 1783, when the Massachusetts courts finally declared slavery unconstitutional in the case of *Commonwealth v. Jennison*.

In February 1783, as Massachusetts was ending slavery and the Revolution was coming to an end, Belinda petitioned the Massachusetts legislature, assembled as a general court, for a portion of the rents and profits of the Royall estate. PRINCE HALL, a local black abolitionist who had personally petitioned the legislature on several occasions, probably helped her author the petition. It is unclear what other individuals or ideas may have influenced her action, although Boston blacks and a local Patriot pamphleteer named James Swan had promoted biblical justifications for restitution to the slaves in the years before the Revolution. After recounting her suffering as a result of slavery and the slave trade, and noting her advanced age and extreme poverty, she used the bulk of the petition to explain her reasons for seeking a pension, noting that she had labored in slavery for Royall for nearly half a century. Drawing on emerging capitalist notions, she observed that, despite her years of unpaid labor, she was "denied the enjoyment of one morsel of that immense wealth, a part whereof hath been accumulated by her own industry, and the whole augmented by her servitude" (Carretta, 143).

She pleaded with the legislature to grant her a pension out of the wealth of the Royall estate. Moved by her argument, the legislature granted her a £15 annual pension. In 1787, after the estate had failed to continue payment of the pension, she again petitioned the legislature to order that the payments be resumed. Her request was granted. Finally, in 1790, the executor of the Royall estate refused to continue payment "without a further interposition" by the legislature. Belinda petitioned a third time and a legislative committee determined the pension was still in "full force." Nothing further is known of Belinda's life after 1790.

Belinda's initial petition had a separate life in the public sphere, reaching readers on both sides of the Atlantic. It was reprinted verbatim in the 18 June 1783 issue of the *New Jersey Gazette*, a popular newspaper in the Middle Atlantic states. Two months later it circulated through a few British periodicals under the heading "The Complaint of Belinda, an African." Rewritten into a first-person slave narrative for use in the emerging British antislavery campaign, the latter version added a tale of rape to the list of sufferings in the original petition. There was another flurry of interest in Belinda's case when Matthew Carey published the petition in his widely-circulated *American Museum* magazine in 1787.

The petition has been remembered and reinterpreted by writers as diverse as the pioneering historian WILLIAM COOPER NELL in his *Colored Patriots of the American Revolution* (1855) and the former U.S. poet laureate RITA DOVE in her 1982 poem entitled "Belinda's Petition." Both of these writers and others have viewed the petition as a suit for freedom. By the early twenty-first century, however, scholars increasingly understood the petition as an early call for personal restitution for time spent in bondage. The anthropologist Stephanie Shaw labeled it "perhaps the earliest example of reparations for the slave trade and slavery" (Finkenbine, 96).

Further Reading
Carretta, Vincent, ed. *Unchained Voices: An Anthology of Black Authors in the English-Speaking World of the Eighteenth Century* (1996).
Finkenbine, Roy E. "Belinda's Petition: Reparations for Slavery in Revolutionary Massachusetts," *William and Mary Quarterly* 54 (Jan. 2007): 95–104.
ROY E. FINKENBINE

BELL, Al (1940/41–) record executive, producer, and activist, was born Alvertis Isbell in Brinkley, Arkansas, in 1940 or 1941. In 1945 his family moved to Little Rock, where Bell later graduated with a bachelor's degree in Political Science from the city's Philander Smith College, following this with uncompleted ministerial training; he worked as a disc jockey throughout high school and college. In 1959 Bell began working at workshops run by the Southern Christian Leadership Conference (SCLC) and Dr. MARTIN LUTHER KING JR. His SCLC involvement was short-lived, which Bell attributed to a difference in philosophy, explaining that King's strategy of non-violent confrontation differed from his belief in the power of black capitalist entrepreneurship in effecting social change.

Bell then worked full time at several radio stations, first at WLOK in Memphis, where his laid-back style helped boost ratings, and then at WUST in Washington, D.C., where he introduced releases by the fledgling Memphis label Stax Records. He soon became station manager and also produced releases by local R&B artists. In 1965, Stax—now requiring expanded advertising to support its nationally marketed hit recordings—hired the charismatic, ambitious Bell as its national promotions director. From his first days with the label Bell's charm and contacts helped push Stax toward new heights of exposure and profitability; 1966 and 1967 would be peak years for the company, and Bell would soon parlay his success into an increasingly prominent role. In 1967 the label's owner, Jim Stewart, promoted Bell to executive vice-president, and from then on Bell would become arguably the most important force within the company.

The year 1968 was a tumultuous one for Stax. In December 1967, OTIS REDDING—the label's biggest star—was killed in a plane crash. In April 1968 Dr. King was assassinated in Memphis. The same year also saw Atlantic Records break its distribution deal with Stax, with Atlantic seizing most of Stax's catalog and severing all business connections. This devastated the already weakened company, and it was during this crucial period that Bell's leadership proved vital.

Over the next several years, and not without controversy, Bell reinvented Stax Records. His goals were a tidy encapsulation of the cultural and economic goals of much of the era's Black Power rhetoric: he sought to help the company achieve financial autonomy, while simultaneously using its music and influence to advance causes of black equality and opportunity. He gained 10 percent ownership in the company in 1968, and soon held controlling interest, making Stax black owned for the first time in its history. From his first days at the label, Bell had pushed toward the diversification of Stax releases, attempting to carve out success in nearly every musical format, even those which the label and its first leaders had previously ignored. Some of these attempts, like comedy releases from RICHARD PRYOR, proved more successful than others (such as, for example, Bell's repeated attempts to find a successful white artist). Stax also helped promote MELVIN VAN PEEBLES's groundbreaking film *Sweet Sweetback's Baadasssss Song*, predicting the huge success of the Stax artist ISAAC HAYES' *Shaft* soundtrack. Musically, Bell hoped to employ a "crossover" strategy similar to that perfected by Detroit's Motown Records. Though Bell loved all the music made at Stax, and as promotions director helped codify the notion of "the Memphis sound," he encouraged Stax artists to constantly explore, rather than stick to what he sometimes derisively referred to as "that 'Bama music," the funky mixture of gospel and blues that characterized Stax's early creative approach (Bowman, 152). While apparently paradoxical, Bell's black-nationalist concept of uplift through economic independence did not render inconsistent his notions of pursuing a mainstream, white audience. Two key events of Bell's tenure exhibit this clearly. In May 1969, Bell oversaw the simultaneous release of twenty-seven LPs and thirty singles. Bell's goal was twofold: this decision—known most for the breakout success of Isaac Hayes's *Hot Buttered Soul*—sought to instantly create a new, Stax-controlled catalog and also to reorient the company toward the release of LPs. As the Stax historian Rob Bowman has argued, the suggestion that R&B audiences would purchase LPs was not a consensus view, and Bell's decision to do this was an example of both his genius and, perhaps, his madness (Bowman, 178–180). Bell's other triumph came in August 1972, at the "Wattstax" concert, where the Stax roster performed for 90,000 people in Los Angeles. Commemorating the 1965 Watts uprisings, and spotlighting both the top Stax artists of the day and several key figures in Black Power politics, most famously the Reverend JESSE JACKSON, *Wattstax* was released as a successful film in 1973. While many, including some company stalwarts, felt that Bell's personal vision ultimately overpowered the communal spirit of 1960s-era Stax, no one denies the magnitude of Bell's importance in the history of the label's success. After the disasters of 1968, Stax under Bell became more commercially successful than ever before. Throughout his time as head of Stax, black organizations like Jesse Jackson's PUSH, as well as industry groups such as the National Association of Radio and Television Announcers (NATRA), honored Bell's leadership.

Despite these achievements, Bell will also be remembered as the head of Stax at its final collapse in the mid-1970s. After a succession of bad business deals—among them one with Union Planters Bank—Stax's unstable finances finally brought about its downfall in 1975. Bell deserves some blame for this, though probably not all. After the closing, Bell was indicted for fraud, and activists including Jesse Jackson leaped to his defense. The historian Rob Bowman has argued that, while charges of racism leveled against Bell's accusers likely have some merit, Stax's incredibly tangled finances suggest that such accusations were not entirely based on race (Bowman, 358–360). Bell was ultimately cleared of all charges, though the combined effect of Stax's closing and the fraud case greatly depleted the financial resources of Bell and his wife Lydia Isbell.

Bell remained active in music throughout the 1980s and 1990s. He helped release Tag Team's "Whoomp! (There It Is)" and Duice's "Dazzey Duks," two hugely successful hip-hop singles of the early 1990s. He also continued to play a role in helping to preserve the legacy of Stax Records. Although there are many who blame Bell and his decisions for the company's collapse, Bell—through his belief in the dual Black Power pillars of economic strength and cultural nationalism—helped not only to save Stax Records at an hour of crisis but also to remake the company into a vibrant force that helped define the soul music of the 1970s.

Further Reading
Bowman, Rob. *Soulsville, U.S.A.: The Story of Stax Records* (1997).
Guralnick, Peter. *Sweet Soul Music: Rhythm and Blues and the Southern Dream of Freedom* (1986).
CHARLES L. HUGHES

BELL, Bobby Lee (17 June 1940–), professional football player, was one of six children born to Pink Bell, a textile millworker, and Janelee Cole, a domestic worker, in Shelby, North Carolina. As a boy, Bell worked alongside his father at the textile mill in Shelby, located in rural Cleveland County, moving bolts of fabric produced from the local commodity cotton. Cleveland County was known for producing more than eighty thousand bales of cotton per year during the 1940s. It was one of the largest cotton producing mill towns in North Carolina, as well as one of the richest. Bell enjoyed sports as a child, and he became a standout athlete at nearby Cleveland High School, where he received all-state honors as quarterback. Bell's excellent football skills and standout ability on the playing field made him one of the top athletes in the nation in 1958 and 1959, which made college football coaches like Jim Tatum nervous. As the head football coach at the University of North Carolina, a school in the segregated Atlantic Coast Conference, Tatum was not interested in having Bell play for the Tarheels; he actually campaigned to have the all-state quarterback recruited away from schools that would play against ACC teams. This push to relocate the best high school football player in the state of North Carolina netted Bell a football scholarship to the University of Minnesota in 1959.

As a freshman at the University of Minnesota, Bell played quarterback on the freshman team. After Bell's first year, his athletic ability and intelligence were quickly recognized by head coach Murray Warmath as valuable assets to the team. According to Bell, during his sophomore year Warmath called him into his office one day and said, "We want quick and strong guys so we're going to switch you to offensive tackle" (Hall of Fame interview with Bobby Bell). While playing on the offensive line, Bell was the long snapper for punts, extra points, and field goals, developing a skill he would later utilize as a member of the Kansas City Chiefs. But it was as a defensive tackle that the gifted athlete excelled. From 1961 to 1962, Bell blossomed as the premier defensive tackle in the country, garnering first-team honors in the Big Ten Conference and All-American honors. Having a nose for the ball and outstanding football instincts, Bell, along with teammate Carl Eller—a future National Football League (NFL) Hall of Famer—anchored the Minnesota defensive line for two seasons, helping the once last-place

Gophers to achieve national success. Bell's play contributed to Minnesota's back-to-back Rose Bowl appearances and helped them win the coveted college bowl game in 1962. In that year, Bell's final season as a Gopher, he won the Outland Trophy as college football's most outstanding lineman and played on the College All-Star team that defeated the two-time NFL champion Green Bay Packers.

The college All-Star and highly sought-after All-American prospect was drafted in 1963 by the Los Angeles Rams in the second round of the NFL draft, and in the seventh round by the Dallas Texans in the upstart American Football League (AFL) draft. The six-foot-four, 230-pound Bell chose to play with the rebel league founded by Lamar Hunt, owner of the Dallas Texans. Becoming acclimated to the professional game alongside teammates such as defensive tackle JUNIOUS "BUCK" BUCHANAN, Bell became one of the AFL's top defensive players as a defensive end. Buchanan would state that Bell was the "best all-around football player" he had ever seen ("Gladiator," Pro Football Hall of Fame). In only his second year in the league, Bell won All-AFL honors for his ability to rush the passer and create havoc on the field. Hank Stram, the head coach of the Dallas Texans (which changed its name to the Kansas City Chiefs in 1963) recognized the depth of Bell's abilities and designed a defense that would allow the gifted athlete to thrive as an All-Pro linebacker. Stram's revolutionary "stack" defense permitted Bell to roam the line of scrimmage, as well as to drop into the secondary from his lineman position. Bell blossomed as the prototype linebacker by utilizing his exceptional quickness and agility to cover running backs out of the backfield and his speed to rush the passer. His productivity and resilience would come to define the featured position on future Kansas City Chiefs teams.

Bell's knowledge of the game of football became his biggest asset. It allowed him to flourish athletically and to create opportunities for the big plays for which he was known. By his third season, Bell had fully made the transition to outside linebacker, grabbing four interceptions, scoring one touchdown, and causing problems for offensive coordinators who were trying to figure out how to control the play maker. Over the span of his career Bell would intercept twenty-six passes and score six touchdowns, while netting nearly five hundred yards in offense. Bell also recovered fifteen fumbles, scoring twice, and he once returned a kickoff fifty-three yards for a touchdown.

From 1965 to 1971, Bell was voted to either the All-AFL or All-NFL teams, playing in the last six AFL All-Star games (1964, 1965, 1966, 1967, 1968, 1969) and the first three AFC-NFC Pro Bowls (1970, 1971, 1972). In the 1969 divisional play-off game against the New York Jets, Bell used his intelligence and football instincts to help his team advance to Super Bowl IV. Late in the third quarter Bell's performance solidified a Chiefs victory. As the game unfolded and anticipating a run fake, Bell played his instincts by dropping in between Jets quarterback Joe

Namath and the running back Matt Snell. Bell disrupted the play and dashed the plans of Namath, the MVP of Super Bowl III, to return to the championship game. The Kansas City Chiefs would go on to play the Minnesota Vikings in Super Bowl IV, beating the Vikings 23-7. In 1974, Bell retired after playing in 168 consecutive outings over a period of twelve seasons with the Chiefs, never missing a game. As an athlete, Bell will be remembered as a fierce competitor who could change the game from wherever he lined up on the field. In that same year, Bell became a full-time employee of the General Motors Corporation, marketing automotive parts and services.

In 1983, Bell became the first Kansas City Chiefs player to be elected to the Pro Football Hall of Fame; only Lamar Hunt, the owner and founder of the Chiefs and the founder of the AFL, would precede him. Bell was enshrined in the College Football Hall of Fame in 1991 and in the Missouri Sports Hall of Fame in 1995.

Bell moved to Lee's Summit, Missouri, in 1982. He became a member of the Kansas City Chiefs Ambassadors in 1989, and became an active member of the NFL Alumni Association in 1987. Bell has three children—Bobby Jr., Tracy, and Joshua—from his two marriages.

Further Reading

Effrat, Louis. "Unbeaten Gophers Inflict First Loss on Hawkeyes," *New York Times* (6 Nov. 1960).
McKenzie, Michael. *Arrowhead: Home of the Chiefs* (1997).
Smith, Don R. *NFL Pro Football Hall Of Fame All-Time Greats* (1988).
"Warfield and Bell Gain Hall of Fame," *New York Times* (2 Feb. 1983).

PELLOM MCDANIELS III

BELL, Cool Papa (17 May 1903–7 Mar. 1991), baseball player and manager, was born James Thomas Bell in Starkville, Mississippi, the son of Jonas Bell, a farmer whose father was an American Indian, and Mary Nichols. James had six siblings, two sisters and four brothers, and said that his mother taught him to be an honest, clean-living man who cared about other people.

He was reared in the Oktoc community near Starkville and began playing pickup games on the local sandlots while attending the local school through the eighth grade. There was neither a high school nor gainful employment in his hometown, so in 1920 Bell moved to St. Louis, Missouri, to live with his older brothers and attend high school, completing two years before ending his formal education. Soon after arriving in St. Louis, he met Clarabelle Thompson, and they were married in September 1920. The marriage lasted seventy years but was childless.

The young husband worked for the Independent Packing Company and played baseball with the semipro Compton Hill Cubs and the East St. Louis Cubs. At this stage of his career, Bell was a promising, left-handed pitcher with a varied repertoire of pitches that included a screwball, a curve, and a knuckleball. He was scouted and signed in 1922 by the St. Louis Stars of the Negro National League for ninety dollars a month. In his rookie season he acquired the colorful nickname by which he was known forever afterward. In a crucial game situation, Bell struck out the great OSCAR CHARLESTON, the best hitter in the Negro Leagues at the time and a future Hall-of-Famer. The manager Bill Gatewood, impressed by the youngster's poise under pressure, applied the appellation "Cool Papa" to his protégé, and the name stuck.

In 1924, after an arm injury ended his pitching career, Cool Papa became a full-time outfielder, where he could use his incredible speed to the greatest advantage. He played a shallow center field and routinely demonstrated extraordinary range in the field by making sensational catches. A natural right-handed batter, he learned to switch-hit to better utilize his speed from the left side of the batter's box. He was so fast going from the batter's box to first base that if he bunted and the ball bounced twice, the fielders would say "Put it in your pocket" because there was no chance to get him out. When JACKIE ROBINSON played in the Negro Leagues with the Kansas City Monarchs, he was a shortstop, but knowledgeable observers knew that it was not his best position and that if he wanted to break into the major leagues he would have to change position. To demonstrate this to him, Cool Papa would hit ground balls to Robinson's right and beat the throw to first base.

Once clocked at twelve seconds circling the bases, Cool Papa is recognized as the fastest player ever to play the game. He was so swift that some players said that it looked like his feet did not even touch the ground. His incredible speed also made him an omnipresent base-stealing threat, and in 1933 he was credited with 175 stolen bases in a 200-game season. He sometimes took two bases on a bunt or scored from second base on a sacrifice fly.

While his speed was real, it was often exaggerated. SATCHEL PAIGE, the legendary pitcher and a skilled raconteur known to embellish stories, said that Cool Papa was so fast that he could turn off the light switch and be in bed with the covers pulled up to his chin before the room got dark. Cool Papa confirmed that he had demonstrated this skill but added a detail that Paige had conveniently omitted: the light switch was faulty, which resulted in a delay before the light went out. In later years, the boxer MUHAMMAD ALI claimed for himself the ability to perform the same feat.

During his ten seasons in St. Louis, Bell consistently batted well over .300, with his best year coming in 1926, when he batted .362, with fifteen home runs and twenty-three stolen bases in the eighty-five-game season; moreover, the Stars won Negro National League pennants in 1928, 1930, and 1931. Following the 1931 season, both the franchise and the league fell victim to the economics of the Great Depression and disbanded. With the demise of the league, the 1932 season was one of chaos, as players scrambled to earn a spot on the roster of a surviving solvent franchise.

Cool Papa Bell, the fastest man in baseball, rounding the bases in an undated photograph. (National Baseball Hall of Fame.)

Cool Papa was no exception and played with three teams, the Detroit Wolves, the Kansas City Monarchs, and the Homestead Grays.

In 1933 he joined owner WILLIAM AUGUSTUS GREENLEE's Pittsburgh Crawfords, and for the next four years Bell continued to bat over .300 each season, as the Crawfords contended for the championship of the new Negro National League. In 1933 Greenlee, who was league president, claimed a disputed championship, and in 1934 the team again finished strong but missed the play-offs. In 1935 the Crawfords defeated the New York Cubans in a seven-game play-off for an undisputed title, and they repeated as champions in 1936. That season was interrupted when the league sent a select All-Star team to participate in the Denver Post Tournament, which they won with ease, as Bell batted .450 and topped the tournament in stolen bases. During each of his four seasons with the Crawfords, Bell was voted to start in the East-West All-Star game, where he always played centerfield and batted leadoff.

In 1937 Cool Papa left the Crawfords and spent the next five years in Latin America. In his first season he helped the dictator Rafael Trujillo's All-Stars win the 1937 championship in the Dominican Republic. Bell later said that the players were told that if they didn't win the championship they would be executed. In 1938 he went to Mexico, where he remained for the next four seasons. After two years with Tampico, where he batted .356 and .354, he split the 1940 season between Torreon and Veracruz and had his best year in Mexico, winning the Triple Crown with a batting average of .437, twelve home runs, and seventy-nine RBI. He also led in hits with 167 and in triples with fifteen in the eighty-nine-game season, as Veracruz won the pennant. Cool Papa played with Monterrey in 1941 and ended with a .367 career batting average in the Mexican League.

During his long baseball career, Cool Papa supplemented his summer income by playing in integrated winter baseball leagues in California and Cuba. In California he had a .368 career batting average for a dozen intermittent winters between 1922 and 1945, and in 1933–1934 he led the league with a .362 batting average. In 1928 he played the first of three consecutive winters in Cuba with Cienfuegas and batted .325, while leading the league in home runs, stolen bases, and runs scored. He returned to Cuba for the

1940–1941 season, playing with Almendares in his final season, to finish with a career .292 batting average in the Cuban winter league.

In 1942 Cool Papa returned to the United States, joined the Chicago American Giants of the Negro American League, and began a string of three additional appearances in the East-West All-Star game. In 1943 he joined the Homestead Grays, the dominant team in the Negro National League, and batted .356 as the Grays won the pennant and defeated the Negro American League's Birmingham Black Barons in the Negro World Series. In 1944 he batted .373, and the Grays defended their Negro League championship by defeating Birmingham in a Negro World Series rematch. The following year he batted .302, as the Grays won another pennant but were swept in the World Series by the Cleveland Buckeyes. Cool Papa's last year with the Grays was 1946, during which he batted .396. He later said that he had won the batting title that year but "gave" it to MONTE IRVIN to enhance his chances to play in the major leagues.

For the next four years Cool Papa was a playing manager with lesser teams, the Detroit Senators in 1947 and the Kansas City Stars, a farm team for the Monarchs, from 1948 through 1950. He finished his Negro Leagues career with a lifetime .341 batting average and also had a .391 average in exhibition games against major leaguers. In 1951 he became a part-time scout for the St. Louis Browns, until the franchise moved to Baltimore in 1954. After leaving baseball he worked as a custodian and night security officer at St. Louis City Hall until he retired around 1970.

In 1974 Cool Papa Bell was inducted into the National Baseball Hall of Fame in Cooperstown, New York. He died of a heart attack in St. Louis, Missouri in 1991, only a few weeks after his beloved wife, Clarabelle.

For a quarter-century, Bell showcased his exceptional speed and all-around excellence on baseball diamonds throughout the United States and Latin America, demonstrating that African Americans could compete successfully against white athletes. His career contributed significantly to the eventual elimination of baseball's color line.

Further Reading
Holway, John. *Voices from the Great Black Baseball Leagues* (1975).
Peterson, Robert. *Only the Ball Was White* (1970).
Riley, James A. *The Biographical Encyclopedia of the Negro Baseball Leagues* (1994).

JAMES A. RILEY

BELL, Derrick Albert, Jr. (6 Nov. 1930–), lawyer and educator, was born in Pittsburgh, Pennsylvania, to Derrick A. Bell Sr. and Ada Elizabeth Bell. Bell was born during the Great Depression and grew up in the city's black neighborhood known as "the Hill." Bell's father was employed as a porter in a Pittsburgh department store and also earned extra money through the underground numbers racket. In 1939 Bell Sr. hit the number for $700 and at the urging of his wife purchased a three-bedroom home in a more prosperous neighborhood. Eventually, Bell's father opened his own business hauling refuse.

Throughout his early life, Bell had a newspaper route that provided him with spending money and made him aware of the rich diversity of Pittsburgh's middle-class black world. He met lawyers, doctors, laborers, ministers, and postal workers all living and working in the same segregated neighborhoods. It was at the urging of one of those black customers, Judge HOMER S. BROWN, that Bell first expressed an interest in becoming a lawyer.

Bell graduated in 1948 from Schenley High School in Pittsburgh, and like his three siblings, attended college. His parents' hard work paid off, too; they were able to actually pay for their children's education with their own money. Following high school, Bell attended Duquesne University in Pittsburgh and joined the ROTC. Following college, he served two years in the military, in Korea from 1952 to 1954. After his military service, Bell was accepted at the University of Pittsburgh School of Law. It was in law school that he began to excel intellectually. He also became interested in civil rights and was selected for law review after his first year, writing a number of articles for that publication. His interest in civil rights began to grow as he learned more about prominent black attorneys like CHARLES HAMILTON HOUSTON and THURGOOD MARSHALL.

Upon graduation, Bell realized that jobs were scarce in Pittsburgh for black law graduates, so he took a job as a lawyer at the Department of Justice. It did not last long. The Department of Justice asked Bell to resign his membership in the NAACP because it was a conflict of interest. Bell refused and was reassigned to meaningless work within the agency. He resigned from the Department of Justice in 1959 in protest. These actions foreshadowed his life's work as a dedicated civil rights advocate and educator in the area of racial justice.

He returned to his hometown of Pittsburgh and became head of the local NAACP, where he organized local efforts to try to integrate the city. In 1960 Thurgood Marshall, head of the NAACP Legal Defense Fund, offered him a job as an attorney. Bell soon was working with the legal giants of the civil rights era— Thurgood Marshall, Jack Greenberg, ROBERT LEE CARTER, CONSTANCE BAKER MOTLEY, and JAMES MADISON NABRIT JR.—to try to implement the mandate of the famous *Brown v. Board of Education* case through the courts. Bell litigated hundreds of school desegregation cases in the South.

Bell remained at the NAACP until 1965, when he took a position as an administrator with the Department of Health, Education, and Welfare. Here he was deputy director at the agency in charge of civil rights. In 1968 he was hired to teach at UCLA's Western Center on Law and Poverty. In 1969 he was hired to teach at Harvard Law School, and in 1971 he became the law school's first black tenured law professor. His biggest contribution to the field of civil rights law and racial issues in the law occurred at Harvard, where he developed a course on civil rights law and in 1973 published the standard textbook for the course, *Race, Racism, and American Law*, which was adopted by law schools throughout the country.

Bell spent eleven years teaching at Harvard, where he won the respect of his colleagues. After a visiting professorship at the University of Washington Law School in Seattle, he was named dean of the University of Oregon School of Law in 1980, but his years there proved to be contentious. He had hoped that more persons of color would be hired for teaching positions at the school, but he could not bring about the changes he was seeking. When the law school's faculty hiring committee refused to authorize him to hire an Asian American woman faculty member (after two white male candidates had turned down the position), Bell concluded that he could no longer tolerate the slow pace of change. He resigned and returned to Harvard Law School only to confront similar problems.

In 1987 Bell published a book of nonfiction parables, *And We Are Not Saved: The Elusive Quest for Racial Justice*, followed by *Faces at the Bottom of the Well: The Permanence of Racism* in 1993. As he began his writing career, Bell also began protesting Harvard Law School's refusal to hire a woman of color as a tenured law professor. His decision not to teach until Harvard offered tenure to a woman of color received intense press coverage. Ultimately, the protest, which lasted from 1990 to 1992 failed; the school did not offer tenure to a woman of color and Bell was fired. He documented his efforts in his 1994 memoir, *Confronting Authority: Reflections of an Ardent Protestor*. Bell had embarked on the protest around the time his wife, Jewel Bell, was diagnosed with cancer. Sadly, she died in 1990. The couple had three sons, Derrick III, Douglass Du Bois, and Carter Robeson.

Following his failed protest at Harvard, in 1991 Bell joined the faculty at New York University School of Law and subsequently produced several more books. In 1996 his book *Gospel Choirs* appeared; *Afrolantica Legacies* appeared in 1998, and *Ethical Ambition: Living a Life of Meaning and Worth* followed in 2002. Finally, Bell published *Silent Covenants: "Brown v. Board of Education" and the Unfulfilled Hopes for Racial Reform* in 2004. Bell received many honorary degrees for his tireless work on racial justice issues, and his textbook on civil rights law remained a key text in that field well into the twenty-first century.

Further Reading

Essien, Victor. "Race in the Academy: Moving Beyond Diversity and toward the Incorporation of Faculty of Color in Predominantly White Colleges and Universities," *Journal of Black Studies*, vol. 34, no. 1 (Sep. 2003): 63–71.

Gilmore, Brian. "American Racial and Legal History According to Derrick Bell," *Crisis* 112 (Sep./Oct. 2005): 40.

BRIAN GILMORE

BELL, James Madison (3 Apr. 1826–1902), abolitionist, poet, and lecturer, was born in Gallipolis, Ohio. His parents' identities are unknown. At age sixteen, in 1842, he moved to Cincinnati. While there, in 1848, he married Louisiana Sanderlin (or Sanderline), with whom he had several children. He also learned the plastering trade from his brother-in-law, George Knight. Bell worked as a plasterer during the day and attended Cincinnati High School for Colored People at night. Founded in 1844 by Reverend Hiram S. Gilmore, the school had a connection to Oberlin College and was said to have given impetus to the sentiment found in *Uncle Tom's Cabin* and the cause of human freedom. Through his studies Bell was thoroughly indoctrinated into the principles of radical abolitionism.

In 1854 Bell moved his family to Chatham, Ontario, Canada, feeling that he would be freer under the authority of the British government. While continuing his trade he became involved in political activities and met and befriended John Brown. As his ally, Bell raised money and enlisted men to support Brown's raid on Harpers Ferry. He probably was one of the last people to see Brown before the raid took place.

In 1860 Bell moved to San Francisco, California, where he became involved in the fight to ensure equal education for local black children. He also took a leading and active role at various state conventions protesting laws that discriminated against blacks. At one such convention, held by ministers of the African Methodist Episcopal (AME) Church, Bell addressed the role of the church and its relationship to the state. (He was an active member and steward of the AME Church in San Francisco.)

Although far removed from the battlefield, he worked as a crusader for abolition during the Civil War. He wrote some of his most rousing poems while living in California, including "Emancipation," "Lincoln," and "The Dawn of Freedom." His works were long, comprising as many as 950 lines, and were meant to be recited. However, while Bell is known as a poet today, poetry came second to his activism during his lifetime.

Bell left California and moved to Toledo, Ohio, in 1865. He arrived at the time of emancipation and began to work with the freedmen, focusing his energies on the struggle for civil rights. He later went to Canada to visit his family and eventually moved them to Toledo. He continued to be active in the AME Church, serving as superintendent of the Sunday school and as a lay worker. Active briefly in Republican politics, Bell was elected as a delegate from Lucas County to the state convention and as a delegate at large from the state of Ohio to the Republican National Convention in both 1868 and 1872. He was a vocal and enthusiastic supporter of the nomination of Ulysses S. Grant at both conventions.

Bell traveled frequently, preaching a doctrine of human liberty, enjoining blacks to use their freedom responsibly, and instructing freedmen in their political and civic duties, often reciting his long poems as the method of instruction. Bishop B. W. ARNETT, a friend who worked with Bell in the church, often traveled with him as he gave public readings of his poetry and lectured on educational and legal rights for black Americans. According to Arnett, no one instructed people better or had a more imposing manner than Bell. "Many a young man who was not an honor to his race and a blessing to his people received the first spark of inspiration for true greatness" while listening to his poems (Arnett, 10).

Bell addressed many issues in his poems, including slavery, war, emancipation, and Reconstruction, often referencing historical figures, such as John Brown, or events of historical significance. Although he tended to vary the lengths of stanzas, his poems have been described as "almost identical and dull" and "without any distinctive literary quality." Many of Bell's poems were published individually, though they were eventually compiled in Arnett's *The Poetical Works of James Madison Bell* (1901).

One of Bell's long poems, "The Progress of Liberty" (1866), was written for the third anniversary of the Emancipation Proclamation. Its 850 lines review the Civil War, the triumph of liberty, and the martyrdom of Abraham Lincoln:

> The bondsman's gloomy night has passed;
> The slavery of this land is dead;
> No tyrant's power, however vast,
> Can wake it from its gory bed.
>
> . . .
>
> Though slavery's dead, yet there remains
> A work for those from whom the chains
> Today are falling one by one;
> Nor should they deem their labor done,
> Nor shrink the task, however hard,
> While it insures a great reward,
> And bids them on its might depend
> For perfect freedom in the end.

Bell also used poems to encourage blacks to be model citizens:

> In this yourselves must take the lead;
> You must yourselves first elevate;
> Till then the world will ne'er concede
> Your claims to manhood's high estate.

In addition, Bell used his works—and the reading of them—to denounce laws and policies that he deemed to be detrimental to blacks. He is said to have triumphed in his "daring, vigorous satire of President Andrew Johnson" in the poem "Modern Moses, or 'My Policy' Man" (1867). Called his "most inventive and readable work" because of its "shrewd humor and irony, concrete topicality and personal emotion" (Sherman, 192), the poem ridicules Johnson from a personal as well as political perspective. It portrays the president as a Judas who betrayed the people by vetoing the Freedmen's Bureau Bill:

> Mark when that bill for the supply
> Of starving millions met his eye;
> A breadless, clotheless, houseless throng.

> Thus rendered by his nation's wrong.
> Does he the bill in haste receive
> And sign, their suff'rings to relieve?
>
> . . .
>
> Then he in their deep hour of grief,
> Did them relieve and kept his vow;
> When with a dark and wrinkled brow,
> He stamped his veto on their prayer,
> And doomed the suppliants to despair.

In *From Slavery to Freedom*, the historian JOHN HOPE FRANKLIN argues that the overwhelming acclaim of the poet PAUL LAURENCE DUNBAR probably overshadowed the works of Bell and other black poets of his era. If not for Dunbar's fame, Bell might have been more highly regarded as a poet during an age that was critical to the political, social, and cultural development of black Americans.

Further Reading
Arnett, Bishop B. W. *The Poetical Works of James Madison Bell* (1901).
Sherman, Joan R. *African American Poetry of the Nineteenth Century: An Anthology* (1992).

MAMIE E. LOCKE

BELL, Mary A. (1 May 1852–?), slave narrative author, was born Mary Rice to SPOTSWOOD RICE, an enslaved tobacco roller, and a slave woman perhaps named Caroline on a large plantation near Glasgow, Missouri. In addition to Mary, Caroline and Spotswood Rice had three sons and two daughters, who lived with their mother on a Missouri riverside plantation owned by Katherine Diggs. Spotswood Rice lived and worked on Benjamin Lewis's plantation nearby. Interviewed by the Federal Writers Project in St. Louis in 1937 Bell recalled that "slavery was a mighty hard life." Her narrative is significant in that it was one of the few of the over two thousand recorded for the Federal Writers Project in which one black woman interviewed another about her life in slavery. The historian Paul Escott's analysis of several hundred WPA narratives found that former slaves interviewed by black women reported significantly higher levels of dissatisfaction with life under slavery. Black female interviewers were more than twice as likely as white male interviewers to report rapes on a plantation and to elicit negative appraisals of their subjects' masters, and were three times more likely than were white female interviewers to record recollections of white masters fathering slave children. Bell's narrative is indeed strongly critical of slavery and of slaveowners, as well as one of the most eloquent in its depiction of slave resistance to bondage.

When Bell was only seven years old her mistress hired her out to a Presbyterian minister to look after his three children. In addition young Mary Bell was placed on a pony to ride out to the minister's large farm and call the field hands to dinner. The following year Diggs hired her out to a baker, again to look after his children and to perform various chores around the house.

"Neither family was nice to me," Bell recalled. Difficult as her own life was, Bell noted that life for her parents under slavery was even worse since they were only allowed to visit each other twice a week, on Wednesdays and Saturdays. She recalled that on those rare visits her mother often had to remove Spotswood Rice's bloody clothes and bathe and grease the injuries he received from whippings by his master's black overseer. Bell's narrative reveals her considerable pride in her father's skills as a tobacco roller and leader of the slave community. She expresses an even greater admiration for her father's defiance of his master, first by learning to read and write, and then by leading eleven of Lewis's best slaves to freedom. Although Bell recalled that her father ran off to Kansas City, Missouri, to join the Union forces, U.S. Army records show that he did not travel that far, enlisting close to his daughter's home in Glasgow in February 1864.

Bell was finally reunited with her father and mother at the end of the Civil War in 1865 at the Benton Barracks Hospital in St. Louis. While her father worked at the Barracks as a nurse, Mary helped her mother to take in laundry. A desire to reconnect the family ties broken by slavery was common to millions of emancipated slaves, as was the goal of gaining an education. Bell shared both. When she was thirteen she attended school for the first time, spending six months in classes at Benton Barracks, where, she recalled, "I was very apt and learned fast." So fast, in fact, that she found herself traveling throughout St. Louis in the late 1860s and early 1870s, attending different schools for six months to three years at a time, to further her education.

Bell converted to the African Methodist Episcopal (AME) Church in St. Louis in 1866, and later, in 1882, she married a man named Bell (his first name is unknown), with whom she had seven children, and who died in May 1896. Although she did not earn enough money to buy a home until 1916, when she was sixty-four years old, Bell was able to purchase her home outright within six and a half years, partly from her widow's pension.

Compared to many former slaves interviewed as part of the federal government's Slave Narrative Project, Bell enjoyed a relatively comfortable retirement, though her life in working-class St. Louis was not without its disappointments. At least five of her children preceded her in death. At the time of her interview in 1937 she had only a daughter, Virginia Miller, who lived next door to her in St. Louis, and a son, William A. Bell, at that time serving in the army in the Philippines. Immensely proud of her son's military service, Bell concluded her 1937 interview by also praising her father, brother, husband, and indeed any "man who will fight for his rights, and any person who wants to be something."

Further Reading

Interview of Mary A. Bell. St. Louis, Missouri, 19 August 1937, WPA Slave Narrative Project, volume 11, *Arkansas Narratives, Part 7 and Missouri Narratives.*

Berlin, Ira, et al. *Remembering Slavery: African Americans Talk About Their Personal Experiences of Slavery and Freedom* (1998).
Escott, Paul. *Slavery Remembered: A Record of Twentieth Century Slave Narratives* (1979).

STEVEN J. NIVEN

BELL, Mary A. (2 July 1873–20 Sept. 1941), artist, was born in Washington, D.C., the daughter of James F. Bell and Susanna County, probably laborers. Little is known about Bell's early life. She presumably attended segregated schools. It is unlikely that she ever received artistic training; she declared that she drew "without human teaching." She probably worked as a domestic servant, laundress, or seamstress, beginning in her teenage years, and she may have traveled extensively. Bell said she "lived all around" before World War I. Since she does not appear in early-twentieth-century city directories or census records in Washington, D.C., or Boston, Massachusetts, and because she apparently never married or had children, it is likely that she resided with her various employers.

By the mid-1920s Bell was working for Edward Peter Pierce, justice of the Supreme Judicial Court of Massachusetts from 1914 to 1937, and Adele Dutaud Pierce, his wife, as a live-in domestic servant in Boston and in their summer home in Georgetown, Maine. Bell may have also worked on occasion for the sculptor Gaston Lachaise and his wife, Isabel. Isabel Lachaise and Adele Pierce were sisters, and Lachaise family papers indicate they both had a fondness for their maid. Bell maintained a friendly written correspondence with both families, signing letters "your humble servant" after she left their employment sometime in the mid-1930s.

Around 1936 Bell moved into a lodging house in Boston. Her artistic career blossomed when she was in her sixties, and she produced at least 140 drawings between 1936 and 1939. Apparently self-taught, Bell usually drew at night after working odd jobs. Most of her wax crayon and colored pencil drawings on tissue paper are delicate, fanciful courtship scenes of well-dressed white couples in elegant parlors or luxurious gardens. Yet there are also depictions of Creole beauties, regal Ethiopians, burlesque performers, penitent sinners, and loving mothers. A small narrative label in flowing script glued to the top center of a fastidiously constructed double-tissue border announces the title of each stage-like scene.

Bell regularly featured women in her work, explaining that "a woman is the cream of the earth and everybody likes cream, so I put a woman in all my drawings." Typically, a large-scale woman and a small man float in between plants and multiple horizon lines or small household furnishings, the latter perhaps traced from magazines. One exemplary work is *Proposing*, which depicts a beautiful woman seated in a parlor amid tiny floating furniture, including a grand piano, a swag lamp, and a fringed hook rug. A Catholic who declared that God, rather than she, created her drawings—as do many self-taught artists—Bell occasionally included an oval portrait of the Virgin Mary in the background, as she does in *Proposing*. Bell explained that the Mother of God appeared in all of her drawings initially "just to introduce her to my friends; now they all know HER and I don't need to put her in pictures."

Another notable work is *American Mixtures of the Ethiopian Race*. Here three women prance in a floral landscape. Two wear fashionable clothing, elaborate coiffures, and sparkling jewelry. The largest and fanciest figure is also the lightest skinned. Bell reflects contemporary notions of hierarchical skin tones by inscribing: "The girl in the center is Octoroon. The girl on the left, the Creole type. The [girl on the] right is the so-called Chocolate type." The darkest-skinned woman wears a miserable sack and has unruly hair. Bell may have identified with her; the artist's monogram, a floral bell, appears just below the hem of her dress.

Such charming images depicted on fragile materials delighted a small group of patrons, mostly in the Boston area, who excitedly shared Bell's work, priced at just fifty cents each, with one another. After Gaston Lachaise died in 1935, Isabel introduced Bell's art to her grandniece Ruth Pierce, a journalist, and the artist Kate Buss. Buss in turn sent Bell's drawings to Gertrude Stein in Paris and to the New York writer and photographer Carl Van Vechten. Van Vechten's friend, the publicist Mark Lutz of Philadelphia, also became a patron, as did the art critic Henry McBride. McBride then convinced the artist Florine Stettheimer to purchase several pieces. Additionally some of Isabel Lachaise's other friends took Bell's drawings on vacation to share abroad. All admired Bell's flamboyant images of women and flowers, dreamlike spaces, vivid colors, and charming narratives.

For Stein and Van Vechten, Bell was all the more exotic and attractive because of her race and outsider status. Both befriended and supported African American writers and performers. Van Vechten, a bisexual, was known for his photographs of Harlemites, and Stein consented to an all-black cast for the performance of her operatic *Four Saints in Three Acts*. Further, African American writers commended her short story "Melanctha" for its nonpatronizing attitude toward black people. Stein also collected work by both modern masters and self-taught artists and even planned an exhibition of American folk art in Paris in 1939. World War II, however, prevented this event.

While Bell did not associate with other artists and never exhibited her art, she hoped that her drawings might lead to some renown and racial uplift. She wrote to Van Vechten, who purchased more than one hundred of her drawings, that she was reincarnated and that whispering spirits told her to send out her drawings and "make yourself known to the world." In 1936 Bell took six works to a movie producer, explaining that she wanted the glory of the Ethiopian race to be known to the world. The producer, apparently amused by the ambition of an elderly black domestic, informed her that her marvelous colors could not possibly be duplicated. Soon thereafter she realized she had been duped when she received a photographic postcard of one of her drawings made by Van Vechten.

Pleased with Van Vechten's patronage, Bell offered to sign her works any way he wished, and she adopted a monogram in the shape of a floral bell at his suggestion. Yet when he and Lutz paid Bell a surprise visit in 1938, she refused to see them for unknown reasons. She also denied Van Vechten's request to photograph her, stating that she would not be photographed until she was on "Ethiopian soil." While stereotypes about a racial hierarchy according to skin color are evident in the artist's work—she believed the most beautiful women were the lightest—Bell was proud of her racial heritage. She included flags and jewelry with the Pan-African colors (red, black, green, and gold or yellow) in her art and took interest in the career of Haile Selassie, emperor of Ethiopia.

Plagued with failing eyesight and asthma, Bell also suffered from smoke inhalation from a fire in her apartment, which forced her to move across the street in May 1938. She then hoped to secure a four-room apartment near the Charles River so she could have a gallery of her own. Soon, however, she lost her most loyal patrons. Two of Van Vechten's friends, Edward Pierce and JAMES WELDON JOHNSON, died in 1938. That year Van Vechten officially donated his entire collection of black memorabilia to the Beinecke Rare Book and Manuscript Library at Yale University in honor of Johnson.

By mid-December 1940 Bell was institutionalized at the Boston State Hospital, a public mental health facility. She had predicted her tragic demise two years earlier: "Fate has decreed a cruel ending for me." Bell died in the facility of heart disease and the hardening of the arteries, complicated by psychosis. It is not known how long she was mentally ill or whether the condition affected her art. Destitute, Bell was buried in a pauper's grave across the street from the hospital.

Recognized by such luminaries as Van Vechten, Lachaise, Stein, and Stettheimer in her own time, Bell's charming and provocative works and letters continue to offer a rare glimpse into the world of an intriguing, self-taught African American artist. While virtually unknown to the mainstream history of art, her works are significant for their fresh vision and their social commentary on escapist romance, black skin tones, religion, and Pan-African overtones. Exhibitions of Bell's drawings were held at the Beinecke Library (1945), the Galerie Brusberg in Berlin, Germany (1986), the Chicago International Art Exposition (1987), and the Yale University Art Gallery (1991).

Further Reading

Bell's papers are in the James Weldon Johnson Memorial Collection of American Negro Arts and Letters, Beinecke Rare Book and Manuscript Library, Yale University, New Haven, Connecticut.

THERESA LEININGER-MILLER

BELL, Philip Alexander (1808?–25 April 1889), newspaper editor and civil rights activist, was born in New York City, the third of three children, to Alexander Bell and Letty (maiden name unknown). A stutterer, the young Bell turned to writing to express himself, honing his natural talents under the teachers at New York City's African Free School, an institution respected for such alumni as the Shakespearean actor IRA ALDRIDGE and the Episcopal priest and Pan-Africanist ALEXANDER CRUMMELL. After finishing school, Bell set out to make journalism his life's work, hoping to use the press to advance black interests.

On 25 January 1831 Bell attended a meeting of the Colored Citizens of New York at the Boyer Lodge Room. The meeting's attendees rejected the idea of black colonization in Liberia, West Africa—a plan of the American Colonization Society—saying that blacks absolutely claimed "this country, the place of our birth, and not Africa, as our mother country." A few months later, Bell was one of New York's representatives at the First Annual Convention of the People of Colour, held in Philadelphia in 1831, to discuss colonization, the abolition of slavery, and ways of achieving equality for "every freeman born in this country." Bell attended a second Philadelphia conven-

Philip Alexander Bell, journalist and civil rights activist who campaigned actively for equal rights on both the East and West Coast. (Schomburg Center for Research in Black Culture, New York Public Library.)

tion in 1832, which revisited the previous year's proposal, the resettlement of former slaves in Canada, instead of Liberia. Throughout his journalistic career, Bell regularly attended similar conventions as a delegate from New York or, later, from San Francisco.

As an activist and writer in 1837, Bell joined with CHARLES RAY to establish New York's *Weekly Advocate*, soon renamed the *Colored American*. Bell used the paper to underscore his basic themes: opposition to colonization, an end to slavery, and equal rights. After the paper's demise, he articulated the same themes in the Philadelphia *Elevator* and the New York *Anglo-African*. Not content with just writing his message, Bell also directed the New York Intelligence Office, where he helped escaped slaves to find work or to flee to Canada.

During the 1840s and 1850s, Bell had established himself as an important newspaperman and an advocate for East Coast blacks. Meanwhile, on the West Coast, California was undergoing transformation from a Mexican province to a state. Its new status encouraged free blacks and former slaves to migrate there, as did Bell's friend, the activist and future judge MIFFLIN WISTAR GIBBS. Sometime in 1859 or early 1860 Bell decided to move to San Francisco, California, arriving in 1860.

Almost immediately, Bell joined the black community's efforts to eliminate California state statutes that prevented blacks from testifying and acting as witnesses in court cases involving whites. To end such laws and to provide a voice for the community, Bell and PETER ANDERSON established the San Francisco *Pacific Appeal* in 1862. In one of his earliest editorials, Bell wrote, "Our paper is devoted to the interests of the Colored People of California and to their moral, intellectual and political advancement [and] . . . will advocate their rights, their claims to humanity and justice; it will oppose the wrongs inflicted on them." In another editorial, Bell assessed African American life:

Exiles in our native land, aliens in the country that gave us birth, outlaws for no crime, proscribed without offence, amenable to the laws without being protected by them, thus we stand, innocent victims of an unholy and unrighteous prejudice—truly our condition is most deplorable. (*Pacific Appeal*, 12 April 1862)

Bell and Anderson soon disagreed over editorial policy, forcing Bell to quit the paper in July 1862. Bell remained in the newspaper business, however, as an agent for New York's *Anglo-African*, while continuing his effort to overturn the discriminatory testimony and witness laws. His struggle proved successful in March 1863, when Governor Leland Stanford signed a measure repealing these laws. For Bell, however, the struggle for rights did not stop there; African Americans needed equal education and the right to vote. To help achieve those ends, Bell established his own newspaper, the *Elevator*, in April 1865. Working in conjunction with the Colored State Convention of 1865, Bell and the delegates sent a petition to the California

State Legislature requesting voting rights. When the California state senate tabled it, Bell responded, "We will continue to repeal slander and denounce injustice and oppression . . . and fearlessly contend for our inalienable rights." In other *Elevator* editorials, Bell explained community goals succinctly:

To "set us right before the law."
To "give us the common right of citizens—in *political franchise*, in the school system."
To "give us in common with the other races, civil liberties" and "equal advantages with them in the development of common resources of the country."
To end the United States as exclusively a "white man's country."
To provide "equal laws for our safeguard and protection."

Bell spent considerable time from 1865 to 1867 working to gain the right to vote for African Americans, but then a new challenge emerged. For many years, black children in San Francisco had attended a separate elementary school, staffed by black teachers, in a building located on Broadway Street. In 1868 the San Francisco school board decided to close the school's Broadway building, replace its black teachers, and move the students to an inferior facility at the old Greenwich Street School. Bell responded that black teachers "feel an interest in the education of their race," and parents showed their resolve by boycotting the school. Of 209 school-age children, only twenty attended the Greenwich School. This equal-education fight dragged on for several years, until Bell convinced superintendent of schools James Denman to open a new school on Taylor and Vallejo streets. This much-improved facility, however, still did not satisfy Bell or the black parents. They pushed to have children attend the regular grammar and high schools in an integrated environment. Finally in 1875 the school board acquiesced, and both white and black students began attending the same schools.

The decade of the 1870s brought further changes and challenges. Once the federal government passed the Fifteenth Amendment, blacks in California could vote, but Bell realized that they also needed to become politically involved. Although he supported the Republican Party of Lincoln, Bell urged his readers to vote not for a party's candidate, but for the most qualified individual. In the late 1870s he warned African Americans to be wary of Denis Kearney's Workingmen's Party and its anti-Chinese platform, not because he was sympathetic to the Chinese, but because he feared repercussions for African Americans. In 1878 Bell supported the National Labor Party, and at its state convention in San Francisco, he held the position of sergeant-at-arms. Bell realized that the problems of workers—white, black, and Asian—overshadowed group identity; he simply wanted all workers to benefit from the land, and from economic, social, and political reforms through effective political leadership.

Philip Bell had other talents besides political activism. With his stuttering under control, he appeared as an actor in the Colored Amateur Company productions of *Ion* and *Pizarro*. As a literary critic, he wrote reviews of both white and black community productions of Shakespeare's *Richard III*, *As You Like It*, and *The Merchant of Venice*. In a review of the latter, Bell commented, "I have always sympathized with Shylock, have considered him 'more sinned against than sinning.'"

The late 1870s and early 1880s saw a still vigorous Bell continuing his efforts toward achieving equal rights and "elevating the character of our race." In the mid-1880s, however, his health began to decline, forcing him to retire. During his newspaper career Bell had made very little money, and since he never married or had children, he had to depend for his support on the charity of local women. Bell never fully regained his health, and he died in San Francisco in 1889. Judge Mifflin W. Gibbs described Bell as "proud in his humanity and intellectually great as a journalist," but perhaps the best summation of Bell's life comes in his own words, "Action is necessary. Prompt and immediate. Agitate! Agitate! Agitate!"

Further Reading
The best sources of information on the life and activities of Bell are the files of the New York *Colored American* and *Anglo-African* and the San Francisco *Pacific Appeal* and the *Elevator* newspapers.
Montesano, Philip M. *Some Aspects of the Free Negro Question in San Francisco, 1849–1870* (1973).
Penn, I. Garland. *The Afro-American Press and Its Editors* (1891).

Obituaries: *San Francisco Bulletin*, 26 and 27 Apr. 1889.

PHILIP M. MONTESANO

BELL, Robert Mack (6 July 1943–), jurist and civil rights activist, was born in Rocky Mount, North Carolina, the son of Thomas Bell, a construction worker, and Rosa Lee (Jordan) Bell, a health-care practitioner and the daughter of sharecroppers. In the mid-1940s Robert M. Bell, his parents, and two older brothers moved to Baltimore, Maryland, where he entered public schools.

As a sixteen-year-old student at Baltimore's Dunbar High School, Bell was recruited by the Civic Interest Group, a student integrationist organization, along with classmates and students from the historically black Morgan State College, to enter whites-only restaurants and request service. Years later Bell recalled that at the time he did not tell his mother what he was doing because he considered it a "high risk" undertaking (Cox).

On 17 June 1960, some five months after the historic sit-in demonstrations at a segregated Woolworth's lunch counter in Greensboro, North Carolina, Bell and eleven other students walked into Hooper's Restaurant in downtown Baltimore, requested service, were turned down, but refused to leave. The students were subsequently arrested, convicted of violating the trespass law, and fined ten dollars each. The judgment was appealed by a legal team that included the National Association for the Advancement of Colored People (NAACP) legal counsel Juanita Jackson Mitchell and the future United States Supreme Court justice THURGOOD MARSHALL.

At the end of that summer Bell returned to Dunbar High School, where he was president of the class of 1961 and finished first among its 196 graduates. He has said that one of the people he has most admired throughout his life was the vice president of that high school class, REGINALD FRANCIS LEWIS, who years later became the chairman and chief executive officer of TLC Beatrice International, the largest black-owned business in the United States. Following high school graduation Bell entered Morgan State College, but after his first semester was diagnosed with tuberculosis. He withdrew from college and was hospitalized for nearly a year.

In 1962 the Maryland Court of Appeals upheld the lower court conviction of Bell and his fellow sit-in demonstrators. The case, which was to become known as *Bell v. Maryland,* was appealed to the United States Supreme Court. By the time it was argued there, on 14 and 15 October 1963, both the Baltimore city council and the Maryland general assembly had enacted laws prohibiting the denial of public accommodations based on race.

On 22 June 1964, however, the U.S. Supreme Court, by a 5-4 decision, declined to rule that city and state public accommodations laws nullified the trespass laws of those respective jurisdictions and remanded the case to the Maryland courts. One of the dissenters, Justice William O. Douglas, pronounced the refusal to grant public accommodations to African Americans "a relic of slavery." Justice Douglas wrote, "When the state police, the state prosecutor, and the state courts unite to convict Negroes for renouncing that relic of slavery, the 'state' violates the Fourteenth Amendment" (*Baltimore Sun,* 27 Oct. 1996).

On 22 October 1964 the Maryland Court of Appeals surprisingly upheld the convictions of the Hooper's Restaurant demonstrators on grounds that the Maryland and Baltimore public accommodations laws were not intended to repeal the state and city trespass laws. The decision was rendered three months after President Lyndon B. Johnson signed the Federal Civil Rights Act of 1964, which included a prohibition against the denial of a public service to a customer on the basis of race.

On 23 November 1964 Bell's legal team filed a petition with the Maryland Court of Appeals seeking reconsideration of its decision, contending that there was "a substantial likelihood that the (U.S.) Supreme Court may hold that the Civil Rights Act of 1964 abates such prosecutions (as the verdict in *Bell v. Maryland)*" (Reynolds). Indeed, on 14 December 1964 the Supreme Court, in deciding *Hamm v. City of Rock Hill,* held that the federal civil rights law did abate all pending prosecutions of those who had been arrested for activity that the law protected. The Maryland Court of Appeals accepted the Bell petition but did not set a hearing date. Without rendering

a written opinion, the state's highest court, on 9 April 1965, almost five years after the arrest of the Hooper's demonstrators, overturned the convictions of Bell and his fellow students.

In 1966 Robert M. Bell graduated from Morgan State College, second in his class of 450, with a degree in History and Political Science. He was subsequently recruited by Harvard Law School, where he was an instant celebrity of sorts. One former Harvard Law School student recalled that Bell frequently would be pointed out in hallways as "Bob Bell of *Bell v. Maryland*" (*Baltimore Sun,* 24 Oct. 1996). Law students who have their names attached to cases argued before the Supreme Court are few and far between.

Following graduation from Harvard Law School in 1969, Bell became the first African American hired by Piper and Marbury, one of Maryland's leading law firms. In 1975 the Maryland governor Marvin Mandel appointed Bell to a judgeship on the District Court of Maryland, Baltimore City, where, at the age of thirty-one, he was the youngest ever to serve. In 1980 Governor Harry Hughes named Bell to the Circuit Court of Maryland for Baltimore. In 1984 he was appointed to the Maryland Court of Special Appeals, where he served until 1991, at which time he was named to fill a vacancy on the Maryland Court of Appeals, the court that twice upheld trespassing convictions against him before finally overturning the verdict and technically ending de facto segregation in the State of Maryland.

On 23 October 1996 Governor Parris N. Glendening appointed Bell to be the first African American chief judge of the Maryland Court of Appeals, replacing the retiring chief judge Robert C. Murphy, who, three and a half decades earlier, as a deputy state attorney general, represented Maryland in the Supreme Court case known as *Bell v. Maryland.*

Further Reading
Cox, Daniel. "Going the Second Mile," *Equal Justice* 3.3 (Fall, 2004).
Hylton, Wil S. "Burden of Proof," *Baltimore Magazine* (Mar. 1997).
Reynolds, William L. "The Legal History of the Great Sit-in Case of *Bell v. Maryland,*" *Maryland Law Review* 61.4 (2002).
Smith, C. Fraser. "Bell's Sweet Victory: New Top Judge Overcomes Segregation," *Baltimore Sun,* 24 and 27 Oct. 1996.

HAROLD N. BURDETT

BELL, Travers, Jr. (31 Jan. 1941–25 Jan. 1988), investment banker and entrepreneur, was born in Chicago, Illinois, the third of four children of Travers Bell Sr., a clerk at a brokerage firm, and Iona St. Ange, a teaching aide. Growing up on the tough streets of Chicago's South Side could often be rough, and Bell would later credit his experiences for giving him the wherewithal to survive and succeed on Wall Street later in his life.

After graduating from high school, Bell planned to go to a teachers' college. At the time his father was working in the backroom of Dempsey-Tegeler, a Midwestern brokerage firm. One summer Bell needed money, so his father got him a job as a messenger at the firm. On Bell's first day on the job, a manager asked him to deliver a briefcase to a company across the street. While walking to the destination, Bell peeked into the briefcase and saw what appeared to be worn and crumpled papers. Upon arrival, he handed it over and in return received a check to the company for $175,000. Bell realized that this was a business where people actually paid for paper if it was stock certificates that represented ownership in companies. This fascinated him and soon he decided that he would make his career on Wall Street.

Bell threw himself into his work. He worked fifteen to seventeen hours a day, trying to learn about the securities industry by studying various materials and closely watching senior officials at the firm. Unlike most other blacks who had preceded him as messengers, he did not stay in the mailroom for long, thanks to Jerome Tegeler, the cofounder and driving force of the firm. One day Tegeler approached the young man and sat him down for a chat. "Travers, I wanted to help your father, but I couldn't because nobody was ready for that yet [having a black man move up because of his race]. However, I don't care anymore. You obviously learn real fast and want to learn even more, so I am going to do something many people are not going to like: I am going to teach you this business." With his mentor guiding him, Bell quickly rose through the ranks. In 1963 Dempsey-Tegeler bought the firm Strauss, Blosser, and McDowell, which had about fifteen offices around the United States. At age twenty-three, Bell was named the operations manager of the whole firm, and he moved to St. Louis, Missouri, the location of Dempsey's headquarters, and began studying economics and business at Washington University in his free time.

After graduating in 1967, Bell became vice president in charge of operations at a small firm called Fusz Schmelzle. As he acquired more experience in all aspects of the securities business, Bell began planning to open up his own firm; however, when he tried to raise capital he was denied at every turn because many were unwilling to invest in a black-owned firm. Then he heard that another African American stockbroker named Willie Daniels was trying to get a firm started on the East Coast. Bell joined Daniels in New York City in 1970, but their ambitions were tempered because of a lack of financing, difficulties in getting over regulatory hurdles, and a slow period in the securities market.

After nearly two years, they had their big breakthrough. On 24 June 1971, Daniels & Bell, Inc., became the first black-owned member firm in the 179-year history of the New York Stock Exchange. Despite this milestone, significant obstacles immediately confronted the firm. The American economy was disintegrating, and Wall Street's business was deteriorating. In just a few years, hundreds of brokerage firms had closed their doors. It was a tough time for all companies, but it was especially hard for a young, black-owned firm. Although there was very little prejudice on the floor of NYSE because it is a buy and sell institution and thus more numbers oriented than relationship oriented, Daniels & Bell had trouble getting into the lucrative business of corporate finance, in which corporations use Wall Street firms to raise money by issuing bonds or stocks. Because their histories and relationships were not rooted in the powerful networks on Wall Street, Daniels & Bell was shut out of the "old boys network" where these deals were made. They thus had little access to the corporate clubs where business titans socialized and formed relationships. Bell's solution was to enter the municipal finance business and raise money for cities and states as an increasing number of black elected officials across the country could give them a fair opportunity to pitch their ideas and proposals. In 1972 Daniels & Bell led a $1.2 million bond issue for Mound Bayou, Mississippi, the oldest black municipality in the United States. Around this time, Daniels left the firm for reasons that are unclear.

Moving forward, Bell began to travel all across the country to talk with elected officials and pitch his belief that minority-owned firms should be given a chance to participate in the business of municipalities. He established close relationships with many elected officials, such as Chicago Mayor HAROLD WASHINGTON and Los Angeles Mayor TOM BRADLEY, and slowly garnered more business. One of Bell's biggest deals came in 1984, when the state of Connecticut chose Daniels & Bell to comanage a $5.5 billion transportation infrastructure renewal financing program. After that the firm received a number of lucrative deals. In 1986 the firm participated in $9 billion worth of financings, ranking as one of the top twenty municipal houses on Wall Street. The firm had also attracted a number of noteworthy corporate clients such as Exxon, General Electric, and Chase Manhattan Bank. As a result, Bell is credited with opening up areas of finance for other minorities on Wall Street.

In addition to his work on Wall Street, Bell had bought a candy maker named Cocoline Chocolate Company in 1974. It ranked as one of *Black Enterprise* magazine's Top 100 businesses for more than a decade. He also was the principal stockholder in Freedom National Bank, financial adviser to the African Development Bank, and chair of the New York District of the Securities Industry Association.

In 1988 Bell, who had a history of heart problems, died of a massive heart attack in his New York City apartment. He was forty-six years old. Because Daniels & Bell was so dependent on his relationships and ability, its business began to decline almost immediately. Though it eventually closed its doors in 1994, Bell's legacy lives on. Both the Securities Industry Association and the National Association of Securities Professionals created the Travers Bell Award to honor his lasting contributions to the world of finance.

Further Reading

Bell, Gregory S. *In the Black: A History of African Americans on Wall Street* (2001).

Dingle, Derek. "Travers Bell: Breaking Barriers on Wall Street," *Black Enterprise* (Apr. 2005).

Pershing, Amy C. "Travers Bell," *Institutional Investor* (June 1987).

Wayne, Leslie. "An Empire in Black Business," *New York Times*, 18 Apr. 1982.

GREGORY S. BELL

BELLAMY, Sherry (12 Oct. 1952–), attorney, was born Sherry Franchesca Bellamy in Harlem, New York, the youngest of seven children of Athelston Alhama Bellamy and Mary Elizabeth Reeves. Sherry's father, born and raised in Harlem, was a career military officer who served with the Tuskegee Airmen and eventually rose to the rank of captain in the U.S. Air Force. After retiring from the military he became a court officer and court clerk in the Civil Court of the City of New York. Sherry's mother was born and raised on a race-horse breeding farm outside Charlottesville, Virginia. Sherry grew up in Harlem and graduated from Cardinal Spellman High School, a Roman Catholic high school whose graduates include many successful minority judges, attorneys, and other professionals.

In 1974 Bellamy graduated from Swarthmore College in Swarthmore, Pennsylvania, with a BA in Political Science. She later received her juris doctor in 1977 from Yale Law School. During that same year she married George Alexander Bumbray Jr., an architect who attended Howard University and completed his bachelor of arts degree at Yale School of Architecture. The two met in New Haven shortly after George completed two master's degrees in Architecture and Environmental Design at Yale. They had three children together.

During her time at Swarthmore and Yale, Bellamy worked with Dr. KENNETH CLARK, the psychologist who provided evidence in support of *Brown v. Board of Education*, the landmark 1954 U.S. Supreme Court decision. Bellamy also studied under Charles Black, who during his tenure as a professor at Columbia Law School had authored the briefs in *Brown v. Board of Education*. She was also fortunate to intern with Haywood Burns, founder of the National Conference of Black Lawyers and the first African American dean of a law school in New York State, as well as MARIAN WRIGHT EDELMAN, founder of the Children's Defense Fund.

Bellamy began her own legal career in 1977 as a family and children's rights attorney with the New Haven Legal Assistance Association (NHLAA) in Connecticut, which provided legal services to the poor. At NHLAA Bellamy was instrumental in the creation of a unit for the civil representation of children, which represented children in cases involving neglect, abuse, rights to education for the handicapped, and other matters before state and federal courts in Connecticut.

After four years in nonprofit service Bellamy became an associate at law firms in New York and Washington, D.C. From 1985 to 1991, while at Jones, Day, Reavis & Pogue, an internationally recognized law firm that specialized in business, government regulation, litigation, and tax, she specialized in telecommunications law at a time when the entire telecommunications industry was undergoing dramatic changes. Her success continued as a corporate attorney for Bell Atlantic beginning in 1991, which coincided with the first major overhaul of telecommunications law in almost sixty-two years. In 1992 she became vice president and general counsel of Bell Atlantic-Washington, D.C., and in 1997 she became president and chief executive officer of Bell Atlantic-Maryland—the first African American woman to advance to senior management within the Bell Atlantic corporation.

Three years later, Bellamy became vice president and associate general counsel for the newly formed Verizon Communications (a merger of the telephone giants Bell Atlantic and GTE), overseeing state regulatory matters for the East Coast. In 2006 she was promoted to vice president and deputy general counsel of Verizon Business, a division of Verizon formed after the acquisition of MCI Communications. Verizon was at that time a leader in delivering broadband, voice, wireless, and video communications to mass market, business, government, and wholesale customers in the United States and in seventy-five countries across six continents. At Verizon Business, Bellamy oversaw the company's litigation and regulatory matters throughout the United States.

Bellamy maintained a connection with the African American community and recognized that she was given opportunities that her parents and other previous generations of blacks had never enjoyed. In 2003, commenting on affirmative action, she wrote, "I feel neither stigma nor concern about benefiting from the only privilege that American society has ever bestowed upon the descendants of African slaves. I recognize that without the affirmative action practiced at Swarthmore College in 1969, I would never have been in a position to achieve what I have been fortunate enough to achieve." Bellamy rejected the assumption that affirmative action explained her success and instead stated that she focused on the tasks at hand to deliver results. As a person committed to justice, Bellamy served on numerous boards and professional and business organizations, including John Hopkins Medicine, the Swarthmore College Board of Managers, and the Kennedy Krieger Institute, devoted to the treatment, education, and study of children with brain injuries. She was the recipient of various awards, and was named a Distinguished Woman in Business and one of Maryland's Top 100 Women. In 2005 she received an honorary degree of humane letters from Rosemont College in Pennsylvania.

Further Reading

Bentley, Kenneth W. *Woman of Courage II* (1998).

Neely, Esme. "Bellamy Takes on Greatest Challenge," *Baltimore Business Journal* (29 Sept. 1997).

GREER C. BOSWORTH

BELLINGER, Charles (15 Apr. 1875–14 June 1937), entrepreneur and political organizer, was born to Louisa and Theodore Bellinger, a blacksmith in Lockhart, a small town in Caldwell County in south central Texas. As a teenager he began to work in Lockhart, Texas, for Jeff Howard, who owned a saloon. There he became a dealer for card games that involved betting.

Using his own savings along with loans he acquired from Howard and the Pearl Brewery, Bellinger moved to San Antonio, where by 1906 he had opened his own saloon. His success as a gambler grew into a regional and national reputation, with trips to Chicago and New York to gamble. As an entrepreneur he diversified his investments by adding a real estate office, a construction company, a café, a pool room, a barbershop, a theater, a baseball team, a lottery, and a taxi service. When Prohibition came in the 1920s rumors suggested he had a hand in bootlegging, although Bellinger always denied it. Perhaps most important in terms of his growing political aspirations Bellinger began to make loans available to the black community. When he extended this possibility to several churches he increased his influence with both preachers and their congregations. As Bellinger's economic status improved, his family also grew. Of the twelve children born to Bellinger and his wife, Celeste Pelliman, only three daughters and two sons reached adulthood. Following a divorce from his first wife, he married Addie Scott.

As early as 1910 Bellinger became involved in San Antonio and Bexar County politics. He helped organize African American voters to support a series of local officials, who in turn responded to the concerns of the black community and its leaders. In Texas the dominant Democrats, through the legislature, had created a state poll tax, effectively disenfranchising many working class voters, including most blacks and Hispanics. The Democratic Party also used a white primary to exclude African Americans from its candidate selection process. Local elections often followed a nonpartisan format, however, that allowed anyone who paid a poll tax to participate. To increase black political participation as well as his own influence, Bellinger paid poll taxes for African Americans and placed the receipts in a safe until election day. He also made clear to voters which candidates would respond favorably to the voters' interests. For the black community he had become the "political boss," who according to some estimates influenced up to five thousand voters by the 1930s.

The first candidate Bellinger supported was John W. Tobin, who served as county sheriff and later as mayor of San Antonio through most of the period from 1900 to 1927. When local government leaders allowed black voters into the Democratic Party primary in 1922 it stirred opposition and led the state legislature to require a white primary. In response African Americans initiated a series of court cases that resulted in the Supreme Court's 1944 determination in *Smith v. Allwright* at last outlawing the white primary. By 1918 Bellinger had increased his role in local politics and become the most influential figure in the black community, even before the death of John Grumbles, the local president of the NAACP, in 1926. Bellinger also threw his weight into mayoral politics, supporting C. M. Chambers from 1929 to 1933, and C. K. Quinn in the 1930s, which resulted in improvements to African American neighborhoods, including street paving and lighting, city sewer lines, an improved public library branch and auditorium, as well as better parks and schools. During the Depression of the 1930s Bellinger also sought public assistance for black citizens who had lost jobs.

Some white reformers, usually those with paternalistic views, became frustrated with what they saw as corruption, machine politics, boss rule, and a lack of influence for themselves. This view was shared by some middle-class blacks, who also suspected that Bellinger chose not to challenge segregation because it allowed him to more easily organize African American voters. When the editors of the black newspaper the *Inquirer* refused to print a Bellinger political ad in 1931, he launched a new paper, the *Register*, with his son Valmo as editor. The *Register* soon pushed its older competitor out of business. The white reformer Maury Maverick, a Democratic congressman who opposed lynching and favored equal pay for African Americans, nevertheless claimed corruption in local government and focused on Bellinger's role in it. Charges followed in 1936 that Bellinger had not paid enough income tax. His conviction brought a fine and an eighteen-month federal prison term. After Bellinger suffered a heart attack, however, Valmo and local Democratic leaders successfully lobbied President Franklin Roosevelt to pardon him. The physical and psychological strain had been too much, and after a second heart attack he died in San Antonio. Valmo Bellinger continued the *Register* and some business activities, but achieved only partial success in assuming his father's political role, which had made Charles Bellinger the most important African American leader in San Antonio during the first half of the twentieth century.

Further Reading

Barr, Alwyn. *Black Texans: A History of African Americans in Texas, 1528–1995* (1996).
Mason, Kenneth. *African Americans and Race Relations in San Antonio, Texas, 1867–1937* (1998).
Taylor, Quintard. *In Search of the Racial Frontier: African Americans in the American West, 1528–1990* (1998).

Obituary: *Houston Informer,* 16 June 1937.

ALWYN BARR

BELTON, Ethel Lee (18 Apr. 1897–1984), teacher, civil rights activist, plaintiff in *Belton v. Gebhart* (1952), a companion case to *Brown v. Board of Education* (1954), was born in Hazelhurst, Georgia, the daughter of Glover and Ida Hall.

Around 1948, almost a decade after her husband Louis passed away, Ethel Belton moved with her seven children to Claymont, Delaware, a suburban community northwest of Wilmington, Delaware, to join her extended family. There she taught general education in a one-room school. Her daughter, Ethel Louise Belton, was eleven years old at the time of the move and was later assigned to Howard High School—the only free, public school for blacks in the entire state at the time. Located in Wilmington, it was a fifty-minute, nine-mile commute for Ethel Louise, who had a congenital heart condition. Although Claymont High School, the school for white children in the community, was but a short walk away, the state constitution mandated that black and white students attend racially segregated schools. Nonetheless, Belton pressed school officials to admit her daughter.

Belton's initial motivation for seeking her daughter's admission to Claymont was born not out of any deep-seated desire to overthrow Jim Crow segregation. She was interested, as she mentioned in a letter to the state board of education and as she later testified before the Delaware Court of Chancery, in enrolling her daughter in Claymont High School because of its proximity and the fact that she was a resident of the district. In her testimony before Judge Collins J. Seitz, she later asserted:

Well, first of all I live in the community of Claymont. I work in Claymont. I shop there, and I help to support the community in general, and I see no reasons of why my child should leave Claymont and travel all the way to Wilmington to attend high school when there is a public

School Integration. From left to right: Linda Brown Smith, Harry Briggs Jr., Ethel Louise Belton Brown, and Spottswood Bolling Jr. during a press conference at Hotel Americana ten years after *Brown v. Board of Education*, 9 June 1964. (Library of Congress, New York World-Telegram and the Sun Newspaper Photograph Collection/Al Ravenna, photographer.)

high school right in Claymont. (Testimony of Witnesses, NAACP Papers, Group II, Box 139: 36–37)

Having exhausted all administrative remedies, she approached LOUIS REDDING, the local attorney for the NAACP, and with his assistance she filed suit along with four other groups of black parents from neighboring communities in Wilmington, Claymont, Newark, and New Castle against the state board of education.

Redding, along with his co-counsel, Jack Greenberg, successfully argued her case, along with one other (*Bulah v. Gebhart*, 1952) in the Delaware Court of Chancery. The state appealed the decision to the Delaware Supreme Court, lost, and applied for a *writ of certiorari* from the U.S. Supreme Court. The high court then agreed to hear the case along with four others from South Carolina, Virginia, Kansas, and the District of Columbia in what came to be known as *Brown v. Board of Education*. In that landmark 1954 case Chief Justice Earl Warren ruled that racially segregated education was in violation of the equal protection clause of the Fourteenth Amendment.

On 4 September 1952 the Claymont School Board admitted, over the objections of the state attorney general, eleven of the twelve child plaintiffs to Claymont High School. But Ethel Louise Belton never made the transfer. She was a junior at Howard by the time the Delaware Supreme Court demanded the admission of the black students to the white school, and she chose to complete her coursework at Howard. That Ethel Louise was a plaintiff in such an important case but failed to take advantage of the opportunity to attend desegregated schools spoke to some of the problems inherent in this particular kind of civil rights activism. First, litigation was often a painfully slow process and students sometimes aged out of the schools in which they sought admission. Ethel Louise also had a fondness for the faculty at Howard and quite naturally wished to graduate with her friends. This desire highlighted a long-standing tension within African American communities between loyalties to historically black educational institutions that had nurtured generations of black students and commitments to desegregation and the promises afforded in often better-resourced schools that had been reserved for white students.

Further Reading

Copies of Ethel Belton's correspondence with the state board of education are located in the papers of the State Board of Education/Department of Public Instruction at the Delaware State Archives. Copies of court transcript are located in National Association for the Advancement of Colored People Collection in the Library of Congress, Washington, D.C.

Irons, Peter. *Jim Crow's Children: The Broken Promise of the Brown Decision* (2002).

Kluger, Richard. *Simple Justice: The History of Brown v. Board of Education and Black America's Struggle for Equality* (1975).

Peters, William. "The Schools That Broke the Color Line," *Redbook: The Magazine for Young Adults* (Oct. 1954, NAACP Papers, Library of Congress).

BRETT GADSDEN

BEMAN, Amos Gerry (1812–1874), clergyman and abolitionist, was born in Colchester, Connecticut, the son of Jehiel C. Beman, a clergyman. Nothing is known of his mother. He grew up and received a basic education in Middletown, Connecticut, where his father was pastor of the African church. A Wesleyan University student, L. P. Dole, volunteered to tutor Beman after the university refused his application for admission because he was an African American. Dole and Beman suffered ridicule and harassment from other students, and an anonymous threat of bodily harm from "Twelve of Us" caused Beman to give up the effort after six months. He went to Hartford, where he taught school for four years, and around 1836 he briefly attended the Oneida Institute in New York.

Beman was ordained as a Congregational minister in 1839. At about this time he married a woman whose name is not known. In 1841 he became the first named African American pastor of Temple Street African Church in New Haven, Connecticut, where he remained for seventeen years. Here he gained respect and support throughout the city from both blacks and whites. The church became a center for social, educational, and benevolent activities for the African American community. The Temple Street Church became the Dixwell Avenue Church and in the early twenty-first century was the oldest existing African American Congregational church in the nation.

Beman was an avid supporter of temperance throughout his life. His father had organized the Home Temperance Society of Middletown African Americans in 1833, and the younger Beman served as its secretary. He was also a participant in the founding of the Connecticut Temperance Society and served two years as its president. He was a leader in 1842 in effecting a merger of the African American temperance associations in Connecticut, Massachusetts, New York, and New Jersey into the States' Delavan Union Temperance Society of Colored People and was the principal speaker at its convention in 1845. For about a year, in 1842, Beman edited *Zion's Wesleyan*, a newspaper that provided a voice for temperance, abolition, and other reforms.

Beman was an ardent abolitionist and a member of the American Anti-Slavery Society from its founding in 1833. In 1840, with the great schism among antislavery supporters resulting from differences on women's rights, politics, and the role of the churches in the antislavery movement, Beman withdrew from the American Anti-Slavery Society. He then became one of the eight African Americans—his father was another—at the founding convention of the American and Foreign Anti-Slavery Society, for which he served as assistant secretary. In great demand as an antislavery speaker, Beman traveled more than five thousand miles between January and August 1856, crisscrossing the Northeast and making trips into Canada and Illinois. In his churches he held regular concerts for the enslaved, which combined protest, agitation, and prayer. Beman also was a frequent contributor to FREDERICK DOUGLASS's newspapers, the *North Star* and *Frederick Douglass' Paper*.

Civil and political rights for free African Americans also received Beman's attention and energy. He carried on a long campaign to get suffrage rights in Connecticut, and he was a leader in the Negro Convention Movement. He served as president of the national conventions that met in Buffalo in 1843 and in Philadelphia in 1854 and as vice president of the meeting that met in Rochester in 1853. It was at the Buffalo meeting that HENRY HIGHLAND GARNET gave his famous address in which he called on the slaves to rise in revolt. Beman stepped down from the chair and spoke for more than an hour against Garnet's address. Beman carried a majority of the convention with him in not endorsing force and violence. However, after John Brown's raid and capture, Beman assisted in a prayer meeting for him at the Siloan Presbyterian Church in Brooklyn, New York.

In 1841 Beman was one of the founders and served as the first secretary of the Union Missionary Society, established by African Americans to support antislavery missionary work at home and abroad. When that society joined with other organizations in 1846 to organize the American Missionary Association (AMA), Beman became a supporter and active worker for the new evangelical abolitionist organization.

In the winter of 1856–1857 Beman's wife and two of their four children died from typhoid fever. After about a year he remarried, this time to a white woman whose name is not known. As a result he lost favor with his New Haven congregation and submitted his resignation in 1858 to accept a call to the Abyssinian Congregational Church in Portland, Maine. This church was small and poor, although it was the only church serving a community of four hundred African Americans. To supplement the small salary pledged by the church, the AMA commissioned Beman as a city missionary. When the church failed to raise the pledged salary, and he again encountered resentment against his wife, he petitioned the AMA for a full-time commission and received an appointment in 1859 as the association's fundraising agent for New England. That year at a meeting in Brooklyn he was elected president of the Evangelical Association of Colored Ministers of Congregational and Presbyterian Churches.

Beman was a hard worker for the AMA, covering a territory from Maine to Sag Harbor, Long Island, and visiting both white and black churches of any denomination that would admit him as an agent of an abolitionist society. He usually prefaced his appeals with lectures on such topics as "The Origin and History of the African Race" and "What the Colored People Can under God Do for Themselves." Nevertheless his collections were small. Either he resigned or his commission was allowed to expire, and in 1863 he became pastor of a struggling Congregational church in Jamaica, Long Island. There his second wife died. In 1865 he went to be pastor of Mount Zion Congregational Church in Cleveland, Ohio. He married again in 1871.

Beman died in Pittsfield, Massachusetts, where he was pastor of the Second Congregational Church, which he had helped in establishing a quarter-century before.

Further Reading

The Beman Collection at the Beinecke Rare Book and Manuscript Library at Yale University contains clippings, pamphlets, and scrapbooks that Amos Beman organized and annotated. There are seventy-two letters and reports written by Beman from 1841 to 1869 in the American Missionary Association Archives at the Amistad Research Center at Tulane University.

Swift, David E. *Black Prophets of Justice: Activist Clergy before the Civil War* (1989).

Warner, Robert A. "Amos Gerry Beman—1812–1874: A Memoir of a Forgotten Leader," *Journal of Negro History* 22 (Apr. 1937): 200–221.

CLIFTON H. JOHNSON

BEMAN, Jehiel C. (1789?–21 Dec. 1858), shoemaker, clergyman, and abolitionist, was born in Chatham, Connecticut, to Sarah Gerry and Cesar Beman, a manumitted slave and Revolutionary War veteran who may have chosen his surname to indicate his freedom to "be a man." By 1809 Jehiel had moved to Colchester, Connecticut, and married Fanny Condol, with whom he fathered seven children, including the noted abolitionist AMOS G. BEMAN. Jehiel worked in Colchester as a shoemaker and Methodist exhorter until 1830, when he moved to Middletown, Connecticut, to pastor the city's Cross Street African Methodist Episcopal Zion (AMEZ) Church. On 11 August of that same year Jehiel's first wife died, and he married Nancy Scott on 17 October. In 1832 he left Cross Street after being appointed an itinerant missionary by the annual AMEZ conference, but he remained in Middletown as a preacher, shoemaker, and reformer until 1838, at which time he moved to Boston to pastor the new First AMEZ Church.

In the 1830s Beman's activities revolved around abolitionism, temperance, and his church. Like other AMEZ leaders Beman favored separate black churches. Upon traveling to Providence in 1837 he reported "finding many who worship in white churches desirous to worship by themselves" and helped organize an independent congregation. Beman denounced white Christians who urged black congregants to "sit in the corners," receive communion last, and "wait for the crumbs after the white brethren have partaken" (*Colored American*, 23 Sept. 1837).

Beman's denunciation of prejudice in white churches dovetailed with his antislavery principles. He joined rising calls for immediate emancipation in the 1830s, and when William Lloyd Garrison founded the *Liberator* in Boston in 1831, Beman, who served as the paper's subscription agent in Middletown, was one of the many black abolitionists whose support kept the paper afloat in its early years. Beman signed the founding declaration of the American Anti-Slavery Society (AASS) in 1833 and helped organize AASS auxiliaries in Connecticut.

Beman was also deeply involved in the temperance movement. He believed, with many other abolitionists, that black Northerners could counteract prejudice and undermine racist defenses of slavery by pursuing "moral reform." Beman approved more than once of the "wisdom to live down oppression" (*Colored American*, 27 Jan. 1838). At one annual meeting of the AASS he sponsored a resolution encouraging education, entrepreneurship, and moral improvement in free black communities. Beman pursued those goals in Connecticut by founding a Middletown temperance society in 1833 and a state temperance society for African Americans in 1836.

Beman continued his activism as an AMEZ minister in Boston. He was involved in local protests mounted by Boston's activist community, signing a petition on behalf of the fugitive slave George Latimer in 1842, as well as a petition against school segregation in 1844. Under his leadership the First AMEZ Church grew rapidly, moving into a new building in 1841 and attracting into its pews many of the city's black abolitionists. The church also served as a center for community events, such as First of August ceremonies celebrating British emancipation.

But in Boston, Beman also became embroiled in controversy. His church experienced some dissension when JULIA FOOTE, a female preacher, claimed that Beman had refused to let her speak in his church. Beman's opposition to Foote was partly caused by her doctrinal heterodoxy but might also have been partly caused by conservative views about women. Many of Beman's African American contemporaries identified social uplift with masculine virtues, a broad cultural tendency implicitly suggested by Beman's own surname. To live down oppression also meant, as Beman put it, "to live the man" (*New York Emancipator*, 16 Nov. 1837).

A larger but not unrelated controversy arose in 1839 when Beman parted ways with Garrison and the AASS. Since 1837 tensions had increased between Boston's evangelical abolitionists and the Garrisonians, who defended female lecturers, opposed political abolitionism, and often espoused heretical religious beliefs. In 1839 Garrison's detractors founded the Massachusetts Abolition Society to oppose the local AASS auxiliary and offered Beman a job as agent for an African American employment service. Beman accepted, a move consistent with his belief in the need for separate black businesses and education. Garrisonians vilified Beman for desertion, but he responded that he had not found work with them—implying, as increasing numbers of black abolitionists did in the 1840s, that jobs in Garrisonian organizations were still closed to African Americans because of latent prejudices among their officers.

Yet the controversy was about more than a job. Beman probably agreed with those who thought that the Garrisonians' radical views on gender and religion were hampering the antislavery cause. In 1840 when a group led by Lewis Tappan seceded from the AASS to form the American and Foreign Anti-Slavery Society, Beman joined them. Thus when his name appeared with other Tappanites on an 1844 petition defending capital punishment—which leading Garrisonians opposed—the *Liberator* called Beman, one of its earliest supporters, "the colored cat's-paw of the clerical seceders from the anti-slavery platform" (*Liberator*, 23 Feb. 1844).

Beman left Boston not long afterward, returning to Middletown in 1844 or 1845. There he resumed his leadership role in the local community, presiding over temperance meetings and state conventions of black activists. In 1844 he traveled to Baltimore and Washington, D.C., to attend an AMEZ conference, and after touring the capital he wrote of "sighing to think that my father faced the cannon's mouth for this country's liberty" (*Boston Morning Chronicle*, 15 Aug. 1844). In the 1850s Beman supported antislavery politicians and suffrage for the state's black citizens. He lectured on behalf of the Free Soil Party in 1852 and attended the national conventions of black abolitionists held in 1853 and 1855. Evidence suggests that Beman also assisted fugitive slaves in Connecticut.

In 1856 Beman's second wife, Nancy, died, and his own death followed two years later in New Haven. But Beman's legacy—as a reformer committed to uplift, as a clergyman committed to independence, and as a committed abolitionist—lived on, primarily in the careers of his sons, Leverett Beman and Amos G. Beman.

Further Reading

Some of Beman's writings can be found in the micro-filmed edition of the *Black Abolitionist Papers* (1981), edited by George E. Carter and C. Peter Ripley.

Horton, James O., and Lois E. Horton. *Black Bostonians: Family Life and Community Struggle in the Antebellum North* (1979).

Housley, Kathleen. "'Yours for the Oppressed': The Life of Jehiel C. Beman," *Journal of Negro History* 77.1 (Winter 1992).

Jacobs, Donald M., ed. *Courage and Conscience: Black and White Abolitionists in Boston* (1993).

James, Jennifer Lee. "Jehiel C. Beman: A Leader of the Northern Free Black Community," *Journal of Negro History* 82.1 (Winter 1997).

W. CALEB MCDANIEL

BENBERRY, Cuesta Ray (8 Sept. 1923–23 Aug. 2007), quilt historian and researcher, was born in Cincinnati to Walter Ray Sr., a dining car steward for the Southern Railway Company, and Marie Jones, a seamstress and homemaker. After age six, following her mother's death, Benberry and her older brother, Walter Jr., lived in Saint Louis with their maternal grandmother, Letha Jennings.

After earning a BA in 1945 from Stowe Teachers College (later Harris-Stowe State University) in Saint Louis, she married George L. Benberry in 1951. The couple had one son, George Jr., born in 1953. Benberry spent about forty years as a teacher, reading specialist, and librarian for the Saint Louis public

school system. She went on to get a certificate of Library Science, also from Stowe, in 1967, and a masters of Education in 1973 from the University of Missouri, Saint Louis.

Benberry's interest in quilting began during a trip to her husband's family in rural Paducah, Kentucky. Her mother-in-law, Minnie Benberry, was a quilter. Minnie and other quilters in the area shared with Benberry their newest quilts, which they called by different names. Benberry began to study the history of the names of the patterns. Her investigations would have an impact on American quilt history for decades.

In the early 1950s Benberry began corresponding with quilters across America and Canada. She joined quilt pattern "round robins," an exchange wherein participants mailed quilt patterns to everyone else in the group, thus enlarging all the members' collections. Benberry collected patterns for their beauty and cataloged them to document their origins and various regional names. In time, her collection of quilt pattern blocks would number eight hundred. In 1965 Benberry designed an original quilt block, *Kennedy's Eternal Flame*, which later the same year received an honorable mention from *Aunt Kate's Quilting Bee Magazine*.

Quilting publications at the time were generally simple, photocopied newsletters. The first, more formal, magazine-style quilt publication started in 1969 with *Nimble Needle Treasures*, a quarterly that featured reprinted quilt patterns and articles on quilt history. From 1970 to 1975 Benberry regularly contributed to the quarterly.

Benberry outlined her seven-year effort to confirm a quilt legend about a black woman MARTHA ANN RICKS, who made Queen Victoria a quilt in 1892 ("A Quilt for Queen Victoria," *Quilter's Newsletter Magazine*, Feb. 1987, 24–25). Benberry was able to accurately determine, with the assistance of her extensive network of quilters, the name of the eight-pointed *Evening Star* pattern used in a cradle quilt sold at the 1836 Boston Female Anti-Slavery Society Ladies Fair ("A Quilt Research Surprise," *Quilters Newsletter Magazine*, July/Aug. 1981, 34–35). Over the years her articles on quilt history and quilt patterns appeared in many periodicals, including *American Quilter Magazine*, *Canada Quilts*, *Center for the History of American Needlework Magazine*, *Essence Magazine*, *International Review of African American Art*, *Lady's Circle Patchwork Quilts*, and *Quilter's Newsletter Magazine*. At her request, Benberry's articles often ran without bylines.

America's bicentennial in 1976 and an attendant emphasis on the study of Americans' various cultural heritages provided the impetus for Benberry's research into African American quilt history. Beginning her study through interviews with older quilters, she then moved to nonquilting sources such as antislavery journals, slave narratives, nineteenth-century autobiographies of black people, newspapers, farm journals, the Work Progress Administration's (WPA's) Federal Writers' Project narratives, and women's history books to gain insights into the quilts and motivations of early black quilters.

In 1980 Benberry wrote the landmark "Afro-American Women and Quilts: An Introductory Essay," one of the first articles to place black women's needlework in the context of American quilt history (*Uncovering 1980*, ed. Sally Garoutte, 64–67). She insisted in her essay that a complete picture should include quilts made by slaves, quilts made in traditional European styles, quilts made in African traditions, and those with black images made by white quilters. Also in 1980 Benberry stitched her only quilt, *Afro-American Women and Quilts*, a sampler quilt featuring twelve blocks, each block representing an African American–made quilt she had learned about during her years of research.

In 1983 Benberry was inducted into the Quilters Hall of Fame for her thirty-year investigative contributions to quilt history and pattern collecting. In her acceptance speech Benberry said, "What I see as the quilt investigator's obligation is the expansion and enrichment of quilt information, undergirded by accuracy and truth, set in a frame of serious scholarship" ("Hall of Fame '83," *Quilters' Journal*, no. 23, 1983, 18). Three years later she answered an advertisement from CAROLYN MAZLOOMI in the February 1986 issue of *Quilter's Newsletter Magazine* requesting correspondence with other African American quilters. Benberry became a founding member of the Women of Color Quilters Network (WOCQN), an outgrowth of the advertisement. She was also a frequent contributor to the *Women of Color Quilters Network Newsletter*, available in the Museum of Arts and Design library in New York City.

Benberry traveled to London in 1986 for the opening of an exhibit featuring the quilts of the Zamani Soweto Sisters Council of South Africa. She gave the opening lecture to the exhibit. In addition, the mayor of Brixton presented Benberry and the Zamani Soweto Sisters with the keys to this London neighborhood for bringing the quilt program to the community.

Over the years Benberry shared her expertise generously, lecturing on African American quilt history, pattern history, and the role of the quilt historian at more than one hundred venues since 1980. A charter member of the American Quilt Study Group, she presented papers at some of the group's conferences, and her appearance on the popular Home and Garden Television (HGTV) network program *Simply Quilts* (1998) reached a wide audience. Benberry served on the board of directors for the American Quilt Study Group (1983–1986) and Art Saint Louis (1995) as well as on the advisory board of the Elder Craftsmen of New York (1989–1994). Her publications include *Always There: The African American Presence in American Quilting* (1992); *A Patchwork of Pieces: An Anthology of Early Quilt Stories 1845–1940* (1993), edited with Carol Pinney Crabb; *Twentieth Century Quilts, 1900–1970: Women Make Their Mark* (1997), with Joyce Gross; *A Piece of My Soul: Quilts by Black Arkansans* (2000); and *Love of Quilts: A Treasury of Classic Quilting Stories* (2004), with Carol Pinney Crabb.

Esteemed for her accumulated knowledge, in 1993 Benberry curated the exhibit Hear My Quilt: 150 Years of African American Quilt Making, which opened at the Saint Louis Art Museum. The following year the museum purchased the quilt *Jo Baker's Birthday*, created by FAITH RINGGOLD in Benberry's honor. In 2004 the Anyone Can Fly Foundation presented Benberry with its first Senior Scholar Lifetime Achievement Award for her life's work—researching the quilt art of the African diaspora. In the same year, she donated her extensive collection of rare quilt history books, patterns, exhibit catalogs, and ephemera materials amassed after fifty years of research to the American Folk Art Museum Library in New York. Benberry continued to encourage and inspire other established and budding researchers until she passed away.

Further Reading

Blair, Margot Carter. "An Interview with Cuesta Benberry," *The Flying Needle* (Feb. 1985).
Center for the Quilt Online. http//www.centerforthequilt.org See 2002 video interview with Benberry.
Doering, Henry, ed. *Book of Buffs, Masters, Mavens, and Uncommon Experts* (1980).
Kogan, Lee, and James Mitchell. "Update: The Library," *Folk Art* (Winter 2004/2005).
"The Meeting Place: Cuesta Benberry," *Quilter's Newsletter Magazine* (Feb. 1980).

KYRA E. HICKS

BENGA, Ota. *See* Otabenga.

BENJAMIN, Bennie (4 November 1907–2 May 1989), musician and songwriter, was born Claude Augustus Benjamin in Christiansted, St. Croix, Virgin Islands (then Danish West Indies), the son of Joseph Benjamin and Euphrasia Seteon (spelled Shöin on his Anglican baptismal certificate). Benjamin's early life was difficult. His father was a fisherman who died when Benjamin was an infant, and changes in the shipping industry, hurricanes, and World War I pushed the economy of the Virgin Islands into decline. After graduating from Virgin Islands High School in 1925, he abandoned his early hopes of becoming a physician for lack of tuition to enter medical school, and worked as a tailor and cabinetmaker instead. In 1927 he moved to New York City in search of better opportunity.

Inspired by a local island musician, Louis Stakemann, Benjamin had taught himself ukulele and banjo (by ear) as a youth. Upon arriving in New York, he added guitar to his skills at Hy Smith's School of Music, and after just six months of training he could read music and play well enough to begin performing in dance orchestras. He developed a distinctive guitar solo style that interspersed chords in his melodic lines and this earned him a job with Napoleon's Orchestra at the Savoy Ballroom where he played for five years (c. 1928–1933). He also toured with the vaudeville act Olson and Johnson and played at the Cotton

Club. Yet despite these prominent gigs, he struggled to make a living and worked odd jobs to stay afloat financially.

Beginning about 1935, Benjamin tried songwriting in the mainstream Tin Pan Alley idiom, but was unable to publish a single song. In 1938 he joined with Sol Marcus, and along with Eddie Seiler and EDDIE DURHAM, revised a tune Benjamin had previously shopped around to publishers unsuccessfully to create the smash hit "I Don't Want to Set the World on Fire" in 1941. Introduced by the African American group HARLAN LEONARD's Kansas City Rockets, the song next hit number four on the pop charts as performed by the Ink Spots and rose to number one when Horace Heidt's version captured the mood of the country after the Pearl Harbor attack. It won a 1941 *Billboard Magazine* Top Songwriter's Award for its creators. Seiler, Marcus, and Benjamin hit number one again soon after in 1942 with "When the Lights Go on Again (All over the World)," as performed by Vaughn Monroe, which used the imagery of World War II blackouts to express the hope for peace.

Benjamin enlisted in the United States Army Air Corps as an entertainment specialist on 5 September 1942 and was stationed at Mitchel Field in New York. During three years of service he played guitar and produced camp shows (writing songs, casting talent, directing, etc.). He wed Martha Flores on 25 September 1944; they remained married until her death in 1983. He was honorably discharged at the rank of corporal on 21 September 1945.

Returning to civilian life, he joined with George David Weiss to form the most successful partnership of his career. This team produced twenty hit songs in ten years, including "Oh What It Seemed to Be" (1945; 1946, number 1 Pop with Frankie Carle and number 1 Pop with Frank Sinatra), "Rumors Are Flying" (1946, number 1 Pop, Frankie Carle and Les Paul), and "Wheel of Fortune" (1952, number 1 Pop, Kay Starr). "Wheel of Fortune" sold over 1 million copies of sheet music and gave its name to an early television game show (1952–1953) that rewarded good Samaritans with a spin of a prize wheel. Other hits by the pair included "Strictly Instrumental" (1942), "I Want to Thank Your Folks" (1946, number 21, Perry Como), "Surrender" (1946, number 2, Perry Como; later Elvis Presley, 1961), "I Don't See Me in Your Eyes Anymore" (1949, number 6), "Can Anyone Explain" (1950, number 5, Ames Brothers), "Can Anyone Explain? (No, No, No)" (1950, number 7, Ames Brothers), "Echoes" (1950, number 18, Jo Stafford and Gordon MacRae), "Jet" (1951, number 20, NAT KING COLE), "These Things I Offer You" (1951, SARAH VAUGHAN), and "Cross Over the Bridge" (1954, number 2, Patti Page). The pair was named the top songwriting team of 1946 by *Billboard Magazine,* and Disney commissioned them to pen the title songs for the movies *Fun and Fancy Free* (1947) and *Melody Time* (1948).

Benjamin reportedly had a hand in more than a hundred songs that registered on the *Billboard* charts.

He approached his work as a professional art, observing that "songwriting is a craft, an art, a gift—like a vocation to medicine or law or any other profession" (*Virgin Islands Daily News*, 29 April 1968). His songs have little direct reference to African American idioms but are rather in the popular mainstream styles of the day. His lyrics focus on the subject of love with an undercurrent of innocent sensuality. Like other Tin Pan Alley songs, dramatic emphasis has shifted to the chorus, with a brief introduction to set the stage. Unobtrusive rhyme and clever word choice enchant the listener. Although his tuneful melodies are easily sung by amateurs, their subtlety engages professional interpreters as well. Rhythmic variations keep the melody fresh as it spins out with gentle syncopations and triplet inflections. Wide intervallic leaps are used with deliberate expressive intent, especially at the song's climax. In sum, Benjamin's songs are masterful realizations of the popular idiom.

Around 1950 Benjamin founded his own publishing company; after his 1955 split with Weiss, he again teamed with Sol Marcus. This pair created such songs as "Fabulous Character" (1955, Sarah Vaughan), "I Am Blessed" (NINA SIMONE), "Our Love (Will See Us Through)" (Nina Simone), "Lonely Man (1960, Elvis Presley), and "Don't Let Me Be Misunderstood" (1965, number 15, The Animals).

Evoking classic themes of love and capturing the energy of their time, Benjamin's songs often appear in movie soundtracks. For example, "Anyone (Could Fall in Love with You)" was sung by Elvis Presley in the 1964 movie *Kissin' Cousins*. The fact that four and five decades later, films continued to include his songs reveals their ability to connect with audiences. These long-lived songs and their respective films include "Wheel of Fortune" (*Household Saints*, 1993; *L.A. Confidential*, 1997), "Don't Let Me Be Misunderstood" (*Layer Cake*, 2004; *The Banger Sisters*, 2002), and "I Don't Want to Set the World on Fire" (*Iris*, 2001; *Ask the Dust*, 2006).

By 1965 his company was known as Benjamin Publishing, and by 1968 Benjamin was sole owner of Bennie Benjamin Music. He was a member of the American Society of Composers, Authors and Publishers (ASCAP), the National Academy of Popular Music, and the Songwriters Guild of America. He also served on the council of the American Guild of Authors and Composers. In 1979 he won an ASCAP Award for "I'll Never Be Free," and that same year he was honored at the dedication of St. Thomas's Reichhold Center for the Arts. Five years later, in 1984, he was inducted into the Songwriters Hall of Fame.

As he became more affluent, Benjamin invested to support the Virgin Islands, buying real estate and becoming the largest stockholder in the West Indies Bank and Trust. Benjamin sponsored benefits for the March of Dimes, the Red Cross, and various leagues and associations such as the Queensboro Tuberculosis and Health Association. In 1963 New York Congressman ADAM CLAYTON POWELL JR. persuaded President John F. Kennedy to appoint Benjamin a member of the board of directors of the Virgin Islands Corporation.

Benjamin died after a long illness in New York City at the age of eighty-one. Lacking children, his last will and testament created the Bennie and Martha Benjamin Foundation to support medical training and clinics in the Virgin Islands. Established in 1990 the foundation gave its first grant for medical equipment in 1992 and began awarding annual scholarships to students pursuing careers in healthcare who are committed to working in the islands. As of 2006 the foundation had donated almost $1.7 million to Virgin Island hospitals, students, and nonprofits.

Further Reading
Benjamin's personal papers are held in the Schomburg Center for Research in Black Culture (New York Public Library, New York City).
Hughes, Langston. *Famous Negro Music Makers* (1955).
Moolenaar, Ruth. *Profiles of Outstanding Virgin Islanders* (1992).

MARK CLAGUE

BENJAMIN, Fred (8 Sept. 1944–), dancer, choreographer, and educator, was born in Boston, Massachusetts, to a theatrical and musical family. One of New York's most superb and demanding jazz teachers, as well as an excellent choreographer, Benjamin began his career at the age of four, studying with Elma Lewis at her well-respected School of Fine Arts. Two years later, he started studying ballet, a requirement for all of Lewis's students, no matter which style they chose to focus on. When peer pressure led Benjamin to stop dancing briefly—a not uncommon situation for young male dancers—he shifted to acting, taking classes at Boston Children's Theatre. Two years later he returned to Lewis's school and found something new: George Howard, a teacher of Haitian dance. Still a child, Benjamin knew instantly that "that's the thing I wanted to do, with the drums and everything. It was so exciting to me" (Hall, 3).

Lewis provided Benjamin with a thorough grounding in a wide range of techniques—ballet, jazz, and what is commonly referred to as "ethnic dance"—that set the stage for his future work as a choreographer. And she offered yet more inspiration by taking Benjamin and a small group of pupils to New York City to expose them to other teachers and performances. While there Benjamin had the opportunity to study with such master jazz instructors as Luigi and Matt Mattox, as well as in the American Ballet Theatre's school, which he later attended on a partial scholarship after graduating from high school.

At nineteen Benjamin joined the company of TALLEY BEATTY, who was a former Dunham dancer and one of the major figures in African American dance. Benjamin remained with the company for three years, finding in Beatty a powerful influence and one who also fused various styles into a cohesive whole. Many years later, following Beatty's death in 1995, Benjamin created *Beattyville* for Philadanco as a trib-

ute to his mentor. One of Benjamin's most successful works, it became a staple in the company's repertoire.

In 1968, shortly after Beatty's company dissolved, Benjamin formed his own dance troupe, the Fred Benjamin Dance Company. Initially he had not intended to become a company director, but Elma Lewis asked him to do a piece for her and he agreed, using some of the dancers who were then performing with him in a production of *Hello, Dolly!* on Broadway. At that point he began to realize that he needed a "larger canvas" to reach his artistic goals (Hall, 8); that small collection of friends formed the original core of his company, which eventually appeared on such TV shows as *Soul*.

Benjamin described his company's technique as modern jazz, and he, as well as others, referred to his works as soul ballets, many of which have been set to popular music by singers like PATTI LABELLE and GLADYS KNIGHT. His choreography created movement that was full of power, often with very long elegant lines: in Benjamin's words, dances that were "sensual, linear, and entertaining," but at the same time rhythmic, with jazz isolations that allowed the body to move polyrhythmically (*Attitude*, 11).

In November 1975, Benjamin scarcely eluded death when thieves attacked and stabbed him six times outside his New York apartment. His response was to create a dance, "Travels Just Outside the House" about the experience. He told the *New York Times* dance reviewer Anna Kisselgoff that in spite of the trauma, the dancers of his studio stayed together and kept the company running, and that their solidarity inspired Benjamin and kept him from becoming bitter.

Benjamin's influence extended in two different directions: first, as a teacher in such studios as the famed New York's Clark Center for the Performing Arts, the Steps studios, and June Lewis, he trained a generation of dancers who went on to modern dance companies (including ALVIN AILEY) and Broadway. Always demanding, Benjamin challenged his students with complex, professional-level combinations. Second, he strove to bring his work to the community and expose as many people as possible to dance; during the late 1970s and early 1980s, he participated in the Harlem Cultural Council's annual Dance Mobile series, which presented free performances outdoors in a non-theatrical setting.

The Fred Benjamin Dance Company dissolved in 1990, when it was restructured as the Tally/Benjamin Project. Benjamin served as chair of the jazz department and faculty adviser of the Alvin Ailey American Dance Center. He also worked internationally, and taught dance in the Netherlands, Japan, and Belgium, among other places.

Further Reading
The Dance Research Division of the New York Public Library at Lincoln Center maintains a clippings file on Fred Benjamin.
Emery, Lynne Fauley. *Black Dance From 1619 to Today* (1988).

Hall, Noel. "Interview with Fred Benjamin," for the Oral History Project, Dance Division, New York Public Library. Conducted 6 Oct. 1989.

Lewis, Julinda. "Fred Benjamin: A Tyrant Matures," *Attitude* (Sept./Oct. 1983).

Perpener, John O., III. *African-American Concert Dance: The Harlem Renaissance and Beyond* (2001).

KAREN BACKSTEIN

BENJAMIN, Robert Charles O'Hara (31 Mar. 1855–2 Oct. 1900), journalist and lawyer, was born on the island of Saint Kitts in the West Indies. Details about his early life, including the names of his parents and the nature of his education, are unknown. In the fall of 1869 he arrived in New York, where he worked as soliciting agent for the *New York Star* and then as city editor for the *Progressive American*. Benjamin apparently became a U.S. citizen in the early 1870s, and in 1876 he gave speeches in support of Rutherford B. Hayes, the Republican candidate for president. He was rewarded with a position as a letter carrier in New York City but quit after nine months and moved to Kentucky, where he taught school. While there Benjamin also took up the study of law. He continued his studies after being named principal of a school in Decatur, Alabama, and he was admitted to the bar at Nashville, Tennessee, in January 1880.

Before and after his admission to the bar, the peripatetic Benjamin continued his career in journalism. In total he edited or owned (or both edited and owned) at least eleven black newspapers, including the *Colored Citizen* of Pittsburgh, the *Chronicle* of Evansville, Illinois, the *Nashville Free Lance*—where, as contributing editor, he wrote under the name "Cicero"—the *Negro American* of Birmingham, Alabama, the *Los Angeles Observer*, and the *San Francisco Sentinel*. When Benjamin worked at each of these papers is unclear. He was apparently in Birmingham in 1887, in Los Angeles in 1888, and in San Francisco in 1891. He also worked for the *Daily Sun*, a white-owned newspaper in Los Angeles.

In addition to his journalism, Benjamin also published a number of books and pamphlets that reflected his wide range of interests. In 1883 he published *Poetic Gems*, a small collection of poetry, and in 1888 he published *Life of Toussaint L'Ouverture*. He was perhaps best known for *Southern Outrages: A Statistical Record of Lawless Doings* (1894). In 1886 Benjamin traveled to Canada on a speaking tour.

For twenty years Benjamin maintained a legal practice in the cities where he edited newspapers. One of his cases received widespread publicity: in 1884 in Richmond, Virginia, he won an acquittal of a black woman charged with murder. At a time when most white newspapers spoke of blacks in derogatory and racist terms, Benjamin's skills as a lawyer drew favorable comment from white newspapers in Richmond, Los Angeles, and Lexington, Kentucky.

Benjamin did not, however, court white favor, although he well understood the risk that African Americans ran in challenging whites in civil rights, politics, and race relations. Benjamin was a vocal critic of racial discrimination and went much further than most black leaders; instead of simply denouncing Jim Crow legislation, he urged blacks to defend themselves when attacked by whites. Such an outspoken attitude led to Benjamin's being forced to leave Brinkley, Arkansas, in 1879 and Birmingham in 1887. Irvine Garland Penn, author of *The Afro-American Press and Its Editors* (1891), said of Benjamin: "He is fearless in his editorial expression; and the fact that he is a negro does not lead him to withhold his opinions upon the live issues of the day, but to give them in a courageous manner."

In December 1892 Benjamin married Lula M. Robinson; they had a son and a daughter. The family settled in Lexington, Kentucky, in 1897. To the dismay of some whites, Benjamin quickly became involved in local politics. On 2 October 1900 he argued with Michael Moynahan, a Democratic precinct worker, over the white man's harassment of blacks who wished to register to vote. Late that evening Moynahan killed Benjamin. At the examining trial several days later Moynahan pleaded not guilty by reason of self-defense. The judge accepted Moynahan's claim and dismissed the case, even though Benjamin had been shot in the back.

Further Reading

A few letters written by Benjamin can be found in the Booker T. Washington Papers at the Library of Congress.

Simmons, William J. *Men of Mark: Eminent, Progressive, and Rising* (1887).

GEORGE C. WRIGHT

BEN JOCHANNAN, Yosef Alfredo Antonio (31 Dec. 1918–), historian, Egyptologist, educator, and Pan-Africanist, known popularly as "Dr. Ben," was born in Gondar, Ethiopia, the son of Krstan ben Jochannan, a lawyer and diplomat, and Tulia Matta, a native of Puerto Rico, who was a homemaker and midwife. Both parents were Jewish: his father was a member of a Jewish Ethiopian people then called the "Falasha," or Beta Israel, and his mother was descended from Spanish Sephardic Jews. The couple met in Madrid, Spain, where Matta was attending college and the elder ben Jochannan was a diplomatic attaché. Soon after their marriage, they traveled from Spain to Ethiopia where their son, Yosef, was born.

Ben Jochannan spent his earliest years in Ethiopia, but after age five he was raised in the Americas. He said in later interviews that, in the 1920s, the Ethiopian government sent his father to Brazil to help develop the coffee trade of that country. They lived for about a year in Rio de Janeiro before a 1928 coup in Ethiopia saw the overthrow of Empress Zauditu and the consolidation of power under Emperor Haile Selassie. After the change in political leadership, the family decided not to return to Ethiopia but instead settled permanently in Puerto Rico. Yosef was raised primarily in the town of Fajardo, located on the eastern side of Puerto Rico, and the nearby islands of St. Croix and St. Thomas, where Matta had additional relatives. He was thus fluent in both Spanish and English from an early age.

After secondary school on the island, ben Jochannan attended the University of Puerto Rico at Rio Piedras. He first studied law, but later switched to civil engineering, graduating with a bachelor of science degree in 1939. In his senior year of college ben Jochannan wrote and self-published a booklet titled *Nosotros los Hebreos Negros* (We the Black Hebrews) about his experience growing up black and Jewish on a predominately Catholic island where at the time people of African ancestry were commonly viewed as inferior (Gates and Appiah, *Africana*, 457). His father, a well-educated man fluent in several languages, spoke often with his son about the significance of Ethiopia's ancient past. However, at school and in the community, the young ben Jochannan frequently heard the view that Africa was a backward and wretched continent. Because of this, shortly after he graduated from the university, his father sent him to visit his grandparents in Ethiopia, where he stayed for several months. To get there, ben Jochannan traveled by ship to Egypt, then took a train through that country to Ethiopia, and thus, he said, began a lifelong fascination with Africa's 4,000-mile-long Nile Valley.

Upon his return to Puerto Rico, ben Jochannan worked briefly as a lawyer. But his prosecution of a criminal case against a friend of his father's soon brought him into conflict with his father who, after the man was convicted, asked him to leave the island. In 1941, he traveled to New York City where he initially stayed with his maternal uncle, CASPER HOLSTEIN, a self-made millionaire and philanthropist who had become rich from the Harlem "numbers racket." Holstein was one of the largest contributors to MARCUS GARVEY's Universal Negro Improvement Association, and was also politically active in his native Virgin Islands. Through his uncle, ben Jochannan gained a unique insight into the rich cultural milieu of black New York, including its lively street life, informal "numbers" lotteries, street-corner preachers, and politics. At the time, Harlem was an epicenter of African American activism in support of Ethiopia, which had been invaded and occupied by Italy under Benito Mussolini during World War II. Although the occupation ended the year he arrived in New York, ben Jochannan joined such affinity groups as the Ethiopian World Federation and African Nationals in America.

Ben Jochannan initially found work as a draftsman, but he was drawn to the study of Africa, especially its ancient history. Though his students and supporters later referred to him as "Dr. Ben," the precise trajectory of his formal education remains unclear, partly because of conflicting claims he made over the years in interviews and in published works. He claimed to have obtained a doctorate in Cultural Anthropology at the University of Havana (1940) and to have done doctoral research at the University of Barcelona in Spain (1941). Whatever his educational training may

have been, ben Jochannan began to speak on Harlem street corners, mostly about African history, taking part in a tradition of public speechmaking that was one of the neighborhood's unique attributes, joining such noteworthy contemporaries as Arthur Reid, Carlos Cooks, and Wentworth Matthew. He came to know several of Harlem's leading intellectuals and historians such as JOHN HENRIK CLARKE, J. A. ROGERS, John G. Jackson, and RICHARD B. MOORE, all of whom were members of the Harlem History Club. In 1947, he returned to Ethiopia, again spending a portion of the voyage in Egypt.

During the late 1940s, ben Jochannan met and befriended a young man known as "Detroit Red," who used to hustle on the corner below his Harlem office. Their friendship deepened after "Red" was arrested, joined the Nation of Islam in prison, and returned to Harlem as MALCOLM X, and it continued until Malcolm's assassination in 1965.

Through this early period of his life in the United States, ben Jochannan maintained the Jewish faith of his upbringing, attending Harlem's Commandment Keeper's Ethiopian Hebrew Congregation led by rabbi WENTWORTH A. MATTHEW, as well as other synagogues. But in New York, he continued to struggle, as he had in Puerto Rico, with the prevailing societal presumption that tended to question his identity as an African Jew; while, at the same time, his study of ancient Egyptian history and spiritual practices was having an ever increasing impact on his thinking. As he later wrote in several of his books, his differences with other Jews and his intense identification with the African American struggle eventually caused his "complete break with Western man's Talmudic Judaism" (*Africa: Mother of Western Civilization* [1971], 585).

In the 1950s, ben Jochannan worked as a researcher for UNESCO and with the Zanzibar mission to the United Nations, work that he continued to do until that country merged with Tanganyika to become Tanzania in 1961. During this period, ben Jochannan also began teaching as an adjunct professor in New York, mostly as a lecturer on African history at such schools as Marymount College at Tarrytown and at Columbia Teacher's College.

In 1957, ben Jochannan led a group of nine African American educators to Egypt because he wanted to show them evidence of his contention that sites such as Abu Simbel, the temple of Isis at Philae Island, and the royal tombs of the Valley of the Kings were the remains of ancient black civilizations. This trip was the first of dozens of similar tours that he led, sometimes twice a year, of scholars and ordinary citizens alike. These trips not only facilitated his own study and writing, but they came to be a major part of his legacy as a teacher. He estimated that he led several thousand African Americans to Egypt, Sudan, and Ethiopia over the next four decades.

In 1960, ben Jochannan self-published his first work produced in the United States, an early version of *Black Man of the Nile*, which he sold for $5 a copy at LEWIS MICHAUX's National Memorial African Bookstore on Lenox Avenue.

In 1961, he married Gertrude England, of St. Croix. The couple would go on to have nine daughters and three sons. They also adopted six other children. Throughout his career as a writer and teacher, ben Jochannan remained a fixture of the Harlem community where he raised his family. When Harlem was engulfed by several days of social unrest during the summer of 1964, after the police slaying of a local teenager, ben Jochannan was one of several Harlem activists who met with the New York mayors Robert Wagner and, later, John Lindsay to address systemic problems facing the black community in New York (*New York Times*, 19 Feb. 1966).

As a historian and anthropologist, ben Jochannan would return to the Nile Valley more than fifty times and self-publish forty-two books—mostly on African pre-history, the civilizations of Egypt, Sudan, and Ethiopia, and on religion. His work argued that the creators of ancient Egyptian civilization—the builders of the pyramids, the Sphinx, and cities and lodges—were black Africans who first migrated north from the Central Rift Valley of present-day Tanzania and Uganda. He claimed that mainstream publishers refused to publish his work, saying that there was not sufficient public interest in them and that the publishers had no way to fact-check his claims.

His self-published books were known for their tendentious tone and, perhaps, crude presentation that included newspaper clippings, hand-drawn maps, and an informal, idiosyncratic writing style. However, these shortcomings did not reflect a disregard for academic standards such as citation, footnotes, and bibliography, which he supplied extensively. His work drew criticism for its assertions about the role of blacks in Egyptian history and was dismissed for its slipshod editing. Despite this, ben Jochannan frequently said that he did not seek the approval of other scholars but deliberately chose to write in a manner that could be readily absorbed by both lay readers and researchers with little more than a middle-school education (Alexander, 9). He also steadfastly criticized the overall presentation of African history in American universities and museums.

In the late 1960s, ben Jochannan worked briefly as a writer for a New York publishing company, W.H. Sadlier, where he wrote textbooks on African history such as *Southern Lands* (1969). Beginning in 1973, he served as an adjunct professor of History and Egyptology at Cornell University's Africana Research Center, where his longtime friend and colleague John Henrik Clarke was teaching. He taught there for fifteen years, a period during which he also served as a visiting lecturer at the Faculty of Languages at Al Azhar University in Cairo, Egypt. In 1979, after another of his tours to Egypt, he traveled to the South Pacific where he lectured in Papua New Guinea about the native population's origins on the African continent. In 1984, he became one of six founding members of the Association for the Study of Classical African Civilization (ASCAC), an organization of black scholars focusing on the ancient African world. The other founders were John Henrik Clarke, Asa G. Hilliard III, Jacob H. Carruthers, Leonard Jeffries, and MAULANA KARENGA.

Ben Jochannan was a popular and sought-after lecturer on college campuses nationally and internationally, celebrated for his direct, polemical style and wit. This popularity also drew criticism as when, in 1993, Mary Lefkowitz, a Wellesley classics professor, mentioned him prominently in a Wall Street Journal editorial that fueled an acerbic national debate about "Afrocentrism" in academia (*Wall Street Journal*, 7 Apr. 1993).

Outside of academia, however, ben Jochannan's reputation remained high, particularly among many black laypeople. He could be frequently spotted around Harlem where residents greeted him warmly as "Dr. Ben!," regaled him with personal stories, and posed for photographs with him. A lifelong bibliophile, ben Jochannan had amassed a personal library of over 15,000 books chronicling African and African American history.

His other most widely circulated books are *African Origins of the Major "Western Religions"* (1970), *Africa: Mother of Western Civilization* (1971), and *Our Black Seminarians & Black Clergy without a Black Theology* (1978). Ben Jochannan was a key influence on a generation of students, historians, and educators such as Asa G. Hilliard III, MOLEFI ASANTE, Jacob H. Carruthers, and Maulana Karenga.

Further Reading

The Schomburg Center for Research in Black Culture's Hatch-Billops Collection includes an audio interview with Yosef ben Jochannan from 1972.

Ben Jochannan, Yosef A. A. *Africa: Mother of Western Civilization* (1988).

Alexander, E. Curtis. *Doc Ben Speaks Out* (interview; 1982).

JODY BENJAMIN

BENNETT, Gwendolyn (8 July 1902–30 May 1981), writer and artist, was born in Giddings, Texas, the daughter of Joshua Robin Bennett and Mayme F. Abernathy, teachers on an Indian reservation. In 1906 the family moved to Washington, D.C., where Gwendolyn's father studied law and her mother worked as a manicurist and hairdresser. When her parents divorced, her mother won custody, but her father kidnapped the seven-year-old Gwendolyn. The two, with Gwendolyn's stepmother, lived in hiding in various towns along the East Coast and in Pennsylvania before finally settling in New York.

At Brooklyn's Girls' High (1918–1921) Bennett participated in the drama and literary societies—the first African American to do so—and won first place in an art contest. She attended fine arts classes at Columbia University (1921) and the Pratt Institute, from which she graduated in 1924. While she was still an undergraduate, her poems "Nocturne" and

"Heritage" were published in *Crisis* (Nov. 1923) and *Opportunity* (Dec. 1923), respectively.

Bennett's poetry generally dealt with racial uplift and pride in her African heritage. "To Usward," published in both *Opportunity* and *Crisis* in May 1924, was a tribute to the new generation and a call to those who have "a song to sing." She also produced symbolist-inspired and romantic lyrics, such as "Quatrains" (1927). It expressed the tension Bennett experienced, torn between art and literature:

Brushes and paints are all I have
To speak the music in my soul
While silently there laughs at me
A copper jar beside a pale green bowl.

Over the next nine years, twenty-two of Bennett's poems appeared in *Opportunity, Crisis, Palms,* and *Gypsy.* Additional poems were published in WILLIAM STANLEY BEAUMONT BRAITHWAITE's *Anthology of Magazine Verse for 1927 and Yearbook of American Poetry* (1927), COUNTÉE CULLEN's *Caroling Dusk* (1927), and JAMES WELDON JOHNSON's *The Book of American Negro Poetry* (1931).

Bennett also created cover illustrations for *Crisis* in December 1923 and March 1924; the latter, *Pipes of Pan,* was a line drawing of a young African American man listening to music produced by nymphs and satyrs. Her covers for *Opportunity* appeared in January and July 1926 and December 1930. She also produced oil landscapes, but she rarely exhibited her work publicly.

In 1924 Bennett began teaching design, watercolor, and crafts at Howard University in Washington, D.C., and was reunited with her mother. The following year, on a $1,000 Delta Sigma Theta sorority fellowship, she studied art in Paris at the Académies de la Grande Chaumière, Julian, and Colarossi and at the École du Panthéon. She published two short stories, "Wedding Day," published in *Fire!!* (1926), and "Tokens," published in CHARLES SPURGEON JOHNSON's *Ebony and Topaz: A Collectanea* (1927). Both express the isolation and loneliness she experienced in Paris and feature African American expatriates who remained in France after serving in World War I.

After Bennett returned to Washington, D.C., in 1926, her father died, and she lost most of the paintings and batiks she had produced abroad in a fire in her stepmother's home. She then spent two years (1927–1928) writing "The Ebony Flute," a "literary and social chit-chat" column for *Opportunity,* for which she had also written book reviews. During the summer of 1927 she taught art classes at Nashville's Tennessee Agricultural and Industrial State College. The same year she served as editor for the magazine *Black Opals.*

In 1928 Bennett received a scholarship to study art at the Barnes Foundation in Merion, Pennsylvania. That year she married Alfred Jackson and moved to Eustis, Florida, where her husband had a medical practice. Unhappy in the segregated South, Bennett gained sixty pounds in four years and wrote little. The couple moved to Hempstead, Long Island, in 1932, and Bennett took a job with the Department of Information and Education of the Welfare Council of New York writing feature articles that appeared in the *Amsterdam News,* the *New York Age,* the *Baltimore Afro-American,* and *Better Times.*

After Jackson died in 1936, Bennett lived alternately with her stepmother and with the sculptor AUGUSTA SAVAGE in New York. She worked as a teacher, then as a project supervisor in the Federal Art Teaching Project. When Savage resigned as director of the Harlem Community Art Center, a Federal Art Project endeavor, in 1939, Bennett took that position. She was also active in the Harlem Artists Guild, the National Negro Congress, the Artists Union, the Negro People's Theater, and the Negro Playwright's Company, serving on the board of directors of the last.

In 1941 Bennett gave a series of lectures on African American arts at the School for Democracy; she also married a white Harvard graduate and fellow teacher, Richard Crosscup. Three years later Bennett was suspended from the Harlem Community Art Center by the House Un-American Activities Committee (HUAC) for her leftist sympathies. She then cofounded and directed the George Carver Community School, an adult education center for African Americans in Harlem. HUAC investigated the school, and it closed in 1947. From the end of the 1940s until the late 1960s, Bennett worked for the Consumers Union as a correspondent.

Upon their retirement in 1968, Bennett and her husband moved to Kutztown, Pennsylvania, and opened an antique store. Bennett died of congestive heart failure in Reading, Pennsylvania. Although she was a minor writer and artist, Bennett contributed significantly to the New Negro movement with her editing, teaching, and leadership, aiding the careers of such better-known colleagues as AARON DOUGLAS, LANGSTON HUGHES, and Cullen.

Further Reading
Bennett's papers are in the Schomburg Center for Research in Black Culture and History at the New York Public Library.

Govan, Sandra. "After the Renaissance: Gwendolyn Bennett and the WPA Years," *MidAtlantic Writers Association* 3 (Dec. 1988).

Primeau, Ronald. "Frank Horne and the Second Echelon Poets of the Harlem Renaissance," in *The Harlem Renaissance Remembered,* ed. Arna Bontemps (1972).

THERESA LEININGER-MILLER

BENNETT, Hal (21 Apr. 1930–8 Sept. 2004), writer and journalist, was born George Harold Bennett in Buckingham, Virginia, the seventh of eight children born to Charles E. Bennett Sr. and Minnie P. (Bryant) Bennett, of whom little else is known. His family moved north to Orange, New Jersey, during the Great Migration, though he often spent his childhood summers in Buckingham. At age sixteen, Bennett worked part time as a features writer for the

Newark (N.J.) Herald News. He attended Orange High School, graduating as class valedictorian, and had dreams of becoming a concert pianist.

After high school Bennett joined the air force and was stationed in Korea, where he was a writer for the Public Information Division and an editor for a military newspaper. When he was discharged in 1952, he continued his journalism career as the fiction editor for *African American News* in Baltimore, Maryland, and then became a partner in an unsuccessful newspaper in Westbury, Long Island.

Later, ill from ulcers and wanting to use his G.I. Bill, he left for Mexico to attend Mexico City College. He received two grants from the Centro Mexicano de Escritores (The Mexican Writer's Center) and was helped by the writer Margaret Shedd, who was director of the Writer's Center at Mexico City College. In 1961 he published a book of poetry, *The Mexico City Poems/House on Hay Street.*

In 1966, at age thirty-six, Bennett published his first novel, *A Wilderness of Vines,* written, according to him, with the constant strains of Beethoven's *Ninth Symphony* in his mind. This first novel won him a fellowship at the Bread Loaf Writer's Conference in Vermont during the summer of 1966. Over the next ten years he would publish a total of five novels and many short stories. The novels, besides *A Wilderness of Vines,* include *The Black Wine* (1968), *Lord of Dark Places* (1970), *Wait until the Evening* (1974), and *Seventh Heaven* (1976).

The major settings for these novels and stories were the fictional towns of Burnside, Virginia (Buckingham), and Cousinville, New Jersey (a combination of Newark and Orange). Bennett's fiction traced the migration of blacks from the rural South to the urban North and ranged in time from 1919 until Watergate in 1972, though his was not naturalistic or sociological literature. His characters were often macabre: preachers who glorify sexuality, a mad and vindictive teenager, a grandmother who kills her husband, a son who plots to kill his father, and a father who kills his baby. While it was a literature that dealt with and revealed the traumas of black life, it did so in subversive, irreverent ways. Most often Bennett's work was described as satire; he zeroed in on the disparity between what was and what should be without sparing anyone. For instance, in *Wilderness of Vines* he mocked the racism that existed among blacks based on their degrees of blackness.

Sometimes Bennett was compared to William Faulkner (he himself said that his influences included Southern Gothic writers like Eudora Welty, Carson McCullers, and Harper Lee, as well as Faulkner) in that he created a mythological landscape and that many of his characters reappeared in numerous stories. In 1973 he won the Faulkner Award for fiction. But he could be more outrageous and more profane than Faulkner or any of the other Southern Gothic writers. Critics, including his former teacher Margaret Shedd, sometimes faulted Bennett for being too sexually explicit. In speaking of his own literary technique, he stated, "I think there are times when we need to distort in order to see reality" (Newman, 368).

In 1977 Bennett published *Insanity Runs in Our Family,* a collection of his short stories. One of these stories, "Dotson Gerber Resurrected," which had first appeared in a 1970 issue of *Playboy,* had won him the accolade as that year's most promising young writer in the same magazine. It was also republished in the 1971 edition of *Best American Short Stories.*

In 1979 Bennett's novel-writing took a radical turn. Responding to what he said was a remark he had heard, that black writers were only capable of writing about their own pain, he decided to write popular fiction under pseudonyms to prove that he could imagine anything and write like anybody he wanted to. His first attempt, under the name Harriet Janeway, was a woman's romance novel titled *This Passionate Land.*

During the 1980s Bennett spent a good deal of time in San Miguel de Allende, Mexico, and began writing a series of men's adventure novels, sometimes two a year. No doubt this made him some money, but it also made his point. The series (titled the Justin Perry Series), was written under the name John D. Revere, and began in 1983 with *The Assassin.* It was followed by *Vatican Kill* (1983), *Born to Kill* (1984), *Death's Running Mate* (1985), and *Stud Service* (1985).

Bennett also continued to write literary short stories. He wrote "The Salamander Kind" in 1984 for *Callaloo* literary magazine and won the Callaloo Award for Fiction for the story. He also wrote "Miss Askew on Ice" in 1987 for *Callaloo,* "Chewing Gum" for *Black American Literature Forum* (1987), and "Wings of the Dove" (1989) also for *Black American Literature Forum.*

In a 1987 interview, Bennett said that he was working on a new literary novel, *The Bank Walkers,* as well as a new collection of short stories. Neither ever appeared. Bennett died in the Menlo Park Veterans Home in Edison, New Jersey.

Further Reading

Newman, Katherine. "An Evening with Hal Bennett: An Interview," *Black American Literature Forum* (Winter 1987).

Walcott, Ronald. "Hal Bennett," in *Dictionary of Literary Biography,* volume 33: *Afro-American Fiction Writers after 1955* (1984).

WILLIAM P. TOTH

BENNETT, Lerone, Jr. (17 Oct. 1928–), journalist, editor, and social historian, was born in Clarksdale, Mississippi, to Lerone Bennett Sr., a chauffeur, and Alma Reed Bennett, a restaurant cook. Bennett's family later moved to Jackson, Mississippi, where Bennett went to public school. He was born into a family that emphasized the importance of education; his grandmother made college obtainable for each of her thirteen children, and it was expected that Bennett would have that option, too. Surprisingly, he failed his first year of formal schooling. With her son at her side, his mother confronted the principal and the teacher before deciding to enroll her son in a better school. This experience helped Bennett understand that education is an accessible and necessary tool needed to combat racism. An avid reader, he was inspired by his teachers, particularly Mrs. M. D. Manning, to develop an interest in history.

While in his early years he also became interested in journalism, reportedly writing his first article at age eleven. He observed how employees worked at both the *Jackson Advocate* and the *Mississippi Enterprise*, black newspapers in Jackson, where he eventually became a gofer and newsboy. Bennett once said,

Before I was ten, I fell in love with the word. I believed the word was one of the few weapons available to save my life and my people's lives. (Dawkins, 13)

During his teen years Bennett played clarinet and saxophone and edited his high school's yearbook and newspaper. After he graduated from Lenier High School in Jackson, he entered the historically black Morehouse College in Atlanta, Georgia. While there, he edited the school newspaper and found his professors, as well as the president of Morehouse, Dr. BEN-JAMIN MAYS, particularly inspiring and influential. In 1949 he graduated Phi Beta Kappa with a bachelor's degree in Journalism. He enrolled in graduate school at Atlanta University that same year. Once interested in pursuing a career in law, he worked as a reporter for the *Atlanta Daily World* newspaper, one of the oldest black-owned papers in Atlanta, from 1949 to 1952. In 1952 he became the paper's city editor.

The following year he met JOHN H. JOHNSON, who in 1945 had founded *Ebony* magazine. Johnson was interested in attracting the best professionals in the publishing industry to his publishing company. He chose Bennett in 1953 to work as an associate editor at *Jet* magazine. This was a major turning point for Bennett, beginning an alliance with Johnson's company that would span over fifty years. In 1954 Bennett became an associate editor at *Ebony*. Two years later he married Gloria Sylvester, and the couple had four children, including one set of twins. Bennett became *Ebony* magazine's first senior editor in 1958. He also was a visiting professor of history at Northwestern University from 1968 to 1969 and a senior fellow of the Institute of the Black World in 1969.

Bennett's first book, *Before the Mayflower: A History of Black America, 1619–1962*, based on articles written for *Ebony* in 1959, helped launch the book division of John H. Johnson's publishing house. Though the book did not garner immediate success, it eventually sold over one million copies and, from its 1962 publication, was revised and updated. *Before the Mayflower*'s companion volume, *The Shaping of Black America: The Struggles and Triumphs of African-Americans, 1619 to the 1990s*, was published in 1975. It had two sections: "Foundations," which focused on the early stages of America's development, including the arrival of Africans in 1619, and "Directions," an exploration of black labor and capital. In 1964 *What Manner of Man: A Biography of Martin Luther King,*

Jr. 1929–1968 was published. That same year, Dr. MARTIN LUTHER KING JR., who had graduated from Morehouse a year before Bennett, won the Nobel Peace Prize, and in 1965 the Society of Midland Authors recognized Bennett's publication with the Patron Saints Award. The book focused on King's life from his birth in Atlanta, through his rise as a civil rights leader, until 1964, when he was named "Man of the Year" by *Time* magazine.

Bennett's other publications include *The Negro Mood, and Other Essays* (1964); *Confrontation: Black and White* (1965); *Black Power U.S.A.: The Human Side of Reconstruction, 1867–1877* (1967); *Pioneers in Protest* (1968); *The Challenge of Blackness* (1972); and *Wade in the Water: Great Moments in Black History* (1979). Bennett also co-wrote *Succeeding against the Odds* (1993), an autobiography of the publisher and entrepreneur John H. Johnson. His most controversial work, *Forced into Glory: Abraham Lincoln's White Dream* (2000), developed from an equally controversial essay in a 1968 issue of *Ebony*, "Was Abe Lincoln a White Supremacist?" Both works investigated the myths that surrounded Lincoln's participation in the demise of slavery. Bennett is often regarded as fair in his criticism of depictions of historical people and events. In 2003 he spoke out against offensive comments made about ROSA PARKS in the box-office hit *Barbershop* (2002). Using the pages of *Ebony* magazine, he told a more accurate story of the civil rights movement and Parks's participation in it.

Bennett also published fiction and poetry in a number of books, magazines, and journals. In 1987 he became executive editor of *Ebony*. He considered retiring from the position in 2003 after fifty years of working as a journalist, but decided against it when Johnson, chairman of *Ebony*, and LINDA JOHNSON RICE, the magazine's president and CEO, asked him not to retire.

Among Bennett's numerous awards and honors include the Literature Award of the American Academy of Arts and Letters in 1978, the Salute to Greatness Award for his contributions to civil rights efforts in 1996, the American Book Award's Lifetime Achievement Award in 2002, the CARTER G. WOODSON Lifetime Achievement Award in 2003, as well as numerous honorary doctorate degrees. After retiring in 2005, Bennett became executive editor emeritus, devoting most of his time to lecturing and working on several books.

Further Reading

Abbott, Dorothy. *Mississippi Writers: Reflections of Childhood and Youth* (1985).
Dawkins, Wayne. "Black America's Popular Historian," in *Black Issues Book Review*, (Jan./Feb. 2004).

KAAVONIA HINTON

BENNETT, Louise (7 Sept. 1919–26 July 2006), poet, short story writer, mythologist, and folklorist, was born in Kingston, Jamaica, to Cornelius A. Bennett, a baker, and Kerene Robinson Bennett, a seamstress. Bennett's father died when she was just seven years old, leaving her mother to support the family. Bennett received a typical colonial education at St. Simon's College (1933–1936) and Excelsior High School (1936–1938), which greatly influenced her later interest in elevating and legitimizing traditional Jamaican culture. Though in high school Bennett began writing poetry in English, she later switched to writing in West Indian English, which linguists would eventually come to recognize as a language rather than just a dialect.

Bennett also began performing versions of her poems to audiences in high school and her success caught the attention of Eric Coverley, who would later become Bennett's husband. Coverley, a draftsman and impresario, organized a popular Christmas concert in Jamaica at which Bennett made her professional debut in 1938. In 1940 Bennett published her first book of poetry, *Dialect Verses*. She also studied journalism in the late 1930s and began to do social work in 1943. Her volume *Jamaican Dialect Verses* was published in 1942, her work *Jamaican Humour in Dialect* in 1943, and her *Anancy Stories and Poems in Dialect* in 1944.

In recognition of her artistic abilities Bennett received a British Council scholarship to attend the Royal Academy of Dramatic Art in London and left for England in 1945. While there she worked for the BBC and had a weekly variety show called *Caribbean Carnival* (1945–1946) and a later show called *West Indian Guest Night* (1950–1953). Bennett moved to the United States in 1953, spending two years in New York, New Jersey, and Connecticut pursuing a career in radio and acting, performing at St. Martin's Little Theater in Harlem, singing folk songs at the Village Vanguard in Greenwich Village, and directing the folk musical *Day in Jamaica* with Coverley. Bennett and Coverley married on 30 May 1954, and the couple returned to Jamaica that same year.

Bennett worked for the Jamaica Social Welfare Commission as a drama officer from 1955 to 1959 and as director from 1959 to 1963, this latter position affording her the opportunity to travel around the island and further study Jamaican myth and folklore. During these years she produced several recordings, including *Jamaican Folk Songs* (1954), *Jamaican Singing Games* (1954), *Children's Jamaican Songs and Games* (1957), and *West Indies Festival of Arts* (1958). Bennett also served as a lecturer at the University of the West Indies in Kingston from 1955 to 1969, where she taught drama and Jamaican folklore.

After 1963 Bennett was a frequent performer on radio, television, and the stage, and from 1970 to 1982 she hosted a weekly children's television show called *Ring Ding*, through which she hoped to pass down Jamaican folklore to the young people of the island and to instill in them a sense of pride in their culture and history. The story of Brer Anancy, the African spider hero of many Jamaican folk tales, was a frequent feature of the show and Bennett also featured Anancy in many of her own publications, including *Anancy and Miss Lou* (1979).

Bennett's *Selected Poems* appeared in 1982 and went on to become one of her most popular works. Her poems often took the form of the ballad quatrain and while this form did give her poetry some structure on the page, the underlying orality of her work remained its most distinctive feature—her poems were meant to be heard. She made use of repetition and sharp images and often alluded to a variety of literary sources, from English literature to Jamaican folk songs. Constant throughout all her work, however, was the value she placed on traditional Jamaican culture and language.

Although Bennett was primarily thought of as a performer and an entertainer, as she stated in a 1968 interview, "I did start to write before I started to perform!" She lamented, "I have been set apart by other creative writers a long time ago because of the language I speak and work in. From the beginning nobody ever recognised me as a writer. . . . Up to now a lot of people don't even think I write. They say, 'Oh, you just stand up and say these things!'" She continued, "My work does lend itself so much to performance because it is oral in its tradition, legendary. People are not as accustomed to reading the dialect as they are to listening to it, and I found it a wonderful medium for the stage" (Scott, 98).

As one of the first West Indian poets to make extensive use of dialect and one of the leading Jamaican folklorists, Bennett had an undeniable influence on Caribbean poetry. As the critic Mervyn Morris noted, "In the final analysis, what most strongly recommends the work of Louise Bennett is not the sanity and generosity implicit in her creations, nor her steady and determined promotion of things Jamaican, but the fact that, for the last 40 years, her uncommon talent has been, for many people, a considerable source of pleasure" (Morris, xix). And, in Bennett's own words, "I think I speak to all Jamaica" (Scott, 100).

Bennett and Coverley lived their final years in Canada, where she nursed her husband through years of ill health until he died at age ninety-one. Bennett herself died in Toronto, survived by her stepson, Fabian Coverley, and three step-grandsons.

Further Reading
Hoenisch, Michael E. "Louise Bennett," *Dictionary of Literary Biography*, vol. 117 (1992).
"Louise (Simone) Bennett." *Contemporary Authors Online* (2003).
Morris, Mervyn. Introduction to *Selected Poems* by Louise Bennett (1987).
Rickards, Colin. "Bennett, (Simone) Louise," *Contemporary Poets*, 6th ed. (1996).
Scott, Dennis. "Bennett on Bennett," *Caribbean Quarterly* 14, no. 1–2 (1968).

Obituary: *New York Times*, 29 July 2006.
MALINDA WILLIAMS

BENSON, Al (30 June 1908–6 Sept. 1978), disc jockey, impresario, and businessman, was born Arthur Bernard Leaner in Jackson, Mississippi. An ambitious young man, Benson sang with the family band, performed in black vaudeville, and produced shows at Jackson's black theater, the Alamo. He also attended Jackson Normal College. In the 1920s he moved to Chicago but returned to Jackson to weather the Great Depression. As the pains of the Depression eased, Benson moved back to Chicago, where he worked as a probation officer, a railroad cook, an interviewer for the Works Progress Administration (WPA), and a preacher before making his name as one of Chicago's leading radio personalities. He lived in Chicago with his wife, Norma, and their daughters, Arleta and Bertina, until he retired in 1967.

Benson began his radio career as Reverend Arthur Leaner, hosting a fifteen-minute Sunday morning broadcast from his storefront church on Chicago's South Side. When station owners objected to his selling of advertising on his religious broadcasts, Reverend Leaner adopted the name Al Benson and became a commercial disc jockey. By 1948 he was broadcasting ten hours a day on WGES, WAAF, and WJJD in Chicago. As Charles Walton relates in "Al Benson: The Godfather of Chicago Black Radio," it wasn't long before people across the city were tuning in to hear him say, "Good afternoon, ladies and gentlemen, this is your Old Swingmaster Al Benson bringing you sixty minutes of red hot, beat me down, swing tunes of the day, and that's for sure" (Walton, 1).

Benson became a disc jockey at a time when few blacks were heard on the radio. Since most owners and announcers were white and most radio content was directed at whites, the representations of African Americans heard on the radio often perpetuated the kinds of racist stereotypes popularized by blackface minstrelsy. One of the most popular shows of early radio was *The Amos 'n' Andy Show* in which the white entertainers Freeman Gosden and Charles Correll caricatured black dialect and culture with their contemporary reincarnation of Zip Coon, nineteenth-century minstrelsy's urban huckster, and Jim Crow, his country simpleton partner. Early African American radio announcers like Jack Cooper and Eddie Honesty challenged the stereotypes of Amos and Andy: they embraced middle class manners and propriety in their speech and musical choices and rejected black dialect and rural working class music like the blues. While this strategy countered prevailing stereotypes and opened doors for a few black announcers, it did not speak to the rapidly growing number of working-class African Americans migrating to Chicago from the rural South. Benson's mix of urban blues and down-home talk did. By 1948 a *Chicago Tribune* poll had voted him the most popular disc jockey in the city and in 1949 the *Chicago Defender* appointed him honorary mayor of Bronzeville, the thriving African American district of Chicago. At this time DJs were independent contractors who bought airtime from stations. As his popularity grew Benson was buying more airtime than he could cover by himself, and he employed numerous "satellite" disc jockeys, many of whom, like Big Bill Hill and Purvis Spann, also went on to successful careers in radio.

Benson did not appeal just to Chicago's new immigrants: he also appealed to advertisers. DJs made most of their money endorsing products, and Benson was a consummate pitchman. He was also one of the first to show that African Americans provided an important market. In his prime he counted many local businesses among his clients, along with Budweiser, Coca-Cola, Ace Beer, and California Swiss Colony Wine. His patronage and on-air commentary could make or break a nightclub, and his influence granted him—and consequently other blacks—entrée to previously segregated establishments.

Though best known as a radio personality, Benson also worked in Chicago's live music and recording industries. He hosted weekly rhythm and blues concerts at Chicago's Regal Theatre, often presiding in brightly colored custom suits. His recording career started in 1948 when he cut several tracks at the Pershing Hotel, followed shortly by recordings of the Benson All-Star Orchestra. He went on to start three record labels: Old Swing-Master, Parrot, and Blue Lake. The short-lived Old Swing-Master label that Benson started with Egmont Sonderling issued mostly jazz and rhythm and blues recordings acquired from defunct local labels like Rhumboogie and Planet. The Parrot and Blue Lake labels were started several years later and featured jazz, gospel, blues, and rhythm and blues. Many of Benson's musicians were unknowns, but he also worked with famous and soon-to-be-famous artists like COLEMAN HAWKINS, AHMAD JAMAL, ALBERT KING, and JIMMY RUSHING. Benson's involvement in radio and recording led to claims that he was plugging his own recordings unfairly. Though Benson always maintained that he simply played records that he liked, he had the power to make a record a hit simply by playing it on his show. And it was not uncommon for recording companies to own radio stations that served as outlets for their products. Indeed, the relationships between independent record labels and small radio stations made it possible for many black musicians to find a place on the airwaves.

Benson's power, wealth, and prestige also afforded him many opportunities to advance the cause of civil rights. Besides making the sounds of African American speech and music acceptable on the radio, he frequently editorialized in favor of the civil rights movement. He also brought many African Americans into the broadcasting industry. In a particularly memorable gesture, he hired an airplane to drop copies of the U.S. Constitution on the Mississippi State Capitol on the eve of the 1956 presidential election "to wake up the citizens of Mississippi" (Spaulding, 81).

But by the late 1950s radio was experiencing major changes and Benson's influence began to fade. The sounds of the Old Swingmaster were being supplanted by new forms of African American music and popular culture—forms of expression that entered radio through the door Benson had opened. Benson's down-home patter began to sound old-fashioned in comparison to the more urban and sophisticated approaches of disc jockeys like Oscar Brown Jr. and Roy Wood, and younger audiences preferred the sounds of soul singers like Jerry Butler to the blues records that Benson played. Shakeups also rocked the industry, especially after revelations that record companies had been paying disc jockeys to play their records. While not illegal, the resulting payola scandal led to a loss of power for DJs. Stations switched to prescribed music formats, placing programming choices in the hands of executives and station managers. Advertising solicitation also shifted from DJs to station managers. Consequently the business opportunities that allowed Benson to become a millionaire all but disappeared. By the late 1960s the post–World War II immigrants Benson had spoken to and for were retiring and their children were creating new forms of music and radio. In 1967, facing declining health and diminishing popularity, he left broadcasting. After a brief return to preaching he and his wife retired to Michigan where he succumbed to pneumonia, leaving others like his daughter Arleta to continue the tradition of black radio, a tradition he helped to invent.

Further Reading

Barlow, William. *Voice Over: The Making Of Black Radio* (1999).

Spaulding, Norman. *History of Black Oriented Radio in Chicago, 1929–1963*. Ph.D. thesis, University of Illinois at Urbana (1981).

Walton, Charles. "Al Benson: The Godfather of Chicago Black Radio." Available online at www.jazzinchicago. org/Internal/ Articles/tabid/43/ctl/ArticleView/mid/ 522/ articleId/ 81/AlBensonTheGodfatherofChicago BlackRadio. aspx.

Williams, Gilbert A. *Legendary Pioneers of Black Radio* (1998).

Obituaries: *Chicago Sun-Times*, 8 Sept. 1978; *Jet*, 28 Sept. 1978.

JOHN HARRIS-BEHLING

BENTLEY, Gladys (12 Aug. 1907–18 Jan. 1960), blues singer and pianist, was born Gladys Alberta Bentley in Philadelphia, Pennsylvania, the eldest of four children of George L. Bentley and Mary C. Mote, a native of Trinidad. The Bentley family was very poor. Later a lesbian, Bentley acknowledged that even as a child she felt more comfortable in boys' clothing than in girls' clothing; however, it was when Bentley developed a long-term crush on one of her female schoolteachers that her classmates began to ridicule her and her parents began to take Bentley from doctor to doctor in an effort to "fix" her. Finally at age sixteen Bentley left Philadelphia and traveled to Harlem, New York, where she quickly became immersed in the Harlem Renaissance and its "don't ask, don't tell" attitude about sexuality. Bentley became just one of many homosexual or bisexual celebrities, joining the likes of LANGSTON HUGHES, ETHEL WATERS, BESSIE SMITH, and MA RAINEY. Though Bessie Smith may have been the "Queen of the Blues," Bentley was known as the "Brown Bomber of Sophisticated Songs."

In Harlem, Bentley found acceptance among the participants in the "sporting life," which favored gambling, rent parties, female impersonators, sex shows, drugs, and alcohol. She began performing at the sporting life events, quickly becoming extremely popular. It was not uncommon to find Bentley, a talented pianist, playing and singing all night long at a piano. Writing to COUNTÉE CULLEN, a friend said of Bentley, "When Gladys sings '*St. James Infirmary*,' it makes you weep your heart out" (Duberman, 324).

Bentley's first major job was at the Mad House, which later became Barbara's Exclusive Club. Starting at thirty-five dollars a week, Bentley soon received a hundred dollars a week when Carl Van Vechten and others began crowding into the clubs to see her perform. As Bentley's popularity increased, she moved on to clubs such as the Cotton Club, Connie's Inn, and the Clam House. Weighing anywhere from two hundred and fifty to three hundred pounds she dressed in a tuxedo with tails and top hat, and her manly style of dress quickly became a feature of her shows. She was even more famous for her raunchy lyrics, full of sexual innuendos that she interpolated into the popular songs of the day. Bentley was so convincing as a man that the artist ROMARE BEARDEN thought that she was a female impersonator. In fact, she did sometimes perform under the name "Bobby Minton." Bentley was one of the few openly lesbian performers, flirting outrageously with the women in her audiences.

In 1928 Bentley began recording for Okeh Records, eventually making a total of eight records. Some of her more famous songs include "How Long, How Long Blues," "Worried Blues," "How Much Can I Stand?" and "Moanful Wailin' Blues." Bentley was at the height of her popularity during the 1920s and 1930s. In 1931 she was celebrated in Blair Nile's novel *Strange Brother*, being the basis of the character Sybil. Carl Van Vechten's book *Parties* and Clement Woods's book *Deep River* were reported to have characters based on the larger-than-life Gladys Bentley (Faderman, 1991). It was also in the early 1930s that Bentley married her white female lover in a much-publicized civil ceremony in New Jersey.

Advantages of the show business lifestyle for lesbians was the ability to earn a decent living, limit contact with men, and work within a predominantly female social world. During the early 1930s Bentley moved on to the New York jazz scene, performing primarily at the Ubangi Club on Fifty-second Street. By the late 1930s the Depression and Harlem's loss of fashionable status became contributing factors in her decision to move to California. There she lived with and cared for her elderly mother and sang at such gay clubs as Hollywood's Rose Room, Mona's in San Francisco, and Joaquin's El Rancho in Los Angeles. She began experiencing problems with the police while at Joaquin's El Rancho and at Mona's in early 1940. The clubs were required to obtain special permits that allowed Bentley to perform her act in men's clothing instead of women's clothing (*Gay and Lesbian Biography*, 1997). By the 1950s and the

McCarthy era, Bentley was forced to perform in women's clothing and came under the scrutiny of the U.S. House Committee on Un-American Activities because of her same-sex marriage in New Jersey.

In 1945 Bentley made five recordings for the Excelsior label, including *Thrill Me till I Get My Fill*, *Find Out What He Likes*, and *Notoriety Papa*. She also worked with the Washboard Serenaders on the Victor label. In a 1952 interview with *Ebony* magazine, Bentley claimed to have overcome her lesbianism through the ingestion of female hormones and announced that she was happily married to a male newspaper columnist named J. T. Gibson. When interviewed, Gibson denied that a wedding had taken place. Bentley was married for a brief time to a cook named Charles Roberts. Bentley was forty-five and Roberts twenty-nine; on the marriage certificate she stated that she was thirty-five.

During the 1950s Bentley performed twice on Groucho Marx's live television show *You Bet Your Life*. Bentley also recorded a record for the Flame label. It was at this time that she became an active member in a Hollywood church called the Temple of Love in Christ. In the late 1950s Bentley began to study to become a minister, but she died during an influenza epidemic before she was able to become ordained. In 1992 Rosetta Records, a small feminist label, reissued five of Bentley's songs on a disc titled *Mean Mothers: Independent Women Blues, Volume 1*. In 2004 Sony Music released a DVD set titled *You Bet Your Life: The Best Episodes*, which includes a 1958 performance of Bentley singing "Them There Eyes."

Further Reading

Duberman, Martin Bauml. *Hidden from the History: Reclaiming the Gay and Lesbian Past* (1989).

Faderman, Lillian. *Odd Girls and Twilight Lovers: A History of Lesbian Life in Twentieth-century America* (1991).

Rodger, Gillian. *GLBTQ: An Encyclopedia of Gay, Lesbian, Bisexual, Transgender & Queer Culture* (2002), also available online at http://www.glbtq.com.

Tyrkus, Michael, ed. "Gladys Bentley (1907–1960): Classic Blues Singer," *St. James Press Gay and Lesbian Biography* (1997).

ANNE K. DRISCOLL

BERNHARDT, Clyde (11 July 1905–20 May 1986), jazz trombonist and singer, was born Clyde Edric Barnhardt in Gold Hill, North Carolina, the son of Washington Michael Barnhardt, a miner, and Elizabeth Mauney. When Clyde was a child, he added Barron to his name because his grandmother in slavery had been lent to a family named Barron who treated her kindly. He changed the spelling of his surname in 1930 on the advice of a psychic. Thus his full name became Clyde Edric Barron Bernhardt or Clyde E. B. Bernhardt.

In 1912, after his father suffered a heart attack and left mining, Bernhardt helped to peddle goods from a wagon. The family moved to New Hope (later absorbed into Badin), North Carolina, and in 1915 his father died. Bernhardt attended school for three months each year while holding various jobs, including work at Alcoa Aluminum in 1918. The following year his mother took the family to Harrisburg, Pennsylvania, and then to Steeltown, Pennsylvania. Bernhardt returned to Badin in November 1919 with the intent of resuming work at Alcoa, but instead he secured a better job, becoming a messenger boy for Western Union. After rejoining his mother and siblings in Steeltown in April 1921, he quit school, having reached eighth grade. He held various jobs over the next several years.

Although Bernhardt had been attracted to music in his preschool years, only in 1922 did he purchase a trombone and begin serious studies with teachers in Pennsylvania and Ohio, when his mother relocated the family and he moved out on his own. By 1925 he was working professionally, and in 1928, after affiliations with several little-known bandleaders, Bernhardt joined the Whitman Sisters—Alice Whitman and her sisters Essie, Mable, and Alberta—in their show in Harlem and toured with them until June 1929. In March 1931 he joined the cornetist KING OLIVER's band, touring for eight months. With Oliver's encouragement Bernhardt began doubling as a blues singer. In 1931 he thought that he had married a woman named Barbara, known as "Bobby" (maiden name unknown), only to discover a few months later that she was already married. He never attempted marriage again.

Bernhardt joined Marion Hardy's Alabamians in New York City in November 1931. He worked with Billy Fowler's band from September 1932 to April 1933, a gig that included jobs accompanying the pianist and singer FATS WALLER. Bernhardt was a member of Vernon Andrade's dance orchestra from 1934 to 1937, and in September 1934 he made his first recordings, "Ain't It Nice?" and "Functionizin'," with Alex Hill's band. As a member of the pianist Edgar Hayes's big band from February 1937, Bernhardt performed in Europe in 1938 and made annual tours accompanying the dancer BILL ROBINSON; he also worked with the pianist HORACE HENDERSON's big band in 1941.

After leaving Hayes, Bernhardt toured briefly with Waller's big band, but he was bored by the lack of challenging parts or solos. In September 1942 he joined the pianist JAY MCSHANN's big band, touring until July 1943. He played in the tenor saxophonist Cecil Scott's band at the Ubangi Club in New York City for five months. In 1944 he joined the orchestra of the pianist LUIS RUSSELL, who featured Bernhardt as a singer, most notably in well-received performances at the Apollo Theater in Harlem. Bernhardt suffered from bronchitis and was obliged to quit Russell's band in October. For the remainder of 1944 he worked with the pianist CLAUDE HOPKINS's band at the Club Zanzibar in New York. He joined the Bascomb Brothers' orchestra in 1945, and he spent the first four months of 1946 with Scott again.

From 1946 to 1948 Bernhardt for the first time led his own group, the Blue Blazers. He rejoined Russell from 1948 to 1951 while also working with other bands. In 1952 he began recording under the pseudonym Ed Barron, and he had a hit rhythm and blues song with his own "Cracklin' Bread," but he was cheated out of royalties by the record company. From 1952 to 1970 he played in Joe Garland's dance orchestra. During the course of this lengthy affiliation he resumed day work and general studies. He passed the high school equivalency examination in 1963 and then took a job as a custodian in Newark, New Jersey.

Interest in Bernhardt's musical activities was rekindled by a series of articles published by Derrick Stewart-Baxter in 1967 and 1968 and by a recording that Stewart-Baxter produced in the latter year and issued in 1971. Bernhardt retired as a custodian in February 1972 and vacationed for a few weeks in England, where he was treated as a musical celebrity. He worked with the bassist Hayes Alvis's band later that year, shortly before Alvis died. Bernhardt recorded his own albums *Blues and Jazz from Harlem* (1972) and *More Blues and Jazz from Harlem* (1973), the latter with the Harlem Blues and Jazz Band of which he eventually became the sole leader. A heart attack interrupted his new career in 1974, but he recovered and resumed playing and singing, touring Europe annually from 1976 to 1979 with his band. He spent his final years from 1979 onward as a member of drummer Barry Martyn's Legends of Jazz. Bernhardt died in Newark.

Though Bernhardt was not an important jazz or rhythm and blues performer, he is important for his detailed, levelheaded reminiscences of dozens of African American entertainers, including valuable essays on less well-known performers such as the Whitman Sisters, Hardy and his Alabamians, Andrade, Scott, and the Bascomb Brothers, among others, as well as important jazz musicians such as McShann and Russell. Bernhardt's several published recollections of a forceful, responsible, talented, shrewd King Oliver in late career provide an especially welcome antidote to the romantic but pathetic portrait of Oliver popularized in the famous early jazz book *Jazzmen* (1939).

Further Reading

Bernhardt, Clyde E. B. "Talking about King Oliver: An Oral History Excerpt," *Annual Review of Jazz Studies* 1 (1982).

Bernhardt, Clyde E. B., with Sheldon Harris. *I Remember: Eighty Years of Black Entertainment, Big Bands, and the Blues* (1986).

Gaster, Gilbert. "Clyde Bernhardt," *Storyville*, no. 44 (1 Dec. 1972).

Stewart-Baxter, Derricks, with Clyde E. B. Bernhardt. "The Clyde Bernhardt Story," *Jazz Journal* 20 (Sept. and Oct. 1967) and 21 (Jan. and Feb. 1968).

Obituary: *New York Times*, 31 May 1986.

BARRY KERNFELD

BERRY, Chu (13 Sept. 1908–30 Oct. 1941), tenor saxophonist, was born Leon Brown Berry in Wheeling, West Virginia. His parents' names and occupations are unknown. He played alto saxophone in high school and at West Virginia State College, which he attended for three years.

In 1929 Sammy Stewart hired Berry to play tenor in his Chicago band. In 1930 Berry moved to New York City and worked in several groups, including bands led by Benny Carter, Charlie Johnson, Spike Hughes, and Teddy Hill. An early highlight was a May 1933 recording for Hughes that included COLEMAN HAWKINS, with the two tenor giants striving to surpass each other in tunes like "Fanfare." Berry recorded with a variety of groups during the second half of the 1930s, including those led by Gene Krupa, Benny Goodman, RED ALLEN, HOT LIPS PAGE, and Wingy Manone. His superb work with various TEDDY WILSON groups is typified by his beautiful solo in BILLIE HOLIDAY's 1935 recording of "Twenty-Four Hours a Day," with Wilson's orchestra. Berry also played and recorded with the COUNT BASIE orchestra for a short while, soloing to particularly good effect in the 1939 Basie classic, "Lady Be Good."

Berry recorded much of his most important work with the FLETCHER HENDERSON orchestra in 1935 and 1936 and with CAB CALLOWAY from 1937 to 1941. He established his reputation with Henderson; Berry wrote "Christopher Columbus," one of the band's biggest hits, and played propulsive solos on pieces like "Sing, Sing, Sing." With Calloway he soloed in practically every recorded performance by the band and was featured more often than any other player; he swapped arrangements with other groups, such as the CHICK WEBB band, and was personally responsible for keeping the group steeped in good music. Examples of Berry's stellar work can be found in tunes like "Ghost of a Chance," "Lonesome Nights," and "Bye Bye Blues," and especially in his near-perfect solo in the 1939 recording of "Pluckin' the Bass."

While starring with the Calloway band, Berry also performed and recorded widely with his own groups. He recorded several sessions with his close friend ROY ELDRIDGE. Among the best of these sides are four outstanding tunes that the two musicians waxed for Commodore Records in 1938 (under the name Chu Berry and His Little Jazz Ensemble), in which Berry and Eldridge proved perfect foils for each other, particularly at the fast tempos at which both excelled. The Berry version of "Body and Soul" recorded at this time remains one of the few to rival the classic Coleman Hawkins rendition.

Berry's short life and compressed recording career provide a particularly accessible portrait of his playing style. From the beginning Hawkins loomed as Berry's major influence—hardly an unusual situation, since Hawkins did so for nearly every other tenor player until LESTER YOUNG appeared. But Berry was more successful in carving out a clear stylistic niche for himself than any of the others. He had a less rounded, less "voluptuous" sound than Hawkins had (though it was fuller than Young's) and was not as melodically imaginative as the older master, but Berry also had "a more emotive vibrato and a strange crying sound in his frequently-used upper register" (Carr, 40). He possessed a propulsive sense of swing and excelled at fast tempos that showed "an unerring sense of time" and a sophisticated "melodic-harmonic conception." On ballads Berry often played in double tempo with a wide, fast vibrato to compensate for his less warm tone. Toward the end of his life he grew less bombastic and more reflective in his ballad playing. Ballads such as "A Ghost of a Chance" and "Lonesome Nights," both recorded with the Calloway band in 1940, and "On the Sunny Side of the Street," from his own 1941 session with Chu Berry and His Jazz Ensemble, illustrate this more subtle, sophisticated approach to balladry.

When Berry died in a car accident in Conneaut, Ohio, Calloway said that it was "like losing a brother, someone I had joked with and hollered at. There was a quiet around the band for weeks and we left his chair empty" (Carr, 40). Berry had what some described as a "tubby and chuckling" personality. His friendship with Eldridge is legendary. The two often played together at after-hours jam sessions, taking on all comers and cutting them mercilessly. Musically Berry just seemed to be coming into his own. A few months before Berry's death, Hawkins ranked him among his favorite tenor players, second only to BEN WEBSTER. Though long all but forgotten, Berry's music made something of a comeback in the 1970s and 1980s, influencing younger players like Frank Lowe.

Further Reading

Carr, Ian, Digby Fairweather, and Brian Priestley, eds. *Jazz: The Essential Companion* (1987).
Schuller, Gunther. *The Swing Era: The Development of Jazz, 1930–1945* (1989).

Obituary: *New York Times*, 31 Oct. 1941.

Discography

Morgenstern, Dan. *The Complete Commodore Jazz Recordings, Vol. 1* (Mosaic, 1988).
Piazza, Tom. *The Guide to Classic Recorded Jazz* (1995).
RONALD P. DUFOUR

BERRY, Chuck (18 Oct. 1926–), singer, songwriter, and guitarist, was born Charles Edward Anderson Berry in St. Louis, Missouri, the fourth of six children of Henry William Berry, a carpenter and handyman, and Martha Bell Banks. The industrious Henry Berry instilled in his son a hunger for material success and a prodigious capacity for hard work, traits that were not entirely apparent in Berry as a youth. Martha Berry, a skilled pianist and accomplished singer, passed on to her son her love for music. By the time he was a teenager, however, Berry preferred jazz, blues, and the "beautiful harmony of country music" to his mother's Baptist hymns (Berry, 14).

In 1944 Berry and two friends hatched an ill-considered plan to drive across the country to California. They soon ran out of money and committed a series of armed robberies in an attempt to return home. All three were arrested, convicted, and given ten-year sentences. In prison, Berry began to take music seriously, cofounding a gospel quartet and a rhythm and blues band popular with both black and white inmates. The quartet sang during services in the prison chapel and met with such success that prison officials allowed the group to sing for African American church congregations in Kansas City and St. Louis.

Berry was released on parole in 1947, and returned to St. Louis. In 1948 he married Themetta Suggs, with whom he had four children. While working menial day jobs, he studied guitar with Ira Harris, who laid the foundation of his guitar-playing style. The recordings of the guitarists CHARLIE CHRISTIAN, T-BONE WALKER, and Carl Hogan, who played in LOUIS JORDAN's band, further shaped his sound. NAT KING COLE, MUDDY WATERS, and BIO JOE TURNER were among the singers whose diverse styles he sometimes emulated. Berry's taste, although eclectic, was firmly rooted in both the urban blues and rhythm and blues of the era.

By 1952 Berry was playing regularly in local St. Louis clubs and had developed a reputation as a capable sideman, whose flamboyant stage presence and willingness to indulge in "little gimmicks," such as singing country and western songs, delighted

Churk Berry, performing his "duck walk" on stage, 4 April 1980. (AP Images.)

audiences. Among those who noticed the rising blues-man was the pianist JOHNNIE JOHNSON, leader of a pop-ular trio whose repertoire included blues, rhythm and blues, and popular songs. When one of Johnson's side-man was indisposed, Johnson asked Berry to sit in with the band at the Cosmopolitan Club in East St. Louis.

Audiences at the Cosmopolitan Club responded enthusiastically to Berry and the club's owner imme-diately asked Johnson to hire him permanently. John-son readily agreed, explaining that Berry's showman-ship "brought something to the group that was missin'" (Pegg, 25). Berry's performance with John-son's trio on New Year's Eve 1952 marked the begin-ning of a remarkable musical collaboration that pro-duced "Roll Over Beethoven" (1956), "School Day" (1957), and "Rock and Roll Music" (1957), which, more than any other songs, defined the new musical genre of rock and roll. Although Johnson helped to shape the melodies, and his powerful left hand sup-plied much of the songs' rhythmic drive, the men were not equal partners. The lyrics were Berry's alone, and he was the sole author of songs such as "Maybellene" (1955), his first hit, and "Johnny B. Goode" (1958), one of the most honored songs in rock and roll history.

Within a few years, Berry's role in the trio over-shadowed Johnson's, and he began to look beyond St. Louis's African American nightclubs toward a wider audience. In 1955 he visited Chicago, hoping to build on his local success by signing a recording contract. The blues musician Muddy Waters, whom Berry met after a concert, directed him to Leonard Chess, who ran a small independent record company. Like many of the era's independent labels, Chess Records pro-duced the African American music that major labels tended to ignore. Chess agreed to record "Maybel-lene," a song similar to the country and western nov-elties that Berry often sang, and "Wee Wee Hours," a standard blues tune.

"Maybellene" fired Leonard Chess's imagination. He knew that young white consumers, bored with the music that major labels produced, were searching for something new. Many had gravitated toward rhythm and blues, which, beyond its musical excellence, pos-sessed the lure of the forbidden.

Independent labels courted this emerging market; and disk jockeys, such as Alan Freed, who began call-ing the music "rock and roll," expanded it. Chess be-lieved that "Maybellene," with its fusion of country and western and rhythm and blues, was the perfect song for the times. It proved to be a dazzling success.

Like most of Berry's songs, "Maybellene" sold well to both whites and blacks. Like all of his songs, it was an exercise in "signifyin'," drawing on African Amer-ican vernacular forms to speak, simultaneously, in more than one voice. While whites heard something both familiar and unexpected—a frenetic homage to country and western—African Americans heard an affectionate parody. The song reached number two on *Billboard* magazine's pop chart (the "white" chart) and number one on the rhythm and blues chart (the

"black" chart). "Maybellene" amalgamated black and white musical styles, exalted cars, girls, and—implicitly—sex, and moved the electric guitar to cen-ter stage, creating a musical template that generations of rock and roll musicians would follow.

Determined to repeat the success of "Maybellene," Berry began the process of transforming himself from a competent bluesman into a brilliant rock and roller. With one eye on the cash register and the other on his growing legions of young white fans, he wrote songs that were, above all, marketable. Although producing great art was the least of his concerns, many of the songs that Berry wrote between 1955 and the early 1960s were nothing less than miniature masterpieces. His lyrics blended irony, parody, and literal-minded observation into a coherent whole. His music, while grounded in rhythm and blues, continued to draw on country and western and other popular forms.

In late 1959 and early 1960, Berry's string of suc-cesses ended when he was arraigned on two counts of having violated the White Slave Traffic Act (Mann Act), a federal statute. The federal prosecutor in St. Louis alleged that Berry had, on two separate occa-sions during concert tours, transported Joan Mathis Bates, a white woman in her late teens, and Janice Norine Escalanti, a fourteen-year-old Native Ameri-can girl, across state lines for immoral purposes. When the case involving Bates went to trial, both she and Berry admitted to having had a consensual sex-ual relationship, and Bates added that she was in love with him. The jury acquitted Berry, noting that the charges involved a voluntary relationship between two adults.

The Escalanti case, however, ended in a conviction. The jury accepted Escalanti's testimony that she and Berry had engaged in consensual sexual relations on several occasions. The fact that the relationship was consensual had no impact on the charges; prosecu-tors were only required to prove that, after transport-ing Escalanti across state lines, Berry's behavior had been "immoral." While Berry denied that he had had a sexual relationship with Escalanti, he proved a ner-vous and unconvincing witness. The behavior of trial judge George Moore, who repeatedly interjected re-marks of a racial nature into the proceedings, com-pounded Berry's difficulties. Berry appealed his con-viction, arguing that Moore's hostile and prejudicial conduct had deprived him of a fair trial. A federal ap-pellate court agreed, and sent the case back to the dis-trict court. However, in 1961 Berry was convicted a second time, and entered federal prison in 1962.

By the time Berry was released in 1963, his music had begun to sound old-fashioned. Even though songs that he wrote in prison, such as "Promised Land" (1964), rank among his best, his career as a recording artist was waning. Berry enjoyed a brief revival in 1972, when he scored his first number one hit on the pop chart with the trifling, double-entendre–filled "My Ding-A-Ling." Although he rarely recorded after this point, Berry continued to tour, often with great success, well into his seventies.

In 2000 Johnny Johnson sued Berry, claiming that he had never received credit for cowriting many of the songs that Berry recorded in the 1950s and that he had thereby been defrauded of millions of dollars in royalties. Parts of the case were dismissed in 2001, with the court ruling that it would be impossible for Johnson to prove that he had cowritten the songs. The court also noted that because so much time had passed, many potential witnesses had died and that the memories of others had faded. In addition, Johnson had admitted in the *St. Louis Post-Dispatch* that he spent much of the 1950s in an alcoholic fog, rendering his testimony suspect. Although the precise nature of the relationship between the two men is likely to remain disputed, Johnson's role was almost certainly that of an arranger of Berry's musical ideas.

In his later years, Berry accrued honors that acknowledged his central role in reshaping popular music. He is a member of the Blues Foundation Hall of Fame, the National Academy of Popular Music Songwriter's Hall of Fame, and, in 1986 he was among the first artists inducted into the Rock and Roll Hall of Fame.

Further Reading
Berry, Chuck. *Chuck Berry: The Autobiography* (1987).
Collis, John. *Chuck Berry: The Biography* (2002).
Pegg, Bruce. *Brown Eyed Handsome Man: The Life and Hard Times of Chuck Berry, an Unauthorized Biography* (2002).

Discography
Rothwell, Fred. *Long Distance Information: Chuck Berry's Recorded Legacy* (2001).

JOHN EDWIN MASON

BERRY, Halle (14 Aug. 1966–), film actress and model, was born Halle Maria Berry in Cleveland, Ohio, the daughter of Jerome Berry, a hospital attendant, and Judith Hawkins, a psychiatric nurse. Her father, an alcoholic, abandoned the family when she was four, leaving her mother to raise Halle and her sister Heidi, first in predominantly black inner-city Cleveland and later in that city's white suburbs. Berry's childhood was troubled, in part because of the economic hardship of growing up in a single-parent household. But as the light-skinned child of an interracial couple—her mother was white, her father African American—she also endured racial taunts from both blacks and whites. Fellow students called her "zebra" and on one occasion left an Oreo cookie in her school locker. Berry never had any doubts about her own identity, however, and states on her Web site that her "race" is African American and English.

An extremely shy teenager, Berry craved acceptance from her peers and worked energetically to be the most active and popular young woman at her high school. As a cheerleader, editor of the school newspaper, an honor student, and class president, she appeared to have succeeded, but when fellow students accused her of stuffing the ballot box in the voting for prom queen, she was forced to share the title with a white student. Although this reversal suggested to Berry that whites would not accept a standard of beauty that included people of color, her success in beauty pageants suggested otherwise. By the mid-1980s an African American woman as flawlessly beautiful as Halle Berry could win Miss Teen Ohio and Miss Ohio. As a runner-up in the 1986 Miss U.S.A. pageant, Berry, then a student at Cleveland's Cuyahoga Community College traveled to London to represent the United States in Miss World, the leading international beauty contest. Although Miss Trinidad & Tobago won the title, Berry placed sixth and created a sensation by appearing in the "national costume" segment of the pageant wearing a skimpy bikini with strands of beads and shooting stars. The outfit was purported to express "America's advancement in space," but it drew the ire of other contestants such as Miss Holland, who wore the traditionally bulky and much less revealing Dutch costume with clogs.

Berry found participation in beauty pageants an ideal preparation for a career in Hollywood, since it taught her how to lose and not be devastated. Considered too short at five feet six inches to be a runway model, she won bit parts in the television sitcoms

Halle Berry, at the induction ceremony of her star on the Hollywood Walk of Fame in Los Angeles, 3 April 2007. (AP Images.)

Amen and *A Different World*, but she was rejected at her first audition for a major television role in *Charlie's Angels '88*. She did win a regular spot as a teenage model in 1989's short-lived sitcom on ABC, *Living Dolls*, but increasingly found that her stunning looks and beauty pageant past kept her from landing the serious acting roles she desired. A minor but critically praised role as a crack addict in SPIKE LEE's *Jungle Fever* (1991) signaled a change in her fortunes. That performance marked Berry's first, but by no means last, effort to overcome critics, including Lee himself initially, who could not envision her as anything less than glamorous. In preparation for the role, she interviewed drug addicts and refused to bathe for ten days before shooting. Her next role, as a radio producer on the prime-time soap opera *Knots Landing*, was much less gritty, but it did ensure greater exposure and led to a series of prominent appearances in the film comedies *Strictly Business* and *Boomerang* (1992) and the television miniseries of ALEX HALEY's *Queen* (1993).

In the 1990s Berry became one of the most bankable actors in Hollywood, appearing in popular, though not critically acclaimed movies such as *Fatherhood* (1993), *The Flintstones* (1994), and *Executive Decision* (1996). She received favorable reviews for these parts, but the praise—the film critic Roger Ebert described her as "so warm and charming you want to cuddle her"—may have reinforced the view in Hollywood that she was best suited to light roles. At the same time, Berry's beauty and poise earned her an MTV award in 1993 for "most desirable female," an assessment shared by *People* magazine, which since 1992 has consistently listed her among the most beautiful and best dressed women in the world, and by the manufacturers of Revlon makeup, who named her their main spokesmodel in 1996. In an age of celebrity, when fashion has come to mean as much to the corporate world and consumers as films and television, such accolades have greatly enhanced Berry's fame, fortune, and clout. Indeed, in 2002 the *Wall Street Journal* reported that the financially ailing Revlon Company was relying on a line of Halle Berry cosmetics as the primary means of halting its plummeting profits and share price.

Berry's growing fame and celebrity came at the price of endless media scrutiny. Her 1993 marriage to David Justice, a right fielder for the Atlanta Braves, delighted the tabloids, who printed scores of articles on the glamorous newlyweds, but the couple's troubled relationship and acrimonious divorce three years later was like manna from heaven for the *National Enquirer* and the *Star*. Though she continued to play an increasing variety of film roles, including a drug-addicted mother forced to give up her child to adoption by white parents in *Losing Isaiah* (1995), Berry's personal life provided greater publicity than her movies. In February 2000 a judge placed her on three years probation and ordered her to pay $13,500 in fines and perform 200 hours community service for leaving the scene of a traffic accident. Berry enjoyed better press in 2001, when she married the singer Eric Benet and became stepmother to his daughter, India. However, Berry and Benet separated in 2003, and in April 2004, Berry filed for divorce.

Her first leading role, as DOROTHY DANDRIDGE in the television drama *Introducing Dorothy Dandridge* (1999), gave Berry the critical success she had long craved and won her an Emmy Award for outstanding lead actress. As a longtime admirer of Dandridge, Berry co-produced the biopic and lobbied hard to publicize this HBO film about an African American actress renowned for her poise and beauty who suffered from depression and several unhappy and tempestuous relationships. Although Berry never faced the full force of Jim Crow segregation, she strongly identified with Dandridge's determination to broaden the diversity of roles open to women of color.

The parallel with Dandridge continued with Berry's performance in *Monster's Ball* (2001), when she became the first black woman to win the Academy Award for best actress; in 1955, nearly half a century earlier, Dandridge had been the first African American nominated in that category. Some critics ridiculed the speech in which Berry accepted her award in the name of "every nameless, faceless woman of color that now has a chance because this door tonight has been opened." They noted that actresses like HATTIE MCDANIEL and Dandridge, let alone thousands of unsung women in the civil rights movement, had already given that door an almighty push. Yet Berry was hardly the first Oscar-winning actress—or actor, for that matter—to be overcome by gushing hyperbole in receiving their profession's highest award. Others, including the members of the Academy, praised her portrayal of a poor southern black woman struggling to raise a son after the execution of her husband, and her complex relationship with one of his white executioners. In *The Nation* Michael Eric Dyson, a prominent black academic, lauded Berry's bravery in using her speech to speak up for "ordinary brothers and sisters."

Following her Oscar triumph, Berry became one of the highest paid actresses in Hollywood. She starred as Storm in the critically and commercially successful *X-Men* trilogy and had a voiceover role in the animated hit *Robots*. In the James Bond film *Die Another Day*, Berry revived memories of Ursula Andress with her role as Giacinta "Jinx" Johnson. Less successful was Berry's eponymous role in *Catwoman* (2004). Widely panned, Berry's performance earned her the unfortunate worst actress award in the 2005 Golden Raspberry Foundation Awards, though she displayed self-deprecation and a great sense of humor in turning up to collect her "Razzie."

Berry's breakthrough in winning an Academy Award and the sharp criticisms of her acceptance speech captured the ambiguities facing prominent African Americans at the beginning of the twenty-first century. Black American talents and achievements were recognized and rewarded by America's dominant culture as never before, yet that same culture continued to debate those successes in highly racialized ways.

Further Reading

Dyson, Michael Eric. "Oscar Opens the Door," *The Nation*, 15 Apr. 2002.
Farley, Christopher J. *Introducing Halle Berry* (2002).
Norment, Lynn. "Halle's Big Year," *Ebony* (Nov. 2002).

STEVEN J. NIVEN

BERRY, Lawrence S. (?–1871), political activist and journalist, was a slave who belonged to an influential antebellum lawyer from South Alabama. Little else is known about his life prior to the Civil War; however, it is known that during the early years of the Civil War, Berry was sent to toil in a hazardous saltworks that the Confederacy operated in Clarke County. Berry survived three years of intense labor there, and he emerged from the ordeal more experienced, as well as more militant, than many of the other African Americans he knew. After moving to the Gulf Coast city of Mobile, Berry became a member of the vanguard of black leaders who would help the state's black masses achieve legal and psychological freedom in the aftermath of the Civil War.

The Union victory and the federal effort to alter the legal status of black people deepened white Alabamians' resistance to change. State lawmakers were particularly devoted to preserving the status quo. In September 1865 delegates to a state constitutional convention adopted a body of laws that voided secession, repudiated the Confederate debt, and ratified section one of the Thirteenth Amendment, abolishing slavery. (Section two, which gave congressmen the power to enforce the amendment through appropriate legislation, was rejected.) Delegates also decided that representatives to Alabama's legislature would serve two-year terms and that only white men would be able to become legislators. A census for 1866 was approved, but representation would be based on the calculated population of white Alabamians only. Henceforth blacks would be allowed to serve as witnesses in open-court criminal cases that involved whites, which existing state law prevented, but marriage between whites and blacks would be forbidden. And because of a split between wealthy white planters (who thought that they could control black voters) and small merchants and farmers (who opposed black suffrage), a proposal for universal manhood suffrage was tabled.

On the heels of the constitutional convention, Berry and E. C. Branch, a white Republican from the North, organized a black convention to encourage political activism. The conference was held in Mobile from 20 to 22 November, with almost sixty black men in attendance. Most of them were ministers from the central and southern regions of the state, and E. S. Winn, an African Methodist Episcopal Zion (AMEZ) Church elder, presided. He and the other black delegates realized that that their newly acquired freedom presented tremendous opportunities and obligations. This, they agreed, was a task that they could achieve with God's help. The men therefore resolved to work hard to promote peace, goodwill, and friendship among all persons (especially the southern whites with whom their lot was cast), but they refused to relinquish any human or civil right. Over the next two years, Berry's influence grew. As a traveling (later general) agent and board member of the *Mobile Nationalist*, Alabama's first unofficial Republican newspaper, he encouraged black people to utilize the legal privileges that they had been afforded by the Thirteenth Amendment, the Civil Rights Act of 1866, and similar measures. A prominent AMEZ layman and one of Mobile's most respected union, or Loyal Leaguer, organizers, Berry led movements to integrate the port city's police force, municipal boards, and streetcars. When white carriers refused to treat black passengers fairly, Berry utilized the federal civil rights act and filed charges against company executives.

Another statewide freemen's convention, led by Branch and Berry, was held on 4 March 1867, just two days after the First Reconstruction Act was passed. Among the matters addressed by convention leaders were white domination and black voters' supposed ignorance. In an extremely concise statement, Berry proclaimed that black Alabamians were smart enough to understand their newfound rights and privileges and were determined to enjoy them. Berry reiterated this point when he and Branch held a third statewide freedmen's conference from 1 to 4 May 1867.

Berry served on the resolutions committee, where he and his companions supported integrated public schools as well as relief programs for elderly and homeless people. The committee congratulated the Freedmen's Bureau for its work on behalf of black Alabamians, asked the central government to address the abuses that former slave owners and federal soldiers were carrying out against free persons, and drafted a resolution calling each delegate a member to the state and national Republican parties and thus eligible for any privilege that membership or federal law afforded. Specifically, the delegates wanted the same rights and privileges that white Republicans enjoyed, including holding public office, sitting on juries, riding on public conveyances, and sitting at public tables and places of amusement alongside other lawful citizens. In one of the strongest political pronouncements that any group of black Alabamians had ever made, Berry and other members of the resolutions committee called these inalienable rights that any respectful citizen should be able to enjoy freely.

In 1867 Mobile city officials opened a soup kitchen to aid the impoverished. The Freedmen's Bureau offered financial assistance, and Berry was hired to help coordinate activities. Blacks throughout the city praised him for his involvement, but they criticized Berry for opposing an all-black national labor convention that was in the works. According to Berry, segregated meetings would hamper black progress and was at odds with the intent of Reconstruction, but numerous black Mobilians disagreed. Consequently Berry changed his position, arguing that the racial history of the nation justified segregated meetings.

Ulysses S. Grant's presidential election in 1868 proved momentous for Berry and other black Republicans. At the state level William H. Smith, a white Republican, was elected governor, and a free public school system was established. In the wake of their victories, a cadre of influential black Mobilians was able to secure legislation allowing them to remove Mobile's mayor and municipal board members. Among the governor's appointments was Berry, who became an alderman. The same year Berry founded a school and opened a grocery store with two other prominent blacks.

The next two years were quite eventful for Berry. In 1869, he became embroiled in a sectarian and ethnic dispute about the composition of the county school board. The following year he supported a plan to allow the city physician to treat destitute citizens, especially blacks, led an official inquiry into police pay, and called on the state government to reform the chain-gang system for prisoners. Berry also backed free public schools and an economic subsidy scheme that might have benefited his black constituency if Governor Smith had been reelected in November 1870. However Smith was defeated by a Democrat named Robert Lindsay.

Lindsay's victory ushered in Alabama's first—and Mobile's only—restoration of Democratic (or home) rule. For the remainder of the nineteenth century, every major political office in Mobile was held by a Democrat. Among the politicians affected by the Democratic reemergence was Berry, who quickly fell on hard times. By January 1871 he was unemployed, having been removed from his sergeant-at-arms post in the Alabama House, and he was impoverished. Without property, money, a wife, or a job, Berry withdrew money from a joint banking account that he and two of his business partners had opened—without their knowledge—and squandered the money. He then began to wander the streets of Mobile, drinking heavily, until one Saturday morning his body was found in a small, run-down dwelling behind a tenement building on Conception Street. His throat was slit, and it was not determined whether he was murdered or if he had committed suicide.

Further Reading

Bailey, Richard. *Neither Carpetbaggers nor Scalawags: Black Officeholders during the Reconstruction of Alabama, 1867–1878* (1995).
Fitzgerald, Michael. *The Union League Movement in the Deep South: Politics and Agricultural Change during Reconstruction* (1989).
Fitzgerald, Michael. *Urban Emancipation: Popular Politics in Reconstruction Mobile, 1860–1890* (2002).
Foner, Eric. *Freedom's Lawmakers: A Directory of Black Officeholders during Reconstruction* (1996).

BERTIS ENGLISH

BERRY, Leonidas (20 July 1902–4 Dec. 1995), physician and public service and church activist, was born Leonidas Harris Berry on a tobacco farm in Woodsdale, North Carolina, the son of the Reverend Llewellyn Longfellow Berry, general secretary of the Department of Home and Foreign Missions of the African Methodist Episcopal (AME) Church, and Beulah Harris. Leonidas acquired the desire to become a doctor at the age of five, when a distinguished-looking local doctor treated a small wound on his foot. The young boy was impressed by this "miraculous" event. His aspiration to go to medical school intensified while he was attending Booker T. Washington High School in Norfolk, Virginia. In 1924 Berry graduated from Wilberforce University and went on to obtain the SB in 1925 from the University of Chicago. In 1930 he also received his medical degree from the University of Chicago's Rush Medical College. Berry continued his medical training, earning an MS in Pathology at the University of Illinois Medical School in 1933. He completed his internship at Freedmen's Hospital (1929–1930), one of the nation's first black hospitals, and then his residency at Cook County Hospital in Chicago (1931–1935).

For most of his career, Berry resided in Chicago, becoming a nationally and internationally recognized clinician. His practice and research were centered at Chicago's Provident, Michael Reese, and Cook County Hospitals. From 1935 until 1970 Berry was a mainstay of the physician staff at Provident. This institution, which had been founded by DANIEL HALE WILLIAMS, was one of the nation's leading black hospitals. In 1946 Berry became the first black physician admitted to the staff at Michael Reese. At Cook County he was the first black internist, rising from assistant to senior attending physician during his long affiliation with this institution (1946–1976). He also served as clinical professor in medicine at the University of Illinois from 1960 until 1975.

Beginning in the 1930s Berry developed into a leader in the emerging specialty of gastroenterology. This branch of medicine focuses on the physiology and pathology of the stomach and intestines as well as their interconnected organs, such as the liver, esophagus, gallbladder, and pancreas. Berry's clinical accomplishments were at the forefront of his specialty. He became an international authority on digestive diseases and the technique of endoscopy. Berry helped revolutionize his field when he became the first American doctor to employ the fiberoptic gastro-camera to examine the inside of the digestive tract. The use of this instrument became increasingly refined, enabling physicians to diagnose at much earlier stages various diseases, especially cancers, of the gastrointestinal organs. He invented the Eder-Berry gastrobiopsy scope, a device that made it possible to retrieve tissue samples from the stomach for microscopic study. This instrument has been exhibited at the Smithsonian Institution in Washington, D.C.

In addition to his extraordinary clinical achievements, Berry was a superb medical academician.

During the course of his career, he authored or co-authored twelve books and eighty-four medical research articles and presented more than 180 medical lectures, exhibitions, and academic papers nationally and internationally. In 1941 Berry presented a research paper before the gastroenterology and proctology section at the American Medical Association's (AMA) annual convention in Cleveland, Ohio, the first time a black physician made a national presentation before this prestigious group.

The church activities and travels of Berry's father and mother deeply impressed him throughout his early life—so much so that Berry's autobiography, *I Wouldn't Take Nothin' for My Journey* (1981), was written primarily as a memoir dedicated to his parents and their lives. Even while achieving his clinical and academic successes, Berry, raised in the swirl of his parents' church work and community service, never lost touch with the traditional ideals of the black American community—ideals that emphasize charitable work and resistance to racial discrimination. He realized these ideals by expanding his duties and resources at the hospitals and medical schools where he worked, as well as by taking on leadership positions in AME Church and community organizations. From the early 1950s Berry served as president of the mostly black Cook County Physicians Association. He led a citywide movement to set up medical services for young drug addicts and to prevent the spread of drug addiction. His plan involved organizing medical counseling clinics and follow-up services for drug addicts—a plan that became a program that he administered for eight years with finances provided by the Illinois state legislature and the Illinois Department of Public Health.

In 1965 Berry served as president of the National Medical Association (NMA), the nation's premier organization established for black physicians. The highlight of his tenure was spearheading the NMA's activities to integrate the AMA. At this time the AMA still maintained segregated local chapters throughout the nation. In addresses to his NMA constituents, Berry described his disdain for this discriminatory barrier faced by black doctors. He called this practice "a senseless social embargo . . . against licensed and practicing physicians based upon a criterion of race in some [AMA] societies and tokenism in others" (Morais, 220). In order to place the NMA on higher ground regarding the integration of physician associations, at the August 1965 annual convention, the association passed Berry's proposal that the NMA recruit white physicians. At the convention's press conference, Berry stated his rationale clearly: "We cannot remain a segregated [medical] society when we are pressing for integration ourselves" (Morais, 196).

Under Berry's leadership the NMA next held a series of formal meetings with AMA officials and trustees. These meetings, which took place between September 1965 and August 1966, resulted in the adoption of several cooperative measures. First, the two organizations agreed to increase recruitment efforts to attract more black Americans into medical careers. Second, the AMA resolved to appoint more black members of the two organizations to high-standing councils and committees of the AMA. Finally, the AMA appointed a special committee of the AMA board of trustees to serve as a watchdog body to work against segregation in local chapters and physician practices. The committee contacted segregated local chapters to persuade them to comply voluntarily with the AMA's national resolutions prohibiting racial discrimination in local societies, hospitals, and medical care.

Berry also was a deeply committed "churchman" for the AME Church. He strove to use his church ties to work with other denominations on projects for community betterment. For example, for many years Berry served as the medical director of the Health Commission of the AME Church. In this capacity, in the mid-1960s he developed means to support the integration drive in Cairo, Illinois. In response to Ku Klux Klan activities and entrenched neighborhood poverty, local community activists in Cairo launched an antiracism campaign known as the Black United Front. Berry organized a "flying health service to Cairo" called the Flying Black Doctors to assist the Cairo activists. Berry's group of thirty-two physicians, nurses, and technicians flew down to Cairo and gave medical exams to some three hundred persons. The Cairo activities of the Flying Black Doctors attracted the attention of the national news media, including NBC's famed television news show, *The Huntley-Brinkley Report*, with Chet Huntley and David Brinkley.

Berry liked to refer to himself as a "multidimensional doctor." In his autobiography he emphasizes that although he was a successful clinician, he was most pleased that he had never given in to the tendency to become too "circumscribed and perhaps obsessed with the pursuit of excellence in . . . matters purely medical" (405). Berry viewed his medical and public service achievements as much more than solo endeavors. Instead, he believed that they were the direct outgrowth of family and religious influences that stemmed from the slave communities of the pre–Civil War United States. In his autobiography Berry writes: "The success of my career [was] a high water mark in the destiny of the Berry family in its long odyssey through the generations. The strength of Afro-American culture to a great extent lies in the unique common bonds which tie together many [such] successful Black nuclear and multinuclear families in America" (Berry, 407). Berry and his extended family have left a permanent contribution at the highest levels of American and black American medical science and religious life.

Further Reading

The papers of Leonidas H. Berry, 1907–1982, are located in the Modern Manuscripts Collection, History of Medicine Division, National Library of Medicine, Bethesda, Maryland. There is also a body of

Berry's personal papers at the Schomburg Manuscripts and Rare Books Collection, New York Public Library, New York City, under the title Leonidas H. Berry Papers, 1932–1988.

Berry, Leonidas H. *I Wouldn't Take Nothin' for My Journey: Two Centuries of an Afro-American Minister's Family* (1981).

Morais, H. M. *The History of the Negro in Medicine* (1968).

Obituary: *New York Times* (Late Edition), 12 December 1995.

DAVID MCBRIDE

BERRY, Mary Frances (17 Feb. 1938–), scholar and civil rights advocate, was born in Nashville, Tennessee, to George Berry, a laborer, and Frances Southall, a beautician. She was the middle child between two brothers. After attending public schools in Nashville, she entered Howard University where she received her bachelor of arts degree in 1961 and her master of arts degree in 1962. During the 1962–1963 academic year she was a teaching fellow at Howard University, after which she moved to Ann Arbor, Michigan, to pursue a doctorate in history at the University of Michigan. She served as a teaching assistant during the 1965–1966 academic year and, after completing work on her PhD in 1966, was appointed assistant professor in the Department of History. In 1968 she was promoted to associate professor. Simultaneously she pursued the study of law and in 1970 received her JD degree from the University of Michigan Law School.

Berry rapidly rose through the ranks of academia, serving as acting director, then director of the Afroamerican Studies program at the University of Colorado from 1970 to 1974. She also acted as provost of the school's Division of Behavioral and Social Sciences and Education in 1974, and as chancellor in 1976 and 1977. From 1976 through 1980 she held the rank of professor in the Department of History, although with the election of President Jimmy Carter in 1976, she took a leave of absence to enter government service. She became a member of his administration, serving as assistant secretary of education in the Department of Health, Education, and Welfare from April 1977 through January 1980. In this post Berry headed the Education Division, administering a substantial annual budget. She oversaw a number of programs, including those of the National Institute of Education, the Office of Education, the Fund for the Improvement of Postsecondary Education, the Institute of Museum and Library Services, and the National Center for Education Statistics. Her years in Washington prompted her departure from Colorado, where she had faced criticism from the faculty of the University of Colorado for her role in granting amnesty to student protestors. Berry returned to Howard University, where she was professor in the Department of History and Law from 1980 through 1987. In 1987 she was appointed Geraldine R. Segal Professor of American Social Thought at the University of Pennsylvania.

In 1980 the Carter administration appointed her to the United States Commission on Civil Rights. The 1957 Civil Rights Act, the first civil rights bill passed by Congress in more than eighty years, created the commission. The commission's objective was to investigate complaints regarding civil rights abuses, hold hearings, and generate briefings, reports, and papers on the state of civil rights in the country for the benefit of lawmakers and the education of the public.

From 1980 to 1982 Berry served as the commission's vice-chairperson. During the 1980s the commission assumed a broad mantle; a number of reports and hearings addressed a spectrum of issues. Her persistence in advocating for civil rights during the Reagan administration—he twice tried to fire her—earned Berry a reputation in Washington as a fierce iconoclast, as did her strong condemnation of the Reverend LOUIS FARRAKHAN at the time of his Million Man March in 1995.

On 19 November 1993 President Clinton appointed Berry as chairperson of the commission and in January of 1999 reappointed her. Working with state advisory committees, the commission, under Berry's leadership, conducted a number of studies and generated reports and recommendations regard-

Mary Frances Berry, chairwoman of the U.S. Commission on Civil Rights, speaking in Washington, D.C., on 7 December 2001. (AP Images.)

ing civil rights issues across the nation, including police misconduct in West Virginia, civil rights issues facing Arab Americans after the terrorist attacks of 11 September 2001, and problems faced by women business owners. Berry continued to serve as a lightning rod for controversy, disappointing some supporters on the political left for her silence in the wake of Clinton's 1996 welfare reform act. Meanwhile, congressional oversight of the commission raised questions of its financial management, leading to allegations of mismanagement, which Berry and some of her supporters attributed to racism. In 1999 Berry's actions in quelling protest at Pacifica Radio, a left-leaning network of radio stations whose board she had headed since 1997, caused many to accuse her of censorship.

Following the 2000 presidential election, a major portion of the commission's attention came to focus on problems attending African American access to the ballot. In a report issued in June 2001, Berry stated that the consequences of Florida's voting problems during the 2000 election "fell most harshly on African Americans." The Civil Rights Commission held a series of meetings in Florida, listening to testimony from blacks who were blocked from voting and from various other parties involved in the debacle. African Americans made up 11 percent of the Florida electorate but cast 54 percent of the votes that were ultimately discarded. The commission found that the problem was nationwide: of the almost 2 million votes thrown out for one reason or another, more than half were cast by African Americans.

Following the Florida hearings Berry argued strongly before Congress on the need for electoral reform. As the 2004 presidential election neared, Berry renewed the call for oversight of the Florida electoral process. The Civil Rights Commission itself lacked enforcement powers of any sort, so Berry held hearings intended to create public awareness of obstacles to free and equal voting.

Even while guiding the Civil Rights Commission, Berry continued to be a productive scholar. Her books include *Black Resistance, White Law: A History of Constitutional Racism in America* (1971), *Why ERA Failed: Politics, Women's Rights and the Amending Process of the Constitution* (1986), *Long Memory: The Black Experience in America* (with John W. Blassingame, 1982), *The Pig Farmer's Daughter and Other Tales of American Justice: Episodes of Racism and Sexism in the Courts From 1865 to the Present* (1999), and *The Politics of Parenthood: Child Care, Women's Rights, and the Myth of the Good Mother* (1993).

The recipient of more than thirty honorary degrees, Berry also received a number of awards. Honorary degrees were conferred by, among others, the University of Akron (1977), Benedict College (1979), Grambling State University (1979), Bethune-Cookman (1980), Clark College (1980), Oberlin College (1983), and Colby College (1986). Her awards include the NAACP's Roy Wilkins Award, the Rosa Parks Award of the Southern Christian Leader-

ship Conference, the *Ebony* Black Achievement Award, and a *Ms.* Woman of the Year Award. Berry was a member of the U.S. Commission on Civil Rights from 1980 to 2004, serving as chair from 1993 to 2004.

Further Reading

Neuman, Johanna. "Civil Rights Panel Changes May Cause Clash," *Los Angeles Times* (4 Dec. 2004).
Smith, Jessie Carney. *Notable Black American Women* (1992).

JOHN R. HOWARD

BERRY, Nyas (18 Aug. 1913–5 Oct. 1951), **James Berry** (c. 1915–28 Jan. 1969), and **Warren Berry** (25 Dec. 1922–10 Aug. 1996), dancers, were the sons of Redna (maiden name unknown) and Ananias Berry, whose occupations are unknown. Nyas, whose given name was Ananias, and James were both born in New Orleans, Louisiana, and Warren was born in Denver, Colorado.

In 1919 Nyas and James began performing together, touring the church circuit in Chicago as elocutionists reciting poems by PAUL LAURENCE DUNBAR. After the family moved to Denver, the two elder brothers branched out and began playing carnivals. Their father, a religious man, had forbidden them to dance, but Nyas had memorized dances he had seen other performers do and had built upon them himself. He persuaded his father to let him enter an amateur dance contest, in which he floored the audience. The theater manager offered Nyas $75 a week; the elder Ananias insisted that Nyas and James continue as a team.

The brothers then put together an act based on the widely acclaimed BERT WILLIAMS and GEORGE WALKER, the most famous African American show business performance team of their time. Nyas and James named their act the Miniature Williams and Walker. In the mid-1920s the Berry family moved to Hollywood, California, where James danced at parties given by silent film stars, such as Mary Pickford and Clara Bow. The brothers also appeared in *Our Gang* comedies. Toward the end of the decade they opened as a duo, the Berry Brothers, with the already legendary DUKE ELLINGTON at Harlem's Cotton Club. Although the famous nightclub would remain their home base for the next four and a half years, they toured and performed in other groundbreaking shows. In 1929 they traveled to London and were featured performers in Lew Leslie's popular and highly acclaimed all–African American revue *Blackbirds of 1928*. They were the first African American act at the Copacabana in 1929. They appeared in *Rhythmania* at the Cotton Club and *Rhapsody in Black* in 1931. When Radio City Music Hall had its grand opening on 27 December 1932, the Berry Brothers were on the bill.

In 1934 Nyas left the act and married VALAIDA SNOW, a popular African American entertainer. During this time Warren, the youngest brother, was pulled out of school and formal dance classes and drafted into the act. James taught his younger brother every move of the Berry Brothers' act, and soon this new duo was performing steadily. When Nyas's marriage dissolved, he talked his brothers into forming a Berry Brothers act with three Berrys. Nyas also persuaded them to move back to Hollywood. The Berry Brothers enjoyed tremendous success in their newly formed trio and appeared extensively throughout the United States on stage, in clubs, and in film as well as throughout Europe. The brothers possessed three distinct personalities and styles: Nyas was the king of the strut, James was the comedian and singer, and Warren was the solid dancer and acrobat. Their act remained virtually unchanged for over twenty years. In addition to their work in the 1941 musical film *Lady Be Good*, the Berrys also appeared in *Panama Hattie* (1942), *Boarding House Blues* (1948), and *You're My Everything* (1949). Their club engagements over the years included the Apollo Theater, the Zanzibar Café, and the Savoy Ballroom in New York; the Moulin Rouge in Paris; and the Rio Cabana in Chicago.

In 1938, at the downtown Cotton Club, a legendary competition took place between the Berry Brothers and the Nicholas Brothers, another great dance act. The Berrys devised a memorable finish in which Nyas and James ran up side stairways onto an elevated balcony and took a flying leap twelve feet out and over the heads of the entire CAB CALLOWAY orchestra, while Warren, on the stage below, completed a flip-flop twist. On the last note of the music, all three landed simultaneously in splits. "People talked about that for a long time!" recalled Warren.

The secret of the Berry Brothers' success was timing, precision, and dynamics. They were masters of the "freeze and melt," the sparkling contrast between posed immobility and sudden flashing action. The act that the three brothers perfected stayed their act for over twenty years. This repetition was common throughout vaudeville, when acts toured the country year after year. During that time, audiences wanted to see exactly the same familiar act with no changes. When the Berry Brothers contemplated using a new song or creating a new dance routine, the bookers dissuaded them. Resigned, the Berrys kept their act intact until Nyas's death of heart failure at the age of thirty-nine in New York. Warren and James performed together and then as solo acts individually for a time, but a hip injury Warren had suffered as a teen finally disabled him. In 1969 James died in New York of complications of arteriosclerosis. Warren worked for over fifteen years as a film editor for Screen Gems in New York City. During his last years he worked in Los Angeles on several unpublished scripts; he died in Los Angeles.

The Berrys are remembered as one of the greatest dance acts in the history of the American stage and cinema in the twentieth century. At a time when tap dancers were "a dime a dozen," these brothers combined their talents to form a unique act that remains unsurpassed. Ironically, they never wore taps on their shoes because their work with canes and their acrobatics required leather-soled shoes for safety. Their mixture of the cakewalk strut, tap dancing, thrilling acrobatics, and amazing cane work was a winning and lasting formula.

Further Reading
Frank, Rusty E. *TAP! The Greatest Tap Dance Stars and Their Stories, 1900–1955* (1990; repr., 1994).
Stearns, Marshall, and Jean Stearns. *Jazz Dance: The Story of American Vernacular Dance* (1968; repr., 1994).

Obituaries: Nyas Berry, *New York Age*, 13 Oct. 1951; James Berry, *New York Amsterdam News*, 8 Feb. 1969; and Warren Berry, *Los Angeles Times*, 16 Aug. 1996.

RUSTY E. FRANK

BERRY, Theodore M. (8 Nov. 1905–15 Oct. 2000), first black mayor of Cincinnati, Ohio, was born in Maysville, Kentucky, to a white farmer whom he never knew and Cora Berry. When he was a toddler, Berry's mother brought him to Cincinnati, where they settled in the emerging African American community in the city's West End. Severely hearing impaired and with difficulty speaking, his mother earned little as a domestic, and Berry's sister Anna, fifteen years his senior, eventually assembled the family in her own household.

Berry attended the segregated Harriet Beecher Stowe Elementary School and graduated from the racially mixed Woodward High School in 1924 as valedictorian, the first black student in Cincinnati to achieve that honor in an integrated high school. Berry received his bachelor of arts degree from the University of Cincinnati in 1928 and his juris doctorate from the UC College of Law in 1931. He worked his way through school by selling newspapers and later working in the steel mills in nearby Newport, Kentucky.

Soon after graduation from law school, Berry became president of the Cincinnati branch of the National Association for the Advancement of Colored People (NAACP), a post he held from 1932 to 1938 and again from 1943 to 1946. Thereafter he served at various times as an officer or board member for the NAACP Cincinnati Branch, the Ohio NAACP state chapter, and the national organization. In June 1938 Berry married Johnnie Mae Newton, and the couple had three children, Faith Daryl, Gail Estelle, and Theodore Newton.

In 1939 Berry became Hamilton County's first black assistant prosecutor—a Republican Party political appointment. In 1942, when he went to work in Washington, D.C., in the federal Office of War Information, he became a Democrat. Upon returning to Cincinnati, Berry resumed his private law practice and his work with the NAACP and ran unsuccessfully as an independent for the Cincinnati City Council in 1947. During that campaign, however, Berry's outspoken support for the proportional representation system of voting then used to elect Cincinnati's city council played a crucial role in helping defeat a Republican-led repeal effort as he reminded black Cincinnatians that proportional representation had allowed them to elect an African American council member in every election since 1931.

Subsequently, Berry was elected to the city council in 1949 on the local Charter Party ticket. This put two blacks, including a Republican incumbent, on the nine-member council for the first time. Berry served on the council from 1949 to 1957, 1963 to 1965, and 1971 to 1975, during the last of which he also served as the city's first black mayor. As a city council member, Berry continued his civil rights activism. In 1953 he worked with civic housing reformers to legislate a ban on racial discrimination in housing to be constructed as part of the city's first postwar urban renewal project, and in 1953 and 1954 he attempted, unsuccessfully, to use Cincinnati's control of the waterworks that supplied the growing suburbs of Hamilton County as a tool to force developers to open a major housing development (later named the City of Forest Park) to African American residents.

Berry lost his 1957 bid for reelection after a successful Republican-led campaign to repeal proportional representation, a campaign widely believed to have prevailed because of white fears that Berry might become mayor. Indeed, Berry had been the top vote-getter of the majority party in the November 1955 election, which by local tradition would have made him mayor. Instead Berry had chosen to step aside in favor of a white council member from his party. With a larger black population and greater support from white voters, Berry was reelected to the council in 1963. He served until he was appointed Assistant Director for Community Action Programs in the federal Office of Economic Opportunity in 1965, which occurred, in part, because of his instrumental role in the early creation of Cincinnati's Community Action Program.

Berry resumed his private practice of law in Cincinnati in 1969. In 1971 he returned to the city council by appointment to fill a seat vacated by the death of a black incumbent. In council elections later that year, he was the top vote-getter in the Charter Party half of the majority Charter-Democratic coalition and as a result became mayor in December 1972, a position he held until he retired from political office in 1975. Berry remained active in Cincinnati municipal politics, including supporting younger black office seekers like Marian Spencer, whom he saw elected as the first woman president of the local NAACP branch, and then as the first black woman elected to the Cincinnati city council in 1983. Berry also continued to work for the reinstatement of proportional representation in the election of city council. While some local activists argued for a combined district/at-large method to assure a fair proportion of blacks on council, Berry worked to persuade the federal courts that the 1957 Republican attack on proportional representation had been racially motivated

and had illegally denied Cincinnati blacks fair representation. Berry and his allies lost the suit in 1993, but Cincinnati finally saw the election of African Americans to its city council starting in the 1990s in numbers roughly proportionate to the city's black population.

In addition to Berry's political career and service to the NAACP, he played important roles in other civil rights organizations, including as president of the Ohio Committee for Civil Rights Legislation (1949–1965), which organized for state fair-employment (enacted 1959) and fair-housing legislation (enacted 1965). Between 1949 and 1958 he helped a group of black war veterans purchase, finance, and build a small subdivision in an otherwise white area of northern Hamilton County. In addition he worked with the North Avondale Neighborhood Association (founded in 1960), which helped that neighborhood make a successful transition from an upper-middle-class white neighborhood to an upper-middle-class integrated neighborhood. That same year he helped found Housing Opportunities Made Equal, which lobbied for local and state fair housing legislation and after 1965 worked to enforce Ohio's fair housing law and then federal fair housing law.

By the early 1990s Berry's age and health had begun to limit his participation in civic life. His death in 2000 was accompanied by accolades from a broad range of Cincinnatians, reflecting the decency, honesty, and effectiveness for which Berry had been known throughout his career.

Further Reading
This article was drawn primarily from materials in the Theodore M. Berry Collection, Department of Archives and Rare Books, University of Cincinnati Libraries. Additional material came from the Theodore M. Berry Collection, Cincinnati Historical Society Library. Berry appears prominently in the papers of a number of other Cincinnati organizations including the Better Housing League, Housing Opportunities Made Equal, and the Cincinnati Human Relations Commission, all at the University of Cincinnati, and in the Urban League of Greater Cincinnati Collection and the Cincinnati Development Committee Collection at the Cincinnati Historical Society Library. Numerous articles are available in Cincinnati newspapers indexed at http://newsdex.cincinnatilibrary.org. His obituary is available on line at the *New York Times* (http://www.nytimes.com), and in the *Cincinnati Enquirer* and the *Cincinnati Post* at http://www.cincinnati.com. There is no complete biography of Berry available. The Cincinnati Historical Society Library's Web site has a brief biography and a guide to other resources about him at http://library.cincymuseum.org/aag/bio/berry.html.

CHARLES F. CASEY-LEININGER

BESSENT, Hattie (26 Dec. 1926–), nursing educator and administrator, was born in Jacksonville, Florida. Little information is available about her parents or other aspects of her personal background. When she was nine years old Bessent lost her mother.

Her grandmother then raised her, instilling in her a strong belief that self-giving is the measure of personal worth. After graduating from high school in Jacksonville, Bessent worked as a laboratory and X-ray technician, an unusual job for a black woman of her time and place but one that led to her groundbreaking career in nursing.

During and after slavery, African Americans, especially women, often served as lay healers and tenders of the sick. Starting in the nineteenth century, as nursing became a more formally organized profession, the "color line" sliced through it. Even though black communities urgently needed more health care, black nurses were denied membership in the American Nurses Association (ANA), educational opportunities, and all but the lowest-paid, least prestigious jobs, usually in private duty work. In 1908 the National Association of Colored Graduate Nurses (NACGN) was founded to strive for professional equality, particularly for the desegregation of the ANA, the largest professional association. By the time of Hattie Bessent's birth, black nurses had created their own basic training programs but were still excluded from many good jobs, graduate education, and specialist training. This was still true in 1949, when the ANA finally accepted black members and the NACGN chose to disband, its chief mission having been attained.

Against this difficult yet newly promising historical backdrop, Bessent sought her BS in Nursing Education from Florida A&M University. After graduating in 1959 Bessent became the first black nursing head of any psychiatric unit in Jacksonville. She then earned an MSN in Psychiatric Nursing from Indiana University in 1962 and spent five years as assistant professor of this specialty at Florida A&M University. With her EdD in Psychological Foundations of Education, obtained in 1970 at the University of Florida, Bessent became the first African American nurse in her home state to receive a doctorate. She was also a registered nurse (RN) and a fellow of the American Academy of Nursing (FAAN).

During the early to mid-1970s Bessent taught and researched on the nursing school faculties of the University of Florida and Vanderbilt University. In 1976 she became Vanderbilt's first African American nursing dean. From 1977 to 1992 Bessent directed the ANA's nationwide Ethnic Minority Fellowship Program (EMFP). Since 1974 the EMFP has offered doctoral fellowships in psychiatric nursing and related fields to African, Native, Asian, and Hispanic Americans. Psychiatric nursing addresses not only conditions like posttraumatic stress disorder and depression but also substance abuse and, since the 1980s, HIV and AIDS. Along with poverty and inadequate health care access, these problems have continued to disproportionately burden people of color. The EMFP increased minority representation, leadership, and wisdom in psychiatric nursing clinical practice, administration, teaching, research, and policy work. As EMFP director Bessent raised millions of dollars from private foundations and government agencies.

Through her congressional policy internships, many fellows witnessed the legislative process firsthand and better understood its day-to-day effects on health care workers and patients. Bessent regularly visited the fellows at each of the fifty-plus universities where they then were enrolled. She stressed the importance of assertiveness training, mentoring, and networking in their development as professionals. She also helped them with job placement, recruited new fellows, and raised awareness of the EMFP and diversity issues among nursing faculty and other health professionals. U.S. Senator Daniel Inouye of Hawaii praised her in the *Congressional Record* as "an outstanding role model for both her professional colleagues and for future generations of minority students. She has ... demonstrated the positive long-term consequences of being actively involved in the political process. ... Very few can match her accomplishments and dedication" (Inouye, S15443–S15444).

After her retirement as EMFP director, Bessent wrote *Strategies for Recruitment, Retention, and Graduation of Minority Nurses in Colleges of Nursing* (1997), *Minority Nurses in the New Century* (2002), and *Soul of Leadership* (2005). She continued to publish articles in professional journals and make presentations at scientific sessions of the World Federation of Mental Health. In 2002 the American Nurses Foundation of the ANA appointed her director of a new initiative to train minority nurse leaders at historically black colleges and universities. Bessent hoped that this training would empower minority nurses to skillfully challenge racial and ethnic disparities in health care and teach their patients how to do the same.

Along with the ANA, Hattie Bessent involved herself in such groups as the W. K. Kellogg Foundation's Project LEAD, the American Educational Research Association, the Association for Supervision and Curriculum Development, the National League for Nursing, the Delta Sigma Theta sorority, the Alachua County Mental Health Association, and the Gainesville Human Relations Board. She was awarded a lifetime membership by the National Black Nurses Association and the first honorary membership in the Association of Black Nursing Faculty. She was the first African American southerner inducted into the honorary nursing organizations Phi Delta Kappa, Sigma Theta Tau, and Pi Lambda Theta. Her other honors include a Career Teachers Grant; appointments by President Jimmy Carter to his Task Force for the Friendship Treaty to China and his Commission on Mental Health (1977); Distinguished Alumna Award, Florida A&M University (1980); Serwa Award, Virginia Chapter, National Coalition of 100 Black Women (1990); an honorary doctorate of science degree, Hunter College (2002); and the ANA's Mary Mahoney Award (2004).

The onetime ethnic minority fellow Beverly Malone aptly described Hattie Bessent as a "fighting spirit with a clear sense of mission"(Inouye, S15443-S15444).When she became one of the first black women to head the American Nurses Association, from 1996 to 2000, Malone expressed gratitude for Bessent's mentorship. In the opening years of the twenty-first century Bessent persisted as a leader in the long and still unfinished struggle for equality in the nursing profession and in health care access. Thanks to Bessent, Malone, and hundreds of other nursing leaders gained the opportunity to thrive and succeed in their profession, improve the life chances of the poor and minority Americans they serve, and cultivate still more nursing leaders of color.

Further Reading
Carnegie, M. Elizabeth. *The Path We Tread: Blacks in Nursing Worldwide, 1854–1994,* 3d ed. (1995).

Inouye, Daniel. "Tribute to Dr. Hattie Bessent for 16 Years of Placing Minority Nurse Interns on Capitol Hill," *Congressional Record,* 30 Oct. 1991, available online at http://thomas.loc.gov.

Taylor, Cheryl. "Bessent, Hattie," in *Black Women in America,* 1st ed., ed. Darlene Clark Hine (1993).

MARY KRANE DERR

BEST, Denzil (27 Apr. 1917–25 May 1965), jazz drummer and composer, was born Denzil de Costa Best in New York City, the son of immigrant parents from Barbados; his mother was Josephine Best (his father's name is unknown). Denzil Best married Arline Riley (date unknown), with whom he had two daughters. Best began studying piano when he was six years old but later learned trumpet, which he played professionally in the mid-1930s with the drummer Chris Columbus (Joe Morris). By the end of the decade Best became associated with several seminal bop musicians playing at Minton's nightclub in New York, including THELONIOUS MONK, KENNY CLARKE, and house bandleader Joe Guy. Because of a lung disorder, Best stopped playing trumpet in 1941, returned to the piano, and later played string bass and drums.

After having worked as a drummer with locally led New York City bands (Saxie Payne, Eddie Williams, Leon Gross), Best made several recordings with the saxophonist BEN WEBSTER in September 1943. The next year he played drums on several recordings made by a number of well-known jazz musicians, including COLEMAN HAWKINS (replacing Jimmy Crawford), ILLINOIS JACQUET, CHARLIE SHAVERS, Clyde Hart, and MARY LOU WILLIAMS.

In 1947 Best was coleader on several quartet recordings with Webster before joining the bassist Chubby Jackson (with Conte Candoli, Frank Socolow, Terry Gibbs, and Lou Levy) on a Scandinavian tour. Throughout the late 1940s and into the 1950s Best played and recorded with swing-era musicians such as BUCK CLAYTON, TEDDY WILSON, Shavers, Jimmy Jones, STUFF SMITH, and Jack Teagarden. From 1949 to 1952 he played with the George Shearing quintet and helped originate the unique mellow sound that identified the group.

Best fractured his legs in an automobile accident in 1952 and was in temporary retirement until October of the next year, when he joined Artie Shaw's last Gramercy Five band, recording with the group in February and March 1954. Best then played with Erroll Garner in 1955–1956, recording on the pianist's milestone album *Concert by the Sea* (1955; Columbia CL883). During the late 1950s Best suffered from calcium deposits in his wrists, and although he continued to perform (with Lee Evans, Cecil Young, NINA SIMONE, Tyree Glenn, and Stuff Smith), his affliction seriously curtailed his professional career, and he worked sparingly during the 1960s. He died in New York City from head injuries that he received in a fall down a flight of subway stairs.

Best was one of several bop-era drummers who personified the subtle, understated style of accompaniment drumming first demonstrated by JO JONES and Dave Tough and later by Connie Kay and Chuck Flores. His playing, characterized by his facile brushwork on the recordings that he made with Shearing and Garner, was in sharp contrast to the forceful style of most bop drummers of this period.

Although well known as a drummer, Best will most likely be remembered for his several compositions that have become bop standards. These include "Allen's Alley" ("Wee"), recorded first by Coleman Hawkins; "Dee Dee's Dance," recorded by Clyde Hart and Chubby Jackson; "Move," recorded by MILES DAVIS and later FATS NAVARRO; "Nothing but D Best," recorded by Shearing; and "Bemsha Swing," written with and recorded by Monk in 1952.

Further Reading
Gilter, Ira. *Jazz Masters of the Forties* (1966).

Harris, Pat. "None Better than Best with a Brush," *Down Beat* 18, no. 8 (Apr. 1951): 18.

Stewart, Doug. "The Forgotten Ones: Denzil Best," *Jazz Journal International* 39, no. 11 (1986): 18.

T. DENNIS BROWN

BETHEA, Rainey (16 Oct. 1913?–14 Aug. 1936), the last person publicly executed in the United States, was born Joseph Rainey Bethea in Roanoke, Virginia, to Rainey Bethea and Ella Louise Huggins. Most press reports of his execution state that Bethea Jr. was twenty-two at the time of his arrest, though he also claimed at times that he had been born in 1909. Since Bethea Jr.'s father would have been only fifteen years old in 1909, it appears more likely that the 1913 date is correct. The younger Bethea hardly knew his parents. He was still a child when his mother died in 1919 and barely a teenager when his father died seven years later in 1926, leaving Bethea, his sister Ora, and his brother as orphans. Around that time the siblings separated. While his brother remained in Virginia and his sister moved to Nichols, South Carolina, Bethea traveled west to Owensboro, Kentucky.

In 1933 Bethea began doing odd jobs for a white family, in whose basement he lived for a couple of years. Barely literate and with only three years of schooling, he took work where he could find it, but in rural Kentucky at the depth of the Great Depression there were few such opportunities for young black men like Bethea. He turned to a life of petty crime and began drinking heavily. He was fined twenty dollars for breach of the peace in Owensboro in early 1935, and he was indicted on May 31 of that year for stealing two purses at a beauty shop. Upon pleading guilty he was sentenced to one year at the Kentucky State Penitentiary in Eddyville, but he was released on parole on 1 December 1935 after serving the minimum sentence of six months. Upon his return to Owensboro he found work as a laborer and odd-job man for his landlady, earning seven dollars a week and free room and board. Within a month of his release from prison, however, he was arrested again for housebreaking and public drunkenness. Unable to pay a one-hundred-dollar fine, Bethea remained in the Daviess County jail in Owensboro from January to 18 April 1936, when he was released. Since he had broken the terms of his parole, the county authorities ought to have returned him to the Kentucky State Penitentiary, but they failed to do so.

That administrative error proved costly both for Bethea and for Mrs. Lischia Edwards, a white, seventy-year-old widow whose Owensboro home a shoeless and drunken Bethea burgled on 7 June 1936. Having once worked for and boarded near Mrs. Edwards, he knew the basic layout of the home. Although the precise sequence of events is unclear, Bethea was arrested several days later and confessed in custody to having raped and assaulted Mrs. Edwards, who had subsequently died from the assault. Bethea, who frustrated his white, court-appointed lawyers by giving them conflicting accounts, later retracted that confession, but then entered a guilty plea at his trial. Despite that admission, the judge allowed the prosecution to make its case. An all-white jury found Bethea guilty after deliberating for only five minutes.

Condemned to hang on 31 July 1936, Bethea once again claimed his innocence and hired new counsel, five black lawyers from Louisville including CHARLES W. ANDERSON JR. Bethea's new attorneys made several procedural appeals concerning their client's lack of access to counsel, and compared his plight to that of the SCOTTSBORO BOYS, whose inadequate court-appointed counsel the U.S. Supreme Court had condemned in *Powell v. Alabama* (1932). Although Bethea's lawyers won him a temporary stay of execution, the courts swiftly rejected all of his appeals. Kentucky governor Albert B. "Happy" Chandler signed Bethea's death warrant on 6 August 1936, the same day he ordered the execution of John (Pete) Montjoy. Bethea's public hanging was set for the Daviess County courthouse on 14 August 1936.

Several factors resulted in the Bethea case becoming a national cause célèbre. Among these was the issue of interracial sex and the apparent rape of a popular and well-respected white woman by a black male drifter in a small southern town. Indeed, the mood in the wake of Bethea's arrest was such that many in the town expected him to be lynched. Another was that Owensboro had not seen a public hanging for more than eighty years and that Kentucky was now the last state in the Union to perform public executions. Such executions were reserved solely for crimes involving rape, because state lawmakers deemed the electric chair too humane for rapists. In a pattern common throughout the South at that time, Kentuckians condemned to death for rape were invariably African American and their victims white. The atmosphere at several contemporaneous public hangings had resembled the carnival of the SAM HOSE and other public lynchings, during which predominantly white crowds sought a combination of vengeance and souvenir items. To this already combustible mix was added the requirement that the local sheriff perform the execution; Owensboro's sheriff was a white woman, a factor that assured the case newspaper coverage throughout the nation. On the eve of the execution, however, the sheriff deputized a man to perform the task.

By then, accounts of the "hangman in skirts" in respectable newspapers like the *New York Times* and Louisville *Courier-Journal*, as well as in the sensationalist "yellow press," had swelled the crowd at Bethea's hanging to between ten and twenty thousand people. Some of the spectators arrived at the gallows on horseback; most walked, came by car, truck, or train; a few arrived for pre-execution hanging parties and barbecues by airplane. They came from Kentucky, Indiana, and Illinois, but also as far away as Florida and the North. Newspaper accounts of the execution differ. The *New York Times* and other out-of-town newspapers reported that an angry white crowd jeered as a Roman Catholic priest read Bethea his last rites and that following the hanging the mob stormed the gallows, tearing Bethea's clothes and even the hangman's hood for souvenirs. Local newspapers disputed those accounts, claiming the crowd had observed the execution in respectful silence, and that the national press, denied the spectacle of a "hangman in skirts," decided to condemn a savage redneck mob instead. Whatever the precise sequence of events, the controversy surrounding the hanging of Rainey Bethea persuaded Kentucky to join the rest of the country in abolishing public executions.

Further Reading

Ryan, Perry T. *The Last Public Execution in America* (1992).

Wright, George C. *Racial Violence in Kentucky, 1865–1940: Lynchings, Mob Rule, and "Legal Lynchings"* (1990).

STEVEN J. NIVEN

BETHUNE, Mary McLeod (10 July 1875–18 May 1955), organizer of black women and advocate for social justice, was born Mary Jane McLeod in Mayesville, South Carolina, the child of the former slaves Samuel McLeod and Patsy McIntosh, farmers.

After attending a school operated by the Presbyterian Board of Missions for Freedmen, she entered Scotia Seminary (later Barber-Scotia College) in Concord, North Carolina, in 1888 and graduated in May 1894. She spent the next year at Dwight Moody's evangelical Institute for Home and Foreign Missions in Chicago, Illinois. In 1898 she married Albertus Bethune. They both taught briefly at Kindell Institute in Sumter, South Carolina. The marriage was not happy. They had one child and separated late in 1907. After teaching in a number of schools, Bethune founded the Daytona Normal and Industrial Institute for Training Negro Girls in Daytona, Florida, in 1904. Twenty years later the school merged with a boys' school, the Cookman Institute, and was renamed Bethune-Cookman College in 1929. Explaining why she founded the training school, Bethune remarked, "Many homeless girls have been sheltered there and trained physically, mentally and spiritually. They have been helped and sent out to serve, to pass their blessings on to other needy children."

In addition to her career as an educator, Bethune helped found some of the most significant organizations in black America. In 1920 Bethune became vice president of the National Urban League and helped create the women's section of its Commission on Interracial Cooperation. From 1924 to 1928 she also served as the president of the National Association of Colored

Mary McLeod Bethune, organizer of black women and advocate for social justice, 6 April 1949. (Library of Congress/Carl Van Vechten.)

Women. In 1935, as founder and president of the National Council of Negro Women, Bethune forged a coalition of hundreds of black women's organizations across the country. She served from 1936 to 1950 as president of the Association for the Study of Negro Life and History, later known as the Association for the Study of Afro-American Life and History. In 1935 the National Association for the Advancement of Colored People awarded Bethune its highest honor, the Spingarn Medal. She received honorary degrees from ten universities, the Medal of Honor and Merit from Haiti (1949), and the Star of Africa Award from Liberia (1952). In 1938 she participated along with liberal white southerners in the annual meetings of the Southern Conference for Human Welfare.

Bethune's involvement in national government began in the 1920s during the Calvin Coolidge and Herbert Hoover presidential administrations, when she participated in child welfare conferences. In June 1936 Bethune became administrative assistant and, in January 1939, director in charge of Negro Affairs in the New Deal National Youth Administration (NYA). This made her the first black woman in U.S. history to occupy such a high-level federal position. Bethune was responsible for helping vast numbers of unemployed sixteen- to twenty-four-year-old black youths find jobs in private industry and in vocational training projects. The agency created work-relief programs that opened opportunities for thousands of black youths, which enabled countless black communities to survive the Depression. She served in this office until the NYA was closed in 1944.

During her service in the Franklin D. Roosevelt administration, Bethune organized a small but influential group of black officials who became known as the Black Cabinet. Prominent among them were WILLIAM HENRY HASTIE of the Department of the Interior and the War Department and ROBERT WEAVER, who served in the Department of the Interior and several manpower agencies. The Black Cabinet did more than advise the president; it articulated a black agenda for social change, beginning with demands for greater benefit from New Deal programs and equal employment opportunities.

In 1937 in Washington, D.C., Bethune orchestrated the National Conference on the Problems of the Negro and Negro Youth, which focused on concerns ranging from better housing and health care for African Americans to equal protection under the law. As an outspoken advocate for black civil rights, she fought for federal anti–poll tax and antilynching legislation. Bethune's influence during the New Deal was further strengthened by her friendship with First Lady Eleanor Roosevelt.

During World War II, Bethune was special assistant to the secretary of war and assistant director of the Women's Army Corps. In this post she set up the first officer candidate schools for the corps. Throughout the war she pressed President Roosevelt and other governmental and military officials to make use of the many black women eager to serve in the national defense program; she also lobbied for increased appointments of black women to federal bureaus. After the war she continued to lecture and to write newspaper and magazine columns and articles until her death in Daytona Beach, Florida.

Urged by the National Council of Negro Women, the federal government dedicated the Mary McLeod Bethune Memorial Statue at Lincoln Park in southeastern Washington, D.C., on 10 July 1974. Bethune's life and work provide one of the major links between the social reform efforts of post-Reconstruction black women and the political protest activities of the generation emerging after World War II. The many strands of black women's struggle for education, political rights, racial pride, sexual autonomy, and liberation are united in the writings, speeches, and organization work of Bethune.

Further Reading
Holt, Rackman. *Mary McLeod Bethune: A Biography* (1964).
Ross, B. Joyce. "Mary McLeod Bethune and the National Youth Administration: A Case Study of Power Relationships in the Black Cabinet of Franklin D. Roosevelt," *Journal of Negro History* 60 (Jan. 1975): 1–28.
Smith, Elaine M. "Mary McLeod Bethune and the National Youth Administration," in *Clio Was a Woman: Studies in the History of American Women* (1980).
Obituary: *New York Times*, 19 May 1955.

DARLENE CLARK HINE

BETHUNE, Thomas. *See* Blind Tom.

BETTIS, Jerome (16 Feb. 1972–), football player, was born Jerome Abram Bettis in Detroit, Michigan, the youngest of three children of Gladys and Johnnie Bettis. Throughout his childhood, Bettis was more interested in bowling than in football, because his mother, an accredited bowling instructor, encouraged bowling as a safe family hobby to deter her children from getting into trouble in their native Detroit. Bettis took up football in tenth grade, which disappointed his mother, who many years later remarked to a reporter from the Pittsburgh (PA) *Tribune-Review* (18 Jan. 2006) that she "hated the dreaded sport of football." However, Bettis was inspired to play partly because he hoped to earn a scholarship to ease the financial burden on his parents. During this early stage of his football career the Reggie McKenzie Football Camp, which was provided free of charge during the summer, aided Bettis significantly, and McKenzie, a former standout offensive linemen with the Buffalo Bills, helped to mold the young man into the 1990 Gatorade Circle of Champions Michigan Player of the Year by the time he was a senior at Detroit's Mackenzie High School. Bettis played on both sides of the ball as a linebacker on defense and as a running back on offense.

Bettis was heavily recruited coming out of high school, but he eventually settled on Notre Dame, where he went on to have a tremendous college career, rushing 337 times for 1,912 yards, a 5.7 yards per carry average. He gave credit to Lou Holtz, his college coach, for motivating him and preparing him for the NFL, claiming at a 2004 College Football Hall of Fame luncheon that "Coach Holtz always made sure he found a way to keep you going." The Notre Dame student newspaper gave him a nickname that defined him for the rest of his college and professional career: "The Bus."

Bettis's successful college career drew the attention of the National Football League, and in 1993, he entered the NFL Draft. He was drafted in the first round by the St. Louis Rams and wasted no time proving himself to be an NFL-caliber running back. He silenced early critics who wondered if his size made him better suited for the heavier fullback position and earned a plethora of honors after becoming the first Rams rookie running back since Eric Dickerson in 1983 to top 1,000 yards in a season, running for 1,429 yards on 294 carries. He was voted the 1993 Rookie of the Year by the Associated Press, *Pro Football Weekly*, the *Sporting News*, and the Pro Football Writers' Association, and he finished just 57 yards behind EMMITT SMITH for the NFL rushing title. Over the next couple years, however, Bettis fell out of favor with the Rams. In 1994, he again topped 1,000 yards, but by 1995 his carries were down to 183 from 319 in 1994. The Rams had lost faith in him and were looking to go in a different direction with the running back, and Bettis needed a change of scenery to jumpstart his career. Both Bettis and the Rams got their wish in 1996 when Bettis was traded to the Pittsburgh Steelers in a draft-day trade sometimes called the trade of the decade by football observers.

Bettis was revitalized in Pittsburgh, saying he felt like he was running downhill for his new team, and in 1996, his first year with the Steelers, he surpassed his rookie total rushing for 1,431 yards. He was also voted NFL Comeback Player of the Year for 1996. In 1997 Bettis followed up his amazing first year in Pittsburgh with his best statistical season as a pro when he rushed for 1,665 yards and removed all doubt about his viability as a starting NFL running back. He carried the majority of the load for the Steelers from 1996 to 2001, leading the Steelers to the AFC Championship game in 2001, where they lost to the eventual Super Bowl champions, the New England Patriots. Starting in 2001, Bettis accepted a reduced role in the offense but was nevertheless central to the Steelers play-off runs in 2002, 2004, and, perhaps most significantly, the Steelers' fifth Super Bowl title in 2005. The Steelers' desire for Bettis to retire as a champion became the rallying cry for the unlikely 2005 world champions. Often featuring Bettis in short yardage situations and in the fourth quarter, the 2005 Steelers reeled off nine straight wins to get Bettis home to Detroit for the Super Bowl. Bettis led the team onto the field before the 2005 Super Bowl and was greeted with a strong ovation from the heavily partisan Super Bowl crowd. He earned a place as one of the Steelers' all-time greats, not just through his play, but by his unselfish mentoring of young running backs, his willingness to take significant pay cuts to stick with the Steelers, and his tireless community activism.

Bettis never forgot what the Reggie McKenzie football camp meant to him as a tenth grader and teamed up with McKenzie to help teach more than six hundred kids each summer about football and to help mentor them about life decisions. The McKenzie football camp became just one of many branches of Bettis' foundation, called The Bus Stops Here. The foundation provided scholarships to his old high school, donated football cleats to local high schools, and endowed a scholarship program at Notre Dame. In 2006, Bettis began the Cyber Bus Computer Literacy Program, which allowed underprivileged children to get valuable hands-on experience with computers. He partnered with the city of Pittsburgh in 2006 to renovate an inner-city park and made plans to help renovate the football field at Mackenzie High School.

Throughout his career, Bettis remained a positive role model both on and off the football field. He is almost assured a spot in the Hall of Fame with his 13,662 career rushing yards and has surpassed NFL greats such as Eric Dickerson, JIM BROWN, and Marcus Allen along the way. He made the Pro Bowl six times: in 1993, 1994, 1996, 1997, 2001, and 2005. However, what Bettis may be remembered most for is his community-first spirit and his good nature. Among his many honors for work off the gridiron was his selection as Pittsburgh Dapper Dan Man of the Year award in 1997 and the 2002 NFL Walter Payton Man of the Year award, both for his contributions to the community. Bettis married Trameka Boykin on 8 July 2006 and had one daughter, Jada, born in 2005.

Further Reading

Barger, James, ed. *Decade of Power: The Pittsburgh Steelers in the Cowher Era* (2002).

Schmalzbauer, Adam. *The History of the Pittsburgh Steelers* (2005).

"Fueling the Bus," Pittsburgh (PA) *Tribune-Review* (18 Jan. 2006). Available at http://www.pittsburghlive.com/x/pittsburghtrib/living/fooddrink/cookbookreviews/s_414466.html

"Jerome Bettis Tells College Football Luncheon Crowd How 'The Bus' Got Rolling" (23 Apr. 2004). Available at http://www.collegefootball.org/news.php?id=369
                                         DANIEL A. DALRYMPLE

BEVEL, James (19 Oct. 1936–), civil rights activist, was born in Itta Bena, Mississippi, to Dennis and Illie Bevel (originally Beverly, from James's white great-grandfather). His father, a farmer and lay minister nicknamed "Crazy Dennis Bevel" by local whites for his unwillingness to suffer the indignities of Jim Crow, served as an early model for James about how to live according to one's personal code. As a black landowner in Humphreys County, Dennis was a target for white repression, and the loss of his prop-erty scarred the family deeply. After his parents divorced James's childhood was divided between rural Mississippi and Cleveland, Ohio. He served in the U.S. Navy and then worked as a bricklayer's assistant in a Cleveland steel mill and moonlighted in a musical group. While making good money, and spending much of it in Cleveland's nightclubs, a neighbor prevailed upon him to join her at church. Here Bevel first heard the voice of God.

Stirred by this experience Bevel enrolled at American Baptist Theological Seminary in Nashville, Tennessee, in January 1957. He soon became well known around campus for his gorgeous singing voice, powerful preaching ability, deep-rooted evangelical beliefs, fondness for and skill at intellectual debate, and singular charisma. Although he pursued his studies and female students with equal ardor, Bevel was drawn into far different extracurricular activities. Late-1950s Nashville was a small but important incubator for civil rights activism, due chiefly to the presence of the Reverend JAMES LAWSON, a former Methodist missionary and representative of the Fellowship of Reconciliation (FOR). Steeped in the philosophy and techniques of nonviolent direct action, Lawson attracted local college students—mostly blacks, but also a handful of whites—to his workshops, which taught nonviolence as a radical form of Christianity that could liberate both blacks and whites from the sin of segregation. Participants in these workshops included the future civil rights activists DIANE NASH, JOHN LEWIS, MARION BARRY, and Bernard Lafayette, among others. Although initially skeptical Bevel became a fervent believer in Lawson's teachings, especially with Lawson's use of the Gandhian example. Bevel had read the Russian novelist and Christian pacifist Leo Tolstoy in the navy, and taken together these influences suggested to Bevel that nonviolent direct action was the logical manifestation of Christian witness, redemptive suffering, and social justice combined.

Lawson's workshops culminated in a sustained and successful sit-in campaign against Nashville's downtown lunch counters in early 1960. Although part of a wider campaign of lunch-counter protests across the South, the Nashvillians won particular attention for their nonviolent discipline and profession of Christian ideals. The group's influence continued after Bevel and his peers met with similar-minded activists from across the South to form the Student Nonviolent Coordinating Committee (SNCC). Bevel and the Nashvillians were regarded with both awe and derision. Some admired what they perceived as a confidence borne from experience, while others derided them as fanatic Christians devoted to nonviolence as a way of life. Such differences of opinion, particularly as the Nashvillians argued with a more pragmatic contingent from Atlanta that saw nonviolence as one tactic among many, would be a considerable source of creative tension within SNCC in subsequent years.

After helping found SNCC Bevel played a critical role in local and national movement activities. In 1961 he assisted the campaign to desegregate downtown Nashville with "stand-ins" outside movie theaters. That year he also joined other Nashvillians in reviving the Freedom Rides to integrate interstate travel accommodations, which the South kept segregated in violation of federal law. The rides resulted in Bevel's imprisonment in Mississippi; after his release he began grassroots organizing in Jackson, Laurel, and elsewhere in the state. He also married fellow activist Diane Nash in fall 1961; they would divorce four years later after having two children. Working both with SNCC and the Southern Christian Leadership Conference (SCLC), Bevel rose quickly in the latter organization, becoming by 1963 a member of the executive staff in addition to a field secretary. In 1964 he was named director of direct action and unofficially served as MARTIN LUTHER KING JR.'s conduit to the younger SNCC activists while continuing to fulfill his reputation as a daring strategist and skilled organizer, which he attributed to voices of divine inspiration. Perhaps most famously, Bevel orchestrated the 1963 Children's Crusade march in Birmingham, Alabama. By using children as protestors, Bevel revived the SCLC's flagging campaign and kept the city at the forefront of national headlines. Although many were aghast at the sight of children demonstrating, dramatic film of Police Commissioner Bull Connor's use of water hoses on black bystanders served the SCLC's cause. Many also credited Bevel as being one of several who inspired the 1963 March on Washington. In September 1963 while organizing in Edenton, North Carolina, Bevel and Nash were shaken by the Klan bombing of Birmingham's Sixteenth Street Baptist Church that killed DENISE MCNAIR, CAROLE ROBERTSON, CYNTHIA WESLEY, and ADDIE MAE COLLINS. The couple returned to the Deep South and redoubled their efforts, particularly in devising the blueprint for SCLC's campaign in Selma, Alabama, for a voting rights bill. In Selma, Bevel directed the Selma-to-Montgomery March and endured a vicious beating and imprisonment that nearly killed him.

With the movement's focus widening as the 1960s continued, Bevel remained active on all fronts. He remained central to the SCLC's work for open housing in Chicago, lobbied Martin Luther King Jr. to oppose the Vietnam War, and worked on behalf of the antiwar and disarmament movements. After King's assassination in 1968 Bevel's eccentric qualities became increasingly erratic, and his opinionated outbursts, combined with his moralistic pronouncements, continued to rankle other members of the SCLC. He was especially fervent in insisting that the SCLC assist the defense of King's murderer, James Earl Ray. Worries about his mental health arose in 1970 after a lecture to Spelman College co-eds degenerated into a weekend where he quarantined himself in a hotel room, ruined the walls with a marker in outlining a sermon, and challenged listeners to drink his urine to prove their commitment. Nonetheless Bevel continued his political and social activism in myriad ways. Through the 1970s he worked extensively on programs addressing mental health, poverty, and economic devel-

opment, based mostly but not exclusively in Chicago. He ran a failed campaign to be the Republican congressman from his Chicago district in 1984. Eight years later he served as the vice presidential candidate on the perennial political gadfly Lyndon LaRouche's ticket. In the mid-1990s he was a catalyst for LOUIS FARRAKHAN's Million Man March.

Although his idiosyncrasies have perhaps overshadowed his role in history, Bevel was among the first rank of leaders in the modern African American freedom struggle. His talents combined a shrewd tactical cunning with the unyielding and passionate belief of a religious prophet. Outspoken and unconventionally brilliant, his activist career is emblematic of the civil rights movement's mix of strategy and belief.

Further Reading
Halberstam, David. *The Children* (1998).
Houston, Benjamin. "The Nashville Way: A Southern City Confronts Racial Change, 1945–1975," PhD diss., University of Florida (2006).
Kryn, Randall L. "James L. Bevel: The Strategist of the 1960s Civil Rights Movement," in *We Shall Overcome: The Civil Rights Movement in the United States in the 1950's and 1960's*, ed. David J. Garrow (1989).
Lewis, John. *Walking with the Wind: A Memoir of the Movement* (1998).

BENJAMIN HOUSTON

BEY, James Hawthorne (17 Apr. 1913–8 Apr. 2004), musician, composer, educator, priest, and artist, was born James Hawthorne in Yamassee, South Carolina, to Mary Hugee and Roland Hawthorne. When he was still a boy he and his family moved to New Jersey, then to New York City—first to Brooklyn and later to Harlem. In Brooklyn James and his parents lived with his grandparents, and his grandfather encouraged him to join the church choir.

His musical talents became more evident after his move to Harlem, when he began to study dance and percussion with Isame Andrews, a specialist in African music and dance and a student of ASADATA DAFORA. Attracting notice with his vocal skills, Hawthorne was admitted to both the EVA JESSYE and the FRANCIS HALL JOHNSON choirs. In the mid- to late 1930s he studied African drum making and performance, especially the ashiko drum, with Moses Miannes (Mianns), a Nigerian who had come to the United States to perform at the 1934 Chicago World's Fair.

Shortly before the beginning of World War II, Hawthorne married Louise Smith. He then enlisted in the military, serving in the United Stated Navy where he had the rank of Mate First Class. He saw action at Pearl Harbor when his ship was attacked and he earned an Asiatic Pacific One Star Victory Medal for his courage in battle. On his return to the United Sates he enrolled in a cosmetology school and began a family. He and his wife had three children—a son, David, and two daughters, Denise and Carolyn.

James Hawthorne's interest in African culture led him to the Moorish Science Temple and after joining he changed his name to Bey. By the 1950s he had developed a reputation for his knowledge and proficiency in African percussion, gospel, jazz, and other genres of African American music. His rich, deep bass voice continued to attract attention and in 1953 EVA JESSYE engaged him as a cast member for the international tour of *Porgy and Bess*, starring LEONTYNE PRICE, CAB CALLOWAY, and WILLIAM WARFIELD. The company traveled across Europe to great acclaim.

Returning to New York Bey began an extensive recording career, which included collaborations with HARRY BELAFONTE, ART BLAKEY, Herbie Mann, Babatunde Olatunji, MAX ROACH, PHAROAH SANDERS, Randy Weston, and many other renowned musicians. His career as a performer continued to blossom during the 1960s, taking him to premier jazz and concert venues throughout the United States performing with Belafonte, Clifford Jordan, Herbie Mann, Miriam Makeba, and the World Saxophone Quartet. Between 1958 and 1998 he performed on twenty-three recordings under five different names (Baba Hawthorne Bey, Chief Bey, Chief James Hawthorne Bey, Hawthorne Bey, and James Bey). However, Bey never let success interfere with his commitment to his people; he found time to return again and again to community centers, churches, schools, and local events to share his spirit and his talent. Always honing his skills, Bey developed a new way of tying and securing the skins on the heads of djembe drums, a technique that has been adopted by a number of African drum makers.

Bey had an affinity for dance as well as music and was engaged with a number of dance companies such as the ALVIN AILEY Dance Theatre, Charles Moore Dance Company, and the Syvilla Fort Dance Company. He performed extensively with PEARL PRIMUS, touring with her troupe in South America and Africa in addition to their appearances in the United States. While on tour in West Africa with Primus he was recognized by the Araba of Lagos, Fagbeni Ajaiku, who honored him with the title of Chief. Back in the United States, Bey organized a music group named Egbe Ife (Society of Love), which became a training ground for young percussionists; a number of his students went on to develop successful careers. From 1973–1975 he was in the cast of the Broadway musical *Raisin*, his role being *African Drummer*. On 17 April 1973 Bey married Barbara Ann Coleman, also known as Barbara Kenyatta, with whom he spent the rest of his life.

As Bey continued to seek connections to his African heritage that would fulfill his spiritual, intellectual, and creative destiny, he discovered Orisha Worship. In 1976 he became an initiated priest of Sango and his wife Barbara became a priest of Yemoja in the Yoruba Lucumi religious tradition. As a priest, Bey was generous with his time and energy—providing spiritual guidance to many people from all walks of life who recognized his sincere character and sought his counsel. He was fiercely honest, deeply aware of his own human weaknesses, extremely loving toward his family, and courageous in defense of his people. These qualities made him an exemplary leader in his community, where he was recognized as a revered elder and was often asked to give blessings, pour libations, lead prayer, and expound on Yoruba Lucumi religious teachings. Eventually he established Ile Omo Olofi, a religious house, with his wife Barbara and many godchildren.

Always interested in teaching and sharing information, Bey was a frequent guest speaker at such institutions as Duke University, City College, Drake University, Medgar Evers College, Princeton University, Temple University, the University of Hartford, and New York University. Interested also in reaching out to children, in the 1990s he accepted a position to teach shekere at Intermediate School 246, in Brooklyn.

Even at the age of ninety, after being diagnosed with stomach cancer, he continued his activities. Just months before his death, he performed in a drum symposium at New York University. By the time of his death, he had been the subject of many celebrations and tributes of all kinds in honor of his life. Hundreds attended his funeral at Friendship Missionary Baptist Church in Brooklyn, New York; he was buried on 14 April 2004 at Calverton National Cemetery, Long Island, New York. Just days later, on 17 April 2004, on the day that would have been his ninety-first birthday and the couple's thirty-first anniversary, his wife died. He was survived by his son, David, and daughters, Carol, Denise, and Ayodele, as well as four grandchildren and abundant godchildren, students, and friends.

Further Reading

James Hawthorne Bey's son, David Hawthorne, maintains Chief Bey's papers and archives, including recordings, photographs, and performance videos.

Frazier, E. "Rhythm (A Tribute to Chief Bey, P.J. and Drummers of the World)," *Essence*, vol. 5 (2002).

Olatunji, Babatunde, with Robert Atkinson, and Akinsola Akiwowo. *The Beat of My Drum, An Autobiography* (2005).

Obituaries: *Amsterdam News*, 14 April, 2004; *Associated Press, New York Times*, 13 April, 2004.

Discography

Bey, Chief, and Ile Omo Olofi. *Explorations II* (Mapleshade, 1995).

Ilori, Solomon. *African Highlife* (Blue Note, 1963).

Mann, Herbie. *At the Village Gate* (Atlantic, 1961).

Olatunji, Babatunde. *Drums of Passion* (Columbia, 1959).

Olatunji, Babatunde. *More Drums of Passion* (Columbia, 1966).

Saunders, Pharoah. *Izipho Zam* (Strata East, 1969).

World Saxophone Quartet. *Metamorphosis* (Elektra/Nonesuch, 1990).

SUSAN RICHARDSON-SANABRIA

BHARUCHA-REID, Albert Turner (13 Nov. 1927–26 Feb. 1985), mathematician, was born in Hampton, Virginia, the son of William Thaddeus Reid, who taught electricity at Hampton Institute's trade school, and Elaine Brown. Albert had a brother,

William M., and a sister, Cora Mae. His strong interest in biology and mathematics led him to enroll at Iowa State University, where such joint disciplinary programs were encouraged. After obtaining his bachelor of science degree in 1949, Reid continued at Iowa State in the graduate program for mathematics and biology, but he left for the University of Chicago in 1950. There he studied mathematical biology, mathematics, probability and statistics, and physics, and he served as a research assistant in the mathematical biology program. In 1953 Reid accepted a position as a research associate in mathematical statistics at Columbia University. He did not complete the PhD program at Chicago or Columbia because he did not believe that a doctorate was necessary to become a competent researcher in the mathematical sciences. This view was reinforced by the continuing publication of his work in significant research journals.

On 7 June 1954 Reid married Rodabe Phiroze Bharucha and from then on hyphenated his name to Bharucha-Reid. The couple had two children, Kurush in 1955, and Rustum in 1965.

In 1955 Bharucha-Reid took a yearlong appointment as assistant research statistician (equivalent to assistant professor) in the statistics department at the University of California at Berkeley. The following year he took a teaching position at the University of Oregon, where he remained until 1961. During the 1958–1959 academic year he continued his research efforts as a fellow at the Mathematical Institute of the Polish Academy of Sciences in Warsaw, Poland. In 1961 Bharucha-Reid accepted a position as associate professor of mathematics at Wayne State University in Detroit. Two years later he took a yearlong leave from the university to travel to Madras, India, as a visiting professor on the faculty of applied mathematics in the Institute of Mathematical Sciences.

In 1965 he was promoted to full professor of mathematics at Wayne State, and he subsequently served there as director of the Center for Research in Probability from 1967 to 1981, as acting chair of the mathematics department from 1972 to 1973, and as dean and associate provost for graduate studies from 1976 to 1981. During this time he also held visiting professorships at the University of Wisconsin's Mathematics Research Center, from 1966 to 1967, and at the Georgia Institute of Technology, from 1973 to 1974. In 1981 Bharucha-Reid began working at the Georgia Institute of Technology in Atlanta as a professor in the School of Mathematics. In 1983 he left that position to assume duties at Atlanta University as distinguished professor of mathematics.

Bharucha-Reid's research covered a wide range of topics in mathematical biology, pure mathematics, physics, probability, and statistics. From 1953 to 1955 he engaged in research on two air force projects at Columbia University that involved him in basic research into stochastic processes and stochastic theories or epidemics. He continued this research during 1955 and 1956 at the University of California, Berkeley. From 1956 to 1962 he was director of an Army Research Office project concerned with stochastic processes and related statistical problems at the University of Oregon and Wayne State University. From 1962 to 1964 he was co-principal investigator for a National Science Foundation grant on stochastic processes and mathematical physics at Wayne, and he continued from 1966 to 1969 as director of a National Institutes of Health grant on stochastic processes in biology. Other Wayne projects included a National Science Foundation grant, from 1969 to 1971, on probability measures and random equations, and an Army Research office grant, from 1977 to 1981, on computational solution of random integral equations.

During his brief tenure at Atlanta University, from 1983 to 1985, Bharucha-Reid was active in the new graduate program for master of science in physics, and he made significant contributions to the research programs in computational and plasma physics. Two of his last papers were concerned with the numerical solutions of a random singular integral equation appearing in crack problems and the effect of random loading on the mechanics of fatigue and crack growth in solids.

Bharucha-Reid published his first book, *Elements of the Theory of Markov Processes and Their Applications*, in 1960. It provided one of the first concise introductions to the area of probabilistic analysis, and for many years it was successful as a textbook and guide for self-study. During his career he published more than seventy papers and wrote seven books on topics in the stochastic theory of epidemics, Markov processes, random integral and polynomial equations, and computational methods. His last book, with M. Sambandham, *Random Polynomials*, was published posthumously in 1986.

Bharucha-Reid traveled widely through North America, Europe, and India, and presented lectures at many universities, international conferences, and workshops. He served as editor of the *Journal of Integral Equations and Applications*, and associate editor for *Nonlinear Analysis* and the *Bulletin of Mathematical Biology*. He was on the editorial board of the *Journal of Mathematical and Physical Sciences* and was a member of the reviewing staff for *Mathematical Reviews* and *Zentralblatt für Mathematik*. He was also editor for the North-Holland series in Probability and Applied Mathematics.

Bharucha-Reid held active membership in numerous professional organizations, including the American Mathematical Society, the Polish Mathematical Society, the American Association for the Advancement of Science, the Institute of Mathematical Statistics, the Society for Mathematical Biology, and the Society for Industrial and Applied Mathematics. His other professional responsibilities included serving as vice president of the International Association for Mathematical Geology, from 1972 to 1976, member of the Russian Translation Committee of the American

Mathematical Society and the Institute of Mathematical Statistics, from 1973 to 1981, and member of the American Mathematical Society's Committee on Academic Freedom, Tenure, and Employment Security, from 1977 to 1981.

Bharucha-Reid had fourteen students earn their doctoral degrees under his direction at Wayne State University, and many of them went on to enjoy successful careers as both academicians and researchers. Having benefited greatly from both his teaching and research abilities, most of his students published jointly with Bharucha-Reid, and several became major research collaborators, in particular, Dhandapani Kannan and Mark J. Christensen. A significant collaborator, who was not a student of Bharucha-Reid's, was M. Sambandham, who published several papers with him and coauthored a book on random polynomials.

Albert Turner Bharucha-Reid died at his home in Atlanta. His distinguished career as both a pure and applied research mathematician extended over three and a half decades, and his many contributions to research, student training and mentoring, and academic leadership were acknowledged by the large number of honors and awards he received throughout his life. In particular, he was granted an honorary doctorate of science from Syracuse University in 1984 and the National Association of Mathematicians established an annual lecture series in his name.

Further Reading

Bharucha-Reid's papers are housed at the Amistad Research Center, Tulane University, New Orleans, Louisiana.

Krapp, Kristine, ed. *Notable Black American Scientists* (1999).

Mickens, Ronald E. "Albert Turner Bharucha-Reid," *Physics Today* (Dec. 1985).

Newell, Virginia K., ed. *Black Mathematicians and Their Works* (1980).

Sammons, Vivian O. *Blacks in Science and Medicine* (1989).

RONALD E. MICKENS

BIASSOU, Jorge (Georges) (c. 1760–c. 1801), Haitian revolutionary, was born a slave in Cap Français (or Guarico, in Spanish), on the northern coast of Saint Domingue, in modern Haiti. Spanish documents give his parents' names as Carlos and Diana, and Biassou and his mother were the slaves of the Holy Fathers of Charity in Cap Français, where Biassou's mother worked in the Hospital of the Holy Fathers of Charity, probably as a laundress or cook. Biassou's father's owner and occupation are unknown.

In 1791 Biassou joined Boukman Dutty, a slave driver and coachman considered by the slaves to be a religious leader, and Jean-François, also a slave from the Northern Plains of Saint Domingue, in leading the largest slave revolt in the Western Hemisphere on the richest sugar colony of its day, French Saint Domingue. Boukman was killed in November of 1791, only three months into the revolt, and Biassou

and Jean-François assumed command of the rebel slave forces of the North. Jean-François decorated himself with the Cross of St. Louis, an aristocratic military order. Biassou titled himself the Viceroy of the Conquered Territories, and Toussaint-Louverture, a freeman who had once been a slave on the Bréda plantation, became aide and physician to Biassou's large army of forty thousand men, all former slaves.

Unable to feed and supply such a large force for very long, Jean-François and Biassou attempted to secure the general amnesty promised in late 1791 by the French Assembly. This decree promised to forgive "acts of revolution" for rebels who "returned to order" (Dubois, 125). They sued for peace in exchange for their own freedom and political rights and those of their families and officers, but the reactionary planters of Saint Domingue unwisely rejected their offer. Biassou angrily ordered the execution of all his white prisoners, vowing that they would pay "for the insolence of the [Colonial] Assembly which has dared to write to me with so little respect" (Landers, 209). Toussaint stayed his superior's order, but the bloody fighting continued.

In the spring of 1793 England and Spain both declared war on France and began to court Biassou and Jean-François, whose troops by that time were almost in a starving state. Commissioner Léger Félicité Sonthonax, one of three civil commissioners sent to represent the new French Republic in Saint Domingue, also offered freedom and alliance in the name of the French Republic, but some rebels considered this a trick and believed only a king could make and keep such a promise. Jean-François and Biassou allegedly responded, "Since the beginning of the world we have obeyed the will of a king. We have lost the king of France but we are dear to him of Spain who constantly shows us reward and assistance. We therefore cannot recognize you until you have enthroned a king" (Landers, 210).

Spain designated its new armies of risen slaves the Black Auxiliaries of Charles IV. The Spanish captain general and governor of Santo Domingo (the Spanish name for Saint Domingue) ceremoniously decorated Jean-François, Biassou, and Toussaint with gold medals bearing the likeness of the king and presented them with documents expressing the gratitude and confidence of the Spanish government. Newly supplied and under a Spanish flag, the forces of Jean-François, Biassou, and Toussaint fought many bloody battles against the French, but when the French Assembly finally abolished slavery in May of 1794, Toussaint broke with the Spaniards and offered his services and loyalty to the French Republic. Jean-François and Biassou remained loyal to Spain.

In 1795 Spain and the directory of the French Republic, the ruling body of the new French Republic, finally concluded a peace treaty by which Spain ceded western Hispaniola to the French and agreed to disband the Black Auxiliaries of Carlos IV. On the last day of December 1795, the exiled black troops sailed away for Havana, Cuba, on a small flotilla of four ships, but Cuban officials refused to let them disembark. After much angry correspondence, Jean-François and twelve of his military subordinates, along with their extended families, totaling 136 persons, sailed away from Havana for Cádiz, Spain. The remainder of Jean-François's troops was dispersed to various parts of Central America. In January of 1796 Biassou traveled with his immediate household of five, his slave, and seventeen other dependents to Spanish-held St. Augustine, Florida.

Biassou had enjoyed a position of command for five years before he settled in Florida, and his proud demeanor immediately alienated the Spanish governor, who had arranged lodging for Biassou and his immediate family and sent two nights' supper to the house, only to have Biassou complain that he had not been invited to dine at the governor's home. The black general walked the streets of St. Augustine in fine clothes trimmed in gold, a silver-trimmed saber, and a fancy ivory and silver dagger. The gold medal of Charles IV must also have impressed the townspeople, but the governor wrote, "The slave owners have viewed his arrival with great disgust, for they fear he will set a bad example for the rest of his class" (Landers, 212). Only three months after arriving, Biassou's brother-in-law and military heir, Sergeant Juan Jorge Jacobo, married Rafaela Witten, the daughter of PRINCE WITTEN. Like Biassou and Jorge Jacobo, Witten was a member of the free black militia and had served with distinction in 1795 against invaders sponsored by the French revolutionary Edmond Charles Genet, first minister of the French Republic to the United States.

The marriage of Biassou's heir, Jorge, and Witten's daughter, Rafaela, thus united the leading families of both groups of blacks who had allied with the cause of the Spanish king against the forces of French republicanism. Previously, no black militiaman in Florida who served in Spain had held a rank higher than sergeant, but by virtue of his service in Santo Domingo, Biassou still used the title of general. His elevated title thus raised the status of Florida's black militia. Biassou and his troops proved able defenders of Spanish interests in the next decades. In 1800 the Seminole Indians launched a series of violent attacks on outlying plantations; Biassou led the troops in expeditions against the raiders and in border patrols until his sudden illness and death in July of 1801.

When Biassou died, his bereaved family and followers arranged a wake and buried him the following day with full honors in St. Augustine's Tolomato Cemetery. Despite rumors about his possible practice of vodun (the Afro-syncretic religion also known as vodou) in Santo Domingo, in his last years Biassou had apparently been baptized and so he received a full Catholic burial. After an elaborate mass that included songs, tolling bells, candles, and burning incense, Florida's governor and other persons of distinction accompanied Biassou's cortege to the graveyard. They were accompanied by drummers and an honor guard of twenty members of Biassou's troops, who discharged a volley of gunfire at the grave site. The obligations of military corporatism outweighed any racial distinctions in this ceremony, the public notary attesting that "every effort was made to accord him the decency due an officer Spain had recognized for military heroism" (Landers, 133). The parish priest entered Biassou in the death register as "the renowned *caudillo* (or military leader) of the black royalists of Santo Domingo" (Landers, *A Turbulent Time*, 169).

Further Reading
Dubois, Laurent. *Avengers of the New World: The Story of the Haitian Revolution* (2004).
Gaspar, David Barry, and David Patrick Geggus, eds. *A Turbulent Time: The French Revolution and the Greater Caribbean* (1997).
Geggus, David. *Haitian Revolutionary Studies* (2002).
James, C. L. R. *Black Jacobins: Toussaint L'Ouverture and the San Domingo Revolution* (1963).
Landers, Jane. *Black Society in Spanish Florida* (1999).
Landers, Jane. "Rebellion and Royalism in Spanish Florida: The French Revolution on Spain's Northern Colonial Frontier," in *A Turbulent Time*, eds. David Barry Gaspar and David Patrick Geggus (1997).

JANE G. LANDERS

BIBB, Henry Walton (10 May 1815–1 Aug. 1854), author, editor, and antislavery lecturer, was born into slavery on the plantation of David White of Shelby County, Kentucky, the son of James Bibb, a slaveholding planter and state senator, and Mildred Jackson. White began hiring Bibb out as a laborer on several neighboring plantations before he had reached the age of ten. The constant change in living situations throughout his childhood, combined with the inhumane treatment he often received at the hands of strangers, set a pattern for life that he would later refer to in his autobiography as "my manner of living on the road." Bibb was sold more than six times between 1832 and 1840 and was forced to relocate to at least seven states throughout the South; later, as a free man, his campaign for abolition took him throughout eastern Canada and the northern United States. But such early instability also made the young Bibb both self-sufficient and resourceful, two characteristics that were useful against the day-to-day assault of slavery: "The only weapon of self defense that I could use successfully," he wrote, "was that of deception."

In 1833 Bibb met and married Malinda, a slave on William Gatewood's plantation in nearby Oldham County, Kentucky, and the following year she gave birth to Mary Frances, their only child to survive infancy. At about this time Gatewood purchased Bibb from the Whites in the vain hope that uniting the young family would pacify their desire for freedom. Living less than ten miles from the Ohio River, Bibb made his first escape from slavery by crossing the river into Madison, Indiana, in the winter of 1837. He boarded a steamboat bound for Cincinnati, escaping the notice of authorities because he was "so near the color of a slaveholder," a trait deemed undesirable by prospective slave buyers and for which he endured prolonged incarcerations at various slave markets. Bibb situated this first escape historically as "the commencement of what was called the underground railroad to Canada." Less than a year after achieving freedom, Bibb returned to Kentucky for his wife and daughter. He was captured and taken to the Louisville slave market, from which he again escaped, returning to Perrysburg, Ohio.

In July 1839 Bibb once more undertook to free his wife and child. Betrayed by another slave, Bibb was again taken to Louisville for sale; this time his wife and child accompanied him on the auction block. While awaiting sale, Bibb received the rudiments of an education from white felons in the prison, where he was forced to work at hard labor for a summer. Finally, a speculator purchased the Bibbs for resale at the lucrative markets of New Orleans. After being bought by Deacon Francis Whitfield of Claiborn Parish, Louisiana, Bibb and his family suffered unimaginable cruelty. They were physically beaten and literally overworked to the point of death, and they nearly perished for lack of food and adequate shelter. Bibb attempted two escapes from Whitfield, preferring that his family risk the perils of the surrounding Red River swamps than endure eighteen-hour days in the cotton fields.

The final escape attempt resulted in Bibb's permanent separation from his family in December 1840. First staked down and beaten nearly to death after his capture, Bibb was then sold to two professional gamblers. These men took him through Texas and Arkansas and into "Indian Territory," where they sold him to a Cherokee slave owner on the frontier of white settlement in what is probably present-day Oklahoma or southeastern Kansas. There Bibb received what he considered his only humane treatment in slavery. Because he was allotted a modicum of independence and respect, and because he was reluctant to desert his master, who was then terminally ill, Bibb delayed his final escape from slavery by a year, departing the night of his master's death. He traveled through wilderness, occasionally stumbling onto Indian encampments, before crossing into Missouri, where his route took him east along the Osage River into Jefferson City. From there he traveled by steamboat through St. Louis to Cincinnati and on to freedom in 1841.

In Detroit in the winter of 1842, Bibb briefly attended the school of the Reverend William C. Monroe, receiving his only formal education. Bibb's work as what he called an "advocate of liberty" began in earnest soon after his final escape from slavery; for the next decade he epitomized the black abolitionist, making his voice heard through lectures, a slave narrative, and the independent press. Like his contemporaries FREDERICK DOUGLASS, WILLIAM WELLS BROWN, and WILLIAM AND ELLEN CRAFT, Bibb was among a first generation of African American fugitives from the South who used their firsthand experience in slavery as a compelling testimony against the atrocities of the southern institution.

Although his highly regarded *Narrative of the Life and Adventures of Henry Bibb, An American Slave* was not published until the spring of 1849, Bibb began telling the story of his life before antislavery crowds in Adrian, Michigan, in May 1844. His story proved so poignant in its depiction of human suffering and endurance, so heroic in its accounts of ingenious escapes, and so romantic in its adventures in the territories of the West that the Detroit Liberty Association undertook a full-scale investigation to allay public incredulity, an unprecedented response to a nineteenth-century slave narrative. Through correspondence with Bibb's former associates, "slave owners, slave dealers, fugitives from slavery, political friends and political foes," the committee found the facts of Bibb's account "corroborated beyond all question."

Lecturing for the Michigan Liberty Party, Bibb was sent to Ohio to speak along the north side of the Mason-Dixon Line, a region notorious for its proslavery sympathies. Bibb returned to the South one final time in the winter of 1845 in search of his wife and daughter. While visiting his mother in Kentucky, Bibb learned that his wife and daughter's escape from certain death on Whitfield's plantation came at the expense of their marriage; Malinda had been forced to become the mistress of a white southerner. In 1848, on a sabbatical from lecturing, Bibb met and married Mary E. Miles, an African American abolitionist from Boston. It is not known whether they had children. With the passage of the 1850 Fugitive Slave Law, the Bibbs fled to Sandwich, western Canada, where, in January 1851, Henry and Mary established the *Voice of the Fugitive*. This publication was a biweekly antislavery journal that reported on the condition of fugitives and advocated the abolition of slavery, black colonization to Canada, temperance, black education, and the development of black commercial enterprises.

With the aid of the black abolitionists JAMES T. HOLLY and J. T. Fisher, Bibb organized the North American League, an organization evolving out of the North American Convention of Colored People, held in Toronto and over which Bibb presided in September 1851. The league was meant to promote colonization to Canada and to serve as the central authority for blacks in the Americas. Although the league survived but a few short months, Bibb continued to work toward colonization, encouraging Michigan philanthropists a year later to help form the Refugee Home Society—a joint-stock company for the purpose of acquiring and selling Canadian farmland to black emigrants—to which Bibb attached his journal as its official organ. Tension among prominent black Canadians, however, brought about the society's demise. Bibb died in Windsor, Ontario, Canada, without realizing his vision for an African American colony.

Further Reading

Andrews, William L. *To Tell a Free Story: The First Century of Afro-American Autobiography, 1760–1865* (1988).

Hite, Roger W. "Voice of a Fugitive: Henry Bibb and Ante-bellum Black Separatism," *Journal of Black Studies* 4 (Mar. 1974): 269–284.

Quarles, Benjamin. *Black Abolitionists* (1969).

Ripley, C. Peter, ed. *The Black Abolitionist Papers*, vols. 3–4 (1985, 1991).

Silverman, Jason H. *Unwelcome Guests: Canada West's Response to American Fugitive Slaves, 1800–1865* (1985).

GREGORY S. JACKSON

BIBB, Joseph Dandridge (21 Sept. 1895–Dec. 1966), editor, writer, publisher, lawyer, and government official, was born in Montgomery, Alabama, the son of Viola (Lovett) Bibb and Joseph D. Bibb, an African Methodist Episcopal (AME) minister and a prominent teacher and advocate for the employment of black teachers. Bibb used his earnings from working in the railroad industry and southern factories to pay for his college education; he attended Atlanta University, Livingstone College, and Howard University, and completed his legal training at Yale and Harvard Universities.

After the completion of his formal education, Bibb moved to Chicago, the destination of thousands of job-seeking African Americans from the South. This mass exodus from the South—the Great Migration—saw blacks pour into urban areas between 1915 and 1925. Chicago and other cities such as Detroit and New York saw their black populations double and triple; these cities offered relative freedom from the violence and lack of opportunity in the South, but it was still hard for blacks to find work. Consequently, African Americans created their own newspapers to address issues such as racial discrimination, violence, and poor living conditions. Black newspapers, however, continued to urge southern blacks to migrate to the North.

Realizing the growing need to empower black citizens and to address black issues, Bibb, along with William Linton, started the *Chicago Whip* in 1919 with a mere twenty-five cents. The *Whip* appeared on the scene when black newspapers were experiencing a renaissance in Chicago, one of the nation's most racially polarized cities. Such newspapers included the *Chicago Conservator* (1878–1914), the *Chicago Defender* (1905–present), and the *Chicago Bee* (1925–1947). Published weekly, the *Whip* reached a circulation of 65,000 within its first year, second only to the *Chicago Defender*. Throughout its twenty-year existence, the paper campaigned for black rights and often featured the civil rights leader MARCUS GARVEY. In his editorials Bibb urged complete integration and the hiring of black workers. Because of this, the paper was considered to be militant by politicians and members of the mainstream press; Bibb later recalled how he was labeled "Red, radical, revolutionary" (*Ebony*, Jan. 1956). While writing for the *Whip*, Bibb also practiced law, and in 1922 he married Goldie Thompson. In 1929

the *Whip* promoted the successful "Don't Buy Where You Can't Work" campaign to combat the practices of white-owned businesses that wouldn't hire blacks. Other black newspapers throughout the country publicized similar boycotts. The *Whip* was liquidated during the Depression in 1939, and Bibb began working as managing editor of the Chicago edition of the *Pittsburgh Courier*, a popular black newspaper that published local and national editions. As an editor, he continued the spirit of the *Whip* in his columns on black civil rights.

Known for his biting editorials on behalf of civil rights, Bibb was also a staunch and loyal Republican, and this made him something of an anomaly at a time when most African Americans were gradually shifting their loyalty from the Republican to the Democratic party, seen as more committed to racial equality. For more than twenty-five years, Bibb served as a writer and speaker for the National Republican Committee. In 1952 Bibb was vocal about what he perceived as a smear campaign against then-vice presidential candidate Richard Nixon by Democratic campaigners to deter blacks from voting for Nixon and Dwight Eisenhower for president. Bibb urged the Republican Party to reach out to black voters.

During his campaign for governor of Illinois in 1952, the Republican candidate William G. Stratton had promised to appoint the first African American to state cabinet. Upon his 1953 inauguration Stratton named Bibb director of public safety. This made the fifty-seven-year-old Bibb the first African American to hold a cabinet post in Illinois and in any state since Reconstruction. Many saw this as a cynical move to court black voters. Nonetheless, Bibb described his new role as overseeing the "well-being and protection of the citizens of Illinois and visitors within its borders" (*Ebony*, Jan. 1956).

Bibb had to give up his law career and newspaper column for the state job, which paid $12,000 a year. From 1953 to 1961 Bibb served as director of public safety, overseeing four state penitentiaries, the state police, all state parole agents, and the Division of Criminal Investigation and Identification. Bibb reduced the prison population and pushed for prison reform and the efficiency of crime labs. He answered letters from inmates and investigated their complaints. When Bibb took office, Illinois had one of the largest populations in the United States, and traffic problems were becoming more of an issue. Bibb researched new techniques to control safety and noise on the Illinois expressways and pushed for a sixty-five-mile-per-hour speed limit in the state.

As the first black department director in the state of Illinois, Bibb restructured the Department of Public Safety to make it more efficient. But his major contributions are embodied in the written word—in his editorials and columns in the *Chicago Whip* and *Pittsburgh Courier*. Bibb remains an important figure in the history of the black newspapers that exhaustively fought for the rights and safety of black citizens.

Further Reading
"'Mr. Public Safety' Joseph Bibb is Guardian of Illinois Life and Property," *Ebony* (Jan. 1956)
Jet (Sept. 1967)

MARTHA PITTS

BIBB, Leon (7 Feb. 1922–), singer and actor, was born Charles Leon Arthello Bibb in Louisville, Kentucky. His father, also Leon Bibb, worked as a mail carrier and his mother, Elizabeth (McCloskey) Bibb, was a homemaker, although she sometimes assisted her mother, a domestic servant. Bibb's grandparents were born in slavery, and his forbears worked as slaves on vegetable plantations in western Kentucky. When he was a young child Bibb's aunt taught him spirituals, some of which he continued to sing throughout his career. His aunt recognized his vocal talent early, and she gave him a vision beyond the heavily segregated world of the South of the 1920s and 1930s by telling the young Bibb about ROLAND HAYES, a black concert singer who moved to Europe when he could not find career opportunities in the United States because of his race, and later returned to perform at Carnegie Hall. Bibb continued to sing in choruses in school and choirs at church, and in more informal groups with his friends during his teenage years.

After high school he attended Louisville Municipal College and was a soloist with the college glee club until he joined the army, where he was chosen for training as part of an all-black unit called the Tuskegee Airmen, the first African American pilots in the U.S. military who served with great distinction in World War II. Music was still on his mind, however, and immediately after his military service ended, Bibb headed to New York City to study voice.

Arriving in the city with just a few dollars in his pocket, he took a variety of jobs to support himself while searching for a way into music. He worked in restaurants, in the animation business, and in a factory making parts for radar equipment. At the invitation of an acquaintance, he attended a theater performance of *Othello* with PAUL ROBESON in the lead role. Bibb had the chance to meet Robeson, and the encounter sparked a lifelong friendship and a mentorship for the younger man.

It did not, however, lead to immediate work opportunities in singing. That came when Bibb responded to a newspaper advertisement seeking "Colored Singers." Asked over the telephone if he was colored, Bibb replied that no, he was a Negro, and was invited to come down to audition. At that time Bibb's professional experience consisted of winning a talent contest at the Apollo Theater. As a result of that audition he was chosen to appear in the original cast of *Annie Get Your Gun*, which starred Ethel Merman and opened on Broadway in 1946.

The show was the first of a number of successful and increasingly prominent roles Bibb enjoyed in the New York theater. He sang in the chorus and joined the touring company of *Finian's Rainbow*, which saw art comment on life with a subplot concerning a racist southern senator who through a mistaken magic spell has to experience life as a black man. At this time, in the late 1940s and early 1950s, there were few roles for blacks on Broadway or off, and Bibb had uneven success in finding work. One of his highest-profile roles was in *Lost in the Stars*, a 1949 piece based on the work of South African writer Alan Paton and written by Kurt Weill and Maxwell Anderson.

Bibb also took roles in Off-Broadway projects, including the play *Sandhog*, and he worked in non-singing parts as well, including an appearance in the drama *Flight into Egypt*. Still, he could not earn a steady income with his acting roles. Considering ways to supplement his income, he created a singing repertoire comprising English and Irish folk ballads, the spirituals he remembered from his Kentucky childhood, and chain gang and prison songs. His timing was right; soon the folk music revival would capture the country's interest, with stars such as the Weavers, the Freedom Singers, and ODETTA, quickly followed on by the next generation of folk-based singers including Bob Dylan, Joan Baez, and Carolyn Hester. Bibb's folk repertoire, classically trained voice, and theater-honed professionalism engaged audiences and also caught the ears of organizers of the first Newport (Rhode Island) Folk Festival, who were drawing on their contacts in the New York city music scene to put together one of the first major festivals featuring contemporary folk singers, coffeehouse stars, and traditional artists all at the same venue. Bibb's eclectic mix of songs and his polished tenor also attracted interest from executives at Vanguard Recording Society, a company that had begun by focusing on classical music but, in part because of the owners' support for the social justice causes of the day, was moving into folk and protest music. Bibb was recorded live performing four songs at the Newport Folk Festival and subsequently released a number of albums with Vanguard and other labels.

The spirituals and prison songs Bibb recorded came into sharper focus as the singer lent his voice and presence to civil rights actions during the 1960s. On the personal side, Bibb had married during the 1950s and had three children, son Eric (who would go on to become a respected blues musician) and daughter Doria, who were twins, and daughter Amy. As the 1960s progressed, however, his first marriage dissolved. He continued to make his living through music and also took occasional roles in film, including an appearance in *For the Love of Ivy* with SIDNEY POITIER in 1968. Bibb often opened for comedians, and while on tour with BILL COSBY in 1971 Bibb visited Vancouver and decided to move there. In addition to recording and performing, Bibb founded Step Ahead, a program designed to start students and teachers talking about racism and bullying, and talking with each other about how to address these issues in their communities.

Further Reading
There are no archives or published biographies of Mr. Bibb. A personal interview with Mr. Bibb was conducted by telephone to obtain some of the material

for this entry. Liner notes for his early recordings many be found in archival collections, and the program notes from *Live at the Newport Folk Festival, Volume One*, also provide a short biography.

Discography
A Family Affair (Jericho Beach 2002).
Roots of Folk (Vanguard 2002).

KERRY DEXTER

BIGARD, Barney (3 Mar. 1906–27 June 1980), jazz musician, was born Albany Leon Bigard in New Orleans, Louisiana, the son of Alexander Louis Bigard and Emanuella Marquez. Little is known of his family except that it produced musicians: his older brother Alex was a drummer, his uncle Emile was a violinist who played with musicians like KING OLIVER and KID ORY, and his cousin Anatie ("Natty") Dominique was a trumpet player and bandleader. Bigard studied clarinet under LORENZO TIO JR., whose students included JOHNNY DODDS, ALBERT NICHOLAS, OMER SIMEON, and Jimmie Noone.

Raised mostly by his grandparents, Bigard worked in the cigar factory of his uncle Ulysses as a boy and also as a photoengraver, and he played music mostly with parade bands. At the age of sixteen, however, Bigard joined Albert Nicholas's band as a tenor saxophonist. He continued playing the tenor with other New Orleans bands, including LUIS RUSSELL's. In 1924, on the recommendations of Russell and Nicholas, King Oliver asked Bigard to join his band in Chicago, and so, like many other young New Orleans musicians of the day, he left town and headed north. Bigard's first wife, Arthemise or Artemise (maiden name unknown), whom he married in about 1924, accompanied him to Chicago. They had four children, but the couple drifted apart, and the marriage ended some years later.

Bigard joined King Oliver's Dixie Syncopators as a tenor saxophonist, later switching to clarinet. While in Chicago he recorded with Oliver, LOUIS ARMSTRONG, JELLY ROLL MORTON, and Johnny Dodds. A young DOC CHEATHAM, at the time a budding saxophonist before he took up the trumpet, heard Bigard play in Chicago; Cheatham said years later, "I thought he was the greatest tenor player I ever heard in my life!" (Dance, 307). It was with the clarinet, however, that Bigard's talent was fully realized. His sound is usually described as warm, clear, liquid, or woody, and his style as fluid or articulate. Bigard's playing employed the full range of the instrument but with a particular resonance in the lower register, which some critics have ascribed to the fact that unlike most clarinetists he used the older Albert fingering system instead of the newer Boehm system. Haywood Henry, as a young sax and clarinet player, first heard Bigard playing with DUKE ELLINGTON in 1930 and remembered that "Barney Bigard was my model from the first. I loved his sound and the way he flowed on the clarinet. What he played always made a lot of sense, and he always told a story" (Dance, 207).

Bigard played with the Oliver band, both in Chicago at the Plantation Café and on tour, until the summer of 1927, when, after a brief stint with Charlie Elgar's Creole Orchestra in Milwaukee, he went on to New York City to join a group led by Luis Russell. Bigard was spotted by WELLMAN BRAUD, the bassist for the Duke Ellington Orchestra, which was playing in Harlem at the Cotton Club. In January 1928 Ellington asked Bigard to join his band as the replacement for Rudy Jackson. Bigard remained with Ellington for fifteen years as a featured player on clarinet, working with such outstanding jazz musicians as COOTIE WILLIAMS, JOHNNY HODGES, SONNY GREER, HARRY CARNEY, and Sam Nanton. Bigard contributed his distinctive New Orleans voice to the Ellington sound, and in return Ellington, as he did with other key musicians, wrote Bigard's voice into many of his classic arrangements, such as "C-Jam Blues," "Azure," "Caravan," "Harlem Air Shaft," and "Clarinet Lament." Bigard claimed to have written one of the band's signature pieces, "Mood Indigo," based partly on a melody borrowed from Lorenzo Tio Jr., although the published score bears Ellington's name and seems to give him credit for its composition.

In a highly segregated era, Ellington's band was an all-black group playing for all-white audiences. Bigard's obituary in the *New York Times* noted that "because he was fair-skinned, Mr. Bigard often purchased food for members of the Ellington band when the musicians toured in the Deep South during the years of the Jim Crow racial practices." Also, when the Ellington orchestra played on screen in a 1930 Amos 'n' Andy film titled *Check and Double Check*, Bigard and the band's valve trombonist, Juan Tizol, both being very light-skinned, were required to appear in blackface.

From 1931 on, Ellington and his group were on the road much of the time. Finally, tired of constant touring, which he found grueling—especially after 1941, when the war disrupted transportation schedules—Bigard left the Ellington orchestra in 1942 and headed to the West Coast, where he played with local groups, briefly formed a small band with Kid Ory on trombone and CHARLIE MINGUS on bass, and did studio work. Also in 1942 he married Dorothy Edgecombe. He returned to New York in 1944 and for a few months led his own group at the Onyx Club on Fifty-second Street. Then in 1944 or 1945 he returned to California, where he played with Kid Ory. In 1947 Bigard appeared in the film *New Orleans* with Armstrong. After the filming, Armstrong asked him to join Jack Teagarden, COZY COLE, and Velma Middleton in a small Dixieland group to be called Louis Armstrong's All Stars. Bigard stayed with the All Stars for five years, making many tours and records, and later he rejoined the group twice for shorter stints. By 1962 he had retired from full-time playing but continued to appear for brief engagements, concerts, and festivals, leading his own bands or playing with groups headed by Cozy Cole, Ben Pollack, JOHNNY ST. CYR, Muggsy Spanier, REX STEWART,

EARL HINES, Art Hodes, Eddie Condon, and Wild Bill Davison.

Bigard died in Culver City, California. Over a period of sixty years he had been a quintessential sideman, playing in big bands and small, Dixieland and swing, associated with many of the great jazz figures of the first half of the twentieth century. Bigard was in that group of fine young New Orleans clarinetists—among them Albert Nicholas, BUSTER BAILEY, Omer Simeon, EDMOND HALL, SIDNEY BECHET, and GEORGE LEWIS—who brought their style of music north after World War I and helped spread the gospel of jazz. A French critic, Jacques Morgantini, assessed Bigard's accomplishments this way: "Apart from those multiple qualities as an instrumentalist, improviser, and swingman . . . Barney Bigard possessed the remarkable talent of being able to adapt the typically New Orleans clarinet style to the big band context" (album notes, *Barney Bigard Story*, Jazz Archives, no. 12).

Further Reading

Bigard, Barney, with Barry Martyn. *With Louis and the Duke* (1985).

Dance, Stanley. *The World of Swing* (1974).

Obituary: *New York Times*, 28 June 1980.

BRUCE R. CARRICK

BIGGERS, John (13 Apr. 1924–25 Jan. 2001), artist and educator, later known as John "Anansa" Thomas Biggers, was born in Gastonia, North Carolina, to Cora Biggers, a homemaker who excelled in sewing and quiltmaking, and Paul Biggers, an educator, preacher, carpenter, and farmer. The youngest of seven children, John learned to appreciate the creativity, industry, and struggle of African American families in the example of his parents. When his father died in 1937, John was only thirteen. Cora Biggers took a job as a matron in an orphanage for black children and sent John and his brother Joe to Lincoln Academy, a boarding school that prepared black students to be teachers and ministers.

Biggers's artistic self-discovery began in 1941 when he enrolled at a black college in Virginia—Hampton Institute (later Hampton University). Although he intended to study the practical trade of plumbing, he ultimately majored in art because he was encouraged by his professor and mentor, Victor Lowenfeld, an Austrian Jewish psychologist and artist who had recently escaped Nazi persecution. Lowenfeld was the former director of an African art museum in Vienna, and he used Hampton's African art collection to teach African social, aesthetic, and spiritual values and their relevance to the lives of African Americans. Through his relationship with Lowenfeld, Biggers was inspired to learn about the art and culture of his ancestral heritage and to work from his life experiences. Describing his changing perspective about art, he reflected, "I began to see art not primarily as an individual expression of talent, but as a responsibility to reflect the spirit and style of the Negro people" (John Biggers et al., *Black Art in Houston*,

7–8). His early paintings revealed this devotion to conveying the tenacity and dignity of African Americans. *Mother and Child* (1943) celebrated black women as pillars of communal and family life, and *Gleaners* (1943) showed the diligence and commitment of regular working people. Other works criticized the effects of racist laws and the impoverished conditions in which blacks lived. *Crossing the Bridge* (1942) showed African Americans striving for a better life, and *Crucifixion* (1942) attacked the racist oppression of blacks in the South.

At Hampton University Biggers was exposed to a variety of artists and art historical movements that defined his philosophy and early style. He was most impressed by the works of American regionalists such as Grant Wood, Thomas Hart Benton, and Harry Sternberg, and by the Mexican muralists Diego Rivera, David Alfaro Siqueiros, and Jose Clemente Orozco. He also studied the figures of the Harlem Renaissance, most notably, the writers W. E. B. Du BOIS and ALAIN LOCKE, and the artists WILLIAM ELLISWORTH ARTIS, HALE A. WOODRUFF, ELIZABETH CATLETT, and CHARLES WHITE. White and Catlett visited Hampton, and they became mentors to and friends of Biggers; White painted Biggers into his campus mural *The Contribution of the Negro to American Democracy*.

In 1943 Biggers was drafted into the still-segregated U.S. Navy, where he served for two years as a visual arts specialist under the supervision of Joe Gilliard, his former ceramics teacher at Hampton. After his discharge in 1945 Biggers returned to Hampton for a semester, then followed Lowenfeld to Pennsylvania State University, where he received all three of his degrees: BS and MS degrees in 1948, and PhD in Education in 1954. Also at Pennsylvania he met Hazel Hales, an accounting major, and in 1948 they married. In 1949 the couple moved to Houston, where Biggers had accepted a position to establish an art department at Texas Southern University, then called Texas State University for Negroes. Initially he encountered many challenges. As a result of the segregated and substandard education for southern blacks, the majority of his students were barely literate, and he was frustrated in attempts to introduce art history to his curriculum, in addition to the foundations of creating art. Further, he lacked the supplies, equipment, and adequate studio space to set up his department, and the school administration was antagonistic to his ideas and requests. Describing the institutional reaction to his interest in digging for the African roots of African American culture, Biggers wrote, "The great majority of American blacks thought I was crazy. . . . These included members of my own department. Paris, London, and Rome were the foreign cities that our teachers, as well as most of those from other universities, wanted to visit" (John Biggers et al., 16). Despite these obstacles, he persevered with the philosophic approach he developed at Hampton, and encouraged students to paint from their own insights and their identification with black cultural heritage.

Biggers soon adopted a workshop approach to teaching: the students were considered apprentices and the program fostered their personal growth, understanding of art materials, and exploration of black cultural heritage. The methodology of "learning by doing" is exemplified by Biggers's mural program for art majors in which every senior student was expected to complete a mural on campus; in the early 2000s there were 114 such murals on the Texas Southern campus (John Biggers et al., 17). Having built the art department from the ground up, with allies in fellow faculty members and artists Joseph Mack and Carroll Simms, Biggers held his position at Texas Southern for thirty-four years.

In 1957 Biggers received a UNESCO grant to study art and culture in West Africa. With his wife, Hazel, he spent six months living in Ghana, Benin (then called Dahomey), Nigeria, and Togo, where he documented his experiences and observations in photographs, writing, and sketches. One of the first African American artists to travel extensively in Africa, he was particularly enthralled with the activity of marketplaces, the sanctity of shrines, and the daily life of fishermen, women, and children. Biggers's style of representation was transformed by the trip to Africa, and his subsequent work was less narrative and more symbolic, for it included African emblems and complex layers of geometric patterning. Using his research and sketches, he created a visual diary, *Ananse: The Web of Life in Africa* (1962), which included eighty-nine drawings and accompanying text. Biggers said that he chose to focus on the spider Ananse, the heroic trickster of Ashanti proverbs, because "God gave Ananse the meaning of order. . . . This is symbolized by his web, which stands also for the sun and its rays, and the sun personifies God" (*Ananse*, title page). Inspired by the powerful symbol of the ananse, this series of drawings expresses the interconnectedness of African communal life. Perhaps this is why he later changed his own name to John "Anansa" Thomas Biggers (although the exact date of the name change is unknown).

Biggers created over twenty-three murals that make visible the contributions of African Americans and their heritage in a monumental form of public art. Before he retired from Texas Southern University in 1983, he made a fifty-foot mural as a legacy to the school and a source of inspiration for future generations of African American artists. Entitled *Family Unity,* the mural showed the human cycle of life and the persistence of cultural continuity. He later used a detail of the mural for his lithograph *The Upper Room.* By the early 1990s Biggers was including Native American, Asian, and African cultural symbols in works that suggested the unity of humankind and the interconnectedness of human beings, nature, and the universe.

From 1995 to 1997 Biggers's work was celebrated in a major traveling retrospective hosted by seven art museums across the United States: Museum of Fine Arts, Houston; Cincinnati Art Museum; Hampton University Museum; North Carolina Museum of Art; Wadsworth Atheneum, Hartford, Connecticut; Museum of Fine Arts, Boston; and California Afro-American Museum, Los Angeles. The exhibition included his prints, drawings, and paintings. He died in his Houston home at the age of seventy-six. He left behind a prolific legacy of murals and paintings that celebrated African American and African life. Remarkably, he spent a lifetime developing dual careers as both an outstanding artist and a groundbreaking educator. Like the songs of an African storyteller, Biggers's art keeps alive the histories of African American people and their vital connection with African heritage.

Further Reading
Biggers, John. *Ananse: The Web of Life in Africa* (1996).
Biggers, John, Carroll Simms, and John Edward Meems. *Black Art in Houston: The Texas Southern Experience* (1978).
Ritter, Rebecca E. *Five Decades: John Biggers and the Hampton Art Tradition* (1990).
Roberts, Kristin Schreiber. *Framing John Biggers'* Shotguns *(1987): African American Art and Identity* (1997).
Wardlaw, Alvia J., with essays by Edmund Barry Gaither, Alison de Lima Greene, and Robert Farris Thompson. *The Art of John Biggers: View from the Upper Room* (1995).
Obituary: *New York Times,* 30 Jan. 2001.
SOPHIE SANDERS

BIGGIE SMALLS. *See* Notorious B. I. G. (Christopher Wallace).

BIGGS, Bradley (29 Aug. 1920–16 Nov. 2004), soldier, author, and educator, was born in Newark, New Jersey, to Bradley Biggs, a bootlegger, and Julia DeFreece, a domestic. The couple divorced when Bradley was an infant, and he recalled his childhood as one of abject poverty. His mother struggled to earn enough to support him and his younger brother Burton, and the family lived in public housing.

In his high school years, consumed by a desire to escape his harsh surroundings, Biggs developed two interests that helped define his path: flying and athletics. As a member of the Falcon Aeronautical Club of East Orange, New Jersey—the first and perhaps only black flying club in the East—he was exposed to the basics of flight and the mechanics of airplanes. At a burly six feet three inches tall, he was also able to use his athleticism to win a place on the New York Brown Bombers professional football club. Sensing an opportunity to advance himself, however, he quit in 1939 to join the United States Army. Biggs would later speak of this decision as one motivated not only by a desire to escape the ghetto but also as a way to create more opportunities for people like himself.

Segregation was still rigidly enforced in the military at the time, and Biggs was assigned to a black infantry unit. Given his interest in aeronautics, he enthusiastically campaigned throughout the war for an assignment in an airborne division. Blacks were considered incapable of handling all but the most menial duties, a prejudice that provided stiff resistance to his ambition. However, an executive officer at the Army's Parachute School in Fort Benning, Georgia, happened to be a former football star at West Point. He and Biggs shared a love of the game, and the officer was fond of him personally. As a result, Biggs, a commissioned second lieutenant, was a logical choice when the military brass planned to experiment with creating a black airborne infantry unit. In 1943 he received an order to report to Fort Benning, Georgia, and begin airborne training with twenty-two other black servicemen. He was the officer of the unit, the 555th Parachute Infantry Battalion, known as the "Triple Nickels." Under Biggs's command, Walter Morris became the first black soldier to receive airborne training.

The unit quickly dispelled the idea that blacks were incapable of succeeding in the same roles as white soldiers. Nevertheless, bigotry kept them from seeing combat duty. They served as "smoke jumpers" who parachuted into blazing forest fires on the West Coast set by Japanese bombs carried across the Pacific by balloons. The hazardous duty resulted in the highest casualty rate of any non-combat unit in World War II. Biggs and his men had successfully penetrated an elite segment of the military five years before the army would formally desegregate.

Where others saw segregation in the army, Biggs saw opportunities. He worked relentlessly for the betterment of black soldiers until the military desegregated in 1948. He continued his career with decorated combat duty in Korea from 1950 to 1951 and a post in Germany at the end of that conflict. While stationed in Germany he completed several programs at Tennessee A&I (later Tennessee State) and at the University of Nevada before receiving his degree from the University of Maryland. He retired in 1960 as a lieutenant colonel and became active in the University of Maryland overseas learning program for servicemen and the U.S. Army Education System, helping numerous soldiers under his command complete college programs.

When Biggs returned to the United States in 1960, a director from the Maryland program solicited his help in establishing a new college near Middletown, Connecticut. Biggs personally scouted a location with his private plane, and Middlesex Community College opened in 1968 with Biggs as its first dean of faculty and administration. While continuing to teach and serve in administrative roles at the college, he was also recruited to serve as deputy commissioner of public works for the State of Connecticut. In 1977 he moved to Boston to serve as both an administrator for the Boston Housing Authority, drawing on his childhood experiences in public housing, and for the Department of Health and Hospitals. Seemingly tireless, he also founded Biggs International Development Corporation to perform municipal public works.

He could not shake his love of education, however. In 1978 he moved to Miami to teach at Florida International University, where he became vice president for administrative affairs in 1983. In the midst of these responsibilities he somehow found time to earn two additional degrees—a master's degree in 1969, and a master of arts for teachers in 1973, both from Wesleyan University—and build a family. He married Kunigunde "Gunde" Elsinger, a teacher, in July 1960, and they raised two children: Bradley III, a clinical psychologist, and Carina, an oncologist. To finish his career, he authored two books: *Gavin* (1980), a biography of Lieutenant General James M. Gavin, the white officer who worked with Biggs to integrate the 555th into the Eighty-second Airborne, and *Triple Nickels: America's First All-Black Paratroop Unit* (1986). He returned to Connecticut in his later years, remaining active in the community and with educational institutions. Most of all, he cherished time with his wife of more than four decades. He died of heart failure in Middletown, near the college he almost single-handedly founded.

Further Reading
Biggs, Bradley. *Gavin* (1980).
Biggs, Bradley. *Triple Nickels: America's First All-Black Paratroop Unit* (1986).
Obituary: *Hartford Courant*, 12 Dec. 2004.

EDWARD M. BURMILA

BILALI (c. 1760–1855), Muslim leader and plantation manager, was born in Africa, sold into slavery, and transported to the Bahamas and then to Sapelo Island, Georgia. His name is also given as Bilali Mahomet and Bul-Ali. Almost nothing is known about Bilali's life in Africa, but his fellow Fula or Peul (originally Malian) friend, SALIH BILALI, who was enslaved on the neighboring island of Saint Simons, said that Bilali came from the village of Timbo, in Futa Jallon (later Guinea). This was an important Muslim educational and political community and the homeland of another Fula, IBRAHIMA ABD AL-RAHMAN, who was enslaved in Mississippi. Bilali's strict adherence to Muslim ways and the book he wrote in Arabic show that he paid attention to his teachers in Africa. In the Bahamas Bilali married at least one of his four known wives before being brought to Georgia around 1802. He had a proud bearing and insisted on the use of his African name. ("Bilali" was popular in West Africa as it was the name of the Prophet Muhammad's first *muezzin* or caller to prayer, a black African former slave and one of the first converts to Islam.) He reportedly persisted in dressing as he had in Africa in a robe and fez; he also prayed facing the east, followed Muslim dietary rules and prohibitions, and held himself aloof from non-Muslims.

Bilali is believed to have been buried with a Koran, prayer beads, and a prayer rug. He must have been an extraordinarily strong person to hold on to these items through the Middle Passage, during which most captives were stripped of their possessions. This seemingly unlikely possibility is not far-fetched since the single extant artifact from Bilali's possessions, his once mysterious book, known about for some time until bequeathed by Bilali to a friendly white writer in the late 1850s, written on eighteenth-century Venetian paper often traded on the coast of Africa, was found in America rather than Africa. Writing his book was Bilali's attempt, around 1830, after at least thirty-five years of slavery, to set down in Arabic some of the rituals required of the followers of Muhammad found on Sapelo Island.

The thirteen-page manuscript was not taken seriously until 1940, and linguists have as of this writing not translated the complete text. Despite apparent corrections and annotations by another hand, the main text admits numerous misspellings and other probable errors. It is possible, however, according to some readers, in light of other manuscripts from West Africa, that Bilali was using phonetic Arabic letters to write his own language, Fulfulde or Pular. Two unpolished pages offer rules about praying, four are still not translated, two describe ablution practices before prayer, while the next five pages include repetitive assertions on keeping the faith, hope in being accepted as a servant of God, and rules about when to pray.

Using skills he had probably learned or practiced in Futa Jallon, Bilali became the only manager needed to run the five-hundred-slave Sea Island plantation on which he lived. His politically prominent and agriculturally adventurous purchaser, Thomas Spalding, a sometime lawyer, wrote occasional newspaper articles—but none have been found about Bilali. Their plantation hosted several once-famous domestic and foreign travelers. Some of these travelers were Aaron Burr, shortly after he had killed Alexander Hamilton in a duel; John D. Legare, editor of the important *Southern Agriculturist* journal; the British wanderers Basil and Margaret Hall; the actress Fanny Kemble; the scientist Charles Lyell; the courtier Amelia Murray; and Sweden's Fredrika Bremer. The travelers wrote positively about their visits and the good slave relations they saw, but though they marveled at how well the place was run, even though the master left for weeks at a time, no one mentioned Bilali or his role as the de facto manager in the absence of whites.

The first-known published notice of Bilali in 1829, written by the slaver Zephaniah Kingsley, does not include names but clearly refers to Bilali and Salih Bilali. He wrote that both had saved their slave charges in 1815 and 1824, and that both were Muslims. As a matter of fact, near the end of the War of 1812, Sapelo Island was in danger of being raided by the British, but the raid did not occur, so Bilali did not have to employ the eighty muskets his master left with him to fend off the invaders. However, the pending danger allowed Bilali, according to tradition, to declare: "I will answer for every negro of the true faith, but not for the Christian dogs you own" (Coulter, *Thomas Spalding of Sapelo*, 1940). (Salih Bilali had less luck in saving his slaves on his plantation on Saint Simons, as some two hundred fled to or were taken away by the British.) In the terrible hurricane of 1824, however, both Muslim leaders seemed to have been responsible for saving their fellow slaves while whites went inland and many coastal people were lost elsewhere.

Bilali was described in 1850—the year his master died—by a neighbor, Georgia B. Conrad, as being old, black, tall, well-formed, good-featured, and the father of many Muslim children. It was not only his children who were servants of Allah; Bilali seems also to have been the leader, *imam* or *amir*, of Sapelo's own Muslim community, which he strove to keep on the right path. Not long before he died, he gave his "book" to Francis Goulding, a local white writer—unable, apparently, to find literate Muslims or African Americans. It may be seen today in the University of Georgia library.

Few whites, including Goulding, paid serious attention to this remarkable man and his story. The famed storyteller Joel Chandler Harris borrowed tales of Bilali from several sources and tenderly recast them in the language of his black servants for the amusement of whites. Harris never allowed his narrator, Uncle Remus, to say anything positive about strong, independent African Americans—though elsewhere Harris, stressing the *Arabic* as if Bilali and others were merely visitors in Africa, wrote positively about "Arabic-Africans." It would be a long time before Americans would accept black African agency and literacy. Consistent with contemporary notices that omitted anything about slave religious practices, Harris considered Arabs to be a light-skinned, improved mixed-race of people. He wrote two books, *The Story of Aaron, the Son of Ben Ali* and *Aaron in the Wildwoods*, with an "Arabic-African" hero who was called the son of "Bul Ali" and made to despise black Africans—misrepresenting the religious attitude as a racial attitude of black African Muslims like Bilali.

In the late 1930s, interviewers of former slaves on Sapelo Island were told stories about Bilali, his religious practices, artifacts, offspring, and others who maintained Muslim names and traditions for at least two generations. Later descendents of Sapelo Island slaves told the historian William McFeely about Bilali "the powerful 'old man,'" and in the late 1990s a descendant named Cornelia Walker Bailey told even more about Bilali and about the island's Baptist church whose members cover their heads, seat men and women separately, and all pray facing the east—as Muslims do around the world.

Bilali lived an extraordinary life. He was a renowned plantation manager, a practicing if not official *imam*, literate in Arabic, and a misused model for the hero of two books by Joel Chandler Harris. His life sheds light on the intelligence, strength, and dignity of enslaved people, many of whom have been all but forgotten in history.

Further Reading
Austin, Allan D. *African Muslims in Antebellum America: Transatlantic Stories and Spiritual Struggles* (1997).

Bailey, Cornelia, with Christena Bledsoe. *God, Dr. Buzzard, and the Bolito Man: A Saltwater Geechee Talks about Life on Sapelo Island* (2000).

Diouf, Sylviane A. *Servants of Allah: African Muslims Enslaved in the Americas* (1998).

Judy, Ronald A. T. *(Dis)Forming the American Canon: African-Arabic Slave Narratives and the Vernacular* (1993).

Martin, Bradford G. "Sapelo Island's Arabic Document . . . in Context," *Georgia Historical Quarterly* (Fall 1994).

McFeely, William S. *Sapelo's People: A Long Walk into Freedom* (1994).

Savannah Unit of the Georgia Writers Project of the Works Projects Administration. *Drums and Shadows: Survival Studies among the Georgia Coastal Negroes, 1940* (1986).

ALLAN D. AUSTIN

BILALI, Salih. *See* Salih Bilali.

BILLINGSLEY, Orzell, Jr. (24 Oct. 1924–13 Dec. 2001), civil rights attorney and political activist, was born in Birmingham, Alabama. One of three sons, he attended Birmingham public schools, including the city's first and oldest, and, at one time, the South's largest African American high school, Industrial (A. H. Parker) High.

After graduating from high school Billingsley attended two highly respected, historically black institutions of higher learning. The first was Talladega College, a private liberal arts college located in Alabama, fifty miles east of Birmingham. He graduated with high honors in 1946 and headed for Washington, D.C., where he attended Howard University School of Law. He earned his law degree there in 1950. Afterward, he returned to Alabama, where he was admitted to the Alabama state bar in 1951, one of the first ten African Americans to do so.

Instantly, Billingsley threw himself behind the post–World War II fight for full black citizenship in America. Always blunt, doggedly direct, and determined, he took no quarter with his opponents in the courtroom. Consequently, he served as either the chief or co-counsel in a number of major court cases. He served as one of the lead lawyers for MARTIN LUTHER KING JR. and the Montgomery Improvement Association during the historic 1955 Montgomery bus boycott. He also represented ROSA PARKS, whose refusal to surrender her seat to a white man triggered the boycott. Equally important, however, is that he represented the impoverished. As a result, he often did not receive any pay for his legal services.

Billingsley's perhaps most notable case began in 1957. His client, the Alabama native Caliph Washington, had been charged with capital murder by an all-white jury for the accidental death of a white police officer with whom he had scuffled. During the scuffle, the officer was killed when his own gun was accidentally discharged. Although it would take four trials and fifteen years, Billingsley eventually won an acquittal for his client in 1972. Washington, indeed, was

only one of at least twenty men whose lives Billingsley saved by serving as their defense attorney. Billingsley's defense of Washington was also notable for helping to end the practice of selecting all-white juries in Jefferson County.

The Washington case also led to the historic *Reynolds v. Sims* (1964) U.S. Supreme Court case and its monumental "one man, one vote" decision. Some legal commentators rank that decision higher in importance than *Brown v. Board of Education* (1954).

Billingsley, who in 1963 demanded that Alabama's racist 1901 state constitution be replaced, gradually became a central figure in the legal life of his native state, serving as general counsel for the Alabama Cities, as a consultant for corporations, credit unions, and cooperatives, and as a Recorder's Court judge. He was also a municipal judge in Roosevelt City, an all-black town near Birmingham, that was one of the more than twenty small towns in Alabama that he organized and helped found in the 1960s and 1970s by soliciting financial assistance from the federal government and private corporations.

Billingsley was also active in electoral politics. In 1960, five years before the passage of the Voting Rights Act, he cofounded and became the president of the Alabama Democratic Conference (ADC), the first statewide black political organization in Alabama. Over time, the ADC became recognized as one of the most powerful African American political organizations in the nation. Birmingham served as its stronghold, but Billingsley traveled extensively and dangerously throughout Alabama's racially divided Black Belt region promoting the organization and its program.

As ADC president, Billingsley butted heads with the Alabama Democratic Party (ADP), then still dominated by segregationist whites. Primarily he did so by demanding that the ADP remove the "white supremacy" phrase from its official emblem and that African Americans have greater involvement in the ADP's activities. He also stressed the importance of political mass education and the need for more African American leaders to run for public and party office.

More a leader than a follower, Billingsley founded the Alabama Unit of the Southern Democratic Conference, and was general counsel for the National Democratic Party of Alabama (NDPA), serving as one of its delegates at the 1968 Democratic National Convention.

A staunch supporter of black economic development, Billingsley organized many corporations, including the Alabama Afro Contractors Association. He also served on the board of directors of both the Alabama State Conference of Counties and the Jefferson County Commission for Economic Opportunity. Moreover, he became a member of the Democratic Executive Commission of Jefferson County, the first black elected to that position.

Highly respected in both legal and political circles during the turbulent era of the civil rights movement, Billingsley would sometimes receive phone calls directly from either President Lyndon B. Johnson or his predecessor, John F. Kennedy. Both often called him to receive updates about the state of race relations in Alabama. So greatly impressed was Kennedy with Billingsley's legal expertise that, reportedly, he requested that Billingsley be appointed as attorney general. Various credible sources have also stated that Billingsley ranked high as a candidate for becoming America's first African American United States Supreme Court justice, prior to his fellow Howard law school alumnus and friend THURGOOD MARSHALL. Orzell Billingsley Jr. died in Birmingham, Alabama, after a long illness.

Further Reading
The Orzell Billingsley Jr. Papers are located in the Department of Archives and Manuscripts, Linn-Henley Research Library, Birmingham Public Library, Birmingham, Alabama.
Chestnut, J. L., Jr., and Julia Cass. *Black in Selma: The Uncommon Life of J. L. Chestnut, Jr.* (1990).
Johnson, John W. *Historic U.S. Court Cases, 1619–1990: An Encyclopedia* (1992).

Obituary: *Birmingham News,* 19 Dec. 2001.

J. D. JACKSON

BILLOPS, Camille (12 Aug. 1933–), ceramist, sculptor, filmmaker, and cofounder (with her husband, James Hatch) of the Hatch-Billops Collection, an archive of African American cultural history, was born in Los Angeles, California, to Lucius Billops, a cook and merchant seaman, and Alma Gilmore, a dressmaker, maid, and aircraft assembly worker. Billops graduated from Catholic Girls High School in 1952, and in 1954 she began her studies at the University of Southern California. She majored in occupational therapy, which included drawing, sculpture, and ceramics. She transferred to Los Angeles State College in 1956 after she became pregnant, and then she changed her major to special education. Billops worked during the day as a bank bookkeeper and maintained a full academic workload in the evening. At the end of 1956 her daughter, Christa, was born, and Billops put her up for adoption. This was an experience she would explore in her 1992 autobiographical documentary, *Finding Christa.* After graduating from Los Angeles State College in 1960, Billops taught special-needs children at Huntington Park Grammar School in California.

In 1960 Camille Billops's stepsister, Josie Dotson, a student of UCLA theater professor James Hatch, introduced Billops to C. Bernard Jackson. Jackson led a multiracial chorus in Echo Park, which was under the auspices of the Los Angeles City Bureau of Music. In 1960 she was in the chorus of the Jackson and Hatch collaboration, *Fly Blackbird.* Billops had acted professionally once before, appearing in Otto Preminger's 1954 film *Carmen Jones* as an extra. Other participants in this production were Dotson, George Takei, and Francis Ford Coppola, who was a lighting and carpentry technician. In 1961 *Fly Blackbird* was produced in New York and won an Obie for Best Off-Broadway Play.

In 1961 Billops began studying sculpture at the Chouinard Art Institute in Los Angeles. At Chouinard she worked with the Dutch artist Heino. She also studied privately with Artpod Damjan, a Hungarian artist who had produced large-scale sculptures in Budapest.

In 1962, when Hatch (then in a relationship with Billops) received a three-year Fulbright grant to teach at the High Cinema Institute in Cairo, Egypt, she accompanied him. At this time Egypt was the center of the Pan Africanism that inspired the American civil rights movement. They met and became acquaintances of W. E. B. DU BOIS, his stepson David DuBois, and Maya Make, who later took the name MAYA ANGELOU. Billops and Hatch completed their first collaboration during her second visit to Cairo in 1964: *Poems for Niggers and Crackers,* a satirical collection coauthored by Hatch and Ibrahim Ibn Ismail and illustrated by Billops.

Billops returned to Los Angeles in 1963. With recommendations from the artist CHARLES WHITE and the writer JOHN OLIVER KILLENS, she received a grant from the Huntington Hartford Foundation. The same year that Billops received the Huntington Hartford grant, four African American girls were killed in the bombing of the Sixteenth Street Baptist Church in Birmingham, Alabama. ROBERT F. WILLIAMS's book, *Negro With Guns,* was published in 1962 and launched the black self-defense movement; among the new organizations inspired by Williams's book was the Black Panther Party for Self Defense. In the tumultuous 1960s, Billops was among the artists producing politically relevant art—or "angry art," as she called it in an interview with the artist and art historian Samella Lewis. With the Huntington Hartford grant Billops produced two ceramic bas-reliefs, the *Birmingham Bombing* and *Marian Anderson.*

Billops returned to Egypt in 1964 and had her first solo exhibition at the Gallery Ahkenaton in 1965. Billops and Hatch returned to the United States in mid-1965, and Leo Hamalian, a writer and friend, helped Hatch get a teaching position at the City College in New York and Billops entered the MFA graduate art program at Hunter College. One of the first African American artists she met in New York was the painter Vivian E. Browne, who was also from California. Upon graduation Billops taught at the Goddard Riverside Community Center and was a substitute teacher in Spanish Harlem. The July 1965 riots in Newark, New Jersey, brought the problems that black Americans faced to the attention of mainstream America. The riots in the Watts section of Los Angeles the following month also focused national attention on inequity in employment and housing, and exposed recurring police brutality.

In 1967 Billops and Hatch traveled to India where Billops made drawings for masks and costumes and designed sets for the traveling production of *America Hurrah* by Jean-Claude van Itallie. The couple returned to New York in 1968 and acquired their first loft, where they presented plays, poetry readings, and exhibitions. Early plays produced in the loft on

Eleventh Street include *Son of Zen* by Lee-Joo For from Kuala Lampur, Malaysia, and *If It Do Not Die, It Do Not Die,* a 1971 piece by Hatch and Larry Garvin about the Black Panthers. During this time, Billops met BENNY ANDREWS, who showed her how to hang and display an exhibition.

In 1970, while teaching in the City University of New York system, the lack of material on black playwrights, plays, and black theater history available for Hatch's theater classes precipitated the creation of the Hatch-Billops Collection—an assembly of art, artifacts, literature, oral histories, and interviews. Hatch also collaborated with the black-theater scholar and playwright Ted Shine to publish *Black Theatre USA, 45 Plays by Black Americans 1847–1974.* The Hatch-Billops Collection was incorporated in 1975 with a mission to accrue material to document the contributions of African American artists and activists. As part of their cultural mission Billops and Hatch inaugurated in 1981 the "Artist and Influence" series of interviews with artists, writers, cultural activists, filmmakers, and other cultural producers, publishing them in a yearly journal of the same name.

In the early 1980s Billops created and exhibited large-scale figural sculptures based on her family. *Smoke and Blue, 1986* referenced her parents by their nicknames, while *George and Phine, 1987* were inspired by her uncle and aunt who lived in Red Bank, New Jersey. *The Story of Mom, 1981* was inspired by her godmother's life, and its decorative characteristics resembled those in her color etching, *Firefighter.* The sale of Billops's sculpture, prints, and drawings helped fund her documentary films. Billops film, *Suzanne, Suzanne* (1982) was selected for the Museum of Modern Art's New Director New Film Series. *Older Women and Love* (1987) was followed by *Finding Christa*, which won the Grand Jury Prize at the Sundance Film Festival in 1992. *Finding Christa* is about finding the daughter Billops gave up for adoption in 1960. Two years later she completed the satirical play *KKK Boutique Ain't Just Rednecks.* In 1997 Camille Billops and James Hatch received an Obie for Distinguished Contributions to Off-Broadway theater. *A String of Pearls* (2000) was chosen as the Diaspora Film at the Toronto Film Festival. In 2003 Billops designed the sets for the New York experimental theater La Mama's production of the musical *Klub Ka: The Blues Legend*, based on Suzanne Noguere and James Hatch's book, *The Stone House: A Blues Legend.*

Further Reading
Estell, Kenneth. *African America: Portrait of a People* (1994).
Harris, Michael D. *Colored Pictures: Race and Visual Representation* (2003).
Henkes, Robert. *The Art of Black American Women: Works of Twenty-Four Artists of the Twentieth Century* (1993).
Moore, Sylvia, ed. *Gumbo Ya Ya: Anthology of Contemporary African American Women Artists* (1995).
Riggs, Thomas, ed. *St. James Guide to Black Artists* (1997).

CYNTHIA HAWKINS

BILLY (fl. 1781), a mixed race slave, also known as Will or William, was the subject of an alleged treason case during the American Revolution. Nothing is known about Billy's birth, family, or childhood.

The Billy, or Will, of the treason case was the slave of Colonel John Tayloe, a resident of Richmond County, Virginia. Billy and others were arrested and convicted of seizing an armed vessel on 2 April 1781 to wage war against Virginia. He was condemned to death by the court of Oyer and Terminer in Prince William County on 8 May. Henry Lee and William Carr, dissenting justices, noted that he was not a citizen and owed no allegiance to Virginia. Furthermore, Billy argued that others had forced him onto the vessel, and there was no evidence that he had gone aboard voluntarily.

Only Governor Thomas Jefferson could grant Billy a reprieve. Jefferson was profoundly ambivalent about the institution of slavery; his actions and writings reveal his often contradictory impulses. Like many planters, Jefferson had a financial interest in perpetuating slavery and believed in the innate inferiority of Africans. He owned many slaves and offered a reward for the return of his escaped slave Sandy in 1769. Yet as a member of Virginia's House of Burgesses, Jefferson also sought, albeit unsuccessfully, to permit slaveholders to free their slaves without approval of the legislature. When granting his own slaves freedom, he exiled them to the wilderness, providing them with the wherewithal for survival. In his draft of the Declaration of Independence, Jefferson condemned the king of England for his involvement in the African slave trade.

When deciding whether to grant Billy a reprieve, Jefferson had to consider his own ambivalence toward slavery as well as Lord Dunmore's 1775 proclamation urging slaves and indentured servants to escape behind British lines to freedom. Even though he considered Dunmore's proclamation an attempt by the king to incite racial massacres, Jefferson did not let his fears of a slave uprising or the loss of thirty of his own slaves to the British deter him from seeking justice for Billy. In May 1781, after accepting the opinion of Mann Page, one of Tayloe's executors, Jefferson signed a temporary reprieve for Billy. After a joint resolution of the Virginia house and senate on 14 June 1781, Billy was granted a permanent reprieve. He was free to return to the anonymity he had known before his brief encounter with American justice.

The case is more significant for what it says about the ambivalence toward slavery of Jefferson and other Virginians than for the light it sheds on the life of Billy, or Will. Ironically, in 1710 another slave named Will had a brief flirtation with history. This earlier Will was freed for "his fidelity . . . in discovering a conspiracy of diverse negros . . . for levying war" in Virginia.

Further Reading
Boyd, Julian P., ed. *The Papers of Thomas Jefferson*, vol. 5 (1952).
Catterall, Helen Tunnicliff, ed. *Judicial Cases concerning American Slavery and the Negro*, vol. 1 (1926).

Higginbotham, A. Leon, Jr. *In the Matter of Color: The Colonial Period*. Race and the American Legal Process series (1978).

Mellon, Matthew T. *Early American Views on Negro Slavery* (1969).

WILLIAM SERAILE

BINGA, Jesse (10 Apr. 1865–13 June 1950), businessman, banker, and real estate investor, was born in Detroit, Michigan, the son of Robert Binga Jr., a barber, and Adelphia Powers, a builder and real estate owner. Nearly all sources cite William W. Binga as Jesse Binga's father, but all are based on a December 1927 article by Inez V. Cantley in *Crisis*, which may not be reliable. A family member, Anthony J. Binga Sr., after conducting research in the census records from the Courts of Records of the Dominion of Canada, claimed that Jesse Binga's father was Robert Binga Jr. *Who's Who in Colored America* (1928–1929) also names Robert Binga as Jesse Binga's father.

The Binga family owned and managed real estate properties, and, according to a number of sources, it was Adelphia Binga who possessed most of the family's business acumen. As a youngster, Jesse helped his mother collect rents on the family's tenement properties along what was called "Binga Row." Tenants were mostly black migrants on their way to and from Canada.

Jesse dropped out of high school after only two years to learn the barber trade from his father. During this period he also worked for a young black attorney. In 1885 Binga left Detroit and set out on his own, working his way across the northwest with the goal of becoming an entrepreneur. After working as a barber in Kansas City, Missouri, St. Paul, Minnesota, and Missoula, Montana, Binga opened his own barbershops in Tacoma and Seattle, Washington. Each venture, however, was short-lived. In Oakland, California, Binga worked first as a barber and then as a porter for the Southern Pacific Railroad. Later, while in Ogden, Utah, he invested in a land deal on a former Indian reservation. The venture was profitable enough that, by the time he arrived in Chicago in 1893, Binga had sufficient capital to begin building his own empire.

Binga opened his first real estate office on State Street in 1898 and continued to prosper for the next three decades by acquiring rental properties throughout Chicago's South Side, regardless of racial restrictions. Binga would purchase the homes of more affluent whites who were fleeing the encroaching black population and then subdivide the houses into smaller units, which he would rent to single black men and families. In 1905 he leased a seven-story building on State Street and opened it to black tenants. Despite hostile reactions to his practice of "block busting" to bring black tenants into formerly white areas, Binga and others like him met housing needs that were not otherwise being addressed. Chicago's African American population, which had grown rapidly since 1900, could no longer be con-

tained within the traditional black ghetto. Thus Binga's business activities served a crucial social need while at the same time turning a nice profit. By 1907 he was one of the most prosperous African American real estate agents in the city. A year later he opened the Binga Bank in a newly constructed office building on State Street. It was the first private bank in the North to be owned or controlled by blacks.

In 1912 Binga married Eudora Johnson, sister of John "Mushmouth" Johnson, the gambling kingpin of the South Side. Apparently Eudora Johnson was neither young nor attractive, and many Chicagoans were convinced that the handsome Binga married her for her money. Whatever the truth, at the time of their marriage she had inherited from her father after his death in 1906 an estate worth $200,000, which greatly enhanced Binga's economic prospects. According to Anthony J. Binga Sr., the couple had two children. Anthony Binga also claimed to have found a record of a second marriage in the U.S. Census records, but details are unknown.

Binga's bank and his personal fortune grew impressively in the wake of the massive black migration to northern cities in the years just before and after World War I, but white resentment in Chicago grew apace. His properties were vandalized on several occasions, and during the so-called Red Summer of 1919 both his real estate office and his home were bombed. Nonetheless at one point in the mid-1920s Binga owned 1,200 leaseholds on flats and residences, and by 1926 the *Chicago Broad Ax* was reporting that he owned more frontage on State Street south of Twelfth Street than anyone else.

All of this made possible the opening of Binga State Bank in January 1921. The bank's board of directors was composed of the leading African American businessmen in the community, and the *Broad Ax* viewed the bank's opening as a "history-making event among colored people residing in Chicago." By 1924 Binga had increased the capital and surplus of Binga State Bank to $235,000. He also opened the Binga Safe Deposit Company and organized a black insurance firm. However, although he had acquired a state charter for the bank, Binga continued to be its largest shareholder and ran the bank as if it were a private, solely owned corporation—practices for which he was later severely criticized.

The pinnacle of Binga's success came in 1929 when he constructed the Binga Arcade, a five-story building and ballroom at the corner of Thirty-fifth and State streets. Once the center of black business in Chicago, the area had badly deteriorated. Binga hoped that his development would help to revitalize the area, but instead his empire soon began to unravel. When the Binga State Bank failed in 1930, Binga lost his personal fortune of $400,000 as well as the savings of thousands of black Chicagoans. Although the Great Depression was partly to blame for the failure, the state banking examiner concluded that Binga had managed the financial institution in an illegal and unwise manner. Convicted of embezzlement in 1933, Binga was sentenced to ten years in prison; appeals delayed the start of his sentence until 1935.

Despite his mixed reputation in the community and even though many had lost their life savings when the bank failed, leading African Americans organized a petition to secure Binga's freedom. The effort was successful, and he was released from prison in 1938. Stripped of his former prominence, Binga spent the remainder of his life working as a custodian at St. Anselm's Catholic Church (having earlier converted to the faith). He died in Chicago after a fall at his nephew's home.

Binga's efforts to develop Chicago's black community brought him both praise and censure from the city's black and white communities. He was lauded for his business acumen and for his philanthropy, but he was also criticized for rent gouging and for having a hard-driving personality. Many years after Binga's death, the eminent African American leader EARL DICKERSON remembered Binga as "a mean son-of-a-bitch." In many ways Binga's career reflected the complex web of hope and despair that characterized the city's black business community during the early decades of the twentieth century.

Further Reading
Binga, Anthony J., Sr. "Jesse Binga: Founder and President, Binga State Bank, Chicago, Illinois," *Journal of the Afro-American History and Genealogy Society* 2, no. 4 (1981).
Harris, Abram L. *The Negro as Capitalist* (1936).
Major, Gerri. *Black Society* (1976).
Osthaus, Carl. "The Rise and Fall of Jesse Binga, Black Banker," *Journal of Negro History* 58 (Jan. 1973).

Obituaries: *Chicago Herald American*, 14 June 1950; *Chicago Defender*, 24 June 1950.

JOHN N. INGHAM

BINGHAM, Howard (29 May 1939–), photographer and writer, was born in Jackson, Mississippi, the eldest son of eight children of Willie Everrett Bingham, a minister and baggage handler, and Emmaline Bingham, a homemaker whose maiden name is not now known. At the age of four, Bingham and his family moved from Mississippi to Los Angeles. Young Bingham was inspired by his photographer neighbors and developed a strong interest in photography. While attending Compton Junior College in the late 1950s, Bingham, a music major, enrolled in a photography course, for which he received a failing grade. Although he eventually left college, he continued to pursue photography and began an apprenticeship at the *Los Angeles Sentinel*, one of the largest black-owned newspapers in the United States. After one month at the *Sentinel*, he was hired as a staff photographer.

In 1962 the *Sentinel* sent Bingham to cover a press conference in Los Angeles for a new young boxer named Cassius Clay. Later that day, Bingham ran into Clay and his brother and offered them a tour of the city. This meeting would be the beginning of a friendship that spanned decades. In his book MUHAMMAD

ALI: A Thirty Year Journey, Bingham recounted his experiences photographing his close friend. Bingham not only captured images of the boxer but also accompanied Ali during travel and personal appearances. In 1963 Bingham met GORDON PARKS in Los Angeles while Parks was there to shoot pictures of MALCOLM X. Parks mentored Bingham and influenced the scope of his photography, even contributing an introduction to one of Bingham's books.

While working at the *Sentinel*, Bingham pursued a number of freelance jobs that eventually led to his firing after eighteen months at the newspaper. By the time of his termination from the *Sentinel*, however, Bingham had acquired the contacts necessary to move onto the next phase of his career.

One of his assignments was to provide coverage of the Watts riots during the summer of 1966. *Life* magazine would later contract him to cover riots nationally, making him only the second black photographer to do contract work with the publication. He would also cover the 1968 National Democratic Convention in Chicago.

Traveling the country, Bingham captured American life, including representations that did not often garner front-page coverage. Bingham partnered with the writer Dick Hall in 1969 for a critically acclaimed photo essay of Mound Bayou, Mississippi. The essay told the story of an all-black town that was founded by former slaves in 1887 and remains one of the poorest communities in the country. Bingham gave a voice to Mound Bayou's citizens, who struggled to acquire basic amenities, such as clean, running water.

Although Bingham struggled with a severe stutter, he charmed and connected with people, including some significant historical figures of the twentieth century. In June 1968, he was one of the few photographers allowed access into the world of the Black Panthers: he photographed the group's leaders as well as its weapons cache. Although the photos were meant for a *Life* magazine feature that never ran, Bingham's work from that project was used in Gilbert Moore's book, *A Special Rage* (1971). Bingham also photographed MARTIN LUTHER KING JR., Elvis, the Beatles, and Nelson Mandela, his work appearing in issues of *Time*, *Sports Illustrated*, *Look*, *People*, *Newsweek*, and *Ebony*.

In 1969, while still traveling with Ali, Bingham met BILL COSBY on the set of his television show, *I Spy*. Blacks were not then allowed to join the Camera Guild (later the International Cinematographers' Guild), but Cosby later invited Bingham to shoot stills for his next television show, *The Bill Cosby Show*. As a non-union photographer Bingham could not work on the set. As a result, a white union cameraman was present on the set as Bingham worked, photographing the show. Cosby wrote a letter urging the union to extend an offer of membership to Bingham; soon after he became the first black members admitted to the cameramen's union. He was a still photographer for many films, including *The Candidate* (1972), *All the President's Men* (1976), and *Ghost Dad* (1990).

Bingham married Carolyn L. Turner in 1972; they would have two sons, Damon Howard and Dustin Lenoid, and divorced in 1986.

In 2001 Bingham served as an executive producer for the motion picture *Ali*. He was instrumental in the development of the film, which took eleven years to make. In *Ali*, Bingham was played by Jeffrey Wright. Bingham sought to ensure the depiction of Ali's life was accurate and remained as close to true events as possible.

Bingham's work and commitment to social change was recognized with a number of awards. In 1997 he received the International Award from the American Society of Photographers/Professional Photographers of America, and Photographer of the Year from the Photographic Marketing Distribution Association. Fusing his craft and commitment to the community, Bingham had an endowment established in his name to provide financial aid to minority photography students through the Eastman Kodak Company at the Rochester (N.Y.) Institute of Technology. In 2002 *Main Event: The Ali/Foreman Extravaganza through the Lens of Howard L. Bingham* was a featured exhibition at the Smithsonian Anacostia Community Museum in Washington, D.C.

Further Reading

Brada, Kristien. "Howard Bingham: Chronicles of a Celebrated Boxer," *Petersen's Photographic* (Mar. 1998).
Deford, Frank. "The Best of Friends," *Sports Illustrated* (13 July 1998).
Kelly, David. Review of *Muhammad Ali*. *New York Times Book Review*, 21 Nov. 1993.

LISA KAY DAVIS

BIRTHA, Becky (11 Oct. 1948–), poet and author, was born in Hampton, Virginia, the youngest daughter of Herbert Marshall Birtha, whose occupation is not known, and Jessie (Moore) Birtha, a librarian. She was named after her great-grandmother, Rebecca Burford, who had been a slave, and was possibly of Irish, Cherokee, and Catawba heritage. When she was three, Birtha's family moved to Salisbury, Maryland, but she mainly grew up in the Germantown section of Philadelphia, Pennsylvania, where the family moved in 1951. Birtha's mother introduced her daughters to the works of major African American writers, but she also grew up with such children's book classics as those written by Laura Ingalls Wilder, Edith Nesbitt, and Edward Eager; her favorite book was *A Little Princess* (1905) by Frances Hodgson Burnett. She took her first creative writing class at the public Philadelphia School for Girls, where she won a first prize for poetry in fifth grade. She began college at Case Western Reserve University, then moved in 1969 to Berkeley, California, but returned to school the following year to graduate from the State University of New York in Buffalo, with a degree in Children's Studies. In 1984 Birtha received an MFA in Creative Writing from Vermont College, and went on to teach at Goddard College and Bryn Mawr College.

Birtha described herself as a Quaker lesbian feminist writer, having declared her sexual identity in 1976. Many short stories in her published collections, *For Nights Like This One: Stories of Loving Women* (1983) and *Lovers' Choice* (1987), have a strong focus on African American women's lives and lesbian communities. But these collections also attest to her keen sensitivity to children, as someone who worked in her early years as a camp counselor, a day-care worker, and a pre-school teacher, and this sustained interest in children's issues would continue to define the shape of her life. In "Ice Castle," her most widely known short story, published in *Lovers' Choice*, Birtha depicts a black lesbian poet, Maurie, whose fascination with European children's books complicates her adult identity as an African American writer. In this story Maurie must grapple with a similar but larger conflict in her private life, in having to find a way of reconciling what seems to her an irrational attraction she feels toward a young white woman.

Representative of the plot twists and open-endedness often seen in Birtha's work, and particularly of her masterful use of metaphor and imagery, the principal characters in "Ice Castle" wander forever in the whiteness of the snow. Emphasizing the value that lies in the process of confronting difficult questions, rather than in finding closure, the short story opens up a space for thinking about the complexity of one's racial and sexual identity that shifts depending on interpretation and context, resonating with the central concerns of major women writers like AUDRE LORDE, Paula Gunn Allen, and Gloría Anzaldúa.

Birtha lent her voice to many readings, conferences, and workshops throughout her career, and her interests ranged from serving on the editorial board of the Lesbian-Feminist Study Clearinghouse, established in 1978 by Carolyn Fontaine at the University of Pittsburgh, to working for the National Adoption Center and Freddie Mac Foundation's program, *Wednesday's Child*.

Birtha gained significant recognition for her writing over the years, winning an Individual Fellowship in Literature from the Pennsylvania Council for the Arts in 1985, a Creative Writing Fellowship in Literature from the National Endowment of the Arts in 1988, a Pushcart Prize that same year, and a Pew fellowship in the Arts in 1993. Her works appeared in nineteen anthologies and over fifty journals and periodicals such as the *Iowa Review*, *Sinister Wisdom*, *Conditions*, *off our backs*, and *Sojourner*. Most notably, her poem "Maria de Las Rosas" was included in *Home Girls: A Black Feminist Anthology* (1983) edited by the literary critic BARBARA SMITH, a landmark anthology influential in forging the aesthetics and politics of black feminist literature. Joining her voice with African American women writers such as ALICE WALKER, Cheryl Clarke, and Michelle Cliff, Birtha's poem thrives within a distinctive heritage of black feminism rooted in the home and the neighborhood. "Maria de las Rosas," about a young black lesbian woman bringing cream-colored brambly wild roses to a housewife across town and walking home with a single fragrant red rose given to her in friendly exchange, conveys a vital sense of acceptance that surrounds the awakening of the girl's lesbian sexuality. In a poem about a bond between two women that reaches across racial, ethnic, and sexual identity, Birtha's vision powerfully reflects black feminism's global purview and its urgent concern with the simultaneous oppression that affects the lives of women belonging to the Third World.

In 1991, as she published her first collection of poetry, *The Forbidden Poems*, Birtha adopted a daughter, Tasha Alfrieda Birtha. She was awarded the Golden Kite Award for her first book written for children, *Grandmama's Pride* (2005).

Further Reading

Brownworth, Victoria A. "The Mother's Tongue: Poet Becky Birtha Gives Voice to the Experience of Parenting," *Advocate* (23 Apr. 1991).

Ferrera, Miranda H., ed. "Becky Birtha," *The Writers Directory*, 19th ed. (2003).

Mark, Rebecca. "Becky Birtha (1948–)," in *Contemporary Lesbian Writers of the United States* (1993).

Pullin, Faith. "Acts of Reclamation," *Times Literary Supplement*, 3–9 June 1988.

Roberts, J. R., comp. *Black Lesbians: An Annotated Bibliography* (1981).

REI MAGOSAKI

BISHOP, Stephen (1821?–1857), slave and guide, achieved fame in the decades preceding the Civil War. Nothing is known of his parents or early life, but it is known that Bishop was a slave belonging to Kentucky lawyer Franklin Gorin, who in the 1830s purchased Mammoth Cave for $5,000. Previous cave guides had been local white men, but Gorin either saw something promising in the teenaged Bishop or reasoned that he could save money by training a slave to do the same work. Either way, beginning in the spring of 1838 Bishop received training from the previous guide and quickly took to the job, learning the several miles of trail and numerous pits, rock formations, and other attractions of his underground place of employment.

Bishop was allowed to spend many hours exploring the cave on his own. In the fall of 1838 he penetrated a confusing maze of trails known as the Labyrinth and discovered a formerly unseen vertical shaft that came to be known as Gorin's Dome. More important, he devised a way to cross Bottomless Pit, a chasm that had previously marked the end of the trail for visitors to the cave. That same year Bishop discovered the River Styx—the first time water had been found within Mammoth Cave. He also captured specimens of the bizarre eyeless fish that inhabited the river, bringing additional attention to the geological and biological treasures located at the site. As a result of Bishop's daring expeditions, many more miles of tunnel were opened to exploration and Mammoth Cave's fame began to spread beyond Kentucky and its neighboring states.

Franklin Gorin did not have the funds to develop Mammoth into a first-class tourist destination, and in 1839 John Croghan, a wealthy physician from Louisville, Kentucky, purchased the cave—and Bishop—from their previous owner. Croghan invested heavily in his new property, building a fashionable, large hotel and working with the state of Kentucky to improve the roads leading to the cave. He brought in two other young slaves to join Bishop on the guide staff, and Bishop taught them everything he had learned. Among the increasing number of visitors to the cave were geologists, biologists, and other scientists, who requested Bishop as their guide. Bishop appears to have learned from his visitors as much as he taught them, for he became an expert on the processes of stalactite and stalagmite formation, the action of water upon the limestone rock that made up the main structure of the cave, and the life cycles of the animals living within it. He learned to read and taught himself still more.

In winter 1842 Croghan took Bishop with him to Locust Grove, his farm outside of Louisville. There Bishop spent days drawing from memory a map of the many miles of trail that had been discovered since the previous map was drawn in 1835. Bishop's map became part of a book about Mammoth Cave that Croghan published as a souvenir and publicity device. Possibly during his stay at Locust Grove, Bishop met Charlotte, a young female slave also owned by Croghan. They were married in 1843; later that year their son, Thomas Bishop, was born.

Bishop continued to guide visitors through the cave for the next fourteen years. Travel writers reported on

Stephen Bishop, renowned guide to Mammoth Cave, Kentucky. Illustrated in Hovey's *Mammoth Cave*, 1882. (Library of Congress.)

his extensive knowledge of the many attractions of the cave, but they also lauded his sense of humor and easy familiarity with visitors from many walks of life. "His great talent was a knowledge of man," Franklin Gorin once wrote about Bishop. Among the celebrities and royalty who visited Mammoth due to Bishop's discoveries and requested him as a guide were the Swedish singer Jenny Lind, the Norwegian violinist Ole Bull, Prince Alexis of Russia, and Dom Pedro, the emperor of Brazil.

In 1849 John Croghan died. His will directed that after three years his slaves be allowed to hire themselves out for pay, and that four years following that they should all be manumitted. Bishop, who had been studying the law, reportedly considered moving to Liberia to become a lawyer, but ultimately stayed in Kentucky and invested money in a piece of land near Mammoth Cave. He died under unknown circumstances and is buried in the Old Guides' Cemetery, within what is now Mammoth Cave National Park. His monument, donated decades later by the Pittsburgh businessman James Mellon, was created from a discarded stone that had been engraved for a Union soldier but never paid for. It carries (incorrectly) 1859 as the year of death. Bishop's widow remarried another cave guide; it is not known what became of Thomas, their son.

As of 2007, with more than 350 miles of mapped trails, Mammoth Cave was the most extensive cave system in the world, and the national park was toured by nearly two million visitors a year.

Further Reading
Bullitt, Alexander Clark. *Rambles in the Mammoth Cave, During the Year 1844, By A Visitor* (1845, 1985).
Brucker, Roger W., and Richard A. Watson. *The Longest Cave* (1976).

ELIZABETH MITCHELL

BIVINS, Horace Wayman (6 May 1866–?), decorated soldier and expert marksman, was born in Pungoteague, Accomack County, Virginia, the eighth of nine children born to Severn and Elizabeth Bivins. His father was a farmer who was also active in religious and educational endeavors. Four years before Horace Bivins was born, his father provided the money for the first church and schoolhouse for freed slaves built on the eastern shore of Virginia. The Accomack County census of 1870 said of Bivins's mother only that she "keeps house."

Bivins worked on his parents' farm until the age of fifteen, when he was put in charge of another farm near Keller Station, Virginia. Three years later he entered Hampton School as a work student and received his first military training. "Having a very great desire for adventure and to see the wild West," as Bivins later put it (Cashin, 58), he enlisted in the U.S. Army on 7 November 1887. After training in Missouri, Bivins was assigned to Troop E of the Tenth Cavalry, which he joined at Fort Grant, Arizona Territory, in June 1888. Over the next four years, Bivins later told a newspaper reporter, "My troop took a prominent part in the campaigns against Geronimo, Apache Kid, and other Indian chieftains of the southwest."

It was during his service in Arizona that Bivins took up shooting, placing second in a troop of sixty men the first time he ever shot a rifle during target practice. He was soon made a sharpshooter. His regiment was ordered to Montana in 1892, where he kept up his shooting record. He represented his troop in 1892, 1893, and 1894 at departmental competitions, and in 1894 he carried off the first army gold medal in carbine competition at Fort Sheridan, Illinois, where he also won two other gold medals.

In 1896 Buffalo Bill Cody, a buffalo hunter and flamboyant showman, offered Bivins a position in his Wild West show, shooting against Annie Oakley. Cody was said to have sought a furlough for Bivins and offered him one hundred dollars a month, but Bivins was in line to become an ordnance officer and said he preferred the army routine to circus life. Bivins's regiment was ordered south when war with Spain was declared in April 1898. The regiment left Montana in April, proceeded to Wisconsin, then south by train. Bivins said they were greeted by "great ovations all along the line" (Cashin, 61), but the welcome grew considerably more muted as they entered the South, where the Jim Crow laws astonished many of the black troopers. They arrived in Cuba in mid-June and were involved in much hard fighting and marching, often side by side with the First Volunteer Cavalry, perhaps more famously known as the Rough Riders. At the battle of Las Guasimas, elements of the Tenth Cavalry, including Bivins, saved the Rough Riders from a near disaster after they had been ambushed by Spanish troops. At the battle of San Juan Hill, Bivins, by then a sergeant, rendered notable service operating a Hotchkiss gun, a small artillery piece from which he was credited with single-handedly firing seventy-two shells, even after he had been wounded. He was awarded a Silver Star for his actions. After more service stateside and then a brief return to Cuba, Bivins's regiment was sent to the Philippines in April 1901 to "pacify" insurrectionist natives in the northeastern part of the main island.

He served there for a year before being transferred back to Montana, where he renewed a relationship with Claudia Browning of Billings, Montana, whom he had met during his earlier service in that state. In March 1904 he married Browning, a native of Deadwood, South Dakota. They lived at Fort Missoula, Montana, until 1906, when he was ordered back to the Philippines. His second tour of duty there was quiet enough that he was able to devote himself to collecting Philippine birds, shells, fossils, and other curios. He later donated artifacts to museums in Montana, California, and Minnesota. From 1908 to 1913, at which time he retired from active service as an ordnance sergeant, Bivins was transferred from fort to fort all over the country. With double-time for foreign service in Cuba and the Philippines, Bivins upon his retirement was given credit for thirty years in the regular army.

He settled down in Billings after his retirement, where he and his wife reared two sons and a daughter, and where Bivins was known for his flourishing vegetable gardens. His wife was an active member of the African Methodist Episcopal (AME) Church, vice president of the Montana Federation of Negro Women, a member of the Society of Eastern Montana Pioneers, and secretary of the Billings Federation of Women's Clubs. Bivins was recalled to active service in 1918, after the United States entered World War I, assigned by the War Department to the ordnance department in Newport News, Virginia. In June of that year the African republic of Liberia, founded in 1821 as a settlement for freed U.S. slaves, offered Bivins a commission to train 115,000 men who were going to fight against the Germans in West Africa, but Bivins declined. Bivins was soon made a captain of infantry, serving as a supply officer and then head of a labor battalion at a detention camp in Fort Dix, New Jersey. He retired from the army for good in 1919. He had thirty-two years of credit with the army and, coincidentally, had won thirty-two army medals.

He studied taxidermy after the war and followed that trade for many years. A newspaper article in 1935 described him as "industrious, sober and studious," and said he was six feet tall with broad, square-set shoulders (*Billings Gazette*, 3 Mar. 1935). Claudia Bivins died in 1943, and in 1949 it was reported in a newspaper article that Bivins had recently left Montana to live in Philadelphia, Pennsylvania. It is unknown whether Bivins ever returned to Montana or whether he died in Philadelphia.

Further Reading.
Cashin, Herschel V., et al. *Under Fire with the Tenth U.S. Cavalry* (1899).

EDWARD A. KEMMICK

BLACK HERMAN. *See* Rucker, Benjamin H. "Black Herman."

BLACK, John Lincoln (17 Aug. 1931–18 June 2004), stationary engineer, labor union president, was born John Lincoln Black in Burgin, Kentucky, the second child of Robert Lincoln Black, a laborer, and Bertha Ann Ball Boggs Black. After his birth the Black family moved to Keene, Kentucky, to live with John's paternal grandmother. Within a few years Bertha Black became ill with tuberculosis and sickle cell anemia, so young John was sent to live with his father's relatives while his older sister and younger brother remained with the family. After the death of his mother in 1934 Black continued to live with his great-aunt Martha while his two siblings, Anna Mae and Wallace, lived with their paternal grandmother. After the death of his great-aunt, John moved to Cincinnati and joined his father, stepmother, and siblings. John Black attended the Cincinnati public schools—the all-black Harriet Beecher Stowe Elementary School founded by Jennie Porter; Bloom Ju-

nior High; and William Woodward High School, from which he graduated in 1949.

After high school he enrolled at the University of Kentucky but transferred to the University of Cincinnati before enlisting in the U.S. Army on 1 February 1950. Training at Fort Benning, Georgia, and Fort Bragg, North Carolina, Black was a member of Battery B 376th Airborne Field Artillery Battalion. During his military service he was promoted to sergeant and awarded the Parachute/Glider Badge; he received an honorable discharge on 15 March 1953. Black married Edna Earl McNeil of Holly Springs, North Carolina, a mother of two children, on 17 March 1953, and moved to Cincinnati. Together they had eleven children. In December 1955 Black gained employment as a janitor with the Cincinnati public schools eight days after ROSA PARKS was arrested for refusing to relinquish her seat on a bus in Montgomery, Alabama. After ten years as a janitor and working a second and sometimes a third job, Black began to study stationary engineering with the tutorial assistance of his cousin James Vinegar. He also took classes at the Ohio College of Applied Science in Cincinnati. In 1965 he received his state license for steam fireman boiler operator and was promoted to steam fireman and sent to Woodward High School. On 25 January 1971 he received his state license for stationary engineering, 3rd class. In 1973 he was promoted to Engineer/Custodian 4 and two years later was promoted to Plant Operator 6 at the School for the Creative and Performing Arts, where he remained for nineteen years. As plant operator he was in charge of the entire physical plant of the school facility. Overseeing the custodial, maintenance, and mechanical operations of the building, Black worked long hours and nearly every day of the week. Nine years later he was promoted to Plant Operator 7.

On 2 February 1967 he joined the International Union of Operating Engineers Local #20, of which he became a loyal member. Black embraced the union idea passed on to him by his father, a unionized forklift operator and clerk at the Cincinnati based Milling Machine Company (later Cincinnati Milacron). Black served as a chief steward of members working for the public schools and in 1975 became steward for Cincinnati public school engineers. He quickly moved up the ranks, becoming a member of Local #20 executive board, a trustee, and then an auditor. In 1978 Black was elected vice president of the local—he was just the second African American elected to that position in the local—and served for twelve years. During his term the local had a strike at the University of Cincinnati, which lasted for one week and involved grievances with contract issues. The strike was settled as the agreement with the University met Local #20 members' demands. The local had a long relationship with the university. Starting in 1966 the local established an apprenticeship program with the university as signatory and sanctioned by the Department of Labor. This program, similar to a co-op education program where students would get course credit for on-the-job work or apprenticeship, offered 144 hours per year on-the-job training in the physical plant, matriculation in the core courses of the university, and after four years the conferral of a bachelor's degree in Stationary Engineering. Black saw this as an opportunity for African American applicants. He actively recruited from the African American community in order to provide opportunities to an alternative engineering program at the university. He was also able to increase the number of African Americans in the stationary engineer field and in the ranks of Local #20.

In 1991 Black was elected president of Local #20, making him the first African American to hold such an office in the IUOE Local. In that position Black oversaw contract negotiations with the Cincinnati public schools and was able to increase the educational opportunities for prospective stationary engineers by instituting tutorial classes directly under his supervision.

Excluded from most labor unions for much of the early twentieth century, African American union activities increased in the postwar era. During the civil rights era African Americans in Local #20 moved quickly into officer positions. John Black worked for the Cincinnati public schools for thirty-eight years and was a member of the International Union of Operating Engineers Local #20 for twenty-six years. He served as an officer of the local for over fifteen years. His term as the first African American president of Local #20 ended July 1993. He retired from the Cincinnati public schools on 1 August 1993. After retirement Black volunteered with the Hamilton County Board of Elections, Democratic County Central Committee, and was steward of the Democratic Party 7th Ward. John L. Black died of cardiac arrest in Cincinnati.

Further Reading

The information for this article was gathered from the Personnel Records, Human Resources Department, Cincinnati Public Schools; and Archives, International Union of Operating Engineers, Local #20, Cincinnati, Ohio. The John L. Black papers are held in a private family collection in Cincinnati, Ohio.

Mason, Patrick L. *African Americans, Labor and Society: Organizing for a New Agenda* (2001).

SAMUEL W. BLACK

BLACK, Leonard (8 Mar. 1822–28 Apr. 1883), minister and author, was born a slave in Anne Arundel County, Maryland, about sixty miles from Baltimore. He is best known for his narrative, published in 1847, which describes his time in slavery, his escape, and his call to the ministry.

Though Black served several owners in his early life, he was eventually brought back to Maryland to live with his original owner, where he was reunited with his four brothers. Within six months of meeting them again, three of his brothers escaped, encouraging him to escape when he could. While enslaved in Baltimore, Black had the urge to read, and though he bought books on several occasions, his master found them and either burned them or gave them to his son. Black is quick in his narrative to make the observation that in this case the education of a white child was not simply gained at the expense of the slaves' education but was quite literally bought for them by slaves.

Ten terrible years passed after his brothers left before Black became inspired by the Bible to escape enslavement, though his escape plan was almost ruined by a fellow slave who reported his plan to the owner. In 1837 Black managed to make it all the way to Boston, where he began to inquire after his brothers, only to be led eventually to Portland, Maine, and the home of George Black, a man who was not his brother, but who welcomed him as one nonetheless. There Black began to learn to read, gained employment, became a Christian, and fell in love with George Black's daughter. He followed the Black family back to Boston, where he married. In time he moved with his wife to Providence, Rhode Island.

Black's narrative describes his more than twenty years in slavery, under several cruel masters, as brutal and demoralizing. He had a keen awareness of the slave owners' lack of economic logic, evident in the treatment of their slaves. Though he acknowledged that it may make sense to feed a slave as little as possible, he knew that hunger made them need to steal and that the punishments he received made it impossible for him to work.

One of the major points of his narrative concerned the distortion of Christianity in the South, such that white people could be considered Christians and own slaves at the same time. Black also outlined the contradictions and faulty logic of white southern pro-slavery advocates, but he was equally critical of white northerners who not only allowed slavery to exist but also profited from its continuance through industry that relied on the products of slave labor from the South. Typical of many slave narrative authors of the time, Black, in hindsight, judged the white men he met based on their adherence (or lack of adherence) to the Christian scriptures.

Filled with biblical references to Hagar, Judas, Joseph, and Ahab, Black's narrative also chronicles his conversion to Christianity and his work as a minister. In Providence he worked for the Reverend Doctor Francis Wayland, then president of Brown University and later founder of Wayland Seminary in Washington, D.C. After being tutored by Wayland, Black believed that he was ready to preach, but the minister and other church committee members declined his request on the supposed grounds that his education was deficient. Black subsequently despaired and temporarily abandoned his desire to preach until a horse accident left him immobile and unable to care for his family. He then had a vision that compelled him to make a commitment to preach the word of God upon his recovery.

Based on that promise he left Providence to search for a church. When he arrived in Nantucket, Massachusetts, he found a congregation with no preacher, a vacancy he succeeded in filling after delivering only one sermon before it. In Nantucket he raised the money to rebuild that church and also served as a missionary to the Native Americans.

Admittedly written as a means to earn money to invest in his education, Black's narrative is the source from which we know the most about the author's life. However, Black's life and achievements did not end with the publication of his life story. He later served as a member of the 25th New York Volunteer Infantry during the Civil War, and he voyaged to England, Scotland, and France in 1867. Ultimately, Black's greater significance relates less to his narrative (which is fairly typical of the genre and not widely read) but to his wide-reaching ministry.

During his time as a minister, Black served in Stonington and New Haven, Connecticut, as well as in Buffalo and Brooklyn, New York. In 1873 he moved to Virginia, first preaching in Norfolk before moving on to Petersburg to be the minister of a Baptist congregation there and to double the congregation during his tenure.

When Black died in1883, he was mourned by more than five thousand people at one of the largest funerals held up to that time in Petersburg. His grave is in Petersburg's People's Memorial Cemetery, an African American burial ground, and it is marked with a monument in memory of his service to the community.

Further Reading
Black, Leonard. *The Life and Sufferings of Leonard Black, A Fugitive from Slavery, Written by Himself* (1847).
Bragg, George F. *Men of Maryland* (1925).
                                                    LAURA MURPHY

BLACKBURN, Alpha (16 Sept. 1939–), designer, businesswoman, and civic leader, was born Alpha Coles in Lynchburg, Virginia, the youngest of eight children of Alphonso Carroll Coles and Minnie Pugh Coles. Growing up, Blackburn attended a segregated school system, and went on to win a scholarship to Howard University, from which she graduated with honors, attaining a bachelor of arts in Design and a master of fine arts in painting and Art History. In 1964 she moved to Indianapolis, Indiana, with her husband, WALTER SCOTT BLACKBURN, who had completed his degree in architecture at Howard. She commenced work as a freelance designer of clothing and interiors.

Blackburn's petite figure and radiant good looks created opportunities for her to model, and she accepted a steady job at the prestigious L. S. Ayres & Company in downtown Indianapolis. Concurrently, she hosted a half-hour daily talk show from 1972 to 1978, *Indy Today*, on WISH-TV (a CBS affiliate), followed by a half-hour weekly talk show *Indiana Illustrated*, from 1978 to 1981 on WTHR-TV (an NBC affiliate). From 1980 to 1990 Blackburn was fashion editor for *Indianapolis Monthly* magazine. From 1980 to 2000 Blackburn was vice president of her husband's firm, Blackburn Architects, Inc., designing interiors and working with the company's architects to choose exterior colors and materials. In 1988 she incorporated a line of designer products as Alpha, Inc.

The Indianapolis Museum of Art commissioned Blackburn to design the "Dress of the Century" to present at its centennial celebration. Also in 1983 Blackburn was the recipient of Harvey's Bristol Cream nationwide Tribute to the Black Designer. Blackburn designed uniforms for the National Football League's Indianapolis Colts and the National Basketball Association's Indiana Pacers cheerleaders, and for Indianapolis's Methodist Hospital nurses. A featured designer and commentator for more than two hundred fashion shows and line showings, Blackburn received more than a dozen citations and awards as Designer of the Year. In 1985 the Indiana State Museum mounted *Alpha, An Original*, a twenty-year retrospective of her work as a fashion designer. Blackburn's "one-of-a-kind" gowns for clients are built on her philosophy that a design reflecting its owner is more important than one that mirrors the designer's artistry.

Blackburn's national clients included the singer Kenny Lattimore and the journalist and commentator TAVIS SMILEY. Her notable design projects include the National Underground Freedom Center in Cincinnati, Ohio; the Purdue University Black Culture Center in West Lafayette, Indiana; and, in Indianapolis, the renovation of the historic Madame Walker Theatre Center, the Lilly Endowment Building, offices of the Indiana State Housing Board and Indiana Arts Commission, and CONSECO Field House. Blackburn is respected because she is responsive to her clients' needs while introducing them to creative possibilities that reflect their personal styles. She believes that "Nothing falls into place. You have to put it into place."

Blackburn assumed the position of president and CEO of Blackburn Architects, Inc., in 2000, just prior to the death of her husband. With his designs firmly in place, she oversaw completion of the National Underground Railroad Freedom Center on the site between the Reds and Bengals stadiums along Cincinnati's Ohio River front. Alpha Blackburn had initially served as spokesperson for the firm, presenting a daring vision to win the 1998 competition. Turning from a traditional museum model of artifacts and labels, Blackburn Architects dramatized the site to create metaphors through structure and embellishment and present material culture and information in the context of past, present, and future. Even before the National Underground Railroad Freedom Center opened on 22 August 2004, Blackburn began plans for the creation of the Indiana Museum of African American History, scheduled to open in 2009, adjacent to the NCAA Hall of Champions in White River State Park in Indianapolis. As chair of the museum's founding board, she assumed the dual roles of spearheading the fundraising and overseeing completion of the $52 million structure designed by Blackburn Architects. The limestone and metal building, which will feature a ninety-foot tower shingled with multicolored glass, bears little resemblance to the curvilinear, interconnected three-pavilion Freedom Center structure. While the Freedom Center's purpose is to explore universal issues surrounding the quest for freedom, the Indiana Museum is primarily focused on collecting, documenting, preserving, and educating the public about the history, life, and culture of African Americans in Indiana and beyond.

Blackburn has been a major fund-raiser for the United Negro College Fund. An American Society of Interior Design Allied member and American Institute of Architects (AIA) associate member, she serves on the AIA Diversity Task Force. She has been a juror of regional and university architectural competitions and has guest lectured on architecture at Miami University of Ohio and Ball State University. She is on the advisory committee of Ball State and Indiana University–Purdue University in Indianapolis. In 1983 Soroptimist International of Indianapolis, Inc., honored Blackburn for Outstanding Contributions to the Arts in Indiana. A commissioner of the Indiana Civil Rights Commission since 1987 and its chair since 1990, Blackburn has chaired the Indiana Business Hall of Fame, sat on the Indiana Cultural Tourism Commission, and served as technical adviser and co-coordinator of art in Indianapolis's airport. In 1993 she was named a distinguished alumna of Howard University. She is a recipient of the Hoosier Heritage Civic Leadership Award, Trailblazer Award, presented by Indiana Black Expo, and was chosen as one of five Indiana "Renaissance Women." She is a recipient of the Prodigy of Indianapolis Award for outstanding commitment to nonprofit organizations and charitable causes, and has served on numerous corporate boards.

Further Reading
Hagen, Patricia. "Circle of Life," *Indianapolis Woman,* vol. 12, no. 2 (Feb. 2005): 36-41.
Slaughter, Ronnetta S. "Alpha," *Indianapolis Recorder,* 14 Apr. 2000, section C.
Way, Deborah. "Alpha's Bet," *Indianapolis Monthly,* vol. 25, no. 1 (Sept. 2001): 162-167, 250.

RITA KOHN

BLACKBURN, Robert Hamilton (12 Dec. 1920–21 Apr. 2003), master printer, artist, educator, and founder of the Printmaking Workshop, was born in Summit, New Jersey, the son of Jeannette Chambers Blackburn and Archibald Blackburn of Jamaica, West Indies. Robert, also known as Bob, had a younger sister, Gertrude, and a half brother. His father, although trained as a minister, found employment with the Lackawanna Railroad in Summit. When Blackburn was two, the family moved to rural Elmira, New York. Blackburn fondly recalled his early childhood in the rural town, where he listened to the train whistle from his bedroom window, attended church every Sunday, and won a toy car as a prize for a drawing he had done. During the Depression, when Blackburn was seven, his family moved to Harlem, where he attended public schools from 1932 to 1936.

At Frederick Douglass Junior High School, Blackburn was influenced by his teacher, the poet COUNTÉE CULLEN, who sparked his interest in literature and the history of art. Blackburn served as the art editor of the *Pilot,* the school paper, and was awarded the FREDERICK DOUGLASS Guidance and Art medals in 1936. Three years earlier he had met CHARLES HENRY ALSTON, a painter and sculptor, and enrolled in his Harlem Arts Workshop, a Public Works Art Project-sponsored program at the New York Public Library. Alston proved to be a major influence on Blackburn as a mentor and teacher, as were Ronald Joseph, another teacher at the Harlem Arts Workshop who introduced him to Chinese art, and Henry W. Bannarn, a sculptor. While Blackburn was initially too young to qualify for the $23.80 weekly project pay, he met and was influenced by a number of emerging artists and thinkers, including JACOB ARMSTEAD LAWRENCE, Sara Murrell, Norman Lewis, Ad Bates, ROMARE BEARDEN, and RICHARD WRIGHT. In the 1930s Blackburn was a member of the Harlem Artists Guild, founded by AUGUSTA SAVAGE, and he took classes at her Uptown Art Laboratory along with Lawrence and GWENDOLYN KNIGHT. Blackburn also attended after-school classes at the Harlem YMCA's Arts and Crafts Department (1934–1935), working with painters Richard W. Lindsey and Rex Gorleigh, as well as the sculptor WILLIAM ELLISWORTH ARTIS. He assisted Artis on a mural for the boys' recreation hall and received the YMCA's John Wanamaker Medal, the Spingarn Award, the Robert Pious Award, the Poussant Award, and the G. J. Pinckney Award.

In 1936 Blackburn entered DeWitt Clinton High School, where he was the art editor for the school's literary magazine, the *Magpie,* in which he published his poetry, stories, and prints. Among his fellow contributors to the *Magpie* were Richard Avedon, JAMES BALDWIN, and Sidney "Paddy" Chayefsky. While in high school Blackburn also attended the Harlem Community Art Center (HCAC). Directed by AUGUSTA SAVAGE, and later GWENDOLYN BENNETT, HCAC grew to be the largest WPA program in the country. At HCAC, Blackburn recalled hearing a lecture by the abstract painter Vaclav Vytlacil, one of several white artists who worked in this predominantly black circle (who would later become an important influence at the Art Students League). Another was Riva Helfond, a WPA artist, who first introduced Blackburn to lithography, etching, woodblock, and silk screening in 1938. Blackburn subsequently published twelve editions of lithographs, some in the *Magpie,* and entered into juried exhibits with the assistance of the Harmon Foundation. ALAIN LEROY LOCKE, his Howard University colleague, and JAMES AMOS PORTER, were among the many critics who praised Blackburn's drawings and lithographs from this period.

Knowing that his family could not fund a college education during the Depression, Blackburn was determined to find ways to make his livelihood in art. He was a scholarship student at the Art Students

League from 1940 to 1943, where he was instructed by Vytlacil and printmaker Will Barnet. In 1943 Blackburn graduated from the league, and for four years he worked as a freelance graphic artist for the Harmon Foundation, the China Institute of America, and Associated American Artists. In 1945 Blackburn moved from Harlem to downtown Manhattan, where he shared a loft with the painter ERNEST CRICHLOW. Two years later Blackburn purchased a lithographic press and began printing for other artists and taught three classes a week. In 1948 he officially opened the Creative Graphic Workshop. Although this workshop did not turn a profit, it provided Blackburn with studio space and enabled him to collaborate with a range of artists, including John Von Wicht, Ronald Joseph, Larry Potter, Tom Laidman, Stella Wright, Peter Bradley, and ELDZIER CORTOR.

In 1949 he also began printing for Cooper Union School of Art students. He did this job for twenty years before being offered a teaching position in the mid-1960s. Blackburn also taught printmaking at Brooklyn College, Maryland Institute College of Art, New York University, Pratt Institute, Rutgers University School of Visual Arts, and Columbia University (where he was a faculty member from 1970 to 1990). In the early 1950s, Blackburn studied drawing with Wallace Harrison and made plein air ink sketches with Ronald Joseph. In April 1952 *ARTnews* magazine highlighted his technical achievements and collaboration with Will Barnet on a suite of color lithographs created from 1951 to 1952.

The following year Blackburn left the workshop in charge of a group of artist-friends and traveled to Europe on a John Hay Whitney Traveling Fellowship. He spent six months in Paris, working with André Lhote, an important Cubist painter, and spent a year touring Europe. From 1957 to 1963 Blackburn was employed as the first master printer at ULAE (Universal Limited Art Editions), Long Island, New York, founded by Tatyana and Maurice Grosman. Blackburn printed the first seventy-nine editions of lithographs for major American artists, including Helen Frankenthaler, Grace Hartigan, Jasper Johns, Robert Rauschenberg, and Larry Rivers. After six years with ULAE, Blackburn returned as director to the Printmaking Workshop. In 1971 the PMW was incorporated as a nonprofit institution, eventually offering scholarships, international fellowships, and community programs to students of all ages in support of its mission to encourage and support creativity and training in the field of printmaking. Blackburn served as director, teacher, master printer, and friend to generations of artists working there.

Blackburn's most productive and mature period as a lithographer was the late 1950s through 1971, when his work was influenced by Cubism, as well as abstract expressionism and color field painting with the focus on abstraction, gesture, and color. Blackburn's experimentation and technical achievements in color lithography greatly affected the work of well-known ULAE artists and contributed to the popularity of the medium and print boom of the 1960s in the United States. Blackburn was unique among African American artists in terms of his artistic development from representation to abstraction and emphasis on the flat, two-dimensional surface of the printmaking stone. In 1971, the year PMW was incorporated as a nonprofit, Blackburn also created a board of trustees. While at ULAE he kept PMW running and eventually returned to full-time director. During the 1970s and 1980s, after ULAE, Blackburn, after twenty-five years of producing lithography, made the woodcut his primary medium. In both small- and large-scale woodcuts, Blackburn continued to maintain "his command of color, his sense of improvisation, and his control of compelling abstract balances" (Cullen, "A Life in Print").

The Printmaking Workshop has been described as "... the oldest continuously operating non-profit, artist-run printmaking studio in the country" (Cullen, "A Life in Print"). As an educational and artistic cooperative, it helped to produce the work of thousands of culturally diverse artists, promoting cultural exchange and advancement in the fields of art and education. Blackburn's passion for collaboration and cooperative learning was ignited by his experiences growing up in the artistic milieu of the late Harlem Renaissance and the WPA-sponsored art centers. He recreated the benefits of those experiences through his own workshop, which came to mentor artists in the same process. As director of the Printmaking Workshop, his interest in fostering the careers of young artists and creating a center for creative expression took precedence over his own artistic career. In spite of this, Blackburn created an outstanding body of work exhibited internationally and in the collections of the Library of Congress, the Brooklyn Museum, the Bronx Museum, the United Negro College Fund, the Baltimore Museum of Art, Asilah Museum (Morocco), and the Tel Aviv Museum. In 1997 more than 2,500 artworks from the Printmaking Workshop Print Collection, formed by donations from participating artists, were transferred to the Library of Congress, in Washington, D.C.

Blackburn received numerous awards, including the Skowhegan Governor's Award for Lifetime Service (1987), the New York Governor's Award (1988), the Mayor of New York City's Award of Honor for Arts and Culture (1992), the John T. and Catherine D. MacArthur Foundation Fellowship (1992), Lifetime Achievement Awards from the College Art Association and the National Fine Print Association (2002); and six honorary doctoral degrees.

Further Reading

Billops, Camille, and James V. Hatch. "Bob Blackburn (1920–2003)," *Artist and Influence*, V, XXII (2003).

Cullen, Deborah. "Appreciation: Robert Blackburn (1920–2003): A Printmaker's Printmaker," *American Art*, vol. 17, no. 3 (2003).

Cummings, Paul. "Interview with Bob Blackburn in the Printmaking Workshop," Archives of American Art, 4 December 1970.

Gaither, Edmund. "Millennium Portrait: Robert Blackburn," *American Visions* (Feb. 2000).

Parris, Nina. *Through a Master Printer: Robert Blackburn and the Printmaking Workshop*, Columbia Museum Exhibition Catalog (March–May, 1985).

York, Hildreth. "Bob Blackburn and the Printmaking Workshop," *Black American Literature Forum*, vol. 20, no. 1/2 (Spring–Summer 1986).

Obituaries: *New York Times*, 25 Apr. 2003 and *Art in America* (June 2003).

LENA HYUN

BLACKBURN, Walter Scott (21 Feb. 1938–9 Aug. 2000), architect and civic leader, was born in Indianapolis, Indiana, the son of the Reverend Cleo W. Blackburn, executive director of Flanner House, a social service center for Indianapolis's black community, president of Jarvis Christian College, and executive director and CEO of the Board of Fundamental Education (BFE), which received a national charter in 1954. Cleo Blackburn was born in Port Gibson, Mississippi, the son of a slave. At Butler University he earned a degree in social work and was ordained a minister of the Christian Church (Disciples of Christ). After earning a master's degree in Sociology at Fisk University in Nashville, Tennessee, Cleo Blackburn was director of research and records at Tuskegee Institute, Alabama. He returned to Indianapolis in 1936. In 2000 he was recognized posthumously as one of the fifty most influential people of the twentieth century in Indianapolis. Walter Blackburn's mother, Fannie Scott Blackburn, a civic leader, was born in Lynchburg, Virginia.

After attending Purdue University for two years, Walter Blackburn transferred to Howard University to obtain a degree in architecture. At Howard University he met and married Alpha Coles (ALPHA BLACKBURN), an artist, art historian, and designer. The couple would have two sons and a daughter. In 1964 they moved to Indianapolis, where Blackburn's first commission came from a Shortridge High School classmate for a funeral home, and commissions for house additions came from his mother's friends. His initial practice was established in partnership with David Snyder. In 1981 Blackburn Architects, Inc., was formed with five employees. The firm garnered praise for its award-winning, distinctive, and elegant rest stops along Indiana's interstates, police and fire stations, schools and churches. Blackburn's breakthrough came in 1984 with an award-winning, innovative design for inner-city housing and a high-profile commission, with Browning and Day, for the Hoosier Dome (later the RCA Dome), home of the National Football League's Indianapolis Colts.

During the next dozen years Blackburn Architects became one of Indianapolis's largest firms, with twenty-eight employees. It won eight major awards and amassed a roster of work stretching into the twenty-first century. Throughout, Blackburn maintained his focus on a high level of aesthetics to inject natural light, beauty, excitement, open space, and connections to community. Blackburn Architects' signature is its portals: brightly and diversely colored entrances that clearly announce the purpose of the structure as well as dramatic exits. Blackburn's Artsgarden, a 12,500-square-foot glass-clad public space, strikes a bold pose in downtown Indianapolis's skyline and spans the intersection of Illinois and Washington streets (known variously as the National Road and U.S. 40). Like his concept for a loggia to unify a new Indiana Government Center with the 1880 Statehouse, 500 Place Office Building seemingly floating along Indianapolis's downtown canal, and the College Avenue Branch Library in the shape of a boat, the Artsgarden is a destination drawing visitors and residents alike.

The commission of his lifetime came in 1998, when Blackburn was fighting the resurgence of the cancer that had been in remission. For the National Underground Railroad Freedom Center along Cincinnati's Ohio River front, Blackburn led a team of designers to encapsulate the significance of the African American migration within an inspiring setting. Multiple winding paths from the river lead to the building's carefully articulated entry, leading to a curvilinear structure. Inside, the perilous journey reverberates throughout interactive exhibits. Three pavilions, signifying Courage, Cooperation, and Perseverance, challenge visitors to consider ongoing universal issues about loss and maintenance of freedom. Also in 1998 he returned to Purdue University to design a Black Cultural Center, featuring elements of traditional African architecture, serving to invite and include everyone.

Blackburn's multifaceted civic life paralleled his professional philosophy of service. A fellow of the American Institute of Architects, he held multiple positions of leadership, including president of Indianapolis and Indiana chapters and vice president of the national AIA board of directors. He was twice awarded Indiana's highest civilian honor, named a distinguished alumnus of Howard University, and received an honorary doctorate from Purdue University's School of Engineering and Technology. He was visiting professor of architecture at Ball State University; a trustee of Rose Hulman Institute of Technology, Terre Haute, Indiana, and Bethany College, West Virginia; and a member of the Dean's Advisory Board for Indiana University–Purdue University, Indianapolis. He was appointed by President Ronald Reagan to the General Services Administration Review Board Region V. He was chairman of the Indiana State Housing Board, a commissioner of the Indiana Arts Commission, and on boards of the American Pianists Association, Indianapolis Opera Company, Second Century Society of the Indianapolis Museum of Art, Indianapolis Arts Council, and founded the Central Indiana Business Development Coalition. A National Kool Achiever awardee, he also was designated by the City of Indianapolis an Outstanding Role Model. He was a life member of the NAACP and the honoraries Sigma Pi Phi and Tau Beta Pi.

Blackburn died in Indianapolis.

Further Reading
Obituary: *Indianapolis Star*, 10 Aug. 2000.

RITA KOHN

BLACKMAN, Pompey (c. 1756–20 May 1790), soldier, served in the militia and Continental army during the American Revolution. Blackman also went by the name of Pompey Fortune, and after the Revolution he used the name Pompey Freeman and often shortened his name to Pomp. Blackman enlisted at Concord, Massachusetts, in 1775 in a regiment commanded by Colonel Samuel Gerrish. His place of origin and civil status are unknown, but given the later change of his name to Freeman it seems probable that he had been a slave. His enlistment therefore may have been illegal, because the Massachusetts Committee of Safety had passed a resolution on 20 May 1775 that forbade slave enlistments. Later acts forbade service by any African American, but clearly Massachusetts continued to violate its own laws on this issue, because African American troops were found in numerous Massachusetts regiments in significant numbers. On 27 January 1777 Massachusetts legislators finally came to terms with the facts on the ground in a law that gave only Quakers exemption from enlistment. On 28 April 1778 the legislature at last passed a law that explicitly allowed for black enlistment.

Blackman fought in the first actions of the Revolution at Lexington and Concord on 19 April 1775. He served under a series of officers, first Captain John Woods and then Captain John Baker and Captain Joseph Pettengill. Blackman went on to serve under Captain John Bridge in Colonel Eleazar Brooks's militia regiment. In 1776 he served under Captain Charles Miles in a Massachusetts militia regiment under the overall command of Colonel Jonathan Reed that reinforced colonial forces at Fort Ticonderoga. New England often recruited African Americans to fill out regiments, but doing this was far less prevalent elsewhere in the colonies. The effect of the Revolution on slavery in Massachusetts was great; most slaves were freed during or after the Revolution, particularly those who served in the military, and Massachusetts was the only state not to number any slaves in its population in the first U.S. census, of 1790.

The Continental army raised by the Continental Congress was multiracial, but soon after George Washington took command in the spring of 1775 he ordered recruiting officers not to enlist African Americans. In a council of war on 8 October 1775 Washington and other prominent officers decided unanimously to bar all slaves and by a wide majority to bar all African Americans from enlisting in the Continental army. Washington quickly reversed this decision, though, given the manpower shortages of the Continental army. African Americans in the Continental army had on average longer enlistment periods than their white counterparts. As the war went on, states increasingly turned to African Americans to deal with manpower shortages in their regiments, and many Continental army officers began to realize the competence of African American soldiers.

In 1777 Blackman joined the Continental army when he took on a three-year enlistment in the Fifteenth Massachusetts, a regiment commanded by Colonel Timothy Bigelow. Blackman served under Captain Edmund Munroe. With this regiment Blackman fought at Saratoga in the autumn of 1777, a battle that led to the defeat and capture of the British general John Burgoyne and his army, an event that proved instrumental in gaining French support for the American war effort. With the rest of the army Blackman wintered at Valley Forge from 1777 to 1778, where the weather and incompetence on the part of American supply officers led to the suffering of the enlisted men. Blackman also fought at the Battle of Monmouth on 28 June 1778 when Captain Munroe was killed. At Monmouth, Washington attacked the rear of the British army of Sir Henry Clinton, though neither of the two held the field at the end of the day. Monmouth was the last major action of the war in the northern theater. After 1778 Blackman served in Rhode Island for a brief period. He was discharged from his regiment on 10 March 1780.

After his wartime service Blackman returned to Massachusetts. He filed an intent to marry Susanna Bay of Holliston, Massachusetts, in 1781, but the marriage never took place. Blackman moved back to Lexington and was admitted to the local congregational church in 1782. Some sources indicate that he died in Lexington on 1 January 1783, but it appears that he made his way to New Hampshire. In Jaffrey, New Hampshire, he worked as a tanner under a free black friend, AMOS FORTUNE, whom Blackman had designated as his legal representative during his wartime service. Loan documents for funds given by Fortune to a Pomp Freeman indicate his presence there. Another black veteran of the American Revolution, Christopher Mann, witnessed the loan document. Blackman continued to live in New Hampshire until his death on 20 May 1790.

The experience of individuals like Blackman as African American soldiers in the Revolution was used by black abolitionists like WILLIAM COOPER NELL in their works to justify claims for equality. In addition, advocates for African American participation in the armed forces of the United States used the experience and heroism of Blackman and others to argue that a multiracial fighting force was not a departure from American military tradition, because it was present at the very inception of the republic.

Further Reading
Greene, Robert Ewell. *Black Courage, 1775–1783: Documentation of Black Participation in the American Revolution* (1984).

Johnson, Edward Austin. *A School History of the Negro Race in America from 1619 to 1890* (1911).

Knoblock, Glenn A. *"Strong and Brave Fellows": New Hampshire's Black Soldiers and Sailors of the American Revolution, 1775–1784* (2003).

National Society Daughters of the American Revolution. *Minority Revolutionary War Service: Massachusetts, 1775–1783* (1999).

Nell, William Cooper. *Services of Colored American in the Wars of 1776 and 1812* (1851).

M. KELLY BEAUCHAMP

BLACKWELL, David (24 Apr. 1919–), mathematician and professor, was born David Harold Blackwell in Centralia, Illinois, the oldest of four children, to Grover Blackwell, a locomotive mechanic for the Illinois Central Railroad, and Mabel Johnson. Although much of Blackwell's hometown was segregated, he attended an integrated elementary school. He first became interested in mathematics in high school where, although not particularly interested in algebra or trigonometry, he immediately took an interest in geometry—the scientific study of the properties and relations of lines, surfaces, and solids in space. Later in his life Blackwell credited his high school geometry instructor for showing him the beauty and the usefulness of mathematics. He joined his high school's mathematics club where his instructor pushed students to submit solutions to the *School Science and Mathematics Journal*, which published one of Blackwell's solutions. It was with geometry that Blackwell first began to apply mathematical methods and formulas to games such as "crosses" in order to determine the probability of winning for the first player.

David Blackwell, an innovator in statistical analysis, game theory, and mathematical decision-making. (Schomburg Center for Research in Black Culture, New York Public Library.)

When Blackwell entered college at the age of sixteen, he intended at first to become an elementary school teacher. In 1938 he earned an AB degree from the University of Illinois at Urbana-Champaign and went on to receive an AM in 1939 and a PhD in 1941. Here, his interest in probability and statistics emerged and flourished. His dissertation, written under the direction of Joseph L. Doob, was entitled "Some Properties of Markoff Chains." When he completed the PhD, Blackwell was only twenty-two years old and was only the seventh African American to receive a PhD in Mathematics.

After completing the PhD, Blackwell accepted a Rosenwald Postdoctoral Fellowship at the Institute for Advanced Study in Princeton, prompting outrage from some in the university community who vehemently opposed the appointment of an African American to this position at Princeton, which had not yet even enrolled African American students. The University's president, Harold D. Dodds, admonished the institute for making such an appointment against the wishes of the university community and sought unsuccessfully to block Blackwell's appointment.

Perhaps because of his experience in the Ivy League, Blackwell seemed to be aware of the limited opportunities for African American scholars in higher academia, and with the exception of an application and interview at the University of California at Berkeley, he applied for faculty positions at only historically black colleges and universities. After one year at Princeton he took short-term professorships at Southern University in Baton Rouge, Louisiana, and Clark Atlanta University.

In 1944 Blackwell joined the faculty of Howard University as an assistant professor at a time when the Washington, D.C., institution was a mecca for black scholars, including the historian RAYFORD W. LOGAN, the philosopher ALAIN LOCKE, and the sociologist E. FRANKLIN FRAZIER. Shortly after arriving at Howard, Blackwell married Ann Madison, and in just three years he had risen to the rank of full professor and chairman of the mathematics department.

At Howard, Blackwell also launched his career as a widely recognized and honored researcher in mathematics. Hearing a lecture and attending a subsequent meeting with the well-known statistician Abe Girshick stimulated Blackwell's interest in statistics and sequential analysis. Even while teaching and chairing the Department of Mathematics at Howard, Blackwell published over twenty research papers in mathematical statistics. Between 1948 and 1950 his interest in the theory of games—the method of applying logic to determine which of several available strategies is likely to maximize one's gain or minimize one's loss in a game or military solution—was revived by three summers of work at the Rand Corporation. Blackwell became particularly interested in the art of dueling with pistols and in determining the most statistically advantageous moment for a dueler to shoot. In the midst of the cold war, such statistical analyses of games became useful and pertinent for the federal government in thinking about U.S. military strategy, and Blackwell's work and Blackwell himself became a leader in the field of statistical analysis and game theory. In 1950–1951 Blackwell spent one year as a visiting professor of statistics at Stanford University.

All of Blackwell's work in game theory (including the art of dueling and the statistical analysis of bluffing as a strategy in poker) culminated in 1954 when he and Abe Girshick jointly wrote *Theory of Games and Statistical Decisions.* This book served as a mathematical textbook for students in statistical decision functions. Building upon the prior works of John von Neumann and A. Wald in the statistical and conceptual aspects of decision theory and theory of games, Blackwell and Girshick developed new and innovative concepts of mathematical decision making that were later used in military tactics, the business world, and engineering.

By the time of the book's publication in 1954, Blackwell's career was rising rapidly. Shortly after he gave an address on concepts of probability at the International Congress of Mathematicians in Amsterdam, he was offered and accepted a position as professor of statistics at the University of California at Berkeley. Serving as chair of the Berkeley statistics department from 1957 to 1961, Blackwell continued to be a prolific academic writer, publishing over fifty articles in the field of statistical analysis. Prominent appointments and accolades soon followed. In 1955 he was elected president of the Institute of Mathematical Statistics, and later served as president for the International Association for Statistics in Physical Sciences and the Bernoulli Society, and vice president of the International Statistical Institute, the American Statistical Association, and the American Mathematical Society.

In 1965 Blackwell became the first African American named to the National Academy of Sciences (NAS), a body used by the federal government and other agencies to investigate, experiment, and report on scientific matters. (Remarkably, nearly three decades later in 1996, *The Journal of Blacks in Higher Education* found that Blackwell had been joined by only two further black inductees at the NAS, the chemist PERCY LAVON JULIAN and the sociologist WILLIAM JULIUS WILSON.) In 1979 Blackwell received the prestigious von Neumann Theory Prize from the Operations Research Society of America for his work in dynamic programming, and in 1986 Blackwell received the R. A. Fisher Award from the Committee of Presidents of Statistical Societies. All of these awards and prizes acknowledged the continued relevance of his research in statistical analysis and game theory. In addition to being known as one of the world's best mathematicians, his scholarly work and professional activities have brought Blackwell honorary degrees from Howard, Harvard, Yale, the University of Illinois, Carnegie-Mellon, the University of Southern California, Michigan State, Syracuse, Southern Illinois University, the University of Warwick in England, and the National University of Lesotho. Blackwell retired from Berkeley in 1989, although he remained on the faculty as professor emeritus and continued to publish in mathematical journals. Blackwell has also advised over fifty graduate students. Blackwell's legacy in teaching and researching, and the pathbreaking trail he made for African Americans in the mathematics field, makes him one of this century's most notable figures in this highly specialized area.

Further Reading
Blackwell, David, et al. *Theory of Games and Statistical Decisions* (1954).
DeGroot, Morris H. "A Conversation with David Blackwell," *Statistical Science.* Feb. 1986: 40–53.
Guillen, Michael. "Normal, against the Odds," *New York Times,* 30 June 1985.
Martin, Donald A. "The Determinacy of Blackwell Games," *Journal of Symbolic Logic,* Dec. 1998: 1565–1581.
"The Mathematics of Poker Strategy," *New York Times,* 25 Dec. 1949.
"National Academy of Sciences: Nearly as White as a Posh Country Club in Alabama," *Journal of Blacks in Higher Education* (Summer 1996): 18–19.

KEITH WAILOO
RICHARD MIZELLE

BLACKWELL, Ed (10 Oct. 1929–8 Oct. 1992), jazz drummer, was born Edward Joseph in New Orleans, Louisiana, to unknown parents. He grew up steeped in his hometown's musical tradition, influenced by two tap-dancing siblings to take up the drums. New Orleans percussionists like PAUL BARBARIN were Blackwell's earliest models, making him one of several future avant-gardists whose roots were in jazz's oldest traditions.

In 1951 Blackwell relocated to Los Angeles, where he played in the rhythm and blues outfits of Plas and Raymond Johnson. More significantly he made the acquaintance the saxophonist ORNETTE COLEMAN, with whom he would be associated for his entire career. Coleman, also working with various degrees of success in the Los Angeles rhythm and blues scene, sought to introduce an unprecedented degree of melodic, harmonic, and rhythmic freedom into jazz. This new approach required an almost telepathic bond between band members, as interaction was governed by little more than improvisational ingenuity. In Blackwell, Coleman found not only a sympathetic collaborator but also a stylist whose loose-limbed, melodic sound provided the perfect complement for his plaintive, emotive alto.

It would be nearly a decade, however, before the rest of the world became aware of Coleman and Blackwell's unique rapport. In search of steady gigs, Blackwell moved first to Texas in 1953 before returning to his native New Orleans in 1956. Meanwhile, Coleman assembled a quartet with BILLY HIGGINS on drums, which arrived in New York in 1959 and was hailed as a revolution in jazz.

Blackwell rejoined Coleman in 1960, in time to appear on the canonical Atlantic recordings *This is Our*

Music and *Free Jazz* that year and *Ornette on Tenor* in 1961. Each of these albums was, in its own right, a major statement on the future of jazz. *Free Jazz* in particular gained such notoriety that its title became shorthand for an entire musical movement. This single, continuous piece, which sported a reproduction of a Jackson Pollock painting as its cover art, consisted of a double-quartet lineup in which Blackwell's exuberant playing was mirrored by Higgins's more fluid style. On all three albums, however, Blackwell's barebones drumming, which relied heavily on dance-like rhythms on the tom-toms and a deep-seated sense of swing, spurred Coleman's rootsy avant-garde to new expressive heights. *Ornette on Tenor* made the link between past and present almost tangible, as Coleman's evocation of the tenor's bluesy heritage brought out the New Orleans second-line heritage that was such an essential part of Blackwell's playing.

During this same period Blackwell performed at the Five Spot with a quintet co-led by the reedman ERIC DOLPHY (who appeared on *Free Jazz*) and the trumpeter BOOKER LITTLE, a forward-looking band arguably the equal of Coleman's ensembles. Work with the pianist Randy Weston and tenor ARCHIE SHEPP also demonstrated Blackwell's preeminent standing in the jazz world, as he showed his ability to excel in settings not directly indebted to Coleman's musical language.

Yet throughout the sixties and seventies Blackwell continued to be identified with Coleman's musical universe. He recorded several classic albums with DON CHERRY, best known as Coleman's trumpeter; their duo sessions, which yielded the two-part *Mu* (1969), are regarded as indispensable examples of interplay and spontaneous invention. In 1975 Blackwell entered academia, joining Connecticut's Wesleyan University as an artist in residence where he found some much-needed professional and financial stability in a particularly lean era for avant-garde jazz musicians.

In 1976 Blackwell joined up with fellow Coleman alumni Cherry, Dewey Redman (tenor), and Charlie Haden (bass) to form Old and New Dreams, an aptly named project devoted to performing Coleman's songbook and new compositions in the Coleman vein. While certainly a celebration of Coleman's legacy, this quintet's lively, engrossing performances proved that this idiom was anything but dated. And although Coleman cast a long, imposing shadow over Old and New Dreams, showcasing these musicians apart from the man himself underscored just how instrumental these sidemen had been in forging a sound that had been largely collective in nature. As both a tribute to their musical guru and an assertion of their own historical importance, Old and New Dreams struck the ideal balance between nostalgia and urgency, making it the ideal vehicle for former vanguardists at a crossroads.

Old and New Dreams served as a lodestar for these Coleman alumni throughout the eighties, and Blackwell was no exception. By the eighties the drummer and his onetime partners in the revolution had all become elder statesmen. For younger musicians, playing with Blackwell became an honor, and he became a regular on the festival circuit. Luckily, Blackwell himself was still every bit the creative force, making these late career efforts easily the equal of his earlier, seminal work in the Coleman orbit.

Blackwell was dogged by ill health throughout the eighties, as kidney problems (which required he undergo dialysis three times a day) limited his recordings and performances. His mounting health-care costs also posed a significant problem for a career jazz musician, but were alleviate somewhat by a series of high-profile benefits. Blackwell's skills remained undiminished; in 1992 he finally recorded as a leader, teaming with Redman for the joyous trio outing *Walls-Bridges*. Months later, his Ed Blackwell Project headlined the Bay Area's Eddie Moore Memorial Jazz Festival, leading to two albums' worth of spirited live blowing (released in 1992 and 1994 as *What It Is?* and *What It Be Like?*, respectively). But despite his continued excellence behind the drum kit, Blackwell's illness eventually caught up with him, and he passed away in Hartford, Connecticut, due to complications arising from his kidney ailments.

Further Reading

Palmer, Robert. "Ed Blackwell: Crescent City Thumper," *Downbeat* (19 May 1977).
Wilmer, Valerie. *As Serious As Your Life: The Story of the New Jazz* (1977).

Obituary: *New York Times*, 9 Oct. 1992.

Discography

Coleman, Ornette, *This Is Our Music* (Atlantic, 1960)
Dolphy, Eric, *At the Five Spot Volume 1* (New Jazz, 1961)
Old and New Dreams, *Old and New Dreams* (Black Saint, 1979)

NATHANIEL FRIEDMAN

BLACKWELL, Lucien Edward (1 Aug. 1931–24 Jan. 2003), politician, was born the son of Thomas Williams Blackwell, a grocery store owner, and Mary Ellen Blackwell in Whitsett, Pennsylvania. Blackwell was one of eleven children. After completing high school in 1949 he matriculated at St. Joseph's College in Philadelphia, Pennsylvania. He left college and worked as a dock worker. In 1953 he joined the U.S. Army and served in the Korean War. After a year he was discharged and returned to his previous job on the waterfront. He participated in labor activities and served as trustee, vice president, and business agent of Local 1332 of the International Longshoremen's Association (ILA). In 1973 he became president of the local chapter of the ILA, a position he retained until 1991.

Blackwell married Jannie L. Blackwell, a former schoolteacher, around 1973. At the time he was a single father with six children from a previous marriage. Blackwell's labor work led him to enter politics in

1973, and that year he was elected as a Democratic representative to the Pennsylvania legislature. There he was instrumental in establishing the Crisis Intervention Network to deal with gang crimes. He left state for local politics when he was elected to the Philadelphia city council in 1974.

Throughout his long tenure as councilman (1974–1991) Blackwell remained devoted to issues related to employment, housing, human rights, and public assistance. He sponsored ordinances that guaranteed quotas of work contracted by the city to minority-owned and women-led enterprises. He even undertook a six-week fast to protest the lack of maintenance and security in the public housing projects. He contributed to the organization of better public assistance for the homeless. Blackwell chaired the finance committee of the city council and the Philadelphia Gas Commission. His work on the finance committee led the city to divest its pension funds from financial institutions doing business in apartheid-era South Africa. By then LEON H. SULLIVAN, pastor of Mt. Zion Baptist Church (1950–1988), had made Philadelphia a center of activism against the apartheid system in South Africa.

Blackwell drafted ordinances authorizing the building of the Pennsylvania Convention Center and worked as a commissioner for the Delaware Port Authority. He ran unsuccessfully for mayor in 1979 and 1991. JESSE JACKSON chose him as the Pennsylvania coordinator of his 1988 presidential campaign. As councilman Blackwell served as mentor to John F. Street, who later became the second black mayor of Philadelphia in 2000. In 1991 Blackwell was elected to Congress and his wife, Jannie Blackwell, took his seat on the city council. His congressional district included west Philadelphia and sections of Delaware County.

Experienced in labor issues, Blackwell pursued the same interests in Congress. He introduced a bill for a thirty-hour workweek in order to allow more people to find employment during the 1990s recession. He sponsored bills meant to protect the credit ratings of the unemployed. As a member of the U.S. Committee on the Budget he strongly supported President Bill Clinton's economic policies. Blackwell was elected to one more Congressional term in 1992. He lost in the Democratic Primary election to CHAKA FATTAH in 1994 and then worked as a lobbyist for the city of Philadelphia. Blackwell later held the chairmanship of two African American organizations, Black Elected Officials and United Black Ward Leaders of Philadelphia. In late 2002 he was appointed to the transition team for Pennsylvania governor-elect Edward Rendell. Just before his death he worked as chairman of St. Hill and Associates, a debt-collection firm. He died in Philadelphia and is remembered as an outstanding advocate for the poor and the homeless. In addition to his wife his political legacy was carried by his son, Thomas Blackwell, who was elected to the Pennsylvania House of Representatives in 2004.

Further Reading
Carey, Charles W. *African-American Political Leaders* (2004).

Obituary: *Philadelphia Inquirer*, 25 Jan. 2003.

DAVID MICHEL

BLACKWELL, Otis (16 Feb. 1932–6 May 2002), songwriter and musician, was born in Brooklyn, New York. Information on his family and early life is fragmented at best, but it is known that Blackwell was a musical child and learned to play the piano while he was young.

Upon leaving school at the end of the 1940s, Blackwell held jobs in a New York theater as a floor sweeper and as a laundry clothes presser. In 1952 his musical talents helped him win a talent contest at Harlem's Apollo Theater, arguably the capital of live black entertainment during the era of the chitlin circuit, the circuit of African American performance venues that supplied black performers with their steadiest and most stable source of employment. Blackwell subsequently signed a deal with RCA Victor Records, under the tutelage of the producer Joe Davis. Davis left RCA a year later to form Jay-Dee Records, and Blackwell followed his mentor to the new label. He recorded several sides for Jay-Dee, but none achieved much chart success. Perhaps most prominent among Blackwell's early recordings was his song "Daddy Rolling Stone," a pulsating R&B groove that would later become popular through versions by the Jamaican singer Derrick Martin and the British rock band the Who. Throughout the early 1950s Blackwell continued to record songs for Jay-Dee, RCA, and Groove Records, but his most outstanding accomplishments in the music business would not come in front of the microphone, but as a songwriter.

Blackwell's breakthrough, and period of greatest success, came during the rock and roll explosion of the late 1950s, when he became a part of New York's prosperous community of tunesmiths that provided hits for a variety of black (and later white) artists. Blackwell not only distinguished himself through his talent, but also through the fact that he combined influences from both black and white musical spaces, linking music which—though popular across the color line—had rarely been combined by a professional songwriter to such a clear and effective extent. Blackwell was influenced by the blues and jazz singers of the era, but he also consistently acknowledged a debt to country and western culture, from recorded country music to the westerns of Gene Autry and Tex Ritter that Blackwell viewed regularly at his local cinema. Throughout his career, Blackwell maintained a connection with his cowboy heroes, from his affection for cowboy hats and boots to his ease at crafting country-influenced hits for both white and black artists. Though notably talented, Blackwell was not alone in his ability to bridge the gap between two genres that, symbolically at least, remained separated by a gulf of racial tension and cultural segregation. From country's interracial origins, through the genre-busting country work of R&B artists like RAY CHARLES or BOBBY WOMACK, to the involvement of southern soul musicians in the pioneering "Nashville sound" country of the 1960s, these two genres are closely intertwined, and Blackwell's work is a testament to this long-standing relationship.

On Christmas Eve 1955 Blackwell sold six of his songs, through a tape of homemade demo recordings, to the publisher Moe Gale for $150. Among the songs in this initial group was "Fever," which would become first an R&B hit for the blues singer Little Willie John and then a pop smash for the sultry white crooner Peggy Lee, and "Don't Be Cruel," which a young Elvis Presley recorded as his first national single release for RCA Victor in 1956, and which became one of Presley's first hits. This initial success led to Presley recording several of Blackwell's songs. The connection between Blackwell and Presley produced the number one record "All Shook Up" (1957) and the hits "Return to Sender" (1962) and "One Broken Heart for Sale" (1963).

Apart from the songs themselves—which perhaps more than any other early Presley recordings capture the singer's energetic blend of pop, country, and R&B elements—Presley was also influenced by Blackwell's vocal style and arrangements (which the pop star heard on Blackwell's demo versions of the material), and he incorporated many of Blackwell's characteristics into his own versions. Also, Presley's business arrangements often got him listed as a cowriter on Blackwell's compositions, a common (though semi-legal) form of compensation for pop singers who chose to record a particular song. (Presley never met Blackwell, never claimed to have actually written the songs, and has since been removed from the songwriter's credit. Blackwell never publicly expressed any resentment toward Presley or any other white artist he was associated with.)

Through the early 1960s Blackwell provided songs for many artists, both black and white; occasionally Blackwell would use the pseudonym John Davenport when copyrighting his songs, a move which some have theorized was an attempt to remove any racial stigma that his "black-sounding" real name may have caused. Blackwell's songs for wild rockabilly star Jerry Lee Lewis are second only to his work with Presley in terms of success; Blackwell wrote three hits for Lewis, most famously the number one hit "Great Balls of Fire." Like the Presley recordings, Lewis's versions of these Blackwell compositions demonstrate the way that early rock and roll blurred the lines between what constituted "white" and "black" music. An interracial coterie of the era's luminaries would record Blackwell's songs over the next several years.

Later in his career, Blackwell's famous catalog songs were recorded by white artists like Tanya Tucker and James Taylor (who revived Blackwell's hit for Jimmy Jones, "Handy Man"), and by black artists like Ray Charles and OTIS REDDING. Blackwell him-self recorded an album in 1976, tellingly titled *These Are My Songs!*, for Inner City Records, and he recorded a tribute to Elvis Presley (titled *The #1 King of Rock and Roll*) in 1977. In 1986 Blackwell was inducted into the Nashville Songwriters Hall of Fame, and he joined the National Academy of Popular Music Songwriters' Hall of Fame in 1991. In 1992 he was the subject of a tribute album, called *Brace Yourself!*, featuring popular artists like Kris Kristofferson, Deborah Harry, and Ronnie Spector.

Otis Blackwell died in 2002, leaving his longtime wife, Mamie Wiggins Blackwell, and seven children, and he is buried in Nashville, Tennessee. Blackwell, who copyrighted more than one thousand songs and is one of the most successful songwriters of the late 1950s, left a body of work that speaks to the excitement and possibility of a time when music's racial lines were not entirely intransigent, and when a country-loving black man from New York could provide hits for rockers, pop crooners, country singers, and R&B performers. Although Blackwell's financial reward from his esteemed catalog never matched his creative success, his name is firmly, justifiably etched in the history of American popular music.

Further Reading
Dahl, Bill. "Otis Blackwell," *All Music Guide to Soul: The Definitive Guide to R&B and Soul*, ed. Vladimir Bogdanov (2003).
Guralnick, Peter. *Last Train to Memphis: The Rise of Elvis Presley* (1994).

Obituary: *New York Times*, 9 May 2002.

Discography
All Shook Up (Shanachie Records 9204).
These Are My Songs! (Inner City Records 1032).
                                                CHARLES L. HUGHES

BLACKWELL, Randolph Talmadge (10 Mar. 1927–21 May 1981), attorney, educator, and civil rights activist, was born in Greensboro, North Carolina, the son of Joe Blackwell and Blanche Mary Donnell. Randolph attended the city's public schools for African Americans and earned a BS in Sociology from North Carolina Agricultural and Technical University in Greensboro in 1949. Four years later he earned a JD degree from Howard University in Washington, D.C. In December 1954 Blackwell married Elizabeth Knox; the couple had one child. After teaching economics for a year at Alabama Agricultural and Mechanical College in Normal, Alabama, Blackwell became an associate professor of social sciences at Winston-Salem State Teachers College in North Carolina.

Because of Blackwell's legal background, WILEY BRANTON, the director of the Voter Education Project (VEP), hired Blackwell as its field director in 1962. Secretly encouraged by the Kennedy administration, the VEP was launched in April 1962 with funding from private foundations. Sheltered under the tax-exempt status of the Southern Regional Council, the

VEP encouraged voter registration among African Americans throughout the South by regranting funds to civil rights organizations to underwrite their voter registration efforts. In Mississippi, where only 5 percent of eligible black adults were registered, the prospect of funding from the VEP encouraged the civil rights organizations to establish the Council of Federated Organizations (COFO) to coordinate voter registration efforts among African Americans. Faced with the threat of being jailed, beaten, bombed, or even killed at the hands of determined white opposition, voter registration workers produced only 3,228 newly registered black voters in 1962, despite $50,000 worth of funding from the VEP.

On 28 February 1963, eight days after an arsonist torched four black businesses in order to destroy COFO's voter registration office in Greenwood, Mississippi, Blackwell met with COFO organizers there. While Blackwell was at the office, Jimmy Travis, a COFO worker, reported that three white men in a Buick with no license plates had staked out the office. Travis then drove Blackwell and the civil rights activist ROBERT MOSES out of Greenwood toward Greenville. The Buick followed them. Seven miles out of Greenwood, white night-riders pulled up beside them and fired on their car. Hit in both the shoulder and the back of the neck, Travis slumped into Moses's lap as he pulled the car to a halt. Two days later, doctors at a Jackson hospital removed a bullet from Travis's spine. Branton quickly wired Attorney General Robert Kennedy with a demand for "immediate action by the federal government" in Greenwood. An appeal to MARTIN LUTHER KING JR.'s Southern Christian Leadership Conference (SCLC) brought trained voter education workers to Greenwood for citizenship education classes. Blackwell revisited Greenwood in March 1963 and found twenty to thirty people working in the COFO office, helping with canvassing and with voter registration, organizing clothing and food distribution, coordinating youth work, arranging both mass meetings and Sunday speaking engagements, and establishing citizenship schools.

When WYATT TEE WALKER left the staff of the SCLC in July 1964, ANDREW YOUNG became his successor, and Blackwell succeeded Young as program director. One of the few laymen to serve on the SCLC's executive staff, Blackwell attempted to restructure the organization by employing various administrative techniques meant to establish clear lines of authority, thus avoiding the confusion and antagonism that had previously permeated the SCLC. Blackwell suggested separating the organization into specific departments with designated department heads who reported to Blackwell, who in turn answered to Young. The proposal had little effect because charismatic preachers on the executive staff vied for control of the field staff and resented having to answer to anyone but King.

Blackwell was the SCLC's program director during the Alabama voting rights campaign that led to the march from Selma to Montgomery. After marchers were attacked on Selma's Edmund Pettus Bridge on "Bloody Sunday," 7 March 1965, Blackwell sent two hundred telegrams in King's name inviting religious leaders from across the nation to join him for the march from Selma. By 9 March, 450 white clergymen had gathered in Selma for the march to Montgomery. After the march, however, Blackwell found little enthusiasm in black Selma for the SCLC's continued presence there because of its staff's poor relationships with local community leaders.

In addition to fighting such external battles as the one in Selma, Blackwell was also plagued by internal battles within the SCLC. Blackwell doubted the ability of the SCLC executive staff member HOSEA WILLIAMS to manage its VEP-funded Southern Community Organization and Political Education (SCOPE) project in the summer of 1965. Later his worst fears were confirmed by SCOPE's incompetence, by Williams's misconduct and mismanagement, and by the incredible waste of the organization as a whole. Blackwell accused Williams of "empire building" and begged King to end the program immediately. "It has cost freedom contributors ten times what it should have," Blackwell wrote. "The operation has raised suspicion of financial dishonesty." Later Blackwell told King that "the conflict between myself and Mr. Williams . . . goes to the bottom of the philosophy of the organization. It raises in a very serious way the question of whether we can at this point develop the structural discipline needed" (Fairclough, 269). Although Blackwell agreed with Williams that the SCLC should maintain its focus on the South rather than open a campaign in a major northern city like Chicago, by October he was talking about leaving the SCLC. In February 1966 Blackwell's conflict with Williams was so intense that Blackwell appealed to King for the resolution of a whole series of issues within the organization, and by August of that year Blackwell had taken a leave of absence. SCLC staff turmoil worsened after Blackwell's departure, and King regretted not having dealt with his complaints and feared that Blackwell would not return to the SCLC staff. As late as June 1967 the SCLC's SEPTIMA CLARK urged King to bring Blackwell back to the organization to ease his personal burdens and to bring more discipline to the staff.

When Blackwell left the SCLC in 1966, he founded Southern Rural Action, Incorporated, an organization based in Atlanta that sought to develop black businesses and economic cooperatives. He was the director of this organization until 1977, when he became the director of the Department of Commerce's Office of Minority Business Enterprise in Washington, D.C. In 1979 Blackwell returned to Atlanta as director of the Office of Minority Enterprise Program and Development. He remained in that position until his death from cancer in Atlanta. A recipient of the Martin Luther King Jr. Peace Prize in 1976, Blackwell was also a member of the board of directors of the Martin Luther King Jr. Center for

Nonviolent Social Change and of Southern Rural Action.

Further Reading

Blackwell's papers are at the Martin Luther King Jr. Center for Nonviolent Social Change in Atlanta, Georgia.

Fairclough, Adam. *To Redeem the Soul of America: The Southern Christian Leadership Conference and Martin Luther King, Jr.* (1987).

Garrow, David J. *Bearing the Cross: Martin Luther King, Jr., and the Southern Christian Leadership Conference* (1986).

Lawson, Steven F. *Black Ballots: Voting Rights in the South, 1944–1969* (1976).

Peake, Thomas R. *Keeping the Dream Alive: A History of the Southern Christian Leadership Conference from King to the Nineteen-Eighties* (1987).

Obituaries: *Atlanta Constitution*, 22 May 1981; *New York Times*, 23 May 1981.

RALPH E. LUKER

BLACKWELL, Unita Z. (18 Mar. 1933–), civil rights activist and mayor, was born in Lula, Mississippi, the daughter of sharecroppers in Coahoma County, Mississippi. Her father had to leave Mississippi when he refused to obey his plantation owner's order to send his young daughter Unita to the fields to pick cotton. He found work in an icehouse in a neighboring state. Her mother was illiterate and determined that her children would learn to read and write. In the Mississippi Delta, everyone was required to pick and chop cotton, and the schools closed down to allow for this work except for two or three months a year. Consequently, Unita Blackwell and her sister took the ferry across the Mississippi River to West Helena, Arkansas. She lived with her aunt for eight months of the year and attended Westside Junior High School, where she completed the eighth grade. Later, she received her high school equivalency diploma. Blackwell spent her younger years picking cotton—as much as three hundred bales a day. After she married, she and her husband went to Florida to pick tomatoes and work in a canning plant. She moved to Mayersville, Mississippi, in 1962 and picked cotton, while her husband worked for U.S. industries.

In 1964 she became a field worker for the Student Nonviolent Coordinating Committee under the supervision of STOKELY CARMICHAEL. She was in charge of voter registration in the Second Congressional District in Mississippi, and, along with seven other people, she registered to vote in Issaquena County. She became a close friend of FANNIE LOU HAMER, and they both became founding members of the Mississippi Freedom Democratic Party (MFDP), formed in 1964 to challenge the white supremacist Democratic Party in Mississippi. Along with Hamer, Blackwell was an MFDP delegate to the 1964 Democratic national convention in Atlantic City. Members of the MFDP challenged the seating of the all-white delegates from Mississippi, and Blackwell, Hamer, and others testified before the credentials committee. When Hamer presented her fa-

mous testimony before the committee, President Lyndon Johnson called a press conference to prevent television coverage of the powerful and inspirational speaker from Mississippi. After much political wrangling, the MFDP was awarded only two delegate seats, which the members refused.

In the summer of 1965 the MFDP marched on the state legislature in Jackson to support Governor Paul Johnson's request that the legislators repeal Mississippi's discriminatory voting laws. Over half of the five hundred demonstrators were in their teens. Police arrested more than two hundred of the marchers, including Blackwell, placing them in the stockyards of the state fairgrounds, where many of the women were tortured. Blackwell herself was imprisoned for eleven days (University of Southern Mississippi oral history interview, 35–36).

Blackwell continued to press for change in the Delta. In 1965 she demanded that the school board provide decent facilities, teachers, and books for her son's school. The board refused to hear the demands, and Blackwell sued for desegregation of the schools in *Sharkey and Issaquena County Consolidated Line v. Blackwell*. The black principal followed the orders of the school board and refused to cooperate and, in Blackwell's view, left them with no alternative but to sue. "Desegregation of school was not one [of] our favorites," she recalled. "Our thing was to have good schools, didn't care what color they were. . . . We was asking for books; we was asking for fixing of the schools, that they would be just as nice" (University of Southern Mississippi oral history interview, 44). She won her case.

Undaunted by intimidation, Blackwell continued her struggle for justice. In the winter of 1965 and 1966 poor people in the Delta were hungry and cold. Indeed, two people froze to death. Conditions were made worse when planters evicted sharecroppers for registering to vote and participating in civil rights activities; the planters then saw to it that officials denied the evicted sharecroppers access to the federal food commodity program. With no food to eat and no place to live, sharecroppers formed the Mississippi Freedom Labor Union in January of 1965. The union launched a strike, and domestic workers, tractor drivers, and field hands walked off of their jobs all over the Delta.

As evictions and starvation continued, the union members Blackwell, Ida Mae Lawrence, and Isaac Foster, in the face of the federal government's refusal to answer their plea for help, decided to set up their own community and government. They led over seventy men, women, and children onto the empty Greenville Air Base, consisting of two thousand acres and three thousand buildings. There Blackwell eloquently expressed the goals of the group: "I feel that the federal government have proven that it don't care about poor people. Everything that we have asked for through these years has been handed down on paper. It's never been a reality. We the poor people of Mississippi is tired," she continued. "We're going to build for ourselves, because we don't have a government that represents us." A group of Air Police removed the squatters after thirty hours, but Blackwell and others had forced national attention on the dire poverty that many lived in and the limits of federal programs to address poor peoples' concerns.

Blackwell continued her efforts on behalf of poor people, becoming a national spokesperson on the issues of community economic development and low-income housing. In 1967, along with Hamer, ANNIE DEVINE, and AMZIE MOORE, she helped organize the Mississippi Action for Community Education Inc. (MACE) "to build and strengthen local human capacities and indigenous community development efforts" in the Mississippi Delta. MACE has trained local community organizers and leaders; conducts literacy, job training, career development, and arts education programs; and sponsors the Mississippi Delta Blues and Heritage Festival. In the late 1960s and early 1970s Blackwell worked with the National Council of Negro Women as a community-development specialist, establishing cooperative ventures in ownership of low-income housing. In 1983 she received a master's degree in Regional Planning from the University of Massachusetts at Amherst.

Blackwell has remained politically active on both a local and a national level. In 1976 she was elected mayor of Mayersville, becoming the first African American to hold mayoral office in Mississippi. In 1979 she attended President Jimmy Carter's Energy Summit at Camp David, and in 1984 she addressed the National Democratic Convention in San Francisco. In 1989 she chaired the National Mayor's Conference and, in 1991, the Black Women's Mayor's Conference. From 1976 to 1983 she was president of the U.S.-China Peoples' Friendship Association and traveled to China on numerous occasions. She has traveled extensively throughout Asia, Central America, and Europe.

In recognition of her achievements, in 1992 Blackwell was awarded the prized MacArthur Fellowship, also called the "genius" award, and the University of Massachusetts invited her to become the Eleanor Bateman Alumni Scholar. Her fighting spirit and faith in humanity persists. In 2000 she observed: "It seems like the whole century has been about overcoming. Fighting and then overcoming. You had women's suffrage, and apartheid and segregation. And we blacks lived in that lock-in, and somehow survived. How, I do not know. Nothing but a God I say. The whole era was full of hate, but we're trying to overcome it, and we're headed for something new, I just feel it. Maybe we are the group of people, the blacks in America, that brought everyone to their worst, and then to their best. Including ourselves" (UMASS Online Magazine).

Further Reading
The most extensive source of information on Blackwell is her interview, located in the Civil Rights in Mississippi Digital Archive, McCain Library and Archives, University of Southern Mississippi. Blackwell herself authored a memoir in 2006. See also the Mississippi Action for Community Education Inc. Web site, and UMASS Online Magazine (Winter 2000).

"My Whole World Was My Kinfolks," UMASS Online Magazine (Winter 2000).
"Mississippi Freedom Labor Union, 1965 Origins," and "We Have No Government," in Black Protest: History, Documents, and Analyses, 1619 to the Present, ed. Jo Ann Grant, 498–505.
Blackwell, Unita, and Joanne Prichard Morris. Bare-footin': Life Lessons from the Road to Freedom (2006).
Dittmer, John. Local People: The Struggle for Civil Rights in Mississippi (1994).
Mills, Kay. This Little Light of Mine: The Life of Fannie Lou Hamer (1993).
Payne, Charles. I've Got the Light of Freedom: The Organizing Tradition and the Mississippi Freedom Struggle (1995).

NAN ELIZABETH WOODRUFF

BLAIR, Norval (1829–1916), farmer, patriarch, and founder of the Sully County Colored Colony, Dakota Territory (South Dakota became a state in 1889), was born in slavery, probably in Tennessee, and was freed at Emancipation. He married Mary Elizabeth Bagby Blair, reported to be half Cherokee. With their six adult children they founded South Dakota's only successful black agricultural colony. Five years out of slavery the family was farming near Morris, Illinois, about fifty miles southwest of Chicago. With substantial personal property, they held their land "free and clear." An oral tradition among South Dakota African Americans suggests that Blair's successful bloodline of fast horses, his unseemly prosperity, and his interest in expanding his lands aroused jealousy among his white neighbors in Illinois, prompting him to consider relocating to Dakota Territory.

Sully County, just east of present-day Pierre, South Dakota, opened for settlement in April 1883. The following year Norval Blair sent two of his sons, Benjamin P. and Patrick Henry Blair, to reconnoiter and, if suitable, to purchase land where the clan could relocate. The Blair sons were personable, educated, and enthusiastic about Sully County, and they were well accepted by other speculators. They chose a home site with an excellent water supply not far from the village of Fairbank. Norval Blair brought the rest of the family to Sully County the following year, along with seeds, livestock, and a string of fine Morgan foundation stock intended for breeding purposes. Settlers to the Northern Great Plains, well into the twentieth century, often brought fine equine breed stock, since horses provided both transportation and power for the arduous work of breaking the prairie to agriculture. Morgan horses, developed in the early 1800s by Justin Morgan, were especially prized as carriage horses for their strength, speed, and beauty. Their bloodlines were foundation stock for American standardbreds, Tennessee Walkers, and other fine breeds.

The Blair family built a comfortable home and lived quietly in Sully County for more than twenty years, successfully farming the difficult and unforgiving land. They continued to breed their Morgan racing stock, which developed a considerable reputation throughout the Midwest. The Blairs' most famous horse was Johnny Bee, which held the state record for speed from 1907 to 1909.

In 1906 Norval Blair, with his sons and daughter Elizabeth (Betty), joined other black South Dakotans in the Northwestern Homestead Movement, a statewide effort to encourage black immigration to farming colonies in the state. Local black families throughout the state pledged to assist and sponsor the newcomers, and the Blair family offered 1,700 acres on their land for an agricultural college to train African American farmers in local farming techniques. Homesteaders from all backgrounds, tempted by the availability of free farmland on the Northern Great Plains, especially west of the Missouri River, found that pioneering unbroken land in a harsh country was difficult, challenging, and discouraging. Snowbound winters, sweltering summers, grasshopper plagues, tough and unyielding unbroken prairie, hailstorms, drought and unpredictable weather patterns, isolation, and falling grain prices proved too much for all but the most hearty and determined. Although the college never materialized, the colony did. Over the next twenty-five years, more than two hundred African Americans experienced Sully County farm life, some with considerable success, and all with the active encouragement of the Blairs.

Betty Blair became a real estate saleswoman for the King Real Estate Company, Iowa land speculators. Most of the black settlers purchased their land from "Miss Betty." The settlers ranged in age from very young couples with young children to elderly couples accompanied by their grown children. Although the population varied over the years, the community was close-knit and was centered on the country school that also served as a church. Like other Great Plains farms, the colony did not survive the Dust Bowl and Depression of the 1930s, although a few farms remained through the 1940s. A maintained cemetery on the original Blair farm is the last resting place of Norval and Mary Blair and others of the Sully County Colored Colony. The cemetery, now located on a private ranch, is maintained in perpetuity by the terms of the property's deed.

Further Reading
Linde, Martha. *Western Dakota Horse Stories* (1989).
Saxman, Michelle C. "To Better Oneself: Sully County's African American 'Colony,'" in *South Dakota History* 34, no. 4 (Winter 2004): 319–328.
Sully County Centennial History Book Committee. *100 Years of a Proud People, 1883–1983: A History of Sully County* (1983).
Sully County Old Settlers Association. *The History of Sully County* (1939).
Thompson, Harry, Editor. *A New South Dakota History* (2005). See especially the chapters "Farming, Dependency and Depopulation" and "African Americans," the latter by Betti C. VanEpps-Taylor.
VanEpps-Taylor, Betti C. *Forgotten Americans: African Americans in South Dakota* (forthcoming 2007).
                                    BETTI CAROL VANEPPS-TAYLOR

BLAKE, Eubie (7 Feb. 1883–12 Feb. 1983), composer and pianist, was born James Hubert Blake in Baltimore, Maryland, the son of John Sumner Blake, a stevedore, and Emily Johnston, a launderer. His father was a Civil War veteran, and both parents were former slaves. While the young Blake was a mediocre student during several years of public schooling, he showed early signs of musical interest and talent, picking out tunes on an organ in a department store at about age six. As a result, his parents rented an organ for twenty-five cents a week, and he soon began basic keyboard lessons with Margaret Marshall, a neighbor and church organist. At about age twelve he learned cornet and buck dancing and was earning pocket change singing with friends on the street. When he was thirteen, he received encouragement from the ragtime pianist Jesse Pickett, whom he had watched through the window of a bawdy house in order to learn his fingering. By 1898 he had steady work as a piano player in Aggie Shelton's sporting house, a job that necessitated the lad's sneaking out of his home at night, after his parents went to bed. The objections of his deeply religious mother when she learned of his new career were overcome only by the pragmatism of his sporadically employed father, once he discovered how much his son was making in tips.

In 1899 (the year SCOTT JOPLIN's famous "Maple Leaf Rag" appeared), Blake wrote his first rag, "Charleston Rag" (although he would not be able to notate it until some years later). In 1902 he performed as a buck dancer in the traveling minstrel show *In Old Kentucky*, playing briefly in New York City. In 1907, after playing in several clubs in Baltimore, he became a pianist at the Goldfield Hotel, built by his friend and the new world lightweight boxing champion JOE GANS. The elegant Goldfield was one of the first establishments in Baltimore where blacks and whites mixed, and there Blake acquired a personal grace and polish that would impress his admirers for the rest of his life. Already an excellent player, he learned from watching the conservatory-trained "One-Leg Willie" Joseph, whom he often cited as the best piano player he had ever heard. While at the Goldfield, Blake studied composition with the Baltimore musician Llewellyn Wilson, and at about the same time he began playing summers in Atlantic City, where he met such keyboard luminaries as WILLIE "THE LION" SMITH, LUCKEY ROBERTS, and JAMES P. JOHNSON. In July 1910 he married Avis Lee, the daughter of a black society family in Baltimore and a classically trained pianist.

In 1915 Blake met the singer and lyricist NOBLE SISSLE, and they quickly began a songwriting collaboration that would last for decades. One of their songs of that year, "It's All Your Fault," achieved success when it was introduced by Sophie Tucker. Sissle and Blake also performed in New York with JAMES REESE EUROPE's Society Orchestra. While Sissle and Europe were in the service during World War I, Blake performed in vaudeville with Henry "Broadway" Jones. After the war Sissle and Blake formed a vaudeville act

Eubie Blake, the veteran jazz, pianist, performs during his surprise birthday party, New York's Waldorf-Astoria Hotel, 7 February 1976. (AP Images.)

called the Dixie Duo, which became quite successful. In an era when blacks were expected to shuffle and speak in dialect, they dressed elegantly in tuxedos, and they were one of the first black acts to perform before white audiences without burnt cork. By 1917 Blake also had begun recording on both disks and piano rolls.

In 1920 Sissle and Blake met the successful comedy and dance team of Flournoy Miller and Aubrey Lyles, who suggested combining forces to produce a show. The result was the all-black *Shuffle Along*, which opened on Broadway in 1921 and for which Blake was composer and conductor. The score included what would become one of his best-known songs, "I'm Just Wild about Harry." Mounted on a shoestring budget, the musical met with critical acclaim and popular success, running for 504 performances in New York, followed by an extensive three-company tour of the United States. The show had a tremendous effect on musical theater, stirring interest in jazz dance, fostering faster paced shows with more syncopated rhythms, and paving the way in general for more black musicals and black performers. *Shuffle Along* was a springboard for the careers of several of its cast members, including JOSEPHINE BAKER, ADELAIDE HALL, FLORENCE MILLS, and PAUL ROBESON.

Sissle and Blake worked for ten years as songwriters for the prestigious Witmark publishing firm. In 1922, through Julius Witmark, they were able to join ASCAP (American Society of Composers, Authors, and Pub-

lishers), which did not at that time include many blacks. They also appeared in an early sound film in 1923, *Sissle and Blake's Snappy Songs*, produced by the electronics pioneer Lee De Forest. In 1924 they created an ambitious new show, *The Chocolate Dandies*. Unable to match the success of *Shuffle Along*, the lavish production lost money, but Blake was proud of its score and considered it his best.

The team returned to vaudeville, ending their long collaboration with a successful eight-month tour of Great Britain in 1925–1926. The two broke up when Sissle, attracted by opportunities in Europe, returned to work there; Blake, delighted to be back home in New York, refused to accompany him. Over the next few years Blake collaborated with Harry Creamer to produce a few songs and shows; reunited with "Broadway" Jones to perform the shortened "tab show" *Shuffle Along Jr.* in vaudeville (1928–1929); and teamed with the lyricist ANDY RAZAF to write songs for *Lew Leslie's Blackbirds of 1930*, including "Memories of You," later popularized by Benny Goodman. After Lyles's death in 1932, Sissle and Blake reunited with Miller to create *Shuffle Along of 1933*, but the show failed, in part because of the Depression. The remainder of the decade saw Blake collaborating with the lyricist Milton Reddie on a series of shows, including the Works Progress Administration–produced *Swing It* in 1937, and with Razaf on several floor shows and "industrials" (promotional shows). Blake's wife died of tuberculosis in 1939, but despite his grief he managed to complete, with Razaf, the show *Tan Manhattan*.

During World War II, Blake toured with United Service Organizations shows and worked with other collaborators. In 1945 he married Marion Gant Tyler, a business executive and former showgirl in several black musicals. She took over management of his financial affairs and saw to the raising of his ASCAP rating to an appropriate level, enhancing their financial security considerably.

After the war, at the age of sixty-three, Blake took the opportunity to attend New York University, where he studied the Schillinger system of composition. He graduated with a degree in music in 1950. Meanwhile, the presidential race of 1948 stirred renewed interest in "I'm Just Wild about Harry" when Harry Truman adopted it as a campaign song. This resulted in a reuniting of Sissle and Blake and in a revival in 1952 of *Shuffle Along*. Unfortunately, the producers' attempts to completely rewrite the show had the effect of eviscerating it, and the restaging closed after only four performances.

Following a few years of relative retirement, during which Blake wrote out some of his earlier pieces, a resurgence of popular interest in ragtime in the 1950s and again in the 1970s thrust him back into the spotlight for the last decades of his life. Several commemorative recordings appeared, most notably, *The Eighty-six Years of Eubie Blake*, a two-record retrospective with Noble Sissle for Columbia in 1969. In 1972 he started Eubie Blake Music, a record company featuring his own music. He was much in demand as a speaker and performer, impressing audiences with his still considerable pianistic technique as well as his energy, audience rapport, and charm as a raconteur. Appearances included the St. Louis Ragfest, the Newport Jazz Festival, the *Tonight Show*, a solo concert at Town Hall in New York City, and a concert in his honor by Arthur Fiedler and the Boston Pops in 1973, with Blake as soloist. In 1974 Jean-Cristophe Averty produced a four-hour documentary film on Blake's life and music for French television. The musical revue *Eubie!*, featuring twenty-three of his numbers, opened on Broadway in 1978 and ran for a year. Blake was awarded the Presidential Medal of Freedom at the White House in 1981.

Blake's wife, Marion, died in June 1982; he left no children by either of his marriages. A few months after his wife's death, his hundredth birthday was feted with performances of his music, but he was ill with pneumonia and unable to attend. He died five days later in New York City.

Over a long career as pianist, composer, and conductor, Blake left a legacy of more than two thousand compositions in various styles. His earliest pieces were piano rags, often of such extreme difficulty that they were simplified for publication. As a ragtime composer and player, he, along with such figures as Luckey Roberts and James P. Johnson, was a key influence on the Harlem stride-piano school of the

1930s. In the field of show music, Blake moved beyond the confines of ragtime, producing songs that combined rhythmic energy with an appealing lyricism. Particularly notable was his involvement with the successful *Shuffle Along*, which put blacks back on the Broadway stage after an absence of more than ten years. Over his lifetime he displayed a marked openness to musical growth, learning from "all music, particularly the music of Mozart, Chopin, Tchaikovsky, Victor Herbert, Gershwin, Debussy, and Strauss," and, indeed, some of his less well known pieces show these influences. Finally, his role in later years as an energetic "elder statesman of ragtime" provided a historical link to a time long gone as well as inspiration to many younger fans.

Further Reading
Blake's papers are at the Maryland Historical Society in Baltimore.
Jasen, David A., and Trebor Jay Tichenor. *Rags and Ragtime: A Musical History* (1978).
Kimball, Robert, and William Bolcom. *Reminiscing with Sissle and Blake* (1973).
Rose, Al. *Eubie Blake* (1979).
Southern, Eileen. *The Music of Black Americans: A History* (1971; 2d ed., 1983).

WILLIAM G. ELLIOTT

BLAKE, Robert (c. 1836–?), Medal of Honor winner, was born into slavery in Santee, South Carolina. When war came he was a slave on the Arthur Blake Plantation on the South Santee River, McClellanville, South Carolina, possibly the same plantation on which he was born. The Blake Plantation, one of many rice plantations in the area, was no small affair; according to the 1860 census it had 538 enslaved men and women and was the twelfth largest plantation in the country. When the Union navy invaded the coastal areas of South Carolina, it not only created widespread panic among slave-holders but also influenced many of those who were enslaved to emancipate themselves and flee to freedom. In May 1862, with the Union navy off the coast of South Carolina, Robert Blake and four others, Prince, Michael, Jack, and Captain Blake, fled the Blake Plantation. All were picked up by the Union navy's *Gem of the Sea* off Georgetown, South Carolina, and would soon thereafter enlist in the Union navy as "contrabands."

The importance of contraband sailors to the manning of the Union navy during the Civil War was considerable. Of the estimated eighteen thousand African Americans that served in the Union navy during the war, only four thousand (of those whose native state is known) were born in free states. The remainder, over eleven thousand, including men such as Robert Blake and ROBERT SMALLS, were born in slave states, with the likelihood that only a fraction of this number was born free. Over one thousand former slaves alone enlisted in the South Atlantic Blockade Squadron from South Carolina, Georgia, and Florida.

African American sailors who entered the Union navy from slave states were called "contrabands" because they were legally considered part of the property seizures made against belligerents of the United States (that is, any slave owner), an idea conceived early in the war by General Benjamin Butler. Legally, the status of these individuals was ambiguous until they were formally made free through Abraham Lincoln's Emancipation Proclamation on 1 January 1863. Prior to this time those formerly enslaved individuals that were either "captured" or were "self-emancipated" and sought refuge with Union forces were often set up in temporary camps and employed by the government, or enlisted to serve in the military.

Robert Blake would choose the later of the options listed above and immediately joined the Union navy, enlisting as a "First Class Boy" on 15 June 1862 aboard the *Gem of the Sea*. He listed his birthplace as Santee, South Carolina, his age twenty-six, and his height at five feet six inches. Enlisting along with Robert were the other men that escaped from the Blake Plantation. One of them, Captain Blake, was called "a good pilot of all the inland creeks and rivers from the South Santee to Savannah" (King, 5). Because all slaves from the plantation carried the last name of their master, it is unknown if Robert and Captain Blake were related. Even lacking a family connection, it may be that Robert learned a bit about sailoring from Blake and, as events would later prove, turned out to be a fine addition to the Union navy.

Upon joining, Robert Blake served on the *Gem of the Sea* until 1 October 1862, at which time he was transferred for duty on the steamer *Norwich*. He would continue on this vessel for the next year, taking part in the ship's actions as part of the South Atlantic Blockade Squadron. Every indication is that Robert Blake was a diligent sailor, enjoying his newfound freedom by practicing his duties faithfully. He would experience his first fighting on 10 March 1863 when the *Norwich* escorted Union transports up the St. John's River and shelled Confederate positions near Jacksonville, Florida. Among the fellow contrabands serving with Blake at this time was Frederick Gardiner, a Jacksonville river pilot.

On 1 October 1863 Robert Blake was temporarily assigned for duty on board the *Marblehead*. The transfer may have been occasioned by the ship's pending operations off the coast of South Carolina, an area familiar to Blake. Whatever the reason, Blake's transfer would soon prove prophetic. Several months later, on Christmas day, the *Marblehead* was in operation on the Stono River off Legareville, South Carolina, and engaged Confederate positions on John's Island. The action was heavy and the *Marblehead* was hit twenty times by Confederate artillery. The ship's commander, Richard W. Meade Jr., however, could not help but notice the actions of the contraband Robert Blake. He would later report that Blake "excited my admiration by the cool and brave manner in which he served the rifle gun" (Quarles, 231). In the end, the men of the *Marblehead* prevailed and the Confederates retreated from the island, leaving their

munitions behind. For his action on 25 December 1863 Robert Blake was awarded the Medal of Honor, the first African American sailor to be so honored.

Following this historic achievement Robert Blake continued in the Union navy, and was later advanced in rate from "boy" to seaman. Just six days after the action on the Stono River he returned to duty aboard the *Norwich*; here he would serve until his naval service ended on 31 March 1865. Blake was mustered out of the service aboard the bark *Gem of the Sea*, the ship on which he had first gained his freedom. After the war the exact fate of Robert Blake is uncertain. It is unknown whether he kept the last name of Blake or, like so many newly freed slaves, shed the name of his former master and took on a new identity. Perhaps he is the same Robert Blake that lived in King William County, Acquinton Township, Virginia, after the war and married, had a family, and worked as a farmer into the 1880s. Whatever his final fate Robert Blake, who transformed himself from a slave to a sailor defending his newfound freedom and that of countless others, will always have an honored place in America's hall of heroes.

Further Reading

King, Lisa Y. "They Called Us Bluejackets," *International Journal of Naval History* 1.1 (Apr. 2002).
Quarles, Benjamin. *The Negro in the Civil War* (1953).
Reidy, Joseph P. "Black Men in Navy Blue during the Civil War," *Prologue Magazine* 33.3 (Fall 2001).
United States Navy. *Medal of Honor, 1861–1949: The Navy* (1950).

GLENN ALLEN KNOBLOCK

BLAKELY, Allison (31 Mar. 1940–), historian, author, and university professor, was born in Clinton, Alabama, to Ed Walton and Alice Blakely, sharecroppers. When Blakely was young his mother moved north to secure better employment, and he was raised by a great aunt in the coal-mining town of Preco, near Birmingham. In 1946 his mother returned to Alabama and moved him and his older sister to Oregon, where Alice Blakely had worked as a seamstress and in the Portland shipyards during World War II.

An avid reader since his early years, Blakely particularly enjoyed Russian literature and studied the Russian language in both high school and college. His interest in revolutions and popular democracy further stimulated his interest in Russian history. He received a BA from the University of Oregon in 1962, where he majored in history and was elected to Phi Beta Kappa. He also graduated as a Distinguished Military Graduate in the Army Reserve Officers Training Corps (ROTC). Blakely then pursued graduate studies in Russian and modern European history at the University of California at Berkeley, where he received his MA and PhD degrees in 1964 and 1971, respectively. These studies, however, were interrupted by his fulfillment of a two-year military service ROTC obligation. He served as an army intelligence officer and attained the rank of captain during the Vietnam War. Wounded in combat, Blakely was awarded both a

Bronze Star and a Purple Heart in 1968. That same year, he married Shirley Ann Reynolds, a nutritional scientist. They had two children.

A recipient of the Woodrow Wilson Fellowship that encouraged fellows to consider teaching at historically black colleges and universities (HBCUs), Blakely was recruited to teach Russian history at Howard University in 1971, after having taught one year as an instructor in the Western civilization program at Stanford University. During three decades at Howard, Blakely rose in the academic ranks, becoming a full professor and also serving in various high academic and administrative posts that included associate dean of the College of Arts and Sciences and director of the honors program. As a professor of European history at Howard University he developed a particular interest in the interconnections between European history and the African diaspora. Professor Blakely's scholarly interests were also stimulated by both his own personal background—an African American who lived mostly in predominantly white areas since leaving his native Alabama at the age of six—and his interest in comparative history, revolutionary change, and the evolution of color prejudice.

His first book, *Russia and the Negro: Blacks in Russian History and Thought* (1986), was widely and generally positively reviewed in both general and Russian historical journals and was awarded the American Book Award from the Before Columbus Foundation in 1988. This unique work examines the historical Russian attitudes toward Africans, the black diaspora, native Russians of African descent (for example, Alexander Pushkin), and the experiences of numerous African American writers and political activists who either lived in Russia or were active in the international communist movement.

His interest in comparative history and revolution further spurred him to do research at the International Institute for Social History in Amsterdam. While in the Netherlands, Blakely became acutely aware of the racism directed against recent immigrants from the former Dutch colony of Surinam who had moved to Holland after their country became independent. Since the Dutch strongly perceived themselves as both liberal and tolerant, Blakely thought it would be a "fascinating case study" to examine their historical attitudes toward blacks. In 1988 he authored *Blacks in the Dutch World: The Evolution of Racial Imagery in a Modern Society*, an extensive survey of the depiction of blacks in Dutch folklore, painting, literature, and religion since the fifteenth century. This pathbreaking work received much praise—although not without criticism—from African, Dutch, and other European historians. Writing in the *Journal of Interdisciplinary History*, a reviewer described the book as "provocative and exceptionally well written—a significant contribution to the history of Dutch overseas expansion," while a University of Utrecht professor observed in the *Journal of African History* that "Blakely detects facts about Dutch culture and society which somehow elude many Dutch historians."

Blakely's writings influenced a generation of African diaspora scholars. In the last decades of the twentieth century and the first years of the twenty-first century his seminal studies have been acknowledged in works written by scholars in Japan, England, Holland, and other European countries, as well as the United States. The editor of *The Russian Review* noted that one of Blakely's articles published in that influential publication was a "landmark" in redefining the issues in the American historiography of Russia. Fluent in Dutch and Russian and working also extensively with French and German sources, Blakely complemented his books through the publication of numerous journal articles, book chapters and conference papers. In 2001 Boston University recruited Blakely for a joint appointment as professor of European and comparative history and professor of African American studies. In 2003 he was designated as the first incumbent of the newly endowed George and Joyce Wein Professorship in African American studies. His teaching career included visiting professorships at Spelman College and the École des Hautes Études en Sciences Sociales in Paris and affiliations with Johns Hopkins University and the University of Leiden in the Netherlands. Blakely received many academic fellowships, grants, and honors, including the Ford Foundation Postdoctoral Fellowship, the Fulbright-Hays Research Fellowship, the National Defense Foreign Language Fellowship, the National Endowment for the Humanities Traveling Fellowship, and the Mellon Fellowship at the Aspen Institute. An elected senator of the Phi Beta Kappa Society, he also served on the editorial board of its quarterly journal, the *American Scholar*. In 2006 he became the president of this prestigious academic honor society.

Blakely's career was inspired by a number of influences, but especially that of his mother Alice, a deeply religious woman who valued education, though she herself only reached the sixth grade. She instilled in him pride in his background and taught him not to "hate people although you may hate the bad things people do." In 1997 Allison Blakely endowed the Alice Blakely Brink Memorial Scholarship to help needy students attend the University of Oregon.

Further Reading

Blakely, Allison. "American Influences on Russian Reformist Thought in the Era of the French Revolution," *The Russian Review* 52 (Oct. 1993).

Jordan, Winthrop. "Allison Blakely. *Blacks in the Dutch World: The Evolution of Racial Imagery in a Modern Society*," *American Historical Review*, vol. 99, no. 4 (1994).

Kuitenbrouwer, Maarten. "*Blacks in the Dutch World: The Evolution of Racial Imagery in a Modern Society* by Allison Blakely," *Journal of African History*, vol. 36, no. 3 (1995).

Postma, Johannes. "*Blacks in the Dutch World: The Evolution of Racial Imagery in a Modern Society* by Allison Blakely," *Journal of Interdisciplinary History*, vol. 26, no. 4 (1996).

DONALD ALTSCHILLER

BLAKELY, Nora Brooks (8 Sept.1951–), teacher, poet, playwright, and artistic director of a theater company, was born Nora Brooks Blakely in Chicago, one of two children of poet GWENDOLYN BROOKS and Henry Blakely, a poet, auto mechanic, and insurance adjuster. Blakely's mother was a leading figure in the Black Arts Movement, the poet laureate of Illinois, and the first African American to receive the Pulitzer Prize, which she did in 1950, just a year before Nora's birth. Nora's father was the author of *A Windy Place*, a 1974 collection of poetry, and he later founded the Perspectivists, a group of black Chicago writers. As a child, Nora displayed a natural ability and love for reading and writing, no doubt cultivated by her parents' passion for the same.

A propensity for teaching emerged early as well; at the age of three Blakely rounded up the children of her South Side Chicago neighborhood and taught lessons in the pretend classroom in her backyard. Her parents emphasized learning and knowledge, and they taught their daughter the importance of understanding and being able to articulate her beliefs. For instance, Blakely remembers once announcing that she supported John F. Kennedy for president, a preference in line with the rest of her family's views, but her parents would not accept this as justification; they pressed her to explain her inclination with solid reasons and logic (Kent, 148).

Blakely was educated at Hirsch High School in Chicago and graduated in 1968. After a short tour of France and England, she enrolled at the University of Illinois. While in college she had the opportunity to further her foreign travels, studying briefly at the University of Dar es Salaam in Tanzania. Blakely received her BA in Education from the University of Illinois at the age of twenty and, in her own words, "assumed that I was going to be teaching until they rolled me out of the classroom in a wheelchair" (Whitaker, 122). After receiving her degree she taught in the Chicago public school systems for eight years, but she eventually became frustrated with a lack of administrative support and failed attempts at reaching some of the more apathetic, undisciplined students.

When the negatives began to eclipse the rewards of teaching, Blakely turned to an alternative venue through which she knew she could have an impact on young people: the theater. In 1982 she founded the Chocolate Chips Theatre Company of Chicago. Her training and previous performance experience at such prestigious groups as Chicago's Kuumba Theatre and the Muntu Dance Theatre of Chicago had prepared Blakely for directing her own theater company. Chocolate Chips first consisted of a traveling troupe of teen performers, but it soon progressed to a professional adult company with a scheduled season. Making stops around the Midwest, but mostly performing in the Chicago area, the company dedicated itself to bringing the vibrancy of African American culture alive on stage for children, teenagers, and adults. Their productions celebrated African American folklore and history and explored the contemporary experiences of blacks, in both national and local contexts; the company strove to use theater as a forum to encourage young people to read and write as well. Blakely kept her mother's legacy alive through her mother's work, with Chocolate Chips frequently performing *A Day in Bronzeville: Black Life through the Eyes of Gwendolyn Brooks*. This production was a stage adaptation of her mother's first volume of poetry, *A Street in Bronzeville* (1945), and featured song and poetry as dialogue for children aged three through twelve. Gwendolyn Brooks passed away on 3 December 2000 at the age of eighty-three, and Blakely is said to have placed a pen in her hand as she died (*Chicago Tribune*, 4 Dec. 2000).

From that time Blakely continued her mother's role as an active citizen of the city of Chicago, both through her own work and in carrying on her mother's legacy. She served as an Illinois Arts Council artist-in-residence, read her own work throughout the city, taught writing, and conducted creative-performance workshops to students of all ages, from preschool to adult. Active in many of the state of Illinois's efforts to honor their late poet laureate, Blakely unveiled the plaque at the 2003 ceremony commemorating the naming of the Illinois state library after the poet and speaking at scholarly conferences on her mother's work. She served as managing artistic director of Chocolate Chips and wrote many of their productions, including *Brother, Man,* a play for teenagers and adults that identifies and counteracts negative stereotypes of black men, and *Moyenda and the Golden Heart,* which details the quest of an African man in a fictional African village. Her poetry appeared in the collection *The Woman That I Am: The Literature and Culture of Contemporary Women of Color* (1994). Blakely once said of her mother:

Gwendolyn Brooks introduced and shared experiences . . . entrances to the lives of people you might, otherwise, never know. Gwendolyn, whether as manic parent, literary midwife, or life mapper, opened places for people—new doorways and mindpaths. And, after all, isn't that what a mother is supposed to do? (Madhubuti)

Blakely also continued her mother's tradition of opening new "mindpaths," using theater as her forum to introduce the young people of Chicago to the lives of people such as Moyenda and those characters of her mother's *Bronzeville*. Blakely's work at Chocolate Chips helped children and adults alike celebrate African American culture through song, movement, and literacy.

Further Reading
Brooks, Gwendolyn. *Report from Part One* (1972).
Brooks, Gwendolyn. *Report from Part Two* (1996).
Kent, George E. *A Life of Gwendolyn Brooks* (1990).
Madhubuti, Haki. *Chicken Bones: A Journal* (2003). This online journal is found at http://www.nathanielturner.com/gweninmontgomery.htm.
Whitaker, Charles. "The Disappearing Black Teacher: Blacks Leaving Careers in Education," *Ebony* (Jan. 1989).

CASEY KAYSER

BLAKEY, Art (11 Oct. 1919–16 Oct. 1990), jazz drummer and bandleader, was born Art William Blakey in Pittsburgh, Pennsylvania, the son of Burtrum Blakey, a barber, and Marie Roddericker. His father left home shortly after Blakey was born, and his mother died the next year. Consequently, he was raised by a cousin, Sarah Oliver Parran, who worked at the Jones and Laughlin Steel Mill in Pittsburgh. He moved out of the home at age thirteen to work in the steel mills and in 1938 married Clarice Stuart, the first of three wives. His other wives were Diana Bates and Ann Arnold. Blakey had at least ten children (the exact number is unknown), the last of whom was born in 1986.

As a teenager Blakey taught himself to play the piano and performed in local dance bands, but he later switched to drums. Like many of his contemporaries, Blakey initially adapted the stylistic drumming techniques of well-known swing era drummers, including CHICK WEBB, SID CATLETT, and Ray Bauduc, to whom he frequently paid tribute. As a result, his earliest playing experiences away from Pittsburgh centered around ensembles fronted by well-known, big-band leaders.

Although some sources indicate Blakey first worked with the FLETCHER HENDERSON Orchestra in 1939, it seems unlikely. The drummer Pete Suggs joined the Henderson band in June 1937 and remained with him until the group disbanded two years later, when Henderson became an arranger and pianist for the Benny Goodman band. However, Blakey did join a newly formed Henderson band in the spring of 1943 after playing with MARY LOU WILLIAMS's twelve-piece band and briefly leading his own group at a small Boston nightclub in 1942.

During the early 1940s Blakey was assimilating the innovative bop drumming styles of KENNY CLARKE and MAX ROACH, as evidenced by his selection as drummer for the BILLY ECKSTINE big band organized in 1944. This group (with the trumpeter DIZZY GILLESPIE as musical director) started at the Club Plantation in St. Louis and was among the first big bands to play bebop-influenced arrangements. Although somewhat unsuccessful as a commercial venture, the band rehearsed and recorded from 1944 to 1947. Blakey's playing with this ensemble indicates that regardless of the bebop bent of the repertoire, he played mainly late, swing-style drums. But it was during his tenure with Eckstine that Blakey came in contact with several major bop luminaries, including Gillespie, CHARLIE PARKER, MILES DAVIS, DEXTER GORDON, and Kenny Dorham. His association with these musicians placed him firmly in the bop camp, where he remained throughout his career. After the dissolution of Eckstine's band, Blakey joined THELONIOUS MONK for the pianist's first Blue Note recordings in 1947; theirs was a complementary collaboration that continued off and on for the next decade. That same year Blakey organized a rehearsal band, the Seventeen Messengers, and in December made several recordings for Blue Note with his octet, Art Blakey's Jazz Messengers, which included Dorham on trumpet. This group was the first to bear the name through which Blakey would later become famous.

In 1948 Blakey made a brief, nonmusical trip to Africa, at which time he converted to the Islamic religion, changing his name to Abdullah Ibn Buhaina. By mid-1948 he had returned to the United States, recording once again with Monk that July and with the saxophonist James Moody in October. The next year he joined LUCKY MILLINDER's R&B–based band and recorded with him in February. Although Blakey never recorded under his Muslim name, several of his children share this name with him, and later he was known to his musical friends as "Bu."

During the early 1950s Blakey solidified his bop drumming style by playing with well-known bop musicians such as Parker, Davis, Buddy DeFranco, CLIFFORD BROWN, Percy Heath, and HORACE SILVER. In the mid-1950s Blakey and Silver formed the first of the acclaimed Jazz Messengers ensembles that initially included Dorham, HANK MOBLEY, and Doug Watkins. When Silver left in 1956, Blakey retained leadership of the group that with constantly changing personnel became an important conduit through which many young, talented jazz musicians would pass. For the next twenty-odd years the Jazz Messengers' alumni comprised a list of virtual "who's who" in modern jazz, including Donald Byrd, Bill Hardman, JACKIE McLEAN, Junior Mance, LEE MORGAN, Benny Golson, BOBBY TIMMONS, Mobley, WAYNE SHORTER, Curtis Fuller, Freddie Hubbard, Cedar Walton, Reggie Workman, Keith Jarrett, Chuck Mangione, McCOY

Art Blakey, percussionist and leader of the Jazz Messengers, 30 November 1955. (AP Images.)

TYNER, WOODY SHAW, Joanne Brackeen, Steve Turré, WYNTON MARSALIS, and Branford Marsalis.

Despite impaired hearing, which ultimately left him deaf, Blakey continued to perform with the Jazz Messengers until shortly before his death in New York City. Throughout his dynamic and influential career he worked with nearly every major bop figure of the last half of the twentieth century, and his Jazz Messengers ensembles provided a training ground for dozens more. He was inducted into the *Down Beat* Jazz Hall of Fame in 1981, and the Jazz Messengers received a Grammy Award for Best Jazz Instrumental Group Performance in 1984. The group recorded several film soundtracks (mainly overseas) from 1959 to 1972, and a documentary film, *Art Blakey: The Jazz Messenger* (Rhapsody Films), containing interviews with Blakey and other musicians as well as performances by the Jazz Messengers, was released in 1988. Blakey also appears in a jazz video series produced by Sony called *Art Blakey and the Jazz Messengers: Jazz at the Smithsonian* (1982).

Blakey's recorded legacy spans forty years and documents his prodigious and prolific career as drummer and leader. His earliest big-band recordings with Eckstine (De Luxe 2001, 1944) demonstrate an advanced swing style comparable to the best of the late swing era drummers. Although his early Monk recordings (*The Complete Blue Note Recordings of Thelonious Monk*, Mosaic, MR4-101) are clearly bop-oriented, he retains some of his earlier swing characteristics. By the beginning of the 1950s, however, several of Blakey's well-defined playing characteristics emerge, including his heavy and constant high-hat rhythm and effective use of both bass drum and high-hat as additional independent rhythmic resources, which identify him as a progressive and influential bop drummer.

The Jazz Messengers' recordings are numerous and contain performances of varying degrees of success; however, Blakey's playing remains somewhat consistent, regardless of whom he is accompanying. The most impressive of the Messengers' playing is in a collection of recordings the group made in 1960 (*The Complete Blue Note Recordings of the 1960 Jazz Messengers*, Mosaic, MD6-141). Here, the group, consisting of Lee Morgan, Wayne Shorter, Bobby Timmons, Jymie Merritt, and Blakey, demonstrates exceptional talent and produces some of the Messengers' most memorable numbers, including Blakey's signature tune, "Night in Tunisia," composed by Gillespie. Later Messenger recordings with such notables as Jarrett and Mangione (*The Best of Art Blakey*, EmArcy 848245-2 CD, 1979) and the Marsalis brothers (*Keystone 3*, Concord CJ 196/CCD 4196, 1980), provide excellent examples of the continued influence Blakey's leadership had on the growth of jazz in the last quarter of the twentieth century.

The harshest criticism of Blakey's playing was directed at his loud, often overpowering drumming style, which developed in the 1950s and may have contributed to his early hearing loss. Nevertheless, he could also be a sensitive and unobtrusive drummer, as many of his ballad accompaniments demonstrate. Furthermore, his frequently recorded, unaccompanied, improvised drum solo pieces provide numerous examples of his imaginative and flashy, but somewhat musically misdirected, solo ability.

Further Reading
Goldberg, Joe. *Jazz Masters of the Fifties* (1965).
Harricks, Raymond, et al. *These Jazzmen of Our Times* (1959).
Stewart, Zan. "Art Blakey in His Prime," *Down Beat* (July 1985).
Taylor, Arthur. *Notes and Tones: Musician to Musician Interviews* (1977).
Obituary: *New York Times,* 17 Oct. 1990.

Discography
The Best of Art Blakey (EmArcy 848245-2 CD, 1979).
The Complete Blue Note Recordings of the 1960 Jazz Messengers (Mosaic, MD6-141, 1960).

T. DENNIS BROWN

BLAKEY, Theodore Robert (31 Aug. 1925–14 Oct. 2004), historian of African Americans in South Dakota, civic leader, entrepreneur, and philanthropist, was born in Yankton, South Dakota, the youngest of eleven children of Henry and Mary (Fristoe) Blakey. The large, extended Blakey clan began migrating from Missouri to South Dakota in 1904, where they acquired land and built a profitable and respected truck gardening business. Young Blakey completed eighth grade in country school and worked in the family business. Beginning in the mid-1960s Blakey returned to school at Springfield State College (which later closed), where he obtained his GED and completed advanced training in building maintenance and pest control. On 22 October 1948 he married Dorothy Edwards in Athabaska, Alberta, Canada; the couple had three children.

Blakey was an ambitious, self-taught businessman with a keen interest in civic activities and public service. Of his three successful businesses, Blakey's Janitorial Services, established in 1956, provided jobs for both blacks and whites and led to leadership in the South Dakota Custodians' Association, which he reorganized and improved. In 1968 he added a pest control business, and in 1975 he established Ted Blakey's Bail Bonds.

Active in public service, Blakey joined the Jaycees and became the first African American to be named to the post of international senator. He was one of two blacks elected president of state Kiwanis organizations. He earned highest rank as a thirty-third-degree PRINCE HALL Mason, and was also an active Republican, serving as delegate to three national and eleven state Republican conventions, where he was well known and widely respected. In 1963 the South Dakota governor Archie Gubbrud appointed him commissioner of the state Emancipation Proclamation Committee, dedicated to passage of a constitutional amendment to eliminate the poll tax. Blakey mobilized black leaders in the state who helped bring the issue to a successful state vote. South Dakota approved the Twenty-fourth Amendment to the constitution, which was ratified in 1964. Moving into the civil rights struggle, Blakey led statewide efforts to ease removal of local Jim Crow customs, which had since become illegal with the passage of civil rights legislation.

Blakey remained active in Yankton's Allen Chapel, the state's oldest black church, which was built in 1885 by former slaves, proudly serving a devoted congregation of African Methodist Episcopalians (AME). When the congregation dwindled and the building fell into disrepair, Blakey began a statewide effort to preserve the building and the history of African Americans in the upper Midwest. Through his efforts the building was saved and deeded to a local preservation organization. In 1981 Dorothy Blakey passed away, and ten years later he married Chessie Wheeler, who preceded him in death. In 1996 Governor William Janklow named Blakey South Dakota black historian, an honor he held until his death.

In 1997 Blakey became the second African American inducted into the South Dakota Hall of Fame, a prestigious statewide organization with a museum and organizational headquarters in Chamberlain, dedicated to honoring prominent South Dakotans. The first African American inducted was Leonard (Bud) Williams the previous year. (Williams, who retired as a lieutenant colonel after a distinguished career in World War II and Korea, also served as mayor in his hometown of Mitchell.) Also in 1997, Blakey was honored by his fellow Yanktonians in a citywide celebration as Citizen of the Year. In 1998 he was named grand master of the South Dakota IOOF, the first African American to lead a state lodge.

Blakey died at the age of seventy-nine, much beloved by his town and his many friends in the state.

Further Reading
Blakey, Theodore Robert. "Early Black Residents," and "Blakey, Ted," in *Yankton County History* (1986).
Blakey, Theodore Robert, with Mary Lovey Kinney Blakey. Interview by Sara Bernson, 1 June 1976. Transcription of tape-recorded interview #1718, 171, University of South Dakota.
Erdman, Patricia A. "Dakota Images: Theodore R. (Ted) Blakey," in *South Dakota History*, vol. 34, no. 4 (Winter 2004).

BETTI CAROL VANEPPS-TAYLOR

BLAND, James Allen (22 Oct. 1854–5 May 1911), minstrel performer and composer, was born in Flushing, Long Island, New York, the son of Allen M. Bland, an incipient lawyer, and Lidia Ann Cromwell of Brandywine, Delaware, of an emancipated family. Bland's father, whose family had been free for several generations, attended law school at Howard University in Washington, D.C., and in 1867 became the first black to be appointed an examiner in the U.S. Patent Office.

James Bland entered Howard University as a prelaw student in 1870 at the urging of his father, but the subject and the life associated with it did not appeal to him. Instead he was attracted to the minstrel show that was approaching its peak during the 1870s. He played the guitar, danced the steps, sang the minstrel songs, and, most important, composed songs for the shows. A free black man who attended college for two years, Bland had to learn from the workers at Howard University, mostly former slaves, something of the actions and the speech of plantation blacks. He was a good actor and a sweet singer and projected himself successfully into the minstrel milieu. In 1875 he left home to tour as a professional minstrel with the Black Diamond troupe of Boston; later he joined the Bohee Brothers, Sprague's Georgia Minstrels, and Haverly's Genuine Colored Minstrels.

It was with Haverly's group that Bland traveled in 1881 to London, where they played with great success at Her Majesty's Theatre. After a highly profitable year the Haverly troupe returned to the United States, but Bland and several others remained and enjoyed great success as music hall performers in England and Scotland. It was said that the Prince of Wales (Edward VII) showed special favor to Bland and once presented the actor with a gold-headed ebony cane. With these successes the performer-composer was able to indulge in lavish living (which sadly did not provide for his comforts in later life). Bland's career continued flourishing throughout the 1880s and part of the 1890s.

By 1901, however, Bland was back in the United States. He toured with W. S. Cleveland's Colossal Colored Carnival Minstrels, where he was billed as "the eccentric original James Bland." He and Tom McIntosh were called "the two greatest comedians of their race." In 1898 he appeared briefly with Black Patti's Troubadours. The minstrel show days were over, however, replaced in the public's affection by the musical comedy.

Bland made one try at writing a musical show, *The Sporting Girl*, but it was not a success. He had referred to himself as "the best Ethiopian song writer in the world," a knack that did not carry over into the new musical comedy. Many had called him "the Negro Stephen Foster," yet in the early 1900s even Foster himself was not a great success. By 1911 Bland was in Philadelphia—out of fame, out of work, and out of money. He died there of pneumonia and was buried in an unmarked grave in the Merion graveyard for blacks. Only in 1939 did James Francis Cooke, editor of the magazine *The Etude*, find his grave (with the help of Bland's sister) and arrange for a proper gravestone, which was erected in 1946. Bland never married, so far as is known.

James Bland's name has been kept alive by his music. The number of his compositions—minstrel songs, a few marching songs, a campaign song or two (for example, "The Missouri Hound Dog")—has been estimated at seven hundred, but this seems a considerable overestimate. The number of Bland's copyright deposits in the Library of Congress has been counted at only thirty-eight. (No doubt, of course, many songs and pieces were tossed off for particular occasions and did not always get published or even copyrighted.)

In 1875 Bland had written his best-known song, "Carry Me Back to Old Virginny," which as "Carry Me Back to Old Virginia" became the official state song of Virginia in 1940. Among his other best-known songs were "In the Evening by the Moonlight" (followed by "In the Morning by the Bright Light"), "Oh, Dem Golden Slippers" (which he sang with a special dance routine), "Dancing on de Kitchen Floor," "The Colored Hop," and "Dandy Black Brigade." Many of Bland's songs were sung not only by him and other members of his troupe but also by members of other troupes. His songs had a combination of sentiment and lyric appeal that exemplified the spirit of the black minstrel show, which ironically was forwarded primarily by white performers in blackface makeup.

Further Reading
Materials relating to Bland are in the Jesse E. Moorland Collection at Howard University.
Daly, John J. *A Song in His Heart* (1951).
Haywood, Charles. "James A. Bland, Prince of the Colored Songwriters." Published by the Flushing Historical Society as *A Discourse Delivered before the Flushing Historical Society* (1944).
Hughes, Langston. "James A. Bland: Minstrel Composer, 1854–1911," in *Famous Negro Music Makers* (1955).
Miller, Kelly. "The Negro 'Stephen Foster': The First Published Biography of James A. Bland," *The Etude* (July 1939).
Southern, Eileen. *The Music of Black Americans: A History* (1971; rev. eds., 1983, 1997).
WILLIAM LICHTENWANGER

BLANKS, Birleanna (18 Feb. 1889–12 Aug. 1968), vaudeville entertainer and singer, was born in Iowa but grew up in East St. Louis, Illinois. Her mother, Amanda Billups, was a Native American, and her father, Addison Blanks, was an African American.

After her studies were complete, Blanks first taught school in her hometown; however, she soon spread her wings as a professional entertainer, performing around the country and appearing in shows in Chicago and New York City. She began her career in a touring vaudeville act, dancing and singing with her sister, Arsceola Blanks, in the late 1910s. Her sister married Leonard Harper and formed Harper & Blanks, another vaudeville act; Birleanna married the baseball player Chesley Cunningham (the date of the marriage is unknown).

In 1919 Blanks made her debut in Harlem at the Lafayette Theatre, where she sang in *Over the Top*. This musical comedy was the first Billy King show in which she performed for the Harlem theater. That same year she appeared in a few more of the company's shows, including *They're Off* and *Exploits in Africa*. In 1921 she appeared in King's *New Americans: A Trip Round the World* and *Derby Day in Dixie*.

The Lafayette Theatre was a landmark in its time for being one of the first theaters to allow integrated seating. In addition it was known for its acting troupe, the Lafayette Players, which presented dramatic plays to black audiences. These dramatic plays starred black actors, an uncommon choice in casting at a time when blacks were known primarily for their singing and dancing in comedies. Anita Bush, the founder of the Lafayette Players, wanted to prove that black people were capable of acting in serious as well as in comedic roles. The Lafayette Theatre also catered to new playwrights in the 1910s and 1920s by producing new plays. One of the playwrights that benefited from this opportunity was Billy King, the playwright whose shows Birleanna Blanks performed in at the Lafayette.

In her mid-thirties, having made a name for herself with the Billy King Stock Company, Blanks went on to sing in other production companies such as the Panama Amusement Company in Chicago, Illinois, and the Harlem Producing Company. Around 1923 she became a member of the Three Dixie Songbirds, singing with AMANDA RANDOLPH and Hilda Perlina in Chicago nightclubs. She then performed with this group in the 1925–1926 run of *Lucky Sambo* with Mae Barnes. During this time Blanks recorded "Mason Dixon Blues" and other songs with Paramount, singing with the FLETCHER HENDERSON Orchestra.

For unknown reasons Blanks left the music industry to seek other job opportunities and did not perform in any shows or record any songs after 1928. As in the experiences of many actors and singers, the Depression possibly was a factor in her absence from the theater and music scene. At the age of seventy-nine Birleanna Blanks died of cancer in New York City at the Florence Nightingale Nursing Home. She was buried at the Woodlawn Cemetery in the Bronx.

Half Native American and half African American, Blanks was a singer who led the way for mixed-race women in the entertainment business. With her vaudeville acts, musical comedy roles, and Paramount recordings, she served as a model of success for women of future generations.

Further Reading
Harris, Sheldon. "Birleanna Blanks," in *Blues Who's Who: A Biographical Dictionary of Blues Singers* (1979).
Kellner, Bruce. "Birleanna Blanks," in *The Harlem Renaissance: A Historical Dictionary* (1984).
Peterson, Bernard L., Jr. *The African American Theatre Directory, 1816–1960: A Comprehensive Guide to Early Black Theatre Organizations, Companies, Theatres, and Performing Groups* (1997).
Southern, Eileen. *The Music of Black Americans: A History* (1997).
ALLISON KELLAR

BLANTON, Jimmy (18 Nov. 1918–30 July 1942), bass player, was born James Blanton in Chattanooga, Tennessee. Little is known about his parents except that his mother was a pianist and bandleader. Blanton is widely regarded as the most outstanding bass player of the late 1930s and early 1940s, almost single-handedly revolutionizing jazz bass playing both technically and conceptually. As a child Blanton studied violin, making his first public appearance at age eight. Showing exceptional talent and a serious interest in music, he learned music theory from an uncle and later switched to string bass while studying at Tennessee State College (1934–1937). Precociously gifted on this instrument, Blanton was soon playing with local bands. In 1937 he moved to St. Louis to play with the Jeter-Pillars Orchestra and FATE MARABLE's Mississippi riverboat bands.

In late 1939 Blanton was heard by DUKE ELLINGTON, who immediately asked him to join the famous Ellington orchestra. Along with the tenor saxophonist BEN WEBSTER, Blanton contributed significantly to a revitalization of the Ellington orchestra, particularly with regard to its deep, rich sound and its strong sense of swing. Blanton recorded prolifically during his relatively brief tenure with the band, including a remarkable series of six bass and piano duets with Ellington, a format unprecedented in the early 1940s and hardly ever tried again since then. Within a short time Blanton came to be regarded as the leading bass player in jazz. His influence is to a large extent attributable to the happy circumstance that his playing was superbly recorded by new microphone and recording techniques, giving the bass a distinctive prominence on recordings. During his years with Ellington, Blanton also frequently played at Minton's Playhouse in Harlem in informal jam sessions that were crucial in the development of the bop style.

In late 1941 signs of the illness—later diagnosed as tuberculosis—that caused Blanton's death began to show, forcing him to leave the Ellington orchestra and retire to a sanatorium in Los Angeles, California, where he died within a few months. He was never married.

Blanton's contribution to the development of jazz, particularly with regard to the full emancipation of the rhythm section, is immeasurable. He expanded jazz bass techniques by considerably extending the upper range of the bass; by developing greater agility in his solos and "walking" bass lines, both in his right-hand pizzicato dexterity and in his left-hand nimbleness; by approaching improvisation more as a horn (brass or saxophone) player would; and by creating more harmonically explorative and wide-ranging (not just scalar) bass lines. In these ways Blanton contributed significantly to the greater musical independence of the rhythm section, thereby freeing him to make substantial contributions melodically, harmonically, contrapuntally, and texturally.

As the first major soloist on the bass, Blanton elevated the instrument to a new and higher status. His strong, well-focused sound and his highly original walking bass lines, often exploring the uppermost range of the instrument, profoundly influenced all subsequent important jazz bass players long after his death—especially Ray Brown, George Duvivier, OSCAR PETTIFORD, Milt Hinton, Eddie Safranski, Chubby Jackson, and CHARLES MINGUS, among others.

Further Reading

Carrère, Claude. *Pitter Panther Patter: Les bassistes de Duke Ellington* (1975).
Ellington, Duke. *Music Is My Mistress* (1973).
Schuller, Gunther. *Swing Era* (1989).

GUNTHER SCHULLER

BLANTON, John W. (25 Jan. 1922–7 May 2003), mechanical engineer and rocket scientist, was born John W. Blanton in Louisville, Kentucky, the son of John O. and Carolyn Blanton.

Blanton attended Purdue University in Indiana, graduating with a bachelor's degree in Mechanical Engineering in 1943. He began his career at Bell Aircraft Corporation in Buffalo, New York, where he worked from 1943 to 1945 and from 1950 through 1956. Initially involved in the research and development of gas and rocket engines, Blanton helped develop the X-1, which on 14 October 1947 became the first aircraft to break the sound barrier in a human-operated, level flight.

Two years after marrying Corinne Jones of Mississippi in 1943, Blanton was named the chief engineer of thermo and fluid dynamics at Frederick Flader Incorporated, in Buffalo, New York, where he worked for five years. In 1956 he joined General Electric in Evendale, Ohio, and continued to make significant advances in transonic and supersonic compressor technology. Blanton's career evolved to include more management and marketing opportunities after he was named general manager of General Electric's Aircraft Engine Field Programs in 1974, and he eventually became responsible for all of General Electric's propulsion products, working mostly with jet engines. For two years, before he retired in 1982, he served as general manager of commercial advanced engines and technical programs.

Blanton is also distinguished by the significant contributions he made to his local community, where he served on several public and private boards, including the Cincinnati Zoo, the Ohio Governor's Coordinating Council on Drug Abuse, and the Community Chest. Leadership positions he held include chair of the Cincinnati-Dayton Section of the American Institute of Aeronautics and Astronautics, president of the Urban League Board of Greater Cincinnati, and vice president of the Dan Beard Council of the Boy Scouts of America. As one of the founding members of the Southwest Ohio Regional Transit Authority, and as its president from 1973 to 1979, Blanton was actively involved in preserving and maintaining the Queen City Metro System at a critical juncture in its history as it faced several financial crises. Blanton continued to receive notable recognition throughout his life by two principal institutions, Purdue University and General Electric. In 1968 his alma mater inducted Blanton into its Old Masters Program, conferred upon him the Distinguished Engineering Alumnus Award in 1973, and elected him a member of the Engineering Dean's Visiting Committee from 1976 to 1979. For his public service, General Electric presented Blanton with the Gerald L. Phillippe Award in 1981 and inducted him into its Aircraft Engine's Propulsion Hall of Fame in 1991.

Survived by his wife and one child, Dr. John W. Blanton Jr., a onetime assistant clinical professor of pediatrics at Yale University, John Blanton Sr. was buried in Cincinnati, Ohio. Blanton was an instrumental figure as both an engineer and marketing director in the early stages of jet engines and rocket science.

Further Reading
Sammons, Vivian. *Blacks in Science and Medicine* (1989).

Obituary: *Cincinnati Enquirer*, 11 May 2003.

WILLIAM A. MORGAN

BLAYTON, Jesse Bee (6 Dec. 1897–13 Sept. 1977), business leader and educator, born in rural Fallis, Oklahoma territory, to Lester Blayton, a Baptist preacher and Mattie E. Carter, a schoolteacher. Despite having only a fourth-grade education Mattie Blayton was a schoolteacher who continually underscored the importance of academic achievement. Blayton's father, the mixed-race, illiterate son of a Creek Indian, was a shaman before becoming a preacher. Blayton attended federally funded elementary and high schools for Native Americans in Meridian, Oklahoma. Later in life he reported that he had been unaware of the poverty of his childhood, though he noted that the only job he had ever hated was when his parents rented him and the family mule out by the day to work in the fields.

With his parents' encouragement Blayton attended Langston University, working menial jobs to cover his costs. His education was interrupted when he volunteered for the U.S. Army during World War I; he served in France from 1918 to 1919 and reached the rank of sergeant major. During his service he learned about the accounting field, and after graduating from Langston he attended the Walton School of Commerce in Chicago, from which he graduated in 1923. While in school he married Willa Mae Daniels on 27 December 1920; they had two children. After finishing his second degree Blayton moved to Atlanta, where he worked as an accountant and auditor for several black-owned insurance companies, including the Standard Life Insurance Company, where he worked for the prominent Atlanta entrepreneur HEMAN PERRY.

Blayton became a certified public accountant in 1928 after passing the challenging CPA examination. He was forced to do so in Illinois because the test sites in Georgia would not accommodate an African American. He was only the fourth African American in the country to earn a CPA, and the first in the Deep South. He soon opened his own accounting firm, Blayton and Company CPAs, where he was known as "Chief" by the many employees, both men and women, whom he trained to follow in his professional footsteps.

He began his career as a professor two years later when he joined the faculty of Morehouse College in Atlanta. Soon thereafter, JOHN HOPE, the president of Morehouse, led the creation of Atlanta University, the first institution in the South to provide graduate education to African Americans. Blayton joined Atlanta University as the Carnegie Professor of Business Administration, and he soon became a key figure in the cadre of Atlanta University professors who actively encouraged African Americans to enter business. The African American historian E. FRANKLIN FRAZIER severely criticized their efforts as illusory, insignificant, and counterproductive to racial progress (Frazier, 154–155). But Blayton was a firm believer in the premise that only black-owned business would create solid opportunities for well-educated black Americans, and he published articles and gave speeches on the importance of black-owned business throughout his career. Because of Blayton's influence, Atlanta University offered more accounting courses than any other black college or university, and many promising African American students were drawn to Atlanta to study with him. He provided education and training to many of the first African American CPAs across the United States, becoming known as the "Dean of Negro Accountants."

Blayton practiced what he preached: he was a successful entrepreneur. In 1925 he and fourteen friends contributed one hundred dollars each to form the Mutual Federal Savings and Loan Association of Atlanta. This association, which grew to over 10 million dollars in assets by 1959, played a major role in enabling African American Atlantans to own their own homes. With his wife, he formed the Blayton Accounting Laboratories in 1927 to provide education to bookkeepers and accountants working in small black-owned businesses.

Blayton formed a partnership known as Blamiya, Inc., with two of his closest business colleagues, Lorimer D. Milton and Clayton A. Yates. Their several ventures included purchasing Citizens Trust Company in 1933, which soon became one of the largest black-owned banks in the United States. In addition to providing loans to small black-owned businesses that often found their access to capital quite limited, Citizens Trust helped develop new neighborhoods, including Hunter Hills and Collier Heights, for Atlanta's growing black elite. When the Federal Housing Administration and Works Progress Administration built new homes for the growing black middle class in Atlanta in the early 1940s, Citizens Trust provided the loans.

In 1938 Blayton became part owner of the first black-owned night club in Atlanta, the Top Hat, which lured the top black acts of the mid-century. The club admitted only white patrons on Saturday nights but was open to African Americans the rest of the week. Blayton achieved another first in 1949 when he bought Atlanta radio station WERD, making it the first black-owned and operated radio station in the United States. His business acumen was widely recognized; in 1956 he was featured in an article on African American business in *Fortune* magazine.

Even as he expanded his business holdings and teaching, Blayton continued his own education, attending the Graduate School of Business at the University of Chicago in the summers of 1933 through 1935 and earning an LLB from the American Extension School of Law in 1936. He was also active in the civic arena: he was a trustee of the Ebenezer Baptist Church, president of the Atlanta Negro Chamber of Commerce, and chairman of the Atlanta Urban League from 1956 to 1967. In 1964 he became the first African American to serve on the Atlanta Housing Authority board.

The advent of the civil rights movement had an effect on Blayton's CPA firm, whose clients grew to include the Montgomery Improvement Association and the Southern Christian Leadership Conference. When the Alabama authorities charged MARTIN LUTHER KING JR. with felony tax evasion, Blayton unraveled the young minister's tangled finances and provided testimony that helped get him acquitted. The movement also contracted his business. Most of his firm's major clients in the 1930s through the 1960s were small black colleges, but during the Johnson Administration more federal funding was provided to these schools and, simultaneously, state funding increased as states tried to preserve the illusion of equality in order to maintain their justification for segregation. As these schools grew, white influence on their leadership increased, and many new board members insisted that the schools hire major white-owned firms to conduct their audits.

After his retirement from teaching in 1969 Blayton remained active in his business undertakings until he died of a heart attack in an Atlanta barbershop where he often socialized. Because of his prominence, several obituaries mistakenly identified him as the first black CPA in the United States. He was eulogized by BENJAMIN E. MAYS, president of Morehouse, who recognized Blayton's many firsts, and by the Reverend MARTIN LUTHER KING SR.

Further Reading

Branch, Taylor. *Parting the Waters: America in the King Years 1954–63* (1988).
Frazier, E. Franklin. *Black Bourgeoisie* (1957).
Hammond, Theresa. *A White-Collar Profession: African American Certified Public Accountants since 1921* (2002).
Hughes, Emmet John. "The Negro's New Economic Life," *Fortune* (Sept. 1956).
Seder, John, and Berkeley Burrell. *Getting It Together: Black Businessmen in America* (1971).

Obituaries: *Atlanta Journal-Constitution,* 16 Sept. 1977; *Atlanta Daily World,* 15 Sept. 1977; *Jet,* 29 Sept. 1977.

THERESA A. HAMMOND

BLEDSOE, Jules (29 Dec. 1897–14 July 1943), baritone, was born Julius Lorenzo Cobb Bledsoe in Waco, Texas, the son of Henry L. Bledsoe and Jessie Cobb, occupations unknown. Following his parents' separation in 1899, Jules lived with his maternal grandmother, a midwife and nurse, who encouraged him to appreciate music. After graduating magna cum laude in 1918 from Bishop College in Marshall, Texas, Bledsoe began graduate medical studies at Columbia University, withdrawing after the death of his mother in 1920 to dedicate himself to singing. In 1924 he presented his debut recital at Aeolian Hall in New York.

Bledsoe's first major stage role was as Tizan in the racially mixed opera *Deep River* by Frank Harling and Laurence Stalling in 1926. That same year he performed in the premiere of Louis Gruenberg's *The Creation* (conducted by Serge Koussevitzky in New York) and worked as an actor at the Provincetown Playhouse. Bledsoe is best known for creating the role of Joe in 1927 in Jerome Kern's *Show Boat,* which ran for two years at the Ziegfeld Theater. (Bledsoe later estimated that he had sung "Old Man River" twenty thousand times.) In 1929 Bledsoe recorded "Lonesome Road" and "Old Man River" to be added to the soundtrack of the 1929 silent film of *Show Boat.* On screen he was represented by the black actor and comedian STEPIN FETCHIT. In 1925 he appeared at the Gallo Theater in New York as Amonasro in the third act of Verdi's *Aida,* performing with members of the New York Philharmonic. In that year he also began a two-year tour of *Show Boat,* followed by a Carnegie Hall recital and concerts in Europe.

In 1932 Bledsoe sang in the Cleveland performance of *Tom-Tom,* an opera by SHIRLEY GRAHAM [DU BOIS], later the wife of W. E. B. DU BOIS. He then returned to the role of Amonasro in Cleveland and New York, with occasional vaudeville and radio engagements. He performed the *Aida* role in Amsterdam the next season and toured Europe in *The Emperor Jones.* Beginning in 1934, Bledsoe performed in New York, adding to his repertoire the major baritone roles of *Carmen, Faust,* and *Boris Godunov.* His recitals and radio broadcasts, however, included spirituals and even blues.

In 1935 Bledsoe participated in charity events in New York, helping to raise money for the Metropolitan Opera—though because of his race he was not even considered for employment by that company—for out-of-work actors, and for pacifist causes. He also returned to Europe to work in musicals. By 1936 he composed and performed his own song cycle, *African Suite,* with Amsterdam's Concertgebouw Orchestra, conducted by Willem Mengelberg.

Bledsoe's plans to leave his home in Roxbury, New York, to return to Europe were thwarted by the outbreak of war in 1939. He spent the remainder of his career largely in recitals to benefit patriotic or humanitarian causes, although he did appear in several films: *Safari* (1940), *Santa Fe Trail* (1940), *Western Union* (1941), and *Drums of the Congo* (1942). He died of a cerebral hemorrhage in Hollywood, where he had been promoting the sale of war bonds. His funeral was held the next week at his boyhood church, New Hope Baptist, in Waco, Texas. He never married.

Although cast in opera for several "race" roles in the United States, Bledsoe was also successful in European productions in roles that were not race-based. Reviews indicate that he was a major vocal talent with an outstanding ability to communicate. One New

York critic observed in 1926, "He has a baritone voice of truly exceptional quality. He is a singer who can pick the heart right out of your body—if you don't look out. And in the second act [of *Deep River*] he showed last night that he is a very fine actor as well." A Parisian critic, praising Bledsoe in 1931, said, "If he remained absolutely what he is, he would be unique in the history of song."

Among Bledsoe's compositions, in addition to the *African Suite*, are arrangements of spirituals for voice and piano, *Ode to America* for baritone and chorus—dedicated to Franklin Roosevelt and first performed in a 1941 broadcast hosted by Eleanor Roosevelt—and the opera *Bondage*, after Harriet Beecher Stowe's *Uncle Tom's Cabin* (never produced).

Bledsoe's career was distinguished by his opera performances, particularly in Europe. American performance opportunities sometimes allied him with figures of the Harlem Renaissance and of vaudeville. Few other black concert artists during this period were able to sustain careers, the major exceptions being ROLAND HAYES, MARIAN ANDERSON, and PAUL ROBESON (who followed Bledsoe as Joe in *Show Boat*).

In 1939 Bledsoe wrote to a former classmate, "I have to be very careful not to injure my prestige. I have had to refuse lesser offers already this year. Most people don't understand that an artist is like a piece of merchandise, which has to be maintained and kept around a certain value, or else . . . the downward grade is begun."

Further Reading
The Jules Bledsoe Papers are in the Texas Collection of Baylor University Library, Waco, Texas. The vertical file of the Schomburg Research Center at the New York Public Library contains newspaper clippings.
Geary, Lynnette G. "Jules Bledsoe: The Original 'Ol' Man River,'" *Black Perspective in Music* 17, no. 1/2 (1989): 27–54.

Obituary: *Waco Tribune*, 21 July 1943.

DOMINIQUE-RENÉ DE LERMA

BLIND BOONE (17 Mar. 1864 or 17 May 1864–4 Oct. 1927), pianist and composer, was born John William Boone in a Union army camp in Miami, Missouri, to Rachel Boone, an army cook and former slave to descendants of Daniel Boone, and to a white bugler for the Seventh Missouri State Militia, Company I, suggested by the historian Mike Shaw to have been Private William S. Belcher (Shaw, 2005). Although Boone's early biographer, Melissa Fuell, referred to Boone as having had five brothers—Ricely, Edward, Sam, Tom, and Harry (Fuell, 137)—according to Shaw it is likely that, except for a half brother, Edward (alternately referred to in census records as both Wyatt and Edward), all were step siblings via Rachel Boone's 17 May 1871 marriage to James Harrison Hendrick (a.k.a. Harrison Hendrix).

"Little Willie," as the newborn John William was called, and his mother soon moved to Warrensburg, Missouri, where at the age of six months the infant developed "brain fever," variously diagnosed in sources as encephalitis, meningitis, or *Opthalmia neonatorum* (Batterson, 23–24), a condition that required his eyes to be removed and his eyelids sewed shut. The resulting loss of sight, rather than undermining the boy's happiness and self-esteem, only fueled an upbeat sense of purpose that was to become a hallmark of Boone's adult character and onstage persona.

Little Willie's penchant for music first manifested itself in his vocal imitations of the sounds of animals and nature, his rhythmic beating on a tin pan to accompany his singing, and his early facility on the tin whistle and harmonica, both of which he played in a seven-piece street band he formed with friends by the age of five. The group's local popularity exposed Boone's talent to the same members of Warrensburg white society for whom his mother was a domestic servant, and who in 1873 contributed money to send him, as a nine-year-old, to the St. Louis School for the Blind (known in Boone's day as the Missouri Institute for the Education of the Blind).

There Boone proved an inattentive student. As punishment he was demoted to the school's trade department, where he made brooms, and soon became fascinated by a nearby piano and the students studying it. One of them, Enoch Donley, became his first piano teacher. So fast was Boone's progress under Donley that within a year he was asked to perform regularly for the school superintendent. He further expanded his repertoire during summers, playing at church services and socials.

In Boone's second year at the school, however, a policy of racial segregation was instituted by a new administration that left the boy both despondent and ostracized from the white student body that, up to then, had so readily embraced him. Stripped of his sense of belonging, the budding musician began to take frequent all-night excursions to hear ragtime in St. Louis, a behavior that led to his expulsion from the school after only two and a half years.

Too ashamed to confront his family in Warrensburg, Boone remained in St. Louis, panhandling on Franklin Avenue and Morgan Street in the heart of the city's tenderloin district. Soon, however, he was returned to his mother by his stepfather, Harrison Hendrix, and to the police after Mark Cromwell, a local gambler, attempted to offer the boy as barter in a card game.

Back in Warrensburg, Little Willie's wanderlust won out again. In exchange for travel fare he began singing and playing harmonica on trains traversing the Midwest. Between Glasgow and Mexico, Missouri, he formed a trio with fellow itinerant musicians Tom Johnson, a Sedalia banjo player, and Ben Franklin, a tea cup artist. Boone also played in the black churches of Glasgow and Fayette.

A turning point in Boone's career was his appearance on an 1879 Christmas concert at the Second Baptist Church in Columbia, Missouri, where he met John Lange Jr., a former slave who, as a building contractor and philanthropist, had amassed considerable wealth constructing roads, public schools, and churches, providing, in the process, much-needed jobs for the local African American community. So impressed was Lange with Boone's pianism that he offered to become the young musician's agent. The subsequent agreement between the parties, guaranteeing Boone's mother $10 per month until her son reached twenty-one and the pianist equal partnership thereafter, was the beginning of a long relationship between musician and manager.

Aware of his client's need for further artistic development, Lange initially kept Boone out of the limelight, arranging first for him to study with a professor (probably Anna Heuermann) at Christian College in Columbia, who introduced the boy to the music of Bach, Beethoven, and Brahms, and later with Mrs. M. R. Samson of the Iowa State Teachers' College. Boone's official coming-out party did not occur until 3 March 1880, the date of an impromptu play-off that Lange was able to orchestrate at Garth Hall in Columbia between his protégé and the celebrated Georgia pianist and former slave Thomas Wiggins, known more popularly as BLIND TOM. After the local favorite purportedly matched Wiggins note for note, it was reported that a humiliated Blind Tom "disappeared backstage. He left town the next day and never again crossed Boone's path" (*Kansas City Times*, 6 Feb. 1950).

Wiggins's influence on Boone's career, however, was profound. Boone's programs, like his predecessor's, not only featured performances of his own compositions, transcriptions of well-known operas, and mainstream classical works by Beethoven, Chopin, Liszt, Thalberg, and the New Orleans pianist LOUIS MOREAU GOTTSCHALK (the first person to compose concert music influenced by African American culture), but also several of Blind Tom's signature stunts—for example imitating various musical instruments and mechanical devices on the keyboard; rendering three songs at once, one in the right hand, another in the left, and the third vocally, each in a different key; and playing back clusters of random notes and an original piece performed moments earlier by a local pianist onstage. *Marshfield Tornado*, a musical recreation of the catastrophic storm that struck Marshfield, Missouri, on 18 April 1880, and Boone's most popular work (unfortunately never recorded or published), was, no doubt, inspired by *Battle of Manassas*, one of several Blind Tom selections in Boone's repertoire. Even "Blind John," an early stage name Boone adopted but later abandoned, was an homage to Wiggins.

However, the Boone Concert Company, officially established in 1880, also departed significantly from the Blind Tom model. Its motto, "Merit, Not Sympathy, Wins" discouraged the kind of sordid attention to the star's infirmity that had served as such an effective drawing card in Wiggins's career. An activist impulse, in fact, lay at the core of the Boone Company mission. By exposing both blacks and whites in the audience to African American–inspired music, Boone and Lange sought to break down those racial barriers that had been so zealously exploited by Blind Tom's handlers. In what Boone liked to characterize as "putting cookies on the lower shelf so that everyone can get at them" (Batterson, 55), the Missourian played camp meeting tunes, coon songs, negro spirituals, and ragtime on every program. The first instrumentalist to bring such fare into the concert hall (preceded only by the Fisk Jubilee Singers), Boone was an important link between nineteenth-century rural black folk music and the more urban jazz and popular music that would emerge in the twentieth. And by incorporating a violinist, a banjo player, and a well-trained singer (Melissa Fuell among them) into each performance, the Blind Boone Concert Company could be viewed, along with the minstrel show, as a precursor of the traveling "revues" that would become a staple of black music in the post–World War II era. Even the jewel-encrusted pocket watch, numerous gold rings, and diamond-studded cross the pianist always wore alongside a dazzling array of secret society pins (proudly displayed military-style on his vest in order to draw attention to the many fraternal organizations of which he was a member) anticipated the sartorial splendor of show business to come.

Further distinguishing Boone from Blind Tom is the greater extent to which the Missourian's own music drew upon black culture. Among Boone's seventeen published solo piano works (including four waltzes, a polka, a serenade, a spinning song, as well as four character pieces), six—his *Southern Rag Medley Nos. 1 and 2*; *Caprice de Concert: Melodies de Negres Nos. 1 and 2*; *Danse des Negres: Caprice de Concert* and *Theme and Variations on Stephen Foster's "Old Folks At Home"*—are direct outgrowths of African American music. The same is true of six of his eight published songs—"Dat Mornin' In De Sky," "Dinah's Barbecue," "When I Meet Dat Coon Tonight," "Whar Shill We Go When de Great Day Comes?," "Melons Cool and Green," and "Geo'gia Melon." And, if Edward A. Berlin's suggestion is correct that the "Alabama Bound" section of *Southern Rag Melody, No. 2* (1909) may have been the first published boogie-woogie (Berlin, 155), Boone, in turn, could be credited as the first to draw the connection, in print, between ragtime and the blues.

Following its inaugural concert in 1880 at the Columbia courthouse, the Boone Company's early tours were marred by a shortage of funds, three fires, two train wrecks, and racial segregation of the Jim Crow era. In some cities Lange had to organize two concerts, one for whites, the second for blacks. But Boone's assumption of full partnership in 1885 and his 1889 marriage to Lange's sister, Eugenia, coincided with the company's peak period. Between 1885 and 1916 Boone and Lange toured the Western and Midwestern United States, Canada, and Mexico virtually non-stop, traveling ten months out of the year, giving six concerts a week, and, between them, taking in $150 to $600 a night. The signing in 1912 of a contract with the QRS Company allowed Boone to become the first African American to make piano rolls and one of the first musicians of any color to make "hand-played" rolls, directly recorded, using the latest technology, from actual performances by the artist.

Lange's death at the age of seventy-five, which came on 23 July 1916 of a cerebral hemorrhage and shock arising from an automobile accident (Shaw, pers. comm.) was an emotional and commercial blow from which Boone never recovered. Although the pianist, as sole owner of the company, hired John and Marguerite Day and then Wayne B. Allen as managerial assistants, competition over the next decade from movies, radio, and other emerging forms of entertainment made bookings increasingly difficult to secure. By the 1920s Boone's nightly net income had plummeted to between $50 and $70. Other than a tour of the East in the 1919–1920 season, during which the pianist performed at Harvard and Yale as well as in Boston, New York, and Washington, D.C., engagements during this final period were mostly limited to smaller towns in the Midwest. Contemplating retirement and convalescing in Warrensburg from a case of "dropsy," Boone suffered a heart attack and died in the backyard of his stepbrother Sam Hendrix's home. He was buried at Columbia Cemetery in a grave that remained unmarked until 1971.

Preceded by Louis Moreau Gottschalk and later Blind Tom, Blind Boone will be remembered as the last of a trio of overlapping nineteenth-century classical pianist/composers, each a musical descendent of his immediate predecessor. All three were influenced by African American culture, and were seminal figures in the development of twentieth-century popular music in the United States.

Further Reading

Batterson, Jack A. *Blind Boone: Missouri's Ragtime Pioneer* (1998).
Berlin, Edward A. *Ragtime: A Musical and Cultural History* (1980).
Fuell, Miss Melissa. *Blind Boone: His Early Life and His Achievements* (1915).
Shaw, Mike. *Compass*, Newsletter of the Boone Society, Inc. (July 2005).

Obituary: *New York Times*, 5 Oct. 1927.

Discography

Marshfield Tornado: John Davis Plays Blind Boone (Newport Classic Ltd., NPD 85678).
Merit, Not Sympathy Wins: Blind Boone's Strains from the Flat Branch (The Blind Boone Renovation Group).

JOHN DAVIS

BLIND TOM (25 May 1849–13 June 1908), pianist and composer, was born Thomas Greene Wiggins to Domingo Wiggins and Charity Greene, field slaves on the Wiley Jones Plantation in Harris County, Georgia. In 1850 Tom, his parents, and two brothers were auctioned off to General James Neil Bethune, a prominent attorney and anti-abolitionist newspaper publisher from Columbus, Georgia. The discovery two years later of the toddler, newly renamed Thomas Greene Bethune, blind from birth, possibly mentally impaired, and unusually captivated by random sounds, playing one of the general's daughter's piano

pieces "totally 'stonished us," according to Charity (*New York Times*, 27 Nov. 1886).

The general, however, viewed Tom's unforeseen musical ability as an opportunity. Eulogized in 1895 as "almost the pioneer free trader in this country" and "the first editor in the south to openly advocate secession" (*New York Times*, 21 Jan. 1895), Bethune saw the potential for this helpless, prodigiously talented boy to become a symbol of what Bethune would argue were "sufficient reasons why we should keep our slaves as they are . . . a class of laborers . . . incapable of taking care of themselves, and controlled by individuals who are not only capable of taking care of them but interested in doing it" (*Corner Stone*, 3 Feb. 1859). Soon Tom would be even more valuable to him as a cash cow.

Ensuring Tom's musical success became Bethune's top priority. Otherwise uneducated, Tom began his piano studies under Mary, the eldest Bethune daughter. Her expertise was soon eclipsed, and more professionally recognized teachers were engaged. Tom's acute ear, phenomenal auditory memory, and natural keyboard facility allowed him to assimilate the repertoire they favored so quickly that in 1857 Bethune produced a debut for the eight-year-old at Colum-

Blind Tom, pianist, composer, and slave, had a phenomenal memory for music and began giving concerts at the age of eight. (Courtesy of John Davis.)

bus's Temperance Hall that led to numerous other concerts around the state of Georgia. But the death in May 1858 of Bethune's wife, Frances, and the increasingly active role the Georgia attorney was assuming in the emerging debate over states' rights made it impossible for the general to stay on as Tom's manager. So, in 1859, he leased Tom out for three years to the Savannah impresario Perry Oliver, whose savvy promotion of the pianist paid dividends well in excess of the fifteen thousand dollars Bethune received in return.

Trading on long-standing racial stereotypes and on the public's fascination with the freak show during this period, Oliver advertised Tom as "The Wonder Negro Child . . . whose feats at the piano baffle the most scientific and learned men in the land" (*New Orleans Times Picayune*, 5 Feb. 1861). Further fueling the carnival atmosphere was the incorporation of an onstage master of ceremonies, a by-request format, and a series of sensational pianistic and extra-musical stunts designed to shift attention away from the legitimate aspects of the boy's talent. Still guaranteed were concert performances rendered "with all the taste, expression, and feeling of the most distinguished artist" (*New Orleans Times Picayune*, 5 Feb. 1861) of compositions by Bach, Beethoven, Chopin, Gottschalk, Liszt, Mendelssohn, Meyerbeer, Rossini, Thalberg, Verdi, and even Wiggins himself, chosen by members of the audience off a list of eighty-two items drawn from the pianist's purported repertoire of seven thousand established works. But these mainstream pieces increasingly gave way to a series of sensational pianistic and extra-musical stunts. Among these stunts were Tom's flawless re-creations of original compositions played moments earlier by a local pianist onstage; performances of complicated classical works with his back to the piano; on-the-spot improvisations of an accompaniment to any piece presented, even one he had never heard before; and simultaneous renderings of three different songs, one using the right hand, another using the left, and the third sung, each in a different key. Other program innovations were Tom's recitations of texts in foreign languages he could not even speak and famous political speeches of the era in the same rhythm and pitch pattern in which they were originally uttered. A final otherworldly touch was the verbal introduction by Tom of each of his own compositions in the third person.

Significant in this era before recordings was the deal Oliver cut in 1860 with Horace Waters in New York and Oliver Ditson in Boston to publish "Oliver Galop" and "Virginia Polka," the first of nineteen solo piano pieces by Wiggins to make it into print. On the surface, most of Tom's keyboard works come off as run-of-the-mill rehashings of nineteenth-century European dance and concert music—waltzes, gallops, a mazurka, a polka, a theme and variations, and a nocturne. A deeper probing, however, reveals in them sophisticated compositional materials and evocative imagery that offer a window onto Wiggins's unique and insular world. "The Rainstorm" (composed when Wiggins was just five years old), "Cyclone Galop," "Voice of the Waves," "Water in the Moonlight," and "Daylight" all grew out of Tom's documented fascination with sounds of nature. The hypnotic ostinato of mechanical devices, yet another of Tom's obsessions, was realized musically by him in both "Sewing Song: Imitation of a Sewing Machine" and "Battle of Manassas," Wiggins's signature piece. Based on a firsthand account by one of Bethune's sons of that important Confederate victory, "Manassas" employed tone clusters and mouthed effects, materials not adopted again by composers until the twentieth century.

Leading up to the Civil War, the annual revenue from Wiggins's concerts and the sale of his sheet music reached $100,000, equivalent today to $1.5 million per year, making Blind Tom undoubtedly the nineteenth century's most highly compensated pianist. Wiggins, of course, saw almost none of this money, as it was deposited directly into the Bethune bank account. So widespread had the pianist's reputation become under Oliver that in 1860 he gave a command performance for the president at the White House, the first African American to do so.

Traveling became so difficult after the beginning of the Civil War that in 1861 Oliver and Bethune were forced to void the final year of their contract. Wiggins, however, continued to give concerts south of the Mason-Dixon Line, ironically often arranged by Bethune for the benefit of the Confederate war machine. In response to Abraham Lincoln's 1863 Emancipation Proclamation, the general persuaded Wiggins's parents to sign an indenture agreement in 1864. This arrangement bound their son to his former owner for the next five years in exchange for "a good home and subsistence and $500 a year" for the parents and "$20 per month and two percent of the net proceeds" for Tom (*Cincinnati Daily Commercial*, 20 June 1865). It was at this time that "Blind Tom," the stage name assigned to Wiggins, first appeared in broadsides and newspapers advertising his concerts.

The Confederate surrender in 1865, however, opened the door for Bethune's guardianship to be challenged. That year, in fact, a habeas corpus petition was filed against Bethune in a Cincinnati court, not by Tom's parents but by Tabbs Gross, a former slave turned show business promoter, known publicly as "the Barnum of the African Race." The six-day trial, covered nationally in the press, culminated on 26 June 1865 in a controversial verdict leaving Wiggins in the care of General Bethune.

Blind Tom's only tour of France and England, the following year, earned his handlers an additional $100,000 and written testimonials by Ignaz Moscheles and Charles Hallé, the first praise of Tom's ability from pianists of international repute. That year, too, the French physician and educator Edouard Seguin included a profile of Blind Tom's behavior in his seminal work on autism, *Idiocy and Its Treatment by the Physiological Method* (1866). Whether Wiggins had a mental disorder is a question that may never be fully answered.

Increasingly dependent on income from Tom's concerts after the war, Bethune decided in 1868 to move his immediate family and Tom to a more centrally located base of operations in Warrenton, Virginia, just forty miles southwest of Washington, D.C. The general's indenture contract with Wiggins's parents was soon to expire, but with Domingo recently dead and Charity still living in Georgia, no one was present to object when, in 1870, Bethune had a Virginia probate judge declare Tom mentally incompetent and name Bethune's son John as Wiggins's new legal guardian.

In 1875 John Bethune, acting as Wiggins's manager, moved with Tom to New York City, where in 1882 John married Eliza Stutzbach, owner of the boardinghouse he and the pianist shared in Greenwich Village. The bloom was soon off the rose, and in 1884 annulment proceedings were initiated against the bride, characterized in John's will as "a heartless adventuress who sought to absorb my estate" (*New York Times*, 23 Mar. 1884). Before any resolution could be worked out, John Bethune was accidentally killed while attempting to board a moving train in Wilmington, Delaware.

The repercussions for Wiggins were enormous. Eliza Bethune, finding that she had been frozen out of her deceased husband's will, persuaded Tom's mother to file a second habeas corpus petition in 1885 against General Bethune, with the understanding that, should Charity prevail, guardianship of Tom would be turned over to Eliza herself. Exactly that improbable scenario played out when, on 30 July 1887, Judge Hugh L. Bond, a federal judge in Baltimore, extricated Thomas Wiggins from the thirty-eight-year custody of Bethune and his immediate family.

Reports that Wiggins lapsed into a self-imposed semiretirement for the last twenty years of his life, as a silent protest against his forced separation from his former owner, appear exaggerated. Clearly, he was distraught over the new arrangement, but he continued to give concerts, albeit not at the same tireless pace as before, and to compose new pieces for publication, their copyright now assigned to Eliza Bethune. Wiggins's occasional absence from the stage, however, did spawn both rumors of his death, most notably in the 1889 flood of Johnstown, Pennsylvania, and the appearance of various Blind Tom impersonators on the nascent vaudeville circuit. Retired in 1908 and well on his way to musical obscurity, Wiggins suffered a stroke and died at age fifty-nine in Hoboken, New Jersey, where he had moved from Manhattan with Eliza in 1903. His body was taken to the Evergreens Cemetery in Brooklyn for burial in a grave that remained unmarked until 1 July 2002. Blind Tom may have been the first in a long line of black musicians, including many of the bluesmen that followed him, to have been canonized and exploited in life and marginalized and all but forgotten in death.

Further Reading
Jay, Ricky. *Learned Pigs and Fireproof Women* (1986).
Riis, Thomas L. "The Legacy of a Prodigy Lost in Mystery," *New York Times*, 5 Mar. 2000.
Southall, Geneva Handy. *Blind Tom, the Black Pianist-Composer, Continually Enslaved* (1999).

Obituary: *New York Times*, 16 June 1908.

Discography
John Davis Plays Blind Tom (Newport Classic Ltd. NPD 85660).

JOHN DAVIS

BLOCK, Samuel (17 July 1939–13 Apr. 2000) civil rights activist, was born in Cleveland, Mississippi, the son of Sam Block, a cotton compress laborer, and Alma Shacklefoot Block, a domestic worker. After graduating from high school, Block enlisted in the Air Force but was discharged for medical reasons. He attended Marlboro College in Vermont for two years, then returned to Mississippi and enrolled at Mississippi Vocational College (later Mississippi Valley State University). When he was expelled for civil rights activities, the veteran National Association for the Advancement of Colored People (NAACP) activist AMZIE MOORE encouraged Block to set up citizenship education classes around Cleveland. ROBERT MOSES, leader of Mississippi voter registration efforts, then recruited Block to work for the Student Nonviolent Coordinating Committee (SNCC).

On 17 June 1962 Block arrived alone in Greenwood, a stronghold of the segregationist White Citizens' Council. In an interview with Joe Sinsheimer in *Southern Exposure*, Block described his first efforts at community organizing:

I would go canvassing, just talking to people in the community about voter education and registration, sort of testing the pulse of the people. Hanging out in the pool halls, wherever people were, the laundromat, run around the grocery stores, meeting people.

Fifteen people showed up for his first meeting at the Elks hall. Whites soon discovered what Block was up to and pressured his hosts. The Elks withdrew the use of their hall and his landlady evicted him. For a week Block slept in an abandoned car in a junkyard. Despite these setbacks, he slowly gained support in the community. The Reverend Aaron Johnson allowed a meeting in his First Christian Church where Block led the singing of freedom songs. He told Sinsheimer that the next day people "asked me when we were going to have another meeting and sing those songs. And I began to see the music itself as an important organizing tool." After a second meeting Block led a group of twenty-one people to the courthouse. Their presence prompted Leflore County registrar Martha Lamb to summon the sheriff, who confronted Block. JAMES FORMAN recounted their exchange in *The Making of Black Revolutionaries*: "I don't want to see you in town any more. . . . Pack your clothes and get out and don't never come back," the sheriff demanded. Block boldly replied, "Sheriff, if you don't want to see me here . . . the best thing for you to do is to pack *your* clothes and leave, get out of town, 'cause I'm here to stay." That night Block noticed a gang of armed white men in the street outside the SNCC office. He and two companions escaped out of a second story window. When they returned the next morning they found the door broken and the office vandalized.

In October county commissioners stopped the distribution of federal surplus food in reprisal for black voter registration activities. SNCC organizers appealed to northern supporters, who delivered truckloads of food and clothing. Block and WAZIR PEACOCK coordinated the distribution of goods to poverty stricken families. Although the amount collected was not nearly enough to feed those in need, it was a powerful stimulus for voter registration.

Block endured constant harassment and assaults. Shortly after arriving in Greenwood he was beaten by three white men. On 20 February 1963 four buildings near the SNCC office were burned. Block told a reporter the fire was in retaliation for voter registration activities. Two days later he was arrested and charged with making a false statement—his seventh arrest in eight months. On 28 February a car without license plates fired into a carload of SNCC workers, critically wounding Jimmy Travis. On 6 March a shotgun blast struck the car in which Block, Peacock, and two young women were sitting. No one was seriously injured.

Despite this violence, voter registration activities increased. In the first three weeks of March more than 250 blacks attempted to register. In *I've Got the Light of Freedom*, Charles M. Payne attributed the growth of the Greenwood movement, in large part, to "the sheer courage and persistence of the young organizers." Sam Block, he observed, "had patiently earned the respect and admiration of a great many people."

Following Greenwood, Block continued voter registration work in Holmes and Humphreys counties. By early 1964, however, Block was showing symptoms of "battle fatigue." The historian John Dittmer wrote in *Local People*, "Eighteen months of beatings and jailings, along with disagreements with other staff members, had taken their toll." One area of conflict was the recruitment of outside volunteers for the Freedom Summer project. Block argued that the presence of inexperienced northern students would undermine the indigenous movement he had helped build. In June 1964 he was brutally beaten by a state trooper in Columbus, Mississippi, suffering permanent damage to one eye.

Block left Mississippi and settled in California where he launched business ventures to manufacture a sealant for flat tires and nutritional supplements. From 1984 to 1988 he served time in federal prison following a conviction on wire fraud charges. His marriage to Peggy Marye ended in divorce. They had one daughter. He remained active in civil rights causes in Los Angeles until his death due to complications from diabetes.

The largely unsung work of young organizers like Sam Block built the grass roots movement that toppled Jim Crow. They faced the entrenched power of segregationists and risked their lives daily to bring basic civil rights to African Americans in the Deep South.

Further Reading

Dittmer, John. *Local People: The Struggle for Civil Rights in Mississippi* (1994).

Forman, James. *The Making of Black Revolutionaries* (1972).

Payne, Charles M. *I've Got the Light of Freedom: The Organizing Tradition and the Mississippi Freedom Struggle* (1995).

Sinsheimer, Joe. "Never Turn Back: An Interview with Sam Block," *Southern Exposure* (Summer 1987) 37–50.

Obituary: *New York Times*, 22 April 2000.

PAUL T. MURRAY

BLOCKER, Sarah (27 Oct. 1857–15 Apr. 1944), educator, was born Sarah Ann Blocker in Edgefield, South Carolina, one of the five children of Sarah A. Stewart of Delaware and Isaiah Blocker of Edgefield, South Carolina. Nothing is known about her early childhood. Blocker briefly attended Atlanta University and enrolled in teacher education classes. At the age of twenty-two, Sarah Blocker moved to Live Oak, Florida, where she taught at the Florida Baptist Institute, a school established by African American Christian ministers of the First Bethlehem Baptist Association of West Florida in 1879.

Resistance and hostility toward African Americans in Live Oak resulted in escalating violence. Blocker herself was almost wounded in a shooting incident in 1892. Blocker's determination remained steadfast, however. In 1892 she cofounded the Florida Baptist Academy, an elementary and secondary educational institution for African American girls and boys. She was assisted in this project by the reverends Matthew W. Gilbert and J. T. Brown of the Bethel Institutional Baptist Church in Jacksonville, Florida, who helped her secured financial assistance from the American Home Mission Society.

The academy, which began operation in the basement of the Bethel Baptist Church, relocated to east Jacksonville's Campbell Addition, an African American community, in 1894, where the institution purchased a large three-story building in December. Blocker's fund-raising, administrative, and management skills substantially contributed to the growth and economic prosperity of the institution, including its recognition as the site where JOHN ROSAMOND JOHNSON and JAMES WELDON JOHNSON composed the song "Lift Every Voice and Sing," which was first performed by the school's students in 1902. She served as assistant to the president of the academy, as secretary to the institute, and as principal of the normal department. She also served as dean of women, and she chaired all of the institution's committees. Blocker recommended the selection of NATHAN WHITE COLLIER as Florida Baptist Academy president, a post in which he served from 1896 until 1941. Collier's leadership transformed the institution and earned him recognition as one of the most revered African American educators in the state of Florida. Blocker mobilized women in Jacksonville to endorse a fund-raising venture for the institution, eventually raising two thousand dollars.

The institution briefly adopted the name of Florida Baptist College in the early 1900s but reclaimed its original name of Florida Baptist Academy until 1918. Blocker participated in educational conferences and was an active member of the Florida Teachers Association. In 1918 the academy relocated to St. Augustine, Florida, where Blocker remained in leadership positions at the school, serving as ex officio chair of all committees, orchestrating faculty activities, and counseling the students. In 1918 the Florida Baptist Academy changed its name to the Florida Normal and Industrial Institute. In 1931 the school received accreditation as a junior college from the Southern Association of Colleges and Secondary Schools and the Florida State Department of Education. Blocker continued to train African American teachers who then taught at local schools throughout the state. Two of her best-known students include the writer ZORA NEALE HURSTON and the social worker EARTHA MARY MAGDALENE WHITE. Blocker worked for the YWCA and the War Camp Community Agency at Newport News, Virginia, during World War II, assisting in providing housing and basic services to local communities.

In April 1941 Blocker terminated her appointment with the War Camp Community Agency and returned to the Florida Normal and Industrial Institute as dean of women. Her timely return was crucial to the institution following President Collier's death several months before. The institution experienced mounting debts, which accumulated as Collier's illness prevented him from engaging in fund-raising activities. Blocker's leadership at this pivotal time was instrumental in the merger of Live Oak's Florida Baptist Institute, which changed its name to Florida Memorial College in 1918, and the Florida Baptist Academy to form the Florida Normal and Industrial Memorial Institute in 1941. The merger brought increased financial support from Baptist organizations and national recognition for the institution. Blocker became the vice president of Florida Normal and Industrial Institute. Despite her ailing health, which played a role in her release from official administrative duties in 1942, Blocker continued to provide valuable assistance to the school's newly elected president, WILLIAM HERBERT GRAY JR. Parents sought her supervision of their daughters and her intervention on financial and academic matters. Blocker's commitment and dedication to the institution were duly noted when she was honored at the fifteenth anniversary of the Florida Normal and Industrial Institute, at which she was presented with the institution's Loving Cup of Appreciation award for her help in developing the institution. She was honored again in 1943, on the occasion of the school's fifty-first anniversary.

Blocker remained very active in the Woman's American Baptist Home Mission Society, which honored her posthumously in 1957. Throughout her life she was affiliated with the First Baptist Church. Blocker was buried on the Florida Normal and Industrial Institute campus when she died in 1944. Her grave was moved to Woodlawn Cemetery in West Augustine, Florida, when the college moved to Miami in 1967. After several name changes, the institution became known as the Florida Memorial College. The only historically black college in Miami, Florida Memorial College honored Blocker with a posthumous honorary doctorate and by naming its classroom building the Sarah A. Blocker Hall. Each year the school issues one of its female students its highest honor, the Sarah Blocker Meritorious Service Award. In 2004 Sarah Blocker was inducted into the Florida Women's Hall of Fame.

Further Reading
Colburn, David R. *Racial Change and Community Crisis: St. Augustine, Florida, 1877–1980* (1985).
McKinney, George Patterson, and Richard I. McKinney. *History of the Black Baptists of Florida, 1850-1985* (1987).

ROSE C. THEVENIN

BLOCKSON, Charles L. (16 Dec. 1933–), African American history scholar, was born in Norristown, Pennsylvania, to Charles E. Blockson and Annie Parker, who preached the importance of learning African American history to him from his earliest youth. Blockson's interest in African American history was sparked when he took umbrage at the racist comments of his fourth-grade teacher. When his teacher said to him, "Negroes have no history; they are meant only to serve white people," Blockson vowed to learn as much as possible about black history and to educate both blacks and whites on the effect that people of African descent had on America (Sinnette, Coates, and Battle, 119). His family encouraged him in this pursuit, and he began collecting items connected to black history at the age of ten.

Blockson attended Pennsylvania State University, where he was recognized for his outstanding athletic performance in football and track and field. He set records for Penn State in shot put and discus, and his performance as a fullback on the football team earned him the nickname Blockbuster Blockson. He graduated from Penn State in 1956. He declined a chance to play for the New York Giants, and after briefly serving in the military, Blockson began a teaching career in Pennsylvania's Norristown Area School District, focusing on American history and multicultural and diversity education, particularly African American studies. Blockson was married to Elizabeth Parker, but the union, which produced a daughter, Noelle, ended in divorce.

Blockson went on to become recognized as one of America's foremost scholars on the Underground Railroad, which indeed had played a significant role in Blockson's family history: his great-grandfather had been liberated from slavery and guided to Canada by the Railroad. Charles L. Blockson's poem,

"The Ballad of the Underground Railroad," published in *Jump Up and Say! A Collection of Black Storytelling* in 1995, describes the various participants in and effect of the Railroad. The poem describes the diversity of the Railroad's participants and praises their courage in a metered, rhymed structure. Blockson took his interest in the Railroad to the political sphere, campaigning successfully for passage of the National Underground Railroad Network to Freedom Act in 1998. The act led to further legislation, eventually resulting in the National Park Service's increased involvement in preserving historical sites connected to the Underground Railroad.

Blockson also pioneered the study of African Americans in Pennsylvania. He wrote numerous books and essays on the subject, including *Pennsylvania's Black History* (1975), one of the first books to provide an in-depth look at the history of African Americans in a northern state. This book not only described the leading black intellectuals, artists, and activists in Pennsylvania's history but it also provided information on the major landmarks connected to the black experience, such as meeting houses for abolitionists and stops on the Underground Railroad. In 1977 he published *Black Genealogy* in collaboration with Ron Fry, in response to the widespread problems encountered by many African Americans in discovering their family history before their ancestors were transported to the United States as slaves. *Black Genealogy* discussed information sources ranging from public records connected to the slave trade to the analysis of facial characteristics to estimate the locations of one's African ancestors, all in an attempt to make genealogy accessible to the average person.

Blockson was most widely known for his work as an antiquarian of African American artifacts, and earned a reputation for being a leading force in bringing black history to a wider audience. Throughout his life he added to his eclectic collection of items connected to the African American experience. Most of the items in the collection were printed materials—books, musical compositions, newspapers, posters, prints, and photographs—but the collection also included artwork, sports memorabilia, and other rare and unique items such as busts and statues of prominent African Americans and handcrafted Bibles. Some notable pieces included first editions by W. E. B. DU BOIS and PHILLIS WHEATLEY, and letters by the Haitian revolutionaries Toussaint L'Overture and Henri Christophe.

One of the most represented subjects in the collection was PAUL ROBESON, the performer, athlete, and activist whom Blockson considered to be one of his heroes. More than three thousand items in the collection pertain to Robeson, including programs from his plays, autographed books, and voice recordings. Robeson himself was a collector of artifacts connected to black history. When Blockson met Robeson in the late 1960s Robeson inspired Blockson to follow his example and continue to safeguard African American history.

In 1984 Blockson donated his collection to Temple University in Philadelphia and became curator of the collection. At that point the collection contained more than 150,000 items, needed five large rooms to house it, and expanded outside of American history to cover black history across the world. Some items were four centuries old. Blockson declared that he sincerely hoped that making the collection accessible to the wider public would "help eliminate ignorance, because in many ways it is the worst form of slavery" (*The Temple News*, 21 Feb. 2002). He retired from his position as curator on 31 December 2006.

Blockson received numerous accolades for his work, including several honorary degrees and the Before Columbus Foundation's Lifetime Achievement Award. He served as president of the Pennsylvania Abolition Society and was a member of the American Antiquarian Society, the Historical Society of Pennsylvania, and the NAACP. Blockson also was a driving force in a project to celebrate the history of African Americans in Philadelphia during the late twentieth and early twenty-first centuries by installing historical markers honoring notable people, places, and events around the city. Some of the honorees were Underground Railroad sites and the homes of prominent abolitionists. His memoir *Damn Rare: The Memoirs of an African-American Bibliophile* was published in 1998.

Further Reading

Goss, Linda, and Clay Goss, eds. *Jump Up and Say! A Collection of Black Storytelling* (1995).
Sinnette, Elinor Des Verney, W. Paul Coates, and Thomas C. Battle, eds. *Black Bibliophiles and Collectors: Preservers of Black History* (1990).
Stewart, Jeffrey C. *Paul Robeson: Artist and Citizen* (1998).

CHRIS CHAN

BLOUNT, Mel (10 Apr. 1948–) football player, was born Melvin Carnell Blount in Vidalia, Georgia. Blount was the youngest of eleven children who grew up in rural Georgia in extreme poverty, often going barefoot and living in a home with no indoor plumbing. Blount's father, a deeply religious man, instilled values in his children through hard work and high expectations, and Blount recalled that some of the most satisfying moments of his childhood came from doing chores for his father and earning his praise. Blount learned football from his seven older brothers, who played a rough brand of football in which Blount excelled at an early age. In high school Blount proved that he was a gifted athlete on the football field and beyond. He was a multiple-sports star, running track as well as playing baseball, basketball, and football. Blount made such an impression in high school that by the time he graduated in 1966 he was offered a football scholarship to Southern University in Baton Rouge, Louisiana.

Blount had a tremendous college career playing for Southern's football team. In the late 1960s he was twice named to the Southwestern Athletic Conference's first team, and in 1968 he was named the conference's Most Valuable Player. Blount was versatile and could play both safety and cornerback so well that he was named to the Pro Scouts' All-American team to play both positions. Blount graduated with a BA in Physical Education in 1970.

It was also in 1970 that Blount got a chance to prove himself on football's biggest stage: the National Football League (NFL). Based on his solid career at Southern, Blount was drafted in the third round of the 1970 NFL draft, the fifty-third pick overall by the Pittsburgh Steelers. Throughout the 1970s and early 1980s, Blount was instrumental in turning the Steelers from a perennially losing team into play-off regulars and four-time Super Bowl champions. Blount started nine games for the Steelers in his rookie year. He realized even more playing time in his second year, and by his third year was a full-time starter at cornerback for the Steelers, adept at playing both man-to-man and zone coverages. Blount never used blazing speed to achieve NFL success, but he was able to break up passes and make interceptions through impeccable positioning and fierce intimidation. Perhaps the best bump-and-run corner of all time, he developed both a keen understanding of offensive patterns and a punishing style that forced receivers to work for every catch. Blount was known as the prototype cornerback of his era, and his strong defensive style, which he employed so skillfully to break up passes and intimidate receivers, was partly responsible for eventual NFL rule changes that prevented much of the contact between receivers and cornerbacks. These rule changes served the goal of player safety, but they were also meant to help receivers who had a difficult time getting open against physical cornerbacks such as Blount.

Blount earned a series of accolades throughout his career. In 1975, he led the league in interceptions with eleven, and he was named the National Football League's Most Valuable Player. He was named All-Pro in 1975, 1977, and 1981, and he played in five Pro Bowls in 1976, 1977, 1979, 1980, and 1982. Blount played in six American Football Conference Championship Games, winning four of them. He was also on all four Pittsburgh Steelers Super Bowl winning teams, in 1974, 1975, 1978, and 1979. His key interception in the 1974 Super Bowl helped the Steelers to their first championship. Finally, Blount had fifty-seven career interceptions, the most in Steelers history.

Blount retired from the NFL in 1983, but his career was not soon forgotten. He was enshrined in the NFL Hall of Fame in his first year of eligibility, 1989. Also in 1989 Blount was inducted into the Louisiana Sports Hall of Fame, and one year later, in 1990, he was inducted into the Georgia Sports Hall of Fame. From 1983 to 1990, the NFL employed him as the director of player relations.

Although Blount remained active in football following his retirement, he was not content to simply fade into NFL lore, and he pursued other interests and goals. Even during his glory years Blount recognized that football would only be a part of his life and that he needed to find some other outlet to be his "life's work." Blount and his brother Clinton looked to their childhood to find a way to give back, and they decided to open up two licensed youth homes. One was located in Blount's hometown of Vidalia, and the other was to be located in Taylorstown, Pennsylvania. Unfortunately, the plans for the Mel Blount Youth Home in Taylorstown met with some racist resistance because many Taylorstown residents claimed that the home would be a harm to the community. However, in 1989, at a meeting called to debate the merits of awarding Blount the permit to build his youth home, he received some support from the community and was finally able to open it. In 1993, Blount published an account of the harrowing experience in a book titled *The Cross Burns Brightly: A Hall of Famer Tackles Racism and Adversity to Help Troubled Boys*.

Following his retirement from the NFL, Blount won numerous awards for his commitment to bettering the community. In 1990 he won an NAACP Human Rights Award, a Service Award from the Boy Scouts of America, and a Peoplehood Award from the National Conference of Christians and Jews. In 1996 he won a Martin Luther King Jr. Humanitarian Award, and in 1997 he was inducted into the World Sports Humanitarian Hall of Fame. In 2002, Blount was awarded the prestigious NFL Alumni Order of the Leather Helmet and Community Service Award. The recognition by so many varied sources reaffirms Blount's commitment to community service and to giving back. Throughout his career Blount proved that with a strong work ethic anything is possible, and after his retirement, he has taught that philosophy to young people in need.

Further Reading
Blount, Roy, Jr. *About Three Bricks Shy—and the Load Filled Up: The Story of the Greatest Football Team Ever* (2004).
Chastain, Bill. *Steel Dynasty: The Team that Changed the NFL* (2005).
Mendelson, Abby. *The Pittsburgh Steelers: The Official Team History* (2006).
Sahadi, Lou. *Super Steelers: The Making of a Dynasty* (1980).
Wexell, Jim. *Tales from Behind the Steel Curtain* (2004).

DANIEL A. DALRYMPLE

BLUE, Daniel T., Jr. (18 Apr. 1949–), lawyer and the first black Speaker of the North Carolina House of Representatives, was born in Lumberton, Robeson County, North Carolina, to Daniel T. Blue Sr. and Allene Morris. Blue excelled in school and later attended North Carolina Central University in Durham, North Carolina, where he earned a BS degree in Mathematics. There he emerged not only as a leader in academics but also in campus politics. Blue furthered his career by receiving his JD degree in Law from Duke University School of Law, where again he distinguished himself and graduated in 1973. He held the certification of the National Institute for Trial Advocacy and served four times as a faculty member of that institute.

When Blue was hired by the firm of Sanford, Adams, McCullough & Beard, he became one of the first blacks to integrate a major North Carolina law firm. However, a desire to own his own practice inspired him to form a firm with several associates in 1976. He was later motivated to run for public office, and in 1980 Blue was elected to the Twenty-first Representative District (Wake County) in the North Carolina House of Representatives. He went on to be elected to ten terms and held several leadership posts in the house, including chair of the Judiciary and Appropriations Committee. From 1983 to 1985 Blue chaired the North Carolina Criminal Code Revision Study Committee. He also served as chair of the Law and Justice Committee of the National Conference of State Legislators. Among his greatest achievements was his term as chair of the Legislative Black Caucus (1984 to 1989), where he advocated for racial equality and inclusiveness for African Americans in the political process.

On 30 January 1991 Blue was elected the first African American speaker of the North Carolina House of Representatives, and he was elected to this office in January 1993. He served the state of North Carolina with distinction as speaker of the house until January 1995. In 2002 he ran unsuccessfully as a candidate for the U.S. Senate seat formerly held by the U.S. senator Jesse Helms from North Carolina. He later returned to serve as a managing partner of the firm Thigpen, Blue, Stephens & Fellers in Raleigh, North Carolina, and was a visiting instructor at the Terry Sanford Institute of Public Policy at Duke University. In November 2006 Blue was appointed by the governor of North Carolina to fill the unexpired term of Representative Bernard Allen and was able to use his votes and eventually took his seat to serve a full term in January 2007.

Blue was consistently recognized by his peers in the state and country as one of America's outstanding and politically gifted leaders. He was actively involved in the national political scene and was a member of the State Democratic Executive Committee. He served on the executive committees of the Southern Legislative Conference, the State and Local Legal Center in Washington, D.C., and as president of the National Conference of State Legislatures (NCSL). In 1984 he was a coordinator of the Mondale/Ferraro campaign in North Carolina. He was chair of the JESSE JACKSON campaign in North Carolina in 1988, and after the Democratic National Convention he served as co-chair of the Dukakis/Bentsen campaign in the state. He served twice as chair of the Clinton/Gore campaign for North Carolina.

Blue was a member of the Executive Council for the Association of Governing Boards for Colleges and Universities in Washington, D.C., the NCSL Board of Directors of the Foundation for State Legislatures, and the Democratic National Committee. Blue was also a member of the board of trustees of Duke University.

During his distinguished career Blue received numerous awards, including, in 1985, the Outstanding Legislator Award of the North Carolina Association of Trial Lawyers and the Outstanding Community Service Award of the North Carolina Association of Black Lawyers. In 1991 he received the ADAM CLAYTON POWELL Leadership Award by the Congressional Black Caucus, and in 1993 he received the Leadership Award by the National Association for Equal Opportunity in Higher Education. He also received numerous honorary doctorate degrees. Blue was recognized by many organizations, churches, and civic groups for his various contributions to the community, state, and nation.

Blue was a member of the American Bar Association, the North Carolina Association of Black Lawyers, the North Carolina Bar Association, Alpha Phi Alpha Fraternity, Inc., the Raleigh Wake Citizens Association, and the Kiwanis Club. In January 1995 North Carolina Central University received a gift from the C. D. Spangler Foundation, which fully endowed the Daniel T. Blue Jr. Chair in Political Science in Blue's honor. Blue lived in Raleigh and was married to Edna Earle Smith; the couple had three children.

Further Reading
Crow, Jeffrey J., Paul D. Escott, and Flora J. Hatley. *A History of African Americans in North Carolina* (2002).
ANDRE D. VANN

BLUFORD, Guion (Guy) Stewart, Jr. (22 Nov. 1942–), engineer, astronaut, and the first African American in space, was born Guion Stewart Bluford Jr. in Philadelphia, Pennsylvania, the eldest son of Lolita Bluford, a public school special educator, and Guion Bluford Sr., a mechanical engineer. Guion Jr. was raised in a middle class, racially mixed neighborhood in West Philadelphia. Both parents instilled strong values and a powerful work ethic in him and his two younger brothers, Eugene and Kenneth. The boys were encouraged to never allow skin color to deter them from obtaining a successful career.

Throughout his youth the introverted Bluford, though well spoken, was quiet and often struggled with schoolwork. Many teachers did not see much potential in him, and indeed one school counselor went so far as to notify his parents that their son was not college potential and advised him to choose a different avenue after his graduation from Overbrook High School. Yet behind his quiet demeanor was an active and intelligent mind. Bluford was interested in math and science, and enjoyed playing chess and building model planes. He was active in the Boy Scouts and achieved the rank of Eagle Scout, but more than anything he was interested in flight. Influenced by his father's work as an engineer Bluford was so intrigued with the process of flight that he decided to become an aerospace engineer.

Thanks to the development of the National Aeronautics and Space Administration (NASA) during Bluford's youth in the 1950s and 1960s, space exploration had become a viable career field. Upon graduation from high school in 1960 Bluford enrolled at Penn State University, majoring in aerospace engineering; he was the only African American in the engineering school. Bluford immersed himself in subjects like calculus, statistics, and physics, actively overcoming the scholastic struggles of his

Guion Steward Bluford Jr., the first African American to travel into space, speaking at the University of Cincinnati on 17 May 1984. (AP Images.)

youth. He was an active member of the Air Force ROTC program, and earned the Phi Delta Kappa leadership award in 1962. When he completed his studies at Penn State in 1964 he enlisted in the air force and was sent to Williams Air Force Base in Arizona to train as a pilot.

Bluford's entry into the air force led to two new beginnings. In addition to his training as a certified F-4C pilot he also became a husband and father. After marrying Linda Tull, whom he had met at Penn State during his senior year, Bluford's two sons, Guion III and James Trevor, were born in 1964 and 1965, respectively. Bluford was called for combat duty in Vietnam in 1967 to join the 557th Tactical Fighter Squadron stationed in Cah Ranh Bay. As a member of the 557th Bluford flew 144 combat missions from 1967 until 1972. He was awarded ten air force Air Medals, including the Vietnam Cross of Gallantry, as well as Vietnam Campaign and Service medals. When his combat duty was complete he moved on to Sheppard Air Force Base in Texas to teach aspiring pilots how to fly.

Bluford also continued his academic pursuits, enrolling in the Air Force Institute of Technology, where he earned an MS in Aerospace Engineering in 1974 and a PhD in Aerospace Engineering with a minor in Laser Physics in 1978. That same year Bluford decided to apply to the NASA program with hope of getting back in the air and possibly seeing outer space. Over 8,800 applications were submitted to NASA,

and only 35 people were chosen to become new members of the space program. The quiet boy from West Philadelphia who had grown into an established pilot and engineer was one of the 35 people chosen from the highly competitive process. His training as a mission specialist began in 1979, studying topics like advanced engineering mechanics, navigation, geology, and oceanography. In early 1982 he learned he would be part of a space mission the following year. As a mission specialist of a five-member crew, Bluford would become the first African American in space.

To Bluford, the prospect of going into space was a fulfillment of a lifelong dream and a testament to the hard work he endured from his days as a youth. He never sought the spotlight of being the "first." But as news spread Bluford became a point of interest for the entire country, especially the African American community. Nearly 250 prominent African Americans from various professions attended the launch, including Dr. DOROTHY HEIGHT (the president of the National Council of Negro Women), BILL COSBY (the actor and entertainer), WILT CHAMBERLAIN (the professional basketball star and fellow graduate of Overbrook High School), and C. ALFRED ANDERSON (the "father of black aviation" who trained the Tuskegee Airmen). Bluford's flight was also significant because it was the first space launch and landing to take place at night. The crew made successful liftoff on 30 August 1983 at 2:32 A.M. from Kennedy Space Center. Among Bluford's responsibilities on the weeklong mission were to launch a $45 million communications satellite that belonged to India and conduct experiments on the separation of body cells and fluids in space. The STS-8 *Challenger* shuttle landed successfully in California on 5 September 1983.

Bluford would go on to make three successive flights into space on 30 October 1985, 28 April 1991, and 2 December 1992. Over his four missions Bluford compiled 688 total hours in space. He subsequently retired from NASA in 1993 to become vice president and general manager of the Engineering Services Division of NYMA Inc. of Greenbelt, Maryland. Throughout the late 1990s Bluford was employed in numerous executive positions in the aerospace, engineering, and information technology fields. As of 2006 he was serving as president of the Aerospace Technology Group in Cleveland, Ohio. Bluford was recognized by many organizations for his accomplishments throughout his professional career. Among his numerous awards and recognitions were the *Ebony* Black Achievement Award and NAACP Image Award, 1983; Black Engineer of the Year, 1991; Induction into the International Space Hall of Fame, 1997; and over ten honorary doctoral degrees.

Further Reading

Gilbert, Betty Kaplan, Miriam Sawyer, and Carolina M. Fannon. *Distinguished African Americans in Aviation and Space* (2002).

Jeffrey, Laura S. *Guion Bluford: A Space Biography* (1998).

Phelps, J. Alfred. *They Had a Dream: The Story of African American Astronauts* (1994).

Schraff, Anne. *American Heroes of Exploration and Flight* (1996).

JOHN BRYAN GARTRELL

BLUNDEN, Jeraldyne (10 Dec. 1940–22 Nov. 1999), dancer and choreographer, was born Jeraldyne Kilborn in Dayton, Ohio, the daughter of Elijah Kilborn, an insurance agent, and Winifred Keith, who worked at Wright Patterson Air Force Base. Her mother played the piano, and her father had an artistic nature, which included writing poetry and soft-shoe dancing. Although Dayton was geographically divided along racial lines at the time, Jeraldyne attended Irving Public School, which was not segregated, and Roosevelt High, which was all white when she entered and fully integrated by the time she graduated. Segregation had never been the official policy of Dayton, and African Americans freely shopped in department stores, although there were no black employees except for cleaning help. Jeraldyne's grandmother was one of the first blacks to build her own home.

Beginning at the age of eight, Blunden trained in classical ballet with Josephine Schwartz, who, with her sister Hermene, was considered the premier dance teacher in Dayton. Their company, the Dayton Ballet, was one of the first regional ballet companies in the United States. A group of mothers had previously invited "Miss Jo" to teach at Linden House, a black community center, where she conducted classes three days a week, thereby breaking racial boundaries. Schwartz and her sister were to become Blunden's role models and greatest supporters. Choreography, improvisation, and modern dance were part of the training given by the Schwartz sisters, and Blunden actually started to create dances while still in elementary school. Eventually the Schwartzes helped Blunden obtain scholarships to study dance outside of Ohio. When Schwartz formed the Linden Dance Company, Blunden was one of ten girls in the group, which rehearsed in a church on Saturday mornings. The ballet company rehearsed at the same time and place.

At thirteen Blunden was a well-trained and obviously talented dancer, and she went to the Schwartz sisters' main studio, where, although she was African American, she was accepted by the other students because of her abilities. Even before *Lincoln's Portrait*, a racially integrated production of the sisters, she danced with the Dayton Ballet Company, but always as a guest and never with a partner. For several years she went to New York City to take the annual Christmas course at the School of American Ballet. At fifteen she danced and briefly toured with Karamu, a black company from Cleveland. Blunden enrolled at Connecticut College, choosing it because of its dance program, but returned home after three weeks. She attended Central State College for two years, planning to major in elementary education, but did not graduate. In 1959 she married Charles Blunden; they had two children. She spent the summers of 1958 and 1959 at the American Dance Festival in Connecticut on a scholarship. There she was exposed to the Horton, Graham, Cunningham, and Limón modern dance techniques, saw the three latter companies perform, and learned repertoire from Helen Tamiris. The first year she was the only black student; the second year there was one other. During this time she also went to New York City on weekends to study ballet with Karel Shook.

While still in college, Blunden taught dance classes at the Linden Center. In 1963 she was asked to direct the program. This formed the basis for her own school, Dayton Contemporary Dance, which she modeled on that of her mentors. She sent her young students to study on scholarship at the American Dance Festival, the ALVIN AILEY American Dance Center, and ARTHUR MITCHELL's Dance Theatre of Harlem. The small performing group, which was started as an outlet for these students, turned professional in 1968. When the company performed Blunden's ballet *Flite* at the Northeast Regional Ballet Association in 1973, the Dayton Contemporary Dance Company became the first African American troupe to gain membership in that organization.

Blunden's company performed works by the invited artists Eleo Pomare, TALLEY BEATTY, Donald McKayle, ULYSSES DOVE, and Lynn Taylor Corbett, among others, with an emphasis on preserving works that were in danger of being lost, particularly those by black choreographers. Hers was the first predominantly black company in the nation to acquire a dance by Merce Cunningham. The company performed throughout the United States, receiving recognition for its vitality and varied repertoire.

Blunden, who gave up performing to devote herself to teaching, felt that ballet was the basis for all dance. When she taught, however, it was a modern class based on the Horton technique, borrowing from Graham, Limón, and others.

Blunden died in Dayton. She was honored with a MacArthur Foundation grant (1994), the *Dance Magazine* Award (1998), a Lifetime Achievement Award from the National Black Arts Festival (1998), and a Dance USA Honors Award (1999). These accolades were for her energy, her warm humor, and her fierce determination to showcase the contributions of black choreographers and performers to American modern dance. Jennifer Dunning noted that Blunden had mixed feelings about that role, quoting Blunden: "What I do is from a black perspective. But people who are sure of themselves don't bother with that." Before her death Blunden arranged for her daughter, Debbie Blunden-Diggs, and Kevin Ward to take over as codirectors of the Dayton Contemporary Dance Company.

Further Reading

Blunden, Jeraldyne. "Board Spotlight," *Dance/USA Journal* 2, no. 1 (Summer 1994).

Blunden, Jeraldyne. "Remembering the Membership Evaluation," *Dance Magazine* (Oct. 1944).

Hering, Doris. "The Future of Dance Is in Dayton?" *Dance Magazine* (Dec. 1993).

Obituary: *New York Times*, 24 Nov. 1999.

DAWN LILLE

BLYDEN, Edward Wilmot (3 Aug. 1832–12 Feb. 1912), educator, diplomat, and advocate of Pan-Africanism, was born on the island of St. Thomas, part of the present-day Virgin Islands, the son of Romeo Blyden, a tailor, and Judith (maiden name unknown), a schoolteacher. The family lived in a predominantly Jewish, English-speaking community in the capital, Charlotte Amalie. Blyden went to the local primary school but also received private tutoring from his father. In 1842 the Blydens left St. Thomas for Porto Bello, Venezuela, where Blyden showed his facility for learning foreign languages. By 1844 the family had returned home to St. Thomas. Blyden attended school only in the morning, and in the afternoons he served a five-year apprenticeship as a tailor. In 1845 the Blyden family met the Reverend John P. Knox, a famous white American minister who had assumed pastorship of the Dutch Reformed Church in St. Thomas, where the Blydens were members. Knox quickly became Blyden's mentor and encouraged his academic studies and oratorical skills. Because of Knox's influence, Blyden decided to become a clergyman, an aspiration his parents supported.

In May 1850 Blyden accompanied Mrs. John Knox to the United States and attempted to enroll in Rutgers Theological College, which was Reverend Knox's alma mater, but was refused admission because he was black. Blyden's attempts to gain admission to other theological colleges also failed. During this time he met important white Presbyterian clergymen, such as John B. Pinney, Walter Lowrie, and William Coppinger, who became his lifelong supporters. All three men were involved with the American Colonization Society. They convinced Blyden to go to Liberia, which had become an independent nation in 1847.

Blyden left the United States for Liberia on 21 December 1850 and arrived at Monrovia on 26 January 1851. Initially, he worked as a part-time clerk for a merchant and resumed his studies at Alexander High School, a new Presbyterian institution headed by the Reverend D. A. Wilson, a graduate of Princeton Theological Seminary. Blyden's intellectual abilities impressed Wilson, who then persuaded Knox to support Blyden as a full-time student. By 1853 Blyden was a lay preacher, and by 1854 he was a tutor at his high school and acted as principal during Wilson's frequent absences due to illness. Blyden published one of the first of his many provocative pamphlets on African affairs, *A Voice from Bleeding Africa*, in 1856, the year he married Sarah Yates, the mixed-race niece of B. P. Yates, the vice president of Liberia. Their marriage was an unhappy one, though they had two children. Blyden blamed his marital troubles on his wife's loyalty to what he termed the "mulatto clique"

Edward Wilmot Blyden, Liberian intellectual, nationalist, and advocate of Pan-Africanism, who tried to convince blacks throughout the diaspora to repatriate, c. 1855. (Library of Congress, American Colonization Society Records, 1972–1964.)

that dominated Liberian politics. However, other important reasons for the marriage's collapse were financial problems due to Blyden's insufficient income and his wife's lack of interest in her husband's intellectual pursuits. In 1858 he was ordained a Presbyterian minister, succeeding Wilson as principal of Alexander High School.

Throughout the 1860s and 1870s Blyden became intensely involved in the educational and political affairs of Liberia. In 1861 he was appointed Liberian educational commissioner and traveled to the United States and Britain on a lecture and fund-raising tour. He encouraged African Americans to immigrate to Liberia, "back home to the Fatherland," where he contended they could live free from slavery and racial inequality. From 1860 to 1871 he taught classics at Liberia College; he was also the Liberian secretary of state (1864–1866). In 1871 Blyden was forced to leave Liberia temporarily for Sierra Leone after a coup d'état against the EDWARD ROYE administration (1870–1871) endangered his life. He returned to Liberia in 1872 to become principal of Alexander High School again, a post he held until 1878. As the Liberian ambassador to the Court of St. James's in Britain from 1877 to 1879, Blyden unsuccessfully tried to win financial support for Liberia from Britain. He then served as president of Liberia College (1880–1884) and was minister of the interior

(1880–1882). In 1885 he ran unsuccessfully for president of Liberia, though he had left the country to live in Sierra Leone.

From the late 1880s to the early 1900s Blyden wrote his most important work on Pan-Africanism, *Christianity, Islam, and the Negro Race* (1887), and maintained his diplomatic and educational commitments. The Liberian government again appointed him ambassador to the Court of St. James's in 1892, and he served as a special envoy to London and Paris in 1905. From 1901 to 1906 he was director of Mohammedan education in Sierra Leone. Poor and frail, he underwent an operation for an aneurysm in the knee at the Royal Southern Hospital in Liverpool, England, in 1909. His friends in the Colonial Office in London helped secure a small pension for him in 1910. He died in Sierra Leone two years later. His funeral service represented the unity he tried to forge among Africans during his lifetime: it was a Christian service in which Muslim men bore his coffin from his residence. His long career as an educator, diplomat, and proponent of Pan-Africanism attracted scholarly attention from African, Caribbean, and African American historians, biographers, and political scientists.

Further Reading

Cole, Julius Ojo. *Edward Wilmot Blyden: An Interpretation* (1935).
Esedebe, P. *Pan Africanism: The Idea and the Movement, 1776–1963* (1982).
Lynch, Hollis. *Edward Wilmot Blyden: Pan-Negro Patriot* (1967).
Moses, Wilson. *The Golden Age of Black Nationalism, 1850–1925* (1978).

KIMBERLY WELCH

BLYTHE, Arthur (7 May 1940–), composer, alto saxophonist, bandleader, and teacher, was born Arthur Murray Blythe in Los Angeles, California, the son of Charles Blythe, an auto mechanic, and Nancy Blythe. Blythe's first musical inspiration was the rhythm and blues music he heard on local jukeboxes. His mother's passion for the music of JOHNNY HODGES, EARL BOSTIC, and Tab Smith led her to purchase an alto saxophone for Blythe, despite his desire to play trombone. Upon receiving his first saxophone at the age of nine, Blythe began to play in school bands, and at the age of thirteen he was performing in a local blues band. Blythe's early experience with rhythm and blues had a strong influence on his powerful, penetrating alto sound and on his composition's tendencies to utilize ostinatos and dance rhythms. As a teenager, Blythe studied alto saxophone with Daniel Jackson, a former RAY CHARLES sideman, and Kirtland Bradford, a former lead alto saxophonist with JIMMIE LUNCEFORD's orchestra. At the age of sixteen, Blythe was exposed to the music of THELONIOUS MONK, an experience that inaugurated his career in jazz.

After attending high school in San Diego and splitting time between family there and in Los Angeles, Blythe returned full time to Los Angeles in 1960.

There he met the like-minded pianist HORACE TAPSCOTT, and the two of them formed a working musical partnership that would last a decade and a half. In 1961, Blythe and Tapscott founded the Underground Musicians Association (UMGA, also known as the UGMAA—the Union of God's Musicians and Artists Ascension), an organization dedicated to furthering the aesthetic and economic aims of creative musicians and to keeping alive the history and performance of music within the black community. Part of a nationwide trend toward greater artistic independence for African American artists and the forging of closer ties between art and the social and political goals of African American communities, the UMGA was the West Coast version of organizations like New York's Black Arts Movement, Chicago's Association for the Advancement of Creative Musicians (AACM), and St. Louis's Black Artist's Group (BAG). In his work with Horace Tapscott and the UMGA, and in his teaching of jazz workshops at the Malcolm X Center (1961–1963), Blythe was at the center of the progressive wing of the Los Angeles jazz community in the sixties and early seventies.

In 1969 Blythe made his recording debut on a Horace Tapscott album titled *The Giant is Awakened*. The album was well received, but it failed to gain wide notice and did little to further Blythe's career. Tiring of the Los Angeles music world and its limited opportunities for his style of performance, Blythe moved to New York in 1974 and soon became a central figure in the vibrant downtown loft scene that served as a hothouse for the jazz avant-garde of the period. His playing attracted much attention, and he quickly found himself playing in Chico Hamilton's band (1974–1977), and recording with Gil Evans, Hamilton, and JULIUS HEMPHILL. In 1977 Blythe made his first recordings as a bandleader, taking a six-piece ensemble (including tuba and cello) into the studio to record *The Grip* and *Metamorphosis* for India Navigation, a small independent label known for promoting adventurous jazz. Blythe soon attracted the attention of the major labels, and in 1979, he signed with Columbia Records.

The first album that Blythe recorded for Columbia, *In the Tradition* (1978), received widespread critical acclaim and marked Blythe as a major figure in the jazz scene. Recorded at a time when the aggressively avant-garde jazz of the 1970s seemed to be running out of steam, *In the Tradition* signaled a new willingness in the jazz community to turn to the music's less recent past for inspiration. It included performances of compositions by DUKE ELLINGTON, FATS WALLER, and JOHN COLTRANE as well as originals by Blythe. The album and the live performances of the band, which came to be known as In the Tradition, were instrumental in inaugurating a movement in jazz that placed emphasis on the music's roots and historical continuity. This movement had its conservative revivalist elements, exemplified by the music and attitudes of WYNTON MARSALIS, but Blythe was always more eclectic and more open-minded in his utilization of the jazz tradition than Marsalis and the other younger figures whose popularity and acclaim overshadowed Blythe's in the second half of the 1980s.

Throughout the 1980s, Blythe played and recorded both with In the Tradition and in a decidedly less traditional quintet made up of tuba, cello, electric guitar, drums, and his own alto. This ability to create innovative and vibrantly moving music in a wide variety of contexts was a hallmark of Blythe's career and of his approach to jazz. Blythe ended his association with Columbia in 1988. His departure led to his commercial decline, but not to a slackening of his seemingly ceaseless creativity. During the 1990s and into the first decade of the twenty-first century, Blythe continued to lead his own ensembles and to work in a variety of contexts, fostering musical interchanges with virtually all of the significant jazz artists of the period; he made recordings with David Murray, the World Saxophone Quartet, Jack DeJohnette, LESTER BOWIE, Chico Freeman, James Newton, Joey Baron and BILLY HART.

Blythe is an important figure in the history of jazz. Ranking with CHARLIE PARKER, Johnny Hodges, and CANNONBALL ADDERLEY as one of the tradition's major alto saxophone stylists, Blythe's work as a composer and bandleader is no less important. His constant exploration of the possibilities of group counterpoint and nontraditional instrumentation has expanded the vocabulary of jazz. An eloquent synthesis of innovation and tradition, Blythe's body of recordings is remarkable for its diversity, exuberant emotional intelligence, and consistently high level of musicianship. Perhaps the most eloquent testimony to Blythe's significance is the lengthy poem that AMIRI BARAKA dedicated to him in 1980: "In the Tradition: For Black Arthur Blythe."

Further Reading
Baraka, Amiri, "In the Tradition: For Black Arthur Blythe," in *Transbluency: The Selected Poems of Amiri Baraka/LeRoi Jones (1961–1995)* (1995).
Francis Davis. "Apples, Oranges, and Arthur Blythe," in *In the Moment: Jazz in the 1980s* (1996).
Kernfeld, Barry, ed. "Blythe, Arthur," in *The New Grove Dictionary of Jazz* (2002).
Levenson, Jeff. "Arthur Blythe's Creative Challenge," *Downbeat* (October 1987).

Discography
In the Tradition (Columbia, 1978).
Lenox Avenue Breakdown (Columbia, 1979).
Retroflection (Enja, 1994).

BRUCE BARNHART

BLYTHE, Jimmy (20 May 1901–21 June 1931), jazz pianist, composer, and bandleader, was born James Louis Blythe in Keene, Kentucky, about twelve miles southwest of Lexington, the youngest of five children of Richard Blythe and Rena (or Arena) (Stovall) Blythe. When Jimmy was around ten, the family moved to Lexington, where his father worked at different times as a laborer, houseman, and janitor.

Jimmy left home about 1918 and moved to Chicago's South Side, staying at first with his older sister Effie. The South Side—the cultural heart of Chicago's black community—was to remain Blythe's base for the rest of his life. Soon after the move Blythe went to study with Clarence M. Jones, a classically trained black pianist who had set up a music studio in the South Side. The musically versatile Jones, who was a skilled jazz, blues, classical performer, as well as a successful composer, seems to have been a strong influence on Blythe. Other than his study with Jones, nothing is known of Blythe's musical activities before 1922.

Blythe's reputation rests almost entirely on his recordings. His career is unique for an African American musician of the era, with roughly 500 recordings squeezed into a ten-year period (even more celebrated performers like DUKE ELLINGTON and LOUIS ARMSTRONG were not so intensively recorded at this time). Beginning in 1922 with piano-roll recordings for the Columbia Music Roll Company of Chicago, Blythe recorded extensively for this medium. Although the total number of rolls recorded will never be known (as roll recordings were not always attributed), they probably reached 300. He recorded both for the home market and also for coin-operated "nickelodeons" that were popular in bars and similar public establishments. Piano rolls are often denigrated by critics and historians for their seemingly mechanical quality (the particular system that Blythe recorded on removed dynamics, pedaling, and nuances of rhythm from his performances). Despite this, many of Blythe's rolls transcend their limitations and at their best are as exciting as any recorded jazz of the 1920s. An example is the 1923 roll of "Barney Google" (Columbia 607), a light popular song of the day. After playing through the song once he unexpectedly inserted a hot blues chorus, which, though entirely unrelated to the earlier material, enormously builds up tension.

In April 1924 Blythe began making phonograph records, initially for the Paramount label. Paramount had recently entered the booming race record market (records marketed to blacks) and actively acquired a stable of jazz and blues performers. Blythe operated as a house pianist for the company, recording a total of 105 sides. At first he mainly worked as an accompanist for female vaudeville blues singers in the Paramount roster, such as GERTRUDE "MA" RAINEY, Priscilla Stewart, and Sodarisa Miller. Around November 1924 he also began to record small-band jazz with a series of trio performances featuring the clarinetist Jimmy O'Bryant. As his reputation as a jazz performer spread Blythe began recording for some of the other leading companies of the era: Vocalion beginning in 1926, and Okeh and Gennett in 1927. With his group the State Street Ramblers, which included some of the leading jazz instrumentalists of the period, he recorded on Gennett between 1927 and 1931 what are probably his most famous issues. There are, however, dozens of other recordings, less well known but just as rewarding. An example is "Bow to Your Papa" (Champion 16451), a piano duet played with his nephew Charlie

Clark (the same performers also recorded the work on piano roll under the title "Regal Stomp," Capitol A-roll 2360). Made in Blythe's last recording session less than two months before his death, "Bow to Your Papa" is an idiosyncratic yet remarkably integrated performance for an unusual medium.

Blythe performed actively in the 1920s, though this part of his career is poorly documented. Some have reported him playing at Mamie Ponce's, a tavern a few doors south of the better-known Dreamland Café, and he probably represented a number of successful jazz pianists playing regularly in entertainment venues on Chicago's South Side. An important associate seems to have been the singer Alex (also known as Bob) Robinson, the husband of Paramount employee Aletha Dickerson, with whom Blythe recorded and composed. A 1926 article in the *Chicago Defender* newspaper mentioned the duo giving twice-weekly radio broadcasts on Chicago's KYW station.

Blythe, a fluent and able composer, created dozens of songs and instrumental numbers for recording and performing. His most enduring song was probably "Mecca Flat Blues," co-composed with Robinson, which was recorded by the boogie-woogie pianist AL-BERT AMMONS in the 1930s and which appeared in the *Paramount Book of the Blues* in 1927. Blythe's only other works published in his lifetime appeared through the agency of Axel Christensen, a Chicago-based white piano pedagogue with whom he owned a chain of piano-teaching schools. Christensen published Blythe's boogie-woogie composition "Chicago Stomps" in 1927 under the name "Walking Blues," and included it in his jazz teaching method (in the 1930s, when boogie-woogie caught on, he changed the title to "Boogie Woogie Blues"). Christensen also published a series of five piano *Syncophonics* claiming himself as the composer; the evidence, however, indicates that at least two of the set (numbers four and five) were Blythe material. An earlier Christensen publication, "Pomeranian Blues" (1924), was probably also by Blythe.

Little personal information is available about Blythe. His friend Lathair Stevens, who was to be one of his pallbearers, apparently remembered him as slight and stout, a description borne out by Blythe's only known photograph, which first appeared in an advertisement in a 1926 *Defender*. Blythe was married by 1924 but nothing is known of his wife Janice, and they had no children.

Blythe's sudden death from meningitis cut short the career of an important popular composer and musician: he had just turned thirty. Yet his achievement within his short career was remarkable. Not only was he the most prolific African American recording artist of the 1920s but he was also one of the most creative. His style is a highly individual blend of the most important genres of the day: jazz, blues, and novelty piano, often underpinned by a strong barrelhouse feel. Always superbly crafted, his compositions anticipated the stride piano style of EARL HINES and FATS WALLER that would become standard in the 1930s. His "Chicago Stomps," recorded for Paramount in 1924 and on piano roll (and published by Christensen), is the earliest known boogie-woogie composition (that is, using left-hand riffs throughout the entire piece), and the intermittent use of left-handed boogie-woogie riffs is a recurring feature of his style. Perhaps his greatest gift was his ability as an accompanist and bandleader to put his fellow musicians at ease, allowing them to play at their most relaxed and creative. For this reason Blythe was responsible for some of the most exhilarating jazz recordings of the 1920s. Despite his enormous talent Blythe has been little recognized or appreciated by jazz historians. A modest man, he did little in the way of self-promotion. The drummer BABY DODDS described him as "a very quiet fellow, not the boisterous type at all." He was a consummate studio musician deserving a central place in the canon of jazz history.

Further Reading
Dodds, Baby. *The Baby Dodds Story as Told to Larry Gara* (rev. ed., 1992).
Montgomery, Michael. Liner notes for *Jimmy Blythe in Chronological Order, 1924–1931* (1994).
Silvester, Peter. *A Left Hand Like God: The Story of Boogie-Woogie* (1988).

PETER MUIR

BO DIDDLEY. *See* Diddley, Bo.

BOEN, William (c. 1735–12 June 1824), a Quaker, was born a slave near Rancocas, New Jersey, and was sometimes known as William Bowen or "Heston." His owner treated him well, and Boen was allowed to learn to read and write. As a boy, Boen was afraid of dying during an Indian attack because of all of the stories circulating among the neighbors about others that were killed by Indians. Whenever he worked in the woods alone, he was on constant guard for Indian arrows. He felt he was not yet ready to die until he accepted what was within him that made him do good and reject evil, as the Quakers he was growing up around had done. The Society of Friends is a Christian sect founded by George Fox in 1660 that rejects formal sacraments, a formal creed, priesthood, and violence. They are also known as Quakers and are recognized by their plain speech, dress, pacifism, opposition to slavery, and philanthropy. Boen decided to follow this path of good, honest, and just living. From that time onward he felt he had two masters, one, God, and the other, the man who owned him. This realization affected every aspect of his life from that point onward, including his everyday work.

One day while out chopping down trees as requested by his master, he felt God telling him not to chop down a particular tree. He decided not to chop it down, leaving the one tree standing and chopping down the rest as requested. His master never asked why he did this; he just chopped that one tree down himself. Boen took this as a sign that God would take care of him if he followed God's path and devoted himself to a life of good.

ANECDOTES AND MEMOIRS

OF

WILLIAM BOEN,

A COLOURED MAN,

WHO LIVED AND DIED NEAR MOUNT HOLLY, NEW JERSEY.

TO WHICH IS ADDED,

The Testimony of Friends of Mount Holly
monthly meeting concerning him.

Philadelphia:
PRINTED BY JOHN RICHARDS,
No. 129 North Third Street.
1834.

William Boen memorial produced by the Mount
Holly Society of Friends, among whom he lived until
his death in 1824. (University of North Carolina.)

While still a young man, he made the acquaintance
of John Woolman, who was a Quaker and member of
the Society of Friends. Boen became interested in the
Friends and began attending their meetings and
studying their demeanor. Before long, he was a
Quaker in most respects—except he was still not an
official member of the Society of Friends.

Offered his freedom at the age of twenty-eight by
his master, Boen accepted and became a freeman by
the age of thirty. It was felt that his master's decision
was influenced by John Woolman, who spoke out
against slavery and encouraged all Quakers to free
their slaves. He and many other Quakers felt that
slavery and slave owning went against the very heart
of the Quaker way of life and beliefs. Two years later
Boen married Dinah (Dido), a servant in the house
of Joseph Burr. They were married in a Society of
Friends ceremony on 3 May 1763 arranged by John
Woolman at Burr's house, even though neither was
officially a member of the Society of Friends. The

marriage certificate was signed by both Quaker and
African American witnesses. Shortly after their wedding, Boen applied for membership in the Society of
Friends but was denied because of his race. He was
encouraged to stay true to his faith and was invited to
continue attending meetings. He continued his studies and also preached to other African Americans.

Boen worked hard enough to acquire a home and
property where his family lived comfortably in or
around Mount Holly. Dinah is reported to have died in
1811 while they were living in Philadelphia, Pennsylvania. No mention is made of when or why they moved
to that particular city. After Dinah's death, Boen returned to the area where he grew up. In 1814 he finally
was made a member of the Society of Friends. He was
seen as a pious, hardworking, honest, and pleasant
man. He exhibited these and other Quaker qualities
through his words and actions. Throughout his life he
refused to wear any clothes or use any articles that
were produced through slave labor. He was particular
about not using plural language instead of *thou* and
thee in the name of social equality, as was the custom of
Quakers of that time. As a Quaker, he was opposed to
war and greed and spoke against both.

As he grew older, his hair and long beard became
white. He did not wear dyed clothing bleached of natural color, which contrasted with his dark skin. He
lived his adult life relatively free of sickness. At the age
of eighty-six, he was still able to recount his life in detail. His health began to fail at the age of eighty-seven,
but his mental faculties stayed sharp until his death.
He died quietly at the age of ninety on 12 June 1824.
His death was marked by a memorial meeting given
by the Mount Holly monthly meeting of Friends, and
the memorial speech was read at the Yearly Meeting
of Friends in Philadelphia in 1829.

Further Reading

Boen, William. *Anecdotes and Memoirs of William Boen, a
Colored Man, Who Lived and Died Near Mount Holly,
New Jersey. To Which Is Added, the Testimony of Friends of
Mount Holly Monthly Meeting Concerning Him* (1834).
Cadbury, Henry. "Negro Membership in the Society of
Friends (1)," *Journal of Negro History* (1936).
Child, Lydia Maria. *The Freedman's Book* (1866).
Griscom, Lloyd E. "The Historic County of Burling-
ton" (1973 [cited 2 Apr. 2007]).
Ives, Kenneth. *Black Quakers: Brief Biographies* (1991).
Woolman, John. *The Journals of John Woolman* (1922).

DARSHELL SILVA

BOGAN, Lucille (Bessie Jackson) (1 Apr.
1897–10 Aug. 1948), blues singer, was born Lucille
Anderson in Amory, Mississippi. Although little is
known of her early life, she was raised in Birmingham,
Alabama, where her family moved early on in search
of work in the numerous steel and coal mills. She was
married to Nazareth Lee Bogan Sr., a locomotive fireman, in about 1914 and had a son, Nazareth Lee Bogan Jr., in 1916 and a stepdaughter, Ira Betty Bogan,
in 1911. In addition, she was the aunt of trumpeter
and pianist Thomas "Big Music" Anderson.

Bogan began her recording career in 1923 with a session for Okeh Records in New York City. Pianist Henry Callens accompanied her. The tracks she recorded were more vaudeville oriented than they were blues, and they reflect the major influence of BESSIE SMITH, IDA COX, and other vaudeville artists. Bogan's style is distinct, however. Like the other classic blues vocalists, her vocal approach and lyrical subject matter reflect her own unique positioning in larger social and political currents. She addresses and responds to current events, economic realities, and romantic and sexual relationships in ways that reflect her standpoint as a black woman. Unlike Cox, whose early musical training was in an African Methodist choir, or even Smith, who toured on the Theater Owners' Booking Association vaudeville circuit early in her career, Bogan apparently had strong ties to Alabama's black criminal underworld, and trained in brothels, barrelhouses, and juke joints. The sexually candid and earthy style she honed in these contexts becomes particularly apparent with the Brunswick recordings of the 1930s (around the time she adopted the name Bessie Jackson).

Shortly after her 1923 session in New York, Bogan again recorded for Okeh, this time in Atlanta. Eddie Heywood Sr. accompanied her on more vaudeville-inspired blues sides. While these did not sell well, they are notable as the first "territory" recordings (i.e., recorded outside of New York or Chicago) made by an African American blues artist. In 1927, she ventured to record again in Chicago for the Paramount label. Will Ezell accompanied her on most of these sides, except for "Sweet Petunia," which featured Alex Channey on piano. This song, in which the female protagonist expresses her love for a "big fat man" nicknamed Tunie, was a modest hit. In 1928 and 1930, Bogan returned to Chicago to record for Brunswick. These sides featured TAMPA RED and COW COW DAVENPORT in supporting roles. Several of the sides she recorded on these sessions were reissued as inexpensive singles by the American Record Corporation (later subsumed by Columbia) during the Depression. Bogan first adopted the name Bessie Jackson on these 1932 reissues. They became popular, and several were remade by other artists. LEROY CARR, Bumble Bee Slim, SONNY BOY WILLIAMSON, and others recorded "Sloppy Drunk Blues." Georgia White took up "Alley Boogie," and Tampa Red and B. B. KING redid "Black Angel Blues."

The success of her "Bessie Jackson" reissues was an important juncture in Bogan's professional life. Her ARC reissues released under the name Bessie Jackson sold better than any of her previous recordings. This may have been the result of their affordability and the sexually themed material. Because of the success, Bogan continued to record under that name, and she continued to explore explicit sexuality in her lyrics. She recorded exclusively as Bessie Jackson between 1933 and 1935. Her approach was fresh, frank, and intelligent, and her thinly veiled euphemisms and double entendres were original. As a result, her lyrics are shocking, even by contemporary standards, but

they also document a range of issues that affected black women's lives. Finally, Walter Roland joined her on piano. While Roland was not as technically skilled as some of her past accompanists were, Roland's rolling barrelhouse and boogie-woogie–inflected style was the perfect accompaniment to Bogan's blossoming southern, down-home style.

The success of their partnership resulted in several recording sessions and well-known sides. They collaborated in July 1933, July and August 1934, and March 1935 (blues singer and guitarist JOSH WHITE is also featured on this session). "Groceries on the Shelf," "Down in Boogie Alley," "B.D. Woman's Blues," and "Shave 'Em Dry" (infamous for its unambiguous lyrics: "I got nipples on my titties / big as the end of my thumb. / I got somethin' 'tween my legs / would make a dead man come") are some of the tracks they produced together.

"Groceries on the Shelf," recorded in 1933 is a good example of the ways in which Bogan's songs could provide commentary on multiple levels. On one level, food euphemisms abound as stand-ins for sex and sexual activity. Piggly Wiggly, the first self-service grocery store, was founded in 1916 and quickly grew in popularity with chains opening across the South throughout the 1920s. Here, Bogan uses the store (and its business model) as a metaphor for sexual transactions:

> My name is Piggly Wiggly, and I swear you can help yourself,
> My name is Piggly Wiggly and I swear you can help yourself,
> And you've got to have your greenback, and it don't take nothin' else.

The metaphor is artfully extended throughout the song in a way that makes clear the protagonist's terms but that also expresses ambivalence over the rapid takeover of the stores and the threat they posed to smaller local stores:

> You can go to your five, you can go to your ten-cent store,
> You can go to your five, you can go to your ten-cent store,
> But if you come to my Piggly Wiggly, you won't go back there no more.

Bogan stopped recording in 1935 and moved back to Birmingham. While there, she managed the group in which her son played bass, Bogan's Birmingham Busters. She and her husband divorced in 1941, and she moved to Los Angeles shortly thereafter and remained active as a songwriter until her death in 1948 of coronary sclerosis. She is buried at the Lincoln Memorial Park Cemetery in Los Angeles.

While not as well known as Bessie Smith or Ida Cox, Bogan ranks with these artists as a major performer and songwriter in the classic blues style of the 1920s and 1930s. As her recording career extended from 1923 to 1935, she was one of the last of the great vaudeville-inspired, big-voiced blues vocalists to be recorded.

Further Reading

Bourgeois, Ann Stong. *Blueswomen: Profiles and Lyrics, 1920–1945* (1996).

Harris, Sheldon. *The Blues Who's Who: A Biographical Dictionary of Blues Singers* (1979).

Harrison, Daphne. *Black Pearls: Blues Queens of the 1920s* (1990).

Komara, Edward, ed. *Encyclopedia of the Blues* (2006).

Spottswood, Dick. Liner notes, *Shave 'Em Dry: The Best of Lucille Bogan* (2002).

MONICA HAIRSTON

BOGGS, James (28 May 1919–22 July 1993), autoworker, Black Power militant, and community activist, was born in Marion Junction, Alabama, a small town near Selma in the highly segregated Dallas County. James was the youngest of four children born to Ernest Boggs, a blacksmith and iron ore worker who died when James was eight, and Leila Boggs, a domestic worker and cook. He attended elementary school in Marion Junction and throughout his life proudly retained his "Alabamese" diction. After graduating in 1937 from Dunbar High School in Bessemer, near Birmingham, he hopped a freight train to Detroit, pursuing his brothers William and Jesse, and hoping to find a job like his uncle's at Budd Wheel. When no work materialized, Boggs rode the rails to the Pacific Northwest before returning South in 1938 to marry his childhood sweetheart Annie McKinley, with whom he fathered seven children. That year he returned permanently to Detroit, securing road-building Works Projects Administration (WPA) relief work and then entering the George Washington Trade School. As production accelerated with the approach of World War II he secured industrial employment in 1940 as a template maker at Chrysler's Jefferson plant, where he remained until he retired twenty-eight years later.

Participation in the United Auto Workers (UAW) labor union, Boggs said, gave him his "real organizing skills—in strikes, wildcats, picketing, goon squads, stuff like that" (Moon, 153). Union activism also introduced him to the political left. Boggs sometimes claimed to have joined the Communist Party, which he may have done during the war, when he supported the UAW faction led by George Addes and R. J. Thomas. By the mid-1940s, however, he was searching for something more radical, and he became associated with anti-Stalinist leftists in the Socialist Workers Party (SWP) and the Industrial Workers of the World. In the late 1940s Boggs served on a fair employment practices committee created to challenge racial discrimination in and near the plant. The committee pushed for seniority as the criterion for admission to skilled trades and, beginning in 1949, joined with the Detroit branch of the National Association for the Advancement of Colored People (NAACP) to launch direct-action protests against restaurants on Woodward Avenue that were violating a state law prohibiting discrimination in public accommodations.

By the early 1950s Boggs had grown close to Correspondence, a small group that had recently left the SWP, where it had been called the Johnson-Forest Tendency after the party names of its leaders, C. L. R. JAMES ("Johnson") and Raya Dunayevskaya ("Forest"). In 1952 Correspondence opened a Third Layer School in New York City that reflected its passion for the primacy of working people. The school was premised on Lenin's observation that a revolutionary party contains three layers: a first of Marxist theoreticians, a second of experienced labor activists, and a third of raw workers and peasants. Johnson-Forest worried that these strata would crystallize, reproducing the division between manual and intellectual labor and opening the door to a "state capitalist" bureaucracy rather than socialism. To prevent that, the leadership needed to listen attentively to the rank-and-file-workers—to be tutored, as it were, by the untutored. Boggs was invited to the Third Layer School to explain shop-floor realities while the group's intellectuals took notes with what Dunayevskaya termed a "full fountain pen." This was a microcosm of the role Boggs later performed for the American left throughout the 1960s. At the school, he met Grace Lee, whom he married in 1954.

Lee (b. 1915), the daughter of a prominent New York Chinese American restaurateur, held degrees in philosophy from Barnard (BA, 1935) and Bryn Mawr (MA, 1937; PhD, 1940). Her political commitments fueled her desire "to become a movement activist in the black community" (Grace Lee Boggs, 89). In June 1953 she moved to Detroit, where Correspondence had its headquarters. Boggs's first marriage had ended in divorce in 1953, and he proposed to Lee after dinner at her house, on their first date. From the moment they were married by a justice of the peace in Toledo, Ohio, the Boggses were an indomitable team. They coauthored numerous publications, especially in the heightened feminist atmosphere of the 1970s, but even work published under James Boggs's name suggested Grace Lee Boggs's involvement. Their marriage, she reveals, challenged them both:

I did follow Jimmy at first, consciously and openly, because he was so rooted in reality and in his community and knew so many things about politics that you can't get out of books. After about ten years I began to struggle more with him because I had begun to feel more rooted myself and also because I was concerned that the young people around us would get the wrong idea about how women should relate to men. Then we began arguing so vigorously that people around us often had to switch their eyes from one side to the other as if at a tennis or Ping-Pong match. (Grace Lee Boggs, 79–80)

Throughout the 1950s, while working two jobs, as janitor and autoworker, to meet his child support payments, Boggs remained a dedicated labor activist. He participated in a rank-and-file caucus critical of the UAW leadership and was elected to his local's steering committee but resigned in protest over its closed meetings. By 1962 disaffection with the union and enthusiasm about the civil rights upturn led the Boggses to break with C. L. R. James's Marxism.

Their conclusions that automation was making labor superfluous and that unions were being absorbed into the capitalist system (a widely shared idea among 1960s leftists) informed Boggs's first book, *The American Revolution: Pages from a Negro Worker's Notebook* (1963). Published first as an issue of *Monthly Review,* whose editor Paul M. Sweezy suggested its title, *The American Revolution* maintained that black Americans, together with countries like Cuba and China, not unions, were the new catalysts of change. Especially because it bore the imprimatur of a black worker, the book was embraced by new-left students already dismissive of the labor movement, a disdain many would reconsider by the 1970s.

Boggs was an early Black Power advocate, collaborating with the Reverend ALBERT BUFORD CLEAGE JR., Max Stanford, and other Detroit militants, and organizing the Detroit meeting where MALCOLM X gave his "Message to the grass roots" speech in 1963. Boggs favored black-only organizations but opposed nostalgia for Africa: "Our destiny is right in this country," he declared. Against the fantasy of a separate nation within the United States, the Boggses in 1965 raised the slogan, "The city is the black man's land." They held that inner cities were colonies dominated by an absentee white power structure of landlords, merchants, school administrators, and police, and that urban dwellers should fight for self-determination. The 1967 Detroit uprising, however, prompted them to distinguish between rebellion and revolution. *Manifesto for a Black Revolutionary Party* (1969) and *Racism and the Class Struggle* (1970) portrayed the black proletariat, particularly street youth, as the dynamic revolutionary force, depicted white workers as racist, roundly criticized "black capitalism," and called for a black vanguard party.

By the mid-1970s the Boggses had concluded that black militancy, like labor before it, had sold out to self-interested careerism and reformist politics. In a 1983 article in *Monthly Review* Boggs reflected that the black liberation movement of the 1960s had been blind to reality in "the United States, where blacks are only a section of the population and where therefore blackness cannot be the basis for a total struggle for power." In *Revolution and Evolution in the Twentieth Century* (1974) and *Conversations in Maine* (1978), the Boggses espoused a multicultural revolutionary humanism attuned to American conditions and informed by a dialectical view of reality as constantly changing. The collapse of radicalism in the black community, they argued, gave wider play to violence, drug abuse, and vandalism, requiring a reassertion of such values as trust, respect, and discipline. The Boggs pamphlet *But What about the Workers?* (1973), coauthored with the black autoworker James Hocker, argued that the United States is technologically and materially advanced but politically and socially backward, so that radicals who raised economic demands alone, such as welfare or wages, merely fostered the selfishness of capitalism.

Such thinking inspired the creation of a small interracial group, the National Organization for an American Revolution, that the Boggses led from 1978 to 1987. However, conditions in Detroit's black community drew most of their attention. From their home on Field Street, they objected to developers' gentrification projects, which included plans to construct a stadium building and introduce casino gambling to the city. Instead, the Boggses posed alternative solutions to disinvestment in the age of multinational capitalism. For example, in 1992 they initiated "Detroit Summer" to bring out-of-town and local youths together to rehabilitate houses, plant gardens, paint murals, and march against crack dealers. A lively vernacular speaker, Boggs emulated Malcolm X's chiding, denying that oppression was an excuse for irresponsibility, urging blacks not to see themselves as victims, and rejecting "biological" thinking that places skin color above beliefs. He championed self-reliance, perseverance, and pride in creative work. To the end, James Boggs remained deeply committed to the struggle for black liberation. Even as he battled the cancer that would take his life, he rewrote the final line of the civil rights anthem by insisting "We shall overcome *today.*"

Further Reading
The James and Grace Lee Boggs Collection is housed in the Archives of Labor and Urban Affairs in the Walter P. Reuther Library at Wayne State University in Detroit, Michigan.

Boggs, Grace Lee. *Living for Change* (1998).
Moon, Elaine Latzman. *Untold Tales, Unsung Heroes: An Oral History of Detroit's African American Community, 1918–1967* (1994).
Mullens, Bill. *Afro-Orientalism* (2004).
Nicholas, Xavier. *Questions of the American Revolution: Conversations with James Boggs* (1976).

Obituary: *Detroit Free Press,* 24 July 1993.

CHRISTOPHER PHELPS

BOGLE, Donald E. (13 July 1944–), film and television historian, was born in Philadelphia to Roslyn, a homemaker and arts advocate, and John Dudley Bogle, vice president and advertising director of the *Philadelphia Tribune,* the oldest continually published black newspaper in the country. Bogle's father was educated at the Virginia Theological Seminary where his maternal grandfather, Robert Clisson Woods, had also been president. His father had studied history and was a charismatic speaker on behalf of African Americans' civil rights. Bogle's mother decided against college and eloped with John Bogle when she was a teenager. Because of her upbringing in a highly educated family, however, she had developed a deep knowledge and appreciation for the arts and culture, which she passed on to her children.

While Bogle was still an infant, his large family moved to a suburb of Philadelphia, and he grew up in a predominately white, middle-class community. Bogle's father died when he was still young, but his mother raised the family on her own.

As a child, Bogle suffered from asthma, which frequently limited his physical activities. As a result, he read books in his family's library and watched a lot of television. He was particularly fascinated with films featuring black actors, some of whom his parents spoke about at the family dinner table. In the preface to his first book, *Toms, Coons, Mulattos, Mammies & Bucks*, Bogle wrote about the first movie he had ever seen with an all-black cast, "I decided one gloomy rainy afternoon to run away from home and go to live at the movies. By chance, the movie I went to 'live at' was something called *Carmen Jones*. In no conceivable way has my life been the same since."

After graduating from a mostly white high school, Bogle acceded to his mother's wishes and attended the historically black Lincoln University. There he studied literature under professors H. Alfred Farrell, Lou Putnam, and Edward Groff, who had a vast knowledge of movie history and encouraged Bogle's cinema interests. After graduating with honors, Bogle briefly pursued a master's degree in Creative Writing at Indiana University, but he left the program after one year. He moved to New York City where he took graduate courses at Columbia University. Before completing a degree, he left again, this time to take a job as a story editor for Otto Preminger, the acclaimed director of *Carmen Jones* and *Porgy and Bess*. Through Preminger, Bogle heard firsthand accounts and assessments about black Hollywood, particularly about the actress DOROTHY DANDRIDGE. In addition to having directed the Oscar-nominated actress in two of his most memorable films, Preminger had been romantically involved with Dandridge before her death from an accidental suicide in 1965. By this time, Bogle was already formulating an idea to write about the history and contributions of African Americans in Hollywood cinema. He was influenced by the writings of several cultural critics, particularly AMIRI BARAKA's (Leroi Jones) *Blues People*, ALBERT MURRAY's *Stomping the Blues,* and by the film criticism of Pauline Kael. He was also influenced by the cultural criticism of STERLING BROWN and L. D. REDDICK.

After nine months of working for Preminger, Bogle moved to Chicago where he worked as a journalist for *Ebony* magazine. Bantam Books offered Bogle a contract to write what later became *Toms, Coons, Mulattos, Mammies & Bucks: An Interpretive History of Blacks in American Films* (1973). He spent four years researching the book, tracking down rare films, such as a 1934 edition of John Stahl's *Imitation of Life*, and also interviewing dozens of black film stars, including several who had worked for the independent black director OSCAR MICHEAUX. He also spoke with other industry notables, such as King Vidor, who made one of the first Hollywood sound movies with an African American cast, *Hallelujah!*, which starred NINA MAE MCKINNEY. Bogle's aim with the book had been not only to catalog and analyze common portrayals of blacks in American films but also to decode the ways in which some black performers subverted the narrow, sometimes demeaning roles offered to them in Hollywood and how African American audiences responded. It was one of the first books by an American writer to document and analyze the experience and contributions of black actors and filmmakers in the twentieth-century development of the Hollywood film industry, and the study quickly became a classic.

Buoyed by the book's success, Bogle taught briefly at his alma mater, Lincoln University, and also lectured around the country for several years. Bogle's second book, published in 1980, was *Brown Sugar: Eighty Years of America's Black Female Superstars.* That survey was later reproduced as a four-part, four-hour television documentary for PBS by German Educational Television for which Bogle wrote the scripts and served as executive producer. The documentary series won an award from the American Women in Radio & Television. Immediately on the heels of the documentary, Bogle wrote a 510-page encyclopedia, *Blacks in American Films and Television*, which was published in 1988.

Throughout his career, Bogle was hampered by debilitating migraine headaches that sometimes left him immobile for days at a time. He became known as an intensely reclusive person who, although he interviewed others for a living, rarely felt comfortable discussing his own life. Occasionally, he had difficulty getting publishers interested in his book ideas that typically centered around black Hollywood. He said, for example, that several publishers passed on his idea to write a biography of Dandridge, who had been largely forgotten by mainstream America at that point, until a black-owned house, Amistad Press, took the project on. The resulting 613-page book, *Dorothy Dandridge: A Biography*, brought the actor's life and career to the attention of a new generation of film enthusiasts.

Bogle went on to publish a history of blacks in television, *Primetime Blues* (2001), and another on black Hollywood, *Bright Boulevards, Bold Dreams* (2005), which garnered excellent reviews and earned Bogle the 2006 Hurston-Wright Legacy Finalist Award in Non-Fiction.

Between writing projects, Bogle appeared as a commentator in numerous documentaries about film and television, including the RICHARD PRYOR–executive-produced *Mo' Funny (A History of Black Humor)*, SPIKE LEE's *Jim Brown: All-American*, and the American Movie Classics channel's *Small Steps . . . Big Strides*. He also hosted Turner Classic Movies' groundbreaking 38-film series *Race and Hollywood*, which won the cable industry's Vision Award in 2007. Bogle has served on the board of the Film Forum in New York City and taught film history at Rutgers University, the University of Pennsylvania, and New York University. He has also curated a major retrospective on the career of SIDNEY POITIER at the American Museum of the Moving Image and another on the career of Lee, who has referred to him as "our most noted black cinema historian."

Further Reading

Bogle, Donald. *Toms, Coons, Mulattoes, Mammies & Bucks: An Interpretive History of Blacks in American Films* (1973).

Jackson, Ronald L., II, and Sonja M. Brown Givens. *Black Pioneers in Communication Research* (2006).

JODY BENJAMIN

BOHANNON, Horace (22 Aug. 1922–14 May 2003), pilot, Tuskegee Airman, civil servant, teacher, and juvenile probation officer, was born in Atlanta, Georgia, the youngest child of Georgia Crane and Earl Bohannon, occupations unknown. Bohannon was the youngest of ten children, although only his oldest sister and a brother were alive when Bohannon was born. One of his greatest influences growing up was his mother, who taught him the importance of principles, hard work, and honesty.

Bohannon began working at eight years of age in a hardware store. His next job was working on a laundry truck. It was the laundry job that ultimately led Bohannon to his dream of becoming an aviator. Bohannon stopped twice a week at Atlanta's Candler Field (later William B. Hartsfield Airport). While picking up the aviators' laundry he listened to the pilots discussing their flights, the difficulties of flying in adverse weather conditions, and other matters that inspired him to become a pilot. From the start people were negative about his aspiration. One white Georgia pilot told Bohannon, "Horace, I know you like that stuff, but I think you are wasting your time. There is no chance in the world that you could work around them [airplanes] or be one of the pilots" (Moye, 58–71). Bohannon would not let the prevailing racial attitude stop him from his dream of becoming a pilot.

Bohannon graduated from BOOKER T. WASHINGTON High School in 1939, at that time the only high school for blacks in Atlanta. He attended Lincoln University in Chester County, Pennsylvania, where he studied to become a teacher from 1939 to 1942. It was at Lincoln that he got his first opportunity to train as a pilot. However, at the end of Bohannon's junior year he was forced to return to Atlanta to work and earn money for his senior year.

Upon returning to Atlanta, Bohannon was recommended for a job as a carpenter's helper in Alabama where the Tuskegee Air Base was being built. While helping to build the airbase he learned that the United States Army was testing for instructor pilots in Atlanta at the Butler Street YMCA. Over 200 men of all races took the test, but only Bohannon and one other man passed.

Unfortunately delays and interruptions forced Bohannon to find other jobs to fill in gaps in the training. He worked as a timekeeper at Tuskegee's airfield, recording the time each plane took off and when it returned so the pilots were credited with the correct number of flight hours. Eventually he became frustrated with the interruptions in training and living hand-to-mouth and returned to Atlanta, where he became a cab driver for the company Harlem Cab. Bohannon was able to average about $70 working three days a week. It was a tremendous sum of money for a black man at that time, especially in comparison to a black porter who made only $11 every two weeks.

In the summer of 1943 Bohannon met Ora Jean Whyte, who became his wife in November 1943. The couple had a son and two daughters. It was Whyte's influence that led Bohannon back to Lincoln University, where much to his surprise he received a draft notice. Bohannon was drafted in to army air corps on 15 October 1943. He attended primary flight training at Moton Field in Tuskegee, Alabama, which was the only army air corps primary flight training facility for black pilots during World War II.

After finishing primary flight training Bohannon moved on to Tuskegee Army Air Field, the base at which Bohannon worked as a carpenter. Bohannon graduated on 20 December 1944 in Class SE-44-J, SE standing for "single engine plane," 44 indicating the year the class graduated, and J, the tenth letter of the alphabet, indicating that it was the tenth graduating class of the year. After graduation Bohannon was sent to Godman Field in Walterboro, South Carolina, for training on how to fly the P-40. He was scheduled to deploy to Europe, but when the fighting ended Bohannon began training to fly in the South Pacific against Japan. However, the war ended before Bohannon got the chance to fly in combat.

Bohannon was discharged from the army air corps not long after in 1945. Like many other black veterans Bohannon returned to the civilian world with the hopes that the situation of black people would improve. Finding few opportunities for work, he went back to driving cabs.

Because blacks were not allowed to join the American Legion as fully-fledged members, Bohannon helped set up the Georgia Veterans League (GVL). The GVL eventually became affiliated with the American Veteran's Committee, which accepted members regardless of race. In 1946 or 1947 Bohannon began working for the Southern Regional Council (SRC), an Atlanta-based civil rights organization. It was while working for the SRC that Bohannon met Dr. George Mitchell, director of the Veterans Education Program for the Southern Regional Council. Mitchell wanted to use blacks as contact officers and representatives for the Veterans Administration. Bohannon spent the next year and a half working for the Veterans Education Program.

Bohannon returned to Lincoln University in January 1948 and graduated with a degree in teaching on 8 June 1948. He worked as a teacher for two years at Atlanta's John Hope School and the English Avenue School. During the summer Bohannon supplemented his family's income by working for the post office. Teaching proved to be unable to hold Bohannon's interest and he quickly became frustrated with the post office's blatant discrimination against blacks.

In 1952 Bohannon took an examination to become a probation officer for the Fulton County Juvenile

Court. Bohannon worked for the Fulton County Juvenile Court until 1961, when he began looking for another job after refusing to attend a segregated Christmas party given by one of the Fulton County Juvenile Court judges.

Bohannon interviewed for a job at the post office and became a training officer for the states of North Carolina, South Carolina, and Florida. From there he moved on to other civil service positions, including contract compliance position with the United States Navy and finally to the Department of Health, Education, and Welfare (HEW).

While at HEW, Bohannon assisted six states, including Mississippi, to comply with federal desegregation laws. Despite the high quality of his work and the mandate of the agency for which he worked, Bohannon regularly faced discrimination from within the organization and from other government employees. In Charleston, South Carolina, during the early 1960s Bohannon worked with the Medical University of South Carolina (MUSC) to establish a plan and set the dates for desegregating MUSC's offices; but when it was time to implement the plan South Carolina Senator Strom Thurmond told the hospital they did not have to implement the agreement.

Frustrated with the situation, Bohannon accepted a job offered by his former boss from his navy contract compliance position. Bohannon was made manager of Special Projects for the Maritime Administration. He worked there until he retired in 1981.

Even after retiring Bohannon was much in demand as a speaker during Black History Month. He remained active in the Atlanta community, raising money for various groups and organizations. Bohannon died of congestive heart failure at age eighty in Atlanta.

Further Reading

Brooks, Jennifer E. "Winning the Peace: Georgia Veterans and the Struggle to Define the Political Legacy of World War II," in *The Journal of Southern History* 66 (Aug. 2000).

Moye, J. Todd. "I Never Quit Dreaming about It; Horace Bohannon, the Tuskegee Airmen, and the Dream of Flight," in *Atlanta History* 47½ (2005).

Onkst, David H. "First a Negro . . . Incidentally a Veteran: Black World War Two Veterans and the G.I. Bill of Rights in the Deep South, 1944–1948," in *Journal of Social History* (Spring 1998).

Obituary: *Atlanta Journal-Constitution*, 19 May 2003.

ANNE K. DRISCOLL

BOJANGLES. *See* Robinson, Bill.

BOLDEN, Buddy (6 Sept. 1877–4 Nov. 1931), jazz musician, was born Charles Joseph Bolden in New Orleans, Louisiana, the son of Westmore Bolden, a drayman, and Alice Harrison. Although Bolden is one of the earliest known figures in the development of jazz in New Orleans, there was little factual information about him until the publication in 1978 of Donald M. Marquis's *In Search of Buddy Bolden*. In this admirable piece of investigative research, Marquis dispels much of the rumor that had grown around Bolden's life in New Orleans and establishes him as an important member of the founding generation of jazz musicians. Marquis confirms that Bolden was not a barber and did not own a barbershop, as popularly believed, although he apparently spent considerable time at barbershops, which served as musicians' meeting places, where information on jobs could be exchanged. Nor did he edit a "scandal sheet" called the *Cricket*. He did drink a lot, played a loud cornet, and was eventually committed to an asylum for erratic behavior resulting from chronic alcoholism.

Like most other New Orleans musicians of that period, Bolden pursued a part-time career performing jazz (then called ragtime). Not until 1902 did city directories begin listing him as a "musician." Before that year he was identified as a "plasterer" and resided in his family's uptown home on First Street in New Orleans. Sufficient documentation and testimony exist to verify that in about 1895 Bolden became active as a cornetist and bandleader at various indoor and outdoor locations in New Orleans. These venues included Lincoln and Johnson parks, Longshoreman's Hall, and Tulane University in the uptown area; the Milneburg and West End resorts on Lake Pontchartrain; the Masonic Hall in Algiers; the Fairgrounds Race Track; and a number of "social clubs" whose halls lined the Perdido–South Rampart Street area. The period from 1897 to 1906 marked the prime of Bolden's tenure as a jazz musician—a time when he enjoyed a sort of preeminence among other players for his boldness and audacity and the barrelhouse nature of his music.

Essentially an "uptown" musician, Bolden had limited contact with the more learned downtown musicians and performed primarily for black audiences. As an untutored musician with little if any formal education, and as one who played mostly by ear, he made music of the "rough blues" variety used to accompany the "slow drag" and other enticing dances of prostitutes. The downtown Creoles called it "honky tonk" music, and Bolden's repertoire was reputed to be particularly coarse. According to Marquis, it appealed "especially to a liberated, post–Civil War generation of young blacks." One number in particular, "Buddy Bolden's Blues," also known as "Funky Butt," was popular enough to cause Union Sons Hall (a location where Bolden's band frequently played) to be commonly referred to as Funky Butt Hall in his honor.

The principal difficulty in assessing the musical contributions of Bolden stems from the total absence of audio recordings. Although he was active during a period when early recordings were being made, no cylinders or records of his playing are known to exist. The search for a cylinder allegedly made by Bolden and his band in the late 1890s, and first reported by one of Bolden's sidemen, Willie Cornish, to the *Jazzmen* editor Charles Edward Smith in 1939, proved fruitless. The only photograph (the original now lost) of Bolden shows him with a six-piece ensemble that included cornet, trombone, two clarinets, guitar, and string bass. Nonetheless, legendary accounts abound of his playing and bandleading and even his lifestyle.

As his celebrity as a cornetist and bandleader grew, so did his appetite for high living. Even as early as 1895 he had become a "ladies' man," known to have consorted with the sporting crowd and prostitutes, one of whom, Hattie Oliver, gave birth to his illegitimate son. Their common-law marriage lasted only a few years, and in 1902 Bolden met Nora Bass and entered into a second common-law marriage that produced his only daughter. The Boldens' domestic environment was anything but tranquil, as contemporary police records and testimony from family members attest. Early in 1906 Bolden began suffering severe headaches, fits of depression, and episodes of violent behavior—all apparently related to his excessive drinking. An attack on his mother-in-law on 27 March, during which he struck her in the head with a water pitcher, led to his arrest and detainment by police, initiating the only apparent newspaper coverage he was to receive during his lifetime. Continued episodes of depression and violent behavior left him in a deranged state that placed him in conflict with many of his former musical cohorts as well as members of his family. Finally, in April 1907, having been confined to the house of detention, Bolden was moved to the state hospital for the insane in Jackson, Louisiana. There he lived out the remaining twenty-four years of his life, separated from his family and largely forgotten for the role he had played as one of the earliest identifiable jazz pioneers.

Further Reading
Marquis, Donald M. *In Search of Buddy Bolden* (1978).
CHARLES BLANCQ

BOLDEN, Charles F., Jr. (19 Aug. 1946–), astronaut, test pilot, military and NASA adviser, was born in Columbia, South Carolina, to Charles Frank Bolden Sr. and Ethel M. Bolden, both teachers. A child during the early years of the civil rights movement, Bolden was encouraged by his parents and teachers to pursue his dream of becoming a pilot, despite the fact that there were few opportunities at the time for African Americans to fly.

After graduating with honors from C. A. Johnson High School in Columbia in 1964, Bolden entered the U.S. Naval Academy at Annapolis, Maryland; he graduated with a BS in Electrical Science in 1968. Following graduation he married Alexis (Jackie) Walker. The couple would later have a son Anthony, born in 1971 and a daughter, Kelly, born in 1976.

In 1968 Bolden accepted a commission in the Marine Corps. Quickly rising to the rank of second lieutenant, Bolden, who had completed two years of military flight training, became a naval aviator in 1970. He served as a fighter pilot during the Vietnam War,

carrying out more than one hundred missions in 1972 and 1973, flying an A-6A Intruder, an attack plane that carries a pilot and a bombardier-navigator.

After the war, Bolden served as a marine recruiting officer in California for two years (1973–1975), and then completed three years of other assignments at the Marine Corps Air Station El Toro; during this time he earned his MA in Systems Management from the University of Southern California in 1977. Bolden had toyed with the idea of applying to NASA to be an astronaut, but he felt he lacked the test-pilot experience necessary to be accepted into the program. In an effort to gain more flying experience, he enrolled in the U.S. Naval Test Pilot School at Patuxent River, Maryland. By the time he graduated in 1979, Bolden had logged more than 6,000 hours of flight time, and was assigned to the Systems Engineering and Strike Aircraft Test Directorates of the Naval Air Test Center, also at Patuxent River.

In 1980 Bolden was accepted into NASA's space shuttle program (STS). On 12 January 1986 he became the second African American to pilot a space shuttle (Frederick Drew Gregory had been NASA's first African American pilot in 1978), when he manned the controls of the shuttle *Columbia* on STS-61C. This was a science-oriented mission in which various astrophysics experiments were performed and a communications satellite was launched. Only ten days after *Columbia* had landed, on 28 January 1986, the *Challenger* space shuttle exploded soon after liftoff. Bolden led the investigative team that would determine the cause of the disaster: faulty O-ring seals in a solid-rocket booster.

Shuttle flights resumed in 1988. Bolden's next space shuttle flight was a historic one: On 24 April 1990 he piloted the *Discovery* on mission STS-31, which deployed the Hubble Space Telescope. This mission also set a record for the highest orbit—400 miles above the Earth—captured with IMAX cameras that offered the public a glimpse of life on a space shuttle.

Bolden commanded and piloted his next shuttle mission on 24 March 1992 aboard the *Atlantis*. An international science mission, with astronauts from NASA, the European Space Agency, and Japan, STS-45 carried out experiments on Earth's atmosphere, land masses, and oceans.

By 1992, however, NASA was confronted with a damaged public image and severe budget cutbacks. Charges of mismanagement led to the hiring of a new director, Daniel Goldin. Impressed with Bolden's work in the aftermath of the *Challenger* explosion, Goldin appointed Bolden to be NASA's assistant deputy administrator. Bolden was responsible for reporting to Congress on efficiency—or the lack thereof—within NASA. After this appointment, Bolden made his final shuttle flight as commander aboard the *Discovery*, on science mission STS-60, which launched on 3 February 1994.

After the mission had returned safely to Earth, Bolden left NASA, having logged more than 680 hours in space, and in June 1994 he returned to active duty in the U.S. Marine Corps, where he finished out the year as deputy commandant of the U.S. Naval Academy. For the next two years, Bolden served as the Assistant Wing Commander, Third Marine Aircraft Wing in Miramar, California, and in July 1997 was assigned to Japan to be Deputy Commanding General, I MEF (1st Marine Expeditionary Force), in the Pacific.

In 1998 President Bill Clinton was concerned that Saddam Hussein was violating the American- and British-mandated no-fly zone in northern Iraq; as a result, Bolden was called back from Japan. From February to June 1998 he served as Commanding General, I MEF (FWD) (Marine Expeditionary Force, Forward), in support of Operation Desert Thunder in Kuwait.

In July 1998 Bolden was promoted to the rank of major general and resumed his previous duties as the deputy commander of the U.S. forces in Japan. In August 2000 he became commanding general of the Third Marine Aircraft Wing.

On 31 January 2002 President George W. Bush nominated Bolden to be deputy administrator of NASA, but Bolden turned down the post. He retired from the marine corps in August 2002 after thirty-four years of service, and he also received a certificate of appreciation from President Bush and a Distinguished Service Medal. Bolden became a director of the Marathon Oil Corporation in 2003.

In addition to his Distinguished Service Medal, Bolden's awards include three NASA Exceptional Service Medals for 1988, 1989, and 1991, the NASA Outstanding Leadership Medal in 1992, and such military awards as the Defense Superior Service Medal, the Defense Meritorious Service Medal, the Distinguished Flying Cross, the Air Medal, and the Strike/Flight Medal. He was honored with the University of Southern California Alumni Award of Merit for 1989 and received honorary degrees from the University of South Carolina, Winthrop College, Johnson C. Smith University, and San Diego State University.

Further Reading
Bigelow, Barbara Carlisle, ed. *Contemporary Black Biography* (1994).
Burns, Khephra, and William Miles. *Black Stars in Orbit: NASA's African-American Astronauts* (1995).
Phelps, J. Alfred. *They Had a Dream: The Story of African-American Astronauts* (1994).
Spangenburg, Ray, and Kit Moser. "Bolden, Charles," *African Americans in Science, Math, and Invention, A to Z of African Americans* (2003).
Wellford, Alison. "Charles F. Bolden, Jr.," *Notable Black American Scientists* (1990).

JOSEPHA SHERMAN

BOLDEN, Ethel Martin (14 Dec. 1918–20 Oct. 2002), teacher, librarian, and community leader, was born Ethel Evangeline Veronica Martin in Charleston, South Carolina, the only girl of four children born to Thomas Jerry Martin, a laborer, and Ethel Sinkler Martin, a schoolteacher. Martin's youth was spent in constant transition because of family loss. Her father relocated to Chicago in search of employment and died in a streetcar accident. In 1927 her mother died of natural causes while working at the Fairwold School for Colored Girls in Columbia, South Carolina. Having lost both parents by the age of six, Martin was initially reared by her paternal grandmother, Sara Martin, who was an educator at Saint Simon Episcopal Mission in Peak, South Carolina. Ethel Martin later lived with her aunt, Dora Dillard, a seamstress in Columbia, South Carolina. Both women had a lasting influence on Martin. Her grandmother exposed her to books and PAUL LAURENCE DUNBAR's poetry. Growing up in her aunt's interracial neighborhood of Edgewood near downtown Columbia left Martin with a belief that blacks and whites could live and interact in a peaceable manner.

Martin attended the all-black Booker T. Washington High School in the Wheeler Hill section of Columbia. She graduated in 1936 and continued her education at Barber Scotia Junior College, a historically black institution in Concord, North Carolina. Working at her first job under the tutelage of the librarian Robbie L. Goodloe, Martin became enamored with the library environment and set her sights on joining the profession. Upon her graduation in 1938, she matriculated at Johnson C. Smith College in Charlotte, North Carolina, graduating in 1940 with a BA in English. Martin returned to Columbia to teach fourth grade at Waverly Elementary School. In 1941 she married her childhood sweetheart, Charles Frank Bolden. The couple had two sons, Charles Jr. and Warren.

Ethel Bolden's dream of becoming a librarian came true through an opportunity provided by John Whiteman, a Waverly Elementary administrator, who expressed interest in establishing a school library. This motivated Bolden to take library courses at neighboring Allen University and Benedict College. With her acquired knowledge, she established the first elementary library in an all-black Richland School District One public school in 1946. Within a twelve-year span, Bolden created libraries at two more African American schools, Carver Elementary and C. A. Johnson High School. Despite her accomplishments, she felt the need to acquire a master's degree in library science. The major obstacle was that the nearest accredited library school that admitted blacks was Atlanta University in Georgia. With the cooperation of her husband, who agreed to take care of their sons, Bolden was able to attend the college beginning in 1954. Mentored by VIRGINIA LACY JONES, the library school's dean, Bolden finished her course work in Atlanta in 1957. She returned home the following year to write her thesis on another pioneer librarian, Sara Dart Butler, who established Dart Hall Branch Library in Charleston. Bolden earned her MA in Library Service in 1959 and soon became the head librarian at Columbia's W. A. Perry Junior High School.

When Columbia dismantled its segregated school system in 1968, Bolden was hired at the formerly all-white Dreher High School. She became the first African American head librarian in a desegregated Richland District One school.

In addition to pursuing a career as a librarian, Bolden was determined to improve the social conditions of Columbia residents. Throughout the Jim Crow era, Bolden was instrumental in providing religious and cultural programs for African American youth. She did this by creating programs through her church, Northminster United Presbyterian, and her membership with the Gamma Nu (Beta Zeta) Omega Chapter of the Alpha Kappa Alpha Sorority, the Columbia chapters of the Pan-Hellenic Council, and Jack and Jill of America. Professionally Bolden chaired the librarian section of the Palmetto State Teachers' Association (PSTA), the South Carolina African American teachers' organization, in 1964. She was also an integral force for interracial cooperation in the Columbia branch of the South Carolina Council on Human Relations, a private, biracial, and interfaith association established in 1954. One of Bolden's proudest affiliations was with Columbia's Community Relations Council, established by Mayor Lester Bates during the 1960s to prevent violent racial unrest and rioting that prevailed throughout other cities in the Southeast. Bolden was among one hundred black and white business and professional leaders on the council who utilized methods of community dialogue for the city's peaceful integration.

Bolden was actively involved in integrating numerous institutional and civic organizations. She often was the only African American to serve on community boards during the 1950s through the 1970s. She was one of fifteen members, and the only African American woman, who served on the Richland County Public Library Board of Trustee's (RCPL) in 1977. Within a fifteen-year period, Bolden oversaw relocation plans for three branches and new construction plans for the main branch in downtown Columbia. She was also in constant demand as a motivational speaker, as she fondly spoke to youths about the virtues of reading, African American history, and obtaining an education. She also talked about her son, who had become a NASA astronaut in 1980. Bolden retired from Dreher High in 1982, having served a thirty-eight-year tenure as teacher and librarian.

During her lifetime Bolden served on over thirty institutional, civic, and religious boards. She also received numerous awards for her civil rights involvement and volunteerism. In 2002 she was honored with the Order of the Palmetto, the state's highest award, given for lifetime achievement and service.

Further Reading

Ethel Bolden's papers are at the South Carolina Library, Manuscripts Division, University of South Carolina, Columbia.

Mayo, Georgette. "'A Voice in the Wilderness': Ethel Evangeline Martin Bolden; Pioneer Librarian," master's thesis, University of South Carolina, Columbia (2005).

Williams, Robert V. "Interview with Ethel Bolden," in *Speaking of History: The Words of South Carolina Librarians* (1988).

GEORGETTE MAYO

BOLDEN, Frank E. (24 Dec. 1912–28 Aug. 2003), journalist and historian, was born Franklin Eugene Bolden Jr. in Washington County, Pennsylvania, the eldest of three sons of Franklin Eugene Bolden Sr., the first black mail carrier in the city of Washington, Pennsylvania, and Mary Woods Bolden. Frank Bolden's parents instilled in him the importance of education and achievement at an early age. His father often told him, "When you're average, you are just as far from the bottom as you are from the top" (Rouvalis, *Post-Gazette*). With that mentality, Bolden's life was anything but average.

Bolden attended the Washington public school system and graduated from high school in 1930. He went on to attend the University of Pittsburgh, where he was the first African American to play in the university's varsity marching and concert bands. He said in a documentary film about his life that his audition for the band was twice as hard as what was required of white members. While in college, Bolden also became one of the first three black students to perform in the Cap and Gown drama club. He joined Alpha Phi Alpha national fraternity in 1931. Bolden graduated in 1934, earning a BS with honors in Education. Bolden intended to enroll in the university's medical school, but racism kept him out. Upon visiting the school's dean, Bolden was told that his transcript was impeccable and he would be admitted that day if only he were white. At the time, the university refused to admit blacks to the medical school. Bolden instead chose to pursue his doctorate in biological studies. He was inducted into Phi Sigma, an honorary biology society, and was a member of the Pennsylvania Academy of Science, with publications in 1936 and 1938. Bolden, who was also the first black graduate assistant to teach in Pitt's biology department, had a teaching certificate and tried to apply for a teaching position with the Pittsburgh public schools. He was again denied entry because the system did not hire black teachers.

Bolden had no formal training in journalism, but around 1935 a friend who worked for the *Pittsburgh Courier*, one of the most renowned black newspapers in the country, asked him if he wanted to work part-time as a sportswriter. He primarily covered the Pittsburgh Crawfords and Homestead Grays, both Negro League baseball teams, and boxing. His talent attracted the attention of editors at the paper as well as its publisher, ROBERT L. VANN. As his career grew, Bolden would become well known for what were later coined "Bolden-isms," phrases he used to describe his subjects. For instance, he referred to black soldiers serving in World War II as "Tan Yanks" because he said he was tired of calling them "Negro Soldiers" in his articles. He called numbers runners "digitarians," and prostitutes were members of the "nocturnal sisterhood." Bolden's career at the *Courier* spanned twenty-seven years and included positions as columnist, feature writer, copy desk editor, and eventually city editor, a post he held from 1956 to 1962. In between his work at the *Courier,* around 1940, Bolden worked late afternoons and evenings as a bacteriologist for the county's Department of Public Health.

Pittsburgh's Hill District, which was one of the most famous African American neighborhoods in the country between the 1930s and 1950s, was Bolden's beat. He covered the neighborhood's nightlife, political, social, and cultural events. He was especially interested in stories of everyday people and their good works. This idea of spotlighting unsung heroes would continue through Bolden's tenure as city editor at the *Courier.* His articles would also speak out against discriminatory practices and ill treatment against blacks. He was an outspoken critic of Pittsburgh's urban renewal plans that destroyed the Hill District in the late 1950s.

During World War II Bolden was eager to unearth stories of the black troops fighting for freedom abroad. In 1942 he became one of the first two blacks accredited by the War Department as a war correspondent. His first assignments were to cover the mobilization of black troops including the Ninety-second and Ninety-third Infantry Divisions at Fort Huachuca, Arizona (which included the Buffalo Soldiers), and aviation training at the Tuskegee Institute in Alabama. He went overseas to cover the China-Burma-India theater of operations for the National Negro Publishers Association (later called the National Newspaper Publishers Association). His goal was to counter reports in the white press that painted black soldiers as cowards who would retreat in combat. Instead, Bolden's stories showed black troops who fought with dignity and courage. He also documented the exploits of the black engineering troops who built the Ledo Road (later Stilwell Road) in Burma. The National Negro Publishers Association distributed his articles to the *Courier* and to other black publications around the country.

In the course of one year, beginning with the Tehran Conference in 1943, Bolden landed a bevy of interviews with several twentieth-century world leaders. At the conference, he interviewed President Franklin Delano Roosevelt, Premier Joseph Stalin, and Prime Minister Winston Churchill. The conference was held to strengthen the cooperation of the United States, Great Britain, and the Soviet Union in World War II. Later, Bolden traveled to India to interview Muhammad Ali Jinnah, the founder of Pakistan, and the Indian leaders Mohandas K. Gandhi and Jawaharlal Nehru. Bolden was invited to stay in the homes of both Gandhi and Nehru; he stayed fifteen days with Gandhi and twelve days with Nehru. Bolden also interviewed General and Madame Chiang Kai-Shek in China. Bolden was the first African American journalist to set foot in India, Burma, and China.

Bolden's war reporting was cited by the War Department for Distinguished Reporting during World War II. When he returned from overseas, he was offered jobs at *Life* and the *New York Times,* but he settled back into the *Courier.* Bolden said he did not think he would have had as much of an influence on civil rights working at a white publication. Upon his return to the *Courier,* he produced an impressive series of articles that traced the complete histories of eight prominent African American families in the Pittsburgh region. In 1960 he married Nancy Travis, and the two were married forty-three years until Bolden's death. They had no children.

Bolden left the *Courier* in 1962 after the paper's financial failure left him and fellow employees without pensions. He went on to work briefly at the *New York Times,* the *Christian Science Monitor,* and at NBC News on the *Huntley-Brinkley Report.* By 1963 he had returned to Pittsburgh to accept a job with the Pittsburgh Board of Education as associate director of information services and community relations. His main task was to promote the board's desegregation policy. He took a leave of absence from the board in 1964 to cover the Democratic and Republican conventions for NBC News. At the Republican National Convention he scooped other national news outlets by scoring an exclusive interview with the Republican presidential candidate Barry Goldwater. Bolden retired from the board of education in 1978 with a pension after seventeen years of service.

While in retirement, Bolden raised prizewinning African violets and orchids and bred champion show dogs. He coauthored a book, *Legacy in Bricks and Mortar: African-American Landmarks in Allegheny County* (1995), and continued to work as a lecturer, historian, consultant, and senior archivist for the Honorable K. LEROY IRVIS, Speaker of the House of Representatives, Commonwealth of Pennsylvania. Bolden was also deeply concerned with the education and welfare of young people and devoted much of his time to boards and organizations serving their needs. He received numerous honors and awards, including the prestigious George Polk Career Award in Journalism, the Legacy Award from the National Association of Black Journalists, and the Heritage Award from the Tuskegee Airmen. Bolden died in Pittsburgh at the age of ninety. The following year, in 2004, he was honored posthumously with a Pennsylvania State Historical Marker erected on the former site of the *Courier* office in Pittsburgh's Hill District.

Further Reading

Rosenwald, Mike. "The Bold(en) Story," *Pitt Magazine,* vol. 14, no. 3. (Sept. 2001): 31–35.

Obituary: Rouvalis, Christina. "Reporter, Raconteur Frank Bolden Dies at 90," *Pittsburgh Post-Gazette,* 29 Aug. 2003.

MICHELLE K. MASSIE

BOLDEN, Melvin R. (28 Jan. 1919–29 Jan. 2000), artist and political activist, was born in Baltimore, Maryland. In 1937 Bolden received a four-year scholarship to the Philadelphia Museum School of Art, where he majored in illustration and advertising design. Upon his graduation he became an artist and layout designer for a top advertising agency in Philadelphia. His duties included prep work for original work by Norman Rockwell. In fact Bolden and Rockwell became close friends, and it was Rockwell who "encouraged Bolden to use neighbors and local townspeople as models for his art," according to a New Hampshire Circle of Friends flyer.

After World War II Mel Bolden moved to New York and became a full-time illustrator, working first for black newspapers, then for such general magazines as *Fortune, Saturday Review, Colliers, Saturday Evening Post, Boy's Life,* as well as for major newspapers like the *New York Times* and the *New York Herald Tribune.* In 1949 Bolden married the actress Gwendolyn Claire Hale, and the two spent their honeymoon in New Hampshire. Falling in love with the New Hampshire countryside, the Boldens moved to the state in 1954, residing near the state capital of Concord.

Once in New Hampshire, Bolden continued his successful artistic career, but also took up an active interest in New Hampshire and local politics and community affairs. As chairman of the Merrimack County Democratic Party in the 1960s, he was the first black chairman ever in the state, and possibly in the nation. Bolden's interest in politics was also expressed in artistic form; in 1983 he co-wrote and illustrated a book of political cartoons entitled *The New Hampshire Presidential Primary Rulebook* with David Wysocki and Charles Russell. Because his political achievements came in a predominantly white state, they are seldom remembered today, but are nonetheless significant and mirrored locally what was going on nationally during the civil rights era.

Mel Bolden's interest in community activism was also far reaching; he was a founding member of the New Hampshire Circle of Friends, a group devoted to celebrating racial diversity in a state whose black population has been historically low, and also became an educator, teaching at New England College in Henniker and the New Hampshire Art Institute in Manchester.

Bolden, however, will probably be best remembered for his outstanding artistic career, during which he gained the title of "dean" of African American illustrators. Among his best known works, in addition to his magazine illustrations, are President Jimmy Carter's 1973 White House Christmas card, a portrait of Dr. MARTIN LUTHER KING JR. that would be displayed in the Portsmouth, New Hampshire, city hall, his series on jazz and big band musicians, and his moving portrait of Christa McAuliffe, the New Hampshire teacher-astronaut lost in the explosion of the space-shuttle *Challenger* in 1986, which became part of the Smithsonian Air and Space Museum's permanent collection. Even after his death Bolden's works gained critical acclaim; in 2004 his dramatic paintings of combat in World War II, including the Tuskegee Airmen of the 99th Pursuit Squadron and their air battles over Europe, were displayed at the newly opened National World War II Memorial in Washington, D.C.

Further Reading
Wysocki, David, with Mel Bolden and Charles Russell. *New Hampshire Presidential Primary Rulebook* (1983).
GLENN ALLEN KNOBLOCK

BOLIN, Jane Matilda (11 Apr. 1908–8 Jan. 2007), attorney and jurist, was born in Poughkeepsie, New York, the youngest daughter of Matilda Emery and Gaius C. Bolin, an attorney and the first black graduate of Williams College. Bolin's mother died when she was eight years old, leaving her father solely responsible for her upbringing. Consequently, she spent a good deal of time in his office around the law books as he worked, absorbing a feel for the law. She later commented that "those leather bound books just intrigued me"(Margolick). Even as a child she was aware of events in the larger world. In 1919, when she was eleven years old, a series of antiblack race riots swept across the nation during what became known as the "red summer." Two years later, the black population of Tulsa, Oklahoma, was driven from the city and the community burned. Apart from the Tulsa race riot more than 120 blacks were lynched during 1921 and 1922, and in 1923 the black community in Rosewood, Florida, was burned and its population scattered. Bolin regularly read *The Crisis*, the journal of the NAACP, as a child and was well aware of the nation's tormented racial scene. Looking back on that period years later, she would comment, "It is easy to imagine how a young, protected child who sees portrayals of brutality is forever scarred and becomes determined to contribute in her own small way to social justice" (*New York Times* 10 Jan. 2007).

Graduating from Poughkeepsie High School in 1924, she entered Wellesley College in Massachusetts, one of only two black freshmen in her class. Her experiences at Wellesley shaped her later sensibilities. The racial isolation was profound. Years later she would recall that she did develop some genuine friendships at Wellesley, but that her time there was largely a lonely experience, in which she was ignored outside the classroom. Despite the isolation and the lack of encouragement from her professors, she graduated in 1928 as a "Wellesley Scholar," one of the top twenty students in her class. Her adviser tried to discourage her from pursuing an interest in law, indicating that there was no future for a black woman in the legal profession. Nevertheless, she applied to Yale Law School and was accepted. Upon learning of her interest in law, her father also sought to dissuade her from pursuing a legal career. He wanted Bolin to go into teaching, a profession he saw as less likely to expose her to the brutal and ugly side of life; but when she persisted, he relented.

In the fall of 1928 she entered Yale Law School, one of only three women (and the only black woman) in her class. She graduated three years later as the first black woman to receive a law degree from Yale. Decades after graduation she commented on rudeness directed at her by some of the southerners in her class.

Upon graduating from Yale, she joined her brother and father in their Poughkeepsie, New York, law firm. Her older brother, Gaius Jr., had graduated from New York University Law School in 1927. In 1933 Bolin married fellow attorney Ralph Mizzell and moved to New York City, believing that she had a better chance of achieving her life-long goals there than in Poughkeepsie.

Bolin was a Republican, and like many blacks of her era, her loyalty to the GOP was tied to that party's actions during the Civil War and Reconstruction eras. In 1937 she ran on the Republican ticket for the New York State Assembly, and even though she lost she came to the attention of New York's popular mayor, Fiorello LaGuardia, who appointed her to the city law department as an assistant corporation council. Two years later, on 22 July 1939 LaGuardia appointed her to fill an unexpired term on the city's domestic relations court (renamed the family court in 1962), making her the fist black woman in the United States to serve as a judge. Within a few years of the appointment, twin events occurred that tested her capacity to survive the intense and often hostile scrutiny her position brought.

A son, Yorke Mizzell, was born to Bolin and her husband in 1941, but shortly thereafter Ralph Mizzell died, leaving her a widow and a thirty-five-year-old single mother with a demanding, high-profile job. Years later, she commented, "I don't think I short-changed anybody but myself—I didn't get all the sleep I needed and I didn't get to travel as much as I would have liked, but I felt my first obligation was to my child" (*New York Times*, 8 Dec. 1978).

Despite her personal challenges, she set in motion major changes in how the court did business. Her comment on one of those changes was succinct, "When I came in the one or two black probation officers handled only black families—I had that changed"(*New York Times*, 8 Dec. 1978). Probation officers were assigned without regard to race or religion. In addition, she commented, "They used to put N or PR on the front of every petition to indicate if the family was black or Puerto Rican . . . because the agencies that the families were referred to were segregated"(*New York Times*, 8 Dec. 1978). Along with two other judges, she lobbied successfully for change. Any private agency receiving public funds had to accept children without regard to race or ethnicity.

During a career spanning forty years, Judge Bolin presided over cases involving major crimes committed by juveniles such as robbery and murder; she also handled child neglect and abandonment cases, spouse abuse cases, and adoptions. She despaired of ever fully understanding the parade of violent young-sters coming before her, but drew comfort from those instances where she knew that her decisions had helped a particular person who might have otherwise ended up in worse trouble. "There are no easy answers," she observed, when asked about the violent young people coming before her day after day, "I get distressed and dismayed when I hear psychiatrists and social workers handing out easy answers, saying its because of the wars children have seen, or the violent programs on television, or its because violence is as American as apple pie. Those answers are just too facile, and I can't accept any of them"(*New York Times*, 8 Dec. 1978).

She remained vigilant about issues of equity in her workplace, even after almost four decades on the job. A colleague recalled that in the 1970s when legal assistants were first assigned to family court judges, Judge Bolin ensured that some of the first assistants were African American.

Community service was vitally important to Bolin. She served on the board of directors of a number of organizations, including the Child Welfare League of America, the Neighborhood Children's Center, and the Wiltwyck School for Boys. She was also an active member of the NAACP.

In December of 1978 Judge Bolin reluctantly retired, having reached the mandatory retirement age of seventy. Thereafter she worked as a volunteer in the New York City school system and served on the State Board of Regents. Jane Bolin died on 8 January 2007 in Queens, New York, at the age of ninety-eight.

Further Reading
Klemesrud, Judy. "A Remarkable Judge, a Reluctant Retirement," *New York Times*, 8 Dec. 1978.
Margolick, David. "At the Bar," *New York Times*, 14 May 1993.

Obituary: *New York Times*, 10 Jan. 2007.

JOHN R. HOWARD

BOND, Horace Mann (8 Nov. 1904–21 Dec. 1972), college professor and administrator, was born in Nashville, Tennessee, the son of James Bond, a Congregationalist minister, and Jane Alice Browne, a graduate of Oberlin College and a schoolteacher. Horace Bond's paternal grandmother, Jane Arthur Bond, was a slave who raised two sons by herself. These two sons, Bond's father and his uncle, Henry, both earned college degrees and embarked on professional careers. Three of Bond's four siblings earned college degrees, and his cousins on his father's side also distinguished themselves academically. This family achievement was important to Horace Bond, because it exemplified the way in which numerous scholars of his generation were nurtured within the African American community. He published a book on the family origins of African American scholars near the end of his life, *Black American Scholars: A Study of Their Beginnings* (1972).

Bond was an intellectually precocious child. He was educated at schools attached to colleges and

Horace Mann Bond (right), with W. E. B. Du Bois (left), E. Franklin Frazier, his daughter Jane Marguerite, and his son Julian Bond. (Courtesy of Julian Bond.)

universities in towns where his father served as a minister—Talladega, Alabama, and Atlanta, Georgia. He finished high school at the age of fourteen at the Lincoln Institute in Shelbyville, Kentucky. He then attended Lincoln University (Pennsylvania) and graduated at the age of eighteen in the class of 1923. He stayed on at Lincoln for a year as a teaching assistant, attended graduate school for a summer at Pennsylvania State College (later Pennsylvania State University), and earned master's (1926) and doctoral (1936) degrees from the University of Chicago. Bond married Julia Washington in 1929; they had three children. Their second child, JULIAN BOND, became famous as a member of the student civil rights movement in the 1960s and served as a Georgia state legislator.

Bond's major field was education, and he specialized in both the history of education and the sociology of education in his graduate studies. He served on the faculties of Langston University in Oklahoma, Alabama State College in Montgomery, Fisk University in Nashville, and Dillard University in New Orleans between 1926 and 1935. He also was chairman of the education department at Fisk and the founding aca-

demic dean at Dillard. In the first two decades of his academic career he was closely associated with the Julius Rosenwald Fund and its president, Edwin Embree. In part because of this relationship, he was chosen as president of Fort Valley (Georgia) State College in 1939. He served in that position until 1945, when he became president of his alma mater, Lincoln University. Bond remained as president of Lincoln until 1957, when he resigned amid controversy over a plan to increase the number of white students at the institution; his relations with older, white faculty, many of whom had taught him as an undergraduate and had difficulty seeing their former student as their superior; and his frequent trips away from campus. He then moved to Atlanta University, where he served as dean of the School of Education for five years and then as director of its Bureau of Educational and Social Research. He retired in 1971 and died in Atlanta one year later.

Bond was the author of six books and numerous articles. In the 1920s he published articles critical of the racial bias in tests assessing intelligence quotient (IQ). His two most enduring books were published in the 1930s, *The Education of the Negro in the American*

Social Order (1934), a study of the inferior conditions in black schools and colleges, and *Negro Education in Alabama: A Study in Cotton and Steel* (1939), an economic interpretation of educational conditions for blacks in Alabama. His articles from the 1930s until the end of his life were published in both academic and popular journals, and he made numerous speeches to black church and civic groups in his later years. His scholarly output was a lifelong concern for Bond, but it diminished in the 1940s and 1950s as he took on the duties of a college president. Bond worked as a historian for the National Association for the Advancement of Colored People as it prepared a legal brief answering historical questions asked by the U.S. Supreme Court in deliberating the famous *Brown v. Board of Education* (1954) school desegregation case.

Bond became particularly interested in Africa and Africans in the late 1940s, and he took nearly twenty trips to that continent in the 1940s and 1950s. He was a founder of the American Society for African Culture and was active in numerous groups that advocated cooperation between Africans and African Americans. He developed the Institute for African Studies at Lincoln University and made sure that African students were welcome at Lincoln and were supported financially whenever possible. In this regard he built on a long-standing commitment of Lincoln to Africa and Africans. Bond was especially interested in Liberia, Nigeria, and Ghana. During Bond's university presidency, the Gold Coast (later called Ghana) political leader and Lincoln alumnus Kwame Nkrumah was awarded an honorary doctorate from Lincoln.

During his career Bond carefully balanced concern for personal survival and professional advancement with a pursuit of social and political activism on behalf of his race that often risked reprisals. He was a representative of the middle generation of African American intellectuals that followed the generation of W. E. B. Du Bois and Booker T. Washington of the early twentieth century and preceded the civil rights activists of the 1960s. He was one of the first of his race to be recognized for his professional academic accomplishments and also was one of the first to head an institution of higher learning.

Further Reading

Bond's papers are in the Archives and Manuscripts Division, University of Massachusetts (Amherst) Library.

Urban, Wayne J. *Black Scholar: Horace Mann Bond, 1904–1972* (1992).

Urban, Wayne J. "The Black Scholar and Intelligence Testing: The Case of Horace Mann Bond," *Journal of the History of the Behavioral Sciences* 25 (1989): 323–334.

Urban, Wayne J. "Philanthropy and the Black Scholar: The Case of Horace Mann Bond," *Journal of Negro Education* 58 (1989): 478–493.

Williams, Roger. *The Bonds: An American Family* (1971).

Wayne J. Urban

BOND, John Robert (May 1846–Jun. 1905), sailor, Civil War veteran, and laborer, was born in Liverpool, England, to James Bond, a carter in that city's dockland, and Eliza Kelly. As one of the British Empire's major port cities, Liverpool was home to many migrants. James Bond was of African descent, though it is unclear how long he and his family had lived in England. Kelly was an immigrant from Ireland, probably of the Roman Catholic faith, but the child was baptized as an Anglican, the established state church in England, which was perhaps also James Bond's faith.

Though we know few details of his early life, it is probable that Bond witnessed discrimination and violence against both black and Irish immigrants. Shortly after Bond's birth the family moved to the Toxteth section of Liverpool, then as now the city's most ethnically diverse and desperately poor neighborhood. It is not known whether he attended school, but he was unable to read and write. Like most of his contemporaries in Toxteth, the teenaged Bond had few economic opportunities other than to find a job at sea or on the docks like his father had done. By 1862 those opportunities appear to have narrowed even further, in part because of the U.S. Navy's blockade of cotton grown in the Confederate States of America. That year, with work hard to find on the Liverpool docks and in the nearby Lancashire cotton mills, sixteen-year-old John Bond signed on as an apprentice seaman on the *Pactolus*, a steamer engaged in the salt codfish trade. Probably during his voyage across the Atlantic, Bond lost his right index finger and part of his right middle finger, though it is uncertain as to whether this was the result of a shipboard accident or as punishment.

The *Pactolus* arrived in New Bedford, Massachusetts, then the world's busiest whaling center, in September 1862. Bond remained there for nine months, most likely working as a dockland laborer, before enlisting for one year in the U.S. Navy. Britain was neutral in the American Civil War, but Bond, though born in Britain, could not be. Although he had just arrived in the United States, Bond family folklore has it that Bond joined the Union forces to further the abolitionist cause of black folk in his new home. Claiming that he was twenty-two years of age, he served on the *Ohio*, an elderly vessel that had earlier been used to suppress the illegal international slave trade. The vessel had an interracial, international, and nonsegregated crew. As on other U.S. Navy ships, blacks and whites of the same rank received the same pay. Bond and his fellow black sailors—none of whom were officers—nonetheless faced racist treatment and attacks on board ship.

In July 1863 Bond disembarked at Boston Harbor and transferred from the *Ohio* to the *Cambridge*, a much faster, recently built gunboat famed for its exploits in capturing Confederate blockade runners. The *Cambridge* patrolled the coast of New England and traveled as far south as the North Carolina port of Beaufort, which was then in Union hands. Much of Bond's early service, however, was spent in port.

Given the high rates of disease and violence among the bored and restless seamen while in port, the ship's enforced stay in the Union-controlled port of Portsmouth, Virginia, was almost as dangerous for the crew as were its infrequent cruises along the Atlantic coast.

In January 1864 the *Cambridge* set out to patrol the waters off Wilmington, North Carolina, the Confederacy's best-protected Atlantic port. In February of that year John Bond was part of a small detachment of sailors sent by the *Cambridge*'s captain, William Spicer, to investigate Confederate blockade runners who had run aground near barrier islands off the Wilmington coast. The occupants of two U.S. Navy dinghies sent from the *Cambridge*, which included Bond, were fired on by Confederate snipers hidden behind sand dunes on one of the barrier islands. As the Union sailors scrambled to return to the safety of the *Cambridge*, one of the snipers fired a rifle ball at Bond. The ball hit the young sailor in his right chest and shoulder, narrowly missing his heart and other vital organs, but smashing his shoulder blade and piercing one of his lungs. Bond bled heavily. None of the men on the USS *Cambridge*, including Bond, were rewarded with medals for their actions on that day.

For John Bond, as for most other soldiers and sailors wounded in the Civil War, the period immediately following his injury proved crucial. Only one-third of those who suffered similar wounds survived; most died as a result of infection, which was often caused by the incompetence of military surgeons and extremely poor hygiene in battle conditions. Perhaps because he was young and healthy, Bond was one of the more fortunate casualties, even though he remained on board the *Cambridge* in the chilly and choppy February waters of the North Atlantic. The ship's physician had few medicines other than whiskey, but that, and vigorous cleansing of Bond's wounds, proved enough to save him. After ten days aboard the *Cambridge*, Bond was taken to Hammond Hospital, a Union-run facility in Beaufort, North Carolina, where many of the patients suffered from highly contagious diseases like typhoid and smallpox. Bond survived, however, and left Hammond Hospital in May 1864, embarking on a perilous coastal journey past the barrier islands of Cape Hatteras and into the Great Dismal Swamp Canal, stopping finally at Portsmouth, Virginia, where he was admitted to the Union hospital. Bond's injuries were such that his right arm no longer functioned properly, but again he survived the poorly sanitized, under-equipped, and overcrowded conditions.

Bond's recuperation was undoubtedly aided by the help of a local woman, Emma Thomas, who was born into slavery near the James River in Isle of Wight, Virginia, in 1846, the same year as Bond's birth. In 1863 Thomas had joined the vast exodus of Virginia slaves who had sought freedom in Union-controlled cities, first in Norfolk, and then in Portsmouth, where she brought fruit to recovering Union troops and met John Bond. Thomas contin-

ued to look after Bond in Norfolk following his honorable discharge in June 1864, and the couple began courting. They married on 21 June 1865 at Norfolk's Bute Street Baptist Church, where Emma Thomas was a member. The Bonds had four children. John Percy, known as Percy, was born in 1868, and John Robert, known as Bob, eight years later. Daughters Lena Emma and Mary Ellen, known as Tooty, were born in 1879 and 1887, respectively. Another child survived only two days.

Finding himself again in a seaport, John Bond probably found work in the docks at Portsmouth or Norfolk. Although he also received a Union pension of eight dollars per month, Bond's job prospects were limited by his war wounds and by the narrowing opportunities for blacks in Virginia after 1870. That year the Bonds left Virginia for Worcester, Massachusetts, where John found a job, working a six-day, sixty-hour week as a fireman in the boiler room of the Bay State House, one of the state's finest and most fashionable hotels. There was little fine or fashionable about the Bonds's cramped quarters, a couple of miles away in the working-class southern section of Worcester. Bond's job required him to spend many nights away from his family, which settled rather uneasily in a town with relatively few black people. Bond never converted to his wife's Baptist faith and remained an Anglican, attending both the well-heeled All Saints Episcopal Church and St. Matthews Episcopal Church, whose congregants included many recent working-class English immigrants to Worcester but numbered few blacks.

Following the 1873 depression, the family moved to Hyde Park, Massachusetts, a community nine miles south of Boston that, unlike Worcester, but like John's native Liverpool and Emma's Norfolk, was close to the sea. During the Civil War, Hyde Park had also been home to the famed colored infantry regiments, the Fifty-fourth and Fifty-fifth Massachusetts. A sizeable number of black Civil War veterans also made Hyde Park a more congenial home to John Bond than had Worcester. Bond befriended several neighbors who had served in black regiments, and he became active in the Grand Army of the Republic (GAR), the leading Union veterans' organization. Although the GAR was an interracial body dominated by whites, it flourished in Massachusetts in part because of the leadership of black veterans like Amos Webber of Worcester and JAMES TROTTER of Hyde Park. By 1880, probably with the assistance of the GAR, Bond found work as a janitor at the Damon Grammar School, a short distance from his home in Hyde Park. Combined with John's increased Navy pension, the Bonds gradually moved from poverty to a relatively comfortable working-class existence by the 1890s. John Bond had also learned to read and write by the time he began working as a janitor, again, perhaps through the efforts of the GAR.

By 1884, at any rate, Bond had acquired sufficient writing skills to apply for American citizenship. Once granted he began to pay the state's two-dollar-a-year poll tax and was eligible to vote and serve on local juries. He later found work as Hyde Park's town constable, responsible for lighting and dousing streetlamps, and again as a janitor. Throughout the 1890s Bond was active in the local and statewide activities of the GAR, as well as an all-black group, the Massachusetts Colored Veterans Assembly. Bond was also active in the Oddfellows and Prince Hall Masons and in the Episcopal church. In June 1905 he died of rectal cancer at his Hyde Park home. Although Bond had been a faithful congregant at the smaller and more humble Episcopal Church of the Good Shepherd in Dedham, his funeral was held at Hyde Park's more prestigious Episcopal Christ Church, so as to accommodate the many mourners and the honor guard of Bond's fellow veterans and Masons.

Further Reading
Alexander, Adele Logan. *Homelands and Waterways: The American Journey of the Bond Family, 1846–1926* (1999).

STEVEN J. NIVEN

BOND, Julian (14 Jan. 1940–), activist and politician, was born Horace Julian Bond in Nashville, Tennessee, the second of three children of Julia Washington, a librarian, and HORACE MANN BOND. He grew up in the relatively insulated environment of the black college campus, a crossroads for leading black intellectuals and artists during the segregation era. Horace Mann Bond, a prominent scholar and educator, was president of Fort Valley State College in Georgia at the time of Julian's birth. In 1945 he became the first African American president of Lincoln University, outside of Philadelphia. When Julian was a child, his father and W. E. B. DU BOIS had a mock ceremony dedicating him to a life of scholarship. His life took a different course, but reflected the influence of both men.

In 1957 Horace Mann Bond became dean of the Atlanta University School of Education, and the family moved to Georgia. Bond's first real introduction to life under segregation in the Deep South coincided with the courageous efforts of nine students in Little Rock to integrate Central High School, an episode that, Bond later recalled, "set a high standard of bravery and behavior" for him and his contemporaries. Bond was in his junior year at Morehouse College in Atlanta, Georgia, in February 1960 when four college students in Greensboro took seats at the lunch counter in the local Woolworth's in defiance of segregation laws, sparking a wave of similar protests across the South. Bond and his classmate Lonnie King organized students in Atlanta, and initiated their protest with a full-page ad in the city newspapers. "An Appeal for Human Rights," coauthored by Bond, put a stark spotlight on the racial segregation and discrimination that confined black lives and opportunities. It was followed by a campaign of direct action targeting segregation in public places. Bond was among the protesters arrested. In April he attended a meeting with fellow student activists in Raleigh, North Car-

Julian Bond, testifying at a legislative hearing before a Special Committee in Atlanta, Georgia, 10 January 1966. (AP Images.)

olina, and founded the Student Nonviolent Coordinating Committee (SNCC).

In the spring of 1961 Bond dropped out of Morehouse College, became communications director for SNCC, and married Alice Clopton, a student at Spelman College in Atlanta. Operating out of a sparse office on Auburn Avenue, Bond had a WATS line that provided continuous telephone contact with SNCC field workers across the South, often as events unfolded. Short but frequent visits to areas of SNCC activity also exposed him to the texture and range of movement activism. He churned out press releases documenting the battles being waged in cities and rural areas, which black newspapers around the country routinely printed. The reach of Bond's network, along with his talent as a writer and his cool yet engaging demeanor ensured his success as the propagandist for the movement. White journalists were drawn to him as a source. He also edited the *Student Voice*, SNCC's newspaper, and was a founder and managing editor of the *Atlanta Inquirer*, established in 1961 as an alternative to the conservative black publication *Atlanta Daily World*. In 1964 Bond took his first trip to Africa. Bond, along with fellow SNCC activists John Lewis and ROBERT P. MOSES, went as guests of the entertainer HARRY BELAFONTE. It was an extraordinary personal experience. Treated like visiting dignitaries in Guinea, they gained an appreciation of the broader significance of the civil rights movement in the American South.

The Civil Rights Acts of 1964 and 1965 dismantled state-mandated segregation and provided for federal enforcement of voting rights, removing the underpinnings of the South's caste system. In the aftermath of these legislative victories, Bond concentrated his efforts on expanding black political participation through voter registration, electing black candidates to office, and securing black representation in the state's Democratic Party. He ran a grassroots campaign for the Georgia House of Representatives from a poor district in Atlanta, winning with what was proportionately the highest voter turnout in the state. Five other black men and one black woman were also elected to the Georgia state legislature in November 1965, becoming the first blacks to serve in that body since 1907. Georgia's House of Representatives, however, refused to seat Bond because of his public opposition to the Vietnam War, as expressed in an SNCC policy statement. After a yearlong legal fight, a unanimous decision by the U.S. Supreme Court upheld Bond's right to free speech and compelled the Georgia House to seat him. Bond went on to serve in the Georgia legislature for the next twenty years, with four terms in the House and six in the Georgia Senate.

In 1968 Bond cochaired the Georgia Loyal National delegation to the Democratic convention in Chicago. His group challenged the regular delegation for virtually excluding black participation in the selection of delegates, in violation of rules set by the Democratic Party in the aftermath of the 1964 challenge by the Mississippi Freedom Democratic Party. They succeeded in securing half of the seats assigned to the Georgia delegation, causing most of the regular delegates to walk out. In a convention where Mayor William Daley came to rival the worst southern demagogues and police battled protesters in the streets, Julian Bond captured the hopes of many. He was, noted one observer, "the most charismatic figure at the convention" and a symbol of the civil rights movement. Shouts of "We want Julian" erupted from the floor of the convention as his name was placed in nomination for vice president, the first time either major party had nominated an African American. Bond requested that his name be withdrawn since, at age twenty-eight, he was seven years shy of the legal age. Chicago secured Bond's standing as one of the best-known figures of the civil rights movement. In constant demand as a speaker, particularly on college campuses, he traveled around the country, addressing the persistent problems of racial inequality and economic injustice. He promoted the enduring lesson of the movement; that it was individuals working steadily in their communities who changed the South and the nation.

Bond's own efforts remained anchored in Georgia and in the South at large. During the 1970s, while John Lewis was head of the Voter Education Project, the two men took weeklong tours to towns and rural areas around the region, promoting voter registration. Bond authored a pamphlet highlighting the campaign experiences of black elected officials for the Southern Regional Council, which served as a "how to" guide on running for local office. He cofounded the Southern Election Fund to raise and distribute money to rural black candidates. Bond considered running in the presidential primaries in 1976 as a way to get more black delegates elected to the Democratic convention. In 1978 Bond was elected president of the Atlanta branch of the National Association for the Advancement of Colored People and served in that post for more than a decade. In 1986 he resigned from the Georgia Senate to run for Congress from Atlanta. In a four-way race, he won with 47 percent of the vote and faced his longtime friend John Lewis in a runoff. Bond carried the majority of black voters in the hotly contested race, but white precincts gave Lewis the edge, and he won the election. That year Bond and his wife Alice separated; they divorced three years later. In 1990 Bond moved to Washington, D.C., and married Pamela Horowitz.

Through lectures, radio and television commentary, and occasional essays, Bond maintained a high profile as a serious and cogent commentator on issues of race and their impact on society. From 1980 to 1997 he was host of the syndicated television program *America's Black Forum*. Sometimes referred to as the "voice" of the civil rights movement, he served as narrator for countless documentaries, most notably the public television series *Eyes on the Prize*, which aired in 1987 and 1990 and became the standard film-documentary history of the civil rights movement. Well known for his sense of humor, Bond turned up as guest host on *Saturday Night Live* in the late seventies.

As he neared fifty, Bond took a path that his father and W. E. B. Du Bois had imagined for him decades earlier. After a series of visiting appointments at several colleges, including Harvard University and the University of Pennsylvania, he secured permanent positions on the faculties of the University of Virginia and American University, teaching courses on a variety of topics concerning the civil rights movement, black politics, and the African American experience. In 1998 he was elected chairman of the national board of the NAACP, the organization founded by Du Bois nearly a century earlier. In a telephone interview on 22 May 2007. Bond commented, "After the 1960s, the NAACP was the only soldier standing" in terms of civil rights organizations. He attributed this in part to its grassroots apparatus, and the continuing relevance of its mission to fight racial discrimination and advance social justice. The position provided Bond with a national platform for raising issues, holding political leaders of both major parties to account, and supporting the efforts of people around the country in the ongoing struggle to realize the promise of the civil rights movement.

Further Reading

Neary, John. *Julian Bond: Black Rebel* (1971).

Tuck, Stephen. *Beyond Atlanta: The Struggle for Racial Equality in Georgia, 1940–1980* (2001).

Williams, Roger M. *The Bonds: An American Family* (1971).

PATRICIA SULLIVAN

BOND, Scott (1852–?), farmer and entrepreneur, was born near Canton, Mississippi, the only child of Wesley Rutledge and Anne Maben. Rutledge was the nephew of William H. Goodlow, the owner of the estate where Anne Maben was a house slave. Wesley worked as the manager of the house for his aunt and uncle. At birth Bond was given the surname Winfield, and at the age of eighteen months he was sent with his mother to Collierville, Tennessee, where they lived until he was five years old. Subsequently, they were sent to work on the Bond farm in Cross County, Arkansas. In Arkansas Anne Maben met and married William Bond, who gave Scott Bond his surname.

The family remained on the Bond farm until the conclusion of the Civil War, when, only months after gaining her freedom, Anne Maben died, leaving Bond in the care of his stepfather. Bond, his stepfather, and half brothers remained as sharecroppers on the Bond farm until 1872 when they moved to Madison, Arkansas, where William Bond purchased a small farm. Scott Bond remained there with his family, working as a sharecropper until 1874. In 1875 he moved eighteen miles away to become an independent sharecropper on the Allen farm, which he selected for its particularly fertile soil.

In his first year at the Allen farm, he rented twelve acres. Bond cultivated this land by himself and was able to make a small profit; this profit enabled him to rent thirty-five acres and hire a farmhand in 1876. After a second successful year the widow Allen insisted that Bond rent and cultivate the entire 2,200-acre farm. The farm was in a state of disrepair and heavily populated by squatters. Mrs. Allen recognized this and, trusting Bond, decided to do everything possible to get the entire farm under his control. She loaned him money to buy seeds and tools and allowed Bond to pay his rent after the harvest season. Bond secured the farm, rid it of squatters, and built a fence around the entire 2,200 acres. At the end of his first year Bond had made a profit of $2,500.

In addition to his farming success, Scott Bond met and married Maggie Nash of Forrest City, Arkansas, in 1877, with whom he had eleven children, all boys. When his seventh child was born, Bond decided that, after living on the Allen farm for eleven years, it was time to buy his own farm and work for himself. Bond bought a 320-acre farm in Madison, Arkansas, for two dollars an acre and moved back to Madison, where he farmed successfully for two years. In contrast, the Allen farm saw two crop failures and was inundated with silt from repeated flooding; some thought the farm ruined. Remembering Bond's success and having collected no rent for two years, Mrs. Allen decided to offer the Allen farm for sale to Bond.

Bond purchased the farm with his partner T. O. Fitzpatrick, a prominent white businessman, for five thousand dollars. Bond continued to improve his own farm in Madison while renting out his interest in the Allen farm to Fitzpatrick. After five years Bond sold his share of the farm to Fitzpatrick. In the same year that he had bought the Allen farm, Bond had also purchased the Madison Mercantile Company, with which he established a profitable retail business, selling supplies to area farms.

Bond took the money from the sale of the Allen farm and bought seven farms that adjoined his Madison property. These farms became available when a group of about three hundred African Americans from the Madison area joined the back-to-Africa movement and left the country. While the fate of most of these emigrants remains unknown, several eventually returned to Madison destitute but determined to recapture their past prosperity. One such man was Taylor Swift, whom Scott Bond helped to reestablish by giving him a mule and land to rent at a reduced rate. By 1893 Scott Bond owned approximately twelve hundred acres of farmland, much of which bordered the Rock Island Railroad, making it easy for him to ship goods to and from his farms. In the years that followed, Bond not only employed laborers to expand the amount of land he cultivated, he also diversified his business ventures. The most profitable of these new ventures were ginning cotton and selling gravel.

Before building his first cotton gin, Bond approached Ed Berry of Madison, who already owned a small gin. Bond offered to buy out a half interest in Berry's gin if they could agree to put it out of service and build a modern, steam-powered one as partners. Berry refused to partner with Bond and vowed to do everything in his power to prevent him from being able to build a gin. Bond decided that he would simply build the gin himself. He contacted three companies that sold steam powered gins and arranged for their agents to have a joint meeting to discuss price. Bond played each company against the others, so he was able to purchase a gin from the Continental Gin Company at a steep discount. Ed Berry did not stand in the way of Bond buying or building the gin machinery and structure, but he did seek an injunction to prevent Bond from building a railroad platform to load his cotton. Bond anticipated this and had the contractor lay out all the materials for the 150-foot platform so that it could be assembled in two hours. In this way the platform was built before Berry could have Bond served with injunction papers from the court. Once built, the gin was a huge success, pumping money into all aspects of the local economy and allowing local farmers to see an increase in their profits.

Seeing how this cotton gin had invigorated and improved the lives of the African American farmers in Madison, Bond decided to build a gin in another town. He picked Edmondson, Arkansas, an African American town that had only two non-steam-powered cotton gins. On arriving in the town, he addressed a town meeting with his business proposition. He let the residents vote on whether they should become stockholders or whether Bond should undertake this venture himself. The town voted to let Bond be the sole owner of the gin. Bond's second gin ran so successfully that after two years the Richmond Cotton Oil Company approached him about leasing its gin in

Widener, Arkansas. Bond accepted this lease and subsequently operated three gins at peak capacity.

The second major venture that Bond undertook was to set up business selling gravel to the local railroad. Bond was given the idea for this venture when he was approached by a Memphis businessman about purchasing gravel from his land. Bond was interested and agreed to sign a contract for two dollars per carload. Unfortunately, when the man from Memphis found out that there would be a five-dollar-per-car charge to use the railroad bridge to get to Memphis, his interest was withdrawn. However, the Rock Island Railroad, whose tracks ran near the bed, was expanding, and the railroad owners expressed an interest in obtaining the gravel. Unfortunately for Bond, he was only able to obtain a price of fifty cents per car. He agreed but retained the right to cancel the contract at any time. Using the possible cancellation of the contract as leverage, he was eventually able to raise the price per car to ninety cents. In addition, he renegotiated with the railroad for a twenty-thousand-dollar contract paid in advance, which allowed him to build a steam-powered excavator and loader that would load a rail car in seven minutes.

Word of Scott Bond's success reached BOOKER T. WASHINGTON, who requested that Bond speak at the Tuskegee Institute about farming. Bond accepted this invitation. The next year, 1911, Washington requested that Bond speak to the National Negro Business League. Bond agreed, and in return Washington spoke in Madison the same year.

Bond's success was a result of his agricultural skill, which allowed him to form the capital necessary to take on additional business ventures. His skill was formally recognized in 1917 when he was awarded a Tuskegee Institute certificate for his agricultural knowledge. Bond began his life as a slave, became free after the Civil War, and through hard work and sound investments was able to preside over property that was valued at $250,000 when he died in 1933. At their height his farms totaled more than twelve hundred acres and employed around eight hundred people who also lived on the land.

Further Reading
Rudd, Dan A., and Theo Bond. *From Slavery to Wealth, the Life of Scott Bond: The Rewards of Honesty, Industry, Economy, and Perseverance* (1917).

JACOB ANDREW FREEDMAN

BONDS, Barry Lamar (24 July 1964–), baseball player, was born in Riverside, California, the first of four children born to Patricia and Bobby Bonds, a baseball player. In 1968 Bobby Bonds was called up to join the San Francisco Giants. The Bonds family moved to the San Francisco Bay Area city of San Carlos. By the time Bonds was five, he was spending his leisure time in the Giants' Candlestick Park locker room with some of the greatest baseball players of the time, among them WILLIE MAYS, who adopted him as his godson.

Though an outstanding hitter and base stealer, Bobby Bonds was traded frequently in his career, and had a tense relationship with the press. Young Bonds was deeply affected by his father's treatment at the hands of apparently unsympathetic sports reporters, something that would greatly shape his own relationship with reporters in years to come. Although his father played for teams around the country, Bonds's family stayed in San Mateo, California. Perhaps owing to his father's long periods away from home, Bonds later recalled being much closer to his mother than to his father as a child.

Bonds excelled in athletics while growing up and eventually starred in football, basketball, and baseball at Junipero Serra High School in San Mateo. As a baseball player he showed considerable talent and was drafted out of high school by the San Francisco Giants in 1982 but decided instead to accept a baseball scholarship to Arizona State University, where he helped lead the Sun Devils to the College World Series in 1983 and 1984.

After Bonds's junior season at Arizona State, he elected to enter the baseball draft once more. This time he was picked by the Pittsburgh Pirates in 1985. He signed with the Pirates shortly thereafter and was sent to the team's single-A franchise in Prince William of the Carolina League in 1985 and later to its AAA franchise in Hawaii in 1986.

Barry Bonds, hitting his 73rd home run of the season against the Los Angeles Dodgers at Pacific Bell Park in San Francisco, 7 October 2001. In 2007 Bonds overtook Hank Aaron as the all-time career leader in home runs. (AP Images.)

Bonds played less than two months in Hawaii before being called up to play for the Pirates. Pittsburgh had been struggling and hoped to rebuild the team around a talented group of rookies, at the center of which was Bonds. His career in Pittsburgh began slowly. Manager Jim Leyland decided to take advantage of Bonds's speed and assign him to the position of leadoff hitter, but Bonds had difficulty fitting into this role and it was not until 1988 that he was able to finish a season with a batting average over .280. That same year Bonds married his first wife, Susann "Sun" Branco, in Montreal. They would eventually have two children, son Nikolai and daughter Shikari.

The 1990 season was Bonds's first big year. Hitting .311 with thirty-four home runs and 103 runs batted in, he led the Pirates to the play-offs and won the first of six National League Most Valuable Player awards. Yet during the play-offs that year Bonds performed poorly. Sportswriters started to tag him as a player who folded in clutch situations. Bonds also became the target of media scorn the following February when he became involved in a public shouting match with Leyland during spring training. Leyland had grown impatient when Bonds acted irritably toward the press and the coaching staff. Although Bonds greatly admired Leyland, the incident was one of the first to establish a public image of Bonds as a player with a petulant attitude.

During the 1991 and 1992 seasons Bonds led the Pirates to consecutive play-off appearances, and each time his team came up just short of victory. In 1993 his contract with Pittsburgh expired, and Bonds entered the free agent market, signing with the San Francisco Giants under the management of longtime family friend Dusty Baker. Although he enjoyed a spectacular first year with San Francisco, Bonds became a symbol of arrogance for many fans. Often short tempered with reporters, Bonds came to be portrayed by many writers as a symbol of what many fans and critics perceived as the widespread greed and insensitivity of Major League Baseball players. In 1994 Bonds separated from his wife, Sun. Earlier in the year, she had called the Atherton, California, police to their home and had told authorities that Bonds had thrown her against a car, grabbed her around the neck, and thrown her partway down a set of stairs. Charges were later dropped owing to lack of evidence and the unwillingness of Sun Bonds to cooperate. The incident received widespread media attention over the next year. In 1998 Bonds married Liz Watson and together they had a daughter, Aisha Lynn. Two years later Bonds helped lead his team to the play-offs, and in 2001 he exploded for seventy-three home runs, breaking a single season record set by Mark McGwire of the St. Louis Cardinals only three years earlier. In 2002 Bonds shed his reputation as a poor postseason performer, leading his team to game seven of the World Series. The Giants lost the series to the California Angels four games to three, but Bonds was the team's top performer, batting .471 and hit-

ting four home runs. At the beginning of the 2004 season Bonds hit his 661st home run, passing his godfather Willie Mays. On 28 May 2006 Bonds hit his 715th career home run, moving him ahead of Babe Ruth and placing him second only to HANK AARON, who hit 755 home runs while playing in the major leagues.

In 2004 four people affiliated with a drug lab called the Bay Area Laboratory Co-operative, or BALCO, were indicted for illegally producing and distributing steroids and human growth hormones. The indicted included Bonds's longtime friend and personal trainer Greg Anderson, along with BALCO founder Victor Conte Jr., vice president James J. Valente, and the track coach Remi Korchemny. Leaked grand jury testimony revealed that Bonds had used rubs that contained steroids. He said that he did not know that these items were illegal performance-enhancing drugs. Nevertheless, he yet again became a symbol in the game, this time of an era in baseball marked by widespread steroid use and doping scandals.

When, on 7 August 2007, in the fifth inning of a home game against the Washington Nationals, Bonds hit his record-breaking 756th home run, Bonds's alleged involvement with steroids served for many fans and baseball pundits to taint that record. At a press conference following the game, however, Bonds was adamant. "This record is not tainted at all, at all. Period," he told journalists (Jack Curry, "Bonds Hits No. 756 to Break Aaron's Record," *New York Times,* 8 Aug. 2007). In a pre-recorded video broadcast, Hank Aaron congratulated the new home run leader for his "skill, longevity, and determination." However, not even Aaron's blessing could silence Bonds's critics or put the steroid issue to rest, and on 15 November 2007 a federal grand jury indicted Bonds on four counts of perjury and one count of obstruction of justice.

Further Reading

Bloom, John. *Barry Bonds: A Biography* (2004).
Fainaru-Wada, Marc, and Lance Williams. *Game of Shadows: Barry Bonds, BALCO, and the Steroids Scandal That Rocked Professional Sports* (2006).
Grann, David. "Baseball Without Metaphor," *New York Times Magazine,* 1 Sep. 2002.
Pearlman, Jeff. *Love Me, Hate Me: Barry Bonds and the Making of an Antihero* (2006).
Suchon, Josh. *This Gracious Season: Barry Bonds and the Greatest Year in Baseball* (2002).

JOHN BLOOM

BONDS, Margaret Jeannette Allison (3 Mar. 1913–26 Apr. 1972), composer, pianist, and teacher, was born in Chicago, Illinois, the daughter of Dr. MONROE ALPHEUS MAJORS, a pioneering black physician, medical researcher, and author, and Estelle C. Bonds, a music teacher and organist. Although legally born Majors, she used her mother's maiden name (Bonds) in her youth and throughout her professional life. She grew up in intellectually stimulating surroundings; her mother held Sunday afternoon salons at which young black Chicago musicians, writers, and

Margaret Bonds, a composer and pianist who fused European musical Romanticism with the varied strands of her African American heritage to form a distinctive musical corpus, October 1956. (Library of Congress/Carl Van Vechten.)

artists gathered and where visiting musicians and artists were always welcomed.

Bonds first displayed musical talent in her piano composition "Marquette Street Blues," written at the age of five. She then began studying piano with local teachers, and by the time she was in high school she was taking lessons in piano and composition with FLORENCE B. PRICE and WILLIAM LEVI DAWSON, two of the first black American symphonic composers, both of whom were professionally active in Chicago. Bonds later remarked that through her mother's circle she had "actual contact with all the living composers of African descent." As a young girl she served as the pianist at the Berean Baptist Church, where her mother was organist. One of several black Chicago churches that fostered performances of classical music, Berean Baptist was the home of a black community orchestra led by Harrison Farrell.

When Bonds was a teenager, the singer Abbie Mitchell introduced her to the European art song and to songs by American black composers, especially those of HENRY T. BURLEIGH. At about the same time Bonds ran across the first published poem of LANGSTON HUGHES, "The Negro Speaks of Rivers,"

which made a great impact on her and which she later set to music. Bonds set many of Hughes's texts and also collaborated with him in theater works, such as *Shakespeare in Harlem* (1959).

Bonds studied with Emily Boettscher Bogue at Northwestern University, where she received bachelor of music and master of music degrees (1933, 1934). While still a student, she received the Wanamaker Foundation Prize for her song "Sea Ghost" (1932). In 1933 she became the first black American soloist to perform with the Chicago Symphony, playing John Alden Carpenter's *Concertino*. Bonds was also the soloist in a performance of Florence Price's piano concerto at the 1933 World's Fair. During the 1930s Bonds performed frequently in the United States and Canada, and she also founded and taught at the Allied Arts Academy in Chicago, an institution devoted to the teaching of ballet and music to black children.

In 1939 Bonds moved to New York City, where she became more active as a composer and arranger and where she served as an editor in the CLARENCE WILLIAMS music publishing firm. For a time she composed pop music; her most famous hits were collaborations—with ANDY RAZAFAR for "Peachtree Street" (1939) and with Hal Dickinson for "Spring Will Be So Sad" (1940). Her popular songs were recorded by Glenn Miller, Charley Spivak, and Woody Herman. In New York she studied both piano (with Djane Herz) and composition (with Robert Starer) at the Juilliard School of Music. She also studied composition with Roy Harris. She made her Town Hall debut as a pianist in 1952. Bonds taught at the American Music Wing in New York and was music director for such theaters as the East Side Settlement House, the White Barn Theater, and the Stage of Youth. She promoted the works of black American musicians and composers by organizing a chamber music society and establishing a sight-singing program at Harlem's Mount Calvary Baptist Church. She married Lawrence Richardson in 1940, and the couple had one child. In 1968 she moved to Los Angeles, where she taught at the Inner City Institute and Repertory Theater and worked as an arranger for the Los Angeles Jubilee Singers.

John Lovell Jr., in *Black Song: The Forge and the Flame* (1972), described Bonds as one of the most significant twentieth-century arrangers of traditional spirituals, along with Burleigh and WILL MARION COOK, all of whose arrangements cultivated widespread appreciation of the repertoire. Bonds arranged spirituals throughout her career, many for solo voice and piano, and some as choral pieces; the singer LEONTYNE PRICE commissioned and recorded Bonds's arrangement of "He's Got the Whole World in His Hands." Other compositions of Bonds's, such as the piano piece *Troubled Water* (1967, also set later for cello and piano), were often strongly steeped in the spiritual idiom.

Bonds's forty-two art songs include "The Pasture" (1958) and "Stopping by the Woods on a Snowy Evening" (1963)—both set to texts of Robert

Frost—and "Three Dream Portraits" (1959) and "To a Brown Girl, Dead" (1956), perhaps her best-known songs, both settings of Langston Hughes poems. Bonds's major choral works include the *Ballad of the Brown King* (1954, to text by Hughes), which has been performed annually in many black churches, and a Mass in D Minor for chorus and orchestra or organ (1959). The *Montgomery Variations*, dedicated to MARTIN LUTHER KING JR. and composed at the time of the march on Montgomery in 1965, was her most successful orchestral piece. Bonds's last work, "Credo," for baritone, chorus, and orchestra (text by W. E. B. DU BOIS), was performed the month after her death by the Los Angeles Philharmonic, conducted by Zubin Mehta. Bonds died in Los Angeles.

Bonds was recognized during her lifetime with many commissions and awards, including a Distinguished Alumna Award from Northwestern University (1967). Although much of her music is still in manuscript, there is a renewed interest in making the music more available for performance, especially her piano music and songs. Some of Bonds's most significant works were her modern Shakespearean musical theater works (*Shakespeare in Harlem* and *Romey and Julie*), as well as other dramatic musicals and ballets, which brought her music to a broad audience. These important works were not published, however, and the manuscripts remain in the hands of the family.

Bonds's close friendship and collaboration with Langston Hughes, as well as her many settings of his poems (from "The Negro Speaks of Rivers" to the 1964 choral work "Fields of Wonder"), resulted in a significant body of work that exemplifies the close mutual interaction of poet and composer in expressing African American ethnic identity. Bonds's many programmatic works for piano and for orchestra also speak of the black experience through their use of spiritual materials, jazz harmonies and rhythms, and social themes. Her music fuses European romanticism with the varied strands of her African American heritage to form a distinctive musical corpus, although access to her most extended works has been limited since her death.

Further Reading
Bonds's papers and manuscripts are owned and held by her daughter, Djane Richardson, in New York.
Bonds, Margaret. "A Reminiscence," in *The Negro in Music and Art*, ed. Lindsay Patterson (1967).
Walker-Hill, Helen, ed. *Black Women Composers: A Century of Piano Music (1893–1990)* (1992).
Obituaries: *New York Times*, 29 Apr. 1972; *Variety*, 10 May 1972; *Jet*, 18 May 1972; *Chicago Defender*, 13 Jan. 1973.

Discography
Hitchcock, H. Wiley, and Stanley Sadie, eds. *New Grove Dictionary of American Music* (1986).
Tischler, Alice. *Fifteen Black American Composers with a Bibliography of Their Works* (1981).
                                        BARBARA G. JACKSON

BONNER, Marita Odette (16 June 1898–6 Dec. 1971), educator and author, was born in Boston, Massachusetts, the daughter of Joseph Bonner, a machinist and laborer, and Mary A. Nowell. Educated in the Brookline, Massachusetts, public schools, Bonner applied to Radcliffe College at the urging of her high school adviser and was one of the few African American students accepted for admission. She majored in English and comparative literature and founded the Radcliffe chapter of Delta Sigma Theta, a black sorority. A gifted pianist and student of musical composition, Bonner won the Radcliffe song competition in 1918 and 1922. Bonner also studied German, a language in which she became fluent. During her last year in college she taught English at a Cambridge high school. After graduating with a BA in 1922, she taught at the Bluefield Colored Institute in Bluefield, Virginia, until 1924 and at Armstrong High School in Washington, D.C., from 1924 to 1930, when she married William Almy Occomy, a Brown graduate. The couple moved to Chicago, where they raised three children.

Bonner began writing in high school, contributing pieces to the student magazine, the *Sagamore*. At Radcliffe she was selected to study writing under Charles Townsend Copeland. Copeland, who encouraged her to write fiction, advised Bonner not to be "bitter"—advice that she thought clichéd and consequently ignored. During her literary career she published short stories, essays, and plays, most of which examined the debilitating effects of economic, racial, and sexual prejudice on black Americans. Bonner's first publication, a short story called "The Hands," was published in *Opportunity* in August 1925, and her award-winning essay "On Being Young—A Woman—and Colored" was published in December of that year in *Crisis*; these two magazines continued to publish her work. In the essay, Bonner examines the triple jeopardy facing black women writers and answers Copeland when she addresses "white friends who have never had to draw breath in a Jim-Crow train. Who never had petty putrid insult[s] dragged over them."

She continues these themes in her other writings. In her 1928 essay "The Young Blood Hungers," a haunting refrain captures the anger and despair of a generation facing economic slavery and brutal racism. In her short story "Nothing New" she introduces Frye Street, a fictional neighborhood in Chicago that she describes as running "from freckled-face tow heads to yellow Orientals; from broad Italy to broad Georgia; from hooked noses to square black noses.... Like muddy water in a brook" (*Crisis*, 1926). She later returned to this neighborhood for many of her stories. Although multiethnic, black Frye Street does not have the same opportunities as white Frye Street.

While living in Washington, D.C., Bonner wrote and published several works that won awards from *Crisis*, including "Drab Rambles" (1927) and "The Young Blood Hungers" (1928). She was also an active member of the S Street literary salon of black writers established by the poet and playwright GEORGIA DOUGLAS JOHNSON. During this time Bonner wrote and published three plays: *The Pot-Maker: A Play to Be Read* (1927), *The Purple Flower* (1928), and *Exit an Illusion* (1929); the latter two also won *Crisis* awards. In her introduction to *Nine Plays by Black Women* (1986), Margaret Wilkerson calls Bonner's *The Purple Flower* a black quest for freedom and happiness in a racist society and "perhaps the most provocative play" of the first half of the twentieth century.

After her marriage and subsequent move to Chicago, Bonner took a three-year break from publishing, and when she returned she devoted herself exclusively to fiction, publishing her stories under her married name. These stories offer a vivid portrait of black Chicago and its strained interactions with other minorities and with a racist white society. Her first work was a three-part narrative titled "A Possible Triad on Black Notes," published in the July, August, and September 1933 issues of *Opportunity*. "Tin Can," a two-part narrative, won the 1933 *Opportunity* literary prize for fiction and was published in the July and August 1934 issues of that magazine. These stories and the eight that followed all show the destructiveness of the urban environment on a people suffering from economic slavery and enforced poverty. All set on Frye Street in Chicago, these stories work together, as critics have noted, much the same way that James Joyce's *Dubliners* stories work; Bonner may have intended this, as shown by the heading to her story "Corner Store": "Three Tales of Living: From 'The Black Map' (A book Entirely Unwritten)" (*Opportunity*, 1933).

Bonner's literary career ended in 1941, the year in which she and her husband joined the First Church of Christ, Scientist. Although the church tenets did not conflict with her writing, Bonner nonetheless devoted her intellectual energy to the church rather than to a literary career. After her children were all in school, Bonner resumed teaching. The Chicago Board of Education, dismissing both her Radcliffe degree and her prior teaching experience, required that she take education classes that she passed easily. She taught at Phillips High School from 1944 to 1949 and at the Dolittle School from 1950 to 1963, where she taught mentally and educationally disadvantaged students. Bonner's daughter, Joyce Occomy Stricklin, remembers her mother—a woman who approached everything she did "with every fiber of her being"—frequently spending her evenings calling students' parents to offer encouragement and advice: "She believed in her students and was convinced that lack of love and attention were the most serious handicaps they faced" (Flynn and Stricklin, ix).

Bonner died of complications after a fire in her Chicago apartment. She left behind a notebook containing six completed but unpublished stories. All her works have since been collected in one volume, *Frye Street and Environs: The Collected Works of Marita Bonner* (1987), by Joyce Flynn and Joyce Occomy Stricklin. In her introduction Flynn writes, "Bonner's works offer the perspective of an educated black female consciousness on a rapidly changing America between the world wars." Bonner was a thematic associate of JESSIE FAUST, NELLA LARSEN, and ZORA NEALE HURSTON and the literary foremother of many black writers, including RICHARD WRIGHT, ALICE WALKER, and TONI MORRISON.

Further Reading

A notebook of previously unpublished stories and Bonner's letters are in the Arthur and Elizabeth Schlesinger Library at Radcliffe College.

Flynn, Joyce, and Joyce Occomy Stricklin, eds. *Frye Street and Environs: The Collected Works of Marita Bonner* (1987).

Peterson, Bernard L., Jr. *Early Black American Playwrights and Dramatic Writers* (1990).

Roses, Lorraine Elena, and Ruth Elizabeth Randolph. "Marita Bonner: In Search of Other Mothers' Gardens," *Black American Literature Forum* 21 (Spring–Summer 1987): 165–183.

ALTHEA E. RHODES

BONTEMPS, Arna Wendell (13 Oct. 1902–4 June 1973), writer, was born in Alexandria, Louisiana, the son of Paul Bismark Bontemps, a bricklayer, and Maria Carolina Pembroke, a schoolteacher. He was reared in Los Angeles, where his family moved when he was three. He graduated from Pacific Union College in Angwin, California, in 1923.

Arna Bontemps, poet, novelist, historian, and librarian who played a major role in shaping modern African American literature, 15 August 1939. (Library of Congress/Carl Van Vechten.)

Bontemps then moved to Harlem, New York, where the Harlem Renaissance had already attracted the attention of West Coast intellectuals. He found a teaching job at the Harlem Academy in 1924 and began to publish poetry. He won the Alexander Pushkin Prize from *Opportunity*, a journal published by the National Urban League, in 1926 and 1927 and *The Crisis* (official journal of the NAACP) Poetry Prize in 1926. His career soon intersected that of the poet LANGSTON HUGHES, with whom he became a close friend and sometime collaborator. In Harlem, Bontemps also came to know COUNTÉE CULLEN, W. E. B. DU BOIS, ZORA NEALE HURSTON, JAMES WELDON JOHNSON, CLAUDE MCKAY, and JEAN TOOMER.

In 1926 Bontemps married Alberta Johnson; they had six children. In 1931, as the Depression deepened, Bontemps left the Harlem Academy and moved to Huntsville, Alabama, where he taught for three years at Oakwood Junior College. By the early 1930s Bontemps had begun to publish fiction as well as poetry. His first novel, *God Sends Sunday*, was published in 1931, and an early short story, "A Summer Tragedy," won the *Opportunity* Short Story Prize in 1932. *God Sends Sunday* is typical of the Harlem Renaissance. Little Augie, a black jockey, earns money easily and spends it recklessly. When his luck as a jockey runs out, he drifts through the black sporting world. Slight in plot, the novel is most appreciated for its poetic style, its re-creation of the black idiom, and the depth of its characterization. While most reviewers praised it, Du Bois found it "sordid" and compared it with other "decadent" books of the Harlem Renaissance, such as Carl Van Vechten's *Nigger Heaven* (1926) and McKay's *Home to Harlem* (1928). But Bontemps thought enough of the basic story to collaborate with Cullen on *St. Louis Woman* (1946), a dramatic adaptation of the book.

Bontemps's next novel would be on a much more serious theme, but he first attempted another genre. In collaboration with Hughes, he wrote *Popo and Fifina* (1932), the first of his many children's books. A travel book for children, it introduced readers to Haitian life by describing the lives of a boy named Popo and his sister Fifina. Bontemps followed his initial success in the new field with *You Can't Pet a Possum* (1934), a story of a boy and his dog in rural Alabama.

Northern Alabama in the early 1930s proved inhospitable to an African American writer and intellectual. The SCOTTSBORO BOYS were being tried in Decatur, just thirty miles from Huntsville. Friends visited Bontemps on their way to protest the trial, and the combination of his out-of-state visitors and the fact that he was ordering books by mail worried the administration of the school. Bontemps claimed in later years that he was ordered to demonstrate his break with the world of radical politics by burning a number of books from his private library—works by Johnson, Du Bois, and FREDERICK DOUGLASS. Bontemps refused. Instead, he resigned and moved back to California, where he and his family moved in with his parents.

In 1936 Bontemps published *Black Thunder*, his finest work in any genre. Based on historical research, *Black Thunder* tells the story of GABRIEL PROSSER's rebellion near Richmond, Virginia, in 1800. Prosser, an uneducated fieldworker and coachman, planned to lead a slave army equipped with makeshift weapons on a raid against the armory in Richmond. Once armed with real muskets, the rebels would defend themselves against all attackers. Betrayed by another slave and hampered by a freak storm, the rebels were crushed, and Prosser was hanged. But in Bontemps's version of the affair, whites won a Pyrrhic victory; they were forced to recognize the human potential of slaves.

Although *Black Thunder* was well reviewed by both black and mainstream journals, such as the *Saturday Review of Literature*, the royalties were not sufficient to support Bontemps's family in Chicago, where they had moved just before publication. Bontemps taught briefly in Chicago at the Shiloh Academy and then accepted a job with the WPA Illinois Writers' Project. In 1938, after publishing another children's book, *Sad-Faced Boy* (1937), he received a Rosenwald Fellowship to work on what became his last novel, *Drums at Dusk* (1939), based on the Haitian rebellion led by Toussaint-Louverture. Although the book was more widely reviewed than his previous novels, the critics were divided, some seeing it as suffering from a sensational and melodramatic plot, others praising its characterizations.

The disappointing reception of the book and the poor royalties it earned convinced Bontemps that "it was fruitless for a Negro in the United States to address serious writing to my generation, and . . . to consider the alternative of trying to reach young readers not yet hardened or grown insensitive to man's inhumanity to man" ("Introduction," x). Henceforth Bontemps addressed most of his books to youthful audiences. He wrote *The Fast Sooner Hound* (1942) in collaboration with Jack Conroy, whom he had met through the Illinois Writers' Project.

In 1943 Bontemps earned his master's degree in Library Science from the University of Chicago. The necessity of earning a living then took him to Fisk University, where he became head librarian, a post he held until 1964. Thereafter he returned to Fisk from time to time. He also accepted positions at the Chicago Circle campus of the University of Illinois and at Yale University, where he served as curator of the James Weldon Johnson Collection of Negro Arts and Letters.

During these years Bontemps produced an astonishing variety and number of books. His children's books include *Slappy Hooper* (1946) and *Sam Patch* (1951), which he wrote in collaboration with Conroy, *Lonesome Boy* (1955), and *Mr. Kelso's Lion* (1970). At the same time he wrote biographies of Douglass, GEORGE WASHINGTON CARVER, and BOOKER T. WASHINGTON for teenage readers; *Golden Slippers* (1941), an anthology of poetry for young readers; *Famous Negro Athletes* (1964); *Chariot in the Sky* (1951), the story of the Fisk Jubilee Singers; and *The Story of the Negro* (1948).

For adults Bontemps and Hughes edited *The Poetry of the Negro* (1949) and *The Book of Negro Folklore* (1958). With Conroy, Bontemps wrote *They Seek a City* (1945), a history of African American migration in the United States, which they revised and published in 1966 as *Anyplace but Here*. Bontemps's historical interests also led him to write *One Hundred Years of Negro Freedom* (1961) and to edit *Great Slave Narratives* (1969) and *The Harlem Renaissance Remembered* (1972). He also edited a popular anthology, *American Negro Poetry* (1963), just in time for the black reawakening of the 1960s.

Bontemps had been forced by the reception of his work to put his more creative writing on hold after 1939, but the 1960s encouraged him to return to it. He collected his poetry in a slim volume, *Personals* (1963), and wrote an introduction for *Black Thunder* when it was republished in 1968 in a paperback edition. At the time of his death, he was completing the collection of his short fiction in *The Old South* (1973). Bontemps died at his home in Nashville.

Bontemps excelled in no single literary genre. A noteworthy poet, he published only one volume of his verse. As a writer of fiction, he is best known for a single novel, written in midcareer and rediscovered in his old age. Yet the impact of his work as poet, novelist, historian, children's writer, editor, and librarian is far greater than the sum of its parts. He played a major role in shaping modern African American literature and had a wide-ranging influence on African American culture of the latter half of the twentieth century.

Further Reading

The major collections of Bontemps's papers are at Fisk University; the George Arents Research Library, Syracuse University; and the James Weldon Johnson Collection, Beinecke Rare Book Room and Manuscript Library, Yale University.

Bontemps, Arna. "Introduction," in *Black Thunder* (1968).

Bontemps, Arna. "Preface," in *Personals* (1963).

Bontemps, Arna. "Why I Returned," in *The Old South* (1973).

Fleming, Robert E. *James Weldon Johnson and Arna Wendell Bontemps: A Reference Guide* (1978).

Gwin, Minrose C. "Arna Bontemps," in *American Poets, 1880–1945*, ed. Peter Quartermain (1986).

Jones, Kirkland C. "Arna Bontemps," in *Afro-American Writers from the Harlem Renaissance to 1940*, ed. Trudier Harris (1987).

O'Brien, John. *Interviews with Black Writers* (1973).

ROBERT E. FLEMING

BOOKER, James Carroll, III (17 Dec. 1939–8 Nov. 1983), classical, jazz, and rhythm and blues pianist, was born in New Orleans, Louisiana, to James Carroll Booker Jr., a minister, and Ora Champagne Booker, a hairdresser. A child prodigy on the piano, Booker professed to have played the instrument as an infant. As a result of his father's ill health, his family moved to nearby Bay St. Louis, Mississippi, in the early 1940s. At the age of seven, while at a Catholic grade school, Booker took his first formal piano lessons. Following his father's death in 1953, Booker returned to New Orleans, entering high school in the fall of that year. He made an immediate impression on fellow classmates (including a young Aaron Neville), and began playing in local bands. Booker made his first appearance on a professional recording at the age of fifteen, performing on DAVE BARTHOLOMEW's 1954 "Hambone" for the Chess label.

In 1957 Booker graduated from high school and performed in clubs as a backing musician for artists such as JOE TEX, Huey Smith, and Shirley Lee. He also made regular appearances as "Little" Booker at the notorious Dew Drop Inn, where he gained notice for his lightning-fast runs across the piano keys. In 1959 he entered Southern University, which he attended for more than a year, until offers to play piano lured him onto the road as a touring musician for LITTLE RICHARD and FATS DOMINO.

In 1960 Booker recorded "Gonzo," a blistering instrumental that sold more than one hundred thousand records, establishing him as a distinctive and skillful stylist. The record's B-side, "Cool Turkey," signaled an emerging trait of Booker's music—sly drug references that eventually would dominate his work. During the late 1950s he had started using heroin, a habit he picked up from the clientele that frequented the Dew Drop Inn. While the success of "Gonzo," which reached number forty-three on the *Billboard* pop charts, garnered Booker increasing attention from other musicians, Booker remained throughout his career largely unknown to audiences outside of New Orleans.

In 1962–1963 he toured successively with LIONEL LEO HAMPTON, Little Richard, and Earl King. After his mother died in late 1965, Booker composed "Ora," a soulful elegy that became a mainstay of his repertoire. The following year his sister Betty Jean died of breast cancer. Booker left New Orleans for New York City in 1967, joining the Neville Brothers and other Crescent City transplants in the vibrant downtown Manhattan music scene. He worked as a session player on albums by ARETHA FRANKLIN and RAY CHARLES, and toured in support of saxophonist KING CURTIS. He also appeared on Fats Domino's *Fats Is Back*, which featured Booker's stellar organ and piano accompaniment.

Booker returned to New Orleans in early 1970, but he was arrested for possession of cocaine and sentenced to two years at the state penitentiary in Angola. During his incarceration he worked in the prison library, taught fellow inmates how to read, studied Eastern philosophy, began to practice yoga, and played in the prison's rhythm and blues band. He also began to exhibit early signs of psychological problems, primarily paranoid delusions, that would plague him for the rest of his life.

After serving almost a year of his sentence, Booker gained release and moved to Los Angeles, where he renewed his career as a session musician. His obscure recordings with his fellow New Orleans performer Dr. John later became legendary among aficionados, but it was his work with rock and roll stars the Doobie Brothers, Jerry Garcia of the Grateful Dead, and the former Beatle Ringo Starr that provided him with financial, if not personal, stability. During a recording session with Starr, Booker got involved in a dispute over drugs, which led to a physically violent encounter resulting in the loss of his left eye. Convinced that Starr had ordered the assault on him, Booker began wearing an eye patch emblazoned with a large blue star. Still addicted to heroin and drinking heavily, Booker returned to New Orleans in 1975 and began performing at local night spots: Rosy's, the Maple Leaf, and the Toulouse Theatre.

In late 1975, with the help of his manager John Parsons, Booker attempted to get control of his finances as well as his drug and alcohol problems. He volunteered at local halfway houses and youth centers, yet his behavior grew increasingly bizarre. His stage shows became wildly unpredictable, with moments of brilliance and clarity—in which he seamlessly blended classical music with jazz and boogie-woogie—giving way to extreme mood swings and paranoid outbursts. His career, however, continued to progress. An acclaimed performance at the 1975 New Orleans Jazz and Heritage Festival drew the interest of a German promoter who arranged for Booker to play, in 1976, his first solo European tour. Foreign audiences greeted him with enormous accolades, dubbing him the "piano prince" of New Orleans. Combining mournful ballads with freewheeling rave-ups, Booker created music in a stream-of-consciousness manner, playing any tune that occurred to him—often improvising new arrangements on the spot. A typical performance might include a medley that comprised one of his signature songs, "On the Sunny Side of the Street," followed by elements of Tchaikovsky, the Beatles, and ragtime. His virtuosity thrilled European audiences and led to the release of his first long-playing album, *Junco Partner*, released in 1976, on Island Records.

After performing in front of large, appreciative European audiences throughout the late 1970s, Booker returned to New Orleans and took a regular gig as the lobby entertainment at the Toulouse Theatre. His mental health continued to decline, and by 1980 his performances had become rife with psychological turmoil. He incorporated into songs his long-standing belief that the CIA was following him, openly criticized local drug enforcement, and failed to fulfill recording obligations. Booker also periodically checked himself into a local hospital mental ward, where he played piano for the doctors on duty.

In 1983 Booker cut his final album, *Classified*, for Rounder Records. His drug and alcohol addictions intensified, and, attempting to remove himself from the influences of nightclubs, he took a job as a file clerk for the New Orleans Department of Economic Analysis. His drug abuse continued, however, and after one year he was fired. In November of that year,

Booker died of heart failure in the waiting room of Charity Hospital in New Orleans.

James Carroll Booker's unparalleled skill at the piano drew acclaim from critics and fans around the world. Many notable New Orleans musicians—the Neville Brothers, the Marsalis family, ALLEN TOUSSAINT, and Dr. John—cited his enormous influence. Booker's dexterity and imaginative approach to his instrument made him unique, as did his ability to cross genres with ease. Largely unknown outside of jazz aficionado circles, James Carroll Booker's influence on the New Orleans piano sound nevertheless remained a timeless tribute to his artistry.

Further Reading

Berry, Jason, Tad Jones, and Jonathan Foose. *Up from the Cradle of Jazz: New Orleans Music since World War II* (1992).
Booker, James Carroll, III. *The James Booker Collection* (2000).
Johnson, Pableaux. *Legends of New Orleans* (2001).

Discography

Classified (Rounder 612036).
Gonzo: More Than All the 45's (Night Train International 7084).
Junco Partner (Hannibal 1359).
Resurrection of the Bayou Maharajah (Rounder 612118).

BRENTON E. RIFFEL

BOOKER, Joseph Albert (26 Dec. 1859–9 Sept. 1925), college president, minister, journalist, and agriculturalist, was born a slave in Portland, Arkansas, to Albert Clark Book and Mary Punsard. Booker was orphaned at three years of age; his mother died when he was one year old and his father was whipped to death two years later, having been found guilty of teaching others how to read. At the end of the Civil War Booker's grandmother sent him to a school established to educate freed slaves.

Booker excelled in school. By the time he was seventeen he had earned the right to open his own subscription school; subscription schools were established during a time before the wide availability of public schools. Parents paid a monthly fee for their children to attend these institutions. Booker saved his money from teaching in order to attend college. He attended Branch Normal School (later the University of Arkansas at Pine Bluff) in Pine Bluff, Arkansas, from 1878 to 1881.

Booker transferred to Roger Williams College in Nashville, Tennessee, and graduated in 1886. While studying at Roger Williams, Booker supported himself by washing dishes, chopping wood, and starting the fires at college. He managed to excel at mathematics and in Latin, and upon his graduation was asked to lead Arkansas Baptist College.

At the time Booker became president in 1887, Arkansas Baptist College had only fifteen students and its classes were scattered throughout various local churches. By 1902 the school had its own campus on High Street in Little Rock, Arkansas, its own farm (the Griggs Industrial Farm), and employed nine teachers.

During his thirty-two-year tenure Booker served as editor of a church newspaper, as a missionary preacher traveling through many southern states, and on local and national Baptist organizations.

On 28 June 1887 Booker married Mary Jane Caver, a teacher, of Helena, Arkansas. Together the couple had eight children. It was said that, in spite of all of his activities, Booker enjoyed spending as much time as possible with his family. One of his daughters became an accomplished musician and taught at Arkansas Baptist College. Other children entered various professions such as law and education.

Booker received his AM degree in 1889 and his doctorate from State University at Louisville, Kentucky, in 1901. In his later years he served on many state and national boards and traveled throughout the United States and Europe. Booker remained a loyal member of the Republican Party, was a member of the Negro National Life Insurance Company, the Southern Sociological Congress, Searchlight, Owl, and Lotus. Additionally, as did so many other men of his social class, he joined several fraternal orders, such as the International Order of Twelves, Knights of Pythias, Freemasons, and Mosaic Templars. Booker died on 9 September 1926, from a heart attack, while attending the National Baptist Convention in Fort Worth, Texas.

Further Reading

Bacote, Samuel William. *Who's Who among Colored Baptists of the United States*, vol. 1 (1913).

Gibson, John W., and William H. Crogman. *The Colored American from Slavery to Honorable Citizenship* (1902).

Hartshorn, William Newton. *An Era of Progress and Promise, 1863–1910* (1910).

Penn, Irvine Garland. *The Afro American Press and Its Editors* (1891).

Peques, A. W. *Our Baptist Ministers and Schools* (1892).

Pipken, J. J. *The Story of a Rising Race: The Negro in Revelation, in History, and in Citizenship* (1902).

Richardson, Clement. The *National Cyclopedia of the Colored Race* (1919).

Richings, George F. *An Album of Negro Educators* (1900).

Richings, George F. *Evidences of Progress among Colored People* (1896).

KECIA BROWN

BOOKER, Kinney Ibis (21 Mar. 1913–1 Mar. 2006), survivor of the 1921 Tulsa, Oklahoma, riot, was one of five children born to Hood Booker, a chauffeur and mechanic, and his wife. Kinney Booker graduated from the segregated Booker T. Washington High School in Tulsa and from Xavier University in New Orleans. Though he was only seven years old when the Tulsa riot broke out on the evening of 31 May 1921, his recollections of the event were central to the Tulsa Race Riot Commission's discussions in the late 1990s and early 2000s. He was quoted extensively in media sources about it, from the *New York Times* to the *Los Angeles Times* to *Nightline* to National Public Radio.

The Tulsa riot began after rumors of an impending lynching of a young African American man circulated in both white and black communities in Tulsa. When some African American veterans of World War I appeared at the Tulsa Courthouse to prevent the lynching, there was a confrontation with police officers and the riot ensued. Before it ended about noon the next day, most of the African American section of Tulsa was burned to the ground.

Booker recalled being awakened by his parents in the early morning hours of 1 June 1921 and hiding in the attic of his parents' house with his mother and sister. He heard men searching their house. Presumably they were the special deputies and members of the mob that were going house to house to arrest everyone they could in Greenwood, the African American section of Tulsa, and bring them to detention centers in the city. When the riot began, the Tulsa police department hastily deputized hundreds of men to help put down the riot. Booker also remembered bullets—perhaps fired by airplanes or, perhaps more likely, by people on neighboring Standpipe Hill—hitting the roof of their house. He recalled hearing his father beg the men not to burn the house to no avail. Booker's house, along with about thirty-five blocks of Greenwood, burned that morning. Booker, his sister, and mother escaped the house shortly after it was set on fire. In a *60 Minutes* television interview in 1999, Booker remembered that his sister asked, "Kinney, is the world on fire?" to which he replied, "I don't know, but we in trouble, deep trouble." They were taken into custody and brought to the Tulsa Convention Center (later the Brady Theater) on the edge of Greenwood.

In the aftermath of the riot Greenwood residents were released from custody only when they could present a white employer or friend to vouch for them. They were then issued green tags that had their name and their employer's name printed on them. Shortly after the riot ended the Booker family was released into the custody of a Tulsa oilman named Homer F. Wilcox, who employed Hood Booker as a chauffeur and mechanic. The Bookers lived in the Wilcox's basement for a time.

The Bookers also lived temporarily in a tent in Greenwood. Shortly after the riot ended the city passed a fire code ordinance, which required the use of fireproof material for rebuilding in the burned area. Toward the end of the summer of 1921, as it became apparent that the use of fireproof materials was prohibitively expensive, Greenwood residents won a lawsuit in the Tulsa County Court that allowed them to rebuild using whatever materials they wanted.

After graduating from Xavier University in New Orleans, Booker played in jazz bands and worked for sixteen years for the U.S. Postal Service as a railroad clerk in Oklahoma and California. For thirty years he taught music in the Los Angeles school system, before retiring to Tulsa where he was a constant presence at meetings of the Tulsa Riot Commission, established in 1997 upon the recommendation of the state representative Don Ross, who grew up in Greenwood after the riot.

As the riot commission gained increasing national attention Booker spoke frequently to the media. He was quoted in 1999 as saying that he had been angry for many years about the riot and even refused to tell his children about it. Eventually, however, Booker overcame his anger. He realized the importance of the memory of the riot as a reminder of the continuing presence of racism and as a warning to future generations. He spoke frequently in favor of reparations being paid to survivors of the riot, though he expressed doubts that it would ever happen. Nevertheless he continued to speak about the riot and, according to many people who knew him, Booker's dignified resolution and his warm personality helped to keep the issue of reparations alive and to make sure that the riot received the attention it deserved in American memory.

In 2003, after it became apparent that neither the city nor the state would pay reparations, Booker was a plaintiff in a lawsuit filed by a distinguished team of lawyers, including Harvard Law School professor Charles Ogletree and Los Angeles lawyer Johnnie Cochran, and with assistance from a distinguished group of expert witnesses, including history professor Leon Litwack of the University of California, Berkeley. The suit, *Alexander v. Oklahoma*, sought financial compensation for the actions of Tulsa and Oklahoma officials in the riot. A key part of the lawsuit was the desire to remember the riot and to get an official acknowledgment of the long-forgotten role of the Tulsa police and their special deputies in the riot, thus affirming that it was not just a white mob that destroyed Greenwood, but a mob working with and supported by the authorities. Booker told *People* magazine in 2003 that "No one has ever taken responsibility for what happened, but because of the lawsuit people are going to have to face it now."

The lawsuit was dismissed on technical grounds in 2004 by the federal district court in Tulsa, in an opinion that acknowledged the culpability and negligence of Tulsa officials. The lower court's decision was affirmed by the United States Court of Appeals, and the United States Supreme Court refused to hear the case.

Booker died in Tulsa. His sister, Dorothy Boulding, survived him, as did one daughter, Darlene Miller, of Savannah, Georgia.

Further Reading

Brophy, Alfred L. *Reconstructing the Dreamland: The Tulsa Riot of 1921—Race, Reparations, Reconciliation* (2002).

Brophy, Alfred L. "The Tulsa Race Riot Commission, Apology, and Reparation: Understanding the Functions and Limitations of a Historical Truth Commission," in *Taking Wrongs Seriously: Apology and Reconciliation*, eds. Elazar Barkan and Alexander Karn (2006).

ALFRED L. BROPHY

BOONE, Clinton Caldwell, Sr. (c. 1878–3 July 1939), minister, author, physician, dentist, and missionary, was born in Winton, North Carolina. His father, Lemuel Washington Boone (1827–1878), was a prominent minister and politician, and one of the original trustees of Shaw University.

Boone received his early education at Waters Normal and Industrial Institute in Winton. From 1896 to 1899 he attended Richmond Theological Seminary in Richmond, Virginia. In 1899, when the seminary merged with Wayland Seminary College of Meridian Hill in Washington, D.C., to form Virginia Union University and moved to its new Richmond campus at North Lombardy Street, Boone finished his senior year and became part of the university's first graduating class in 1900; he received the bachelor's of divinity degree.

During his final year at Virginia Union, Boone met Eva Roberta Coles from Charlottesville, Virginia, who studied at the neighboring African American women's institution, Hartshorn Memorial College, from which she graduated in 1899. Eva Coles taught school in Charlottesville while Boone completed his studies, and they were engaged to be married. Clinton Boone was the first missionary named by the newly established Lott Carey Baptist Mission Convention, in partnership with the Missionary Union of Boston and the American Baptist Foreign Mission Society, under the auspices of the Northern Baptist Convention. He was assigned to the station at Palaballa (sometimes called Mpalaballa) in what was then the Congo Free State, now the Republic of the Congo.

On 16 January 1901 Boone and Eva Coles were married and soon took up residence at the Palaballa mission, some three hundred miles inland from the Atlantic Ocean. Though EVA ROBERTA BOONE and CLINTON BOONE proved to be an extraordinarily committed and hardworking team, their eighteen months together at Palaballa were touched by tragedy. Their infant son died, and on 8 December 1902 Eva herself succumbed to what seems to have been the effects of a poisonous insect or snake bite. Widowed and isolated from familiar surroundings, Boone continued the work alone, often trekking through hundreds of miles of dangerous territory to baptize, officiate, and minister to the local population, until his service in the Congo came to an end in 1906.

Boone then returned to the United States to take medical courses at the Leonard Medical School of Shaw University. He earned his MD, and immediately upon graduation in 1912 he journeyed to Liberia as a qualified medical missionary. There he served for nearly a year on an interim basis as secretary to the U.S. diplomatic staff in the capital at Monrovia. In 1918 he became pastor of the oldest Baptist church in Liberia, Providence Baptist Church in Monrovia, founded by Lott Carey in 1822.

In 1919 Boone took a leave of absence and returned to the United States in order to study at the Bodee Dental School in New York City, with the purpose of fulfilling what he perceived as a dire need of his parishioners. The only dentist in Liberia had died the previous year in the great influenza epidemic. Back in Richmond, Boone met Rachel A. Tharps, who had graduated from Hartshorn Memorial College in 1911 and was teaching in the Richmond public schools. She became his second wife and in 1920 traveled with him to Liberia, where he continued his pastoral duties at Providence Baptist Church. He served on the Board of Managers of the Liberia Missionary and Educational Convention, and his wife ran the Mission School, which had an enrollment of ninety-one students. The couple had two children, both born in Monrovia. Their son, Dr. Clinton Caldwell Boone Jr., was born on 23 February 1922 and served as pastor at the Union Baptist Church in Hempstead, New York, from 1957 to 2003 and as commissioner of the Department of Occupational Resources for the town of Hempstead. Their daughter, Dr. Rachel Hannah Celestine Boone Keith, born on 30 May 1924, became a noted medical practitioner in Detroit and the wife of Judge DAMON J. KEITH of the United States Court of Appeals for the Sixth Circuit.

Returning once more to Richmond in 1926, the Boone family settled in the old Navy Hill neighborhood on the city's north side. Mrs. Boone resumed teaching, and Dr. Boone ministered to congregations in Richmond and Petersburg, and also published two autobiographical accounts of his missionary career: *Congo as I Saw It* and *Liberia as I Know It*, in 1927 and 1929, respectively. The first was dedicated to Eva, and the second was dedicated to Rachel, who died of tuberculosis in 1938.

On 3 July 1939, while swimming in the James River at the Elder Solomon Michaux's Beach near Jamestown, Virginia, Boone was pulled away by a strong tidal current and drowned. He had been a pillar of support for the missionary movement, and his two published books, with their notable tone of humanity, their meticulous descriptions of the Congo's geography, natural history, and society, and their account of Liberia's history, were instrumental in arousing increased interest in ongoing evangelizing efforts and providing a valuable primary insight into early twentieth-century Baptist missions to Africa.

Further Reading
Boone, Clinton Caldwell, Sr. *Congo as I Saw It* (1927).
Boone, Clinton Caldwell, Sr. *Liberia as I Know It* (1929).
Fisher, Miles Mark. *Virginia Union University and Some of Her Achievements* (1924).
Freeman, Edward A. *The Epoch of the Baptists and the Foreign Mission Board, National Baptist Convention, USA, Inc.* (1954).
Jacobs, Sylvia M., ed. *Black Americans and the Missionary Movement in Africa* (1982).
Whitted, J. A. *The Reformed Reader: A History of the Negro Baptists of North Carolina* (1908).

Obituaries: *Richmond Afro-American*, 8 July 1939 and 15 July 1939.

RAYMOND PIERRE HYLTON

BOONE, Eva Roberta (or Mae) Coles (8 Jan. 1880–8 Dec. 1902), teacher and missionary, was born Eva Coles in Charlottesville, Virginia. Nothing is known about her parents or her early years. She is sometimes confused with Elizabeth Coles, and her parents are often erroneously listed as John J. Coles and Lucy A. Henry Coles, who married in 1886 and went to Liberia as missionaries in 1887.

Eva Coles was one of the first young women to attend Hartshorn Memorial College in Richmond, Virginia. This institution had been established in 1883 by northern white Baptists as the world's first college for African American females (Spelman College in Atlanta did not become a college until 1924, and Bennett College in North Carolina was coeducational until 1926). Hartshorn was established by the American Baptist Home Mission Society (ABHMS) through the donation of Joseph C. Hartshorn of Rhode Island as a memorial to his late wife. The first classes at Hartshorn were held in 1883 in the basement of Ebenezer Baptist Church. Then the college moved its campus to the northwest corner of Leigh and Lombardy streets. After its relocation, Hartshorn took both day and boarding students and offered its young women a solid academic curriculum based on that of Wellesley College. A close-knit family atmosphere stressed Christian life and values and community service. In 1892 Hartshorn gave the first bachelor's degrees ever conferred at an African American female college, and Coles graduated in May of 1899.

It is likely that Coles met her future husband, CLINTON C. BOONE, in Richmond. On 11 February 1899, Coles joined others in the groundbreaking ceremony of the newly founded all-male Virginia Union University in Richmond. The ABHMS proposed a National Theological Institute to provide education and training so that recently freed black men could enter the Baptist ministry. Separate branches of the National Theological Institute were set up in Washington, D.C., and Richmond, Virginia. Classes began at both National Theological Institutes in 1867. In Washington, the school became known as Wayland Seminary, named in commemoration of Francis Wayland, former president of Brown University and a leader in the antislavery struggle. The first and only president of Wayland was George Mellen Prentiss King, who administered the school for thirty years, from 1867 to 1897. In Richmond, efforts at establishing a theological school for black men were more difficult, but classes at Colver Institute in Richmond also began in 1867. In 1899 the Richmond Theological Institute (formerly Colver Institute) joined with Wayland Seminary of Washington, D.C., to form Virginia Union University (VUU) at Richmond.

Clinton Boone completed Waters Normal Institute in Winton, North Carolina, and graduated from the theological seminary at Richmond's Virginia Union University with a BD degree on 21 May 1900. After his graduation, Clinton Boone served as a traveling agent for the Foreign Mission Board of North Carolina of the National Baptist Convention (NBC) and the LOTT CAREY Baptist Foreign Mission Convention. After graduating from Hartshorn, Eva Coles taught for a year and a half at a school (probably on an elementary level) in her hometown of Charlottesville. On 16 January 1901 Clinton Boone and Eva Coles were married.

In its early years the Lott Carey Convention (LCC) cooperated with other black Baptist boards that were engaged in foreign mission work. On 31 August 1900 the Women's Auxiliary to the LCC was founded. Surprisingly, though, considering the attitude of the founders concerning cooperation with whites, in 1900 the LCC agreed to join the white American Baptist Missionary Union to mutually support Clinton and Eva Boone. On 8 April 1901 Clinton Boone was appointed a missionary to Africa, and he and his wife sailed from New York on 13 April 1901 to the Congo Free State (later known as the Belgian Congo, as of this writing known as Democratic Republic of the Congo) under the auspices of the American Baptist Missionary Union (later known as the American Baptist Churches U.S.A.) in cooperation with the Lott Carey Baptist Foreign Mission Convention. The couple was stationed at Palabala, the oldest station in Africa for the American Baptist Missionary Union.

Eva Boone's husband preached and taught the Congolese people in their own language. Boone was stationed at Palabala for a little more than a year and a half before her death. During her first year at the station, Eva Boone took charge of the infant classes held at the day school. Through the teaching methods that she probably had learned in Charlottesville she conducted the kindergarten classes. She convinced thirty to forty young children to attend school daily, many of whom did not understand or see the value of this Western education. Boone was also one of the first missionaries in the Congo to advance the idea of a sewing school for women. Despite the fact that most African women saw sewing as men's work, she was able to enroll more than forty in a sewing class. Since missionary women also were expected to do some medical work with women and children, she was sometimes put in charge of administering medical treatment to women and children at the mission station.

Boone made many friends among the Congolese people as a result of her kind words and loving disposition. The villagers respected her and the work that she was doing. They affectionately called her Mama Bunu, a nickname that probably referred to her efforts in getting the women to sew. (For the Bunu Yoruba people of central Nigeria, cloth is a symbol of continuing social relations and identities, and the Bunu mark every critical juncture in an individual's life—from birthing ceremonies to funeral celebrations—with handwoven cloth).

Although the Boones won the respect of many Congolese, fate was unkind to them. The couple endured heartrending hardships and sorrow, which tragically included the loss of their own baby. Boone

herself then fell gravely ill from a poisonous bite from a worm or snake. The village women held a vigil around her house during her illness, but after several weeks of sickness, Boone died on the morning of 8 December 1902, one month shy of her twenty-third birthday, and she was buried at Palabala Station. Boone's contributions continue to be cherished and honored at Virginia Union University.

Further Reading
Boone, Clinton Caldwell, Sr. *Congo as I Saw It* (1927).
Freeman, Edward A. *The Epoch of Negro Baptists and the Foreign Mission Board* (1953).

SYLVIA M. JACOBS

BOONE, Sarah (fl. 1890s), inventor, lived in New Haven, Connecticut, in the early 1890s. Little is known of her early life; it is not known who her parents were or where she was born. She was, however, one of the first African American women to receive a patent from the United States Patent Office in the nineteenth century. On 26 April 1892 Sarah Boone received her patent for an improved ironing board. As a result, Boone became the fourth African American woman to apply for and receive a patent for a new invention and the first person to receive a patent for an ironing board design.

Those who have written about Boone and her improved ironing board note that her invention was a significant improvement over existing devices. According to James Brodie, before Boone's "ironing board, this task normally required taking a plank and placing it between two chairs or simply using the dining table" (Brodie, 70). Women would place clothes across the plank and press them with an iron heated on the hearth. Biographers have also noted improvements to earlier ironing technologies found in Boone's design, including a narrow part for ironing sleeves, collapsible leg supports, and a padded cover.

Boone's patent application describes a complex design intended for a specific purpose. "My invention relates to an improvement in ironing-boards, the object being to produce a cheap, simple, convenient, and highly effective device, particularly adapted to be used in ironing the sleeves and bodies of ladies' garments" (U.S. Patent 473,653). Not only was Boone's ironing board particularly useful for ironing sleeves, it was also specifically designed for ironing the curved sleeves and waistlines of nineteenth-century dresses.

According to her patent specifications, Boone's ironing board consisted of a narrow board with its edges curved so that the outside and inside seams of a sleeve could be fitted around it and more easily pressed. The curved edges of the ironing board were "most pronounced . . . at the 'elbow-point' . . . of the sleeve." In addition to the curved surface, Boone's ironing board was supported at one end by a fixed stand and "at its opposite end with a movable support attached to it by a hinge and arranged in line with the board." While the fixed stand provided support, the hinged support allowed the board to be easily adjusted for ironing the various seams of the same garment. This allowed one to efficiently and skillfully, iron the inner and outer curved seams of a garment's sleeves or waistline. Boone described the function of the adjustable support: "When the board is to be used for pressing inside seams, the movable support is turned down . . . and then co-operates with the transverse support in maintaining the board in this position. For ironing or pressing outside seams the board is reversed."

Boone's application also considered possible variations on its design and the flexibility of its usefulness. She recognized that the design intended to ease pressing of the seams of sleeves would be useful in working with curved seams wherever they occurred. By including alternative uses and variations on her design in the patent application, Boone protected herself against future patent infringements. Further reinforcing the breadth of her patent design, Boone notes in her application, "I would have it understood that I do not limit myself to the exact form herein shown and described, but hold myself at liberty to make such changes and alterations as fairly fall within the spirit and scope of my invention."

Through her invention and patenting of an improved ironing board, Sarah Boone made a historic contribution to American society and culture. While women's inventions over the centuries have ranged from household items to heating furnaces to missile guidance systems, many, like Sarah Boone's ironing board, fell within the range of domestic tasks often performed by women in their own homes or in the homes of an employer. Women, Boone among them, found creative ways to improve the efficiency and quality of their workdays when they invented new technologies or improved on existing ones.

Further Reading

Boone, Sarah. Letter of Application and Letter Patent No. 473,653 (26 Apr. 1892).
Baker, H. R. "The Negro Inventor," in *Twentieth Century Negro Literature*, ed. Daniel Wallace Culp (1902).
Brodie, James Michael. *Created Equal: The Lives and Ideas of Black American Innovators* (1993).
Sluby, Patricia C. "Black Women and Invention," *Sage: A Scholarly Journal on Black Women*, vol. VI, no. 2 (Fall 1989): 33–35.
Vare, Ethlie Ann, and Greg Ptacek. *Patently Female: From AZT to TV Dinners, Stories of Women Inventors and Their Breakthrough Ideas* (2002).

PAMELA C. EDWARDS

BOOTHE, Charles Octavius (13 June 1845–1924), Baptist minister, missionary, and author, was born Charles Octavius Boothe in Mobile County, Alabama, to a Georgia-born slave woman belonging to and carried west by the slave owner Nathan Howard Sr. Little is known of Boothe's Georgian parents, but he proudly claimed that his great-grandmother and stepgrandfather were Africans. Boothe's description of his ancestors reflects his lifelong pride in his African heritage, but he was equally

effusive about the spiritual influence that these Christian elders had on his life. His earliest recollections included his stepgrandfather's prayer life and singing of hymns and "the saintly face and pure life of my grandmother, to whom white and black went for prayer and for comfort in the times of their sorrows." These early familial Christian influences were further reinforced by attending a "Baptist church in the forest, where white and colored people sat together to commune and to wash each other's feet" (Boothe, 9).

An intelligent and precocious child, Boothe learned the alphabet at age three by studying imprinted letters on a tin plate. Later he gained literacy under the tutelage of teachers boarding in the home of Nathan Howard Jr., thus beginning a love affair with the written word, particularly the Bible. As a teenage slave, Boothe worked as an office boy in the Clark County, Mississippi, law office of Colonel James S. Terrel, an experience that afforded him even greater access to books. Clearly, Boothe encountered greater leniency from whites during slavery than most African Americans did; of James Terrel he could even write, "I think I can say that the Colonel and I really loved each other." However, Boothe was still a slave, and he was therefore exposed to "life's sterner facts," such as the apparent absence of a father and the separation from his remaining family upon moving to the home of Nathan Howard Jr. (Boothe, 10). Still, his early positive experiences with many educated whites and Christianity shaped the remainder of his life.

By 1860 a childhood filled with prayer and "refreshing seasons of love and joy" led Boothe to "an experience of grace which so strengthened me as to fix me on the side of the people of God" (Boothe, 10). Boothe followed his conversion with formal baptism in March 1866 and was ordained as a Baptist minister at the Saint Louis Street Church of Mobile, Alabama, in December 1868. Already engaged in educating his fellow African Americans as a teacher for the Freedmen's Bureau in 1867, Boothe's ordination cemented his course on a lifelong journey of ministry and public service. In 1877 Boothe served as the first pastor for the now-legendary Dexter Avenue Church of Montgomery, Alabama, turning a former slave trader's pen into a house of God. He was an early and active participant in the Colored Baptist Convention of Alabama, serving at various times as convention clerk, editorial assistant to the convention newspaper the *Baptist Pioneer*, instructor of ministers' and deacons' institutes, president of the denomination's Selma University, and state missionary.

At some point between 1877 and 1882 Boothe attended Meharry College in Nashville, Tennessee, where he studied medicine and most likely met and married Mattie Alice Roach, a Baptist minister's daughter and graduate of Roger Williams University of the same city. The thirty-five-year marriage complemented Boothe's ministry because Mattie was also an educator and served as the first president of the Colored Women's Christian Temperance Union of Alabama. The couple had eight children, of whom only four lived to maturity. Later Boothe served as pastor for the First Colored Baptist Church, Meridian, Mississippi, until he resigned in 1892.

Throughout his ministry Boothe urged African Americans to develop a "ripened manhood, out of which shall [grow] great enterprises, manned by unity, wisdom, wealth and righteousness" (Boothe, 267). Although Boothe described slavery as harmful and "dark times" (Boothe, 13), he also believed that God used whites to elevate African Americans into Christian civilization and unabashedly praised the achievements of white society as goals worthy of emulation. Accordingly, Boothe did not hesitate to build relationships across the color line and worked closely with the white Alabama Baptist Convention and the American Baptist Home Missionary Society at various times from the 1880s until 1917. In fact, Boothe dedicated his 1890 theological primer, *Plain Theology for Plain People*, to the memory of a dear white friend and fellow Christian laborer, the Reverend Harry Woodsmall of Indiana. In return, whites praised Boothe, describing him as "a graceful speaker, a gifted preacher" whose "services have been of distinguished value" (Cathcart, 114–115). Boothe's appeal to whites in part reflected his willingness openly to criticize African Americans for behavior that he deemed unchristian or counterproductive, a trait that he shared with BOOKER T. WASHINGTON. Indeed, he embraced Washington's philosophy of racial progress begetting civic inclusion and worked closely with Washington as a teacher at Tuskegee Institute's Phelps Hall Bible Training School beginning in 1893.

Although Boothe grossly misjudged white willingness to accept African Americans as equals, he believed that he sought the best for his race. Boothe saw his chastisement of blacks as a wake-up call, and he fashioned himself as a teacher who demanded much from his most promising pupils. Calling for greater race pride, his *Cyclopedia of the Colored Baptists of Alabama: Their Leaders and Their Work* (1895) reflects this tone in declaring, "Because we made it to the top of one mountain, we could therefore make it to the top of another" (Boothe, 54). Self-criticism aside, Boothe also challenged white Alabamians' bigotry and denial of African American opportunities. In 1901 he joined Washington in challenging the Alabama Constitutional Convention's intention to disfranchise African American voters, and in 1913 he investigated the treatment of black prisoners in state camps and mines. He also served his community as a practicing physician in Birmingham and as a teacher at Alabama A&M University. For these reasons he remained a valued, multitalented member of his community until his death in Detroit.

Further Reading

Boothe, Charles Octavius. *The Cyclopedia of the Colored Baptists of Alabama: Their Leaders and Their Work* (1895).

Cathcart, William, ed. "Boothe, Rev. C. O.," in *The Baptist Encyclopedia: A Dictionary of the Doctrines, Ordinances, Usages, Confessions of Faith, Sufferings, Labors, and Successes, and of the General History of the Baptist Denomination in all Lands, with Numerous Biographical Sketches of Distinguished American and Foreign Baptists, and a Supplement* (1883).

Crowther, Edward R. "Charles Octavius Boothe: An Alabama Apostle of 'Uplift,'" *The Journal of Negro History* 78, no. 2 (Spring 1993):110–116.

Crowther, Edward R. "Interracial Cooperative Missions among Blacks by Alabama Baptists, 1868–1882," *The Journal of Negro History* 80, no. 3 (Summer 1995):131–139.

DANIEL L. FOUNTAIN

BORDE, Percival (31 Dec. 1922–31 Aug. 1979), Afro-Caribbean dancer and choreographer, was born Percival Sebastian Borde in Port of Spain, Trinidad, the son of George Paul Borde, a veterinarian, and Augustine Francis Lambie. Borde grew up in Trinidad, where he finished secondary schooling at Queens Royal College and took an appointment with the Trinidad Railway Company. Around 1942 he began formal research on Afro-Caribbean dance and performed with the Little Carib Dance Theatre. In 1949 he married Joyce Guppy, with whom he had one child. The year of their divorce is unknown.

Borde took easily to dancing and the study of dance as a function of Caribbean culture. In the early 1950s he acted as director of the Little Carib Theatre in Trinidad. In 1953 he met the noted American anthropologist and dancer PEARL PRIMUS, who was conducting field research in Caribbean folklore. Primus convinced Borde to immigrate to the United States as a dancer and teacher of West Indian dance at her New York City school. Borde developed courses in traditional Caribbean dance forms for the Pearl Primus School and began performing with the Pearl Primus Dance Company. Shortly thereafter he and Primus were married (date unknown). The couple had one child.

Performing success with Primus's modern dance company brought Borde appearances on television and the popular stage. He appeared on Broadway as the African Chief in Joyce Cary's 1956 play *Mr. Johnson*. In 1956 and 1957 he toured with the Primus dance company throughout Europe. Borde brought his own self-named dance troupe to the St. Marks Playhouse in New York City on 23 September 1958. He performed his own works and dances created for him by Primus, who acted as the artistic director of the company. John Martin, dance critic for the *New York Times* and a longtime supporter of Primus's dance anthropology, called the concert an "unusually well unified and atmospheric presentation, unpretentious in manner but with a wealth of knowledge behind it." Raves also came from the African American press, and Borde's arrival as a leading male figure in Afro-dance was confirmed. In 1959 the separate Borde and Primus companies combined to form the Pearl Primus and Percival Borde Dance Company.

Borde's performances always included ethnographic dance characterizations of several African American archetypes. For instance, his four-part 1958 program titled *Earth Magician* included portrayals of an Aztec warrior, a giant Watusi, a Yoruba chief, and a Shango priest. Borde performed sections of this program throughout his career, honing the authenticity of his dance movements through research and study. His performance style was consistently described as dynamic yet elegant, his strong physicality offset by his striking good looks. Martin described him as "light and easy of movement, with strength, admirable control and authority."

In 1959 Borde and Primus toured Africa and performed in Ethiopia, Ghana, Mali, Kenya, Nigeria, and Liberia, which held special import for the couple. It was in Liberia that Borde was named Jangbanolima, or "a man who lives to dance," by Chief Sondifu Sonni during an official adoption ritual. Also in 1959 Borde and Primus became the directors of the Performing Arts Center of Monrovia, Liberia. They remained in Liberia until November 1961. During this time Borde wrote articles for the *Liberian Age* and was active in the Liberian Chamber of Commerce. He was awarded the Gold Medal of Liberia for his work in the dance of the African diaspora.

After returning to the United States, Borde produced *Talking Drums of Africa*, an education-in-theschools program sponsored by the New York State Department of Education. He was active in the Congress on Research in Dance, a dance scholars' organization, and served on its board of directors. He also continued to work in the theater, serving as the resident choreographer for the Negro Ensemble Company's 1969 season.

Borde completed a bachelor's degree (1975) and coursework toward a master's degree at the School of the Arts at New York University. He taught movement courses there, at Columbia University Teachers College, and at the State University of New York at Binghamton, where he was an associate professor of theater arts and black studies. Borde's highly popular courses offered participatory, dance-based studies of Afro-Caribbean culture, which emphasized the connections between dance, ritual, and everyday life. He often reminded his students, "Just as one should prepare oneself to enter a temple, one should prepare to dance" (*Wichita Eagle*, 20 Aug. 1969).

Borde died of a heart attack backstage at the Perry Street Theater in New York City immediately after performing "Impinyuza," the strutting Watusi solo he had danced for more than two decades.

Borde's masculine stage presence and dynamic performance style helped widen interest in concert African American dance forms. His work continued the efforts of the dancer-choreographers Primus and KATHERINE DUNHAM in the insertion of ceremonial, anthropologically researched dance on the concert stage. After his death, Primus characterized Borde as "the outstanding exponent of African influences on Caribbean culture."

Further Reading
The Dance Collection of the New York Library for the Performing Arts at Lincoln Center holds a file of newspaper reviews of Borde's performances. The New York Public Library's Schomburg Center for Research in Black Culture holds listings of materials from the black press.

Obituary: *New York Times*, 5 Sept. 1979.

THOMAS F. DEFRANTZ

BOSTIC, Earl (25 Apr. 1913–28 Oct. 1965), alto saxophonist, was born in Tulsa, Oklahoma. Details about his parents are unknown. Bostic played clarinet in school and saxophone with the local Boy Scouts. By 1930 or 1931 when he left Tulsa to tour with Terrence Holder's Twelve Clouds of Joy, Bostic was already a saxophone virtuoso. Fellow saxophonist Buddy Tate recalls that Bostic was asked to join the band because of his dexterity and maturity as a soloist. Holder's band members then informally tested Bostic's ability to read difficult music: skipping the opportunity to rehearse, Bostic counted off an impossibly fast tempo and played the piece on first sight with such skill that only he and the drummer made it through to the end. "We let him alone after that," Tate said.

Sometime in the early 1930s Bostic spent a year at Creighton University in Omaha, Nebraska, playing by day in an ROTC band and by night with jazz groups. He was briefly a member of BENNIE MOTEN's band early in 1933. Later that year he enrolled at Xavier University in New Orleans to study music theory, harmony, and various instruments; again he played with military bands at school and jazz groups in the city. One year later he left to work mainly with lesser-known bands, although in 1935–1936 he played and arranged for a band led by Charlie Creath and FATE MARABLE.

After moving to New York at the beginning of 1938, Bostic joined DON REDMAN's band in April, played briefly with Edgar Hayes's orchestra, and then led his own band at Small's Paradise in Harlem intermittently from 1939 to the early 1940s. In this group he occasionally played trumpet, guitar, or baritone sax in addition to his alto sax. During these years he also contributed his best-known composition and arrangement, "Let Me Off Uptown," to Gene Krupa's big band, which recorded it in 1941, and he was a member of HOT LIPS PAGE's group in 1941 and again around 1943. From June 1943 to August 1944 Bostic played and wrote for LIONEL HAMPTON's big band. He left to resume leading a group at Small's. In September 1944 he recorded several sides with Page, including "Good for Stompin'" and "Fish for Supper." His solos on these recordings reveal an alto saxophonist with a full-bodied tone, a precise articulation of notes, and considerable technique, but an uncertain sense of melodic architecture, with the result that sometimes he relied on stiff, étude-like figurations. Ironically, in light of what was to come, the worst of these solos was in a blues piece, "You Need

Coachin'," which finds Bostic so busy with technique that he sounds out of touch with characteristic blues timbres, melodies, and emotions.

For the remainder of his career Bostic led bands. In the mid- to late 1940s he changed his stylistic orientation by adopting a ferocious, gritty, vocalized tone; by playing simple, singable melodies—although many tunes still left room for improvising; by using the catchy dance rhythms of contemporary rhythm and blues; and by basing the group's sound on a twangy electric guitar and smooth-toned vibraphone—the vibes perhaps inspired by his year with Hampton, but used in a less aggressive style. Early recordings in this vein were done for the Gotham label, including "That's the Groovy Thing" (1946), "8:45 Stomp," and "Temptation" (probably late 1947). After signing with the King label (which reissued these titles) in 1949, the new approach came to fruition with a recording of "Flamingo," which held the top position on the rhythm and blues popularity chart for twenty weeks in 1951. Other hit records included "Sleep" (also 1951), "Moonglow" and "Ain't Misbehavin'" (both 1952), and "Blue Skies" (1954); incidentally, the 1952 sides included a young JOHN COLTRANE in the band.

Bostic toured the country, and it is a testimony to his unusually high level of success in rhythm and blues and jazz that for several years he was able to take six-week vacations. In 1956 he suffered a serious heart attack that, apart from recordings, rendered him inactive. He resumed touring in 1959, but he soon became ill again. After years of semiretirement, he began an engagement in October 1965 in Rochester, New York, only to die there two days after suffering another heart attack.

Tate summarized Bostic's career: "Oh man, he could read. . . . He was a virtuoso. . . . He could play . . . way out, progressive, but he made it big, just playing the melody. That's what people wanted to hear." It might be added that, in pursuing this path, Bostic discovered a musicality that had sometimes been lacking in the earlier part of his career. By the mid-1980s Bostic was felt to be a "forgotten" man (Schonfield), but with the reissue in the late 1980s and 1990s of much of his work for the King label, it is possible for new generations of listeners to discover his best music.

Further Reading
Cage, Ruth. "Rhythm & Blues Notes," *Down Beat*, 29 Dec. 1954.
Chilton, John. *Who's Who of Jazz: Storyville to Swing Street*, 4th ed. (1985).
Schonfield, Victor. "The Forgotten Ones: Earl Bostic," *Jazz Journal International* 37 (Nov. 1984): 10–11.

Obituary: *Down Beat*, 2 Dec. 1965.

BARRY KERNFELD

BOSTON, Absalom (1785–6 June 1855), prosperous businessman, whaling captain, and community leader, whose court case against Nantucket led to the integration of the public schools, was a member of one of the largest and most influential black families on the island. His father was Seneca Boston, a manumitted slave, who was a self-employed weaver. His mother was a Wampanoag Indian named Thankful Micah. They had four sons and one daughter. Absalom Boston, the third-born, went to sea, as did many of Nantucket's young men, signing onto the whale ship *Thomas* in 1809 when he was twenty-four. Little is known about his early education. Anna Gardner, in her memoir *Harvest Gleanings*, mentions him visiting her family and hints that it may have been her mother, Hannah Macy Gardner, who taught the young man to read.

Shortly before he went to sea, Boston married his first wife, Mary Spywood, about whom little is known. He returned to land because of the deaths of his father and his eldest brother, Freeborn; he was left the sole supporter of the family, which included his mother, Thankful; his brother's widow, Mary; and her two young children. Boston's wife died in 1813, leaving him with four-year-old Charles. In 1814 he married a widow, Phebe Spriggins, née Williams, in the South Congregational Church (later Unitarian), as there were no separate black churches on the island at that time. Their union produced three more children: an unnamed baby who died at birth, Henry, and Caroline.

Two years later he returned to the sea. This time he went as Captain Boston, the captain and master of the whale ship *Industry* with an all-black crew. This was a rare event in maritime history. The landmark voyage became the subject of a song that included the lyrics: "AF Boston was commander and him we will obey. . . ." It ends with the promise that, should Boston ever captain another ship, the crew would sign up again (Nantucket Historical Association Archives). Whaling was a risky business, however, and the *Industry*'s voyage proved a financial failure, forcing Boston to auction his ship upon returning to Nantucket. He remained on land for the rest of his life, although he continued to invest in whaling ventures.

The failure of the *Industry* was only a temporary setback for the enterprising Boston, who continued to prosper on Nantucket and became a successful businessman and entrepreneur. By 1812 town records show him venturing into real estate, a business in which he was active throughout his life, successfully buying and selling properties in the segregated community of New Guinea, sometimes known as Newtown, where most of the African Americans of Nantucket lived. He also made mortgage loans to others in the New Guinea community, and when he turned thirty-five, he was granted a license for a public house and inn in New Guinea. His inn was frequented by transient sailors passing through the island. His wealth enabled him to contribute to the improvement of life for the African American community on the island. Around 1825 he helped found the island's first black church, which still stands on the corner of York and Pleasant streets. The African Meeting House, as it is now called, was also used as a one-room school for black children, and the trustees rented the building to the town to use a primary school until 1838.

Absalom's second wife died in 1826 at thirty-two years of age, leaving him once again with motherless children. He remarried within a year, this time to Hannah Cook of Dartmouth, Massachusetts, and together they had five more children, Phebe Ann, Absalom Jr., Oliver, Thomas, and Sarah.

Boston continued to prosper. In 1827 he paid for an ad in the local newspaper offering a reward for the recovery of a French-made silver watch, and in 1833 the local newspaper reported that a "gang of foreign vagabonds" had burgled his house and taken forty to fifty dollars in silver coins; few of the island's blacks would have such money readily at hand. His influence in the community grew with his affluence; a notice in the local paper in 1840 listed him as "attorney" for the executor of a will and in 1844 he served as the executor for the will of an Abel Norcross, a mariner. When the whale ship *Loper*, with an all-black crew under the command of a white captain, Obed Starbuck, returned from a particularly successful voyage in the Pacific in 1830, Boston led a triumphant parade through the main streets of Nantucket. He also became increasingly active in reform and politics. In 1826, he placed a notice in the local paper that Jacob Perry, at the time a minister and a teacher at the African School, would deliver a "discourse against slavery" at the Meeting House. In 1839 Boston became the first African American on Nantucket to run for public office, one of thirty to run for the five-member board of selectmen. He also ran to be a fire warden, but he failed to win either position.

An eight-year battle began in 1838 to integrate the public schools after seventeen-year-old EUNICE ROSS qualified to attend the all-white high school but was denied entrance. There were frequent but unsuccessful attempts at the annual town meetings during the time period to integrate the public schools. The trustees of the African Meeting House refused to let the town continue to use their facility as a primary school, protesting the exclusion of black children from the town's upper-level schools. This forced the school committee to build a new primary school in New Guinea. (It was during this time that Boston made his unsuccessful bid for the board of selectmen.) During the controversy, the library closed its doors to blacks and to abolition meetings. In 1842 the New Guinea community wrote an address to the town, which was printed in the local newspapers, as well as in the *Liberator*, complaining "that for a mere accident, the difference of complexion, we are denied the right of privilege of education in common with our fellow citizens; we must pronounce it to be *unkind, unjust*." That summer, emotions connected with school integration resulted in an explosive antislavery convention that culminated in riots, necessitating visiting abolitionist speakers, including William Lloyd Garrison and CHARLES LENOX REMOND, to leave the island.

That same year, Nantucket voted to build a third grammar school not far from the New Guinea neighborhood, and controversy intensified as to whether black children, including Boston's daughter Phebe Ann, would be admitted to the new school. Boston put his name up for the school committee that year with nine other black Nantucketers, none of whom was elected. He continued to seek public office almost every year during the school integration controversy. He ran for assessor in 1843, for the school committee again in 1844, for highway surveyor in 1845, and for fire warden again in 1846. He won none of these elections.

In 1843 abolitionists were elected to the school committee, and they integrated the public schools despite a vote at the annual town meeting directing maintenance of the status quo in the schools. Anecdotal evidence suggests that Phebe Ann Boston and others were admitted to integrated grammar schools. The integration was short-lived, however, as the abolitionists lost their positions on the school committee at the next annual town meeting. That newly elected school committee forcibly expelled black students from all the schools, except the one that had been built on York Street. The students were humiliated, called to the front of the class and made to leave in the middle of the school day. With Absalom Boston as one of their leaders, the New Guinea community began a two-year boycott of the public schools. There is some evidence that a classroom was set up during that time by local abolitionists, who pressed for school integration at the next annual town meeting. Failing there, the integrationists turned to the state legislature for redress. Boston, along with his wife and oldest daughter, signed one of the petitions that eventually led to the passage of a law in 1845, stating that any student unlawfully excluded from a public school had the right to recover damages in court.

Boston, on behalf of Phebe Ann, now seventeen, began legal procedures against the town based on the new legislation. She had applied to one of the town's upper-level schools—it is unclear whether grammar school or high school—in June 1845 and had been refused admittance. A special town meeting was convened in September 1845, according to the Nantucket town records, "to see what order the town will take, in relation to an action brought by Phebe Ann Boston, by her Father . . . for depriving her of the advantage of Public School Instruction." The case went from the Court of Common Pleas to the Supreme Judicial Court, which caused a delay of almost a year.

In the meantime, the Great Fire of 1846 destroyed much of the downtown of Nantucket, devastating the economy of the island, as the wharves and most of Main Street went up in smoke. Luckily for the New Guinea community, the fire did not make it as far as their neighborhood, although several black businesses were destroyed in the center of town. The fire may have changed the voters' attitude regarding school integration on Nantucket. At the next annual town meeting, they rejected the segregationist town officers and voted in a solid abolitionist school committee. Their first act was to reintegrate the schools. Boston dropped his lawsuit, and Phebe Ann was admitted to an integrated school. Unfortunately, in 1849, not long after completing her education, she died at age twenty-one from dysentery.

Her father retired from public activities. He had lost seven of his ten children and two of his three wives. One son, Oliver, a mariner, enlisted in the navy during the Civil War. Another son, Thomas, lived in Boston and Washington, D.C., supporting himself in a variety of ways, from giving music lessons to banking. At the age of sixty-nine, Absalom Boston died in Nantucket in 1855, the year the commonwealth legally integrated public education. He left a large estate valued at more than one thousand dollars, including several houses, a shop, and an inn.

Further Reading
Karttunen, Francis. *The Other Islanders: People Who Pulled Nantucket's Oars* (2005).
Nantucket Historical Association Archives.
White, Barbara. *The African School: The African School and the Integration of Nantucket Public Schools, 1825–1847* (1978).

BARBARA A. WHITE

BOTTOMS, Lawrence Wendell (9 Apr. 1908–1 Sept. 1994), pastor, theologian, and churchman, was born in Selma, Alabama, the son of Wilbur McDonald Bottoms, a teacher, and Gussie Adolphus Shivers. While his mother's family had been Methodists, his father was a Reformed Presbyterian who graduated from Wilberforce College in Ohio and answered a call to teach at the Knox Academy in Selma. This school was operated by the Reformed Presbyterian Church of Selma, and it was upon taking this post that Wilbur Bottoms met and married Shivers. Lawrence was raised in a highly unusual situation, for neither the school nor the church was segregated. Whites who taught at the school also lived on the school property and attended the church as members alongside African American teachers and other members in the congregation. At times the church had a white pastor, and at other times the pastor was African American.

Lawrence continued his education in Pennsylvania, first at Geneva College from 1929 to 1931 and then at the Reformed Presbyterian Theological Seminary in Pittsburgh from 1932 to 1935. During his college years, Bottoms came to believe that the key to racial reconciliation lay in a strong sense of personhood with a firm identity that began inwardly, that rose above culture, and that was not imposed by others. During his time as a seminary student, Bottoms married Elizabeth Loutisha Stallworth, a schoolteacher from Selma, in September 1933. Reverend Bottoms was licensed to preach in May 1934, and even before graduation from the seminary in 1935 he often returned to Selma to fill the Reformed Presbyterian pulpit there. He was ordained in November 1936. Bottoms left the Selma church and the Reformed

Presbyterian denomination in 1938 and became pastor of Grace Presbyterian Church in Louisville, Kentucky. Bottoms's new pulpit had the distinction of being the only African American church in the Louisville Presbytery, a regional division of the Presbyterian Church, U.S. (PCUS), denomination, more commonly known as the Southern Presbyterian Church, which remained crippled by the legacy of segregation. Bottoms was pastor of Grace Presbyterian until 1949. During these years, he and his wife raised their four children.

For many years Bottoms worked for change within the denomination. From 1953 to 1964 he was secretary of the Department of Negro Work for the PCUS. He was the first African American moderator of the Presbytery of Louisville and the first African American moderator of the Synod of Kentucky, serving in 1963 and 1964. He served as assistant secretary of the Division of Home Mission, Board of Church Extension (PCUS), from 1964 to 1966. From 1966 to 1969 he served as associate secretary of the Division of Education and Research, Board of Church Extension (PCUS), and from 1969 to 1973 he was coordinator of the Support Services, Board of National Ministries (PCUS). As pastor of the Oakhurst Presbyterian Church in Decatur, Georgia, from 1973 to 1975, Bottoms became the first African American to serve as moderator of the General Assembly of the Southern Presbyterian Church. Elected on the first ballot in a three-way race for the denomination's top leadership position, he won that election by an overwhelming majority. As a young commissioner to the assembly, he was not allowed to eat in the dining hall because of his race; however, some thirty-five years later he was widely received as one of the church's key leaders.

In his final years, Bottoms served as president of the Christian Council of Metropolitan Atlanta (1980) and as associate pastor of the Morningside Presbyterian Church. Bottoms received the 1960 Distinguished Service Award from Geneva College, honorary doctor of divinity degrees from Davis and Elkins College, Stillman College, and Oglethorpe University, the doctor of humane letters from Tarkio College, and the doctor of laws degree from Geneva College. During his ministry Bottoms helped to plant African American congregations throughout the South. By 1993 he was listed as honorably retired, and he died in 1994 while residing in the Atlanta area.

Further Reading
Brackenridge, R. Douglas. "Lawrence W. Bottoms: The Church, Black Presbyterians and Personhood," *Journal of Presbyterian History* (Spring 1978).
Presbyterian Church (U.S.A.). *All-Black Governing Bodies: The History and Contributions of All-Black Governing Bodies in the Predecessor Denominations of the Presbyterian Church (U.S.A.)* (1996).

WAYNE SPARKMAN

BOUCHET, Edward Alexander (15 Sept. 1852–28 Oct. 1918), educator and scientist, was born in New Haven, Connecticut, the youngest of four children of William Francis Bouchet, a janitor, and Susan Cooley. Part of New Haven's black community, the Bouchets were active members of the Temple Street Congregational Church, which was a stopping point for fugitive slaves along the Underground Railroad. During the 1850s and 1860s New Haven had only three schools that black children could attend. Edward was enrolled in the Artisan Street Colored School, a small (only thirty seats), ungraded school with one teacher, Sarah Wilson, who played a crucial role in nurturing Bouchet's academic abilities and his desire to learn.

In 1868 Bouchet was accepted into Hopkins Grammar School, a private institution that prepared young men for the classical and scientific departments at Yale College. He graduated first in his class at Hopkins and four years later, when he graduated from Yale in 1874, he ranked sixth in a class of 124. On the basis of this exceptional performance, Bouchet became the first black student in the nation to be nominated to Phi Beta Kappa. In the fall of 1874 he returned to Yale with the encouragement and financial support of Alfred Cope, a Philadelphia philanthropist. In 1876 Bouchet successfully completed his dissertation on the new subject of geometrical optics, becoming the first black person to earn a PhD from an American university as well as the sixth American of any race to earn a PhD in Physics.

In 1876 Bouchet moved to Philadelphia to teach at the Institute for Colored Youth (ICY), the city's only high school for black students. ICY had been founded by the Society of Friends because African Americans had historically been denied admittance to Philadelphia's white high schools. Members of the ICY board of managers like Cope, Bouchet's Yale benefactor, believed firmly in the value of a classical education and were convinced that blacks were capable of unlimited educational achievement. In 1874 Cope had provided forty thousand dollars to establish a new science program at ICY, and soon thereafter recruited Bouchet to teach and administer the program.

Although Philadelphia was as segregated as any southern city, it offered a supportive environment for a man of Bouchet's abilities. The city's black population, the largest in the North, had made considerable progress in education during the decades preceding his arrival. As early as 1849 half the city's black population was active in one or more of the many literary societies established by the black community. After the Civil War the ICY played an important role in training the thousands of black teachers that were needed throughout the country to provide freedmen with the education they sought.

Bouchet joined St. Thomas's Church, the oldest black Episcopal church in the country, served on the vestry, and was church secretary for many years. The bishop also appointed Bouchet to be a lay reader, which gave Bouchet the opportunity to take a more active part in church services. Bouchet took his scientific interests and abilities beyond the ICY into the broader black community, giving public lectures on various scientific topics. He was also a member of the Franklin Institute, a foundation for the promotion of the mechanic arts, chartered in 1824. Bouchet maintained his ties with Yale through the local chapter of the Yale Alumni Association, attending all meetings and annual dinners.

By the turn of the century, a new set of ICY managers emerged, more receptive to the industrial education philosophy of BOOKER T. WASHINGTON than to academic education for blacks. In their efforts to redirect the school's programs, the all-white board fired all the teachers, including Bouchet, in 1902 and replaced them with instructors committed to industrial education.

Over the next fourteen years Bouchet held five or six positions in different parts of the country. Until November 1903 he taught math and physics in St. Louis at Sumner High School, the first high school for blacks west of the Mississippi. He then spent seven months as the business manager for the Provident Hospital in St. Louis (November 1903–May 1904), followed by a term as a United States inspector of customs at the Louisiana Purchase Exposition held in St. Louis (June 1904–October 1906). In October 1906 Bouchet secured a teaching and administrative position at St. Paul's Normal and Industrial School in Lawrenceville, Virginia. In 1908 he became principal of Lincoln High School of Gallipolis, Ohio, where he remained until 1913, when an attack of arteriosclerosis compelled him to resign and return to New Haven. Undocumented information has Bouchet returning to teaching at Bishop College in Marshall, Texas, but illness once again forced him to retire in 1916. He returned to New Haven, where he died in his boyhood home at 94 Bradley Street. He had never married or had children.

Bouchet had the misfortune of being a talented and educated black man who lived in a segregated society that refused to recognize his particular genius and thus hindered him from conducting scientific research and achieving professional recognition. Segregation produced isolation as Bouchet spent his career in high schools with limited resources and poorly equipped labs. Even with Bouchet's superior qualifications, no white college would have considered him for a position on its faculty. Completely excluded from any means of utilizing his education and talent, Bouchet languished in obscurity. The ascendance of industrial education also served to limit his opportunities, since his academic training in the natural sciences made him unattractive as a candidate at the increasing number of black institutions that adopted a vocational curriculum.

The absurdity of the claims made by some proponents of vocational education concerning the innate inability of blacks to undertake an academic education could not have been more obvious to Bouchet. From his own accomplishments and those of his students, it never occurred to Bouchet that blacks could not master the fields of classical education or excel in science. In the face of personal setbacks and a changing public mood on black education, Bouchet maintained his standards and never altered his educational ideals.

Further Reading
Some of Bouchet's writings and those of his classmates are available in the Yale University Manuscripts and Archives, Sterling Memorial Library.
"Edward A. Bouchet, Ph.D." *Negro History Bulletin* 31 (Dec. 1968).
Mickens, Ronald E. "Edward A. Bouchet: The First Black Ph.D." *Black Collegian* 8, no. 4 (Mar.–Apr. 1978).
Perkins, Linda M. *Fanny Jackson Coppin and the Institute for Colored Youth, 1865–1902* (1987).

Obituary: *Bulletin of Yale University, Obituary Record of Yale Graduates, 1918–1919*, no. 11 (1919).

H. KENNETH BECHTEL

BOUEY, Harrison N. (4 Aug. 1849–1909), educator, clergyman, missionary, and community leader, was born in Columbia County, Georgia, the son of Lewis Bouey, a carpenter, and Maria, a cook. The couple had no other children. Bouey spent his early life in Augusta, Georgia, where he was apprenticed to learn the painter's trade and attended night school. He passed the examination to become licensed as a teacher and taught in the public schools of Augusta for two years. From 1870 to 1873 he attended the Baptist Theological School in Augusta, an institution that later moved to Atlanta and in 1913 was renamed Morehouse College. Upon graduation he moved to Ridge Springs, South Carolina, where he became principal of a school and taught there for two years.

Bouey's work as an educational and community leader brought him into politics in 1874. He was elected to a two-year term as probate judge in Edgefield County, South Carolina. He moved from Ridge Springs to the county seat, Edgefield Court House, where he took a call as minister to the Macedonia Baptist Church.

In 1876 white Democrats in South Carolina determined to take back control of local and state offices from black and white Republicans. Edgefield County in particular served as a model for radical extralegal actions by former Confederates to defeat the county's black majority. An all-out battle between black militiamen and members of white rifle clubs in Hamburg, on the Georgia border of Edgefield County, in early July 1876 left eight men dead, seven of whom were black, and launched a frenzy of legal and political activity to prepare for the fall elections. More than seven hundred armed and mounted Democrats wearing red shirts rode through the streets of Edgefield County to intimidate black voters before the election, despite the presence of two companies of federal troops. On voting day, 7 November, hundreds of black voters were turned away from the polls, and when votes were counted, there were two thousand more ballots than eligible voters in the county. Harrison Bouey claimed he was elected as county sheriff, but was counted out through election fraud.

The Republican Party contested the elections in Edgefield and neighboring Barnwell and Laurens counties. Tension and confusion followed the corrupt elections until April 1877 when President Rutherford B. Hayes withdrew federal troops, finally ending Reconstruction in the state. Black Republicans felt betrayed by the federal government for leaving them at the mercies of white Democrats. Given this situation, it is no surprise that some black leaders, such as Bouey, began talk of leaving not just South Carolina or the South, but the United States.

Claiming to speak for a large number of black families in Edgefield County who wished to immigrate to Liberia, on 23 May 1877 Bouey wrote to the American Colonization Society office in Washington, D.C., and to Bishop HENRY MCNEAL TURNER in Atlanta, the black leader most associated with the back-to-Africa movement. The American Colonization Society had founded Liberia to receive black American expatriates. Black South Carolinians in several other counties also began to organize for an exodus to Liberia. Later in the spring Bouey traveled to Charleston to serve as a juror in the United States District Court, and there he linked up with other black leaders interested in African migration, including B. F. Porter, the pastor of Morris Brown African Methodist Episcopal (AME) Church. In July they formed the Liberian Exodus Joint Stock Steamship Company, selling stock at ten dollars a share to raise money for the expedition. Porter was named the president and Bouey the secretary of the company. By early 1878 the company had raised six thousand dollars and in February purchased a sailing ship, the bark *Azor*. The ship was consecrated at a ceremony in March in Charleston attended by five thousand people, including black dignitaries such as MARTIN ROBISON DELANY and Bishop Turner.

On 21 April the *Azor* sailed from Charleston, carrying Harrison Bouey and 274 other emigrants. The largest number hailed from Edgefield, Barnwell, and Clarendon counties, with several others from Charleston and east central Georgia. By most standards the expedition was a failure. The ship was quickly overloaded, so 175 passengers were left on the dock to await a second voyage, which never materialized. The officers had stored insufficient food and water for the monthlong voyage, and poor diet and cramped quarters took a toll; twenty-three passengers died and were buried at sea, and six more died soon after their arrival in Africa. After leaving the emigrants in the capital, Monrovia, the *Azor* returned to Charleston empty of freight but with plenty of debt. The company never made another voyage, and the *Azor* was sold in November 1879 to pay the company's remaining debts. In the next month eighteen of the emigrants returned to South Carolina, bringing stories of extreme poverty of the emigrants who remained in Liberia to add to the bad publicity for the endeavor. Several of the *Azor* passengers settled in Royesville, to the north of Monrovia, and some prospered in Liberia.

Bouey labored as a Baptist minister in Monrovia, traveled throughout the country to organize the National Baptist Convention, and did some missionary work in the western part of Liberia among the Gola people. He returned to the United States in 1881 and served as the agent of the Liberian Baptist Convention, working to promote missions to Africa among the black Baptist churches.

In April 1882 he married Laura P. Logan, of Charleston, South Carolina, and the couple lived in Selma, Alabama, where Bouey worked as a Sunday School missionary, financial agent of Selma University, and then corresponding secretary for the Alabama Baptist Mission Board. He later served as associate editor and business manager of the *Baptist Pioneer*, published in Selma. He also served on the board for the national Baptist Foreign Mission Convention. He returned to Liberia as a missionary sometime shortly after 1902 and died there in 1909.

Further Reading

Foner, Eric. *Freedom's Lawmakers: A Directory of Black Officeholders during Reconstruction* (1993).

Tindall, George Brown. *South Carolina Negroes, 1877–1900* (1952).

Williams, Walter L. *Black Americans and the Evangelization of Africa, 1877–1900* (1982).

KENNETH C. BARNES

BOUSFIELD, Midian Othello (22 Aug. 1885–16 Feb. 1948), physician, was born in Tipton, Missouri, the son of Willard Hayman Bousfield, a barber, and Cornelia Catherine Gilbert. From the start Bousfield exemplified what W. E. B. DU BOIS meant by the term "talented tenth." Awarded a bachelor's degree from the University of Kansas in 1907, Bousfield earned his MD two years later from Northwestern University in Chicago and did an internship at Howard University's Freedmen's Hospital in 1910. He was lured back to Kansas City for his initial medical practice following an unlikely adventure in Brazil, where, when medical prospects dimmed, he took up prospecting for gold. Bousfield soon felt a need for a larger stage, and in 1914, with his new bride, Maudelle Tanner Brown, he shifted his base to Chicago. There he embarked on a career of astounding breadth that took him to leadership positions in the business, health, medical, philanthropic, educational, and military worlds of Chicago and beyond. He and his wife had one child.

Bousfield's first success was in the black business sphere. Perhaps perceiving the larger influence of a corporate career, in 1919 he gave up an affiliation with a fledgling black railroad union and helped found the Liberty Life Insurance Company, remaining on as medical director and vice president. A decade later, as president, he guided the company through a merger and a reorganization as the Supreme Liberty Life Insurance Company. For the next four years he led the new firm as both medical director and chair of its executive committee.

But the worlds of health, medicine, and philanthropy absorbed most of Bousfield's energy, and his primary interests there lay in improving the opportunities and quality of black physicians and the health care of black citizens, especially the underserved majority in the South. His great chance to promote those interests came in 1934, when the Chicago-based Julius Rosenwald Fund named him its director of Negro health.

Although the appointment was due mostly to Bousfield's stature as a business leader, the post itself was largely one he created by cultivating the Rosenwald medical director, Michael M. Davis, and convincing him of the need and possibilities for Rosenwald involvement in black health issues. Largely at Bousfield's initiative, the fund (both before and after 1934) launched projects aimed at improving black hospitals and nurses' training and creating openings for black doctors within southern health agencies, in part by using the lure of Rosenwald money for their initial salaries. By 1942, when the fund ceased operations, the color line in southern public medicine had been substantially breeched and the black profession greatly strengthened.

For Bousfield 1933–1934 proved a take-off year apart from the Rosenwald post. It also brought him the presidency of the all-black National Medical Association, making him for a time the leading spokesman of black medicine. Moreover the year provided him an influential, inside forum from which to exert that prestige to good ends through the annual meeting of the American Public Health Association (APHA), where Bousfield became its first black speaker. He did not mince words. It was simply "inconceivable," Bousfield said, that anything but racism could account for the fact that health officers could "so complacently review, year after year, the unfavorable vital statistical reports of one-tenth of the population and make no special effort to correct them" (210). Members must shed their racist blinders and start solving blacks' health problems, using black professionals as partners. For the first time the APHA got the African American perspective and learned to its surprise that "darky" dialect stories and racial disdain raised barriers to black community participation in vital health work. Thanks in part to Bousfield, a new racial sensitivity among health professionals had begun.

Despite such bluntness, Bousfield never lost his ties to white leadership. Whether this was due to his reputation in business or his visibility as an Episcopal layman (surely a mark of acceptability to whites), Bousfield nonetheless continued to enjoy opportunities to serve the African American community from the upper reaches of the white establishment. In 1939 the Democratic boss Edward J. Kelly named Bousfield the first black member on Chicago's board of education, a move black Chicago had been urging for twenty-five years. In 1942 Bousfield got a national call: to take charge of the U.S. Army hospital at Fort Huachuca, Arizona. The army's first all-black hospital, it would also be under the direction of the medical corp's first black colonel. Not only did his leadership give black physicians new opportunities, but the quality of their care was so patently good that neighboring whites sought out Fort Huachuca in preference to their own white facility.

One final creative venture remained. In 1946 Bousfield helped organize the Provident Medical Associates, a group of well-heeled (but progressive) Chicago black doctors, whose purpose was to fund the education of aspiring medical specialists and in the process break another racial barrier in American medicine. Upon Bousfield's death in Chicago, a momentum was building that in little more than a decade and a half would demolish the structure of medical segregation, thanks substantially to his efforts. Ironically, it was Bousfield's separate but (truly) equal strategy that helped bring on integration, for his approach helped ensure the quality the black medical profession needed to convince white physicians that integration was an acceptable next step.

Bousfield's career is significant for two reasons apart from his own professional contributions. It demonstrated that African Americans—North and South—were making large strides toward equality well before the civil rights movement, even before World War II. It further showed that a conservative approach to social change, that is, stressing gradualism and reliance on the white power structure for help, did bring some results. Bousfield did associate publicly and early on with black unionism through work with the Railway Men's International Association, and he was a key leader in the National Urban League. Perhaps most importantly, he spoke bluntly to white professionals when straight talk seemed a surer course than tact and cajolery.

Further Reading
Bousfield, Midian Othello. "Reaching the Negro Community," *American Journal of Public Health* 24 (Mar. 1934).
Beardsley, Edward H. *A History of Neglect: Health Care for Blacks and Mill Workers in the Twentieth-Century South* (1987).
Obituaries: *Chicago Daily News*, 17 Feb. 1948; *Journal of the National Medical Association* 40 (May 1948).
E. H. BEARDSLEY

BOUTELLE, Frazier Augustus (12 Sept. 1840–12 Feb. 1924), military officer and conservationist, was born in Troy, New York, the son of James Boutelle of Fitchburg, Massachusetts, and Emeline Lamb Boutelle. Little is known of his childhood and adolescent years. However, at age twenty-one, possibly passing as white, Boutelle began his ascent through the ranks of the military to become a highly decorated officer, including earning the rank of adjutant general.

On 15 August 1861 Boutelle enlisted in the Fifth New York Calvary Regiment. On 4 November 1862 he was promoted from quartermaster sergeant to second lieutenant. Boutelle and his regiment were then assigned to Pennsylvania to battle against Robert E. Lee's Confederate forces. During the Gettysburg campaign Boutelle was injured when he fell from his horse during a charge on Hanover on 30 June 1863. Because of his injuries Boutelle was assigned to the First Brigade, Third Calvary Division on 17 January 1864 as an ambulance driver. During his stint as an ambulance driver, Boutelle's former commanding officer, Captain Theodore A. Boice, was captured, resulting in Boutelle's being recruited as the replacement to lead the Fifth New York Calvary Regiment. Boutelle remained with the regiment until 10 July 1865.

After the dissolution of New York Calvary, Boutelle enlisted in the regular U.S. Army. Upon enlisting, Boutelle lost his rank from a volunteer regiment and was deemed a private on 12 February 1866. However, he received the commission of sergeant major followed by the rank of second lieutenant on 8 May 1869. After being transferred to Fort Klamath, Oregon, Boutelle and his regiment were instructed to escort the Modoc tribe to a reservation as was outlined in a Senate treaty approved on 14 October 1864. Upon contact between the regiment and the Modoc tribe, a gunfight erupted between Boutelle and Scarface Charley of the Modoc tribe. As a result of the skirmish, the war between the Modoc tribe and the United States began. For his participation in what became known as the Modoc War, Boutelle was cited for his bravery in the Lost River engagement at Lava Beds, Oregon.

On 30 May 1888 Boutelle was promoted to the rank of captain and the following year was named head of Yellowstone National Park. Boutelle began his tenure, replacing Captain Moses Harris, at Yellowstone National Park on 1 June 1889. As head of the park Boutelle sought to reduce the number of forest fires, protect the Snake and Missouri rivers, and stock the park with various types of fish. He also devised procedures that limited the number of parasites in the park's waters. Boutelle garnered mass support with his measures to protect the bison herds throughout the Northwest. He urged Congress to pass and enact laws protecting the bison from slaughter, ordered the elimination of animals in the park that preyed on bison, deer, and elk, and provided the National Zoological Park in Washington, D.C., with animals that were captured in Yellowstone.

Although he was recommended for promotion to brevet major on 1 July 1830, Boutelle chose to retire from the U.S. Army, but he was not mustered out of service until 27 August 1895. Before retirement Boutelle accepted the post of brigadier general of Washington State. As brigadier general he streamlined the National Guard and its procedures. Before his four-year term had expired, Boutelle was removed from his position by Governor John R. Rogers. It has been suggested that Boutelle was forced out of his post once news of his African American genealogy reached the governor. He ended his tenure in Washington State on 13 January 1897. During the ensuing years Boutelle remained active by serving as an army recruiter from 1 August 1905 to 20 September 1918. During his retirement Boutelle was once again promoted, earning the rank of colonel.

Boutelle married Mary Adolphine Augusto Haydon on 12 October 1873. They had one son, Henry Moss Boutelle, born 17 June 1875. Henry Boutelle was killed in action in Manila, the Philippines, on 2 November 1899. Colonel Frazier A. Boutelle died on 12 February 1924 in Seattle. He was survived by his wife. As a soldier Boutelle displayed qualities that led to his ascension through the ranks of the U.S. Army, assured by his willingness to hide his African American ancestry. As a conservationist Boutelle helped to establish laws that protected and enriched the splendor of Yellowstone National Forest.

Further Reading
Johnson, Charles, Jr. "Frazier A. Boutelle: Military Career of a Black Soldier," *Journal of the Afro-American Historical and Genealogical Society* 3 (1982).
Quinn, Arthur. *Hell with the Fire Out: A History of the Modoc War* (1997).

MICHAEL J. RISTICH

BOWDEN, Artemisia (1879–18 Aug. 1969), Texas school administrator and civic leader, was born in Albany, Georgia, the eldest of five children of Milas and Mary Bowden, former slaves. When Bowden was sixteen years old her mother died, and her father sent her to St. Augustine's Normal, Industrial, and Collegiate School (later St. Augustine's College) in Raleigh, North Carolina, where she graduated in 1900. There Bowden came into contact with educated African American Episcopalian role models.

Having gained two years of teaching experience in North Carolina, Bowden moved to San Antonio, Texas, to accept the position of chief administrator and primary teacher of St. Philip's Normal and Industrial School. St. Philip's had been founded in 1898 for the Episcopalian Church by Bishop James Steptoe Johnston, the son of a Mississippi plantation owner. Initially operating as a day school, St. Philip's consisted of two classrooms where sewing was taught to African American girls. For the next fifty-two years Bowden dedicated her life to providing the educational and cultural and economic needs of the African American community in San Antonio. As principal her first charge was to organize the school into three departments, primary, grammar, and industrial. Later she increased the staff of instructors and expanded the course work in each department. Boarding facilities were added, a normal and a music department were added, and an off-campus kindergarten was organized. By 1908 the school's enrollment had reached a high of 117 students. However, in 1913 the enrollment fell to eighty-five, and the school continued to be underfunded by the diocese and was on the brink of financial ruin.

Retaining a vision of the school as a great institution of learning, Bowden took on the responsibility for fund-raising, in addition to her teaching and administrative duties. Not afraid to ask anyone she thought would give her a donation, she raised funds to make an initial payment to buy approximately four acres, including a two-story brick house and two frame buildings in east San Antonio. In 1918 the school occupied its new location, and by 1921 St. Philip's began receiving approximately two thousand dollars annually from the American Church Institute for Negroes, an Episcopal organization. With financial security in place, Bowden set a new goal: to establish St. Philip's as a junior college. In 1927, with the support of the mayor, the Chamber of Commerce, and a number of African American organizations and business people, St. Philip's Junior College and Industrial School became a reality. Bowden's title changed from principal to president of the newly established junior college.

The Great Depression brought new challenges for Bowden and her beloved St. Philip's Junior College. By 1940 the Episcopal Church relinquished all ties to the college, leaving it again at the brink of financial ruin. Bowden refused to allow the school to die and began a campaign to have the San Antonio Board of Education assume responsibility for the school. Since 1926 the board had operated a publicly funded junior college for whites only. Although African Americans living in San Antonio helped support the college through taxes they paid, none was allowed admission. Reluctantly, in 1942, the San Antonio Board of Education incorporated St. Philip's into the municipal junior college system, operating it as a branch of San Antonio Junior College. The president of San Antonio Junior College also administered the St. Philip's branch, and Bowden became the school's dean.

Bowden did graduate work during the summers at Columbia University, Pennsylvania's Cheyney State Teachers College, the New York School of Social Work, and the University of Colorado. In 1952 she received an honorary doctorate from Tillotson College in Austin, Texas. Bowden held memberships in the National Association of College Women's Clubs and several state and national associations for professional educators. In 1947 she was named to the Texas Commission on Interracial Relations. The National Council of Negro Women cited Bowden as one of the ten most outstanding women educators in the country. A member of Delta Sigma Theta Sorority, Inc., Bowden was recognized by a number of local organizations for her lifetime of service, including Zeta Phi Beta Sorority, Inc., which in 1955 named her Woman of the Year. An elementary school in San Antonio and the San Antonio chapter of the Business and Professional Women, Inc., were named in her honor. St. Philip's College honored her with an endowed scholarship in her name and with the Bowden Administration Building located on campus.

Bowden devoted her time not only to St. Philip's but also to civic projects benefiting African Americans in greater San Antonio. She is given primary credit for securing Lindberg Park for African American residents, establishing the East End Settlement

House, and the introduction of an African American nursing unit in Robert B. Green Hospital. She was a member of the Southern Conference of Christians and Jews and of St. Philip's Episcopal Church in San Antonio. At the time of her retirement in 1954 Bowden was given the title dean emeritus. Although Bowden never married and had no children, her life touched many and continued to assure that generations would obtain a valuable education in San Antonio. St. Philip's College would grow into a multi-campus institution of the Alamo Community College District, joining three other colleges: San Antonio College, Palo Alto College, and Northwest Vista College. It became one of the fastest growing colleges in the southwest. With a student population per semester that exceeded eight thousand, it ranked as one of the largest of the 160 historically black colleges and universities. Bowden died in San Antonio.

Further Reading

Eckerman, Jo. "Artemisia Bowden: Dedicated Dreamer," *Texas Passages* (Winter 1987).

St. Philip's College, available online at http://www.accd.edu/spc/main/history.aspx.

LINDA EVERETT MOYÉ

BOWE, Riddick (10 Aug. 1967–), boxer and activist, was born Riddick Lamont Bowe in the Brownsville neighborhood of Brooklyn, New York, the twelfth of thirteen children of Dorothy Bowe, a factory worker. Little is known of Bowe's father, whose first name is believed to have been Jake, as he left the family when Bowe was very young. Brownsville was notable for its high crime rate and poverty, forces that affected Bowe directly. Several of his brothers spent time in prison, and his sister Brenda was assaulted and robbed of a welfare check, dying of injuries sustained in the incident. Bowe stayed clear of such troubles, and as a teenager began training at the New Bedford-Stuyvesant Boxing Club. He married Judith (her maiden name is unknown) in 1986 and shortly afterward she gave birth to the first of their five children (Riddick Jr., Riddicia, Brenda, Julius, and Diamond). He graduated from Thomas Jefferson High School that same year.

Success in the ring came early for Bowe. As an amateur he won four New York Golden Gloves titles in addition to a gold medal as a light heavyweight in the 1985 World Junior Championships. It was not until the 1988 Olympics in Seoul, South Korea, that Bowe experienced his first setback as a boxer, losing the gold-medal bout in the super heavyweight division to the Canadian boxer Lennox Lewis.

Bowe turned professional following the 1988 Olympics. He hired veteran trainer Eddie Futch, who had helped many boxers realize their potential and win titles. Under Futch's tutelage, Bowe accumulated an impressive record, going 21-0 in his first two years as a professional fighter.

In November 1992 Bowe fought the undisputed World Heavyweight Champion EVANDER HOLYFIELD.

Riddick Bowe, reacts after defeating Marcus Rhode at Fire Lake Casino in Shawnee, Oklahoma, 25 September 2004. (AP Images.)

This dramatic fight, won in the eleventh round by Bowe, became an instant classic and revived the public's previously dwindling interest in boxing. With the victory Bowe became the sport's unified champion, his status acknowledged by all three of boxing's major governing bodies: the World Boxing Council (WBC), the World Boxing Association (WBA), and the International Boxing Federation (IBF).

Charismatic and politically active, Bowe met with world leaders such as Pope John Paul II, Nelson Mandela, and President Bill Clinton. He supported a wide range of causes, including the anti-apartheid movement, ending world hunger, and raising awareness of the perils of drug addiction. Despite all the philanthropy he was participating in, some sportswriters believed his passion and ambition had waned upon achieving boxing's ultimate distinction as undisputed world heavyweight champion.

Because of a breakdown in negotiations between Bowe's management and that of Lennox Lewis's, Bowe lost his WBC title belt after failing to fight the top-ranked challenger; Lewis became the WBC heavyweight champion by default. The seemingly unflappable Bowe discarded his WBC championship belt into a trashcan at a London press conference, one of many controversial actions that would take place during his career. His championship reign was also marred by a lack of quality title defenses. He lost his IBF and WBA belts in a rematch with Holyfield in November 1993. The fight was a close one, despite the fact that Bowe had not prepared as thoroughly as he had for their first bout and was noticeably overweight. Bowe would have problems with his weight throughout his career. His dislike of training and his love of food proved to be an unfortunate combination; between fights his weight would rise significantly, leaving him either flabby or, in those instances where he lost the extra weight on a crash diet, weakened.

Bowe's career was marked by several strange and controversial moments. In a bout with Buster Mathis Jr. in August 1994, Bowe struck his opponent with an unsportsmanlike blow as Mathis was on one knee, regrouping from a knockdown. The fight was ruled a no-contest by the New Jersey Boxing Commission. Violence would occasionally erupt outside of the ring as well, as Bowe engaged in violent altercations with other boxers at pre-fight press conferences and weigh-ins. Prior to these events, Bowe had been known for being good-natured with a sense of humor, characteristics that sportswriters and commentators frequently contrasted with fellow Brownsville native and prizefighter MICHAEL GERARD TYSON.

Bowe fought Holyfield a third time, in November 1995, winning the fight in the eighth round, despite being knocked down for the first time in his career. Despite all his successes, he did not figure prominently in the title picture after losing his belts. He did win the belt of a smaller organization, the World Boxing Organization, by defeating Herbie Hide in March 1995, making him a champion again; but the major belts remained beyond his grasp. Bowe's inability to get into the ring with key contenders for the major boxing titles may have been out of retribution for the cutthroat negotiating style of his manager and promoter, Eugene Roderick "Rock" Newman.

In July 1996 Bowe would once again see controversy in the ring and violence outside it with a bout at Madison Square Garden. Following a bloody fight in which Bowe's opponent, Andrew Golota, had been disqualified for punching below the belt, the arena erupted into violence and a riot ensued. This was blamed largely on Bowe's rowdy corner crew and Newman's inability to control them. The boxers had a rematch in December of 1996, and once again the fight ended in a disqualification for Golota. Between the two bouts Bowe's longtime trainer, Eddie Futch, quit. Bowe had been overweight and underprepared for his first fight with Golota, and Futch had grown tired of the fighter's lack of discipline. Bowe himself retired in May 1997.

In February of 1997 Bowe joined the U.S. Marine Corps. He lasted a total of eleven days, completing just three days of basic training. It was also in 1997 that his marriage broke up; his wife and their five children moved to Cornelius, North Carolina. A year later Bowe, attempting to reunite his family, abducted Judy Bowe and their children at knifepoint from their home. Bowe was apprehended and forced to go through a mental health evaluation and serve eighteen months in jail. The relative leniency of the sentence was due in part to a plea deal, and in part to the testimony of several doctors that Bowe had sustained brain damage as a boxer. Bowe had initially received an even lighter thirty-day sentence for kidnapping from North Carolina; assault charges in Maryland (where Bowe lived) were set aside. The North Carolina sentence was twice rejected by an appeals court; in 2003 Bowe was sentenced to eighteen months in prison. Bowe and his wife divorced in 1998.

In 2000 Riddick married Terri Blakney. He was arrested on a domestic violence charge of second-degree assault against his wife in 2003, shortly before he was to start serving the North Carolina prison term.

He staged a boxing comeback in September 2004 with a victory over Marcus Rhode, and had a narrow victory over Billy Zumbrum in April 2005. He filed for bankruptcy in October 2005.

Further Reading
Myler, Thomas. *The Sweet Science Goes Sour: How Scandal Brought Boxing to Its Knees* (2006).
Sugar, Bert Randolph. *Boxing's Greatest Fighters* (2006).
                                   THOMAS EDWARD GUASTELLO

BOWEN, John Wesley Edward (3 Dec. 1855–20 July 1933), Methodist educator and theologian, was born in New Orleans, Louisiana, the son of Edward Bowen and Rose Simon. John's father was a carpenter from Maryland who was enslaved when he moved to New Orleans. After purchasing his own freedom, Edward Bowen bought that of his wife and son in 1858 and served in the Union army during the Civil War. After the war, young J. W. E. Bowen studied at the Union Normal School in New Orleans and at New Orleans University, which was founded by the Methodist Episcopal Church for the education of freedmen. Bowen received a bachelor's degree with the university's first graduating class in 1878. Eight years later, New Orleans University awarded him a master's degree. From 1878 to 1882 Bowen taught mathematics and ancient languages at Central Tennessee College in Nashville.

In 1882 Bowen began theological studies at Boston University. While he was a theological student he was also the pastor of Revere Street Methodist Episcopal Church in Boston. Bowen earned a bachelor of sacred theology degree in 1885, and soon after he became pastor of Saint John's Methodist Episcopal Church in Newark, New Jersey. He continued graduate study in theology, and he married Ariel Serena Hedges of Baltimore, Maryland, in 1886; they had four children. Bowen was the second African American to earn a PhD in the United States when Boston University conferred the degree on him in 1887. After leaving Saint John's in 1888, Bowen went on to serve as pastor of Centennial Methodist Episcopal Church in Baltimore and of Asbury Methodist Episcopal Church in Washington, D.C.

At Centennial Church he conducted a notable revival in which more than seven hundred people claimed conversion. He also served as professor of church history and systematic theology at Baltimore's Morgan College from 1888 to 1892 and as professor of Hebrew at Howard University in Washington, D.C., from 1890 to 1891. From 1889 to 1893 Bowen was also a member and examiner for the American Institute of Sacred Literature. In 1892 he published *What Shall the Harvest Be? A National Sermon; or, A Series of Plain Talks to the Colored People of America, on Their Problems*. He represented the

Methodist Episcopal Church at conferences of world Methodism in Washington, D.C., in 1891 and in London in 1901.

In 1892, after leaving his posts at Centennial and Asbury, Bowen became a field secretary for the Freedmen's Aid Society of the Methodist Episcopal Church. He left the Freedmen's Aid Society in 1893, however, to become professor of historical theology at Gammon Theological Seminary in Atlanta, Georgia. As the first African American professor at the school—founded in 1883 by the Methodist Episcopal Church for the preparation of African American clergymen—Bowen was awarded an honorary doctor of divinity degree by Gammon in 1893. As secretary of the seminary's Stewart Missionary Foundation for Africa, he also edited its periodical, the *Stewart Missionary Magazine.*

In October 1895, after praising BOOKER T. WASHINGTON's emphasis on industrial education and the work ethic in Washington's address to Atlanta's Cotton States' Exposition a month earlier, Bowen delivered his own address, "An appeal to the king," on "Negro Day" at the exposition. In December 1895 Bowen organized an important three-day conference on Africa that was held in conjunction with the exposition; he published its proceedings as *Africa and the American Negro: Addresses and Proceedings of the Congress on Africa . . . in Connection with the Cotton States . . . Exposition, Dec. 13–15, 1895* (1896). Subsequently, however, Bowen distanced himself from Washington by defending liberal arts education for leadership and joined W. E. B. DU BOIS in protesting state legislation to segregate railroad transportation and limit funds for black public schools to taxes paid by black people.

In 1896 Bowen was elected a delegate to the quadrennial general conference of the Methodist Episcopal Church, a position that he retained until 1912. As the most distinguished African American clergyman in the Methodist Episcopal Church, Bowen received many votes for the episcopacy at the general conferences in 1896, 1900, and 1904. As a member of the Board of Control of the Methodist Episcopal Church's Epworth League, he organized a national conference in Atlanta on the Christian education of African American youth. With I. GARLAND PENN, Bowen also edited and published its proceedings, *The United Negro, . . . Addresses and Proceedings: The Negro Young People's Christian and Educational Congress, Held August 6–11, 1902* (1902).

In January 1904 Bowen and JESSE MAX BARBER launched the *Voice of the Negro,* a literary journal addressed to a national audience of African Americans. In September 1905 they endorsed the Niagara Movement, which was organized by Du Bois and others to protest African Americans' loss of civil rights; months later they promoted the organization of the Georgia Equal Rights League, which had similar objectives. At the peak of its circulation in 1906 the *Voice of the Negro* claimed twelve to fifteen thousand subscribers.

After the death of his first wife in 1904, Bowen married Irene L. Smallwood in 1906. They had no children. That same year Bowen became the president of Gammon Theological Seminary. In September, however, his inaugural year was shadowed by a severe race riot in which white rioters brutally attacked black people in Atlanta. Bowen opened the seminary to shelter black refugees from the riot. Three days after the rioting began Bowen himself was beaten and arrested by Atlanta's white police. Barber fled the city, taking the *Voice of the Negro* with him to Chicago, where he continued its publication as the *Voice* for a year without Bowen's assistance.

Bowen survived the Atlanta race riot and served as president of Gammon until 1910, when its administration was merged with that of Clark University. He became vice president of the merged institution and continued as professor of historical theology. A lecturer on the Chautauqua circuit, Bowen was an active member of the American Historical Association, the American Negro Academy, and the National Association for the Advancement of Colored People. The frustration of African American hopes for leadership in the church eventually led to Bowen's publication of *An Appeal for Negro Bishops, but No Separation* in 1912. When the Methodist Episcopal Church finally determined to elect its first two African American bishops in 1920, however, it chose younger men, Robert Elijah Jones and Matthew Wesley Clair. Bowen retired as head of the church history department at Gammon in 1926 but continued to teach until 1932, when he became an emeritus professor. He died in Atlanta. Throughout a distinguished career Bowen was an eloquent example of an African American Christian intellectual.

Further Reading

The J. W. E. Bowen Papers are in the Gammon Theological Seminary Archives at the Atlanta University Center's Woodruff Library.

Harlan, Louis R. "Booker T. Washington and the *Voice of the Negro,* 1904–1907," *Journal of Southern History* 45 (Feb. 1979): 45–62.

Luker, Ralph E. *The Social Gospel in Black and White: American Racial Reform, 1885–1912* (1991).

Meier, August. *Negro Thought in America 1880–1915: Racial Ideologies in the Age of Booker T. Washington* (1963).

Moss, Alfred A., Jr. *The American Negro Academy: Voice of the Talented Tenth* (1981).

Obituaries: *Atlanta Constitution,* 21 July 1933; J. R. Van Pelt, "John Wesley Edward Bowen," *Journal of Negro History* 14 (Apr. 1934): 217–221.

RALPH E. LUKER

BOWEN, Ruth Jean (1924–), business owner and entertainment promoter, was born in Danville, Virginia, to Claude Carlton and Marion Baskerville, about whom little is known. Ruth attended the Westmoreland Elementary School and Langston High School in Danville. Ruth's family moved to New York City when she was a teenager, and she graduated from

Girls High School in Brooklyn. After attending New York University for two years, she met and fell in love with Wallace "Billy" Bowen, a member of the popular Ink Spots, one of the few entertainment groups in the 1940s and 1950s to break the race barrier and perform for white audiences across the United States. Bowen left school and she and Billy were married until his death in 1982.

Bowen managed the daily office responsibilities of her husband's business. She also traveled the United States with the Ink Spots during their concert tours. During the 1940s the Bowens and the members of the Ink Spots often experienced the sting of segregation when they were denied hotel rooms or forced to lodge in special back rooms designated for "coloreds only." While on tour in Pittsburgh, Bowen's husband introduced her to the legendary blues singer DINAH WASHINGTON. The two women quickly became friends and eventually Bowen became Washington's publicist.

Bowen's endeavors as a publicist were successful, and she soon also became Washington's manager. Washington's booking agent taught Bowen everything about the entertainment industry—from how to handle correspondence to how to book acts. After Bowen noticed that the earning potential of black entertainers was limited because of the social restrictions placed on where they could perform in the United States, she began to book Washington for European concerts, a successful stroke that solidified her reputation as an entertainment booking agent.

In 1959 Bowen and Washington became business partners, opening the Queen Artists booking agency. After Washington won a Grammy Award that same year for "What a Difference a Day Makes," Bowen had to hire office staff so that she could personally manage Washington's growing career. While the two were on the road for concert venues, Washington often referred new acts to Bowen, including popular groups like the Dells and the dancer LOLA FALANA.

Queen Booking grew quickly and Bowen found that she had to train her office staff to become talent-booking agents. The agency was responsible for booking acts in big theaters like the Apollo in Harlem and the Regal in Chicago, and many popular jazz clubs across the United States. Bowen trained her staff—which was both black and white—in the art of entertainment booking. Queen Booking handled the publicity and bookings for popular acts like EARL BOSTIC, KENNY BURRELL, and the Basin Street East Nightclub. When Washington died in 1963, the Queen Booking agency employed thirty workers and managed more than 100 acts. The company name was soon changed to Queen Booking Corporation (QBC). Within five years the company had become the largest black-owned entertainment agency in the United States. Its client base had expanded beyond music groups to include other acts like comedians, gospel choirs, and rock bands. Bowen was able to demand and receive top venues and pay for her clients—even from nightclubs that had developed reputations for discrimination against African Americans.

Despite the fact that Bowen had excelled in a traditionally male industry, she found that occasionally she still had to prove herself. Club owners were sometimes not as accommodating to her as they were to male counterparts. For example, sometimes she would only be given one chance to successfully book an act before losing all other booking opportunities. With the growth in popularity of rock and roll and rhythm and blues, QBC began to handle both black and white artists. Bowen had a reputation as a tough negotiator for all of her acts—black and white. Her philosophy was that if the same money was being paid, then the same respect and comforts should be provided, and she did not compromise. Despite the obstacles Bowen faced, she was able to build QBC into an industry powerhouse with a net worth of $3 million. She received further recognition in 1973 when the Manhattan borough president PERCY SUTTON issued a proclamation and declared it "Ruth Bowen Day." Among the top entertainers managed by QBC were ARETHA FRANKLIN, PATTI LABELLE, the O'Jays, SMOKEY ROBINSON, STEVIE WONDER, MARVIN GAYE, IKE and TINA TURNER, the Ohio Players, AL GREEN, RAY CHARLES, SHIRLEY CAESAR, the Mighty Clouds of Joy, and RICHARD PRYOR.

Further Reading

Cohodas, Nadine. *Queen: The Life and Music of Dinah Washington* (2004).

Hine, Darlene Clark, ed. *Black Women in America: An Historical Encyclopedia* (1993).

Who's Who Among Black Americans, 1994/95, 8th edition (1993).

ANGELA BLACK

BOWEN, Uvelia Atkins (23 Apr. 1922–), educator and community activist, was born Uvelia Atkins in Middlesex County, Virginia. She attended public elementary schools in Middlesex County, and in 1940 she graduated from the Rappahannock Industrial Academy, a private high school in Essex County. Atkins graduated in 1945 from Virginia Union University, in Richmond, where she majored in English and was vice president of the YWCA, secretary of Kappa Gamma Chi, and a member of the NAACP. She married the Reverend Walter Duncan Bowen, a Presbyterian pastor, in Philadelphia, Pennsylvania, in 1954. The couple did not have any children, and throughout their lives they worked with inner-city young people. She received a master of social service degree from Bryn Mawr College in 1957.

From 1951 to 1965 Bowen worked in Philadelphia for the United Neighbors Association, a multi-program agency that provided services to city residents; she was the association's first woman assistant director from 1959 through 1965. During the years 1961 through 1964, she served as the national chair of the United Presbyterian Women's Target: Youth in a Troubled World. Often considered a forerunner to the federal government's War on Poverty program of the late 1960s, it established tutoring and mentoring programs as well as employment and housing initiatives.

In 1967 Bowen founded HEART—the Household Employment Association for Reevaluation and Training in Philadelphia—at a time when household employment was the third largest occupation for women and usually the only employment women of color could obtain. It also was the poorest paid. HEART worked to establish policies to upgrade the status of household employment, including the education of employers about fair work practices. The association's goal as stated in its literature involved training both the employer and the employee so that "equity and dignity in the home existed for employees and employer." HEART aimed at developing a work relationship between employer and employee characterized by communication and professionalism. In addition, HEART opened a licensed, private trade school for community education, job development, and placement counseling. The school selected, trained, and placed workers as professional technicians in households, and by 1971 had become a national training center for people interested in establishing programs to upgrade the service occupations.

Bowen also wrote *What Is a Day's Work?*, published by HEART in 1970, which argued that greater respect should be accorded to household work and that the relationship between household employee and employer should be redressed. She wrote about specific new policies for the employee-employer household work relationship regarding work hours, wages, sick leave, vacations, and work assignments. She detailed twenty-two employment categories, from cleaning technician with light laundry, geriatrics assistant, foods technician, and party aide. She changed the name of caretakers of the elderly to "geriatrics assistants," housekeeper to "cleaning technician," cook to "foods technician," and party waitress to "party aide." Other aspects of the book included the rights and responsibilities of both the employee and employer with a focus on policies that create a balanced employer-employee relationship. Employees' needs are also discussed in the book, including neighborhood-based day care for employees' children. The final chapter examined the role of the employer as a supervisor and suggested guidelines for determining what should be considered a realistic "day's work." Bowen's second book, *Thursday's People on the Move!*, was published by HEART in 1971 and is a teaching tool for organizations interested in upgrading work policies in the service occupations. The first section outlined HEART's policies and procedures for recruiting, training, and counseling household employees. The second section discussed job development, placement counseling, and community education. Instructive case histories were included along with open-ended discussion questions.

In 1974 Bowen founded the International Congress of Virginia Union University Women Graduates. The goals of the congress were to create a registry of female graduates from the university and to provide a resource to help new graduates. Also in 1974 she founded Personnel Resources Inc., a private

trade school that trained students in household employment. Despite politically motivated criticism as reported in the *Philadelphia Inquirer* in 1988 when the Philadelphia Housing Authority was instructed by HUD to investigate documentation of a grant to Personnel Resources Inc., Bowen continued her work in upgrading policies for employees in the service occupations. She was named an Outstanding Professional in Human Services in 1974 and 1975 by the American Academy of Human Services. From 1977 through 1981 she served as a member of the Board of Trustees at Temple University in Philadelphia. She also established the Youth Assistance Endowment in memory of her husband when he died in 1997.

In 2000 Bowen received the Presidential Award for Exemplary Service from the National Association of Social Workers, which was presented to her for "exemplary service and excellence in social work education."

Further Reading
The papers of Uvelia Atkins Bowen are at the Archives and Special Collections Library, L. Douglas Wilder Library, Virginia Union University in Richmond, Virginia.
"Bad Housekeeping PHA Is Squandering More Than Money," *Philadelphia Inquirer*, 25 Oct. 1988.
Loeb, Vernon. "HUD Wants to See Data on City Housekeeping Course," *Philadelphia Inquirer*, 21 Oct. 1988.
National Association of Social Workers, Inc. NASW News, available online at http://www.socialworkers.org/pubs/news.

LINDA SPENCER

BOWERS, Thomas J. (1826–4 Oct. 1885), tenor, was born in Philadelphia, Pennsylvania, the son of John Bowers, a prominent member of Philadelphia's black elite and vestryman at St. Thomas's African Episcopal Church, and Henrietta Bowers (c. 1795–1868). Widowed in October 1844, his mother was a member of St. Thomas's congregation for more than fifty years. The 1860 federal census listed her occupation as cook. Bowers learned to play pianoforte and organ from his elder brother, John C. Bowers, and at the age of eighteen became organist at St. Thomas's. Although his parents encouraged their children's musical abilities at home and in church, they looked unfavorably on public performances of music. As a consequence, Bowers declined an offer to join the popular Philadelphia band led by FRANCIS JOHNSON.

Despite his parents' objections, however, in 1854 Bowers made his first public performance as a vocalist at Sansom Street Hall in Philadelphia. He appeared as the student of ELIZABETH TAYLOR GREENFIELD, a well-known singer with an extraordinary range who had been given the sobriquet "Black Swan." During her career Greenfield sang in the United States, Canada, and Great Britain, where she made a command performance for Queen Victoria. Bowers received high praise for the Sansom Street

Hall performance and other concerts in Philadelphia, and subsequently he and Greenfield embarked on a tour of New York State and Canada, where they garnered excellent reviews. While on tour in Hamilton, Ontario, Bowers successfully defied that city's segregationist policy, refusing to perform unless six black ticket holders were permitted to take their seats. Bowers's opposition to performing before segregated audiences continued throughout the tour as well as during the remainder of his career. Politically active in Philadelphia, he was a supporter of the anti-colonization movement, which opposed the emigration of free blacks and slaves from the United States to Africa, and was later elected a delegate to the National Convention of Colored Men in 1865.

Because of his remarkable singing abilities, Bowers was dubbed the "colored Mario" or "American Mario" after the famous Italian opera singer of the nineteenth century, Mario (Giovanni Matteo, Cavaliere de Candia). In response he adopted the stage name Mareo. Bowers performed in a number of states during his career. Continuing to sing publicly on occasion into middle age, he sang "The Star-spangled Banner" upon request at the opening of the first grammar school for African American children in Philadelphia in 1876. His repertoire included ballads as well as many of the popular solos for tenors from the operas and oratorios of the period. He hoped that his performances would prove to whites that black musicians were not minstrels—popular entertainers, both black and white, who performed a caricatured version of African American songs and dances while made up in blackface—but were capable of performing music from the classical repertoire as well as white musicians. Along with his sister, Sarah Sedgewick Bowers, who was also a professional singer known as the "Colored Nightingale," Bowers was an outstanding example of the gifted black classical performers of the nineteenth century. In addition to his musical performances, Bowers worked as a tailor, and then became a prosperous coal merchant. Around 1850 he married Lucenia (Serenia?) Bowers, and they had one daughter, Adelia (Alice?). He died in Philadelphia in 1885.

Further Reading
Southern, Eileen. *The Music of Black Americans: A History* (1971, 3d ed. 1997).
Trotter, James Monroe. *Music and Some Highly Musical People* (1881, repr. 1968).
Obituary: *New York Times*, 5 Oct. 1885.
                                                   WILLIAM S. WALKER

BOWIE, Lester (11 Oct. 1941–8 Nov. 1999), jazz trumpeter, composer, and cofounder of the Art Ensemble of Chicago, was born William Lester Bowie Jr. in Frederick, Maryland, and raised in St. Louis, Missouri, the eldest son of the cornetist W. Lester Bowie Sr. and Earxie Lee Willingham, who worked for the Social Security Administration. Bowie came from a musical family; in 1911 in Bartonsville, Maryland, his grandfather founded the Bartonsville Cornet Band, which included several uncles; his father directed school bands in Little Rock, Arkansas, and St. Louis; and his brothers Byron and Joseph became professional musicians. As a baby Bowie played with his father's cornet mouthpiece, at five he started playing the trumpet, and as a teenager he joined the musicians' union and worked regularly with St. Louis R&B musicians like ALBERT KING and IKE TURNER.

In spite of his early musical success, Bowie did not expect to make music his life, and after graduating from high school in 1958 he enlisted in the air force for four years. He served with the military police, performing in his spare time. During his military service he learned that he preferred playing music to being a soldier, so after he was discharged, he studied music first at Lincoln University in Missouri, and then a year later at North Texas State. After a year in Texas he returned to St. Louis, where he began performing full time with blues and R&B musicians and touring occasionally with circus bands.

Bowie developed a workmanlike philosophy. Reflecting on the diversity of his musical experiences, he told his interviewer Bob Bernotas: "You have to learn how to feed yourself with the instrument, period. And that entails playing everything you can" (Bernotas, 23). At the same time his love of jazz continued to grow. He was influenced by bebop and post-bop musicians, but even stronger was the influence of earlier trumpeters like BUBBER MILEY, COOTIE WILLIAMS, and especially LOUIS ARMSTRONG; these players spoke directly to his sense of playful exploration and showmanship. Bowie was well versed in the jazz tradition, but he was not content to reproduce the music of the past. He thought of jazz as a way of life that embraced innovation and exploration, one that sought to move beyond the classic performers and composers of the past while honoring their accomplishments. This philosophy led him to develop his own unique and highly personal musical voice. He experimented with other young, avant-garde musicians including Oliver Lake and JULIUS HEMPHILL, who later helped found the Black Artists' Group in St. Louis.

In 1965 Bowie moved to Chicago, where he became music director for R&B singer Fontella Bass. They married and had four children together. Chicago was home to many great blues and R&B musicians such as JERRY BUTLER and JACKIE WILSON and influential recording studios such as Chess Records, so Bowie was able to earn a good living in the city. Chicago's growing free jazz scene also drew him. In 1966 Bowie began performing with a group led by Roscoe Mitchell and he joined Chicago's black avant-garde collective, the Association for the Advancement of Creative Musicians (AACM), becoming the organization's second president. The AACM embraced free improvisation, African musical practices, and aspects of ritual and theater. At times AACM members seemed to reject standard jazz characteristics like popular song forms, functional harmony, swing rhythm, and a clear distinction between a soloist and the rhythm section. Many condemned their music as the end of jazz. On the 1966 Roscoe Mitchell Art Ensemble recording, *Congliptious,* Bowie addressed this issue. His piece "Jazz Death?" opens with the question, "Isn't jazz, as we know it, dead yet?" His answer is an unaccompanied improvisation in which he plays his way through the history of jazz trumpet styles, incorporating them into the avant-garde performance practices of the AACM. At the end of the piece Bowie says, "Well, I guess that depends on what you know," presenting the music of the AACM and the Art Ensemble of the Chicago not as the end of jazz but as a legitimate continuation of jazz's spirit of innovation.

In 1969 Bowie, saxophonist Roscoe Mitchell, bassist Malachi Favors Maghostut, and saxophonist Joseph Jarman moved to Paris, where they were later joined by their fellow AACM member and percussionist Famoudou Don Moye. Previously, in Chicago, the group had rehearsed constantly but performed infrequently; in Europe, where they became known as the Art Ensemble of Chicago (AEC), they found themselves in constant demand. Their groundbreaking improvisations included brass band–flavored melodies, African-inspired percussion work, and "little instruments" like whistles, bells, and toys, as well as aspects of performance art. The musicians wore face paint, African robes, and costumes, heightening the ritual aspects of their performance. In the spirit of experimentation and irony, Bowie frequently appeared in a white lab coat, his long goatee waxed into two devilish points.

Having established himself as a leading voice in experimental jazz, Bowie returned to the United States in 1971. He moved to Jamaica in 1975 and returned to the United States in 1976. He and Bass divorced, and he married photographer Deborah Neeley in 1979. Though Bowie and Neeley settled in the Bronx, he maintained close ties with Chicago musicians. He continued to play with the AEC until his death, but he became involved in many other projects; in 1978 he joined drummer Jack DeJohnette's quartet New Directions; in 1979 he organized the fifty-nine-piece Sho'Nuff Orchestra; and in 1982 he formed the New York Hot Trumpet Repertory Company, which included Olu Dara and WYNTON MARSALIS. (Bowie and Marsalis parted ways, and Marsalis would go on to represent a very different approach to the jazz tradition.) In 1983 he renamed the Hot Trumpets Lester Bowie's Brass Fantasy. The group played original compositions as well as songs by the Spice Girls, Marilyn Manson, and Puccini, offering succinct expressions of Bowie's iconoclastic yet all-embracing philosophy of music in album titles such as *Avant Pop* (1986) and *Serious Fun* (1989). In the 1980s Bowie also led From the Root to the Source, a quintet plus three gospel singers (including Fontella Bass), which blended jazz, pop, and gospel; in the 1990s Bowie formed the New York Organ Ensemble.

In describing his music, Bowie said: "People ask me, 'What kind of music do you play?' I tell them free jazz—free to play whatever I feel like" (Green, 86). Indeed, he drew inspiration from a broad range of African American musical expressions that included not only early and mainstream jazz but also sources as diverse as doo-wop, soul, the *Howdy Doody* theme song, and African musical traditions. He was among the first avant-garde trumpeters to use and expand upon the wails, growls, and sneers of early trumpeters like Bubber Miley and Cootie Williams, adapting those techniques to the performance of free jazz and bringing to the trumpet the kind of sonic flexibility that came so readily to avant-garde saxophonists. Some, like Wynton Marsalis, trumpeter and artistic director of Jazz at Lincoln Center, and Ken Burns, director of the epic documentary *Jazz,* seek to understand jazz as a collection of canonical composers, compositions, and practices. Lester Bowie's eclecticism and his humorous, ironic, and unorthodox improvisations suggest alternative, more open-ended histories of jazz that, in the twenty-first century, continue to inspire new generations of jazz musicians, including trumpet players such as Dave Douglas and Corey Wilkes, who replaced Bowie in the AEC after his death.

Further Reading
Bernotas, Bob. "Lester Bowie," *Jazz Player* (Oct./Nov. 1995).
Green, Tony. "Profile: Lester Bowie," *Jazziz Magazine* (Mar. 1996).
Jordan, Phillippa, and Rafi Zabor. "Lester Bowie: Roots, Research, and the Carnival Chef," in *The Jazz Musician,* eds. Mark Rowland and Tony Scherman (1994).
Livingston, Tim. "Interview: Lester Bowie," *Cadence* (Jan. 2001).
Obituaries: *New York Times,* Arts section, 11 Nov. 1999; *Village Voice,* 8–14 Dec. 1999.

JOHN HARRIS-BEHLING

BOWLES, Eva Del Vakia (24 Jan. 1875–14 June 1943), organization leader, was born in Albany, Athens County, Ohio, the daughter of John Hawkes Bowles and Mary Jane Porter. Unlike most African Americans born during the Reconstruction era, Bowles grew up in comfortable circumstances. Her grandfather John R. Bowles served as a chaplain for the all-black Fifty-fifth Massachusetts Infantry and later became the first black teacher hired by the Ohio Public School Fund. Her father was the first black postal clerk in Columbus, Ohio.

Bowles was educated in Columbus at a business college and attended summer courses at Ohio State University. After a short teaching career in Kentucky, North Carolina, and Virginia, she was recruited in 1905 to work in New York City as secretary of the Colored Young Women's Christian Association (later affiliated with the New York City YWCA as the 137th Street branch in Harlem). This position made her the "first employed Negro YWCA Secretary in the country." In 1908 she received training in social work at Columbia University School of Philanthropy.

In 1913, after a brief return to Columbus, where she worked as a caseworker, Bowles returned to New

York as secretary of the newly formed Subcommittee for Colored Work of the YWCA national board. The position had been created in recognition of the fast-growing interest in association work among urban black women. Among Bowles's responsibilities was helping the organization accommodate its black membership without jeopardizing the support of whites. At a time when many whites supported race separation, this was no easy task.

At the time of Bowles's appointment, the national board had fourteen local "colored" affiliates. For the most part, these associations were organized by black club women to provide services similar to those offered by white YWCAs—namely lodging and club activities for young single women who moved into cities to work. Black women were routinely excluded from white facilities. Furthermore, although local black and white associations were affiliated with the national board, there was often little communication between the local organizations. Bowles's solution was to create a structure whereby there would be only one YWCA in each city. Because the black associations were usually smaller and less financially stable, they became branches of the larger, white organization.

Although this arrangement made black women accountable to white women, Bowles insisted that the volunteers and staff of the black branches be in charge of day-to-day operations and fund-raising. In addition she regularly scheduled skills and leadership training opportunities for black volunteers and staff. Bowles believed that integration was inevitable. She felt that this structure would provide a way for the two races to become accustomed to working together and that black women would have the opportunity to prove their administrative and decision-making abilities.

World War I offered a unique opportunity for the YWCA when the national board was granted $4 million by the U.S. War Department Commission on Training Camp Activities to work with women and girls on the home front. The War Work Council of the YWCA set aside $200,000 for projects with African Americans, and Bowles was made secretary in charge of expanding services to black women. Under this mandate, the association was able to open recreation centers, industrial work centers, and fifteen hostess houses (facilities that provided entertainment for soldiers and sometimes lodging for their families) near army installations. By the end of the war, black women were being served in forty-five cities, and the association had over thirty-nine thousand black members. Most notable was the use of funds leftover from the war effort to build a much-needed association facility in Washington, D.C., to accommodate the city's growing black population. Bowles's accomplishments during the war so impressed former president Theodore Roosevelt that he designated $4,000 of his Nobel Peace Prize to be dispersed according to her directions.

To accomplish this expansion of work during the war, Bowles sought the support of the network of prominent black club women in the National Association of Colored Women. She later used the influence of this group to press the national board for more equitable representation for black women on local and national committees and boards. This move resulted in significant steps toward more biracial cooperation in student and community associations. Furthermore black women gained their first representative on the national board in 1924.

After the war, Bowles concentrated on the improvement of race relations within the national association. As secretary of the Council on Colored Work, she increased the number of black staff employed by the national board to nine at headquarters and three in the field. Under her leadership, the board led other organizations in negotiations to hold nationally sponsored conventions and meetings only in cities that would guarantee that all members, regardless of race, could be accommodated. She also worked tirelessly as an advocate of the international work of the association, especially in Africa and the Caribbean. She became disillusioned with the YWCA, however, and resigned in 1932, charging that a recent reorganization would "diminish participation of Negroes in the policy making of the Association" by dispersing black staff in a way that she felt decreased their effectiveness in behalf of the specific needs of black women.

Bowles did not confine her interest in race work to the YWCA. She was an active volunteer in such important organizations as the Urban League, the National Interracial Conference, the American Interracial Peace Committee, the National Association for the Advancement of Colored People, the National League of Women Voters, the Commission of Church and Race Relations of the Federal Council of Churches, and her denominational Episcopalian Women's Interracial Council.

After her resignation from the YWCA, Bowles worked briefly as an executive of the National Colored Merchants Association, sponsored by the National Business League. Then, after returning to her native Ohio, she served for a brief time as acting secretary of the West End branch of the YWCA of Cincinnati. During the 1940 presidential campaign, she became the Harlem organizer for the Wendell Willkie Republican organization. She died in Richmond, Virginia.

Further Reading

Information on Bowles's work is on microfilm in the national board YWCA archives under Colored Work, Interracial Work, and War Work Council.
Olcott, Jane, ed. *The Work of Colored Women* (1919).

Obituaries: *Norfolk Journal and Guide*, 19 June 1943; *Woman's Press*, Sept. 1943.

ADRIENNE LASH JONES

BOWMAN, James E., Jr. (5 Feb. 1923–), pathologist and geneticist, was born in Washington, D.C., the oldest of six children born to James E. Bowman, a dentist, and Peterson Bowman, a homemaker. Bowman completed his undergraduate and medical school education in Washington, receiving a BS in 1943 and an MD in 1946, both from Howard University. After completing an internship at the Freedman's Hospital in Washington, D.C. (1946–1947), Bowman moved to St. Luke's Hospital in Chicago for a residency in pathology (1947–1950). It was during his residency that he met his future wife, Barbara Taylor, a Chicago native who was then completing her undergraduate degree at Sarah Lawrence College in Bronxville, New York. The couple married in 1950, the same year that Bowman was made chairman of the department of pathology at Chicago's Provident Hospital, a primarily African American institution (1950–1953).

From 1953 until 1955 Bowman served as a captain in the U.S. Army Medical Corps with an appointment as chief of the pathology branch of the Medical Nutrition Laboratory at Fitzsimmons Army Hospital in Denver, Colorado. Bowman's career then took a turn pioneered by many other black doctors and scientists before him: he went abroad in search of further opportunities. He and he wife spent the next six years in Iran, where Bowman held appointments at Namazaee Hospital (chairman, department of pathology, 1955–1961) and Pahlavi University (associate professor and professor of pathology, 1957–1961), both in Shiraz, Iran. Bowman's exposure to the particular set of diseases, mainly favism, experienced by Iranian patients stimulated his growing interest in population genetics, particularly the distribution of inherited metabolic and blood disorders. After leaving Iran in 1961 Bowman spent the following year as a special research fellow in biometry and genetics at the University of London's Galton Laboratory, a leading research center for the study of what was then known as inborn errors of metabolism.

Bowman published several papers in the early 1960s on the origins of favism, an inherited disease in which patients lack glucose-6-phosphate dehydrogenase, an enzyme necessary for the normal functioning of hemoglobin. The enzyme deficiency can cause a sudden destruction of red blood cells after eating certain legumes—particularly fava beans, a staple of the Iranian diet. Bowman's research in genetic blood disorders was taking place during a revolution in biochemistry and genetic medicine. In 1948 Linus Pauling had demonstrated that sickle cell anemia is caused by a protein abnormality in hemoglobin. Proteins are the molecules that carry out most of the biological processes within the cell. The structure of a protein is determined by its sequence of amino acids, which in turn is specified by the DNA sequence that codes for the specific protein. Because proteins' functions are tied so closely to their structure, a single point change in the DNA sequence (a mutation) can have a dramatic effect on cellular function. In 1956 a new era of molecular medicine was born when researchers located the point mutation that caused sickle cell anemia. These findings explained that any number of in-

herited blood diseases had specific genetic origins; for Bowman they established a research agenda for the rest of his career.

In 1962 Bowman and his wife returned to Chicago to accept an appointment as medical director of the Blood Bank (1962–1972) and assistant professor of medicine and pathology at the University of Chicago. He became associate professor in 1967 and full professor in 1972. Bowman occupied a number of leadership positions at the University of Chicago, including director of laboratories (1971–1981), director of the Comprehensive Sickle Cell Center (1973–1974), and liaison officer for International Activities (1969–1971), the Committee on Appointment Inequities (1971–1975), and University Senate (1971–1974).

As head of one of the country's leading sickle cell treatment centers Bowman soon became involved in debates within both the black and scientific communities about the benefits and limits of genetic screening programs. As genetic screening tests became available for diseases such as sickle cell anemia, PKU, and Tay-Sachs, some states began making these tests mandatory for marriage and admission to public schools. Although many physicians, including Bowman, were enthusiastic about the possibilities of this research for human health, some in the black community pointed a skeptical finger at the long association of genetics with scientific racism and eugenics. In the late 1970s, for example, the Du Pont Company required genetic screening as a pre-employment test and refused to hire workers with sickle cell. These debates only intensified with the launch of the Human Genome Project—a massive effort to sequence the entire human genome—in 1990. Throughout the 1980s and 1990s Bowman served on a number of national committees and policy boards on genetics, including, most visibly, the National Institutes of Health's (NIH) Working Group on Ethical, Legal, and Social Issues (1995–1998). With Robert F. Murray, a professor of pediatrics and medicine at Howard University, Bowman authored what would become the standard textbook on genetic variation in persons of African heritage, *Genetic Variation and Disorders in Peoples of African Origin* (1990).

Bowman's interest in international population genetics and scientific issues continued throughout his career, with over ninety publications on genetic variation in populations in Iran, Turkey, Taiwan, the United States, Ghana, Nigeria, Cameroon, Uganda, Ethiopia, Mexico, and South Vietnam. Bowman was a fellow of the College of American Pathologists, the American Society of Clinical Pathologists, the Royal Society of Tropical Medicine and Hygiene, and the Hastings Center. He held memberships in thirteen scientific societies in pathology, hematology, genetics, ethics, anthropology, clinical research, and ethics. He retired in 1993 and was named professor emeritus in the departments of pathology and medicine at the University of Chicago. In 2006 his daughter, Valerie Jarrett, was named chair of the University of Chicago Medical Center Board.

Further Reading

Much of the information for this entry was gathered through personal correspondence with its subject, 16 Feb. 2007.

Bowman, James E., and Robert F. Murray Jr. *Genetic Variation and Disorders in Peoples of African Origin* (1990).

American Men and Women of Science, 22d ed. (2005).

Harris, Ron. "Tampering with Genes: A New Threat to Blacks?" *Ebony* (Sept. 1980).

AUDRA J. WOLFE

BOWMAN, Laura (3 Oct. 1881–29 Mar. 1957), actor and singer, was born Laura Bradford in Quincy, Illinois, the daughter of a Dutch mother and a father with mixed black and white parentage. She grew up in Cincinnati, where she sang in church choirs. Her early family life was difficult, and her father arranged her marriage at sixteen to Henry Ward Bowman, a railroad porter. The unhappy marriage lasted only two years. In 1902 Bowman's dream of a singing career began with her professional debut as a member of the chorus in the Midwest tour of the Williams and Walker Company's production of *In Dahomey*. The show went on to New York and in 1903 toured England, where it also played at Buckingham Palace for the ninth birthday of the Prince of Wales, Edward VIII.

During the tour of *In Dahomey* Bowman fell in love with PETE HAMPTON, another performer in the show. Soon after arriving in England the original company broke up, and Bowman and Hampton decided not to join the new one. Instead, they formed the Darktown Entertainers quartet with singers WILL GARLAND and Fred Douglas. Performing everything from grand opera to lullabies, the Darktown Entertainers appeared on stage in Germany, Hungary, Austria, France, Switzerland, and Russia. When increasing political unrest forced the group to leave Russia, they returned to London and disbanded. Bowman and Hampton, now in a common-law marriage, returned to the United States, where Bowman appeared in the chorus of *The Southerns* during its thirty-two-week run in New York. Then the couple returned to London to join the second company of *In Dahomey*, this time with Bowman as one of the show's principal actors. After the show closed, Bowman and Hampton worked as a duet throughout Europe and purchased a house in England in 1910. But with war approaching, the British government ordered all foreigners to leave the country. Extremely ill on the voyage home, Hampton died shortly after their arrival.

In 1916, just weeks after Hampton's death, Bowman joined the Lafayette Players, the well-known stock acting troupe from Harlem, New York. She appeared in numerous dramatic and musical productions, often receiving positive reviews from critics. There she also met and fell in love with actor Sidney Kirkpatrick. Because the Lafayette Players management did not want married couples in the company, Bowman and Kirkpatrick eventually left. They married and formed a duo that performed in Boston, Philadelphia, and Washington, D.C. Settling for a time in Indianapolis, Kirkpatrick's hometown, the light-skinned couple circumvented racial prejudice that prohibited African Americans from performing in many of the town's venues by billing themselves as the Hawaiian Duet. During this time Bowman also made her screen debut in the African American independent filmmaker OSCAR MICHEAUX's *The Brute* (1920), an association that would continue into the early 1940s.

In 1923 Bowman and Kirkpatrick moved to New York, where they became involved with the Ethiopian Art Players. Bowman took on the role of Aunt Nancy in the Broadway production of *The Chip Woman's Fortune* by the black playwright WILLIS RICHARDSON. She also played Herodias to Kirkpatrick's Herod in Oscar Wilde's *Salome*, as well as the role of Aemilia in a jazz version of Shakespeare's *Comedy of Errors*. After the company disbanded, Bowman and Kirkpatrick performed in Indianapolis shortly before rejoining the Lafayette Players. By this time, the couple's popularity convinced the troupe's management to put aside the stipulation against married actors. Bowman's role, in 1928, was as the wife of the lead character in thirty-two performances of *Meek Mose*, written by actor and playwright FRANK H. WILSON. Although the production received fairly negative reviews, Bowman was uniformly praised for her part.

While in New York, Bowman established the National Art School, which taught drama to aspiring African American actors and staged performances at churches, schools, and social events. When the Lafayette Players moved to Los Angeles in August 1928, Bowman and Kirkpatrick followed. The company, after good attendance and reviews at the outset, soon struggled to fill seats and in January 1932 disbanded. Joining the JUANITA HALL Singers, Bowman and Kirkpatrick sang in several films, including *Dixie Anna* and *Check and Double Check*.

The couple moved back to New York City, where Bowman appeared in *Sentinels* in 1931 and *The Tree* in 1932 on Broadway. As had happened earlier in her career, the shows received bad reviews, but Bowman's performances were applauded. Although her roles were based on the black mammy stereotype, by the early thirties she had established herself as a legitimate actor on the stage.

Bowman and Kirkpatrick traveled to Los Angeles briefly to join the revived Lafayette Players in 1932. The troupe lasted only three weeks, but she remained in Los Angeles for several months. There she made *Ten Minutes to Live* (1932), with Micheaux, and had a role in the film *Drums of Voodoo* (released 1934). By the end of 1932 Bowman and Kirkpatrick were back in New York performing their duo act. Soon after their return Kirkpatrick died suddenly from a heart attack, leaving Bowman widowed for the second time.

Despite her personal tragedy Bowman continued to work, and just weeks after her husband's death played Auntie Hagar in the all-black cast of *Louisiana*. She also began to drink heavily, and while at a

Harlem bar frequented by black performers, she met her next husband, LeRoi Antoine, a Haitian immigrant twenty-three years younger than Bowman, with aspirations to become an opera singer. Bowman and Antoine married soon after they met in 1933.

During the remainder of the 1930s Bowman appeared in stage, screen, and radio productions. After *Drums of Voodoo* was released, the original Broadway cast restaged a production of *Louisiana*, with Bowman once again as Auntie Hagar. She also appeared in the short-lived *Yesterday's Orchid* (1934). She played Edgar Allan Poe's housekeeper in *Plumes in the Dust*, which opened in Washington, D.C., in 1936 before moving to New York's Forty-sixth Street Theatre. Critics singled out Bowman for her well-executed role as Parthenia, the Conjur woman in 1938's *Conjur*, which featured an all-black cast. The following year she once again played the stereotypical role of domestic servant, this time in a short-lived production of *Please, Mrs. Garibaldi.*

As a radio actor, Bowman could be heard on numerous shows, including *Southernaires, Personal Column on the Air,* and *Pores and Drums* as well as radio soap operas such as *Stella Dallas* and *Pretty Kitty Kelly.* Indeed, her radio performances became a steady source of income during the 1930s. In 1938 she had a role in Micheaux's film *God's Stepchildren.* Bowman and Antoine decided to move to Los Angeles to help his career as an actor, and in 1940 Bowman played the leading role of Dr. Helen Jackson in the movie *Son of Ingagi,* notable as the first all-black horror film. In the same year she also appeared in *The Notorious Elinor Lee,* another independent film by Micheaux.

An amateur theater group Bowman created during the early 1940s landed her work on radio, and the group's show—often featuring biblical stories—became widely popular. The venture paid little but kept Bowman busy until the mid-1940s, when she began acting again. Her role in the Hollywood production of *Decision* led to a role in a new postwar drama, *Jeb,* in New York. She played the mother of a black World War II hero who struggles with racial prejudice after returning to the South at the end of the war. Opening on 7 February 1946 at the Locust Street Theatre in Philadelphia, it enjoyed a short run on Broadway. Afterward Bowman was invited to perform with a company touring with *Anna Lucasta.* With more than nine hundred performances, the play was an overwhelming success, and the company took it to Europe. Bowman remained in the United States and continued with the play on the "subway circuit"—the Bronx, Brooklyn, Atlantic City, and other nearby locations. After four years as Theresa in *Anna Lucasta,* she returned to Los Angeles when the show finally closed. The role of Theresa was her last.

In 1951, shortly after arriving in Los Angeles, Bowman, by then weighing more than two hundred pounds, suffered a stroke that confined her to a wheelchair for the rest of her life. Although she had made a significant amount of money during her career, she had no savings during her last years. For the next six years Antoine attended dutifully to his bedridden wife. Bowman died at her home in Los Angeles at the age of seventy-six. In her obituary the *New York Times* noted, "It was said of Miss Bowman that she played in about every country that had a theatre." In 1961 Antoine published her biography, *Achievement: The Life of Laura Bowman,* "as told by Laura Bowman to her husband."

Further Reading
Sampson, Henry T. *Blacks in Black and White: A Source Book on Black Films* (1977).
Tanner, Jo A. *Dusky Maidens: The Odyssey of the Early Black Dramatic Actress* (1992).

MARY ANNE BOELCSKEVY

BOWSER, David Bustill (1820–30 June 1900), commercial painter, artist, and activist, was born in Philadelphia, Pennsylvania, the only known child of Jeremiah Bowser from Maryland and Rachel Bustill, daughter of the prosperous black abolitionist and educator Cyrus Bustill. The intermarriage among the region's free black Quaker families headed by Cyrus Bustill, Robert Douglass Sr., Jeremiah Bowser, and David Mapps created a dynamic force that benefited all African Americans and particularly spurred David's personal growth and accomplishments. Jeremiah, a member of the Benezet Philosophical Society, served as a steward on the Liverpool lines and, later, it seems he was the proprietor of an oyster house near the intersection of 4th and Cherry Streets, where David Bowser first hung up his sign as a commercial painter. Later, the Bowser family moved to the Northern Liberties section of Philadelphia, into a house at 481 North 4th Street where Bowser remained for the rest of his life. Many members of the Bustill, Douglass, and Bowser families lived and worked within or near Northern Liberties and attended local meetings of the Society of Friends (Quakers).

Bowser was taught by Cyrus's granddaughter SARAH MAPPS DOUGLASS (his cousin), who was herself a well-known artist and activist. Having demonstrated a talent for painting, David was apprenticed at the age of eleven to Sarah's younger brother, Robert Douglass Jr. Robert began his professional life as a barber, like his father, but having been instructed in art both in Philadelphia and London, he later earned his living in Philadelphia as a sign painter and artist. Bowser also learned hairdressing in the lucrative family business, and he made his way across America for several years plying the trade. When he returned to Philadelphia, Bowser was perhaps emboldened in pursuing a painting career by the Register of Trade of the Colored People (1838), a measure initiated by the Pennsylvania Abolition Society to encourage the employment of black artisans. He accepted commissions during the 1840s, 1850s, and 1860s to design banners, signs, and paraphernalia for various institutions, including volunteer fire companies and fire insurance businesses.

Some of his early ornamental works and his marine and landscape paintings were displayed in various exhibitions at the Philadelphia Museum, the Franklin Institute, and the Colored American Institute. Pictorial banners were his specialty, and his commissions during the Civil War included flags for all eleven units of the United States Colored Troops. These banners depicted black soldiers engaged in battle, usually in an allegorical setting. The abolitionist activism preceding the Civil War and the northern support for slave emancipation encouraged Bowser to turn his hand to portraits of cultural heroes. He had entertained the revolutionary abolitionist John Brown at his home, and he painted a portrait of Brown from life in 1858. Yet another Brown portrait, which he painted after 1860, commemorated the raid on Harpers Ferry. In addition Bowser received commissions for more than twenty portraits of Abraham Lincoln: two well-known examples are a hand-painted photograph for the black Philadelphia businessman and abolitionist ROBERT PURVIS, and an oil painting showing Lincoln freeing a kneeling female slave (1863?).

In addition to conceptualizing African American social empowerment and military achievement and bolstering the authority of white abolitionists, Bowser was directly involved in several causes. He aided in the escape of slaves; he was instrumental in helping to abolish Philadelphia's segregated streetcars; and he belonged to several African American reform groups. In 1853 he attended the thirtieth meeting of the American Moral Reform Society, which was held in Rochester, New York. This organization had been founded in Philadelphia in 1837 under the auspices of JAMES FORTEN and WILLIAM WHIPPER for the promotion of African American education, temperance, economy, and universal liberty. Its mandate to integrate all Americans under the banner of universal Christian love evidently guided Bowser's subsequent activism and explains his profound distrust of the colonization movement. Bowser was also a member of the Philadelphia delegation to the Pennsylvania Equal Rights League in 1865. Although he was probably married twice, it seems that only his second wife, a dressmaker by trade, named Elizabeth H. S. (1833–1908) bore children: these were Raphield Bowser, born in 1858, an artist, and Ida E. Bowser, born in 1869, the first woman to graduate with a degree in music from the University of Pennsylvania.

Black fraternal and social orders serving to create community bonds and to ensure the provision of mutual aid became popular during his lifetime. Bowser may well have joined the black Freemasons, but his primary commitment was to the Grand Order of Odd Fellows (an African American offshoot of the British fraternal society of Odd Fellows) to which he was initiated in 1844. His cousin Joseph Cassey Bustill, who is thought to have helped frame the Fifteenth Amendment to the Constitution, belonged to the same lodge. After 1871, when the volunteer fire companies lost their professional standing, the Odd Fellows became Bowser's primary market for banners and regalia. He held several high-ranking offices during his membership, including grand master, deputy grand master, grand director, and grand secretary. His motivations for this lifelong involvement in fraternal activity doubtless included family ties, a devotion to the welfare of African Americans, a love of ritual, a need for egalitarian religious fellowship, and the development of business contacts. His fraternal contacts assured him of a secure, if not an exceptionally profitable, niche in Philadelphia society despite the building pressure of nineteenth-century racism, which ignited several anti-black riots.

Bowser died in Philadelphia at his home, his obituary appearing in several major newspapers. Little remains of his substantial commercial output, but some portraits, photographs of his banners and flags, and a number of painted hats, which all attest to his talent, can still be seen in various museums. In an era of increasing racism, job discrimination, and, for many years, black disenfranchisement, Bowser held firm to his faith in African Americans' achievement and in their right to be integrated into mainstream American society, which seemed determined to exclude even the most gifted.

Further Reading
Details about Bowser and his extended family can be researched in the Dorsey Collection, Cheyney University, Cheyney, Pennsylvania, and in the Bustill-Bowser-Asbury Collection, Moorland-Spingarn Research Center, Howard University, Washington, D.C.
Jones, Steven Loring. "A Keen Sense of the Artistic: African American Material Culture in 19th-Century Philadelphia," *International Review of African Art,* vol. 12 (1995): 4–29, esp. 16–22.

SUSAN B. IWANISZIW

BOWSER, Mary Elizabeth (1839?–?), Union spy during the Civil War, was born a slave on the Richmond, Virginia, plantation of John Van Lew, a wealthy hardware merchant. Very little is known about her early life. Upon Van Lew's death in 1843 or 1851, his wife and daughter, Elizabeth, manumitted his slaves and bought and freed a number of their family members, Mary among them. Like most of their former slaves, Mary remained a servant in the Van Lew household, staying with the family until the late 1850s. Noting her intellectual talent, Elizabeth, a staunch abolitionist and Quaker, sent Mary to the Quaker School for Negroes in Philadelphia to be educated.

Mary returned from Philadelphia after graduating to marry Wilson Bowser, a free black man. The ceremony was held on 16 April 1861, just days after the Civil War began. What made the ceremony so unusual was that the parishioners of the church were primarily white. The couple settled outside Richmond. There is no record of any children. Even after her marriage, Bowser was in close contact with the Van Lew family, clearly sharing their political goals. As a result, their wartime record was very much intertwined, and information about Bowser can be gleaned through the records of Elizabeth Van Lew.

Despite her abolitionist sentiments, Elizabeth Van Lew was a prominent figure in Richmond. Shunned by many before the war began, her loyalty to the Union during the war earned her further enmity. Unlike other spies, Van Lew used this enmity as a cover for her serious efforts on behalf of the Union. Adopting a distracted, muttering personae, she was dubbed "Crazy Bet." During the war, Van Lew helped manage a spy system in the Confederate capitol, went regularly to the Libby Prison with food and medicine, and helped escapees of all kinds, hiding them in a secret room in her mansion.

Perhaps Van Lew's most trusted and successful source of information was Mary Bowser. Like Van Lew, Bowser had considerable acting skills. In order to get access to top-secret information, Bowser became "Ellen Bond," a slow-thinking, but able, servant. Van Lew urged a friend to take Bowser along to help out at functions held by Varina Davis, the wife of the Confederate president, Jefferson Davis. Bowser was eventually hired fulltime, and worked in the Davis household until just before the end of the war.

At the Davis's house, Mary worked as a servant, cleaning and serving meals. Given the racial prejudice of the day, and the way in which servants were trained to act and seem invisible, Mary was able to glean considerable information simply by doing her work. That she was literate, and could thus read the documents she had access to—and, in that way, better interpret the conversations she was hearing—could only have been a bonus. Jefferson Davis, apparently, came to know that there was a leak in his house, but until late in the war no suspicion fell on Mary.

Richmond's formal spymaster was Thomas McNiven, a baker whose business was located on North Eighth Street. Given his profession, he was a hub for information. His bakery was an unexceptional destination for his agents, and McNiven was regularly out and about town, driving through Richmond making deliveries. When he came to the Davis household, Mary could daily—without suspicion—greet him at his wagon and talk briefly. In 1904, just before he died, McNiven reported his wartime activities to his daughter, Jeannette B. McNiven, and her nephew, Robert W. Waitt Jr., chronicled them in 1952. According to McNiven, Bowser was the source of the most crucial information available, "as she was working right in the Davis home and had a photographic mind. Everything she saw on the rebel president's desk, she could repeat word for word. Unlike most slaves, she could read and write. She made a point of always coming out to my wagon when I made deliveries at the Davis' home to drop information" (quoted in Waitt, Thomas McNiven Papers).

By the last days of the Confederacy, suspicion did fall on Mary—it is not known how or why—and she chose to flee in January 1865. Her last act as a Union spy and sympathizer was an attempt to burn down the Confederate White House, but this was not successful.

After the war ended, the federal government, in an attempt to protect the postwar lives of its Southern spies, destroyed the records—including those of McNiven's and Van Lew's activities—that could more precisely detail the information Bowser passed on to General Ulysses S. Grant throughout 1863 and 1864. The journal that Bowser later wrote chronicling her wartime work was also lost when family members inadvertently discarded it in 1952. The Bowser family rarely discussed her work, given Richmond's political climate and the continuing attitudes toward Union sympathizers. There is no record of Bowser's postwar life, and no date for her death.

Bowser is among a number of African American women spies who worked on the Union side during the Civil War. Given the nature of the profession, we may never know how many women engaged in undercover spy operations, both planned and unplanned. Harriet Tubman is the most well known, especially for her scouting expeditions in South Carolina and Florida that resulted in the freedom of hundreds of slaves. In 1995 the U.S. government honored Mary Elizabeth Bowser for her work in the Civil War with an induction into the Military Intelligence Corps Hall of Fame in Fort Huachuca, Arizona.

Further Reading

Coleman, Penny. *Spies! Women in the Civil War* (1992).
Forbes, Ella. *African American Women During the Civil War* (1998).
Kane, Harnett T. *Spies for the Blue and Gray* (1954).
Lebsock, Suzanne. *A Share of Honor: Virginia Women 1600–1945* (1984).
Van Lew, Elizabeth. *A Yankee Spy in Richmond: The Civil War Diary of "Crazy Bet" Van Lew*, ed. David D. Ryan (2001).
Varon, Elizabeth. *Southern Lady, Yankee Spy: the True Story of Elizabeth Van Lew, a Union Agent in the Heart of the Confederacy* (2003).

LYDE CULLEN SIZER

BOWSER, Rosa (7 Jan. 1855–7 Feb. 1931), educator and community leader, was born in Amelia County, Virginia, probably a slave, to Henry Dixon, a carpenter, and Augusta Hawkins Dixon, a domestic servant. After emancipation she moved with her family to Richmond, where they were active in the First African Baptist Church and where she would teach Sunday school for the next half century. Bowser completed her education at Richmond Colored Normal School, where she was taught by the school's founder, Rabza Morse Manly, a noted educator throughout the South.

In 1872 Bowser began her teaching career at Richmond's Navy Hill School. She became the first black woman appointed to teach in Richmond public schools and continued to teach until her marriage to James Herndon Bowser on 4 September 1878. Their only child, Oswald Barrington Herndon Bowser, who became a well-known physician in Richmond, was born two years later. Her husband died in 1881, and in 1883 Bowser returned to the Navy Hill School.

The following year she began teaching at Baker Street School, where she would remain until her retirement in 1923.

Bowser is believed to have organized Richmond's first night school for black men in 1896. In the nineteenth century former slaves lobbied for universal education and the creation of black schools, aware that schooling for blacks was the primary vehicle to achieve economic independence. The night school Bowser created allowed men to work and still receive basic literacy instruction during evening hours.

Outside the classroom, Bowser participated in several church and civic organizations. From 1890 to 1892 she served as president of the Virginia State Teachers Association, an organization of professional African American educators who lobbied for equal salaries and better facilities. In August 1895 she helped to found the Richmond Women's League at a time when black women had launched a national campaign to denounce lynching. As the first president of the organization, Bowser oversaw a campaign that generated more than five hundred dollars for the defense of three black Lunenburg women charged with murder. She also worked in collaboration with national figures such as MARY ELIZA CHURCH TERRELL and MAGGIE LENA WALKER in support of the treatment of tuberculosis and the creation of kindergartens for African American children. She participated in the founding of the National Association of Colored Women (NACW) in 1896 and was once nominated—though not elected—to be president of the organization. Bowser also helped to found the Virginia State Federation of Colored Women's Clubs in 1908 and became the first chairperson of the Women's Missionary and Educational Society of Virginia.

Working in these civic organizations, Bowser bore witness to the community consciousness and black agency that afforded blacks a sense of dignity in the face of social and political repression. In the Jim Crow South, black educational institutions, when they existed at all, were extremely underfunded and neglected. Black citizens paid property taxes to finance schools but, because of insufficient aid from public school authorities, they were forced to raise more money among themselves. Bowser's service exemplified black commitment to provide schooling to as many people as possible.

As an active member of the NACW, whose motto was "Lifting as We Climb," Bowser worked to improve the conditions of black homes. She believed that improving black homes and families would foster the advancement of the entire black community. NACW women held classes on housekeeping and childrearing and advocated temperance. The NACW also supported passage of the Nineteenth Amendment, which guaranteed women the right to vote and helped make the 1920s antilynching campaign an issue of national prominence. The organization remains an integral part of the black community and, among other things, awards annual college scholarships to young black students.

In recognition of Bowser's lifelong commitment to the people of Richmond, the first branch of the Richmond Public Library system for African American patrons was named in her honor on 2 December 1925. Six years later Bowser died of complications from diabetes at her home in Richmond. In 1976 the National Biscuit Company (now Nabisco) awarded Bowser posthumous national recognition by including her in its Bicentennial Salute to Twenty-four Outstanding Black Educators.

Further Reading

Lebsock, Suzanne. *Murder in Virginia: Southern Justice on Trial* (2003).
Lee, Lauranett. "More Than an Image: Black Women Reformers in Richmond, Virginia, 1910–1928," master's thesis, Virginia State University (1993).
"Rosa D. Bowser: Talent to Spare, Talent to Share," *Richmond Literature and History Quarterly* (Fall 1978).

CRYSTAL RENÉE SANDERS

BOYD, Gerald M. (3 Oct. 1950–23 Nov. 2006), journalist, was born in St. Louis, Missouri, the second of three children of Odessa and Rufus Boyd. Boyd's mother died from sickle cell anemia when he was a small child, so he and his older brother, Gary, were raised by their paternal grandmother, Evie, while maternal relatives in California raised Boyd's sister, Ruth. Boyd attended Soldan High School in St. Louis, playing clarinet and writing for the school paper. He supplemented his grandmother's pension by bagging groceries at Cooper's, a neighborhood mom-and-pop store. As a high school student Boyd became interested in journalism while attending Upward Bound, a program that helped prepare him for college, doing layout and writing editorials on a paper produced at Webster College in suburban St. Louis.

Boyd attended the University of Missouri at Columbia from 1969 to 1973 on a journalism scholarship. There Boyd and fellow student Sheila Rule founded *Blackout*, a minority-run paper. Boyd's scholarship guaranteed him a job at the *St. Louis Post-Dispatch* upon graduation, and Boyd joined the paper as a copy clerk while still a college student. While at the *Post-Dispatch*, Boyd and George Curry, a *Post-Dispatch* reporter, cofounded the Greater St. Louis Association of Black Journalists in 1977 and created seven-week journalism workshops for black high school students. Boyd also taught journalism at Howard University and was an instructor at the University of Missouri's journalism workshop for minority students. In 1977 he was named Sigma Delta Chi's journalist of the year, and in 1979 he became a Nieman Fellow at Harvard—the youngest journalist so chosen.

While in St. Louis, Boyd reported on city hall and wrote on housing and consumer affairs. In 1978 he was assigned to the paper's Washington bureau, which gave him the opportunity to cover Congress, the 1980 presidential campaign, and the early years of the Ronald Reagan White House. Few minorities

Gerald Boyd, walking to a meeting with fellow *New York Times* editor Howell Raines in New York, 14 May 2003. (AP Images.)

covered the White House in the early 1980s, something Boyd believed helped him to receive an inordinate amount of attention from the president.

Boyd joined the *New York Times*'s Washington bureau in 1983, covering then vice president George H. W. Bush during the 1984 presidential campaign. Boyd was promoted to White House correspondent following Reagan's reelection, and he covered the Iran-contra affair and the subsequent shake-up in the administration, including Chief of Staff Donald Regan's resignation. Boyd reported on George H. W. Bush's presidential nomination, campaign, and election in 1988, and he produced numerous articles on Bush's appointees and the administration's plans.

In 1991 Boyd was named special assistant to the managing editor of the *Times*, then worked as chief editor in the Washington bureau and on the national and metropolitan news desks. As metropolitan editor Boyd oversaw a significant expansion and reorganization of that department, directing coverage of the 1993 World Trade Center bombing, for which the *Times* earned a Pulitzer Prize in 1994 for spot news reporting. Boyd was promoted to assistant managing editor in 1993 and to deputy managing editor in 1997. In the latter role he supervised the *Times*'s reporting on metropolitan, Washington, national, and foreign news, and he oversaw the layout of the front page. Boyd was co-senior editor of the *Times*'s 2001 series "How Race Is Lived in America," for which the paper won the Pulitzer for national reporting. The National Association of Black Journalists honored Boyd as Journalist of the Year in 2001.

Executive editor Howell Raines named Boyd managing editor—the second highest position at the *New York Times*—in 2001, and Boyd took over less than a

week before the 11 September terrorist attacks. The *Times* won six Pulitzers for its coverage of 9/11 and its aftermath, and Boyd pointed to helping lead the *Times* newsroom during that tragedy as his proudest moment as a journalist.

Boyd's tenure as managing editor was short-lived: in June 2003 he and Raines resigned after Jayson Blair, a twenty-seven-year-old *Times* reporter, was revealed to have fabricated stories and plagiarized. Following his resignation from the *Times*, Boyd wrote a syndicated column for Universal Press Syndicate, worked briefly as a consultant to Columbia University's Graduate School of Journalism, and wrote his memoir.

Boyd was married to Sheila Rule, a St. Louis neighbor and colleague at the *Times*. That marriage ended in divorce, as did his marriage to the newscaster Jacqueline Adams. Boyd and the journalist Robin Stone married in 1996, and they had a son, Zachary. Boyd died from complications of lung cancer.

Further Reading

Boyd, Gerald. "My Story," in *Reaching Generation Next*, ed. Lisa Frazier Page (2003).
Poniewozik, James. "Mutiny at the *Times*," *Time* (16 June 2003).

Obituaries: *New York Times*, 24 Nov. 2006 and 1 Dec. 2006.

DAVID SCHROEDER

BOYD, Henry Allen (15 Apr. 1876–28 May 1959), publisher, entrepreneur, and banker, was born to RICHARD HENRY BOYD, a publisher, and the former Harriet Moore in Grimes County, Texas, one of nine children. Henry Allen went to public school in Palestine, Texas, and attended the West Union Baptist Church. The Boyd family later moved to San Antonio and Henry found work at the local postal office. He became the first black to be hired as a postal clerk in San Antonio. He married Lula M. Smith, who bore him a daughter, Katherine. Lula did not live long after her daughter's birth. In 1908 he married again, this time to Georgia Ann Bradford. Around the early 1900s Henry Allen moved to Nashville, Tennessee, at the request of his father who had preceded him there. R. H. Boyd was making a name for himself in Nashville as founder and secretary-treasurer of the National Baptist Publishing Board (NBPB), a publisher of Sunday school literature, hymnals, and Christian education materials for black Baptists. Until 1896 nearly all black Baptists had bought their materials from the white American Baptist Publication Society (ABPS). After the creation of the National Baptist Convention (NBC) in 1895, black ministers asked the ABPS to hire black writers. The ABPS failed to comply, and the result was the NBPB, a reflection of the growing efforts of post-Emancipation blacks to gain respect from whites while affirming their own self-reliance.

About 1905, to generate a steady flow of sales, R. H. Boyd created the Sunday School Congress, an annual convention to train Sunday school workers. Through it the NBPB made itself indispensable to the churches affiliated with the NBC. When Boyd arrived in Nashville, his father made him assistant secretary-treasurer and secretary of the Sunday School Congress. He quickly immersed himself in the operation of what would become the largest black publishing enterprise in America. Boyd, who became an ordained minister in 1904, became involved in all his father's business activities. In addition to the NBPB, R. H. Boyd had opened and ran several moneymaking enterprises: the Citizens Savings Trust and Bank Company (1904); the *Globe*, a weekly secular newspaper, and its parent company, the Globe Publishing Company (1905); the National Negro Doll Company; and the National Baptist Church Supply Company. Boyd's father also published two other papers, the *Clarion* and the *National Baptist-Union Review*.

Both Boyds addressed social issues and in 1907 they led a protest when President Theodore Roosevelt visited Nashville but ignored the black community. The *Globe*, the official paper of the Republican Party in the county, supported the successful campaign of William H. Taft for president in 1908. The next year father and son successfully lobbied the state legislature for the creation of a school for black teachers, which became the Tennessee Agricultural and Industrial State Normal School for Negroes (later Tennessee State University). In 1910 Boyd used his influence as editor of the *Globe* to help raise funds for a new building for the local black YMCA.

In 1915 a major controversy split the black Baptist community. The NBC incorporated and tried to take control of the NBPB by pursuing its legal case all the way to the Tennessee Supreme Court. Right before founding the publishing house, R. H. Boyd had been elected corresponding secretary of the NBC's Home Mission Board (HMB) and it was as such that he encouraged the denomination to authorize the creation of the NBPB, which printed and sold Christian literature to churches affiliated with the NBC. He served on the HMB until he resigned in 1914. Because Boyd did not share his publishing profits with the NBC, many NBC leaders thought that he was manipulating the denomination for personal gain. The NBC lost the case, however, because Boyd's father had incorporated as a private, nonprofit corporation that was independent of the NBC. As a result the pro-NBPB faction seceded from the NBC and founded the National Baptist Convention of America (NBCA). The Sunday School Congress survived the split and continued to serve as a promotion outlet for the NBPB.

Boyd supported the United States's entrance into World War I through the *Globe*. Many African Americans supported the war out of patriotism and thought that black participation in the war effort would force the government to grant civil rights to the black minority at home. Boyd visited Camp Meade, an army camp in Maryland that trained black soldiers, and published articles and photographs about black trainees and black units fighting the war abroad. When Boyd's father died in 1922 the NBPB through its board of directors elected Boyd as secretary-treasurer.

He inherited all of his father's leadership positions and remained active in social work. During the twenties he protested black lynching in Texas and Alabama. He was elected president of the local Lincoln-Douglass Voters' League that recruited voters for the Republican Party. As a seasoned political observer and activist he used the *Globe* to attract thousands of new black voters for the Republican Party.

The NBPB's stature increased when in 1925 the NBCA signed a joint agreement with the Lott Carey Baptist Foreign Mission Convention (LCBFMC), a black Baptist organization founded in 1897 to support missionary work in Africa. This agreement meant that the publishing house would be able to sell materials to LCFMC workers. A shrewd manager, Boyd in 1930 added correspondence theological courses to extend his client base. To further increase business he traveled widely so that by 1934 he was supplying materials to 20,000 Sunday schools and 8,000 churches. Boyd also contributed to the outstanding growth of the Citizens Bank that was managing $300,000 in deposits by 1940. During World War II Henry Allen led a successful campaign that landed 1 million dollars' worth of deposits in the Citizens Bank's coffers.

After World War II the NBPB hired and trained veterans to work as art preservationists and printers, a practice in keeping with the Boyd family's interest in the social uplift of the black race. By the 1950s both the doll company and church supply subsidiaries had closed. Higher prices led the NBPB to connect with the Protestant-Church Owned Publishers of America to buy paper at lower rates.

Boyd's second wife died in 1952. As Boyd grew older he relinquished his duties to his nephew, Theophilus Bartholomew Boyd Jr., who was made assistant secretary-treasurer and who would replace Henry Allen upon his demise. At the time of Henry Allen's death the NBPB's assets were worth nearly $900,000. In 1960 the *Globe* ceased publication. Henry Allen's funeral was held at Tennessee State University upon request of the school's president. His greatest accomplishment is to have kept the NBPB and the Citizens Bank in operation through the years. Through these two institutions Henry Allen significantly affected black America both during and after his association with his father.

Further Reading
Lovett, Bobby L. *A Black Man's Dream: The First 100 Years, Richard Henry Boyd and the National Baptist Publishing Board* (1993).

DAVID MICHEL

BOYD, Richard Henry (15 Mar. 1843–23 Aug. 1922), Baptist minister, was born Dick Gray in Noxubee County, Mississippi, the son of Indiana, a slave woman; nothing is known of his father's identity, but the surname Gray is the same as the owner of the plantation. When the master died, Boyd accompanied members of the Gray family to Washington County in western Texas. During the Civil War he served his new master in the Confederate camps until he was sent back to Texas, where he was given responsibility for managing the Gray plantation. After the war he left the plantation and took on several occupations in Texas, including that of cattleman. Having had no formal education in his early years, it was not until the mid-1860s that he learned to read and write.

In 1867 he changed his name to Richard Henry Boyd, and two years later he enrolled at Bishop College in Marshall, Texas. Although he did not complete his studies, he was ordained a Baptist minister. In 1868 Boyd married Laura Thomas, who died shortly thereafter. In 1871 he married Harriett "Hattie" Albertine Moore. At least five children resulted from the two marriages.

During the 1870s and 1880s Boyd became a leader of the black Baptist community in Texas. He formed and led congregations throughout the state, aided in organizing the Texas Negro Baptist Convention (TNBC), and became the convention's education secretary.

Boyd's influential role in American religious history is best understood against the background of racial conflict among the major Baptist denominations in the late nineteenth century. At the 1892 meeting of the TNBC, Boyd opposed a plan that would have allowed the northern and predominantly white American Baptist Home Mission Society (ABHMS) to consolidate schools for black freedmen; the plan would have given oversight of the publication and dissemination of Baptist school literature to the American Baptist Publication Society (ABPS), which declined to publish the writings of black ministers. Some black Baptists viewed Boyd's opposition as escalating the issue of race. Boyd's vision of a publishing house that served black educational needs eventually led him and his supporters to separate from the TNBC in 1893 and form the General Missionary Baptist Convention (GMBC), with Boyd serving as superintendent for the new convention's missions program.

Resigning his pastorate of Mount Zion Church in San Antonio, Texas, Boyd worked to create a central repository from which to disseminate Sunday school materials to black churches in the GMBC. He achieved this aim by skillfully negotiating with the Southern Baptist Convention's Sunday School Board for the delivery of materials. Boyd's efforts lessened the dependency of black Baptist Sunday schools on the ABPS's literature and distribution network and eventually decreased the influence of white northern Baptists in the affairs of southern black Baptists. He was criticized by some black Baptists, who believed he had diminished the prospect for cooperation and undermined the Fortress Monroe Agreement, a cooperative pact between the Southern Baptist Convention and the ABHMS.

Throughout 1895 Boyd strengthened his position. He prompted a convening of Sunday school teachers and superintendents in Grimes County, Texas, where he convinced church officials to direct their requests for Sunday school materials to his newly established repository. He also received the endorsement of the Palestine Baptist Association of Texas and was able to convince many at a Palestine Sunday school convention of the importance of having a black publishing house.

Boyd's influence grew when he represented the Texas delegation from the GMBC at the predominantly black National Baptist Convention, U.S.A. (NBC-U.S.A.) in St. Louis, Missouri, in 1896. His proposal to establish a publishing board capable of producing materials on a national scale for the black Baptist population was initially rejected by supporters of the ABPS and by people within the TNBC who opposed his efforts. However, the TNBC's Home Mission Board, to which Boyd had been elected corresponding secretary, accepted Boyd's idea to establish a committee in charge of printing Sunday school materials. On Boyd's recommendation, the committee was granted board status by the convention and was named the National Baptist Publishing Board (NBPB). Boyd became the new board's corresponding secretary and treasurer.

In October 1896 Boyd resigned his position as the GMBC's superintendent of missions and proceeded to establish the operations of the NBPB in Nashville, Tennessee. By 1897 the board had begun printing Sunday school materials copyrighted in Boyd's name. In 1898 he obtained a state charter and incorporated the NBPB in Tennessee.

Although Boyd resigned his position as corresponding secretary of the NBC-U.S.A.'s Home Mission Board in 1914, his chartering of the NBPB had heated up a long-simmering conflict over the control and legal ownership of the publishing board's operations and copyrights that culminated at a meeting of the National Baptist Convention, U.S.A., in Chicago in 1915. The courts of Tennessee ruled in Boyd's favor, the NBC-U.S.A. having failed to support its legal claims over the publishing board. The conflict, however, led Boyd and his supporters to organize an "unincorporated" faction of the National Baptist Convention in 1915, now known as the National Baptist Convention of America (NBCA). In 1916 the NBCA declared that the NBPB was an independent legal entity and hence was not owned by or subject to the control of any convention.

From its inception in 1896 to 1922 Boyd served as secretary and treasurer for the NBPB. From 1905 the NBPB held annual congresses of Sunday school leaders and teachers, and by 1909 it had established service training for Baptist teachers.

Boyd also became a successful businessman in Nashville. He founded the National Negro Doll Company in 1911 to manufacture dolls with African American features; he helped establish and was president (1904–1922) of Nashville's One Cent Savings Bank, a savings and loan bank for African Americans; he helped organize and became the president in 1906 of the Globe Publishing Company, which produced the *Globe* newspaper primarily for African American readers; and he served as a national vice president of the National Negro Business League. Boyd died in Nashville.

Further Reading

Boyd, Richard Henry. *A Story of the National Baptist Publishing Board: The Why, How, When, Where, and by Whom It Was Established* (1915).

Lovett, Bobby L. *A Black Man's Dream: The First One Hundred Years* (1993).

Montgomery, William E. *Under Their Own Vine and Fig Tree: The African-American Church in the South, 1865–1900* (1993).

Tyms, James D. *The Rise of Religious Education among Negro Baptists* (1979).

Washington, James Melvin. *Frustrated Fellowship: The Black Baptist Quest for Social Power* (1986).

Obituary: *Nashville Banner*, 24 Aug. 1922.

ZIPPORAH G. GLASS

BOYER, Frances (1871–1949), teacher, farmer, and entrepreneur, was born Frances Marion Boyer in Pelham, Georgia, the son of Henry Boyer, a former slave and one-time teamster for the U.S. Army. Nothing is known of Boyer's mother. In 1846 the elder Boyer passed through the Pecos Valley region of south-central New Mexico. Impressed by the wide-open spaces the elder Boyer returned to his home in Georgia and reportedly spoke regularly about returning to New Mexico with his family and friends. Henry Boyer was never able to realize his dream, but his youngest son Frank, one of eight children, probably went well beyond anything his father had thought of doing when he later founded Blackdom, one of the first all-black towns in New Mexico, albeit one of the last founded in nineteenth-century America. Frank Boyer was educated at the Atlanta Baptist Seminary, and later received his bachelor's degree in teacher's education from Morehouse College, Atlanta. He also took advanced classes at Fisk College, Nashville.

Pelham, Georgia, was home for the Boyer family and also the place from which Frances Boyer began his long walk with a brother-in-law, Daniel Keyes. By means of the Homestead Act of 1863, which allowed a person to homestead up to 160 acres, Frank and his wife, Ella, whom he had met in 1892 while at a summer teaching session at Atlanta University, had discussed using this as an opportunity. This, combined with his father's love of the land he had traveled during his army days, apparently convinced Boyer that it might be possible to begin a utopian community for blacks in the wide-open spaces of New Mexico. Boyer and Keyes left Georgia in January 1900, walking and working their way west until October of the same year. Odd jobs covered part of their expenses, but it is also reported that they danced for drunken cowboys or other travelers they met. Upon their arrival in New Mexico, which was a territory until 1912, Boyer and Keyes were able to find work with ranchers in the area around Roswell and Dexter, in the southeastern part of the state. Boyer also worked as a bellhop in a Roswell hotel for a time.

Ella and the Boyer children came to New Mexico in 1901, which was also the time that Frank Boyer and Daniel Keyes were visiting surrounding states to promote their idea of Blackdom to other black citizens. One of Boyer's employers was successful in drilling a well that hit artesian water at six hundred feet, nearly ten times deeper than other drillers had gone. This discovery turned the Roswell area into a temporary boomtown, since it helped make Roswell, at least for a while, a garden area. It was also in 1901 that Boyer was able to secure a loan and drill for water in the area chosen for Blackdom. An artesian well was soon operating, and Blackdom was on its way to becoming a dream fulfilled.

Things went well for Boyer at first, with crops of hay and apples plentiful. Other black homesteaders began to arrive, many of whom stayed with the Boyers until they could establish themselves. Blackdom began to grow, and in 1903 Boyer and Keyes, along with several other residents, signed the articles of incorporation for the Blackdom town site. It was not until 1920, however, that the actual town site was dedicated, ironically not long before Blackdom itself ceased to exist. The town site comprised about 40 acres, with 166 lots, each 35 x 100 feet. All of the home sites were set around a public square and park, and most streets were apparently named after noted African Americans of the era. The actual Blackdom settlement, which grew up around the Boyer homestead, entailed 15,000 acres and was home to black and white families that settled there under the various land laws of the time. A store, post office (from at least 1913 to 1920), hotel, school, and two churches soon sprang up. A one-sheet newspaper was also printed for a short time. Population estimates vary from three hundred to five hundred at Blackdom's high point.

Historical texts do not note any major problems between black and white residents, and it was noted that both races celebrated Juneteenth, the annual commemoration of the abolition of slavery in Texas. However, the town failed when the apple crops proved unreliable and the wells, overdrilled for the aquifer, ran dry.

Francis and Ella Boyer, who eventually had ten children, finally left Blackdom in 1921, and relocated briefly in Pacheco, New Mexico. Here again they were probably the first black settlers in the area, and one more move to what would later become Vado, New Mexico, just south of Las Cruces, brought the Boyer's and their eventual ten children to their last stop. They were also successful in helping approximately fifty other black families settle in the area. Both Frank and Ella became involved in education in the area, starting the Paul L. Dunbar School. Their farm was also the first to grow cotton successfully in New Mexico, where it remains a major crop for southern New Mexico farmers. Frank and Ella both died in Vado. Blackdom itself lasted until 1925. The site is now noted on a state historical marker, located about eighteen miles south of present-day Roswell.

Further Reading
Baton, Maisha, and Henry Walt. *A History of Blackdom, N.M., in the Context of the African American Post Civil War Colonization Movement* (1996).
Fleming, Elvis. "Lillian Westfield Collins Blackdom, N.M., Interview for the Chaves County Historical Society," in *Roundup on the Pecos* (1985).

JEFF BERG

BOYKIN, Keith (28 Aug. 1965–), civil rights and gay rights advocate, was born in St. Louis, Missouri, to Bill Boykin, a bus driver and salesman, and Shirley, a federal employee. Shortly after the birth of his sister Krystal in 1966, the family moved from inner-city St. Louis to the predominantly white suburb of Florissant, Missouri. As he grew up, Boykin displayed an interest in politics, becoming student body president in the fifth grade and dreaming of the White House.

Boykin's parents separated when he was in elementary school, and both left the St. Louis area in 1980. Boykin moved with his father and sister to Clearwater, Florida, where his father opened a black beauty-supply business. Boykin attended Countryside High School, where as a senior he was elected student government president, and graduated in 1983. He enrolled in Dartmouth College in Hanover, New Hampshire, that fall, and joined the track team and in his junior year was editor in chief of the campus newspaper, the *Dartmouth*. He graduated with a degree in Government in 1987 and subsequently moved to Boston to work on the Michael Dukakis presidential campaign until November 1988, after which he joined his father at his new home in Atlanta, Georgia, and worked as a high school teacher while applying to law school. Boykin enrolled in Harvard Law School in 1989, where he served as general editor of the *Harvard Civil Rights–Civil Liberties Law Review*, and graduated in 1992. As a law student, he was also one of eleven plaintiffs in a 1990 suit against Harvard Law School protesting its lack of minority and female faculty hiring, even arguing a portion of the case in court. The case was dismissed on appeal by the Massachusetts Supreme Judicial Court in 1992.

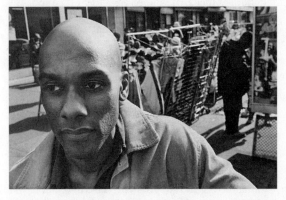

Keith Boykin, author and commentator on issues of race and sexual orientation, near his home in Harlem, New York, 2 March 2004. (AP Images.)

Boykin came out as gay in 1991, and as he gave up a lucrative job with a San Francisco law firm to work on Bill Clinton's presidential campaign after law school, he gradually intensified his commitment to gay and lesbian as well as African American civil rights issues. After Clinton's election, Boykin was hired in January 1993 as a special assistant and was later promoted to director of specialty press, a position in which he coordinated communications between the administration and minority publications. The highest-ranked openly gay official in the White House, Boykin helped organize a historic April 1993 meeting between President Clinton and gay and lesbian community leaders.

In the course of his work, Boykin became frustrated by what he considered the inaccurate portrayal of race and sexuality in the media, and he left his position in 1995 to work on his first book, *One More River to Cross: Black and Gay in America* (1996). Based on Boykin's own experience and dozens of interviews across the country, the book revealed the alienation often felt by black gays and lesbians, given racism within the gay community and denial or anti-gay harassment in the black community and the black church. Boykin asserted that despite these tensions and despite the differences in the civil rights goals of African Americans and gays, both groups share a common struggle for equality.

From 1995 to 1998 Boykin was executive director of the National Black Lesbian and Gay Leadership Forum in Los Angeles, California. His second book, *Respecting the Soul: Daily Reflections for Black Lesbians and Gays*, was published in 1999 and won the 1999 Lambda Literary Award for Spirituality. He was an adjunct professor of political science at American University in Washington, D.C., from 1999 to 2001, winning the School of Public Affairs award for outstanding adjunct professor in 2000. In 2001 Boykin moved to New York City where he founded the National Black Justice Coalition, an antiracism and anti-homophobia advocacy group for black gays, lesbians, bisexuals, and transgendered men and women and their supporters. He later became president of its board of directors.

Boykin's advocacy work included challenging negative images of black gays and lesbians in the media. In August 2004 he was featured on the Showtime television network reality series *American Candidate*, in which ten contestants organized mock presidential campaigns. He also published his third book, *Beyond the Down Low: Sex, Lies, and Denial in Black America* (2005), which became a *New York Times* best-seller. The book was written in response to the phenomenon of the "down low," widely publicized in books such as J. L. King's *On the Down Low: A Journey into the Lives of "Straight" Black Men Who Sleep with Men* (2004), in which African American men in heterosexual relationships engage in clandestine, often risky, homosexual encounters. Boykin criticized the implications that the down low occurs only among African Americans and that black men are to blame for rising rates of HIV infection among black women. Boykin urged a more honest account of the means by which HIV spreads in the African American community and public policy initiatives to provide better prevention and treatment.

Born on the second anniversary of the 1963 March on Washington and MARTIN LUTHER KING JR.'s call for a racially integrated America in his "I have a dream" speech, Boykin used his work to reflect both the continuation and the expansion of the goals of the civil rights movement since the 1960s. Gays and lesbians joined African Americans, Latinos, Native Americans, and women in applying the language and techniques of that movement to their own demands for equality. Boykin suggested that the dream is incomplete without a society that confers the same rights to all people, regardless of their sexual orientation.

Further Reading

Boykin, Keith. *One More River to Cross: Black and Gay in America* (1996).

Graham, Chad. "The Other Presidential Race," *The Advocate*, 17 Aug. 2004.

Strong, Lester. "Fighting Demons," *A&U Magazine* (Jan. 2005).

FRANCESCA GAMBER

BOYNTON ROBINSON, Amelia (18 Aug. 1911–), civil rights and voting rights activist, was born in Savannah, Georgia, the seventh of ten children born to Anna Eliza Hicks and George Platts, the latter of whom owned and operated a wood supply business for years before moving to Philadelphia, Pennsylvania, and engaging in real estate.

Amelia Platt's childhood was idyllic; she was raised in Savannah and its outskirts in an affectionate middle-class family and community that encouraged her aspirations. She graduated from Tuskegee Institute (later Tuskegee University) in 1927, later adding course work from colleges in Tennessee, Virginia, and Georgia. She briefly taught school in Georgia before being named home demonstration agent for the Dallas County, Alabama, Cooperative Extension Service. In the early 1930s she served alongside Samuel William "Bill" Boynton, who was the county agent for Dallas County. The Cooperative Extension Service at that time was segregated by both race and gender in the South, with black home demonstration agents teaching farm women ways to improve their lives, and black county agents instructing farm men in agricultural improvements. Although the work was intended to assist farmers in improving their economic lot, the combination of the entrenched poverty brought on by tenant farming and the racial caste system hindered the efforts of extension agents. Platts was shocked by the racial and economic oppression in Dallas County, a startling contrast to her own middle-class background.

In 1936 Platts left home demonstration work to marry Boynton, who worked in real estate and insur-

ance after retiring from the extension service in 1949. The Boyntons had two sons, William and Bruce. William Boynton worked for the postal service, and later in real estate. Bruce Boynton, as a college student, was arrested in 1958 for challenging segregation in a restaurant. *Boynton v. Virginia* was decided by the Supreme Court in 1960 in Boynton's favor. He later became a lawyer.

Both Boyntons were registered voters in the 1930s, and both were strong advocates for voter registration. Bill Boynton served openly in the Fourth Congressional District for Registration and Voting for nearly twenty years, and was president of the Dallas County Voters League, coaching many African Americans in preparation for registration. He also served as NAACP president for Selma in the 1950s. He used his expertise gained as a county agent to press for improved economic conditions for black farmers, assisting individuals in finding loans for land purchases. Keenly aware and frustrated with the roadblocks to economic and political advancement for blacks, Boynton testified before Congress in 1955 about the hindrances to the enjoyment of civil rights.

By the early 1960s both Boyntons were assisting the Justice Department by supplying evidence of voter intimidation, and they assisted Bernard Lafayette of the Student Nonviolent Coordinating Committee (SNCC) in encouraging voter registration. The Dallas County Voters League found it difficult to overcome local black fears of recrimination should they register to vote, but Lafayette chipped away at such fears by enlisting youth from Selma schools to attend meetings and marches. The first of these mass meetings was held as a memorial service for Bill Boynton on his death in 1963, and proved an effective means through which to raise local interest in voter registration.

As more SNCC volunteers arrived in Selma, and as mass meetings were followed by marches and arrests, in July 1964 Circuit Judge James A. Hare reacted by slapping an injunction on civil rights leaders and participants, prohibiting more than three of them from gathering in public meetings. Prior to the injunction, Amelia Boynton ran for office on the Democratic ticket in the race for the Fourth Congressional District. She lost in the primary but heightened her visibility in both the black and white communities. Although prohibited from attending public meetings by the injunction, Boynton continued working for voter registration.

In response to the shutdown in free expression brought about by Judge Hare's order, Boynton wrote to MARTIN LUTHER KING JR. and the Southern Christian Leadership Conference (SCLC), asking them to come to Selma. King agreed, established a headquarters in Boynton's office, and set about turning Selma's local resistance to voter registration into a nationally recognized problem. The injunction was quashed in early 1965, and demonstrations resumed. In January 1965, while assisting African Americans who waited in long lines to register to vote, Boynton was accosted and arrested by Sheriff Jim Clark. The photographs of Clark's rough handling of Boynton made national press. Tensions in Selma grew as King was arrested in February 1965 and briefly held in jail.

White response to the heightened civil rights activities often included acts of violence, one instance of which was the killing of JIMMIE LEE JACKSON during a civil rights march in nearby Marion. To protest Jackson's death, SNCC leaders decided to walk to Montgomery, about fifty miles from Selma, to carry their grievances to Governor George Wallace. On Sunday, 7 March 1965, Boynton and about six hundred other protesters began peacefully walking out of Selma, heading across the Edmund Pettus Bridge at the end of town. At the base of the bridge the marchers were confronted by state and local police, some on horseback, who ordered them to turn around and head back into Selma. Barely waiting for a response, police charged the crowd, clubbing and tear-gassing many individuals, including Boynton, who was struck unconscious. News coverage of the "Bloody Sunday" attack prompted President Lyndon Johnson's decision to ask Congress to pass the 1965 Voting Rights Act. This law transcended local efforts by ensuring federal intervention in districts where there was significant evidence of voting rights fraud.

In 1968 Amelia Boynton worked with the ill-fated Poor People's Campaign and Resurrection City in Washington, D.C., which was an attempt by Martin Luther King Jr. to draw attention to poverty. She later joined the Schiller Institute, founded by Lyndon LaRouche, to attack injustice on a national and international level.

Further Reading

Robinson, Amelia Boynton. *Bridge across Jordan* (1979, rev. 1991).

Branch, Taylor. *Parting the Waters: America in the King Years, 1954–1963* (1989).

Branch, Taylor. *Pillar of Fire: America in the King Years, 1963–1965* (1999).

Chestnut, J. L., Jr., and Julia Cass. *Black in Selma: The Uncommon Life of J. L. Chestnut, Jr.* (1990).

MARY A. WAALKES

BOZEMAN, Sylvia Trimble (1 Aug. 1947–), mathematician, was born Sylvia Trimble in Camp Hill, Alabama, the daughter of Horace Edward Trimble Sr., an insurance agent, and Robbie Jones Trimble. She had four siblings, three brothers and one sister. She attended the segregated public schools in her rural hometown, and was motivated by the standards and values instilled in her by her parents. Early in her education, Bozeman's parents helped her develop confidence that she was capable of accomplishing her goals. Though her father worked with numerical calculations in his career, it was her mother who encouraged Bozeman to pursue her interest in mathematics. Her enthusiasm for the subject grew into advanced mathematical knowledge when her high school mathematics teacher, Frank Holley, returned after school to

teach trigonometry to a small group of students because the course was not part of the school's curriculum. Her excellence in mathematics and other subjects led to Bozeman's honor as class valedictorian upon graduating from Edward Bell High School in 1964.

Following graduation, Bozeman entered the historically black Alabama Agricultural and Mechanical University in Huntsville, where she majored in mathematics. Encouraged by Howard Foster, the head of the department of math and physics, she contributed to a computer research project sponsored by the National Aeronautics and Space Administration (NASA). Additionally, Trimble participated in a summer research program at Harvard University, where she learned the early computer programming language FORTRAN. In 1968, after serving as student government vice president, Trimble graduated second in her class from Alabama A&M University with a bachelor of science degree in Mathematics.

Several weeks after graduating, Sylvia Trimble married Robert Bozeman, a fellow mathematics student whom she met during her freshman year in college. The newlyweds moved to Nashville, Tennessee, where they both enrolled in graduate school at Vanderbilt University to study mathematics. In 1970 Sylvia Bozeman graduated from Vanderbilt with her master of science degree in Mathematics. While her husband pursued his doctorate at Vanderbilt, Bozeman worked at Vanderbilt as an instructor of mathematics for two years. In 1972 she served as an Upward Bound math instructor at Tennessee State University. A year later the Bozeman family, which had expanded to include two young children, moved to Atlanta, Georgia, when Bozeman's husband earned his PhD. With her husband as a newly appointed professor at historically black, all-male Morehouse College, Sylvia Bozeman was hired by Spelman College, its female counterpart.

As an instructor of math at Spelman, Bozeman recognized the need to earn a doctorate degree to further her career. With the support of mentors, including ETTA ZUBER FALCONER, head of the math department at Spelman, Bozeman took a leave of absence to enroll in a doctoral program at Emory University in Atlanta. She studied functional analysis, an area of mathematics that merges algebra and topological geometry. Under the tutelage of her academic adviser, Luis Kramarz, Sylvia Bozeman earned her PhD in 1980. Her dissertation was titled "Representations of Generalized Inverses of Fredholm Operators." Immediately following graduation, Bozeman returned to Spelman College as an assistant professor of mathematics. In 1982 she became the head of the mathematics department and held that post for eleven years. She was promoted to associate professor in 1984 and full professor in 1991. In 1998 Bozeman was promoted to associate provost for science and mathematics at Spelman College.

From 1980 to 1984 the National Science Foundation and the U.S. Office of Army Research funded Bozeman's continued research on functional analysis.

In 1986 Bozeman received a grant from NASA to study a computer-based subject, image processing. Because of her strong work in this area, Bozeman was awarded the White House Initiative Faculty Award for Excellence in Science and Technology in 1988. That same year Bozeman was granted the Tenneco United Negro College Fund's Excellence in Teaching Award. Her recognition for distinction continued with her election to Phi Beta Kappa, an academic honor society, and to Pi Mu Epsilon, the honorary national mathematics society.

In addition to her academic achievements, Bozeman participated in professional organizations. She served as the vice president of the National Association of Mathematicians from 1984 to 1988. In 1989 Bozeman became the first African American to be elected to the board of governors of the Mathematics Association of America, the largest mathematics organization of college and university professors. In 1993 Bozeman was appointed project director for the Center for Scientific Applications of Mathematics, Spelman College's initiative to increase African American participation in the sciences. This project also affected high school mathematics by exposing high school math teachers to innovations in mathematics and mathematics instruction.

In the mid-1990s Lee Lorch, the eminent mathematician and human rights activist, introduced Sylvia Bozeman to Rhonda Hughes. Hughes was a mathematics professor at Bryn Mawr College in Pennsylvania. Sharing common circumstances—both were mathematicians at small liberal arts, historically female colleges, and both recognized a need to increase the participation of women in mathematics—Bozeman and Hughes collaborated to develop the Enhancing Diversity in Graduate Education (EDGE) program. In 1998 EDGE was created to improve opportunities for women who wished to earn graduate degrees in the mathematical sciences.

Further Reading

Hine, Darlene Clark. *Black Women in America: An Historical Encyclopedia* (1993).
Morrow, Charlene, and Teri Peri, eds. *Notable Women in Mathematics: A Biographical Dictionary* (1998).
Proffitt, Pamela. *Notable Women Scientists* (1999).

COURTNEY A. HOWARD

BRACE, Jeffrey (1742?–1827), slave, sailor, soldier, and farmer, was born Boyrereau Brinch, the seventh of eight children (four boys and four girls) born to Whryn Brinch, the son of Yarrah Brinch, and of Whryn Douden Wrogan, the daughter of Grassee Youghgon. He lived in the city of Deauyah in the kingdom of Bow-woo, which was probably situated in the Niger River basin, in the area that would later become Mali. In 1758, when he was around the age of sixteen, Boyrereau was abducted by slave traders, transported to Barbados, and sold to Captain Isaac Mills of New Haven, Connecticut, who trained him for British naval service. Like thousands of other slaves and freed Africans in the Caribbean, Brace (as he would come to be called years later, after his manumission. This may have been an anglicized version of Brinch) was forced to labor aboard ship during the Seven Years' War. He remained at sea for two years, and Mills renamed him Jeffrey after the British commander Sir Jeffrey Amherst, in recognition of his bravery but lack of prudence in battle.

Though he was wounded in a skirmish, Brace continued on voyages to Ireland, Georgia, Nova Scotia, New York, Rhode Island, and Boston. In the fall of 1763 Mills sold him to John Burrell, a sadistic Puritan from Milford, Connecticut. For the next five years Brace passed from one cruel Yankee owner to another until he was purchased by an elderly widow, Mary Stiles, around 1768. A devout grandmother from Woodbury, Connecticut, Stiles taught Brace how to read and write. Upon her death he passed into the hands of her son, Benjamin Stiles, a prominent lawyer and politician.

In 1777 Brace enlisted in the Revolutionary army in hopes of gaining his manumission. He fought for more than five years and was honorably discharged with a badge of merit in 1783. A year later, under community pressure, Stiles consented to Brace's manumission. Brace went to Vermont, which through its 1777 constitution became the first state to abolish adult slavery. The Vermont constitution also established universal male suffrage.

Arriving in Poultney in 1784, Brace found southern Vermont rich in both promise and disappointment. Initially, he said, "I enjoyed the pleasures of a freeman; my food was sweet, my labor pleasure: and one bright gleam of life seemed to shine upon me" (Brace, 166–167). He worked hard and earned more than a subsistence, but periodically he found himself cheated out of promised wages and victimized by broken contracts. Eventually he bought land in Poultney and then went to the neighboring town of Dorset to attempt to earn enough money to farm his land. While working in John Manley's tavern in Dorset, Brace met and married Susannah (or Susan) Dublin, whom he described as "a native African female, who possessed a reciprocal abhorrence to slavery." As a couple, Jeffrey and Susan contributed to a growing New England patchwork of abolitionist Africans who remembered and valued their cultural origins.

Through hard work and persistence, the Braces achieved moderate success, but the peace and material comfort they deserved were never fully realized. The most painful problem they encountered stemmed from Vermont's pervasive racism and its entrenched practice of exploiting children, especially black children. Susan had two children from her first marriage, a twelve-year-old boy, whose name is not known, and a young girl named Bersheba. Coveting these children as servants, two powerful white citizens, Elizabeth Powell of Manchester and Archibald Dixon of Poultney, forced the Brace children into indenture.

The couple also had children of their own. Although the exact number is uncertain, the 1790 U.S.

census lists five free people of color in the Poultney household of "Jeffrey Bran," which suggests that they had three children by 1790. They may have had more later on. Around 1795 they returned to Poultney to clear their land, which was rocky and full of trees. Compounding their hardships was a jealous, spiteful neighbor who harassed them relentlessly for seven years, finally threatening to "bind out" (that is, force into indenture) their children. Faced with this threat Brace decided to sell his farm and move to northern Vermont. After attempting to settle in other villages, Jeffrey and his son-in-law eventually purchased land in a small village named Georgia, on the fertile shores of Lake Champlain. Here they cleared a farm and prospered for a while. In 1804 a grandson, most likely his first, was born in the neighboring town of Saint Albans. On 19 March 1807 Susan Brace died.

In 1810 Jeffrey Brace, who became blind in his late sixties, narrated his life story to Benjamin Prentiss, a white lawyer who, despite his education, was poor and obscure. Published under the title *The Blind African Slave, or Memoirs of Boyrereau Brinch, Nicknamed Jeffrey Brace*, the memoir elicited almost no recorded reader or critical responses. In an 1852 biography of an African preacher from Vermont named Charles Bowles, the biographer John Lewis provided a rare glimpse into a racially mixed abolitionist community in Vermont. Lewis suggested that through storytelling and moral suasion, "Brother Jeffrey Brace" helped shape the political climate of Vermont, which by the mid-nineteenth century was the most antislavery state in America.

On 18 March 1818 the U.S. Congress passed an act to provide pensions for eligible Revolutionary War veterans. On 4 April Jeffrey Brace filed a pension application, which was rejected on the grounds that the War Department could not find his service record. He had forgotten that he had enlisted under the name of Stiles. The Franklin County judge of probate, Seth Wetmore, became his impassioned advocate, but it was three years before Brace, on 11 July 1821, received a pension of $8 a month, plus arrears totaling $328.23. This money was most likely sufficient to make his final six years of life materially comfortable.

Jeffrey Brace died in Georgia, Vermont, and was memorialized in Poultney, where the 9 May 1827 *Northern Spectator* published an unusually long, laudatory obituary, saying in part:

DIED

In Georgia, Vt., Jeffrey Brace, an African, well known by the appellation of "Old Jeff," supposed to be nearly 100 years old. . . . He had for many years been totally blind, yet his mental powers appeared to be hardly impaired. The powers of his memory were frequently tested by repeating whole chapters of the scriptures nearly verbatim. He was formerly a resident of this town.

Despite his accomplishments and regional reputation, Brace and his memoir virtually vanished from history until the dawn of the twenty-first century.

Further Reading

Brace, Jeffrey. *The Blind African Slave, or Memoirs of Boyrereau Brinch, Nicknamed Jeffrey Brace*, ed. Benjamin F. Prentiss (1810; 2004).

Obituary: *Northern Spectator*, 9 May 1827.

KARI J. WINTER

BRADFORD, Alex (23 Jan. 1927–15 Feb. 1978), composer, singer, and choir director, was born in Bessemer, Alabama, a town with a rich musical tradition of blues, gospel, and male quartets. His mother, Olivia Bradford Spann, worked as a hairdresser, among other occupations, and his father, Alex Bradford Sr., was an ore miner. Bradford exhibited early musical talent, performing on stage at the age of four. This experience, reinforced by his brief attendance at a church that embraced more exuberant displays of emotion and livelier music than did the Baptist church of his mother (who put a halt to her son's foray), initiated his lifelong love for theater. He soaked up the performance styles of local showmen like Prophet Jones, and national gospel stars like ARIZONA DRANES, MAHALIA JACKSON (whom he later accompanied on piano), and Queen C. Anderson, who traveled to Bessemer during the town's annual gospel event. Spann sent her teenaged son to school in New York for one year and then to an African American private school in Alabama, where he led other students in the performance of blues and gospel and acquired the title "Professor" because he taught as a student.

After graduating from high school and serving in the army during World War II, Bradford moved to Chicago in 1947, where he proceeded to perform both blues and gospel. His first big break came a few years later when Willie Web invited him to join his gospel group and soon after recorded Bradford's arrangement of the hymn "Every Day and Every Hour." The encouraging reception of this song inspired him to form his own vocal group, the all-male Bradford Specials. Their first release, "Too Close to Heaven" (1953), was written by Bradford and sold over a million copies. During the 1950s Bradford performed and recorded with luminaries like SALLIE MARTIN, ROBERTA MARTIN, DELOIS BARRETT CAMPBELL, Maceo Woods, and CLARA WARD. While Chicago was the epicenter of gospel during this time, Bradford moved to New York City to escape the inhibiting control exerted over the sacred music scene by the city's most established performers.

Like older gospel legend SISTER ROSETTA SHARPE, Bradford disrupted boundaries by performing sacred music in decidedly non-religious settings. In his mid-twenties he performed at Chicago's famous Regal Theater in a midnight show, along with other blues and gospel performers, in what one newspaper labeled as "flesh entertainment" because it included nearly-nude female dancers (*Chicago Defender*, 28 Nov. 1953). He later claimed to have appeared at Harlem's Apollo Theater more than any other gospel singer. His unparalleled flamboyancy and theatricality, which he accentuated through colorful robes and stoles, made some people question whether his primary motivation was religious faith or self-aggrandizement. The gospel historian Anthony Heilbut asserted that Bradford was "a born star, the cynosure of all eyes" (*Gospel Sound*, 146). Attesting to his penchant for publicity, his first marriage took place in February 1956 in the Bronx funeral home owned by his bride, Susan Cannon, and attracted hundreds of onlookers.

Bradford's second vocal group, the Men of Song, helped to popularize gospel among white audiences by appearing at the 1959 Newport Jazz Festival, the Indiana Jazz Festival, and on the Mike Wallace television show. The *Chicago Defender* noted that he was "widely regarded as America's leading male gospel singer" (18 Sept. 1961). In addition to the sacred compositions for his own group he wrote popular songs for RAY CHARLES and LAVERN BAKER, and the National Baptist Convention awarded him a trophy as "America's Top Gospel Writer." His distinctive baritone voice, known for its gravelly timbre and wide range, influenced the vocal styling of other well-known singers like SAM COOKE.

In 1961 Bradford performed in and wrote music for *The Black Nativity*, the first of several gospel plays in which he participated. Based on poetry by LANGSTON HUGHES and directed by VINNETTE CARROLL, the play opened in New York and was a smash hit on its European, Asian, and Australian tours. Along with that of the gospel legend MARION WILLIAMS, Bradford's performance in the play helped to popularize gospel music outside the African American community. According to his second wife, Alberta Carter Bradford, who served as musical conductor and pianist for the play and with whom he had two daughters, the cast performed for the Dutch, Danish, and British royal families and for many celebrities, like DUKE ELLINGTON and the Beatles. When asked about the appropriateness of bringing religious expression into the commercial theater, Bradford, who had become an ordained minister, responded, "The church was in fact the first theater, and theater is an extension of the pulpit. The play came from the church and it was from the church that Satan took the dance. These are the Biblical facts" (*New York Times*, 11 Sept. 1977).

Although typically not outspoken on social issues Bradford did protest certain personal experiences with racism. As a teenager in Bessemer he refused to be disrespected at work by a belligerent white man, which prompted his mother to send him away to New York for safety. In 1958, on a delayed cross-country airline trip, Bradford and his vocal group were denied accommodations at a motel in Chicago. He responded by suing the airline and motel for fifty thousand dollars and taking his story to the *Chicago Defender*. Over the years he performed at various benefits and church-sponsored events. For some his extravagant musical style symbolized black pride. Months before he died he formed the Creative Movement Repertory Company in Newark, New Jersey, which, similar to the WILLA SAUNDERS JONES Passion play in Chicago, offered young African Americans an opportunity to develop their dancing, music, and theatrical skills.

Bradford remained active in theater until the time of his death. In 1972 he received an Obie Award for his performance in the gospel musical *Don't Bother Me, I Can't Cope* and wrote many of the songs for Vinnette Carroll's *Your Arms Too Short To Box with God* (1976). His own gospel musical, *Don't Cry, Mary*, opened shortly before he suffered a stroke, dying two weeks later in New York's Beth Israel Hospital. Professor Alex Bradford will be remembered as a remarkably versatile showman who helped to popularize gospel music by packaging his extraordinary musical talents in the flashiest and most audacious displays of religious fervor.

Further Reading

Boyer, Horace. *The Golden Age of Gospel* (2000).
Dunning, Jennifer. "His Music Celebrates the Gospel Truth," *New York Times*, 11 Sept. 1977.
Heilbut, Anthony. *The Gospel Sound: Good News and Bad Times* (2004).
"Prof. Bradford Set for 'Jubilee Showcase,'" *Chicago Defender*, 8 Feb. 1964.
"Singers to Sue Motel, TWA for $50,000, Charge Bias," *Chicago Defender*, 25 Mar. 1958.

Obituary: *New York Times*, 16 Feb. 1978.

BRIAN HALLSTOOS

BRADFORD, Perry (14 Feb. 1895–20 Apr. 1970), blues and vaudeville songwriter, publisher, and musical director, was born John Henry Perry Bradford in Montgomery, Alabama, the son of Adam Bradford, a bricklayer and tile setter, and Bella (maiden name unknown), a cook. Standard reference books give his year of birth as 1893, but Bradford's autobiography gives 1895. Early in his youth Bradford learned to play piano by ear. In 1901 his family moved to Atlanta, where his mother cooked meals for prisoners in the adjacent Fulton Street jail. There he was exposed to the inmates' blues and folk singing. Bradford attended Molly Pope School through the sixth grade and claimed to have attended Atlanta University for three years, there being no local high school. This is chronologically inconsistent, however, with his claim to have joined Allen's New Orleans Minstrels in the fall of 1907, traveling to New Orleans for Mardi Gras performances in February 1908 and then moving on to Oklahoma.

After working as a pianist in Chicago, Bradford toured widely from about 1909 to 1918 with Jeanette Taylor in a song-and-dance act billed as Bradford and Jeanette. His nickname "Mule" came from his being featured in a piano and vocal vaudeville song titled "Whoa, Mule," although the jazz dance historians Marshall and Jean Stearns point out that the name also fit Bradford's personality. Bradford learned countless dances from local performers as he toured. When appropriate he memorialized the best dances in lyrics to songs such as "The Bullfrog Hop" (c. 1909) and "Rules and Regulations" (printed in 1911). A shrewd entrepreneur, he initially published his songs as sheet music to be sold after performances. This informal method of distribution was caused in part by the racist structure of the publishing industry, which put roadblocks in the paths of aspiring African American songwriters. (Compare the experiences of the lyricist and composer ANDY RAZAF.) Bradford's financial situation improved slightly with the commercial publication of "Scratchin' the Gravel" (1917) and "The Original Black Bottom Dance" (1919). During these final years of the decade he produced and performed in the musical revues *Sergeant Ham of the 13th District* (1917 and 1919), *Made in Harlem* (at the Lincoln Theatre in New York, 1918)—for which he wrote "Harlem Blues"—and *Darktown after Dark* (1919). Around 1918 Bradford married his first wife, Marion Dickerson, who took Taylor's place in the revues; details of his subsequent marriage or marriages are unknown.

In 1920 Bradford initiated a revolution in popular music. After several companies had turned him down, Bradford convinced Fred Hager of Okeh records to take a chance in spite of racist warnings "not to have any truck with colored girls in the recording field" (Bradford, 118). In February the African American singer MAMIE SMITH recorded for Okeh Bradford's songs "That Thing Called Love" and "You Can't Keep a Good Man Down," accompanied by a white band; these were not immediately released, owing to an industry-wide patent dispute that was still half a year from settlement. In August, with an African American band, the Jazz Hounds, that was put together hastily, Smith recorded "It's Right Here for You" and "Crazy Blues." "Crazy Blues" became a huge hit, selling perhaps more than a million copies. It initiated the 1920s craze for female blues singers and more broadly opened up the field of recording to African Americans, not only in general markets but also in a newly created market: race records.

In 1921 Bradford organized tours for Smith, directed further recording sessions, and established his own publishing company. He quickly made five-figure sums in royalties, and when a Columbia Records lawyer, unaware of the immediate success of "Crazy Blues," offered to make the song a big hit if Bradford would waive his rights to royalties, Bradford made the classic reply, "The only thing Perry Bradford waives is the American flag" (Bradford, 155). Also in 1921 the singer ETHEL WATERS featured Bradford's song "Messin' Around" on the Theater Owners' Booking Association circuit, and Bradford himself performed in the show *Put and Take* (1921). But all did not go smoothly in this year. Bradford reached an out-of-court settlement for having previously sold "Crazy Blues" (a retitled version of "Harlem Blues") to other publishers under the alternative titles "The Broken Hearted Blues" and "Wicked Blues." Also, a series of financial and touring disputes with Smith's husband and her boyfriend led Bradford to switch from Okeh to Columbia to promote the singer EDITH WILSON, who recorded Bradford's "Evil Blues" in 1922. The

same year he was sued for publishing a song owned by another publisher, was convicted of this charge and also of having witnesses commit perjury while testifying on his behalf, and was sentenced to four months in prison.

Among his achievements in the 1920s Bradford claimed to have taught the Black Bottom dance to Ethel Ridley, who introduced it in Irvin C. Miller's show *Dinah* (1923). From this point on his star descended quickly. He assembled great musicians such as LOUIS ARMSTRONG, JAMES P. JOHNSON, and BUSTER BAILEY for undistinguished recordings made from 1923 to 1927 under the name of Perry Bradford's Jazz Phools, and in 1927 he introduced his song "All I Had Is Gone." He also wrote lyrics to the musical revue *Messin' Around* (1929). He seems to have made no further impact, however, apart from a hit song recorded by LOUIS JORDAN's new band in 1939, "Keep a Knockin' (But You Can't Come In)." The singer and songwriter NOBLE SISSLE asserts: "The industry, especially some of the publishers, finally had Perry's terrific catalog of 1,400 songs black-balled from being recorded because he would not sell out to them. They practically broke him. His only brother Negro publisher, CLARENCE WILLIAMS, offered him the same fate. He had to sell out to a white publisher" (Bradford, 10). Bradford lived on relief and worked in New York as a mailman at Queens General Hospital, where he died after having spent his last years in ill health and confined to a nursing home.

As a musician Bradford was no match for the pianist and composer JELLY ROLL MORTON, but they resembled one another in crucial ways. Both were aggressive, perceptive self-promoters who backed up brash claims with documented achievements. Touring the country during the developmental years of blues and jazz, they absorbed and disseminated what they heard, thus helping to create an international music from scattered rural and urban folkways. Both were inflexibly hardheaded and after a period of great success—Bradford's financial and sociocultural, Morton's artistic—found themselves left behind as they stuck doggedly to musical styles that had fallen out of fashion.

Bradford's autobiography is a sustained outburst against his having been left out of early histories of blues and jazz and also against what was in his (probably incorrect) opinion an overestimation of the significance of New Orleans jazzmen in comparison to African American jazz musicians in other places. Although he distorts history as much as he repairs it, his essential arguments have been taken into account in most subsequent studies, and the great significance of his personal contribution to the music's flowering is now widely acknowledged.

Further Reading

Bradford, Perry. *Born with the Blues: Perry Bradford's Own Story, The True Story of the Pioneering Blues Singers and Musicians in the Early Days of Jazz* (1965).

Charters, Samuel B., and Leonard Kunstadt. *Jazz: A History of the New York Scene* (1962; rpt. 1981, 1984).
Stearns, Marshall, and Jean Stearns. *Jazz Dance: The Story of American Vernacular Dance* (1968).

BARRY KERNFELD

BRADLEY, Aaron Alpeora (1815?–Oct. 1882), Reconstruction politician, was born in Edgefield District, South Carolina, the son of unknown slaves on the plantation of Francis Pickens, a prominent politician. Little is known of Bradley's youth and early manhood other than that he was a shoemaker for a time in Augusta, Georgia, and that he escaped slavery and made his way to the North, apparently during the 1830s. He lived for a time in New York and in Boston. In Boston he not only met abolitionists but also studied the law and eventually became a practicing attorney.

The Civil War opened new horizons. Bradley returned south late in 1865 and settled in Savannah, Georgia, intending, it seems, to open a law practice and a school. Drawn inexorably to the public arena, he began to champion the cause of freed people who were resisting President Andrew Johnson's policy of restoring plantation land to its antebellum owners. Bradley's advocacy took the form of leading mass public demonstrations as well as petitioning authorities in Washington. Military officials in Georgia deemed his spirited criticism of government policies seditious, convicted him of the charge of sedition before a military tribunal, and permitted him to leave the state in lieu of a year's imprisonment. When he returned to Savannah from Boston late in 1866, he resumed his role as champion of the freed people with the same militancy that he had earlier displayed. He immediately took up the cause of rice-plantation laborers, who were locked in a dispute with both the antebellum plantation owners and the Freedmen's Bureau over rights to the land; both sides threatened to use armed force to gain their objectives.

Despite his ambivalent relationship with military authorities, Bradley had no doubt that federal power—military as well as executive, legislative, and judicial—was essential for revolutionizing the South. Accordingly, he appealed to federal officials both broadly to protect freed people in what he termed the "free enjoyment of Equal Rights and Immunities" and narrowly to redress an assortment of pressing grievances. One representative campaign aimed to remove from office the mayor of Savannah, a former Confederate colonel who treated former slaves with undisguised contempt. Although often unpolished and by turns brazen and elliptical, Bradley's numerous petitions articulated the political aspirations of his constituents in the language of constitutional rights.

For Bradley and like-minded political activists throughout the South, the Reconstruction acts of March 1867 marked a milestone in the struggle to revolutionize the political system. The acts granted suffrage to black men and required elections for delegates to write new constitutions for the former Confederate states. Bradley put his name forward as a candidate, won the hearty support of the voters in his black-majority district, and assumed his seat in the constitutional convention that met in Atlanta from December 1867 to February 1868. By downplaying his constituents' demands to press for a redistribution of plantation land and by supporting the package of debtor relief and homestead-exemption measures tailored to the needs of white yeoman farmers, Bradley aligned himself behind the state's Republican leadership. He seemed to defer to the Republican strategy of appealing to potential white voters (although he never said so directly). At the same time his black constituency grew broader—including urban laborers who showed less interest in land grants than plantation laborers had shown—and he surely began to see more realistically how slim the prospects of legislating land reform at the state level were. Despite his loyalty, Republicans raised neither hand nor voice in his defense when Democratic delegates maneuvered to expel him from the convention on grounds of a past criminal conviction on a morals charge in New York City in 1851. Unfazed, his constituents promptly elected him to the state senate, only to see him, together with every other black senator, driven from that body as well. Bradley ran unsuccessfully for Congress in 1868 and 1870 but reclaimed his state senate seat in January of 1870, when federal authorities initiated Georgia's third postwar reconstruction.

For the next two years Bradley labored on behalf of his working-class constituents, introducing various bills to lower taxes, shorten the workday for urban workers, and guarantee civil and political rights. Increasingly convinced that state officials cared more about preserving the trappings of office than about satisfying the freed people's needs, Bradley castigated the Republican governor Rufus B. Bullock and party regulars in Savannah, who were backpedaling before a Democratic onslaught. At the same time Bradley petitioned Washington officials to grant him a sinecure. Appointed a special customs inspector in 1872, he soon politicked his way out of favor and out of his position.

When Georgia Democrats assumed full control over the state government in 1872, Bradley grew increasingly disenchanted. In his search to realize Reconstruction ideals, he advocated a strategy of migration to Florida in the mid-1870s and to Kansas at the end of the decade. Frustrated by his inability to garner support for the Kansas exodus among black Georgians, he headed west on his own in 1882, making it to Saint Louis, where he died without any known descendants. Whether he ever married is unknown.

Assessing Bradley's role in Reconstruction requires an appreciation of his role as a leader in a mass movement for radical social change. He consistently identified his political agenda with that of ordinary former slaves, especially the field laborers on coastal rice plantations and the semiskilled and unskilled workers in Savannah. Their collective demand that constitutional rights be extended to all citizens regardless of color or former condition of servitude was frustrated at the time, but it resurfaced with unstoppable force in the twentieth-century civil rights movement.

Further Reading
Reidy, Joseph P. "Aaron A. Bradley: Voice of Black Labor in the Georgia Lowcountry," in *Southern Black Leaders of the Reconstruction Era*, ed. Howard N. Rabinowitz (1982).

Obituary: *Savannah Morning News*, 25 Oct. 1882.

JOSEPH P. REIDY

BRADLEY, Buddy (1908–1972), choreographer and jazz tap dancer, was born Clarence Bradley in Harrisburg, Pennsylvania. His parents' names and occupations are unknown. His father died when he was quite young, and his religious mother brought him up strictly. After seeing the tap dancers Jack Wiggins and Clarence "Dancing" Dotson at a local theater, Bradley learned to do the time step on one foot by age eight. He taught himself the Charleston, the strut, the drag, the shuffle, and a vast assortment of African American vernacular dances.

After his mother died when he was fourteen, Bradley went to live with a brother-in-law in Utica, New York, and worked as a hotel busboy. A few months later he ran away to New York City and lived at a Harlem boardinghouse inhabited by many show people, especially dancers. With a group of other youngsters that included Derby Wilson, who became a well-known tap dancer, Bradley learned how to tap dance in a blind alley next to Connie's Inn in Harlem and picked up flash and acrobatic steps as a chorus boy both at the downtown Kentucky Club and at Connie's Inn. In 1926 he made his stage debut as a dancer in a FLORENCE MILLS revue at the Lincoln Square Theatre.

Around 1928, at the Billy Pierce Dance Studios off Broadway, Bradley found himself tailoring routines for specific dancers—from gangsters' molls to Broadway stars—for $250 a routine. His dance formula was radically new: he simplified rhythms for the feet while sculpting the body into shapes from African American social dance, blending easy tap dance and jazz dance into routines that rose to a climax and finished gracefully. Well paid but known only in show-business circles, Bradley created dozens of dance routines for white stars of Broadway musicals—stars such as Adele Astaire, Ruby Keeler, and Eleanor Powell—although his name never appeared on any program. It was the custom that so long as the dance director, who grouped scenes and coached the stars, got his pay, there was no need for program credit. Bradley coached Tom Patricola, Ann Pennington, and Francis Williams in the Black Bottom musical numbers in George White's *Scandals* (1926). In 1928 he re-choreographed the entire production of *Greenwich Village Follies*, even though Busby Berkeley's name remained as choreographer on the program. Bradley created routines and sometimes staged complete scenes for Mae West, Gilda Gray, Irene Delroy, Jack Donahue, and Paul

Draper in shows such as *Ziegfeld Follies* (1929) and Erroll Carroll's *Vanities* (1924). The "High Yaller" routine from the "Moanin' Low" number in *The Little Show* (1929), which established Clifton Webb as one of the hottest dancers since EARL "SNAKE HIPS" TUCKER, was choreographed by Bradley.

Inspired by the music of the day, Bradley ignored the melody and translated the accents of improvising jazz-musician soloists into dance patterns that were new to Broadway. Bradley received the first full choreographic credit in his career in 1930 in London with *Evergreen*, a new Rodgers and Hart musical at the Adelphi Theatre. His choreography for C. B. Cochran's 1931 revue catapulted him into English musical theater. In the 1930s alone, Bradley choreographed more than thirty musical productions in London, including *Revels in Rhythm* (1931), *Words and Music* (1932), *Mother of Pearl* (1933), *Tulip Time* (1935), Cochran's 1936 revue *Follow the Sun*, and Lew Leslie's *Blackbirds of 1936*. *Evergreen*, which was made into a film in 1934, launched him into the emerging English film industry.

In simplifying dance steps, Bradley used the body to express rather than to accompany the music; and although he simplified rhythms, he never sacrificed the distinctive accents of rhythm tap. Bradley collaborated with Frederick Ashton in creating the first English jazz ballet, *High Yellow* (1932), which featured Alicia Markova. He also created a cabaret act for the ballet dancers Vera Zorina and Anton Dolin, and he collaborated with Agnes de Mille on *Words and Music* (1934), with Antony Tudor on *Lights Up!* (1940), and with George Balanchine on Cochran's 1930 revue.

Bradley lived in London for thirty-eight years, working in Europe as a teacher, choreographer, and producer of musical revues, films, and television shows. By 1950 the Buddy Bradley Dance School in London had more than five hundred students. It remained in operation until 1968, when he returned to New York, where he died. He was survived by his wife Dorothy (maiden name unknown).

Bradley was a key figure in the transplantation of African American jazz and tap dance onto the American and English musical theater stage. "His dance ideas were well ahead of his time, and knowing performers of the musical comedy stage flocked to him," Bradley's obituary in *Variety* (26 July 1972) stated. "He was personally popular in the profession, together with respect given to his creative choreography."

Further Reading
"Buddy Bradley: Nimble Ex-Harlemite Runs Most Successful School in England," *Ebony* (July 1950).
Hill, Constance Valis. "Buddy Bradley: The 'Invisible' Man of Broadway Brings Jazz Tap to London," *Proceedings of Society of Dance History Scholars* (14–15 Feb. 1992).
Stearns, Marshall, and Jean Stearns. *Jazz Dance: The Story of American Vernacular Dance* (1968).

Obituary: *Variety,* 26 July 1972.

CONSTANCE VALIS HILL

BRADLEY, David (7 Sept. 1950–), writer and educator, was born David Henry Bradley Jr in Bedford, Pennsylvania, the only son of Reverend David Henry Bradley Sr. and Harriette M. (Jackson) Bradley. His family has been closely involved with the black church for three generations, as he told an interviewer in 1992: "I'm a super preacher's kid. My great-grandfather was a preacher, my grandfather and granduncle were preachers, my father was a preacher. This is the first generation of my family since we liberated ourselves from slavery where there hasn't been a preacher" (Bonetti, 69). This familiarity with the black church and with preachers would influence his work and inspire his characters.

After he graduated from Bedford Area High School in 1968, Bradley entered the University of Pennsylvania. He graduated in 1972 with a bachelor of arts, summa cum laude, in Creative Writing, and was awarded a Thouron British-American Exchange Scholarship for King's College at the University of London, where he received his master of arts in 1974 in Area Studies, particularly nineteenth-century American history. This interest in history was apparent in Bradley's novel *The Chaneysville Incident* (1981), which was inspired by his mother's discovery of thirteen unmarked graves near Chaneysville while she was researching local history for Bedford County's 1969 bicentennial. After his return from England, Bradley spent a short period in editing and teaching, after which he settled at Temple University in Philadelphia, Pennsylvania, where he taught from 1976 to 1996.

Bradley's first novel, *South Street* (1975), drew on the African American oral tradition, celebrating the vernacular culture of Bradley's unemployed working-class characters. The novel was set in the 1970s in South Street, close to central Philadelphia. Taking place in a black bar, a black church, and a hotel lobby, it was structured around a series of vignettes exploring the lives of black ghetto dwellers, ranging from unemployed prostitutes, hustlers, and henchmen to bartenders, preachers, janitors, and winos. The protagonist was Adlai Stevenson Brown, a black, middle-class, educated poet, who temporarily moved to South Street in order to live with the proletariat and to experience the conditions of the black poor. An outsider to South Street, he was viewed with suspicion. His interaction with South Street's working classes revealed his feelings of inadequacy and alienation. Through this class dynamic the novel played on identity politics and shed light on class hierarchy and racial divisions.

While *South Street* received little critical attention, Bradley's second novel, *The Chaneysville Incident*, established him as an important voice in African American fiction. The novel won the 1982 PEN/Faulkner Award and an Academy Award from the American Academy and Institute of Arts and Letters and prompted comparisons to the works of RALPH ELLISON, JAMES BALDWIN, and TONI MORRISON.

The novel told the story of John Washington, a successful African American historian, and his attempt to resolve the mystery of his father's death, which was linked to the deaths of a group of runaway slaves. The novel fashioned a continuous dialogue with the past that was informed by the present, constantly moving between rural Pennsylvania in the 1970s where John was currently investigating the death of his father, Moses Washington, and nineteenth-century America, to which John traced his family's history. His family's past, which intersected with and illuminated significant aspects of African American history, became the impetus for John's self-exploration and formation of a new cultural and racial identity.

There was a tendency among critics to focus on the novel's treatment of African American history, and to fail to emphasize the novel's cultural implications. Although Bradley's narrative was shaped by storytelling, and the oral tradition was privileged in the novel, the role of written history and narrative was never displaced or dismissed. John Washington's quest for personal and cultural identity was further complicated by his relationship with Judith, the white girlfriend whom John initially kept at a distance and refused to trust. A shift occurred toward the close of the narrative; racial and gender relationships became reconfigured as Judith moved to the center of Bradley's narrative. She entered John's world imaginatively, becoming both his audience and a contributor to his story.

In addition to his fictional work, Bradley also contributed essays, book reviews and interviews to a diverse range of scholarly periodicals, magazines, and newspapers, including *The Village Voice, Savvy, Signature*, the *Washington Post, Book World, Esquire, Callaloo, The New Yorker, Time Magazine, Philadelphia Magazine, New York Arts Journal*, the *New York Times Book Review, Southern Review*, and the *Los Angeles Times Book Review*. He was also awarded a Guggenheim Fellowship for fiction in 1989, and a National Endowment for the Arts Literature Fellowship for creative non-fiction. In 2003 Bradley became director of the creative writing program at the University of Oregon.

Further Reading

Blake, Susan L., and James A. Miller. "The Business of Writing: An Interview With David Bradley," *Callaloo* 21 (1984).

Bonetti, Kay. "An Interview with David Bradley," *Missouri Review* 15 (1992).

Brigham, Cathy. "Identity, Masculinity, and Desire in David Bradley's Fiction," *Contemporary Literature* 36 (1995).

Ensslen, Claus. "Fictionalizing History: David Bradley's *The Chaneysville Incident*," *Callaloo* 35 (1988).

Hogue, W. Laurence. "Problematizing History," *College Language Association Journal* 38 (1995).

Wilson, Matthew. "The African American Historian: David Bradley's *The Chaneysville Incident*," *African American Review* 29 (1995).

MAHA MAROUAN

BRADLEY, Edward (22 June 1941–9 Nov. 2006), journalist, was born Edward Rudolph Bradley Jr. in Philadelphia, Pennsylvania, to Edward Bradley Sr., a businessman, and Gladys Bradley. After his parents divorced, Bradley, an only child, lived in Philadelphia with his mother during the school year and with his father in Detroit during the summer. He graduated from Cheyney State College in 1964 with an education degree and taught elementary school in Philadelphia while working as an unpaid jazz disc jockey at the radio station WDAS. Bradley's career break as a reporter came during the race riots in the summer of 1965.

After leaving a club in the early morning, Bradley heard reports that rioting had broken out in the northernmost part of the city, but WDAS did not have reporters to cover the events. Bradley took the initiative, picked up a tape recorder and a station engineer, and headed out to cover the rioting himself. He took a job as a full-time news reporter for New York's WCBS radio in 1967 and remained at the station through 1971. He next took his savings and went to Paris to live as an author, but when his savings ran out, Bradley found part-time work late in 1971 as a stringer for CBS News. He moved to the network's Saigon bureau full time in 1972 and was wounded while on assignment in 1973. Bradley was reassigned to the Washington bureau in 1974, but asked to return to Southeast Asia in 1975 to cover the fall of Saigon at the end of the Vietnam War. His coverage of Cambodian refugees was given a George Polk Award for Foreign Television Reporting, one of the most respected awards given to print and broadcast journalists.

Bradley was hired to report on Jimmy Carter's campaign and went on to become the first black White

Edward Bradley at the Republican National Convention in the Joe Louis Arena in Detroit, July 1980. (AP Images.)

House correspondent, covering the Carter administration from 1976 to 1978. He took over the evening anchor position on the *CBS Sunday Evening News* from 1976 to 1981 and became a principal correspondent for *CBS Reports* in 1978. It was on the latter assignment that he famously reported on Indochinese political refugees escaping from their homelands by boat. Bradley also received honors for his report on the state of integration in public schools mandated by the U.S. Supreme Court in *Brown v. The Topeka Board of Education* in the special *Blacks in America: With All Deliberate Speed. CBS News* executive Don Hewitt lured Bradley away from the nightly news to work on *60 Minutes*, the news magazine show that featured Harry Reasoner, Mike Wallace, and Morley Safer.

During the following years his reporting was marked by prestigious industry awards, including the Robert F. Kennedy Journalism Award in 1995, the George Foster Peabody Award in 1997, the 2000 Paul White Award given by the Radio/News Directors Association, and the Denver Press Club's Damon Runyon Award for career journalistic excellence in 2003. Bradley marked a milestone in the 2005–2006 television season, celebrating his twenty-fifth year as a correspondent on *60 Minutes*. He won several Alfred I. duPont-Columbia University awards as well as nineteen Emmys given by the National Academy of Television Arts and Sciences, including an Emmy for lifetime achievement. Bradley also received Peabody, Overseas Press Club (the Edward R. Murrow Award), Capital Press Club National Media, and Ohio State awards for his broadcasting work. His hour-long features covered controversial topics, and he gained interviews with people who rarely spoke to reporters. Bradley reported on the AIDS crisis in Africa before it was widely covered, the shockingly high level of violence in American cities, and manufacturing defects that led to the recall of a quarter of a million Audi automobiles.

Bradley's biographical pieces showed his appreciation of the human condition, and his personal interview style successfully illuminated personalities ranging from cultural stars to ordinary people who had overcome physical challenges. He was an ardent jazz and gospel music fan and enjoyed attending concerts and interviewing singers and instrumental musicians. His report on the singer LENA HORNE, for which Bradley earned an Emmy, remained his lifelong favorite. His weekly broadcasts *Jazz at Lincoln Center Radio with Ed Bradley* were heard on 240 public radio stations. The Oklahoma City bomber Timothy McVeigh gave Bradley his only televised interview in 2000, and the convicted killer and book author Jack Henry Abbott agreed to an interview that Bradley later said was his most difficult.

Bradley's legacy includes mentoring a new generation of black newscasters, including CHARLAYNE HUNTER-GAULT, former journalist for the *New York Times*, *The McNeil/Lehrer News Hour*, and National Public Radio. One of the first black correspondents to maintain a high-profile presence on network news,

Bradley was given a National Association for the Advancement of Colored People Anniversary Award.

Bradley was married three times but had no children. His first marriage to Diane Jefferson ended in divorce, as did his second marriage to singer Priscilla Coolidge in 1984. Bradley married his companion of several years, Patricia Blanchet, in 2004.

Years before his third marriage Bradley contracted lymphocytic leukemia. He hid his condition from colleagues and friends and continued to work. He underwent quintuple bypass heart surgery in 2003 but resumed work at a breakneck pace, turning out more reports than any other *60 Minutes* correspondent.

Despite a sudden downturn in his condition in October 2006 when his illness became unmanageable by medication, he was able to complete a final assignment for *60 Minutes* before entering a New York hospital.

Further Reading

Campbell, Richard. *"60 Minutes" and the News: A Mythology for Middle America* (1991).
Coffey, Frank. *"60 Minutes": 35 Years of Television's Finest Hour* (1993).
Hewitt, Don. *Minute by Minute* (1985).
Madsen, Axel. *"60 Minutes": The Power and the Politics of America's Most Popular TV News Show* (1984).

Obituary: *Washington Post*, 9 Nov. 2006.

PAMELA LEE GRAY

BRADLEY, Thomas (29 Dec. 1917–29 Sep. 1998), mayor of Los Angeles, was born in a log cabin on a cotton plantation near Calvert, in Robertson County, Texas, the son of Lee Thomas Bradley and Crenner Hawkins, sharecroppers. Calvert had thrived in the late nineteenth century, buoyed by the cottonseed industry and the Southern Pacific Railroad, but its economy had declined by the time of Thomas's birth. Life for sharecroppers like the Bradleys was precarious—little better, in fact, than it had been for Lee's father, a slave in the Carolinas. They knew the certainty of picking cotton for eighteen hours a day and the annual uncertainty of the price of that cotton. Heavily indebted to white landlords, Lee and Crenner struggled to provide their family with vital necessities, such as food and health care; five of their children died in infancy. Like many southern blacks in the 1920s, the Bradley family saw only one answer to the restrictions of Jim Crow: migration, first to Dallas; then briefly to Arizona, where even the six-year-old Tom picked cotton for a while; and, finally, in 1924, to Los Angeles.

The Bradleys struggled in their new home. Unable to find steady employment in Los Angeles, Lee served as a crewman on Pacific Coast ocean liners. Crenner found work as a maid, and Tom's elder brother dropped out of school to work on farms in Orange County. Even so, as a boyhood friend of Tom's recalled, the Bradleys "were poorer than a lot of folks were poor" (Sonenshine, 59). His parents' enforced absences left Tom as the de facto head of the household. As a teenager, he had to balance the family budget, negotiate sibling rivalries, and take care of his handicapped younger brother, experiences that he would later draw upon as a politician. Although Crenner relied heavily on Tom, she was also determined that her son, a studious child, should take advantage of the educational opportunities available to him in the Los Angeles school system. A combination of academic success and prowess on the track brought him to Polytechnic High School, one of the best schools in the city. As one of the few black students at Poly, and one of the poorest, Tom faced discrimination, but he quickly earned a reputation as a mediator, often called on by the administration to ease tensions among the diverse student body. Those skills and his high profile as the captain of the track team and as a star football player helped Tom win his first political campaign, as president of the Poly Boys' League. They also helped him win a full athletic scholarship to the University of California, Los Angeles (UCLA) in 1937.

Bradley thrived at UCLA. He continued to star on the track and also played football on a team that included the future baseball legend JACKIE ROBINSON. Fraternity politics occupied much of Bradley's time in college; his membership in Kappa Alpha Psi helped him create a network of black professionals who would later back his political ambitions. Bradley continued to help his family in the summertime by shoveling scrap iron, gardening, and working as a photographer for the comedian Jimmy Durante. That connection to Hollywood would later prove invaluable in Los Angeles politics. In 1940, his junior year, Bradley took the Los Angeles Police Department (LAPD) entrance exam, placed near the top, and decided to leave UCLA to join the police force. With a steady income of $170 a month, Bradley felt secure enough to propose marriage to Ethel Arnold, a fellow member of the New Hope Baptist Church; they married in May 1941. Tragically, their first child died the day she was born, the Bradleys' first wedding anniversary. Two daughters were born later.

Although Bradley had broken racial barriers at UCLA with ease, the LAPD presented a far greater challenge. Only three of his seventy-one colleagues at the police academy and one hundred of the four thousand members of the force were black, a situation that changed little in Bradley's twenty years on the force. By the time he resigned in 1961, Bradley had risen to lieutenant, the highest rank held by an African American on the force at that time. Bradley did much to improve race relations, most notably in his role as head of the LAPD's community-relations detail. Bradley's superiors, however, resisted his efforts to bolster the image of the force in nonwhite neighborhoods. In 1960 Police Chief William Parker vetoed Bradley's unilateral decision to integrate the radio cars in his division. That reversal undermined the lieutenant's authority and also suggested that reform of the LAPD—and the city's other racist institutions—would have to come from outside.

After Bradley resigned from the police force, he became increasingly active in the Democratic Party, and in 1961 he was elected city councilman for Los Angeles's ethnically diverse Tenth District, defeating his white opponent by a 2-to-1 margin. The Tenth District did not include Watts, but when that neighborhood rebelled against police brutality, overcrowding, and high unemployment in August 1965, Bradley emerged as the leader of all Angelenos opposed to the policies of Mayor Sam Yorty and Chief Parker. Parker inflamed black opinion by blaming the riots on "monkeys in a zoo." Yorty was less offensive, but equally inaccurate, in reproaching "Communists for agitating Negroes with propaganda over past police brutality" (Payne and Ratzan, 73).

Bradley knew from his own experience on the force that police brutality was no myth, and over the next four years he became the most visible critic of the LAPD excesses and the most vocal proponent of increased federal and local efforts to improve equal economic opportunity. In 1969 Bradley challenged Yorty for the position of mayor. The election was racially divisive, though most of the mud was flung by Yorty, who disingenuously, but successfully, linked the moderate Bradley to militants such as the Black Panther ELDRIDGE CLEAVER. Bradley chose not to respond in kind, a stance that some commentators viewed as a tactical error. In a rematch in 1973 Bradley won easily. Yorty again tried to paint his opponent as an extremist, but this time Bradley responded with a television campaign that highlighted his police experience and charming, far-from-militant demeanor. Bradley energized his base of African American voters, made gains among Asians and Latinos, and won over significant sections of the city's white business community, most notably in Hollywood. Yorty had misread the electoral dynamics of an increasingly diverse Los Angeles.

Over the next twenty years Bradley tried to govern the city as inclusively as he had run his campaign; this was no easy task, given the city's rapid growth and the increasing diversity of its population. In his first term in office Bradley attempted to redevelop the crumbling downtown of Los Angeles. He skillfully deployed state and federal funds to bring jobs to depressed neighborhoods, but the antitax crusade of the late 1970s wreaked havoc with any meaningful effort to use government to solve the city's problems. In 1978 Californians approved Proposition Thirteen, a referendum measure that cut property taxes and

Thomas Bradley campaigning in Los Angeles, 1973. (AP Images.)

drastically reduced the revenues available to local governments. Given that Bradley had already cut property taxes in 1976, the revenue loss proved devastating to those impoverished Angelenos most dependent on government services. Downtown business leaders, however, were delighted by what they saw as Bradley's fiscal rectitude and worked closely with him in the late 1970s and 1980s on his three flagship projects: revitalization of the downtown business district, expansion of the Los Angeles International Airport, and bringing the Olympic Games to the city in 1984. The latter undertaking was particularly rewarding to Bradley, the UCLA track star who, as a child, had read avidly about the ancient games and who, as a teenager, had peered through the L.A. Coliseum fence to catch a glimpse of the 1932 Olympians. Despite a Soviet boycott, the Los Angeles Olympics, the first privately funded games, proved to be a resounding commercial success. That year Bradley was the recipient of the NAACP's Spingarn Medal.

Bradley succeeded in diversifying the city workforce, but the deep-rooted racism of the LAPD proved intractable. After 1978 he faced a formidable foe in Daryl Gates, the new police chief. In the 1980s a rash of police shootings and beatings of minorities provoked anger in the black community, not only at Gates but also at Bradley for failing to fire him. Constitutionally, however, the mayor did not have the power to do so. The 1991 police beating of a black motorist, RODNEY KING, videotaped by a bystander and later relayed worldwide on television, however, was the final straw for Bradley, who worked behind the scenes to remove Gates. The acquittal of King's attackers in 1992 was an "outrage," Bradley told a news conference.

Many of the citizens of South Central, Los Angeles, agreed. Within hours of the acquittal, the city experienced its greatest civil unrest since the Watts riot. More than fifty people were killed, four hundred were injured, and seventeen thousand were arrested. Property damage amounted to $1 billion. In his last year in office, Bradley worked hard to bring the city's fractious communities together. Although all races had participated in the riots, relations between African Americans and Korean Americans were particularly fraught, since many of the black rioters had targeted Korean shopkeepers. While Bradley had his share of political disappointments, notably his defeat in two gubernatorial campaigns in 1982 and 1986 and a 1989 financial disclosure scandal, the South Central riots would remain the low point of his career. Bradley had earned a law degree at Southwestern University while still a policeman, and on leaving office in 1993 he practiced law until he suffered a heart attack and a stroke in 1996. He died of a heart attack two years later in Los Angeles.

Mourners at Bradley's funeral recalled his electoral victories and losses and agreed upon his warmth, courtliness, and charm. Bradley's abiding legacy, however, was an ability to craft and to maintain for two decades a broad, multiracial, and ideologically diverse political coalition in one of the world's most fragmented cities.

Further Reading
The Mayor Tom Bradley Administrative Papers (1973–1993) at the Department of Special Collections of the UCLA Library provide the most comprehensive introduction to his five terms as mayor and include some materials on his earlier career. The UCLA Oral History Program, also at the Department of Special Collections of the UCLA Library, has interviews with Bradley and many of his contemporaries in Los Angeles and California politics.
Davis, Mike. *City of Quartz: Excavating the Future in Los Angeles* (1992).
Payne, J. Gregory, and Scott C. Ratzan. *Tom Bradley: The Impossible Dream* (1986).
Sonenshine, Raphael J. *Politics in Black and White: Race and Power in Los Angeles* (1993).
Obituaries: *New York Times* and *Los Angeles Times*, 30 Sept. 1998.

STEVEN J. NIVEN

BRADSHAW, Tiny (23 Sept. 1905–26 Nov. 1958), singer, drummer, and bandleader, was born Myron Carlton Bradshaw in Youngstown, Ohio. His parents' names are unknown. He played the drums from the age of ten and soon after was performing professionally as a drummer and vocalist. Early in his career he served as the drummer of the Jump Johnson Band in Buffalo, New York. He attended Wilberforce University in Wilberforce, Ohio, and majored in psychology. Before forming his own big band in 1934, he sang with Horace Henderson's Collegians, and in New York he either drummed or sang with Marion Hardy's Alabamians, the Savoy Bearcats, Mills Blue Rhythm Band (1932–1933), and LUIS RUSSELL (1933–1934).

Bradshaw's own band enjoyed long engagements in the ballrooms and nightclubs of Harlem (notably the Savoy and the Apollo), Philadelphia, and Chicago and toured throughout the United States and Europe, making its reputation with powerful, blues-based jazz. His band was introduced to the public at the Renaissance Ballroom in New York City in 1934. That same year it landed a recording contract with Decca and earned nationwide recognition. The performances and recordings of this ensemble typically featured the highly energized singing of its leader—a combination of blues belting, scat improvisations, and patter reminiscent of CAB CALLOWAY, whom Bradshaw was known to greatly admire. In 1935 the teenage ELLA FITZGERALD won an amateur contest at the Harlem Opera House, earning her a week of performances with the newly popular Bradshaw band. These performances with Bradshaw at the Harlem Opera House resulted in her first mention in the press and her introduction to the bandleader CHICK WEBB, with whom she catapulted to national fame. A high rate of turnover in band membership suggests the continual financial and artistic challenges that Brad-

Tiny Bradshaw, singer, drummer, and bandleader, March 1942. (Library of Congress/Carl Van Vechten.)

In his assessment of Bradshaw's early work, Gunther Schuller praised the bandleader's own jazz-oriented singing and the consistent quality of the solos of the trumpeter Shad Collins and the alto saxophonist Procope as well as the effective integration of improvised solos into arrangements. Yet Schuller faulted the formulaic nature of the arrangements themselves. Putting Bradshaw's big band in the context of its era, Schuller wrote, "Bradshaw and his band were a rhythmically exciting, hard-swinging group, perhaps not exactly ahead of its time in that respect, but certainly undeviatingly committed to a strong propulsive swing as the essence of jazz—at a time when so many bands could not swing at all or reserved it only for special up-tempo instrumental numbers" (423–424). Summarizing Bradshaw's achievements, Schuller continued, "With jazz and the blues always at his side, he was swinging long *before* swing arrived in full force and long *after* it had disappeared" (425).

Further Reading
McCarthy, Albert. *Big Band Jazz* (1974).
Schuller, Gunther. *The Swing Era: The Development of Jazz, 1930–1945* (1989).

Discography
Garrod, Charles. *Tiny Bradshaw and His Orchestra* (1994).
Mohr, Kurt. *Discography of Tiny Bradshaw* (1961).
MICHAEL J. BUDDS

shaw faced over a fifteen-year period. Such constant changes in personnel, however, also reveal Bradshaw's uncanny ability to identify talent, especially among alto saxophonists. At one time or another his lineup included RUSSELL PROCOPE, BILL JOHNSON, George Dorsey, Bobby Plater, SONNY STITT, and GIGI GRYCE. With Plater and Edward Johnson, Bradshaw composed the evergreen riff song "Jersey Bounce" (1942), which was popularized initially by Glenn Miller and later by Benny Goodman. During World War II, with the rank of major, Bradshaw led a large military show band that performed for the troops both at home and overseas. In 1945 he made a USO-sponsored tour of Japan and in the same year made his last big band recordings.

After World War II Bradshaw downsized his ensemble and shifted its emphasis to the rhythm and blues idiom, in which he achieved great popularity during the 1950s. Between 1949 and 1958 he was affiliated with the King label as leader, piano soloist, and accompanist. In the "jump" tradition he issued approximately sixty recordings and scored several hits, including "Big Town" with rhythm and blues vocalist Roy Brown and "Soft" (1953). Bradshaw's hard-driving instrumental pieces and novelty songs were among the models imitated by early rock and roll singers. Toward the end of his life, Bradshaw settled in Chicago, where he worked regularly until two strokes brought his thirty-five-year entertainment career to a close. He died in Cincinnati, Ohio.

BRADY, St. Elmo (22 Dec. 1884–25 Dec. 1966), chemist and educator, was born in Louisville, Kentucky, the eldest son of Thomas Brady, a tobacco factory laborer, and Celester Brady, both of whom were born free around the time of the Civil War. Brady's father, himself illiterate, made sure that all of his children attended school. St. Elmo Brady graduated from high school with honors before enrolling at Fisk University in Nashville, Tennessee, in 1904. At Fisk, he studied with Thomas W. Talley, who was regarded as one of the best chemistry teachers in the black college system.

After graduating from Fisk in 1908 Brady accepted a teaching position at the Tuskegee Institute in Alabama. He quickly became friends with both BOOKER T. WASHINGTON, the institute's first president and leading advocate, and GEORGE WASHINGTON CARVER, the scientist famous for his agricultural research on peanuts, soybeans, sweet potatoes, and pecans. Brady was deeply impressed with both men and strived thereafter to emulate their dedication to education, service, and improving opportunities for their race. It was at Tuskegee that Brady also met his wife, Myrtle Travis.

In 1913 Brady broke new ground when he left Tuskegee to pursue a graduate degree at the University of Illinois. In 1916 he became the first African American to receive a PhD in Chemistry and one of only a very few African Americans to hold a PhD in any scientific field. Brady's research on the divalent oxygen atom was completed under the supervision of Clarence G. Derick in the prestigious Noyes Laboratory. The Noyes Lab was the site of a number of chemical achievements, including the development of nuclear magnetic resonance spectroscopy, the invention of high-intensity X-ray tubes, and the birth of the polymer industry. Brady broke additional barriers at Illinois, becoming the first African American to join Phi Lambda Upsilon, the chemistry honor society, and one of the first African Americans to be accepted into Sigma Xi, the science honor society.

Partially because of connections established during his time at Illinois, Brady was offered a position in industry after he completed his degree; however, he was also offered a new position at Tuskegee. As Brady would later recount to SAMUEL PROCTOR MASSIE JR., another pathbreaking African American chemist, he faced a choice between financial success and duty: "Here I was, an ambitious young man, who had all of the advantages of a great university, contact with great minds, and the use of all modern equipment. Was I willing to forget these and go back to a school in the heart of Alabama, where I wouldn't even have a Bunsen burner?" (Massie). In the end he returned to Tuskegee in 1916 as head of the division of science.

After four years at Tuskegee, Brady left to become the head of the chemistry department at Howard University in Washington, D.C. Brady's experience at Howard (1920–1927) set the pattern for his appointment at Fisk University (1927–1952). Brady developed a strong undergraduate curriculum, strengthened the faculty, and laid plans for new buildings and laboratories. At Howard and Fisk, Brady also established graduate degree programs.

The bulk of Brady's career was spent at Fisk, his alma mater. The chemistry building he built, later named the Talley-Brady Building, was the first modern laboratory at a black college devoted entirely to chemistry. A strong believer in the importance of research, Brady established an infrared spectroscopy program at Fisk, open to faculty from all colleges and universities, and ensured that his faculty's labs were stocked with modern equipment and instrumentation.

Although Brady thrived at Fisk, his personal life suffered. His wife, Myrtle, was unable to find employment in Nashville. A teacher, she preferred to live and work in Washington, D.C., where she raised their only son, St. Elmo Jr. Having spent much of the previous twenty-five years shuttling back and forth between Washington and Nashville in the segregated South, Brady moved back to Washington upon his retirement from Fisk in 1952. He had planned to stay there, but he found it difficult to refuse a request for help from the president of Tougaloo College in Mississippi, and accepted a position there from approximately 1956 to 1961. As he had at Howard and Fisk, Brady established a fully functioning chemistry department at Tougaloo, where none had existed before.

In a career that spanned more than forty years, Brady personally supervised the work of hundreds of young African American chemists. Primarily remembered as an administrator and teacher, he also maintained a modest research program on the chemical characteristics of native southern plants in the model of his mentor, George Washington Carver. Brady died on Christmas Day at his home in Washington, D.C., at the age of eighty-two.

Further Reading

Information about St. Elmo Brady's family was reconstructed from records in the 1860, 1870, 1880, 1900, 1910, and 1920 federal census.

Feldman, Martin R. "St. Elmo Brady, 1884–1966: American Chemist," in *Notable Twentieth-century Scientists*, ed. Emily J. McMurray (1995).

Massie, Samuel Proctor, Jr. "St. Elmo Brady: The Lengthened Shadow," *Chemistry* 43 (1970).

AUDRA J. WOLFE

BRAGG, George Freeman, Jr. (25 Jan. 1863–12 Mar. 1940), Episcopal clergyman, was born in Warrenton, North Carolina, the son of George Freeman Bragg Sr. and Mary Bragg (maiden name unknown). He was two years old when the family moved to Petersburg, Virginia, where he studied at the elementary school and at St. Stephen's Parish and Normal School. His family helped found St. Stephen's Church for Negroes in 1867. At age six he was employed as a valet by John Hampden Chamberlayne, editor of the *Petersburg Index*. In 1879 he entered a school founded by Major Giles B. Cooke, a former chaplain on Robert E. Lee's staff; the school had become a branch of Virginia Theological Seminary. The next year he was suspended for not being "humble" but was appointed a page in the Virginia legislature by the Readjuster Party. After a severe case of typhoid fever and a period of teaching school in 1885, he returned to his theological studies at Cooke's school, renamed the Bishop Paine Divinity and Industrial School. He was ordained deacon on 12 January 1887 and priest on 19 December 1888 by Bishop Francis M. Whittle. He married Nellie Hill in 1887; they had four children.

Bragg's parish ministry began in 1887 at St. Luke's Church in Norfolk, Virginia, where within four years he built a new church and rectory, renovated a school, organized the Holy Innocents (which became Grace Church), and founded the Industrial School for Colored Girls. After becoming rector of St. James First African Church in Baltimore, Maryland, in 1891, he opened St. James Mission in Portsmouth, Virginia. Under his leadership, St. James Church became self-supporting, purchased a rectory, and built a new church. By 1931 there were five hundred communicants, and the church made annual charitable contributions of a thousand dollars. At least four young men entered the priesthood under Bragg's guidance. In addition, he established the Maryland Home for Friendless Colored Children and was associated with St. Mary's Home for Boys and St. Katharine's Home for Little Girls. For thirty-five

George Freeman Bragg Jr. (seated) with two of his sons, also clergymen, in an undated photograph. (University of North Carolina at Chapel Hill Libraries, Rare Book Collection.)

years he was general secretary of the Conference of Church Workers among Colored People and a special chaplain to the bishop of the diocese of Maryland.

Beyond his service within his denomination, Bragg performed many duties. In 1884 he was honorary commissioner to the New Orleans Exposition. Virginia's governor Fitzhugh Lee appointed him a curator to the Hampton Normal and Agriculture Institute in 1887. He also served as chaplain to the second battalion of Virginia Colored Militia. In Maryland he was on the board of managers for the House of Reformation for Colored Boys and a member of the State Inter-Racial Commission. He started the Committee of Twelve, a group of black leaders, including BOOKER T. WASHINGTON and W. E. B. DU BOIS, that campaigned against the Poe Amendment, designed to disfranchise blacks in Maryland. He led the fight to have Negro teachers assigned to Negro schools in Baltimore. In 1905 he joined the Niagara Movement, a forerunner of the NAACP, and became a supporter of Du Bois, its founder.

Bragg's early association with the *Petersburg Index* had generated a lifelong interest in journalism. At age nineteen he had begun publishing the *Virginia Lancet*, a pro-Republican paper involved in Virginia politics. In 1886 he founded a new paper, the *Afro-American Churchman*, published, he said, in the interests of the Colored Episcopal church. Also that year he founded the *Afro-American Ledger*, which he later merged with the *Baltimore Afro-American*. The *Church Advocate* served for many years as the unofficial organ of the Conference of Church Workers among Colored People and was filled with biographical sketches of clergy, histories of local black Episcopal churches, and

commentary on the continuing struggles of blacks in the Episcopal Church. In later years it served as a parish paper for Bragg's church. The *Maryland Home* was a monthly, published to promote the Maryland Home for Friendless Colored Children.

Some of his published works, all of which contain biographical data, are *The Colored Harvest in the Old Virginia Diocese* (1901), *Afro-American Church Work and Workers* (1904), *The Story of Old St. Stephen's, Petersburg, Va.* (1906), *The First Negro Priest on Southern Soil* (1909), *Bond Slave of Christ* (1912), *Men of Maryland* (rev. ed., 1925), *The Pathfinder Absalom Jones* (1929), and *Heroes of the Eastern Shore* (1939). A major work still of prime importance is *History of the Afro-American Group of the Episcopal Church* (1922). Many of these volumes were printed on Bragg's own printing press, under the imprint of the Church Advocate Press.

Race relations would be improved, Bragg believed, by morally sensitive, educated people of both races, and he did not hesitate to denounce racial discrimination within his own denomination. Petitions for his selection to the episcopate were made in 1911 and 1917, but he was not elected. He died in Baltimore.

Further Reading

Bragg's papers are in the Schomburg Center for Research in Black Culture of the New York Public Library; the Moorland-Spingarn Research Center, Howard University, Washington, D.C.; and Virginia State University, Petersburg.

Brydon, George M. *The Episcopal Church among the Negroes of Virginia* (1937).

Burkett, Randall K., et al., eds. *Black Biography, 1790–1950: A Cumulative Index* (3 vols., 1991).

Suggs, Henry L., ed. *The Black Press in the South* (1983).

FREDERICK V. MILLS

BRAGG, Janet (24 Mar. 1907–11 Apr. 1993), aviator, nurse, and nursing home proprietor, was born Janet Harmon in Griffin, Georgia, the daughter of Cordia Batts and Samuel Harmon, a brick contractor. The Batts family had long been established in Griffin. Janet's maternal grandfather was a freed slave of Spanish descent, and her maternal grandmother was a Cherokee. Janet's grandfather had built the house in which she and her siblings were born; her mother had been born in the same house. The youngest of seven children, Janet had a happy childhood, enjoying sports and games and excelling at school. In an interview conducted at the University of Arizona as part of a project called "African Americans in Aviation in Arizona," Bragg reminisced: "We were a very happy family. We were not a rich family, only rich in love."

Independence was encouraged in the Harmon household. The children were allowed to attend any church they chose. They were also encouraged to work up to their potential academically, regardless of gender. In her autobiography, *Soaring above Setbacks* (1996), Bragg recalled her father saying, "If Jack can do it, so can Jill." This statement bolstered Bragg's courage, leading her to believe, "I could do anything I set my sights on." She transferred from public elementary school to St. Stephen's Episcopal School, which provided a better education in those days of strict segregation. She chose to attend an Episcopal boarding school, Fort Valley Episcopal High School, in Fort Valley, Georgia, where she did well in math, science, and sports.

Bragg next attended Spelman Seminary (later Spelman College), a historically black women's college in Atlanta, Georgia, where she majored in nursing. Her training took place at MacVicar Hospital on the Spelman campus. MacVicar's nursing program was selective and demanding, and Bragg was but one of two out of an entering class of twelve who survived the probationary period. The hospital had no interns, so nursing students assisted in operations and performed other procedures customarily handled by interns. As a result they received first-rate training. Bragg received her registered nurse degree in 1929.

After her graduation from Spelman, Bragg worked as a nurse in the segregated department of a hospital in her hometown, but she left after a month because of the inferior care offered to black patients. She moved to Rockford, Illinois, to live with a sister. While there, she passed the Illinois nurses' license test. Unable to find professional employment in Rockford, she moved to Chicago, where she became a nurse at Wilson Hospital. About 1931, while working at Wilson, she met and married Evans Waterford; they had no children. The marriage lasted only a few years (five, according to one source), but she kept the name Waterford until she married again.

In 1933 Bragg's father died. Bragg took on the support of her mother and two nieces, who moved into her Chicago home. She left the hospital for a better-paying nursing job in a medical office. Graduate work in pediatric nursing at the Cook County School of Nursing and a graduate certificate in public health administration from Loyola University led to a more lucrative position as health inspector for the Metropolitan Burial Insurance Company. She could now afford to pursue her dream of learning to fly.

Bragg wrote in her autobiography: "I saw a billboard with a bird . . . nurturing her young fledglings into the flying world. It read, 'Birds Learn to Fly. Why Can't You?' . . . It was so beautiful." In 1933 she enrolled in the Aeronautical University ground school. The black aviation pioneers JOHN ROBINSON and CORNELIUS COFFEY instructed her in meteorology, aeronautics, aircraft maintenance, and aircraft mechanics. Because the school owned no airplanes, it offered no actual flight instruction. Such instruction cost $15 an hour, so Bragg decided that it made more sense financially to purchase her own plane, which she could then rent to others. The plane, which cost $600, was the first of three she would own.

Finding an airfield where she and other aspiring black flyers would be permitted to learn to fly proved impossible. Black pilots were not allowed to fly out of airports used by whites. If they truly wanted to fly, they needed to build their own airfields. The class at the ground school, with the aid of Robinson and Coffey, formed the Challenger Aero Club. The group purchased land and built an airfield with their own hands in the small all-black town of Robbins, Illinois. In the spring of 1934, in her own plane and from the airfield that she had helped build, Bragg learned to fly. After thirty-five solo hours, she passed the test for the private pilot's license. In addition to her other activities, in the 1930s Bragg wrote a weekly column, "Negro Aviation," in the *Chicago Defender* under the byline Janet Waterford.

In 1939 the federal government announced the Civilian Pilot Training Program (CPTP) for whites only. Black pilots, civil rights organizations, and prominent politicians lobbied successfully to have the race restriction removed. African Americans would be trained, but separate from whites and in different facilities.

In 1943, during World War II, Bragg and several other black women applied for appointments with the Women's Auxiliary Service Pilots (WASPS). The interviewer rejected Bragg outright, and her appeal was unsuccessful. She then applied to the military nurse corps but was informed that the quota for black nurses was filled.

Unable to join the war effort, Bragg went to the CPTP school at Tuskegee, Alabama, to obtain her commercial pilot's license. After successfully completing her written work, she took and passed her flight test, but a bigoted instructor refused to issue her license. Bragg returned to Chicago, where she passed the test with ease, the first black woman to do so.

Flying was a hobby, and Bragg continued to work as a health inspector until an opportunity arose to start her own business. Bragg and her brother had arranged to purchase a property, but her brother backed out. A friend suggested that she turn the property into a health-care facility for patients on welfare. With the aid of cousins from Georgia, Bragg's venture grew into a nursing home business that eventually housed sixty patients. She married Sumner Bragg late in 1951, and he joined her in running the business. They operated several nursing homes successfully until their joint retirement in 1972. They had no children.

Bragg befriended several Ethiopian students studying in the United States, traveling with them and showing them around. For her helpfulness she was invited to Ethiopia to meet the emperor, Haile Selassie, in 1955. In the 1970s she traveled widely in Africa, leading tour groups. In 1986, after the death of Sumner Bragg, she moved permanently to Arizona, where the Braggs had been spending their winters.

Bragg's achievements were recognized during her later years. Invited to appear at aviation events around the country, she received many awards and honors. She was also active in such civic organizations as the Tucson, Arizona, Urban League, Habitat for Humanity, and the Adopt-a-Scholar Program at

Pima College in Tucson. She died in Blue Island, Illinois, a suburb of Chicago. She wrote in her autobiography, "I think I've had a wonderful life."

Further Reading
Bragg, Janet. *Soaring above Setbacks* (1996).
Hine, Darlene Clark. *Black Women in America* (1993).

Obituaries: *Jet*, 5 May 1993; *Chicago Defender*, 15 April 1993.

MIRIAM SAWYER

BRAITHWAITE, William Stanley Beaumont (6 Dec. 1878–8 June 1962), poet, critic, and anthologist, was born in Boston, Massachusetts, the son of William Smith Braithwaite and Emma DeWolfe. Of his two avocations—American poetry and the status of the American Negro—the second clearly had its origins in an unusual cultural heritage. The Braithwaite family, of mixed black and white descent, was wealthy and held prominent positions in British Guiana. Braithwaite's father studied medicine in London but quit because of apparent mental strain and moved to Boston, where he married DeWolfe, whose family had been in slavery. His father remained aloof from neighbors, educating his children at home. Braithwaite's autobiography mentions no employment held by his father, whose death, when his son was eight years old, left the family destitute.

William Stanley Braithwaite, poet, critic, and anthologist, c. 1915. (Library of Congress, National Association for the Advancement of Colored People Records.)

Braithwaite's mother was forced into menial employment, and at the age of twelve, so was Braithwaite. After showing interest in reading, he was given a job as a typesetter, where exposure to the poetry of John Keats fixed the course of his life: "Keats had created in me an aspiration that became the most passionate urgency in my life, and Wordsworth and Burns nourished it into an ambition that developed into a fanatical determination" (Butcher, 174). Braithwaite read widely and completed a volume of poetry before he was twenty-one, but a series of disappointments made him aware of the tremendous racial barriers he would have to overcome as an African American in order to make a living in the literary field. He became determined to prove that a black poet could be successful despite the fact that he was black—without being forced into a special category as a Negro writer. With this resolve he developed a Keatsian theory of poetry: "It is not the feeling of contemplative anxiety aroused by the philosophic or moral imagination that gives to poetry its highest value, but the agitated wonder awakened in the spirit of the reader by the sudden evocation of magic" (Butcher, 29–30). Braithwaite's attempted evocations of sheer beauty show virtually no awareness of his racial heritage or of the social problems confronting black Americans, and as a result he has often been criticized or dismissed by those concerned with black literature. It should be remembered, however, that Braithwaite frequently championed black writers, offered his guidance to writers of the Harlem Renaissance, and analyzed the position of black writers in essays such as "The Negro in American Literature."

In "The Negro in American Literature" he traces the treatment of black people in American literature by both black and white writers from *Uncle Tom's Cabin* through the mid-1920s. He does not praise authors whose work shows no signs of race but whose work transcends the racial. Of JAMES WELDON JOHNSON he says, "Mr. Johnson's work is based upon a broader contemplation of life, life that is not wholly confined within any racial experience, but through the racial he made articulate that universality of the emotions felt by all mankind" (Butcher, 77). Of JEAN TOOMER's *Cane* he writes: "So objective is it, that we feel that it is a mere accident that birth or association has thrown him into contact with the life he has written about. He would write just as well . . . about the peasants of Russia, or the peasants of Ireland" (83). Although Braithwaite's poetry is not a reflection of his black heritage, he admired writers whose work went beyond their black heritage to universal human experience.

In 1903, with his career still before him, he married Emma Kelly; the couple had seven children. A few months after his marriage, he dedicated himself full time to literature. His first volume, *Lyrics of Life and Love* (1904), was published by subscription. In 1906 he began writing reviews and criticism for the staid but influential *Boston Evening Transcript*. The collections of the year's best poetry that he published there developed into an annual anthology of magazine verse that appeared from 1913 until 1929.

Braithwaite was an important guiding force during the emergence of modern poetry in the United States. He recognized the genius of Edwin Arlington Robinson before the turn of the century and became a close friend. Among the others whose careers he advanced was Robert Frost, whom he first praised in 1915. He was receptive to imagism, although he did not share the American poet and editor Harriet Monroe's enthusiasm for Ezra Pound.

In spite of his influence, Braithwaite was hampered by financial difficulties. He published his yearbooks at his own expense, and he was unable to publish a projected anthology of Negro poetry. His *Poetry Journal*, begun only months after Monroe's *Poetry*, failed after a few issues. It was not until 1935, when he accepted a professorship at Atlanta University, that he enjoyed financial security. He taught ten years before retiring to Harlem, where he produced *Selected Poems* (1948) and *The Bewitched Parsonage: The Story of the Brontës* (1950). He died at his home in New York City.

It is doubtful that Braithwaite will be remembered as a poet. His *Selected Poems* is a very slim volume, and the poetry is fragile and overly delicate. Between this volume and his first appeared only one other, *The House of Falling Leaves* (1908). His work rarely appears in anthologies. Philip Butcher, editor of *The William Stanley Braithwaite Reader*, predicts that "William Stanley Braithwaite's stature is sure to grow as scholars give attention to the records of his life and work" (7). If Braithwaite is remembered, it will be as an important critical voice of the early twentieth century.

Further Reading
Forty libraries have papers relating to Braithwaite. The major collections are at Harvard University and Syracuse University.

Bardolph, Richard. *The Negro Vanguard* (1971).

Butcher, Philip, ed. *The William Stanley Braithwaite Reader* (1972).

Redding, J. Saunders. *To Make a Poet Black* (1939).

Obituary: *New York Times*, 9 June 1962.

DALTON GROSS
MARYJEAN GROSS

BRANCH, Frederick Clinton (1923–10 Apr. 2005), first black marine officer and distinguished educator, was born in Hamlet, North Carolina, the son of a Methodist minister. Little is known of his parents or his early education, but he was educated in New York state public schools and attended Temple University in Philadelphia, Pennsylvania, until he was drafted into the U.S. Marine Corps in 1943. Branch completed basic training at the segregated Marine Corp Recruit Depot for black recruits known as Montford Point, located on a desolate portion of Camp Lejeune in North Carolina. Following basic training, Branch served overseas as part of the Fifty-first Defense Battalion, a supply unit stationed on a Pacific island near the International Dateline. While in the Pacific, Branch applied to the navy's V-12 commissioning program for college draftees and was accepted. After participating in the V-12 program he attended the Sixteenth Platoon Leaders Class at the Marine Corps Officer Candidate School in Quantico, Virginia.

On 10 November 1945, the 170th birthday of the U.S. Marine Corps, Branch became the first African American officer in marine corps history. Following his commissioning he commanded an all-black reserve unit in Philadelphia. During the Korean War, Branch commanded an integrated anti-aircraft training platoon at Camp Pendleton in California. He married Camilla "Peggy" Robinson around 1950. Although he was promoted to captain in 1955 he resigned his commission in order to begin a career in education.

After earning a degree in Physics from Temple University Branch began a thirty-five year career in the Philadelphia school system. During his tenure he was awarded a geology fellowship at Princeton University and a Shell Oil Merit Fellowship to Cornell University to study chemistry. In addition Branch served as a curriculum writer for the school system. More than merely a groundbreaking figure in the marine corps, Branch was also a consummate professional educator.

On 7 July 1997 the marine corps dedicated a building in honor of Branch at its Officer Candidate School in Quantico, Virginia, in recognition of his achievements as a U.S. marine and professional educator. Frederick Clinton Branch died in 2005 and was buried at Quantico National Cemetery with full military honors. Shortly after his death in North Carolina the senators Elizabeth Dole and Richard Burr sponsored a U.S. Senate resolution commemorating Branch's life and achievements.

Further Reading
Some of the information for this article was found in the Marine Corps Files, courtesy of the History and Museums Division, U.S. Marine Corps.

Danelo, David. "Branching Out," *U.S. Naval Institute's Proceedings* (June 2005).

Davis, Mark. "How a Philadelphia Man Reshaped the History of the Marine Corps," *Philadelphia Inquirer*, 1 Aug. 1997.

Gilliam, Gregory. "Standing Alone," *Marines Magazine* (Sept. 1997).

CHARLES EDWARD WILES IV

BRANCH, Mary Elizabeth (20 May 1881–6 July 1944), educator, was born in Farmville, Virginia, the daughter of Tazewell Branch, a former slave who served in the Virginia legislature and worked as a shoemaker and tax collector, and Harriett Lacey, a domestic worker. Although she learned to read at home, Branch began her quest for formal education when she was thirteen. Because her mother did laundry for students and teachers at State College in Farmville, Branch often made trips to the school to pick up or deliver clothes; in time she herself became a maid in the college library. Exposed for the first time to a wide variety of books and knowledge, she was determined to obtain her own education. Within a few years she had earned a high school diploma from the normal school of Virginia State College, a land-grant college for black students in Petersburg, where she also took teacher education classes.

Eager to share her knowledge, Branch accepted a position as an English teacher at an elementary school in Blackstone, Virginia, soon after completing her secondary education. After a few years she returned to Virginia State, where she taught English for twenty years and also served as housing director for both men's and women's dormitories. While at Virginia State, Branch spent her summers continuing her own education. She studied at the University of Pennsylvania and at Columbia University, as well as at the University of Chicago, where she earned a bachelor's degree in Philosophy in 1922 and a master's degree in English in 1925. She also began, but did not complete, a doctorate in Education.

In the late 1920s Branch moved to Kansas City, Kansas, to teach social studies at Sumner Junior College. After one year she moved to St. Louis to serve as dean of girls at Vashon High School, then the largest school in the United States for black girls. Working at Vashon—located in a poor urban neighborhood—was challenging, but it paid well and provided Branch with a prominent position within black education circles. By 1930 the American Missionary Association (AMA) had noted her work and invited her to become president of its Tillotson College in Austin, Texas. Branch initially declined two offers from the association, but she accepted after the third request. Noting that many white teachers had gone to the South after the Civil War to help newly freed slaves, Branch determined that accepting the presidency of Tillotson could be no more difficult than that. In taking her new position in 1930 she became the first black woman to serve as a college president in Texas.

The task ahead of her was a formidable one. Chartered by the AMA in 1877 and opened in 1881, Tillotson College was declining when Branch was hired to lead it. Originally established as one of several AMA schools for former slaves throughout the South, the school had prospered for many years; it provided industrial and traditional education at the elementary and secondary levels and then achieved collegiate status in 1909. By 1930, however, black migration out of Texas and poor administrative leadership had deeply hurt the school. It was reduced to a junior college in 1925, and in 1926 it converted to a women's college; its enrollment at that time dropped below 150 students.

Branch arrived at Tillotson on 1 July 1930 and found a few run-down buildings on a physically unkempt campus. She appreciated the challenge that awaited her and took advantage of the AMA's promise to let her run the school with minimal interference.

Branch quickly established a five-year plan for Tillotson, with immediate goals to improve the physical plant and increase enrollment. Radical and activist in her approach, Branch directed her attention to every aspect of the campus. She was responsible for vastly expanding the library's holdings—often shopping at used bookstores to acquire volumes—renovating several old buildings, and adding numerous others. She solicited donations and initiated a long-term fundraising program for the physical plant. The campus was landscaped, the high school program was dropped, the faculty was doubled, and the minimum requirement for faculty was raised to a master's degree. To attract more students, Branch sent teachers throughout the Southwest, added scholarships, and invited high school girls to special events on the campus. In 1935 she returned Tillotson to its coeducational status. By this time enrollment had increased to more than two hundred students, and it topped five hundred students by the time of her death.

Branch understood the importance of outside recognition for her college. She secured Tillotson's senior college ranking by the Texas Board of Education in 1931, gained its membership in the American Association of Colleges in 1936, and garnered an "A" rating for it from the Southern Association of Colleges and Secondary Schools in 1943. Branch was an early supporter of the United Negro College Fund, founded in 1944, and made Tillotson one of its first affiliates.

At the same time that she rejuvenated Tillotson and ensured its survival, Branch took a prominent role in the Austin community. She served in 1943 as president of the Austin chapter of the National Association for the Advancement of Colored People, was a member of the state's Commission on Interracial Cooperation, and served on the state's Negro Advisory Board for the National Youth Administration from 1935. In this capacity she worked closely with Lyndon Johnson, then the state's Youth Administration director, and established two freshmen college centers under the auspices of Tillotson to encourage unemployed black youth to further their education. Such efforts, she wrote to Johnson, "bolstered up the self-respect of those young folks" (Winegarten, 183). She participated in a local book club and women's club and was a regular walker on Tillotson's twenty-three-acre campus.

Branch's efforts garnered nationwide attention. For her work at Tillotson, Virginia State College gave her an honorary doctorate of pedagogy, and Howard University presented her with an honorary doctor of laws degree. Never one to be satisfied with past accomplishments, Branch continued to push for needed improvements at Tillotson. She initiated shared faculty and speakers programs with Samuel Huston College, a black Methodist Episcopal college also located in Austin. These arrangements ultimately led to the merger of the two schools into Huston-Tillotson College in 1952. Branch had died in Camden, New Jersey, eight years earlier.

Mary Elizabeth Branch gave singular attention to Tillotson College and moved the college from almost certain failure to exemplary success. Described by those who knew her as frank and at times even brusque, she was also recognized as one who loved her institution and loved those who shared its life with her. Her interest in the welfare of her students was extensive and included her adoption of one female pupil as her own daughter. She never married. One of only a few black women college presidents in the United States in the 1930s and 1940s, Branch was an inspiring leader for her students, a talented and successful college administrator, and a visionary for the direction of black education in the South.

Further Reading

Branch's papers are in the archives of the Downs-Jones Library at Huston-Tillotson College in Austin, Texas.

Brown, Olive D., and Michael R. Heintze. "Mary Branch: Private College Educator," in *Black Leaders: Texans for Their Times*, ed. Alwyn Barr and Robert A. Calvert (1981).

Winegarten, Ruthe. *Black Texas Women: 150 Years of Trial and Triumph* (1995).

DEBBIE MAULDIN COTTRELL

BRANCH, Wallace (29 Oct. 1945–6 Sept. 2004), historian, collector, archivist, photographer, and entrepreneur, was born Wallace Michael Branch in Brooklyn, New York, one of two sons of Byrd Branch, an entrepreneur who operated a cleaning and tailoring business in New York City and held down a thirty-five-year job at the weekly newspaper *Irish Echo* to support his family, and Vera Barbour Branch. In Brooklyn, Branch and his family lived a solid middle-class lifestyle, making their home in a four-floor brownstone home that they owned.

Branch was born with sickle cell anemia, a hereditary, incurable, chronic disorder with which patients suffer severe pain and tissue and organ damage as a result of oxygen and nutrient deficiencies. At the time of Branch's birth, information about and treatment of the disease were limited. According to his family, doctors who treated Branch as a child never gave him much hope for survival. At fourteen Branch became so ill that he had to have a bone marrow transplant. In 1983, in an effort to help others with the disease, Branch's mother, Vera, founded the Connecticut chapter of the Sickle Cell Disease Association of America, a nonprofit organization providing support and education for sickle cell patients and their families. The family took regular recreational excursions together. It was on one of these trips, to Atlantic City, New Jersey, that the family was blindsided by tragedy. Sixteen-year-old Calvin, Branch's brother, died in a drowning accident. After years of mentally preparing for Wallace to die prematurely, he and his parents were not equipped to handle the death of his healthy, vibrant brother.

Wallace Branch attended grammar and high school in Brooklyn before enrolling at Monroe College, where he earned an associate's degree. After graduating from the Germain School of Photography in New York City, Branch began a career as a professional photographer. In 1977 he received a job offer from a CBS affiliate, WFSB-TV Channel 3. He accepted the position and moved to Hartford, Connecticut, where he spent the next fifteen years as a news photographer for the station, capturing local and regional news events and social activities. Branch was married for a short time in the early 1980s to Gladys Adams. The couple had no children and the union ended in divorce.

In 1992 Branch left Channel 3 and started his own business, Empire Photo and Video Studios, in Hartford, Connecticut, and New York. He specialized in portrait photography as well as business and special-event photography. He took many photos of politicians and entertainers, and was a photographer for events sponsored by the Essence Awards and Black Entertainment Television.

When not taking pictures Branch was collecting them. A self-proclaimed historian, he accumulated photos, news and magazine articles, and other items of historical significance. He was particularly interested in black memorabilia and was an advocate of the importance of chronicling cultural history. Branch amassed a huge collection of items and co-founded the Black Historians, in Hartford which maintained a mobile historical exhibit that it displayed at public venues. He gave speeches about the collection and black history in general. He co-organized a Black Historian exhibit at the Hartford Public Library called *Upon Reflection: A Half-Century of African American Cultural Highlights*, which was displayed in the summer of 2003. Branch held membership in the Photographers Association of America and the Charter Oak Photographic Society and was a founding member of the Russwurm Wells Society, a local black history group for enthusiasts.

In 1991 Branch traveled to Caux, Switzerland, to videotape performers at a peace conference of international ambassadors and heads of state. In 1996 he traveled to China, documenting his trip with an impressive collection of photos.

Defying longevity odds dictated by a devastating incurable disease (sickle cell patients generally live approximately forty years with the disease), Branch so rarely complained about the pain he endured that many friends and associates never knew he was sick until the years just before his death. Those years were the most difficult for him, yet he still managed to care for his ailing father, who died mere months before he did. Wallace Branch died from complications of sickle cell disease at the age of fifty-eight.

Further Reading

Icon Health Publications. *The Official Patient's Sourcebook on Sickle Cell Anemia* (Jan. 2005).

Obituaries: *Hartford Courant*, 9 Sept. 2004; *Hartford Inquirer*, 15 Sept. 2004.

NANCY T. ROBINSON

BRANCHE, George Clayton (10 Jan. 1896–10 Sept. 1956), physician, was born in Louisburg, North Carolina, the son of the Reverend Joel Branche and Hanna Shaw. He attended the Mary Potter Academy in Oxford, North Carolina. The Branche home was located near this Presbyterian school; George Branche enjoyed playing on the campus, and he acquired his early education there.

After his high school graduation in 1913, Branche enrolled at Lincoln University in Pennsylvania, where he participated as an athlete. He graduated in 1917 and served in World War I as a master sergeant. After the armistice he focused on medicine as a career. Branche graduated from the Boston University Medical School in 1923, and he was an intern at the Boston Psychopathic Hospital.

While Branche was in medical school, federal officials sought a site to establish a hospital for black veterans. African American World War I veterans suffered from treatment at inferior hospitals or were neglected. Health care for many black Americans was poor, and few black physicians were available to serve the vast population. Government leaders sought a southern town in which to build a black veteran's hospital, but only black citizens from Tuskegee, Alabama, expressed interest in the project.

The Tuskegee Veterans Administration (VA) Hospital was approved in 1921 and initially had a white staff. White area residents opposed black physicians' securing control of the facility and threatened violence if they did so. Black medical professionals were disappointed that promises made by government officials to place black physicians in leadership positions at the hospital were not kept. General Frank T. Hines, director of the Veterans Bureau, and leaders of the National Medical Association had selected promising physicians to replace the white physicians at the hospital. After it was announced in 1923 that six black physicians, including Branche, would soon arrive, some local whites responded by burning crosses.

Branche moved to Tuskegee in November 1923 as a junior medical officer at the hospital. He served on rotations and treated patients in general medicine, neuropsychiatry, and tuberculosis wards. In 1927 he was accepted for postgraduate study in neuropsychiatry in New York City, and later he returned to be chief of Neuropsychiatric Service at the Tuskegee VA Hospital.

Perhaps Branche's most significant work involved the development of new treatments for neurosyphilis occurring in blacks. He had experimented unsatisfactorily from 1928 with the tertian strain of malaria to treat neurosyphilis. In November 1932 he inoculated seven patients with the quartan strain of malaria as a possible treatment for neurosyphilis. Branche considered the results favorable. He first discussed his work at the 1934 American Psychiatric Association meeting. After inoculating thirty-six patients with the quartan strain, he had experienced a 91 percent success rate as compared to a 14 percent rate with the tertian strain injected into twenty-two patients. Psy-

chiatric professionals considered his quartan treatment as some of the most outstanding research performed at Tuskegee.

Branche read his paper "Therapeutic Quartan Malaria in the Treatment of Neurosyphilis among Negroes" at the 1939 American Psychiatric Association meeting in Chicago. During panel discussion his peers agreed that his work was a "real contribution." Dr. Walter L. Bruetsch of Indianapolis, Indiana, remarked that "the work of Dr. Branche and his associates in Tuskegee represents an admirable contribution and has an important practical application. It also comes at the right moment" because most hospitals at that time were dealing with treatment of malaria. "I believe it is one of the best contributions which have been made in recent years in the treatment of neurosyphilis," Bruetsch concluded (*Journal of the National Medical Association* [1941]: 84–85).

Physicians traveled to Tuskegee to learn Branche's method, and the treatment was quickly adopted. Branche explained that treatment with the tertian type of malaria had failed in blacks because he believed that they had acquired immunity because of the "entrenched endemic nature of tertian malaria in the South." Dr. TOUSSAINT TOURGEE TILDON, the African American manager of the Tuskegee VA Hospital, said that "Dr. Branche's greatest single attainment was the contribution he made when he gave to the medical profession and to the world an improved method of treating neurosyphilis by means of quartan malaria" (*Journal of the National Medical Association* [1958]: 140).

Branche's work took place during the same period as what came to be known as the Tuskegee Syphilis Experiment, in which the Public Health Service allowed African American men with syphilis to remain untreated so that the effects of the disease could be studied. In the years since the experiment came to light in 1970, scholars have grappled with questions over the culpability of the black medical professionals who collaborated with the PHS, which used Tuskegee facilities for much of its work.

World War II interrupted Branche's work. Serving as assistant clinical director from 1941, he embarked on a tour of duty as a lieutenant colonel in the U.S. Army Medical Corps in February 1944. When he was discharged in May 1946, Branche returned to Tuskegee as director of Professional Services.

Branche was a fellow of the American Psychiatric Association and a diplomate of the American Board of Psychiatry and Neurology. He was a member of the American Board of Neuropsychiatry, the National Medical Association, the American Association for the Advancement of Science, and the Association of Military Surgeons of the United States. Branche earned many honors, including the 1944 E. S. Jones Award for research in medical science from the John A. Andrews Clinical Society at Tuskegee Institute. He was named "Omega Man of the Year" in 1954 by Iota Omega Chapter of Omega Psi Phi fraternity.

Branche had married Lillian V. Davidson in 1924; they had two sons, who both became doctors, and a daughter. Branche was active in civic organizations and helped to establish the Presbyterian church at Tuskegee, as well as establish athletic teams, including baseball, basketball, and tennis, at the Tuskegee Institute. After a year's illness, Branche died at the Tuskegee VA Hospital, where he had devoted thirty-three years on staff. He was buried at Arlington National Cemetery.

Further Reading

Barker, Prince P. "Psychiatry at the Tuskegee VA Hospital in Retrospect," *Journal of the National Medical Association* 54 (Mar. 1962): 152–153.

Daniel, Pete. "Black Power in the 1920s: The Case of Tuskegee Veterans Hospital," *Journal of Southern History* 36 (1970): 368–388.

ELIZABETH D. SCHAFER

BRANDON, Barbara (1960–), cartoonist, was born in Brooklyn, New York, the youngest of three children of BRUMSIC BRANDON Jr., a pioneering black cartoonist and creator of the long-running comic strip *Luther*, which debuted in the late 1960s and was syndicated by the Los Angeles Times Syndicate in 1971.

As a young girl growing up in New Cassel, Long Island, Brandon often assisted her father with his work. Later she studied illustration in the College of Visual and Performing Arts at Syracuse University, but left six credits short of completing her degree. At age twenty-four Brandon created her own comic strip called *Where I'm Coming From*, which featured the faces of a diverse group of nine African American women friends.

Although her characters' perspectives were quintessentially African American, the cartoonist stressed that the voices were universal reflections on life and love. The characters were talking heads without bodies. Women are "too often summed up by our body parts," she said. "I'm saying 'We have opinions,' and 'Look me in the eye and talk to me'" (*New York Times*, 19 July 1992).

Although the strip was originally created for and sold to a fledgling black women's magazine called *Elan* in 1982, the publication folded before Brandon's work ever appeared. Moving back to Brooklyn in 1983, Brandon next approached *Essence* magazine. While her strip was not accepted for publication, she was offered a job as a beauty and fashion writer, which she accepted. She went on to work at the magazine for more than five years.

In 1988 Brumsic Brandon referred his daughter to the *Detroit Free Press*, where editors were looking for African American cartoonists. As *Free Press* editor Marty Claus noted in explaining her motives, "My community happens to be largely black, and we know young readers turn to the comic pages." *Where I'm Coming From* first ran in the *Free Press* in 1989 and continued to make regular Sunday appearances. Then in September of 1991 it appeared for the first time as an acquisition of the Universal Press Syndicate, making Brandon the first black female syndicated cartoonist—and only the eighth black cartoonist of either gender—to be published in the mainstream American press (in the 1930s JACKIE ORMES's strip *Torchy Brown* had appeared in the African American press, making her the first black woman cartoonist to have her work syndicated).

Encouraged by Universal Press Syndicate to feature political and racial themes in her strip, Brandon incorporated musings about the MARTIN LUTHER KING JR. holiday, CLARENCE THOMAS's appointment to the U.S. Supreme Court in 1991, and the RODNEY KING verdict and subsequent uprisings in Los Angeles in 1992. Brandon also made use of culturally specific references to black hair care, music, and history, saying that she thought it was more important to be "thought-provoking than funny" (*New York Times*, 19 July 1992). Brandon added that she was primarily concerned "with recording the experiences black women are having in this country and how some of us are feeling about them."

In the early 1990s it appeared that Brandon was "poised for wide recognition," as the *New York Times* (19 July 1992) put it. There were plans for marketing her characters on greeting cards, coffee mugs, and T-shirts, and in 1993 a collection of her strips, *Where I'm Coming From*, was published in book form by Andrews & McMeel. A second collection, *Where I'm Still Coming From*, appeared in 1994.

Yet there were still challenges facing professional black cartoon artists, who in the early 1990s still numbered fewer than a hundred. As Brandon remarked, as late as the 1960s, illustrations of African Americans were still mostly caricatures drawn by white people, images of "big lips and pickanniny heads" (*New York Times*, 19 July 1992). In 1996 such tensions came to a head when *The New Yorker* magazine commissioned but failed to publish a number of works by black cartoonists for its special double issue, "Black in America" (29 April/6 May 1996). Although illustrations were solicited from as many as nine black artists for the special issue, including Brandon, all but one of the African American–oriented images chosen were created by white artists. The magazine's editors reportedly felt nervous about some of the submissions, fearing that they might be controversial. Brandon handled the rejection with the even-tempered grace that seemed to define her public persona over the years, saying that she was proud to be among those whose work they considered too difficult.

In May 1997 Brandon married the musician Monte Croft and became Barbara Brandon-Croft. Their son, Chase, was born in October 1998.

In 1999 the cartoon landscape took a dramatic turn when twenty-four-year-old African American cartoonist AARON McGRUDER made his debut with *The Boondocks*, a highly politicized comic strip featuring a young, would-be black nationalist named Huey (after the Black Panther HUEY P. NEWTON). The strip, acquired by the Universal Press Syndicate, enjoyed major success in hundreds of mainstream newspapers across the country, and again it looked as though the fortunes for black cartoonists might be improving.

Meanwhile Brandon-Croft accepted work as a freelance researcher and fact-checker for magazines to make ends meet, as her comic strip work did not earn more than $30,000 a year. In 2002, after living in Brooklyn for nearly two decades, she relocated with her family to Queens, New York. Then, in March 2005, Brandon-Croft announced that she would end her comic strip after sixteen years of publication as her client list had declined dramatically. That same year, however, the cartoonist signed a development deal with Universal Press Syndicate to design a daily comic strip.

Further Reading
Adell, Sandra, ed. *Dictionary of Twentieth-Century Culture* (1996).
"Barbara Brandon is First Black Female Cartoonist Nationally Syndicated," *Jet* (26 Aug. 1991).
"Crusaders with Pen And Ink—African Americans Cartoonists," *Ebony* (Jan. 1993).
Hine, Darlene Clark, ed. *Black Women in America* (1993).
Lindin, Amy. "A Comic Strip For Us," *Essence* (Mar. 1990).
Rule, Sheila. "The 'Girls' Talking with a Black Perspective," *New York Times*, 19 July 1992.

KRISTAL BRENT ZOOK

BRANDON, Brumsic, Jr. (10 Apr. 1927–), artist and creator of *Luther,* one of the first comic strips with African American characters to be widely published in U.S. newspapers, was born in Washington, D.C., two blocks north of Union Station, then the national capital's major transportation center. Brumsic Brandon Sr. worked there as a railway porter. Brandon Jr.'s mother, the former Pearl Brooks, was a stock clerk and maid at the Kann's Department Store.

At Charles Young Platoon Elementary School, Brandon was a high achiever who loved to draw, which inspired him to pursue art as a career. In 1942, when he entered Armstrong Technical High School, he took nearly every painting, sketching, and sculpture course. Also, at the urging of teachers, he added courses in drafting, which later made him more employable. Brandon graduated in February 1945, intent on becoming a comic strip artist, but instead he became one of the first African Americans recommended for an appointment to the United States Naval Academy in Annapolis, Maryland.

The Reverend ADAM CLAYTON POWELL JR., a freshman Democratic congressman from New York's Twenty-second District in Harlem who made a political career knocking down racial barriers, was responsible for nominating Brandon and WESLEY A. BROWN, a Maryland native, for academy enrollment. Powell told the young men they might be rejected, but the navy would have to answer some tough questions

if they passed the admissions test. Brown passed, becoming Annapolis's first African American graduate. Brandon, however, flunked, largely because his passion was art. In fall 1945 he entered the art program at New York University.

An honor student, Brandon made extra money with sales of gag cartoons to pulp magazines such as *Pack o' Fun*. After less than a year he left school to be a full-time cartoonist. Around 1947 the price of paper shot up because of post–World War II shortages, contributing to the demise of the pulp magazine industry. Comics were the first sections dropped, so Brandon went home to Washington, D.C.

He took a job as a mail sorter on the night shift in the United States Post Office. As the U.S. Army bulked its ranks for the Korean conflict, Brandon was drafted in 1950. He was a sergeant in the all-black 594th Field Artillery battalion, part of the U.S. occupation forces in postwar Germany. After he was discharged, Brandon went back to his wife, Rita Broughton, a Howard University graduate, who worked for the government, whom he had married in 1950 in Washington. They raised two daughters, Linda, an entertainment attorney, and BARBARA BRANDON, who gained prominence as a cartoonist, and a son, Brumsic III, who taught in Westbury, Long Island, New York.

Cartoons were in Brandon's heart and mind, but he was unable to pay his bills as a cartoonist. He worked through a swift series of jobs, as an IBM machine operator, a statistical draftsman, and a technical illustrator for John R. O'Brien and Associates Incorporated, a professional services company. He drew exploded views of diesel and aircraft engine parts. In 1957 Brandon, with his wife, eldest daughter, and son, moved to New York City again for a full-time job with Bray Studios. The job gave him a chance to learn the basics of animation from Max Fleischer, a pioneer and innovator in animation who brought Betty Boop, Popeye, and Superman to the silver screen. Brandon worked at Bray Studios until 1970, when his now famous comic strip *Luther* rose to prominence.

While employed at Bray, Brandon continued to draw cartoons on his own time. He experimented with a variety of characters. Some of his worst efforts included early strips that featured an abstract figure and an inventor. The early strips matured into gag cartoons that took on issues of race. In 1963 Brandon became a regular contributor to *Freedomways,* a black-run quarterly magazine that showcased works by the best human rights advocates, thinkers, and artists of the sixties, seventies, and eighties. He stayed on as a contributing editor until the publication's demise in 1986.

In 1968 his cartoons in *Freedomways* drew the attention of editors at Newsday Specials, the syndication service of Long Island's daily newspaper, which asked Brandon to develop a comic strip. That year, on the evening of 4 April, on a hotel balcony in Memphis, the Reverend MARTIN LUTHER KING JR. was assassinated. Riots broke out throughout the nation.

Luther was born; Brandon named the strip and its main character to honor the late civil rights leader. Still, the comic strip's success did not come easily. Newsday Specials' editors changed their minds.

Brandon continued to develop the idea, nonetheless. Luther, a boy who lived in a black, working-class neighborhood, strove to understand the world around him. By 1960s' standards the cartoons were edgy. Brandon's cast of children included Hardcore, a militant outsider; Oreo, whose white mind-set was only thinly disguised by black skin; and their white teacher, Miss Backlash, who represented a faceless, oppressive power structure. The strip debuted in 1968 in the *Manhattan Tribune,* a weekly newspaper owned by William F. Haddad and distributed on New York City's Upper West Side. Soon the Los Angeles Times Syndicate picked up *Luther* and distributed the comic until 1986.

Offers flowed in, and suddenly *Luther* seemed to blossom. Between 1969 and 1976 publisher Paul S. Eriksson released six volumes of *Luther* comic strips—*Luther, from Inner City* (1969); *Luther Tells It* (1970); *Luther Raps* (1971); *Right On, Luther!* (1971); *Outta Sight, Luther!* (1972); and *Luther's Got Class* (1976). At the same time, Joya Sherrill, a former jazz singer and host of *Time for Joya* (later renamed *Joya's Fun School*), a New York children's television show, called on him to draw pictures for the stories and various art projects. Known as "Mr. BB," he was on the show until 1982. Richard Nixon's White House called, too. The insightfulness of *Luther* earned him a place at the White House Conference on Children in 1970.

Brandon's television work expanded during the mid-1970s. He wrote and illustrated several *Luther* segments for *Vegetable Soup,* a children's show produced by the New York State Department of Education. African American publishers wooed him as well. In 1974 Brandon developed *Black Cat's Bebop Fables* as a newspaper strip distributed to 125 black newspapers throughout the country through Black Media. Brandon stayed with the distributor, later called Black Resources, until 1999. He also showcased a television version of the cartoons on *Vegetable Soup.* The jazz icon DIZZY GILLESPIE narrated the stories. In 1995 thirty-two of his pen and ink drawings were added to the Library of Congress's permanent collection African American Odyssey: A Quest for Full Citizenship. He considered the inclusion to be his highest honor, although many of his cartoons are in Pelican Books' Best Editorial Cartoons of the Year from 1996 to 2003.

Further Reading
Robinson, Matt. *The Six Button Dragon* (1971).
Strömberg, Frederik. *Black Images in the Comics: A Visual History* (2003).

VINCENT F. A. GOLPHIN

BRANSON, Herman Russell (14 Aug. 1914–7 June 1995), physicist, educator, and academic administrator, was born in Pocahontas, Virginia, the son of Harry P. Branson, a coal miner, and Gertrude Brown. In 1928, after several years at his local elementary school, Herman enrolled at Dunbar High School in Washington, D.C., one of the nation's preeminent black secondary schools. He was encouraged in this move by a young black physician, William Henry Welch, who practiced in Pocahontas and who rented lodgings from young Branson's grandmother.

At Dunbar, Branson was introduced to studies in Latin, advanced mathematics, and other disciplines to which he would not have been exposed in his local high school. After graduating as valedictorian in 1932, he enrolled at the University of Pittsburgh with a view to studying medicine, partly because his great-uncle had been trained as a physician there. Branson completed the premedical program in two years and still found time to immerse himself in a wide range of science courses. "Physics could answer more questions than any other science," he later recalled, "so I decided physics was what I'd go into—but I really liked biology and chemistry, so as an undergraduate I took almost enough for a major in four fields: biology, chemistry, math, and physics" (Manning interview).

When the University of Pittsburgh turned down his application to the medical school in 1934—they had no intention of admitting blacks at the time, he was convinced—he transferred to all-black Virginia State College, where he majored in physics, graduating summa cum laude in 1936. His eclectic mix of scientific interests as an undergraduate foreshadowed the versatile, interdisciplinary character of his later research.

In 1936 Branson enrolled as a doctoral student in physics at the University of Cincinnati. He chose Cincinnati in part because he had relatives with whom he could live in the city, but also because the university had an excellent physics department, including the faculty member Boris Podolsky, known for his work in quantum mechanics. Podolsky was a primary mentor, but Branson—still intent on shaping his program in multidisciplinary ways—took courses in other fields as well, for example with Harris Hancock, a mathematician specializing in the theory of elliptic functions. Branson earned a PhD in Physics in 1939, and that year he married Corolynne Gray of Cincinnati; they had two children, Corolynne Gertrude and Herman Edward, both physicians.

His first academic appointment was at Dillard University, where he served as instructor in mathematics and physics from 1939 to 1941. Part of that period was spent as a Rosenwald Fellow in physics at the University of Chicago; the Rosenwald fellowships had been established by the Julius Rosenwald Fund in 1936 to support advanced study for "Negroes of unusual talents and abilities in any field of work." In 1941 Branson was appointed assistant professor of physics and chemistry at Howard University; he was assistant professor of physics, 1942–1944, professor of physics, 1944–1968, and department head, 1955–1968.

At Howard, Branson embarked on a lifelong commitment to improving science education for African Americans. He developed a physics undergraduate major and a graduate program there in the 1940s, when physics in black colleges and universities was thought of primarily as a service course for premedical majors, rather than as a discipline in its own right. In 1942 and 1943 he published several articles on blacks in science and technology, particularly addressing issues relating to research, education, and the war effort, as in "The Role of the Negro College in the Preparation of Technical Personnel for the War Effort" (*Journal of Negro Education* 11 [July 1942]); "Physics Training for the Negro Student" (*American Journal of Physics* 10 [Aug. 1942]); and "Contribution of Natural Sciences to the Development of Attitudes" (*Quarterly Review of Higher Education Among Negroes* 11 [Jan. 1943]). After the war he continued to address the role of blacks in the sciences and published two notable articles: "The Negro in Scientific Research" (*Negro History Bulletin* 15 [Apr. 1952]), and "The Negro Scientist" (in *The Negro in Science*, ed. Julius H. Taylor [1955]).

The next decade was a time of remarkable productivity in Branson's scientific research as well. He pioneered the use of integral equations in describing processes in biological systems, published as "A Mathematical Description of Metabolizing Systems" (*Bulletin of Mathematical Biophysics* 8 [1946]; 9 [1947]). He was also among the first to use radioactive phosphorus (^{32}P), mathematical methods, and electron microscopy in the study of sickle cell anemia blood cells (*Science* 115 [25 Jan. 1952]). Another innovative line of research brought him to the intersection between biology and information theory. He calculated, for example, the information content of several protein molecules in "Information Theory and the Structure of Proteins" (in *Information Theory in Biology*, ed. Henry Quastler [1953]).

Most important of all, and least recognized, is his contribution to early discoveries about the structure of proteins. In the late 1940s, working as a National Research Council senior fellow with Linus Pauling and others at the California Institute of Technology, Branson helped discover the "alpha-helix," the first clear vision of three-dimensional order in proteins. He established and solved the relevant spatial equations and demonstrated the hydrogen-bonded helical structure of certain amino acids. The "alpha helix," announced in a paper coauthored by Branson, Pauling, and Robert B. Corey, "The Structure of Proteins: Two Hydrogen-Bonded Helical Configurations of the Polypeptide Chain" (*Proceedings of the National Academy of Sciences* 37 [1951]), ranks as one of the most important discoveries in the history of biology in the twentieth century, anticipating the helical structure of DNA. Pauling was awarded the Nobel Prize in Chemistry for the achievement in 1954, while Branson's role has been all but forgotten.

After nearly three decades at Howard University, Branson served as president of Central State University, Wilberforce, Ohio, from 1968 to 1970, and of Lincoln University, from 1970 to 1985. His leadership at these two historically black institutions reflected his ongoing commitment to educational opportunity for African Americans. In the spring of 1970 he led a group of fifteen black college and university presidents to a White House meeting with President Richard Nixon, laying out the frustration felt by blacks nationwide toward the administration's policies; Nixon responded with a 30 percent increase in federal aid for historically black educational institutions.

Following his retirement as president of Lincoln University in 1985, Branson directed the Pre-College Science and Mathematics Program at Howard University, bringing high school seniors into mentoring relationships with professional scientists. He worked hard throughout his career to raise public awareness about the role and potential of scientific careers for blacks. "The civil rights struggle is quite a recent thing," he said in a 1966 interview, "and until we provide Negroes with suitable opportunity from the time they are born, we are not going to have as many Negro physicists as numerically we should." An early critic of "black studies" as a discrete academic discipline, he feared that such programs would emphasize emotion at the expense of intellectual rigor and distract attention from more practical goals.

In 1969 Branson became a cofounder of the National Association for Equal Opportunity in Higher Education and from 1970 to 1973 he served as its president. He was elected to membership in the Institute of Medicine, National Academy of Sciences in 1975. His stellar accomplishments over a life of service distinguished him as both a scholar and administrator.

Further Reading

Important archival sources for Branson's career may be found in the Moorland-Spingarn Research Center at Howard University, the Julius Rosenwald Fund Archives in the Fisk University Library Special Collections, Nashville, Tennessee, and in the Lincoln University Archives, Lincoln University, Pennsylvania. Oral histories conducted by Kenneth R. Manning in 1976 are held at the Massachusetts Institute of Technology. There is no published biography.

Hodes, Bernard. "The Negro in Physics—An Interview with Herman Branson," *Physics Today* 19 (Sept. 1966): 72–73.

Obituaries: *New York Times*, 13 June 1995; *Jet*, 26 June 1995.

PHILIP ALEXANDER

BRANTON, Wiley Austin (13 Dec. 1923–15 Dec. 1988), lawyer and civil rights activist, was born in Pine Bluff, Arkansas, to Pauline Wiley and Leo Branton, who operated a taxicab company. The family was of mixed race on both sides, and Wiley Branton attended segregated public schools through the twelfth grade, benefiting from the fact that Pine Bluff was one of the few Arkansas towns offering a high school education to African Americans.

The Wiley and Branton families were prominent in the Pine Bluff African American community and were respected in the white community. Wiley's maternal grandfather was a charter member of Pine Bluff's chapter of the NAACP. His grandmother, Effa Wiley, was a community activist who had a great influence on Wiley's early development. He accompanied her on neighborhood visits to troubled homes and to meetings and conferences of black groups where problems of segregation and unequal treatment were discussed. From her, Wiley learned compassion for others and absorbed a sense of duty and obligation to his community.

Wiley Branton was drafted into the segregated U.S. Army in 1943 for service in World War II. At that time, military leaders discounted, and even objected, to the participation of black soldiers in fighting units. African Americans usually found themselves performing the most menial jobs in the camps under the supervision of white officers. Branton scored well on the Army General Classification Test used to determine the working ability of new soldiers. He was sent for special training in drafting and then was assigned to the segregated 1894th Engineering Aviation Battalion at MacDill Field, Florida. By the end of 1943 Wiley had been promoted to sergeant. Three months later he received training as an intelligence specialist and was made an operations NCO. By mid-April 1944, however, Branton was being investigated for disaffection by the army. He and another soldier had sent a letter condemning the treatment of black soldiers to President Franklin D. Roosevelt, the War Department, and to a number of African American publications. The investigation was extensive but apparently came to nothing as his service record contains no mention of it. Branton's unit was sent to Okinawa, Japan, in March 1945, arriving after the Battle of Okinawa was officially over. He spent a year on Okinawa Island, engaged in surveying and serving as a construction foreman and technician in building airfields in preparation for the invasion of Japan. Branton left Okinawa in February 1946 and was honorably discharged at Camp Chaffee, Arkansas, as a master sergeant on 17 March 1946.

Branton returned from service determined to work against segregation. He took up management of his family's taxicab company and also became active in the Pine Bluff NAACP, particularly with regard to issues of voter education and registration work, which he believed were the key to changing southern society. Branton married Lucille McKee of Memphis, Tennessee, in January 1948. The couple delayed their honeymoon so that Branton could accompany a classmate whom he had convinced to test the University of Arkansas' claim that its law school would accept qualified African Americans if they tried to register. The friend, Silas H. Hunt, was admitted to the law school in January 1948.

In the summer of 1948 Branton's civil rights work led to his arrest and conviction for violating an Arkansas law, when he used a copy of a voting ballot to teach people how to mark their ballots when they voted. In 1950, having earned sufficient academic credits from Arkansas Agricultural, Mechanical & Normal College at Pine Bluff (later the University of Arkansas at Pine Bluff), Branton entered law school. Three years later he received a law degree from the University of Arkansas at Fayetteville. During law school he continued to manage the taxicab company, the proceeds of which supported his family, which included his four children.

Within three years of admission to the bar, Branton was representing black clients in civil rights matters. The case that brought him to national prominence was the suit against the school board of Little Rock, Arkansas, on behalf of African American parents and children seeking to integrate the city's schools following the U.S. Supreme Court's 1954 decision in *Brown v. Board of Education*. Branton served as lead attorney, although he worked with lawyers, including THURGOOD MARSHALL, from both the NAACP and the NAACP Legal Defense and Education Fund. During the court battles, and the publicity and segregationist defiance that accompanied them, Branton and Marshall became fast friends.

In 1962 Branton was asked to become executive director of the Voter Education Project (VEP), a foundation-funded entity created to distribute grants to local and national Negro organizations that would educate and register Southern African Americans to vote. His family, which now included six children, moved with him to Atlanta, Georgia. Two and a half years later VEP had registered more than six hundred thousand new black voters, despite having its workers beaten, jailed, and otherwise punished by white segregationists. Branton was called upon many times to use his legal and advocacy skills in their defense.

In 1965 Branton's reputation led Vice President Hubert H. Humphrey to ask Branton to work with him on the President's Council on Equal Opportunity, which was created to coordinate the federal government's implementation of the 1964 Civil Rights Act. When President Lyndon B. Johnson abolished the council in September 1965, he asked Branton to become his representative within the Department of Justice to work on achieving the goals of the 1965 Voting Rights Act. Branton spent two years acting as liaison between the government and civil rights groups.

In 1967 Branton left the Department of Justice to become executive director of the United Planning Organization, Washington, D.C.'s, antipoverty program. For two years he used his skills and contacts to provide education, job training, and other social services to the district's poorest residents. When President Richard M. Nixon slashed antipoverty funding, Branton accepted the invitation of labor leader and president of the United Automobile Workers Union, Walter Reuther, to begin the Alliance for Labor Action (ALA) in July 1969. The ALA was to be an antipoverty program funded by union dues to improve the lives of workers. It was a unique idea, but its progress was cut short by Reuther's death in an airplane accident in 1970.

Branton then went into private practice with a black law firm in Washington, D.C., and he stepped up his involvement in professional activities and groups. He served on the Washington, D.C., Home Rule Committee, which made efforts to allow D.C. residents to govern themselves. Historically, D.C. was governed by congressional committees and had no voting rights as to the people who administered the city. As a member of the Lawyers' Committee for Civil Rights Under Law, he helped to defeat the nomination of Robert Bork to the U.S. Supreme Court in 1987. He served as the grand sire archon (an office equivalent to president) of Sigma Phi Pi, a black fraternity of professional men.

In 1977 Branton was named dean of Howard University School of Law. Supreme Court Justice Thurgood Marshall delivered the address at Branton's investiture. Branton hoped to return the school to its glory days, when it was a beacon of legal training for civil rights lawyers. While his six-year effort improved the school's standing among other law schools, its former prominence in civil rights could not be regained. During this period Branton was a member of the Judicial Nomination Commission of the District of Columbia and was on the Council of Legal Education for the American Bar Association.

In 1983 he left Howard Law School to join the Washington, D.C., office of the Chicago firm Sidley & Austin, where he maintained a general practice not too different from those of prior years, except that he also worked on cases involving major firm clients, such as AT&T. He represented CORETTA SCOTT KING when the U.S. senator Jesse Helms tried to open FBI files on MARTIN LUTHER KING JR. in 1983. After only one year as an associate, Branton was made a partner with the firm. It was during this period of his life that he began receiving honors from his peers for the length and breadth of his civil rights work.

In an interview nine months before his death, Branton said, "If I had to do it all over again, I would do exactly what I did." As advice for young people, Branton stated, "You've got to work damn hard. You've got to be better than the next guy, white or black. Your words have to mean something. You've got to be honest in your dealings. . . . And you have to enjoy what you're doing. I genuinely enjoy what I do. In addition to it being a profession, it has become a hobby. I'm always dabbling in law or reading law. I love it" (Adelman, 114).

Further Reading

Branton's papers are on deposit at the Moorland-Spingarn Research Center, Howard University, Washington, D.C.

Adelman, Ken. "You Can Change Their Hearts," *The Washingtonian* (Mar. 1988).

Kilpatrick, Judith. "Wiley Austin Branton, A Role Model for All Times," *Howard University Law Journal* (2005).

Kilpatrick, Judith. "Wiley Austin Branton and the Voting Rights Struggle," *UALR Law Review* 26.641 (Summer 2004).

Obituary: *New York Times*, 17 Dec. 1988.

JUDITH KILPATRICK

BRASHEAR, Carl Maxie (19 Jan. 1931–25 July 2006), U.S. Navy diver, was born in Tonieville, Larue County, Kentucky, the son of McDonald and Gonzell Brashear, sharecroppers. He attended the Tonieville Elementary School until he reached the seventh grade, in 1946, when he decided to quit school and go to work as an attendant at a filling station. He was dissatisfied with that job, however, and began to explore other areas of interest. In 1948, at the age of seventeen, Carl Brashear joined the U.S. Navy. His enlistment coincided with President Harry Truman's executive order to desegregate all branches of the armed forces. Brashear felt comfortable in his new position, and, being a proud member of the U.S. Navy, went on to complete the education he had abandoned in elementary school by earning his GED in 1960. His first marriage, to Junette Wilcoxson in 1952, ended in divorce in 1972.

Upon enlisting in the navy in 1948, Brashear entered the Naval Training Center Beach Master Unit at

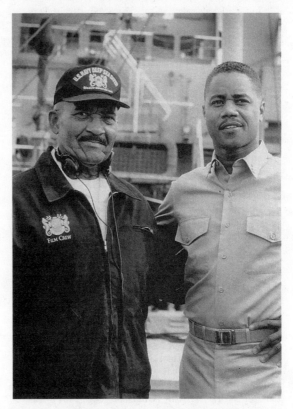

Carl Maxie Brashear, the U.S. Navy's first African American master diver, posing with Cuba Gooding Jr., the actor who portrayed him in the 2000 film *Men of Honor*. (Library of Congress.)

Great Lakes, Illinois. He completed the course of training for salvage diver in 1951 with the intention of becoming a boatswain's mate. He possessed the physical ability and stamina needed by a diver and did well academically. In 1954 he graduated from diving school, becoming a U.S. Navy diver. Brashear was promoted to senior chief boatswain's mate (E-7) in 1960 and was assigned to the aircraft carrier *Tripoli.* There he learned to dive from the carrier's deck by observing navy divers. So impressed was Brashear by these maneuvers that he decided that he would attempt to become the first African American navy deep-sea diver. Brashear applied to diving school several times before he was accepted. Once admitted, he was forced to endure many racial obstacles and comments. Upon his arrival at the Deep Sea Diving Program in Bayonne, New Jersey, the training instructor mistook him for the cook and directed him to the mess hall. On another occasion one officer commented that the navy did not have any "colored" deep-sea divers, to which Brashear politely responded that the navy was about to have one. Ignoring the racist remarks, Brashear concentrated on his training and, as a result, earned his way from salvage diver to first- and second-class diver to saturation diver and finally, in October 1979, to the pinnacle of success, master diver. Brashear was the first African American to attend and graduate from the U.S. Navy Diving and Salvage School. His second marriage, to Hattie R. Elam in 1980, ended in 1983.

In 1966 Brashear was involved in what is known as the Curv accident (Curv was an acronym for Cable-controlled Underwater Recovery Vehicle). In January of that year a hydrogen bomb was lost off the coast of Palomares, Spain, as a result of a collision between two U.S. Air Force planes; one plane was a B-2 and the other was a KC-139 (tanker). The navy was called in to find and recover the bomb, and Brashear, onboard the carrier *Hoist,* was assigned this critical mission. On 23 March, during the recovery process, a towing cable broke, causing a mechanical device to strike Brashear in his left leg just below the knee, almost severing his leg. Brashear was sent to the Naval Hospital in Portsmouth, Virginia, where doctors, after trying to save his leg, were forced to amputate. Despite his terrible injury, Brashear accepted the loss as a challenge and immediately started therapy. He remained at the Navy Regional Medical Center in Virginia from May 1966 to March 1967, during which time he began the strenuous rehabilitation process. In March 1967 Brashear was released from the hospital and then set out to convince the navy that he could continue with his diving career. He was assigned to the Harbor Clearance Unit Two, Diving School, to begin training to return to full active duty as a navy diver. In April 1968 Brashear became the first amputee to be certified as a diver, and in 1970 he became the first African American U.S. Navy master diver, eventually achieving the rank of master chief boatswain's mate in 1971. Brashear's final marriage was to Jeannette A. Burndage in 1985, ending two years later. He was the father of four children. In

2000 a movie, *Men of Honor,* starring Cuba Gooding Jr. as Brashear, was made about his life.

Carl Brashear received many citations, decorations, and medals for his dedicated service in the navy. He was awarded the Navy and Marine Corps Medal for Heroism in Saving Lives, the Good Conduct medals (eight awards), the Navy Commendation Medal, the Navy Achievement Medal, the National Defense Medal, the China Services Medal, and the Korean Service Medal. He retired from the U.S. Navy in 1979 as a master chief petty officer (E9) and master diver. Brashear died of respiratory and heart failure at the Portsmouth Naval Medical Center.

Further Reading
Stillwell, Paul. *The Reminiscences of Master Chief Boatswain's Mate Carl Brashear* (1998).
U.S. Naval Institute's Oral History of Carl Brashear (interview).

Obituaries: *Virginian Pilot,* 26 July 2006; *Navy Newsstand,* 30 July 2006.

AGNES KANE CALLUM

BRAUD, Wellman (25 Jan. 1891–29 Oct. 1966), jazz bassist, was born Wellman Breaux in Saint James Parish, Louisiana. Nothing is known of his parents except that they were of Creole heritage, and it is not known when he anglicized his name. Braud began playing violin at age seven and later took up guitar. His earliest work was with string trios playing on the streets of New Orleans. During the 1910s he worked regularly at Tom Anderson's cabaret, probably playing guitar in a group with the violinist ARMAND J. PIRON while also playing drums and trombone in various ad hoc brass bands.

In 1917 Braud moved to Chicago, where he began playing bass and toured with John Wickliffe's band, later joining the Original Creole Band (or Orchestra) at the Pekin Café as a replacement for Ed Garland. When Braud joined the band the other members included the cornetist "Sugar" Johnny Smith, the clarinetist Lawrence Duhé, the trombonist Roy Palmer, the guitarist Louis Keppard, and the drummer Tubby Hall. In 1918 the clarinetist SIDNEY BECHET was added to the group, which during Braud's stay also worked at the Dreamland and De Luxe cafés. From 1920 to 1922 Braud was with Charlie Elgar's orchestra, most likely at the Dreamland, and from March to May 1923 he doubled on trombone and bass with WILL VODERY's orchestra in the *Plantation Revue* in London.

Later in 1923 he moved to New York, where he worked with the vaudevillian clarinetist and bandleader Wilbur Sweatman. In early 1925 Braud and Bechet joined the ten-piece orchestra of the *Seven-Eleven* revue, with which they played in vaudeville and burlesque houses in Newark, Baltimore, Washington, D.C., Boston, and Providence, before opening at New York's Columbia Theater. After leaving *Seven-Eleven,* Braud joined the *Lucky Sambo* revue and remained with it through early 1927.

In mid-1927 Braud joined DUKE ELLINGTON's Kentucky Club orchestra and made his first recordings with the band in October. Among the many titles that he recorded with Ellington over the next few years, those most revealing of his prominently featured capabilities are, from 1927, "Washington Wobble"—his debut solo performance, which may be the first example of the "walking bass" style, with its four beats to the bar; from 1928, "Diga Diga Doo," "Move Over," "Hot and Bothered," and "Bandanna Babies"; and from 1930, "Flaming Youth," "Saturday Night Function," "High Life," "Hot Feet," "Stevedore Stomp," "Saratoga Swing," "Freeze and Melt," "Cotton Club Stomp," "Ring Dem Bells," and "Old Man Blues."

Although Braud's technically advanced style of alternately picking and slapping the strings of his bass provided an undeniably powerful lift to the sound of Ellington's late 1920s "jungle-style" band, particularly on fast stomp tempos, by the early 1930s Ellington wanted to cultivate a smoother, more sophisticated sound and rhythm. Braud's inability to read music proved no impediment, for he could play any of Ellington's arrangements by ear. But his seemingly dated, New Orleans–style rhythmic conception was no longer what Ellington wanted. Not wishing to fire the mild-mannered older man, Ellington devised a scheme by which Braud would leave the band of his own will, his pride intact. In November 1934 Ellington added the younger, more modern-thinking bassist Billy Taylor to the fold, and the following March Braud quit, probably never realizing how he had been eased out. Ellington, though, must have seen the potential in having two bassists in the band, because in May 1935 he hired the equally young Hayes Alvis as an adjunct to Taylor.

In mid-1935 Braud worked briefly at the Vodvil Club in Harlem in a band that he had formed with the New Orleans clarinetist Jimmie Noone, and when that ended he spent some time working with the drummer Kaiser Marshall at a club in New Jersey. Later in the year he joined the Spirits of Rhythm, a novelty vocal and instrumental group, as both bassist and manager, but he also worked sporadically with his own trios through 1937. In March 1938 he recorded with the trumpeter HOT LIPS PAGE and may have played engagements with Page's band as well.

Either during or after his stay with pianist Edgar Hayes's orchestra in 1939, Braud participated in two important recording dates with JELLY ROLL MORTON's New Orleans Jazzmen in September. In these sessions he was reunited with old hometown friends such as the clarinetist ALBERT NICHOLAS, the drummer ZUTTY SINGLETON, and, most significantly, Sidney Bechet, the most formidable soprano saxophonist alive. In January 1940 Braud recorded three more dates with Morton, once again with Nicholas and Singleton but now also with the New Orleans trumpeter HENRY "RED" ALLEN.

The next few months were even more fruitful. In March and April 1940 Braud recorded with the Bechet-Spanier Big Four, which produced one of the most perfectly realized jazz recording groups of all time, and in May he participated in the reunion of Bechet and LOUIS ARMSTRONG for Decca's *New Orleans Jazz* album. As a more or less regular member of Bechet's working bands, Braud was present in three of Bechet's dates for Victor between June 1940 and September 1941. Meanwhile he continued playing engagements with his quartet at Nick's in Greenwich Village, at the Log Cabin in Fonda, New York, and at BILL "BOJANGLES" ROBINSON's Mimo Club in Harlem.

In 1943 and 1944 Braud worked in the swing bands of the saxophonists Al Sears and Garvin Bushell, but in 1944 he also began operating a poolroom and a meat-marketing business in New York, playing music only on weekends. In January 1947 Braud and Bechet appeared at a Town Hall concert produced by the clarinetist Mezz Mezzrow to promote his autobiography *Really the Blues*, and in September Braud replaced the bassist POPS FOSTER in a recording date with the Mezzrow-Bechet Quintet for the clarinetist and author's King Jazz label.

Braud was also the New Orleans trumpeter BUNK JOHNSON's choice for three recording dates in December that ultimately appeared on a Columbia album called *The Last Testament*. In early 1956 Braud joined the equally venerable New Orleans trombonist KID ORY's band in California and toured Europe with the band later in the year. In 1958 Braud settled in Los Angeles, where in 1960 he worked in the clarinetist Joe Darensbourg's band. After recovering from a mild heart attack in the summer of 1961, Braud sat in with the Ellington band in the fall and later worked with the traditional jazz singer Barbara Dane. Braud worked only infrequently after that, including a tour in Oregon in the fall of 1966. He died in Los Angeles.

Further Reading
Schuller, Gunther. *Early Jazz: Its Roots and Musical Development* (1968).
Schuller, Gunther. *The Swing Era: The Development of Jazz, 1930–1945* (1989).
Stewart, Rex. *Jazz Masters of the Thirties* (1972).

Discography
Bruyninckx, Walter. *Traditional Jazz Discography, 1897–1988* (5 vols., 1989).

JACK SOHMER

BRAUN, Carol Moseley. *See* Moseley Braun, Carol.

BRAWLEY, Benjamin (22 Apr. 1882–1 Feb. 1939), educator and author, was born Benjamin Griffith Brawley in Columbia, South Carolina, the son of Margaret Saphronia Dickerson and EDWARD McKNIGHT BRAWLEY, a prosperous Baptist minister and president of a small Alabama college. Brawley was an exceptionally bright boy, and the family's frequent moves never interfered with his learning. Up until the third grade he was tutored at home by his mother, but he also attended schools in Nashville, Tennessee, and Petersburg, Virginia. During summers, when he was not studying the classics, Latin, and Greek at home, he earned money by doing odd jobs, working on a tobacco farm in Connecticut or in a printing office. One summer he drove a buggy for a white doctor—and studied Greek while the doctor was out. At age twelve he was sent to Virginia to be tutored in Greek and he also studied the language with his father.

By age thirteen Brawley had excelled so much in his studies that he was sent to the preparatory program at Atlanta Baptist College (later Morehouse College). He was surprised and disappointed on his arrival to note that most of the older students there knew nothing of classical literature, much less Greek or Latin. His classmates were equally surprised to find such a young man in their midst, but they soon discovered just how valuable an asset he was. Aware of his intellectual and grammatical prowess, they brought their compositions to him before passing them on to their instructors. Brawley excelled outside the classroom as well. He played football, managed the baseball team, and cofounded the school newspaper, the *Athenaeum* (later the *Maroon Tiger*), for which he wrote numerous articles and poems. Brawley is also said to have initiated the first debate among African American colleges when his Morehouse team challenged another group from Talladega College.

In 1901 Brawley graduated with honors from Atlanta Baptist College and immediately took a teaching position, for five months at thirty-five dollars a month, in a one-room school in Georgetown, Florida, but then, in 1902, he took a teaching job at his alma mater, where he stayed until 1910. During his years at Atlanta Baptist College, he also earned his BA (1906) from the University of Chicago and his MA (1908) from Harvard by taking mostly summer courses. Then he accepted a professorship at Howard University and while teaching there met Hilda Damaris Prowd, who became his wife in 1912. They had no children. After only two years at Howard, he returned to Atlanta Baptist, where, in addition to teaching, he became the college's first dean and where his teaching techniques became legendary.

Brawley considered teaching to be a divine profession that should be used to bring students "into the knowledge of truth," the success of which depended as much upon the efforts of the teacher as on those of the student. He expected of his students the same high academic and moral standards that he had learned as a child, and he stressed that teaching should take into account the whole student—his or her physical, emotional, economic, and moral background. Brawley would commonly make students memorize long passages from classical literature, and he returned any compositions with even the slightest degree of sloppiness or imprecision, marking them with terse comments like "Too carelessly written to be carefully read" (Parker, *Phylon* [1949], 18). A traditionalist first, last, and always, Brawley was also dissatisfied with the state of education in the country, which emphasized materialism and innovation rather than rote learning.

Although Brawley still earned his primary living as a teacher, he also began to turn seriously toward another profession. He had written articles for his school paper and other publications for several years, but from 1921 on he produced at least ten books and about one hundred newspaper and magazine articles, book reviews, editorials, and other efforts. Whether he was writing about African American life and culture, as in *A Social History of the American Negro* (1921), or more literary topics, as in *A New Survey of English Literature* (1925), Brawley stressed two major themes: first, that literature must rest on a sound artistic and moral basis, and second, that it should present not just the struggles of individuals and races, but "a mirror of our hopes and dreams" as well (*The Negro Genius* [1937], 196). He was particularly saddened that most novels and short stories about African Americans that came out of Harlem and other places in the 1920s depicted characters as comic or appealed to readers' lower natures. "We are simply asking," he wrote in *The Negro Genius*, "that those writers of fiction who deal with the Negro shall be thoroughly honest with themselves" (206). Only by strict adherence to these high ideals, Brawley believed, could the lot of his own race be improved and race relations be dealt with honestly.

In 1920, after many years at Morehouse, Brawley went to the African Republic of Liberia to conduct an educational survey. Shortly after his return in early 1921, he followed in his father's footsteps and became an ordained Baptist minister at the Messiah Congregation in Brockton, Massachusetts. After only a year, however, he found the congregation's type of Christianity not to his liking and resigned. Brawley returned to teaching, first at Shaw University in North Carolina, where his father, by then in failing health, taught theology, and then, in 1931, at Howard, where he stayed until the end of his life. In 1936 he published *PAUL LAURENCE DUNBAR: Poet of His People*. He died at his home in Washington, D.C., from complications following a stroke.

Brawley's impeccable academic credentials and high standards earned him the respect of almost all his students, although that respect was shown in unusual ways. One story goes that a student came to class carrying under his arm a bundle wrapped in newspaper, which everyone assumed was laundry. Instead, the student had carefully wrapped his essay in the bundle to be sure that it met Brawley's exacting standards. Brawley's techniques, coupled with his difficulty in abiding by any standards other than his own, earned him his share of criticism, but far more often than not they achieved desirable results.

Further Reading

The Brawley papers are at the Moorland-Spingarn Research Center at Howard University. A complete bibliography of Brawley's published works appears in *North Carolina Historical Review* 34 (Apr. 1957): 165–175.

Parker, John W. "Benjamin Brawley and the American Cultural Tradition." *Phylon* 16 (1955): 183–194.
Phylon Profile XIX. "Benjamin Brawley—Teacher and Scholar." *Phylon* 10 (1949): 15–24.
Price, Charlotte S. *Richard Le Gallienne as Collected by Benjamin Griffith Brawley* (1973).

Obituaries: *New York Times*, 7 Feb. 1939; *The Crisis* 46 (1939).

ROGER A. SCHUPPERT

BRAWLEY, Edward McKnight (18 Mar. 1851–13 Jan. 1923), Baptist minister, educator, and editor, was born in Charleston, South Carolina, the son of free African American parents, Ann L. (maiden name unknown) and James M. Brawley. Brawley's parents took a keen interest in the education and professional development of their son, providing him private schooling in Charleston, sending him at the age of ten to Philadelphia to attend grammar school and the Institute for Colored Youth, and apprenticing him to a shoemaker in Charleston from 1866 to 1869. He enrolled as the first theological student at Howard University for a few months in 1870 but then transferred to Bucknell University in Lewisburg, Pennsylvania, in January 1871. The first African American student at Bucknell, Brawley completed his education with the encouragement and financial support of a white couple named Griffith and with his own work teaching vocal music and preaching during school vacations. The white Baptist church in Lewisburg with which he had affiliated ordained him to the ministry the day after his graduation, 1 July 1875; he was examined by a board composed largely of professors and other learned individuals. In 1878 he received an AM from Bucknell and, in 1885, an honorary doctor of divinity degree from the State University in Louisville, Kentucky.

Brawley's first marriage in 1877 lasted only a year; his wife, Mary W. Warrick, and their baby both died. His second marriage, to Margaret Dickerson in 1879, produced four children; one of them, BENJAMIN BRAWLEY, became a renowned historian and author.

Immediately after Brawley left Bucknell, the predominantly white, northern-based American Baptist Publication Society (ABPS) appointed him as a Sunday school missionary, or agent, for his home state of South Carolina. There he found little organization among the black Baptists. He set about establishing new Baptist associations and reorganizing existing ones, as well as encouraging the founding of Sunday school conventions at the state Baptist regional or associational levels. After two years the first statewide Sunday school convention among African American Baptists was held, with Brawley serving as corresponding secretary and financial agent. Brawley also helped black Baptists organize African missions, and South Carolina sent its first missionary, HARRISON N. BOUEY, to Africa in the late 1870s. Not only did Brawley strengthen denominational structures in the state but he also raised considerable funds for Benedict College in South Carolina.

Eight years of strenuous work in South Carolina took their toll on Brawley's health. Following his doctor's advice despite the ABPS's strong desire that he continue his duties, in 1883 Brawley traveled to Alabama to assume the presidency of Alabama Baptist Normal and Theological School (later Selma University), a position that he had declined several times before. Once again Brawley's service was successful. He upgraded the school's standards and collegiate rank, and the first class graduated in May 1884. Fiercely committed to education, Brawley, like many other early educators both black and white, gave as much as half of his income to needy students.

With his wife's health in decline, Brawley returned to South Carolina after two years to preside over a school that he had helped to establish, Morris College. In 1912 he assumed the pastorship of White Rock Baptist Church in Durham, North Carolina. Around 1920 he became professor of biblical history and evangelism at Baptist-supported Shaw University in Raleigh, North Carolina, serving there until his death.

Brawley was highly valued as a speaker and lecturer. He was also an accomplished writer and editor. At different points in his career he edited the *Baptist Pioneer* in South Carolina, the weekly *Baptist Tribune*, and the monthly *Evangel*. Ever concerned about raising the educational standards of both ministers and the laity, he wrote *Sin and Salvation*, which focused on evangelism, and his most significant work, *The Negro Baptist Pulpit: A Collection of Sermons and Papers* (1890; repr. 1971). Of the twenty-eight sermons and addresses in the latter work, Brawley authored four. Throughout his career he also published numerous sermons, speeches, and addresses.

In addition to his church, educational, and publishing work, Brawley left a theological and philosophical legacy of one committed to uplifting the African American race by moral and spiritual education. Furthermore, Brawley passionately supported cooperation with sympathetic whites as a way to advance the race, believing that all racial sentiments should be subordinate to the greater principle of building up American Christianity. That position often placed him at odds with African American leaders who were increasingly restless with the racial parochialism and paternalism of their white benefactors. Whereas some African American Christians, including Brawley, emphasized the necessity of continued white financial assistance, the more independent complained of the stifling effect that these whites had on the development of racial responsibility and self-respect. Nonetheless, Brawley's contributions to denominational organization, church leadership, education, and publishing left an impressive mark on American religious history.

Further Reading
Brawley, Edward McKnight. *The Negro Baptist Pulpit: A Collection of Sermons and Papers* (1890; repr. 1971).
Pegues, Albert W. *Our Baptist Ministers and Schools* (1892).

Simmons, William J. *Men of Mark: Eminent, Progressive, and Rising* (1887; repr. 1968).

Washington, James M. *Frustrated Fellowship: The Black Baptist Quest for Social Power* (1986).

SANDY DWAYNE MARTIN

BRAWLEY, James P. (26 Sept. 1894–3 Dec. 1986), college president and lay Methodist Church leader, was born James Phillip Brawley in Lockhart, Texas, the son of Thomas H. Brawley and Emma Storey. Despite being born in the Jim Crow era, Brawley received a college education, graduating from Samuel Houston College in 1920. He did graduate work at the University of Chicago and Northwestern University, where he received his MA in Religious Education in 1925 and his PhD in Education in 1941.

Brawley took his first teaching position in 1922 at Rust College in Holly Springs, Mississippi, a school founded by the Methodist Episcopal Church's Freedmen's Aid Society following the Civil War. He moved from Rust College to Clark College in Atlanta, Georgia, in 1925, where he taught education and religious education. Clark College was another Freedmen's Aid Society school that had traditionally emphasized the training of ministers and teachers. Brawley became the college academic dean there in 1926 and also served as registrar. One of his first accomplishments was to regularize the recording of student grades, determine whether all graduate requirements were fulfilled, and create transcripts, which was a vital step for students to receive Georgia teacher certification. Brawley married Georgia L. Williams, an English teacher, on 20 June 1929, and the marriage lasted until his death; they had no children.

During the Great Depression, Clark College, like other historically black colleges in the South, struggled to keep its doors open. However, the college strengthened its curriculum and eliminated precollegiate programs to increase its academic standing. This period in the college's history culminated with a coalition of philanthropic support by the Methodist General Education Board (successor to the Freedmen's Aid Society) and private gifts, making it possible for Clark to move from its location just south of Atlanta to a new site adjacent to Atlanta University and its affiliated institutions, Morehouse and Spelman colleges (and later Morris Brown). The new facility opened in 1941, the year Brawley became president of Clark College.

A committed Methodist layman, Brawley was a delegate, in 1939, to the Uniting Conference of the Northern Methodist Episcopal Church; the Methodist Episcopal Church, South; and the Methodist Protestant Church. The purpose of this conference was to create a new Methodist Church to heal the division between Northern and Southern Methodists that began over slavery in 1844. Although most African American Methodists were members of the African Methodist Episcopal Church (AME), the African Methodist Episcopal Zion Church, or the Colored Methodist Episcopal Church (after 1954, the Christian Methodist Episcopal Church), for black Methodists who were members of the Northern Methodist Episcopal Church, the Uniting Conference was a humiliating experience, because the newly created Methodist Church put all black Methodists into a separate jurisdictional conference called the Central Jurisdiction. For the first time, these black Methodists were able to elect their own bishops and had representation on church councils and agencies, but the Central Jurisdiction was a bitter reminder that white Methodists still did not accept African American members as equals, or even as members of the same denomination.

Brawley served as a lay delegate to the Methodist General Conferences in 1948, 1952, 1956, 1960, and 1964. In the Central Jurisdiction, he chaired self-studies in 1952 and 1956 that assessed the problems of the jurisdiction and the prospects for racial change within the Methodist Church. He also wrote numerous articles for the Central Jurisdiction's newspaper advocating racial inclusiveness.

In 1956 the Methodist Church General Conference established an interjurisdictional commission of seventy members to review church race relations. Brawley served as the chair of the Central Jurisdiction representatives on that commission, which held hearings in all regions of the country. It recommended to the 1960 General Conference that desegregation proceed using Amendment IX to the church constitution, which had been ratified by Methodist annual conferences in 1958. Amendment IX provided a way to abolish the Central Jurisdiction by transferring black Methodist church and annual conferences out of the Central Jurisdiction into overlapping regional annual and jurisdictional conferences. Brawley supported desegregation, but in the commission's deliberations he opposed establishing a target date for the abolition of the Central Jurisdiction. Brawley, while anxious to see desegregation begin, wanted the church to make a greater commitment to change in order to prevent token desegregation.

Desegregation also presented new challenges to historically black colleges, which found themselves being judged by the standards of white institutions, whether they had comparable financial resources or not. Clark College was among the first fifteen African American colleges accredited by the Southern Association of Schools and Colleges when it began receiving these institutions into full membership in 1957. During the 1960 student sit-ins, Brawley joined with other black college presidents in Atlanta to support the students. While he was very concerned about the safety of the protesting students and refused to cancel classes, he urged faculty members to make allowances for student participants. When white business leaders urged him to discipline student demonstrators, Brawley instead praised the students' courage and condemned further segregation by the businesses.

Between 1960 and 1964 Brawley served as vice chair of another Methodist commission regarding race, the Commission of Thirty-six. The purpose of this commission was to speed the use of Amendment IX, but its first plan to accomplish this encountered black Methodist opposition. At a special meeting of Central Jurisdiction's leaders in March 1962 held in Cincinnati, Ohio, Brawley gave the keynote speech. He stressed that white Methodists were trying to speed the use of Amendment IX in other parts of the country while there was no plan to ensure eventual desegregation in the South. Moreover, the church had not convinced its African Americans that it was committed to abolish all areas of segregation, including church-related institutions. In 1963 Brawley wrote a memorandum to the entire Commission of Thirty-six outlining why the Central Jurisdiction still held back from using Amendment IX. At the 1964 General Conference held in Pittsburgh, Pennsylvania, the Methodist Church took actions to answer many of the concerns outlined by Brawley. The Central Jurisdiction met for the last time in 1967.

After his retirement as president of Clark College in 1965, Brawley wrote two books about African American higher education. *Two Centuries of Methodist Concern: Bondage, Freedom, and Education of Black People* (1974) chronicled the Methodists' work in higher education for African Americans. In 1977 he completed *The Clark College Legacy: An Interpretive History of Relevant Education, 1869–1975*. Brawley died on 3 December 1985 in Atlanta, Georgia. In September 1984 the Atlanta City Council honored him by renaming Chestnut Street, a major street that runs adjacent to Clark College and Atlanta University, James P. Brawley Drive.

As a college dean and president in the early and mid-twentieth century, Brawley was part of a small group of influential African American educational leaders. Although Brawley was not as well known as other African American college presidents such as JOHN HOPE, he was remarkably adept at moving a small and relatively weak institution into a position of strength.

Brawley's leadership guided Clark College through difficult times to make it a strong African American educational institution. His successful stewardship of resources and his recruitment of talented faculty, such as the young sociologist CHARLES ERIC LINCOLN, eventually contributed to the merger of Clark College and Atlanta University in 1987 that created Clark Atlanta University. More than any other African American lay Methodist, Brawley worked to develop a policy of racial inclusiveness that reached through all levels of the church. Born and educated in the Jim Crow South, he prepared more than a generation of African American leaders for the day when civil rights would create new opportunities in American society and in Methodism. He was a model of industry and moral rectitude, and he never wavered in his faith in a desegregated society or in his belief that education was the key to African American success.

Further Reading

An extensive collection of Brawley's papers is available at the Atlanta University Center Archives. These papers cover his career as an educator, a Methodist layman, and a resident of Atlanta, Georgia.

Murray, Peter C. *Methodists and the Crucible of Race, 1930-1975* (2004).

PETER C. MURRAY

BRAXTON, Anthony (Delano) (4 June 1945–), composer and multi-instrumentalist specializing in alto saxophone and contrabass clarinet, was born in Chicago to Clarence Dunbar Braxton Sr., a railroad worker, and Julia Samuels Braxton. Braxton experienced a rich childhood centered in Chicago's Washington Park neighborhood. His parents and his stepfather, Lawrence Fouche, imbued Braxton and his siblings with values of tolerance and perseverance. Exposed to a wide range of popular media, Braxton developed an early interest in rock and roll, particularly CHUCK BERRY and FRANKIE LYMON, and he sang in his Baptist church's choir. He had begun to play clarinet at about the age of eleven, and in high school became interested in jazz and the alto sax. In 1959 he entered the Chicago Vocational High School, in part because of his interest in technology.

Through his teens, Braxton studied both jazz and European classical music at the Chicago School of Music of Roosevelt University. In 1963 he graduated from high school and enrolled in Wilson Junior College, where he met musicians like Jack DeJohnette, Henry Threadgill, Joseph Jarman, and Roscoe Mitchell. He was drafted into the U.S. military in 1963 and became a member of the army band, stationed at Fort Sheridan in Highland Park, Illinois. He returned to Chicago regularly to continue his musical pursuits, practicing up to six hours a day, and intermittently taking courses in music history and theory at Roosevelt from 1964 to 1968.

Early on Braxton nurtured an interest in free jazz and musicians like JOHN COLTRANE. In 1965–1966, while stationed in Korea, he discovered the music of Arnold Schoenberg, which emphasized line and rhythm, qualities he saw as central to the African American musical heritage. Returning to Chicago in the fall of 1966, he joined the Association for Advancement of Creative Musicians (AACM) under the sponsorship of Roscoe Mitchell, a core member of the group. MUHAL RICHARD ABRAMS, the organization's key figure, became an important mentor and influence. Braxton also extended his study of European composers like Schoenberg, Edgar Varese, Anton Webern, and particularly John Cage. He became politically active, joining the Congress of Racial Equality (CORE) and reading widely in philosophy, religion, and radical political literature, sources that helped shape his musical style. Philosophically, he accentuated the spiritual basis of modernist jazz language, a "sacred-sonic linkage" (Radano, 69) between the spiritual and the world of sound. He also came under the influence of musicians like JACKIE

McLean, Lee Konitz, Warne Marsh, and Paul Desmond. In 1966 Braxton made his first appearance on record, on Abrams's *Levels and Degrees of Light*. In 1967 he formed his own group, Creative Construction Company, a trio with violinist Leroy Jenkins and trumpeter Leo Smith. In 1968 he released his first album under his own name, *3 Compositions for New Jazz*, with Jenkins, Smith, and Abrams on piano. Considered one of the more innovative recordings of the period, it overturned some of the most basic assumptions of jazz practice.

Nevertheless, Braxton received little critical attention and less work. He was forced to take jobs at a Pepsi-Cola bottling plant and at the Roosevelt University library. In 1969 he and several other members of the AACM moved to Paris, where he enjoyed some public success and critical acclaim, although on the whole neither listeners nor critics understood or appreciated his music. In 1970 he returned to New York, where he briefly joined Musica Elettronica Viva, an Italian improvisational ensemble. He also joined Circle, the avant-garde group that included pianist Chick Corea, bassist Dave Holland, and drummer Jack DeJohnette. In appearances and recordings with the group, Braxton pursued a black-based modernism that extended the association of art and the sacred, honoring the tradition, yet testing its boundaries. While performing with Circle in London in 1971, he also recorded some of his own compositions on *The Complete Braxton*, a recording that reflected the integration of improvisation and modernist compositional material.

In 1968 Braxton recorded *For Alto*, a double-record set that was the first-ever recording of solo alto saxophone improvisations. The album is filled with instrumental shouts and screeches and other experiments in sound, phrasing that revealed the influence of Coltrane, and a lyricism that affirmed the legacy of Desmond. A critical success, the recording also brought a measure of financial stability, allowing Braxton to devote more time to composition. Throughout the 1970s he maintained a working quartet with drummer Barry Altschul, bassist Holland, and either trombonist George Lewis or trumpeter Kenny Wheeler; this group appeared on the Arista albums recorded in the mid-1970s that confirmed Braxton's status as the leading avant-garde figure of his day. By 1974 Braxton had married Nickie Singer, who became his creative partner, copying scores, doing the photography for some of his albums, and creating costumes for projects like the Trillium operas.

Though Braxton would record for the Arista label at least in part to gain financial independence and support his family (the couple would have three children, and Braxton had another from an earlier relationship), his albums *New York, Fall 1974* (1974), *Five Pieces* (1975), and *Creative Orchestra Music* (1976) were creative gems. *New York, Fall 1974*, a collection of six- and seven-minute compositions that ranged from boppish improvisations to modernist sound ex-

periments, sold more than twenty thousand copies, and *Creative Orchestra Music* won *Down Beat* magazine's Best Album Award for 1977, highlighted by its parodic, celebratory parade march.

The success of these albums allowed Braxton to record more of his own concert music, though mostly at his own expense. And the resultant albums for Arista, *For Trio* (1977), *For Four Orchestras* (1978), and *For Two Pianos* (1980), though aesthetically triumphant, were much less successful both commercially and critically. Braxton viewed jazz as only part of what he did; *Four Orchestras*, for instance, was the first of a projected series for six, eight, and up to one hundred orchestras playing in different cities, linked by satellite. Other recordings from the period emanated from the jazz tradition. These included recordings for HatHut with Max Roach, *Birth and Rebirth* and *Two in One* (both 1979); a second solo recording, *Alto Saxophone Improvisations* (1979, Arista); and *Performance 9-1-79* (HatArt) with a new group of the trombonist Ray Anderson, the violinist John Lindberg, and the bassist Thurman Barker. Braxton also played with a variety of European avant-garde groups, including Company and the Globe Unity Orchestra, and he made the first of a series of recordings with synthesizer player and composer Richard Teitelbaum.

Braxton lived and worked in New Haven from 1983 to 1985, joined the faculty at Mills College in 1986, and was appointed to a tenured position at Wesleyan University in 1990. From 1985 to 1994 he led a quartet with Marilyn Crispell on piano, Gerry Hemingway on drums and percussion, and Mark Dresser on bass. The group toured and recorded extensively. Their most notable recordings are a series of concerts in England at Coventry, London, and Birmingham, and at Willisau in Germany, which showcased musicians with a seemingly telepathic anticipation of each other's musical direction. This was avant-garde music both virtuosic and accessible even to the mildly adventurous. He continued his interest in large-scale ensembles with 1989's *Eugene*, perhaps his most approachable large piece, and he recorded albums with British avant-garde saxophonist Evan Parker and trombonist Paul Rutherford.

Braxton also continued to explore the African American tradition in a "stylist" fashion, taking the music of past masters and reimagining it, on long series of recordings: 1985's *Seven Standards*, a tribute to Charlie Parker, Miles Davis, and Thelonious Monk; *Six Monk Compositions*, a 1987 tribute; a 1989 album of Lennie Tristano compositions, recorded as a tribute to Tristano's student Warne Marsh; the 1993 sextet recording of the *Charlie Parker Project;* and the quartet album *Nine Standards* (1993), a profound statement on the music of John Coltrane. Most unusual, perhaps, is *14 Compositions* (1996), consisting of fourteen tunes from the first half of the century, including "Rosetta" and "Stardust."

In 1994 Braxton was awarded a MacArthur Grant; he used a portion of the award to establish the

New York–based, nonprofit Tri-Centric Foundation. He also began to play the piano in concerts and on a series of small-group recordings, and in 1995 he recorded a solo piano album. Also in 1995 Braxton began to compose his "Ghost Trance Music," a style that involved interaction between notated and improvised materials and sought to bring together Native American and Eastern ritual, often creating a dream-like, meditative atmosphere. In 1997 he founded his own label, Braxton House, on which he released recordings of ensembles of varied sizes, often with Wesleyan students, and pieces that embraced his fondness for multimedia experiments, such as "Composition No. 102 for Orchestra and Puppet Theatre." During these years he also composed a two-act musical, and he embarked on a projected series of thirty-six operas, Trillium. These works were satirical portrayals of a Western culture undermined by materialism, contrasted with African American and world group cultures that remain rooted in spiritual values. He continued to record prolifically during the first years of the twenty-first century.

As an improviser, performer, and composer, Braxton explored the widest possible range of musical styles, from the earliest days of jazz to Schoenberg and the aleatory music of John Cage, and moved beyond them to create his own restructuralist music that drew new musical maps for the future. He wrote music for seemingly every possible performance combination, from solo instruments to huge ensembles, and he explored the integration of music with puppetry, theater, video, and cinema. Intellectually and in practice, he completely rejected the validity and constraint of traditional musical categories. His work was rooted in the African American musical tradition, in the conception of black music as the embodiment of the African American collective memory. For Braxton, music was far more than a duplication or extension of the past. Music was a force for social change, a creator of alternative universes.

Further Reading

Lock, Graham. *Blutopia: Visions of the Future and Revisions of the Past in the Works of Sun Ra, Duke Ellington, and Anthony Braxton* (1999).
Lock, Graham. *Forces in Motion: The Music and Thoughts of Anthony Braxton* (1998).
Radano, Ronald. *New Musical Figurations: Anthony Braxton's Cultural Critique* (1994).

RONALD DUFOUR

BRAZIER, Arthur (22 July 1921–), community organizer and Pentecostal bishop, was born in a Hyde Park apartment on Chicago's South Side. His parents were among the waves of African Americans who migrated from the South to the North in pursuit of greater economic opportunity and social mobility during the Great Migration. His mother, Geneva, was a household domestic and lay Pentecostal preacher, eventually leading the Universal Church of Christ in Chicago. His father, Robert, was a maintenance man at the Hyde Park Laundry Company from 1921 to 1940. One of five children, Brazier grew up in a highly segregated black community, since restrictive covenants bound blacks to certain areas of the city.

From his early teenage years, Brazier worked whenever he wasn't in school, first as a milkman's helper for the Bowman Dairy Company and later as a parking attendant at the Chicago World's Fair in 1933 and 1934. During the Depression, Brazier was forced to drop out of Wendell Phillips High School after only one year to work at the laundry with his father and to take a job as a delivery boy for a drugstore. When he was drafted into the army in 1942, he saw it as an opportunity to see the world and escape the poverty of his urban environment.

His experience in the army (1942–1945) was transformative. While stationed with an all-black unit (the 2033d Quarter Master Unit attached to the Fifty-second Air Service Group) in Ripley, Tennessee, Brazier had his first encounter with southern-style Jim Crow. Although clear racial borders demarcated Chicago, Brazier was struck by the difference between the socially accepted segregation in the North and the legally enforced segregation he found in the South. However, when Brazier toured in Burma and India with the army, he was shocked to find even more extreme levels of poverty and social stratification. "India gave me my first glimpse of what life must have been like during the time of Christ," Brazier explained (Dortch, 29). Brazier's experiences in South Asia not only cultivated his appreciation for American opportunity but also made him more acutely aware of oppression and class divisions in other countries.

After he left the army, Brazier worked as a welder, a molder's helper at Western Electric, and a postal carrier. Throughout this fifteen-year period, Brazier also cultivated his professional profile as a minister. In 1947 he was baptized at the Apostolic Pentecostal Church of Morgan Park. That same year he met his wife, Esther Isabel Holmes, with whom he had four children: Lola, Byrson, Janice, and Rosalyn. In 1960 he left the United States Postal Service to enter the ministry full time. Although Brazier believed in the driving theological principles of Pentecostalism, he was constantly at war with his parents' conservative Pentecostalism, which emphasized external behavior and constructed elaborate prohibitions against smoking, certain types of clothing, makeup, and dancing. Brazier disdained such exclusionary regulations and developed his own progressive Pentecostalism after attending evening classes at the Moody Bible Institute from 1955 to 1961, where he gained a critical understanding of the Bible. Unlike most Pentecostals, who tend to eschew involvement with worldly matters, Brazier believed that those bent on personal salvation could not ignore the problems of the world. "The soul cannot be dealt with as a separate entity divorced from the body," Brazier wrote (*Black Self-determination*, 133). He pointed to Jesus's concern for the poor to argue that if an individual needed food or housing or clothing, he or she could not be expected to work toward salvation (*Black Self-determination*, 130).

Brazier also decided to enter political life against the counsel of his own tradition because he believed that Jesus modeled a theology that demanded spiritual salvation combined with worldly restoration. Upon graduation from Moody Bible Institute, Brazier began the aggressive implementation of his spiritual mission. He took a position at the Apostolic Church of God in the Woodlawn area of town. Located near the University of Chicago, Woodlawn was on a steady decline, experiencing increased levels of crime, poverty, and unemployment. Without a vigorous community response, Woodlawn would become a major slum. Saul Alinsky, the famed community organizer and founder of the Industrial Areas Foundation (IAF), had targeted Woodlawn as the next cite for IAF mobilization. IAF provided technical services to community residents who wanted to organize themselves. During a chance encounter at the Apostolic Church of God, one of Alinsky's operatives saw Brazier at work among his congregants and subsequently introduced the two men. Brazier began working with a local IAF-backed group, the Temporary Woodlawn Organization (TWO) and soon became the official spokesman for TWO. TWO functioned as an operational center for several community institutions and social welfare organizations. During the early 1960s TWO focused on three issues: preventing the University of Chicago from land development in Woodlawn; squelching the growing gang wars between the Blackstone Rangers and the East Side Disciples; and protesting school and housing segregation. TWO attracted national acclaim and was described by one journalist as "the most impressive experiment affecting the Negro anywhere in the U.S." (*Fortune* [Mar. 1962], 140).

According to Brazier, the people of Woodlawn did not need to fight for political power; they simply needed to claim the power that was already theirs. "Nobody, including the government, has the right to make plans and dictate arrangements for whole populations," he announced in a 1961 TWO press release. "We are not asking for our rights. We are asking them to respect our rights, and we are telling them that if they do not respect our rights we will defend ourselves against them." This combination of political pragmatism and righteous rage won Brazier a large following in his own community and respect from the city's political leaders. As spokesman and eventually president of TWO, Brazier never demanded anything beyond the scope of the law. He focused on bringing desegregation and economic opportunity to one small community. This focus brought grassroots success, but little national recognition to Brazier. When MARTIN LUTHER KING JR. came to lead the Chicago Freedom Movement (CFM) in the summer of 1966, Brazier and TWO participated in his marches, yet continued to protect their relationship with Mayor

Daley and their local accomplishments. King's disappointment with the CFM is usefully contrasted with Brazier's persistent local success. Whereas King arrived in Chicago without much northern denominational familiarity or sensitivity to the urban political machine, Brazier was a rapacious precinct worker, respected in the dominating evangelical black churches as well as in city hall.

In 1969 Brazier authored a study of TWO and outlined his faith in black self-determination. "America cannot keep down thirty million people who are moving up, without destroying the entire nation in the process," he concluded (*Black Self-determination*, 147). Throughout the 1970s and 1980s Brazier continued to fight for better conditions in the Woodlawn community. He chaired the Woodlawn Preservation and Investment Corporation and the Fund for Community Redevelopment and Revitalization. Later he was vice president of the Center for Community Change, a Washington, D.C., think tank that provided technical assistance through the Community Development Corporation on large-scale housing and commercial projects throughout the country. However, Brazier never forgot his Chicago congregation. Founded on Easter Sunday 1963 the Apostolic Church of God grew to more than eighteen thousand parishioners by 2004. With his emphasis on spiritual salvation and material ministry, Brazier was pivotal in the church's growth and continued development. Named bishop of the Pentecostal Assemblies of the World in 1976, Brazier established himself as a key figure in the rapid growth of African American Pentecostalism.

Further Reading

Brazier, Arthur. *Black Self-determination: The Story of the Woodlawn Organization* (1969).
Brazier, Arthur. *From Milk to Meat: A Primer for Christian Living* (1996).
Anderson, Alan B., and George W. Pickering. *Confronting the Color Line: The Broken Promise of the Civil Rights Movement in Chicago* (1986).
Dortch, Sammie M. *When God Calls: A Biography of Bishop Arthur Brazier* (1996).
Fish, John. *Black Power/White Control: The Struggle of the Woodlawn Organization in Chicago* (1973).
Ralph, James, Jr. *Northern Protest: Martin Luther King Jr., Chicago, and the Civil Rights Movement* (1993).

KATHRYN LOFTON

BREEDLOVE, Sarah. *See* Walker, Madam C. J.

BRENT, Linda. *See* Jacobs, Harriet.

BREWER, John Mason (24 Mar. 1896–24 Jan. 1975), teacher, historian, and folklorist, was born in Goliad, Texas, one of five children of John Henry Brewer, a cattle drover, and Minnie Tate Brewer, a teacher. John Mason grew up with his three sisters, Jewel, Marguerite, Gladys, and his brother Claude in a household that provided a fertile environment for his imagination. His father told exciting stories about his adventures on the cattle drives from the Media Luna Ranch in Texas to the cattle market in Kansas. His mother, a teacher in Texas for over forty years, read the poetry of PAUL LAURENCE DUNBAR to John Mason during his early childhood. As an adult poet, Dr. Brewer would write dialect verse in the manner of Dunbar. Dr. Brewer's love for the oral tradition in African American culture was also nurtured by his grandfathers, Joe Brewer and Pinckney Mitchell, who told him folktales. John Mason developed a strong interest in folklore and devoted more than forty years of his life to gathering, collecting, and preserving folklore in Texas and elsewhere in the South.

When Brewer was seven years old, his family moved to Austin, Texas, to take advantage of the schools and to pursue better job opportunities. He graduated from Austin's black high school and enrolled at Wiley College in Marshall, Texas. He received a bachelor of arts degree in 1917 and taught school in Austin for a year. Then in 1918 he joined the American Expeditionary Forces and was sent to France with the rank of corporal. Fluent in French, Spanish, and Italian, Brewer served as an interpreter for his brigade officers. After the war, he accepted a principalship in Fort Worth, Texas, but he left that post in 1924 to take a job with an oil company in Denver, Colorado, where he wrote for the company's trade journal. However, he soon lost interest in that job and returned to teaching, serving briefly as a principal in Shreveport, Louisiana.

Brewer devoted over fifty years of his life to teaching, mostly at the college level. In the 1920s and 1930s he taught creating writing at Tillotson College in Austin, and Romance languages at Samuel Huston College, also in Austin; the two institutions would later merge to become Huston-Tillotson University. Brewer taught one year (1942) at Claflin College in Orangeburg, South Carolina, and then returned to Austin. From 1943 to 1959 he served as chair of the Department of English at Huston-Tillotson College (later University); from 1959 to 1969 he taught English at Livingston College in Salisbury, North Carolina. From 1969 until his death in 1975 Brewer served as distinguished visiting professor of English at East Texas State University (later Texas A&M University at Commerce). His students from the East Texas State period remembered him as a brilliant, entertaining lecturer. Brewer and his wife, Ruth Helen, frequently invited students to their home near campus for socials and weekend parties. He was one of the most popular professors at East Texas State, and his classes were always fully enrolled.

Brewer's engagement with folklore as an academic discipline began in 1932 when he sought advice from J. Frank Dobie. A noted professor and author, Dobie was also secretary of the Texas Folklore Society. After reading Brewer's shoebox full of folktales, Dobie arranged to have the tales published in the Texas Folklore Society's annual yearbook. Brewer joined the Texas Folklore Society, launching his long and distin-

guished career as a folklorist. He published his work in four of the Texas Folklore Society's yearbooks. Brewer's professional affiliations also included membership in the American Folklore Society, which elected him second vice-president.

In 1933 he began his formal study of folklore under Dr. Stith Thompson at the University of Indiana, where he earned his master of arts degree in 1950. Brewer's master's thesis, entitled "Negro Preacher Tales of the Brazos Bottoms," was published by the University of Texas Press in 1953 (and republished, in an expanded version, in 1976). Paul Quinn College in Waco, Texas, awarded Brewer an honorary Doctor of Literature at its August Convocation in 1951. As an expression of his appreciation, Brewer established the Minnie Tate Brewer Creative Writing and Oral Literature Prize at Paul Quinn College.

Although Brewer never learned to drive an automobile, beginning in 1925 he managed to collect folklore in Texas as well as in the Carolinas and throughout the South. He also pursued an interest in African American history, and he enjoyed writing poetry. His 1936 book, *The Negro in Texas*, remains a classic in Texas history. *Negrito: Negro Dialect Poems*, published in 1932, reflected his early exposure to the dialect poetry of Paul Laurence Dunbar. In 1945 Brewer published *Humorous Folktales of the South Carolina Negro*. But his best-known collection, *The Word on the Brazos: Negro Preacher Tales from the Brazos Bottoms of Texas*, illustrated by JOHN BIGGERS, was published by the University of Texas Press in 1953. In the Brazos Bottoms, the Holy Bible was known as "the Word." J. Frank Dobie, Brewer's friend and mentor, praised the collection for the humanity that informs the characters. In his brief introduction to the collection, Brewer compared the preacher tales to medieval exempla, narratives that illustrated or confirmed a moral or lesson. The tales also revealed the humorous side of the Brazos Bottom Negroes, especially in the comic anecdotes that poked fun at preachers who craved status and control over the folk.

The fifty-six tales in *The Word on the Brazos* covered a variety of themes, touching on cultural history, the trickster figure, and values. The tales stood as a testament to the survival of blacks in the Brazos Bottoms and celebrated the richness of their culture. Like ZORA NEALE HURSTON, Brewer developed an excellent ear for a variety of African American dialects. He captured the nuances of the oral performance in tales such as "A Sermon, a Cat, and a Churn." In that tale, the speaker recalled the harsh working conditions that prevailed on the plantations after Emancipation. Brewer's transcription went beyond the quaint spellings that characterized black dialect recorded by less able folklorists. Brewer's rendering of the dialect not only recorded the sounds of the speech but also conveyed a sense of the speech rhythms typical of the blacks in the Brazos Bottoms. In another tale, entitled "Mulatto Boys and the Religious Test," light-skinned black men passed for white in order to get better jobs. The trickster figure was highlighted in "The Preacher who Walked on Water," a satirical tale about a preacher who devised a scheme to make his parishioners believe he could walk on water. However, the preacher's trick was exposed when pranksters removed his submerged platform, causing him to sink when he stepped into the water. The tales in *The Word on the Brazos* were entertaining, to be sure, but they also documented the social and cultural history of the African Americans who lived in the Brazos Bottoms in the early twentieth century.

In 1958 Brewer published another major collection of tales titled *Dog Ghosts and other Texas Negro Tales*. Illustrated again by Brewer's friend, Dr. John Biggers, an art professor at Texas Southern University, *Dog Ghosts* featured tales on a variety of subjects, including slavery, animals, ranch life, religion, and dog ghosts and spirits. There were sixty-three tales in the collection, but only eighteen tales dealt specifically with dog ghosts. Like *The Word on the Brazos,* the *Dog Ghosts* collection was a repository of cultural history, social history, and values. The dog ghost tales usually concerned deceased family members who came back from the dead in the form of a dog to assist the living. For example, in "The Oak Cliff Dog Ghost" a man's dead wife returned every year on the day she died and brought him a ten-dollar bill. Although *Dog Ghosts and Other Stories* explored serious topics such as slavery, the humorous tone made the tales a pleasure to read.

Brewer published several books of folklore in addition to *The Word on the Brazos* and *Dog Ghosts and Other Stories.* These included the delightful *Aunt Dicy Tales* (1956), *Worser Days and Better Times* (1964), and an anthology, *American Negro Folklore* (1968), for which he received the Chicago Book Fair Award, and he was among the Texas writers who received the Twenty-first Annual Writers Roundup award in 1969. Brewer also published many scholarly essays and newspaper articles. Dr. J. Mason Brewer left an impressive body of work that deserves further study. Dr. Brewer died in Fort Worth.

Further Reading

Byrd, James W. *J. Mason Brewer: Negro Folklorist*. Southwestern Writers Series, no. 12. (1967).

Byrd, James W. "In Memory of John Mason Brewer (1896–1975)," *CLA Journal* 18 (June 1975).

Thomas, Lorenzo. "The African-American Folktale and J. Mason Brewer," in *Juneteenth Texas: Essays in African American Folklore*, eds. Francis E. Abernethy, et al. (1996).

Turner, Darwin T. "J. Mason Brewer: Vignettes," *CLA Journal* 18 (June 1975).

ELVIN HOLT

BREWSTER, William Herbert (2 July 1897?–15 Oct. 1987), gospel composer and pastor, was born into a family of sharecroppers in Somerville, Tennessee. Although Brewster stemmed from a humble background, he managed to study a wide variety of subjects, including theology, law, and Hebrew. After graduating from Roger Williams College in 1922 he moved to Memphis, Tennessee. By 1930 Brewster had begun a lifelong tenure as pastor of the East Trigg Baptist Church. A major aspect of Brewster's early ministry centered on the founding of theology schools, and these centers of learning helped to establish his voice as one of moral authority and spiritual guidance in religious circles.

By the time Brewster began seriously publishing his songs in the 1940s, he had gained over a decade of experience in his pastoral role. This experience provided a wellspring of material for songs that often relayed Old Testament stories and were enjoyed by African American congregations across the United States. Drawing on the gospel blues style of Thomas Dorsey, Brewster composed "I'm Leaning and Depending on the Lord" in 1939 and published it two years later. During this time, he made it a priority to write scripts and songs for pageants and biblical dramas, genres to which he had been exposed through attendance at National Baptist Conventions. His best-known biblical drama, a historical piece titled *From Auction Block to Glory*, was written in 1941. This play represented a move away from a primary reliance on Negro spirituals and toward the use of modern gospel music in African American religious dramas. Brewster was the first to compose gospel songs specifically for biblical plays that appeared before a racially mixed, national audience. His success in writing music and scripts for black religious pageants would have a profound impact on American writers such as LANGSTON HUGHES, OSSIE DAVIS, and Micki Grant.

Brewster refined many compositional devices that distinguished his gospel songs from those of his predecessors. By creatively manipulating the rhythm of a melodic line, changing tempos from one section of a piece to another, and occasionally employing a waltz time feel—as he did in "Surely God Is Able"—Brewster was able to maximize the emotional effect his songs had on listeners. His most often cited compositional contribution is the use of a repetitive section, known as the "vamp" or "drive," which provided a relatively stable harmonic texture on which singers could improvise mini-sermons as a song grew in intensity. Such vamp sections were particularly popular among the many Holiness congregations within the Memphis-based African American Pentecostal organization, the Church of God in Christ.

By 1943 several vocal ensembles began to embrace Brewster's compositions and incorporate them into their repertoires. Brewster himself also put together vocal groups to perform his songs, and he often showcased a talented young singer named "Queen" Candace Anderson, who would influence legendary singers such as CLARA WARD and MAHALIA JACKSON. The Brewsteraires, featuring Anderson, were heard regularly on African American radio stations such as WDIA, which also ran Brewster's program, *Camp Meeting in the Air.* Singers such as Dorothy Love Coates, the Soul Stirrers, and Elvis

Presley also credited Brewster's radio programs with influencing their musical and professional development. The gospel singer Mahalia Jackson became an immediate sensation after recording Brewster's "Move on up a Little Higher" in 1948. Eventually, the song sold 2 million copies, becoming the first million-selling recording in the history of gospel music. The following year, Brewster's prosperity continued, as Clara Ward's rendition of "Surely God Is Able" also sold over 1 million copies. Throughout the subsequent decade and a half, Clara Ward and the Ward Sisters built their career on Brewster's compositions. Their versions of pieces such as "God's Amazing Love," "The Old Landmark," and "How I Got Over" were enormous hits with African American audiences.

The 1940s and 1950s were Brewster's most fruitful decades, and he composed several songs that would eventually become gospel classics. He achieved unprecedented fame and became the most prolific and influential gospel songwriter of the post–World War II era. Along with LUCIE CAMPBELL, Brewster was also a pivotal figure who facilitated a stylistic transition from the jubilee style of quartet singing to the modern brand of sacred song that flourished during gospel's golden age from 1940 to 1960. He became one of the first gospel superstars, influencing generations of audiences and performers through songs that provided expressive vehicles for both amateur and professional gospel performers.

Often hailed as the greatest American gospel songwriter, Brewster was admired by both his contemporaries and successors, who sometimes referred to him affectionately as "Old Man" Brewster. His songs are appreciated for their lyrical and musical content, as well as their implicit social and political messages, which predated the civil rights movement of the 1960s. Indeed, songs such as "I'm Climbing Higher and Higher" speak to the need for social uplift and justice while resonating with Christian aspirations to reach heaven. For his many contributions to the musical and social landscapes of American society, Brewster was honored by the Smithsonian in 1982. He continued to work as pastor of East Trigg Baptist Church and as musical mentor to countless others until his death.

Further Reading

Boyer, Horace Clarence. *How Sweet the Sound: The Golden Age of Gospel* (1995).

Cusic, Don. *The Sound of Light: A History of Gospel Music* (1990).

Darden, Robert. *People Get Ready!: A New History of Black Gospel Music* (2004).

Heilbut, Anthony. *The Gospel Sound: Good News and Bad Times* (1971).

Lornell, Kip. *Happy in the Service of the Lord: African-American Sacred Vocal Harmony Quartets in Memphis* (1995).

Reagan, Bernice Johnson, ed. *We'll Understand It Better By and By: Pioneering African American Gospel Composers* (1992).

MELVIN L. BUTLER

BRICE, Carol Lovette (16 Apr. 1918–15 Feb. 1985), contralto concert singer, recording artist, and professor, was born in Indianapolis, Indiana, the youngest of four children born to the Reverend Dr. John Brice, a 1904 graduate of Knoxville College who served as a chaplain during World War I. He was a Congregationalist minister and served as vice president and religious director at Palmer Memorial Institute for thirty years, retiring in 1950. Her mother, Ella Hawkins, also of Knoxville College, was an educator and musician who taught history and pursued a career as a singer. She spent so much time on the road that Brice and her siblings were taken by her father when she was only eighteen months old to Sedalia, North Carolina, and placed in the custody of her first cousin, Dr. CHARLOTTE HAWKINS BROWN, whom Brice called "Aunt." Dr. Brown was the founder and president of Palmer Memorial Institute. The institute was the only finishing school for blacks in the United States. By the age of three Brice's singing voice was exceptional, and as an early student at Palmer she toured the country with the Sedalia Singers.

In 1930, at the age of thirteen, Brice won a cup for the best contralto voice at a North Carolina music festival. The following year she appeared with the Sedalia Singers at Town Hall in New York City and later performed in such places as Symphony Hall in Boston and the White House. The group served as the major fund-raising arm of Palmer Memorial Institute and it performed traditional Negro spirituals.

Brice graduated from the high school department of the institute in 1933 and completed Palmer Memorial Institute Junior College in 1935. There she became acquainted with numerous luminaries who visited the school, including W. E. B. DU BOIS, MARY MCLEOD BETHUNE, MARIAN ANDERSON, and First Lady Eleanor Roosevelt. With the aid of a Palmer Memorial Institute supporter and benefactress, Carrie L. Stone, Brice journeyed to Talladega College in Alabama, where she majored in music, studied under the noted voice teacher Frank G. Harrison, gave numerous concerts, joined the Alpha Kappa Alpha sorority, and received a bachelor of music degree. Upon graduation from Talladega she went to New York City, where her mother, who was now divorced, and her brother Jonathan were residing. She was a fellowship recipient to the Juilliard School of Music in New York (from 1939 to 1943), where she came under the tutelage of Francis Rogers.

In the summer of 1939 Brice received wide acclaim when she performed with BILL "BOJANGLES" ROBINSON in the musical *The Hot Mikado* at the New York World's Fair. There she met her future husband, Cornelius Wiley "Neil" Scott, a baritone in the chorus; they had two children before his death in 1967.

In the 1940s, as a versatile contralto Brice was able to attain recognition that was not as readily available to other black musicians at that time. Her voice was often compared to that of Marion Anderson and other giants of her day, and as an African American singer she succeeded in many firsts. She had the pleasure in

January 1941 to sing at the third inauguration of President Franklin D. Roosevelt, which was one of the first times an African American performed at an inauguration. She was the first black singer to earn the prestigious Naumberg Foundation Award for young performers in 1943, a prize that included a recital at Town Hall in New York City on 13 March 1945. From here her career blossomed as she began to receive wide acclaim, not only as a contralto but also on stage. After the Town Hall concert, she performed with the Pittsburg Orchestra in 1945, with the Boston Symphony in 1946, and with the San Francisco Symphony in 1948. During the summer of 1950 she toured in South and Central America, singing in Puerto Rico, Curaçau, Venezuela, Brazil, Argentina, Ecuador, Chile, and Panama. From 1944 until 1977 she sang in recitals across the United States, most often accompanied on the piano by her brother, Jonathan.

In 1958 Brice formed a trio with her brothers Eugene, also a graduate of Juilliard, who performed in numerous Broadway productions, and Jonathan, who sang with the Robert Shaw Chorale and the New York City Opera. They called themselves the Brice Trio, and in 1958 they performed at Town Hall.

Brice's Broadway career included the roles of Addie in *Regina* (1959), Maude in *Finian's Rainbow* (1960), Queenie in *Showboat* (1961), HARRIET TUBMAN in *Gentlemen, Be Seated* (1963), and Maria in *Porgy and Bess* (1961, 1976). She was a member of the Vienna Volksoper from 1967 until 1971. Brice made a number of outstanding and much-praised recordings, as she was among the first black classical artists to record extensively in the United States. Her most noted recordings include Gustav Mahler's "Songs of a Wayfarer," with Fritz Reiner and the Pittsburg Orchestra; Falla's *El Amor Brujo*; *The Grass Harp* by Claibe Richardson; and her Grammy-winning recording of *Porgy and Bess* in 1976.

In 1968 Brice met the baritone Thomas Carey during a tour for the U.S. State Department in France. They were married the following year and together performed in *Porgy and Bess* throughout the world. Brice received numerous awards for her pioneering spirit and commitment to singing. In 1948 she was honored as the outstanding "Negro woman musician" by the National Council of Negro Women; in 1954 she was chosen one of Long Island, New York's, "Women of the Year." In 1955 her alma mater, Talladega College, awarded her with an honorary doctor of humane letters; in 1963 she was presented the Emancipation Proclamation Award by the National Association of Negro Musicians; and in 1965 she and her two brothers were honored at the Fifth Annual Founder's Day Program of the National Association of Negro Musicians, Eastern Region.

In 1973 Brice was appointed associate professor of music at the University of Oklahoma. In 1974 she and her husband founded the Cimarron Circuit Opera Company, which prospered under their leadership. In 1977 both Brice and Carey were named

Oklahoma Musicians of the Year. Carol Brice died of cancer.

Further Reading
The Carol Brice Papers are at the Amistad Research Center at Tulane University in New Orleans, Louisiana. Also, a significant vertical file has been maintained at the Charlotte Hawkins Brown Museum at Historic Palmer Memorial Institute in Sedalia, North Carolina.
Burns-Vann, Tracey, and Andre D. Vann. *Sedalia and the Palmer Memorial Institute,* Black America Series (2004).
Marteena, Constance H. *The Lengthening Shadow of a Woman: A Biography of Charlotte Hawkins Brown* (1977).
Nettles, Darryl G. *African American Concert Singers before 1950* (2003).
Wadelington, Charles W., and Richard K. Knapp. *Charlotte Hawkins Brown and Palmer Memorial Institute: What One Young African American Woman Could Do* (1999).

ANDRE D. VANN

BRICKTOP (14 Aug. 1894–31 Jan. 1984), entertainer and nightclub operator, was born in Alderson, West Virginia, the daughter of Thomas Smith, a barber, and Hattie E. (maiden name unknown), a domestic worker. Christened Ada Beatrice Queen Victoria Louise Virginia, because her parents did not wish to disappoint the various neighbors and friends who offered suggestions for naming her, Bricktop received her nickname because of her red hair when she was in her late twenties from Barron Wilkins, owner of a nightclub called Barron's Exclusive Club in Prohibition-era Harlem.

Bricktop's father died when she was four, and her mother moved with the children to Chicago to be near relatives. Hattie Smith worked as a domestic in Chicago, and her children attended school. Bricktop showed early musical talent and interest in perform-

Bricktop, expatriate who ran nightclubs in Paris and Rome frequented by American celebrities, June 1934. (Library of Congress/Carl Van Vechten.)

ing. She made her stage debut as a preschooler, playing the part of Eliza's son Harry in a production of *Uncle Tom's Cabin* at the Haymarket Theatre. As an adolescent, she had the opportunity to perform onstage again when she was hired as part of the chorus for a show at the Pekin Theatre. She quit school at age sixteen to pursue a career as an entertainer, first touring with (Flournoy) Miller and (Aubrey) Lyles, a well-known black comedy team.

After the Miller and Lyles show folded, Bricktop toured with a variety of black vaudeville acts across the northern half of the United States. In the early 1920s she returned to Chicago and worked as a saloon performer at Roy Jones's and the Cafe Champ, owned by heavyweight champion JACK JOHNSON. In 1922 she went to Harlem, where she worked in Connie's Inn, among other nightclubs, and received her nickname. In 1924 she was invited to work in Paris at Le Grand Duc, a tiny club in Montmartre managed by EUGÈNE BULLARD, an African American pilot who had distinguished himself during World War I in the French Foreign Legion and the Lafayette Escadrille.

Never a great song stylist, Bricktop attracted the attention of white Americans in Paris because of her charming personality and her ability to make them feel at home. T. S. Eliot wrote a poem for her. F. Scott Fitzgerald liked to say, "My greatest claim to fame is that I discovered Bricktop before Cole Porter." But it was her discovery by Porter, who later wrote the song "Miss Otis Regrets" for her, that put the imprimatur of acceptance upon her. Under Porter's aegis, Bricktop became a darling of the American celebrity set in Paris. By the fall of 1926, Bricktop had opened the first Bricktop's nightclub in Paris, catering to such American luminaries as Fitzgerald, Elsa Maxwell, Tallulah Bankhead, Ernest Hemingway, and Barbara Hutton, and to international celebrities like the Aga Khan. "Everybody belonged, or else they didn't bother coming to Bricktop's more than once," she wrote in her autobiography.

A succession of Bricktop's nightclubs followed, both in Paris and, in the summertime, at Biarritz, where Bricktop claimed to have cradled the romance of the Duke of Windsor and the American divorcée Wallis Simpson. Among the careers she nurtured was that of the British-born black singer MABEL MERCER.

The stock market crash in the United States in October 1929 had no effect, at first, on the "gay" life in Paris. In December 1929 Bricktop married Peter Duconge, an African American saxophonist from New Orleans, and the two purchased a country home in Bougival, outside Paris. Childless, each led an independent life, as well as sharing a life together. Some years after their marriage, however, Peter had an affair with a young African American singer whom Bricktop had taken under her wing in Paris. On learning of her husband's infidelity, Bricktop refused to sleep with him again, although she never divorced him. He died in 1967.

In 1939, as war in Europe and the invasion of France seemed imminent, the Duchess of Windsor (the former Wallis Simpson) and Lady Mendl (Elsie de Wolfe) helped Bricktop escape from Paris to New York, where her friend Mabel Mercer had already relocated. Mercer managed to find a niche as a singer in New York cabarets, but Bricktop's special talents as a self-described "saloonkeeper par excellence" went unappreciated. Bankrolled by the tobacco heiress Doris Duke, she relocated to Mexico City, where she successfully ran clubs until the war in Europe was over. In 1943 she converted to Catholicism and remained a devout Catholic for the rest of her life.

Returning to Paris in 1950, she found her old stomping grounds much changed, as was the clientele. After trying and failing to revive the prewar atmosphere, Bricktop removed to Rome, where on the Via Veneto from 1951 to 1965 she re-created the feeling of the old Bricktop's for a new celebrity crowd, primarily American film stars. The romance of Richard Burton and Elizabeth Taylor first made the gossip columns when they were seen together at the Rome Bricktop's during the filming of *Cleopatra*. To Bricktop, her career in Rome was secondary to the golden years in Paris, and she never fully accepted the Hollywood film stars as the nouveau royalty.

When Bricktop's older sister Blonzetta became ill in 1965, Bricktop returned to Chicago to nurse her and, after her death, went back to straighten out her affairs. Blonzetta left Bricktop a substantial inheritance. In her early seventies, Bricktop moved to Los Angeles, returned briefly to Europe, and then in 1970 settled in New York City. She made a recording of "So Long, Baby" with Cy Coleman, briefly ran a club owned by Huntington Hartford and then one called Soerabaja, and appeared from time to time at clubs in Chicago, at the Playboy Club in London, and at "21" in New York. Ill health caused her to cease working in 1979.

In August 1983 Bricktop published her autobiography, *Bricktop*, written with Jim Haskins. Five months later she died in New York City. To the end she was a lady of the dawn who drank only champagne and expected a rose from every male visitor.

Further Reading

Bricktop's papers are in the collection of the Schomburg Center for Research in Black Culture of the New York Public Library.
Boyle, Kay, and Robert Altman. *Being Geniuses Together, 1920–1930* (1968).
Haskins, Jim. *Mabel Mercer: A Life* (1968).
Obituary: *Rolling Stone*, 29 Mar. 1984.

JIM HASKINS

BRIDGEWATER, Cecil (10 Oct. 1942–), jazz trumpeter, composer, arranger, and educator, was born Cecil Vernon Bridgewater in Urbana, Illinois, into a family of musicians. His mother, Erma Pauline Scott Bridgewater, was the daughter of Ramon Mack Scott, who sang, played saxophone, piano, and drums, and led a band called Mack Scott and the Foot Warmers, in which Erma played piano for a time. Bridgewater's father, Cecil Bernard Bridgewater, played trumpet in the U.S. Navy band during World War II, and he was stationed at Great Lakes Naval Base with other African American musicians such as CLARK TERRY, Marshall Royal, Jerome Richardson, and others. Bridgewater's grandfather, Preston Bridgewater, played trumpet and cornet professionally with the circus.

When Cecil Bridgewater was a student at Marquette Grade School in Champaign, Illinois, the school's band director noticed his potential and encouraged his parents to find a private trumpet teacher for their son. Haskell Sexton, then head of the trumpet section at the University of Illinois School of Music, became Bridgewater's musical mentor from the time Bridgewater was thirteen years old through his high school and college years. Sexton took Bridgewater through the European classical tradition for trumpet and symphony orchestra, and even though Sexton admitted that he did not know much about the jazz tradition, he taught Bridgewater how to practice.

Bridgewater enlisted in the U.S. Army in 1964 and was accepted into the 25th Infantry Army Band. Eventually, Bridgewater ended up in Vietnam, stationed at Cu Chi, home of some of the famous network of hidden tunnels built by the North Vietnamese northwest of Saigon. He completed his stint in the army band in 1966. From 1968 to 1970 Bridgewater toured the Soviet Union and Europe with the University of Illinois band. In 1969 he formed the Bridgewater Brothers Band with his brother, the saxophonist Ronald Scott Bridgewater. They played and recorded together on and off until about 1989. Among these recordings was "Lightning and Thunder" (Denon, 1977) and "Bridgewater Brothers Generation Suite" (Denon, 1978).

In 1970 Bridgewater married Denise Eileen Garrett, a jazz singer who became known as DEE DEE BRIDGEWATER, and moved to New York City, where he joined the THAD JONES/Mel Lewis Jazz Orchestra, which he played in until 1976. This move put Bridgewater right in the middle of the "Loft Jazz" scene, where musicians were finding new places to create and play jazz outside of the mainstream venues. The Collective Black Artists (CBA) were renting out halls, publicizing their artistic goals, and creating a space for new jazz artists with the help of established musicians. Bridgewater's first daughter, Tulani Adenike Bridgewater, was born in 1972. Having divorced his first wife in 1975, Bridgewater married again, this time in 1977 to Mattie Bowman, with whom he would have a second daughter, Chelsea Amber Bridgewater.

Over the years, Bridgewater worked with many of the great musicians of the time: HORACE SILVER (in 1970), MAX ROACH (from 1971), ART BLAKEY (in 1972), JIMMY HEATH (from 1974 to 1976), LENA HORNE (from 1982 to 1983), Mercer Ellington (from 1985 to 1986), Grover Mitchell, Richard Davis, and the COUNT BASIE Orchestra with Frank Foster. In 1970 Bridgewater recorded with the pianist Horace

Silver for the Blue Note label on Silver's album *Total Response*, and in 1973 he played with the pianist MC-COY TYNER on his *Song of the New World* and *Inner Voices*. Bridgewater's extensive recorded work with the drummer Max Roach includes *Cecil Bridgewater Nonet Plus* (1992) and *I Love Your Smile* (1993) for Mesa Blue Moon, *To The Max!* (1992) for Enja, and *Max Roach with the New Orchestra of Boston and the So What Brass Quintet* (1993) for Blue Note. In 1997 Bridgewater received a Grammy nomination for his arrangement of the song "Undecided" on Dee Dee Bridgewater's Grammy Award–winning album *Dear Ella*. Bridgewater joined the faculty of the Manhattan School of Music in 1991, and he also received commissions from the Cleveland Chamber Symphony, the Atlanta Arts Festival, the Jazzmobile, and Meet the Composers, which produced the *Cannonball Adderley Suite*, performed in Los Angles in 1994 and in Washington, D.C., in 1998. A consummate educator, Bridgewater's advice to aspiring jazz musicians was that there are two parts to taking care of business if they wanted to play. Part one is being "curious about every aspect of what [you] . . . do so [you] don't make the same mistakes that [your] elders made . . . don't overlook something out of ignorance." Part two of taking care of business was to "create places where the creative process can take place."

Further Reading
Joyce, Mike. "Cecil Bridgewater: Brassman's Holiday," *Washington Post*, 25 June 1993.
Joyce, Mike. "Trumpeter Bridgewater, Unmuted," *Washington Post*, 22 Mar. 2000.
Mathieson, Kenny. *Giant Steps: Bebop and the Creators of Modern Jazz 1945–65* (1999).

SUZANNE CLOUD

BRIDGEWATER, Dee Dee (27 May 1950–), jazz singer, was born Denise Eileen Garrett in Memphis, Tennessee. Her father, Matthew Turner Garrett, was a jazz trumpeter and a teacher at Manassas High School in Memphis. He taught music to BOOKER LITTLE, CHARLES LLOYD, and George Coleman, and during summers played with DINAH WASHINGTON's band. Her mother, Marion Hale Holiday, born in Flint, Michigan, was one of the first African Americans hired at the Flint unemployment office; she also worked as a legal secretary. When her parents divorced, Bridgewater's mother returned to Flint and raised her along with her sister, Rhonda Garrett Whiters.

During her early years in Flint, Bridgewater went to Southwestern High School, and at sixteen she joined an all-girl trio, modeled after the Marvelettes, called the Iridescents and sang in local clubs in Flint. In 1968, when she was eighteen years old, the singer attended Michigan State University in East Lansing and sang in saxophonist Andy Courtridge's group. Bridgewater transferred to the University of Illinois at Urbana-Champaign at the urging of the university's band director. It was there that she met the trumpeter

Dee Dee Bridgewater, performing at London's Barbican Theatre in "Billie and Me," a Billie Holiday tribute concert, 5 April 2004. (AP Images.)

CECIL BRIDGEWATER, who was also a student. In 1969 they toured the Soviet Union and Eastern Europe with the University of Illinois Concert Jazz Band, and in 1970 they moved to New York City when he got a gig with HORACE SILVER's quintet. They married the same year. In 1971, when her husband joined the THAD JONES/Mel Lewis Jazz Orchestra, Dee Dee Bridgewater became its lead vocalist. In 1972 the Bridgewaters had a daughter, Tulani Adenike Bridgewater.

Dee Dee Bridgewater's career took off after her debut with the famed New York jazz orchestra, and she began to perform with some of the legends of the 1940s, 1950s, and 1960s: SONNY ROLLINS, DIZZY GILLESPIE, DEXTER GORDON, and MAX ROACH. In 1974 Bridgewater recorded her classic first album, *Afro Blue*, with Cecil Bridgewater, Ron Bridgewater, George Mraz, and Roland Hanna. The twenty-four-year-old singer was not ready to be pigeon-holed by the jazz community, however, so she auditioned for the original Broadway production of *The Wiz* (an adaptation of the *Wizard of Oz*) and landed the role of Glinda the Good Witch. Her performance earned her the 1975 Tony Award for Best Featured Actress in a Musical.

Bridgewater divorced Cecil Bridgewater that year, and in 1976 she married the film and television director Gilbert Moses. She had a second daughter, China Nicole Moses, in 1978. Dee Dee Bridgewater toured the United States and France from 1983 to 1984 in the Broadway musical *Sophisticated Ladies* and then moved to Paris in 1986. The same year saw her starring in *Lady Day* as Billie Holiday, a role that garnered her a nomination for the Laurence Olivier Award. In 1989 Bridgewater divorced Gilbert Moses.

She returned to jazz in 1990, when she performed at the Montreux Jazz Festival. In 1991 she married the French concert promoter Jean-Marie Durand, and they had a son, Gabriel Morgan Durand, in 1992. In 1994 Bridgewater collaborated with the jazz composer/pianist Horace Silver and released the album *Love and Peace: A Tribute to Horace Silver* in 1995. Her tribute to ELLA FITZGERALD, *Dear Ella*, won Bridgewater a 1998 Grammy Award for best jazz vocal album, and another nomination followed for *Live at Yoshi's* in 2000. She also reconceptualized the music of Kurt Weill on her 2002 album for Verve called *This is New* and recorded a project of French classics called *J'ai Deux Amours* in 2005. She was the host of *JazzSet* for National Public Radio beginning in 2001 and also was one of the United Nations's (U.N.) first ambassadors for the Food and Agriculture Organization (FAO), a movement that grew out of the World Food Summit in 1996 and which pledged to end world hunger by 2015. Dee Dee became an ambassador in 1999 and visited food projects in Senegal. In 2002 she gave the greeting message on the occasion of World Food Day at the U.N. for the FAO. In 2007 Bridgewater released *Red Earth*, which she recorded in Barnako for the Emarcy Label.

Further Reading

Byrnes, Sholto. "Dreadlock Diva; Dee Dee Bridgewater is a Force to be Reckoned With," *The (London, England) Independent*, 10 May 2002.
Hunter, Al. "Don't Stick Her With 'Jazz' Label," *Philadelphia Daily News*, 13 Feb. 2004.
MacNeil, Jason. "Dee Dee Bridgewater: *J'ai Deux Amours*," *PopMatters* (21 Oct. 2005).
Ouellette, Dan "Six Questions With Dee Dee Bridgewater," *Billboard* (24 Sept. 2005).
Schudel, Matt. "Brilliance at Both Ends of the Jazz Universe," *Washington Post*, 7 May 2006.
Thomas, Jo. "Arts in America: A Singer is Returning to a Stage Where it All Began," *New York Times*, 22 Sept. 1998.

SUZANNE CLOUD

BRIGGS, Bunny (22 Feb. 1922–), dancer, was born in Harlem, New York, to Alma Briggs and Bubba Jones. Born out of wedlock, "Baby" Briggs received no first name; however, his grandmother Abrella delighted in the toddler's quickness and nicknamed him "Bunny." The Briggs family gravitated toward entertainment. His mother, Alma, and her brothers held various jobs at Harlem hot spots, and her sister, Gladys, became a dancer (she was sometimes known as Gerry Wiley). The home was frequented by musicians and dancers, who used the space for socializing and rehearsing. The musicians JAMES P. JOHNSON and Kid Lippy practiced on the family's piano and played their rent parties, an important part of African American urban economy and social life, providing an evening of entertainment for a small admission. The Cotton Club performers Mordecai, Wells, and Taylor rehearsed there, exposing Briggs to the rhythms and footwork of tap. Steeped in this atmosphere he became a natural performer, entertaining guests with his delivery of popular dances like the Charleston, Shimmy, Mess Around, and Truckin'. When he was five years old Briggs saw BILL "BOJANGLES" ROBINSON at the Lincoln Theatre. Robinson's charisma and style captivated the child. Backstage, Gladys Briggs, a prominent "end-dancer" in the chorus line, had her nephew perform his rent-party repertoire for Robinson. Charmed, he asked Alma's permission to bring Briggs into his act, but she declined the offer, reluctant to let her five-year-old go on the road. Regardless, this was a life-changing experience for Briggs, who determined to become a tap dancer.

Like most performers of his time, Briggs learned informally, by seeing and doing. While performing on the sidewalk for small change, he was spotted around 1928 by a dancer named Porkchops, who developed an act called Porkchops, Navy, Rice, and Beans with Briggs and two other boys, Juney Miller and Paul White. Briggs started school, attending St. Mark the Evangelist. He was baptized into the Catholic faith as Bernard Morris, after his mother's marriage to Clifton Morris. Neither the marriage nor the name change lasted, but Briggs's devotion to Catholicism would. Performing frequently interfered with school, a problem that would continue until he turned sixteen, the legal age to join the workforce.

In 1932 Briggs came to the attention of the stride pianist and composer LUCKEY ROBERTS. Roberts's Society Entertainers, a premiere society orchestra, was popular with New York's elite. Mentored by Roberts, Briggs began earning an income, and he developed social graces and performance dynamics, learning how to play to an audience to suit the occasion.

In adolescence Briggs began to shape his personal style. Around age fourteen he danced with the jazz trumpeter ERSKINE HAWKINS and his band at the Ubangi Club, where he was partnered with another teen, BABY LAURENCE. Laurence was developing a musicality and rhythmic complexity similar to innovations in jazz drumming. Briggs's concept of tap was completely changed by this musical approach and departure from the trick steps common in tap. Their partnership was cut short when Briggs was discovered to be underage and truant, but the friendship endured. Around age sixteen, working at Small's Paradise and under the guidance of the dancer Brother Ford, Briggs learned to develop material from the steps he knew and to make use of the stage. Briggs never set routines, instead improvising like a jazz

soloist from a repertoire of steps. And like jazz musicians, tap dancers had their own cutting contest, where dancers would compete with each other, demonstrating their virtuosity. Briggs became known as one to beat.

The 1940s brought Briggs into the world of the big bands. His work with EARL "FATHA" HINES, COUNT BASIE, JIMMIE LUNCEFORD, and the Dorsey Brothers furthered his relationship with jazz and jazz musicians, especially his interplay with drummers. From 1945 to 1949 Briggs performed with Charlie Barnet as vocalist as well as tap dancer. His numerous recordings with Barnet included the hit "East Side West Side," also featured in the 1949 film *Charlie Barnet and His Orchestra*. Briggs's years with Barnet honed his professional skills and familiarized him with the music of DUKE ELLINGTON, Barnet's idol.

The 1950s saw a decline in the popularity and commercial viability of tap as theaters closed, jazz venues grew smaller, and television kept audiences at home. Briggs found work in the remaining clubs, theaters, Catskills resorts, television, and occasional appearances with, among others, LOUIS ARMSTRONG and Count Basie. In 1960 Briggs appeared at the Apollo with the Duke Ellington Orchestra. Ellington, who continued to employ dancers, was taken with Briggs's gliding intricacies, dramatic accents, and rapport with his audience. For the next fourteen years Ellington provided an inspiring environment and consistent employment for Briggs, often of historic importance. At the 1962 Newport Jazz Festival, for example, Briggs participated in a presentation titled "The History of the Tap Dance and Its Relationship to Jazz," bringing to life the "lost art," followed by a stunning performance with Baby Laurence and backed by Ellington. In 1963 he performed in *My People*, Ellington's contribution to the centennial celebration of the Emancipation Proclamation, *A Century of Negro Progress Exposition*, at Chicago's McCormick Place. Here Briggs first performed "David Danced before the Lord," an up-tempo arrangement of Ellington's "Come Sunday," inspired by the biblical story of King David. In 1965 he reprised "David Danced" for the finale of Ellington's triumphant First Sacred Concert.

After Ellington's death in 1974 Briggs worked cruise ships and stage shows with the luminaries PEARL BAILEY, Tony Bennett, Jerry Lewis, and SAMMY DAVIS JR. He was featured in the 1979 documentary *No Maps on My Taps*. In 1982 Briggs married the jazz harpist Olivette Miller, the daughter of Flournoy Miller, who coauthored the 1921 musical *Shuffle Along*. The couple moved to Las Vegas, and Briggs continued to perform as a solo act and with Miller.

In the 1980s tap began to experience a revival, creating new opportunities for Briggs, including two 1988 projects with GREGORY HINES: the Emmy-winning *Gregory Hines, Tap Dance in America* and the film *Tap*. From 1989 to 1991 Briggs co-starred in the Broadway review *Black and Blue*, receiving a Tony nomination. A founding member of the International Tap Association, Briggs received an honorary doctorate from the University of Oklahoma, along with eight other tap masters in 2002. That same year Miller died and Briggs settled into retirement. In 2006 he received the International Tap Dance Hall of Fame Award from the American Tap Dance Foundation. During his long career Briggs had contact with virtually every notable entertainer and jazz musician of the twentieth century. He remained active in the tap community, sharing his colorful history and coaching dancers in the fine art of performance.

Further Reading

Frank, Rusty. *Tap!: The Greatest Tap Dance Stars and Their Stories, 1900–1955* (1994).

Radecki, Allana. "Bunny Briggs, A Quality of Heart," *On Tap* 15.2–3 (2004).

Stearns, Marshall, and Jean Stearns. *Jazz Dance: The Story of American Vernacular Dance* (1968).

ALLANA RADECKI

BRIGGS, Cyril Valentine (28 May 1888–18 Oct. 1966), journalist and activist, was born on the Caribbean island of Nevis, the son of Marian M. Huggins, a woman of color, a plantation worker and Louis E. Briggs, a white native of Trinidad and plantation overseer. From childhood Briggs had a stutter that made verbal communication difficult, but he more than compensated through the power of his pen. Butting heads with colonial school administrators, he was dismissed from two primary schools before settling at Ebenezer Wesleyan on the island of St. Kitts; he graduated from this school in 1904. In his autobiographical writings Briggs indicated that despite its challenges, colonial education shaped his later career by introducing him to radical thinkers like the freethinking agnostic Robert Green Ingersoll. After his graduation Briggs embarked on his lifelong career in journalism by becoming a reporter for the *St. Kitts Daily Express* and the *St. Christopher Advertiser.*

Briggs immigrated to the United States on 4 July 1905 and joined a growing West Indian activist community in Harlem. Little is known about his first years in the United States except that he became engaged to Bertha Florence Johnson in Norfolk, Virginia. Johnson moved to New York in 1912, and the couple married on 7 January 1914. In 1912 Briggs became a society reporter for the *New York Amsterdam News*, an African American newspaper founded in 1909. He rose through the ranks at the *Amsterdam News* as sporting editor and editorial writer for three years before he resigned to join the staff of the *Colored American Review*, a black business magazine. He returned to the *Amsterdam News* almost immediately, but his work with the *Colored American Review* launched his career as a radical nationalist journalist. From 1915 to 1919 Briggs published hard-hitting editorials urging African Americans to have race pride and to seek self-determination, notably through the creation of a separate black state. When President Woodrow Wilson argued that post–World War I peace in Europe should rest not on governments but on the rights of European peoples, Briggs published an editorial calling for a separate state within the geographical borders of the United States where the rights of African Americans would be respected.

When the United States entered World War I, Briggs registered for military service, joining the many African Americans who believed that wartime service could counteract white racism. His hopes were dashed with the 2 July 1917 antiblack race riot in East St. Louis, and he became an outspoken opponent of U.S. participation in the war. Southern mobs lynched at least sixteen African American World War I veterans between 1918 and 1920, and summertime race riots were so violent in 1919 that JAMES WELDON JOHNSON, writer and later executive secretary of the NAACP, termed it "Red Summer." Briggs is perhaps best known for organizing the African Blood Brotherhood for African Liberation and Redemption (ABB) in response to this turmoil. The nationalist fraternity recruited men willing to arm themselves against racial violence, fostered pride in African ancestry, and promoted African American participation in a global anticapitalist struggle.

Briggs launched his own paper, the *Crusader*, in September 1918. The mission of the *Crusader* was to advance a movement to "help make the world safe for the Negro" (*Crusader*, Sept. 1918). In choosing these words, Briggs noted the irony of President Wilson calling World War I a war to make the world "safe for democracy" while African Americans still faced oppression on the home front. In early issues Briggs advocated self-pride and armed resistance, and after Red Summer he expressed increasingly anticapitalist and anti-imperialist opinions. His radical views led to a break with the *Amsterdam News* in 1919. From 1919 until the Tulsa race riot of 1921 the *Crusader* acted as the official organ of the Hamitic League of the World, a nationalist organization of which Briggs was a member. In the June 1921 issue he praised black residents who fought back against the white mobs, declared the *Crusader* the official organ of the ABB, and introduced the latter as an above-ground organization.

Dissatisfied with the platforms of mainstream politics, Briggs allied with the Communist Party. He saw communism as a means of ending racial oppression and in an October 1919 editorial wrote, "If to fight for one's rights is to be Bolshevist, then we are Bolshevists and let them make the most of it!" ("Bolshevist!!!" *Crusader*, Oct. 1919). Briggs's allegiance to racial nationalism and class-based communist revolution put him at odds with both African American and Communist Party leaders. His relationship with MARCUS GARVEY, founder of the United Negro Improvement Association, was particularly problematic. Briggs originally sought an alliance with Garvey as a fellow West Indian immigrant in favor of racial self-determination, but a conflict over Garvey's strict anticommunism and a feud over adherents left the men estranged.

The *Crusader* folded due to decreased funding and government anticommunist pressure in 1922, and the ABB disbanded in 1925. Undeterred, Briggs was at the forefront of African American and communist cooperation in the 1920s and helped spur increasing black membership in the Communist Party into the late 1930s. Nevertheless, he maintained his black nationalist views and in 1942 was expelled from the party for holding this line. Briggs is also significant as one of a cadre of West Indian immigrants who took leading roles in an era of post–World War I radicalism and were sometimes referred to as the New Negro movement. Perhaps due to his own international experience, he was a global thinker who garnered inspiration from such disparate sources as his Caribbean upbringing, African history, the Irish independence movement, and Soviet Communism.

Briggs migrated to California and worked as editor of the *California Eagle* from 1945 to 1949. He remained an outspoken radical and in 1958 was called before the House Un-American Activities Committee, where he angered representatives by refusing to offer any information about communism. Instead, he took the opportunity to criticize the slow pace of school desegregation efforts in the South. Briggs died in Los Angeles.

Further Reading

Blake, Gene. "Integration Issue Raised by Witness at Red Quiz," *Los Angeles Times*, 4 Sept. 1958.

Hill, Robert A., and Cyril V. Briggs. *The Crusader* (1987).

James, Winston. *Holding Aloft the Banner of Ethiopia: Caribbean Radicalism in Early Twentieth-Century America* (1998).

Kornweibel, Theodore, Jr. *"Seeing Red": Federal Campaigns against Black Militancy, 1919–1925* (1998).

Makalani, Minkah. "For the Liberation of Black People Everywhere: The African Blood Brotherhood, Black Radicalism, and Pan-African Liberation in the New Negro Movement, 1917–1936," PhD diss., University of Illinois at Urbana-Champaign (2004).

Solomon, Mark. *The Cry Was Unity: Communists and African Americans, 1919–1936* (1998).

AMBER MOULTON-WISEMAN

BRIGGS, Martha Bailey (21 Mar. 1838–28 Mar. 1889), educator and public school administrator, was born in New Bedford, Massachusetts, the only child of Fannie Bassett of Vineyard Haven, Martha's Vineyard, Massachusetts, and John Briggs of Tiverton, Rhode Island. Her parents were married in 1831. Brigg's mother died when she was a young girl, and as a result, she was raised by her father, with the help of an aunt, Mrs. Bailey. John had grown up poor, in a rural area where he was allowed to attend school only in the winter. At about age twelve, he came to the city of New Bedford to work for George Howland, a Quaker and a whaling ship agent. John stayed employed by the Howland family until his death, more than fifty years later. When his daughter was still an infant, John was fitting Howland's whaling ships, the

Java and *Golconda*, and he developed a friendship with another of Howland's workers, an escaped slaved and abolitionist named FREDERICK DOUGLASS. Though his own access to formal schooling was limited, he was known to be a well-read man of high intelligence. His commitment to education and to uplifting members of his race were traits that he passed on to his daughter.

After several years of private tutoring, when she was twelve-and-a-half years old (slightly younger than the required age thirteen), Martha began her studies at New Bedford High School in 1850. She finished with honors and is believed to be the first African American to graduate from the school. Shortly thereafter, she opened a private school for ten or twelve pupils at her father's home on Allen Street in New Bedford. She also offered evening lessons in reading and writing for fugitive and former slaves.

Briggs attended Boston Medical College from 1857 to 1859, with aspirations of becoming a nurse, but she later decided that she preferred teaching. She returned to teaching at private schools in southeastern Massachusetts, including one in Christiantown, Martha's Vineyard, as well as at public schools in Newport, Rhode Island. It is here that she served as governess to the children of GEORGE T. DOWNING, a wealthy African American restaurateur and hotel proprietor whose home was frequented by Frederick Douglass and other notable persons. Downing, an abolitionist and advocate for school desegregation, loaned a building in which Briggs and two other teachers taught school. While teaching in Newport, Briggs was recruited in 1859 by Myrtilla Miner, a white American educator, to teach at her Miner School, also known as the School for Colored Girls, in Washington, D.C. Briggs turned the offer down, reportedly because of her father's concern that with tensions increasing between the North and the South over slavery, Washington, D.C., would not be a safe place for his daughter.

By 1867 Briggs accepted a teaching position in Easton, Maryland, and two years later she applied to teach in the "colored" schools of Georgetown and Washington, D.C. She received an offer to teach in the public schools of Washington, D.C., and served as principal of Anthony Bowen during 1869–1873. She then accepted a position to teach at Howard University, which she did for six years, serving as head of the Normal Department, a department she helped to create during 1873–1879. (Normal schools, often the predecessors to modern-day teacher's colleges or schools of education, were institutions for training teachers and establishing teaching standards or norms.) Briggs left Howard University in 1879 to return to public schools as principal of the Miner Normal School, the same school for which Miner had tried to recruit her some twenty years earlier, and where Douglass served as a board member. She continued her work at the Miner Normal School for four years, graduating some eighty teachers (more than any teacher trainer at the time). Many of her graduates went on to teach for District of Columbia public schools.

Briggs left the Miner Normal School to return to Howard University in 1883, where she served as head of the Normal School until the time of her death. In addition to her administrative roles, Briggs taught French and mathematics, as was noted in Howard University's school catalogues and the Modern Language Association of America's annual conference in 1884–1985. She had been elected president of the Industrial Institute Association of Washington, D.C., an educational organization, and was a member of the Monday Night Literary Club.

Briggs died in Washington, D.C. The District of Columbia Certificate of Death cites the cause of death as a tumor. A memorial service was held on 14 May 1889 by the Bethel Historical and Literary Society, during which she was eulogized as an outstanding educator. Another memorial service was held at Howard University's Andrew Rankin Chapel, in which a tributary marble tablet was inserted into the wall. The tablet is inscribed, "Her works do follow her." She was returned to New Bedford for her burial.

Following her death, the District of Columbia Board of Education named two elementary school buildings in Washington, D.C., in her honor, most notably the Martha B. Briggs Building of the Briggs-Montgomery School. Both school buildings have since been demolished. The Martha Briggs Educational Club, Inc., a member of the National Association of Colored Women's Clubs, Inc., was founded in New Bedford in 1920, and Miner Teachers College (a predecessor of the University of the District of Columbia) celebrated Briggs's service as the third principal of Miner Normal School during its March 1934 Founder's Day program. Briggs is considered a pioneer in the field of teacher education and is regarded as a founder of both the Teachers College of Howard University and Miner Teachers College in Washington, D.C.

Further Reading

Cooke, Paul P. "Martha B. Briggs," in *Black Women in America: An Historical Encyclopedia*, ed. Darlene Clark Hine, Elsa Barkley Brown, and Rosalyn Terborg-Penn (1993).

Gregory, J. Francis. "Martha Bailey Briggs," *Journal of Negro History*, vol. 20, no. 2. (April 1935).

Iturralde, Lucilla Hiomara, and Adrienne Lash Jones. "Martha Bailey Briggs," in *Notable Black American Women, Book II*, ed. Jessie Carney Smith (1996).

Scruggs, Lawson Andrew. *Women of Distinction: Remarkable in Works and Invincible in Character* (1893).

Turner, Geneva C. "For Whom Is Your School Named?" Negro History Bulletin 22 (April 1959).

SIMONE MONIQUE BARNES

BRIMMER, Andrew Felton (13 Sept. 1926–), economist and educator, was born in Newelton, Louisiana, the fourth of five children of Andrew Brimmer Sr., a sharecropper and warehouse worker, and Vellar (Davis) Brimmer. The family abandoned farming when they found it impossible to make a decent living under the crop lien system, an economic arrangement in which farmers borrowed money at high interest rates to work land that they did not own in hopes of sharing profits that rarely materialized. His parents' efforts to escape debt and poverty were young Andrew's first exposure to economic forces and monetary policy.

As a child Andrew was bright and serious. In 1944 he graduated from Tensa Parish Training School, a segregated high school in St. Joseph, Louisiana. Brimmer joined the U.S. Army and served from May 1945 to November 1946, becoming a staff sergeant in the 645th Ordinance Ammunition Company in Hawaii. After the war, he took advantage of the G.I. Bill to enroll at the University of Washington in Seattle. Initially, he was interested in journalism and became an assistant editor of the *Seattle Dispatch* before a professor persuaded him that he might have a more promising career studying the role of money in society. Brimmer switched his major to economics, and when he earned his BA in 1950 he was awarded a John Hay Whitney Foundation fellowship. While continuing his graduate studies at the University of Washington he won a Fulbright Fellowship, which allowed him to study in India at the Delhi School of Economics at the University of Bombay.

After receiving his master's degree in 1951 Brimmer worked for the Wage Stabilization Board in Seattle before entering Harvard University in the fall of 1952. The following year he married Doris Millicent Scott, a graduate student at Radcliffe College. Eventually they would have one child, Esther Diane. From 1953 to 1954 Brimmer worked as a research assistant at the Center for International Studies at the Massachusetts Institute of Technology before getting a job at the Federal Reserve Bank of New York City. While there he took part in a fact-finding mission to the Sudan to determine the feasibility of establishing a central bank in that developing African nation. Brimmer was especially interested in the economic forces that affect poor communities in the United States and in the Third World—particularly the role that banks and insurance companies play in promoting or retarding growth. This became the focus of his dissertation, which earned him a PhD in 1957, and was the basis of several scholarly articles and a book, *Life Insurance Companies in the Capital Market* (1962).

Brimmer held his first academic post at Michigan State University, where he served as an assistant professor from 1958 to 1961. He then joined the Wharton School of Finance at the University of Pennsylvania from 1961 to 1963. In addition to his teaching responsibilities he was a consultant for the Securities Exchange Commission from 1962 to 1963. Brimmer joined the Kennedy Administration in 1963 as deputy assistant secretary to Richard Holton in the Department of Commerce in Washington, D.C. When the U.S. Supreme Court unanimously upheld the constitutionality of the 1964 Civil Rights Act, it cited Brimmer's testimony in its decision. The following year he was promoted to Assistant Secretary for Economic Affairs, and President Lyndon Johnson appointed him to a panel charged with investigating the 1965 Watts riots in Los Angeles, California.

Brimmer became the first African American to serve as a governor on the Federal Reserve Board in 1966, when President Johnson appointed him to a fourteen-year term. To ensure that Brimmer would be confirmed by the Senate, President Johnson invited Senator Russell Long of Louisiana, chair of the Senate Finance Committee, to the White House. Senator Long had been trying to get someone from Louisiana onto the Federal Reserve Board for some time, but when Johnson showed Long a picture of Brimmer, the senator responded, "When they all jump on me because I couldn't get one Louisianan on the FRB, I can say I did get one—a nigger" (Goodwin, Doris Kearns, *Lyndon Johnson and the American Dream* [1991], 186).

As one of the seven governors of the Federal Reserve Board, which exists to ensure the stability of the nation's monetary system, Brimmer supported moderately raising long-term interest rates in order to reduce the liquidity of capital and thereby act as a check on inflation, which had become a major fiscal concern of the 1960s and 1970s. In 1974 Brimmer resigned from the Federal Reserve Board to join the Harvard University Graduate School of Business Administration as the Thomas Henry Carroll Ford Foundation Visiting Professor. From this post Brimmer advised President Ford in 1974, that the best way for him to stimulate the economy and bring the nation out of recession was to cut personal income taxes by 10 percent. Congress implemented many of his recommendations as part of its $22.8 billion tax reduction plan in 1975.

In 1976 Brimmer returned to Washington, D.C., to establish his own economic consulting firm, Brimmer & Co., Inc. While in private practice he continued to write on public policy issues, including the oil crisis of the late 1970s and the looming problem of Third World debt, which often forced poor countries to choose between paying the interest on their loans to the International Monetary Fund or feeding and educating their people. In addition Brimmer maintained his membership in such professional organizations as the American Academy of Arts and Sciences, the Association for the Study of Afro-American Life and History (serving as president from 1970–1973 and again from 1989–1990), the Council of Foreign Relations, Tuskegee University Board of Trustees, the Brookings Institute, the Ford Foundation, the National Urban League, and the Chamber of Commerce of the United States

When EARL GRAVES invited him to join the economic board of *Black Enterprise*, the nation's largest black business magazine, Brimmer began to write a series of articles that assessed the economic health of black America, made strategic recommendations, and tracked investment in Africa. His columns were penetrating and hard-hitting, excoriating the often poor business skills of black businessmen in impoverished neighborhoods, imploring blacks to take better advantage of opportunities to improve their education and skills, and expressing little faith in most government programs. However, Brimmer's essays also exposed patterns of racial bias in banking that made it harder for black people to acquire credit and buy homes. He found that "even when blacks' incomes were well above average . . . they still had the highest rejection rate," causing him to conclude that "a major reason for the lending gap appears to be discrimination" (Brimmer, "The Cost of Bank Bias," *Black Enterprise* 12 [July 1992]: 43).

In 1986 Brimmer published *International Banking and Domestic Economic Policies: Perspectives in Debt and Development* (1986). His reputation for sound business advice had grown, and when the District of Columbia found itself facing bankruptcy and suffering a crisis in confidence under the leadership of Mayor MARION SHEPILOV BARRY JR., President Bill Clinton appointed Brimmer to lead a five-member control board to put the district's finances in order. This was the most controversial job of Brimmer's career. Instead of achieving statehood, which the district had demanded for years, district residents found that Congress had suspended their limited home rule until fiscal responsibility was restored. Although the board was empowered to approve all contracts and budgets, this placed it at odds with Mayor Barry and other elected officials in the district who felt that their authority was being usurped. Moreover, Brimmer was forced to institute painful austerity measures that involved thousands of proposed job cuts in order to reach a balanced budget.

Even ELEANOR HOLMES NORTON, who had initially celebrated Brimmer's appointment, found the board to be too secretive; others described Brimmer's management style as autocratic. By late 1995 Brimmer's relationship with Barry could only be described as poor. Nevertheless, when Brimmer informed FRANKLIN DELANO RAINES, President Clinton's budget director, of his decision to leave the control board in 1998, the district had accrued a surplus of $185 million and was projecting a $300 million surplus by the end of the fiscal year.

Brimmer spent the twilight of his illustrious and pathbreaking career consulting on economic matters, serving on charitable boards, and receiving over twenty-two honorary degrees. Though not autobiographical, Brimmer's published works are nevertheless the best presentation of his economic philosophy. They include: *International Banking and Domestic Economic Policies: Perspectives in Debt and Development* (1986), *Trends, Prospects, and Strategies for Black Economic Progress* (1985), and *Capital Shortage: Real or Imagined?* (1976).

Further Reading

Brimmer's personal papers have not yet been made available to the public. However, periodic reference to his public service can be found among various presidential papers: the Gerald R. Ford Library, Ann

Arbor, Michigan; "Stanley S. Scott" collection contains a few speeches by Brimmer; the Lyndon B. Johnson Library and Museum, at the University of Texas in Austin, Texas, holds papers relating to his appointment to the Federal Reserve Board and information on his role on the commission that investigated the Watts riots; and the William Jefferson Clinton Presidential Library, Little Rock Arkansas, has material on Brimmer's chairmanship of the D.C. control board.

Henneberger, Melinda. "Andrew Brimmer: Prideful Economist is Capital's Local Power Center," *New York Times*, 20 Aug. 1997.

SHOLOMO B. LEVY

BRISCOE, Neliska Ann "Baby" (7 Apr. 1914–25 Aug. 1994), dancer, jazz band leader, and businesswoman, was born in New Orleans, Louisiana, the daughter of Eddie Briscoe, a meatpacker, and Neliska Thomas, a cook and housekeeper born in Mexico. She had two half brothers and a sister who died young. Briscoe's career as an entertainer began early, at about the age of nine, when she performed in a club where her uncle, Escaliere Thomas, was employed part time in the evenings. Soon thereafter Briscoe acquired the nickname "Baby" (sometimes "Babe"), a moniker she retained in her entertainment career even as an adult.

Briscoe performed in New Orleans at the St. Bernard Alley Cabaret, known for its talented jazz band, as an acrobatic dancer in a floor show in which she was the sole child performer, accompanied there in the evenings by her mother after work. A natural on the stage, Briscoe continued to perform as a popular acrobatic dancer and singer in such New Orleans cabarets as the Astoria, Entertainers, and the Owl throughout her early teenage years, often mentioned in newspaper articles as a cabaret's main draw.

The development of jazz music and its historic roots in New Orleans has been well documented. However, the historian Sherrie Tucker noted that while "the musicians credited with bearing, rocking, and nurturing early New Orleans jazz are invariably men[,] . . . women *did* contribute . . . in many and significant ways. . . . They were instrumentalists, vocalists, dancers, and bandleaders" (Tucker, 68). Many of these women and the contributions they made to this uniquely American style of music have been forgotten or "miscast as *precursors* to jazz rather than essential participants in the birth of music" (Tucker, 68). Indeed there were opportunities enough for talented women of color in the many cabarets and nightclubs in New Orleans, and while the life of a performer was often difficult, the performance industry offered an exciting option to women who were otherwise usually limited to employment as a domestic, as was Briscoe's mother.

In February 1931, at age seventeen, the talented Briscoe moved to New York City to pursue a career as a dancer. She was employed at two clubs in the city, one of them Small's Paradise Club. Her time in New York may have ended prematurely when in late November 1931 she was one of two "coloured girls" caught in a gang shootout in a club and suffered a gunshot wound in the arm (*Louisiana Weekly*, 14 Dec. 1931). She was out of work for at least several weeks during her recovery period, and her subsequent activities until 1933 are unknown. In 1933 she returned to her native New Orleans to rise to such renown in the local jazz scene that she later gained the title "the Sweetheart of New Orleans."

In 1933 the pianist Joe Robichaux hired Briscoe to front his band, Robichaux's New Orleans Rhythm Boys, a group consisting at various times of up to fifteen members, including three women: Briscoe, Joan Lunceford, and Ann Cooper. Dressed in what became her trademark tuxedo, Briscoe worked as a tap dancer, entertaining the crowd in front of Robichaux's band during and between musical sets.

Briscoe worked with Robichaux for nearly five years before joining another group, the Harlem Playgirls, in early 1938. Based out of Minneapolis, Minnesota, this African American all-woman band toured the country to popular and critical acclaim, dubbed in club circles variously as "the World's Greatest Sepia Women's Orchestra" and "the American Woman's Foremost Expression in Music." From 1938 to 1940 Briscoe, in her tuxedo, fronted the band as it toured the country, playing at the famed Apollo Theater in New York on Thanksgiving Day in 1938 as well as at smaller venues in such locales as Frederick, Maryland; Cleveland, Ohio; Youngstown, Ohio; and Jackson, Tennessee. The Harlem Playgirls also made numerous appearances at the Tick Tock Tavern in New Orleans. By this time Briscoe was not just a "front" for the band but a true band leader.

Following her two-year tour with the Harlem Playgirls, Briscoe returned to New Orleans, where she met a merchant mariner named David "Val" Mouton. At the peak of her success Briscoe left her career in show business to marry Mouton in 1942. They had two daughters, Avon ("Vonnie") and Debra. Brisco, an energetic advocate for the right to vote, became a registered voter in New Orleans in 1948, unusual at the time for an African American woman. Briscoe divorced her husband in 1950 after enduring physical abuse and even gun threats at his hands.

After Briscoe's divorce she and her daughters lived with her mother on North Tonti Street in New Orleans, and Briscoe became a successful businesswoman. She became a cosmetologist, operated a gift boutique named Avon and Debra's Gift Shop after her daughters, owned a small restaurant, and worked as a seamstress, making ball gowns for Mardi Gras. The same energy that Briscoe applied to her stage show she applied to whatever she did in her private life.

In 1957 Briscoe married Clarence Casimire, whom she had known from her youth. The marriage ceremony was performed by Briscoe's half brother Joseph Mitchell at the Christian Mission Baptist Church he had cofounded in New Orleans. Shortly after their marriage the couple moved to Cleveland with Briscoe's daughters and Casimire's daughter from a previous marriage. Together they had one son. Despite her retirement from the stage, Briscoe never abandoned performing entirely. She took up the saxophone in her sixties, did splits on her seventy-fifth birthday, and danced on her eightieth birthday.

In 1994 Briscoe was hospitalized with bone cancer at St. Alexis Hospital. A nun at the hospital told one of Briscoe's daughters that Briscoe "had talked of being a famous dancer, . . . about wearing a satin tuxedo and conducting an orchestra. The nun added quickly that it was surely the morphine" (Mouton, 27).

Though she was undiscovered for many years, Briscoe's legacy has been reexamined, and through the research efforts of the historian and author Sherrie Tucker and the national park ranger Margie Ortiz, she has gained her rightful place among America's early jazz pioneers. In 2004 Briscoe was included in a feature exhibition celebrating the Women of Jazz at the National Historic Jazz Park in New Orleans.

Further Reading

The Hogan Jazz Archive Collection at Tulane University in New Orleans has information about Briscoe and her only known contemporary recording, singing "When the Sun Goes Down" with Robichaux's band at the Rhythm Club in New Orleans on 20 Mar. 1936. Although recorded by Decca (Master #60838), it was one of four Robichaux songs that were never released in record form to the public. Seventy years later, in 2006, Briscoe's version (a recording of this song with male vocals had been previously released) was made publicly available for the first time on the video *New Orleans Piano Players* by the Jazzology label of New Orleans.

Barker, Danny. *A Life in Jazz*, ed. Alyn Shipton (1986).

Mouton, Debra. "Baby Briscoe Plays the Majestic," *Northern Ohio Live* (Apr. 2004).

Tucker, Sherrie. "Rocking the Cradle of Jazz: These Are the Women Who Changed the Face of Music," *Ms.* (Winter 2004–2005).

GLENN ALLEN KNOBLOCK

BRISTOW, Lonnie Robert (6 Apr. 1930–), physician and organization president, was born in New York City, the son of Lonnie Harlis Bristow, a Baptist minister, and Vivian Wines, a nurse. At age ten Bristow was exposed to the medical profession by his mother, who was an emergency room nurse at Harlem's now defunct Sydenham Hospital. Bristow would observe the hospital staff from a distance while waiting to escort his mother to their apartment. She introduced him to the hospital's African American doctors, who became his role models as he came to believe that a career in medicine was something he could attain. Bristow graduated from the High School of Commerce in Manhattan and entered Morehouse College in Atlanta, Georgia, in 1947. There he became acquainted with fellow student MARTIN LUTHER KING JR.

Two years later Bristow signed up with the U.S. Navy and was on active duty until 1950. He enrolled

at the City College of New York, where he gained notoriety as the football team's quarterback. He graduated with a bachelor of science degree in 1953 and then went on to the New York University College of Medicine where he was awarded an MD in 1957. Bristow's first marriage to Margaret Jeter in 1957 ended in divorce. The couple had one daughter, Mary. In 1961 he married his office manager, Marilyn Hingslage, a union that produced a son, Robert, also a prominent physician, and a second daughter, Elizabeth.

Upon completing an internship at San Francisco City and County Hospital, Bristow was a resident in internal medicine at the U.S. Veterans Administration Hospital in San Francisco, from 1958 to 1960. He held corresponding positions at Francis Delafield Hospital (affiliated with Columbia University) in New York City in 1960 and the U.S. Veterans Administration Hospital in the Bronx in 1961. He returned to northern California to establish his private practice in 1964 and had staff privileges at Brookside Hospital in San Pablo. In 1969 he was elected president of the East Bay Society of Internal Medicine. That same year he managed the political campaigns of three pro-school busing candidates for the Richmond, California, school board. By the mid 1970s he was a fellow of the American College of Physicians and was on the Federated Council of Internal Medicine. In 1976 he headed the California Society of Internal Medicine. From 1979 to 1981 Bristow was a resident in occupational medicine at the University of California at San Francisco School of Medicine. After serving on a number of health and professional committees and commissions, in 1981 he ascended to the presidency of the American Society of Internal Medicine, the most important professional group related to his medical specialty.

Aside from his formidable personal attributes, commitment, and competence, Bristow's success in these predominantly white medical organizations was facilitated, in large part, by the agitation of black doctors pushing for their inclusion as respected, full-fledged members with something to contribute. Exclusion from the white-controlled medical profession and its organizational groups, particularly in the South, led African Americans to form their own groups starting in the late 1880s, most notably the National Medical Association, which was founded in 1895 as a result of the segregationist policy of the American Medical Association (AMA). The country's largest physicians' advocacy group, the AMA was founded in 1847 but only began (officially) accepting African American members in 1948. The AMA was also slow in adopting policies that would boost its black membership or amend its constitution to end racial discrimination in its constituent groups. From 1963 until 1968, when the AMA finally banned such discrimination, its annual meetings were picketed by protesters who were unable to join the national AMA because their regional and state AMA-affiliated organizations remained segregated.

Bristow had joined the AMA in 1957. His climb to the top of the AMA bureaucracy began when he was voted an alternate delegate to the AMA's House of Delegates in 1978. The following year he was placed on the AMA's Council of Medical Services, which he chaired from 1983 to 1985. From 1988 to 1990 he was president of the AMA's Education and Research Foundation. In 1985 he was elected to the fourteen-member Board of Trustees of the American Medical Association, becoming its first-ever African American member. From 1993 to 1994 he served as the board's chair. While on the board he was well known for backing the AMA's health-care reform proposal called Health Access America. Capitalizing on his national exposure and contacts, Bristow ran unopposed to become the AMA president-elect in 1994, representing 295,000 physicians.

As the AMA's first African American president, Bristow became the subject of numerous press stories, including a segment on the popular CBS television news show *60 Minutes*. Bristow downplayed his personal achievements and insisted that the fact that he was black and presiding over the nation's largest and most prestigious medical association should not be the defining legacy of his term in office on the House of Delegates. During his tenure as president he helped to refashion the AMA's public image by emphasizing its role as an agent for the common good. He refused to shy away from controversial positions and confronted the powerful tobacco industry and heath maintenance organizations (HMOs). He challenged the federal government to enact universal health care and advocated measures to expand health education and increase the production of minority race doctors and nurses.

Among the many honors Bristow received were the 1977 Award of Excellence from the California Committee for Political Action, the 1989 Contra Costa Humanitarian of the Year award, California Society of Internal Medicine Most Distinguished Internist award in 1990, and honorary doctorates from Morehouse College, City University of New York, and Wayne State University.

Bristow's speeches and articles on medical ethics and health-care reform were published in popular and scholarly periodicals, including *The Internist*, the *Journal of the American Medical Association*, and the *Annals of the New York Academy of Sciences*. Aside from his AMA duties, Bristow was actively involved in committee work and projects of the Center for Disease Control, the California Department of Prisons, the California Department for Health, the University of California at Berkeley, the Institute of Medicine, the National Council on Health Care Technology, and the Health Care Financing Administration.

In 1998 Bristow officially retired from private medical practice and continued to live in his home in Walnut Creek, California. In 2002 he was selected to chair the Institute of Medicine's Committee on Institutional and Policy-Level Strategies for Increasing the Diversity of the U.S. Health Care Workforce, for which he issued the report "In The Nation's Compelling Interest: Ensuring Diversity in the Health-Care Workforce," published in February 2004 by the National Academic Press.

Further Reading
Jones, Lisa C. "New American Medical Association President, Lonnie R. Bristow," *Ebony* (Aug. 1995).
Libman, Gary. "First Black on AMA Board Makes His Mark," *Los Angeles Times*, 12 Aug. 1985.
Sammons, Vivian O. *Blacks in Science and Medicine* (1990).

ROBERT FIKES JR.

BROADNAX, Wesley Jerome (17 Feb. 1970–), music educator and musician, was born in Marshall, Texas, the son of Maude Irene Jernigan, a home health-care provider, and Leon Broadnax Sr., a truck driver. Wesley Broadnax is the sixth of seven children, having five sisters and one brother. Broadnax began his musical pursuits at age twelve when he took his first trombone lesson. Throughout his middle school and high school years in the Marshall public schools he participated in every band-related program, including marching band (drum major), concert band, jazz band, and various small ensembles. Between 1983 and 1988 he was selected to the All-Area Bands and Orchestras and the All-Region Bands and Orchestras (for Region IV), and he received first division ("superior") medals in the Texas University Interscholastic League Solo and Ensemble Contests. In 1988 he was chosen as bass trombonist for the Texas All-State Symphony Orchestra. Later that year he graduated from Marshall High School, where he won the John Philip Sousa Award for Best Bandsman.

In fall 1988 Broadnax entered Stephen F. Austin State University (SFASU) in Nacogdoches, Texas, where he studied conducting with John L. Whitwell and trombone with William Young, J. Mark Thompson, and Nathaniel Brickens, a leading figure in trombone performance and pedagogy and a past president of the International Trombone Association. Broadnax was awarded the Mel Montgomery Band Scholarship all five years that he attended SFASU, and in 1990 he was selected to Pi Kappa Lambda, a national honorary fraternity for academic and musical achievement. In 1993 he earned a bachelor of music education degree and graduated with honors (magna cum laude).

In August 1993 Broadnax began his professional teaching career, serving for two years as band director for both Wylie Middle School (Wylie, Texas) and Paris High School (Paris, Texas). In fall 1995 he returned to college to pursue advanced studies in conducting at Michigan State University (MSU) in Lansing, where he resumed his work with Whitwell, who left SFASU in 1993 to become director of bands at MSU and who later received a Distinguished Faculty Award there for outstanding teaching. In addition Broadnax studied bass trombone with Curtis Olson and euphonium with Philip Sinder. Throughout his master's degree studies at MSU, Broadnax received the Leonard Falcone Scholarship. In spring 1997 he completed a master of music degree in Wind Conducting. The following fall he began doctoral coursework at MSU and was awarded the Kenneth G. Bloomquist Scholarship for graduate wind conducting. From 1998 to 2000 he was the recipient of a King/Parks/Chavez Future Fellowship. In spring 2000 he completed his dissertation, "The Chamber Music of Joseph Schwantner: How Text Influences Instrumental Music," and he was awarded a doctor of musical arts degree in Wind Conducting.

Shortly after graduation Broadnax became assistant director of bands at MSU, where he led the symphony band, concert band, chamber winds, and Musique 21 (a new music ensemble) and taught undergraduate and graduate courses in conducting and wind literature. He received numerous honors. In spring 2001 he was selected by Pierre Boulez to participate in his symposium on twentieth-century music at Carnegie Hall in New York City, in summer 2002 he was a conducting fellow under the mentorship of Frank Battisti at the world-renowned Tanglewood Music Festival, and in summer 2003 he was a minority scholar fellow at Indiana State University.

As an acclaimed advocate for new music, Broadnax conducted the premieres of works by many notable contemporary composers, including Paul Barsom, Jere Hutcheson, David Maslanka, Joel Puckett, Stephen Rush, Lawrence Singer, Michael Weinstein, Dana Wilson, and Davide Zannoni. He was a guest conductor and presented conducting seminars throughout the United States and a frequent adjudicator and clinician for various state and national band and orchestra festivals. His scholarly work focused on a published analysis of Dana Wilson's "The Avatar: Concerto for Bassoon and Chamber Orchestra" (*Journal of Band Research*, 2007) and in expanding his dissertation research into a book on the influence of text on the instrumental music of Joseph Schwantner.

In addition to his teaching responsibilities at MSU, Broadnax maintained an active performance schedule on bass trombone and euphonium with the West Shore Symphony (Muskegon, Michigan) as well as various appearances throughout Michigan with orchestras in Grand Rapids, Greater Lansing, Jackson, Kalamazoo, and Midland and chamber performances with the West Shore Symphony Brass Trio and the Capitol Brass Quintet (Lansing).

In August 2007 Broadnax left MSU to become an assistant professor of instrumental music education and director of bands at California State University at East Bay in Hayward, California.

DANIEL CHRISTOPHER JACOBSON

BROCK, Lou (18 June 1939–), baseball player, was born Louis Clark Brock in El Dorado, Arkansas, the son of a sharecropping family. When Lou was a child, his mother relocated to Collinston, Louisiana, where he grew up on a cotton plantation. A quiet and shy youth, Brock attended Union High School in Mer Rouge. Upon graduation he accepted an academic scholarship to Southern University in Baton Rouge. He chose to major in math for one simple reason: he had seen his family "duped" by plantation owners year in and year out, leaving the family deep in debt (Halberstam, 151). Despite hard work Brock lost his academic scholarship and turned to sports to stay in school, making the baseball team as a walk-on. He earned an athletic scholarship on the spot when he was given five practice swings in a batting session, three of which went for home runs.

Brock's career in baseball started slowly at Southern University. He broke out in his sophomore year when he hit .545 and sparked Southern to a victory in the National Association of Intercollegiate Athletics (NAIA) World Series, the first black school to win the title. Although major league scouts had paid Brock some attention, one scout in particular maintained a close relationship with him, the Chicago Cubs's JOHN "BUCK" O'NEIL. A renowned Negro League player and a great baseball mind, O'Neil saw in Brock the same skills that had made his friend JAMES "COOL PAPA" BELL one of the greatest players in the Negro Leagues. O'Neil also saw in Brock the same hunger for success as his earlier Cubs protégé, ERNIE BANKS. In 1960 Brock flew to St. Louis with the belief that he was scheduled for a meeting and tryout with the Cardinals organization. However, the meeting never materialized and Brock, low on money, took a bus to Chicago to stay with a friend. There Brock earned a living washing floors while trying to get a tryout with

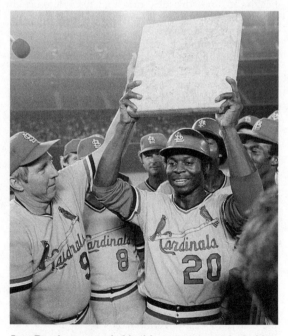

Lou Brock, surrounded by his teammates as he holds second base plate after breaking Ty Cobb's record of 892 stolen bases in San Diego, California, 29 August 1977. (AP Images.)

the two Chicago franchises, the White Sox and the Cubs. In 1961, after two workouts, the Chicago Cubs signed Lou Brock to a contract for $12,000 and paid him a $5,000 bonus.

Brock played one season of minor league ball for the Cubs before being brought up late in the 1961 season. However, his play the next two years at the big league level inspired little confidence among Cubs management. His inexperience and Chicago's unusual coaching system of revolving managers, each with his own ideas as to what Brock should or should not be doing, led to his slow development. By mid-1964, with a journeyman's average and just fifty stolen bases to his credit, the Cubs traded him to the St. Louis Cardinals for the pitcher Ernie Broglio, an eighteen-game winner in 1963. The "Brock for Broglio" deal then seemed like a steal for the Cubs, but has since gone down as one of the most lopsided trades in baseball history; while Broglio won just seven more games in his career, Lou Brock blossomed into a Hall of Famer.

Brock made his debut with the Cardinals on 15 June 1964 and ignited the team. When he joined the Cards they were in fourth place, but they ended the season by winning the National League pennant and subsequently defeating the New York Yankees to win the World Series. One of the keys to Brock's early success in St. Louis was the relaxed attitude of the Cardinals's clubhouse. More importantly, manager Johnny Keane recognized Brock's amazing speed and let him put it to good use. Early on, in a team meeting, Keane told Brock, "I want you to keep running. If I don't tell you to stop running, then no one else on this team does [sic] either, and if someone tries to stop you, then you can tell them where to go" (Halberstam, 141). Indeed, Brock's base-stealing abilities not only helped the Cardinals to win but also revolutionized baseball. His aggressive style of base-running often forced the opposition to make errors. Brock also popularized the "pop-up" style of stealing a base; not only did he go into a base cleats first and deal punishment to fielders but he was also up and on his feet in a hurry, ever-ready to take the next base if the opportunity arose. Brock's steals did not happen just by chance. He was an early proponent of using game film of opposing pitchers, studying their moves and tendencies from 8mm game film shot from the Cardinals dugout. Brock's base-stealing became legendary and he led the league in stolen bases from 1966 to 1969, and 1971 to 1974. In 1974 he shattered the single season record for stolen bases set by Maury Wills, stealing 118 bases. When he retired after the 1979 season Brock held the record for steals with 938. Though this record was eclipsed by RICKY HENDERSON in 1982, Brock remains second all-time in this category.

Not to be forgotten is Lou Brock's hitting ability. He batted over .300 in nine seasons and in 1967 became the first player ever to hit twenty-one home runs and steal over fifty bases in a season. In 1962 Brock hit one of only three home runs that ever went over the center-field wall at New York's Polo Grounds. His stellar career notwithstanding, Brock had his critics in the baseball world. Not a typical lead-off man, Brock struck out often and at his retirement was the career leader with 1,730 strikeouts. However, it was not with his bat and power that Lou Brock made history, but with his legs and his intelligence. He helped his team win the World Series in 1964 and 1968 and was a six-time All Star who was enshrined into the Baseball Hall of Fame in 1985, his first year of eligibility. Brock was also voted as one of the twentieth century's top one hundred players by Major League Baseball.

Following his retirement after the 1979 season Brock remained active both with the St. Louis Cardinals and with the local community. Operating a successful florist business and acting as spring training instructor for the Cardinals, Brock and his wife, Jacqueline, were also both ordained ministers and elders at the Abundant Life Fellowship Church and were well known for their scholarship programs and their work with disadvantaged young people in the St. Louis area.

Further Reading

Brock, Lou. *Biography*. Available online at http://www.loubrock.com.
Brock, Lou. *Stealing Is My Game* (1976).
Bucek, Jeanine, ed. *The Baseball Encyclopedia* (1996).
Halberstam, David. *October 1964* (1994).

GLENN ALLEN KNOBLOCK

BRONSON, James H. (ca. 1838–16 Mar. 1884), Civil War soldier and Medal of Honor recipient, was born in Burrell Township, Pennsylvania. Little is known about Bronson's life before the war except that he was a barber. Perhaps enthusiastic about getting a chance to fight for the Union cause, he journeyed from Pennsylvania to Delaware, Ohio, to enlist in the 127th Ohio Regiment on 4 July 1863. When he joined, James Bronson was in the vanguard of black service in the army; less than two months prior, the War Department had created the Bureau of Colored Troops. This military agency was created to aid in the establishment of black regiments and the enlistment of both black troops and the white officers who would command them. In some cases these regiments were raised entirely under the bureau's guidance. However, as was the case with Bronson's 127th Ohio Regiment, some were raised by individual states and were later incorporated into the Union army. Thus it was that the 127th Ohio would be redesignated in 1863 as the Fifth United States Colored Troop (USCT).

Most of the men in James Bronson's regiment came from Ohio and the surrounding states. Because Ohio was a major link in the Underground Railroad, a number of black soldiers in the 127th Ohio were former slaves, or the children of former slaves, and they made Ohio their home. Camp for the new recruits of the 127th Ohio was established at Delaware, near Columbus, and Colonel James Conine was chosen as its leader. His second in command was Lieutenant Colonel Giles Shurtleff, a graduate of Oberlin College who was sympathetic to the abolitionist movement. Because Conine would not join the regiment until it was sent southward, Shurtleff trained the new recruits, and he chose his company sergeants, including Bronson, MILTON MURRAY HOLLAND, ROBERT PINN, and POWHATTAN BEATTY. These men originally enlisted as privates but were likely promoted based on their aptitude and the respect they commanded among their fellow soldiers; sometimes company sergeants were chosen by vote among the soldiers they would lead. Bronson was not just a soldier; he also served as a musician in the regimental band.

The Fifth USCT departed for the war on 18 November 1863 and first served in Virginia, where Colonel Conine assumed command upon the regiment's arrival in Norfolk. In December the regiment was assigned to duty in North Carolina, where it remained until January 1864, when it returned to Virginia. The Fifth USCT saw little action until it was assigned to the Army of the James, an element of Grant's Union army operating in the James River area of Virginia in May 1864. Bronson and the men of the Fifth USCT saw their first combat during the siege of Petersburg, losing fourteen men during the Battle of the Crater on 30 July 1864. Afterward, the Fifth USCT continued with the Army of the James, stationed opposite the Confederate fortifications around Richmond near New Market Heights. In late September 1864 the Union general Ulysses S. Grant concocted a plan to take four key Confederate forts in the Richmond line by launching simultaneous attacks on both sides of the James River. The attacks would be conducted by a number of USCT units, including the Fifth Regiment. Perhaps fortuitously, the Fifth USCT underwent a command change on the eve of battle. With Colonel Conine injured, Lieutenant Colonel Shurtleff, the man responsible for training the men of the original 127th Ohio, now took command. While awaiting orders to attack, Shurtleff visited with his men and told them, "If you are brave the stigma of diminished pay must be removed and the greater stigma of denying you full and equal rights of citizenship shall also be swept away" (Mercer, 23). That was all the men of the Fifth USCT needed to hear.

The Battle of New Market Heights commenced in the early morning hours of 29 September 1864 and lasted two days. The outcome of the battle was a stalemate, and only one of the objectives was taken. It cost the Union 5,000 casualties, and out of 550 men, the Fifth USCT counted 85 dead and 257 wounded. However, the battle was one of historic proportions, for black soldiers fought with such valor and distinction that they achieved the only success of the battle. They captured Fort Harrison against overwhelming odds. The fighting was so fierce that many white officers, Shurtleff included, were shot down while storming Confederate fortifications, and the outcome of the fighting fell on the shoulders of sergeants who were now in positions of leadership. And lead they did, men like James Bronson, EDWARD RATCLIFF, CHRISTIAN ABRAHAM FLEETWOOD,

SAMUEL GILCHRIST, and three of Bronson's fellow regimental sergeants, Pinn, Holland, and Beatty. Indeed, the actions of USCT soldiers at New Market Heights were so inspired that sixteen men earned the Medal of Honor in the fighting. Two weeks following the battle, Major General Benjamin Butler was inspired to comment that "All these gallant colored soldiers were left in command, all their company officers being killed or wounded, and led them gallantly and meritoriously through the day. For these services they have most honorable mention, and the commanding general will cause a special metal to be struck in honor of these gallant colored soldiers" (Official Records, 168). In addition to receiving the Medal of Honor, Bronson and a number of other men also received the Butler Medal, specifically created by General Butler after this battle to honor those black soldiers who fought bravely and heroically at New Market Heights.

Following this battle, Sergeant James Bronson continued with the Fifth USCT, but with one change; perhaps tired of fighting, he asked that he be allowed to relinquish his rank of sergeant and return to his position in the regimental band. Bronson's request was granted, and he later served in 1864 at the Battle of Fair Oaks, the expeditions to capture Fort Fisher in December 1864–January 1865, and the capture of Wilmington, North Carolina, in 1865. It was possibly while stationed in North Carolina that James Bronson met and married his wife, Ellen, a native of that state. When he was discharged from the Fifth USCT on 20 September 1865 at Carolina City, North Carolina, Bronson's rank was listed as musician.

James Bronson would live for less than twenty years after the Civil War; he resided with his wife and worked as a barber in Salem Boro, Columbiana County, Ohio, for a time before moving back to his native Pennsylvania. At the time of his death at the approximate age of forty-five, Bronson was living near Pittsburgh in Carnegie, Pennsylvania, and he is buried in Chartiers Cemetery in that town.

Further Reading

Mercer, John. "Giles Waldo Shurtleff: Leadership in the Cause of Freedom," available online at http://www.oberlin.edu/external/EOG/shurtleffBio-Mercer.htm.

United States Government Printing Office. *The War of the Rebellion: A Compilation of the Official Records of the Union and Confederate Armies,* vol. 42, series I, part III (1893).

GLENN ALLEN KNOBLOCK

BROOKE, Edward (26 Oct. 1919–), lawyer and U.S. senator, was born Edward William Brooke III in Washington, D.C., to Edward Brooke Jr., an attorney for the Veterans Administration, and Helen Seldon. Growing up in an integrated middle-class neighborhood, Brooke readily absorbed his mother's instruction to respect others and treat all people equally. The Brookes lived relatively free from much of the racism endured by other African Americans. "We never felt hated," his mother recalled (Cutler, 14). Brooke attended Dunbar High School, an elite public school with many middle- and upper-class African American students and then went on to Howard University, where he became president of the school's chapter of the Alpha Phi Alpha fraternity and earned his bachelor's degree in 1941. Following the bombing of Pearl Harbor later that year, Brooke was drafted into an all-black combat unit in the army. He served in many roles, including as a defender of those who had been court-martialed. His tour of duty during World War II took him to Africa and to Italy, and he earned a Bronze Star for leading an attack on a military battery. While in Italy he met his wife, Remigia Ferrair-Scacco, who had served in the underground resistance against the Nazis. The couple married in 1947 and later had two daughters.

Brooke enrolled in law school at Boston University in 1946. He became editor of the law review during his final year of school and went on to earn LLB and LLM degrees. Brooke then practiced law in the Roxbury area of Boston, where he witnessed firsthand the problems African Americans faced regarding housing, education, employment, and health care. At the same time, he worked as legal counsel for the local chapter of the NAACP and served on the board of directors of the Greater Boston Urban League. He lobbied the state legislature for the elimination of segregation in the state's National Guard units and worked on an appeal to the U.S. Supreme Court to outlaw segregation in railroad dining cars. Brooke was also very active in the AMVETS, an organization for World War II veterans, and in 1956 he served as the National Judge Advocate for the group.

In 1950 Brooke's friends persuaded him to run for the state legislature. A Republican in a heavily Demo-

Edward Brooke, at his office in Boston, Massachusetts, 22 January 1964. (AP Images.)

cratic state, he lost the election and vowed never to run for office again, in part because his wife was upset over campaign talk about their mixed marriage. He nonetheless ran for the legislature two years later but lost again. Brooke narrowly lost another election in 1960, this time for secretary of state for Massachusetts. Although he had failed in his quest for political office, Brooke won the respect of numerous leaders in the state's Republican Party and soon accepted an appointment to the Boston Finance Commission. He quickly earned a reputation as a tough crime fighter as he exposed corruption in several city agencies, including the police department.

In 1962 Brooke was elected as Massachusetts attorney general, becoming the first African American ever to win such a statewide position. He first won a difficult primary battle, overcoming strong objections from Republican leaders concerning his liberalism and inexperience, and then went on to win the general election by appealing to white voters on the strength of his personal charm and his record with the Boston Finance Commission. As would be the case throughout his career, Brooke resisted attempts to label him a "black" politician. He commented, "I'm the lawyer for the five million citizens of Massachusetts, not for its . . . Negroes" (Cutler, 117). He did not ignore racial matters, however. While in office Brooke filed a brief in support of a fair housing law and helped draft legislation to forbid employment discrimination by businesses and unions. A firm believer in gradual change through legal means, he clashed with civil rights leaders over their plans to have students boycott school for a day, which would have violated the state's truancy laws, to protest de facto segregation in Boston.

Brooke's triumph as an African American in an overwhelmingly white state propelled him into national Republican debates in 1964. Like other liberal Republicans, Brooke grew alarmed at the conservative movement's efforts to nominate the Arizona senator Barry Goldwater, who had voted against the 1964 Civil Rights Act, as the party's presidential candidate that year. Attending the Republican convention in San Francisco, Brooke urged the party to adopt a strong civil rights plank and seconded the nomination of Governor William Scranton of Pennsylvania, a more moderate candidate on race and other issues, for president. Goldwater withstood the Scranton challenge, and Brooke, like several other northeastern liberals, refused to support the Arizonan that fall. Although Goldwater suffered a crushing defeat in November, Brooke was overwhelmingly reelected as Massachusetts attorney general.

Two years later Brooke won election to the U.S. Senate. The victory marked him as the first black senator since Reconstruction and as the first African American to win a Senate seat by popular vote. As conservatives gained influence within the Republican Party nationally, Brooke continued to support many of President Lyndon Johnson's social-welfare Great Society programs. Brooke even attacked Johnson on occasion for doing too little to combat poverty, and in 1966 he published his views on racial and economic problems facing black Americans in *The Challenge of Change*. He also became deeply involved in debates over the future of the Republican Party. Although he once again refused to make his race an issue, Brooke urged the party to broaden its appeal beyond white, middle-class suburbanites by reaching out to African Americans and other minorities. Many political pundits saw him as a leader who could bring at least some of the black vote back to the party of Abraham Lincoln. Soon after his election, there was speculation among some Republicans, as well as in the media, that Brooke would make an excellent choice for the Republican vice-presidential nomination in 1968.

Brooke was at the center of debates over the racial violence of the mid- and late 1960s. Following enormously destructive riots in the summer of 1967 in Newark, New Jersey, and Detroit, Michigan, President Johnson chose Brooke to serve on his Advisory Commission on Civil Disorders (also known as the Kerner Commission). Brooke toured several riot-torn areas and firmly rejected conservative claims that the riots were the result of communist influence or a conspiracy among radical black leaders. Instead, he insisted that the riots stemmed from social and economic problems related to jobs, housing, education, and health care. At the same time, Brooke held to his beliefs in integration and peaceful change. He worried that the media gave too much attention to more radical black leaders, such as STOKELY CARMICHAEL, and he rejected Black Power, calling it "a turn in the wrong direction" (Cutler, 197). In 1968 Brooke worked closely with Senator Walter Mondale of Minnesota, a liberal Democrat, on behalf of the Fair Housing Act.

During the late 1960s and early 1970s Brooke regularly criticized Richard Nixon's civil rights policies. He blasted the president for his early approach to school desegregation in the South and for not following through on his promise to promote economic development in the inner cities through "black capitalism." Worried that Nixon was too eager to appeal to white southerners and suburbanites, Brooke played a prominent role in successful efforts to defeat Nixon's nominations of the conservatives Clement Haynsworth and G. Harrold Carswell to the Supreme Court. He also opposed the nomination of William H. Rehnquist out of concern about his right-wing views on civil rights, though the Senate confirmed Rehnquist.

Brooke won reelection in 1972 but lost six years later, in part because of press revelations that he had lied about his personal finances in a deposition related to his divorce that year from his wife. Brooke was never charged with any crime, however, and the Senate Ethics Committee absolved him of any wrongdoing. In 1979 he became head of the National Low-Income Housing Coalition, resumed practicing law in Virginia, and married Anne Fleming. The couple had one son, Edward W. Brooke IV. In 2002 Brooke underwent successful surgery for breast can-

cer, and subsequently launched an effort to alert men to the dangers of this relatively rare disease among men. A recipient of the NAACP's Spingarn Medal for black achievement in 1967, and the Presidental Medal of Freedom in 2004, Brooke symbolizes the post–World War II rise of African Americans to prominent political positions, as well as his generation's faith in integration and working through established political and legal channels to achieve change.

Further Reading

Edward Brooke's papers are in the Library of Congress, Washington, D.C.

Brooke, Edward. *Bridging the Divide: My Life* (2006).

Cutler, John. *Ed Brooke: Biography of a Senator* (1972).

TIMOTHY N. THURBER

BROOKS, Carolyn Branch (8 July 1946–), academic dean and scientist, was born Carolyn Daphne Branch in Richmond, Virginia, the second of two daughters born to Shirley Marian Booker Branch and Charles Walker Branch, owners of a grocery store. Shirley Branch earlier held a job at an antique store, while Charles Branch's early job was as a truck driver. Shirley later worked for the Virginia Department of Motor Vehicles. Carolyn's sister Delores was born in 1942, and both children attended segregated public schools in Richmond, Virginia, where Carolyn graduated from Maggie Walker High School as salutatorian. Branch excelled in academics and was encouraged to pursue a college education. With the aid of her teachers, she sought college scholarships because her supportive parents were unable to afford college tuition. Branch, a first-generation college student, chose Tuskegee University after being offered a choice of six scholarships to attend a historically black college or university (HBCU).

Her freshman year, she met her husband, Henry M. Brooks, a senior at Tuskegee, and they married in 1965 during her sophomore year. Brooks had one son, Charles, during her junior year, and another, Marcellus, during her senior year. Despite her busy family life, Brooks completed her BS in Biology in four years, graduating in 1968. Brooks also earned an MS in Biology in 1971 from Tuskegee, where she was mentored by Dr. Howard P. Carter and worked as an undergraduate research assistant and a graduate teaching assistant. Brooks gave birth to a daughter, Alexis, while working on her MS. During this time Brooks developed a keen interest in teaching and research and decided to pursue a PhD and become a college professor.

During her doctoral studies at Ohio State University, she found the social climate much different from that at Tuskegee. While her mentor, Dr. Julius Kreier, was strongly supportive, at an institution with very few African American students, she had to overcome hurdles related to racism. She became an activist to increase minority recruitment and retention in science, and she became a dedicated mentor of students. She persisted in her work with the support and encouragement of her husband. It was during this time that Brooks gave birth to Toni, her second daughter. She received a PhD in Microbiology in 1977, and later in her career she took continuing education courses in molecular biology at Indiana University, University of Minnesota, University of Maryland (Center of Agricultural Biotechnology of MBI), and University of Wisconsin (La Crosse campus).

After she completed her PhD, Brooks pursued her career at HBCUs and advanced steadily upward through the academic ranks. Brooks began as a principal investigator and progressed to acting program director at Kentucky State University (1977–1981). From 1981 to 2007 she worked at the University of Maryland Eastern Shore (UMES). At UMES she began as research assistant professor on USDA-funded research projects. Brooks progressed in various administrative roles until 1995 when she became dean of the School of Agricultural and Natural Sciences, and she subsequently became the research director. In 1997 she was named executive assistant to both the president and the chief of staff at UMES while still holding the positions of dean and research director.

Brooks gained a reputation for her work at HBCUs and the black land grant colleges. At UMES she won recognition for her work in increasing minority participation in the sciences, especially microbiology. She significantly improved the experiences of minority students in the sciences through winning external and university grants, establishing a state-of-the-art research lab, recruiting high school students, working with high school counselors, creating precollege summer programs and the Scientific Enrichment Program for Minority Students, and instituting a graduate education bridge program.

Brooks's three-decade career in higher education was marked with accomplishment in teaching, research, administration, and service. Not only did she become a full professor but she became dean of the School of Agricultural and Natural Sciences at the University of Maryland Eastern Shore and research director of land grant programs. She increased science participation by African American students at Kentucky State University and at the University of Maryland Eastern Shore, and she directed the United States Department of Education–funded Scientific Enrichment Program. In 1998 she became the program codirector of the LOUIS STOKES Alliance for Minority Participation in the Sciences grant, funded by the National Science Foundation, and she remained a passionate mentor. Awards related to her work with students include the Outstanding Educator Award from the Maryland Association for Higher Education (1990), student awards for her dedication and devotion (1989 and 1996), and Advisor of the Year (1995).

Brooks's list of honors and awards includes the 2007 WILLIAM A. HINTON Research Training Award from the American Society for Microbiology. She was also named one of the 2007 recipients of Maryland's Top 100 Women awards and was a recipient of the first annual White House Initiative for Historically Black Colleges and Universities Faculty Award for Excellence in Science and Technology (1988).

Further Reading
The American Academy of Microbiology of the American Society for Microbiology. "William A. Hinton Research Training Award," *Microbe* 2, no. 2 (Feb. 2007).
Kessler, James H., et al. *Distinguished African American Scientists of the 20th Century* (1996).
Maryland's Business and Legal News since 1888, vol. 118, 127 (2 Mar. 2007).

TERRI L. NORRIS

BROOKS, Elizabeth Carter (1867–1951), educator, social activist, and clubwoman, was born in New Bedford, Massachusetts. She was the daughter of a freed slave, Martha D. Webb, who had been sent north to be educated. Her father is unknown.

Elizabeth Carter began her formal education in the New Bedford public school system, where she attended New Bedford High School, the Swain School of Design, and, later, the Harrington Normal Training School. While attending the Harrington Normal Training School for Teachers, Carter started planning a home for the aged. In 1897, true to her convictions as a social activist, she opened the New Bedford Home for the Aged under her direction and financial support. The home welcomed anyone, regardless of race. Carter continued supporting the institution throughout her life, dedicating her time and experience and providing financial support.

Carter was a diligent, committed, and compassionate student, destined to leadership. After finishing high school, Carter journeyed to Brooklyn, New York, where in the 1880s she accepted a teaching position at the Howard Colored Orphanage. During this period she became involved in civic and club activities, which would play an integral role in formulating her perception of the social injustices suffered by African Americans, particularly African American women and girls, and her desire to achieve social equality.

While at the Howard Colored Orphanage, Carter became active in club work. She acquired a wealth of knowledge about administrative functions which helped propel her into leadership positions in several social activist clubs that were designed to improve the lives of African American women, both married and single, while eventually extending assistance to young African American girls.

These social clubs sought to demonstrate that African American women were intelligent and responsible, and that they should be allowed to fill social leadership roles and exercise all the rights and privileges of citizenship. Many educated, middle-class African American women felt it was part of their civic duty to elevate the "uneducated, less fortunate female members of her race"(Davis). Carter joined an elite group of her contemporaries, such as MARY ELIZA CHURCH TERRELL, JOSEPHINE SILONE YATES,

MARGARET MURRAY WASHINGTON, IDA B. WELLS-BARNETT, Lucy Thurman, and MARY MCLEOD BETHUNE, all of whom sought to expand the realm of activities for African American women.

While working as a teacher in Brooklyn, Carter became the first recording secretary for the National Federation of Afro-American Women, which had been formed as a direct result of the First National Conference of Colored Women of America held in Boston in 1895. Through her club work and activities, Carter was instrumental in forming and co-founding the Northeastern Federation of Colored Women's Clubs, later serving as recording secretary and president. Her experience especially in this latter role would prove most beneficial in improving the administrative functions of the National Association of Colored Women and its affiliates across the country. From 1899 to 1904, she served as a recording secretary for the National Association of Colored Women and from 1904 to 1906 she served as its first recording secretary. In 1906 Carter was appointed vice president-at-large, relinquishing this post only when elected as the association's fourth president, holding the office from 1908 to 1912.

During her tenure as president of the National Association of Colored Women, Carter traveled to affiliate clubs across the nation, reviewing and helping to improve their organizational structures. Her diligence and skill resulted in standard organizational procedures for all associate clubs, improvements in financial recording, and the creation of an annual scholarship program for one extraordinary young black female to attend the Educational and Industrial Training School in Daytona, Florida (later Bethune-Cookman College).

After completing her training as a teacher at the Harrington Normal Training School, she became the first African American to graduate from this institution and be appointed to a teaching position in the New Bedford public school system. However, with the outbreak of World War I, the War Work Council summoned her to plan and supervise the erection of the new Phillis Wheatley Building at Rhode Island Avenue and Ninth Streets, N.W., Washington, D.C. After completing this building project Carter returned to teaching until her retirement from the New Bedford public school system, after twenty-nine years of dedicated service.

In 1930 Carter married W. Simpson Brooks, bishop of the African Methodist Episcopal (AME) Church in Texas. The couple returned to Texas, where they built a thriving ministry until his death in 1934. On 14 June 1934 Elizabeth Brooks received an honorary law degree from Wilberforce University in Ohio. Returning to New Bedford, she remained active in missionary and civil rights work. In 1951 she was stricken with a cerebral hemorrhage and taken to St. Luke's Hospital, where she died. For her dedication to advancing education for African Americans, her commitment to caring for the elderly, and her steadfast fight for social equality and justice, the city of New Bedford named an elementary school in her honor, the Elizabeth Carter Brooks School.

Further Reading
Afro-American (Baltimore), 14 Apr. 1926.
Dannett, Sylvia G. L. *Profiles of Negro Womanhood*, vol. 1 (1964).
Davis, Elizabeth Lindsay. *Lifting as They Climb* (1933).
"Elizabeth Carter Brooks," in *Notable Black American Women*, book 1 (1992).
New Bedford Standard Times, 20 June 1948; 13 July 1951.

JANET E. MOORMAN

BROOKS, Gwendolyn (7 June 1917–3 Dec. 2000), poet and novelist, was born Gwendolyn Elizabeth Brooks at her grandmother's home in Topeka, Kansas, the daughter of David Anderson Brooks, a janitor, and Keziah Wims Brooks. When she was two months old, the family settled in Chicago, where she would live the rest of her life. Brooks and her brother had a sheltered upbringing in a cheerful, orderly household. (She would later draw on memories of those years for her poem "a song in the front yard" [1945].) At Forrestville Elementary School, where she learned that light skin and fine hair were valued, this shy child with dark skin and coarse hair felt socially isolated. Her mother, however, encouraged her interest in writing, and Brooks published her first poem in *American Childhood* magazine in 1930.

Later, to escape further isolation at a mostly white high school, she transferred to an all-black school; finally, at the somewhat more integrated Englewood High School, she found a peer group and teachers who encouraged her writing. From then on, she was constantly publishing—in national periodicals and regularly in Chicago's African American newspaper, the *Defender*. With her mother's encouragement, she showed her work to the poets JAMES WELDON JOHNSON, whom she found cold and distant, and LANGSTON HUGHES, with whom she established a long friendship.

Her family struggled financially during the Great Depression, but the year she finished high school Wilson Junior College opened with a low tuition that made it possible for her to earn an associate's degree. After college Brooks endured a series of dead-end jobs, including a humiliating position as a domestic; she later fictionalized that experience in her poem "Bronzeville Woman in a Red Hat" and in a chapter of her novel *Maud Martha*. She also worked several months for a charlatan spiritual healer operating out of the Mecca Building, a once fashionable apartment building that had decayed into a tenement; her experiences therein would later become the basis of her long narrative poem "In the Mecca." Active in the Youth Council of the NAACP, she cofounded a club for young black artists and writers. Through the NAACP, she met fellow poet Henry Blakely, whom she married in 1939; they had two children. Blakely died in 1996.

Gwendolyn Brooks, sitting in the Poet Room of the Library of Congress in Washington, D.C., March 1986. (AP Images.)

Brooks's mature style developed after 1941, when she and her husband joined a South Side poetry workshop run by the white socialite Inez Cunningham Stark. Brooks credited Stark with introducing her to the artistic possibilities available in poetic form and forcing her to submit her work to more rigorous aesthetic judgment. She began winning poetry contests, and book publishers encouraged her to develop more poems about African American life. The title of her first book, *A Street in Bronzeville* (1945), refers to the *Defender*'s name for the African American section of Chicago. The book includes some of her most admired poems, such as "The Sundays of Satin-Legs Smith," a portrait of a Bronzeville dandy; "The Mother," a bold and compassionate poem about abortion; and two poems that present African American perspectives on World War II, "Negro Hero" and "Gay Chaps at the Bar."

Working on poetry, fiction, and book reviews while her son attended school, Brooks wrote *Annie Allen* (1949), which loosely follows the life of the title character, an intelligent, sensitive African American woman. The centerpiece is the poem "The Anniad"; the title alludes to Virgil's ancient epic the *Aeneid*, and the language strives for Virgilian complexity, suggesting

the extraordinary heroism and ingenuity it takes to get through an ordinary life. For that book she became the first African American to receive a Pulitzer Prize.

Ironically, as Brooks was receiving high literary honors, her family was having trouble finding suitable housing. The tiny apartments they lived in are described in many of her poems. Housing for African Americans in Chicago was then limited to one area on the South Side; it had expanded very little over the decades, while its population had increased, nearly doubling in the 1940s. Part of her motivation for writing a novel, therefore, was to earn enough of an advance to be able to put a down payment on a house. The resulting autobiographical novel, *Maud Martha* (1953), is now considered a classic of African American literature, with its intimate, affectionate, and sometimes infuriated view of urban African American life in mid-century, before the rise of the civil rights movement. It portrays, through a series of lyrical scenes and frequent linguistic play, the childhood and young adulthood of an African American woman in Chicago.

Brooks's next collection, *The Bean Eaters* (1960), took an explicitly political turn with such poems as "The Ballad of Rudolph Reed," about the tragic result of a black family's move into a white neighborhood. Her most popular and most often reprinted poem, "We Real Cool," in eight short, infectiously rhythmic lines, introduces seven dropouts bragging about their wild lives despite their expectation of early death. She came to consider this poem her most successful combination of artistry with popular appeal, since, with its clarity and catchiness as well as its frequent inclusion in anthologies, it has spoken to an unusually broad audience.

In 1963 Brooks was offered a teaching position at Chicago's Columbia College. Throughout the 1960s and 1970s she would go on to teach also at Elmhurst College, Northeastern Illinois University, and the University of Wisconsin at Madison, among other schools. Brooks identified 1967 as the turning point in her career. Attending a Black Writers Conference at Fisk University, she was impressed by the contrast between the formal respect for her and the enthusiasm for the more radical AMIRI BARAKA. That striking contrast indicated to her a shift in African American culture from liberal integrationism toward a more militant black nationalism. Returning home, she was asked by the writer and community organizer Walter Bradford to lead a workshop for some members of the Blackstone Rangers street gang who were interested in writing. Although she eventually turned that workshop over to Bradford, she started meeting with black college students (including Don L. Lee [later Haki R. Madhubuti] and Carolyn Rodgers) for workshops in her home. Both these groups resisted Brooks's attempts to teach traditional poetic forms and high cultural aesthetics, insisting rather on a populist aesthetic in tune with their radical politics.

Also in 1967 Brooks read at the dedication of a mural depicting African American cultural heroes, including herself. Afterward, some of her workshop students led her into a local bar, where they gave an impromptu poetry reading, much to the appreciation of the patrons. The literary ambitions of the gang members and the warm reception of the tavern customers opened Brooks's eyes to an audience she had neglected. The events of that year initiated her commitment to the Black Power movement and black cultural nationalism, as well as to the Black Arts Movement, which in the late 1960s and early 1970s encouraged black artists and writers to reject European-derived aesthetics and the production of works for white audiences in favor of African and African American themes and forms for a specifically African American audience.

In 1968 she succeeded Carl Sandburg as poet laureate of Illinois, and, using her own funds, she established an award for young writers in the state. That same year Harper and Row, Brooks's publisher since 1945, brought out the collection *In the Mecca*, which includes her narrative poem set in the Mecca Building, as a tribute to martyred heroes such as MALCOLM X and MEDGAR EVERS, and a sequence of poems about the Blackstone Rangers. Starting with *Riot* (1969), she published new work only with black presses. DUDLEY RANDALL's small but influential Broadside Press in Detroit began publishing chapbooks of her new poetry, two anthologies she edited, and her unconventional autobiography *Report from Part One* (1972). Rather than providing a straightforward narrative of her life, the latter volume offers a collage of anecdotes, comments on her own and others' writing, interviews, photographs, and commentary on her work by other writers. She would publish other chapbooks and the collection *To Disembark* (1981) through Madhubuti's Third World Press and her own imprints.

In 1969 she and her husband separated, and she felt a renewed sense of freedom. She traveled on her own to East Africa, an experience that influenced her sense of American blacks as Africans in the New World. It was during this period that she wrote the first volume of her autobiography and began editing an annual periodical, *The Black Position* (1971–1974). Her mother, however, encouraged Brooks and her husband to reconcile, which they did in 1973; in part to celebrate that reunion, they traveled together to Ghana.

In 1976 Brooks became the first black woman elected to the National Institute of Arts and Letters. She was appointed poetry consultant to the Library of Congress in 1985. By this point, however, much of her early work, except for *Selected Poems* (1963), was out of print, so she self-published her collected works, *Blacks* (1987). Over the years, she received numerous awards, including over fifty honorary doctorates. She died in Chicago.

With passion, clarity, and rich literary craft, Brooks's writings present and comment on urban African American life in the mid- to late twentieth century. As the struggle for racial justice heated up, she became a more overtly political public figure. She was the most prestigious African American poet of her generation, so her conversion in the late 1960s to a radical black politics was an important endorsement of that position. Her decision to publish only with black presses restricted the audience for her later work, but it made concrete her commitment to African American readers and cultural institutions. She successfully married political engagement with the highest quality of artistry and in the latter part of her career sought to present poetry as a cultural practice available to everyone, not just the literary elite. A major figure in American poetry, she used her personal prestige to support and inspire young black writers and to establish publishing institutions that would serve the specific cultural interests of African Americans.

Further Reading
Brooks's papers are at the Bancroft Library, University of California, Berkeley.
Brooks, Gwendolyn. *Report from Part One* (1972).
Brooks, Gwendolyn. *Report from Part Two* (1996).
Bodlen, B. J. *Urban Rage in Bronzeville: Social Commentary in the Poetry of Gwendolyn Brooks* (1998).
Kent, George E. *A Life of Gwendolyn Brooks* (1990).
Melhem, D. H. *Gwendolyn Brooks: Poetry and the Heroic Voice* (1987).
Mootry, Maria K., and Gary Smith, eds. *A Life Distilled: Gwendolyn Brooks, Her Poetry and Fiction* (1987).
Wright, Stephen Caldwell, ed. *On Gwendolyn Brooks: Reliant Contemplation* (1996).
Obituary: *New York Times*, 4 Dec. 2000.

JAMES D. SULLIVAN

BROOKS, Owen (18 Nov. 1928–), civil rights activist, was born Owen Herman Brooks in New York City to West Indian immigrant parents, but was raised by an aunt and uncle in Boston, Massachusetts. His family was conscious of its West Indian identity, and as the civil rights movement developed Brooks also became conscious of his blackness. He joined Boston's NAACP Youth Council in 1942. Attracted to left-wing politics, he became involved in the Progressive Party and Henry Wallace's unsuccessful presidential campaign in 1948. In September 1948 Brooks picketed a Selective Service office in protest against registration for conscription. Drafted into the army in March 1951, he served in the Korean War and spent a year in Savannah, Georgia, witnessing the South's racial problems firsthand.

After leaving the army Brooks returned to Boston, where he earned a degree in electrical engineering from Northeastern University. He met MARTIN LUTHER KING JR., then a doctoral student at Boston University, and also heard MALCOLM X speak in Boston. Though a number of his friends were members of the Nation of Islam, he remained an Episcopalian, like his parents, and an associate in the church. A serious car accident in 1962 put Brooks in the hospital for several months just as the direct-action phase of the civil rights movement was gaining momentum. After his recovery Brooks participated in the March on Washington in August 1963. He also helped organize support for the Student Nonviolent Coordinating Committee (SNCC) in Boston and met FANNIE LOU HAMER, an SNCC worker from the Mississippi Delta, when she came north on an SNCC fund-raising tour.

Brooks's white former pastor, Warren McKenna, spent the summer of 1964 in Mississippi as resident director of the National Council of Churches' (NCC) minister orientation program, which trained clergy volunteers to assist the Mississippi Summer Project. After the project ended McKenna stayed in Mississippi to work for the NCC's Delta Ministry (DM), which in September 1964 began a ten-year program of relief, literacy, voter registration, economic development, and community mobilization primarily in the Delta but with other projects in Hattiesburg and McComb. McKenna tried to recruit Brooks for the DM, which at first had only one African American staff member, but work commitments prevented him from joining until May 1965. In June 1965 Brooks became the DM's project director for Bolivar County, where he worked in voter registration and with the fledgling Mississippi Freedom Labor Union (MFLU), which organized low-paid agricultural workers in an unsuccessful Delta strike for higher wages and union recognition.

In January 1966 Brooks participated in the occupation of the unused Greenville Air Force Base by one hundred civil rights activists, MFLU members, and other displaced plantation workers in an attempt to pressure the state and federal governments to address the Delta poor's economic problems. Although 150 air police forcibly evicted the group and the occupation had no long-term effect, it did help to break logjams in implementing an emergency federal surplus food program in Mississippi and re-funding a federal Head Start program run by the Child Development Group of Mississippi. In June 1966 Brooks helped plan the strategy of the Meredith March, which the leaders of the Southern Christian Leadership Conference, the Congress of Racial Equality, and SNCC undertook to complete after JAMES HOWARD MEREDITH, who had begun a lone "March against Fear" from Memphis to Jackson, Mississippi, was shot and temporarily hospitalized on the second day of his march. Brooks successfully encouraged the civil rights leaders to route the Meredith March through the Delta and also to create a voter registration program in adjoining counties.

Brooks became the DM's acting director in September 1966 and director two years later. He inherited and maintained a DM commitment to create a model agricultural and industrial cooperative for unemployed agricultural families at Wayside, Washington County, called Freedom City. Although its residents built twenty of the projected fifty houses, the experimental community failed to become self-sustaining and consumed much of the DM's staff time and budget. Brooks concentrated his efforts on raising federal loans and foundation and church grants to try to create jobs and modernize the infra-

structure of Mound Bayou, an all–African American town in Bolivar County. While some improvements occurred, they were insufficient to attract industry or stem black migration north.

A drastic budget cut by the cash-strapped NCC forced Brooks to release all but three of the DM's staff in 1971 and end its county projects. The remaining staff focused the organization's efforts on assisting Mound Bayou; aiding ROBERT CLARK, the state's only African American legislator; and providing technical assistance to community organizers and citizenship education groups. The terminated staff, who had run the county projects and objected to Brooks's domineering management style and his growing emphasis on developing independent black economic and political power, complained unsuccessfully to the NCC. Brooks worked closely with Hamer and the Mississippi Freedom Democratic Party, but the party withered as the state's moderate blacks and whites coalesced in the Loyal Democrats of Mississippi, which the national Democratic Party recognized in preference to the regular, segregationist Mississippi Democratic Party.

Brooks enjoyed some success. His efforts helped keep the Delta Community and Health Center in Mound Bayou funded for another ten years after it faced closure in the early 1970s. However, the hospital, like the DM, eventually succumbed to lack of funding. By 1977 the DM was little more than the office Brooks maintained in Greenville, which he kept through much of the 1990s, remaining active in community organizing. Brooks became an aide to MICHAEL ALPHONSO ESPY, Mississippi's first African American congressperson since Reconstruction, and to Espy's successor, BENNIE G. THOMPSON, with whom the DM had worked when he was mayor of Bolton. In the mid-1990s Brooks worked with Greenville youth, trying to combat drug culture. He became an oral historian, assisting Kim Lacy Rogers in interviewing African American community leaders in the Delta for her book *Life and Death in the Delta: African American Narratives of Violence, Resilience, and Social Change* (2006). Brooks also served on the board of the Mississippi ACLU.

Although little known outside Mississippi and only briefly mentioned in accounts of the state's civil rights movement and its aftermath, Brooks was involved in many facets of the struggle for racial equality in Mississippi.

Further Reading

Owen Brooks's interview with Robert Wright, from 18 September 1968, is available in the Ralph J. Bunche Oral History Collection, Oral History Department, Moorland-Spingarn Research Center, Howard University, Washington D.C. An interview by Tom Dent, from 18 August 1978, is available in the Mississippi Oral History Collection, L. Zenobia Coleman Library, Tougaloo College, Tougaloo, Mississippi.

Newman, Mark. *Divine Agitators: The Delta Ministry and Civil Rights in Mississippi* (2004).

MARK NEWMAN

BROOKS, Shelton (4 May 1886–6 Sept. 1975), songwriter, was born Shelton Leroy Brooks in Amesburg, Ontario, near Detroit, to Potter, a Methodist minister, and Laura Brooks. Both of his parents sang and played the organ, and they kept a harmonium (pump organ) in the home. Shelton began experimenting on this while still a small child. Because Shelton was too small to reach the foot pedals, however, an older brother operated them while he played the keyboard. The family moved to the United States while Shelton was a boy, and he began his career in Detroit and Cleveland, honing the performing skills that would later make him a popular entertainer. He migrated to Chicago, the unrivaled hub of African American entertainment in the Midwest, sometime before 1909.

Brooks's first known song, "You Ain't Talking to Me," was published in 1909 by Will Rossiter of Chicago, and Brooks stuck with this firm for most of his publications. The second of these, "Some of These Days," became an enormous hit. Brooks personally persuaded the vaudeville star Sophie Tucker to feature the song in her act at Chicago's Orpheum Theatre; it became a sensation and became Tucker's theme song for the remainder of her long career. Each of her four varying recordings of the song (1911, 1926, 1927, and 1929) became a hit, and a short feature film named for the song was released with Tucker as its star. Brooks followed this song with a number of lesser efforts, including "The Cosey Rag" and "Jean" (1911), "All Night Long" (1912), "At an Old-Time Ball" (1913), and "Rufe Johnson's Harmony Band" (1914). His best and most successful song during these years was "I Wonder Where My Easy Rider's Gone" (1913), which cleverly combined horse racing and romantic subject matter with blues touches. It in turn helped inspire W. C. HANDY's 1914 hit "Yellow Dog Blues," which serves as an answer to Brooks's song and even readapts the chorus of the Brooks song for the verse of Handy's.

Brooks was reputed to be a gifted improviser, and like many vaudevillians, he chose not to write down much of his material. Thus he may well have created numerous songs that did not survive his stage acts. He almost always composed alone, writing both music and lyrics, but occasionally he collaborated with others. For the 1912 "Oh You Georgia Rose," his co-authors were the little-known Johnnie Watters and W. R. Williams. Most of Brooks's songs were published by the major white firms of the day, initially all by Rossiter of Chicago and after 1913 also by some of the New York firms. His "You Ain't No Place but Down South" (1912) was published in Dallas by his African American songwriting peer Chris Smith. Sometime around 1912 Brooks married a woman named Lina; they had one son.

Brooks had his second hit in 1916 with the dance song "Walking the Dog," which lived on as a title and as a concept beyond Brooks's actual piece. GERTRUDE "MA" RAINEY probably used Brooks's music in a dog-walking number that she performed in vaudeville around 1920. Brooks's piece may also have given George Gershwin the idea for an instrumental number of the same name that he wrote some years later. Another Brooks dance hit of the World War I years was "I Want to Shimmie" (1919), which capitalized on a shoulder-shaking dance featured by Gilda Gray and other leading vaudevillians of the period.

It was in 1917 that Brooks had his second universally popular smash hit with "The Darktown Strutters' Ball." Whereas most of Brooks's songs, even the best of them, feature rather weak verses leading to a payoff in the chorus, this one is strong throughout. In both its overall structural integrity and its theme, "The Darktown Strutters' Ball" may have owed something to Irving Berlin's 1911 hit "Alexander's Ragtime Band." An invitation is issued to a potential dancer or audience member to join one or more persons at a musical event, whether as passive listeners or (preferably, in the dance-mad era in which these songs were issued) as dancers, participants. The verse slides smoothly into the infectious chorus, which supplies the rhythmic and harmonic payoff for what preceded it. Among the innumerable jazz and vaudeville artists who recorded "The Darktown Strutters' Ball" were LOUIS ARMSTRONG, CAB CALLOWAY, COLEMAN HAWKINS, FLETCHER HENDERSON, Benny Goodman, ETHEL WATERS, Benny Carter, Artie Shaw, the Quintet of the Hot Club of Paris (featuring Django Reinhardt), the Original Dixieland Jazz Band, Red Nichols, VALAIDA SNOW, and the Original Indiana Five. Brooks himself recorded some duets with the blues singer Sara Martin in 1923 and served in 1926 as an accompanist on some Ethel Waters sides featuring his songs.

By 1920 Brooks's best years as a songwriter were behind him. In 1920 he contributed songs to two shows, *Canary Cottage* and *Miss Nobody from Starland* (neither was a notable success). In 1922 his career got a second wind when he was hired by the producer Lew Leslie to appear in *Plantation Revue*, one of many shows mounted to cash in on the runaway success of the 1921 EUBIE BLAKE–NOBLE SISSLE show *Shuffle Along*. Leslie's shows, which ran at his own Plantation Club, became a major success after he discovered a scintillating young singer-dancer named FLORENCE MILLS. Mills was teamed up with Brooks in the show *From Dover Street to Dixie*, which combined British and African American material. This became a sensation in London, and Mills and Brooks gave a highly successful command performance before King George V, Queen Mary, and the royal family of England.

Although his inspiration was winding down, Brooks remained active through the 1930s. He appeared in a short film for Vitaphone in 1929 and was on radio regularly in the period around 1930. He made cameo appearances in stage productions, including *Brown Buddies* in 1930. His friend W. C. Handy, ever willing to take a chance on African American talent, published Brooks's "Swing That Thing" in 1933 and "After All These Years" in 1936.

Neither song was particularly successful. Brooks appeared in a film entitled *Double Deal* in 1939, and he continued to make stage appearances, including one at the Apollo Theater in 1942. In the same year he was recognized as one of the grand old men of American music at an ASCAP tribute, alongside Irving Berlin, W. C. Handy, and Harold Arlen. By this time he had moved to Los Angeles, where he died at the age of eighty-nine, largely forgotten despite his importance as the creator of popular music standards. The musical style he pioneered had receded several generations into the past.

Further Reading

Jasen, David A., and Gene Jones. *Spreadin' Rhythm Around* (1998).

Morgan, Thomas L., and William Barlow. *From Cakewalks to Concert Halls* (1992).

ELLIOTT S. HURWITT

BROOKS, Tyrone (10 Oct. 1945–) Georgia state legislator and civil rights activist, was born in the back seat of a car rushing from his parents' home in Warrenton, Georgia, to the "colored ward" of the hospital in neighboring Wilkes County. He was the second of three children born to Mose Brooks, a Pullman car porter, and Ruby Cody Brooks, who worked as a clerk in two white-owned Warrenton stores.

Rural Warren County in east-central Georgia was removed from the influence of Atlanta and psychologically distant even from the nearby city of Augusta. Although its population was nearly two-thirds African American at the time of Brooks's birth, black residents experienced all the disadvantages of southern apartheid in the 1940s: political powerlessness, segregated public accommodations, and an unequal share of poverty, to name a few. Brooks recalled that from an early age he was aware of the outside world and the social struggle going on around him. At the home of his maternal grandmother, the younger Brooks read *Ebony*, *Jet*, the *Atlanta Daily World*, the *Pittsburgh Courier*, and *Muhammad Speaks*. "We were being exposed to the world from this little town," Brooks said years later. The combined influences of his father and grandmother, he said, "motivated me to take a keener interest in the civil rights revolution" (interview with Tyrone Brooks, 22 Sept. 2005).

At age fifteen, inspired by the 1960 sit-ins in Greensboro, North Carolina, Brooks and some of his friends decided to take direct action in their hometown. They targeted the segregated school system and the Knox Theatre in downtown Warrenton, where black moviegoers had to view the films from the balcony. "When we started our little campaign in Warrenton to desegregate the school system and the theater and the businesses, we really didn't know what we were doing," Brooks recalled. Their sit-in downstairs at the Knox brought the manager with his flashlight, but no ejection or police action. Brooks said their demonstration outside the county board of education did provoke a response. The police chief brought

them to the jail, where their parents picked them up. After creating a stir with his activism, Brooks was sent to Boggs Academy, a long-established black boarding school in nearby Keysville, to finish his high school education (interview with Brooks).

The Warren County children's crusade came to the attention of civil rights leaders in Atlanta. Two staff members from the Southern Christian Leadership Conference (SCLC), Carl Farris and Willie Bolden, were assigned to Warren County. Farris and Bolden became Brooks's mentors, bringing him along to demonstrations in Albany, Georgia; Birmingham, Alabama; St. Augustine, Florida; and elsewhere. They also introduced Brooks to the Reverend MARTIN LUTHER KING JR., who stopped in Warrenton one day on his way to South Carolina. Brooks and his friends served lemonade to King and his associates, got over their surprise that King was not a tall man, and beamed under his benediction. By 1967 Brooks had joined the SCLC's staff.

"I was just one of those who were caught up in the movement," Brooks said. "You couldn't say no. It was an overwhelming desire to make a contribution to defeating Jim Crow and also to changing the course of our nation. For some of us it became our life." Brooks intended to remain on the SCLC staff only two years. But King's assassination in 1968 sealed his commitment to the movement. Summoned from Georgia to Memphis with the rest of the SCLC staff, Brooks heard the Reverend RALPH ABERNATHY's exhortation to "stay on the team." He remained on the SCLC staff and became a close associate of HOSEA WILLIAMS. When Williams was forced out in 1979 during a struggle for control of the organization, Brooks went with him.

Brooks was soon approached by a group of Atlanta ministers who asked him to run for a seat in the Georgia General Assembly. Brooks considered himself too much of a street radical to be a viable candidate. But he agreed to run, and he won the 1980 election. During his tenure, Brooks pressed for an increase in the number of black judges on Georgia's superior courts, supported the "black max" redistricting plan that increased the number of majority-black election districts in 1992, and led the Georgia Association of Black Elected Officials (GABEO) from obscurity to become an outspoken voice in Georgia's political debates.

Brooks is best known for his nearly two-decade struggle to remove the Confederate battle cross from Georgia's state flag. The Dixie symbol had been placed there by the 1956 general assembly in a symbolic gesture of disdain for integration following the 1954 *Brown v. Board of Education* decision. Brooks drew little support until 1992 when the then governor Zell Miller—looking to clean up Georgia's image in advance of the 1996 Atlanta summer Olympic Games—called for its removal. Miller not only failed but also nearly lost the 1994 election as a result. Miller's successor, Roy Barnes, succeeded in removing the Dixie cross in 2001. Brooks was at the center of the negotiations that led to the successful legislation. Barnes's 2002 election defeat was partly attributed to white discontent over the flag amendment. Barnes's successor, Sonny Perdue, got rid of the flag that Barnes and Brooks created, but did not bring back the Dixie emblem.

From his platform as a lawmaker and as president of GABEO, Brooks became involved in human rights cases throughout Georgia. He spearheaded efforts to reopen the investigation of the mass lynching at Moore's Ford in Walton County, which federal agents failed to solve in 1946. Arrested at least sixty-five times for his civil rights work, Tyrone Brooks stayed true to his roots even while helping to bring about significant changes in his native state.

DON SCHANCHE JR.

BROOKS, Walter Henderson (30 Aug. 1851–6 July 1945), clergyman, temperance leader, and poet, was born in Richmond, Virginia, the son of Albert Royal Brooks and Lucy Goode, slaves. Brooks's father, an enterprising slave, owned his own "snack house" and a livery business that brought him into contact with some of Virginia's wealthiest citizens, including his wife's owner, the German consul Daniel Von Groning. Albert Brooks purchased his wife's freedom in 1862 for eight hundred dollars. Still a slave, Walter Brooks at age seven was sold to the Turpin & Yarborough tobacco firm. He woefully recalled his time there, writing: "It was all I could do to perform the task assigned to my little hands. What I do remember is that I stood in mortal fear of 'the consequences' of failing to do what was required of me." When the Richmond manufacturer fell victim to wartime economic decline, Brooks was allowed to reside with his mother and began working in hotels, boardinghouses, and restaurants. In his youth he acquired the doctrines that served as the foundation for his life's work. He learned temperance from his pastor, the Reverend Robert Ryland, who taught songs at Christmas to curb the consumption of "egg-nog and the drinking of wine in countless homes," and Brooks's parents instilled "lessons of uprightness and sobriety."

After the Union victory in the Civil War, Brooks worked to make a place for himself in the world. In 1866 he entered the preparatory program at Lincoln University, a Presbyterian school founded for African Americans in Pennsylvania. He obtained his college degree in 1872 and one year later earned his theological degree. He joined the Ashmun Presbyterian Church in Lincoln in 1868. When he returned to Richmond after graduation, he changed denominations and was baptized into the First African Baptist Church. In 1874 he married the pastor's daughter, Eva Holmes; they had ten children.

Between 1874 and 1876 Brooks worked with the American Baptist Publication Society as a Sunday school missionary in Virginia. He gained national attention for his views on temperance when he addressed the society at its anniversary meeting in Philadelphia in 1875. His speech, entitled "Facts from the Field," sparked controversy when he "drew a picture of the drinking habits of preachers" in an effort to illustrate the critical need for temperance. That same year Brooks became the chaplain of the Anti-Saloon League of the District of Columbia. He retained this position until 1882.

Brooks's greatest legacy came from his work as a Baptist minister. In 1876 he was formally ordained into the ministry and a year later became pastor of the Second African Baptist Church of Richmond. In 1880 he briefly returned to his missionary work, but by 1882 he had accepted the pastorate of the Nineteenth Street Baptist Church in Washington, D.C. Over the next sixty-three years Brooks established a national reputation. He assisted John W. Cromwell in creating the Virginia Historical and Literary Society and for a time served as vice president in the Bethel Literary and Historical Association in Washington, D.C. Brooks was a trustee of NANNIE BURROUGHS's National Training School for Women and Girls and the Virginia Theological Seminary and College in Lynchburg, Virginia. He supported the black women's club movement, and in 1896 his church was the site of the foundational meeting of the National Association of Colored Women.

Brooks played an important role in efforts to build and maintain a national black Baptist convention. He was chairman of the American National Baptist Convention's Bureau of Education, a black organization founded in 1886, and he continually mediated relationships with national white Baptist conventions. In 1889 the American Baptist Publication Society, in an effort to increase black participation, agreed to accept literary contributions from Brooks and two of his colleagues for its regular publication. The society, however, reneged on its offer when its southern white contingency voiced opposition. The society opted instead to create a special publication for black clergymen, the *Negro Baptist Pulpit*. Although Brooks authored an article for that volume, he and his colleagues were infuriated by this palliative act and predicted that it would typify future relations. Further difficulties led eventually to the formation of a black-controlled denominational body, the National Baptist Convention, U.S.A., in 1895.

Brooks's intellectual capabilities and dedication earned him recognition as an exceptional scholar. He wrote a number of essays on the history and development of black Baptist organizations and their relationships with white Baptists. For the *Journal of Negro History* he wrote "The Evolution of the Negro Baptist Church" (Jan. 1922) and "The Priority of the Silver Bluff Church and Its Promoters" (Apr. 1922). For *The Crisis* he wrote "Unification and Division among Colored Baptists" (May 1925). In his work with the Bethel Literary and Historical Association, he offered a "severe but eloquent criticism" of FREDERICK DOUGLASS's lecture "The Philosophy and History of Reform" that "occasioned a battle royal between him and Mr. Douglass, in which 'Greek met

Greek' with vigorous onslaught and heroic defence [*sic*]." Brooks was a member of the American Negro Academy and a lifelong member of the Association for the Study of Negro Life and History, where he worked closely with CARTER G. WOODSON.

Brooks's first wife died in 1912, and three years later he married Florence H. Swann. Following Florence's death, he married Viola Washington in 1933. Late in his life Brooks established himself as a poet. Two books of his poetry were published, *Original Poems* (1932) and *The Pastor's Voice* (1945). His poems thematically reflect his lifelong concerns for temperance, faith in God, and racial progress.

Brooks, like many black clergy of his time, used the church and his role as pastor for purposes that extended beyond the sacred. He was uncompromising in his struggle to promote education and the use of Christian morals as means to improve the quality of life for black Americans. As racial segregation gained legal precedent and race-related violence reached new heights, Brooks fought for equality and clung to a faith in the American creed that was second only to his faith in God.

Further Reading
Brooks's granddaughter Evelyn Brooks Higginbotham, Harvard University, possesses some of his papers, including a 1935 autobiographical piece, "Memories of a Life Time," some untitled autobiographical notes, and a genealogical "History of the Brooks Family."

Higginbotham, Evelyn Brooks. *Righteous Discontent: The Women's Movement in the Black Baptist Church, 1880–1920* (1993).

Moss, Alfred A. *The American Negro Academy* (1981).

Washington, James Melvin. *Frustrated Fellowship: A Black Baptist Quest for Social Power* (1986).

Woodson, Carter G. "Introduction to Walter Brooks," *The Pastor's Voice* (1945).

Obituaries: *Journal of Negro History*, 30 Oct. 1945; Washington, D.C., *Evening Star*, 8 July 1945.

ADAM BIGGS

BROONZY, Big Bill (26 June 1893?–15 Aug. 1958), blues singer and guitarist, was born William Lee Conley Broonzy in Scott, Bolivar County, Mississippi, the son of Frank Broonzy and Nettie (or Mittie) Belcher, former slaves who became sharecroppers. One of at least sixteen children, including a twin sister, he lived in Mississippi until age eight, when his family moved to Arkansas, near Pine Bluff, to try sharecropping there. As a youngster he made violins out of cornstalks, learning music from an uncle, Jerry Belcher, and a local musician known as See See Rider. He and a friend began playing homemade instruments to entertain local children, though always out of sight of his parents—stern Baptists who frowned on secular music. The parental disapproval eased, however, when he graduated to a real instrument (supposedly bought for him by a white patron) and began earning money as a musician. When he was twelve, the family moved to Scotts Crossing,

Arkansas, where he continued to play, mainly for white dances.

In 1912, however, he joined the Baptist Church, briefly putting music aside to try his hand at preaching. In 1914 (some accounts say 1916) he married a fellow church member, seventeen-year-old Guitrue (or Gertrude) Embria, who allowed him to take up music again, he said later, because it paid more than preaching. In 1918 he was drafted, serving with an army supply company in France. Returning to Arkansas, he grew dissatisfied with life in the South. In early 1920 he left his wife and went to Chicago, where he eventually found work as a Pullman railroad sleeping-car porter. He took guitar lessons from Papa Charlie Jackson, a recording artist who introduced him to the Paramount Records executive J. Mayo Williams. After an unproductive session for Paramount in 1926, Broonzy and the guitarist John Thomas cut four sides in late 1927 and early 1928, launching Broonzy on one of the most prolific recording careers in blues history.

Through the 1930s and 1940s he recorded hundreds of sides for a dozen labels, including the most important blues labels of that era: Bluebird, Columbia, Okeh, and Vocalion. He recorded both as a solo artist and in small-combo formats. He became active on Chicago's house-party circuit and then the tavern and club scene as it developed in the late 1930s and 1940s, working with such artists as MEMPHIS MINNIE and John Lee "SONNY BOY" WILLIAMSON.

As early as 1938 he began making inroads on a new market, participating in John Hammond's *From Spirituals to Swing* programs at Carnegie Hall in New York City—possibly the first appearance of a Mississippi-born blues musician in concert format. He also worked New York's Cafe Society nightclub in 1939 and 1940. In 1941 and 1942 he toured with a Mississippi protégé, the vocalist Lil Green, until she started singing with big rhythm-and-blues bands. On tour in Houston, Texas, Broonzy married a "Creole woman," Rosie Syphen, who returned with him to Chicago, where he plunged back into a steady schedule of club work. They had five children.

Although World War II interrupted his recording career, the interruption apparently did not cause a major financial blow. Partly because he recorded under contract to the music publisher Lester Melrose, not to any specific labels, Broonzy received little more than session fees as a recording artist. He once claimed that he earned a total of only two thousand dollars for the hundreds of songs he had recorded. As a result, even during his tenure as the nominal king of Chicago blues, he always worked nonmusical jobs on the side.

Broonzy returned to the recording studio in 1945, working in a new band format as he tried, with diminishing success, to keep pace with the postwar rhythm-and-blues sound. In 1947 the folklorist Alan Lomax brought Broonzy to New York, along with MEMPHIS SLIM and Sonny Boy Williamson, for a Town Hall concert. The next day, Lomax supervised a recording session at which the three blues artists, identified by pseudonyms (Broonzy's was "Natchez"), played music and talked candidly about life in the South. That session, like the *From Spirituals to Swing* concert, marked another stage in Broonzy's shift from racial/ethnic recording star to interpreter of blues for white audiences.

By the 1950s African American popular musical tastes had passed Broonzy by, and his recordings were more of a documentary or folk music nature. In 1950 and 1951 he briefly left the Chicago blues scene and took a job as a janitor at Iowa State University, where he learned to read and write. Returning to music, Broonzy looked more and more to the predominantly white folk revival audiences for work—for example, touring with the Chicago critic and oral historian Studs Terkel's program *I Come for to Sing*. He also looked to overseas markets and was one of the first artists to bring traditional American blues to British, European, Australian, African, and South American audiences in the 1950s. He appeared in several films and, with his newly acquired literacy, became the first Delta artist to be credited with an autobiography, *Big Bill Blues* (1964), a compilation of anecdotes, tall tales, and recollections originally written as letters to the Belgian enthusiast Yannick Bruynoghe. On tour in England in 1957, Broonzy was forced by health problems to return to Chicago, where he was diagnosed with lung cancer. He died in Chicago.

Big Bill Broonzy's performing career spanned five decades, taking him from the Deep South to Chicago and on to Europe, where he became one of the first and most effective ambassadors for American blues. As a recording artist, he recorded over 250 songs—many of them his own—prior to World War II and hundreds more in the postwar era. He also played as a sideman at countless sessions for other artists. As an instrumentalist, he could handle down-home finger picking or single-string electric styles, and, even late in his career, he could flash techniques that dazzled the guitar-oriented folk-music audience. Although he ended his career singing protest songs and other folk material in coffeehouses and cabarets, Broonzy was the central character in the first generation of Chicago blues musicians and spent most of his adult life performing blues, ragtime, hokum, and pop material for the so-called race market. Because he was one of the first blues artists to work successfully for white audiences, though, Broonzy helped shape the way several generations thought about the blues. Perhaps his most enduring musical influence was on a host of young, white British blues aficionados, notably John Mavall, Eric Clapton, and Jimmy Page, who in the 1960s sparked a blues-inspired "British invasion" of America. Broonzy was elected to the Blues Foundation Hall of Fame in Memphis, Tennessee, in 1980.

Further Reading
Broonzy, Bill. *Big Bill Blues: Big Bill Broonzy's Story as Told to Yannick Bruynoghe* (1964).
Harris, Sheldon. *Blues Who's Who: A Biographical Dictionary of Blues Singers* (1989).
Lomax, Alan. *The Land Where Blues Began* (1993).

Discography
Dixon, Robert M. W., and John Godrich. *Blues and Gospel Records: 1902–1943*, 3d ed. (1982).
Leadbitter, Mike, and Neil Slaven. *Blues Records 1943–1970: A Selective Discography*, vol. 1 (1987).
Oliver, Paul, ed. *The Blackwell Guide to Blues Records* (1989).

BILL MCCULLOCH
BARRY LEE PEARSON

BROTEER (Venture Smith) (1729?–1805), slave, entrepreneur, and autobiographer, was born in Guinea, Africa, to Saungm Furro, a West African prince with three wives. Broteer was the eldest son of the first wife. When he was six years old an "army supplied by whites" captured him and marched him to the coast (Smith, 544). During the capture Broteer had seen his father tortured and killed, a haunting memory that stayed with him for the rest of his life. After being imprisoned for two years Broteer was one of 260 Africans sold into slavery to a Rhode Island slaver named Robertson Mumford, who purchased Broteer for four gallons of rum and a piece of calico cloth. It was Mumford who gave Broteer his American name, Venture, a result, as Broteer recalled in his memoir, of his master "having purchased me with his own private venture" (Smith, 545).

With new slaves in tow Mumford's first stop was Barbados. En route, however, a quarter of his cargo died, having been afflicted with smallpox during the Middle Passage. The remaining slaves were sold to planters there, except for Venture and three others who continued on to Rhode Island. During his time in bondage he lived with various slaveowners along the Atlantic seaboard. He spent a dozen years with Mumford in Rhode Island and on Fischer's Island near Long Island, New York, and at least a dozen more with another master, Thomas Stanton of Stonington Point, Connecticut. His third and final master was Colonel Oliver Smith of Long Island, New York, whose surname he kept after his emancipation. Smith spent his adolescent years working as both a household servant and field hand. In his teenage years he began to resent those who exerted control over him, particularly his master's son James Mumford, who, on one occasion, charged Smith with a pitchfork only to be sent home in tears after Smith got the best of him. As punishment for this act of self-defense Smith was beaten, whipped, and hung on a butcher's gallows for an hour.

Smith survived the gallows and went on to make a life for himself in slavery. He married and had a family. He also saved a considerable sum of money, hiring out his labor as a fisherman, woodsman, and farmer. Because of his work ethic he acquired the reputation as a tireless laborer who could paddle a canoe several miles across the river and back and then cut nine cords of wood—all in a single day. Known also for his size, Smith weighed over three hundred pounds, stood just over six feet tall, and measured six feet around the waist. In his memoir he reported that he "was pretty large and stout," which played to his advantage against his whip-cracking masters (Smith, 544). Once he snatched a whip away from his master and on another occasion he beat his master and his master's brother after they viciously attacked him.

Nearly three decades after his capture in Africa, Smith had saved enough money to buy his freedom. In 1765, at age thirty-six, he paid his enslaver Colonel Oliver Smith seventy-one pounds and two shillings, a sum roughly the cost of four thousand acres of land. At last a free man again he supported himself by whaling, fishing, chopping wood, and hunting. With the money from his labors he saved enough to buy his family's freedom as well. He also purchased three other slaves from their masters and freed them. In 1776 Smith moved his family to East Haddam, Connecticut, where he built a home and employed two black indentured servants. Soon thereafter he acquired more than a hundred acres of land and bought three homes. He supported these endeavors by buying and selling land, running a shipping business, and acting as a creditor by loaning money to both blacks and whites. Of this last pursuit he once complained that he had "been cheated out of considerable money by people" who took "advantage of my ignorance of numbers" (Smith, 556).

In 1798, in his sixty-ninth year, Smith published his memoir, *A Narrative of the Life and Adventures of Venture, a Native of Africa*, a twenty-page account that was republished at least four times in the two centuries after his death. The *Narrative* begins with a preface by the Connecticut schoolteacher and antislavery activist Elisha Niles, the man to whom Smith dictated the memoir and who encouraged Smith to write the account. Accompanying the publication of Smith's memoir was a December advertisement in the *New London Bee* describing Smith as "a negro remarkable for size, strength, industry, fidelity, and well known in the state of Rhode Island, Long Island, and in Stonington, East Haddam, and several other parts" of Connecticut. Among the earliest examples of its kind in the Americas Smith's memoir offers a clear and concise account of his rise from slavery to that of a self-made man. It spans the years just prior to the outbreak of the American Revolution and concludes in 1798. The memoir was, in Niles's words, "a pattern of honesty, prudence and industry to people of his own color"—a true rages-to-riches story that could inspire slaves to revolt (Smith, 539).

Smith died in East Haddam, Connecticut, at the age of seventy-seven. His tombstone reads: "Sacred to the Memory of Venture Smith, African. Though the son of a King, he was kidnapped and sold as a slave, but by his industry he acquired money to purchase his freedom."

Further Reading

Smith, Venture. *A Narrative of the Life and Adventures of Venture, a Native of Africa*. Reprinted in *Early Negro Writing, 1760–1837*, ed. Dorothy Porter (1798; repr. 1971).

Andrews, William L. *To Tell a Free Story: The First Century of Afro-American Autobiography, 1760–1865* (1986).

Caretta, Vince, and Phillip Gould. *Genius and Bondage: Literature of the Early Black Atlantic* (2001).

Kaplan, Sidney. *The Black Presence in the Era of the American Revolution, 1770–1800* (1973).

MATTHEW L. HARRIS

BROWN, Ada (1 May 1890–31 Mar. 1950), singer and actor, was born Ada Scott in Kansas City, Kansas, the daughter of H. W. and Anna Morris Scott. (Some scholars list her as being born on 1 May 1889 in Junction City, Kansas.) Nothing is known about her education, except that she began piano lessons at an early age. She also started singing in the local church choir, developing the voice that the historian Bruce Kellner calls "full, rich, and mellow" (Kellner, 55). Indeed, musical ability ran in Brown's family: Her cousin was renowned ragtime pianist and composer JAMES SYLVESTER SCOTT.

Brown's professional life began in 1910, when she became a performer at Bob Mott's Pekin Theater in Chicago. Barely out of her teens, Brown also performed in clubs in Paris, France, and Berlin, Germany. In the early 1920s Brown joined BENNIE MOTEN's band, which was considered the Midwest's preeminent band. During the 1920s and 1930s Brown sang the blues on both the West Coast and the East Coast, as well as in recording studios in Chicago and St. Louis. She recorded "Evil Mama Blues," "Ill Natured Blues," and "Break o' Day Blues" with Moten's band in September 1923 for the Okeh label. By the end of the 1920s, however, Brown had left the band for the East Coast's vaudeville theater circuit. There she became a popular attraction. She toured with the shows *Step on It* (1922) and *Struttin' Time* (1924), both musical revues written by the African American team of Flournoy Miller and Aubrey Lyle. By 1928, when Brown made her second record, including "Panama Limited Blues" and "Tia Juana Man," critics and audiences alike applauded her sweet voice. Such popularity not only earned her the title the "Queen of the Blues" but also brought her to the stage. Brown's stage appearances at Harlem's Lafayette Theatre included *Plantation Days* (1927), *Bandannaland* (1928), and *Tan Town Tamales* (1930). She also played at the Liberty Theater with BILL "BOJANGLES" ROBINSON in *Brown Buddies* (1930), a musical comedy about African American soldiers in France during World War I. The show had a thin plotline but featured plenty of song and dance.

In 1936 Brown moved to Chicago, where she sang with the FLETCHER HENDERSON Orchestra at the Grand Terrace Café. That same year, along with actor Leigh Whipper and actress FREDI WASHINGTON, Brown helped found the Negro Actors Guild of America in New York City, a benevolent welfare organization for African American performers composed of six committees: finance, administrative, membership, entertainment, sickness, and welfare. Brown's first and only film appearance came in 1943, when she played herself in *Stormy Weather*, the thinly disguised life of Bill "Bojangles" Robinson ("Bill Williamson"). Critics now consider this film, a cinematic survey of African American entertainment from 1918 to 1943, an unusual opportunity for audiences to see African American entertainers prominent in the 1940s. Even into the twenty-first century, Brown's performance in the film was still winning critical accolades. In his 2001 book *Toms, Coons, Mulattoes, Mammies, and Bucks*, DONALD BOGLE writes: "FATS WALLER and Ada Brown provided spicy renditions of 'Ain't Misbehavin' and 'That Ain't Right'"(131).

Before her sudden and unexplained retirement from music in 1945, Brown teamed up with Robinson once again, this time at the Broadway Theater in New York City in *Memphis Bound*. After the show closed, she returned to Kansas City, Kansas (some sources give Kansas City, Missouri, as the location). Brown died at home of kidney disease on 31 March 1950. She is buried in the Westlawn Cemetery in Kansas City, Kansas. Ada Brown belonged to the first generation of African American blues singers. Along with MA RAINEY, BESSIE SMITH, and many others, she helped to make the female blues singer an icon in American culture.

Further Reading

Bogle, Donald. *Toms, Coons, Mulattoes, Mammies, and Bucks: An Interpretive History of Blacks in American Films* (2001).

Kellner, Bruce. *The Harlem Renaissance: A Historical Dictionary for the Era* (1987).

Stewart-Baxter, Derrick. *Ma Rainey and the Classic Blues Singers* (1970).

MARY ANNE BOELCSKEVY

BROWN, Anne (9 Aug. 1912–), concert opera singer and teacher, was the oldest of four girls born to Dr. Harry F. Brown and Mamie Wiggins in Baltimore, Maryland. Her mother was her first music teacher, and mother and daughters would frequently sing around the piano. Anne grew up listening to the recordings of Caruso, Melba, and Schumann-Heink. Toward the end of World War I, when Anne was six years old, she made her concert debut with her younger sister Henrietta singing for returning African American soldiers at Camp Meade in Baltimore. At age twelve Anne began attending Frederick Douglass Senior High School, then the city's only public high school open to blacks. During her high school years, she attended a wider range of concerts including performances by MARIAN ANDERSON and ROLAND HAYES at Baltimore's Lyric Theatre. After graduation from high school Anne hoped to continue her education at the Peabody Conservatory. Her audition was so impressive garnering positive comments until her mother mentioned the fact that Anne and she were black. Because of Anne's light complexion she was naturally assumed to be white. Positive feedback was soon followed by a flat refusal to admit her because of her race. The Peabody Conservatory rectified this mistake in 1998 by honoring Anne Brown with an award for lifetime achievement in music.

The young singer benefited from the intervention of Constance Black, wife of the *Baltimore Sun* newspaper chairman Harry C. Black. She had heard about Anne from her chauffeur, who was a patient of Dr. Harry Brown. His glowing reports of how beautiful his doctor's daughter sang prompted Mrs. Black to request that Anne be driven out to the house to meet her. Anne sang songs from the German classics accompanied by her mother. Black was impressed by the young singer and invited her back on several occasions to perform in her home. Black also encouraged Anne to audition for the Institute of Musical Art of the Juilliard School in New York. Anne's father was initially opposed to his daughter's leaving Baltimore, believing that New York was full of the devil's spawn and did not believe that she would succeed in entering that school. Only after her mother threatened to leave her husband did the father relent. Mother and daughter packed their bags and headed to New York. Anne sang for Frank Damrosch, head of the school, and at the age of sixteen was accepted as a pupil. Entering Juilliard in 1928 Brown studied musical technique for three years. From 1931 to 1934 she won the coveted Margaret McGill three-year tuition scholarship to study opera and singing technique under the musical tutelage of Lucia Dunham. During the first two years of study, she was the only black student. Ruby Elzy, another African American singer, was shortly to gain admittance. Later she would gain prominence playing Serena in *Porgy and Bess* with Brown. Though a soprano, Brown developed her lower range, developing a mezzo-like quality with Dunham's training. In New York Brown felt a freedom from the South's strict racial codes, but in the 1930s the opportunities for a black classically trained singer were limited. Brown did not expect the way to be easy for an African American performer to have a serious musical career. Although ROLAND HAYES, PAUL ROBESON, MARIAN ANDERSON, and Dorothy Maynor had shown it possible to achieve success with a concert career, the world of opera still held its color line. Brown was determined to face this racial stricture and beat it. She received her diploma in voice in 1932 and artist's diploma in 1934.

A couple of years before graduation, she read in a newspaper article that George Gershwin was going to write an opera about black people in North Carolina named *Porgy and Bess*. Brown called Gershwin's secretary and requested an audition. Brown's initial audition with Gershwin was so successful that a long series of meetings with other members of the production team including Gershwin's brother Ira, the director Rouben Mamoulian, and the librettist Dubose Heyward was immediately put into motion. Prior to being offered the role of Bess in *Porgy and Bess*, she took a two-month job singing in London in the chorus of a musical titled *Blackbirds*.

Porgy and Bess premiered in Boston in September 1935, and opened on Broadway at the Alvin Theatre on 10 October 1935. The show opened to mixed reviews and played for 124 times on Broadway before embarking on a three-month tour. In March 1936 Brown refused to perform at the National Theatre in Washington, D.C., unless the theater's racially segregated house policy was abolished. With the help of MARY MCLEOD BETHUNE and RALPH BUNCHE the National Theatre was desegregated. After *Porgy and Bess* moved on, the policy of segregated seating policy was immediately restored.

Throughout the 1940s and 1950s, Brown commanded a European concert repertoire of French and Italian opera arias. After World War II, Todd Duncan and Brown reprised their roles of Porgy and Bess for the Royal Opera in Copenhagen. She toured nationally and internationally, and in 1948 married the Norwegian ski jump champion Thorleif Schelderup. Her performances on the Norwegian stage include *Dido and Aeneas, Member of the Wedding*, and *Amal*. From 1953 to 1955 she lived in Italy, where she studied the vocal technique of bel canto. In the 1960s Brown began teaching at the National Theatre School of Norway. It was during this time that she directed a production of *Porgy and Bess* in France with Avon Long as Sportin' Life. The principals were African American and the chorus was made up of white French singers. In Norway, she continued private coaching. Her students included the Norwegian opera singer Elizabeth Norberg-Schultz and the actress Liv Ullmann. In 1990 Brown was awarded the Oslo Kultur Prisen (Oslo Culture Prize) for her artistic achievements. Among her other awards are Honorary Citizen of New Orleans (1991) and a special plaque from Frederick Douglass Senior High School in Baltimore, Maryland, for superior contributions in the performing arts and bel canto (1998). Brown retired to Norway in the mid-1960s.

Further Reading
Brown, Anne. "I Gave Up My Country for Love," *Ebony* (Nov. 1953).
Hine Darlene, Clark. "Anne Brown" in *Black Women in American Music* (1997).

BARON KELLY

BROWN, Arthur McKimmon (9 Nov. 1867–4 Dec. 1939), physician, was born in Raleigh, North Carolina. Little is known about his family or upbringing. Some sources suggest that Brown briefly attended Shaw University, the Baptist-affiliated postsecondary school for blacks founded in Raleigh in 1865; contemporary accounts indicate that Brown graduated from Cleveland High School in Cleveland, Ohio. Brown pursued undergraduate studies at Lincoln University in Pennsylvania, earning a BA in June 1888. That fall, Brown enrolled in the medical school of the University of Michigan at Ann Arbor. He earned his MD with a special qualification in surgery in 1891. At his graduation, friends from Ann Arbor's Second Baptist Church presented him with a new medical case, as a token of recognition and thanks for his active involvement in the church's choir and social activities during his student days in Ann Arbor.

Brown soon moved to Jefferson County, Alabama, where a local examining board certified him to practice medicine. He initially practiced for three years in Bessemer, located a few miles southwest of Birmingham; but in 1894 he moved his practice to Birmingham proper. Brown quickly became an important figure in that city's black community. He helped establish the Children's Home Hospital, Birmingham's first medical facility specifically for the treatment of African Americans.

In 1898 Brown volunteered for military service in the Spanish-American War. After being ignored in the initial call-ups, apparently because of his race, Brown served as an assistant surgeon to the U.S. Cavalry's Tenth Regiment, an all-black unit created under Congressional authorization in 1866 and popularly known as the "buffalo soldiers" for the unit's exploits in the American West. Brown reported for duty in Cuba in early August 1898 as an assistant surgeon at the rank of first lieutenant, thereby becoming one of the first African Americans to serve as a commissioned medical officer in the U.S. armed forces. He worked briefly at the regimental hospital before returning with his unit to the United States at the end of August 1898. He transferred with much of the Tenth Regiment to Alabama, where he had, in his words, "the privilege to go back to civil life." He was discharged from the U.S. Army in March of 1899.

Brown's activities as a civilian were varied. With Herschel V. Cashin and others, he helped to write a history of the U.S. Army's Tenth Regiment and its exploits during the Spanish-American War; the book, titled *Under Fire*, was published in 1899. He also worked on numerous inventions, including innovations to deep-shaft mining cars, and he operated a drug store in addition to his continuing medical practice. In February 1902 Brown was acknowledged by the state of Alabama as one of only 76 African American men who satisfied the highly restrictive criteria established in the state's new constitution and were thus issued official certificates permitting them to legally cast ballots in Alabama elections.

In 1903 Brown moved to Chicago, Illinois, where he lived part time until at least 1907. Meanwhile, he maintained connections, business activities, and his medical practices in Birmingham and also in Cleveland, Ohio. His broad experience and contacts in the medical profession resulted in his being elected, in 1914, president of the National Medical Association, the principal professional association for African American physicians. After a long career Brown died in Birmingham, Alabama, at the age of seventy-two from complications associated with diabetes. His home in Birmingham, designed by noted local African American architect Wallace A. Rayfield, is still maintained as a community center by the Birmingham Arts Club.

Further Reading

Cashin, Herschel V., et al. *Under Fire with the Tenth U.S. Cavalry* (1899).

Savitt, Todd L. "Entering a White Profession: Black Physicians in the New South, 1880–1920," *Bulletin of the History of Medicine* (Spring 2005).

LAURA M. CALKINS

BROWN, Cecil (3 July 1943–), novelist, playwright, screenwriter, memoirist, folklorist, and educator, was born in Bolton, North Carolina, to Dorothy and Cecil Culphert Brown. His father was in prison until Brown was thirteen, so he and his brother Donald Ray were raised until then by his Uncle Lofton, who recognized and nurtured young Cecil's talent for academics and his facility with words. Brown describes this part of his life as a kind of idyll haunted by the mysterious but terrible situation of his father.

When he was fourteen years old Brown reluctantly moved with his brother and father to Green Swamp, North Carolina, to grow tobacco. Considerably less supportive of Cecil's bookishness, Culphert Brown beat him for reading when he should have been plowing. It was around this time that Brown first encountered the Stagger Lee story, which would be the focus of much of his scholarly research. Friends of his father would sing a version of the ballad, and then tell young Cecil that his father was a bad man like the murderous Stagger Lee (also known as STAGOLEE, Stack Lee, and other variants). It was around this time, too, that Brown at last learned the truth behind his father's imprisonment: he had murdered a man in a fight over a card game. It was also while living in Green Swamp, however, that, having been thrilled by a magic show at school, Brown became a magician himself. An able hypnotist, the young man captivated crowds of peers and adults, and saw a career in magic as a way out of the sharecropping life he hated.

Brown's deliverance came in a different form, however: with a scholarship to Agricultural and Technical State University at Greensboro in 1961. Unsatisfied with the library at Greensboro A&T, Brown transferred to Columbia University, where in 1966 he earned a BA in Comparative Literature. Upon graduating from Columbia he completed a master's degree in English and American Literature at the University of Chicago. The mastery of the traditional, Eurocentric Western canon was an important part of his intellectual and artistic development. Also important were the connections he made there with his fellow writers, like LEROI JONES (later AMIRI BARAKA), ISHMAEL REED, and ELDRIDGE CLEAVER. Together they were at the forefront of a new, politically engaged black art.

In the spring of 1968 Brown was impressed with a speech delivered by Eldridge Cleaver, whose *Soul On Ice* (1967) he admired, at a political rally. The two became close friends and moved to California together. They shared an interest in the oral tradition in black culture and a conviction that the writer was an essential actor in the struggle for equality. Brown was an important part of a vital new school of writers who expanded the purview of American literature to include black voices. The political aspect of this literature was important, but so was its stylistic innovation. In 1968 Brown began to publish his criticism, essays, and interviews in such journals such as the *Negro Digest, Kenyon Review,* and *Evergreen Review.* At this time he was also working on his own novel and teaching at the University of Illinois.

In 1969 Brown published his first novel, *The Lives and Loves of Mr. Jiveass Nigger,* a work that bespoke the mixture of density, political relevance, and aesthetic novelty that would mark all of Brown's work. Linguistically and stylistically playful, with voices vernacular and formal, Brown told the story of a character called George Washington. A black American abroad, Washington made his living catering to the sexual wishes of white European women, retaining a dubious freedom from penury and menial labor. He philosophized about race and literature throughout. In the end, a ghostly narrator counseled him against hopelessness and suicide, warning that if he were not vigilant in representing himself, white sociologists and "experts" would attempt to destroy that which he had brought to light. The book received mixed reviews and gained Brown some notoriety.

Having befriended the comedian RICHARD PRYOR in 1971, Brown began to work in Hollywood as a screenwriter, collaborating with Pryor on the controversial comedy *Which Way Is Up?* From 1977 to 1979 he was engaged as a screenwriter by Warner Brothers and Universal Studios. He drew on his experiences in Hollywood to write his 1982 novel, *Days Without Weather,* a Hollywood satire about the attempts of a black screenwriter to bring a historical film about a slave riot to the screen. His project was continually corrupted and foiled by producers and studios. *Days Without Weather* won the Before Columbus Foundation American Book Award in 1984.

In 1990 Brown returned to academia and to Stagger Lee. He obtained his PhD in African American Literature, Folklore, and Theory of Narrative in 1993 from the University of California at Berkeley. His dissertation was published by Harvard University Press in 2003 as *Stagolee Shot Billy.* In this work Brown wrote elliptically, interspersing various versions of the song with historical facts and historical conjecture. He used the myth of Stagger Lee as a repository of buried historical fact, a folktale that could instruct about race relations, pimps, and politics in turn-of-the-century St. Louis. At the same time, the story in all of its many versions conferred upon Stagger Lee the status of archetype. Brown sorted out what this archetype might represent for black men in America in the age of hip-hop.

Brown was a professor at a number of universities. He pioneered courses on orality, hip hop, and popular culture. He continued writing as well, taking another approach to the Lee mythos in his historical novel *I, Stagolee* in 2005. In 2007 he published a book of academic rabble-rousing called *Dude, Where's My Black Studies Department?,* the extension of a controversial 2004 essay in the *Eastbay Express* that strongly criticized his employer at the time, the University of California, Berkeley. In this work Brown argued that black studies departments had shifted their focus, both in content and hiring practices, to Pan-African and Caribbean studies, and called for a black studies that was engaged more specifically with African American life and employed more African American professors.

Further Reading

Brown, Cecil. *Coming Up Down Home: A Memoir of a Southern Childhood* (1993).

"Cecil Brown," in *Dictionary of Literary Biography, Volume 33: Afro-American Fiction Writers After 1955*, eds. Thadious M. Davis and Trudier Harris (1984).

ANN MCCARTHY

BROWN, Charlotte Eugenia Hawkins (11 June 1883–11 Jan. 1961), educator, was born Lottie Hawkins in Henderson, North Carolina, the daughter of Edmund H. Hight, a brick mason, and Caroline Frances Hawkins. Accounts vary as to whether her father and mother separated before or after her birth, and it is also unclear whether her parents ever married. After her mother married Nelson Willis, Lottie (as she was called until she changed her name to Charlotte Eugenia in high school) relocated with nineteen members of her extended family to Massachusetts in 1888. By joining the widespread migration of African Americans, the family hoped to enjoy greater economic opportunities and a better life. After settling in Cambridge, her stepfather worked odd jobs to support the family, while her mother boarded African American Harvard students, operated a laundry, and babysat. Hawkins began her elementary education at the Allston School in Cambridge, where she befriended two of Henry Wadsworth Longfellow's daughters and excelled in her studies. She also attended Baptist Sunday school, where at the age of twelve she organized a kindergarten department.

Hawkins then attended Cambridge English High and Latin School. During her senior year she met and made a favorable impression upon the former president of Wellesley College, Alice Freeman Palmer. Although Hawkins wanted to attend Radcliffe in order to gain the best possible preparation for a teaching career, her mother urged her to enter teaching immediately. As a compromise, Hawkins entered the Salem Normal School (later Salem State College) in 1900. Having spotted Palmer's name in the school catalog, Hawkins wrote to her in search of advice; her inquiry gained her a letter of recommendation and an offer of financial assistance from Palmer.

A second chance encounter at the beginning of Hawkins's second year at Salem determined the course of her life. After meeting a representative of the American Missionary Association on a train between Salem and Cambridge, she decided to accept an offer to return to her native state and operate a school for the association. Leaving Salem before

Charlotte Eugenia Hawkins Brown, in her doctoral robes, c. 1928. (Charlotte Hawkins Brown Museum at Historic Palmer Memorial Institute, Division of State of Historic Sites and Properties, North Carolina Department of Cultural Resources.)

graduating (she later received credit for her work in the South and was awarded a diploma), she traveled south by train and arrived in McLeansville, North Carolina. After walking four miles to the community of Sedalia, she boarded with a local minister and on 12 October 1901 welcomed fifteen children to the poorly maintained one-room shack that was the Bethany Institute.

Although Hawkins was accepted by the community and encouraged by her accomplishments during the five-month school term, her future in Sedalia looked bleak when the association moved to close all its smaller schools at the end of the school year. Undaunted and determined to complete her work in the community, Hawkins rejected an offer from the association to teach elsewhere and returned north with the goal of raising sufficient funds to open her own school.

Upon returning to Cambridge, she approached Palmer for assistance, only to find her benefactress in poor health and bereft of her fortune. Palmer did, however, provide her with the names of several possible financial contributors. After soliciting funds from these people, Hawkins traveled to the resort community of

Gloucester, Massachusetts, where she gave dramatic recitations and musical performances to raise money. She returned to Sedalia with less than four hundred dollars and, with that money and a donation of fifteen acres of land and an old blacksmith shop, she opened the school on 10 October 1902.

The school, which was named the Palmer Memorial Institute the following summer in honor of her recently deceased mentor, soon became a success story. Inspired by and patterned after BOOKER T. WASHINGTON's Tuskegee Institute, Palmer in its early years emphasized basic instruction and manual training. Students were responsible for daily chores and farm work as well as academics. The school filled a dire need in a state in which educational opportunities for African Americans were few. (No teacher-training institutions existed until the 1930s, and there was no public schooling in the Sedalia area until 1937.) Fund-raising was a constant concern; fortunately, wealthy northerners, such as Charles W. Eliot (who also served as the president of the first board of trustees), Seth Low, and Galen S. Stone, were generous in their support. The American Missionary Association added its resources in 1924, and Hawkins's own fund-raising efforts resulted in a permanent endowment of $250,000.

Despite her many commitments, Hawkins did not neglect her own intellectual development. She took summer and regular courses at Simmons College, Temple University, and Harvard University. It was at the latter that she met Edward S. Brown, whom she married in June 1911. Although he initially returned with Hawkins to Sedalia and taught at Palmer, he left after five years to teach at a similar school in South Carolina, and the marriage ended in divorce. Charlotte Hawkins Brown, though childless, raised several nieces and nephews at her on-campus home, the Canary Cottage. One of her nieces, Maria Hawkins Ellington, became a singer and later married NAT KING COLE.

The Palmer Institute eventually grew to three hundred acres in size and shifted its academic emphasis; in its latter years it became a preparatory school with a focus on high school and junior college–level instruction. While Brown's students remained central in her life, she also engaged in professional activities and social activism. She helped found the North Carolina State Federation of Negro Women's Clubs in 1909 and also served as its president (1915–1936). While she was president, the federation purchased and maintained the Efland Home for Wayward Girls in Orange County, North Carolina; it was the only institution of its type for African American women in the state.

Charlotte Hawkins Brown's interest in interracial harmony led to her work in founding the Commission on Interracial Cooperation in 1919. That same year she published *Mammy: An Appeal to the Heart of the South*, a fictional indictment of the treatment of African Americans during slavery. Fully supportive of civil rights, Brown chafed under the restrictive racial atmosphere of her day and frequently challenged established Jim Crow standards. She refused to ride in segregated elevators and was sometimes ejected from "whites only" Pullman berths. Nonviolent in outlook, she occasionally resorted to lawsuits in order to challenge the discriminatory practices that she encountered during her travels. Despite her outspoken nature, Brown was a firm believer in the social graces. She constantly sought to inculcate manners as well as education into her students and published *The Correct Thing to Do, to Say, and to Wear* in 1941 as a guidebook in this area.

Brown remained busy throughout her life. She was named in 1940 to the North Carolina Council of Defense—one of the first African Americans so nominated—and also served as a member of the Executive Committee of the Home Nursing Council of the American Red Cross during World War II. Although she retired as president of Palmer in October 1952, she retained the post of director of finance until 1955. She died in Greensboro, North Carolina, after a lingering illness.

Charlotte Hawkins Brown is remembered for her pioneering efforts at Palmer Memorial Institute. Given early advantages of education and upbringing, she returned to her native state to provide educational opportunities for her fellow African Americans at a time when those opportunities were not readily available. She succeeded against often overwhelming odds in creating a preparatory school that provided hundreds of students with opportunities for a better life. Although Palmer Institute closed because of financial problems in 1971, its graduates are Brown's greatest legacy.

Further Reading

The papers of Charlotte Eugenia Hawkins Brown are held at the Schlesinger Library of Women in America at Radcliffe College, Cambridge, Massachusetts. Additional material on Brown and on Palmer Institute is available at the Charlotte Hawkins Brown Museum and Historic Site in Sedalia in the W. C. Jackson Library at the University of North Carolina at Greensboro and in the North Carolina Historical Room at the Greensboro Public Library.

Marteena, Constance Hill. *The Lengthening Shadow of a Woman: A Biography of Charlotte Hawkins Brown* (1977).

Wadelington, Charles W., and Richard F. Knapp. *Charlotte Hawkins Brown and Palmer Institute: What One Young African American Woman Could Do* (1999).

Obituary: *New York Times*, 12 Jan. 1961.

EDWARD L. LACH JR.

BROWN, Clara (Aunt Clara) (1803?–26 Oct. 1885), former slave, western pioneer, church founder, businesswoman, and philanthropist, was born in Gallatin, Tennessee—some sources offer a birth date of 1800—and at the age of three was sold with her mother to a planter in Virginia. There, at the age of eighteen, she married a slave named Richard and had several children. When her owner, Ambrose Smith,

Aunt Clara Brown, a freed slave who built a successful laundry business catering to the mining community of Central City, Colorado, in an undated photograph. (AP Images.)

died in 1835 Clara and her children were auctioned off to different slaveholders. Her daughter Margaret was sold to a slaveholder in Kentucky and reportedly died a few years later. Clara lost contact with her son Richard, who was sold repeatedly. Another daughter, Eliza Jane, was sold to a James Covington, also in Kentucky.

Clara was sold again at auction, this time to a Kentucky slaveholder named George Brown, a merchant, and for the next two decades served the Brown family as a house slave. During this time Clara took on the Brown surname and became known as "Aunt" Clara Brown, a name that followed her for the rest of her life. In 1857 George Brown died, and Clara Brown's life shifted dramatically. She received three hundred dollars from the Brown estate and bought her freedom, which was allowed by Brown's will. She left Kentucky immediately (state law mandated that freed slaves had to migrate) for St. Louis, Missouri. Brown may have done some laundry work in St. Louis, but not for long. She moved on to Fort Leavenworth, in the Kansas Territory, right in the midst of a civil war that had exploded over the future of slavery in the western territories.

In the spring of 1859 Brown left Kansas with a wagon train headed west, agreeing to cook and launder in exchange for passage. She arrived in the Denver area in June after eight weeks of grueling travel, thus becoming one of the first black women—and certainly the oldest—free or enslaved, to arrive in the Colorado Territory. Her washtubs in tow, Brown now set about making money to enable her to search for her family. She remained in the area less than a year before moving closer to the mining camps in the Cherry Creek area. It proved to be a wise decision. By 1860 she had become a landowner, "paying $50.00 for a lot in Mountain City. Gilpin County records show that in 1868 she sold that same lot for $500.00, after building a house on the property" (Baker, 32). Brown's assets grew rapidly. Her booming laundry business in Central City, coupled with land and mining investments in several Colorado counties, plus the occasional payment from the county for the board or care of an indigent person, brought her fortune to an estimated ten thousand dollars by 1864. Although Brown belonged to the Central City Presbyterian Church, she used her wealth to support a variety of local congregations. She provided more than one hundred dollars toward the building of the Congregational church and contributed money to the founding of the St. James Methodist Church and even opened her home to its religious services until construction was complete. Five years after her arrival in Colorado, Brown was one of the wealthiest women in the West. Her success remains an astonishing achievement.

In 1865, at the age of sixty-two and with financial security, Brown returned to Kentucky to find her daughter, Eliza Jane. Her search proved fruitless and keenly disappointing. Kentucky and Tennessee were in chaos after the Civil War, and thousands of African Americans were free yet jobless, hungry, and often without homes. Brown gathered a group of emancipated black families and paid for them to travel with her back to Colorado. The twenty to thirty people who traveled by rail to Leavenworth and then by wagon train to Colorado likely cost her more than five thousand dollars. The payoff for Central City did not occur overnight, but in time, as Brown helped find homes and jobs for these families, the contributions of the African American community grew and continued for generations. Brown was the heart of this community.

Brown then shifted her focus to her own business concerns and for the next fourteen years bought and sold land and homes. She signed at least one quit-claim deed to provide land for one of the people she brought from Kentucky. She dealt with claim jumpers and in at least one case went to court to settle a land dispute. Brown's tax records indicate a considerable valuation of property, reaching a high of $2,500 in 1869. By 1872, however, her property valuation had dropped to $1,500. She fell behind in property taxes in 1869, 1870, and 1871, although those taxes were paid in 1874. Yet at the same time, Brown was sending money to several young female students at Oberlin College in Ohio. She continued opening her door to those in need, giving shelter, food, or medical care when asked. Disaster struck in 1873 and again in 1874 when fires swept large areas of Central City. Brown lost a number of rental properties and possessed no insurance to cover her losses.

In 1879, at the age of seventy-six, Clara Brown was called upon again to help people in need. The governor of Colorado suggested that Brown travel to Kansas to survey the dire situation of the so-called Exodusters, the free southern African Americans who were moving into Kansas in huge numbers. She carried a letter of introduction from the governor, authorizing her to ask for aid from the governor of Kansas. It may be that Brown thought that if some of the stranded blacks would be an asset to Colorado they could be brought back to work and live there; however, she returned to Colorado with little fanfare and brought back no one. Existing records indicate that little money donated from anywhere in Colorado went to the Exodusters relief efforts, and the purpose of the mission remains baffling.

By 1882 Brown had moved from her beloved Central City back to Denver. At age seventy-nine and ailing, she lost most if not all of her remaining properties to fraud, failure to pay taxes, and natural disasters. She took up residence in a home of an old friend who charged her no rent. For those who believe in miracles, there was one left for Brown. She was contacted by a stranger who told her that her daughter, Eliza Jane, might be living in Council Bluffs, Iowa. Brown went there in February 1882 and found not only her daughter but also a grandchild. Eliza Jane Brewer, probably in her mid- to late fifties, was widowed and had at least one child, although records are uncertain as to the precise number of her children. The reunion was widely reported in newspapers in Colorado and throughout the Midwest. Her daughter and grandchild returned with Brown to live with her in Denver. But the next three years proved difficult. Brown's health began to fail, and she fell on hard financial times. As word circulated about her poverty, many of those whom Brown had assisted over the many years offered contributions. In January 1884 the pioneer society in Central City invited Brown to its annual banquet. That September the Colorado Society of Pioneers made Brown its first female and first African American member. Although terribly ill, Brown put in an appearance at the September 1885 annual reunion. Brown died at home in Denver, and her funeral service on 29 October was an ecumenical event, held at the Central Presbyterian Church. Hundreds attended the services, including the governor of Colorado, the mayor of Denver, many old pioneers, and most of the Central City African American community. On 10 January 1896 Brown's body was removed to another burial site, a plot owned by Harriet Mason, one of the original members of the group of African Americans Brown brought back from her trip to Kentucky. Posthumous awards and honors preserve the memory of Brown's life, including induction into the Colorado Women's Hall of Fame in 1989 and installation of a stained glass window of Brown's image at the Colorado State Capitol.

Further Reading
Baker, Roger. *Clara: An Ex-slave in Gold Rush Colorado* (2003).

Obituaries: Denver *Republican*, 27, 30 Oct. 1885
MARIAELENA RAYMOND

BROWN, Claude (23 Feb. 1937–2 Feb. 2002), writer, was born in Harlem, New York, the eldest of four children of Henry Lee, a railroad worker, and Ossie Brock, a domestic. Both parents had moved in 1935 from South Carolina to New York, seeking a better life in the North. Brown characterized his father as a man who worked hard, drank too much, enjoyed gospel music (especially when under the influence of alcohol), and whose parenting skills were limited to corporal punishment, which he meted out with great frequency. Brown's mother attended to the material needs of her children and attempted to save their souls by occasionally bringing them to an evangelical preacher who ran a makeshift church in her apartment.

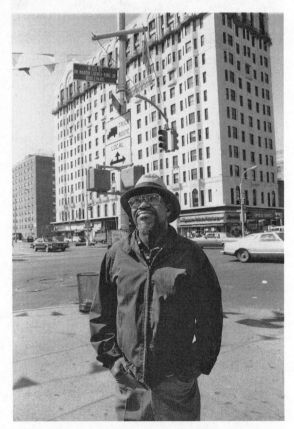

Claude Brown, standing on the corner of 125th Street in Harlem, New York, on 2 March 1986, the twentieth anniversary of the publication of his book *Manchild in the Promised Land*. (AP Images.)

Growing up in a household with two working parents, Brown got much of his upbringing on the streets and thus developed a tough attitude. He recalls that around the age of four he was hit by a bus in some kind of accident in which he was only slightly injured. His father attempted to benefit financially from the incident, but his submissive behavior around the white judge and lawyers in court transformed him in his son's eyes from a "bad nigger," (i.e., a black man who commands respect by being or acting tough), into a "simple-actin' nigger." Brown decided that unlike his posturing father, he was going to be a "bad nigger" all the time.

At the age of five, Brown started school and by December of his first year, had become a truant almost a third of the time. The following year he started stealing—not because he was hungry or destitute but because it was fun. At the age of six he felt deprived for not being allowed to participate in the Harlem riot of 1943. By the age of eight he was staying out all night and had seen a man killed for urinating in the hallway of his building.

Neither his father's beatings nor his mother's pleadings could sway Brown from his early road to perdition. Out of desperation his parents had him admitted to Bellevue Hospital for psychiatric observation to determine if there was any medical explanation for his apparent incorrigibility; none was found. However, each incident of antisocial behavior enhanced Brown's reputation among older juvenile delinquents, and at the age of nine he became one of the youngest members of the Forty Thieves, an apprentice division of the Buccaneers street gang.

In 1948 Brown was sent to the Wiltwyck School in rural Ulster County, New York, an institution for troubled boys. Already having learned to roll reefers and make homemade zip guns, Brown's criminal education continued at Wiltwyck to include the art of picking pockets, as taught by the older boys. But there he also came under the countervailing influence of the school's new director, Ernest Papenek. Papenek's innovative techniques for working with disturbed youth in Austria were soon to earn him great acclaim in the United States through the later achievements of Wiltwyck's most famous alums, Brown and the boxer FLOYD PATTERSON; but at that crossroads in Brown's life Papenek was just the "smartest and the deepest cat" he had ever met, "the best thing that could ever happen to any boy who got into trouble" (Brown, *Manchild*, 85).

In spite of these positive influences, Brown could not resist the attractions of a life of crime during his adolescence. After leaving Wiltwyck, at the age of thirteen, Brown was shot in the stomach during a burglary, and he subsequently divided his time between mischief-making in Harlem and three trips to Warwick, a reform school for hardened teenagers where "we all came out . . . better criminals" (Brown, *Manchild*, 146). If he were not killed first, Brown expected to advance from reform school and serve time with his mentors at Sing Sing or Attica prison. But at Warwick he was encouraged by Mrs. Cohen, the wife of the superintendent, to read the autobiographies of MARY MCLEOD BETHUNE, Albert Einstein, JACKIE ROBINSON, Albert Schweitzer, and others.

When he left Warwick for the last time in July 1953, an epidemic of heroin use, which Brown described as a plague of biblical proportion, was beginning to ravage Harlem. Brown's first experiment with the drug resulted in a physical reaction that was so violent and unpleasant that he never tried it again—though he liberally used cocaine and marijuana. His hustle on the streets consisted of a series of con games perpetrated against the naive and the greedy. At seventeen Brown felt as if he had lived a full and successful career as an outlaw, and in his weariness he wondered if it was not time to "retire." Conventional occupations did not appeal to him; he could never see himself working for "Mr. Charlie" or "Goldburg" (euphemisms for gentile or Jewish businesses) for any length of time. Yet, while attending Washington Irving High School at night, he worked as a watch-crystal fitter, shipping clerk, cosmetics salesman, and at various other odd jobs.

Around 1954 Brown moved from Harlem into an apartment in New York City's Greenwich Village, immersing himself in its bohemian, interracial environment. He became a jazz enthusiast, decided to become a pianist in the bebop tradition of THELONIOUS MONK, and began practicing up to eight hours each day until he played well enough to join a local band. While he had had numerous sexual encounters with black women, who were in his opinion mostly "bitches," he entered into his first serious romantic relationship with a white Jewish woman who played classical piano. He did not think that she was particularly attractive, but "compared with her, most of the colored chicks I'd known seemed crude and hard. They were chicks who you couldn't be but so sweet to, because they weren't sweet themselves. Her voice and manner were warm. She seemed to be more feminine than most of the women I knew, and more of everything a woman was supposed to be" (Brown, *Manchild*, 356). They discussed marriage, but when her parents learned of her relationship with Brown, she was whisked out of the state.

Brown received his high school diploma at the age of twenty-one and then moved back to Harlem in search of a personal sense of community. A friend from his old gang had turned his life around through religion and introduced Brown to the Coptic faith. Brown was intrigued by this black nationalist theology, with its veneration of the Ethiopian emperor Haile Selassie and its interest in mysticism and ancient history. Brown also found himself drawn to the more militant teachings of the Nation of Islam, which seemed to be the only organization in Harlem that was trying to replace the stigma of being black with the confidence of black pride. Brown attended meetings but never formally joined either organization; however, his association with them helped build a bridge to a new way of life.

By the late 1950s Brown knew that he wanted to extricate himself from the conditions that had trapped his brother in a cycle of crime and drug addiction. He hoped to go to college, but without a scholarship that seemed impossible. Brown began to confide in the Reverend William M. James of the Metropolitan Community Methodist Church. James was so impressed with Brown that he secured enough financial assistance to send him to Howard University. There Brown studied with TONI MORRISON, then a little-known writing instructor, and he prepared for a career in the law. During Brown's senior year, Dr. Papenek recommended that Brown could best fulfill a request from *Dissent* magazine for an article about inner-city youth. Bram Cavin, an editor at Crowell-Collier and Macmillan, was so taken with the resulting article that he offered Brown a two thousand dollar advance for a book. Brown wrote frantically, mostly out of a stream of consciousness, and in the fall of 1963 he submitted a fifteen-hundred-page manuscript. The draft languished for six months, until Alan Rinzler discovered it and helped Brown shape and condense it into *Manchild in the Promised Land* (1965). Brown related the brutal truth of his life in Harlem in this straightforward and uncompromising autobiographical novel. *Manchild in the Promised Land* is both a coming-of-age narrative and a eulogy for a generation of young black men perishing in America's ghettos.

Although RICHARD WRIGHT, RALPH ELLISON, ANN PETRY, JAMES BALDWIN, and others had been writing powerfully about the black urban experience for years, reviewers welcomed Brown into this exalted circle. Black magazines and newspapers were disturbed by the often true but negative depictions of black life, and most critics praised Brown's work for its plain, authentic, candid, and uncompromising presentation. Some, however, such as ALBERT MURRAY, scoffed at its lack of sophistication. Perhaps no one was less prepared for the book's success than was Brown. He had married Helen Jones, a telephone operator, while still at Howard, and after graduating in 1965, he was in his first year at Stanford University Law School when he suddenly became famous. He transferred to Rutgers Law School to accommodate frequent invitations to New York book parties; but by 1968, the dream of becoming a lawyer could no longer compete with the reality of being a writer earning sixty thousand dollars a year lecturing about his book.

Brown initially thought of using his popularity to run for the Harlem congressional seat held by ADAM CLAYTON POWELL JR. He never became a formal candidate and eventually felt the need or desire return to writing. *The Children of Ham* (1976) continues in the same tone and style that had won Brown such acclaim ten years earlier, as it recounts the struggles of thirteen Harlemites against poverty, drugs, and crime. But times and literary tastes had changed, reviews were harsh (with the notable exception of one by ARNOLD RAMPERSAD), and sales were disappointing. Brown never completed his third book, though he did write many articles and essays. His marriage ended in divorce, and he moved to New Jersey, where he devoted much of his time to working with troubled youth and prison inmates until he was overcome by lung cancer.

Manchild in the Promised Land was undoubtedly Brown's most enduring work. It sold more than four million copies in fourteen languages and earned a place in the literary canon as a period piece if not as a classic of African American autobiographical writing.

Further Reading
Hartshorne, Thomas L. "Horatio Alger in Harlem: Manchild in the Promised Land," *Journal of American Studies*, vol. 24, no 2 (Aug. 1990): 243-9.
Madhubuti, Haki R. "In Memoriam," *Black Issues in Higher Education Magazine,* vol. 19.1 (Feb. 2002): 26.

Obituaries: *New York Times,* 6 Feb. 2002; *Boston Globe* and *New York Amsterdam News,* 7 Feb. 2002.

SHOLOMO B. LEVY

BROWN, Cleo (8 Dec. 1907–15 Apr. 1995), jazz pianist and singer, was born in Meridian, Mississippi, the daughter of a Baptist minister. The names of her parents are unknown. Some sources set her birth in 1909, while others suggest that she may have been five or more years older than that; the year 1907 is based on Social Security records, where her name is listed as Cleo Patra Brown. Her surname is sometimes spelled Browne.

Cleo began taking piano lessons as early as age four, and she was soon accompanying the choir in her father's church. The family moved to Chicago when Brown was ten years old. Though her father came to disapprove of his daughter's playing, she continued studying piano and, when only fourteen years old, she found a job with a traveling orchestra and went on the road. She worked in South Side Chicago's Three Deuces Club, leading her own group in that club and in other places in Chicago and New York from the late 1920s to perhaps as late as the 1950s. For a time she broadcast her own show on WABC in New York.

Chicago in the 1930s was known for its blues stars, and Brown became part of the crowd that made blues and boogie-woogie the rage at the time. Through her brother, Everett, she got to know and was influenced by the barrelhouse pianist Pinetop Smith, who died in 1929. In March 1935 she recorded a version of "Pinetop's Boogie-woogie" for Decca that made her a star in Chicago. She also recorded during that same session four songs with a quartet that included the drummer Gene Krupa, and later that year she recorded another side with the Decca All Star Revue, including Victor Young and the Scottish-born singer Ella Logan. In her recording sessions through the thirties and forties, Brown performed with other notable musicians, both white and black, including ZUTTY SINGLETON.

Though her recordings spread her influence as a singer and especially a jazz pianist in the 1930s and 1940s, Brown remained a virtual secret from the mainstream jazz world for most of her long life, largely because she retired early from the national scene. It may be that life on the road was too difficult for her, causing her to fall ill from the strain. It was especially difficult for African American women to find places to sleep and eat or simply to exist comfortably on the road. Women players were frequently harassed by audiences and often were forced to sleep in the vehicles they had traveled to their jobs in. That is probably why Brown, at least for a time, chose Los Angeles as her headquarters. The city was becoming a lively mecca for jazz, and many well-known musicians settled in the area. There Brown recorded for the California-based Hot Shot label and then for Capitol Records in 1949. By the late 1940s a string of hits by NAT KING COLE had already done much to establish Capitol's reputation.

In the early 1950s Brown became a Seventh-day Adventist, stopped performing in public, and found work as a nurse. At some point Brown left California; in 1973 she surfaced in Denver, Colorado, where she played and taught piano under the name of C. Patra Brown and then Cleopatra, a name she had always favored for herself. She had become a member of the Seventh-day Adventist Church and played primarily church music—gospel and hymns. In 1987, at age seventy-eight, she played and sang church music, including some of her original compositions, on McPartland's Peabody Prize–winning radio show, *Piano Jazz*. That same year the National Endowment for the Arts awarded her an NEA Jazz Masters fellowship.

A number of women pianists have acknowledged their debt to Brown. According to the singer and pianist NELLIE LUTCHER, such tunes as Brown's "It's a Heavenly Thing" fostered a trend for women to emphasize "a sly, coy, or somewhat risqué humor backed by boogie-woogie piano." In the 1980s the British-born pianist Marian McPartland recalled that Brown's distinctive boogie-woogie style was one of her earliest influences back in the 1930s and 1940s, when she was looking for role models to develop her skills and tastes. McPartland went so far as to say that Brown was one of the few pianists who actually convinced her to make a career for herself in jazz.

A year after Brown's death Audiophile Records released *Living in the Afterglow*, a set of mostly religious songs that she performed with McPartland. The jazz pianist Dave Brubeck, who wrote a tribute to Brown, "Sweet Cleo Brown," in 1957, called her "one of the greatest women pianists," and he noted in a later interview, "When FATS WALLER died, the musicians in that band wanted her to take over, that's how great she was."

Further Reading

Dahl, Linda. *Stormy Weather: The Music and Lives of a Century of Jazzwomen* (1984).

Discography

Lord, Tom. *The Jazz Discography* (1992).
Cleo Brown, 1935–1951 (Melody Jazz Classics, 2002).
The Legendary Cleo Brown (President, 2003).
Living in the Afterglow (Audiophile, 1996).

LESLIE GOURSE

BROWN, Clifford (30 Oct. 1930–26 June 1956), trumpeter, was born in Wilmington, Delaware. Brown's parents' names are unknown. Brown's father was a self-taught musician who played the trumpet, violin, and piano for his own amusement. He kept several instruments around the house. Young Clifford eventually picked up the bugle and demonstrated an aptitude for it. At age twelve Clifford was taken by his father to study with the renowned Wilmington teacher and bandleader Robert Lowery. Clifford spent three years with Lowery, studying jazz harmony, theory, trumpet, piano, vibraphone, and bass and playing in Lowery's big band.

Brown's father bought Brown a trumpet in 1943, the year he entered high school. He studied the trumpet with his high school band director, Harry Andrews, who had done advanced brass study at the University of Michigan. Brown became an outstanding trumpet player under Andrews's tutelage. He perfected octave jumps, developed a beautiful range, and ornamented melodies with little grace notes. These grace notes became a hallmark of his jazz trumpet style. Brown also began writing arrangements for his high school band. He left a lasting impression on Andrews with his brilliant "Carnival of Venice" graduation solo.

Brown showed a DIZZY GILLESPIE bebop trumpet influence all the way through high school. He graduated from high school and enrolled at Delaware State College in 1949. The school did not have a music department, so he studied mathematics. The following year Brown transferred to Maryland State College on a music scholarship. This school had a good fifteen-piece band, which gave Brown playing and arranging experience. While at Maryland State, Brown played a couple of times a month as a member of a Philadelphia house band for jazz concerts. He played with innovators such as the trombonist J. J. JOHNSON, the drummer MAX ROACH, the alto saxophonist ERNIE HENRY, and the trumpeters MILES DAVIS and FATS NAVARRO.

Navarro encouraged Brown and became his major stylistic influence. Navarro's trumpet roots were in the Cuban trumpet tradition and the American bebop style. He was known for his clear articulation, melodic inventiveness, and ringing, bell-like tone. Brown's own melodic inventiveness, clear articulation, and fat, bell-like tone can be traced to Navarro's influence. Gillespie's big band played a date in Wilmington one night in 1949. Benny Harris, one of Gillespie's trumpet players, was late, so Brown got the opportunity to replace Harris for forty-five minutes. Gillespie was impressed and encouraged the youngster to pursue a jazz career.

Brown was seriously injured in a 1950 car crash and was hospitalized from June 1950 to May 1951. Gillespie visited him during this period and encouraged him to resume his trumpet career. Brown left the hospital and played successful gigs on the piano until he was able to resume his trumpet playing. One of his trumpet gigs was with the alto saxophonist CHARLIE "BIRD" PARKER. Brown said of this gig, "Benny Harris was the cause of that one, too. He left Bird shortly after the engagement began so I worked in his place for a week. Bird helped my morale a great deal. One night he took me into a corner and said, 'I don't believe it. I hear what you're saying, but I don't believe it' " (Hentoff, "Clifford Brown").

Brown toured with Chris Powell's rhythm and blues band for a year and a half during 1952 and 1953. He played both trumpet and piano with this group. Brown made his first modern jazz recordings during this period, playing on a Blue Note recording for the alto saxophonist Lou Donaldson. Brown played with the composer-pianist TADD DAMERON in Atlantic City, New Jersey, in 1953 and recorded for Prestige Records with Dameron. During the summer of 1953 the arranger-trumpeter QUINCY JONES was working with the LIONEL HAMPTON Band in Wildwood, New Jersey. Jones begged Hampton to hire three musicians from Dameron's band, which was nearing the end of its Atlantic City engagement: alto saxophonist GIGI GRYCE, tenor saxophonist Benny Golson, and trumpeter Brown. Hampton listened to them and hired all three. Brown stayed with Hampton from July until November 1953. During the band's European tour, Brown recorded several albums with Swedish, French, and American musicians, including Gryce.

Brown freelanced in New York City in 1953 and 1954. He recorded with the drummer ART BLAKEY and the pianist Horace Silver in the band that subsequently became the Jazz Messengers. Brown won the 1954 *Down Beat* magazine Critic's Poll as the new star of the year on trumpet. Late in March 1954 Brown joined MAX ROACH in California to form and colead a new quintet. During this time he met and married a University of California music student named LaRue Watson; they had one child.

The Clifford Brown–Max Roach Quintet became one of the most important jazz combos in history. The quintet's 1954–1955 personnel consisted of Brown on trumpet, Harold Land on tenor saxophone, Richard Powell on piano, George Morrow on bass, and Roach on drums. In January 1956 the tenor saxophonist SONNY ROLLINS replaced Land.

The Brown-Roach quintet established new standards of quality and balance between combo arrangements and improvisations. Roach commented that they desired the quintet "to be interesting musically and emotionally at the same time" (Hentoff, "Roach & Brown, Inc."). The quintet's 1955 and 1956 EmArcy recordings are masterpieces of artistry and creativity. Brown's solos are unequaled in their melodic beauty and emphatic clarity.

Brown introduced a new trumpet style. The nebop trumpeter Gillespie said that "Brown was gifted. And he established a new style, a way of playing the trumpet that was a little different from what we were doing before" (West, 30). Brown's career was short, but it was long enough to influence virtually every major trumpeter that followed him. Brown, Richard Powell, and Powell's wife died in an auto accident on the Pennsylvania Turnpike.

Further Reading

Catalano, Nick. *Clifford Brown: The Life and Art of the Legendary Jazz Trumpeter* (2000).
Hentoff, Nat. "Clifford Brown: The New Dizzy," *Down Beat* (7 Apr. 1954).
Hentoff, Nat. "Roach & Brown, Inc.: Dealers in Jazz," *Down Beat* (4 May 1955).
West, Hollie. "Clifford Brown: Trumpeter's Training," *Down Beat* (July 1980).

MILTON STEWART

BROWN, Corrine (11 Nov. 1942–), U.S. congresswoman, was born in Jacksonville, Florida, where she lived from childhood through her high school years. Brown has not made much information about her early years, her parents, or her personal life known. In 1965 she gave birth to her only daughter, Shantrel, the same year she began college. Brown received a BS in 1969 and a master's degree in Education in 1971 from Florida A&M University. She earned an education specialist degree from the University of Florida in 1974. From 1977 to 1982 Brown worked as a faculty member and guidance counselor at Florida Community College in Jacksonville.

Corrine Brown, voicing her opposition to Governor Jeb Bush's order to end affirmative action and minority set-asides in Florida at a news conference in Orlando on 15 November 1999. Listening is Orlando City Commissioner Daisy Lynum (left). (AP Images.)

As a member of Sigma Gamma Rho Sorority Inc. at Florida A&M, Brown became close friends with her sorority sister Gwendolyn Sawyer-Cherry, who was the first African American woman to serve in the Florida state legislature. Sawyer-Cherry influenced Brown to enter politics, and after Brown lost her first race for a seat in the Florida state legislature in 1980, Sawyer-Cherry encouraged her to try again. Brown followed her advice and remained an active member of the political scene, supporting the Jacksonville Democratic Party. In 1980 she joined the Duval County Democratic Executive Committee. In 1982 Brown was elected as the Seventeenth District Florida state representative in the Florida legislature, a position that she held for ten years.

Following the 1990 U.S. Census, Florida was one of many states influenced by the U.S. Department of Justice to redraw its voting districts. The new crookedly shaped districts were designed to give minority groups majority representation, but they immediately came under criticism as being unconstitutional. The Florida districts would be redrawn two additional times following the 1992 election to comply with a federal court ruling that deemed them unconstitutional. In 1992 Brown campaigned for the U.S. House of Representatives to represent the new black-majority Third District. She endured a tough Democratic primary, facing charges of ethical misconduct from her opponents, but she won in a runoff with 64 percent of the vote. After winning the primary, Brown proclaimed, "This is the year of the woman, so get out of the way, men" (*CQ Weekly*, Jan. 1993). She secured her seat in Congress with 59 percent of the vote in the general election against Republican Don Weidner. Brown was successful in winning each of her bids for reelection thereafter.

Brown's congressional activities focused on improving the lives of Floridians. She sought an assignment on the Transportation and Infrastructure Committee to address the problems of highway congestion and road flooding in eastern Florida. She also used her seat to bring new jobs into Florida. When federal transportation programs were redesigned in 1998, Brown was instrumental in making sure Florida received a 57 percent increase in federal funding. She also worked on the Veteran Affairs and Government Operations Committee to advocate for the interest of military installations around her district and the growing number of military veterans in the Jacksonville area. She maintained memberships in the Congressional Black Caucus, Women's Caucus, Human Rights Caucus, and Progressive Caucus, advocating on behalf of the underprivileged, the unemployed, and the undereducated citizens of her state and the nation. A vocal liberal, Brown consistently supported social programs such as affirmative action and advocated for improved health care for minorities, children, and the elderly.

Brown's advocacy for the poor and disadvantaged, as well as her consistent representation of the interests of Floridians, has at times been overshadowed by her outspoken nature and repeated allegations of ethics violations. After just one hundred days in office, she became the subject of state and federal probes into her staff spending and campaign finance. In 1998 the *St. Petersburg Times* reported that Brown received a ten-thousand-dollar gift from the Reverend Henry Lyons, president of the National Baptist Convention; Brown denied all charges of misconduct. Later that year, the *Times* reported that Brown's daughter, Shantrel, a government lawyer in Washington, had received a luxury car from a West African businessman for whom Brown had lobbied to keep him out of federal prison. Brown again denied the allegations, but further attention to the issue was encouraged by Republicans, and the House Ethics Committee launched its own investigation. After fifteen months, the committee found no evidence of ethical misconduct, but expressed that Brown likely exercised "poor judgment" (Foerstel, *CQ Weekly*, Sept. 2000).

In 2000 Brown became an outspoken advocate for voters' rights, as the United States faced one of the most controversial presidential elections in history. Many Florida voters in 2000, and many minority and senior voters, of particular concern to Brown, were turned away at the polls, and thousands of ballots were miscounted or miscast. As late as 2004 Brown spoke out against the injustice she believed had occurred in Florida in 2000. Her sharp words on the floor of Congress resulted in her speaking privileges being revoked for a day because she violated protocols of decorum. "I come from Florida, where you and others participated in what I call the United States coup d'etat," Brown said. "Over and over again, after the election when you stole the election, you came back here and said, 'Get over it'" (Allen, *CQ Weekly*, July 2004). Brown remained unapologetic, saying, "If they're going to take my words down for telling the truth, that's OK" (Allen, *CQ Weekly*, July 2004). Brown backed a 2002 measure to heighten election standards and continued to push for election reform.

Brown was reelected for an eighth term in the U.S. House of Representatives in November 2006. As a senior House member, she was selected as chair of the Transportation Subcommittee on Railroads, Pipelines, and Hazardous Materials. This position allowed Brown to continue to secure federal funding for the improvement of the Jacksonville and Orlando road and transit projects. Additionally, Brown was selected as the first vice chairwoman of the Congressional Black Caucus. Following her reelection she remained an outspoken critic of the Republican Party, particularly of the Bush administration's economic and foreign policies.

Further Reading

Allen, Jonathan. "Florida on Her Mind: Rep. Brown Invokes 2000, Ignores Decorum," *CQ Weekly* (July 2004).

Anonymous. "Special Report: 103rd Congress House Freshman Profiles Florida—3rd District: Corrine Brown," *CQ Weekly* (Jan. 1993).

Foerstel, Karen. "No Ethics Violations Found in Brown Probe," *CQ Weekly* (Sept. 2000).

Gill, LaVerne McCain. *African American Women in Congress: Forming and Transforming History* (1997).

MONIKA R. ALSTON

BROWN, Dorothy Lavinia (7 Jan. 1919–13 June 2004), surgeon and Tennessee legislator, was born to a single mother, Edna Brown, in Philadelphia, Pennsylvania. When she was five months old, her mother placed her in the Troy Orphanage. In 1932 Brown's mother reclaimed her daughter, but the two clashed and Brown ran away from home. She was subsequently taken in by Samuel Wesley and Lola Redmon. Brown obtained a job as a mother's helper in the W. F. Jarrett home and graduated from high school, possibly Troy High School, about 1937.

Several factors inspired Brown to become a surgeon. As a child, she entered the hospital for the removal of her tonsils and adenoids. She loved the special attention that she received and wanted to duplicate that experience for other patients. Later, in her teens, she attended a performance by the African American opera star MARIAN ANDERSON. Impressed by Anderson's greatness and graciousness, Brown resolved to do something to make other African Americans proud of her. To achieve this dream, she had to overcome the double burden of discrimination based on race and gender.

Brown graduated from Bennett College, a historically black college for women, in Greensboro, North Carolina, in 1941. While in college, she joined the Delta Sigma Theta sorority, with which she remained affiliated throughout her life. Upon graduation she spent two years working in the Rochester (New York) Army Ordnance Department. Brown entered Meharry Medical College, a historically black medical school, in Nashville in 1944. In the 1940s no white southern medical school would accept an African American student despite the black community's strong need for medical professionals.

Dorothy Lavinia Brown, addressing supporters for her mayoral campaign at a news conference in Chicago, 31 August 2006. (AP Images.)

Graduating in the top third of her class, she earned her MD in 1948.

Although Brown served her internship at the historically black Harlem Hospital in New York City, she was denied a residency there because she was a woman. Brown returned to Nashville in 1949 to become a resident at the George W. Hubbard Hospital on the Meharry campus. She completed her residency in 1954. Brown spent the remainder of her medical career in Nashville. One of the first black female surgeons in the country, she became clinical professor of surgery at Meharry Medical College in 1954, chief of surgery at Riverside Hospital in 1957, and an attending physician at several other hospitals in the city. At the time that Brown became a fellow of the American College of Surgeons in the mid-1960s, only two other African American women were fellows.

As a physician in the South in the age of Jim Crow, Brown was well acquainted with the effect of racism on health care for African Americans. Blacks were less healthy than whites and died earlier. They did not receive the quality of medical care provided to whites because of a lack of monetary resources, a lack of trust between blacks and white medical professionals, a refusal on the part of some whites to treat black patients, and a lack of access to quality hospital care. A desire to improve the lives of African Americans may have prompted Brown to enter politics. In 1966 she became the first African American woman to be elected to the Tennessee State Legislature. A Democrat, she was elected to one term in the house of representatives in 1967.

Brown took the politically risky step of attempting to liberalize Tennessee abortion laws. A number of states had begun to reform their abortion laws in the 1960s; Tennessee never joined them. Tennessee law permitted abortions only in cases where the mother's life was in danger. Brown's 1967 bill would have legalized abortions caused by rape or incest. The bill fell two votes short of passage. Brown had better success in pushing through an African American history bill. The legislation required all Tennessee public schools to conduct special programs during Black History Week to recognize accomplishments made by African Americans. Brown ran for a seat in the Tennessee Senate in 1968 but lost. She left the legislature when her house term expired at the end of 1968.

African American women of Brown's generation were taught that they had an obligation to help uplift the black race. Brown's life reflected this teaching. She became the first single woman in Tennessee to adopt a child, doing so in 1956, and she named the child Lola Denise in honor of her foster mother. Brown also served as a member of the board of trustees of Bennett College and remained active in the United Methodist Church. In 1959 she became only the third woman to become a fellow of the American College of Surgeons. In her lifetime, she received honorary degrees from Bennett College and Cumberland University.

Further Reading:
Alpha Kappa Alpha Sorority. *Women in Medicine* (1971).
Neumann, Caryn E. "Status Seekers: Long-established Women's Organizations and the Women's Movement in the United States, 1945–1970s," PhD diss., Ohio State University (2006).

CARYN E. NEUMANN

BROWN, E. C. (Edward Cooper) (1877–28 Jan. 1928), businessman and banker, was born in Philadelphia, Pennsylvania, to Robert Brown, a turnkey in the local jail, and Anne Brown, a homemaker. E. C. Brown was the eldest of three children. He attended the public schools in Philadelphia and after his high school graduation worked for three years as a mail clerk at the financial firm of Bradstreet Mercantile. He took stenography and typewriting classes at the Spencerian Business College in Philadelphia and subsequently worked as a stenographer for the National Railway Company but was soon laid off. Brown then became secretary to a Frank Thompson, who ran a catering business in Florida in the late 1890s. Around 1901 Brown left Thompson and started a real estate business in Newport News, Virginia. By 1908 he was renting more than 300 houses and had more than 800 tenants. On 27 June 1908 he opened the Crown Savings Bank, a private bank catering to African Americans in Newport News, while still holding onto his real estate business. In 1909 Brown founded another private bank for African Americans, the Brown Savings Bank in Norfolk, Virginia. The success of both banks made Brown nationally known within African American business circles. Later it would be discovered that both banks were financially unsound and that Brown was using depositors' funds to finance his real estate deals.

Brown was active in BOOKER T. WASHINGTON's National Negro Business League, which was founded in 1900 and provided a forum for black businesspeople to discuss their successes and problems in business operations. At the league's 1908 meeting Brown described his career in real estate, endorsing Washington's philosophy of black self-help. At that time Brown was treasurer of the Colored Bankers Association, and a member of the National Negro Bankers' Association, which was dissolved around 1916. At the 1919 National Negro Business League meeting Brown cited his success in Virginia as an example of why southern blacks should support black businesses. He also said that he was still the president and a stockholder in the Brown Savings Bank of Norfolk. Despite his popularity among black businessmen and -women, Brown lost a bid to become president of the National Negro Business League in 1921

Brown's lasting accomplishments, however, were made in the North. In 1913, for reasons that are unclear, he returned to Philadelphia to open a real estate office. About this time Brown formed a business partnership with the Philadelphia politician Andrew Steven Jr. In January 1916 they opened a private bank in Philadelphia known as Brown and Stevens. Its advertisements in the *Philadelphia Tribune* beckoned African Americans recently arrived in Philadelphia during the Great Migration. Migrants found the Brown and Stevens Bank attractive because it welcomed small savings accounts and encouraged clients to invest in real estate and black business. In 1917 Brown and other black entrepreneurs established the Payton Apartments Corporation to manage the Payton Apartments—considered a desirable address for members of the black middle class—in Harlem. Around this time Brown married Estelle Smith, although the exact year of the marriage is unclear. The Browns raised Estelle's daughter Suzie.

In July 1918 Brown and Stevens founded the Dunbar Amusement Company to finance a new theater in Philadelphia and in 1919 bought the Quality Amusement Company from Robert Levey of New York City. That company controlled the Lafayette Players Stock Company and the Lafayette Theatre in Harlem. Under Brown the company later acquired the Howard Theatre in Washington, D.C., the Avenue Theatre in Chicago, and the Douglass Theatre in Baltimore. As head of the Quality Amusement Company, Brown featured weekly performances by the Lafayette Players in Philadelphia. They starred in the show *Within the Law*, a comedy-drama, at the grand opening of the Dunbar Theatre in Philadelphia on 29 December 1919. The Dunbar Theatre also featured motion pictures for black audiences such as OSCAR MICHEAUX's *The Symbol of the Unconquered*, released in 1920, vaudeville acts such as the blues singer MAMIE SMITH, and musicals like EUBIE BLAKE and NOBLE SISSLE's *Shuffle Along*.

In 1920 Brown lost his bid to become president of the National Negro Business League. Meanwhile yet more serious setbacks loomed in his financial matters. In July of that year Brown sold his stock in the Quality Amusement Company, which controlled the Lafayette Theatre in New York. Then, citing a two-thousand-dollar weekly deficit, in August 1921 Brown persuaded stockholders in the Dunbar Amusement Company to sell the Dunbar Theatre in Philadelphia to JOHN TRUSTY GIBSON. This was the first time the public became aware of Brown's financial problems. In 1925 there was a run on the Brown and Stevens Bank, forcing it to file for involuntary bankruptcy. As a private bank Brown and Stevens was not subject to oversight by the state banking department that could have identified problems early on. An auditing of the bank's books revealed evidence of inadequate record keeping and fraud. The state auditor alleged that Brown and Stevens used their companies for their own financial gain. Because of the bankruptcy, hundreds of African Americans lost their savings. Brown moved to New York City and set up a real estate business. He remained in the city until his death. An ambitious man with questionable business practices, his business empire collapsed as rapidly as it had risen. Yet Brown's lasting legacy was his promotion of the Lafayette Players and black theaters during the Harlem Renaissance.

Further Reading

Hamilton, Kenneth M., ed. *Records of the National Negro Business League* (c. 1994).

Harris, Abram Lincoln, Jr. *The Negro as Capitalist: A Study of Banking and Business among American Negroes* (1969).

Kellner, Bruce. "E.C. Brown," in *The Harlem Renaissance: A Historical Dictionary for the Era*, ed. Bruce Kellner (1987).

Richardson, Clement, ed. *The National Cyclopedia of the Colored Race*, vol. 1 (1919).

Sampson, Henry T. *Blacks in Blackface: A Source Book on Early Black Musical Shows* (1980).

Obituary: *New York Age*, 28 Jan. 1928.

ERIC LEDELL SMITH

BROWN, Earl (24 July 1903–13 Apr. 1980), politician, journalist, and Negro League professional baseball pitcher, was born in Charlottesville, Virginia, one of four children. His father was a Baptist minister and his mother was a nurse. His mother wanted him to pursue medicine, but Brown was interested in sports and studying social problems. After preparing at Howard Academy in Washington, D.C., Brown went to Harvard.

Brown majored in economics but also played baseball, lettering as a left-handed pitcher. He worked his way through Harvard as a janitor and waiter. During summer breaks he was a Red Cap at Grand Central Station in New York, and also played in the Negro Leagues. In 1923 and 1924 he pitched for the New York Lincoln Giants. Interestingly Harvard, usually aggressive about enforcing early NCAA rules barring athletes from playing professional sports, apparently did not punish Brown when he played in the professional ranks before returning to the Harvard baseball team for his senior year.

Brown suffered discrimination on the baseball team. In April of his senior year Harvard hosted the University of Georgia, which objected to playing against African Americans. Harvard obliged and barred Brown from playing in the two-game series. He did go on to win four games that season, including an impressive twelve strikeout victory over Amherst. After graduating in 1924 Brown went into real estate and continued to play baseball, appearing with the Lincoln Giants and the Harrisburg Giants in 1924 and the Baltimore Black Sox in 1925, before finishing up with the Lincoln Giants in 1926.

Brown taught economics, first at Union University in Virginia, then at Louisville Municipal College, before going into journalism. He married Emma Moseley in 1931. They had no children. He became a reporter for the *New York Herald Tribune* then took a managing editor position at the *Amsterdam News*. While at the *Amsterdam News* Brown wrote an unflattering profile of the boxing great JOE LOUIS for *Life* magazine. The resulting furor got him fired, but he was hired by *Life* and worked there as an editor for many years.

Brown's political career started when he was named a delegate to the 1944 Democratic National Convention. In 1949 the Republican, Democratic, and Liberal parties united to nominate him for the Harlem City Council seat held by BENJAMIN JEFFERSON DAVIS, a Communist then just a year away from being imprisoned for his political beliefs. In this era of growing red-baiting, Brown won easily. During his time in the City Council he took the lead on securing passage for numerous laws fighting discrimination, including the Sharkey-Brown-Isaacs Housing Law, which banned discrimination in private rental housing. This law served as a model for similar ordinances in cities throughout the United States.

In 1958 he was recruited by the Democratic Party to oppose incumbent ADAM CLAYTON POWELL JR. for the Sixteenth Congressional Seat in Harlem. Powell was an extremely popular Congressman who had angered Democratic regulars by openly supporting the Republican Dwight Eisenhower for president in 1956, and Powell was also under federal indictment for income tax evasion. Even with these impediments, Powell was viewed as an overwhelming favorite. The campaign was ugly. Brown accused Powell of "racist tendencies" and "treason to the Democratic Party" for supporting Eisenhower. Powell labeled Brown's charges ridiculous and in turn accused him of "playing Uncle Tom's game" for not protesting southern democrat hostility to civil rights.

As expected, Brown was soundly beaten, but that wasn't the only fallout from that bitter election. A dying Tammany Hall, New York's longtime Democratic political machine, was behind Brown's challenge to Powell, who in turn attacked Brown as a "handpicked Uncle Tom selected by the Tammany plantation bosses to work against his own people." Brown retaliated by claiming that Powell hurt Harlem by refusing to work with Tammany Hall, pointing out Tammany's help in getting a housing discrimination bill passed.

Powell said votes for him were votes "to defeat Tammany," and the *New York Times* agreed, declaring that "the attitude of Negro voters toward Tammany Hall . . . is sure to be tested when those voters go to the polls." Brown's defeat surely hastened Tammany Hall's demise and left him politically damaged. In 1961 he left the city council to join New York's Housing and Redevelopment Board. In 1963 he was named a deputy Manhattan Borough President, with the expectation that he would become Borough President in 1965.

But it was not to be. In addition to acquiring Adam Clayton Powell as a political enemy Brown also angered Councilman J. Raymond Jones by opposing his reelection. When Brown came up for appointment Jones vehemently opposed it, announcing that Brown as Borough President would be "personally obnoxious" to him. Powell also opposed it. They prevailed, and Mayor Robert Wagner chose CONSTANCE BAKER MOTLEY instead of Brown. He took the appointment with good grace, appearing at Motley's swearing-in and joking that if his enemies were successful in forcing him out of politics he could always "get a job with the Mets." Brown was appointed head of New York's Commission on Human Rights but soon retired due to poor health. He suffered from emphysema and died in New York.

Earl Brown was called a political maverick, which is curious. He did take on powerful personages: everyone from Joe Louis at the height of his fame, to Adam Clayton Powell and J. Raymond Jones. But he opposed Powell at the behest of Tammany Hall, and Tammany leader Carmine De Sapio supported him for Borough President. It is hard to call someone who worked with Tammany Hall a maverick.

Brown also made a poor choice politically in aligning himself with Tammany Hall, which was clearly a dying institution during Brown's time. The *New York Times* observed that Brown had weak political skills, describing him as "diffident, not very good at handling a crowd, weak at oratory," with a reputation for snobbishness, derided as "look-down Brown." Although he lacked innate political skills, Brown had considerable political influence, passing seminal civil rights legislation in such an influential locale as New York City.

Further Reading

"City's New Rights Chief: Earl Louis Brown," *New York Times*, 27 May 1965.

Egan, Leo. "Mayor and De Sapio Favor Brown for Borough Post," *New York Times*, 2 Jan. 1961.

Knowles, Clayton. "Dudley Studied for State Court," *New York Times*, 2 Jan. 1961.

Knowles, Clayton. "Mrs. Motley Gets Mayor's Backing as Borough Head," *New York Times*, 17 Feb. 1965.

"Rivals in Harlem Trade Hot Words," *New York Times*, 4 Aug. 1958.

Robinson, Layhmond. "House Campaign Arouses Harlem," *New York Times*, 4 Aug. 1958.

Obituary: *New York Times*, 15 Apr. 1980.

STEPHEN ESCHENBACH

BROWN, Elaine (2 Mar. 1943–), activist and author, was born in Philadelphia, Pennsylvania, the only child of Dorothy Clark, a factory worker, and Dr. Horace Scott, a neurosurgeon who never publicly acknowledged his daughter's existence. As a result Elaine was raised by a single mother.

Elaine Brown grew up in poverty in a row house on York Street in North Philadelphia. Hoping for a better life for her daughter, Dorothy Clark enrolled Elaine in an experimental elementary school, Thaddeus Stevens School of Practice. There she was exposed to the lives of her often privileged, white Jewish classmates, and from an early age she learned to assimilate their habits. She learned to adopt their speech patterns and cadence of voice using words such as "these" instead of "dese" or "he'll be going" instead of "he be goin'." Thus Brown lived in two worlds in which she was able to act "white" while at school and "black" when she was with the girls from her neighborhood. Brown's mother provided her with opportunities not widely available to other children in her neighborhood, such as private piano lessons and

ballet classes. Throughout her adolescence Brown played the piano and composed original songs. In 1957 she was admitted to the prestigious Philadelphia High School for Girls on the basis of her high IQ score. She excelled in Latin and English and graduated in 1961. Brown entered Temple University in Philadelphia but she did not take her course of study seriously, and withdrew in 1962, later taking a job as a service representative at the Philadelphia Electric Company.

In 1965, at age twenty-two, Brown moved to Los Angeles to be a professional songwriter. She began as a waitress at the Pink Pussycat nightclub, where she met the writer Jay Kennedy, with whom she had an affair. It was through her relationship with Kennedy that she became aware of social and political movements of the 1960s. When their relationship ended in 1967 Brown began giving piano lessons to girls living in the Jordan Downs Housing Project in the Watts section of Los Angeles as a part of a tutorial program organized by her friend Beverlee Bruce. It was through her teaching that she became aware of the circumstances of African Americans and realized the need to create conditions for fundamental change in their lives. Bruce introduced her to people in the Black Power movement and she became a member of the Black Congress and was involved with producing the organization's newspaper, *Harambee*. The Black Congress was founded in Los Angeles after the 1965 Watts riots as an umbrella group that represented many of the African American organizations in the area. It consisted of an executive committee on which each member served as a representative from a different organization. The Black Congress served to meet the concerns and interests of African Americans in Southern California. Brown also served on the Executive Committee to the Black Student Alliance, which was a vision of Harry Truly, a professor of sociology at California State University, Los Angeles, who wished to form a union of all-black student unions in the United States to act as a base of power in the black student movement.

In 1967 at a Black Congress Executive Committee meeting she met Earl Anthony, a Central Committee member of the Black Panther Party for Self-defense, working for the HUEY P. NEWTON Legal Defense Fund. The Black Panther Party for Self-defense was formed in 1966 in Oakland, California, by Newton and BOBBY SEALE to further the aims of the civil rights movement to bring equality to African Americans. In April of 1968 Brown joined the Southern California Chapter of the Black Panther Party (BPP). Brown rose through the ranks, learning the Panthers' rhetoric, selling Panther newspapers, and learning to handle firearms. She attended UCLA as part of the High Potential Program for disadvantaged students with a high potential for success, a program organized by Beverlee Bruce. During this time she worked with the party to expand its platform of community Survival Programs in Los Angeles. These Survival Programs, such as the Breakfast Program, which provided free breakfasts to school-age children, and free clinics that provided medical care, were designed to benefit the lives of the black community. Brown assisted in organizing rallies against police brutality and organized financial support among Hollywood personalities such as movie producer Bert Schneider.

An accomplished songwriter, Brown released her first album of original music dedicated to the BPP, *Seize the Time*, in 1969. That year she was appointed deputy minister of information for the chapter. In March 1970 Brown gave birth to her daughter, Ericka Brown, with Masai (Raymond) Hewitt. In June of that year she accompanied the BPP minister of information ELDRIDGE CLEAVER to North Korea to announce the establishment of an International Section of the party. When she returned from the trip she met the chairman of the party, Huey P. Newton, and began a personal and professional relationship that lasted during most of the 1970s. She moved to Oakland in 1971 and assumed duties as editor of the BPP newspaper, the *Black Panther*. Newton appointed her minister of information, filling the vacancy of the expelled Eldridge Cleaver, who felt that the party should put more emphasis on guerrilla activity and less on community programs and spoke out publicly against the party leadership, causing a fracture within the general membership. In assuming that role Brown became the first woman elected to the Central Committee of the party. In 1972 she began recording a second album of original music, *Until We're Free*. To expand the reach of the BPP, Brown ran unsuccessfully in 1972 for a seat on the Oakland City Council.

In 1974, after the 1973 expulsion of Bobby Seale by Newton, Brown was named chairman of the Black Panther Party. In 1974 the already fragmented party was further strained by the arrest and subsequent self-imposed exile to Cuba of Newton. In his absence Newton charged Brown with leadership of the BPP. Brown had inherited an organization weakened by internal rivalries and years of police subversion; surveillance by the FBI and various local police departments became constant, and BPP offices were raided frequently. She also faced great opposition from the members of the party who objected to a woman in a leadership role. As chairman of the Black Panther Party, Brown expanded community Survival Programs in the areas of health care and education, establishing the Intercommunal Youth Institute, a school for children in Oakland. She also ran, again unsuccessfully, for Oakland City Council in 1975. She began installing women for the first time in key administrative positions in the party. In 1977 Newton returned from Cuba to face trial and reassume co-leadership of the BPP. Brown faced the reality of a changed party. Many members questioned the legitimacy of her power since the return of Newton. Newton's drug use increased, and so did his violent temper. After witnessing the result of a particularly brutal discipline of a female member, Brown decided to leave the party and Oakland to move to Los Angeles.

Brown went on to explore a variety of personal and professional interests, including law school. In 1992 she published her autobiography, *A Taste of Power*, chronicling her life in the BPP. In 1996, after living seven years in France, she moved to Atlanta and established the nonprofit organization Fields of Flowers to build an education center for African American and poor children. Brown continued to advocate community concerns and cofounded Mothers Advocating Juvenile Justice in 1997. She also cofounded and became a board member of the National Alliance for Radical Prison Reform, one of the many nonprofit and activist organizations she founded beginning in the mid-1990s. In 2002 she wrote *The Condemnation of Little B*, highlighting the case of Michael Lewis, who was arrested at age thirteen for murder in Atlanta.

Brown entered politics again in 2005 and moved to the poor, predominantly black city of Brunswick, Georgia, to run for mayor. She was later disqualified on a residency requirement. Brown lectured at colleges and universities, in addition to writing and pursuing social activism.

Further Reading

The papers of Elaine Brown are housed at the Manuscript, Archives, and Rare Book Library at Emory University.

Brown, Elaine. *A Taste of Power: A Black Woman's Story* (1992).

Bray, Rosemary L. "A Black Panther's Long Journey," *New York Times Magazine* (31 Jan. 1993).

Steinfeld, Dave, et. al. "What Ever Happened To . . . ," *Essence* 36 1 (May 2005).

WENDY PFLUG

BROWN, Emma V. (c. 1843–Oct. 1902), educator, was born Emmeline Victoria Brown in Georgetown, District of Columbia, the daughter of JOHN MIFFLIN BROWN, a bishop of the African Methodist Episcopal Church, and Emmeline (maiden name unknown), a dressmaker. Emma Brown and her siblings were born and raised in what the racial climate of the period called a "better class of colored." When Brown was still a young girl her father died, and her mother worked to support the family. Brown attended Miss Myrtilla Miner's School for Colored Girls, which opened in 1851 with the goal of training teachers for public schools in the Washington, D.C., area. Brown soon distinguished herself as an outstanding student. When illness forced Miner to take a leave of absence, Brown was recruited to stay on and assist Emily Howland, who had moved from New York to be Miner's replacement. In 1858 Brown ran the school during Howland's temporary absence, and by the summer of 1859 Brown was ready and able to open her own small school (twelve students) in Georgetown. At the insistence and encouragement of Miner and Howland, Brown chose to continue her education and enhance her teaching skills at Oberlin College.

Located in Oberlin, Ohio, Oberlin College was the institution of choice for many African American women. Founded by abolitionists, Oberlin was the first coeducational and interracial college in the country. Accompanied by a friend, Matilda A. Jones, Brown arrived in February 1860 for the spring term and enrolled as a literary degree candidate. Her matriculation at Oberlin was cut short because of long-standing health problems that included a humor in her blood, severe headaches, insomnia, and stress. So determined was Brown to continue her studies, however, that she consented to the drastic treatment of having her head completely shaved in an effort to combat her debilitating headaches. But the combination of complaints proved to be too much for Brown, and she was forced to leave Oberlin in June 1861.

On returning to Washington, D.C., Brown's health gradually improved to the point that, in 1862, she was able to start her own modest school. Armed with a new spirit of abolition and reform Brown became one of a new class of "black schoolmarms" dedicated to educating and improving the lives of newly freed slaves. During the 1860s and 1870s Washington attracted many educators and reformers because it was the first southern city to offer blacks a free, tax-supported school system. On 1 March 1864 the Board of Trustees of Public Schools in Washington opened a black school in Ebenezer Church on Capitol Hill and offered Brown the first teaching position. Brown began with an annual salary of four hundred dollars and forty students. By summer, enrollment reached 130. Brown continued at the school until 1869, when recurring health problems forced her to abandon teaching and secure less stressful work as a clerk in Washington's Pension Office.

During 1870 Brown lived and worked among the black social elite of Charleston, South Carolina, where she taught school, and in Jackson, Mississippi, where she copied the acts of the legislature. Her health renewed, Brown returned to Washington and became the principal of the John F. Cook School on Capitol Hill. Brown received a prestigious appointment in the Washington school district in 1872, when she was named principal of the new Sumner School. The school, named for Senator Charles Sumner, was very modern and had ten classrooms, offices, playrooms, and an auditorium. With a starting annual salary of nine hundred dollars, the appointment was the pinnacle of Brown's teaching career.

In 1879 Emma Brown married Henry P. Montgomery, a former slave from Mississippi, a former Union army soldier, and principal at the John F. Cook School. Because married women were banned from teaching, Brown's career in Washington's school system ended. Her educational interests remained strong, however, and she worked as a corresponding secretary for the Manassas Industrial School in Virginia. Suffering from declining health, Brown died at the age of fifty-eight. Her last known address was Washington, D.C.

Brown was a pioneer and a crusader in the mid- to late-nineteenth-century movement directed toward educating and improving the lives of freedmen.

Whether the subject was astronomy or algebra or botany, Brown taught adults and children to have self-respect and to use education as their chief tool for personal and social betterment.

Further Reading
Lawson, Ellen N., and Marlene Merrill. "Antebellum Black Coeds at Oberlin College," *Oberlin Alumni Magazine* (Jan.–Feb. 1980).
Sterling, Dorothy, ed. *We Are Your Sisters: Black Women in the Nineteenth Century* (1984).

THEA GALLO BECKER

BROWN, Everett (1 Jan. 1902–25 Oct. 1953), actor, was born in Texas. Little is known of his early life or how he came to film. He played, often uncredited, a series of African or South Seas characters in mainstream adventure movies such as *King Kong* and *Tarzan*. He is best remembered for his role as Big Sam in the 1939 movie *Gone with the Wind* and is an example of an actor making the most of what was available to him in a period of segregation and extreme stereotyping in movies.

Brown's first credited movie role was as Nahalo, an island "native" in the 1923 silent movie *South Sea Love*. He continued with roles of this ilk, playing natives or Africans in *Danger Island* (1931), *Hell's Headquarters* (1932), and *Kongo* (1932). That same year he had a small part in *I Am a Fugitive from a Chain Gang*, where he played an American, Sebastian T. Yale, who helps the star, Paul Muni, escape. His next role, in *Nagana* (1933), gave him the chance to play something different: an educated man, willing to sacrifice his life in the pursuit of science. He received a one-line credit in the *New York Times* review of that movie: "Everett Brown makes the most of the role of Nogu" (16 Feb. 1933). In his next role in *King Kong*, in 1933, however, he returned to his demeaning (and often uncredited) characters when he appeared simply as "native in ape costume." Such roles continued in three *Tarzan* films: the 1933 *Tarzan the Fearless*, 1934's *Tarzan and His Mate*, and *Tarzan Escapes*, from 1936. Interspersed throughout his roles as slaves and natives were a few others, such as the Iron Man in *Under Pressure* (1935), a movie about an underwater tunnel project, and then as a convict in the 1935 *Les Misérables*.

At about this time, Brown looked to the race-film industry to expand his choices of roles. Race films were made by all-black or mixed-race production companies. They were specifically geared toward African American audiences, and they offered performers and entertainers a wider range of roles than those being offered by Hollywood at the time. With the "black Clark Gable," Ralph Cooper, Brown played in the all-black cast gangster film *Dark Manhattan* (1937). In 1938 he again acted with Cooper in *The Duke Is Tops* (alternate title: *Bronze Venus*), also LENA HORNE's first feature movie. That same year he also appeared with NINA MAE MCKINNEY in *Gang Smashes,* directed by Cooper.

During this time Brown continued to work in Hollywood films. For example, in 1937 he appeared as "a darky" (uncredited) in *Boys Town* with Spencer Tracy. In 1939 he was in five movies, including the one for which he is best known, *Gone with the Wind*, where he played Big Sam, the foreman of the plantation Tara. While the success of the film gave many African American actors hope that Hollywood would open up for more black talent, such was not the case, and Brown continued landing roles of slaves and natives, including *Congo Maisie* (1940) and *Zanzibar* (1940).

After *Zanzibar*, Brown disappeared from films for eight years, and little is known of his activities from this time. He returned to film in 1949 in *Rope of Sand*, where he again played a native chief (again uncredited). That same year, he was in a Three Stooges film, *Malice in the Palace*, and a movie about a racing horse, *The Great Dan Patch*. Both roles were uncredited. His last role was in 1953, as the Babuka King in *The White Witch Doctor* with Robert Mitchum.

Brown died in Los Angeles and is buried in the Evergreen Cemetery. While he enjoyed a long career in Hollywood, his legacy has gone largely unnoticed by film historians, yet it provides a perfect example of the film industry's inability to see African American performers outside certain roles.

Further Reading

Bogle, Donald. *Bright Boulevards, Bold Dreams: The Story of Black Hollywood* (2005).

Bogle, Donald. *Toms, Coons, Mulattoes, Mammies, and Bucks: An Interpretive History of Blacks in American Films*, 4th ed. (2001).

Cripps, Thomas. *Slow Fade to Black: The Negro in American Film, 1900-1942* (1977).

Sampson, Henry T. *Blacks in Black and White: A Source Book on Black Films*, 2d ed. (1995).

ROBIN JONES

BROWN, Frank London (7 Oct. 1927–12 Mar. 1962), writer, musician, journalist, and civil rights activist, was born in Kansas City, Missouri, to Myra Myrtle and Frank London Brown Sr., the eldest of their three children. In 1939, when Brown was twelve years old, the family relocated to the South Side of Chicago in hopes of better economic opportunities. Brown attended Colman Elementary School and went on to DuSable High School. His adolescence in Chicago's "Black Belt" during the 1940s, which Sterling Stuckey referred to as a "dark nether-world of crime" and "shattered idealism," deeply influenced his artistic and writing career. In the streets of the South Side's slums he learned how to sing and soon discovered a deep passion for music, especially for jazz and blues. Brown is credited with being the first person to recite short stories (as opposed to poetry) to a jazz music accompaniment.

After graduating from high school in 1945, Brown attended Wilberforce University in Ohio; he left without receiving a degree and joined the U.S. Army, serving from 1946 to 1948 and singing baritone in an army band. He married Evelyn Marie Jones on 30 November 1947. The couple had three daughters and a son who died shortly after birth. Brown attended Roosevelt University on the GI Bill and received his BA in Political Science in 1951. He then enrolled at Kent College of Law in Chicago, but decided later to go to the University of Chicago. In 1960 he graduated with a master's degree in Social Science, and followed his doctoral studies in political science as a fellow of the prestigious University of Chicago's Committee on Social Thought. He did not complete his PhD because of his early death in 1962.

While in school and writing, Brown also worked many jobs to feed his family, including stints as a jazz singer, bartender, loan interviewer, machinist, and, most significantly, organizer for the United Packinghouse Workers and other labor unions. After earning his master's degree, Brown was appointed director of the University of Chicago's Union Research Center. Apart from his own objectives in life, one of his major concerns was standing up for the rights of the underprivileged. His leftist social activism during the McCarthy and cold war era testifies to his courage. Some of Brown's actions as a social activist included helping a black man escape from Mississippi after the lynching of EMMETT LOUIS TILL in 1955, which Brown had covered as a journalist. He also actively demonstrated against segregation on Chicago beaches and protested against discrimination in apartment buildings owned by the University of Chicago.

Brown's literary career began while he was still an undergraduate. He contributed several articles and short stories to such publications as the *Chicago Review*, *Down Beat*, *Ebony*, and *Negro Digest*. Brown also authored a short play, *Short Ribs*, and short stories like "A Matter of Time," "McDougal," and "The Ancient Book." Meanwhile, he cultivated his interest in music by not only performing with modern jazz ensembles but also writing about music. He published an interview with jazz musician THELONIOUS MONK, as well as an article on poet GWENDOLYN BROOKS. In 1959 he was made associate editor of *Ebony*. Brown kept actively involved in the literary scene of his time and was friends with such writers as WILLARD FRANCIS MOTLEY. Literati like Gwendolyn Brooks were partially influenced by Brown's style of writing.

His first public success was his award-winning novel *Trumbull Park*, published in 1959. It garnered immediate critical acclaim and brought him recognition as an author and social activist. In the first chapter of *Trumbull Park*, the death of a neighbor girl due to a broken banister prompts Louis "Buggy" Martin and his family to choose to either stay in their dilapidated and rat-infested ghetto building or move to an outlying white area of Chicago. They become one of the first black families to move into Trumbull Park, the first integrated housing project in Chicago during the 1950s. The Martins, like all black tenants, face massive protest, violence, intimidation, and humiliation by their white neighbors. They are forced to live imprisoned under police protection and are only able to leave the building in a patrol wagon, while white people stone their windows and bombs are going off around them.

Trumbull Park is a semiautobiographical work for which Brown drew upon his own experience with race-related violence. Brown, his wife, and children were one of the first black families in "white" Trumbull Park, where they lived from 1954 to 1957 in a constant state of fear. The story of an everyday struggle for better housing conditions can be directly transplanted into the larger context of the civil rights movement, wherein African Americans proudly stood up for their rights. Brown successfully depicted the conditions, daily terrors, and struggles for a better life faced by African Americans during the 1950s, a time when laws were changing in their favor, but law enforcement still favored the white majority. Most reviews praised Brown's vivid characters and psychological insight and cited him as an auspicious author.

In his second novel, *The Myth Maker*, Brown delves into the fatal psychological effects of racism on the individual's mind. In this story racism leads to a deeply felt self-loathing of the protagonist, a drug addict named Ernest Day, who is both an offender and victim. His aggressiveness and longing for self-annihilation, caused by a hostile and racist environment in an indifferent universe, lead him to murder an innocent old man. Day is punished twice, first with a body subject to worldly penalty, and second with the pangs of his own conscience. *The Myth Maker* was often compared to Fyodor Dostoevsky's *Crime and Punishment* for its underlying themes of sin and redemption, crime and punishment. Brown could not find a publisher for this novel in his lifetime.

In 1961 Brown discovered that he suffered from a terminal case of leukemia. His body quickly degenerated while his mind remained vibrant and his creativity undiminished. Brown died at the age of thirty-four at the University of Illinois Educational Research Hospital in Chicago. His second novel, *The Myth Maker*, was published posthumously in 1969, as was a collection of his short stories, *Short Stories of Frank London Brown*, published privately in 1965.

Brown wrote first and foremost about the African American experience in everyday life and consistently demonstrated an insight into the human heart and the needs of black American people. He also wrote and spoke in favor of social protest. Although *Trumbull Park* found public acclaim during Brown's lifetime, his complete works have not yet been fully credited as among the important literary works of the 1950s and early 1960s.

Further Reading

Brooks, Gwendolyn. "Of Frank London Brown: A Tenant of the World," *Negro Digest* 18 (1962).

Hall, James C. "Frank London Brown," in *Oxford Companion to African American Literature*, eds. William Andrews et al. (1997).

Hauke, Kathleen A. "Frank London Brown," in *Dictionary of Literary Biography: Afro-American Writers, 1940-1955*, ed. Trudier Harris (1988).

Stuckey, Sterling. "Frank London Brown," in *Black Voices*, ed. Abraham Chapman (1968).

Tita, Charles. "Frank London Brown," in *Contemporary African American Novelists*, ed. Emmanuel S. Nelson (1999).

Obituary: *New York Times*, 13 Mar. 1962.

BÄRBEL R. BROUWERS

BROWN, Fredi Sears (4 Nov. 1923–), museum cofounder, college equity officer, educator, and community volunteer, was born Fredi Mae Sears in Bradenton, Florida. She was the only daughter of three children born to Mary Miller, a laundress, and Oscar C. Sears Sr., a laborer at a trailer park operated by the local Kiwanis Club. She grew up in a deeply religious community that valued family, friends, and the church, and her father was a deacon and a founding member of St. Mary Baptist Church. Such lived experiences prepared Sears for a life of service.

In 1939 she graduated as valedictorian of her class at Lincoln High School in Bradenton. Upon graduation, she enrolled at Florida A&M College (later University) in Tallahassee, Florida, where in 1944 she earned a bachelor of science degree in Home Economics with minors in Science and English. While at Florida A&M, Sears wrote for the student newspaper, and her extracurricular activities in college would prove to be rewarding, both professionally and personally. Upon graduating in 1944 she moved to Kansas City, Missouri, where she landed the post of assistant advertising manager with the black-owned newspaper *Kansas City Call*. It was at the *Call* that Fredi Sears met Ernest Leroy Brown, the paper's sports editor. During her brief stay in Kansas City, Sears also volunteered as an essay contest editor for the National Negro Newspaper Publishers Association.

Fredi Sears and Ernest Brown were married in 1946, and they eventually had four children. The couple relocated to Detroit, Michigan, where Ernest Brown became the manager of urban affairs with Detroit's Urban League. This new position began for both of the Browns a life of engagement within the city's black communities. Sharing her life-partner's passion for service, Fredi Brown touched many lives. From 1964 to 1974 she counseled teenaged substance abusers and prepared them for the GED test at the Salvation Army's Harbor Light House, established a library for a community center in one of the city's housing developments, organized parents of elementary school children to become more actively involved in the education of their children, taught English to incarcerated women at Louise Groom's Business College, and taught preschoolers at the Unity Church.

It was during their years in Detroit that the Browns were drawn into the world of collecting black memorabilia and materials. Though she did not consider herself a collector, Brown soon found herself accumulating books, posters, artifacts, and other ephemera relating to black life and history, some of which was gathered during her husband's work trips for the Urban League and the Equal Opportunity Commission. These would become the nucleus of the collection housed at the Family Heritage House, an African American Gallery and Resource Center located on the campus of Manatee Community College in Bradenton, Florida. Included in the collection were artifacts, newspaper clippings of the civil rights movement in Detroit, the 1872 edition of William Still's *Underground Railroad*, West African masks, the sixtieth anniversary publication of *The Crisis* magazine, and the 1994 South African presidential election ballot.

Upon Ernest's retirement in 1974, the Browns moved to Bradenton. There Brown became an instructor and Equal Access/Equal Opportunity coordinator at Manatee Community College. Remembering the segregated system that during her youth had barred blacks from attending the school, Brown accepted the opportunity to help bridge the gap between the African American community and the college. While employed at the college, Brown continued her education at the University of South Florida, Sarasota Campus. She earned a master of science in Education in 1981.

Initiatives implemented under Brown's leadership included establishing Future Unlimited Scholarships for minority students, inviting black artists to the community, and providing networking and mentoring opportunities between students and local professionals through the Talking and Touching dialogues. Brown also created community-based study centers. While she was employed at Manatee Junior College, Brown displayed items from her collection of black memorabilia in her office and shared them with students. By the time of her retirement in 1989, Brown had built a sturdy bridge that connected the community with the college.

Reluctant to store their collection in boxes, the Browns sought another space for the books, newspaper clippings, photographs, and audiocassettes on the local, state, and national figures that they had collected over the years. As a result, in 1990, the Family Heritage House was founded in a trailer belonging to the Bradenton Head Start program. By 1999, however, the Browns began to seek another home for their museum, especially as the collection became an important community resource. As a result the Browns once again gained a presence at Manatee Community College, which welcomed the idea of housing the collection because it would serve as a magnet in the college's continued efforts to reach out to the African American community. Local businesses, organizations, and residents demonstrated their support for the Browns when they raised $370,000 for a 2,085-square-foot wing, which would be the new location for the Family Heritage House museum, to be built on to the college's Sara Scott Harlee Library. The doors of the Family Heritage House museum officially opened on 20 September 2000. Ernest Brown died on 26 December 2001, but Fredi Brown continued their work with the collection.

The Family Heritage House indeed became a magnet for the community college. An array of excellent programming activities, which included lectures, jazz concerts, and other performances, and permanent and traveling exhibitions enriched the lives of the county residents. Listed on the Florida Black Heritage Trail and included on the National Park Service Network to Freedom, the Family Heritage House attracted visitors from across the nation.

Brown was the recipient of numerous awards in honor of her influence on the community, including the 2001 Distinguished Alumni Award from the University of South Florida, Sarasota Campus; the 1999 Service to Youth and Community Education awarded by the Links, Inc.; and the 1998 Passing the Torch award, given by Delta Sigma Theta sorority. The Family Heritage House serves as a living monument to the life and service of Fredi Mae Sears Brown.

Further Reading
Some of the information for this entry was gathered during a telephone interview with Brown on 28 Dec. 2006.
Ayres, Annette. "Funding Raised for New MCC Museum," *Bradenton Herald*, 10 Sept. 1999.
Ayres, Annette. "Museum to Get New Home," *Bradenton Herald*, 18 Feb. 1999.
Reddick, Tracie. "Heritage House Opens Doors," *Bradenton Herald*, 21 Sept. 2000.

DOROTHY A. WASHINGTON

BROWN, Grafton Tyler (22 Feb. 1841–2 Mar. 1918), draftsman, lithographer, painter, and entrepreneur, was born free in Harrisburg, Pennsylvania, to Thomas Brown and Wilhelmina (maiden name unknown). Nothing is known about Brown's family or childhood. It appears that in the mid-1850s, Brown moved to San Francisco on the heels of the gold rush. While black fur traders, including EDWARD ROSE and JIM BECKWOURTH, had already explored the West by the mid-1850s, few African Americans were living in California before this time. By 1860, though, close to five thousand blacks had moved to California, including MARY ELLEN PLEASANT and EDMOND WYSINGER. Just what precipitated Brown's decision to move to San Francisco is unknown, but records show that by 1861 he was employed as a draftsman for the commercial lithography firm of Kuchel and Dressel. While his skill is evidenced by the quality work he produced for the firm, Brown must also have been considered a competent businessman, because following the 1866 death of Charles Kuchel he assumed management of the firm. A year later the twenty-six-year-old opened his own business, G. T. Brown and Company, at 520 Clay Street in San Francisco. Brown was a prolific lithographer, known for his keen drafting skills, exactness, and attention to detail.

Brown was exceedingly busy throughout the 1860s and 1870s, producing a host of topographical and street maps, stock certificates, sheet music, letter- and billheads, and advertising materials for banks, municipalities, mining companies, and California companies.

Brown's clients included Levi Strauss Co., Ghirardelli Chocolate & Spice, and the California Fertilizing Company, for whom he designed stock certificates. The image of a stagecoach he designed for Wells Fargo Mining Co. remains the company's logo today. A major component of Brown's business was the production of aerial-view maps of western cities and towns, including Santa Rosa and Oakland, California, and Fort Churchill, Nevada, which he would visit to sketch their major buildings and structures. Brown's 1861 map of Virginia City, Nevada, features individual renderings of thirty of the town's buildings in a border surrounding a bird's-eye view of the city nestled into the hills of Nevada Territory. Brown's hand-tinted lithograph of San Francisco from around 1876 became a standard source, and in 1878 he completed his largest commission, *The Illustrated History of San Mateo County*, which consisted of seventy-two views of ranches and towns in San Mateo County.

The discovery of gold in 1848 and the subsequent Gold Rush transformed California, especially San Francisco. By 1854, 300,000 people from across the United States, Asia, Mexico, South America, and Europe had arrived in California, increasing the state's population from around 13,000 residents in 1848. San Francisco, home to 600 people in 1848, quickly and abruptly grew into a major, racially diverse, boomtown with a population of 50,000 by 1856. Nearly a half-billion dollars' worth of gold passed through the city in the 1850s. A plot of San Francisco real estate that cost $16 in 1847, for instance, sold for $45,000 just eighteen months later. In less than two years the city burned to the ground—and was rebuilt—six times. By 1856, even after the major mining companies had wrested control of the area's mining profits, many gold rushers remained in California, opening banks, shops, saloons, and other businesses that catered to the new population. Lithography, in the years before the universal adoption of photography, was an integral part of this boom, benefiting from and contributing to the settling and commercialization of California and the West. Brown's lithographs, including an 1878 commission scrip for five dollars, an 1879 bank note for the Pioneer Woolen Factory Bank, an 1870s billhead for J. A. Folger & Co., and an 1869 sheet music frontispiece for "Under the Snow," reveal a great deal about the growth, manner, and priorities of California's new businesses.

Brown's work documented the rapid growth of California's cities, ranches, and businesses, as well as other changing conditions. City views, which were used by local businesses on their letterhead and correspondence, also served a broader purpose, advertising the new West as a concrete, solid, and stable environment for entrepreneurial investment. The clarity and meticulousness of Brown's city views articulated the philosophy of westward expansionism and Manifest Destiny. In his 1875 view of the Iron Clad Mine in Nevada County, the indigenous forest has been neatly cleared, replaced by the orderly geometry of main streets and abutting houses, all built by human imagination and hard work.

In 1879 Brown left San Francisco and traveled through the Pacific Northwest, apparently joining an 1882 geological survey of the Cariboo gold mines in British Columbia, Canada, led by Amos Bowman. By 1883 he had settled in Victoria, British Columbia, and was advertising himself in the *Williams British Columbia Directory* as a landscape painter. That same year he held his first, and only documented, exhibition of paintings. While living in British Columbia, he painted many tender and intimate views of Victoria locales, including *Goldstream Falls, B.C.* (1882) and *View of Lake Okanogan, B.C.* (1883). Trips to Washington and Oregon in 1884 and 1885, respectively, yielded paintings of the area's rivers and mountains, including Puget Sound, Mount Hood, Mount Tacoma, and Cascade Cliffs. Brown's new dedication to painting, indicated by his prolific output and his efforts in advertising his work, marked a career shift from commercial lithography to landscape painting. His paintings—pure landscapes devoid of figures or manmade elements—may also reflect a shift in his attitudes toward expansionism. Celebrations of the area's untouched wilderness, particularly the Yellowstone area, which was designated the country's first national park in 1872 partly as a result of the paintings of Thomas Moran, indicate that Brown may have supported the growing conservation movement. In 1886 Brown relocated to Portland, Oregon, where he became an active member of the Portland Art Club. He continued painting, producing larger works, including many of the Grand Canyon.

Around 1892 Brown made yet another dramatic career shift. Settling in St. Paul, Minnesota, he returned to work as a draftsman, first for the U.S. Army Corps of Engineers (from 1892 to 1897) and then the St. Paul Civil Engineering Department (from 1897 to 1910). Whether or not he continued to paint is unknown, since no canvases have survived. Brown died of pneumonia and arteriosclerosis.

In 1972 the Oakland Museum of California mounted an exhibit of Brown's work, focusing primarily on his lithographs. In 2004 Grafton Tyler Brown: Visualizing California and the Pacific Northwest, a traveling exhibition organized by the California African American Museum, included the first serious exhibition of his paintings. Brown's work is held in a number of collections, including the British Archives, Victoria, British Columbia, and the National Museum of American Art, Washington, D.C.

Further Reading
Grafton Tyler Brown: Nineteenth Century American Artist. The Evans-Tibbs Collection (exhibition pamphlet, Spring 1988).
Lewis, Jo Ann. "A Painting Pioneer," *Washington Post*, 2 May 2004.

LISA E. RIVO

BROWN, H. Rap (4 Oct. 1943–), militant political activist and religious leader, was born Hubert Geroid Brown in Baton Rouge, Louisiana, the youngest child

H. Rap Brown, answering a question at a Student Nonviolent Coordinating Committee news conference, 27 July 1967. (Library of Congress.)

and second son of Eddie C. Brown, a laborer for Esso Standard Oil, and Thelma Warren, a teacher. According to his own account, Brown was a rebel from the earliest days against the color biases of his community as well as the authoritarianism and Eurocentric curricula of the schools in Baton Rouge. He identified with youth street culture and its heroes, whose verbal and physical jousting he extolled in his 1970 memoir *Die Nigger Die!* His facility at signifying or "playing the dozens" earned Brown the "Rap" sobriquet that he was to carry throughout the first phase of his public career.

Brown attended Southern University in Baton Rouge from 1961 to 1963 but dropped out to pursue his growing interest in the civil rights movement. Following his brother Ed, whose social activism was also lifelong, he moved to Washington, D.C., and became active in the Nonviolent Action Group (NAG), an affiliate of the Student Nonviolent Coordinating Committee (SNCC), composed largely of Howard University students. Although Brown never enrolled at Howard, he participated increasingly in the group's meetings and demonstrations and became deeply involved in SNCC activities. He worked with the

Mississippi Summer Project and in 1966 was appointed director of the Greene County Project in Alabama, part of the group's campaign to organize black voters and elect black candidates.

Brown was elected chairman of SNCC in 1967, succeeding STOKELY CARMICHAEL at a time when the organization's community-organizing programs were on the wane and as the mainstream media had begun to denounce SNCC's turn to Black Power. Brown's incendiary rhetoric—"They're scared of me with this .45, wait till I get my atomic bomb!" (from the film *King: From Montgomery to Memphis*, 1970)—alienated many of SNCC's former liberal allies, but his denunciations of government racism and corruption struck a chord with disillusioned young African Americans. So, too, did Brown's approving remarks about the July 1967 Detroit riots, in which he urged blacks to stop "trying to love that honky to death . . . shoot him to death, brother. Cause that's what he's out to do to you" (Sitkoff, *Struggle for Black Equality*, 217).

Many commentators, especially whites, understood the "burn, baby, burn" refrain of one of Brown's speeches as an unqualified call to violence. However, his political philosophy was less nihilistic than that phrase might suggest. In fact, Brown stated in that speech in Cambridge, Maryland, that "if America don't come around, we going to burn it down, brother. We going to burn it down, brother, if we don't get our share of it." America, then, could prevent violence by radically redistributing wealth and resources. Yet if violence were to come, Brown reminded his audience—and the journalists and politicians who denounced him for his militancy—that, "violence is as American as cherry pie."

Brown's tenure as SNCC chairman was hampered by numerous arrests and indictments on a variety of charges. His effectiveness was severely undermined by constant litigation. The most consequential of these legal troubles arose out of an uprising in Cambridge, Maryland, where authorities charged him with incitement following his speech there in July 1967. The federal government also charged Brown with unlawful interstate flight to avoid prosecution, violation of the National Firearms Act, arson, and violation of the terms of his bond. Although many of these charges would ultimately be dropped, Brown spent much of his twelve-month tenure as SNCC chairman behind bars. Brown was also appointed the Black Panther Party's minister of justice in 1968, though, with his own legal troubles and SNCC duties, this was largely a titular office. Brown went underground in 1970 rather than stand trial for the incitement to riot charges, and little is known of his activities at that time. He resurfaced in October 1971, when he was captured along with three others in the aftermath of an armed holdup of a New York City nightclub. Although it was not part of the legal defense, supporters claimed that this robbery was directed at drug dealers, whose illegal and immoral profits from exploiting the black community were to be used for the movement. If true, such actions were in line with those of the Black Liberation Army, whose members engaged in similar activities, often with equally unsuccessful results. In any case, Brown, who converted to Islam while imprisoned in the Tombs and changed his name to Jamil Abdullah al-Amin, was convicted of armed robbery and assault with a deadly weapon and sentenced to five to fifteen years in prison. He was paroled in 1976 and moved south, where he lived quietly as the owner of a small neighborhood store in Atlanta's West End. Al-Amin eventually became the imam of a small Muslim community in Atlanta, and in 1993 he published a book of sermons entitled *Revolution by the Book: The Rap Is Live*. His community earned a reputation as a positive force in lowering the incidence of street crime in the neighborhood. However, the group, and al-Amin in particular, seemed to be targets of numerous investigations by police agencies over the years. (During his later murder trial, Atlanta police would accuse them in the press of involvement in a dozen unsolved murders in the neighborhood.) Perhaps the most bizarre episode was a 1995 charge of attempted murder, in which the police alleged that al-Amin shot at a man walking down the street for no apparent reason. This well-publicized case was later dropped when the supposed victim denied that al-Amin was his attacker and later joined the *masjid*, or mosque. Federal authorities also tried to tie members of the *masjid* to the 1993 World Trade Center bombing in New York City, with much press attention. Eventually two *masjid* members were convicted of gunrunning.

On 16 March 2000 two Atlanta police officers, who stated that they were seeking to arrest al-Amin on charges of driving a stolen car and impersonating a police officer, approached his house at ten thirty at night. Both were shot; one was killed. The survivor claimed to have shot his assailant, and a blood trail seemed to confirm his story. Al-Amin was the prime suspect. He fled to Alabama, where he was captured several days later, uninjured and proclaiming his innocence. There were sensational headlines across the country about the bloodthirsty former Black Panther cop killer, while an international campaign supporting al-Amin's right to a fair trial was mounted. Nonetheless, an all-black Fulton County jury found him guilty of murder in March 2002 and sentenced him to life without parole.

Al-Amin's story is unsettling, bizarre, and tragic. He is painted by opponents of social change as a violent murderer with a history of involvement in active violence. His supporters cite a legacy of FBI repression of black activists leading to his ultimate fate as a prisoner for life. Yet al-Amin's SNCC activities, as well as his later leadership of a religious community, clearly display a commitment to humanistic concerns at odds with his status as a convicted murderer.

Further Reading

al-Amin, Jamil Abdullah. *Die Nigger Die!: A Political Autobiography* (1970, 2d ed. 2002).
Carson, Clayborne. *In Struggle: SNCC and the Black Awakening of the 1960s* (1981).

W. S. TKWEME

BROWN, Hallie Quinn (10 Mar. 1845?–16 Sept. 1949), elocutionist, educator, women's and civil rights leader, and writer, was born in Pittsburgh, Pennsylvania, the daughter of Thomas Arthur Brown, a riverboat steward and express agent, and Frances Jane Scroggins, an educated woman who served as an unofficial adviser to the students of Wilberforce University. Thomas Brown was born into slavery in Frederick County, Maryland, the son of a Scottish woman plantation owner and her black overseer. Brown purchased his freedom and that of his sister, brother, and father. By the time of the Civil War, he had amassed a sizable amount of real estate. Hallie's mother, Frances, was also born a slave, the child of her white owner. She was eventually freed by her white grandfather, a former officer in the American Revolution.

Both of Hallie's parents became active in the Underground Railroad. Around 1864, the Browns and their six children moved to Chatham, Ontario, where Thomas worked as a farmer and Hallie began to show

Hallie Quinn Brown, elocutionist and educator. (Duke University.)

a talent for public speaking and performance. The Browns returned to the United States around 1870, settling in Wilberforce, Ohio, where Hallie and her youngest brother enrolled in Wilberforce University, an African Methodist Episcopal (AME) liberal arts school and the first four-year college owned and operated by African Americans in the United States. Wilberforce was at that time under the direction of the AME bishop DANIEL ALEXANDER PAYNE, America's first black college president and a Brown family friend.

Brown graduated with a BS from Wilberforce University in 1873. (The university later gave Brown two honorary degrees, an MS in 1890 and a doctorate in Law in 1936.) Shortly after graduation Brown moved to the South, beginning what would become a lifelong commitment to education and to the advancement of disenfranchised women and African Americans. For more than a decade, in plantations and public schools from Yazoo, Mississippi, to Columbia, South Carolina, Brown taught literacy skills to black children and adults denied education during slavery.

Attracted to its combination of education with entertainment, Brown had joined the Lyceum movement in 1874. The Lyceum, a nineteenth-century movement that fostered adult education in the arts, sciences, history, and public affairs through traveling programs of lectures and concerts, brought Brown's eloquent lectures to a wide audience in the South and Midwest. By the early 1880s Brown was touring with the Lyceum full time. She continued her elocution training at the Chautauqua Lecture School from which, in 1886, she graduated at the top of her class, having completed several summer sessions.

As Brown's eminence and reputation grew, so did her job prospects. From 1885 to 1887 she served as dean of Allen University in Columbia, South Carolina, the first black college in South Carolina, founded in 1870. In 1887 Brown returned to Ohio, where for the next five years she taught in the Dayton public schools and at a night school she founded for migrant African American adults recently relocated from the South. The Tuskegee Normal and Industrial Institute brought Brown to Alabama from 1892 to 1893 to serve as lady principal, or dean of women, under the direction of BOOKER T. WASHINGTON.

Brown's lasting dedication to Wilberforce University began in 1893, when she was hired by her alma mater as professor of elocution. Brown would remain a part of the Wilberforce community, as an English and elocution teacher, trustee, and fund-raiser, until her death. Shortly after her appointment, however, Brown suspended her classroom teaching duties in favor of a series of extensive lecture tours of Europe.

Brown left for Europe in 1894 and remained on tour for much of the next five years. She quickly became an internationally lauded lecturer and performer, speaking on the themes of African American culture, temperance, and women's suffrage. Enamored audiences flocked to experience Brown's lectures on topics like "Negro Folklore and Folksong" and her recitations of the works of PAUL LAURENCE DUNBAR and other African American authors. Brown was a featured speaker in London at the Third Biennial Convention of the World's Woman's Christian Temperance Union in 1895 and a representative to the International Congress of Women held in London in 1899. Having been introduced to the royal family via letter by FREDERICK DOUGLASS in 1894, Brown performed for Queen Victoria on several occasions, even joining the monarch for tea at Windsor Castle and as a guest during the Jubilee Celebration in 1899. Brown was made a member of the exclusive Royal Geographical Society in Edinburgh, and in 1895 she helped form the first British Chautauqua, a Lyceum-style touring educational program, in North Wales.

Brown returned to teaching full time at Wilberforce around the turn of the century but visited Europe once again in 1910 as a representative to the Woman's Missionary Society of the AME Conference held in Edinburgh. For Brown, this trip marked the culmination of over ten years of work with the AME Church and validated her role in the church outside of her association with Wilberforce University. In 1900 Brown had campaigned for the job of AME secretary of education. Although she failed to get the appointment, she remained committed to expanding the role of women in the church. Brown remained in Britain for seven months, raising enough money for Wilberforce to build a new dormitory. Still popular as a lecturer, Brown gave a command performance for King George and Queen Mary and was a dinner guest of the Princess of Wales.

While Brown is remembered for her achievements as an elocutionist, it is her vision of a nationally organized African American women's community that has secured her place in history. Brown was a pioneering force in the formation of the black women's club movement, the development of which saw the establishment of schools, scholarships, museums, elder-care facilities, and political institutions.

Concerned that the achievements of African Americans would be omitted from the exhibitions at the 1893 World's Fair and Columbian Exposition in Chicago, Brown petitioned for a seat on the Board of Lady Managers, the planning committee presiding over the U.S. exhibits. "For two hundred and fifty years the Negro woman of America was bought and sold as chattel," Brown argued. "Twenty-five years of progress find the Afro-American woman advanced beyond the most sanguine expectations. Her development from the darkest slavery and grossest ignorance into light and liberty is one of the marvels of the age. . . . What more is needed? Time and equal chance in the race of life" (*The World's Congress of Representative Women*, May Wright Sewall, ed., 1894). The Board denied Brown's request, explaining that only individuals representing organizations could participate. Provoked by her exclusion and motivated to set up a national organization devoted to and run by black women, Brown cofounded the Colored Women's League of Washington, D.C. Two years later Brown's organization merged with JOSEPHINE ST.

PIERRE RUFFIN's Boston Women's Era Club, becoming the National Federation of Afro-American Women, which was later renamed the National Association of Colored Women (NACW).

Brown served as national president of the NACW from 1920 to 1924 and as honorary president until her death. During her tenure at the NACW, Brown took a leadership role in two projects: the creation and maintenance of a memorial at the former home of Frederick Douglass in Washington, D.C., and the establishment of the Hallie Q. Brown Scholarship Loan Fund for the education of black women, a national program open to college students and postgraduate women, that allots generous loans to be repaid with no interest.

In addition to her work with the NACW, Brown played major roles in several other African American and women's organizations. She served as president of the Ohio State Federation of Colored Women's Clubs from 1905 to 1912 and worked as an organizer for the Women's Christian Temperance Union. Brown lent her support and oratorical skill to a variety of issues. In 1922 she lobbied President Warren Harding and several key U.S. senators in support of a federal antilynching law and worked with the NAACP in its efforts to defeat a national bill outlawing interracial marriages. On another occasion, in an incident reported in the *New York Times*, Brown arrived in Washington, D.C., for the 1925 All-American Musical Festival of the International Council of Women and found the auditorium segregated. In a biting speech condemning the council's racist policy, Brown threatened a boycott by the festival's black performers if segregation continued. When her demands were not met, many of the audience members joined the two hundred black performers in a boycott of the program.

Brown was also engaged in mainstream political organizations. An ardent Republican, she spoke in support of local, state, and national candidates in Ohio, Pennsylvania, Illinois, and Missouri. Brown's Republican activities increased in the 1920s and 1930s, during which time she labored on behalf of the National League of Women Voters and as vice president of the Ohio Council of Republican Women. In 1924 Brown emerged on the national stage, addressing the Republican National Convention in Cleveland. Speaking in support of Warren Harding's nomination, Brown took the opportunity to discuss issues of significance to African Americans. After the convention, Brown directed the Colored Women's Activities at the Republican national campaign headquarters in Chicago and the new National League of Republican Colored Women, which adopted the slogan "We are in politics to stay and we shall be a stay in politics."

Concurrent with her teaching, lecturing, and organizing, Brown worked as a writer, essayist, and anthologist. She published several collections of speeches and prose, including *Bits and Odds: A Choice Selection of Recitations* (1880), *Elocution and Physical Culture* (1910), *First Lessons in Public Speaking* (1920), *The Beautiful: A True Story of Slavery* (1924), *Our Women: Past, Present and Future* (1925), and *Tales My Father Told* (1925). She often wrote of the power and complexity of black America's relationship to language, frequently using black vernacular speech in her writing, and of the importance of African American heritage, family history, and culture. In 1926, when Brown was in her seventies, she published her best-known book, *Homespun Heroines and Other Women of Distinction*, a collection of sixty biographies of black women born in North America between 1740 and 1900.

"Miss Hallie," as Brown was known at Wilberforce, remained active until her death in 1949, near age one hundred. Her legacy continues through the scholarship fund that bears her name; the good works of the Hallie Quinn Brown Community House in St. Paul, Minnesota; and the Hallie Q. Brown Memorial Library at Wilberforce University, a facility that includes a collection of books by and about African Americans.

Further Reading
Brown's unpublished papers are held at the Hallie Q. Brown Memorial Library at Wilberforce University in Wilberforce, Ohio.
Davis, Elizabeth Lindsay, ed. *Lifting as They Climb* (1933, 1996).
Majors, M. A. *Noted Negro Women: Their Triumphs and Activities* (1893).

LISA E. RIVO

BROWN, Henry "Box" (1815?–?), escaped slave, was born on a plantation in Louisa County, Virginia, to unknown parents. As a youth, Brown lived with his parents, four sisters, and three brothers until the family was separated and his master hired him out at age fifteen to work in a tobacco factory in Richmond, Virginia. Brown's autobiography illuminates the vicissitudes of slave life but does not recount any further major events in his own life other than his marriage around 1836 to Nancy, the slave of a bank clerk, with whom he had three children. In August 1848 Nancy's owner sold her and her three children (Brown's children) to a slave trader who took them South. Brown begged his own master to purchase them, but he refused. Brown later wrote in his autobiography: "I went to my *Christian* master . . . but he shoved me away." According to his autobiography, Brown actually saw his wife and children being marched out of town, but they did not see him. Angry over the loss of his family and his master's callous refusal to buy his wife and children, the formerly mild-mannered Brown resolved to liberate himself from "the bloody dealers in the bodies and souls of men."

In response to Brown's prayerful search for a way to freedom, "an idea," he reported, "suddenly flashed across my mind." Brown's revelation was that he have himself nailed into a wooden box and "conveyed as dry goods" via the Adams Express Company from slavery

THE RESURRECTION OF HENRY BOX BROWN AT PHILADELPHIA.
Who escaped from Richmond Va. in a Box. 3 feet long 2½ ft. deep and 2 ft wide.

Henry "Box" Brown, emerging from his box in the office of the Pennsylvania Anti-Slavery Society, in a nineteenth-century broadside published in Boston. (Library of Congress, Broadside Collection.)

in Richmond to freedom in Philadelphia (Brown, 57–58). This plan was carried out with the assistance of two friends, a white abolitionist, Dr. Samuel A. Smith, and James Caesar Anthony Smith, a free black. Brown had met Dr. Smith while singing in an integrated church choir. J. C. A. Smith helped Brown obtain a wooden box—complete with baize lining, air holes, a container of water, and hickory straps—that was constructed by a carpenter, who measured it precisely to hold Brown's five-feet eight-inch, two-hundred-pound body. The crate was addressed to Dr. Smith's friend, William Johnson, an abolitionist on Arch Street in Philadelphia and marked "this side up with care." On 29 March 1849, at four o'clock in the morning, the box was loaded onto a wagon and delivered to the depot, and Brown began his historic, twenty-seven-hour, 350-mile odyssey, some of it upside down and all of it in danger.

The box with its human content eventually found its way to the Anti-Slavery Committee's office on North Fifth Street in Philadelphia. A small, nervous group, including WILLIAM STILL, the African American conductor of Philadelphia's Underground Railroad, pried open the lid to reveal, in "my resurrection from the grave of slavery," the disheveled and battered Henry Brown, who arose and promptly fainted (Brown, 62). Revived by a glass of water, he proceeded to sing Psalm 40, which includes the line "Be pleased, O Lord, to deliver me" (Psalms 40:13). Discovering a

flair for the dramatic, he immediately took the name "Box" to celebrate his new identity as well as his escape.

Brown became an instant celebrity. The novelty of his escape caught the attention of abolitionists around the country. Two months after his escape he sang his psalm before an antislavery convention in Boston. Within months a narrative of his life and escape appeared (mostly written by the abolitionist Charles Stearns). Woodcuts of Brown emerging from his box were printed and reprinted; his story appeared in a children's book that year as well. Brown quickly began a career as an abolitionist speaker and entertainer. He traveled in the North telling his story with his friend J. C. A. Smith, who had left Virginia, selling copies of the 1849 edition of his narrative, and singing not only psalms, but lyrics of his own creation. He cleverly adapted to his own purposes a popular song of the day, Stephen Foster's 1848 ballad "Uncle Ned." The original text begins:

Dere was an old Nigga, dey called him Uncle Ned—
He's dead long ago, long ago!
He had no wool on de top ob his head—
De place where de wool ought to grow.
Chorus
Den lay down de shubble and de hoe,
Hang up de fiddle and de bow;
No more hard work for poor old Ned—
He is gone whar de good Niggas go.

Brown's version begins:

Here you see a man by the name of Henry Brown,
Ran away from the South to the North,
Which he would not have done but they stole all his rights,
But they'll never do the like again.
Chorus
Brown laid down the shovel and the hoe,
Down in the box he did go;
No more slave work for Henry Box Brown,
In the box by *Express* he did go.

Brown later published this parody of "Old Ned" as a broadside which he sold along with his narrative. Not only is Brown's revision witty and entertaining, it also is a window into his mind. He used a song everyone knew, a song with racist lyrics, stereotypical images, and a condescending attitude, all set in a sentimentalized South. Brown subverted the norms and values of a white supremacist society, turning Uncle Ned upside down, as it were, by replacing negative representations with positive ones.

Another way the imaginative and entrepreneurial Brown broadened the appeal and effect of his performance was through the addition of a large didactic panorama, "The Mirror of Liberty," which consisted of thousands of feet of canvas, divided into scores of panels painted with scenes depicting the history of slavery. Josiah Wolcott, a white Massachusetts artist, designed and painted it, perhaps with the assistance of other artists. Brown recruited Benjamin F. Roberts, an African American activist from Boston, to write an accompanying lecture, "The Condition of the Colored People in the United States." To dramatize its message, the panorama showed alternating scenes, one a traditional and romanticized American view and the next an image of the cruelty of slavery—a whipping post, for instance—in the same place. Just as Brown's version of "Uncle Ned" turned a popular ballad into a protest song, so the "Mirror of Liberty" transformed idealized American myths into the realities of a slave society.

It is not known whether Box Brown solicited an author to tell his story or whether he was approached by abolitionists; in either event, Brown submitted his life to Charles Stearns for presentation to the world. A nephew of Brook Farm's Utopian founder, George Ripley, Stearns was a militant antislavery activist. Though earlier a pacifist, he had participated so ardently in the violent struggle between proslavery and antislavery factions in Kansas during the late 1850s known as "Bleeding Kansas" that he lost his pacifism. In Boston in 1849 Stearns published his *Narrative of Henry Box Brown who Escaped from Slavery Enclosed in a Box 3 Feet Long and 2 Wide Written from a Statement of Facts Made by Himself. With Remarks upon the Remedy for Slavery. By Charles Stearns.* The book's problem was Stearns's "Remarks." As well as appearing in a separate essay, they permeated the entire text with Stearns's dogmatic ideology and arrogant and opinionated style. Brown's personal response was to edit or, more likely, to have the book heavily edited at

the first opportunity. Most of Stearns's overblown rhetoric was simply excised.

Brown was forced to leave the United States, even the free North, before he could find his own voice. With the passage of a stronger fugitive slave law in 1850, the North was legally obliged to participate in the recapture and return of escaped slaves. Skirting the threat of arrest in Providence, Rhode Island, Brown immediately left for England. A second edition of his autobiography, with a Manchester 1851 imprint, appeared with a new title: *Narrative of the Life of Henry Box Brown Written by Himself.*

At this point he fell out with J. C. A. Smith, who reported to abolitionists in the United States that Brown had begun to lead a dissolute life, engaging in drinking, swearing, smoking, and "many other things too Bad" to name. By this time, Brown had fully escaped from his life as a slave, and remade himself as a freeman, living under the protection of Queen Victoria. In fact, Brown had become a successful entertainer in England, where he married an English woman, rather than attempting to use his earnings to buy his wife and children out of slavery.

For the rest of the decade Brown toured the British Isles, lecturing on the history of slavery as well as acting and singing. He used a large moving panorama to depict the history of blacks in Africa and America, as he lectured on "African and American Slavery." He often appeared as an "African Prince" as he melded antislavery sentiments and propaganda, popular history, and entertaining theatrical production. In 1862 he developed a new lecture and panorama called the "Grand Moving Mirror of the American War." However, by this time his career as a political speaker was beginning to play itself out, and he moved into other forms of entertainment.

By 1864 he was billed as "Mr. H. Box Brown, the King of all Mesmerisers," although he continued to perform his "Panorama of African and American Slavery." In 1875 the sixty-year-old Brown returned to the United States with his wife and daughter Annie, performing as the magician and mesmerist Prof. H. Box Brown; he toured New England in the mid- and late 1870s with a show called the *African Prince's Drawing-Room Entertainment.* He still advertised himself as the man "whose escape from slavery in 1849 in a box 3 feet 1 inch long, 2 feet wide, 2 feet six inches high, caused such a sensation in the New England States, he having traveled from Richmond, Va., to Philadelphia, a journey of 350 miles, packed as luggage in a box." There is no record of Brown's life after 1878.

Brown's narrative was a dramatic moment in the antislavery movement. His escape was brave and striking; he emerged from the "box" of slavery to become an icon of those who loved liberty. However, there was also a darker side to Brown's story. After Brown's successful escape Samuel Smith tried to help another slave to escape in the same way. But Richmond authorities were now well aware of how Brown had escaped, and Smith was arrested. He would spend six years in the penitentiary. Dr. Smith was feted in the North after his release but soon disappeared from view. It is striking that while Brown was entertaining audiences in Britain, and living the life of a celebrity, the man who literally sent him on to freedom was himself in prison. FREDERICK DOUGLASS was somewhat disdainful of Brown for exposing the way he escaped. In his own *Narrative*, Douglass was careful not to reveal his method, lest someone else be unable to use it, or because it might imperil those who helped him (as happened with Samuel Smith). However, it was hardly Brown's fault that his escape became famous. Abolitionists were thrilled with its novelty and audacity. It was not only Brown himself, but the abolitionists who supported him, who turned the fugitive Henry Brown into "Box" Brown.

Douglass and other abolitionists were also probably disappointed that Brown chose the life of the entertainer instead of the life of the reformer and advocate. However, his career as an entertainer, his marriage to an English woman, and his later return to the United States as a "mesmeriser" also suggest another way of understanding him. While he traded in on the dramatic circumstances of his escape, he refused to be defined in later life as a runaway slave, or even a black person. A talented singer and showman, Brown used freedom to freely recreate himself in a white world as an entertainer/entrepreneur. He made himself free to be who he wanted to be, and not who society or the abolitionist movement expected him to be. He is remembered for his escape, but his later life illustrates the power of freedom for someone once held in bondage.

Further Reading

Brown, Henry Box. *Narrative of the Life of Henry Box Brown Written by Himself* (1851, reprinted 2002 with an Introduction by Richard Newman).
Ruggles, Jeffrey. *The Unboxing of Henry Brown* (2003).

PAUL FINKELMAN
RICHARD NEWMAN

BROWN, Homer S. (23 Sept. 1896–22 May 1977), attorney, judge, and civil rights activist, was born in Huntington, West Virginia, to the Reverend William Roderick Brown and Maria Wiggins Rowlett Brown. He attended Virginia Union University in Richmond and in 1923 earned a law degree from the University of Pittsburgh, graduating third in a class of twenty-two students.

Following his graduation in October 1923, Brown joined the Allegheny County Bar Association and became active in his community to reduce crime and improve the quality of life for youth. He married Wilhelmina Byrd in 1927, and the couple had one son, Byrd Rowlett Brown, who also became a well-known attorney and civil rights activist in Pittsburgh. During the 1930s, when there was an increase in crime as a result of the Great Depression, Brown chaired the Friendly Service Bureau, a committee established to help reduce crime in Pittsburgh. Along with the help of the mayor of Pittsburgh, the committee successfully reduced crime and improved the quality of life for youth within the district—a major feat for that era.

From 1934 to 1950 Brown served in the Pennsylvania House of Representatives. In 1937 he began to pay attention to the Pittsburgh Board of Education's hiring practices, noting that since desegregation rulings, Pittsburgh had refused to hire black teachers. Brown subsequently paved the way for a major lawsuit, and facilitated the hiring of the first black music instructor in a Pittsburgh school. He was voted the most able member of the House in 1943 by the Capital News Correspondents' Association and also named the most outstanding legislator.

In 1945 Brown faced an important struggle to secure human rights for working class residents of Pennsylvania. After conducting extensive research into the hiring practices of Pennsylvania businesses, Brown concluded that the majority of them practiced racial and religious discrimination. As a result of his research, Brown authored Pennsylvania's Fair Employment Practices Act, gaining him notoriety and a victory for the working class citizens of Pennsylvania.

Brown also served as founder and first president of the Pittsburgh chapter of the National Association for the Advancement of Colored People (NAACP) for twenty-four years, and was also the first African American to be appointed to the Board of Education. In 1949 he was elected the first African American Allegheny County Judge, a role that empowered him to facilitate numerous positive changes for the community. In 1956 he was elected to the Court of Common Pleas, and held that position until illness forced him to retire in 1975, two years before his death.

During his years as an attorney and judge, Brown handed down several significant rulings that were subsequently upheld by the Supreme Court of Pennsylvania. For example, in 1968 he decided that the city's "sick tax" on hospitals was unconstitutional, and in 1973 he ruled that prayer should be allowed during graduation ceremonies. Brown became well known and highly respected in his community, often entertaining luminaries such as U.S. Supreme Court Justice THURGOOD MARSHALL It was within this environment that Homer and Wilhelmina nurtured their son, Byrd, to carry on their legacy of civil and political activism in Pittsburgh.

In 1969 the Homer S. Brown Law Association was founded in Brown's honor. The Association represents over 200 African American attorneys. A membership group that supports minority lawyers and tracks hiring progress in Pittsburgh, the association assists local law students and increases legal knowledge within the community. Still quite active in the community, the association continues to monitor hiring practices and support minorities in Pittsburgh.

Besides his work in the Pittsburgh community, Brown was also the member of a number of other organizations. He was a member of the Pennsylvania Governor's Committee on Education in 1960, chaired the Board of Directors of the YMCA, and was a member of the White House Commission on Education in

1955. He was also on the advisory board of the United Nations Educational, Scientific, and Cultural Organization. Brown received honorary Doctor of Law degrees from several universities, including Virginia State College, Lincoln University (Pennsylvania), Virginia Union University, and the University of Pittsburgh.

Homer Brown died at home following a long illness. Both before and following his death, Brown's son, Byrd, complemented his father's important work in the Pittsburgh community, particularly gaining respect for his courage during the civil rights movement. Brown's widow, Wilhelmina Byrd Brown, also a well-known civil and political rights activist, collected and compiled twenty-three volumes of material belonging to her late husband. These volumes are on deposit at Virginia Union University in Richmond.

Further Reading

Who Was Who in America, 1977–1981, vol. 7 (1981).

CHERYL DUDLEY

BROWN, James (3 May 1933–25 Dec. 2006), rhythm-and-blues singer, was born James Joe Brown Jr. in a country shack just outside Barnwell, South Carolina, to Joe Gardner and Susan Behlings. His father did various jobs, while nothing is known about his mother's occupation. Brown was raised in extreme poverty, and his parents separated when he was four; two years later he went to live with his great-aunt, Minnie Walker, in Augusta, Georgia.

Brown's father often sang blues songs in the evening, and when Brown was four, his father gave him a ten-cent harmonica. His earliest years were spent tap

James Brown, who became "The Godfather of Soul," performing with the Famous Flames in 1964. (Library of Congress.)

dancing in the street for spare change. He claimed that his formidable sense of rhythm stemmed from such humble beginnings. A self-taught musician, Brown began to play organ at the age of eight and later acquired a rudimentary knowledge of bass, guitar, saxophone, and trumpet. At eleven Brown won his first talent contest as a singer, and a year later he formed a group he called the Cremona Trio. In those same years Brown was involved in petty crime, shoplifting and stealing car batteries and hubcaps to obtain money for school clothes and food. In 1948, at the age of fifteen, he was caught stealing cars for the second time and was sentenced to eight to sixteen years in the Georgia Juvenile Training Institute in Rome, Georgia, thus ending his formal schooling at the seventh grade. Nicknamed Music Box, Brown formed a gospel quartet in prison.

In 1952, Brown was paroled and went to live in Toccoa, Georgia. There he joined a group formed by Bobby Byrd, whom Brown had met during a baseball game while he was still in prison. Byrd's group originally sang gospel and was known as the Gospel Starlighters. Just before being joined by Brown, they had switched to singing rhythm and blues and consequently had changed their name to the Avons. They would soon be known as the Flames and eventually as James Brown and the Famous Flames. As word of the group's incredibly intense live shows spread throughout the South, they were summoned to Macon, Georgia, by LITTLE RICHARD's manager, Clint Bradley, after Richard became a national star in 1955.

A year later Ralph Bass signed Brown and the Famous Flames to Cincinnati-based King Records, their releases appearing on the subsidiary Federal label. Legend has it that upon hearing the demo recording of "Please Please Please," King's owner, Syd Nathan, fired Bass. Nathan could not believe that anyone would want to buy a record that consisted of six straight eight-bar verses, each of which was made up solely of one bar after one bar call-and-response patterns between Brown and the Flames. What Nathan did not understand, Brown knew from playing the song night after night in concert. Audiences would go crazy over the heightened emotion Brown conveyed, using numerous gospel-derived vocal devices. It took several months, but eventually "Please Please Please" reached the number-six position on *Billboard*'s R&B charts. Brown's debut effort and later singles, such as 1958's "Try Me" and 1960's "Think," were, along with early efforts by RAY CHARLES and SAM COOKE, the first examples of what would become known as soul music.

In 1962 Brown suggested that he wanted to record a live album at the Apollo Theater in New York. Long billed as "The Hardest Working Man in Show Business," Brown was positive that a recorded version of his legendary show would sell in significant numbers. When Nathan refused to finance the recording, Brown paid for it himself. Upon its release in 1963, *Live at the Apollo* climbed all the way to number two on *Billboard*'s LP charts. Such success was pretty well unprecedented for black artists and totally unheard of for live albums.

As the 1960s unfolded and Brown enjoyed a string of successes, American society underwent momentous changes. The civil rights movement had successfully brought about legal desegregation, but as the end of the decade approached most African Americans still found themselves the last hired and first fired, being paid less money than white workers for the same labor, living in inferior housing and sending their children to substandard schools.

As this reality slowly made itself manifest, the mood of black America began to change. In 1966 during the JAMES MEREDITH march in Mississippi, STOKELY CARMICHAEL popularized the phrase "Black Power." A year earlier the predominantly black neighborhood of Watts in Los Angeles had burned in the first of the modern-day race rebellions. In 1967 Newark, New Jersey, and Detroit, Michigan, would also burn. This new militancy no longer asked for equality, nor did it seek to achieve such equality by adopting mainstream (i.e., "white middle class") standards of deportment. Rather, black Americans were encouraged to celebrate and embrace everything black and to assume and demand equality. Inspired by the belief that "black is beautiful," many African Americans began to explore their historical and psychological connections to their African motherland. While some blacks adopted African names and wore African garb, many more began to sport an "Afro" or "natural" haircut.

This re-Africanization of black culture was also reflected in popular music, most radically in the development of funk by James Brown. In the simplest terms, Brown, beginning in 1967 with "Cold Sweat," de-emphasized melody and harmony (for example, by having whole sections of a song with no chord changes and by delivering the lyrics in a voice closer to speaking than singing) while privileging rhythm (by employing more complex syncopated figures and using several different rhythmic patterns simultaneously, creating interlocking grooves). This reconstruction of Brown's music could be interpreted as de-emphasizing parameters favored by white American society while highlighting sub-Saharan African characteristics; this was, in effect, re-Africanizing the music, thus paralleling the re-Africanization of African American society at large at the time.

Brown could be a temperamental and demanding bandleader—his trombonist Fred Wesley once noted that "James was bossy and paranoid." But when it came to performance, Brown was often able to submerge his ego in pursuit of a more democratic, communal sound. Notions of community and solidarity are connoted in "Cold Sweat" in a number of ways. Throughout the performance Brown utters any number of vocables judiciously placed within the rhythmic matrix. In doing so, he projects himself as part of the band rather than as a separate, somehow special, more important front man. Similarly, he can be heard during the performance calling out such things as "Maceo,

Maceo," "Give the drummer some," "Bernard, come on and help him out; play that thing." In this way, Brown conveys a sense of community. He explicitly *names* those who are contributing, recognizing their intrinsic value as individuals and the equality implicit in *collectively* unleashing the spiritual magic of the performance. "Cold Sweat" ends after seven and a half minutes with an extraordinary section in which Brown seems to be shredding his larynx while singing, "I can't, I can't, I can't, I can't stop, I can't stop, I can't stop singing." The effect is cathartic. Brown thus demonstrates an exceptional level of commitment that is not lost on his audience. It is as if he has no choice in the matter.

Within a year Brown had connected funk lyrically to the newly emergent black consciousness, specifically with the song "Say It Loud, I'm Black and I'm Proud." Around that time he made clear that he was "totally committed to black power, the kind that is achieved not through the muzzle of a rifle but through education and economic leverage." Brown believed in the bootstraps philosophy of BOOKER T. WASHINGTON, and like the 1960s civil rights activists JAMES FORMAN and FLOYD MCKISSICK, in 1972 he supported Richard Nixon, whose presidential platform advocated "black capitalism," in the form of federal loans to small black businesses.

Significantly, "Black and Proud" would be Brown's last Top Ten pop hit until 1985's "Living in America." Conversely, this was the beginning of his greatest success on the R&B charts. Between 1968 and 1974 Brown had forty-one R&B hits, thirty-two of which went to the Top Ten. This is extraordinary testimony to the meaning he held for the black community in the United States at the time. It would appear that as Brown's music became understood as more African, it was encoded or at least decoded by blacks and whites as having a value and aesthetic system that was largely outside the experience of most white Americans. Consequently, most white Americans found little they could relate to while, in direct contrast, black Americans embraced funk as one of the most meaningful expressive forms of the time. Brown's music also found a huge audience in Africa in the late 1960s and early 1970s, influencing the Nigerian star Fela Kuti, among other exponents of Afrobeat.

At the same time that Brown was personally dominating the R&B charts in the United States, he built up a stable of artists in his revue whom he recorded for King, Polydor, and his own People label. Among the most successful of these side projects were Vicki Anderson, Lyn Collins, Bobby Byrd, and his backing group, the JB's. Brown seemed to be an endless source of funky grooves, writing hits for himself and his stable of artists while developing legendary bands that included such luminaries as Bootsy Collins, Fred Wesley, Maceo Parker, Pee Wee Ellis, and the drummers Melvin Parker, Jabo Starks, and Clyde Stubblefield.

In the 1980s Brown and funk music fell out of fashion, only to be resurrected and revered by decade's end, owing to the inordinate number of times his earlier hits were sampled by many prominent rap artists. Despite a troubled personal life, Brown endured. He was married three times and rumors of spousal abuse were frequent. So too were his run-ins with the law, for drugs or gun possession, tax evasion, and assault. In one incident, in September 1988, police pursued Brown through South Carolina and Georgia and arrested him on a count of arrest and battery with intent to kill and a series of traffic offenses. Sentenced to six years in prison, Brown was released on probation in February 1991. In 1998 Brown was convicted of another drug-related offense and arrested for domestic violence in 2004.

Brown continued to tour, record, and earn the numerous accolades that might be expected of an elder statesman. He received the Grammy Lifetime Achievement Award in 1992 and was inducted into the Rock and Roll Hall of Fame in 1996. In 2003 he received a Kennedy Center Honor for his achievements and influence in popular music. He was even, in March 1997, recognized by the State Legislature of Georgia, a body not hitherto known for its funkiness. A joint House and Senate resolution declared him "the minister of the new super heavy funk," and credited James Brown with bringing "a spark of energy and excitement to an otherwise listless U.S. music scene." He died of congestive heart failure after being hospitalized for pneumonia, in Atlanta, on 25 December 2006.

Further Reading
Brown, James, and Bruce Tucker. *James Brown: The Godfather of Soul* (1986).
Brown, Geoff. *James Brown: A Biography* (1996).
Rose, Cynthia. *Living in America: The Soul Saga of James Brown* (1990).

ROB BOWMAN

BROWN, Jeannette Elizabeth (13 May 1934–), organic chemist and educator, was born in the Bronx, New York, the only child of Ada May Fox, a homemaker, and Freddie Brown, a maintenance worker who later became a postal worker. Brown's education was obtained in various schools of New York, and she received her high school diploma from New Dorp High School, Staten Island, New York; in 1952. Upon completing high school, she continued her educational pursuits by enrolling at Hunter College of the City University of New York, which was free to eligible high school graduates. In 1956 she graduated with a BA in Chemistry and two years later earned her MS at the University of Minnesota, where she was the first African American woman to receive any degree in chemistry. In her two years at the university, she conducted research titled "A Study of Dye and Ylide Formation in Salts of 9-(p-Dimethylaminophenyl) Fluorene." Her research resulted in a compound that was white at room temperature and pink when heated above room temperature; this compound was possibly one of the very few compounds synthesized that appeared to be both a liquid and a solid and changed appearance at different temperatures. These types of compounds are called liquid crystals. This synthesis by Brown is important because this strange "stuff" called liquid crystals could be produced in large amounts for scientific research and other uses.

By the time she completed her MS, industry in general was just opening up to African Americans. Prior to that period, most African Americans who became chemists worked for the federal government or at historically black colleges and universities since industry was not an option for many. She was hired at CIBA Pharmaceutical Company in 1958 where she worked for several years as a junior chemist. She was the second woman and the third African American hired by the company. After leaving CIBA, she accepted a position as an organic medicinal chemist at Merck Sharp and Dohme Research Laboratories, where she worked from 1969 to 1995 and was fortunate to serve as a member of a team that was very productive and appreciative of her talent and skills. When this team synthesized the Cilastatin sodium component of Primaxin, an antibiotic, Brown shared in the success in many ways. For example, her name was included as one of the authors of the publication about the synthesis, and she was invited to a dinner held for the team by the head of the laboratory to celebrate the success of the team. In addition to the article that she coauthored on this synthesis, she was author or coauthor of fourteen other scientific articles and five patents. One of the patents is in her name only. Her suggestions of new targets for development were respected as she conducted research on other drug candidates for human and animal health. Her tenure at Merck lasted twenty-five years.

In addition to conducting research and publishing her work in scientific journals, Brown served as a member of Merck's Black University Liaison Committee in 1978. This committee was charged with identifying African Americans for employment at Merck and encouraging black students to major in chemistry or biology and to earn graduate degrees. Brown was awarded the Merck Management Award for directing the carrying out of the charge of this committee, especially for her work in improving the chemistry department at Grambling University in Louisiana. From 1993 until 1995, while still employed at Merck, she went on a detail assignment to serve as a visiting professor at the New Jersey Institute of Technology (NJIT), where she helped write the NJIT Alliance for Minority Participation in Science proposal. Additionally, she served as the science adviser to the NJIT Urban Elementary Outreach Program, and she designed, developed, and coordinated the NJIT Trust K–8 Professor Development Program. She also worked in a number of other educational capacities. Brown's appointment at NJIT was on a year-to-year basis as a visiting faculty member. Later, from 1998 to 2002, she served as the director of the Regional Center for the National Science Foundation–funded New Jersey Statewide Systemic Initiative. At this center the staff worked with minority students and their science teachers to increase their knowledge of science so that more students would choose to study science and engineering in college and work in those fields once they completed their studies. The teaching abilities of the teachers were made stronger so that they could help more students and appreciate science better. Also, Brown was responsible for improving mathematics and science education in Essex and Hudson counties, New Jersey, by implementing the programs of the statewide systemic initiative, which were designed to improve the teaching and learning of math and science, and she introduced these programs to teachers and administrators. She did this in her role as the New Jersey regional director of the Statewide Systemic Initiative in Science and Mathematics Education.

Brown became an active member of several professional societies: American Chemical Society (ACS), National Organization for the Professional Advancement of Black Chemists and Chemical Engineers (NOBCChE), Association for Women in Science (AWIS), American Association for the Advancement of Science (AAAS), New York Academy of Sciences, National Science Teachers Association (NSTA), New Jersey Science Teachers Association, New Jersey Science Leadership Association, and National Association of Science Writers. She was also a fellow of the WestEd National Academy for Science and Mathematics Leadership and a 2004 Société de Chimie Industrielle (American Section) fellow of the Chemical Heritage Foundation. As a fellow of the Chemical Heritage Foundation, Brown studied the history of African American women chemists.

Committed to broadening black participation in science and mathematics in the private sector, Brown has visited high schools to talk about the importance of science and mathematics, acting as a role model to students and as a career adviser to teachers and university students. She also has lectured at career-day programs and at special scientific outreach programs, and she has served as an ambassador to the Grambling University department of chemistry. As councilor for the North Jersey Section of ACS for more than twenty-five years beginning in 1982, she has also served as a member of the Women Chemists Committee and a coordinator for the North Jersey Section Metro Women Chemists Committee. Nationally, she was chair of Project SEED from 1986 to 1988—an ACS educational program for disadvantaged high school students—and has worked as a member of the Local Section Activities Committees of ACS starting in 1989. From 2002 to 2006 she served as a member of the PERCY JULIAN Task Force of ACS, and beginning in 2005 she became a member of the Speakers Bureau. She served as a career counselor starting in 1995 and as a reviewer for proposals submitted to the National Science Foundation (NSF). From 1991 to 1998 she also served two terms as a member of the congressionally mandated NSF Committee on Equal Opportunities in Science and Engineering.

In 2001 Brown was among the few chosen to participate in the Iowa State University Women in Chemistry Project—an oral history project for the university's Archives of Women in Science and Engineering. In May 2002, while serving as regional coordinator for the New Jersey Statewide Systemic Initiative (a National Science Foundation–sponsored partnership to improve science and math education in Essex and Hudson counties; the partnership was among schools, colleges and universities, science centers and museums, businesses, and industry) at NJIT, she was presented with the Women Chemists Committee Regional Award for contributions to diversity. In 2004 she was named a scholar of the Chemical Heritage Foundation, where she completed a multimedia project focused on the development of a history of African American women chemists.

In 2005 her alma mater, University of Minnesota, placed her name on the Alumni Wall of Honor. That same year she received the ACS Award for encouraging disadvantaged students into careers in the chemical sciences, sponsored by the Camille and Henry Dreyfus Foundation—she was the second African American woman to receive an ACS award. She generously used the funds from the ACS national award to establish the Freddie and Ada Brown Award for African American and Native American middle and high school students. In 2006 she was presented the North Jersey ACS Harvey Russell Award for support to chemistry teachers. On 18 February 2007 she was one of ten persons honored as an AWIS fellow at the AAAS annual meeting in San Francisco, California.

Further Reading

"ACS 2005 National Award Winners," *Chemical & Engineering News*, 3 Jan. 2005.
"Association for Women in Science Announces Its 2007 Fellows," *AWIS Newsletter*, 18 Feb. 2007.
"Jeannette Brown Receives University of Minnesota Outstanding Achievement Award," *NOBCChE News* (Spring/May 2005).
"Preserving History of African-American Women Chemists," *Women Chemists* (Fall/Winter 2004).
Sweeney, L. (Tanya Zanish-Belcher, curator), "An Interview: Jeannette E. Brown," Women in Chemistry Oral History Project, Archives of Women in Science and Engineering Special Collections Department, Iowa State University (2001).
This article was written by Dr. Margaret E. M. Tolbert in her personal capacity. The views expressed in this article do not necessarily represent the views of the National Science Foundation or the United States.

MARGARET E. M. TOLBERT

BROWN, Jesse (27 Mar. 1944–15 Aug. 2002), disability advocate and cabinet secretary, was born in Detroit, Michigan, but grew up in Chicago. He attended Catholic University in Washington, D.C., and Roosevelt College in Chicago. He graduated from Chicago City College and subsequently enlisted in the U.S. Marine Corps in 1963, serving in the Vietnam War. There he was seriously wounded when an enemy bullet shattered his right arm while he was on patrol in Da Nang, leaving him partially paralyzed. In a real sense, that injury defined the rest of Brown's career.

Upon leaving the Marine Corps in 1966 Brown joined the Disabled American Veterans (DAV), an advocacy group supporting the cause of veterans injured while in military service. The organization had been founded in 1920 and given a congressional charter in 1932 and was the official voice of America's service-connected disabled veterans, representing all of America's disabled veterans, their families, and survivors. Brown worked for the DAV from 1967 until 1988, moving to the organization's national headquarters in Washington, D.C., in 1973. He became the first African American executive director of the DAV and served in that capacity from 1989 until 1993. As executive director he earned the reputation of being the nation's keenest mind regarding veterans' benefits and services.

Because of that reputation, he was tapped by President Bill Clinton to serve as the secretary of veterans affairs in Clinton's first cabinet. During confirmation hearings Brown testified that his background in veterans' advocacy gave him "an intimacy with veterans' issues that can only come from hard work, every day, year in, year out, in a single field" (*Congressional Quarterly Almanac* [1993], 427). While some senators expressed concern that Brown was too close to veterans, warning that he could never please them, Brown was confirmed by voice vote, indicating no real opposition to his nomination. Representative Sonny Montgomery, Democrat of Mississippi, praised the appointment, saying it was the "best possible appointment in these crucial times" (*Washington Post*, 17 Aug. 2002). Brown became the second secretary of the department, which had been created during President George H. W. Bush's administration, and the first African American in the post. His military record made him a perfect choice for Clinton, who had been criticized during the 1992 campaign for avoiding military service during the Vietnam War.

Once in office, Brown became a tireless advocate for American veterans. He was fond of referring to himself as the secretary "for" Veterans and often said that he would win battles with Congress because "we hold the high moral ground" (*Washington Post*, 17 Aug. 2002). During the time that he was secretary, he opposed cuts that the Office of Management and Budget (OMB) had recommended to the president and for four consecutive years increased the budget of the Veteran's Administration (VA) as a percentage of the federal budget. He helped expand benefits for Vietnam and Persian Gulf War veterans who had been prisoners of war, exposed to Agent Orange or mustard gas, or who had suffered posttraumatic stress syndrome. He also increased benefits for women veterans and for children with ailments linked to their parents' service. Brown increased the efficiency of the VA, and even convinced veterans' groups to accept the closure of veterans' medical facilities, something that VA observers had thought nearly impossible. In exchange, however, Brown expanded VA coverage so that physicians were allowed to treat veterans for all of their ailments, not just injuries received in the line of duty.

After leaving office Brown founded Brown and Associates, a planning and marketing consulting firm. His expertise figured prominently in planning and marketing initiatives at a broad variety of companies, both domestic and international. He died in Warrenton, Virginia, following a long battle with amyotrophic lateral sclerosis (ALS), commonly known as Lou Gehrig's disease. More than one thousand mourners, including former president Clinton, then-current and former cabinet officials, lawmakers, and other dignitaries joined friends and family at a service held at Washington National Cathedral. "When we lost Jesse Brown, we lost one of the greatest veterans' advocates I have ever known, and I am deeply saddened by the loss of this great American," said the Senate Veterans' Affairs Committee chairman John D. Rockefeller IV. Brown himself said that he wanted to be remembered as "someone who made a difference in the quality of veterans' lives" (*Washington Post*, 17 Aug. 2002). He left behind a wife, Sylvia, his mother, his two children, and a granddaughter. To honor his service, the DAV established the Jesse Brown Memorial Youth Scholarship program to encourage young volunteers to play active roles in the Department of Veterans Affairs Voluntary Service programs.

Further Reading
Congressional Quarterly Almanac (1993).

Obituary: *Washington Post*, 17 Aug. 2002.
JAMES W. RIDDLESPERGER JR.

BROWN, Jesse Leroy (13 Oct. 1926–4 Dec. 1950), the first black U.S. Navy pilot, was born in Hattiesburg, Mississippi, the son of John Brown, a sharecropper, and Julia Lindsey, a schoolteacher. The family worked from sunup to sundown and lived in a typical, unpainted, pine-board house with one story and a tin roof. Behind the house were a well, an outhouse, chicken and hog pens, and a vegetable garden. John Brown was a deacon in the Baptist church, where the family worshiped each Sunday.

Young Jesse fell in love with flying at age six, when his father took him to an air show, and he marveled at the white wing walkers, parachute jumpers, and acrobatic tricks performed by the pilots of the biwinged aircraft. His father didn't have the two dollars to let his son ride in a cockpit that day, but by the time he was seven Jesse was reading *Popular Aviation* magazine by kerosene lamp late into the night. Jesse was also fascinated by movies of World War I dogfights between American and German planes and decided that he wanted to be a fighter pilot. Whenever a plane from the dirt strip at nearby Palmer's Crossing flew overhead, the youngster would wave at it with his straw hat and yell, "That's where I'm going to be someday."

On Saturday afternoons Jesse could usually be found hiding near the dusty forty-foot-wide, five-hundred-yard runway at Palmer's Crossing. Though

Jesse Leroy Brown, at his graduation from the Naval Aviation Cadet Program in Jacksonville, Florida, 23 October 1948. (National Association for the Advancement of Colored People Records, Library of Congress.)

he was repeatedly chased away by Corley Yates, the field manager and mechanic, nothing could stop Jesse from watching the biplanes rush down the runway. This war between Corley Yates and Jesse Brown went on for years.

Brown's school in Lux, Mississippi, consisted of only one room with eight rows of benches. Students from first grade to eighth grade assembled each day, batting bugs in summer and shivering in winter. The powerful influence of their mother ensured that all five Brown boys were excellent students. In 1938, when Jesse was one bench from finishing Lux, he began to deliver the *Pittsburgh Courier*, a black newspaper that one day ran a long article about the black man's struggle to enter military aviation. Reading it, twelve-year-old Jesse was furious at General Hap Arnold, chief of the U.S. Army Air Corps, who said, "Negro pilots cannot be used in our present Air Corps since this would result in having Negro officers in command of white enlisted men." When the *Courier* editorialized that there was a white belief that black men did not have "the brains or fortitude or aptitude to fly military planes," Jesse cut the article out, nailed it to the wall over his bed, and then wrote a letter to President Franklin Roosevelt asking why black pilots were excluded from the air corps.

Brown attended Eureka High School, making "A" grades, playing football and basketball, and starring in track. Graduating in 1944, he chose to enroll that September at Ohio State University, against the advice of his principal and friends, who wanted him to enroll in a black college in Mississippi. Brown wanted to test his abilities, however, and was prepared to withstand prejudice at the predominantly white university. He majored in engineering and joined the track team, but as always his great interest was flying. There was a navy V-5 program at the university, and Brown took the entrance exam after being told that no African

American had ever entered Selective Flight Training. Three years later, having passed all tests, he prepared for entry into the Naval Air Training Command in Glenview, Illinois, by looking into a mirror and yelling at himself, "Nigger! Nigger! Nigger!" After two weeks of training, Brown made his solo flight in a dual cockpit "Yellow Peril" Stearman, a navy training biplane, executing three perfect landings.

Although his officer instructors often derided him, and though he almost flunked out of the arduous Pre-Flight School at Ottumwa, Iowa, because he couldn't swim, Brown persisted. Though Glenview had been tough, it was easy compared to Pre-Flight, where Brown confronted every possible physical and mental test, the final being in a Dilbert Dunker to simulate an open ocean crash. His preflight instruction then continued at the Pensacola, Florida, Naval Air Station, where he flew a single-wing SNJ trainer to prepare for carrier landings. As the only African American among six-hundred-odd white midshipmen, Brown felt enormous pressure and often faced outright hostility from his instructors. One vowed, "No nigger is going to sit his ass in the cockpit of a Navy fighter." Each day was a struggle, and twice he had to appear before a special board to save his existence at Pensacola because of aerial mistakes.

Brown got some relief from the strain and loneliness when he married nineteen-year-old Daisy Pearl Nix in October 1947, even though that was forbidden by training regulation. If the union were discovered, he would be headed back to Lux within twenty-four hours. He found a home for Daisy in Pensacola through the church. He could talk to her, and they could discreetly meet. Brown struggled on the ground and in the air but finally made his first carrier landing on the USS *Wright* in the Gulf of Mexico on 17 June 1948, flying an SNJ trainer. After five landings, the *Wright*'s loudspeaker rasped, "Midshipman Brown qualified." On 21 October, Brown, flying a Hellcat fighter, a super aircraft of its day, won his gold wings at Jacksonville Naval Air Station. The public information office put out a press release: *First Negro Naval Aviator*, along with a photo. *Life* magazine published his picture. But Daisy Brown, still hidden from the navy, and in her fourth month of pregnancy, couldn't perform the traditional pinning on of his wings.

In mid-January 1949, less than a month after the birth of his daughter, Pamela, Brown left for Quonset Point, Rhode Island, for his first assignment as a fighter pilot with Squadron 32 on the USS *Leyte*. On 26 April he was sworn into the navy as an ensign, and he began flying a Bearcat three to five hours a day. Later that year he began flying a Corsair, the navy's "killer" aircraft of World War II. Since they no longer needed to hide their marriage, the Browns also rented a house in Quonset Point and entered the social life of the air station. It was the happiest time in Brown's life. In June 1950, however, North Korea invaded South Korea, and President Harry Truman decided to take America into the Korean War.

On 4 December 1950 the carriers *Leyte* and *Philippine Sea* were stationed off the northeast coast of North Korea. For three desperate days Brown and his fellow pilots had been ordered to provide maximum air support, day and night, to fifteen thousand U.S. Marines fighting their way along the bloody, body-strewn, ice-bound road to Hungnam, North Korea. More than one hundred thousand Chinese troops surrounded the marines. That morning Brown dressed quickly in long johns, coveralls, a sweater, a rubber antiexposure suit, and fleece-lined boots and gloves and proceeded to his Corsair. He headed for the infamous Chosin Reservoir and the bloody road where marines were dying around the clock. Arriving over land, Brown and his flying partners dropped to five hundred feet to search for targets. As Brown and his comrades passed overhead, Chinese troops lying on their backs unseen in the snow fired upward. When a bullet hit Brown's fuel line, his wingman, Thomas Rudner, flying close by, walked him through the safety procedures they had learned in flight school. Meanwhile, U.S. planes began circling the area, ready to use every single bit of firepower to keep the communists at bay. It did not matter to Brown's fellow pilots that his skin was black. He was simply a gallant shipmate and friend.

Brown crashed uphill, out of control. With his plane skidding over the frozen ground, only his harness kept him from being a punching bag, as the huge engine and four-bladed propeller broke off and careened away, leaving a tangle of steel and wires in the cockpit. His fellow pilots kept circling, watching for a sign of life. Finally, Brown opened the canopy, which had jammed on impact, and waved, but he could not climb out. A piece of steel had jammed his knee in that narrow space, and escape was impossible.

Tom Rudner then made a decision against all combat regulations, one that could have earned him a court-martial for destroying a navy aircraft. He decided to risk his own life and crash land, hoping he could help before Brown's two-hundred-gallon gas tank exploded. Rudner put his Corsair down as close as possible to Brown's plane, knowing that the enemy troops on the rise might shoot both of them. Talking to Brown continually, Rudner packed snow into the area of the smoke and used his own radio to call in a helicopter. Rudner kept talking to Brown while the injured pilot drifted in and out of consciousness. At one point Brown said to Rudner, "Cut my leg off," but Rudner could not. Nor could Charlie Ward, the pilot of a Sikorsky rescue helicopter, because night had fallen, making it impossible for him to see.

A few minutes later, Brown told Rudner, "Tell Daisy how much I love her." He then took a shallow breath, and as his head slumped down on his chest, Rudner and Ward wept.

Aboard the *Leyte* there was shock and disbelief. The African American stewards on board ship had carefully made Brown's bunk each morning and made sure he got the best meals. They wept bitterly as a bugle played taps and marines fired volleys off the stern. Hudner persuaded Captain Sisson, his commanding officer, that Brown would not have approved a mission to recover his dead body if it meant risking the lives of others. Sisson therefore ordered two divisions to give Jesse Brown a "warrior's funeral." Within an hour seven Corsairs (six loaded with napalm), piloted by Brown's friends, took off for Somong-ni. Arriving there, one fighter dropped down to make a run over the two aircraft. The sun was out, and the sky was blue. Brown sat in his cockpit, snow dusting his hair. Then six aircraft loaded with napalm rose to ten thousand feet while the seventh continued to climb, almost straight up, and the radios connecting them heard, "Our Father who art in heaven, hallowed be Thy name." In roaring dives, the Corsairs released their napalm pods, and Brown vanished in sheets of fiery red.

Further Reading
Taylor, Theodore. *The Flight of Jesse Leroy Brown* (1998).

THEODORE TAYLOR

BROWN, Jill (1949–), pilot, who made aviation history when she became the first African American woman to fly for a major passenger airline in the United States, the first to be admitted to the U.S. Navy's flight school, and the first in U.S. military history to qualify as a pilot.

Brown was born in Millersville, Maryland. Her family had taken up aviation as a hobby, and she learned to fly small planes with her parents—Gilbert Brown, who was a former U.S. Air Force instrument mechanic and also owned a building construction business, and Elaine Brown, an art resource teacher in the Baltimore public schools—when she was seventeen years old. For her eighteenth birthday, she received a Cherokee 180D airplane. In 1967 Brown flew her first solo flight in a Piper J-3 Cub. She had always dreamed of becoming a commercial pilot, but her mother advised her otherwise, and on her mother's advice, she majored in home economics at the University of Maryland. After graduation, in 1973, she took a teaching job at Oakmont Regional High School outside Boston, Massachusetts, and kept in touch with a navy recruiter, as the dream of flying still weighed heavily on her mind. She soon realized that it would take more than a degree in home economics to fulfill an urge to be somebody.

Of the 49,694 airplane pilots in the nation in 1970, only 162 were black, and only five of these were women. In 1974 the U.S. Naval Air Force began accepting women for officer's training, and Brown was finally called to try out for naval officer's training school in Newport, Rhode Island. She knew that the military would provide extensive pilot training, so she signed up, but she soon discovered that the military was not yet ready for minorities. According to Brown, she and the navy were not compatible, and she dropped out of the program after six months. She was honorably discharged, but because the military

experience had left a sour taste in her mouth, she decided that she would have to find a way to fund her future pilot training herself.

Brown returned to a teaching post in Baltimore, instructing inner-city youngsters in home economics through the spring of 1976. During a July 1978 interview with *Ebony* magazine, Brown noted that the magazine had played an important part in her success. She said that while reading the April 1976 issue of *Ebony*, she came across a story on Wheeler Airlines in Raleigh, North Carolina. The story in the magazine described how Captain Warren H. Wheeler, a pilot for Piedmont Airlines, was operating the nation's first scheduled, black-owned-and-operated airline during his off-duty hours.

Brown wrote to Captain Wheeler and asked for a job—she even offered to work without pay—then followed up with a telephone call. Wheeler called her back and invited her down to take a check ride with him on a B-737 jet the next day so that they could talk. Brown said that she knew Wheeler didn't need a co-pilot, but he wanted to help her, because he knew that she wanted to fly for a major airline. She started out working for him as a reservationist and was paid a three-hundred-dollar-a-month salary to write tickets, but she flew for free when there was space available. Later she was made resident co-pilot, and she flew extra time in order to earn more hours in the air. While doing this job she logged 1,200 flying hours—the requirement for most major airlines at the time. In May 1978 she became a pilot, flying a Beechcraft 99 for Wheeler. Brown soon realized, however, that she was being assigned to more publicity shots as the first African American female airline pilot than she was to planes, so she resigned and on 2 October 1978 took a job in Detroit flying cargo for Zantop International Airlines.

In an earlier issue of *Ebony*, Brown had read about Evans McKay, an African American who was a vice president of Texas International Airlines. She figured that if Texas International was liberal enough to hire a black vice president, they would be liberal enough to hire a black woman pilot, and they were. When she left Wheeler Airlines, she had been as well qualified as any of the other applicants seeking to enroll in flight-training programs with major airlines, so she began sending out applications. She received an immediate response from Texas International Airlines and was invited for an interview, and she subsequently enrolled in the company's training program. At that time, Brown was one of six women in a class of thirty-eight to graduate as pilots from the Texas International Airlines training program, and her status caught the eyes of the national media. In 1978, still with Texas International, she also became the first African American woman to serve as a captain on a major commercial airline. There were only 110 black pilots flying for the airlines, including the five other women.

When asked about her tenacity during an *Ebony* magazine interview in 1978, Brown responded: "Someone once said that to be a success you must find a need, then fill that need. I felt women would someday have a chance in aviation, and I was determined to be ready for it."

Further Reading
Burgen, Michele. "Backstage," *Ebony* (July 1978).
Burgen, Michele. "Winging It at 25,000 Feet," *Ebony* (Aug. 1978).
Smith, Elizabeth Simpson. *Breakthrough: Women in Aviation* (1981).
Smith, Jessie Carney. *Black Firsts: 2,000 Years of Extraordinary Achievement* (1944).

CLARE J. WASHINGTON

BROWN, Jim (17 Feb. 1936–), athlete, actor, and activist, was born James Nathaniel Brown on Saint Simons Island, Georgia, to Theresa and Swinton Brown, a onetime boxer, who abandoned Theresa and their son two weeks after his birth. A couple of years later Theresa departed for Long Island, New York, to take a domestic job, leaving Jim to be raised by his great-grandmother and grandmother, the latter an alcoholic. By 1944 Theresa had saved enough money to send for Jim, and they were reunited in Manhasset, Long Island, for the first time in six years. Despite the usual friction of being the new kid—he was once accused by his peers of fighting dirty—Brown eventually distinguished himself athletically. He gained the attention of a local policeman, who lent Brown keys to the high school gym so that the youth

Jim Brown, on the field in an undated handout photo. (AP Images.)

could organize Police Boys' Club games whenever he and his friends wanted to play.

At Manhasset High School, Jim became a starter on the football team at the age of fourteen; he also played basketball, track, and baseball. By the end of his senior year he had tallied thirteen varsity letters, earning All-State honors in all but baseball; he averaged thirty-eight points per game in basketball (including a high game score of fifty-five) and 14.9 yards per carry in football. A self-proclaimed "gang warlord" in high school, Brown managed to keep himself on the academic honor roll and graduated in 1953 with more than forty athletic scholarships from which to choose.

Brown decided instead upon Syracuse University in upstate New York. Syracuse had not offered him a scholarship, but a family friend secured enough support from Manhasset businessmen to bankroll his freshman year, confident that he would quickly play his way into a scholarship. He did not accomplish this until his sophomore year, when a teammate's injury opened up a spot for him on the football team. It was a breakout year, as he also scored fifteen points per game in basketball, ran track, and played lacrosse for the first time. In track he competed in the decathlon, placing fifth nationally. Though this was good enough to qualify for the 1956 Olympics, Brown declined, because he felt it was dishonest to devote too much time to anything other than his scholarship sport, football. Altogether he would earn ten letters in three years across four sports; he was named All-American once in football and twice in lacrosse. In the latter sport, he became the first African American to play in the storied North-South game, though he only needed to play part of it to account for half of the North's output, scoring five goals and assisting on two, in a 14–10 victory.

Graduating with a degree in physical education, Brown planned to pursue coaching when his athletic career was over. In the meantime, he ignored repeated advances from major league baseball teams, as well as the Syracuse Nationals in basketball, and he declined a three-year, $150,000 deal offered by a Syracuse promoter to become a professional boxer. He finally decided on a $15,000 deal with the Cleveland Browns of the National Football League (NFL).

As a fullback in 1957 Brown led the league in rushing, totaling 942 yards and leading Cleveland to the Eastern Division Championship while picking up Rookie of the Year honors. The following year he increased his yardage per carry by 1.2 yards to 5.9, scored eighteen touchdowns, and was named Player of the Year. He never missed a game due to injury, and he became such a dominating presence in his sport that he headed a players' revolt against Cleveland's coach, Paul Brown, in 1962. Paul Brown was subsequently fired, and the team's new coach for 1963, Blanton Collier, better utilized his star by designing plays that granted Brown more running room along the line of scrimmage. Brown responded with his best season by collecting more than a mile in total yards (1,863 at 6.5 yards per carry) and scoring fifteen touchdowns; he performed similarly the next year, and Cleveland won the NFL Championship. In 1965, Brown's final season, he averaged more than five yards per carry for the third consecutive year, scored twenty-one touchdowns, and took home his second Most Valuable Player award. He played in the Pro Bowl every single year and led the league in rushing for eight of his nine seasons.

The following autumn, however, saw Brown in Europe, filming a lead role in *The Dirty Dozen* (1967), a big-budget Hollywood picture about American convicts who become highly trained World War II soldiers. He had already appeared two years earlier in *Rio Concho* (1964), and when the Cleveland Browns owner Art Modell threatened to cut him if he did not report to training camp immediately, Brown retired to devote his full energies to a movie career. For *100 Rifles* in 1969 Brown was paid $200,000 and starred opposite Raquel Welch, with whom he filmed the first love scene between a black man and a white woman ever captured in a Hollywood picture. These three movies, along with *Ice Station Zebra* (1968), were his most successful mainstream projects.

As Brown made the transition from football star to movie star, the press became increasingly concerned with his personal life, particularly after his marriage to Sue Jones ended in the late 1960s. The couple, who had married in 1958, had three children. Brown, a regular on the Hollywood social scene, had numerous encounters with the L.A. Police Department—almost all of them involving questionable behavior by both parties—culminating in Brown's arrest when his girlfriend fell from a second-floor balcony during a domestic dispute, though she never pressed charges. A year later Brown was arrested for felonious assault in a hit-and-run traffic incident; the case was dismissed during trial. In 1978 he was found guilty of misdemeanor battery for punching a player on a golf course, and in 1986 he was again arrested in a domestic dispute, though again the charges were dropped.

In the 1960s and 1970s Brown commenced a number of charitable endeavors, most of which centered around the Black Economic Union, a collective of African American business owners dedicated to pooling and recommitting their wealth to projects such as teenage education, job training, and rehabilitation. In 1971 he was inducted into the NFL Hall of Fame, though nearly twenty years later he would threaten to withdraw on behalf of historically neglected black players. (Brown would eventually be inducted into the College Football Hall of Fame and the Lacrosse Hall of Fame, as well.) He continued making movies such as the "blaxploitation" films *Slaughter* (1972) and *Slaughter's Big Rip-Off* (1973) and the all-black western *Take a Hard Ride* (1975), but they failed to match his earlier commercial successes. In the early 1980s Brown started a movie production company, Ocean Productions, with his friend RICHARD PRYOR, but Pryor soon fired him.

In 1973 the Buffalo Bills' O. J. SIMPSON broke Brown's rushing record for a single season, and in

1984 Brown's career rushing record fell to the Chicago Bears' WALTER PAYTON. But Brown's athletic legacy was already established, and four years later he founded the Amer-I-Can Program Inc., a nonprofit organization dedicated to reaching gang members and prisoners; in 1992 Amer-I-Can played an essential role in securing a truce between L.A.'s rival gangs, the Bloods and the Crips. By 2000 Amer-I-Can had spread to twelve cities and built a reputation for developing innovative strategies to rehabilitate prisoners and troubled youths. Brown's own troubles with the authorities continued, however. He was sentenced to three years probation in October 1999 for smashing the car of his second wife, Monique Brown, and in 2002 he served four months in prison for refusing to undergo court-ordered domestic violence counseling. Brown appeared in a few more Hollywood productions, most notably as a defensive coordinator in Oliver Stone's football epic, *Any Given Sunday* (1999). It was an ironic turn for an offensive player of whom one opponent had said, "the best way to tackle Brown is to hold on and wait for help."

Further Reading
Brown, Jim, with Myron Cope. *Off My Chest* (1964).
Brown, Jim, with Steve Delsohn. *Out of Bounds* (1969).
Toback, James. *Jim: The Author's Self-Centered Memoir on the Great Jim Brown* (1971).

DAVID F. SMYDRA JR.

BROWN, Joan Myers (25 Dec. 1931–), dancer, teacher, choreographer, and community activist, was born in Philadelphia, Pennsylvania, the only child of Nellie W. Lewis, a research and chemical engineer during World War II, and Julius T. Myers, a chef. Lewis's determination to pursue her interest in chemistry provided a model of high expectations and self-confidence for Brown that enabled her to venture into a world closed to African Americans in the 1940s and 1950s.

Brown was encouraged by a high school teacher to join an after-school classical ballet dance club and later took lessons in a private studio. Because of de facto desegregation and racism, Brown could not enroll in any of the local dance schools for white students, but this did not stop her from pursuing her dream. Instead she studied a variety of dance forms at the Sydney School of Dance in Philadelphia, a school for black dancers. Upon her graduation from high school Brown pursued a career in dance rather than a more formal education. In 1949 she won a scholarship through her Cotillion performances (formal dance productions). The scholarship allowed Brown to move to New York City in 1950 and to enroll in the KATHERINE DUNHAM School of Dance, where she remained for two years.

Brown then joined the Anjoel Dancers and performed in clubs such as the Latin Casino and others located in Atlantic City, New Jersey. In 1951 Brown married Fred Johnson, but the marriage was short-lived, and the couple divorced shortly after the Korean

War. In 1955 Brown joined the Savar Dancers, an American dance troupe begun in Montreal, Canada, and patterned in the style of the *Creole Follies*, a traveling revue show. In 1958 CAB CALLOWAY recruited the dance troupe to work in his Miami Beach *Cotton Club Revue*. Brown danced with the revue for three years, after which she performed in different revues with Larry Steele and PEARL BAILEY. Brown married Max G. Brown in 1960, and the couple had two daughters, Marlisa and Dannielle, before divorcing in 1981.

Since opportunities for a talented African American classical ballet dancer in the 1950s were few, Brown decided to teach dance to African American children. While continuing to dance and choreograph with the *Club Harlem Revue* in Atlantic City, she founded her first school in 1960. Ten years later she founded the Philadelphia Dance Company, also known as Philadanco, and the accompanying Philadelphia School of Dance Arts.

Philadanco, a pilot for Pennsylvania's Comprehensive Education Training Act (CETA) Program, established an instruction and training model that incorporated successful work ethic and discipline and enabled Brown to pay her dancers. In 1973 Philadanco was one of the first companies to receive a National Endowment for the Arts Expansion Arts grant. One of only six dance companies nationally to pay its dancers fifty-two weeks of the year, Philadanco was also the first African American dance company to do so. Drawing from the work of Katherine Dunham and Lester Horton, the company and school incorporated jazz and African-influenced techniques as well as classical and modern ballet into its dancing.

As the company grew, Brown turned over the choreographic responsibilities to other guest artists, providing opportunities for choreographers who had worked in the business for many years to showcase their talent. Gene Hill Sagan was a favorite choreographer with the company, and his works are considered classics within the company repertoire. Other choreographers included CARMEN DE LAVALLADE, GEOFFREY HOLDER, TALLEY BEATTY, BEBE MILLER, and Ron Brown. *My Science*, a dance set expressly for Philadanco by Miller, examines how the imagination and science act as catalysts for each other. *Mother*, created by Ron Brown, is a celebration of women.

In 1981 the company was the first in Philadelphia to purchase its own corporate headquarters and studio facilities, with funding provided by the NEA, the William Penn Foundation, and through a private donation from the Philadelphia-based music producer Kenny Gamble. In the same year the company was one of only fifteen organizations awarded the National Choreography Planning Grant, and in 1986 the company created the first artist-housing program in the city for its principal dancers. A newly renovated studio housed Philadanco and the Dance Arts School. Further, the renovation of three houses for dancer residencies set into motion the eventual total rehabilitation of the houses located on the street.

In 1988 Brown organized the International Conference on Blacks in Dance, the first such organization of its kind. Brown saw the need for black dance companies to align with each other for creative and financial support. In 1991 the conference became the International Association of Blacks in Dance (IABD), designed to preserve and promote dance by persons of African ancestry or origin through worldwide membership. It was responsible for establishing important dance archives with the National African American Historical and Cultural Museum in Wilberforce, Ohio, and the African American Museum in Philadelphia and Howard University. The IABD continues to serve as a support system for African American dance companies in the United States and abroad.

Brown was responsible for influencing and training hundreds of artists. The Philadelphia Dance Arts School and the performing company were considered safe havens to youths and helped to provide adults with a sense of community. Philadanco performed throughout the United States, Europe, Asia, and the Caribbean as well as at the Kennedy Center and Lincoln Center and the American Dance Festival. It has been involved in collaborations with well-known organizations and performers both inside and outside Philadelphia, including the Philadelphia Orchestra, the DUKE ELLINGTON Orchestra, LOU RAWLS, and TEDDY PENDERGRASS. Individual Philadanco members went on to perform with the ALVIN AILEY Dance Company and in numerous Broadway shows. In 2000 Philadanco was invited to establish permanent residency at the Kimmel Performing Arts Center in Philadelphia.

Brown was recognized by a number of organizations for her artistic accomplishments, community activism, and leadership. Over the years she was honored with a Kennedy Center award, the Theodore L. Hazlett Memorial Award from the Pennsylvania Council on the Arts, and a Philip Morris New Work Fund Award. She also received an honorary doctorate from the University of the Arts in 1994. In addition to her roles at Philadanco, Brown held faculty positions at the University of the Arts, Howard University, and Temple University. Brown's faculty positions provided Philadanco dancers with free or reduced tuition. Reciprocally, students who interned with the company received academic credit. Brown served as a consultant for the Rockefeller Foundation's Arts and Humanities Program along with other foundations and performing arts centers. She was honored as a Dance Living Legend by New York-area presenters in tribute to five nationwide African American pioneer women founders of modern dance companies rooted in black communities. Throughout her career Brown made it her mission to bring the culture, music, history, and heritage of Africans and African Americans to the world.

Further Reading
Clark, Veve, and Sara Johnson. *Kaiso!: Writings by and about Katherine Dunham* (2006).

Defrantz, Thomas F. *Dancing Many Drums: Excavations in African American Dance* (2001).

Emery, Lynne Fauley. *Black Dance in the United States from 1619 to 1970* (1972).

BARBARA TOOMER DAVIS

BROWN, Joe (18 May 1925–21 Nov. 1997), boxer, was born in Baton Rouge, Louisiana. Little is known about his early life or his parents, except that the family lived on the brink of poverty.

Brown worked a number of different jobs—carpentry among them—before beginning his boxing career in 1943 in New Orleans, winning a four-round decision. Almost immediately, however, his participation in the professional sport was cut short when he was drafted to fight in World War II. Brown spent nearly two years in the U.S. Navy—most of it in the Pacific Theater—during which time he continued to box, finally winning the All-Service Lightweight Championship before his discharge in 1945. Following his return to civilian life, in 1946 Brown threw himself back into professional prizefighting, averaging from seven to twelve fights a year, sometimes with only a week's rest between bouts. Despite his enthusiasm and seemingly limitless energy his career did not get off to a particularly auspicious start. From 1946 through 1948 his record was a lackluster fifteen wins (only three by knockout), eight losses, and four draws. Most of his opponents were local New Orleans fighters, but he did manage to land two big fights in 1947. In April of that year he fought and defeated Jimmy Carter, who would go on to win the lightweight championship four years later. One month later he fought the legendary Sandy Saddler, who was less than a year away from winning the featherweight crown. The hard-punching Saddler knocked Brown out in three rounds.

After this slow start, and as he began to fight more of his bouts away from New Orleans, Brown's career began to take off in 1949. Indeed Brown became a well-traveled fighter, boxing in Chicago, St. Paul, Cincinnati, and Philadelphia. He even traveled to Australia for four bouts in 1950. Again maintaining a furious pace Brown won forty-five bouts and lost only eight from 1949 through late 1956. On 2 May 1956 he fought the lightweight champion Wallace "Bud" Smith in a non-title contest held in Houston, Texas, and took a ten-round decision. The performance earned Brown a title shot, and he took full advantage of the opportunity, winning a lopsided decision over Smith in a fifteen-round rematch in August of that year. After nearly eleven years of continuous boxing, and nearly seventy fights, the thirty-year-old Brown—who had by this time acquired the nickname "Old Bones"—was lightweight champion of the world.

Over the course of the next five and a half years Brown successfully defended his title eleven times—a record for consecutive defenses of the lightweight crown that stood for seventeen years. He also fought eleven non-title bouts to maintain his always busy boxing schedule. In spite of his record of success Brown did not achieve the fame and fortune enjoyed by many other champion boxers, in some large part due to the relative quality of Brown's opposition during his years as lightweight king. In his nearly six years as champion Brown mostly fought unknown challengers. Only two of the men he faced were themselves champion boxers: Smith, who Brown knocked out in a 1957 rematch, and Ralph Dupas, who was knocked out in six rounds and very briefly held the junior middleweight champion in 1963. Such lackluster opponents meant that Brown fought most of his championship fights in second- and third-rate venues. For example, Brown never fought in the mecca of boxing, Madison Square Garden. And during a time when boxing was a television staple, Brown's fights in places such as Houston, Denver, or Albuquerque attracted little media attention. In addition Brown's style, while celebrated by boxing purists, lacked the power that sparked fan excitement. He won by knockout in less than 50 percent of his victories. Tall and lanky, Brown frustrated his opponents with odd angles and a tight defense. Those able to penetrate that defense, however, often found Brown susceptible to being floored, as when the unheralded Ray Portilla knocked Brown out in six rounds in a 1960 non-title fight.

In April 1962 the nearly thirty-seven-year-old Brown ran up against the tough former junior welterweight champion, Carlos Ortiz. A decade younger than Brown, Ortiz dominated the fight, winning a fifteen-round decision and ending Brown's run as lightweight champion. Brown never again fought in a world championship fight. Nevertheless he kept fighting for eight more years. A heavily traveled fighter before his loss to Ortiz, he now became an absolute globetrotter. From 1963 through his last fight in 1970 Brown fought in England, Mexico, Argentina, Brazil, Venezuela, Panama, South Africa, Colombia, Puerto Rico, Italy, Finland, and France. As a former champion, Brown still held some appeal to fight promoters, but it was clear that he was now simply an opponent for younger fighters or local favorites. Brown fought forty-six times after the loss to Ortiz, winning just twenty bouts, losing twenty-four, and twice fighting to a draw. Finally in 1970, at the age of forty-five, "Old Bones" stepped away from the ring and announced his retirement.

The International Boxing Hall of Fame opened its doors in 1989, but Brown had to wait another seven years before being inducted in 1996. Just a year after joining the boxing elite, Brown passed away in New Orleans at the age of seventy-two.

Further Reading

Ashe, Arthur R., Jr. *A Hard Road to Glory: A History of the African American Athlete since 1946* (1988).

"Joe 'Old Bones' Brown," in *Encyclopedia of African-American Culture and History*, vol. 1 (1996).

MICHAEL L. KRENN

BROWN, John (1810?–1876), fugitive slave and slave narrative author, was born in Southampton County, Virginia, the son of slaves Joe and Nancy. For most of his life as a slave he was called Fed or Benford. When he was about ten years old he and his mother were moved to nearby Northampton County, North Carolina. Eighteen months later he was sold alone and sent to Georgia, never again to see any of his kinfolk.

Bought by the ambitious and quick-tempered Thomas Stevens, Fed grew to maturity on a farm in central Georgia near the state capital at Milledgeville. Stevens drove his slaves hard, often employing whippings and other brutal punishments. Gradually Stevens accumulated much land and more than twenty slaves, becoming a "planter" by federal census standards. In the 1820s Stevens expanded his family enterprises into DeKalb County, near Cherokee territory in northwestern Georgia, and when these Indians were driven west in the late 1830s, he settled in Cass (later Bartow) County, northwest of modern Atlanta. Fed went with his master, and when Stevens died in 1840 his considerable estate, now including more than forty slaves, was divided among his heirs. Fed became the property of twenty-two-year-old Decature Stevens, an even harsher and more erratic master. Fed determined to escape slavery.

The most influential person in Fed's life, the man who taught him to love freedom, was a slave named John Glasgow. Born a free black in British Guiana, Glasgow became a sailor in the British merchant marine and married an Englishwoman from Liverpool. On a voyage to Savannah, Glasgow made the mistake of going ashore, where Georgia law took effect. As a foreign free black he was interned in the city jail. Several weeks later, when his ship sailed without him, he was sold as a slave. Glasgow became the property of Thomas Stevens. Free all his life, he could not adjust to slavery, and brutal beatings left him crippled. But he planted the image of freedom in England in the mind of the provincial, uneducated young Fed.

Fed finally ran away from Decature Stevens. Caught in Tennessee when his white accomplice betrayed him, he was brought home to face harsh punishment. But in the mid-1840s he ran away again. He had no idea how to reach England, and he ended up in a slave pen in New Orleans with the new name Benford. There he was sold to Theodoric J. "Jepsey" James, who owned rich cotton land in Washington County, Mississippi, and ninety-five slave laborers. The environment was primitive and the work exhausting on the James plantation, and after only three months Benford ran for freedom again.

This time he understood that he could reach free country by heading north up the nearby Mississippi River. Traveling by night and hiding by day, Benford reached St. Louis, Missouri, in three months. Then he crossed over into Illinois, got directions from a free black, and headed for Vandalia. A few days later another black man gave him a free pass made out to John Brown, the name that Benford carried for the rest of his life. After spending two weeks in a black commu-

nity near Terre Haute, Indiana, Brown walked toward Indianapolis and got help from Quakers involved in the Underground Railroad. They sent him on to Marshall, Michigan, where he worked as a carpenter in the black community for a year. Then Brown moved to Detroit, where he joined Cornish miners and worked as a carpenter for eighteen months until his English friends returned home. Brown planned to follow them, but first he went to Canada and worked for almost six months in a sawmill at the Dawn Institute, a vocational training school for runaway slaves from the United States.

In August 1850 Brown sailed on a ship bound for Liverpool and soon rejoined his miner friends in Redruth, Cornwall. After two months he moved to Bristol and then to Heywood in Lancashire, still working as a carpenter. But he encountered strong racism, and in the spring of 1851 he went to London, where he lived for the remainder of his life. There he contacted the British and Foreign Anti-Slavery Society, whose secretary, Louis Alexis Chamerovzow, was particularly impressed with Brown's plain, direct description of American slavery.

The society carefully checked Brown's story for authenticity and then sent him on a speaking tour. British audiences responded well to Brown's story, especially to the sad story of John Glasgow. For a while Brown's speaking fees supplemented his carpentry wages, allowing him to live frugally in a boardinghouse in a working-class area of London. The British and Foreign Anti-Slavery Society's *Anti-Slavery Reporter* ran an account of Glasgow's tragedy on 1 July 1853, and other British journals repeated it. The *Leeds Anti-Slavery Series* covered it in tract 89, and *Frederick Douglass' Paper* and a few other American journals also repeated the story. In 1854 Brown and his abolitionist friends took a notarized account of Glasgow's life to the British Foreign Office, but inquiries by consuls in Charleston and Savannah led nowhere.

A year later the British and Foreign Anti-Slavery Society published *Slave Life in Georgia: A Narrative of the Life, Sufferings, and Escape of John Brown, a Fugitive Slave, Now in England.* This small, 250-page volume included the Glasgow material and also covered Fed–Benford–John Brown's entire life. Brown himself was illiterate, and so Chamerovzow wrote the book in standard middle-class English. However, the story is Brown's, the authentic autobiography of a real man and a real slave.

A second limited edition was soon published, and it was also translated into German. Americans were already familiar with fugitive slave narratives, so *Slave Life* drew little attention in the United States even though it was one of the few narratives that focused on the Deep South. Its limited royalties augmented Brown's income for a while. Soon he married an Englishwoman and became an herbalist in London, where he died. An ordinary man, Brown told an extraordinary story of black bondage in white America.

Further Reading

Brown, John. *Slave Life in Georgia: A Narrative of the Life, Sufferings, and Escape of John Brown, a Fugitive Slave* (1855, repr. 1972, 1991).

Boney, F. N. "The Blue Lizard: Another View of Nat Turner's Country on the Eve of Rebellion," *Phylon* 31 (1970).

Boney, F. N. "Doctor Thomas Hamilton: Two Views of a Gentleman of the Old South," *Phylon* 28 (1967).

Boney, F. N. "Slaves as Guinea Pigs: Georgia and Alabama Episodes," *Alabama Review* 37 (1984).

Boney, F. N. "Thomas Stevens: Antebellum Georgian," *South Atlantic Quarterly* 72 (1973).

F. N. BONEY

BROWN, John Mifflin (8 Sept. 1817–16 Mar. 1893), African Methodist Episcopal (AME) bishop, was born in Cantwell's Bridge, New Castle County, Delaware. Little is known of his family or early childhood. He lived in Cantwell's Bridge until he was ten. He then moved to Wilmington, Delaware, where he lived for two years with the family of William A. Seals, a Quaker. At Cantwell's Bridge, he attended a predominantly white private school. His older sister encouraged him to move to Philadelphia, Pennsylvania, where he lived with and worked for the attorney Henry Chester, who tutored him and provided him with limited religious training. Brown attended St. Thomas Colored Protestant Episcopal Church in Philadelphia.

In January 1836 Brown became a member of Bethel AME Church in Philadelphia and began private studies under the Reverend John M. Gloucester to prepare for the ministry. He also studied barbering and worked as a barber in Poughkeepsie, New York, and New York City between 1836 and 1838. In 1838 he studied at Wesleyan Academy in Wilbraham, Massachusetts. In 1841–1842 he studied at Oberlin College in Ohio but did not complete a degree. He moved to Detroit in 1844 and opened the first school for African American children in that city. After the death of a local AME pastor, Brown was appointed acting minister, serving from 1844 to 1847. His success in the pastorate led to rapid advancement in denominational affairs. He joined the AME Ohio Conference, was ordained a deacon, was assigned to the AME church in Columbus, Ohio, and was appointed principal of Union Seminary, which was the first school owned and operated by the AME Church.

In 1852 Brown became pastor at Allen Station AME Church in Pittsburgh, Pennsylvania, and joined the Indiana Conference. In February of that year he married Mary Louise Lewis; they had eight children. Bishop DANIEL A. PAYNE commissioned Brown to participate in a mission to New Orleans, Louisiana, where, over a five-year period, Brown took responsibility for building the Morris Brown Chapel. He purchased Trinity Chapel and started congregations in Algiers and Covington, serving as pastor of St. James AME Church. During his mission to New Orleans, he was imprisoned five times for allowing slaves to attend religious services. In April 1857 he requested a transfer and was reassigned to Asbury Chapel in Louisville, Kentucky. In May 1858 he was transferred to Bethel AME Church in Baltimore, Maryland. He added seven hundred members to the Baltimore congregation. He also served pastorates at the Ebenezer AME Church and at the Brite Street AME Church in Baltimore.

Brown accompanied Bishops Payne and Wayman on their mission to Virginia and established St. John's AME Church in Norfolk. He was elected corresponding secretary of the Parent Home and Foreign Missionary Society in 1864 and successfully raised over $10,000 to establish AME churches and schools in the southern United States.

In recognition of his exceptional organizational abilities, Brown was elected an AME bishop at the General Conference in Washington, D.C., and was consecrated on 25 May 1868. His first assignment (1868–1872) was to the Seventh Episcopal District (South Carolina, Georgia, Florida, and Alabama). In 1871 he was instrumental in establishing Payne Institute (later Allen University) in south Carolina. He was assigned to the Sixth District (Tennessee, Arkansas, Louisiana, and Texas) from 1872 to 1876, and he organized the west Texas, south Arkansas, west Tennessee, Denver (Colorado), Columbia (South Carolina), and north Georgia conferences and set the groundwork for an AME college in Waco, Texas (later Paul Quinn College). From 1876 to 1880 he served the Third Episcopal District (Baltimore, Virginia, North Carolina, and South Carolina); from 1880 to 1884 he served the First Episcopal District (Philadelphia, New York, New Jersey, and New England); and from 1884 to 1888 he served the Fourth Episcopal District (Missouri, Kansas, Illinois, Iowa, and California). His last assignment (1888–1892) was to the Fourth Episcopal District, which had been restructured to include Indiana, Illinois, Michigan, and Iowa.

In 1878 Brown organized and raised funds for the Liberian Mission Church. He was a supporter of the Back to Africa movement and a strong advocate for the ordination of women. He was a delegate to the World Methodist Ecumenical Conference held in London, England, in 1881 and again in Washington, D.C., in 1891. He died in Washington, D.C.

Brown's nearly twenty-five years as a bishop had a profound impact on his denomination. Bishop Henry Tanner described him as "more of an Episcopal than a Methodist by temperament." Brown's keen organizational skills and abilities as a fundraiser did much to foster the dynamic growth of AME churches throughout the United States, Africa, and the Caribbean.

Further Reading

Campbell, James T. *Songs of Zion: The African Methodist Episcopal Church in the United States and South Africa* (1995).

Dvorak, Katherine L. *An African-American Exodus: The Segregation of the Southern Churches* (1991).

Wright, Richard R. *The Bishops of the African Methodist Episcopal Church* (1963).

Wright, Richard R., ed. *The Centennial Encyclopedia of the African Methodist Episcopal Church, Philadelphia, Pa.* (1916).

STEPHEN D. GLAZIER

BROWN, Lawrence (3 Aug. 1907–5 Sept. 1988), jazz trombonist, was born in Lawrence, Kansas, the son of John M. Brown, a minister in the African Methodist Episcopal Church, and Maggie (maiden name unknown), who played pump organ for the church. When Brown was six the family moved to Oakland, California, where he learned how to play piano, tuba—which he began to play in the Oakland public school system—and violin. He also briefly experimented with alto saxophone before taking up trombone, to which he became intensely devoted after the Browns relocated across the bay to San Francisco.

The family moved to Pasadena, and around 1924 Brown enrolled at Pasadena Junior College for music and premedical studies. Risking his father's disapproval, Brown dropped out of school, moved to north Pasadena on his own, and around 1927 went into jazz as a member of Charlie Echols's seven-piece band at a dime-a-dance venue, the 401 Ballroom. From 1928 to 1931 he worked with the bands of Paul Howard, Curtis Mosby, and LES HITE. The affiliation with Mosby included acting in and recording the soundtrack for the director King Vidor's movie *Hallelujah!* (1929) and performing at Mosby's Apex clubs in Los Angeles (later renamed the Club Alabam) and San Francisco. These affiliations were not continuous, however, because Brown and the drummer (soon to be vibraphonist) LIONEL HAMPTON were also contracted individually to Frank Sebastian's Cotton Club in Los Angeles, where they played under Mosby, Howard, and others, most notably LOUIS ARMSTRONG with Hite's big band in 1931.

In the spring of 1932 Brown joined DUKE ELLINGTON's big band, with which he remained for two decades, except for a brief absence in 1943. His career followed the leader's grueling schedule of far-ranging touring. In 1933 (some sources say 1934 or 1935) Brown married FREDI WASHINGTON, an actress. They divorced some years later, and at an unknown date he married Dorothea Bundrant, whom he also subsequently divorced. Obituaries do not mention any children.

Brown became one of Ellington's principal soloists, featured on recordings of "The Sheik of Araby," "Ducky Wucky" (both 1932), "Slippery Horn" (1933), "Stompy Jones" (1934), "Braggin' in Brass," "Rose of the Rio Grande" (both 1938), "Across the Track Blues" (1940), "Come Sunday" on the *Black, Brown, and Beige* suite (as premiered at Carnegie Hall in January 1943), and his own compositions "Golden Cress" and "On a Turquoise Cloud" (both 1947). Brown may be seen and heard as a soloist in the film short *Salute to Duke Ellington* (1950).

In March 1951 Brown left Ellington to work in the small band of the saxophonist JOHNNY HODGES, with which he recorded the album *Used to Be Duke* (1954).

In the spring of 1955 Brown began to work as a freelancer in New York City, but a year later, when the trombonist Warren Covington resigned as a studio musician for CBS, Brown took his place. He rejoined Ellington in May 1960. Notable recordings include "The Mooche" on *Duke Ellington's Greatest Hits*, from a concert in Paris in 1963, and the album *Popular Duke Ellington* (1966). Brown also was featured again in a film short, *Playback: Duke Ellington* (1963).

Brown left Ellington and retired from music in 1970. Moving to Washington, D.C., he was appointed by President Richard Nixon to the advisory committee of the Kennedy Center. In 1974 he settled in the Los Angeles area and worked as a recording agent for Local 47 of the musicians' union. He had a stroke and not long afterward died in Los Angeles.

Brown explained on several occasions that he wanted to play trombone in a pretty manner, as if it were a cello, not in the blustery sliding fashion popular in early New Orleans jazz. Hence in his first tenure with Ellington, he was featured on romantic melodies, and he also favored clear-toned, nimble lines, as heard in "The Sheik of Araby." From 1961 to the end of his career he supplied a third type of solo for Ellington's orchestra, playing emotive, vocalized, plunger-muted melodies in the manner created by his predecessors BUBBER MILEY and Tricky Sam Nanton.

Further Reading

Dietrich, Kurt. *Duke's 'Bones: Ellington's Great Trombonists* (1995).
Ellington, Duke. *Music Is My Mistress* (1973).

Obituaries: *New York Times*, 9 Sept. 1988; *Jazz Journal International* (Nov. 1988): 16–17.

BARRY KERNFELD

BROWN, Lawrence Benjamin (29 Aug. 1893–25 Dec. 1972), pianist and composer, was born in Jacksonville, Florida, the son of Clark Benjamin Brown, himself the son of a former slave. Little is known of Brown's natural mother, who died when Lawrence was three; from then on, he was raised by his stepmother Cenia Brown.

During his youth Brown took music instruction from the well-respected William Riddick. Exhibiting incredible promise, Brown was sent to Boston to receive further instruction in his primary instrument, piano. In addition to scholarships, Brown financed his education in Boston by working as an elevator operator. In 1916 he made his professional music debut as accompanist for the tenor Sydney Woodward. With this exposure Brown caught the eye of other musicians, including the famed tenor ROLAND HAYES. Brown and Hayes toured abroad from 1918 to 1923 and received great popular acclaim. They had many important engagements, including a performance for the king and queen of England at Buckingham Palace in 1921.

While in England, Brown also took advantage of advanced training at Trinity College in London. There he had composition instruction from Amanda Aldridge, daughter of the great African American actor IRA ALDRIDGE. Brown's interest and talent in composition went beyond piano and vocal arrangements. In 1923 he performed some string arrangements with the famed cellist Beatrice Harrison at Wigmore Hall in England. Brown's profound talent at musical composition and arrangement as well as at singing and piano playing quickly proved him to be one of the most important new figures in the musical world.

Brown used his educational instruction to pursue research into folk songs, paying particular attention to the music of African Americans. His work took him to the southern United States, where he began to absorb the traditional work songs of field workers and laborers. From this research he developed his popular arrangements of hundreds of Negro spirituals, more than thirty of which were published during his lifetime in collections such as JAMES WELDON JOHNSON's *Book of American Negro Spirituals* (1925) and Brown's own *Negro Folk Songs* (1930). Brown is distinguished among arrangers of the spirituals for his attention to detail and investment in preserving the original elements of the songs. Arrangements authored by Brown include "Swing Low, Sweet Chariot," "Joshua Fit de Battle of Jericho," "Ezekiel Saw de Wheel," and "Steal Away." Many of his compositions went on to become very popular.

In 1925 the baritone PAUL ROBESON became the first major singer to perform Brown's spiritual arrangements in concert. Robeson was also the first solo singer to offer an entire concert of spirituals. This practice was continued by other African American singers such as the contralto MARIAN ANDERSON. Robeson's performance of Brown's arrangements at the Greenwich Village Theatre was the spark that generated a forty-year relationship between the two men, professionally and personally. During the 1930s they toured Europe together while Robeson reprised his role as Joe in the Jerome Kern and Oscar Hammerstein II musical *Show Boat*. Their camaraderie on and off the stage was legendary: Robeson's bass-baritone vocal lines were often harmonized by Brown's tenor, and their political work for issues ranging from worker rights to antiapartheid organizing solidified their standing as a powerful artistic force. They performed internationally, including in New York, Paris, London, and Ireland. The pair appeared before European royalty on numerous occasions, including before the Prince of Wales and the king of Spain.

Part of the pair's popularity stemmed from their many recordings. They recorded classics such as "Nobody Knows de Trouble I've Seen," "Sometimes I Feel Like a Motherless Child," and "Joe Hill" for RCA Victor records. In 1939 Brown led the orchestra and chorus for Robeson's CBS recording of "Ballad for Americans," which garnered them international attention. The two men often offered their support and art in service of armed struggles around the globe, including a United Service Organizations (USO) camp tour during World War II. Beyond Negro spirituals and work songs Brown was also a champion of world folk music. In addition to Robeson's detailed and incisive study of the music, it was Brown who investigated this music for inclusion in their repertoire. Brown was often contacted by musicians and conductors for music of obscure folk songs.

Brown had many important relationships with artists and leaders during the course of his lifetime, including with the scholar and writer LLOYD LOUIS BROWN and with the poet and writer LANGSTON HUGHES. Brown was also a confidant for Robeson's wife ESLANDA CARDOZA GOODE ROBESON, who often traveled with the pair. His close relationship with the Robeson family was put to the test after World War II when Robeson came under intense scrutiny for his ties to the Soviet Union. Opportunities to perform abroad were denied after the United States government revoked Robeson's passport in 1950. Despite the passport's later reinstatement, the careers and reputations of both men suffered. Brown retired in 1963 after illness ended Robeson's career. Brown never married and lived the last forty-seven years of his life as a resident of Harlem. In February 1973 he was honored by friends and family with a concert of his works at Saint Martin's Episcopal Church in Harlem.

Further Reading

The Lawrence Benjamin Brown Papers are in New York City at the Schomburg Center for Research in Black Culture.

Green, Jeffrey P. "Roland Hayes in London, 1921," *Black Perspective in Music* (1982).

SHANA L. REDMOND

BROWN, Lawrence, Jr. (19 Sept. 1947–), professional football player and businessman, was born in Clairton, Pennsylvania, the first of three sons of Lawrence Brown, a baggage handler for the Pennsylvania Railroad, and Rosa Lee, a housemaid. The family moved to Pittsburgh, Pennsylvania, when Brown was only two years old. He began playing football in his junior year at Schenley High School in Pittsburgh. He chose football over baseball because he thought he had a better chance to attain a college scholarship in football. Prior to his junior year, Brown played baseball. He said that his father encouraged him to play baseball because it was a game one could play as an organized sport at a young age. His dad loved baseball and was an excellent player in his own right, though he did not play professionally but rather with neighborhood friends.

Brown played fullback in high school primarily because he had good blocking skills. He received honorable mention to the all-city football team. He graduated from high school in 1965. He was offered a scholarship to play football at Kent State University. Instead, his high school football coach suggested that Brown talk to a former Schenley High School football player who had attended Dodge City Junior College in Dodge City, Kansas. Brown did and was convinced to go to Dodge. He was named honorable mention All-American his sophomore year at Dodge and was invited to try out for the varsity football team at Kansas State University; Brown made the team and was given a scholarship. He played his junior and senior years for the Kansas State University football team, serving as a blocking back, and became the featured tailback later in his senior year.

In 1969 Brown was selected by the Washington Redskins in the eighth round of the NFL draft. Soon after Brown was drafted, Vince Lombardi was hired to replace Otto Graham as head coach of the Redskins. One day while reviewing practice and game films in slow motion, Lombardi noticed that Brown was seconds late getting off the snap. Lombardi arranged to give Brown a hearing test, and it was discovered that he was completely deaf in his right ear. Lombardi petitioned the league office for permission to install a hearing aide in Brown's helmet. The request was granted, and soon Brown was the starting running back for the team. The Redskins finished with a 7-5-2 record—their first winning season in thirteen years. That year Brown also made a Pro Bowl appearance. He was chosen for that honor three out of the following four years.

Before the start of the 1970 season, Lombardi died of cancer. Bill Austin, an assistant coach under Lombardi, was named interim coach for the 1970 season. The Redskins finished 6-8, and Austin was fired. Nevertheless, Brown gained 1,125 yards and rushed for 100 yards or more in six different games that year. George Allen was hired as head coach and general manager of the team before the start of the 1971 season.

The remedy was immediate and swift. The Redskins started the 1971 season with five wins in a row. The team made the play-offs for the first time in twenty-six years, compiling a record of 9-4-1. In 1972 Brown led the team to a 11-3 record, gained 1,216 yards (rushing for 100 yards in six different games), and led the Redskins to Super Bowl VII, which they lost 14-7 to the Miami Dolphins in the Los Angeles Coliseum. Brown was also the NFL's most valuable player (MVP) that year. The next season he scored four rushing touchdowns in a game against the Eagles on 16 December 1973. Brown was not afraid to play with injuries, and he got hurt often because of his running style. He literally threw caution to the wind when he ran the ball, often hurdling himself to gain that extra yard.

In an eight-year career Brown was MVP in 1972 and selected to play in the Pro Bowl in 1969, 1970, 1971, and 1972. He carried the ball 1,530 times in his career, gaining 5,875 yards. His best seasons were in 1972, when he gained 1,216 yards, and in 1970, when he gained 1,125 yards. He rushed for 100 yards or more twenty-one times and rushed for 100 yards or more in six games in 1970 and six games in 1972. He also scored four rushing touchdowns in a game against the Eagles on 16 December 1973. It should be noted that the season consisted of fourteen games during Brown's career.

Brown's jersey number 43 was unofficially retired, and he was selected by a special panel as one of the seventy greatest Redskins of all time. The blue-ribbon panel consisted of the former CNN news anchor Bernard Shaw; the Redskins alum Bobby Mitchell; the U.S. senator George Allen of Virginia, son of the Redskins Hall of Fame coach George Allen; the Washington broadcasting legend Ken Beatrice; Noel Epstein, editor of several *Washington Post* histories of the team; the former undersecretary of state Joseph J. Sisco; Phil Hochberg, who retired in 2001 after thirty-eight years as team stadium announcer; the Pro Football Hall of Fame historian Joe Horrigan; the WRC-TV sports director George Michael; the WTEM sports director Andy Pollin; the NFL Films president Steve Sabol; and the WRC-TV news anchor Jim Vance.

Team records held by Brown include second for most yards gained in a career (5,875 yards); fourth for most yards gained in a season (1,216 yards in 1972); most 100-yard games in a season (6 in 1970 and 6 in 1972); second for most touchdown rushes in a career (35); most touchdown rushes in a single game (4 versus the Philadelphia Eagles on 16 Feb. 1973).

After he retired in 1976, Brown worked for E. F. Hutton as a personal financial management adviser. He also worked for twelve years with Xerox and was responsible for business and community relations. He then became vice president of the Michael Companies, Inc., a commercial real estate firm based in Lanham, Maryland, leasing and selling commercial properties.

Influenced by the fact that he was hearing impaired, Brown participated on many committees for the deaf, including the board of directors of the Deafness Research Foundation (1980–1992) and the board of directors of the National Institute on Deafness and Other Communication Disorders (1989–1991). He also served on the board of associates of Galludet University, a school for the deaf in Washington, D.C. (1991–1993).

Brown married Janet, a Washington native, in 1997. The couple had two daughters, Tonya and Lauren.

Further Reading

Brown, Larry, and William Gilde. *I'll Always Get Up* (1973).
Attner, Paul, and Ken Denlinger. *Redskins Country: From Baugh to the Super Bowl* (1983).
Denlinger, Ken. *Washington's Redskins: The Allen Triumph* (1973).
Whittingham, Richard. *Hail Redskins: A Celebration of the Greatest Players, Teams, and Coaches* (2001).

ROBERT JANIS

BROWN, Letitia Christine Woods (24 Oct. 1915–3 Aug. 1976), historian, was born in Tuskegee, Alabama, the daughter of Matthew Woods and Evadne Adams, professors. Her maternal grandfather, Lewis Adams, was born a slave and after the Civil War was instrumental in establishing the Tuskegee Normal School in 1881. Her parents both taught at Tuskegee Institute, continuing the family's commitment to education. Letitia attended Tuskegee Institute High School and graduated with a BS from Tuskegee Institute in 1935. In 1937 she completed her MA at Ohio State University. While working on an advanced degree at Radcliffe College, Letitia married Theodore E. Brown, a labor economist who later worked for the Agency for International Development in the U.S. Department of State. After raising two children and becoming involved in community projects in Mount Vernon, New York, she attended Harvard University, which awarded her a PhD in 1966.

As a historian, Letitia Woods Brown sought to educate people, in a variety of forums, about the African American experience and about race relations. Her career as a teacher began in 1935 when she taught in the segregated Macon County school system in Alabama. She then returned to Tuskegee, where she taught from 1937 to 1940. From 1940 to 1945 she was an instructor at another black college, LeMoyne College in Memphis, and from 1961 to 1970 she taught at Howard University, where she served on several committees, including the committee to establish the Department of Afro-American Studies. In 1968 Brown became a Fulbright professor in Australia at Monash University and at Australia National University. After brief teaching stints at Georgetown University and Goucher College, in 1971 she became the only full-time black faculty member in the College of Arts and Sciences at George Washington University.

Throughout her career, Brown taught courses in U.S. history and African American history. At George Washington University, she promoted interracial educational experiences by encouraging graduate students from George Washington and Howard universities to take courses at both institutions. While at George Washington, Brown also helped develop a course on the history of the District of Columbia. Emphasizing local rather than federal history, the course was a model for other interdisciplinary classes within the university.

Brown also taught outside the traditional classroom setting. In 1961 she instructed the first group of Peace Corps volunteers, who were eventually assigned to Ghana. For teacher in-service projects in Maryland and Virginia, she helped develop educational materials on blacks and other minorities. In 1972–1973 she served as the only historian on the panel of the National Assessment of Educational Progress, which set objectives for congressionally mandated tests for precollege students in social studies. Brown also was a professor at the Federal Executive Institute (1970–1973), after which she conducted training programs for the institute, including at the Department of Agriculture.

Brown's writing reflected broad interests that reached beyond academia to include the local history of the District of Columbia. With Elsie M. Lewis,

Brown wrote *Washington from Banneker to Douglass, 1791–1870* and *Washington in the New Era, 1870–1970*, which accompanied a two-part exhibition in 1971–1972 on African Americans at the National Portrait Gallery, Smithsonian Institution. Brown's major work, *Free Negroes in the District of Columbia, 1790–1846*, was published in 1972. The historian BENJAMIN QUARLES said of the work, "In language as concise and conclusive as the court records she has searched, Professor Brown traces the ways—many of them novel—in which blacks in the District moved from slavery to freedom." Brown's other writing included an essay on residential patterns of African Americans in the District of Columbia and an article entitled "Why and How the Negro in History," published in the fall 1969 issue of the *Journal of Negro Education*.

Brown also promoted awareness of African American history and of racial issues through her work in the local community, both on public history projects and at international history conferences. As vice chair of the Joint Committee on Landmarks of the National Capital, Brown broadened the committee's criteria for designating landmarks by promoting sites important to the history of African American residents, a criterion that had been ignored by previous committees. As consultant to the Capitol Historical Society, she advocated the inclusion of the contributions of many groups, including the slaves who built the structure, in the historical narrative of the Capitol. She served on the Advisory Board of the Schlesinger Library on the History of Women in America at Radcliffe College and helped the library initiate the Black Women Oral History Project, which eventually interviewed seventy-two African American women and published the transcripts in ten volumes in 1990. Brown's work with the Bicentennial Committee on International Conferences of Americanists led to the African Regional American Studies Conference in Lagos, Nigeria, in 1976. She served on the Advisory Committee on Historical Research for the Columbia Historical Society, helping it become more knowledgeable about local African American history, and was a cofounder of the annual conference on Washington, D.C., Historic Studies. Brown's other professional affiliations included membership on the executive board of the National Humanities Institute at Yale University, on the National Archives Advisory Council, and on the review board of the American Historical Association that oversaw the restructuring of that organization in the early 1970s.

Brown died of cancer at her home in Washington, D.C. Throughout her life she used her expertise as a historian in both academic and public arenas to increase awareness of the history of African Americans in the United States. She encouraged the reinterpretation of U.S. history both locally and nationally to include the historical experience of blacks, and she helped redefine the ways in which that history was conceptualized. Brown saw herself as "both historian and futurist. I suppose I shall continue to grapple with it—with a growing awareness that the way we organize and present data helps shape the way people think, that how we teach is as important as what we teach."

Further Reading
Some of Brown's papers are in the Special Collections at the Melvin Gelman Library, George Washington University, Washington, D.C., and at the Radcliffe College Archives at Harvard University.
French, Roderick. "Letitia Woods Brown, 1915–1976," *Records of the Columbia Historical Society of Washington, D.C.* 50 (1980): 522–524.

Obituaries: *New York Times* and *Washington Post*, 5 Aug. 1976.

NORALEE FRANKEL

BROWN, Lloyd Louis (3 Apr. 1913–1 Apr. 2003), writer, editor, and activist, was born Lloyd Louis Dight in St. Paul, Minnesota, the son of Ralph Dight and Magdalena (Paul) Dight. His mother, the German-American daughter of a Union army veteran, died when Brown was four. After his wife's death, Brown's father, a Louisiana-born African American Pullman porter, placed Brown and his three siblings in St. Paul's Crispus Attucks Home. During his upbringing at the residence, which served as both an old folks' home and an orphanage for the city's poor blacks, Brown experienced the desolate conditions of poverty, but he also received nurturing and affirming care from members of the black community. Raised largely by older members of the home, many of them former slaves, he gained an enduring respect and appreciation for the black folk stories and traditions shared with him by the home's elders. Influenced by this early experience, Brown's literary works often reflect the liberating power of black folk traditions in the face of oppression and injustice. Lloyd dropped out of St. Paul's Cretin High School after one year and embarked on a rigorous course of self-education. He studied the works of H. L. Mencken, Omar Khayyám, Toussaint L'Ouverture, and other writings on radical social thought. It was during this time that the sixteen-year-old Brown changed his name from Lloyd Dight to Lloyd Brown in homage to the nineteenth-century abolitionist John Brown.

In 1929 Brown joined the Young Communist League (YCL) and began his career as a labor organizer and political activist. While the threat of repercussions for involvement with the Communist Party under McCarthyism has obscured the relationship between the Communist Party and the African American community, there were many African Americans, from the late 1920s through the 1950s, who believed that Communism would be the best way to secure social, political, and economic equality. In the wake of the stock market crash of 1929 and the ensuing Depression, Brown traveled to Youngstown, Ohio, where he continued working as an organizer during the most turbulent years of the labor union movement. During this time he also traveled to Europe as a freelance journalist to report on the antifascist movement, and in 1933 he went to the Soviet Union to seek international support for the SCOTTSBORO BOYS, the nine young black men who were arrested in the 1930s for allegedly raping two white women. In 1937, Brown married Lily Kashin, an YCL member of Polish-Jewish descent, to whom he remained married until her death in 1996. They had two daughters, Linda and Bonnie.

In October 1940 Brown, along with several others, was convicted of "fraudulent circulation of Communist election petitions" (*Pittsburgh, Pa., Sun Telegraph*, 21 Apr. 1941). While serving a seven-month sentence in Pittsburgh's Alleghany County Jail, Brown met William Jones, a young African American man unjustly imprisoned on charges of murder and sentenced to death. From within the prison, Brown and his fellow detainees formed a defense committee and with the help of an elaborate community network outside the jail, fought to get Jones a new trial. While their efforts resulted in several stays of the execution, it was ultimately to no avail, and Jones was executed on 24 November 1941. Brown based his 1951 novel, *Iron City*, on this experience. According to literary scholar Alan Wald, *Iron City* is "possibly the first black prison novel, and certainly the first depicting the activities of political prisoners in the United States" (*Iron City*, xviii). Unlike the grim portrayals offered in popular protest fiction and epitomized in RICHARD WRIGHT's *Native Son*, *Iron City* celebrated black folk culture and affirmed individual dignity even in the face of the most severe forms of repression.

Brown served in the U.S. Army Air Force from 1942 to 1945, was stationed in Salina, Kansas, and rose to the rank of sergeant. From 1945 to 1952, Brown was managing editor of *New Masses* (later *Masses and Mainstream*), a leftist literary journal that published works by figures such as Wright, LANGSTON HUGHES, JAMES BALDWIN, and RALPH ELLISON. During this time Brown published several short stories, articles and reviews. "God's Chosen People," a fictionalized account of his experiences in the St. Paul orphanage, was listed in the O'Brien collection of *Best Short Stories of 1948*. Brown was especially well known for his scathing review of Ellison's *Invisible Man*. He charged that the novel was "profoundly anti-Negro," and that Ellison was "cut off from the surging mainstream of Negro life" ("The Deep Pit," *Masses and Mainstream*, June 1962). Throughout his career, Brown continued to observe and critique the direction of African American literature and culture. In "Which Way for the Negro Writer," Brown sharply criticized the integration-era tendency for African Americans to abandon black themes, and he insisted on the need for African American writers to render black experiences in black literature (*Masses and Mainstream*, Mar. 1951).

In the 1950s Brown left his editorship at *Masses and Mainstream* to work as a literary collaborator with the radical actor, singer, cultural scholar, and political activist PAUL ROBESON, a position Brown held until

Robeson's death in 1976 Brown wrote columns for Robeson's Harlem newspaper *Freedom,* and the two collaborated on Robeson's 1958 autobiography, *Here I Stand.* Brown also published the 1976 pamphlet *Paul Robeson Rediscovered* and in 1997 a full-length biography, *The Young Paul Robeson: On My Journey Now.* The biography won the 1998 Carey McWilliams Award for Outstanding Scholarly Work in Cultural Diversity. In later years, Brown remained a tireless cultural and social critic. His articles covered topics ranging from politics and police brutality to literature and popular entertainment and appeared in numerous journals including the *New York Amsterdam News, Negro Digest,* the *Nation,* and the *New York Times.*

During the repressive cold war era, Brown remained an unwavering voice of the black pro-Communist left. He challenged African American writers not to abandon black themes in the promise of integration, but to insist on equality while affirming black culture and black identity. At the time of his death in 2003 Brown was working on publishing *Jubilee,* a novel he had begun writing in 1953, exploring the relationship between Communism and the civil rights movements of the 1950s and 1960s

Further Reading

Nelson, Paul, "Orphans and Old Folks," *Minnesota History* (Fall 2001).

Wald, Alan. "Foreword" in Lloyd Brown, *Iron City* (1994).

Washington, Mary Helen. "'Lighting a Match to Kerosene': Lloyd Brown's *Iron City,*" in *The Other Blacklist: African American Writing and Activism in the Cold War* (forthcoming 2008).

Obituaries: *New York Times,* 14 Apr. 2003; *New York Amsterdam News,* 17 Apr. 2003.

SHIRLEY C. MOODY

BROWN, Lucy Manetta Hughes (Apr. 1863–26 June 1911), physician and educator, was born in Mebanesville, North Carolina, one of eight children. Her parents' names are not known. There are no records of Brown's earlier education, but in 1881 she enrolled at Scotia Seminary in Concord, North Carolina, and graduated in 1885. Four years later she married David Brown, a minister, and the following year entered Woman's Medical College of Pennsylvania, founded in 1850 and the first medical school for women in America. When Brown matriculated at the school in 1891, it was one of the best medical colleges in the country.

After graduating from Woman's Medical College of Pennsylvania in 1894 Brown returned to North Carolina and practiced medicine in her home state for two years before going to Charleston, South Carolina, where she became the first female physician of African ancestry in South Carolina. A year later, a fellow alumna from Woman's Medical College, MATILDA ARABELLA EVANS, began a practice in Columbia, South Carolina, and became the second black female physician in the state.

In 1897 Brown and ALONZO CLIFTON MCCLENNAN founded the Cannon Hospital and Training School for Nurses in Charleston, with McClennan as surgeon-in-charge and instructor of surgical nursing and hygiene and Brown as instructor of obstetric and pediatric nursing and head of gynecology and the nursing staff. This partnership not only provided health care for black patients, but also, through the leadership of Brown and McClennan, provided clinical experience for aspiring black nurses. The institution was initially intended to be a training school for nurses, but there were no facilities in Charleston where black nurses could get practical training in a hospital ward, so Brown and McClennan added the hospital.

Cannon Hospital and Training School for Nurses was one of many black hospitals that were established by blacks between 1890 and 1920. In Chicago, a city of fifteen thousand blacks in the 1890s, unless blacks were patients of white doctors, there were no hospitals that would admit them until Provident Hospital was built in 1891. Hospitals for blacks were desperately needed, not only because mortality rates were significantly higher for blacks than for whites but also because white medical professionals were using these statistics as another indication of the racial inferiority of people of African descent. Leaders in the American Public Health Association declared blacks a health threat to society and devoted an entire issue of their official publication, the *American Journal of Public Health,* to the "Negro health problem," featuring articles that portrayed blacks as a medical menace. Frederick Hoffman, chief statistician for Prudential Life Insurance, contributed to the discussion of health status and race by referring to blacks as members of a "dying race" in his book *Race Traits and the Tendencies of the American Negro,* published in 1896. DANIEL HALE WILLIAMS, head of Provident Hospital, aggressively challenged these assumptions, arguing that discrimination, which forced blacks to live in unsanitary and unsafe conditions without access to medical care, was directly responsible for the discrepancy between black and white life expectancies. At a symposium around that time, Williams and eleven other black physicians refuted the "dying race" concept and contended that speculation about the survival of blacks was meaningless and premature without a record of every birth and death in the black race for a period of at least ten years. They questioned the validity of statistics based on the observations and memories of doctors in states like North Carolina, with large black populations, but no board of health in many counties.

A few years after its founding, the Cannon Hospital and Training School began the *Hospital Herald,* which described itself as "a journal devoted to hospital work, nurse training and domestic and public hygiene," with McClennan as editor in chief and Brown as one of two associate editors. The journal not only served as a source of professional and personal information for those who were associated with the school, but it was also an effective promotional tool for procuring much-needed financial support. Within a short time, the work of the institution was known not only in South Carolina but also throughout the South.

Brown was a member of an elite group of nineteenth-century black women who became physicians in spite of prevailing prejudices, so pervasive in the medical profession, against race and gender. Her career had an auspicious beginning, and there were indications that she would have a long and productive professional life as a physician and nursing instructor. But illness forced her into an early retirement in 1904, and she died seven years later.

Further Reading

Papers on file for Lucy Hughes Brown are in the Archives and Special Collections/Black Women Physicians at Drexel University College of Medicine.

Du Bois, W. E. B. *Efforts for Social Betterment among Negro Americans* (1909).

Hine, Darlene Clark. "Co-laborers in the Work of the Lord," in *"Send Us a Lady Physician": Women Doctors in America*, ed. Ruth Abrams (1985).

Morais, Herbert M. *The History of the Negro in Medicine* (1967).

GERALDINE RHOADES BECKFORD

BROWN, Morris (12 Feb. 1770–9 May 1849), African Methodist Episcopal minister and bishop, was born of mixed parentage in Charleston, South Carolina, where he spent his early and middle years. Apparently self-educated, he worked as a boot maker and shoe repairman; he married Maria (maiden name unknown), with whom he had six children. Associated with the city's community of free people of color, Brown earned a reputation for assisting slaves in purchasing their freedom and for teaching and advising both free and enslaved African Americans in the region.

Soon after his religious conversion and his joining of the Methodist Episcopal (ME) Church, Brown was licensed to preach. In that role he had greater access to the slave population as well as to groups of free African Americans. As the number of blacks grew, both generally and within the African church in Charleston, Brown emerged as their leader. As a result of an 1816 dispute over a burial ground, many African church members withdrew from the ME Church. When the opportunity came later that year, Brown's congregation of about 1,400 members transferred to the new African Methodist Episcopal (AME) denomination, centered in Philadelphia and headed by Bishop RICHARD ALLEN. Brown was ordained deacon of the AME Church in 1817 and elder the following year.

The Charleston African Church, by meeting independently of white authorities and supervision, ran afoul of local and state laws intended to control religious gatherings of slaves and free blacks. Consequently, Brown and other ministers of the church served prison sentences in 1818 while protesting the repression of the free exercise of religion. Brown also

Morris Brown, in a portrait that appeared in Daniel Payne's *History of the African Methodist Episcopal Church* (1891); it was also included in James M. Handy's *Scraps of African Methodist Episcopal History* (1902). (Library Company of Philadelphia.)

attended early AME annual and general conferences, where he reported both the difficulties of being harassed by the police and the spectacular growth of the Charleston congregation; it had more than two thousand members by 1822.

That year, 1822, civil authorities uncovered a conspiracy to overthrow slavery associated with the initiative of DENMARK VESEY, a lay class leader in the African church. Betrayed by slaves loyal to their masters, the conspiracy involved six other class leaders from Brown's AME community; the conspiracy ended with 131 arrests and 35 executions. Suspected of knowing about Vesey's plan (though there was no direct evidence), Brown, aided by some local white clergy who advised him to leave, saw his church forced to close. Before the year ended he went north; early in 1823 his family joined him in Philadelphia, where he served as an assistant at the Mother Bethel AME Church and as aide to the aging Bishop Allen. Occasionally he traveled as an itinerant preacher, also organizing new AME congregations. On 25 May 1828 the AME General Conference selected Brown as its second bishop. When Allen died in 1831, Brown became the sole bishop of the denomination, and he became its senior bishop in 1836. Never forgetting his southern experience, Brown was active in the Vigilance Committee of Philadelphia, a public arm of the Underground Railroad for fugitives from slavery.

During Brown's thirteen active years in the episcopacy, the AME Church expanded westward. Brown organized the Pittsburgh Conference in Ohio in 1830 and the Indiana Conference ten years later. By the time of his death the church had congregations in fourteen states and in Canada, organized into six annual conferences, and had more than seventeen thousand members. In 1841 the denomination launched its first periodical, the *A.M.E. Church Magazine*, published until 1848; in it the initial debate was held about the right of women to preach. The AME Church also sent a representative to the 1846 international meeting of the Evangelical Alliance in London.

While in Toronto, Ontario, in 1844, Brown suffered a paralytic stroke, from which he never regained mobility. He even lost his voice in his last months, though it returned briefly just before his death in Philadelphia. By that time his son, Morris Jr., had become a well-known musician in Philadelphia, and the senior Brown had accumulated enough property to support his widow and their five other children.

Not known for literary productions or great preaching, Brown was a practical administrator and effective speaker who kept his message plain and pointed. A portrait shows him to have been a tall man with a large frame, a light complexion, and piercing eyes. His admirers named local churches after him in Philadelphia and Charleston, as well as a denominational college—Morris Brown College—that was founded in Atlanta after the Civil War.

Further Reading

George, Carol V. R. *Segregated Sabbaths: Richard Allen and the Emergence of Independent Black Churches, 1760–1840* (1973).
Wright, Richard R. *The Bishops of the African Methodist Episcopal Church* (1963).
Wright, Richard R., ed. *The Centennial Encyclopedia of the African Methodist Episcopal Church* (1916).

WILL GRAVELY

BROWN, Oscar, Jr. (10 Oct. 1926–29 May 2005), singer, songwriter, actor, activist, playwright, was born Oscar Cicero Brown Jr., the son of Oscar Brown Sr., a lawyer and real estate broker, and Helen Lawrence, a schoolteacher, in Chicago.

Growing up, Brown demonstrated an early attraction to and flair for language. He won elocution contests in school and was drawn to the poetry of LANGSTON HUGHES and COUNTÉE CULLEN as well as to the music of Cole Porter and Oscar Hammerstein. He wrote songs as a teenager and by age fifteen had made his show business debut in the children's radio drama *Secret City*. A year later, having skipped two grades, he enrolled at the University of Wisconsin, only to find that academia was not for him; he was drawn to creative writing but fell short in other subjects and as a consequence drifted from school to school, never graduating. Throughout this period his political sensibilities were also evolving. In 1946 he joined the Communist Party. In 1948 he ran on the Progressive Party ticket for a seat in the Illinois legislature. During this same period he became host of *Negro Newsfront*, a radio presentation that was also the nation's first issue-oriented news program focusing on the black community.

Brown left the show in 1952, the same year he ran for U.S. Congress as a Republican, although he was still a communist and would be for four more years. In 1955 he was drafted into the army and served two years. During that time he began to write songs in earnest. After his discharge he joined his father in the real estate business but never sold a single property; instead he concentrated all of his efforts on songwriting and playwriting. It would be three years before Brown's career was officially launched, then with the assistance of Robert Nemiroff, husband of the playwright LORRAINE HANSBERRY. Nemiroff passed Brown's demonstration tape to an executive at Columbia Records, and Brown signed with the company. His debut album, *Sin and Soul . . . And Then Some*, was released in 1960.

Now considered a classic because of songs like "Signifying Monkey," "Bid 'Em In"—the harrowing tale of a black woman slave sold at an auction—and the trenchant lyrics of his own "Brown Baby," a lullaby written for his newborn son, the album brought Brown immediate recognition. His newfound fame also earned him the attention of Dave Garroway, host of the *Today Show*, who, in an unprecedented move, turned over an entire program to Brown's musical *Kicks and Company*, in what was essentially a backer's audition. While the play never made it to Broadway, Brown went on to share billing with such jazz greats as DIZZY GILLESPIE and JOHN COLTRANE. Moreover, his jazz connections made him the perfect choice to host the short-lived *Jazz Scene USA* in 1962. That same year, he met Jean Pace, a costume designer, who would later become his wife.

The year 1963 found Brown on tour in Europe and wowing the crowds in London with his one-man show. Critics there hailed him a "genius," and "the high priest of hip." But his London success did not follow him back to the United States. His work was too political for some in the recording industry and too angry for others. Refusing to compromise, he bore witness to the struggle against racism and the indomitable spirit of African American life with humor and deep feeling. He also set the stage for the politically conscious artists who came later and is regarded as a progenitor of Afrocentrism. By 1967, however, frustrated by his lack of commercial acceptance, Brown had found an additional outlet for his talents. Working with gang members from Chicago's infamous Blackstone Rangers street gang, he, along with his wife, wrote and produced the theatrical production *Opportunity, Please Knock* that featured over sixty gang members. The following year Richard Hatcher, mayor of Gary, Indiana, invited him to work with youngsters in a talent showcase. The Jackson 5 was one of the acts to emerge from that undertaking.

In 1969 Brown finally reached Broadway with his musical adaptation of Joseph Dolan Tuotti's play *Big Time Buck White*, starring MUHAMMAD ALI. The play enjoyed a brief run, and Brown, disheartened by a theater industry that refused to take risks, turned his attention once again to writing, producing, and performing. In 1972 he returned to the studio and subsequently released three more albums. In 1974, however, he found himself without a recording contract, a circumstance that persisted for twenty years. Still he continued to work. In 1975 he won two local Emmy Awards for a Chicago television special entitled *Oscar Brown is Back in Town*. During this period he was also artist-in-residence at Howard University, Hunter College, and Malcolm X College in Chicago. Finally in 1980 he was tapped to host the PBS special *From Jumpstreet: The Story of Black Music*.

Brown worked throughout the 1990s also, making regular appearances on the television drama *Brewster Place* and the sitcom *Roc*. In 1995 he returned to the recording studio and released *Then and Now*, which included old and new material. But his life was not without its tragedies; in 1996 his son Oscar Brown III, who often played nightclub dates with his father, died in an automobile accident.

Steadfast in his commitment to justice, Brown carried on. He delivered his message to the viewers of the HBO program *RUSSELL SIMMONS Presents Def Poetry*. Just before his death he also received the Pan African Film Festival Lifetime Achievement Award in tandem with the presentation of a documentary about his life, *Music is My Life, Politics is My Mistress*. At the time of his death, Brown's body of work included a dozen operas and plays and more than 1,000 songs, only a fraction of which could be heard on ten albums. He died from complications due to a blood infection.

Further Reading

Brown, Oscar., Jr. *What It Is: Poems and Opinions of Oscar Brown Jr.* (2005).
Harrington, Richard. "The Many Moods of Oscar Brown Jr.: The Singer-Songwriter-Actor Melding Music and Message," *Washington Post*, 8 Mar. 1992.
Saul, Scott. *Freedom Is, Freedom Ain't: Jazz in the Making of the Sixties* (2005).
Wilson, John S. "Oscar Brown Jr. Seeking Audience For His Songs," *New York Times*, 19 Sept. 1980.

Obituary: *Black Issues Book Review*, Nov./Dec. 2005.

Discography

Kicks!: The Best of Oscar Brown Jr. (BGP Records 2004).

ELEANOR D. BRANCH

BROWN, Richard Lonsdale (1893?–1915), landscape painter, was born in Indiana but was raised by his grandparents in Parkersburg, West Virginia. His parents and grandparents sent him to Charlestown Institute where he was trained in house painting. In 1904 he began studying art at West Virginia Colored Institute in Institute, West Virginia. He graduated in 1910 from the academic department, where he was trained in watercolor and where he took painting as an industrial course.

Brown then moved to Pittsburgh, Pennsylvania, where he studied pictures to compare various styles of landscape paintings, after which the Charlestown Institute invited him to teach house painting as a vocational art. Instead, Brown traveled to New York, where he lived on two dollars a week, without lodging. Brown could not afford to both sleep at a hotel and eat. He decided that he should eat, and chose to sleep on the railway cars for brief snatches of time. During the days he would try to sell his artwork to dealers, though with little success, and every evening he would stare at the work in the Metropolitan Museum of Art in New York City. He was especially influenced by Rousseau and Corot.

When art dealers refused to take him seriously because of his color, Brown became discouraged and eventually sought the opinion of his idol, George DeForest Brush, a legendary painter in Greenwich Village, New York. Brown visited Brush in 1911 for a critique of his artwork. Brush hailed Richard Brown an artistic genius and became his mentor. He helped Brown receive a grant from the newly established NAACP, and with it Brown was able to become Brush's student in New York and also to study with him at the Cornish, New Hampshire, Art Colony, during the summer of 1911.

In March 1912 Brown exhibited his impressionist paintings at the Ovington Gallery, owned by the Ovington Brothers Company, in New York. Around this time his paintings were featured on the covers of *The Crisis*, the NAACP's magazine. Brown was featured in both the December 1911 and April 1912 editions. *The Crisis* called its Easter edition the best ever issued because of Brown's cover illustration, which featured an early-spring image dominated by a central tree and with mountains in the distance. The tree is in heavy shadow but with the impression of leaves artistically rendered. "Winter Landscape," on the cover of the Christmas edition of *The Crisis*, featured a snowy scene with a sunset. Dark storm clouds taper to a fading of pink, and snowy hills are in the foreground; the picture is dominated by the sparse grass covered in snow and a few shadowed trees. Both covers show an artist interested in lighting and the isolation of landscapes. Richard Brown went on to work at the Robert Gould Shaw House, where he designed posters for W. E. B. DU BOIS's lectures.

Brown died at the age of twenty-four, without reaching his full potential. While no original works have been located, reproductions can be found at Harvard University, Cambridge, Massachusetts. The art historian John Cuthbert describes Brown's paintings as sharing common features with Frederick Maxfield Parrish and Willard Metcalf, whom Brown may have encountered in Pennsylvania or in Cornish, New Hampshire. Parrish shares the same love for large trees and plays similarly with light and shadow. Metcalf's paintings of winter scenes also use large expanses of snowy ground and large shadowy trees that dominate the painting and give it a feel of loneliness.

Further Reading

"Becomes Famous: Colored Boy of This City Is Ranked as One of the Leading Artists," *Parkersburg Sentinel*, 11 Mar. 1912.

Cuthbert, John A. *Early Art and Artists in West Virginia* (2000).

"Negro Youth Amazes Artists by His Talent," *New York Times*, 17 Mar. 1912.

KIMBERLY L. MALINOWSKI

BROWN, Ron (1 Aug. 1941–3 Apr. 1996), Democratic Party activist and cabinet secretary, was born Ronald Harmon Brown at Freedmen's Hospital in Washington, D.C., the son of William Brown, who worked for the Federal Housing and Home Finance Agency, and Gloria Elexine Carter. The Browns moved to Harlem, New York, in 1947, and Ron grew up in the famed Theresa Hotel, where his father was manager. JOE LOUIS was a frequent guest, and gave young Ron the nickname "Little Brown." Ron showed his entrepreneurial skills at an early age by getting autographs of Louis, SUGAR RAY ROBINSON, and other celebrity guests at the Theresa and selling them for five dollars each to his friends. His parents, both graduates of Howard University, set Ron on a solid path to join the black middle class, which became, in many ways, the social network that would make possible many of his achievements. As a child, he met various politicians, including DAVID DINKINS, Congressman CHARLES RANGEL, and other notables, many of whom became his supporters in his adult life. He was the only black student at the Hunter College elementary school, and he graduated from the Rhodes School, a private preparatory school, in 1958.

Brown attended Middlebury College in Vermont and was the first African American inducted into Sigma Phi Epsilon fraternity—an action which cost the Middlebury chapter its charter in the national

Ron Brown, with President Bill Clinton, at the announcement of his appointment as Commerce Secretary at a news conference in Little Rock, Arkansas, 12 December 1992. (AP Images.)

organization. After graduating with a BA in Political Science in 1962, he married Alma Arrington, a recent graduate of Fisk University from New York. The couple had two children. Brown entered the U.S. Army as a second lieutenant, serving abroad in Germany and Korea, where he was promoted to captain. But rather than continuing a military career, he left the service in early 1967 and began working for the National Urban League (NUL) while pursuing a law degree in the evenings at the St. John's University Law School in New York, graduating in 1970. Motivated in part by the feeling that he had missed being involved in the civil rights movement that was the focus of so much of the African American community in the 1960s, Brown chose to work with the NUL because it was a leading social service and civil rights organization.

Brown began at the NUL as an assistant to Malcolm Puryear, deputy director to executive director WHITNEY YOUNG. Brown's talent was noticed and he rose quickly within the organization. When VERNON JORDAN assumed the role of president and CEO of the NUL after Young's death in 1971, Brown was promoted to general counsel. In October 1973 he was appointed director of the NUL's Washington bureau, which was responsible for maintaining relations with politicians on Capitol Hill and members of the business community in the task of managing the League's agenda. Because of his effectiveness in this role, the League appointed him as liaison for its Commerce and Industry Council.

In 1980, Brown, who had been a district leader of the Democratic party in Westchester County, New York, in 1971, became increasingly interested in national politics and left the National Urban League to join Senator Edward Kennedy's presidential campaign as deputy manager. After Kennedy's unsuccessful presidential bid, the Senate Judiciary Committee hired Brown as its chief counsel, making him the first African American staff director of a major congressional committee. After the Senate passed to Republican control in 1981, Brown took a position at Patton, Boggs and Blow, a prestigious Washington lobbying and law firm. Brown's clients at the firm included Japanese electronics firms, the government of the autocratic Haitian leader Jean-Claude "Baby Doc" Duvalier, and a number of major domestic companies. In 1987 the firm made him a partner.

Brown continued to combine party political work with his lobbying activities, and in 1981 he became general counsel to the Democratic National Committee (DNC). He also was a prominent supporter of JESSE JACKSON's historic presidential bid in 1988, and Jackson invited Brown to serve as director of convention affairs for his presidential campaign. Increasingly, Jackson relied on Brown, rather than on his official campaign manager, as his key strategist in the run up to the Democratic National Convention in Atlanta. After Michael Dukakis became the Democratic presidential nominee at that convention in July 1988, Brown played a key role in cementing a relationship between Dukakis and Jackson, winning the respect of both the establishment and insurgent wings of the Democratic Party. At the convention, Brown also secured for himself a seat on the Party's national executive.

The experience and contacts he made in unifying the often fractious Democratic Party gave Brown the confidence to run for the post of DNC chairman in January 1989. Upon his election in February, he became the first African American to serve in that position. Brown and his staff, especially his political director, Paul Tully, prepared the Democrats to compete in the 1992 election by creating a "coordinated campaign" in which the national party worked closely with state party campaigns. This approach worked to the advantage of the Democratic presidential nominee, Bill Clinton, who campaigned without a strong national organization. Brown's direction of the DNC was also central in building national support for Clinton after his nomination. His choice of New York City as the party's convention site proved controversial, however, because Brown also served on the board and held stock in a company that had just won a $210 million dollar waste treatment contract from the city. Despite such negative publicity, Brown's political and business contacts in New York proved invaluable in helping the Clinton campaign gain access to one of the largest media and financial markets in the country.

Bill Clinton, who often acknowledged that he would not have become president of the United States without Brown's help, appointed Brown as secretary of commerce in 1993. Again, Brown was the first African American to hold that position. Although he had hoped to become secretary of state, Brown settled enthusiastically into his new role, becoming one of the most vigorous secretaries of commerce in history. Believing that he could "really realize something for the American people," he traveled extensively throughout the country and around the globe to boost the standing of American business, securing numerous lucrative agreements for U.S. businesses abroad. During his tenure, a time of rapid economic growth, U.S. exports increased by over 25 percent.

Brown was not without his critics. He came under considerable attack from congressional Republicans who claimed that his trade missions favored Democratic Party supporters. In response, he stressed the bipartisan makeup of his delegations and their success in winning contracts for American firms and jobs for American citizens. Brown was particularly sensitive to the historical exclusion of minority firms and vigorously promoted expanded opportunities for minority businesses. But liberal groups like Common Cause were also critical of Brown's close ties to large corporations. The *New York Times*—hardly part of any vast right-wing conspiracy—ran a series of editorials in 1993 criticizing Brown's lack of full disclosure of his business interests.

Brown was cleared of the bribery charges leveled against him in 1993, but in 1995 Attorney General Janet Reno initiated an investigation into claims that he had submitted misleading financial disclosures and that his son Michael had been paid by an Oklahoma

company in order to gain influence with his father. However, while on a trade mission to Dubrovnik, Croatia, in April 1996, a plane carrying Brown and his delegation of twelve executives of major corporations and fourteen U.S. government employees crashed during a storm in the mountains of Bosnia. At the time of his death, Ron Brown was considered by many to be the most powerful African American in the country.

Further Reading
Brown, Tracey L. *The Life and Times of Ron Brown* (1998).
Holms, Steven A. *Ron Brown: An Uncommon Life* (2001).

Obituary: *New York Times*, 4 April 1996.

RONALD WALTERS

BROWN, Roosevelt "Rosey" (20 Oct. 1932–9 June 2004), Hall of Fame football player, was born in Charlottesville, Virginia, to Roosevelt Brown, a railroad worker, and Catherine Jackson Brown. He attended Jefferson High School, where he played trombone in the school band because his father forbade him from playing football. The football coach saw Brown and decided that a 180-pound thirteen-year-old should be playing football, not trombone. Rosey's father, who was worried because Rosey's uncle had died from a football injury, finally relented after Rosey played a full season injury free in 1945. Brown played four years of high school football, graduating in 1948.

After high school, Brown attended Morgan State University in Baltimore, Maryland, mainly because his high school coach was an alumnus. Brown was a

Roosevelt Brown, during a New York Giants workout at Bear Mountain in New York, 11 September 1958. (AP Images.)

standout lineman on the football team and was named to the 1952 Negro All-America team selected by the Pittsburgh *Courier*. He also wrestled while in college and served as the wrestling team captain for two years. He graduated in 1952 with a BS in Business.

During the 1952 National Football League (NFL) draft, the New York Giants selected Brown in the twenty-seventh round, and he became only the second football player from Morgan State to turn pro. The Giants had not scouted Brown, and in fact no one in the organization had ever seen him play, but they took a chance after someone on the draft team saw his name on the Negro All-America list. After his college graduation, his mother put him on a train to the Giants' training camp with only ten dollars in his pocket—five from her and five from the Giants. When Brown arrived at the training camp at Gustavus Adolphus College in St. Paul, Minnesota, his 6'3", 245-pound frame tucked into a neat dark suit, fedora, and horn-rimmed glasses, team management was not sure if he was a football player. When camp opened, the offensive line coach played Brown against Arnie Weinmeister, arguably one of the best defensive tackles in football, to see what Brown could do. Brown was pounded continuously by Weinmeister, but he kept getting up and even ran laps after practice. His grit, combined with his size and speed, convinced the Giants of his potential. Brown, having never seen a professional football game before, was pretty green and had no idea how the business side of professional football worked. Unlike other rookies at the training camp who were in constant fear of being cut, Brown assumed it was similar to college and that everyone had made the team already. His first coach, Ed Kolman, the former all-league lineman for the Chicago Bears, taught Brown the basics of being a pro lineman, because everything about professional football was new to Brown, even down to the stance the coaches wanted him to use. Kolman also taught Brown that he could not try to play the opponent's game by letting the opponent dictate how he played, but Brown had to play his position his way. The Giants' coaches liked what they saw in Brown and in 1953 named him a starter on their offensive line.

Brown started as the left tackle, one of the hardest and least respected jobs in pro football. He was responsible for protecting the quarterback's blindside, usually toiling away in anonymity while the quarterback received the glory for the team's success. Not only was he a great pass blocker but he also had the speed and agility to run outside and block on running plays. Brown loved to hit people and was a punishing blocker, even taking out multiple defenders on some plays. The Giants used him occasionally on defense, when they needed a big body on goal line stands. Brown also played when he was hurt, missing only a few games over his career despite suffering concussions, broken bones, and torn ligaments.

Brown lived in Teaneck, New Jersey, and was easily recognized around town, mainly because of his affinity for expensive cars. During the off-season, he worked as a salesman for a local brewery, a job he hoped would become full-time after his football days. He was married to Linda Lock and helped raise her two children.

Brown played for the Giants for thirteen seasons before retiring in 1966 because of phlebitis. Over his career he became one of the greatest offensive linemen in the history of pro football. Brown and his contemporary Ron Mix of the San Diego Chargers were the last pulling tackles in the NFL, a job usually reserved for guards. Brown appeared in nine Pro Bowls and was named All-Pro for eight consecutive years (1956–1963). He became the first black captain for the Giants and helped them win six Eastern Conference titles. In 1956 Brown was named the Associated Press Lineman of the Year because he helped lead the Giants to the NFL Championship.

Following his retirement, Brown became one of few linemen and even fewer black football players to successfully transition into coaching. He served as an assistant line coach for the Giants from 1967 to 1968. In 1969 Brown replaced Joe Trible as the head line coach, and he became a scout for the Giants in 1971, a position he held until his death. In 1975 he was inducted into the Pro Football Hall of Fame, a feat rarely accomplished by an offensive lineman. The NFL named him to its 75-year All-Pro team in 1994 and to its All-Time team in 2000. The noted sports broadcaster John Madden named Brown to the All-Madden Millennium team in 1999.

Brown died of a heart attack while gardening outside his home in Columbus, New Jersey. Many former Giants attended his funeral to pay their respects, including Giants' owner Wellington Mara, who called Brown a "great Giant" (*Hackensack Record*, 11 June 2004). Teammate and fellow Hall-of-Fame member Frank Gifford said he owed his career to Brown's ability. Gifford, a running back, recalled the longest run of his career in which Brown made a tremendous block at the line of scrimmage to open a hole for Gifford. When Gifford looked up again, there was Brown out in front making another block. That play was the epitome of the abilities that made Brown a Hall-of-Fame football player and a respected member of the New York Giants organization.

Further Reading

Bechtel, Mark. "A Nimble Giant," *Sports Illustrated* 100 (21 June 2004): 29.
Silverman, Al, ed. *The Specialist in Pro Football* (1965).

Obituaries: *New York Times*, 11 June 2004; *Hackensack (New Jersey) Record*, 11 June 2004.

MICHAEL C. MILLER

BROWN, Roscoe Conkling, Jr. (9 Mar. 1922–), military pilot and educator, was born in Washington, D.C., the elder of two children born to Vivian Brown, a public school teacher, and Dr. Roscoe C. Brown Sr., a dentist and newspaper editor who served in President Franklin D. Roosevelt's "black cabinet." As a young boy Brown lived with his family in Depression-era

Washington, D.C., where economic troubles were as harsh as racial segregation in the city's social spheres. Public education was no exception. But Brown did not allow racial bigotry to stifle his academic interests.

Brown began his formal education at Blanche K. Bruce School, a segregated public institution named after a black U.S. senator from Mississippi elected during Reconstruction. He was fortunate to receive a first-rate education at the academically prestigious Paul Laurence Dunbar High School (formerly the M Street High School), a black public school named after the eminent black poet, and alma mater of famous Washingtonians such as CHARLES RICHARD DREW and CHARLES HAMILTON HOUSTON. Brown excelled in his studies, enjoying Latin, history, and chemistry. After graduation Brown, like many high school graduates of his generation, traveled to the North for his undergraduate studies. Brown became a scholar-athlete at Springfield College, a mostly white liberal arts school located in Massachusetts. He earned letters in football and lacrosse, making him one of the first black athletes to do so, and he graduated as class valedictorian in 1943 with a bachelor of arts in Health, Physical Education, and Chemistry.

With degree in hand, Brown heeded the call of Uncle Sam to fight the Nazi Luftwaffe by enlisting in the U.S. Army Air Corps. Three years before Brown's enlistment, blacks had been unable to join the air corps. All of that changed on 16 September 1940, when President Franklin D. Roosevelt signed the Selective Service and Training Act. This law opened the U.S. Army Air Corps to black enlistees, but on a segregated basis only. So in October 1940 an all-black aviation school was established at Tuskegee Institute, a private historically black college located in central Alabama and founded in 1881 by BOOKER T. WASHINGTON. The aviation group was called the Ninety-ninth Pursuit Squadron. A year before Brown's arrival at Tuskegee, the U.S. Army Air Corps created the One Hundredth Fighter Squadron as part of the 332d Fighter Group. The latter group was known as the "Black Red-tail Angels" by white American pilots. German opponents called them the "Schwartze Voglemenschen," the "Black Birdmen." Brown became a member of the One Hundredth Fighter Squadron of the 332d Fighter Group, where he later assumed the position as commander. On 4 July 1944 the all-black 332d Fighter Group was created through a merger of the existing 99th, 100th, 301st, and 302d squadrons.

From 1943 to 1944 Brown trained at the Tuskegee Army Base in Alabama, at Selfridge Field in Michigan, and Waterboro Air Base in South Carolina. During his training Brown met General BENJAMIN O. DAVIS JR., another black Washingtonian as well as a West Point graduate who became the leader of the Tuskegee Airmen. At Davis's 2002 funeral Brown referred to him as "My hero." Brown flew in sixty-eight combat missions, flying the P-51 Mustang over Germany, Austria, and the Balkans. As a result of the role black soldiers such as Brown played in World War II, President Harry S. Truman signed Executive Order

9981 to integrate the U.S. Armed Services on 26 July 1948. And because of Brown's gallantry to the American cause for freedom, he was one of 150 recipients of the Distinguished Flying Cross and a recipient of the Air Medal with eight Oak Leaf Clusters. He returned to civilian life in 1946, retiring three years later from the military with the rank of captain. Having helped make the world safe for democracy, Brown relocated to New York City, energized and focused on achieving the same ideals in his own country. Higher education was his weapon of choice.

Brown worked as a social investigator in the New York City Department of Welfare, then as a physical education teacher at West Virginia State, a historically black public college. Eager to become a college professor, Brown earned a masters of arts degree in 1949 and a PhD in 1951 from New York University (NYU), specializing in exercise physiology. Brown later used this training to become a founding member of the American College of Sports Medicine in 1954. In 1988 Brown was inducted into the National Sports and Physical Education Hall of Fame. During his tenure as a professor of education at NYU from 1950 to 1977, Brown attained the rank of full professor in 1960 and in 1969 became the director of the Institute of Afro-American Affairs. In addition to his work inside the academy, Brown's film and television projects won him an Emmy Award for Distinguished Program in 1973 for his Black Arts series shown on CBS television. After a long and successful career at NYU, Brown accepted a position as president of the Bronx Community College in 1977 and stayed for sixteen years. In 1993 Brown created the Center for Urban Education Policy at the City University of New York to provide support to systemic school reform. Brown has been the director of the center since 1993.

To honor the service of Dr. Brown and his fellow Tuskegee Airmen during World War II, President George W. Bush awarded the airmen a Congressional Medal of Honor on 29 July 2007. Brown and five other Tuskegee Airmen accepted the medal on behalf of their friends. "We are so overjoyed," said Roscoe Brown Jr. "We are so proud today, and I think America is proud today." The Democratic senator Carl Levin from Michigan and the Democratic congressman CHARLES RANGEL from New York sponsored the legislation to honor the Tuskegee Airmen.

Brown published more than fifty articles during his academic career and received honorary degrees from the College of New Rochelle, Springfield College, the University of the State of New York, and the Regents of the State of New York. An avid believer in strengthening the mind and body, Brown completed nine New York City marathons.

Further Reading
Brown, Roscoe, Jr., and Bryant J. Cratty. New Perspectives of Man in Action (1969).
Brown, Roscoe, Jr., and Gerald S. Kenyon, eds. Classical Studies on Physical Activity (1968).
Ploski, Harry A., and Roscoe Brown, eds. The Negro Almanac (1967).

Superville, Darlene. "Tuskegee Airmen Get Congressional Medal," *USA Today,* 29 Mar. 2007.

GERARD ROBINSON

BROWN, Ruth (12 Jan. 1928–17 Nov. 2006), rhythm and blues performer and actress, was born Ruth Alston Weston, in Portsmouth, Virginia, the eldest of Leonard and Martha Jane (Alston) Weston's seven children. Her father, a skillful athlete who had hoped to become a professional baseball player, found work as a laborer on the Portsmouth docks and worked odd jobs at nights. His weekly wages rarely exceeded $35 per week and barely covered the needs of his growing family. Ruth's mother worked as a domestic. In 1934, when she was six years old, Ruth entered Portsmouth's George Peabody Elementary School and later attended I. C. Norcom High School. Her early years were decidedly urban. She was a weekend regular at Portsmouth's Capitol movie theater, where she cheered on the black action heroes Herb Jeffries and Ralph Cooper, and idolized the young LENA HORNE.

Ruth Weston belonged, however, to that generation of urban African Americans who were born after the Great Migration but who maintained close links to the rural South. During the long summer months of her early school years, the Westons shipped Ruth and her siblings a few miles south to their mother's childhood home in Macon, North Carolina. There the rural blues rhythms of her uncles, who whooped, hollered, shrieked, and shouted across the fields "was soaking in just as surely as the sweat was pouring out," she later recalled (Brown, 30). Her vocal style was also shaped by singing spirituals in Portsmouth's Emmanuel AME church choir, which her father directed, and by performing from age seven onward at weddings and other family functions. In her early teens, she listened to Bing Crosby, Hank Williams, and other white pop and country singers on the radio; Crosby's croon and Williams's yodel and moan would also become part of her vocal repertoire. Jazz and blues performers were rare on most southern radio stations at that time, but in 1942 a visit to some relatives in Harlem, New York, introduced her to recordings by BILLIE HOLIDAY, who along with DINAH WASHINGTON and SARAH VAUGHN greatly influenced her early preference for soulful, jazz-inflected ballads. Around this time Brown began frequenting black nightclubs in nearby Norfolk, Virginia, and was soon performing "The Chattanooga Choo Choo," among other pop standards at United Services Organizations (USO) events in and around Norfolk. She did so in secret, knowing that her father was opposed to his teenage daughter performing secular music, particularly in venues crowded with hundreds of young men who had flocked to the Virginia Tidewater's docks, factories, and military bases in the wake of America's entry into World War II. Despite her father's warnings and occasional beatings, Ruth persisted, even traveling to New York City in 1944, where she won first prize on Amateur Night at Harlem's famed Apollo Theater for her performance of Bing

Ruth Brown, singing in the "Salute to the Blues" concert at Radio City Music Hall, 7 February 2003. (AP Images.)

Crosby's "It Could Happen to You." She declined the offer of a week's engagement at the Apollo, but returned to Virginia considerably emboldened about her prospects as a professional performer. In 1945, after a fight between two of her suitors left one of them dead, Brown, still only seventeen, left Portsmouth to pursue a full-time musical career.

At first she performed mainly on southern military bases, and in her new hometown of Norfolk, where in late 1945 she met and fell in love with Jimmy Earle Brown, a midshipman, singer, and trumpeter. At eighteen, Jimmy was only one year her senior. The couple began performing together as Brown and Brown, even before they married in Elizabeth City, North Carolina, in 1946, but Ruth later found out that Jimmy already had a wife. Although their marriage was annulled, Ruth continued to sing with Brown and his Band of Atomic Swing throughout 1947, retaining her stage name when the couple separated a year later. In early 1948 Ruth Brown performed briefly with the LUCKY MILLINDER band, but was sacked by Millinder for delivering drinks to the band after finishing her spot. Following a brief stint at BLANCHE CALLOWAY'S nightclub in Washington, D.C., Brown signed with Ahmet Ertegun and Herb Abramson's fledgling Atlantic Records in January 1949.

In May 1949 Atlantic released Brown's first single, "So Long," a blues-tinged ballad that displayed the singer's extraordinary vocal range, her moans, shouts, dips, and yelps. For this performance Abramson did not have to ask Brown to sing "like you've got tears in your eyes," as he often did. She was still on crutches and wearing painful leg braces, the consequence of a serious car crash that had left her hospitalized for nine months with two broken legs. By June 1949 "So Long" had climbed to number six on *Billboard*'s rhythm and blues chart, making it one of Atlantic's first major hits. After four unsuccessful follow-up singles, Brown released "Teardrops From My Eyes," a more up-tempo, swinging number that reached the top of the chart in October 1950 and stayed there for the next eleven weeks. Over the next decade "Miss Rhythm," as she came to be known, recorded eleven top ten singles and five number one hits for Atlantic, the most popular being the raunchy "5-10-15 Hours (Of Your Love)" (1952), "(Mama) He Treats Your Daughter Mean" (1953), "Oh What a Dream!" (1954), and "Mambo Baby," Atlantic's contribution to 1954's mambo craze.

"(Mama) He Treats Your Daughter Mean" proved to be Brown's signature recording for Atlantic. It included what Abramson called her "million dollar squeal" and a shouted "-uh!" at the end of "Mama" that LITTLE RICHARD later copied for his classic, "Lucille" (Brown, 123). The song was also to some extent autobiographical, given Brown's continued troubled relationships with men, among them the tenor saxophonist Willis "Gator Tail" Jackson, a serial philanderer; Drew Brown, a heavy drinker, with whom she had a brief affair and a son, Ronald, born in 1955; and Earl Swanson, another tenor sax player, whom she married that year, and with whom she had a son, Earl Jr., in 1956. Swanson also drank heavily, beat Brown several times, and tried to control her career. The couple separated and divorced in the late 1950s.

Although some of Brown's singles crossed over into the lower reaches of the white pop charts, they were more often covered—in a less raunchy and supposedly more palatable fashion—by white singers like Georgia Gibbs and Patti Page. Brown resented that these artists got to perform her hits on *The Ed Sullivan Show* and other nationally syndicated programs, which rarely booked black artists in the early 1950s. The general crossover of rhythm and blues to the white consumer-driven *Billboard* pop chart and radio play began in mid-1954, a few weeks after the Supreme Court's decision in *Brown v. Board of Education*. In some sense, this seismic cultural shift in white musical preferences proved as significant to American race relations as the Court's school integration ruling. It certainly proved profitable for Atlantic, the "House that Ruth [Brown] Built," which was by the mid-1950s in prime position to exploit this new market, with a roster of artists that came to include the Drifters, the Coasters, and ARETHA FRANKLIN.

By the time Ahmet Ertegun sold Atlantic Records to Warner Brothers for $17 million in 1967, Ruth Brown was living on Long Island, New York. She had recently divorced her third husband, Bill Blunt, a policeman, whom she had married in 1963, and who had tried unsuccessfully to stop her from performing. Her successful recording career apparently behind her, she worked briefly as a bus driver, a teacher's aide at a Head Start program, and as a maid, and depended on federal assistance to help raise her children. As was the case with many performers during the early days of the music recording industry, the fruits of Brown's success and popularity had gone largely to her label. Brown had received no royalties—and sometimes as little as sixty-nine dollars per side—for her many hit singles on Atlantic. In need of money she wrote to Ertegun for help, receiving in return a check for $1,000 and a warning that *she* owed money to Atlantic.

In the 1970s Brown's career revived when the comedian REDD FOXX, a friend from her days touring the South with the Band of Atomic Swing, offered her a role on his hit television show, *Sanford and Son* (1972–1977). Foxx later invited her to play the role of MAHALIA JACKSON in his musical about the civil rights movement, *Selma* (1977). She also began to tour again, in Europe, as part of a package put together by Scandinavian rhythm and blues aficionados, before returning to New York in the 1980s, where she appeared Off-Broadway in an adaptation of JAMES BALDWIN's *Amen Corner* (1982) and in the musical *Staggerlee* (1986), based on the life of outlaw STAGOLEE. It was, however, her star turn in *Black and Blue*, a musical about Harlem's famed Cotton Club in the 1920s, that brought Brown back into the national spotlight. She received rave notices for the show's premiere in Paris in 1985 and in 1989 won a Tony Award when the production moved to Broadway. Her popularity was also enhanced by her role as Motormouth Maybelle in John Waters' *Hairspray* (1987) and for her contribution to *That Rhythm Those Blues* (1988), an award-winning documentary. She also won a Grammy in 1990 for her album, *Blues on Broadway*. The standout song on both *Black and Blue* and *Blues on Broadway*, "If I Can't Sell it, I'll Keep Sitting On It," assured her fans that Miss Rhythm had lost none of her earlier sass and spice. In 1993 Brown was inducted into the Rock and Roll Hall of Fame and sang at Bill Clinton's presidential inaugural. In 1996 Brown published her autobiography, *Miss Rhythm*. Despite suffering a stroke in 2000, she continued to tour and perform regularly.

In addition to a career spanning more than six decades, Brown took a leading role in the Rhythm and Blues Foundation, a cooperative she established with the Washington attorney Howell Begle and the singer Bonnie Raitt to educate the public about the pioneering work of early rhythm and blues and rock and roll performers. The Foundation also helped hundreds of performers receive some of the monies owed to them by record companies like Atlantic, whose guiding principle in those days was summed up by its comptroller, Miriam Beinstock: "That's the whole principle of capitalism. You take advantage of people!" (Brown, 261). Atlantic Records eventually promised to endow the

Foundation with $1,500,000. The Foundation also persuaded Atlantic and other record companies to re-calculate the royalties paid to some of their artists in the 1950s and 1960s. Brown eventually received a check for $27,000 and 4.5 percent of the royalties on her old recordings, considerably less than today's rock, pop, and hip-hop performers who receive 10 percent. Many of her fans, however, viewed her settlement as considerably less than a pioneer like Brown deserved. As STEVIE WONDER stated, Ruth Brown "started it all. Wasn't for Ruth there wouldn't be no Aretha [Franklin], wouldn't be *nobody!*" (Brown, 184).

Brown died in Henderson, Nevada, from compli-cations related to a heart attack and stroke she suf-fered in 2006.

Further Reading

Brown, Ruth, and Andrew Yule. *Miss Rhythm: The Auto-biography of Ruth Brown, Rhythm and Blues Legend* (1996).

Ward, Brian. *Just My Soul Responding: Rhythm and Blues, Black Consciousness, and Race Relations* (1999).

Obituary: *New York Times*, 18 Nov. 2006.

STEVEN J. NIVEN